DISCARD

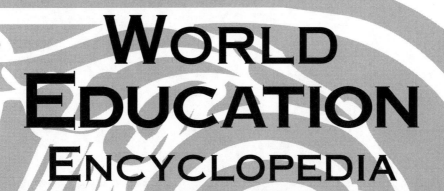

WORLD EDUCATION ENCYCLOPEDIA

A SURVEY OF EDUCATIONAL SYSTEMS WORLDWIDE

SECOND EDITION

VOLUME 1
A–H

WORLD EDUCATION ENCYCLOPEDIA

A SURVEY OF EDUCATIONAL SYSTEMS WORLDWIDE

SECOND EDITION

VOLUME 1
A–H

REBECCA MARLOW-FERGUSON, EDITOR

GALE GROUP
THOMSON LEARNING

Detroit • New York • San Diego • San Francisco
Boston • New Haven, Conn. • Waterville, Maine
London • Munich

WORLD EDUCATION ENCYCLOPEDIA

A SURVEY OF EDUCATIONAL SYSTEMS WORLDWIDE

2ND EDITION

GALE GROUP STAFF

Editor: Rebecca Marlow-Ferguson

Associate Editor: Chris Lopez

Contributing Editors: Jason B. Baldwin, Caryn E. Klebba, Claire Campana, Dawn Conzett DesJardins, Eric Hoss, Kathleen E. Maki-Potts, Jane A. Malonis, Christine Maurer, Amanda C. Quick

Managing Editor: Erin E. Braun

Electronic and Prepress Composition Manager: Mary Beth Trimper

Assistant Manager, Composition Purchasing and Electronic Prepress: Evi Seoud

Buyer: NeKita McKee

Production Design Manager: Kenn Zorn

Art Director: Jennifer Wahi

Permissions Specialist: Margaret A. Chamberlain

Permissions Manager: Maria Franklin

Technical Support Services: Wayne D. Fong

Library of Congress Cataloging-in-Publication Data

World education encyclopedia: a survey of educational systems worldwide / Rebecca Marlow-Ferguson, editor and project coordinator; Chris Lopez, associate editor.—2nd ed.

p. cm.

Includes bibliographical references and index.

Contents: v.1 Afghanistan-Hungary — v.2 Iceland-Rwanda — v.3 Saint Helena- Zimbabwe.
ISBN 0-7876-5577-5 (set: hardcover: alk. paper) — ISBN 0-7876-5578-3 (v.1) —
ISBN 0-7876-5579-1 (v.2) — ISBN 0-7876-5580-5 (v.3)

1. Education—Encyclopedias. I. Marlow-Ferguson, Rebecca. II. Lopez, Chris, 1967-

LB15.W87 2001
370'.3-dc21

2001033159

ISBN 0-7876-5577-5 (Set)
ISBN 0-7876-5578-3 (Volume One)
ISBN 0-7876-5579-1 (Volume Two)
ISBN 0-7876-5580-5 (Volume Three)

Printed in the United States of America

TABLE OF CONTENTS

VOLUME TWO

VOLUME THREE

CONTRIBUTOR NOTES

Andrei G. Aleinikov: President, Mega-Innovative Mind International Institute; Adjunct Professor, Division of Arts and Sciences, *Troy State University Montgomery*

M. June Allard: Ph.D., Chair, Psychology Department, *Worcester State College*

Angela M. Arrey-Wastavino: Associate Director and Professor, Master of Arts in Teaching Program, *Quinnipiac University*

Leena Banerjee: Associate Professor of Psychology, California School of Professional Psychology-Los Angeles, *Alliant International University*

Regsurengiin Bat-Erdene: Doctoral Student, *University of Pittsburgh*; former State Secretary, Ministry of Science, Technology, Education and Culture of Mongolia

Dorota Batog: Secondary School Teacher, Kielce, Poland

Wlodzimierz Batog: Assistant Professor, *Kielce Pedagogical University*, Kielce, Poland

Kimberly A. Battle-Walters: Associate Professor of Social Work, *Azusa Pacific University*

Brigitte H. Bechtold: Professor of Sociology and Director of European Studies and of the Center for Research on Poverty, *Central Michigan University*

Jayne R. Beilke: Associate Professor, Department of Educational Studies, *Ball State University*

Richard W. Benfield: Associate Professor of Geography, Department of Geography, *Central Connecticut State University*, New Britain, Connecticut

S.D. Berkowitz: A.B., Ph.D., Professor, Department of Sociology, *University of Vermont*

Dr. Dallas L. Browne: Chairman, Department of Anthropology, *Southern Illinois University Edwardsville*; Honorary Consul for The United Republic of Tanzania; President of the St. Louis Committee on Foreign Relations

Mark Browning: Associate Professor of English, *Johnson County Community College*

Jo Anne R. Bryant: Professor of English, Division of Arts and Sciences, *Troy State University Montgomery*

Sandra J. Callaghan: Ph.D. Candidate, Urban Studies, *University of Wisconsin-Milwaukee*

Professor Bob Catley: Chair, Department of Political Studies, *University of Otago*, Dunedin, New Zealand

Isabel Cavour: Associate Professor of Spanish, Department of Languages, *University of Dayton*

Rafael Chabrán: Associate Dean for Academic Advisement and First Year Experience and Professor of Spanish, *Whittier College*

Siegfried Christoph: Professor of German, Modern Languages Department, *University of Wisconsin-Parkside*

Linda K. Clemmer: Department of Education, *College of the Ozarks*

Priscilla Coleman: Assistant Professor of Psychology and Education, Department of Psychology, *University of the South*

Mark Connelly: *Milwaukee Area Technical College*

Merrilee A. Cunningham: Ph.D., Department of English, *University of Houston-Downtown*

Stephen Curley: Professor of English, Department of General Academics, *Texas A&M University at Galveston*

LeAnna DeAngelo: Ph.D., Independent Writer and Researcher

Haig Der-Houssikian: *University of Florida*

Emily Dial-Driver: Department of Communications and Fine Arts, *Rogers State University*

Matts G. Djos: Department of Language and Literature, *Mesa State College*

Grigory Dmitriyev: Professor, College of Education, *Georgia Southern University*

Barbara Lakeberg Dridi: Ph.D., Director, *Concordia International Research*

Eric H. du Plessis: Professor of French Studies, Department of Foreign Languages and Literatures, *Radford University*

Deanna Edens: *Eastern Michigan University*

Bonnie W. Epstein: Ph.D., Department of English, *Plymouth State College*

Greg Forehand: Social Work Graduate Student, School of Social Work, *University at Buffalo*

Laurence Armand French: Professor of Psychology and Department Chair, Social Sciences Department, *Western New Mexico University*

Helen H. Frink: Professor of German, *Keene State College*, Keene, New Hampshire

Gerald W. Fry: Professor of International/Intercultural Education and Director of Graduate Studies, Department of Educational Policy and Administration, *University of Minnesota-Twin Cities*

Leon Ginsberg: Carolina Distinguished Professor, College of Social Work, *University of South Carolina*, Columbia, South Carolina

Ellen W. Gorsevski: Ph.D., Faculty Instructor, Department of English, *Washington State University*

Leslie D. Gottesman: Ed.D., Professor of English and Communications, *Golden State University*, San Francisco, California

Roy Neil Graves: Professor of English, Department of English, *The University of Tennessee at Martin*

Matthew Gray: Centre for Arab and Islamic Studies (Middle East and Central Asia), *Australian National University*, Canberra, Australia

Dr. Roger E. Hartley: Department of Public Administration and Policy, *University of Arizona*

Mahboub E. Hashem: Professor of Communication and Director of Graduate Studies, Department of Communication, *Fort Hays State University*

Heather Heckel: *Georgia State University*

Alice S. Horning: Professor of Rhetoric and Linguistics, *Oakland University*

Tonya Huber: Ph.D., Associate Professor of Education, Department of Curriculum and Instruction, *Wichita State University*, Kansas

Mark Hutchinson: Head, History Department, *Southern Cross College*

Beverly J. Inman: Adjunct Instructor, German and History, *Kirkwood Community College*

Mara Iutcovich: Associate Researcher, *Keystone University Research Corporation*

Mark Iutcovich: Ph.D., Research Director, *Keystone University Research Corporation*

Héctor Jaimes: Assistant Professor of Spanish, Department of Foreign Languages and Literatures, North Carolina State University

John J. Janc: Professor of French, *Minnesota State University, Mankato*

Kelihiano Kalolo: Director of Education, Tokelau, *University of Auckland*

Sheikh Umarr Kamarah: Assistant Professor, Department of Languages and Literature, *Virginia State University*

Saliwe M. Kawewe: Ph.D., Associate Professor and Graduate Program Director, School of Social Work, College of Education, *Southern Illinois University at Carbondale*

Howard A. Kerner: Professor of English and Communications, *Polk Community College*

Dr. Young-Key Kim-Renaud: Professor of Korean Language and Culture and International Affairs, Department of East Asian Languages and Literatures, *The George Washington University*

Hasso Kukemelk: Chair, Department of Education, *Tartu University*

Gilles Labrie: Professor of French, Department of Foreign Languages, Literatures, and Cultures, *Central Michigan University*

Donna Langston: Chair Ethnic Studies, *Cal Poly*

V. Celia Lascarides: Ed.D., Independent Scholar

Dr. Chong Jae Lee: Ph.D., Professor, College of Education, *Seoul National University*, Seoul, Korea

Kon-zue Lee: Social Work Graduate Student, School of Social Work, *University at Buffalo*

Olga Leontovich: Director of the Center of American Studies, *Volgograd State Pedagogical University*

John P. Lesko: Ph.D., Applied Linguist, Critical Theorist, and English Languages Specialist, GHQ, *United Arab Emirates Armed Forces*

Timothy Lintner: Assistant Professor of Education, *Columbia College*

Pedro Lopes: Doctorate Student, Department of Romance Languages, *University of North Carolina, Chapel Hill*

Lenor Lopez: Research Assistant for Virginia Davis Nordin

Kristen Loschert: Freelance Writer

Patrick McGuire: Associate Professor of Sociology and Director of the Urban Affairs Center, *University of Toledo*, Toledo, Ohio

Pamela R. McKay: Reference Librarian, *Worcester State College*

Bill T. Manikas: Instructor, History and Political Science, *Gaston College*

Magdaleno Manzanárez: Assistant Professor of Political Sciences, Social Sciences Department, *Western New Mexico University*

Edward H. Matthei: Adjunct Professor, Department of Literature and Languages, *Texas A&M University-Commerce*

Linda Miller Matthei: Associate Professor of Sociology and Anthropology, Department of Sociology and Criminal Justice, *Texas A&M University-Commerce*

Richard E. Mezo: Lecturer, Asian Division, *University of Maryland University College*

Brij Mohan: Professor of Social Work and Former Dean, Director of the Doctoral Program, School of Social Work, *Louisiana State University*

Melanie Moore: Associate Professor of Sociology, *University of Northern Colorado*

Michèle Moragné e Silva: Assistant Professor of English Writing and Rhetoric, School of Humanities, *St. Edward's University*

Richard E. Morehouse: Ph.D., Professor, Department of Psychology and Graduate Faculty, *Viterbo University*, La Crosse, Wisconsin

Minoru Moriguchi: Technical Communication Consultant, Osaka, Japan

Bernard E. Morris: Instructor, Literature and Language Arts, *Modesto Junior College*

Eleanor G. Morris: *Georgia State University*

Gladys Mutangadura: Postdoctoral Research Fellow, Sociology Department, *University of North Carolina*

P. Masila Mutisya: Associate Professor, Department of Middle, Secondary and Special Education, School of Education, *Fayetteville State University*, Fayetteville, North Carolina

Mbulelo Vizikhungo Mzamane: *University of South Australia* and *St. Nichael's College*

Carrie E. Nartker: English Department, *University of Toledo*; Humanities and Social Sciences, *Monroe County Community College*

Ting Ni: Assistant Professor of History, Department of History, *St. Mary's University of Minnesota*

Ashakant Nimbark: Professor of Sociology, *Dowling College*, Oakdale, New York

Petya Nitzova: Lecturer, Department of History, *The University of Oklahoma*

Salome C. Nnoromele: Associate Professor, Department of English, *Eastern Kentucky University*

Virginia Davis Nordin: Educational Policy Studies, College of Education, *University of Kentucky*

Hank Nuwer: Education Author; Adjunct Graduate Faculty, *Ball State University School of Journalism*; Adjunct Professor, *Indiana University School of Journalism*, Indianapolis

Osama M. Obeidat: Institute for International Studies in Education, *University of Pittsburgh*

Henning Salling Olesen: Professor in Adult Education and Director of Graduate School in Life Long Learning, *Roskilde University*, Denmark; Chairman of the *European Society of Research into the Education of Adults (ESREA)*

David Owusu-Ansah: Professor of History, *James Madison University*, Harrisonburg, Virginia

Dr. Karin I. Paasche: Assistant Professor, Department of English Studies, *Salem International University*, Salem, West Virginia

Maria A. Pacino: Ed.D., Chair and Professor, Department of Advanced Studies in Education, School of Education and Behavioral Studies, *Azusa Pacific University*

William A. Paquette: Ph.D., Professor of History, *Tidewater Community College*, Portsmouth, Virginia

Joel Peckham, Jr.: *Hope College*

Morgan Axel Peterson: Associate Professor, *Palomar College*

William Sanborn Pfeiffer: Vice President for Academic Affairs, Professor of Humanities and Technical Communication, *Southern Polytechnic State University*

Zoltán Raffay: Research fellow of the *Transdanubian Research Institute, Center for Regional Studies, Hungarian Academy of Sciences*, Pécs, Hungary

Danielle Raquidel: *University of South Carolina*, Spartanburg

Monica Rector: Ph.D., Associate Professor, Department of Romance Languages, *University of North Carolina, Chapel Hill*

Dr. Jorge Rodríguez-Florido: Lecturer in Mathematics, *Roosevelt University*

James G. Ryan: Ph.D., Associate Professor of U.S. History, Department of General Academics, *Texas A&M University at Galveston*

Jane Sabes: Associate Professor of Political Science, History and Political Science Department, *Andrews University*

Jean-Marie Salien: Professor of French Language and Literature, Department of Modern Languages, *Fort Hays State University*

Meshack M. Sagini: Ph.D., Associate Professor of History of Education, American Government, and Management Studies, Department of Social Sciences and Humanities, *Langston University*, Edmond, Oklahoma

D.R. SarDesai: Emeritus Professor of South and Southeast Asian History, *UCLA*

Samuel Sarri: Ph.D., Economics, Philosophy, and Political Science Professor, *University and Community College System of Nevada*

Charlene Santos: Research Assistant for Virginia Davis Nordin

Carol L. Schmid: Professor of Sociology, *Guilford Technical Community College*

Manoj Sharma: Associate Professor, College of Education, *University of Nebarska at Omaha*

Ronald E. Sheasby: Assistant Professor of Writing, English Department, *Loyola University Chicago*

AnnaMarie L. Sheldon: Independent Researcher

Dr. Marsha L. Shively: Department of English, *Indiana Purdue Universities at Fort Wayne Indiana*

Marco Silva: Doctorate Student, Department of Romance Languages, *University of North Carolina, Chapel Hill*

Franklin H. Silverman: Professor of Speech Pathology, *Marquette University*

Sherman E. Silverman: Professor of Geography, Department of History, Geography and Political Science, *Prince George's Community College*

Terry L. Simpson: Chair, Division of Education, *Maryville College*

Paul D. Starr: Professor of Sociology, *Auburn University*, United States; Professor of Social Sciences, *Zayed University*, Abu Dhabi, United Arab Emirates

Dennis J. Stone: *Florida Coastal School of Law Osmon Petty*; Secretary for the Ministry of Education, St. Kitts and Nevis

Nobuku Tanaka: Research Assistant for Minoru Moriguchi and William Sanborn Pfeiffer

Sanna J. Thompson: Assistant Professor, School of Social Work, *University at Buffalo*

Roben Torosyan: Ph.D., Assistant Director, Adjunct Assistant Professor of Psychology, Straus Thinking and Learning Center, *Pace University*

Karl D. Uitti: The John N. Woodhull Professor of Modern Languages, Department of Romance Languages and Literatures, *Princeton University*

Marta A. Umanzor: Associate Professor, Modern Languages and Literature Department, *Saint Michael's College*

N. Prabha Unnithan: Professor, Department of Sociology, *Colorado State University, Fort Collins*

Nader K. Uthman: Faculty Fellow, Department of Middle Eastern Languages Cultures and Comparative Literature, *Columbia University*; Iraq Sanctions Challenge Delegate, May 1998

Nicole E. Vartanian: Ed.D., Senior Research Associate, Office of the Assistant Secretary, Office of Educational Research and Improvement, U.S. Department of Education

Victoria Villena: Lawyer

Juanita Villena-Alvarez: Associate Professor of French and Spanish, Department of Foreign Languages, *University of South Carolina Beaufort*

Karen Vocke: Assistant Professor, College of Education, *Eastern New Mexico University*, Portales, New Mexico

William J. Wardrope: Ph.D., Assistant Professor of Management, *Southwest Texas State University*

Joseph Watras: Professor of Education, Department of Teacher Education, *University of Dayton*

Thomas W. Webb: Ph.D., Professor Emeritus in Sociology of Education and former Rector, *Roskilde University*, Denmark

John C. Weidman: Professor of Education and of Sociology, *University of Pittsburgh*

Duffy Austin Wilks: Associate Professor, Department of Social Science, *Western Texas College*

Don J. Wyatt: Professor of History, Department of History, *Middlebury College*

Jean Boris Wynn: Ph.D., Assistant Professor of Anthropology, Division of Social Science, *Manchester Community College*

Linda K. Yoder: Associate Professor of English Studies, *Salem International University*, Salem, West Virginia

Michael W. Young: Department of English, *La Roche College*

John A. Zurlo: Professor of English [Asian-African Cultures], *Tarrant County College*, Arlington, Texas

INTRODUCTION

Welcome to the second edition of the *World Education Encyclopedia: A Survey of Educational Systems Worldwide*. In these three volumes, readers will find comparative, in-depth essays on the educational systems of 233 countries and/or territories. *World Education Encyclopedia (WEE)* is unique and valuable to users because in addition to essays on each country's educational system, WEE also contains custom-made graphs and statistical tables, as well as regional maps and an extensive index.

This comprehensive, authoritative source of information allows for easy comparison between essays with a standard format or "rubrics" used whenever possible (see section titled **"Essay Components"**). Each essay also features basic data information—such as official country name, literacy rate, and language(s)—clearly marked with headings at the beginning of each entry. Additionally, *WEE's* contributors include scholars and educators from across the United States and around the world; each essay includes a byline.

NEW FEATURES

Although this is the second edition, *WEE* has been completely reconceptualized and **100 percent revised** from the last edition, which was published in 1988. Differences include:

- All essays have been freshly researched and written for this edition.

- Essays now appear in alphabetical order.

- The standard format has increased consistency, which eases comparison.

- *WEE* includes "new" countries since the last edition due to the dissolution of the Soviet Union and

Yugoslavia; it also includes renamed countries such as Myanmar, which was formerly known as Burma.

- Essays include information, when available, on topics such as new political and educational philosophies, new technologies (including Internet and distance learning), and study abroad programs.

- Essays include custom-made graphs.

- The appendix tables include regional and country statistics.

- *WEE* now includes regional maps.

VOLUME BREAKDOWN

- Volume 1: Afghanistan-Hungary

- Volume 2: Iceland-Rwanda

- Volume 3: Saint Helena-Zimbabwe

CONTENTS OF ESSAYS

Essays in *WEE* were individually researched and written by more than 130 authors. Essays range in size from 235 to nearly 30,000 words. The essays' standard rubrics (see section titled **"Essay Components"**) such as "Constitutional & Legal Foundations" and "Teaching Profession" allow for ease of comparison. Even the smaller essays include such information when applicable.

The **"Essay Components"** section lists all possible rubrics. Please note that authors were allowed to use other subheads than those listed, but the ones we have listed should give the reader a good idea of what to expect under that particular header. For example, the "Constitutional & Legal Foundations" header should contain information on constitutional provisions, laws affecting education, and educational philosophies. The "Teaching Profession" header should contain training and qualifications, salaries, and union and association information.

IMPORTANT TO NOTE

- "Tertiary" and "Higher" are used interchangably throughout *WEE*.

- Statistics presented in "Basic Data," graphs, and tables may differ slightly due to the large number of sources for this information. Additionally, figures presented in "Basic Data," graphs, and tables were not compiled by the authors of the essays, so the text may present somewhat different numbers.

- Common acronyms may not be defined in all essays. Some examples include: GDP (gross domestic product), GNP (gross national product), UNICEF (United Nations Children's Fund), UNESCO (United Nations Educational, Scientific and Cultural Organization), NGO/ONG (non-governmental organization), and USAID (United States Agency for International Development).

APPENDICES

WEE contains two appendices. Appendix 1 contains 16 tables of educational statistics on such topics as male and female literacy rates and the number of teachers for primary, secondary, and tertiary levels. The tables may include regional rankings and percentages, as well as brief explanations of the data gathering methods. **Please note that not all countries appear in these tables since not all countries report the necessary data.** Appendix 2 contains a list of all 233 countries and their corresponding regions, which in turn correspond to the maps that are also included in this section.

GENERAL INDEX

The index contains alphabetic references to items mentioned within the essays such as significant terms, trade and professional associations and organizations, names of individuals and countries, government agencies, significant court cases, and key legislation.

INCLUSION CRITERIA

In determining which countries and/or territories should be included, the editors found it best to rely upon several means, a small portion of which were decidedly subjective. We consulted many Internet sites, as well as other Gale Group products and an advisory board. We included many small countries and/or territories that are,

admittedly, difficult to research, hence, the shorter essays.

In addition, we tried to overlook territorial disputes and political issues when compiling the essay list. For example, Israel and West Bank/Gaza Strip have separate essays, as do Serbia and Montenegro and Indonesia and East Timor.

We also chose to use some more common names such as Lao instead of Lao People's Democratic Republic, Libya instead of Libyan Arab Jamahiriya, and North Korea instead of Korea (Democratic). The official country names are given within the "Basic Data."

Finally, the authors were asked to maintain an objective point of view when compiling their essays.

ADVISORS & ACKNOWLEDGMENTS

The editors would like to sincerely thank the members of the *WEE* advisory board for their assistance:

- Mark Mentges, Education-Psychology Library, University of California, Berkeley, California

- Lynn C. Hattendorf Westney, Associate Professor, Assistant Reference Librarian, Coordinator of Reference Collection Development and Coordinator of CRRC: Career and Resume Resources Collection, The University of Illinois at Chicago, The Richard J. Daley Library, Chicago, Illinois

In addition, the editors wish to express their gratitude to the authors of the essays for their invaluable work and patience.

The editors wish to thank the copyright holders of the excerpted criticism included in this volume and the permissions managers of many book and magazine publishing companies for assisting us in securing reproduction rights. We are also grateful to the staffs of the Detroit Public Library, the Library of Congress, the University of Detroit Mercy Library, Wayne State University Purdy/Kresge Library Complex, and the University of Michigan Libraries for making their resources available to us. Following is a list of the copyright holders who have granted us permission to reproduce material in *WEE*. Every effort has been made to trace copyright, but if omissions have been made, please let us know.

Copyrighted material in *WEE* was reproduced from the following: From *2000 World Development Indicators*. The World Bank, 2000. Copyright 2000 by the International Bank for Reconstruction and Development. All rights reserved. Reproduced by permission.—From *2000 World Development Indicators CD-ROM*. The World Bank, 2000. Copyright 2000 by the International Bank for Reconstruction and Development. All rights reserved. Reproduced by permission.—From *Education at a Glance*. Organisation for Economic Co-Operation and Development (OECD), 2000 edition. (c) OECD 2000. www.oecd.org. Reproduced by permission.—From *The State of the World's Children 2001*. UNICEF, 2001. The United Nations Children's Fund (UNICEF) (c). Reproduced by permission.—From *Statistical Yearbook*. Bernan Press, 1999. Copyright (c) 1999 UNESCO. Reproduced by permission.—From *World Education Report, 2000*. UNESCO, 2000. (c) UNESCO 2000. Reproduced by permission.

All maps were created by Maryland Cartographics on behalf of Gale Group.

COMMENTS & SUGGESTIONS

Comments and suggestions are most welcome. Readers are invited to send their thoughts to:

Editor/World Education Encyclopedia
Gale Group
27500 Drake Rd.
Farmington Hills, MI 48331-3535
Telephone: 248-699-GALE
Toll-free Phone: 800-347-GALE
Toll-free Fax: 800-339-3374
Editor E-mail: rebecca.marlow-ferguson@galegroup.com
Web Site: http://www.galegroup.com

Essay Components

History & Background

Historical Evolution

Political, Social, & Cultural Bases

Constitutional & Legal Foundations

Constitutional Provisions

Laws Affecting Education

Educational Philosophies

Educational System—Overview

Compulsory Education

Age Limits

Enrollment

Female, Minority Enrollment

Academic Year

Language of Instruction

Examination

Grading System

Private Schools

Religious Schools

Instructional Technology (Computers)

Textbooks—Publication, Adoption

Audiovisuals

Curriculum—Development

Foreign Influences on Educational System

Role of Education in Development

Preprimary & Primary Education

General Survey

Curriculum—Examinations

Urban & Rural Schools

Teachers

Repeaters & Dropouts

Secondary Education

General Survey

Curriculum—Examinations, Diplomas

Teachers

Repeaters & Dropouts

Vocational Education

Nonformal Education

Higher Education

Types of—Public & Private

Admission Procedures

Administration

Enrollment

Teaching Styles & Techniques

Finance (Tuition Costs)

Courses, Semesters, Diplomas

Professional Education

Postgraduate Training

Foreign Students

Students Abroad

Role of Libraries

Administration, Finance, & Educational Research

Government Educational Agencies

Ministry/Department of Education

Educational Budgets

Types of Expenditures

National Education Organizations

Educational Research

Nonformal Education

Adult Education

Open Universities

Distance Education (TV, Radio, Internet)

Vocational Education

Teaching Profession

Training & Qualifications
Salaries
Unions & Associations

Summary

General Assessment
International Programs
Needs for Changes—Future

Bibliography

FOREWORD

INTRODUCTION & OVERVIEW

The *World Education Encyclopedia* is designed as a descriptive survey of the national education systems of the world. It is a global report on the state of education in the dawn of the twenty-first century. It describes not so much educational theory (which is of interest only to educators) but the actual working of the systems, which concerns all educated people. In doing so, it defines the levels and characteristics of the systems; their growth, especially since the end of World War II; their legal, political, and social foundations; their contributions to national welfare; their bases and their biases; and their problems and their performance. The *Encyclopedia* analyzes educational systems, but it does not pass judgment.

Education is the largest single activity in the world, involving more than 1 billion students and 50 million teachers at all levels, not counting millions of others in educational support activities. But its importance stems not merely from its size but also from its role as institutionalized knowledge—the principal repository, producer, disseminator, and transmission belt for all forms of knowledge. Education is, in essence, a form of energy that sustains and perpetuates every form of intellectual activity. The most significant feature of global education in the twenty-first century is not so much what the French call *l'explosion scolaire* (pupil explosion), but the *knowledge explosion,* which has expanded the catchment basins of learning so fast that it often takes only a decade for the state of the art in many fields to become obsolete. The modes of communicating that knowledge are also changing and becoming more sophisticated; knowledge can now be dispensed technologically and electronically. Teachers and formal school structures are becoming less important, and the conventional age limits on the learning process are becoming blurred. Change is becoming the only constant in educational systems, as is the adjust-

ment to change; the upgrading of skills is becoming incorporated into the very fabric of instruction. A second notable feature of education is the growing homogenization of curricular materials and the standardization of teaching techniques; it is proper in this sense to speak of a global village school. Education is functioning as a major promoter of the migration of ideas across borders. It is possible now for a student from, say, Papua New Guinea, to go to France or the United States to continue his or her schooling without having to relearn or unlearn anything. Certain educational philosophies have become universally accepted, and when one speaks of innovation, it does not imply so much a radical break with the past or convention as a gradual refinement and an incorporation of ideas whose worth has been proved in other countries. The third significant feature of global education is that it is becoming the cause as well as the result of a growing egalitarianism and democratization in all countries. It is generally accepted that education is an engine of modernization; it can break barriers and raise consciousness in politics and society. Education has spin-offs and ripple effects whose influence extends beyond the classroom—horizontally across all layers of society and vertically across layers of time. While enhancing individual worth and dignity, shared learning also can become a strong bond among individuals, creating new professional and social castes or classes.

Education has long been recognized as the central element in the development of human personality. But in the twenty-first century, it has acquired a new range of functions. It is no longer merely one of the sectors of national life (like agriculture or industry) but a multidimensional process that energizes and pervades all other sectors. As the 1948 UNESCO Declaration stated, "Man is both the end and the instrument of education."

In almost all countries, education is designed to fulfill three well-defined functions:

- *As a Basic Human Need:* people require education not only for the structured information in the core subjects of the curricula but also as a tool for gaining attitudes, values, and skills on which they can build later. The former may be called "surface learning" and the latter "deep learning." Deep learning triggers learning potential and enables students to respond to new opportunities without formal guidance, to participate in society, and to respond to change.

- *As a Means of Meeting Other Basic Needs:* education influences and is, in turn, influenced by other basic needs, and it serves as a catalyst in creating needs where none existed before. This is the upward pull or mobility that raises a country's level of aspirations and expectations. A country's quality of life is the sum total of these aspirations and expectations, and it is directly related to its quality of education.

- *As an Activity that Sustains and Accelerates Economic Development:* education trains and prepares skilled workers at all levels to manage capital, technology, services, and administration in every sector of the economy. First, economists believe that long-term returns on investment in education exceeds returns on alternative kinds of investment, and these returns are not subject to cycles and recessions. Second, through trained personnel, developed methodologies, and institutional settings, education facilitates the advancement of knowledge in pure and applied fields. Third, rapid economic growth, technological advancement, and social change tend to tear down traditional social and religious support systems. Education enables individuals to make the transition to new social orders by providing self-understanding, better knowledge of the choices available, and a critical appreciation of the nature of change itself.

Education, however, operates in every country under a variety of constraints, the most powerful of them being political and economic. Education is most effective when there is a general climate of broadly understood freedom. But experience suggests that even in the absence of such freedoms, education does not necessarily act as an agent for maintaining or reinforcing the status quo. On the other hand, widely diffused educational activities provoke and facilitate change in prevailing sociopolitical conditions by sowing seeds of discontent, by suggesting alternatives, and by generating a clearer understanding of political and social rights. Through the ages, the enemies of freedom have echoed the words of Governor Sir William Berkeley of Virginia in 1671:

> I thank God there are no free schools, and I hope we shall not have them these hundred years, for learning has brought disobedience and heresies and sects into the world. . .and libels against the best government.

The ideal education has always remained elusive in both theory and practice, even more so in the latter. Because education is, by its nature, diverse and responds to the varying needs of learners, it resists neat categorizations. But the key word appears to be "responds," and many efforts have been made in recent years to make education more "responsive" or "relevant" to the needs of changing societies. Many of these efforts were merely trendy and have withered on the vine; the few that gained roots in the system concentrated on modes of delivery rather than on content or format.

Modes of delivering education—formal, informal, and nonformal—are conceived today not as alternatives but as complementaries. Formal education—the institutionalized, graded, and hierarchically structured system covering primary, secondary, and tertiary, or higher, levels—is the most prominent mode of delivery. Informal education—the unorganized, lifelong process by which everyone acquires knowledge, skills, and attitudes through experience, contacts, reading, and watching—is conterminous with life itself but cannot function as a surrogate for formal training and instruction. Its major disadvantage is the lack of a corrective or evaluative mechanism. Nonformal education—the systematic learning activity carried on outside the formal system—provides a second chance to those who have missed formal schooling. It enables the rural and urban poor to acquire a wide array of skills either directly associated or not associated with their work. It provides minimum rather than maximum education and often is associated with development rather than education.

All governments acknowledge their responsibility to provide basic education to children within certain age limits. Universal, free, and compulsory education remains the watchword of all governments enshrined in the constitution and statute books, and in many countries this goal is an attained reality. The nonschooling gap (the differential between the school-age population and the actual enrollment) has narrowed worldwide during the past five decades except in the case of the least developed countries. Even where education is universal and compulsory, it is not equal. A large percentage of students throughout the world are enrolled in elite or private schools. Data on private education is incomplete because of the diversity of the definitions of private institutions. But the idea that the rich tend to send their children to elite schools and the poor to public schools counters the ideal egalitarian thrust of education and reinforces existing social and economic class divisions.

QUALITY OF EDUCATION

Education is one of the most intensely national of activities with lateral roots in a country's culture, religion, society, and politics. In one sense, education may be properly described as an extension of the national psyche. Implied in this assertion of educational nationalism is the concern that education must produce good citizens and must be relevant to national needs. The issue of relevance is derived from the function of education in identifying and sustaining the historical, cultural, and religious ethos of a country. It, therefore, involves rethinking the substance of education to assert the authentic national character. The concept of relevance is sometimes extended to define the educational needs of particular groups within a country, such as women, the handicapped, and ethnics. In countries where a foreign or colonial language is the medium of instruction, national pride requires the use or reactivation of native vernaculars in at least the lower primary grades; however, the use of native languages has generally been counterproductive in an educational sense, denying students access to the vast corpus of learning mainly in Western languages. Linguists also have suggested that many hundreds of African and Asian tongues will die out within the twenty-first century as a result of their exclusion from the classrooms.

EDUCATIONAL PROBLEMS

Despite substantial and impressive quantitative and qualitative progress throughout the past 40 years, education in all countries is beset with 5 major problems: inequalities in educational opportunities, internal inefficiencies, external inefficiencies, management inefficiencies, and financial insufficiencies.

Inequalities in Educational Opportunities: Article 26 of the 1948 United Nations' Universal Declaration of Human Rights states: "Everyone has the right to education. Education shall be free at least in the primary and fundamental stages. . .Technical and professional education shall be made generally available and higher education shall be equally accessible to all on the basis of merit." For the first time in history, education was elevated as an inalienable right of every human being. No government has ever contested this right.

According to available data, at least 1.1 billion people, including 400 million children, are unable to exercise, or have never exercised, this right. In addition, there are unequal educational opportunities within countries,

based on gender, socioeconomic status, ethnic background, and geographic regions. Of the disparities, none is more glaring than discrimination based on gender. In almost all developing countries, not only are more women illiterate, but also there are continuing disparities in the male and female enrollment ratios. The effects of other factors on enrollment (such as regional differences, urban or rural location, socioeconomic status, and ethnic background) are not always clearly distinguishable, since they tend to co-exist. Efforts to expand and equalize educational opportunities face many constraints. The most obvious one is the lack of financial and human resources. Next, geographic conditions (vast distances, low-density population, harsh environments, and poor communications) make the construction of schools, the supply of books and equipment, and the provision of qualified teachers a difficult task. Additionally, cultural and religious prejudices may restrict the education of females, especially in Muslim countries.

Equal access to educational facilities does not necessarily ensure equal use of those resources. Many factors influence the achievement of specific kinds of learning outcomes. Some of them are related to the school environment—curriculum, instruction, teachers, instructional materials, extracurricular programs, and physical facilities. But there are extramural factors as well, such as the student's family, health, and economic status. Disadvantaged children suffer other handicaps for which they are directly compensated only in a few countries.

Internal Inefficiencies: The problem of efficiency deals with the flow of students through the system with a minimum of waste and the quality of learning achieved within the classroom. Wastage in the flow of students is manifested quantitatively in the form of dropouts and repetition, while the quality of learning is determined by inputs and outputs of the educational system.

According to UNESCO, only 40 percent of the first-grade cohort in developing countries reach the fifth grade, the point at which permanent literacy is achieved. The rest simply drop out of school, constituting the detritus of the educational system. The ripple effects of dropping out are felt not only throughout the remaining years of the dropout, but also cumulatively on the job market, where it exerts a downward pull on the general achievement level of job seekers. Even more serious is wastage caused by repetition. The number of children admitted to primary school could be increased by the same percentages with no increase in costs if repetition could be reduced in school systems. Because there is a rough correspondence between the per capita income of a country and the internal efficiency of its educational system, the poorest countries pay most dearly for inefficiency.

Economic profiles of dropouts and repeaters show that these failures are most common among students from low socioeconomic backgrounds. Similarly, they are more prevalent in rural areas than in urban, and they are more prevalent among females than among males. Inefficiencies in student flow are also accompanied by inefficient use of scarce teachers and student space. Many other factors also influence the ratio of students to teachers, such as the size of classes, the weekly teaching load, and the number of class periods. Likewise, there are inefficiencies in the use of space when physical facilities are assigned to classes that are smaller than the norm or when facilities are used only part of the time during which a school is open.

The second aspect of efficiency involves the evaluation of the quality of learning and, hence, is more controversial. It is necessary to start with a definition of the three terms most often used in a discussion of quality of learning: input, output, and outcome. Input refers to factors such as size of class, qualifications of teachers, material facilities, and years of schooling. Output refers to the learning achieved—knowledge, skills, behavior, and attitudes—most commonly measured by tests and examinations. Outcome refers to total value added by the educational system to a country's productive capacity. In short, there is a distinct relationship between what goes into the educational system and what comes out of it and, by enhancing the former, it is possible to upgrade the latter.

Recent studies draw three conclusions on what types of input produce optimal learning:

- Learning is influenced by both out-of-school variables (including educational level of parents, socioeconomic status, nutrition, healthcare, child-rearing patterns and preschool education) and in-school variables (including textbooks and teachers).

- In-school variables often are more influential in this regard than out-of-school variables.

- Positive effects of school input frequently are greater on children from lower socioeconomic background than on those from higher ones.

Improvement of school efficiency thus is seen as a direct consequence of improvements in school inputs, particularly curriculum, teaching styles, instructional materials, and the use of audiovisual and non-print materials.

Curriculum development is considered a principal element of educational reform, although it has not always resolved problems. Where it fails, usually it is confused with the revision of syllabi or the updating of the topic outlines. Because curricular innovations frequently are misunderstood by consumers of the educational system, they are either resisted or ignored. Often, changes in curricula consist simply of replication of programs in other countries. The transition of pilot curriculum projects to nationwide adoption is made without providing for the necessary complementarities (such as teachers, textbooks, and physical resources) and without monitoring and evaluation procedures.

Proper curriculum development involves an assessment of educational objectives, sophisticated analysis and organization of content, and the design and preparation of corresponding textbooks, instructional materials, training courses, and physical facilities. The content of curriculum should reflect the structure of knowledge—that is, the principal concepts, relations, and theories of various disciplines. It also should incorporate the dynamics of the generation of knowledge, such as observation, measurement, classification, induction, deduction, verification, and appreciation. The level of presentation should match the stage of development of the learner; it should draw on the environment of the learner for the demonstration and application of its content. Finally, it should be uniform for a given territorial unit, giving all students equal opportunities to advance to higher levels.

Curriculum reform also extends to improvements in the processes and styles of teaching and learning, involving discovery, experimentation, and practical activities. A sound curriculum maintains a balance between theory and practice, permits learners to interact with physical objects, stimulates curiosity, and drives motivation. It also provides the learner with conceptual structures to assimilate information and a means of communicating and interpreting that information. The expository method is just as effective in imparting knowledge as the discovery method, although the latter is more useful in the development of higher cognitive faculties. A well-devised curriculum also permits the learner to proceed at his or her own pace, neither slowing down, nor being slowed down by, other learners.

Teachers constitute the second major school input. Teaching skills are positively related to student performance. Although teacher qualifications—certification, credentials, educational attainment, and knowledge—are the most frequently used measures of a teacher's classworthiness, skills in specific subjects are just as important. Students have high expectations of their teachers, and the personality traits of teachers should meet and fulfill those expectations. Despite the known effects of teachers on educational efficiency, most developing countries have a high percentage of unqualified teachers and have poorly designed and equipped teacher-training and in-service programs. In many countries, the professional self-image of teachers is adversely affected by the low salaries relative to the remuneration of those who perform comparable work. The profession, therefore, suffers from high turnover, particularly among male teachers.

Textbooks and audiovisual media are the third most consistent determinant of academic achievement. They are also one of the most expensive items in the educational budget. In the more advanced countries, textbooks are provided free to all students, but in the less developed ones, students need to buy them or share copies with other students. A number of conditions make for an efficient program in producing instructional print and non-print instructional materials: consensus on curricula and syllabi; expertise in design, editing, and evaluation of materials; frequent revisions; and the training of teachers in the use of these materials. Audiovisual media improves educational efficiency by improving the quality of instruction in subjects for which qualified teachers are not available by supplementing the curricula and reinforcing the absorption of information by slow learners.

External Inefficiencies: The external efficiency of an educational system involves the interface between academic and vocational education and between school and work. It looks at education as a tool rather than as an end in itself, as a feeder into the economic stream rather than as a reservoir of knowledge, in terms of earning potentials rather than learning potentials.

First, it is universally acknowledged that there can be no economic growth without a trained labor force. The "power" in manpower comes from education. One of the functions of education is to determine, even to forecast, the types of skills required in an economy, to design the best processes for transmitting those skills, and to ensure that, once acquired, those skills are properly deployed and used. The percentage of unemployment in a country is, therefore, a reflection not only of its industrial system but also of its education. Somewhere, the educational planners had miscalculated the absorptive capacity of the job market and had failed to turn off the faucets. As long as diplomas and certificates are passports to jobs, there must be a logical parity between the two; otherwise, education becomes externally inefficient, leading to an enormous waste of human resources.

In a deeper sense, the linkage between work and education performs a more significant function. Work experience and skill acquisition help to form productive habits and attitudes. They introduce students to the fulfillment of work schedules, the discipline of work goals, the demands of subordination to a hierarchy of authority, and the budgeting of time. The school occupies an intermediate place between home, with its intensely personal affections and value systems, and the office or factory with its depersonalized work ethic; the school's job is to mediate between the two. Education also creates and perpetuates a distinction between blue- and white-collar jobs, often granting superiority to managerial work over manual work.

There is strong evidence that education increases the productivity of a national workforce. The social rate of return on education has been estimated at 26.2 percent in primary education, 13.5 percent in secondary education, and 11.3 percent in higher education. Educated workers generally are more achievement-oriented, more self-reliant, more adaptive to new situations and, above all, more trainable. These qualities can be directly imparted by the educational process.

In an effort to provide pre-employment training in broad categories of skills before the majority of students leave school at the end of compulsory education, many governments have diversified the secondary curricula by introducing practical or occupational subjects into an otherwise completely academic program. Two models are prevalent. The first introduces practical subjects (such as industrial arts, home economics, and agriculture) in lower secondary schools to provide prevocational orientation and to help foster positive attitudes toward manual work. The second model includes a general academic stream, plus a specialized occupational stream, usually at the upper secondary level. Diversified schools have been a popular alternative to purely academic ones, but their track records have been patchy because they are complex and expensive, requiring new teachers, new curricula, and new physical facilities. The viability of industrial and technical schools depends to a large extent on the pace of industrial growth; it also depends on the vigor of relationships among schools, employers, and educational planners.

Management Inefficiencies: Educational management is not much different from other forms of management. It is subject to the same personnel and financial constraints and the same kind of scrutiny and standards. Education is the largest public-service establishment in all countries. However, the responsibility for management is often dispersed horizontally among an increasing number of agencies and vertically among central, state, and local authorities, while operational responsibilities devolve on school and college principals, presidents or rectors of universities, and directors of other types of institutions. On the macro level, educational management is determined by considerations of public administration and politics; on the micro level it is affected by prevailing educational management philosophies, bureaucratic inertia and community values. Educational management has a high degree of visibility and accountability—from the legislature and local elected representatives to the parents and concerned religious and social groups. These checks and balances keep the administrators of the educational system on their toes in most countries.

The problems of educational management are of a different order. Simply, there is too much management and too little planning. In many instances education develops as an isolated activity outside the mainstream of policymaking. The knowledge base for policymaking has also been skimpy and often unreliable. Adequate information on economic, demographic, cultural and political conditions and constraints, and the dynamics of the educational system has been lacking. Often goals are set without any regard for clear-cut strategies for achieving them. Too much attention is devoted to quantitative expansion and too little to qualitative change. The core of the educational system appears to be highly resistant to change, and most innovations introduced periodically in modern times have either been transitory or cosmetic or both.

One unmistakable trend in many countries is the growing centralization of educational policymaking. Originally, education was a local responsibility, and most federal constitutions in the world treated it as such. Since the end of World War II, the process has been reversed; central governments have appropriated more and more educational functions formerly exercised at the state and local levels. Even in the United States, where the Constitution delegates educational powers to the individual states, a Federal Department of Education was established in the closing years of the Carter administration against the opposition of the states' rights' advocates. In some countries central government involvement is necessary to preserve the national character of the educational system and to hold back divisive local and parochial interests. The central hegemony over education is moderated to some extent by intermediate links in the chain of educational management, such as school inspectors and school boards with immediate responsibility for the smooth function of the system. Institutions of higher education are semiautonomous in the vast majority of countries and their management is subject to fewer public controls.

Financial Insufficiencies: Money makes the mare go. Education is no exception to this adage. Education competes with other national sectors for its share of the public budget and, more often than not, it loses out to other ministries, such as defense or health. Educational funds also are among the first to be pruned in times of financial crises because educators tend to be less vociferous lobbyists than others.

Financial resources allocated to education are not exclusively from public revenues. They include expenditures borne directly by parents, local communities, religious groups, foreign aid programs, and private philanthropists. As a result it is difficult to estimate the outlay on education in any one country, let alone the world, but it may safely be assumed that public funding covers between 80 and 90 percent of all education expenditures. The most common yardsticks of education expenditures are as a percent of GNP, as a percent of the national budget, and per student. UNESCO has a recommendation of 4 percent for the former, but none for the latter two. Generally, education expenditures represent a proportionately heavier burden on the treasuries of lower-income countries, even though richer countries spend more per student and provide a much better education. There are wide disparities in budgetary allocations. Developing countries spend a larger proportion than developed countries on primary education.

Education is a labor-intensive activity where economies of scale are not possible. Finance, therefore, is likely to prove the major constraint in educational development in the future. Such constraint will operate more stringently in post-compulsory education and will make education in the twenty-first century even more of a pyramid with clearly marked echelons of educational achievement. Primary education will be for all, secondary education for many, and higher education for few.

GLOBALIZATION

Throughout the world globalization is becoming a major factor in the convergence of educational theory and practice. The explosion in electronic methods of conveying information, the creation of a worldwide youth consumer market, and the growing international network of education reform ideas and policy experts are stimulating a globalization of schooling. National economies are now global in their competitive outlook, insatiable in their quest for technological innovation, and crucially dependent upon the availability of human talent. Reliance upon a narrow intellectual elite appears increasingly outmoded. Educated and highly skilled personnel are increasingly viewed as a nation's primary economic resource, as a new strategic raw material for nation-building.

These forces are beginning to reshape the forms of schooling across national boundaries. This globalization will occur simply because values and ideas are spilling over borders, challenging government planners and educational authorities to respond with positive reforms before it is too late. Expansion of the populations served by schools and colleges, centralized curricula, expanded use of standardized tests, growing dependence on government agencies to collect and analyze school performance data, intensified efforts to link colleges and industry, and new techniques of educational evaluation are among the most predictable practical outcomes of the globalization movement. Specific reforms and administrative procedures may vary from nation to nation, depending upon historic patterns, contemporary politics, current resource levels, and operating structures. Within national borders, the watchword will be "to leave no child behind." Internationally, the watchword will be "to leave no nation behind."

Globalization will be achieved incrementally through a series of reforms that will be linked to demographic and social trends. These reforms will have the following components:

- Extension of publicly funded schooling to lower age groups, or preschool

- Greater central government-imposed uniformity in curricula

- Intensified instructional emphasis on science and technology

- Expanded use of standardized examinations and centralized evaluation procedures to measure student achievement and school performance

- Greater monitoring of school outcomes through accountability standards

- Devolution of greater operating authority to schools, bypassing conventional units of local educational governance.

PRESCHOOL EDUCATION

The growing number of mothers in the workplace has created enormous political pressures for the provision of publicly financed or subsidized childcare. This represents a downward institutional expansion of education, as schools are becoming surrogate parents, which is outside their traditional function. Childcare and preschool services are generally provided for children as young as three years of age. There is no agreement on the degree to which content and specific skills should be imposed on children at the preschool stage. The age at which children are capable of learning formally structured materials is debatable. The focus, however, is on school readiness. Early childhood programs are expected to prepare young children for school in a social sense—to train them to follow adult directions, cooperate in a group setting, adhere to schedules, stand in line, and so forth—and they may also incidentally train them in reading and counting.

Early childhood care and education is the first and most essential stage of preschool education. Research shows that the period from 0 to 8 years of age is a critical development time for children involving physical, motor, cognitive, emotional, and social dimensions. Nutritional, physical, psychological, and cognitive deficits incurred by children in these crucial years are cumulative to a much greater extent than at any other time in a life cycle.

In the industrialized world, public provision for early childhood education is both a goal itself and a policy expression of the desire to retain skilled and professional women in the workforce after motherhood. Young women who continue their careers after childbirth are a growing constituency needing preschool facilities and daycare. In the developing world, childhood education is necessary, but for different reasons. Because of the feminization of poverty, most mothers are overworked and extremely poor. The human resources argument for investing in preschool education is much broader than immediate social concerns. Longitudinal studies show that preschool education has a very positive impact on the intelligence, personality, and social skills of young children, which lasts well into adulthood. Investment in this age group gives a higher rate of return over the long haul than investment in any other age group in terms of later healthcare costs or rehabilitation and re-education programs. Childhood education plays an indispensable role in introducing children to school organization, language of instruction (which may be in many cases different from the mother tongue), the universe of print and audiovisuals, and cognitive and expressive behaviors. It also helps to reduce the drop of dropout and repetition later in life.

The developing world accounts for more than four-fifths of the world's children, only less than 1 percent of whom receive daycare. Coverage is weakest for children aged 0 to 3. Most of the programs are run not by the state but by communities, especially women's groups. Such community-managed programs cater to a multiplicity of needs (such as nutrition, basic health, and hygiene) and provide enrichment programs for children through play groups. These programs are low-cost and voluntary and culturally relevant to the children they serve. A large percentage of preschool centers are located in primary schools, but a growing number are private, unlicensed institutions funded by fees paid by parents.

Major differences exist among industrialized countries. Childhood care and education is highly organized in countries such as Israel, Japan, and Sweden, but it is less satisfactory in the United States (and, to a lesser extent, in the United Kingdom) where it is regarded as either a welfare service or a matter of private arrangement. The United States operates a two-tier system: a publicly funded welfare system for poor and minority children and private childcare funded by parents for the middle-class and rich. Only 12 percent of American infants and toddlers receive care in preschools or public centers. Essential aspects of childcare in continental Europe, such as family support or employment entitlements of parents, are weak or absent in U.S. social policy. Among the factors cited to explain the weak commitment to preschool education in the United States are idealization of the family and the maternal role and the consequent reluctance toward social innovation as well as public tolerance of social inequalities. More positively, kindergarten is provided free to all children, and a growing number of employers, including the federal government, are beginning to provide childcare for the children of their employees.

CENTRALIZATION OF EDUCATION

In the twenty-first century, central governments, rather than local officials, will determine what children will learn and what teachers will teach in primary and secondary schools. Detailed directives will cover subject-matter guidelines, content frameworks, lesson plans, teaching modules, reading lists, bibliographies, lecture outlines, illustrative class activities, suggested experiments and field trips, sample examinations, and textbook preferences. These policy objectives may be incorporated as secondary school graduation or college admission requirements or they may cover each particular grade level. Although there will always be room to supplement the curriculum at the discretion of local officials, the intention will be to reduce choice and establish a predictable outcome.

Global convergence has also centralized the collection of comparative international educational data such as that available from UNESCO and its affiliated agencies, including the International Bureau of Education. Educational policymakers will continue to depend on this transnational data on student performance and school achievement to establish comparative benchmarks in their studies of international education.

PRIVATIZATION

Privatization and choice have become the rallying cries of conservative educational planners disappointed with the quality of public education and frustrated with increasingly liberal curricular approaches in public schools. It also represents one area in which education has become intensely politicized. Proponents of privatization seek to render schools more competitive and to provide parents with an expanded range of choices. They claim that educational monopolies tend to become less sensitive to the needs of its clients. A wide spectrum of proposals exist—some more radical and some less so. Advocates of moderate choice would restrict choice merely to the public sector or for a particular set of grades or for parents below a minimum income level. The more radical plans envisage a free market in which parents would receive vouchers with which they could shop around for schools in the public and private sector. Government might regulate such services and might subsidize it through vouchers, but it would not be involved in the educational marketplace.

TEACHER PROFESSIONALIZATION

Teacher professionalization is a major component of global reform movements. It has two dimensions. One is an effort to upgrade the quality of teachers by elevating entry standards. Policy debates on the most effective manner in which to achieve this objective revolves around the level of academic preparation and competency tests. Another trend in professionalization is to expand the range of decision-making permitted to teachers. In settings where teachers are permitted greater measure of discretion, they generally have greater responsibility for selecting curricular materials.

AT-RISK STUDENTS

In every country there exists an educational underclass of at-risk students, a counterpart of the social underclass of criminals and derelicts. Policymakers are concerned about keeping these students in school rather than out of it, with programs designed to combat drugs, delinquency, gangs, guns, and promiscuity. In many European countries, the children of illegal immigrants tend to resist assimilation into the national school systems. This is not strictly a school function, but represents a spillover of social anomie into education that needs to be addressed on a broad scale by sociologists, psychologists, and politicians.

COMPUTER NETWORKING IN EDUCATION

The use of computer networks in education beginning in the 1960s has transformed teaching and learning beyond the era in which print and oral instruction were the sole means of educational delivery. Various forms of computer networking (e-mail, bulletin boards, and electronic conferencing, to mention just a few) have been widely adopted by educators in all developed countries and some developing countries as a means of intensifying and supplementing traditional methods of pedagogy.

They also increase student interaction and peer collaboration both within and between classrooms.

Educational uses of computer networks can be traced to the late 1960s, while the application of e-mail networks for course activities and information exchange began in the early 1970s. Computer conferencing and bulletin board systems, first developed in the early 1970s, were used soon after for educational communications and, by 1981, computer conferencing was used for course delivery.

Computer networking as a classroom adjunct has been adopted at all levels of education. One of its earliest applications was the use of electronic mail to complement classroom activities. Computer conferencing and bulletin board systems were also adopted for information exchange and collaborative projects among learning peers, for sharing assignments, for communicating with the instructor, and for accessing expertise and resources. As early as 1969, Stanford University began delivering mathematics lessons to low-income students in Mississippi, Kentucky, and California via computer networks.

The networked classroom approach links classes in different geographical locations for information exchange and group activities. One of the earliest examples was a network of secondary schools linked by Dartmouth in 1969. The Inter-Cultural Learning Network (ICLN), implemented in 1983, used e-mail to link students in San Diego, California, with peers in Alaska, Japan, Mexico, Puerto Rico, and Israel. The Canadian RAPPI network in 1985-1987 linked school children and teachers in more than 70 regions in Canada, France, Italy, and the United Kingdom. Other examples of school-level networks are the National Geographic KIDSnet, the AT&T Learning Network, Australia's Computer Pals Across the World, and Japan's APICnet. University examples include European Campus 2000, and BESTnet and AFRInet, which link universities in the United States, Africa, Canada, and Latin America.

Since the mid-1980s, networks have been used by universities and adult education institutions to deliver credit and noncredit courses. As early as 1985, the Ontario Institute for Studies in Education (OISE) and the New York School for Social Research began to offer graduate level courses entirely online. Other institutions, such as those associated with the Virtual Classroom Project, developed the use of computer conferencing for undergraduate course delivery. Additionally, full degree or professional programs are offered entirely online.

Distance education institutions and programs use computer conferencing and networking in adjunct and full course delivery mode. The American Open University began using computer conferencing in 1984 to supplement learner-tutor communication and to provide a forum for group discussion. In 1989 the British Open University introduced the first mass-based distance education course that incorporated computer conferencing.

Networks are also used within a broader educational framework, not restricted to curriculum integration. Thousands of specialist forums and user groups support professional collaboration among teachers and educators and provide teacher education and enhancement. Electronic newsletters, special lecture seminars, workshops, formal courses, and other professional development activities are also available online.

Networks offer a variety of community education and support services. The Big Sky Telegraph Network, launched in Montana in 1988, serves rural schools. Public free-nets, such as the Cleveland Free Net, was established in 1986 as a free community computer service in areas such as health, education, technology, government, arts, recreation, and law. In addition, GeoNet supports a consortium of Electronic Village Halls throughout Europe.

The use of computer networking in education has been referred to variously as online education, the virtual classroom, and learning networks. It should be distinguished from other educational applications of computing, such as (1) computer-based or computer-assisted or computer-managed instruction in which a student is tutored by a computer; (2) computer programming in which a computer is instructed to carry out a particular task; and (3) the use of a computer as a tool in such applications, such as word processing or spreadsheets. These applications involve an individualized interaction between a student and a computer and do not facilitate communication among members of a learning community. Learning networks are characterized by human communication and function within an educational environment.

Networked learning shares some characteristics with the traditional face-to-face classroom. However, because the participants may be geographically separated, it also shares some common attributes with distance education. It is a new educational model that is independent of place and asynchronous in interaction among learners. Electronic mail networks support one-to-one (interpersonal) as well as one-to-many (broadcast) communication. Computer conferencing and some bulletin boards support both personal and broadcast modes, as well as group communications. In a group communication environment, topics are discussed, teachers introduce new subjects, and "spaces" are created to facilitate various types of learning activities. Students network with peers, experts, and mentors to ask questions, share information, and engage is discussion, debates, and collaborative work. They may undertake a joint research project, such as a short story or a newspaper. By using networks, students and teachers can form linkages with counterparts in other parts of the world with relative ease and access ideas and perspectives beyond their own locality. Networked learning is not only place-independent, it is also time-independent or asynchronous; class discussions and interaction can occur at any time, 24 hours a day, seven days a week.

Currently, most networks are text-based, although multimedia networking is becoming increasingly common. The text-based nature of learning encourages articulation and response, and the comments of participants encourage group interaction. The availability of a text-based archive provides a form of group memory and also encourages retrospective analysis.

One of the most critical factors in successful learning networks is designing applications. In network learning, just as in face-to-face learning, there is intervention by an expert (the instructor) who organizes the content, sequences the instructional activities, structures task and group interaction, and evaluates the process. Six main types of learning approaches are found in educational computer networks:

- *Ask an Expert,* which provides access to local or global experts in subject areas.

- *Mentorship* in which a professional online mentor in a particular subject area provides ongoing feedback until the apprentice masters the learning task, at which time the mentor "fades away."

- *Tutor Support* in which, in distance learning modes, tutors provide the primary source of instructional support.

- *Peer Interaction,* which may take various forms such as electronic pen pals; special interest group discussions, such as newsgroups; and social interaction, such a virtual café. Often interactions are initiated through public spaces and then move on to the exchange of personal e-mail messages.

- *Structured Group Activity,* which is a curriculum-based approach based on guided coaching. It may be long and structured or short and informal. It may include seminars, small group discussions, learning partnerships and dyads, small work groups, learning circles, simulations and role plays, and debating teams.

- *Access to Network Resources,* which includes global networks such as the Internet, to provide access to online databases and archives as well as thousands of special interest forums. Global networks facilitate communication across national boundaries and build cross-cultural bridges. The main problems in global network-based learning are differences in language and curricula as well as cultural perspectives.

Network learning is now established as a part of the global educational environment. Its popularity is due to a number of factors. The opportunity to control the pace, place, and time of participation is one. Moreover, such features as the opportunity to edit a message and the anonymity afforded by text-based communication encourage students to take a more active role in online discussions. Also, ideas and responses generated by group interaction promote the assimilation of new information and perspectives.

BASIC EDUCATION

While most of the developed world is concerned with the enhancement of the quality of education through technology, the developing world is still struggling with issues related to the provision of primary or basic education to its people. In the immediate post-World War II period, the term "basic" or "fundamental" education was conceived as a panacea to reduce illiteracy in low-income countries. However, the term became discredited in the 1960s and 1970s as a form of inferior education for "colonials." The term was reintroduced into educational discourse in the 1980s and now refers to whatever is necessary for the attainment of minimum knowledge, skills, and values. It covers early childhood education and preschool activities, the primary cycle, and adult literacy activities. Many writers use it as a synonym for primary education, with preprimary and adult education as extensions of basic education. UNESCO adopted this definition in its *Declaration of Human Rights,* which proclaimed universal primary education as one of inalienable rights of a human being.

A series of international UNESCO conferences in the 1960s led to a rapid expansion of universal primary (in many cases also free) education in all developing countries. Resources allotted to education increased beyond the UNESCO-recommended figure of 4 percent, and the gross enrollment ratio grew in some cases to greater than 100 percent. But having reached this plateau, national governments discovered that the simple fact that their citizens were receiving basic education did not have the kind of economic or social impact they had envisioned. They found growing maladjustments between their educational systems and the rapidly changing world around them. In short, basic education was not a panacea, but only a stage in national development. The growing imbalance between large cohorts of young people with secondary qualifications and their limited employment opportunities led to increased popular discontent and also created a lack of confidence in education itself.

Nevertheless, basic or primary education remains the rallying cry of educational planners in developing countries. The universal goal is a minimum literacy rate of 40 percent. The spread of formal primary education impacts development in a number of ways. Better-educated parents tend to have fewer children and to care for and feed their children better, thereby reducing child and infant mortality. They also tend to have aspirations to upward mobility; in particular, educated women want, and are able, to take jobs outside the home. Formal primary education also has an effect upon attitudes toward modernization in general and the use of modern farming practices and technology in particular. Studies have shown that farmers' productivity rates increased for every extra year of primary education. Primary education plays a more diffuse, but no less important, role in social terms and is considered a fundamental requirement for the efficient functioning of a democracy and for strengthening a national cultural identity. Many also see primary education as empowerment, giving a sense of civic rights and participation.

Four major themes have emerged in studies on basic education:

- Differential between the enrollment of boys and girls

- Defining literacy

- Relation between primary education and quality of education

- Basic education and quality of life.

Differential Between Enrollment of Boys & Girls: School enrollment, wastage, and absenteeism are related to class background, ethnicity, income, and gender. The most obvious bias, and the most easily quantifiable, is the differential in the enrollment rates of boys and girls. In developing countries, this is due to the significant contribution of female child labor in domestic work, the concern to control contacts between boys and girls, and the perception that women have nothing to gain from education in patrilineal societies where they are confined to the home. The perceived lack of benefits was accentuated when many countries introduced or raised school fees as part of their adjustment policies. Although the fees are

not large, they are high when considered as a percentage of the average income. If the cost requires the households to choose who is to receive additional schooling, girls suffer because they have fewer chances than boys to receive waged employment, and girls are often thought to be more useful at home.

Defining Literacy: The definition of basic education raises some problems because the primary cycle varies in length and quality between countries. Although universal primary education is generally required to be at least four years in length, students in many countries do not attain functional literacy in these four years. Thus, the provision of universal primary education in itself is no guarantee that literacy rates are advanced in the process.

Relation Between Primary Education & Quality of Education: Quality of education is best assessed by four measures: retentivity, outcome, educational services, and returns on human capital. The first measure, retentivity, is the extent to which schools retain students between the first and fourth years of schooling. There is a substantial dropout in the very first year in Africa and, to a lesser extent, in South America. In more than 50 percent of the countries for which data is available, fewer than 80 percent reach grade 4.

The second measure to assess education is outcome. In many countries, pass rates of examinations for entry to or departure from a particular cycle or transition rates from one level to another are internal to that system and do not indicate the quality of education provided or received. Studies by the International Association for the Evaluation of Educational Achievement suggest that "the quality of education in Sub-Saharan Africa is below world standards." At the same time, the studies show that the relative influence of the home background and socioeconomic circumstances is greater in the Third World than in the developed nations. The apparent importance of school quality relative to impoverished environment may simply be a consequence of social selective enrollment because the least motivated students simply do not attend school.

The third way to assess education measures the quality of educational services, such as textbooks, physical facilities, average class size, double shift teaching, and teacher training. Reduction in these basic services and resources leads to a fall-off in the quality of education.

The fourth way to assess education measures the returns on human capital invested in education. The rapid expansion in the basic education in the immediate post-World War II era was related to the notion that it was the means of social development. This belief was weakened when it was discovered that the number of jobs in the marketplace did not keep pace with the growth in enrollments. Economic betterment has ceased to be the primary motivation for education in many developing countries; it has also led to a "brain drain" in which the brightest graduates go abroad. The returns from employment, either at home or abroad, need to be sufficiently high to sustain the demand for education.

Basic Education & Quality of Life: Until the 1990s it was assumed that basic education has a contagious effect, that is, the presence of educated parents or siblings is sufficient motivation for children to pursue formal education. It has also been assumed that an education leads to a "better" life. Parents normally desire that their children should be better educated than themselves. The social demand for education thus builds up over generations, regardless of other circumstances. But this process obviously does not work well in developing countries because of the poor quality of educational services, as well as the lack of relevance of the school to the community or the job market. The drive toward universal primary education has diluted quality while increasing access. There are also the questions about whether the curriculum of basic education should be terminal or merely a stepping stone to the next level, whether native languages should be the language of instruction, and whether manual labor and/or vocational training should be emphasized in schools.

For many developing countries, attendance at school is a recent Western innovation without roots in local traditions. In most industrialized countries, the primary school is the main instrument of social integration for children, so formal schooling is almost universally accepted as having a fundamental value. This is not the case in many developing countries where the modern school is viewed as antagonistic to religious and secular traditional values.

EDUCATION OF WOMEN

Women's access to educational opportunities is markedly less in the majority of the world's countries— especially so in the developing world. This imbalance is demonstrated clearly in the gap between male and female adult literacy rates, which is more than 20 percentage points in more than 40 countries. The correlation of women's education and fertility is now well-established. The completion of primary education is the determining factor in the demographic transition, that is the transition from a high population and high fertility to low population and low fertility. The world of work is the other major area that has benefited from women's education. For women, literacy represents a liberation from the traditional life cycles to which they are consigned in patriarchal societies. Women and girls in poor countries are locked into a cycle of poverty and early marriages, with illiterate mothers bringing up illiterate daughters who are married off early into a repeat cycle.

In all developed countries, as well as in South America, the male-female disparities in enrollment ratios has effectively disappeared; indeed in many countries, in the second and third levels, the disparity is in favor of females. The only countries where the gap still persists are in Sub-Saharan Africa. In this region, less than one-half of all 6- to 11-year-old girls are in school. In South Asia, the relative figure is more than one-third, and in the Arab states, it is more than one-quarter. Among the in-school factors considered to have an important influence on the attendance of girls is the presence of female teachers, since parents in many countries are reluctant to allow their daughters to be taught by male teachers. The strategic importance of the teaching profession for the advancement of women has been underestimated by policymakers. In almost all countries, teaching is one of the few modern wage-paying occupations relatively free of discriminatory entry conditions for women.

While the concept that both sexes should have equal access to education has become universally accepted, there is more resistance to the concept that men and women should have access to the same types of education or fields of study. Even Western philosophies of education have stressed the separate and distinct nature of women's education, even when they acknowledge that women should be educated at all. At the first level, girls and boys learn pretty much the same things, in a coeducational setting. It is at the secondary level that significant differences emerge, and they become more pronounced at the postsecondary and higher levels.

There exist several international conventions bearing on the types of education offered to the two sexes. The first was the 1960 UNESCO Convention Against Discrimination in Education which, however, maintained that "the establishment or maintenance of separate educational systems or institutions for pupils of the two sexes does not constitute discrimination." Twenty years later, the UN Convention on the Elimination of All Forms of Discrimination Against Women added several important details regarding the process and content of education, especially curricula and examinations, stereotyped roles of men and women, career and vocational guidance, school programs and teaching methods, and sports and physical education. The 1989 UNESCO Convention on Technical and Vocational Education reaffirmed the injunctions against gender-based discrimination.

In most societies, social convention has emphasized gender-based specialization as well as a division of labor between men and women. The basic idea of a social and even biological preference for different types of education for the two sexes has never really disappeared from Western educational thinking. In every country for which data is available, the female share of enrollment in the natural sciences, engineering, and agriculture is less than the female share of the total enrollment in all fields, and the reverse is true in the humanities. The partitioning of sexes among fields of study is so well defined empirically that it would seem to constitute an iron law. Educational psychologists have not determined whether this is a reflection of social or institutional pressures, biologically determined abilities, or culturally determined gender segregation. Recent studies have explored to what extent motivation based on innate abilities rather than discrimination influences subject choices of boys and girls that eventually lead to employment and career paths. That boys and girls behave differently in class, whether in single-sex settings or in coeducational ones, is now well established. In coeducational settings girls typically are observed to be less aggressive than boys in demanding the teacher's attention. Any effort to ensure equality of educational opportunities for girls must grapple with this dilemma in pedagogical as well as psychological terms.

Foreign Students in Tertiary Education: The international or cross-cultural dimension of higher education has grown steadily since the end of World War II. Such growth has enhanced the dominance of Western educational ideas and practices since most of the flow is from developing nations to developed nations. It has also fueled what is known as the "brain drain," since a vast majority of students stay and seek jobs in the host country after completion of their studies. The phenomenon is another aspect of the growing globalization of higher education, but one in which the benefits are unevenly distributed.

A relatively small number of countries enroll the vast majority of foreign students. The United States is the largest host country accounting for 32 percent of the total, followed by the United Kingdom with 16 percent, Germany with 13 percent, France with 11 percent, and Australia with 8 percent. These five receiving countries account for more 80 percent of all foreign students. The rise of English as the global *lingua franca* is responsible for the fact that three English-speaking countries account for more than half of the total. In 1998, some 1.31 million foreign students enrolled in OECD (Organisation for Economic Co-operation and Development) countries, representing all advanced nations. The largest proportion (44 percent) of foreign students is from Asia—led by Japan, Korea, China, Malaysia, and India.

The patterns of student cross-national mobility can be attributed to a variety of push and pull factors, such as language, the academic reputation of particular institutions or programs, the limitations of higher education in the home country, financial incentives, and so on. These patterns also reflect geographical and historical links between countries, future job opportunities, immigration policies, and the presence of co-nationals. The transparency and flexibility of courses and requirements for degrees also count in the choice of institutions.

CONCLUSION

Structured informal educational systems, as we know it, are about 1,000 years old. The second millennium surely will transform them dramatically in every country of the world. Globalization will invigorate both the theory and practice of pedagogy on the one hand and the institutional structures on the other. The *World Education Encyclopedia* provides the backdrop against which these great changes will take place.

—George T. Kurian

A

AFGHANISTAN

BASIC DATA

Official Country Name:	Islamic State of Afghanistan
Region:	East & South Asia
Population:	25,838,797
Language(s):	Pashtu, Afghan Persian (Dari), Uzbek, Turkmen, Balochi, Pashai
Literacy Rate:	31.5%
Compulsory Schooling:	6 years
Educational Enrollment:	Primary: 1,312,197 Secondary: 497,762 Higher: 24,333
Educational Enrollment Rate:	Primary: 49% Secondary: 22%
Teachers:	Secondary: 17,548 Higher: 1,342
Student-Teacher Ratio:	Primary: 58:1 Secondary: 28:1
Female Enrollment Rate:	Primary: 32% Secondary: 12%

HISTORY & BACKGROUND

The Islamic State of Afghanistan is located in South Central Asia. Afghanistan's population was estimated at 26.7 million in 2000, making it South Central Asia's fifth largest populated country, as well as its fifth largest land area (251,772 square miles).

Afghanistan is a land-locked country surrounded by Pakistan and India to the east, Iran to the west, Turkmenistan and Uzbekistan to the north, and Tajikistan and China to the northeast. The Hindu Kush mountain range, with its world-famous Khyber Pass, peaks at about 24,000 feet (7,315 meters). The country's land-locked status played significant roles throughout centuries of historical and social development when invading forces sought control over Asian trading routes and populations.

The people of Afghanistan are called Afghans, although the term originally referred to the country's largest ethnic group, the Pashtuns, who comprised about 38 percent of the 2000 population. The remaining ethnic groups were Tajik (25 percent), Hazara (19 percent) and Uzbek (6 percent). Other ethnic groups, such as Aimaks, Turkmen, and Balochs, comprised the remaining 12 percent. While many Afghans were bilingual, about 50 percent of the population primarily spoke Pashtu, 35 percent spoke Afghan Persian (Dari), and another 11 percent spoke Turkic languages (primarily Uzbek and Turkmen).

The Islamic religion was the tie that bound Afghanistan's ethnically and linguistically diverse population. About 99 percent of Afghans were Muslim, with Sunni Muslim being the dominant sect (84 percent) and Shi'a Muslim being the second largest (15 percent). Since about 80 percent of Afghanistan's population lived outside its cities, religion and kinship formed the basis of most social circles in the male-dominated society.

Political, social, and economic chaos overwhelmed Afghanistan at the close of the twentieth century and continued to plague the war-beleaguered nation into 2001. About one-third of the population fled the country when Russia invaded in 1979—occupying it until anticommunist Islamic Afghan ethnic groups joined forces to expel Russian forces in 1989. During Russian occupation more than 2.5 million people fled to Pakistan, another 1.9 million to Iran, and some 150,000 fled to the United States and other countries. According to the United Nations, at the end of the twentieth century, Afghans were the largest refugee population in the world.

Due to the combination of more than twenty years of civil strife and severe drought conditions, Afghanistan had one of the lowest living standards in the world by 1999 with per person gross national product estimated at US$800. In addition, the country's infant mortality rate (149.7) was the world's third highest, and its overall life expectancy (46 years) was the sixteenth lowest in 2000. Significantly, Afghan women suffered the greatest personal loss of freedom during the latter decades of the twentieth century after the controlling Taliban government placed strict prohibitions on their roles, forbidding them from working or attending schools outside their homes or from interacting with unrelated males.

Prior to the onset of civil war, slightly more than two-thirds of Afghanistan's labor force was employed in agriculture, and about one-half of its gross domestic product was agricultural. In 1996 the country exported $80 million worth of fruit, nut, hand woven carpet, wood, cotton, hides, and pelts as well as precious and semi-precious gem products. Afghanistan's largest export product however, was opium. In fact, according to the U.S. Central Intelligence Agency, Afghanistan was the world's largest producer of illicit opium in 1999. The major political factions accumulated profits from the illegal drug trade.

Although Afghanistan experienced invasions by other civilizations—most notably Alexander the Great (328 B.C.), Genghis Khan (1219 B.C.), Tamerlane (late fourteenth century), and Babur (early sisteenth century)—none of them transformed Afghan society to the extent of the Arabic invasion that brought the Islamic religion to the region in the mid-seventh century. By the end of the ninth century, most Afghans converted to Sunni Islam replacing Buddhism, Hinduism, Zorastrianism, and other religions of previous empires, invaders, and indigenous groups. Even with the wholesale adoption of the Islamic faith, however, Afghanistan remained a loosely organized tribal society until a tribal council elected Ahmad Shah Durrani, a Pashtun, as king in 1747, formally establishing the country and its monarchy.

From 1747 until 1978, all of Afghanistan's rulers were from Durrani's Pashtun extended tribe and, after 1818, all were members of that tribe's Mohammadzai clan. The last member of the Pashtun tribal royal family to rule Afghanistan was Sardar Mohammad Daud, former prime minister and a cousin of King Zahir Shah (who reigned from 1933 to 1973). Daud seized power in a bloodless military coup in 1973. Daud abolished the monarchy, abrogated King Zahir's 1964 constitution, and declared himself the first president and prime minister of the Afghanistan ''republic.''

In April 1978 members of the communist-inspired People's Democratic Party of Afghanistan (PDPA) overthrew Daud, killing him and most of his family. The PDPA attempted to institute broad communist-inspired social reforms that contradicted many deeply held Islamic traditions. Many of PDPA's changes were brutally imposed. Thousands of traditional, religious, and intellectual leaders were tortured, imprisoned, or murdered during the PDPA reign.

In September 1979, Hafizullah Amin seized power, thus igniting further rebellion. Amin refused to heed Soviet advice on how to stabilize the country and its government so, in December 1979, Russia invaded (killing Amin) and installed Babrak Karmal as prime minister. Even with substantial Russian support, however, the Karmal regime was only able to establish limited control in the area surrounding the capital city of Kabul.

CONSTITUTIONAL & LEGAL FOUNDATIONS

In 2000 Afghanistan did not have a constitution, legislative branch, or legal system. The loosely organized political factions tacitly agreed that they would follow Islamic law through local Shari'a (Islamic) courts. The country's 29 provincial governments bore the brunt of responsibility for maintaining and delivering the limited governmental services intermittently available during war years. Afghanistan's lack of central government and related infrastructure at the beginning of 2001 could be traced to the Taliban's keenly agile response to Russia's folly.

To begin with, Russia's ten-year attempt (1979-1989) at dominating Afghanistan was trouble-filled not only because most Afghans opposed any foreign non-Islamic control but also because Afghanistan society was so loosely knit. Centralized governments are easier to topple than scattered governing councils who are able to put forth new leaders almost at will. Afghan freedom fighters—with weapons and training supplied by the United States and other countries—were able to rally the country's many political parties into an allied resistance against the Russian supported Karmal. In 1986 Muhammad Najibullah, the former head of the Afghan secret police, replaced Karmal. But, Najibullah's administration also depended upon Russian support and could not broaden its base of support into Afghanistan society. By 1988 the governments of Pakistan and Afghanistan, with the United States and the Soviet Union serving as guarantors, signed an agreement that settled disagreements between the neighboring countries. The agreement also included the full withdrawal of Russian troops by February 1989 and noninterference in Afghanistan's internal affairs by either Russia or the United States.

The Afghan freedom fighters were not parties to the international agreement, so they refused to accept its terms. War between Afghan factions escalated but Najibullah remained in control until March 1992 when his general, Abdul Rashid Dostman, and Uzbek militia defected. Subsequently, Afghan freedom fighter groups agreed to establish an "Islamic Interim Government" to assume power under the leadership of Professor Sibghatullah Mojaddedi of the Afghanistan National Liberation Front political party for three months. Then, a ten-member leadership council was to be formed under the Islamic Society political party's leader, Professor Burhanuddin Rabbani, for another three months after which time a grand council of Afghan elders and leaders was to convene to designate an interim administration to hold power for up to one year pending elections. When Rabbani prematurely formed his leadership council, Mojaddedi surrendered. Rabbani was elected president of the new leadership council, but fighting between the various political factions continued. In 1993 two accords, the Islamabad naming Gulbuddin Hekmatyar as prime minister and the Jalalabad calling for disarmament, were signed but both failed to bring lasting peace.

In 1994 an unknown fundamentalist Islamic group, the Taliban (Religious Students Movement), most of whom had been exiled, educated and trained in Pakistan, appeared in the southeastern city of Kandahar. The Taliban movement spread rapidly throughout southern Afghanistan and gathered steam when oppositional groups surrendered their arms. In fact, entire provinces surrendered to the movement with very little resistance. By 1995 the majority of the country, including the capital city of Kabul were under Taliban control. In 1996 the Taliban declared itself the legitimate government. At that time the Taliban renamed the country the "Islamic Emirate of Afghanistan."

According to a United Nations Educational, Scientific, and Cultural Organization (UNESCO) report, Afghans supported the Taliban because they appeared to offer freedom from the war-ravaged years of fighting between the various freedom fighter power factions. But, apparent disillusionment with the Taliban set in as their severe interpretation of Islamic law; strict enforcement of keeping women in seclusion and restrictions on female education and employment became more widely apparent. Consequently, the Taliban were unable to firmly establish centralized government controlling all provincial areas of the country. The UN continued to recognize Burhanuddin Rabbani as president and Gulbuddin Hekmatyar as prime minister of Afghanistan in 2000. Also, the Organization of the Islamic Conference left Afghanistan's seat vacant until the legitimacy of its government could be resolved through negotiations among the warring parties.

EDUCATIONAL SYSTEM—OVERVIEW

Unfortunately, Afghanistan's system of formal education, like that of its central government, was in complete disarray by the year 2000. Without a national authority overseeing the distribution of educational funds and program implementation, the level of schooling varied greatly across the country. Any sort of national philosophy ensuring pupil participation, in even the most basic schooling, was virtually nonexistent by the end of the twentieth century. For example, even though Afghanistan's policy of free education was compulsory for children aged 7 to 13, only 22 percent of the country's "school-aged" children were actually attending schools in 1996.

While it is certainly true that the long term effects of Afghanistan's civil war depleted nearly all community resources that might have been available for the critically important function of education, Afghanistan had one of the lowest standards of education in the modern world—even prior to the Russian invasion. Indeed, according to research conducted by the World Education Forum (WEF), by 1980 only 11 percent of the country's population over the age of 25 had any formal schooling and less than one percent had completed primary school.

Even though, as the result of two war decades, Afghanistan's centralized educational infrastructure was nonexistent in 2000, sporadic educational services were provided at local levels whenever and wherever war conditions permitted. Due to the sporadic nature of Afghanistan's provincial education services, consistent and reliable enrollment data was difficult to obtain. The reliability of enrollment data was complicated by the fact that the last official census was conducted in the pre-war years so that all population numbers were estimated. Furthermore, enrollment figures were based on percentage estimates provided by local groups, not upon actual counts. UNESCO collected the most reliable sets of data as part of the WEF program. UNESCO data was collected using "International Standard Classifications of Education" (ISCED). The ISCED terminology replaced older educational terms such as "first," "second," and "third" levels with primary, secondary, and tertiary, respectively.

UNESCO reported there were two types of education providers in Afghanistan in 1999: provincial directorates and nongovernmental organizations, particularly international humanitarian relief agencies such as the United Nations Children's Fund (UNICEF). Taliban-induced law and order did return some degree of stability to the country in the late 1990s, and the number of schools increased dramatically from 2,633 in 1990 to 3,084 in 1999. In 1990 agencies operated 2,044 (77.6 percent) of Afghanistan's schools and provincial director-

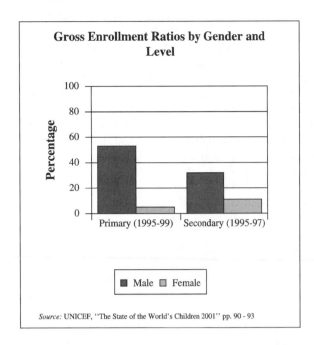

Gross Enrollment Ratios by Gender and Level

Source: UNICEF, "The State of the World's Children 2001" pp. 90 - 93

547, but the number of schools operating in the eastern region increased to 828, to 652 in the southern region, to 449 in the western region, and to 608 in the central region. In 1999 UNICEF estimated that 53 percent of the population lived in central and northern regions, which only had 38 percent of the total number of schools.

Student/teacher ratios were also based on estimates. In schools operated by the provincial directorates, estimates were that class sizes ranged from 13 to 104 students, with an average of 50 students per teacher. In schools operated by humanitarian relief agencies, class sizes ranged from 12 to 51 students, with an average of 30 students per teacher.

PREPRIMARY & PRIMARY EDUCATION

Preprimary education programs were implemented in Afghanistan in 1980. By 1990 the country had 195 centers providing such childcare services. The programs covered children between the ages of three to five. But, by 1999 only one remained open. In effect the 1980's decade of gains in early childhood development program halted and it essentially collapsed.

In spite of the uneven distribution of schools, UNESCO reported that primary schools did operate in all provinces in 1990. Afghanistan's compulsory primary education program generally began at age seven and included six years of schooling. The primary education program took six years (ages seven to twelve).

UNESCO reported that only 35 percent of school-aged boys and 19 percent of school-aged girls were attending primary schools in 1990. The percentage of school-aged boys increased to 46 percent in 1993 and 63 percent in 1995 but declined again to 53 percent in 1999. The percentage of school-aged girls declined in 1993 to 16 percent but increased in 1995 to 32 percent. However, reflecting Taliban prohibitions, by 1999 the percentage of females attending primary schools dramatically declined to only five percent.

Since both the provision of primary educational programs and actual attendance varied so greatly across the country and because supplies and textbooks were in extremely short supply, UNESCO reported that primary educational training focused on literacy and "knowledge about life" during the war years. Teachers provided lessons verbally; students memorized the lessons and recited them back.

In the early war-years, an American University study found that elementary education textbooks in the 1980s were available in all the major languages because the government's stated policy was that all children should be able to learn in their native language.

ates operated 589 (22.4 percent). In 1999 provincial directorates operated 2,015 schools (65.3 percent) and agencies operated 1,069 (34.7 percent).

The main reason agencies operated far fewer schools in Afghanistan in 1999 than they did in 1990 was because UNICEF suspended its assistance to formal education programs in areas under Taliban control after the Taliban issued its 1995 edict prohibiting the education of females. UNICEF did continue supporting schools where equal access was available and in the informal network of home-based schools. In fact, in 1999 agencies were the main provider of education for girls operating 407 (91 percent) of the 446 girls schools. Provincial directorates operated 1,959 (74.7 percent) of the 2,621 boys schools operating in 1999. The ratio of boys' to girls' schools operated by the government's provincial directorates was 50:1 in 1999. The ratio of boys' to girls' schools operated by agencies in 1999 was 1.6:1.

Access to education was severely limited by the availability of schools and the distribution of Afghanistan's population. UNICEF recorded the number of schools operating in five Afghanistan regions: northern, eastern, southern, western, and central in 1990 and in 1999. During the 1990 to 1999 period, the distribution of schools in Afghanistan changed considerably with the number of schools increasing in every region but the northern region. In 1990 there were 739 schools operating in the northern region, 445 operating in the eastern region, 234 in the southern region, 198 in the western region, and 586 in the central region. In 1999 the number of schools operating in the northern region declined to

SECONDARY EDUCATION

Secondary level education (ages 13 to 18) was not compulsory and appeared to be less widely available (if at all) than primary education and nonformal education programs. Although elementary schools were located throughout the country, secondary schools were generally located only in larger cities.

HIGHER EDUCATION

Prior to the war years, Afghanistan had two universities, Kabul University and the University of Nangarhar in Jalabad. Kabul University had been a respected learning center, and its medical faculty was largely responsible for the opening of the University of Nangarhar in 1962. In addition to the two universities, in 1983 there were also seven professional and technical universities.

ADMINISTRATION, FINANCE, & EDUCATIONAL RESEARCH

Given that Afghanistan did not have a centralized educational authority in 2000, no information was available about educational administration or educational research. It appeared that those schools operating in 2000 were organized by local efforts without general, much less financial, support of the Taliban government. The only available information about Afghanistan's educational funding indicated that 87.6 percent of funds were allocated to primary education in 1990. The remaining 12.4 percent was allocated to tertiary education. However, no actual dollar amounts were reported.

Based upon UNESCO definitions of educational programs, it must be assumed that secondary educational programs were not funded in 1990. Further, tertiary education programs probably included nonformal education programs such as vocational training (including teacher training).

NONFORMAL EDUCATION

Only 3 of the 29 provincial directorates (Kabul, Paktya, and Logar) operated nonformal education programs for the out-of-school population. Twelve of the twenty-five nongovernmental relief agencies operated informal education centers. In combination, the provincial directorates and the relief agencies operated informal education centers in 12 of the 29 provinces in 1999.

Both agency and provincial directorates offered gender segregated as well as gender mixed training facilities. Some of the programs only accepted children under the age of 15 who had dropped out of school. Others enrolled persons over the age of 15.

Nonformal education programs were generally of two types, literacy and skill development. The literacy

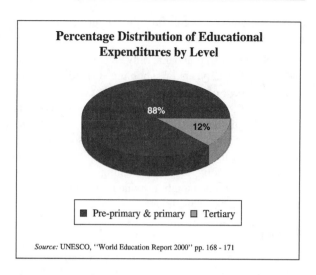

Percentage Distribution of Educational Expenditures by Level

88%

12%

■ Pre-primary & primary □ Tertiary

Source: UNESCO, ''World Education Report 2000'' pp. 168 - 171

program usually lasted six months. Upon completing the literacy program, students could progress to trade apprenticeships lasting from 6 to 18 months. Apprenticeship training programs included bicycle repair, carpentry, shoe making, radio repair, candle making, baking, tailoring, embroidery, welding, watch repair, soap making, vehicle painting, and radio and television repair.

TEACHING PROFESSION

According to the World Education Forum (WEF) the teaching profession was considered a low status occupation in Afghanistan society. An appalling fact of the Afghanistan wars was that thousands of teachers were assassinated and even more assaulted by the warring factions. Accordingly, teacher recruitment was extremely difficult, salaries were very low, and teachers were often not paid for their work. The number of Afghanistan teachers dropped 10.7 percent—from 30,502 in 1979 to 27,230 in 1999. Further, the percentage of female teachers dropped from 59.2 percent in 1990 to 10 percent in 1999.

When UNESCO conducted its study of Afghanistan education, published documents pertaining to the qualifications of Afghanistan's teaching profession could not be located. However, UNESCO did collect its own data that indicated while a national system of teachers colleges existed prior to the Russian invasion, no formal teacher training programs were in existence by 2000. Under the defunct program, teachers received 2 years of preparation in addition to the 12 years of primary and secondary education in order to become academically qualified to teach. In effect, ''academically qualified to teach'' in the Afghanistan context equated to two years of postsecondary classes (college or university) in the U.S. context. In 1999 only 18.8 percent of Afghanistan's male teachers were academically qualified (according to Afghanistan standards) and only 13.8 percent of the female teachers were academically qualified.

UNESCO also found that only 28 percent of teachers had completed 12 years of schooling. Effectively, more than 50 percent of Afghanistan's teachers had not completed the U.S. equivalent of high school (postsecondary school). To fill the void in teacher training programs, humanitarian relief agencies were providing some training courses targeting teachers who had completed less than 12 years of schooling. Agency training courses, ranging from one day to one month, provided training in elementary school teaching methods.

SUMMARY

Even though Afghanistan's policy of free education was compulsory for children aged 7 to 13, only 22 percent of the country's ''school-aged'' children were actually attending schools in 1996. In 1997 UNESCO estimated that 50.8 percent of males and 80.6 percent of females over the age of 15 were illiterate.

The effects of war upon a society are unimaginable to those who have not lived through one. The fact that any educational training took place in Afghanistan during the 1980s and 1990s is testament to the courage and indomitable human spirit of the families and teachers of the provincial directorates and humanitarian relief agencies who were courageous enough to continue teaching and learning. When political, economic, and social stability are returned to Afghanistan—no matter the leadership directing the country—it will take the efforts of all Afghans, men and women, girls and boys, for generations to come, to raise the country out of illiteracy and into a higher standard of living.

BIBLIOGRAPHY

The Central Intelligence Agency (CIA). *The World Factbook 2000.* Directorate of Intelligence, 1 January 2000. Available from http://www.cia.gov/.

Giustozzi, Antonio. *War, Politics, and Society in Afghanistan 1978-1992.* London: Hurst & Company, 2000.

Matinuddin, Kamal. *The Taliban Phenomenon: Afghanistan 1994-1997.* Pakistan: Oxford University Press, 1999.

Nyrop, Richard F., and Donald M. Seekins, eds. *Afghanistan: A Country Study.* The American University, 1986.

Population Reference Bureau. ''World Population Data Sheet.'' Washington, DC, 2000.

United Nations Children's Fund. *The Progress of Nations 2000,* New York: Division of Communication, Division of Evaluation, Policy and Planning, 2000.

United Nations Educational, Scientific, and Cultural Organization. *World Education Report 2000: The Right to Education (Towards education for all throughout life).* New York: UNESCO Publishing, 2000.

World Education Forum. *The EFA 2000 Assessment: Country Reports, Afghanistan.* New York: United Nations Educational, Scientific, and Cultural Organization, 2000.

—*Sandra J. Callaghan*

ALBANIA

BASIC DATA

Official Country Name:	Republic of Albania
Region:	Europe
Population:	3,490,435
Language(s):	Albanian, Greek
Literacy Rate:	93%
Academic Year:	September-June
Number of Primary Schools:	1,782
Compulsory Schooling:	8 years
Public Expenditure on Education:	3.1%
Educational Enrollment:	Primary: 558,101
	Secondary: 89,895
	Higher: 34,257
Educational Enrollment Rate:	Primary: 107%
	Secondary: 38%
	Higher: 12%
Teachers:	Primary: 31,369
	Secondary: 6,321
	Higher: 2,348
Student-Teacher Ratio:	Primary: 18:1
	Secondary: 17:1
Female Enrollment Rate:	Primary: 108%
	Secondary: 38%
	Higher: 14%

HISTORY & BACKGROUND

The Republic of Albania is a southeastern European country on the Adriatic Sea bordered by Greece, Macedonia, Serbia, and Montenegro. Albania occupies an area of 28,752 square kilometers (11,101 square miles). Except for the coastline, the terrain is rugged and mountainous. Forests and woodlands comprise nearly 40 percent of the country. Approximately 21 percent of the nation is arable land. Principal natural resources include petroleum, natural gas, coal, chromium, copper, timber, nickel, and hydropower. Throughout the twentieth century, Albania remained one of the poorest and least developed nations in Europe. Rail service did not exist until 1948. In 2000 the per capita GDP was approximately $1,300 compared to $13,000 in neighboring Greece.

The population in 2000 was estimated at 3.5 million, 98 percent of whom are ethnic Albanians making the country one of the most homogenous nations in the world. The national language is Albanian, a blend of two historic dialects, Gheg and Tosk. The literacy rate is estimated at 98 percent. The population is 70 percent Muslim, 20 percent Albanian Orthodox, and 10 percent Roman Catholic. Mosques and churches reopened in 1990, having been closed in 1967 by the former Communist government. In the 1990s an estimated 300,000 Albanians (10 percent of the population) emigrated with the majority seeking employment in Greece and Italy.

Prior to the twentieth century, Albania was subject to foreign domination. Albanian culture and language were suppressed during a 400-year occupation by the Turks. Albanian language schools were not permitted until the 1880s. During the Balkan War of 1912, Albania declared its independence from the Ottoman Empire but remained a feudal society plagued by pervasive poverty, blood feuds, epidemics, and widespread illiteracy.

In 1939 Italy annexed Albania. Following Italy's surrender to the Allies in 1943, German troops briefly occupied the country. In 1944 Enver Hoxha, a former school teacher and General Secretary of the Communist Party, assumed power and ruled Albania until his death in 1985.

Hoxha's rigidly Stalinist regime was determined to transform Albania from a traditional agrarian society into an industrialized socialist state. All lands and properties were seized by the government. Private ownership was so restricted that Albanians were prohibited from owning personal automobiles until 1991. The Directorate of State Security, the Sigurimi, ruthlessly suppressed dissent. State enterprises were highly centralized. Aided by the Soviets, the government drained swamps, opened vocational schools, built roads, and constructed factories. Despite these accomplishments and an improvement in the general standard of living, Albania remained impoverished and largely dependent on economic aid, advisors, and beneficial trade agreements supplied by other Communist countries.

Refusing to alter Albania's ideological course, Hoxha became successively disillusioned with Communist countries that departed from orthodox Marxist-Leninism. In 1948 he broke relations with neighboring Yugoslavia when Tito rejected Moscow's leadership. In 1961 he severed relations with the Soviet Union, objecting to Khrushchev's de-Stalinization policy. Albania then aligned itself with the People's Republic of China, becoming its sole ally throughout the 1960s. In the 1970s Hoxha denounced China for resuming diplomatic relations with the West. In response, China terminated all trade and economic aid to Albania in 1978. Hoxha, devoid of allies, pursued an isolationist program, maintaining Albania as a bastion of xenophobic Stalinism into the 1980s.

Hoxha's successor Ramiz Alia sought to preserve the Communist system while liberalizing its administration. He opened Albania to foreign investors, expanded diplomatic relations with the West, allowed Albanians to travel abroad, restored religious freedom, and limited the actions of the Sigurimi. But as other Communist governments collapsed throughout Eastern Europe in 1989, Alia recognized the need for change. In 1990 he endorsed the creation of independent political parties, ending 45 years of Communist monopoly. In 1991 Albania restored diplomatic relations with the United States.

In 1992 the Democratic Party won a decisive electoral victory. The new government launched a number of reforms intending to integrate Albania into the European economy. Decades of isolation, however, prevented Albania from developing the social, technological, and educational institutions needed to participate in the free market. The collapse of its highly centralized system caused a severe depression. In 1997 hundreds of thousands of Albanians lost their savings in failed pyramid schemes. In the ensuing unrest, approximately 1,500 Albanians were killed. In 1999 nearly 500,000 ethnic Albanians, victims of ethnic cleansing in Kosovo, sought refuge in Albania, further straining the country's resources. The turmoil in Kosovo, however, focused international attention on Albania, spurring greater interest in assistance and exchange programs.

Albania's educational system reflects the nation's history. The Communist regime saw education as an essential instrument in building a socialist state. The 1946 Communist constitution placed all schools under state authority. The Education Reform Law of 1946 dictated that Marxist-Leninist principles would permeate all textbooks and made the eradication of illiteracy a primary objective of the new school system. In addition to providing seven years of compulsory education and four years of secondary education, the law called for a network of vocational and teacher training schools. In 1949 the government passed a law requiring all illiterate citizens between the ages of 12 and 40 to attend classes in reading and writing. Local people's councils developed special courses for peasants and the armed forces developed similar classes for illiterate military personnel. These compulsory programs were highly successful, raising the literacy rate from an estimated 20 percent in 1945 to more than 95 percent by the mid-1980s. In addition the Hoxha government fused elements of the Gheg and Tosk dialects to create a common language. Though previously denied education, girls were given equal access to all levels of schooling.

In the early 1950s Soviet advisors played a major role in developing Albania's educational system. Schools, vocational programs, and teacher training were modeled on Soviet examples. Following Albania's break with the Soviet Union, Russian elements in the nation's schools were purged. In the 1960s the school system was reorganized into four categories: preschool, a general eight-year program, secondary, and higher education. The eight-year program stressed Marxist ethics and values. Vocational programs placed emphasis on producing highly skilled technical workers. Graduate students were required to complete a nine-month probationary period in industrial production and three months military training.

The democratically elected government views education as important in helping Albania end its cultural, political, and economic isolation and participate in the European economy. The Ministry of Education is seeking, despite the nation's lack of resources, to improve the quality of schools, introduce new teaching methods, and open intellectual discourse with the rest of the world.

CONSTITUTIONAL & LEGAL FOUNDATIONS

In 1998 Albania adopted a new constitution. The Ministry of Education oversees education in Albania and facilitates international cooperation and exchanges in higher education.

The ministry's Higher Education Department reviews foreign credentials. Although Albanian educators and international advisors see a need for greater decentralization, the Ministry of Education retains a high degree of central authority. The Ministry of Education intends to bring Albanian educational standards in line with those of developed European nations.

EDUCATIONAL SYSTEM—OVERVIEW

In the 1990s Albania's educational system underwent major structural reforms as the country struggled to emerge from a half century of isolation and rigid central-

ization. However, efforts to modernize and democratize education have been hampered by the lack of resources, political conflict, and ethnic violence. In 1991 the minister of education reported that nearly one-third of the nation's schools had been vandalized and 15 buildings razed. Underpaid teachers relocated from villages, leaving hundreds of rural schools severely understaffed. Approximately 2,000 teachers fled the country.

Albanian reformers, however, have devoted much of the country's limited education budget to improve instruction, textbooks, and school buildings. Educational exchange programs with other countries have introduced Albanian teachers to European and North American methods and technology.

The educational system consists of preschool (ages 3 to 6), an eight-year compulsory program combining primary (ages 6 to 10) and secondary (ages 11 to 14), and high school (ages 14 to 18). University studies have three levels: the *diplome,* awarded after three to six years of preparation, depending on the discipline; the *Kandidat i Shkencave* degree, awarded after two to three years of post-graduate education; and the *Doktor i Shkencave* degree, granted on the basis of publication, research, and a dissertation.

PREPRIMARY & PRIMARY EDUCATION

Albania has eight years of compulsory education, which begins at age six. Some 59 percent of the nation's preschoolers attend 3,400 kindergartens. There are approximately 1,500 primary schools serving students aged 6 to 10. The 1,700 secondary schools provide education for students aged 11 to 14. Most primary schools, especially in rural areas, are in poor condition and inadequately staffed. Basic supplies, such as books and chalk, are in critically short supply.

SECONDARY EDUCATION

About 70 percent of Albanian children continue their education by attending high school. The objective of the nation's 500 high schools is to prepare students for university education. Due to economic and social instability, however, enrollment rates have fallen since 1990. Traditional vocational and technical programs are obsolete, educational resources inadequate, and classrooms crowded. Conditions in rural areas are especially poor. The government is concerned that if the current 5 percent a year dropout rate continues, the literacy rate may decline.

HIGHER EDUCATION

Albania's institutions of higher learning were founded in the 1950s and were patterned on Soviet designs. The Higher Pedagogic Institute, Higher Polytechnical Institute, and Higher Agricultural Institute were founded in 1951. A team of Soviet educators developed the administration and curriculum of Enver Hoxha University (now the University of Tirana) in 1957. All these highly centralized institutions were greatly influenced by Soviet practices. Although Soviet influence declined markedly after 1960, higher education remained highly politicized. In addition to attending classes, students were required to work in factories or on collective farms. Access to higher education was generally limited to the children of party members.

Today some 27,000 students are enrolled in Albania's six universities: Tirana, Shkoder, Korca, Vlora, Gjirokaster, and Elbasan. Other students attend institutes and academies, including Tirana's fine arts academy. Institutions of higher learning charge tuition though fees are based on family income. In the mid-1990s Albanian students began to study abroad in large numbers—breaking 60 years of intellectual and cultural isolation.

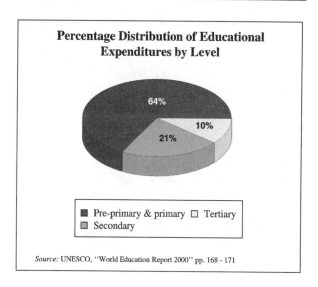

Percentage Distribution of Educational Expenditures by Level

- ■ Pre-primary & primary   □ Tertiary
- ■ Secondary

Source: UNESCO, "World Education Report 2000" pp. 168 - 171

ADMINISTRATION, FINANCE, & EDUCATIONAL RESEARCH

During the Communist era, the administration of education was noted for its high degree of centralization and strict adherence to ideological principles outlined by the party leadership. Since 1991 the democratically elected government has initiated a number of reforms. In 1995 a law was passed that stipulated the importance of civic education to instill democratic values.

Educational research is conducted by the Pedagogical Research Institute. Officials from the Ministry of Education, teachers, and administrators from the Textbook Publishing House have been sent to other nations to research modern educational methods and policies. New textbooks and teachers' manuals have been prepared. Still, limited budgets and the nation's economic instability hamper widespread reform.

NONFORMAL EDUCATION

Albania's nonformal education offerings are limited. Part-time education is available through correspondence courses. Employment-related continuing education courses are offered to diploma-holders with two years of related work experience. Students completing these courses are given a certificate. Albania's lack of resources has restricted the availability of distance learning and alternative delivery systems.

TEACHING PROFESSION

From 1945 to 1992, the teaching profession was disciplined along Communist party guidelines. Courses for teacher preparation stressed Marxist concepts of psychol-

ogy and pedagogy. Teachers were trained to use didactic teaching methods. Individuality and interaction were discouraged. Teachers were viewed as instruments for political indoctrination. After 1992 the Ministry of Education began to encourage teachers to use alternative instructional methods and introduce democratic principles into the curriculum.

Teachers in nursery schools and kindergartens must complete four years at the pedagogical middle school to receive a certificate and the title of educator. Primary school teachers in lower grades must complete three years at a higher education institution. Teachers in upper grades are required to have four years of academic preparation, education courses, and practice training. Secondary school teachers must complete four years in an academic discipline in addition to education courses and practice teaching.

Professors in higher education must hold a degree of Doctor in Sciences and have a background of extensive research and publishing. Docents are experienced instructors or researchers with a Candidate of Sciences degree. Pedagogues and assistants hold diplomas with excellent grades.

SUMMARY

Like many emerging democracies, Albania views education as central to building a new society that can compete in the twenty-first century. Its movement from a totalitarian regime to a democratic society has been hampered by economic and political instability.

BIBLIOGRAPHY

Albania, February 2001. Available from http://countrywatch.altavista.com/.

Albania: Land of the Eagles. *Education,* February 2001. Available from http://www.albania.co.uk/.

Euro Education Net. *Structure of Education System in Albania,* February 2000. Available from http://www.euroeducation.net/prof/albanco.htm/.

International Monetary Fund. *Interim Poverty Reduction Strategy Paper—Albania,* 2000. Available from http://www.imf.org/.

Kaltounis, Theodore. "Democratic Citizenship: Education in Albania." *The Social Studies 90,* 6 (November 1999): 245.

Leach, Jenny, and Bob Moon, "Albania's Open Question." *Times Educational Supplement 4212* (21 March 1997): B3.

—*Mark Connelly*

ALGERIA

BASIC DATA

Official Country Name:	People's Democratic Republic of Algeria
Region:	Africa
Population:	31,193,917
Language(s):	Arabic, French
Literacy Rate:	61.6%
Number of Primary Schools:	15,426
Compulsory Schooling:	9 years
Public Expenditure on Education:	5.1%
Educational Enrollment:	Primary: 4,674,947 Secondary: 2,618,242 Higher: 347,410
Educational Enrollment Rate:	Primary: 107% Secondary: 63% Higher: 12%
Teachers:	Primary: 170,956 Secondary: 151,948 Higher: 19,910
Student-Teacher Ratio:	Primary: 27:1 Secondary: 17:1
Female Enrollment Rate:	Primary: 102% Secondary: 62% Higher: 10%

HISTORY & BACKGROUND

Algeria is the second largest country in Africa, after the Sudan. Located in northern Africa, Algeria is bordered by the Mediterranean on the north, on the west by Morocco and Western Sahara, on the southwest by Mauritania and Mali, on the southeast by Niger, and on the east by Libya and Tunisia. The present boundaries were set during the French conquest in the nineteenth century.

Algeria is rich in oil, and the economy is heavily dependent on hydrocarbons. Petroleum and natural gas and nonfuel minerals such as high-grade iron, oil phosphates, mercury, and zinc account for approximately 50 percent of the budget revenue. The state owns more than 450 of the heavy industrial enterprises, particularly steel, and envisions the creation of private small-and medium-sized businesses in commerce, tourism, and transport.

Algeria is divided into 48 *wilayas* (provinces). Each *wilaya* has a *wilayat* (provincial council) headed by prefects appointed by the president and 1,539 local authorities. The Director of Education for each *wilaya* administers the plans and operations of the schools.

In 2000, the population numbered 31,193,917 people, with 35 percent aged 0 to 14 years, 61 percent aged 15 to 64 years, and 4 percent older than 64. The growth rate in 2000 was estimated at 1.74 percent, down from 3.3 percent in 1988. The mortality rate in children under five years of age was 4.2 percent in 1997; 13 percent were reported to be malnourished. Approximately 90 percent of the inhabitants are concentrated in 12 percent of the land along the coastal area that stretches some 1200 kilometers. More than half (57.2 percent) of Algerians live in urban areas. Approximately 2.5 million Algerians live in France.

The combined Arab-Berber people comprise more than 99 percent of the population (Arabs approximately 80 percent; Berbers 20 percent), with Europeans less than one percent. Islam is the official state religion, with Sunni Muslims numbering over 98 percent of the population. There are also 110,000 Ibadigah Muslims and 150,000 Christians. Together Christians and Jews comprise about one percent of the population.

In 1999, an estimated 23 percent of the population fell below the poverty line and 39 percent were unemployed. Almost 30 percent of the working population holds government positions, 22.0 percent are in agriculture, 16.2 percent in construction and public works, 13.6 percent in industry, 13.5 percent in commerce and services, and 5.2 percent are in transportation and communication.

Algeria derives its name from *Al Jazain,* which is Arabic for "the Islands," referring to the small islands along the coastline of the capitol Algiers. The territory along the Mediterranean coast has recorded early history, but the areas far south in the Sahara do not have written records. The indigenous people of Algeria and the surrounding Mediterranean area were Berbers, the name given the inhabitants from western Egypt to Morocco since ancient times. The origins of the Berbers are obscure, but they are believed to have migrated across North Africa from Asia. The origin of the Berber language is unknown.

Before the arrival of the French in 1830, Algeria was known as the Barbary Coast (a corruption of Berber) and was notorious for the pirates who preyed on Christian shipping. Piracy remained a serious problem until the U.S. Navy defeated a Barbary fleet off the coast of Algiers in 1815, and it was not completely eradicated entirely until the French attached Algeria.

Algerian history is one of repeated invasions. Phoenician traders (900 through 146 B.C.) established Carthage (present day Tunisia) and established and expanded small settlements along the North African coast. They were followed by the Romans (98 through 117 A.D.), who annexed Berber territory to the Roman Empire. In 429, a Germanic tribe of 800,000 Vandals crossed into Africa from Spain and pillaged Carthage. In 533, the Byzantines (429 through 536) raided and sacked the Vandal kingdom. For more than 1,000 years (642 through 1830), Muslim armies invaded from Cairo, bringing Islam to the Berbers. The Spanish (1504 through 1792) constructed outposts and collected tribute. The Ottomans (1554 through 1830) captured Algiers and established it as the center of the Ottoman Empire. The French (1830 through 1962) captured Algeria and annexed the country. Of all the invaders, it is the Muslim and French conquests that have had the greatest lasting impact.

The Muslim expansion into Algeria dates back to the first decades of Islam. The Arabs were tent-dwelling herdsmen; the Muslim invaders of the Barbary Coast stationed Arab leaders and soldiers in towns but did not settle in Algiers. The Berbers, who were highlanders and cultivators, lived in towns and villages in the countryside, which remained essentially Berber.

The Berbers found it advantageous to join the religion of the Muslim rulers and avoid having a minority status. Islam was compatible with Berber society and conversion to Islam provided a sense of identity and belonging. Between the tenth and the fifteenth centuries, Berber-Arab dynasties developed, eventually becoming Algeria, Morocco, and Tunisia (collectively the *Maghreb*). Although the Maghreb (literally, place of sunset) today is considered part of the Arab world, the enduring influence of the Berber population gives it a cultural identity distinct from the Islamic lands to the east, in the *Mashreq* (place of sunrise).

The French forces who invaded Algeria in 1830 encountered fierce resistance. Achieving control of Algeria required the expenditure of a tremendous number of troops and was not complete until 1847. Algeria however, was annexed to France in 1842, after which the French started colonizing the entire country. The French colonists wished to be ruled by the home government rather than by military authorities, and a very close connection with France developed, whereby Algeria came to be regarded as an integral part of France, with representatives in the French parliament. Assimilation, however, was never complete and Algeria enjoyed considerable autonomy.

The colonial authorities imposed a policy of cultural imperialism intended to suppress Algerian cultural identity and to remold the society along French lines. Local culture was actively eliminated, mosques were converted into churches, and old *medinas* (Arab cities) were pulled down and replaced with streets. Prime farming land was appropriated for European settlers. White French settlers controlled most of the political and economic power, and the indigenous peoples became subservient.

As colonization continued, a new Euro-Algerian people came into being, numbering 800,000 by 1954. Of these, half were of Spanish, Italian, Maltese, or of other non-French origin. The 150,000 Algerian Jews were completely politically assimilated into that group. The Muslim population increased from three to nine million.

The rulers appropriated the *habut* lands (the religious foundations constituting the main income for religious institutions, including schools) in 1843, allocating insufficient money to maintain Muslim schools and mosques properly or to provide for adequate numbers of teachers and religious leaders for the growing population. As the colonizers ushered undesired changes into Muslim society, they unintentionally created Muslim resistance—a resistance born of the fear of cultural contamination and resentment of political domination.

From 1882 forward, primary instruction for Europeans and Jews was compulsory; Muslim schools were established at the discretion of the governor general. In 1892, more than five times the money was spent educating Europeans as was spent on Muslims, who had five times as many children of school age. Since few Muslim teachers were trained, European teachers staffed Muslim schools. The curriculum was in French, and there were no Arabic studies. It is estimated that, in 1870, only five percent of Muslim children were in any kind of school.

Early attempts at mixed French and Muslim primary and secondary schools had little success, but after 1920 improvement was achieved. In 1949, French and Muslim primary schools were merged. In 1958, only 12 percent of all children attended school. Few Muslims went beyond primary school.

Under French dominion for well over a century, Algerian independence came in 1962 after an eight-year war. A national assembly was elected and a republic was declared. Three years later, a military junta overthrew the government and ruled for 10 years before new elections were held. The National Liberation Front (FLN), the sole political party in Algeria, was a party of primarily secular socialist policies.

The post independence policy of Arabization that included replacing French with Arabic as the state language led to clashes with the Berber population, who saw French as their "avenue to advancement." At the same time, a grassroots Islamic revivalist movement was created that aimed to establish an Islamic state in Algeria.

After independence, free and compulsory education was guaranteed for all. School enrollment rose from 850,000 in 1963 to 3 million in 1975.

With the steep drop in oil prices in 1986, came a number of changes. The economy moved from a rigid, centralized control and placed a greater emphasis on market forces. Public expenditures in the early 1990s were increased to upgrade education and health care. As the Islamists sought to redefine Algerian identity to be more Arabic, more Muslims questioned the legitimacy of the existing political system, which they perceived as too secular and Western. A 1988 protest against austerity measures and food shortages resulted in government promises to relax the FLN monopoly on political power and to work toward a multiparty system.

In 1992, democratic elections were cancelled just as the militant Islamic Salvation Front (FIS)was headed for a landslide victory. The president resigned and handed power over to the military, which led to a civil war between the government and the Islamic fundamentalists. The FIS laid siege to the secular government, which escalated into the destruction of academic institutions, the assassination of students and scholars, and the exodus of over 1,000 academics from the country. By the 1995 election, the violence had become so widespread that the death toll was placed at 45,000. Bombings even reached Paris.

Reports differ on the effects of a 1999 government offer of amnesty to the FIS. Some sources report that, as a result of the offer, the Islamic Salvation Army disbanded in January 2000 and many of the insurgents surrendered under the amnesty program. However, all violence did not end. Other sources reported that, while some of the rebels responded to the offer and disarmed, the FIS still exists and is suspected of assassinations aimed at derailing peace efforts.

The transition from a state-owned economy and one-party regime to a liberal economy and a multiparty regime was accompanied by violence, both physical and symbolic. Officials of the authoritarian, centralist government that has ruled since independence are products of French education and are seen by many Algerians as a "political-economic mafia." Berbers (more specifically Kabyles), whom the French favored in education and employment, moved into administrative jobs after independence, much to the frustration of lesser-educated Arabs. Political turmoil ensued, as the angry Islamic Salvation Front sought to gain power by imposing fundamentalist ideology to transform Algeria into an Islamic state. At stake in the ongoing violence was the complete re-negotiation of the distribution of power.

The dramatic downturn in international petroleum prices in 1998 led to a decline of more than 25 percent of government revenues from oil and gas, amounting to as much as 60 percent of total revenue. Educational expenditures suffered at a time when educational needs were growing. In 1999 however, a degree of optimism was seen regarding Algeria's economic prospects, thanks to rising petroleum prices, and hopes that a return to domestic political stability would attract foreign investment and form the basis for sustained growth.

Algeria, more formally the Democratic and Popular Republic of Algeria, is a multiparty socialistic state based on French and Islamic law. Suffrage is universal and begins at age 18. The government established the multiparty system in September 1989. One year later, there were an estimated 30 to 50 legal parties. The right to form political parties is guaranteed, provided such parties are not based on differences in religion, language, race, gender, or region.

Language: Three languages are widely spoken. Arabic, the official language, is spoken by 83 percent of the population, although many government and business functions occur in French, which is still widely spoken. Arabic has replaced French as the language of instruction. In 1992, English was introduced in primary schools on an equal footing with French as a first foreign language. Berber, with dialects spoken by approximately 17 percent of the population, was introduced into the schools in 1995.

Two forms of Arabic are used: the classical Arabic of the *Quran* (Koran) and Algerian dialectical Arabic. Classical Arabic is the essential base of written Arabic and formal speech throughout the Arab world. Written Arabic is psychologically and sociologically important as the vehicle of Islam and Arabic culture and as the link with other Arabic countries. It is the repository of a vast religious, scientific, historical, and literary heritage. Berber is primarily a spoken language with approximately 10 dialects, some with considerable borrowing of Arab words. An ancient Berber ceremonial script, *tiffinaugh,* survives in some areas.

Literacy: Prior to French occupation in 1830, the literacy rate in Algeria was 40 percent. After 130 years of French rule, it was even worse, as Algeria was left with one of the lowest literacy rates in the world—as low as 15 percent, according to the United Nations. Illiteracy was attacked in stages, with the greatest emphasis initially placed on developing formal education. The National Center for Literacy Education was established in 1964 to supervise the work of local literacy centers. Literacy is regarded as essential to economic development, and from the beginning, it was a prime objective of the independent government. In 1966, only 7.9 percent of women and 29.9 percent of men were literate. In the 1970s, massive efforts to reduce illiteracy resulted in vast improvements, as nominal literacy rose steadily, reaching 48.6 percent in 1985 (62.7 percent male, 35.0 percent female) and 57.4 percent in 1991 (69.8 percent male, 45.5 percent female). In 2000, literacy rates ranged from 62 to 72 percent (males, 73 to 80 percent; females, 43 to 63 percent). Female literacy is improving, but continues to lag in comparison to males.

Culture: Islamic culture constitutes a comprehensive holistic system of thought and behavior, with an equal emphasis on both the spiritual and physical aspects of life and their integration. All Muslims are equal before God and equal among themselves, an orientation that carries over into their philosophy of education for all. Learning in the Muslim culture, a necessity and a religious duty, occupies a central position in Muslim thought. Muslims often quote The Prophet: ''God eases the way to paradise for him who seeks learning'' and the Quran: ''Seek knowledge from the cradle to the tomb;'' and ''To acquire knowledge is a duty for all Muslims.''

CONSTITUTIONAL & LEGAL FOUNDATIONS

Algeria was under French constitutional rule until independence was gained in 1962. The first Algerian constitution was adopted in 1963, and a second followed in 1976, which was amended in 1988 and 1989 and revised in 1996.

In the 1996 constitution, the preamble emphasized the Arab, Islamic, and Amazigh (Berber) identity of Algeria. The beginning articles of the constitution declared that Algeria was to be democratic and republic, Islam was to be the state religion, and Arabic was to be the national and official language. The constitution established the High Islamic Council (advisory) and prohibited practices contrary to Islamic morality. Although the constitution declared Islam the state religion, *Shari'a* (Islamic law)

was not incorporated into the state's legal system. Sovereignty rested with the people through their elected representatives.

The Constitution guaranteed the right to free education, made fundamental education compulsory, and allocated to the state the power to organize the educational system and legislate the general rules for scientific research. Control of education, originally vested in the Ministry of Education, now rested in two ministries:the Ministry of Higher Education and Scientific Research, and the Ministry of Primary and Secondary Education.

In 1995, the Higher Council for Education was created to improve the efficiency of the educational structure and to link the ministries of Education, Higher Education, and Employment. An Arabization law, implemented in 1998, required governmental and educational functions to be conducted in Arabic. The deadline for Arabization in higher education was extended to July 5, 2000. By that time, officials in government ministries had to acquire at least a minimal facility in literary Arabic. Additionally, the media had to increase the use of Arabic.

Modern day education in Algeria has roots first in Moslem and later in French philosophies. The high value placed on knowledge by the Quran and the Prophet Mohammed provided Muslims with incentives to develop education in order to read and learn the Quran and The Prophet. In the earliest schools at the mosques and in other early Quran schools—and even in private homes—instruction was offered in the Quran, the life of the Prophet, and in the grammar, structures, and forms of the Arabic language.

Maktab or *kuttab* were developed as learning centers for children as were *masjid* and *majlis,* adult study groups associated with mosques. Discussion was part of the learning process at the centers and included topics such as legal matters and poetry, as well as the Prophet's life, sayings, and devotional practices. *Jami,* the Friday mosques, eventually became seats of higher learning. As the Muslims engaged in learning and writing, a number of libraries developed. They were often attached to courts, where collections of books were organized. These large and informal institutions also housed books from other cultural traditions.

From its earliest beginnings, Moslem learning focused on life skills and theological concerns. The Moslem heritage is a philosophy that places high value on education, prescribes it for all Muslims, and uses a comprehensive approach to learning infused with religious teachings. Moslem educational philosophy is based on acquiring self-knowledge, balanced with the recognition of the need for skills to live in the world. The Moslem learning during the medieval period (800 to 1000 A.D.)

was conceived as six sciences: celestial spheres and heavenly bodies, earth and geography, medicine and natural science, crafts and vocations, religion and creeds, and political administration. Throughout the medieval period, Muslim women's education was affected by local cultural factors that imposed constraints on their training and role in society. The tenth century saw organized institutional development supported by the state. By the eleventh century, *medersa* (primary schools) developed into Muslim schools of law and became the primary centers for religious and legal education. They received state support and had endowed professorships and residential facilities. Educational philosophy rested with the intellectuals in informal teaching until the 1880s.

In the early decades of the 1800s, Algerian education was comprised of *quranic* schools, primary schools, and secondary schools (*zaouias*). Jurisprudence, geometry, philology, physics, and astronomy were taught. Higher education institutions did not exist in Algeria and students attended universities in neighboring countries.

Moslems initially withdrew from the French-imposed educational system, a condition that changed when veterans returned from World War I. In 1917, the French made primary education compulsory for boys who lived within two miles of a public Algerian school. The lack of schools and teachers deterred implementation of this decree. In 1944, a plan to enroll one million Algerian boys and girls in primary school by 1964 was introduced. In 1947, Arabic became an official language and was introduced into schools. The destruction of the Moslem schools and the imitation French system imposed by the colonizers left independent Algeria with a strong desire to establish an authentic Algerian system of education. In the way of this major educational change stood a host of impediments.

Political freedom did not bring cultural freedom; the heritage of colonialism was still felt strongly in the educational system. French ideas and influence remained after the departure of French teachers and administrators in 1962. The French left behind a rigid school curriculum complete with very selective formal examinations: *La Sixieme* (primary school, in the sixth year), the *Brevet d'Etudies du Premier Cycle* (secondary school, in the fourth year), the *Probatoire* (secondary school, in the sixth year), and the *Baccalauréat* (secondary school, in the seventh year). The French educational heritage was a highly centralized, rigid structure designed for the elite; a fact-acquisition based system of learning with major exams throughout the curriculum.

Algerian Philosophy: In 1961, African ministers of education met in Addis Ababa and developed a comprehensive educational plan to set the stage for educational change in Algeria. The plan called for universal primary schooling, rapid increases in secondary and higher education enrollments, and major improvements in the quality of education. With Algerian independence the following year, educational opportunities were opened to all people, marking a shift from the French exclusive elitist system to an Algerian system with equal opportunities for all. Education became a right rather than a privilege.

Algerian authorities recognized very early the role of education in economic development. They realized that for Algeria to develop economically, a literate and trained workforce was a necessity. They planned to channel students into scientific and technical fields, which were most needed by the Algerian industrial and managerial sectors.

The departure of French teachers in 1962 left a gap in the classrooms that was first filled by teachers from the quranic schools and medersas. The marked decline in teaching quality however, led authorities to abandon this practice before these teachers became entrenched in the system. Temporary teachers from nearly 50 countries were brought in to fill the void and to try to overcome the complete disarray caused by independence. Enrollment was only 850,000 at that time (1962), but it quickly swelled. The change in philosophy from education for the few to education for the many was admirable, but the pedagogical and human resources necessary to provide a quality education for all simply were not available—Algeria was not prepared for the massive number of students. In the decade following independence, large enrollments meant hastily trained teachers and improvised classrooms, many in the vacated homes of former French residents. The growing enrollments reached 3.0 million by 1975 and 6.5 million by 1991.

The early independence period between 1962 and 1970 was marked by a series of educational reforms using models and philosophies imported from Europe, the United States, and the Middle East. The profusion of imported educational theories and ideas contributed to disorganization and incoherence in the overburdened system. There was a lack of facilities, trained teachers, and instructional materials; confusion caused by differing educational philosophies; rigidity caused by the highly centralized system together; and, unwieldy, large classes. These mounting problems were dealt with on the local level in very sporadic fashion. Critics complained of the lack of long-term planning and integration. A new phenomenon appeared with mass schooling: mass dropouts. These dropouts and other young "un-employeds" developed a kind of antiestablishment attitude and become known as *hittiste* (those who lean on walls).

This period was called the "impossible emancipation" due to the restrictive political, social, economic, and education factors. This period included a lack of teachers, schools, colleges (only one university existed), financing, managers, and educational expertise. Illiteracy remained very high. The productive and the educational sector of the economy operated independently and without coordination or apparent consultation, forcing the industrial sector to develop its own training capabilities and to draw heavily upon foreign technical aid to meet its needs for skilled manpower. Graduates in scientific and technical fields from public institutions often were inappropriately trained for employment in industry. The guarantee of free universal education that led to a massive influx of students brought large problems.

Riding on the economic crest of the oil boom, the decades of the 1970s and 1980s produced educational reforms, which were more carefully planned than previous attempts. The reforms were often based on imported theories. The goals remained the same—to provide equal opportunity for all, with free, or nominally priced, schooling and scholarships. Priority was given to reducing illiteracy. The policies put in place all aimed toward the Arabization of all curricula, the Arabization of the medium of instruction, and the Algerization of the teaching staff. A number of major policy decisions were made as educational structure developed over the years.

In 1976 the National Charter was created. The highly centralized control of Algerian education was codified in this charter. It was intended to politically unify all or nearly all of the educational institutions. By this time, the public education system was virtually the only education provider, in large part because of the diplomas, titles, and certificates it awarded. Algerians are said to value degrees (more than expertise) for social promotion purposes to the point that degrees are said to exercise a "fatal attraction."

In 1977 the Abolition of Private Education was formed. Private education, primarily in the realm of foreign institutions and schools that were often run by Roman Catholic missions, was abolished.

The Polytechnic Curriculum Theory came into existence in 1978. The theory from East Germany was adopted for the first nine years of schooling, which resulted in the creation of the Foundation School. It was intended to reduce dropouts by combining primary school (at the end of which most dropouts occurred) with middle school.

The École Fondamentale et Polytechnique resulted from pressure for more and better education in 1976-1979, and was designed to bridge the gap between academic and practical studies by combining theory with practice. It was aimed at improving the dropout problem, which had reached epidemic proportions. Also in 1979, Technical colleges were ended just when industry needed large numbers of skilled and semiskilled workers.

The Ministry of Vocational Education was created in 1983. It was given the responsibility of developing a national training system to satisfy the skill requirements of the economy and provide training for as many young people as possible.

In 1985 and 1986 additional reforms developed core programs in general secondary education and channeled university students into vocational specializations, exact sciences, or experimental and human sciences. The Carte Universitere defined Algeria's graduate and postgraduate needs to the end of the century, with each higher education center expected to fill its quota of the national trained manpower requirement.

The University of Further Training (l'Université de la Formation Continué) targeted those students who were oriented toward vocational learning but who were not going to earn the baccalauréate. It was a place for students completing six years of primary school (ending at age 12) who were not old enough to work. The university began operating in 1991. The Ministry of Vocational Education was transferred to the Ministry of Education. The carefully planned educational reforms were often not realistic and were rarely realizable. Either the resources to implement them were lacking or the planning was so remote from the realities of the situation that they reflected no real remedy for the target problem. From 1988 on, social and economic conditions and shortcomings in the education system led to the formation of informal, voluntary educational activities.

In 1989 the National Commission was appointed to study educational reforms. The first baccalauréates that used nothing but Arabic instruction were completed.

In 1995 the Higher Education Council was created. It aimed to structure the education system more effectively by linking the work of the ministries of Education, Higher Education, and Employment.

The Arabization Law replaced French as the language of government and education in 1996. In spite of the reforms and intensive efforts to create an Algerian system, education in 1996 was still often described as consisting of the "wholesale adoption of European theories, policies and practices" that critics lamented "failed to connect with Algerian realities and needs."

EDUCATIONAL SYSTEM—OVERVIEW

The educational system is structured into primary foundation school for nine years, followed by secondary education school for three years, and then the tertiary (university) level. Algerian education is still grounded in the French fact-acquisition orientation, and teaching is almost exclusively in the lecture and memorization mode. In 1996, the total enrollment at primary and secondary

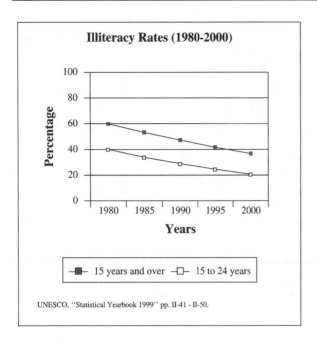

Illiteracy Rates (1980-2000)

Legend: ■ 15 years and over   □ 15 to 24 years

UNESCO, "Statistical Yearbook 1999" pp. II-41 - II-50.

schools was equivalent to 86 percent of the school age population (89 percent of the boys, 82 percent of the girls). Enrollment at primary schools in the relevant age group was 97 percent for boys and 91 percent for girls.

A 1995 UNICEF study reported that early childhood education services for children up to 6 years of age were limited. Fewer than 50,000 children were enrolled, exclusive of those in quranic preschools (quranic schools accommodate large numbers of preschool children.). Of those enrolled, 10 percent of children up to 3 years old were in nurseries and 90 percent of 3 to 6 year olds were in kindergartens. Fifty-five percent of those in kindergarten were urban children. Estimates in 1995 of the percentage of preschool age children enrolled in some form of preschool (including quranic schools) ranged from 3 to 20 percent. Reports from 1995 indicated that no preschool services existed for children with special educational needs except for special sections in kindergartens attached to primary schools for those with hearing impairments. Preprimary schools are conducted in Arabic and are not compulsory.

The Foundation School (École Fondamentale et Polytechnique), replaced the French 10-year compulsory school model with a nine-year model. Primary and middle schools were combined, scientific and technical literacy stressed, and closer connections sought between schooling and work. Classes are taught in Arabic, with French considered the first foreign language. Students are oriented either toward secondary school or toward vocational training.

Primary education (*Enseignement Primaire*) is organized into three cycles, each comprising of three years.

It is compulsory for the nine years between ages 6 and 15. Students completing primary education follow one of three tracks—general, technical or vocational. Students take a final exam (*brevet d'enseignement fondamental*) that they must pass for admission to secondary education.

In 1996, the total enrollment in primary schools included 94 percent of the appropriate age groups (97 percent of the boys, 91 percent of the girls). The ministry reports that in 1996 there were 15,426 state primary schools with 4,674,947 students (46 percent were girls) and 149,958 teachers for the first through the sixth years, and 3,038 middle schools (for those age 7 to 9) with 1,762,761 students, of which 38 percent were girls.

There are two types of secondary education: technical and general. Secondary education (*Enseignement Secondaire*) begins at age 15 and ends when students take the baccalauréat examination before they proceed to one of the universities, state technical institutes, or vocational training centers, or move directly into employment. The academic year is from September to July, with a 15-day break in December and another in March. Schooling is free, although some scholarships are offered by the state for living expenses.

In 1996, enrollment in the secondary schools included 56 percent of the appropriate age groups (58 percent of the boys and 54 percent of the girls). There were 1,033 secondary schools with 52,210 teachers and 853,303 students. Admission to secondary schools is based upon the student's primary school grades and the student quota at each institution, as set by the Ministry of Primary and Secondary Education. Instruction is in Arabic.

Higher education is comprised of universities, national institutes for higher education, engineering schools, and teachers' colleges. The institutions administered by the Ministry of Education produce about 90 percent of the bachelor's degrees. The remaining institutions come under the control of other ministries.

In 1995-1996, a total of 347,410 students enrolled in higher education. Admission is based on the student quota for each institution (set by the ministry) and grades. Allocation to fields of study depends on how well students did in primary subjects in each field. The teaching staff is largely Algerian.

Undergraduate Programs: Admission to undergraduate programs requires the baccalauréat or equivalent (*cours préparatoires aux études superiéres, capacité en droit, etc.*). Some popular fields, such as medicine, have additional requirements. Foreign students are admitted if they meet admission requirements and their parents live in Algeria, or if they receive an Algerian scholarship. Scholarships and room and board are arranged by the

Centres des Oeuvres Scholaires et Universitaires. The academic year lasts from September to July and consists of two semesters, with a 21-day break in January.

There are two levels of higher education: Level Five, lasting five semesters, and Level Six, lasting eight to 12 semesters. Generally, Level Five leads to qualification as a technologist, while Level Six leads to a first degree (*licence*), higher education diploma (*diplomé d'études supériéures*), or other professional degree in medicine, dentistry, pharmacy, and engineering.

Graduate Programs: Graduate student enrollment climbed to 11,987 in 1988-1989, an increase of 998 percent from 1974-1975. Graduate education is designed to train teachers and professors, to answer the need for Arabic in teaching, and to get universities involved in Algeria's development effort. Graduate education is not yet fully developed. Master's (*magister*) programs require a first degree (license) or equivalent and take two years (four semesters). Students spend the first year on course work, directed research, seminars, and one foreign language. The second year is spent writing a thesis. Entrance to doctoral level programs (*doctorat d'état*) requires a master's degree or equivalent. Foreign students are accepted into graduate school if the Ministry of Education authorizes them.

The diploma of magister contains a "mention" of the performance of the student. The possible mentions are: "Passable" when the general average is at least equal to 10/20 and lower than 12/20; "Rather Well" when the general average equals or exceeds 12/20 but is less than 14/20; "Well" when the general average is at least 14/20 and lower than 16/20; and "Very Well" when the general average is equal or higher than 16/20. The general average is calculated by giving equal weighting to the average of the examinations and the thesis defense. Only those who earn the rating of Very Well, Well, and Rather Well can gain admittance to a doctoral program. Doctoral candidates must also complete a thesis reporting original research and an oral thesis defense.

Language: In the postcolonial Arabization program, restoring Arabic as the general language required teaching citizens who had been educated in a foreign language to learn and use their own. The Higher Council for the National Language oversees the Arabization process. Every government organization created an Arabization department to plan lessons for its workers.

In a radical reversal of policy, the Haut-Commissariat a l'amazighité was created (following an eight-month boycott of school by nearly a million students) and Berber dialects (Amazigh) were introduced into the schools in 1995 by decree of the president. This was a tre-

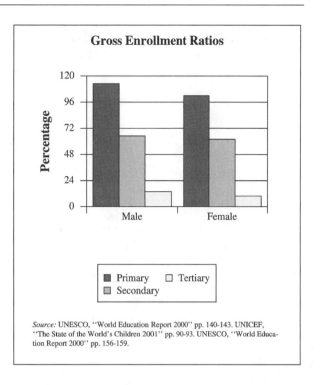

Gross Enrollment Ratios

Source: UNESCO, "World Education Report 2000" pp. 140-143. UNICEF, "The State of the World's Children 2001" pp. 90-93. UNESCO, "World Education Report 2000" pp. 156-159.

mendous political-cultural victory for the Berbers (Amazigh means "free men"). Barely 15 years earlier, scribbling a few words in tiffinagh, the characters of the Berber language, meant a stay in prison. One-third of the 48 provinces introduced pilot classes in Berber in the last year of middle school (ninth year) and the first year of high school (tenth year). Training courses for teachers were organized and exams planned for the *brevet d'enseignement moyen* (middle school certificate) and for the baccalauréat.

PREPRIMARY & PRIMARY EDUCATION

The government pays most of the costs (approximately 83 percent) of nurseries, kindergartens, and community-based centers with parents paying the rest. In private centers, parents pay all the costs. Preschool educational institutions, authorized in 1976 by the Ministry of Labor and Social Works are governed by laws updated in 1983, 1985, 1988, 1990, and 1992. Children in preschool public institutions receive basic instruction regarding nutrition, health care, and education. There is no standardized curriculum; each institution decides on the activities in its program. Children receive around eight hours of services each day, approximately 1,280 hours a year.

In 1996, the total enrollment in primary schools included 94 percent of the appropriate age groups (97 percent of the boys, 91 percent of the girls). The Ministry reported that in 1996 there were 15,426 state primary schools with 4,674,947 students (46 percent were girls)

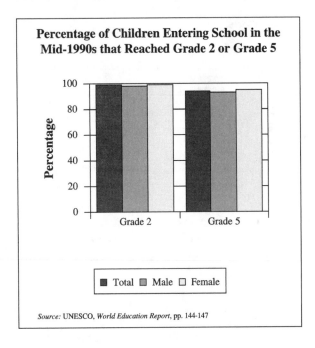

Percentage of Children Entering School in the Mid-1990s that Reached Grade 2 or Grade 5

■ Total ■ Male □ Female

Source: UNESCO, *World Education Report*, pp. 144-147

and 149,958 teachers for the first through the sixth years, and 3,038 middle schools (for those age 7 to 9) with 1,762,761 students (38 percent were girls).

Rural-to-urban inequities exist in the system. The percentage of children enrolled in school is weakest among farmers and seasonal rural workers. In 1990, 9 percent of the students were repeating grades (boys, 11 percent; girls, 7 percent). In 1996, 10 percent of the students were repeating (boys, 13 percent; girls, 8 percent) and nearly 9 percent of all six-year-olds were not in school.

The accepted goal of primary education is to teach children to "practice, research, observe, and discover, as well as depend on themselves in acquiring knowledge and accomplishing their work." Arabic is the language of instruction, but other languages are not excluded.

Primary schools operate on a three cycle system. The curriculum in the first through third year of primary education (basic cycle) for children 6 to 9 years of age provides manual work with education and training tools to develop motor skills and help children understand and adapt to the environment. The second, or "awakening" cycle, is designed for 9- to 12-year-olds and occurs in the fourth through sixth year of education. The educational focus is on reinforcing skills acquired during the first stage plus continued learning in language, mathematics, environment, and religious and national studies. A first foreign language is offered. The third, or training, cycle (also called the middle school) comprises the seventh through the ninth year of education for children 12- to 15-years-old. The curriculum is dedicated to the study of lin-

guistic, social, cultural, religious, and scientific education, as well as mathematics, physics, and various sciences of applied technology. A second foreign language is offered. At the end of the third stage, students take the final *brevet d'enseignement fondamental* (foundation education certificate, or B.E.F). If they pass, they gain access to general secondary schools, technical secondary schools, or technical training programs.

Special Education: Children and young people with special needs are neither registered nor categorized for official purposes under a policy of encouraging integration. Ministerial circulars were developed in the mid-1990s concerning the future education of children with various difficulties, such as sensory impairments or chronic illnesses, such as diabetes or asthma.

Special education takes three forms: special classes in primary schools for children with hearing impairments, courses for students who repeat a year, and transition courses for students who arrive in school late. Special education is the combined responsibility of the Ministry of Education (concerned with pedagogy) and the Ministry of Social Affairs (concerned with administration and resourcing), with some additional responsibility shared by the Ministry of Health. The Office of Special Education within the Ministry of Education administers special education. Administrative decisions are made at national and regional levels. The National Consultative Council is responsible for the coordination of services at the national level. Children with severe handicaps are excluded from the public education system; they are placed directly in special care centers. Special education is financed entirely by the government.

SECONDARY EDUCATION

The first year of secondary education is comprised of a core curriculum in which courses are grouped into three general areas: *accala* (languages and social sciences), *des sciences* (natural and physical sciences and mathematics), and *technologie* (mathematics, physical sciences, design, and technology.) Extracurricular activities, sponsored by the school or parent associations, are important and include music, painting, and sports. Sports, music, and physical education are also part of the curriculum.

Evaluation is systematic within the secondary school and passage to the next level is based on the results obtained on homework and compositions. Parents are told the results of the evaluations periodically by means of regular bulletins containing each professor's observations and a report at the end of the academic year stating whether the student passed, would be repeating, or would be *exclusion* (excluded).

At the end of the first year in secondary school, a decision is made as to whether students enter the general secondary education or technical secondary education program based on the wishes of the students, their academic records, and the exigencies of the academic program. For third-year students who have failed the baccalauréate twice, special classes are offered for a total of 19 hours that are tailored to the particular needs of each student. Remedial courses are given daily in the *lycées* in the evening after normal class hours. The same chance is given to the children returning to the country because they receive a distinct education that permits them to sit for the official exams.

General Secondary Education: The Ministry of Education reports that in 1999, a total of 855,481 students (53 percent girls) were enrolled in secondary education. Students overwhelmingly chose general education (88 percent) over technical education. Some 496,019 students (57 percent girls) were in general education classes while 64,888 students (12 percent girls) were in technical education classes.

General education is considered the most prestigious secondary education and offers five courses of study—exact sciences, natural and life sciences, humanities, foreign language, and religious sciences. The reform of 1985-1986 arranged lessons during the first year of secondary education into core programs to help students identify appropriate specializations by the end of the year. Completion of both technical and general secondary education ends with the baccalauréate examination that determines admission to higher education institutions. Successful completion of general education leads to *le diplome de l'enseignement* (education diploma).

Technical Secondary Education: There are two types of secondary education: technical and general. Students in technical secondary education study electronics, electrical science/technology, mechanical science, public works and engineering, chemistry, and accounting. Technical education is considered less desirable by Algerians even though new fields of study such as information technology, applied biochemistry, and agricultural education have been added, as well as optional classes in foreign languages and design. Students can specialize in the industrial option of technical education or in the commercial option. The teaching staff is mainly Algerian. Successful study in this program ends with a technical baccalauréate diploma (*le diplome du baccalauréat technique*).

Vocational Education: Vocational education in Algeria has a checkered past. Independence from the French found Algeria with no national vocational education policy. Colonial authorities often opened vocational schools as a second-class educational option for the "natives," so not surprisingly, after independence, Algerians expressed a strong distaste for this type of schooling. Also at that time, and for decades to come, the government was the principal employer in the country, and general education was viewed as the appropriate form of training for government employment.

State education initiatives of the 1960s emphasized general education programs, with only limited growth of technical and vocational schools. As late as 1979, only 65 vocational training centers existed, with a combined enrollment of 23,000 students. In the absence of a centralized policy and in spite of slow technical growth in the 1960s and 1970s, technical ministries and public industries developed many training programs to meet the demands for skilled manpower. Most were well managed; the National Petroleum Company's training center (SONATRACH) still functions well. The proliferation of these training programs did result in duplication of effort, however.

In 1983, a Ministry of Vocational Education was created to develop a national training system. Vocational education was expanded and diversified to be available to the large number of students completing primary education but "not qualified by disposition or grades" to continue secondary education.

Vocational education was intended to provide graduates with immediate employment and to provide the country with a trained work force as Algeria concentrated on developing heavy industry. Students were to be trained as apprentices for up to five years. Vocational expansion continued and more than 200 training centers were built, tripling enrollment between 1981 and 1987. In 1990, a total of 325 vocational training schools were in operation and about 200,000 apprentices were in training. Vocational skills were also taught as part of the national service program.

Expansion concentrated on building physical facilities rather than on modern equipment and materials, and without planning for the particular specializations and/or the number of trainees needed. Vocational schools operated without links to specific industries. Vocational training responsibilities were transferred to the Ministry of Education in 1987 when educational philosophy changed. The existing general educational program was refocused toward technical and vocational subjects to change the negative perceptions of technical training and manual labor and to alleviate shortages of skilled workers.

Problems arose in the late 1980s during the worldwide recession. Resources were harder to obtain, training quality declined, and jobs for graduates were scarce. The 1986 drop in oil prices exacerbated the government's financial problems and restricted budget expenditures for education. Only a few training centers actually formed relationships with employers. In spite of decreasing job opportunities, pressure for more vocational training centers increased as a growing school-age population increased the number of dropouts and "push-outs" from the general educational system.

In the early 1990s, Algeria experienced a vocational "crisis." Low student motivation and aptitude were the norm, as those who "couldn't make it" in general education ended up in vocational centers. Low teacher salaries reduced instructional quality as better teachers went to industry. Language difficulties occurred as most instruction in technical subjects was still in French. Finally, poor management and financial constraints compounded all of the other problems.

The oversupply of graduates created a phenomenon of downward vertical substitution, as people with university degrees couldn't get jobs and accepted lower positions. Employers then raised their requirements for those jobs. The lack of systematic, institutionalized job placements meant employment ended up being a very inefficient system of "who you know." A widespread phenomenon of horizontal substitution developed whereby vocational education graduates ended up in positions not related to their training. Poor quality, insufficient funding, and low external efficiency are signs of malfunctions in vocational education, but they are also a normal and logical result of the other role of these schools, that is, the "social parking" function.

The Offices for Practical Works in Vocational Training, created specifically for aiding the production activities of vocational training centers, act as intermediaries between enterprises requiring products and the training centers that provide them. They identify requirements from enterprises, particularly when the demand for products is too large for a single vocational center, fix prices and deadlines, allocate the product demands among various centers, and provide centers with raw materials.

While these offices permit economies of scale from a business perspective, there are educational problems. The main problem is that production and trading concerns very often tend to prevail over pedagogical interests, meaning trainees work on repetitive and monotonous tasks in which the pedagogical dimension is virtually neglected.

HIGHER EDUCATION

Universities are organized into institutes, each of which coordinates several departments. National institutes of higher education, though smaller than the universities, offer degrees in a variety of fields. The engineering schools (*grandes écoles*) include polytechnic, veterinary medicine, architecture and urbanization, agriculture, information, telecommunications, and ocean science. Teachers colleges train teachers for both general and technical secondary schools.

Only the University of Algers predates independence. Founded in 1879 on the French model, it stressed autonomy for the university faculty including designing curricula. The system was unwieldy, with duplication of academic offerings and the complete loss of credits by students changing programs. Not until 1946 did the first Algerian students begin attending the University of Algers, and in 1959, only 600 Algerian students (13 percent of all the university students) were in attendance. Independence in 1962 found university attendance still low, numbering only 2,200 Algerians (from the population of 12 million). Attrition was very high.

The massive influx of students following independence led to the large-scale establishment of universities, university centers, and colleges. Within four years, in 1966, there were six universities, two universities of science and technology, five university centers, one agronomic institute, one veterinary institute, one telecommunications institute, one school of architecture and town planning, and one École Normale Supériéure. Enrollment numbered 160,000 students, with 7,947 academic staff. Additional universities were created and the system was reformed in 1971, with major reforms following in 1988. The universities loosely resemble the French model.

By 2000, enrollment in higher education climbed to 298,767 with 20,026 teachers. The number of universities has risen to nine plus two universities of science and technology, four university centers, and 12 colleges and institutes each coordinating several departments. There is a heavy emphasis on engineering institutes and "hard sciences." The academic year is from September to June. Although the central government coordinates the activities of the institutions, they have a fair degree of autonomy.

The reforms of 1985-1986 were intended to channel higher education students into vocational specializations and exact sciences, or into experimental and human sciences, as such subjects traditionally are nonpolitical. Subjects such as chemistry, biochemistry, and industrial chemistry were to be introduced. The basis for the plan, at least in part, was the perceived requirements of the country in terms of developing industry, agriculture, and the administration, as well as to "form distinguished individuals proud of their cultural heritage, their attempts to change their reality, and their contributions to their country."

The political-religious conflict in Algeria is played out in higher education. When the wave of nationalism of the 1960s and 1970s waned, Islamism took its place. Islamic fundamentalists reigned freely on university campuses in the 1980s. In 2000, Islamic fundamentalists existed as a weakened underground movement on the campuses. They have since been banned from these schools.

In 1987, student riots in Constantine and Setif led to the realization that four main university towns—Algiers, Oran, Constantine, and Annaba—hosted 76 percent of the students in higher education. Efforts were made to find ways of decreasing such large concentrations of students.

After the cancellation of the state elections in 1992, protests by the militants quickly spread to university campuses. Low-level violence started in 1992 (usually arson) and escalated dramatically in succeeding years. The violence resulted in a mass exodus of academics from the country, especially in 1994–1995. Between 1992 and 1997, nearly 1,000 academics fled Algeria and settled in France. Many more tried but failed to secure French visas.

Academics have been the victims of assassination since 1992. Faculty members are not the only targets. Rectors and students have been killed, and female students are threatened. One report states that in 1994, by official count, there were more than 2,725 acts of terrorism, more than 80 teachers assassinated, and more than 600 schools, three university centers, and nine training institutes burned down or blown up. Other victims include Communist Party members, socialists, left-wing secularists, academic and intellectual defenders of cultural freedom, academics and scholars who run research centers or who hold government positions, academics known for their fundamentalist Islamic beliefs, and foreigners.

By some accounts, the toll of violence has reached 40,000 to 50,000 victims. The assassinations are reported to be part of the strategy of Islamic fundamentalists to deter peace efforts and, in the case of foreigners, deter foreign investment. In addition to the assassinations, increasing violations of university freedoms originate from a number of sectors. Police come on campus and arrest fundamentalist teachers and staff and people professing opposition to dictatorship and other ''unpopular'' views. Fundamentalists pressure teachers at all levels with threats (especially foreign-language teachers) to quit teaching. Faculty members are reportedly losing control over their syllabi and careers as well as promotion standards. The Teacher Training Institute library in Algiers was turned into a prayer room, thereby forcing an end to the debates and cultural activities previously held there.

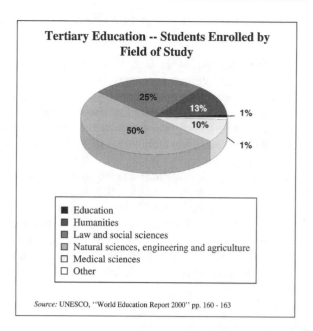

Tertiary Education -- Students Enrolled by Field of Study

25% 13% 1%
50% 10%
1%

- ■ Education
- ■ Humanities
- ■ Law and social sciences
- ▨ Natural sciences, engineering and agriculture
- □ Medical sciences
- □ Other

Source: UNESCO, ''World Education Report 2000'' pp. 160 - 163

University officials are pressured to separate males and females in cafeterias. ''Nosey Parkers'' (university-created security forces) harass students, thwart trade union organizing among faculty, and systematically encroach on union free speech and right of assembly. Universities interfere in the bar exam registrations by providing special dispensations to matriculate without taking the examination.

Universities are characterized by huge classes, aging equipment, out-of-date materials, equipment shortages, inadequate supervisors, and diminishing faculty control. The Arabization that already occurred in the social and human sciences reached the exact sciences in 1997. Without Arabic books and instructional materials, such as software, keyboards, and publications, and given a lack of Arabic-speaking teachers, instruction suffers. Access to the science and technology of western cultures is restricted by language limitations. Poor working conditions, inflation-eroded salaries and poor housing led teachers, professors, and assistants in Oran to strike in 1997, a strike that immediately spread to other universities.

Complementary Education: Some complementary education is found at the foreign cultural centers, where language instruction is available, such as English (Centre Culturel Britannique et Centre Culturel Américain) and French (Centre Culturel Français). With one-third of Algeria's postgraduate students studying abroad in 1992, bilingualism remains a crucial asset. Libraries and documentation services at these centers are frequented and solicited by students who find the public and university libraries, as well as the bookstores, insufficient. Other activities at these centers (not so heavily frequented) include painting, photography, music, theater, and more.

Libraries: Major libraries in Algiers include the University of Algiers library containing 800,000 volumes; the National Library housing 950,000 volumes, with special collections including Africa and the Maghreb; the National Archives of Algeria; and the Department for the Distribution of Scientific and Technical Information at the French Cultural Center in Algiers. A Municipal Library containing 25,000 volumes is located in Constantine. Library holdings at universities include Batna (55,000 volumes), Mentouri (240,000 volumes), D'Oran Es-Senia (200,000 volumes), and Abou Bekr Belkaid (Tlemcen: 66,000 volumes). The university center at Mostaganem holds 75,000 volumes and a number of colleges hold modest collections, as do museums and art galleries.

It is difficult to assess the library resources, given that budget restrictions reportedly have forced many to curtail periodical subscriptions. Semiannually, the National Library issues the national bibliography. Separate lists of periodicals are not issued, nor are lists of periodical articles. The National Library is open eight hours a day. There are three library science institutes and one center that provide special training in scientific and technical information.

Some cultural centers are developing children's libraries. Student use of libraries in cultural centers is high. In Oran, Algiers, and Constantine, there are an estimated 50 readers for every reading location. School libraries are poor or nonexistent. No specific budget is allocated to libraries in Algerian schools. Few public libraries have children's sections, as loaning books to children is unlikely. There are no specialized bookshops for children's literature; few keep a section for children's reading. No publishing house specializes in this field. There is no listing of Algerian writers of children's books or systematic advertisement of children's books.

ADMINISTRATION, FINANCE, & EDUCATIONAL RESEARCH

Government Educational Agencies: Algerian education remains highly centralized even though there is a stated aim of gradual decentralization. The Ministry of National Education is the controlling body. The ministry is charged with all activities relative to the education of children of school age (foundation, general secondary, technical secondary, and tertiary) including the programs, evaluation, orientation, communication, finances, planning, cultural, sports and social activities, legal studies, and personnel.

The central administration of the Ministry of Education is comprised of the Secretary General, the Cabinet,

and the Inspector General, plus various directors. Four regional offices (north, south, east, and west) are concerned with pedagogy, financial, administrative, and cultural affairs, and, at the local level, each of the wilayas has a Director of Education (D.E.) to implement programs and operations.

The Ministry of Higher Education and Research administers the universities and engineering schools (grandes écoles). It also is responsible for teacher's colleges (écoles normales superiéure and école normale superiéure d'enseignement technique) and national institutes for higher education (instituts nationaux d'enseignement superiéure) that train teachers for secondary schools.

The Ministry of Primary and Secondary Education administers preuniversity institutions (foundation and secondary schools). A number of other ministries also contain (specialized) institutes. L'Inspector Générale, created in 1995, is directly under the Minister of Education and is charged with inspecting, controlling, and evaluating local educational institutions. This office coordinates approximately 500 inspectors. There are inspectors concerned with the formation of academic disciplines, lycées and colleges, finances, and scholarly and professional orientation.

A national center (L'office national des examens et concours) prepares the annual exams; another (Le center national de documentation pédagogique) purchases all books and educational documents. CNDP (L'Institut national de recherch, pédagogique) is concerned with pedagogical research and the evaluation of the educational system. The institute is comprised of university professors who serve three-year terms on a scientific council. CNF (Le centre national d'enseignement generalizé) is charged with distance education and audiovisual methods of instruction for people who cannot go to school.

Educational Budgets: The government alone funds education. In 1994, expenditures on education totaled 79,889,000,000 dinars (5.6 percent of the gross national product and 17.6 percent of total government expenditures.) Capital expenditures totaled 10,200,000,000 dinars. In the 1997 budget, 12.5 percent of the administrative budget was allocated to education and training. Priorities were teacher training, the development of technical and scientific teaching programs, and adult literacy and training initiatives.

Algeria received substantial assistance from the World Bank. Between 1973 and 1980, Algeria contracted five education loan agreements for sums totaling US$276 million. The World Bank has continued to provide funds and technical assistance in connection with fundamental reform in education, the latest phase of which occurred in 1992.

Since the 1980s, funds for the purchase of books and the renewal and maintenance of library collections, journal subscriptions, and laboratory equipment have been reduced dramatically. The reductions coincided with swelling enrollments from the post independence baby boom.

Universities were hurt by the country's economic crisis in the 1990s. In particular, the restrictive measures imposed on the operating and equipment budgets of the Algerian state by the International Monetary Fund and the World Bank heavily impacted higher education and scientific research.

Educational Research: Research, an essential ingredient of academic excellence, has returned to the Education Ministry again after a decade of reforms that splintered the national research center, split responsibility for research and higher education, and left academic researchers swamped with teaching assignments. The INRE (*Le center national de formation des cadres de l'éducation*) is expected to participate in educational research and experimentation.

The University of Algers houses the National Documentation and Research Center for Education (*Centre National de Documentation et de Recherche en Pedagogie*), or CNDRP. In addition, the Center for the Coordination of Studies and Research on the Infrastructure and Facilities of the Ministry of Education and on Scientific Research (*Centre de Coordination des Études et des Recherches sur les Infrastructure, les Equipements du Ministére de l'Enseignement et de la Recherche Scientifique*) is located in Algiers. The University d'Algers also hosts the Institut de Psychologie et Sciences de l'Education.

Generally in Algeria, an educational institution is evaluated in terms of quantitative internal criteria such as rates of success, failure, retention and attrition. Rarely are external criteria used such as performance tests, interviews with graduates, employers, and the like.

NONFORMAL EDUCATION

Literacy: Adults who acquire literacy through adult programs have great difficulty retaining it, a problem that also occurs with early school dropouts. Post-literacy programs, therefore, are more than remedial measures for ensuring the retention and stabilization of literacy skills. They are intended as lifelong education aimed at improving the quality of life through the continuation and application of learning. Literacy is viewed as an integral part of continuing education.

Estimates of adult (15 years and older) literacy in 2000 ranged from 62 to 72 percent, with male literacy estimated to be from 73 to 80 percent and female literacy,

48 to 63 percent. The National Centre for Literacy Education came into being in 1964 and adopted the concept of functional literacy education with the intent of providing social, political, and vocational education in addition to traditional reading, writing, and counting literacy education.

Adult Education: Continuing education includes all age groups. It is not limited to vocational instruction. Its aim is continuing progress in all fields. Following independence, teachers in all primary schools were compelled to give part of their time to adult education.

From 1988 on, social factors fostered the development of voluntary educational activities. Conditions such as the growth of unemployment among young people, qualified as well as unqualified; the inflexibility of public schools; the effects of the French-Arabic language conflict on the educational system; and other factors led to voluntary educational activities. Some activities are aimed at making up for the inadequacy of the public schools, others are more lifelong in nature, and some provide complementary training for social groups with religious or political motivation.

Distance Education: There were 3.1 million televisions and 7,000 fax machines in 1997, and there was one Internet provider in 1999 with 2,250 Internet users. Algeria's distance education programs, utilizing 18 television broadcast stations in 1999 (not counting low power stations), are run by CNEG (*Centre National d'Enseignement Généralisé*). CNEG is charged with the organization, administration, and teaching methods of the country's education system. The range and scale of CNEG's operation and activities is extensive. In 1991, it was reported that since the inception of CNEG's distance teaching programs, more than one million people had enrolled in the various courses and programs offered—including many females.

In 1990 there were approximately 100,000 students enrolled at the institution. Regional centers provide nationwide coverage of CNEGs activities. Courses are offered in general and technical education up to the baccalauréate, for certificates and diplomas at various levels, and for specialist (professional) training. Courses in education, humanities, music, arts, languages, social sciences, economics, mathematics, science, medicine, medical jobs and professions, and first aid are taught.

The first American production subtitled in Arabic was broadcast in July 1990 on ENTV, the Algerian television network. Some 85 percent of the programs on ENTV were already in dialectical Arabic and Berber as early as 1992, even though dubbing and subtitling are both difficult and expensive. French broadcasts have declined. Funding comes from the government, student fees, and receipts from the sale of course materials. The media and methods of instruction include printed course materials, local press, audio/video cassettes, radio broadcasts, telephone, and group study.

TEACHING PROFESSION

Training & Qualifications: Primary school teachers are trained at institutes of educational technology (*institute de technologie de l'éducation*). Students graduating from intermediate schools enroll in these institutes for two years, the last year as a student teacher. Success on the terminal examination leads to the certificate of general culture (*certificat de culture generale et professionelle*). Students who obtain a baccalauréate train at the *Institut de Formation de Professeurs École Moyenne* (Middle School Teacher Training Institute) to become middle (third-cycle foundation) schoolteachers. Teachers for special education are recruited from those with teaching experience in regular schools; they can participate in special education training courses lasting for one or two years.

Teachers for general and technical secondary education come from the teachers' colleges (*écoles normales superierures* and *écoles normales d'enseignement technique*) and national institutes for higher education (*institutes nationaux d'enseignement superiéure*). Secondary teachers are more specialized than foundation schoolteachers, either in a particular field such as mathematics or in a more general area such as social science. Entry-level teachers at the universities require at least the third-cycle master's-level qualification. Teacher's salaries are low, which has led to strikes at the universities.

Adult Instruction: Each group of teachers and instructors is given approximately one month of instruction on how to teach adults. Adult instructors fall into three categories. Full-time instructors, considered the best and most likely to try new methods and systems, are viewed as the backbone of the system. Second are the part-time instructors who hold other jobs. They are not under supervision and cannot be required to use specific educational methods, but nevertheless are important. The third type include the workers from different sectors who understand their sector and the workers in it, but who rarely have any training in teaching.

SUMMARY

Arabization in the education system included replacing foreign instructors with Arabic teachers, replacing the Eurocentric curriculum with an Arabic/African one, and replacing French with Arabic as the medium of instruction. Not everyone was pleased with the results. "The Ar-

abization in the schools has actually often been managed under disastrous conditions and has delivered a generation of illiterate bilinguals mastering neither Arabic nor French," say the critics.

Arabization was intended to be the vehicle for creating a national identity. Whether or not this has happened, it has created a number of problems, including linguistic generational differences. Parents, particularly middle class parents educated in French, have difficulty following their children's education and in transmitting to their children the culture and cultural information that they themselves have acquired, thereby depriving children of considerable cultural knowledge.

The most experienced administrators find it difficult to communicate to their young recruits (mostly Arabic speakers) their knowledge and their savoir-faire. The communication difficulties occurring between officials of different generations are due not only to purely linguistic differences, but also to psycho-cultural factors bound up with the linguistic differences.

Additional problems occur at training centers where the teachers are often technicians and qualified workers who most often acquired their knowledge and experience in the French language. The students, however, often have poor command of both French and Arabic.

In higher education, the government sought to ease the transition to Arabic by organizing a summer crash course for French-speaking teachers, promising adequate supplies of Arabic science manuals and a working party to establish new terminology. The decree proved impossible to enforce. Many academics did not take the crash course, much of the teaching material is still in French, and the student level of classical Arabic is often inadequate. There are difficulties for students entering sciences, and in particular, medicine, without adequate knowledge of French. Some of the best secondary students fail or quit.

Literacy rates have steadily risen since independence, reaching between 62 and 72 percent in 2000. These are "nominal" literacy rates, which undoubtedly overestimate functional literacy. Too often individuals barely achieving literacy don't retain it.

The first year for students at a university proves to be terribly overcrowded and the students, who are poorly prepared by the lycées, are left to the least competent staff because fully qualified academics do not take first-year students. Many university teachers began teaching when they were taking graduate courses and eventually became permanent staff members without completing their studies. With the mass exodus of the teachers fleeing the violence, a large part of the experienced teaching staff left just as the student numbers increased from 300,000 to 384,000. The exodus has seriously affected scientific research. The universities are further stressed by huge classes, overstressed infrastructures, inadequate and unskilled supervisors, insufficient and old equipment, and a lack of up-to-date educational and scientific materials.

Vocational education suffers from problems with the language of instruction, poor teaching, haphazard job placement (lack of systematization), lack of industrial linkages, and lack of flexibility. These problems produce graduates with inadequate skills in unwanted areas and the inability to adapt.

Algeria still has the fact-acquisition orientation to instruction. It is woven into the fabric of education. The teachers, as their teachers before them, are themselves products of the lecture-rote memorization system (both a French and Islamic heritage) thereby automatically perpetuating the system. The fact-recall examinations further reinforce this orientation. Teachers teach for the exams and until higher order skills such as critical thinking are measured, the situation will not change. Outdated methods and materials and a lack of internships means that students don't get practical hands-on experience. Knowledge is often out of date, citing 10-year-old computer programs. Students complain of insufficient class hours, as classes are often reduced because of strikes.

Funding is inadequate in every sector. Poor pay deters better students from entering teaching. Absent or obsolete equipment and materials lower instructional quality, as do overcrowded schools, classes, and education conducted in multiple shifts.

The Franco-Arabic language split impacts both vocational and collegiate education. The language skill levels of students and of instructors are factors, as is the availability of manuals and teaching materials in the language of instruction.

Since the late 1980s, every sector of Algerian society has been affected by a deep and on-going crisis of violence. This crisis has touched every aspect of life. It is the most serious problem impacting Algerian education today. The violence is a reaction to grinding poverty and blocked opportunity. It is far more a power struggle than a religious issue, and it will continue until the socioeconomic underpinnings are alleviated. The violence has damaged educational progress on every front.

Education in Algeria is clouded by the civil war. Beyond the human and physical damage is the damage caused by the restrictive direction the Islamists seek to impose. The isolationist approach, evidenced by the violent opposition to all foreign ideas and influences, operates to cripple educational progress. Until the violence and intimidation are curtailed, it is hard to foresee a bright future.

Illiteracy rates are still high, but literacy efforts appear to be working and need to be continued as a priority. There are major problems of educational quality and quantity that need to be addressed. Increased funding is part of the answer, but will not by itself cure the problems of ineffective pedagogy, language splits and fluency, lack of coherence between educational levels, and absence of linkages to the work world and to the users of the system. Rigid bureaucracy is slow to react and out of touch with the realities of the work world. Teacher training needs upgrading with models of better pedagogic techniques through in-service training, distance learning, and improved teaching materials and equipment.

BIBLIOGRAPHY

Boubekeur, Farid. "Des Diplômés Algériens parlent de la formation universitaire." *Mediterranean Journal of Educational Studies (University of Malta) 4, no. 2* (1999): 181-186.

Djerbal, Daho. "Algeria." In theme issue: "From Beijing to Belgrade: Academic Freedom Around the World." *Academe 85, no. 4* (1999): 16-18.

Ellyas, Akram, and Lamia Ellyas. "Algerian Strikers Stay Out." *Times (London) Higher Education Supplement,* 3 January 1997, 9.

Faksh, Mahmud A. *The Future of Islam in the Middle East: Fundamentalism in Egypt, Algeria, and Saudi Arabia.* Westport, CT: Praeger, 1997.

Festing, Sally. "Algeria's Long March Out of the Desert." *Times (London) Higher Education Supplement,* 19 September 1986, 14.

Fetni, Abdullatif. "Literacy and Post-Literacy in the Framework of Continuing Education: The Algerian Experience." In *Learning Strategies for Post-Literacy and Continuing Education in Algeria, Egypt, and Kuwait,* ed. by R. H. Dave, A. Ouane and A.M. Ranaweera, 1-39. UIE Studies on Post-Literacy and Continuing Education, no. 6. Hamburg, Germany: UNESCO Institute for Education, 1987.

Flanz, Gisbert H. "Algeria." In *Constitutions of the Countries of the World,* ed. by Gisbert H. Flanz. Release 97-2. Issued March 1997. Dobbs Ferry, NY: Oceana Publications, 1997.

Henderson, Emma. "Switch to Arabic Adds to Deadlock Over Islam Reform." *Times (London) Higher Education Supplement,* 5 June 1992, 10.

Hughes, Stella. "Student Leader Murdered." *Times (London) Higher Education Supplement,* 24 February 1995, 10.

Metz, Helen Chapin, ed. *Algeria: A Country Study.* 5th ed. Washington, DC: Federal Research Division, Library of Congress, 1994.

Miliani, Mohamed. "Algeria." In *Handbook of World Education: A Comparative Guide to Higher Education and Educational Systems of the World,* ed. by Walter Wickremasinghe, 11-18. Houston, TX: American Collegiate Service, 1991.

――――. "The Circulation of European Educational Theories and Practices: The Algerian Experience." *Mediterranean Journal of Educational Studies (University of Malta) 1, no. 1* (1996): 1-12.

van Oudenhoven, Nico, and Rekha Wazir. "Early Childhood Development and Social Integration: The Mediterranean Experience. A Background Paper." Paper presented at the Health and Social Welfare Conference, Scheveningen, Netherlands, 9-11 December 1997. EBSCOhost, ERIC, ED416970.

Rarrbo, Kamel. *L'Algérie et sa jeunesse: Marginalisations sociales et désarroi culturel.* Paris: Éditions L'Harmattan, 1995.

République Algérienne Démocratique Populaire. "Ministère de l'Education Nationale." 1999-2000, 17 February 2001. Available from http://www.meducation.edu.dz.

――――. "Ministry of Higher Education and Scientific Research—English." 1999, 17 February 2001. Available from http://www.mesrs.edu.dz/.

Salmi, Jamil. "Issues in Strategic Planning for Vocational Education: Lessons from Algeria, Egypt, and Morocco." *Journal of Industrial Teacher Education 28, no. 3* (1991): 46-62.

――――. "Vocational Education in Algeria, Egypt, and Morocco: The Crisis and Its Lessons." *Prospects 20, no. 1* (1990): 95-106.

Singh, Madhu. "School Enterprises: Combining Vocational Learning with Production. International Project on Technical and Vocational Education (UNEVOC)," January 1998. EBSCOhost, ERIC, ED424422.

Turner, Barry, ed. *The Statesman's Yearbook: The Politics, Cultures, and Economies of the World 2001.* 137th ed. New York: St. Martin's Press, 2000.

Wise, Michael, and Anthony Olden, ed. *Information and Libraries in the Arab World.* London: Library Association, 1994.

World Education Report 2000: The Right to Education: Towards Education for All Throughout Life. Paris: United Nations Educational, Scientific, and Cultural Organization, 2000.

—M. June Allard and Pamela R. McKay

AMERICAN SAMOA

BASIC DATA

Official Country Name:	American Samoa
Region:	Oceania
Population:	65,446
Language(s):	Samoan, English
Literacy Rate:	97%

American Samoa is an unincorporated territory of the United States. The capital is Pago Pago, which is located on the island of Tutilla. The islands are located approximately 2200 hundred miles southwest of the Hawaiian Islands.

American Samoa has a total land area of 77 miles that includes 5 inhabited islands and 1 uninhabited coral atoll. The estimated population in 2000 was 65,446 and the literacy rate was 97 percent.

The area came under U.S. control in 1900 and was presided over by the Navy until 1951. In 2001, the Department of the Interior administered American Samoa.

The Director of Education in 2001 was Mr. Silia Sataua, who oversaw more than 14,000 students in the public school system. The system comprises 90 early childhood education centers (preschools for three- and four-year-olds situated in the villages); 22 consolidated elementary schools; and three high schools with three new high schools under construction. American Samoa also has a vocational-technical school and a community college.

Nine parochial schools and a Montessori preschool provide private education; the latter is operated by the Poor Sisters of Nazareth. The church-sponsored schools service approximately 2000 students.

Education is compulsory and free for all children between the ages of 6 and 18. The focus of American Samoan education is "education for export," since the majority of young people relocate to the United States.

The American Samoa Community College is an accredited, open admission, coeducational land grant institution. The two-year institution provides transfer programs, vocational training, programs in adult education and literacy, and Samoan and Pacific studies.

BIBLIOGRAPHY

American Samoa U.S. Territory, 2000. Available from http://www.prel.org/pacific_region/am_samoa/index.html.

The Central Intelligence Agency (CIA). *The World Factbook 2000.* Directorate of Intelligence, 1 January 2000. Available from http://www.cia.gov.

Holmes, Lowell D., and Ellen Rhoads Holmes. *Samoan Village Then and Now,* 2nd ed. New York: Harcourt Brace, 1992.

Public Schools in American Samoa, 1999. Available from http://www.government.as/education.html.

—Morgan Axel Peterson

ANDORRA

BASIC DATA

Official Country Name:	Principality of Andorra
Region:	Europe
Population:	66,824
Language(s):	Catalan, French, Castilian
Literacy Rate:	100%

Andorra, located between France and Spain on the southern slope of the Pyrenees Mountains, is one of Europe's smallest countries. This landlocked country houses a population of approximately 66,000 in an area about two and one half times the size of Washington, DC. The population is 43 percent Spanish, 33 percent Andorran, and 24 percent other ethnic groups. The official language is Catalan, but French and Spanish are also spoken. The Roman Catholic Church is the predominant religious institution. Andorra has a 100 percent literacy rate, an average life expectancy of almost 84 years, a negligible unemployment rate, and no income tax. The country has become prosperous since World War II.

Formal education for Andorran students begins at age 6 and is free and compulsory until age 16. Students attend six years of primary school and four years of secondary school. Instruction is provided in Catalan-, French-, and Spanish-language schools. About 50 percent of the students attend the French-speaking schools and the other 50 percent attend the Spanish or Catalan schools.

Most teachers in Andorra are paid by Spain or France, but the schools are built and maintained by the Andorran government. In 1999, about 15.5 percent of the total government expenditure was allocated to education, youth, and sports.

In 1997-1998, an enrollment of 9,272 students attended Andorra's primary and secondary schools; an additional 1,217 students were enrolled in higher education. Although most higher education is completed in other countries, Andorra does have two graduate schools for nursing and computer science programs.

The number of schools and the percent of the budget spent on education seem to indicate Andorra's interest in the future of its children. With continued emphasis on educational development, Andorra will provide well for the education of its students.

BIBLIOGRAPHY

The Central Intelligence Agency (CIA). *The World Factbook 2000.* Directorate of Intelligence, 1 January 2000. Available from http://www.cia.gov/.

The Europa World Year Book 2000. London: Europa Publications Limited, 2001.

—Linda K. Clemmer

ANGOLA

BASIC DATA

Official Country Name:	Republic of Angola
Region:	Africa
Population:	10,145,267
Language(s):	Portuguese, Bantu, Kikongo, Kimbundo, Umbundo, Chokwe, Mbunda, Oxikuanyama
Literacy Rate:	56%
Academic Year:	January-November
Compulsory Schooling:	8 years
Educational Enrollment:	Primary: 989,443 Secondary: 218,987 Higher: 6,331
Teachers:	Higher: 787

HISTORY & BACKGROUND

Angola is located in southwestern Africa, bordered by the South Atlantic Coast to the west, Namibia to the south, Zambia to the east, and the Democratic Republic of Congo to the north and northeast. The Cabinda Province is separated from the rest of Angola by the Democratic Republic of Congo. Angola boasts 1,600 km of coastline with four major ports and rich natural resources. It is potentially one of Africa's richest countries with impressive oil reserves and gem-quality diamond deposits.

Recorded history of the people of Angola dates back to 6000 B.C., with indications that the Khoi and San peoples populated the area as far back as 25,000 B.C. The Bantu arrived from the north from 800 A.D., but their main influx occurred during the fourteenth century, preceding the arrival of the first Portuguese in 1483. The Bantu established kingdoms and absorbed much of the Khoisan-speaking population, and by the fifteenth century, native Africans numbered close to four million in Angola. The major kingdoms were the Kongo, Loango, Mbundo, with smaller kingdoms such as the Lunda and Ovimbundu. The leader of the most important Kongo kingdom, mani-kongo or King Nzinga Nkuwu, converted to Christianity during early Portuguese contact, and his successor, King Afonso, was also a Christian. Early relationships were mutually beneficial for the Kongo king and the Portuguese, who were also ruled by a monarchy and had a similar social structure from nobility to slaves.

Colonial Rule: The Portuguese colonial period in Angola lasted almost five hundred years, but the Portuguese population itself was quite small for most of the period. In 1845 there were only two thousand Portuguese living in Angola, increasing to forty thousand by 1940. The last twenty years of colonial rule, from 1955-1975, saw the major influx of Portuguese who totaled 340,000 at independence in November 1975. Despite their relatively small numbers, the Portuguese had a tremendous effect on native Angolans and their education. For four hundred years, the Portuguese were heavily involved in the slave trade, and perhaps eight million Angolans were lost to slavery. Economically, the Portuguese developed Angola within separate colonial sectors far removed from most of Angolan society. Initially through slave trade and later through production and exportation of rubber, diamonds, coffee and then oil, the Portuguese developed an economy that used natural resources of the country but did little to include Angolans other than through forced labor even after slavery was abolished in 1878.

Socially the Portuguese also had a great impact on the native population. They reorganized villages and established transportation routes that facilitated exportation while at the same time dividing native groups. Colonial rule allowed and at times encouraged interracial marriage, but there was a distinct separation of population groups according to racial background. *Mestiços* of mixed European and African ancestry were allowed access to more education and other opportunities than *indígenas* Africans, but in the last fifty years of colonial rule, official policies were strictly racially divided and even *mestiços* were denied access to or greatly restricted from holding jobs in the public and private sectors. Despite official statements to the contrary, education of the native Africans from the beginning of colonization was discouraged.

Officially Portuguese colonization valued education within its civilizing mission, but little was accomplished, especially outside of urban centers. Natives who were educated were considered *assimilados* or assimilated into the Portuguese culture and values, and during the later years of colonial rule, the brightest were often sent to Portugal for secondary and/or higher education. Many of these, however, were exposed to "progressive" ideas in Europe and were prevented from returning to Africa for fear of political unrest. The most accurate census figures from 1950 estimated that there were fewer than thirty-one thousand *assimilados* in the entire Angolan population of four million.

Although Portuguese was the language of instruction from the first primary school established by the Jesuits in 1605, in 1921 the Portuguese forbade by decree the use of African languages in the schools. In 1940, the Portuguese ruler Salazar signed the Missionary Accord with the Vatican that made the Roman Catholic missions and their schools the official representatives of the state in Africa. Most students in the early mission schools came from traditional African ruling families, thus creating a small but important educated elite in the country. But until the 1960s, the Catholic missions had limited financial backing, and education declined in Angola. In addition, the Portuguese created the Department of Native Affairs, and they officially separated state-run education of the *assimilados* and the Portuguese from that of rural native Africans, run by Catholic missionaries and called *ensino de adaptação* (adaptation school). A great majority of Africans remained uneducated even after the 1960s when a new emphasis was placed on education by the colonial rulers. During the 1960s many new schools were established, but by some estimates, just slightly more than 2 percent of the Angolan school-age children were admitted. Other figures state that enrollment in primary school rose from 6.3 percent in 1960 to 32 percent in 1970, and secondary-school enrollment rose from 0.6 percent in 1960 to 4.3 percent in 1970, but these figures include both state- and missionary-run schools.

Those students who were in schools followed an educational system similar to that in Portugal with a preprimary year stressing language, and then four years of primary school of two two-year cycles. Secondary school consisted of a two-year cycle and a final three-year cycle.

Most students who began schooling, however, did not complete even the primary school cycles. Adaptation schools run by the missionaries had especially high dropout rates, with 1967-1970 figures showing 95.6 percent of the students not continuing. One of the significant reasons for this was that the majority of teachers at all primary schools had very few qualifications. Secondary schools had many Portuguese teachers, but they, too, had limited success in part because they needed to spend the first years teaching material from the primary level.

As part of the Portuguese university system, the University of General Studies was established in Angola in 1962. English and medical studies took place in Luanda, educational studies were given in Sá da Bandeira, and agronomy and veterinary medicine were at Nova Lisboa. Within ten years, close to three thousand students attended the university, but only a very small percentage of these students were African.

Independence: The first national movement against colonial power took place in 1961; Portugal sent in thousands of army troops and tens of thousands of native Angolans were killed. Many nationalists fled to surrounding countries and in time organized into three main guerilla groups: the National Front for the Liberation of Angola (FNLA), the Popular Movement for the Liberation of Angola (MPLA), and the National Union for the Total Independence of Angola (UNITA). Although each group fought Portuguese colonial rule, they also fought each other and were already close to civil war by November 1975 when Portugal granted independence to the colony. The MPLA, backed by Cuba and the Soviet Union, gained control of Angola after independence. Civil war ensued and eventually the FNLA, supported by China and the United States, dissolved, leaving UNITA with support from South Africa as the primary opposition to the ruling MPLA. Cuba sent in troops in 1975 in response to South African troops crossing the border at Namibia, and over the next fifteen years hundreds of thousands of Angolans lost their lives to civil war. In 1986 the United States backed UNITA against the Marxist MPLA governing party, but in 1991 it was influential in negotiating an eventual peace agreement between UNITA and the MPLA, and Cuba withdrew its troops.

This brief period of peace was shattered in September 1992 when UNITA leader Jonas Savimbi refused to accept MPLA leader José Eduardo dos Santos as president of Angola following elections. Armed conflict resumed, and in May 1993 the United States officially recognized the dos Santos government, removing all support of UNITA. A new peace agreement was signed between dos Santos and Savimbi on November 20, 1994, but sporadic fighting continued until a new national unity government was installed in April 1997. However, in late 1998, UNITA refused to give up territory and resumed fighting against the government. Civil war continued into the new millennium. By March 2001, dos Santos' government had control over most of the country, but fighting continued and civilian lives continued to be lost, notably from the estimated seven million landmines scattered across the countryside.

CONSTITUTIONAL & LEGAL FOUNDATIONS

Angola's 1975 Constitution, revised in 1976 and 1980, guarantees access to education for all. It prohibits discrimination based on color, race, ethnic identity, sex, place of birth, religion, level of education, and economic and social status. It also outlines social goals of combating illiteracy, developing education and a national culture, and respecting all religions while maintaining a clear separation of church and state. National defense requires mandatory military service of men and women over the age of eighteen, which has significant effects on enrollment in higher education.

By all accounts, literacy in Angola was only 10-15 percent at the time of independence. The government initiated a literacy drive in November 1976, giving priority to rural Africans who had been virtually ignored under colonial rule. The National Literacy Commission under the Minister of Education was created to administer the literacy campaign.

The civil war that ensued after independence destroyed much of the country's infrastructure, including the educational system. Most Portuguese instructors left the country, many buildings were destroyed or badly damaged, and instructional materials were scarce. The shortage of qualified teachers was especially pronounced: of the twenty-five thousand primary school teachers in Angola, only two thousand were considered even minimally qualified. At the secondary level, there were only six hundred teachers. To improve these conditions, the First Party Congress in 1977 resolved to institute an eight-year compulsory system of free, basic education for children between the ages of seven and fifteen. Other important educational goals in the early years of independence included, in order of importance, primary education, secondary education, and intermediate and university education.

EDUCATIONAL SYSTEM—OVERVIEW

Marxism-Leninism was declared the basis of Angola's new educational system by the ruling MPLA, but a respect for traditional African values was also retained. Four years of compulsory, free primary education began at age seven, and secondary education began at age eleven, lasting eight years. Missionary schools were nationalized and private or religious organizations were not allowed to conduct schools.

Considerable efforts were made by the government in the first five years of independence to improve the accessibility of education, especially for primary-school aged children. There were fewer than 500,000 students in Angola in 1974, but by 1980 at least 1.6 million children were studying. Enrollment of the relevant age group was up to 80 percent in 1980, but by 1984, it had fallen to 49 percent due to austerity measures and population increases. Government statistics from 1990 show 1,180,008 students enrolled at the primary level, but only 148,137 at the middle and secondary level, with no indication as to the percentage of relevant age group. President dos Santos stated that by January 2000 school equipment had been acquired to meet 42 percent of the country's needs, demonstrating that 1,040,000 children between the ages of six and fourteen were without a school. However, the Ministry of Justice estimates that only about 5 percent of children have had their births registered. Unregistered children do not legally exist and therefore cannot enroll in schools.

Since 1980, education funding has been low, and all areas of education are in dire need of facilities, materials, and teachers. In 1994, for example, 4.4 percent of public expenditure was allocated for education. Civil war has consumed most of the country's financial gains. Of the US$2 billion the government earned in oil and diamond revenues in 1996, US$1.5 billion was spent on arms and military equipment.

During the early 1990s, Angola began gradually moving to a free-market economy, pursuing a policy of liberalization and privatization in industrial economic sectors. The effects could be seen within the educational system as well. Sixteen years after independence, major changes were made in Angola's educational system with Law N.18 that institutionalized private teaching in 1991. In 2001, the Ministry of Education announced that it would require a "symbolic payment" for public education,changing the free education policy that had been in effect since independence.

Basic adult literacy continues to be extremely low, but there are conflicting figures from government and other sources. No reliable census has been taken since 1970 which makes it difficult to assess not only literacy but also other educational needs. Statistics available in 2001 from UNICEF estimate the total population of Angola to be 12.5 million and adult literacy to be 56 percent for males and 29 percent for women. It is unlikely that these figures include population in UNITA-claimed territory. During the mid-1980s, Savimbi established a state-within-a-state with its own educational system that closely resembled that of Portugal. UNITA territory was much smaller but still in existence in 2001.

PREPRIMARY & PRIMARY EDUCATION

Of the estimated 2.5 million Angolan children of preschool age, fewer than twenty thousand attend preschools or day care centers. Preschools were established in 1977 and the government considers them important to compensate for home environments not conducive to early learning. Primary education is made up of three levels; the first is theoretically compulsory and lasts four years. The second and third levels last two years each. There continues to be a severe shortage of schools for Angolan youth, and the government estimates that 60 percent of the school facilities have been destroyed or are in disrepair. Most primary school students can only receive three hours of instruction a day because the schools operate two or three shifts daily. Lack of qualified teachers continues to be an acute problem, as well as high dropout rates, low attendance rates, and promotion rates below 50 percent. Instructional materials, equipment, and even desks and chairs are limited in many areas. Most schooling is only available in provincial capitals because rural areas have been especially hard hit by intense fighting. But even in the nation's capital, Luanda, schools cannot keep up with demand. On February 7, 2001, the start of the new school year in Angola, 45,000 students were to enroll in Luandan schools. The city could only accept 5,000 of them. As many as 100,000 students (primary and secondary) study at private schools in Luanda, but the cost is crippling for most residents.

SECONDARY EDUCATION

For those students who complete the third level of primary education (eighth grade), two alternatives of secondary education are available. Students may follow a three-year course required to enter universities, or they may follow a four-year technical education course. Technical education includes either teacher training for primary teachers or specialized education in areas including business, health, agriculture, fisheries, and mechanics. Secondary education enrollment increased from 105,000 students in 1977 to 151,759 in 1984, but accurate figures for later years have not been available. In 1990, 3.3 percent of boys and 1.7 percent of girls in Luanda were enrolled in secondary education. The percentages in rural areas of the country were estimated to be 0.4 percent for boys and 0.2 percent for girls.

HIGHER EDUCATION

Universidade de Agostinho Neto was established in 1976 in Luanda with affiliated institutions in Huambo (formerly Nova Lisboa) and Lubango (formerly Sá da Bandeira). University enrollment has varied from three thousand to over seven thousand. There are departments of law, education, medicine, economics, science, and civil engineering in Luanda; economics, educational science and law in Lubango; and agronomy, medicine, economics and law in Huambo. Schools have been destroyed in Lubango and Huambo, and those in Luanda have been prone to closure for political reasons and teacher shortages. There is also a severe shortage of laboratory equipment in medical and science schools, affecting teaching and research.

In 1992, the Council of Ministers declared Decree 38-A, extending rights to the Catholic Church to administer a non-profit university. Angola was ''open to fruitful co-operation initiatives that safeguard the full autonomy and identity of the State and the peoples'' and therefore authorized The Episcopal Conference of Angola and São Tomé to create Universidade Católica de Angola. It further acknowledged the university as a corporate public service entity with statutory, scientific, pedagogic, patrimonial, administrative, financial, and disciplinary autonomy. The Catholic University of Angola opened on February 22, 1999 in Luanda with initial funding from Citizens Energy in the United States, Energy Africa, SAGA Petroleum, and Mobil. Initial enrollment was 320 students. The university offers five-year courses in law, economics, management, and computer science. A state-of-the-art computer and Internet center offers computer training for faculty and students with plans for distance learning.

Finally, there are plans underway for the *Universidade Nova de Angola* with funding from the *Eduardo dos Santos Foundation*. This new university will emphasize high-tech training and education and will complement coursework at the *Universidade de Agostinho Neto*. Correspondence courses and distance learning will make courses available to more students in the country. At its foundation is a network of Brazilian universities that will assist in planning, developing curriculum, and continuing student exchanges already in progress.

ADMINISTRATION, FINANCE, & EDUCATIONAL RESEARCH

The Ministry of Education has control over primary and secondary education. It shares responsibility for vocational education with numerous other ministries. The Adult Education Department of the Ministry of Education administers national literacy programs. Accurate financial budgets concerning education expenses are not available; however, from 1980-1994, education was allotted less than 5 percent of public expenditure of the annual budget. Many educational improvement projects, particularly those targeting primary school needs, have been financed through international humanitarian aid. UNICEF's US$18,848,700 appeal for Angola for 2001 included US$2,464,000 allocated for education. The bulk

of the appeal, over $US10 million, was for health and nutrition.

NONFORMAL EDUCATION

Nonformal education is greatly needed in Angola, and it is one area where substantial innovation is occurring. As in all other areas of education, nonformal education lacks financial backing and sufficient teachers, materials, and facilities, but it has continued because of humanitarian aid such as that given by UNICEF and national and international nongovernmental organizations (NGOs). Among important efforts in rural areas have been education projects such as landmine awareness and vocational training for war-injured and landmine victims in tailoring, metalwork, carpentry, and business administration. Urban and rural education projects include literacy education as well as vocational training for targeted populations such as child soldiers (5,000 soldiers in 1997, half of which were demobilized in 1996), street children in Luanda (estimated at 5,000 in 1996), amputees (70,000 in 1996), and internally displaced persons (3.8 million estimated in 2001) who have fled their home areas due to fighting.

The Ministry of Education employs distance learning in two remote education projects to reach students in seven of Angola's eighteen provinces. The initial project in banking served 221 students. Plans have begun to launch a television education network that eventually could be used nationwide. The Adult Education Department initiated a new literacy program in 1999 that hopes to eradicate illiteracy in the country by 2007. Greater effort will be directed to the countryside and particularly to women who have had limited access to education. The literacy program also teaches adults in local vernaculars. Angola has six national languages: Kikongo, Kimbundo, Umbundo, Chokwe, Mbunda and Oxikuanyama. Although Portuguese is the official language and that of instruction, only 27 percent of adult men and 10 percent of women speak the language, greatly limiting their educational and occupational opportunities.

TEACHING PROFESSION

A shortage of qualified teachers has always limited the educational system in Angola, even during colonial days. When the Portuguese left in 1975, other teachers arrived, notably from the Soviet Union and Cuba, but language differences hampered their success. Most native Angolan teachers (75 percent) are only minimally qualified to teach at the primary level having completed only four to six years of school themselves.

Much has been attempted to improve teacher training since independence; however, the teaching profession is in such shambles that it is difficult to retain even poor

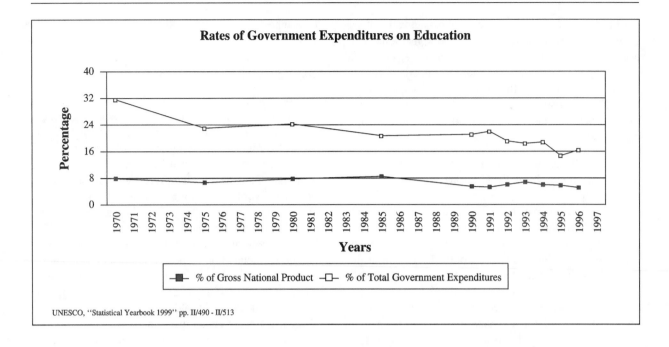

Rates of Government Expenditures on Education

UNESCO, ''Statistical Yearbook 1999'' pp. II/490 - II/513

teachers. Teaching conditions are very difficult, and especially outside of Luanda, it is not uncommon to see many students crammed into a small classroom without books, desks, or even chairs. The government reports an average of thirty-six students per teacher, but tremendous variation exists among provinces, and there are reports of as few as thirty to as many as one hundred primary school students per teacher and classroom in some areas. One of the most challenging aspects of the teaching profession is that teachers are often not paid for up to six months at a time. Not surprisingly, teacher absenteeism is high. Some teachers charge fees directly to families, but few can pay.

A few promising teacher-training programs have been developed by international humanitarian organizations with plans to expand across the country. Future Teachers in central Angola requires one and one-half years of training, a one-year internship, and a commitment to teach in a rural school. The teacher college has 30 networked computers with CD instructional material, especially important because printed material is difficult to obtain.

SUMMARY

The government of Angola has outlined excellent priorities in its efforts to improve the country's extremely poor educational system. But unless armed combat comes to a complete halt, little can be done to improve conditions nationwide. At the very minimum, financial resources must be committed to rehabilitation and construction of schools, acquiring instructional materials and equipment, and in greatly increasing teacher training and

pay. Without tremendously improving literacy, Angola can never develop much beyond the limits of a separate, educated, elite class. However, even more pressing concerns than education compete for government funding. In a nation where half of the population is under 15 years of age and where only one in four children makes it to his or her fifth birthday, basic health and safety of the nation's youth must be improved before education can be given the priority it deserves.

BIBLIOGRAPHY

The Embassy of the Republic of Angola, Washington, D.C. O Pensador. Angolan Mission to the United Nations, March 2001. Available from http://www.angola.org/.

The International Rescue Committee. Recovering From Thirty Years of War: Refugee Women and Children in Angola. Women's Commission for Refugee Women and Children, December 1996. Available from http://www.intrescom.org.

Tvedten, Inge. Angola: Struggle for Peace and Reconstruction. Boulder, CO: Westview Press, 1997.

United Nations. Relief Web. Office for the Coordination of Humanitarian Affairs, 201. Available from http://reliefweb.int/.

United States Committee for Refugees. Country Report: Angola. Worldwide Refugee Information, 2000. Available from http://www.refugees.org/.

United States Library of Congress. Angola: A Country Study. Federal Research Division, February 1989. Available from http://lcweb2.loc.gov/frd/cs/.

—Michèle Moragné e Silva

ANGUILLA

BASIC DATA

Official Country Name:	Anguilla
Region:	Puerto Rico & Lesser Antilles
Population:	11,797
Language(s):	English
Literacy Rate:	95%

HISTORY & BACKGROUND

Anguilla, from the French word *anguille* (eel), is a long, narrow island in the Caribbean Sea. The island, which is about half the size of Washington, DC, is located approximately 150 miles east of Puerto Rico and is the most northerly of the Leeward Islands in the Lesser Antilles. Its length of 16 miles and width of 3.5 miles gives the country a total area of 35 square miles, or 91 square kilometers. The territory also includes Sombrero, Scrub, Seal and Dog Islands, and Prickly Pear Cays. The capital is The Valley, which is located in the center of the island. It is a part of the British West Indies and is a dependent British Crown colony.

Anguilla was colonized by British settlers from St. Christopher (St. Kitts) in 1650 and has been a British territory since that time. In 1882, Anguilla was united with St. Christopher and Nevis as a single British dependent colony. The inhabitants resisted the alliance with several protests and attempts to separate from the association with St. Christopher. Results were finally achieved in 1967 when the Anguillans ejected the St. Christopher policemen and declared the country's independence, refusing to further recognize the authority of the state government of St. Christopher. After two years of negotiations, British troops were sent in to establish control of the island. In 1980, the country was officially separated from Nevis and St. Christopher and placed under direct British rule; in 1982 a new Anguillan constitution was ratified.

In 2000, the Anguillan population was approximately 12,000, of which 26 percent were 14 years of age or less. Birth and death rates in 2000 were moderate with average life expectancy standing at slightly more than 76 years. Most of the inhabitants are of African descent. The official language is English, and Protestant denominations comprise the largest religious groups. The literacy rate, based on the definition of ages 12 and over being able to read and write, stands at 95 percent.

CONSTITUTIONAL & LEGAL FOUNDATIONS

Because Anguilla is a dependent British colony, its government is outlined and administered according to British dictates. The administration of the island is the responsibility of a governor appointed by the monarch of the United Kingdom, an executive council, and a legislative assembly. The territory has a legal system based on English common law, and the country's defense is the responsibility of the United Kingdom. Although Anguillans live under rather poor conditions in some respects, with a 1998 per capita income of approximately US$7,900, they fare better than a number of other Caribbean countries. Low crime rates and virtually no taxation add to the appeal of Anguilla.

EDUCATIONAL SYSTEM—OVERVIEW

Government expenditure on education in 1991 was approximately 17 percent of the total expenditure, and in 1995 the amount rose to more than 18 percent. This amount allows the government to provide free education for children ages 5 to 15. In addition to education, the school health service provides physical screenings for children five to nine years of age, and health educators teach schoolchildren the importance of healthy living. Environmental conditions are also monitored.

While education is free in Anguilla, it is also compulsory from ages 5 through 15. The academic year consists of three terms from mid-September to mid-July. Each term is 13 weeks long. Students receive a summer recess of six weeks, a Christmas break of four weeks, and an Easter break of three weeks. Instruction is given in English, the official language.

The Anguillan education system is based primarily on the British system of education. When students finish their high school education, they take the Caribbean Examination Council (CXC) examination. If they receive four or five passes, including English and math, they may enroll in a program for advanced education. The program is called "6th Form." It is a two-year program that leads to Advanced Levels examinations, which, in turn, can lead to credit in U.S. universities.

Instructional technology and other resources are being implemented in Anguillan schools. In 2000, most schools had a teacher resource room, Internet access, audiovisual materials, copying and facsimile equipment, and e-mail capability. Most of the schools also had individual Web sites. Educators, as well as students, are learning through hands-on courses and workshops to use technology in different formats. One example of technology instruction is found in the Anguillan Library Computer Club. Weekly meetings are held for the purpose of instruction in Windows, Spreadsheets, Basic Programming, and digital cameras. While this instruction is not part of the school curriculum, it is arranged for students during after-school hours.

PREPRIMARY & PRIMARY EDUCATION

In 1988, the country had four privately owned pre-primary schools, all subsidized by the government. In addition, the government has appointed a curricular officer for early childhood education. The officer's responsibility is to develop activities and programs to further student learning at early ages. Because most preprimary teachers are untrained, the government conducts training programs and ensures that teachers are exposed to "in sight" training at centers in Trinidad and Tobago. In 1996/97, the teacher/student ratio was 1:8.

Anguilla has six primary schools whose combined enrollment in 1998 was 1,502. With a total of 77 teachers, the teacher/student ratio was 1:20. The primary curriculum includes the core courses language arts, math, science, and social studies. A co-curriculum includes arts, music, physical education, and technology. Since the early 1990s, emphasis has been placed on preventive education in life skills, drug awareness, and guidance/counseling. Education is also provided for students with mild to moderate learning disabilities through modified curriculum, adapted physical environments, and appropriate teaching methodologies.

SECONDARY EDUCATION

Only one comprehensive (secondary) school exists for students who complete their primary school education. It is located centrally in the capital, The Valley. Enrollment for 1997 totaled 1036, with the majority being female. When students reach the age of 11, they are automatically transferred to the secondary program, whether or not they have completed their primary curriculum. In addition to core courses, curricular changes are under way to include environmental education, home economics, and geography. More than 80 percent of the country's labor force has completed a secondary school education.

HIGHER EDUCATION

Higher education is available at locations outside the country. In 1995, a little more than 7.5 percent of the labor force had received a university education, while 6 percent had an education from a technical college.

NONFORMAL EDUCATION

Adult education is a growing element of the Anguillan education system. The government has appointed a coordinator for adult and continuing education. The government is also moving to establish relations with partners in education to set guidelines to ensure the best use of resources for continuing education. In addition, the Ministry of Education serves as a center for several overseas examinations.

TEACHING PROFESSION

In the mid-1980s, Anguillan schools had a total teaching staff of 92. Seventy-five percent of that number were completely trained teachers. In the late 1990s, about one third of primary teachers were untrained, a small number of whom participated in the Inservice Teachers' Training Program and were referred. The goal in 2000 was to have all teachers trained within ten years. To improve their education, teachers also train through programs such as computer training workshops or camps.

SUMMARY

With a literacy rate of 95 percent, the Anguillan education system is successful. However, rather than remain at that level, the education system continues to move forward. This forward movement has been greatly impacted by innovations in technology and communications. Until 1971, the island had no system of telecommunications. By 2000, the country had a digital telephone exchange, national paging service, cellular telephone service, voicemail, e-mail, and Internet access.

In addition to technological advances, Anguilla has begun to use other educational innovations. The Caribbean Advanced Proficiency Examination is being tested on a pilot basis as a possible replacement for the Cambridge A Level examination. In 1998, Anguilla became the first Caribbean country to introduce Reading Recovery, a school-based intervention for literacy problems, in its primary school system. In 1992, a "Test of Standards" was implemented for grades three, five, and six to set performance norms.

Many reforms and improvements are under way in Anguilla because the government recognizes the deficiencies in its educational system. The inhabitants must continue to work diligently to modernize the education system that serves as a vital component of the country's efforts to improve the quality of life for its citizens.

BIBLIOGRAPHY

Bonk, Mary Rose, ed. *Worldmark Yearbook 2000.* Detroit: Gale Group, 2000.

"Bootcamp 2000." Anguilla Library Computer Club, 12 February 2001. Available from http://www.computerclub.ai/.

Cable & Wireless. "History of Cable and Wireless Anguilla," 2000. Available from http://www.anguillanet.com/.

Carter, Tara. "School Exams in Anguilla." *Bob Green's Anguilla News,* 1998. Available from http://www.news.ai/ref/schoolexams.html.

Cashmore, Ross, and Estelle Cashmore. "Reading Recovery in Anguilla." *Bob Green's Anguilla News,* 1998. Available from http://www.news.ai/ref/reading.html.

The Central Intelligence Agency (CIA). *The World Factbook 2000.* Directorate of Intelligence, 1 January 2000. Available from http://www.cia.gov/.

KPMG (Anguilla) Corporate Services LLC. "About Anguilla," 1999. Available from http://www.kpmg.ai/.

Pan American Health Organization. "Anguilla: Basic Country Health Profiles, Summaries," 1999. Available from http://www.paho.org/.

UNESCO. *EFA 2000 Assessment: Country Reports-Anguilla,* 2001. Available from http://www2.unesco./org/wef.

—Linda K. Clemmer

ANTIGUA & BARBUDA

BASIC DATA

Official Country Name:	Antigua and Barbuda
Region:	Caribbean
Population:	66,422
Language(s):	English
Literacy Rate:	89%

HISTORY & BACKGROUND

The nation of Antigua and Barbuda is located in the Eastern Caribbean, situated strategically in the Leeward Islands, between the Caribbean Sea and the North Atlantic Ocean, east-southeast of Puerto Rico, near maritime transport lanes of major importance to the United States.

The largest of the islands is Antigua, which is about 13 miles across, and spans a total area of about 108 square miles. While the low-lying coral island of Barbuda consists of approximately 62 square miles. The capital, and island's main seaport, is the city of St. John's, which is located on the island of Antigua. Known as the "gateway to the Caribbean," this twin island state also includes Redonda, a small, uninhabited island which only consists of about 6 square miles and is located 32 miles southwest of Antigua. The total land area is about two and a half times the size of Washington, D.C.

In 1493, Christopher Columbus discovered the island, naming it Antigua after the Santa Maria La Antigua church in Seville, Spain where he prayed before leaving on his voyage. In 1632, the British were the first Europeans to colonize the islands and, with the exception of French occupation for a brief period of eight months in 1666, Antigua remained a British colony until 1967. Although it gained its independence on 1 November 1981, Antigua continues to be part of the Commonwealth of Nations and the 157th member of the United Nations (Charisma, 1997).

With a population of nearly 78,000 on Antigua, approximately 30,000 live in and close to the capital of St. John's. Barbuda's population is around 2,000, most of whom reside in Codrington, Barbuda's only city. While most of the population is of African descent, many are from British, American, Portuguese, Syrian, and Lebanese lineage. Antigua is home to many retired Europeans and North Americans, and the annual population growth is about 1.3 percent. The official language of the country is English, although natives also speak a local dialect known as Creole (Charisma, 1997).

Although the economy of Antigua and Barbuda is primarily service and tourism oriented, accounting for approximately 60 percent of the Gross National Product (GDP) and leading the way as the country's most important economic indicator, agriculture remains an important industry as well, although a declining one. Fruit and vegetable production dominate the agricultural scene, but the government has encouraged expansion into livestock, cotton, and export-oriented food crops. Some other crops produced include bananas, pineapples, coconuts, cucumbers, mangoes, and sugarcane.

The agricultural sector is constrained not only by the country's limited water supply (water management is a major environmental concern due to the limited supply of natural fresh water and is further hampered by the clearing of trees to increase crop production, which causes rainfall to run off too quickly), but also by labor shortages that reflect the pull of higher wages in tourism and construction. The growth of construction has been spurred by the tourism industry. Manufacturing industries that thrived during the 1980s are export oriented, producing clothing, furniture, paint, and galvanized sheets.

Antigua and Barbuda's government is a Parliamentary Democracy, a democracy based on the British Parliamentary system, and consists of a Cabinet of Ministers, headed by the Prime Minister. As head of state, Queen Elizabeth II is represented in Antigua and Barbuda by a governor general who acts on the advice of the Prime Minister and the cabinet. It also has a bicameral legislature, which includes a 17-member Senate appointed by the governor general and a 17-member popularly elected House of Representatives. The Prime Minister, leader of the majority party in the House, conducts affairs of state with the cabinet, both of which are responsible to the Parliament. Elections must be held at least every five years but may be called by the Prime Minister at any time. The Constitution was established in 1981 and constitutional safeguards include freedom of speech and freedom of worship, movement, and association, along with freedom of the press. Antigua and Barbuda is a member of the eastern Caribbean court system, and its legal philosophy is based on English law.

EDUCATIONAL SYSTEM—OVERVIEW

Antigua and Barbuda's literacy rate is about 90 percent, one of the highest in the Eastern Caribbean. The non-discriminatory educational system is funded by the state at all levels with nine years of education compulsory. At 5 years old, a child enters the primary school system, progressing to the secondary school system when he/she reaches the age of 11 or 12. Entrance into the secondary system requires successful completion of the common entrance examinations. The state provides full five-year secondary education, where the students are equipped to take what are referred to as Ordinary Level (O'Level) exams, specifically the Caribbean Examination Council or Cambridge University examinations. These exams are also used to prepare the students for college and university level courses. Some of the students take the Advanced Level (A'Level) exams offered by Cambridge University, which gives them entrance into the regional University of the West Indies or, if they desire, to foreign universities.

Through the University of the West Indies, the Antigua State College has offered the First Year university program since 1988, and successful students continue on to complete their final two years of study, leading to the undergraduate or Baccalaureate degree. It also offers students technical vocational training in home management, office practice, refrigeration, electronics, agriculture, and other areas. The University of the West Indies has campuses in Jamaica, Barbados, and Trinidad with areas of study covering natural sciences, which include Math, Biology, Physics, and Chemistry. Studies in the arts, general studies, engineering, tropical agriculture, law, medicine, and computer science are also offered. Antigua hosts a center for the University of the West Indies, which also offers courses to qualified students.

BIBLIOGRAPHY

Antigua Nice Ltd. *Antigua information at Antigua Nice Ltd..* 2001. Available from http://www.antiguanice.com/.

Batt, Tony. ''Antigua Leading Way in Regulating Internet Gambling.'' *Las Vegas Journal Review* (30 April 2001).

Charisma. *Antigua Net: Antigua!* 1997. Available from http://www.antiguanet.net/.

Coutsoukis, Photius. *Antigua and Barbuda Economy.* 1999. Available from http://www.photius.com/.

United States State Department. ''Antigua and Barbuda'' *Background Notes on Countries of the World.* (April 1997).

U.S. Department of State. *Background Notes: Antigua and Barbuda.* April 2000. Available from http://www.state.gov/.

—*Marsha L. Shively*

ARGENTINA

BASIC DATA

Official Country Name:	Argentine Republic
Region:	South America
Population:	36,955,182
Language(s):	Spanish, English, Italian, German, French
Literacy Rate:	96.2%
Academic Year:	March-December
Number of Primary Schools:	22,437
Compulsory Schooling:	10 years
Public Expenditure on Education:	3.5%
Foreign Students in National Universities:	12,678
Libraries:	2,700

Educational Enrollment:	Primary:	5,153,256
	Secondary:	2,594,329
	Higher:	1,069,617
Educational Enrollment Rate:	Primary:	113%
	Secondary:	77%
	Higher:	36%
Teachers:	Primary:	309,081
	Secondary:	125,218
Student-Teacher Ratio:	Primary:	17:1
Female Enrollment Rate:	Primary:	113%
	Secondary:	81%

HISTORY & BACKGROUND

The Republic of Argentina, the second largest country in South America, contains 22 provinces, 1 national territory, and the federal district of Buenos Aires. Argentina's varied topography and the remoteness of some of its regions have played a large role in the development of its educational system, which serves students who live not only in urban centers, but those who live in rural areas as well. Educational facilities range from the largest university in Latin America, to one-room primary schools scattered in remote areas. The largest city, Buenos Aires, has more than 12 million people, 40 percent of the country's total population. In each of the two other major cities, Córdoba and Rosario, reside more than 1 million inhabitants. Eighty-five percent of the population is descended from Europeans, and the remaining ethnic groups consist mostly of *mestizos* and Amerindians. More than 90 percent of the population is Roman Catholic, giving the educational system a strong religious background and influence. The country's official language, Spanish, is common to the whole educational system.

Spanish Jesuits and priests of other orders were among the first to open schools in colonial Argentina. Between 1770 and 1820, the government vigorously promoted popular education, establishing primary schools and commercial, art, agricultural, and nautical schools. At first, enrollment was only 6 percent of the school population in Buenos Aires, and in several provinces no one was enrolled. By the 1800s, secondary and normal (teacher-training) schools had been established in the provincial capitals, but most were still poorly attended. Not until well into the twentieth century did children of poorer families in the remote cities receive more than two or three years of schooling.

Under the Constitution of 1853, a secondary school system was set up along with dozens of primary schools throughout the country. The government also formed the National College of Buenos Aires as a five-year institution devoted to the study of humanities and science. By 1878, Argentina had more than 400 private schools, a third of them private and Catholic. The Catholic Church continues to play an important role in the educational system in 2001.

Between 1868 and 1874, the government established another 1,000 primary schools, reorganized secondary education, and founded schools of agriculture, schools for the handicapped, and the Military College and Naval School. Educators from the United States were brought in to set up teacher-training schools and kindergartens. School enrollment rose from 6 percent of the eligible population to 38 percent in the next decade. Compulsory primary school attendance was also established for ages 6 to 14, and the illiteracy rate for persons 14 and older dropped from 77 percent to 13 percent between 1869 and 1947.

Until World War I, schools were concentrated in the major cities, Buenos Aires, La Plata, Rosario, Santa Fe, and Córdoba. Secondary schools prepared students for entrance to universities and were attended mainly by the children of the well-to-do. The national government opened some rural secondary schools that taught agronomy, animal husbandry, and viticulture, but poorer families still could not afford to send their children to these schools. Middle-class families were not interested in them; they looked to university training in the professions as the only path to success and status for their children. This attitude continues to hamper curricula reform in the schools.

In 1918, a student-led reform movement at the University of Córdoba marked a major turning point in Argentine education. This movement sought to eliminate upper-class privilege, which had kept poorer students out of the university, and to protect the university from governmental intervention. It also aimed at modernizing the university curricula, raising academic standards, and getting rid of incompetent and conservative faculty. Free tuition was established, and poor students were given financial assistance. This manifesto led to the creation of the Argentine University Federation, which included student representatives from the five national universities.

Toward the middle of the twentieth century and after, as teachers' salaries fell and conditions in the schools deteriorated, the schools became the target of the changing policies of a succession of repressive regimes. Perónist ideology was injected into the curricula and textbooks. Teachers who resisted these changes were fired. University autonomy was abolished, and 70 percent of the faculty was dismissed. On the positive side, the government stressed primary and secondary school attendance, reducing illiteracy and increasing the number of skilled young people. Adult education was offered outside the federal capital for the first time ever. Schools and services for shut-ins and handicapped children were established. Schools were exempted from taxation, and efforts were made to make the quality of provincial education equal to that offered in urban centers. More secondary schools and a teacher-training school for girls were founded.

In 1958, legislation authorized the establishment of private universities, and the same year the first small provincial university was opened in the La Plata province. The majority of the private universities were operated by Catholic orders, and the 1958 law gave them and other private universities the authority to grant degrees. These new universities emphasized the traditional professions, law and medicine, avoiding new disciplines, such as sociology and psychology. From 1966 to 1972, the military government began decentralizing the educational system by transferring the schools created by the federal government to the provinces. This transfer would make better use of increasingly scarce resources and reduce overlapping of education systems. After 1983, as political freedom returned to the country, the universities regained autonomy. Entrance exams were again eliminated as a way to equalize educational opportunities. Enrollments nearly doubled in the public universities, causing problems with overcrowding and understaffing.

The changes introduced in the 1960s by some national universities—such as new degrees in the sciences, departmental organization by discipline, and the development of graduate programs—reached only a small sector within the university. The universities continued to offer lengthy degree programs, and part-time professors continued to lecture students who combined studies with outside employment. The problems of this traditional model were aggravated by open admissions and budgetary constraints, which resulted in a very high student dropout rate and a teaching staff made up mostly of part-time personnel with no graduate-level training. The government continued to authorize new institutions, both public and private, and the giant public universities continued to expand their programs without becoming accountable for their academic quality or economic feasibility. More than 100,000 graduates, about 1 in every 10, are employed in teaching and research positions at the universities, making higher education the main employer in the academic labor market.

CONSTITUTIONAL & LEGAL FOUNDATIONS

The responsibility for administering the educational system is shared by the federal government and the 22 provincial governments. This responsibility arises from a number of legal sources, including the National Constitution, the provincial constitutions and laws, and various decrees and resolutions made by national and provincial political leaders since the nineteenth century. Each province addresses education differently, though all of them specify that primary education is free and compulsory, and all deal with school financing.

The Constitution of 1853 stipulated that the National Congress was responsible for general and university education; the provinces, for primary schools. Law number 1420, enacted in 1874, set down the administration of primary schools, inspection, school finance, and so on. Under this law, education from the ages of 6 to 14 is compulsory and free to everyone through the university.

In 1993 a new federal Law, number 24.195, superseded Law 1.420, placing the entire national educational system under legislative control and setting new objectives, academic structure, and content for all levels of education. The Law gives the Ministry of Culture and Education the authority to make policy and control the quality of education. In addition, the Law establishes the means for gathering statistical information on schools, evaluating and regulating teaching quality, and improving school infrastructures.

The federal government established the Federal Educational Pact, made up of members of the national administration, the provinces, and the municipality of Buenos Aires. Among its many principles, the Pact specifies the amount and source of financing that education is to receive. By 2000, the goal was to achieve 100 percent attendance of children 5- to 14-years-old. The Pact members also aimed to eliminate ill-equipped schools and to upgrade school libraries and instructional equipment.

EDUCATIONAL SYSTEM—OVERVIEW

The school year in Argentina runs from March to December and lasts about 200 days. Schools are closed for national holidays, such as Good Friday and Easter, and two weeks in July for vacation. Normally, public elementary schools are in session four and a half hours each weekday. Saturdays are generally reserved for extracurricular school activities. Often, a school will have a morning and afternoon session, allowing pupils and teachers to choose their sessions. Some elementary schools offer evening classes for adults. Bilingual programs are offered in many private elementary schools.

The educational system is divided into four distinct levels. The preprimary level (kindergarten) is not compulsory and enrolls children from 3- to 5-years-old. The primary (elementary) level is compulsory and consists of

7 grades. Pupils at this level must remain until all 7 grades are completed or, in case of repetition of grades, until age 14. Children from 6- to 12-years-old attend primary school along with adults who need instruction on this level. The secondary level is attended by youths from 12- to 17-years-old, or 16 if they are employed and attend night school. Courses of study vary from 3 to 8 years and prepare students for vocational or professional programs. Higher education includes private and national universities and institutions that provide teacher training and advanced training in technical careers.

University education is provided by public universities, either national or provincial, and by private universities. Since 1955, university entrance has been open to all students who have completed secondary school. Some public universities, such as the University of Buenos Aires, require an orientation course or an entrance exam, or both, and many private universities require other qualifications. The traditional university degree is awarded after five or six years of full-time study in a specialized field. Degrees may be obtained for completion of part of a program or for completion of a training program that enables the degree-holder to work in a specific profession. The academic year normally consists of two, four-month terms, and full-time students usually take three classes per term for six hours each week. Lecturing remains the principal method of instruction.

The academic year begins in March and ends in December, although the calendar may vary somewhat from one department to another within the university. The typical university consists of independent schools or colleges in a particular field, such as law or agriculture, and these faculties are free to vary their grading system, calendar, and academic procedures. Universities design their own curricula and degree programs, but the National Authority for University Affairs approves them. Universities communicate with one another by way of the National Interuniversity Council, one for public and another for private universities, both composed of university rectors (presidents). Student unions also influence university policy, but neither the rectors' committees nor the student unions have any official authority over policy.

Universities may award various kinds of degrees. The short-degree program, which takes two or three years to complete, trains a student for a specific area in the workforce, such as computer programming or librarianship. The intermediate degree takes three years and qualifies one for immediate employment in a specific profession or to continue for another two years and earn a license in a particular field.

As with other degree programs, each university determines the length of the program and its curriculum. The medical degree ranges from five to seven years.

Some universities require seven years of study for the same degree that others award in five years. Although most universities require students to take their courses in a prescribed sequence, those who earn a degree are qualified to practice in their field of study, such as law, medicine, or engineering. Wide diversity may be found in grading systems and examinations, dealing with failure, and many other aspects of university affairs.

Since the 1980s, graduate degree programs have proliferated and include master's degrees along with doctoral degrees. Emphasis remains on training for a specific profession rather than on original research, and only about 7 percent pursue a postgraduate education, since a degree qualifies one to work in a profession without it. Increasingly, however, universities are requiring that all candidates for full professor hold an earned doctorate, and many of the professions are giving added importance to graduate degrees. The National Authority for University Affairs approves the degree, but no central authority on the national level oversees graduate programs, so standards vary considerably among the universities. Doctoral programs usually include course work and a thesis that contributes new knowledge to a field of study.

A great discrepancy between urban and rural schools remains. Many of the provinces are geographically isolated, and nearly 50 percent of the country's population lives in metropolitan Buenos Aires, leaving the rural areas with very little power to dictate policy at the national level. Consequently, educational attainment is lower in the rural areas. On the whole, however, many improvements have been made since the return of democratic government in 1983. Rural education has been expanded, more than 17,000 adult schools have been built, and hundreds of secondary schools offer night classes to those in the workforce.

PREPRIMARY & PRIMARY EDUCATION

Preprimary school in Argentina is not mandatory, but from the 1980s, enrollment in preschool increased more rapidly than at any other level. Most preprimary schools are private and serve the children of the upper class. By 1986, Argentina had slightly more than 8,000 preprimary schools. According to a government statement, preprimary school should prepare the child physically, spiritually, and morally, as well as instill orderly habits and obedience. The child learns personal hygiene along with correct posture and graceful movements and is introduced to language skills, arithmetic, writing, and reading. Religion is also part of the child's instruction.

Primary education lasts seven years, at the end of which time the student receives a Certification of Completion. It is, in theory at least, compulsory for children ages 6 through 14. The curriculum includes mathematics,

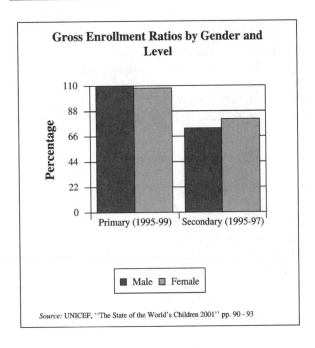

Gross Enrollment Ratios by Gender and Level

Primary (1995-99) Secondary (1995-97)

■ Male □ Female

Source: UNICEF, "The State of the World's Children 2001" pp. 90 - 93

Spanish, social studies, basic science, art, music, and physical education. About 10 percent of the primary schools are private and enroll 18 percent of the age group. Fewer than 50 percent of the students who enroll complete all seven years of the primary curriculum. By the 1990s primary schools numbered more than 21,000. Nearly 18,000 of these were controlled by provincial governments and more than 2,200 schools were private. Almost 5 million children attended the primary level.

In 1977, the official curriculum included language, mathematics, social studies, basic science, aesthetic training (music, art, and handicrafts), and physical education. A revised curriculum in 1978 minimized the curriculum to make it adaptable to different geographical areas. All courses are required, and each course lasts one complete academic year from March to December. The curriculum is developed by a national administrative committee and then approved by the Ministry of Culture and Education.

Only about half of those starting primary level ever reach secondary school. Until 1983, parents from the lower class were not able to afford the private tutoring that the high-school entrance exam required. To make education more equitable, the democratic government in 1983 eliminated the entrance exam and selected students by lottery to attend the desired schools. Students who fail a subject are allowed to take an exam in that subject the following academic year; after a second failure, students must repeat the entire grade. Grade repetition is one of the main causes of school dropouts. The national proportion of students completing the seven years of primary schooling rose steadily from 35 percent in 1960 to around 65 percent in 1990.

SECONDARY EDUCATION

Secondary education is not compulsory but is offered free in federally funded public schools. In 1987, nearly 2 million students were enrolled in secondary programs, about 74 percent of the relative age group. Students may enter secondary programs after successfully completing the seven years of primary school. Secondary education programs, whether academic or commercial, are divided into a basic cycle of three years, followed by a cycle of two or three years. The commercial programs teach accounting, computer science, and the like. A technical-vocational program includes 12 to 15 hours a week in applied workshops. About 85 percent of the students studying at the secondary level are enrolled in academic and commercial programs. Graduates of any secondary program requiring five or more years to complete are eligible for further study at the tertiary level. Students are graded at the end of the year, and they must make up any failures from the previous year; they are not allowed to graduate with any failures on their records.

Students who have completed seven years of primary school may enter any of the technical schools where the programs have an academic core, but stress applied learning and practical skills in workshops. These programs are employment-oriented and vary in the number of hours needed to complete them. Shorter courses prepare students for employment only, with no access to higher education; the longer courses include academic courses and do offer access to higher education. Beginning in the 1990s, graduates of any of these programs could teach their specialization in technical schools. Several secondary schools offer agricultural training in a wide range of specializations, such as irrigation, cultivation of fruit trees and wine production, and so on. Practical experience is required. As in other technical schools, students go through a six-year course of study, at the end of which they can advance to the university or non-university programs.

HIGHER EDUCATION

Students who have completed secondary school may enter a public or private university, a non-university institution, or a military school. Programs are offered by both public and private universities and institutions; postsecondary degree and certificate programs beyond secondary school may require two to seven years to complete and focus on a single area of study.

Argentina has more than 80 public and private universities offering degree programs; they may be mass metropolitan universities or private elite institutions. On the whole, however, all are non-residential universities with their students commuting to class from their homes. The public universities are often plagued by strikes and political conflicts. Academic equipment is generally rather poor, and in many instances the educational technology is rather primitive. The number of graduate-degree programs more than doubled in the 1990s, totaling more than 1,000, and between 10,000 and 15,000 students were enrolled in these programs, up from only 3,000 a decade ago. Forty percent of these graduate programs are master's degree programs.

The private and public sectors cooperate in providing education in geographically isolated areas. If a private institution operates in a community where no public school exists, the national government might pay teachers' salaries, depending on the resources of the community. The largest institutions tend to locate in the Buenos Aires metropolitan area, while in the rest of the country most private institutions are small and operate with the support of the Catholic Church. A new wave of private institution development has taken place since 1989 and is part of the overall privatization policy geared to shift the burden of financing higher education to the private market.

The University of Buenos Aires, in many ways, represents public higher education in Argentina. Since the 1980s, the University's budget has been woefully inadequate, and overcrowding has become a chronic problem. More than 250,000 students are spread among its 12 faculties and 4 schools. The number of professors, both full-time and part-time, cannot keep pace with massive enrollments. Curricula are outmoded, and the University lacks adequate libraries, laboratories, and modern teaching aids. Students and faculty alike must pay for their books and Internet access. Most professors work part time, teaching a course or two per term for token payment. In most of the faculties, fewer than 20 percent are full time, but even full-time faculty members must hold other jobs, since yearly salaries average only about $24,000 for senior faculty. Full-time faculty are evaluated every seven years and must compete for their jobs in an open contest with other applicants. Part-time staff members have no place to meet students or prepare for class. Even many full-time faculty are without offices of their own.

Entering students encounter several obstacles from the beginning. Most of them hold jobs while studying and must take a one-year general-education course that is overcrowded and taught by part-time staff. Sixty percent of those who start this course either drop out or fail the examinations. Even those who survive have virtually no contact with professors until late in their academic program, if then. In some disciplines, such as medicine, the dropout rate approaches 90 percent. Only about 7 percent of those who enroll end up graduating, and the average time for graduation is nine years.

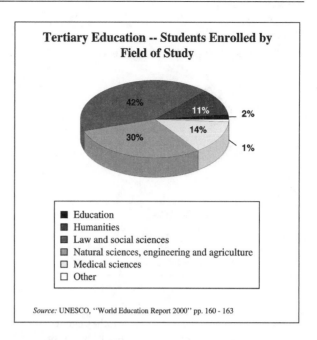

Tertiary Education -- Students Enrolled by Field of Study

- ■ Education
- ■ Humanities
- ■ Law and social sciences
- ▨ Natural sciences, engineering and agriculture
- ☐ Medical sciences
- ☐ Other

Source: UNESCO, ''World Education Report 2000'' pp. 160 - 163

ADMINISTRATION, FINANCE, & EDUCATIONAL RESEARCH

Administration: Two official authorities are responsible for the educational system in Argentina, the national Constitution and the constitutions of the 22 provinces. The highest government office is the Ministry of Culture and Education, whose minister is appointed by the president and sits in the President's Cabinet. The minister oversees the political aspects of the educational system, and the executive functions are performed by the Secretariat of State, Education, and Culture, who works through various Councils. Under these Councils, five directorates work directly with schools in technical and administrative matters, proposing programs, textbooks, and the like. The provincial governments have their own Councils of Education, and various municipalities run a few schools. Private schools are regulated by the same offices as regulate the national schools. The curricula and credentials of teachers in the private schools are approved by one or more national and provincial offices. The certificates and diplomas awarded by private schools must be accredited by federal inspectors.

The complex nature of Argentina's educational system and its divided administrative authority promotes confusion, increases the costs of the system, slows progressive change, and complicates administrative control. For example, before 1992, most secondary and postsecondary education was supervised by at least nine different agencies. The vocational-technical secondary programs and one postsecondary teacher training institute for special programs are supervised by the National

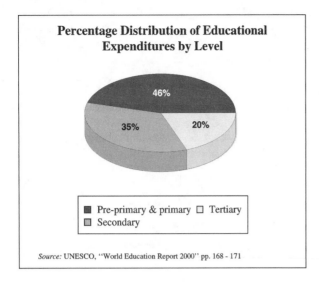

Percentage Distribution of Educational Expenditures by Level

46%
35%
20%

■ Pre-primary & primary □ Tertiary
■ Secondary

Source: UNESCO, "World Education Report 2000" pp. 168 - 171

Council for Technical Education. Another agency supervises 43 agricultural secondary schools throughout Argentina, sharing its authority in some schools with another agency. The National Authority for Artistic Education controls another 60 schools, and National Authorities exist also for adult, special, and physical education.

Private secondary schools and institutions of higher education must apply to the Minister of Education for a review of teaching personnel, facilities, programs of study, and diplomas awarded; they also must submit plans of study for each degree program to the National Authority for University Affairs at the Ministry for approval in order to award official titles.

Financing of Education: The public educational system is financed mainly by the government, which allocates a certain percent of the national budget annually to the Ministry of Education and Culture. In turn, the Ministry finances all public schools, subsidizes private schools teaching the official curriculum, and funds specialized institutions, including the national university system. A few other ministries give some financial support to their own specialized educational establishments. The national Congress determines how much of the annual budget goes to education, and a part of tax revenues goes to education. The largest portion of the education budget goes to public schools, both national and provincial. Allocation to private schools always lags behind these two groups. In 1955, the percentage of the national budget for education was 10 percent. By 1974, it was 17 percent. In 1977, Argentina was spending US$40 per citizen on education; by comparison, the United States in the same year spent $250 per citizen. In 1987, however, allocation to education fell to 9 percent of all government expenditures. Between 1963 and 1988, expenditures decreased at

a rate of 1.5 percent per year, while student enrollment increased annually at 5.9 percent.

University budgets have become the largest single item directly financed through the Ministry of Education. In theory, each university must submit a budget to the Ministry through the inter-university council, which is included in the yearly budge proposal to Congress. Wages and salaries make up more than 90 percent of the total budget.

Private institutions of higher learning are not subsidized by the government, and primary and secondary schools, to receive funding, must meet conditions stipulated by national authorities. School construction is financed in part by special taxes, and many schools are financed by bonds, fines for non-attendance, sales of public lands, and private donations. Technical schools benefit from a special technical education tax levied on certain industrial and commercial businesses and from proceeds derived from the sale of products made in school workshops. Since 1982, technical schools have been funded by the national government but, like other sectors of the educational system, they regularly face financial hardships. To supplement their budgets, they rely on local communities. In some areas, parent organizations help buy school equipment, and some schools exchange services with other schools.

Research: Research is only marginal to the function of the university; teaching is the university's main or, in some cases, its only function. University faculty are not required to conduct research for employment, advancement, or prestige. On the whole, research is left to independent research centers. By 1991, Argentina had 27 publicly financed research institutions, which have been converted into self-supporting private companies and foundations. At the National Council of Scientific and Technical Research, which finances projects for about 8,000 scientists and other researchers throughout the country, scientists earn from US$330 to US$800 a month.

Many independent research centers offer master's programs, sometimes in conjunction with universities. A research center may receive some support from the national government, but it receives most of its funding from private foundations, such as the Ford Foundation; from tuition; or from business grants. Many faculty members in these institutions come from abroad and many of them teach part-time at a university.

Alternative Education: Increasingly, Argentina is gaining a variety of educational institutions that are independent of the traditional four-level framework. A growing number of students enroll in the National

Technological University, primarily a technological institute offering professional training. Established specifically for the working class, this university has 29 campuses throughout the country. Beyond secondary school, a variety of schools offer programs in a broad range of careers. Some offer master's programs in business administration and are designed for professionals with three to five years of experience who work and study part-time. Their relative high cost is usually paid by employers.

The National Authority for Artistic Education, for example, operates about 60 schools throughout the country at the secondary and tertiary levels that offer programs in fine arts, interior design, dance, music, and so on. Entering students must pass an artistic aptitude test and study from three to five years, depending on the program. Often, these students are also enrolled in an academic program at another school. Other tertiary institutions offer two- and four-year courses to those who wish to teach in vocational schools and in three-year courses for nurses and hospital assistants.

All branches of the military offer educational programs, primary schooling to those who have not completed elementary school, and postsecondary schooling to those who have. Curricula generally combine traditional academic disciplines with courses designed to prepare students for military duties or promotion. Both the national government and provincial authorities operate police academies where men and women are trained in a variety of law-enforcement fields. Two-year postsecondary programs train legal aides, security officers, and technical assistants in police law. Schooling that combines basic elementary school with vocational training is also available to prison inmates.

Special-Need Schools: A variety of primary schools serve students with special needs. Home schools offer both free boarding and educational services to abandoned, indigent, or orphaned children. Outdoor schools outside urban centers offer primary education to children with chronic health problems. Special-education schools are available for students with motor, sensory, or mental handicaps. Classes may be held at the student's home, at a hospital, or in a regular school building.

NONFORMAL EDUCATION

Some primary schools are devoted exclusively to those who are beyond school age, providing them with the standard curriculum in the evening to accommodate those who hold jobs. The National Plan for literacy and adult education has established centers offering accelerated primary education to any adult who lacks basic literacy.

TEACHING PROFESSION

Teacher training at the secondary level is furnished by normal schools, which date from 1869. Today, the basic requirement for a teaching career is completion of a five-year normal school. Satisfactory completion earns a person a teaching certificate and permission to teach in a national primary school, or in a provincial school, if local authorities approve the certificate. An additional two years are required for teaching in kindergarten, and four years at secondary teacher-training schools qualify a person for teaching at the secondary level.

In 1956, the Teachers' Statute granted civil service status to teachers and guaranteed them, among other benefits, tenure and seniority, certain holidays, the right to appeal inequitable administrative actions, medical care, and pension rights. In 1961, about 99 percent of the primary teachers had the requisite certification, a record of qualification unmatched in Latin America. In 1967, about 325,000 teachers were employed in the schools. Seventy-two percent of these teachers were in the primary system; 17 percent in the secondary system; and 5 percent in higher education. By 1967, more than 200,000 students, 86 percent of them women, were enrolled in normal schools, up from 75,000 in 1953.

In the late 1960s, the preprimary and primary programs were elevated to the status of a non-university degree program consisting of a two-year course followed by a half year of residency. Students in this program had to have a secondary-school diploma from a normal school. At the same time, some universities began their own teacher-training programs. Since 1968, teachers have been required to attend a university to receive their credentials. Private institutions have also become important teacher-training centers. By 1967, about 140 different kinds of schools provided postsecondary education outside the universities to almost 30,000 students, more than three-quarters of whom were women. Teachers are now trained in a variety of institutions, including provincial, technical, and private institutes and universities. Even with these many avenues to teacher training, not every teacher in an elementary school has been through a teacher-training school. In recent years, teachers have swamped the marketplace, yet qualified teachers are in demand, especially in the remote regions.

SUMMARY

Argentina's educational system has not had a smooth evolution. Many educational reforms have been politically motivated and punitive, and the reforms of one government have been undone by a subsequent government. Political upheavals in 1946, 1955, 1966, and 1973 decimated the teaching profession, each time changing the character of the universities. Progress has been further hampered by the fact that Argentina's educational system is a maze of parallel and overlapping agencies and authorities, each having the power to decide educational affairs. This bureaucratic redundancy is expensive and makes change slow and difficult.

Although Argentina boasts a literacy rate of 94 percent of the population, this figure does not tell the whole truth. Recent studies indicate that as of the year 2000, about 54.0 percent of Argentina's adults had no education beyond primary school, only 14.1 percent had finished secondary school, and only 4.0 percent were university graduates. According to the Ministry of Culture and Education, more than 9 million people have no education past primary school. In recent years, the principal barrier to educational improvement has been inadequate funding, which has resulted in constant tension between the public education sector and the state.

The government abolished entrance examinations in 1983, and within three years the number of students at public universities nearly doubled—to about 635,000 nationwide. At the University of Buenos Aires alone, enrollments rose from 132,000 students in 1984 to 250,000 in 1986. But increased enrollments were not accompanied by budgetary increases, so standards declined sharply and buildings and staff could not keep pace with soaring enrollments. In 1989, about 92 percent of the budget for universities went to salaries, causing many universities to have so little money that they stopped paying their other expenses.

Economic troubles have become the central issue in education and have raised union membership. Collegiate bodies, teaching and non-teaching unions, and students have joined in an almost permanent political fight for university budgets and salaries since 1984, often paralyzing the universities and making consensus on proposed reforms impossible. Enrollments in Argentina's private universities have increased while those of the public institutions have slipped. Observers say one reason is labor conflicts at public institutions, which jeopardizes the completion of studies.

By all accounts, teachers do need to be paid more. Faculty salaries from 1971 to 1990 decreased more rapidly than the wages of civil servants and non-farm workers. A teacher in Buenos Aires receives little more than $300 per month, and teachers in the provinces receive even less. A university lecturer receives about $200 a month for five lectures per week. In some areas of the country, salaries arrive late or teachers are paid with meal tickets. Not surprisingly, the quality of teachers has fallen along with salaries.

The government agrees that increased funding is necessary, but it calls on the universities themselves to

help ease the financial crisis. Universities could generate income by providing the business community with training, scientific, and technology services; students also could pay fees. Making school administrations more efficient and reducing educational bureaucracy are further ways to ease the crisis. In 1991, the government did its part by reducing the staff of 27 universities and of the Ministry of Culture and Education. Public universities also suffer from poor financial management. On average they spend for each student up to three times more than private universities do.

At the same time, the Minister of Education is trying to align university curricula with the reality of the marketplace, revising programs to take into account realistic social needs. Undergraduate programs are too long and, in most cases, impractical. About 30,000 students graduate from Argentine universities each year, yet the labor market can absorb only 4,000. At least 100,000 university graduates have left Argentina in the last 20 years because of a lack of job opportunities.

Argentina's system of higher education is criticized for promoting social inequality. Only 8.3 percent of all university students come from the lowest social stratum. Forty percent of the 18 to 24 age group in Buenos Aires are enrolled in school, whereas only 10 percent of the same age group is enrolled in education in the poorer southern and northern provinces. Urbanization has produced a great discrepancy between urban and rural education.

The proliferation of graduate degree programs in Argentina is causing problems of quality control for the country's higher education system. By 1995, Argentina had more than 80 public and private universities and more than 1,600 non-university institutions, all awarding degrees and diplomas and causing a crisis in organization. The universities are working with the Ministry of Education on a new system to accredit graduate programs, seeking help from other countries in designing and implementing new graduate programs.

Since the country returned to a democratic government in 1983, the educational system has received serious attention at all levels, evidence of which may be seen in some genuine improvements and many positive proposals awaiting implementation. The Federal Education Act of 1993 set forth the government's plan to revamp and revitalize the national educational system. The Act establishes a system for evaluating quality in education and a federal network for permanent teacher education. The Act also speaks of educational reform and restructuring the national educational system. To help ease the budget crisis, an Argentine group has set up the Fund for the Improvement of University Quality, which aims to distribute $224 million over a period of five years to update library collections and facilities, and to provide fellowships for graduate studies in Argentina and abroad. Ministry officials will support efforts by the country's privately financed universities to obtain loans for similar purposes from the World Bank and other agencies.

Argentina continues to be deeply committed to improving the quality of education. Although financing is at the heart of the problems plaguing the educational system, it will take more than money to mend the system. The problems have developed over years of economic and political turmoil and are so deeply rooted in social beliefs and traditions, in the country's size and geographical features, and in the national character that most believe a successful resolution will not be easy, inexpensive, or quick.

BIBLIOGRAPHY

Albornoz, Orlando. *Education and Society in Latin America.* Pittsburgh, PA: University of Pittsburgh Press, 1993.

Altbach, Philip G. "Survival of the Fittest (University of Buenos Aires)." *Change* v. 31 (May-June 1999): 47(2).

Argentina: Reallocating Resources for the Improvement of Education. A World Bank Country Study. Washington, DC: The World Bank, 1991.

Cookson, Peter W., Jr., Alan R. Sadovnik, and Susan F. Semel. *International Handbook of Educational Reform.* New York: Greenwood Press, 1992.

Fischman, Gustavo E. *Imagining Teachers: Rethinking Gender Dynamics in Teacher Education.* New York: Rowman & Littlefield Publishers, Inc., 2000.

Kelly, Cristina Bonasegna. "Argentina Struggles to Insure Quality of Graduate Programs." *The Chronicle of Higher Education* no. 49 (1997): 35-36.

"More Students Than Cash: School Funding and Education Policy in Argentina." *The Economist* (US), 355, no. 12 (2000).

Parrado, Emilio A. "Expansion of Schooling, Economic Growth, and Regional Inequalities in Argentina." *Comparative Education Review* 42 (1998): 338.

Reisberg, Liz A. *Argentina: A Study of the Educational System of Argentina and a Guide to the Academic Placement of Students in Educational Institutions in the United States.* Washington, DC: A World Education Series Publication, 1993.

Shumway, Nicolas. *The Invention of Argentina.* Berkeley and Los Angeles: University of California Press, 1991.

Torres, Carlos Alberto, and Adriana Puiggrós, eds. *Latin American Education: Comparative Perspectives.* Boulder, CO: Westview Press, 1997.

Tulchin, Joseph S., and Allison M. Garland, eds. *Argentina: The Challenges of Modernization.* Wilmington, DE: Scholarly Resources Books, 1998.

Tyler, Lewis A. et al., eds. *International Issues for the Twenty-First Century: Higher Education in Latin America.* Philip G. Altbach, Series Editor. New York and London: Garland Publishing, Inc., 1997.

—Bernard E. Morris

ARMENIA

BASIC DATA

Official Country Name:	Republic of Armenia
Region:	Middle East
Population:	3,344,336
Language(s):	Armenian, Russian
Literacy Rate:	99%
Number of Primary Schools:	1,402
Compulsory Schooling:	11 years
Public Expenditure on Education:	2.0%
Foreign Students in National Universities:	869
Libraries:	1,300
Educational Enrollment:	Primary: 256,475 Secondary: 372,187 Higher: 35,517
Educational Enrollment Rate:	Primary: 87% Secondary: 90% Higher: 12%
Teachers:	Primary: 13,620 Higher: 4,065
Student-Teacher Ratio:	Primary: 19:1
Female Enrollment Rate:	Secondary: 79%

HISTORY & BACKGROUND

Located in Asia Minor, Armenia borders Turkey to the west, Georgia to the north, Azerbaijan (including the disputed Nagorno Karabagh region) to the east and south-west, and Iran to the south. While the historic Armenian kingdom once extended into northeast Turkey and north-west Iran, from the Caspian to the Mediterranean seas, Armenia is the smallest of the 15 former Soviet Socialist republics, at only 29,800 sq km (11,490 sq mi) in size. The population is 3.8 million. Although for centuries most Armenians lived in highlands tending animals, today 68 percent occupy the nation's towns and urban areas.

Education in Armenia has long been regarded as a vital part of the nation's identity and heritage. An ancient culture and mountainous land, Armenia was located at the center of what has been called the "cradle of civilization." Unfortunately, because it was situated between Eastern and Western civilizations, the country was continually caught in the turmoil of war. At the same time, however, its seat astride trade and migration routes between Europe and Asia Minor allowed goods and ideas to pass frequently through the land. Intercourse with China, for example, may have helped bring to the west some of the tools and knowledge that aided in events of the Renaissance such as the discovery of the new world.

Over time, Armenia developed a unique language, extensive literature, and distinctive art and architecture, all the while sustaining several dynasties. In 301 A.D., it was the first nation to adopt Christianity as the official state religion; subsequently, Armenian schooling has been closely connected with the Armenian Apostolic Church at various stages of the nation's history.

Until the fifth century, Armenians wrote in Greek, Aramaic, Syriac, or other alphabets. In 406 A.D., the clergyman Mesrob Mashtots created the original Armenian alphabet of 36 letters (two more were later added). Immediately afterwards, the first Armenian schools opened. They were state-run and accessible to a large population.

In the seventh century, Anania Shirakatsi developed a primary school that marked a milestone in education. Shirakatsi's writing gained renown outside Armenia for pioneering ideas such as tailoring material according to age and emphasizing not only content but methods of teaching.

One of the first institutions of higher education, the Academy of Tatev, was founded in the ninth century. Other schools and tremendous scholarship emerged over the next 400 years in centers of education throughout Armenia. Notably, one of the historic educators and deacons of the time, Hovhannes Sarkavag, was distinguished for arguing that love of the child was central to teaching. Although an invasion by Seljuk Turks in the eleventh century caused the first large-scale emigration of Armenians, universities were founded, such as University of Gladzor

in 1280. The reestablished University of Tatev, celebrated beyond the borders of the country, was referred to as a "Second Athens," with instruction in music, aesthetics, and philosophy. These medieval Armenian institutions conferred degrees of "Archimandrite" and "Rabbi," upon passing of written examinations and defense of theses. From the thirteenth to the fifteenth centuries, libraries issued forth and the first schoolbooks were pioneered.

Just as the West began exploring new lands and engaging new ideas in earnest, the East began to degenerate. By the sixteenth century, increasing numbers of schools were forced to close as the land was invaded repeatedly. Soon, most of Armenia was ravaged and fragmented. With no leader, its people amounted to a small Christian cluster surrounded by Muslims and nomads. For many years, the Armenian culture and its people dispersed, with their cultural life developing primarily in centers abroad, in Moscow, Venice, Tiblisi, and elsewhere.

Yet by the 1800s, Armenian intellectual life began to expand again as contact with Europe grew. Armenians helped build the first printing house in the Middle East in 1638 in Iran. The first novel ever written in spoken Armenian was produced by Khatchadour Abovian (1805-1848), making leisure reading accessible to more than solely the rich or educated. Armenians—at home and abroad—grew an extensive educational system during this time, developing schools, textbooks, teacher training, and educational policies to guide the process of learning across the lifespan.

This cultural and educational revival was aggressively dismantled, however, as Armenians fell victim to one of history's first genocides. In 1894 the Ottoman Turks began a massacre of over 200,000 Armenians which lasted for the next two years. The Russians closed Armenian schools and ordered the confiscation of church property, while the Turks wanted to move Armenians to Mesopotamia. After WWI broke out in 1915, the Young Turk party of the Ottoman Turkish Empire oversaw the systematic elimination of 1.5 million Armenians and the deportation of thousands more in a genocidal campaign that lasted until 1918.

With the advent of a brief period of statehood between 1918-1920, the first Armenian republic was established, building on the progress that had been made decades earlier—and then destroyed—to help create a foundation for today's educational system. By 1920, the institutions of school and church were separated. Over the next 20 years illiteracy was reduced drastically, from 83 percent to 16 percent between 1932 and 1940. Compulsory secondary education evolved in the 1960s with extensive construction and development of preschool, vocational, secondary and higher education systems.

After 1921, the Communist Soviet era dominated and information and literature from non-Communist nations was censored. Stalin's policy of "Russification" discouraged Armenians from preserving traditions and customs of their predecessors. By the 1980s, however, Gorbachev's rise to power brought new notions of reform, namely *glasnost* (openness in the media) and *perestroika* (rebuilding and restoring prosperity).

Just as positive change began to come to the region, however, the nation and its education system suffered the devastating blow of a massive earthquake in 1988. Some 50 villages were hit directly, and more than 500 schools were utterly destroyed. In all, estimates of as many as 50,000 Armenians were killed and 500,000 people left homeless by the earthquake. Conditions in the earthquake region continue to be dire, with tens of thousands of people still living in—and business and schools being conducted in—the temporary housing they were granted at the time of the quake.

Meanwhile, a war had ignited earlier in the year with neighboring Azerbaijan over the small region of Nagorno Karabagh ("mountainous fertile black gardens"), spawned after hundreds of Armenians were raped, maimed, and killed in Sumgait, north of Baku. Although a tenuous cease-fire has been in place since 1993, Azerbaijan and Turkey continue to impose a blockade around Armenia, leaving the nation in a crippling energy crisis and desperate economic condition.

Upon the breakup of the USSR, the Armenian people declared themselves a republic in 1991, for only the second time in nearly 700 years. While the main cities bustle with activity, they badly need modernizing due to lack of state financing for the fledgling nation.

CONSTITUTIONAL & LEGAL FOUNDATIONS

Even amidst difficult economic times, the value of education continues to be held in high regard in Armenia. The present educational system has its roots in the brief period of independence during the formation of the first Republic of Armenia (1918-1920), and was solidified in the ensuing Soviet era of governance (1920-1990).

The significant role of education in the nation's set of priorities can be found within the first chapter of the Constitution of the Republic of Armenia, which outlines the Foundations of Constitutional Order. Article 11 charges the government with the task of supporting the development of Armenian education and cultural life. The Constitution further states that every citizen is entitled to free public secondary education, as well as free higher and specialized education as granted on a competitive basis.

The Ministry of Education and Science manages the general primary, secondary, and higher educational systems in Armenia. Included among its many responsibilities are the implementation of national education policy, the preparation of legislative bills, the enactment of reform measures, the establishment of performance indicators for decision-making, and the control of the system's resources.

During the Soviet era, the entire educational system rested under state control. Since then, the government has crafted decrees and laws to decentralize school administration. As part of the nation's Constitution, the Law of the Republic of Armenia on Education is organized into 54 articles, outlining the State's goals, objectives, and guarantees regarding the nation's educational system. In this regard, the Law defines education as the "process of training and instruction based on the interests of the person, the society, and the state, aimed at the maintenance of knowledge and its transmission to the new generation."

Article 4 situates the foundation of the state educational policy in "the national school, the main goal of which is preparation of persons with adequate professional and all-round (sic) knowledge, educated in the spirit of patriotism, state and humanity." The full system is divided into six areas: preschool, general (elementary and secondary), vocational, higher professional, supplementary education, and postgraduate professional education. Through the national school system is developed "the spiritual and intellectual potential of the Armenian people, maintenance and development of national and universal values." As an ally in these endeavors, "The Armenian Church also has a contribution in this affair."

Article 5 offers the principles embedded in the school system, including national dignity, democracy, universal values, assistance to the Diaspora, secular teaching, and equality between and access to both state and private educational offerings. For its part, the State guarantees citizens the "right to education, irrespective of nationality, race, sex, language, religion, political or other opinions, social origin, economic situation or other circumstances." Beyond these intangible, yet valuable, principles, the government goes so far as to pledge to sustain "regular functioning of the educational system, and creat(e) socioeconomic conditions" conducive to receiving a formal education. Towards this end, the system of secondary education is free, and textbooks are also made available without charge or for nominal rental fees.

In the years since independence, dramatic changes have been made to the national educational system, including new mechanisms for managing individual schools and selecting school directors. Local control over school management has shifted to city governors who appoint school councils that approve costs estimates and financial-economic reports, and also select school directors. While this has been regarded as an effective means of improving school management, the reforms have not sufficiently addressed issues of training and implementation. Steps are being taken to address these issues at the school level via a national program involving the training of school headmasters.

EDUCATIONAL SYSTEM—OVERVIEW

Armenia's public educational system is manifested in four levels of schooling: preprimary (ages three to six), primary (grades one to three), intermediate (grades four to eight) and senior (grades nine to ten). The latter three levels are often grouped in the category of general education. Public schooling is free and compulsory until the age of sixteen, essentially through the senior level. From this point, students undergo testing to help determine their placement and financial support in either vocational study (two-year degrees) or from an extensive array of higher education institutions, both private and public. These are further broken down into baccalaureate (four-year undergraduate degrees), magistracy (two-year Master's degrees), and post-graduate (two-year scientific degrees). In sum, Armenia is home to more than 1,400 schools, not including preschools, kindergartens, and specialized institutions.

Armenian became the primary language of instruction in 1990, replacing Russian in this capacity. As with many of the changes that took hold after independence, teachers were not trained or prepared for this transition, and the quality of instructional delivery was affected. Of course, new textbooks presenting the national curriculum needed to be written and printed to reflect this departure, despite a sharp reduction in school expenditures. School construction and maintenance expenditures also dropped dramatically, and outdated laboratory and technical equipment could not be replaced.

The school year begins for all grade levels on September 1 and is divided into semesters and quarters. It lasts 30 weeks for first grade and 34 weeks for the remaining grades. Classes are held in 45-minute intervals. Armenian language and literature, mathematics, and physical education are taught at every grade level. Russian, other foreign languages, and electives are offered beginning in the second grade and continuing throughout the system. The teaching of natural sciences (including ecology, biology, chemistry, physics, and astrology) begins in grade four, and the teaching of social sciences (including history, geography, economics, political science, and law) begins in fifth grade. Courses in ''culture, nature and work'' (such as music, fine arts, drawing, handwork, and life skills) begin in fifth grade and continue throughout schooling. Military training is reserved for the senior school level. Grades are calculated on a five-point sys-

tem. In most areas of the country, class sizes are set at 25-30 pupils per class at the secondary level, and 15-20 per class in higher education.

To be sure, the educational system continues to undergo a number of reforms, loosely geared toward addressing the quality and relevance of curricula, as well as promoting decentralization and parental involvement. This has required a major overhaul in the system, given that until 1991 the schools followed prescribed Soviet curricula and methods of teaching and learning. In essence, this meant that the same topics and methodologies were employed for all children in all settings, regardless of differences in demographics, abilities, or interests. However, new approaches have been introduced which emphasize the development of problem solving and decision making skills, as well as tailoring educational experiences for students. As one example, a senior school program with advanced study in selected subjects has been introduced.

PREPRIMARY & PRIMARY EDUCATION

Primary education became compulsory in 1932, helping dramatically to reduce illiteracy rates in the nation to nearly nonexistent. The Soviet system created and funded the preschool network in order to accommodate working mothers, who received 1.5 years of maternity leave before they had to return to the workforce. Parents' main contributions went towards clothing and shoes, as the cost of food in the preschools was either free or heavily subsidized. Teachers were held in the highest regard.

After the collapse of the government, funding for preprimary education fell dramatically, forcing many to close and leaving others to deteriorate. In 1997, the government sharply reduced the percentage of the education budget allocation for preschools, using the funds instead to increase spending on basic education and shifting the control of the preprimary system to local municipalities.

Article 17 of the Law on Education lists seven objectives of preschool education: aiding in physical, moral and intellectual development; laying the foundation for native and foreign language development; developing mathematical and other skills; learning rules of behavior and cultural and historical norms; nurturing respect for the Armenian nation; and preparing students for general education. The system is divided between nursery schools (which accommodate children ages one to three) and kindergartens (for children ages three to seven). The schools offer either day care or educational activities, though many combine both of these practices.

While the system relies heavily on strong preprimary schooling—since formal education does not begin until the age of seven—enrollment rates in both preschool and kindergarten began to decline in the late 1980s. Armenia's under-five population numbers approximately 232,000. Although 64,000 children attend preschool and kindergarten in Armenia, this number represents a decrease in attendance; figures show 1989 enrollment rates at 27.8 percent, while the number declined to 15 percent in 1997. Some explanations for this drop in enrollment include both insufficient resources and unprepared local governing bodies abruptly tasked with oversight, leading to a decline in the quality of the system. Further, the high rate of unemployment undoubtedly added to this trend, as many caregivers chose to keep children at home with them instead of sending them off to school. And, by introducing cost into the equation, parents had to decide whether or not it was worthwhile to send their children to preprimary institutions. In 1996, the tuition averaged about 500 dram (roughly $1 USD) a month, but the costs have since risen eight-fold. Private preschools began to emerge in 1999, with 15 schools registered nationally that year.

SECONDARY EDUCATION

Article 18 of the Law on Education expands upon the goals outlined for preschool education, noting that general education in Armenia seeks to develop children's knowledge of nature and the self, understanding of values and politics, and military preparation. More specifically, the focus of elementary school (grades one to three) is on the cultivation of language, mathematics, and work skills, with an eye towards character education. The middle school (grades four to eight) brings in a focus on science and healthy living, as well as helping to develop a sense of independence and self-care in the students. Senior school (grades nine to ten) brings these knowledge bases together and offers supplementary training for students with specialized academic interests. A school can offer a single grade level or multiple grade levels.

Children with special needs (including those who are without families) are either mainstreamed into the school system or are placed in schools designed to accommodate their particular needs. Evening and boarding schools, as well as orphanages, are available for this purpose.

The Armenian parliament is considering a draft law that proposes an expansion of the secondary education system, stretching it to eleven or twelve years. This is in response to additional curricula introduced into the system, increasing the number of subjects available for study by as many as 33 percent. The Ministry of Education and Science believes that this expansion is not only necessary for Armenia's school system to meet international standards, but also the rising standards of the Commonwealth of Independent States.

In total, Armenia's under-eighteen population numbers approximately 1,101,000; nearly 750,000 children attend Armenia's general school system. Elementary school enrollment remains high in Armenia, with schoolchildren achieving literacy at this juncture. However, it is important to recognize the growing number of homeless children and child refugees in Armenia, whose lack of schooling not only adversely impacts their own lives but also affects the larger social fabric of which they are a part.

Two examinations are administered at the end of fourth grade in Armenian and mathematics. Students are re-tested in these content areas at the end of intermediate school, at which time they are also tested in a foreign language. Upon completion of these grade levels and exams, students then choose to pursue either the third level of general education—known as senior school—or else to attend a more specialized vocational school.

Significant curriculum reforms have occurred in the post-Soviet era, offering students (and teachers) new paths of inquiry into subjects and topics they had not previously considered—the most notable of which can be found in the arenas of civics and history. In addition to the scope of the new curricula and textbook materials, these texts offer colorful photos and maps as well as space-appropriate passages, which are radical departures from the previously bland, overcrowded, and imageless layout of books from the Soviet era.

In this spirit, a new civics book was introduced in 1999, dealing with issues including human rights, the Armenian constitution, and the workings of the branches of government. The book, supported by funds from Junior Achievement of Armenia as well as USAID, has attained a formal place in the curriculum and is in its second edition.

In addition, significant changes have been made in the manner which Armenian history is taught in Armenia. While the subject was always included in the curriculum, it was not given much importance, being subsumed into the broader spectrum of global and Soviet history. This approach has changed, largely due to the work of a group of academicians and educators who authored texts for seventh and eight grades as well as high school usage, which ambitiously address the beginnings of Armenian history through the 1990s.

These topics are further explored in a textbook that considers ''The History of the Armenian Question,''which relates to the study of the national struggle for freedom, emancipation, and recognition of the Armenian Genocide. These issues of state and ethnic identity provide students with a rich and introspective base of knowledge that previously was inaccessible to them. Written for a ninth grade class level, the books are used in the curriculum followed by students who chose to pursue a humanities track after completing their eighth grade year. In addition to the textbook, brief (to keep costs down) but comprehensive teacher manuals and professional development seminars were created, offering educators guidance in both content and in methodology. Funding for these materials—which went through a second printing due to high demand—came from both a private donor and the Armenian Educational Foundation.

HIGHER EDUCATION

Higher education is widespread throughout Armenia, with the nation ranking first in educational attainment in the 1989 general census of the former Soviet Union. Adult literacy rates in Armenia remain exceptionally high, with UNICEF figures showing as many as 100 percent of the male population and 99 percent of the female population over the age of fifteen possessing the ability to read and write. Between 1920 and 1986, over 250,000 individuals were trained in the nation's universities. Armenia's private universities enroll some 20,000 students, while public higher education offers schooling to 34,000 students.

While the developing private school system is still working to streamline its accreditation with the Ministry of Education and Science, students are finding these institutions to be valuable options. Partially due to their focus on social sciences, as well as their flexibility regarding enrollment figures, these schools are driving the public universities into an era of reform as well. In this way, the state institutions are moving towards the American three-tiered system, whereby bachelor's, masters, and doctoral degrees are awarded.

Leading public institutions have achieved strong reputations for their contributions to scholarship in their respective fields, including Yerevan State University, the State Engineering University of Armenia, Yerevan State Medical University, the Armenian Academy of Agriculture, Yerevan State Institute for Russian and Foreign Languages, and Yerevan Komitas Conservatory. Funding continues to be an issue for public universities, however. Before independence, these schools were offered free of charge to Armenian students. Now, prospective students must pass an examination to gain entry to the schools, and based upon their scores they are either granted free admission or required to pay tuition. As such, students compete in large numbers for a select few scholarships. With annual tuition in some specialized departments running as high as $1500 USD, students are under great pressure to try to obtain—and maintain—these scholarships. Recipients are reevaluated annually and are only able to continue studying under scholarship if they display academic excellence.

A vital addition to the higher education landscape in Armenia has been the American University of Armenia (AUA). Opened in 1991, AUA offers English-taught graduate-level programs in Business, Engineering, Political Science, Health Sciences and Law, as well as providing training in English as a Foreign Language. Tuition runs nearly $1000 USD annually. Russia followed with a university in Armenia in 1998, and, in 2000, France also opened an Armenian university.

The National Academy of Sciences of Armenia represents the nation's brightest scholars and researchers and includes over fifty scientific and miscellaneous organizations. Founded in 1943, the Academy boasts 116 academicians, 337 doctors of sciences, and 1,152 candidates of sciences. As with other former Soviet republics, however, Armenian universities, technical institutes and research centers suffered a "brain drain" after independence. While this certainly continues to be a concern, the Ministry of Education and Science is taking steps to keep the nation's intelligentsia working in Armenia. In this regard, the Ministry is trying to encourage and develop links and connections to the international research community that allow scholars to integrate their work in the global landscape without having to leave the country to do so. To help support their efforts, the diasporan organization Fund for Armenian Relief has funded over $100,000 in grants to help foster the research projects of Armenian scientists and scholars.

ADMINISTRATION, FINANCE, & EDUCATIONAL RESEARCH

The 1996 decentralization of school and community governance brought additional economic challenges as well as influence by special interest groups. Initially, regional government offices managed all educational activities and appointments, and were given discretionary funds by the central treasury. All of this fell under the supervision of the Ministry of Education and Science. A revised decree in 1997 shifted control to the local Council which oversees spending and appointments.

The financial constraints upon the educational system prove to be perhaps the most daunting issue facing education in Armenia. Alarmingly, per-pupil public expenditures fell from $600 USD in 1985 to an estimated $36 USD in 1998. As a result, various programs have been enacted in an attempt to address the financial needs of the nation's schools and families.

At the same time, a great deal of assistance comes from outside Armenia. Organizations and individuals from the Armenian Diaspora have contributed funds for the construction of school buildings, for example. The Armenian Educational Foundation has created scholarship programs for students and is helping to renovate approximately 100 schools. The Children's Television Workshop includes Armenia on its list of countries that air ''Open Sesame,'' which provides culturally neutral episodes of ''Sesame Street'' dubbed into the Armenian language. In addition, many international organizations offer their support via the purchase of computers and professional development. Further, outside funds have come from organizations such as UNHCR, UNDP, UNICEF, World Bank, Catholic Refugee Services, the Norwegian government, the Armenian Relief Society, the Fund for Armenian Relief, and Aznavour pour L'Armenie. A notable UNICEF-assisted program established textbook rental policy, wherein students pay a nominal fee (150 drams or approximately $.25 USD) to rent each book, which is returned at the end of the school year. Rental fees are banked by the schools and allowed to accrue interest to be used towards the purchase of additional texts every four years.

TEACHING PROFESSION

As with nearly every other aspect of the educational system in Armenia, the teaching profession has undergone dramatic changes since the fall of the Soviet Union. While teachers continue to be respected as professionals, and 80 percent hold degrees from institutions of higher education or professional pedagogical institutes, the post-Soviet corps tends to be less motivated, undergo fewer hours of professional development training, and hold lower status in their communities.

These problems are exaggerated in the rural areas, where conditions are poorer and fewer opportunities exist for educators to supplement their salaries. The workweek averages between twelve and eighteen hours, although many teachers work the low end of the spectrum because they hold other jobs. Their salaries declined from $200 USD a month in the 1980s, down to as low as $10 USD a month in 1993. Further, the teaching force—of which women comprise the vast majority—often goes unpaid for several months on end. As a result, private tutoring has become an unavoidable sideline business for many teachers. In an attempt to address the pressing concern over teacher salaries, the government decided in 1998 to exempt educational institutions from paying income tax, with the intent that some of the funds that would be retained could be used towards increasing teacher salaries at the school level.

Deteriorating conditions in the schools also adversely affect the profession, both in terms of motivation and efficacy. Until 1990, building renovations were completed every five years in all schools. By the 1993-1994 school year, the percentage of schools undergoing repair fell from twenty to five percent. Minor needs often go neglected, leading to the complete disrepair of many buildings. This deprioritization is reflected in the budget, which in 1997 allocated only $2 USD per pupil for reno-

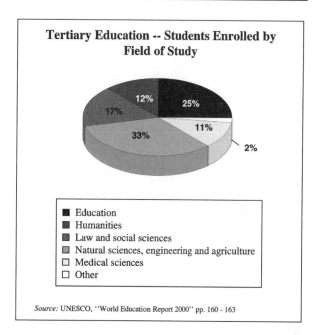

Tertiary Education -- Students Enrolled by Field of Study

- ■ Education
- ■ Humanities
- ■ Law and social sciences
- ▨ Natural sciences, engineering and agriculture
- □ Medical sciences
- □ Other

Source: UNESCO, ''World Education Report 2000'' pp. 160 - 163

vations and did not allow for any repair in 1998 other than in disaster areas.

Another issue of concern lies in the discrepancy in the student-teacher ratio, in that the number of trained teachers is increasing while the student population declines due to a decreasing birth rate and financial pressures that force some children (mostly boys) to leave school to help support their families. This results in a pupil-teacher ratio that is too small for the system to sustain—averaging around 1:10—and had led to measures by the government to rationalize the system and decrease the overall number of teachers.

SUMMARY

Since Armenia acquired independence from the Soviet Union in 1991, funding for education declined drastically as costs rose. The nation decentralized school and community governance in 1997 and shifted control of spending and appointments to local councils to attempt to address financial needs of families. But annual preprimary tuition for a single student now can cost as much as the annual salary of a teacher. Consequently, many children do not enroll in formal schools until age seven. Unfortunately, the teaching profession suffers too, due to decreases in training opportunities, status, salaries, and overall motivation in the post-Soviet era.

Higher education, however, boasts the highest ranking of the former Soviet states in terms of educational attainment. The finest of the nation's scholars and researchers belong to the National Academy of Sciences of Armenia. Also, adult literacy rates hovered at 100 percent through 1999.

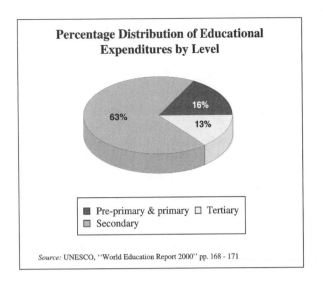

Percentage Distribution of Educational Expenditures by Level

- ■ Pre-primary & primary □ Tertiary
- ▨ Secondary

16%
13%
63%

Source: UNESCO, "World Education Report 2000" pp. 168 - 171

In the midst of this period of inordinate financial strain, Armenia is striving to enact educational innovations to address the shifting sociopolitical realities it faces. Curricula and methods of teaching and learning are being reinvented anew. Many teachers, however, are skeptical of these radical changes and resistant to the reforms that are being thrust upon them. Understandably, they hesitate to simply adopt the succession of changes they have had no role in enacting, at the same time that they are teaching under increasingly difficult circumstances. As a result, there is a notable disconnect between traditional and progressive philosophies of education in Armenia, and educators' voices need to be heard as the nation struggles to resolve the tenuous, interconnected challenges facing the educational and political systems of the nation. Of course, these same teachers need to reflect upon the new and vibrant ways that they can contribute to this process in their individual classrooms—always, of course, with focus on the enrichment of the nation's educational offerings. Ultimately, this will require dialogue on the parts of all stakeholders in the system—teachers, students, parents, policymakers, and administrators—and holds the most promise for establishing a credible and thoughtful program of reform.

To this end, research in adult development has shown that for adults to make any serious life changes (such as those faced by Armenia's teachers), they need first to take ownership of their own personal development. With empathic support and inspired leadership, teachers in Armenia could take charge of recreating their own educational system. At the same time, they could utilize research by Kegan, Lauer, and Torosyan on fostering this development—for themselves as well as their students. One potential approach is to avoid treating issues as separate and disconnected (e.g. "funding," "training," "motivation" in education) and instead identify

the way of thinking that brought about the issues or problems in the first place. Thus an overarching problem such as "poor teacher training" can be seen as being "caused" at least partially by individuals needing a better understanding of how to "listen," "cooperate," and "take leadership." Often, once people can see that such skills form a larger pattern, they can better transfer the abilities to manage other problems that come their way. Moreover, with globalization and the new world economy's emphasis on "ideas" and "entrepreneurs as agents of change," the Armenian people may benefit from creating such a "transformative" (rather than merely "informative") system of education more than ever before.

For its long-term future, Armenia could indeed gain from considering its current status within the Chinese definition of "crisis"—as a time of both "danger" and "opportunity." This turning point carries the stark risk that the nation may initially fall into steep decline, but also brings the very real opportunity ultimately to renew intellectual and cultural resources to meet both the mental and material demands of modern life.

BIBLIOGRAPHY

"Armenia Set to Move to 11-year Secondary Education System." Yerevan, Armenia: Snark Newspaper, 7 February 2001.

Armenian National Commission for UNESCO. *Educational Policy Making During a Situation of National Emergency,* 1994.

Balian, Simon. "ANSEF Awards $110,000 for 22 Research Grants for Armenia." *The Fund for Armenian Relief,* 8 March 2001.

Bournoutian, George. *A History of the Armenian People: Vol. II: 1500 A.D. to the Present.* Costa Mesa, CA: Mazda, 1994.

Bournoutian, George. *A History of the Armenian People: Vol. I: Pre-history to 1500 A.D.* Costa Mesa, CA: Mazda, 1995.

Gabrielian, Richard. "Armenia." *World Education Forum, EFA 2000 Assessment.* UNESCO, 2000. Available from http://www2.unesco.org.

Ghazarian, Salpi Haroutinian. "Back to School: Revamping Armenia's Educational System." *Armenian International Magazine,* February 1998.

Government of Armenia. *Law of the Republic of Armenia on Education.* Yerevan, Armenia: 1 September 2000.

Government of Armenia. *Situation Analysis of Women and Children.* United Nations International Children's Fund (UNICEF), Save the Children Foundation (SCF), 1999.

Kasbarian, Lucine. *Armenia: A Rugged Land, an Enduring People.* Parsippany, NJ: Dillon/Simon & Schuster, 1998.

Kegan, Robert. *In Over Our Heads: The Mental Demands of Modern Life*. Cambridge, MA: Harvard University Press, 1994.

Kegan, Robert, and Lisa Lahey. *How the Way We Talk Can Change the Way We Work: Seven Languages for Transformation*. San Francisco: Jossey Bass, 2001.

Peroumian, Rubina. *The History of the Armenian Question*. Yerevan, Armenia: Hye Edit, 2000.

President of the Republic of Armenia. ''The Constitution,'' 7 July 1995. Available from http://www.president.am.

Republic of Armenia Ministry of Education and Science. *Indicator (Standard) for Secondary Education*. Yerevan, Armenia. 3 March 1998.

Torosyan, Roben. ''Encouraging Consciousness Development in the College Classroom Through Student-Centered Transformative Teaching and Learning.'' Unpublished doctoral dissertation, Teachers College, Columbia University, 2000. Available from http://webpage.pace.edu/rtorosyan.

Torosyan, Roben. ''Applying learning to life: a theoretical framework in context.''Spring 1999.

United Nations International Children's Fund (UNICEF). ''Countries Affected by Armed Conflict.''*UNICEF Annual Report,* 1996. Available from http://www.unicef.org.

—*Nicole E. Vartanian and Roben Torosyan*

ARUBA

BASIC DATA

Official Country Name:	Aruba
Region:	Puerto Rico & Lesser Antilles
Population:	69,539
Language(s):	Dutch, Papiamento, English, Spanish
Literacy Rate:	97%

Aruba, a 74.5 square mile island located in the southern Caribbean Sea, was first inhabited by Arawak Indians and later was discovered by a Spaniard, Alonso de Ojeda.

The chain of dates documenting Aruban governmental history includes: 1499, the date of the Spanish discovery; 1636, when the Dutch took control of the island following the 80 Year War between Spain and Holland; 1805 to 1816, when the English took possession during the Napoleonic Wars; 1816, when the Dutch returned to power; 1986, when as a member of the Netherlands Antilles Federation, Aruba petitioned to automatically become a separate entity; and 1990, when Aruba requested cancellation of the agreement to become totally independent and remained a third part of the Dutch realm. Aruba is a parliamentary democracy and is autonomous in internal affairs, but the Kingdom of the Netherlands is responsible for the island's defense and foreign affairs. Oranjestad is Aruba's capital.

Linked to its Dutch heritage, Aruba's educational system is administered by the Aruban Ministry of Education and requires the high standards maintained by educational institutions in the Netherlands. In 2000, approximately 24 percent of the island's budget was designated to fund education, a designation that purportedly resulted in Aruba having one of the highest levels of education in the Caribbean. The literacy rate is 97 percent. Reflecting the island's rich ethnically-diverse history, although public school instruction is in the official Dutch language, lower grades are taught English and Spanish, and upper-grades have additional language offerings including French and German. Further, the local language, Papiamento, is being progressively introduced in the schools. Papiamento is a combination of Spanish, Dutch, Portuguese, English, French, African, and Arawak Indian languages.

Education became compulsory in 1999. The Compulsory Education Act requires kindergarten beginning at the age of 4; a 6-year primary education beginning at 6 years of age; and a 5-year period of secondary education beginning at age 12. At the preprimary level, there are 4 public and 19 private kindergartens. During the 1998-1999 school year, there were 2,601 kindergarten students and 98 teachers. At the primary level, there were 5 public and 28 private schools (1998-1999: 8,456 students and 397 teachers), as well as 4 special education schools with a total of 291 students and 54 teachers.

Secondary education levels include nine schools offering a four-year preparatory course to middle level professional education (1998-1999: 2,485 students and 141 teachers); and one private school offering a four-year non-university, higher professional education and a six-year preparatory course to university higher education (1998-1999: 1,628 students and 81 teachers). In addition, one school offers lower level, basic professional, technical and vocational education (1998-1999: 1,968 students and 148 teachers).

Middle level professional education includes: one public school offering a four-year middle technical education (1998-1999: 467 students and 36 teachers); one public school three-year secretarial program (337 students and 26 teachers); and two private schools—the Aruba Hotel School (121 students and 9 teachers) and the Colegio Paso Sigur, a school for human services (151 students and 29 teachers).

Institutions of higher learning include a community college and two universities, The University of Aruba (1998-1999: 214 students and 28 teachers) and The Teachers College (180 students and 25 teachers). The University includes a law school and a school of business administration. English-language education, remediation, and advance-standing admissions for degree programs in a number of fields for are provided in Aruba, the United States, and online. For example, the university offers an online two-year health profession program, and scholarship arrangements for specialized professions are available with the United States, Canada, Europe, and South America. A number of Arubans choose to attend higher education institutions in the Netherlands.

Across time, Aruba's economy has been influenced by the discovery of gold in 1824, the discovery of oil in 1924, and by a blossoming tourist industry. An ever increasing population coupled with the rapidly emerging tourist industry impacted education by making clear the need for training institutes, technical organizations, and special-purpose schools. One such special-purpose school, funded in part by the European Common Market Development Fund, is the Aruba Hotel School, which opened in August 1982. The school provides accredited Associate of Science and Associate of Applied Science degrees in Hospitality Management and meets transference criteria for many institutions of higher learning in the United States and the Netherlands.

Other educational institutions include the International School of Aruba, which provides instruction in English for students pre-kindergarten through grade 12. The school follows a general academic, college preparatory, U.S. public school curriculum, and it is accredited by the Southern Association of Colleges and Schools. The institution is incorporated in Aruba and is non-profit, with about 95 percent of the 1999-2000 school year being funded by student tuition. Major contributors to the school include the Coastal Refinery of Houston, Texas, and the PTA. During the 1999-2000 school year, there were 164 students and 26 faculty members.

During the 1990s and into the 2000s, Aruba's Minister of Education and Labor, Mary Wever-Lacle, was instrumental in bringing modern technology into the island's education system, providing classroom computers and distance learning opportunities. These and other initiatives designed to enhance education by meeting the challenges of modern technology continue to reflect the high academic and practical standards of excellence required in Aruba.

BIBLIOGRAPHY

ABC Country Book of Aruba, 2000. Available from www.theodora.com/wfb/aruba_government.

''Aruba Education.'' Changes in L'attitudes, Inc., February 2001. Available from www.aruba-tours.com/info/education.

Aruba Fast Facts. ''Education,'' 2000. Available from www.bestvaluetimeshares.com/arubafacts.

Aruba Hotel School. Educacion Profesional Intermedio, March 2001. Available from aruba4you.com/aruba_hotel_school.

''Aruba History.'' Changes in L'attitudes, Inc., February 2001. Available from www.aruba-tours,com/info/history.

''Aruba Language.'' Changes in L'attitudes, Inc., February 2001. Available from www.aruba-tours.com/info/language.

''Aruba: Ministry of Education and Labor.'' *Washington Times,* March 1999. Available from http://www.washtimes.com/internatlads/aruba/10.

Brender, Karen W., and Elise Rosen. *Foder's Pocket Aruba.* Fodor's Travel Publications, November 2000.

The Central Intelligence Agency (CIA). *The World Factbook 2000.* Directorate of Intelligence, 1 January 2000. Available from http://www.cia.gov/.

Europa World Year Book, 41st Ed. ''Netherlands Dependencies: Aruba,'' 2000.

Global Investment Center. ''Aruba: A Country Study.'' In *World Country Study Guides: Business & Investment Opportunities,* Vol. 199. Washington, DC: International Business Publications, May 2000.

International School of Aruba, 2000. Available from www.state.gov/www/about_state/schools/oaruba.

Schoenhlas, Kai (Compiler). ''Netherlands Antilles & Aruba.'' *World Bibliographical Series,* Vol. 168. California: ABC-CLIO, Inc., 1994.

—*Duffy Austin Wilks*

AUSTRALIA

BASIC DATA

Official Country Name:	Australia
Region:	Oceania
Population:	19,169,083
Language(s):	English, native languages
Literacy Rate:	100%
Academic Year:	January-December
Number of Primary Schools:	8,123
Compulsory Schooling:	10 years
Public Expenditure on Education:	5.4%
Foreign Students in National Universities:	102,284
Educational Enrollment:	Primary: 1,855,789 Secondary: 2,367,692 Higher: 1,041,648
Educational Enrollment Rate:	Primary: 101% Secondary: 148% Higher: 80%
Teachers:	Primary: 103,774
Student-Teacher Ratio:	Primary: 17:1 Secondary: 12:1
Female Enrollment Rate:	Primary: 101% Secondary: 148% Higher: 83%

HISTORY & BACKGROUND

Australia became a country in 1901 as a federation of former British colonies inhabiting the continent of Australia. At Federation, six states emerged out of the six colonies, and they retained the establishment of policy and funding for education. Progressively, the states voluntarily surrendered some of their powers so that by the end of the twentieth century, the federal government played a major role in the educational system. Each state has carried on separate educational policy development, teacher training, and registration procedures.

The Australian population was 19,222,000 in 1999, spread across 7,713,364 square kilometers of land. Australia is closely knit into the world economy and is an active middle power in world politics. Its social policies are driven by an aging population and declining birth rate. Australia is trying to sustain national population growth through migration, which has meant a more diverse population towards which education has to be directed from a tax and income base that is undergoing radical changes in the face of globalization.

The first period of Australian education was dominated by the social and moral needs of a convict society which, from 1810, began to develop a free minority. As an exiled society of adults, the problems were conversion and moral restraint. Consequently, the Anglican church provided the first schoolmaster in the colonial chaplain, Reverend Richard Johnson. His educational efforts came in the form of sermons and bible readings, the literature that came with the first fleet, and a variety of moral and biblical tracts. He also oversaw the first hut schools, one in Sydney in 1789 and another in Parramatta two years later. There was no real model for financing or organizing religion outside of the United Kingdom. Therefore, *glebes* were established (400 acres for support of a minister and 200 for a schoolmaster) in each developing center. Later, this arrangement was formalized in the Church and School Corporation established under Thomas Hobbes Scott in 1825, as part of an attempt to extend to Australia the Anglican monopoly in England by deeding it one-tenth of all surveyed land. The problem with the model was that most land was still unsettled or, if settled, unsurveyed, leaving available finances well behind the expansion of population and demand for education.

The arrival of the Second Fleet increased the number of women in the colony, leading to an ever-expanding number of children to be raised. Female convicts, for whom there was less call for as manual laborers, also tended to be the first teachers in local schools. It was not a promising beginning for education. Scarcity of labor drove up wages and land was easily obtainable, often by grant. A masculine society had good economic and cultural reasons for despising learning, an attitude that remained common enough in the anti-intellectualism of the culture into the post-World War II period.

In 1792, the funding and fortunes of education varied with government patronage. The advent of a number of missionaries fleeing Tahiti in 1798 further strengthened educational endeavors in the colony. They also reinforced the assumption that religion was education. This attitude remained the case for much of the nineteenth century, particularly on the edges of settlement. The clergyman was often the most educated person in the locality. Wherever churches went, schools followed. Local groups out of the growing centers turned to the voluntary society as a model.

By 1814, the state was wholly or partially funding 13 elementary schools in the vast arc from Moreton Bay in the north to Hobart in the south. The spreading edge of settlement (and the dangers of a masculine, frontier society) soon created boarding and girls schools. While student numbers were small, individual instruction and private study was the preferred method. The increase in the number of children (by 1810, there were more than 3000 children, 26 percent of the population, in the colony) meant the adoption of different methods. Crook's Academy, for instance, adopted British charity school methods such as the Lancastrian monitorial system. Larger numbers of students also meant more variety and pressure to provide non-denominational forms of religious instruction. As the formal structures of denominations became more firmly established, however, there was contention over the shape of education, particularly education paid for by public funds. Free settlers who were nonconformist and democratic by spirit came into conflict with the assumptions of the imperial state, wealthy colonialists, and merchants.

The state's aim for education was to inculcate obedience to Christian church principles. For the churches, the definition of *Christian* implied was questionable, and the order of priority was to be reversed. For the state, religion was an instrument for social and moral order; for the churches, religion was a prime objective from which social and moral order were desirable, but not essential side-effects. The Church Acts of 1836 made Anglicanism, Catholicism, Methodism, and Presbyterianism the main forms of Christian worship.

With the crossing of the Blue Mountains in 1813, and the extension of settlement north to Moreton Bay (later Brisbane) and south to Hobart, the far-flung edges of pastoral empires and the accumulation of wealth also raised the need for residential grammar schools to which children could be sent away from their isolated station. These first began as private schools in the classics, largely run by clergymen for additional income, preparing genteel ladies and men who would be capable either of running the family business or returning to Britain to take a profession. The Australian College was founded in 1831, and King's School was founded in 1832. The former folded, but King's lasted, and the Scots school was founded in 1838, beginning a long-running tradition of Presbyterian grammar schools perhaps best typified by Scotch College. St Mary's Seminary, a mixed Catholic seminary and secondary school, was founded by Bishop Polding in 1837. In Tasmania, Queen's School (Anglican, 1842), Launceston CGS (Anglican, 1846), and the Hutchins School (Anglican, 1846) led the way in a system which, under the energetic Bishop Francis Nixon and by the direct intervention of W. E. Gladstone, came to be dominated by Anglican schooling. In Queensland, grammar schools were publicly supported under the Grammar School Act of 1860 in order to fill the rural educational vacuum.

In the 1830s, the central administration was just beginning to struggle with these issues. Its first step sought to break the stranglehold the Churches had on education. As the price of government support for the largely stretched denominational schools each committed to a British geographical parish model, the government proposed the funding of a parallel public system modeled on the Irish National system. Delayed by fierce church-based opposition in the 1830s, and the deep colonial depression of the 1840s, a Board of National Education was set up in 1848 to parallel the Denominational Schools' Board, which administered state aid to the *big four* denominations. In Tasmania, under Eardley-Wilmot and then William Denison, the dominance of Anglicans in a more homogenous population matched with government cost-cutting meant that denominational schools continued to overshadow the public schools. By 1849, there were only 10 public schools (compared to 25 in New South Wales), but 72 Anglican schools and 4 Catholic day schools.

The growth of population in areas too distant to be governed effectively from Sydney introduced even more variety. The 1820s saw Tasmania separate, and the 1830s saw new colonies in Western Australia and South Australia and the urban centers of future Victoria and Queensland founded. These colonies moved more quickly to urban development and equalitarian values in comparison to New South Wales. The cessation of convict transportation to mainland Australia in 1842, while leaving a generational backlog of continuing and former prisoners in the population, firmly declared the colonies for free development.

Some colonies, such as South Australia, never relied on income from convict transportation. Later, the shift to land sales rather than grants also provided colonial governments with the money to expand public infrastructure. In Western Australia, lack of an immediate revenue stream, and a stagnant population, hobbled the development of a public system for more than a decade. The colonial depression further flattened growth through the 1840s, leaving educational initiative in the hands of resurgent, missionary Irish Catholic religious orders.

By 1846, almost all the schools in Perth were Catholic. This led to vigorous educational rivalry by the new government of Andrew Clarke, the foundation of colonial schools in four centers of the huge, underpopulated territory, and a free grammar school in Perth. A similar reaction to Catholic success in Adelaide was, in the 1870s, to produce a centralized State Council of Education, and then a Department of Education along the lines of the one already established in Victoria. These were extended over time and brought under the direction of a General Board of Education, causing the virtual disappearance of smaller private schools. In 1849, both systems received government funding on a population, producing a binary system of education unique in the continent.

By contrast, South Australia was considered to be a "paradise of dissent," reflecting a lower proportion of either Anglicans or Catholics. Its uniqueness lay in the fact that it had a voluntarily-supported school system planned through the South Australian School Society before it was founded. Unfortunately, membership levies did not go through as expected and, without government support, the school was privatized, leaving private schools as the only alternatives in the colony for some years.

The failure of South Australia to produce a stream of philanthropy disappointed the dissenting bourgeois, and government funding, controlled by the Anglicans, was only available on a denominational basis. The public dispute over government funding was so bitter in this colony that the Governor resigned amidst the public turmoil, and "state aid to religion and education remained the single biggest political issue in the colony until its discontinuation in 1851" (Barcan 1980).

German migration saw the opening of a seminary and school in Lobenthal in 1845, and St. Peter's CECS (Anglican) in 1849. By 1850, elementary education and various forms of state aid were functioning successfully in most colonies. High schools or their equivalent were less evident, and advanced education of this type was in private hands in the form of academies or grammar/collegiate schools. Most education suffered from lack of funds and population, competition between church systems in a small market, economic cycles, and popular neglect of educational priorities.

The review of education by Childers in 1851, for instance, found that Victorian schools were not reaching up to a third of children in towns and did not reach up to half of children in suburbs (Barcan 1980). On top of this, Australia was at the other end of the earth from institutions from which either a flow of talented teachers or quality teaching supplies relevant to colonial conditions could come. Private education or sending children back home was an option, but only if one had the money; quality education was a right only for the wealthy.

Two of these problems were solved by the discovery of gold in Victoria and New South Wales in the early 1850s. The population of both colonies virtually tripled, creating movable towns of gold seekers, new domestic demand for foodstuffs and building materials, and new infrastructure, including schools and *Mechanics Institutes*. The problem was that many professionals, including teachers, abandoned their posts for the goldfields, and rising costs made living difficult for those, mainly women, who stayed. In Tasmania, which had no rush, many towns were decimated, and the dominant Anglican schools struggled to keep their doors open as people left for Victoria.

Funding via denominational boards favored the majority Anglican population, and so re-enforced the status quo. South Australia was the first to discontinue funding in 1851, followed by Tasmania and Western Australia, then Queensland, Victoria, and finally in 1872, New South Wales. With the support of non-conformist Christians, especially Congregationalists and Baptists, State educational policy shifted into the hands of liberal idealists, precisely the sort of ideals that were anathema to the Catholic Church in the wake of Vatican I and the Syllabus of Errors. Reports attacking the quality of denominational education by the Anglican Rusden, and liberal William Wilkins, seemed to support their fears.

Universities did not overcome their distance from the schooling system until the rise of public examinations made their services central to public life. The Oxford and Cambridge examinations were used by many schools, and continued to be used in the Theological colleges, as a way of determining entry and matriculation standards. Without a local demand for a large number of public servants, the British universities continued to have the advantage. The University of Melbourne followed the University of London's model, establishing a Matriculation Examination as early as 1855. Sydney established the Junior and Senior Public Examinations in 1867, opening examination centers around the state in succeeding years. The opening of these examinations to women in 1871 acted as a spur to educational provision for women, and girls grammar schools thus spread across the countryside as a precursor to the opening of university courses to women from 1879. Such schools were part of the great surge in institution building that swept across eastern Australia in the long economic boom between 1865 and 1890. Even the universities, though planted in the 1850s, did not begin to grow significantly until this period: their move into examinations thus made them de facto Boards of Examiners for much of the secondary sector from this time on, cementing a critical place in the development of Australian education. The role of public examinations, and the lack of a Catholic tertiary alternative, was a major element in uniting the various systems of education as they developed separate lives from 1880.

The period of 1880-1900 was the period of implementation for these strategies of free, secular, and compulsory education. Making education compulsory did not necessarily mean that students would attend, but the legislative strengthening of education departments in pursuit of the goal of universal literacy was the result. With the extension and bureaucratization of government services generally in Australia, came the irony of democracy producing a stronger and stronger center. In time, education and health would be swept up into an effective welfare system.

The economic boom of the period had several effects. It gave money to the universities with additional resources (often in the form of religiously based colleges) flowing from the great pastoral fortunes made in the period. The same fortunes also endowed the great private grammar schools, even while the small private academies were eliminated through advancing government regulation and service. The systematic expansion of Presbyterian and Methodist Ladies Colleges was a major contributor to the expansion of the grammar school form. They were a concern of the State because they contributed to the provision of advanced education in rural areas. These, together with state agricultural high schools, some of which were residential, began to push the regional country private academies out of existence, though they could never replace correspondence education for the more remote areas. Australian primary and secondary education thus took on a threefold form: Catholic, low-fee-paying, private; Catholic and Protestant grammar schools (such as Trinity and St. Ignatius in Sydney or in Brisbane); and an expanding state system that was finally able to reach out to the distant rural towns. The boom also allowed the rise of a wealthy urban professional class, feeding more pragmatic university courses such as economics, law, and medicine for which schools were founded in all the major universities.

CONSTITUTIONAL & LEGAL FOUNDATIONS

The provisions of relevant Commonwealth and State or Territory Anti-Discrimination and Affirmative Action legislation are set out in the Affirmative Action (Equal Employment Opportunity for Women) Act 1986, The Disability Discrimination Act 1992, The Racial Discrimination Act 1975, and the Sex Discrimination Act 1984. Following the path of teacher education, the process by which other sub-professions (such as nursing) reached the status of professions (through the status of university entrance), was accelerated by the 1990s. This process has further strengthened the links between vocational and professional education and makes the offerings of universities, in many ways, connected with the technical system.

Vocational Education and Training (VET) authorities by the end of the 1980s sought a new formula in Competency Based Training, which effectively stripped teaching of its content-orientation. It reoriented vocation-

al and technical education away from disciplines and towards the needs of particular employers. The focus was outward, on standards rather than content, and on the transformation of knowledge into a commodity in order to sell it into a market. The construction of an Australian Qualifications Framework may be seen as the logical outcome of these trends, whereby the formation of a single great federal system (called, under the Dawkins' scheme, the Unified National System) embracing technical, vocational, and university education, assumed the continuity of all forms of learning in fitting national industry-specific standards. For such discipline- or community-specific areas as clergy training or the human relationship end of medical practice, it has generally been acknowledged that the imposition of such external standards was not always successful and led to considerable heat and public discussion in Australia through the 1990s.

Though Australia has not used monetarist policies to the extent that trademarked the Thatcher government in Britain, there is a simmering discontent over the so called ''economic rationalism'' evident in handling national and intellectual assets on both sides of politics, the Liberal-National Party Coalition, and Australian Labor Party. The rise of non-establishment parties, such as the Greens, Democrats, and even the One Nation Party is further evidence of the fragmentation of Australian opinion over issues such as education. The one common denominator is the opinion that education is important. In 1999, about 88 percent of respondents to a Commonwealth Bank survey put ''ensuring everyone has access to good education'' at the top of all issues surveyed (*Australian* 19 June 2000). Meanwhile, the debate over how to rebuild the social status and effectiveness of teachers within the education system continues, in seeming ignorance of the fact that it is the progressive rationalization of education into an objectified system that assists in the destruction of such social status and effectiveness.

EDUCATIONAL SYSTEM—OVERVIEW

Education is compulsory in all states of Australia from K-10 (between the ages 5 to 15). Effectively, almost all Australian citizens have access to elementary and junior educational provision, under state legislation in the six states (New South, Wales, Victoria, South Australia, Western Australia, Queensland, and Tasmania) and in the Australian Capital Territory, while citizens in the Northern Territory obtain education under Federal funding provisions channeled through the Northern Territory administration.

Education is in English, though most primary schools now have access to community language programs. Italian, Japanese, and Spanish are among the most common in state schools, French and German in several

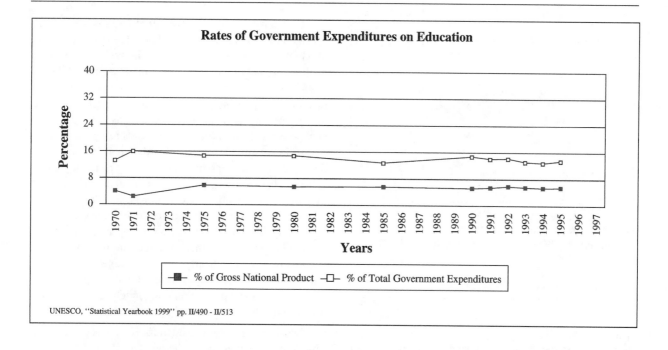

Rates of Government Expenditures on Education

UNESCO, "Statistical Yearbook 1999" pp. II/490 - II/513

of the international language schools in the capital cities, and indigenous languages in Aboriginal schools, particularly in Western Australia, northern Queensland, and the Northern Territory.

Most states, along the lines of a resurgent return to basic policies operate basic skills tests in elementary schools (called primary or public schools in most states). In New South Wales, basic skills tests are run for year 3 and year 5 students. Access to state selective schools is possible in some states through special examination, and there are regular examinations for entry on scholarship to the larger private schools. Internal assessment governs progress through years 7 through 9, and in year 10, there is the equivalent of New South Wale's school certificate offered in most states as a entry point into technical education, apprenticeships, and other vocational training alternatives. Year 12 ends with a higher leaving certificate examination—in New South Wales called the Higher School Certificate, in Victoria the VCE, and in Queensland the Core Skills Test.

The Academic Year runs from the end of January (mid-summer in Australia) across 4 terms, ending towards the middle or latter end of December, allowing for a 5 to 6 week holiday in what are the hot months in most Australian states. Curriculum in most states is set by the State departments of Education, against which (through the system of public examinations at the end of year 10 and year 12) inspectors also assess registration requirements in privately run schools.

The shaping influences on Australian education have been distance and time. Distance, because it was distance that has dictated the economics and socio-cultural devel-

opment of the country. Time, as both the newness of the country and the time to travel for ideas, has been critical in the formation of education policy and thought. Distance and time, significantly, are also the key axes underlying the processes of globalization which are driving educational agendas in Australia.

In the first instance, distance from the expanding centers of world civilizations meant that, until 1788, Aboriginal peoples in Australia could follow traditional mechanisms of customary education unhindered for thousands of years. Aboriginal learning patterns tend to be directed towards community survival, de-emphasizing the individual in favor of customary law, through knowledge of the intricate Aboriginal social system, and ensuring the passing on of communal history and culture in an often difficult natural environment. Their culture emphasized group work, daily vocational skills, and in-depth knowledge of the natural environment. From white settlement in 1788, these values brought Aboriginal children into a direct conflict with individualistic-, time-, and achievement-oriented white education systems.

Despite missionary practice that emphasized bible translation and grammar/vocabulary construction, which has since become a major source for the revival of Aboriginal languages and cultures, and high level recommendations towards bilingual education in the early 1960s, English remained the primary language of instruction for Aboriginal students until 1973. Effectively, this was part of a program of assimilation that was extended by the Australian government to all minority groups in Australia until the promulgation of official multiculturalism in November 1972. The extension of linguistic reviv-

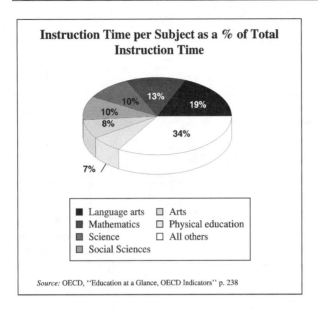

Instruction Time per Subject as a % of Total Instruction Time

13% 19% 34% 10% 10% 8% 7%

■ Language arts □ Arts
■ Mathematics □ Physical education
■ Science □ All others
■ Social Sciences

Source: OECD, "Education at a Glance, OECD Indicators" p. 238

als, teaching in the primary language of students, support for the training of Aboriginal people as teachers, and national organization of Aboriginal and Torres Strait Islanders has greatly assisted in shifting education away from the sort of identity stripping, residential institutions that were the norm for Aboriginal education from the foundation of the Native Institution under Lachlan Macquarie in 1815. A scholar noted:

> the Native Institution was expected to de-Aboriginalise its pupils on a permanent basis. In this it failed, and that was how it was judged. Some colonists realized that Aborigines returned to their own people because there was no place for them in a society which regarded them, educated or not, as the lowest in the scale of humanity, but most colonists were convinced that the Aborigines themselves were inherently unable to profit from education. (Fletcher 1989)

With debate over "the stolen generations" and reconciliation dominating the minds of Australians at the beginning of the twenty-first century, it is important to note the processes by which Australian education became a major tool for social engineering up until the 1970s, and then how it entered into a crisis period of self-redefinition until the beginning of the twenty-first century.

Primary education in South Australia extends from pre-year 1 to year 7, while the southeastern states (New South Wales, Victoria, and Tasmania), run from pre-year 1 to year 6. Secondary education in all states runs to year 12, with differing mechanisms for matriculation to university. Different examinations are used in Victoria and New South Wales. The development of national standards is increasingly putting pressure on these regional variations and increasing cooperation between states at all levels.

In August 1998, there were 9,587 schools enrolling 3,198,655 (61 percent K-6) students, 6,998 (73 percent) of which were government schools. In the face of a slight decline in the number of government schools (1995-1998), the non-government sector continues to grow rapidly (1 to 3 percent per triennium), particularly in the low-fee paying Christian school sector, as much as 8 percent per year (Long 1996). These trends reflect the general drift in Australian society towards private delivery and downsizing; a retreat by sub-cultures from the public sphere in the face of growing social diversity. The impact of parental fears about social trends such as violence, drugs in schools, and retention of traditional values, can be seen by the fact that such schools are strongest in years 8-10, but follow patterns of retention in government schools in K-6. The nearly 100,000 indigenous students enrolled in K-12 are, due to issues of isolation and the inability to mobilize private funding, much more reliant on government funded schools.

Most private school growth for K-12 has occurred in rapid growth, lower-to-middle-class outer suburban areas of Australia's major cities. Their ability to draw on constituency support in addition to government per capita funding of student institutions has meant that non-government schools have better staff-student ratios than government schools, particularly in the wealthier Anglican schools sector. Building growth has not increased at the same rate as population growth, leaving many low-fee paying private schools to struggle with accommodation issues.

Clear distinctions continue between the greater public schools, which are mostly church-based but are in fact private corporations, Catholic systemic schools, low-fee paying Christian schools, and local government schools.

With the improvement of the economy after the economic recession in the late 1980s, retention rates years in grades 10-12 have dropped, from 77 percent to 71 percent (65 percent government and 84 percent non-government). This trend reinforced the lack of a universal tertiary college culture in Australia (ABS, Education and Training 1999).

Higher Education was attempted a number of times through the early history of the various colonies. The Australian College in New South Wales, for instance, was meant to combine K-12 activities with the seeds of future clergy training for the Presbyterian Church. All such institutions failed, however, until the foundation of the University of Sydney in 1852—on deliberately nonsectarian lines. The University of Melbourne followed in 1853, Tasmania (in Hobart) in 1893, Adelaide (established by Act of Parliament in 1874), and Queensland in 1909 (Barcan 1980).

Enrollment figures tended to follow population growth and decline and the policy function of the universities in their home colonies/states. Prior to World War II, universities in Australia tended to be for the children of the professional classes. This status changed radically after World War II with the need to retrain hundreds of thousands of Australian soldiers for civilian life. Post-war migration added additional pressure, leading to an efflorescence of new institutions (Monash, Macquarie, La Trobe, Murdoch, and Flinders), mostly in the suburbs.

By the 1970s, universities had become a major tool for the Australian government that was attempting to redirect national effort away from commodities production and trading towards value added industries and (from the 1980s) the information industries revolutionizing large parts of Asia. Encouraging Australian students into those institutions was a more difficult task, given the lack of a generalized learning culture and the lack of obvious career paths for many of the courses offered.

By March 1998, there were 671,853 students in higher education courses in Australia (about 3.7 percent of the population), of which 72,183 (or 10.0 percent of the total) were classed as overseas students (up from 21,000 in 1989, 5 percent of the total). Some 359,225 of these students were aged 16 to 24, representing 14 percent of the population group. The vast number of the new growth among these students went into business, economics, computer sciences, media, and health. There was a relative decline in numbers going into straight humanities and education subjects. The growth in both the business disciplines and in the proportion of non-resident students, as well as the consolidation of higher education institutions through the 1980s, marked the shift of education from its position as a core community service to a position as a growing export industry that was competing in the global market.

Since 1995, all registered Australian tertiary institutions have been required to tailor their curricula according to the Australian Qualifications Framework (AQF), a normative system dictating standard outcomes rather than content. The AQF replaced the Register of Australian Tertiary Education (operative since 1990). This has meant that the vocational education and training (VET) system (offering diplomas from Certificate 1 to Advanced Diploma) articulates from upper school education and to the university system, which offer knowledge based baccalaureate and higher degrees, but overlap with VET in offering diplomas and Advanced Diplomas in a unified system. It is possible to transfer credit and recognition of prior learning throughout the tertiary system.

The integration of previously separate spheres of education within relatively new and artificial standards-based structures raises two major challenges to education: "The first of these is 'What counts as worthwhile learning?' The second question is 'What may be accepted to confirm that such learning has occurred?' Both of these questions, and the issues they raise . . . must reignite a serious consideration by teacher education faculties of what actually constitutes knowledge.'' (Taylor and Clemans 2000)

Through the 1980s, most states introduced legislation restricting use of the terms like *university* or *degree* to those recognized by the state and falling within the AQF. With state universities, this has not been an issue, since those institutions are largely self-accrediting. Considerable tension developed over the recognition of private providers under the various state Acts. There is not an education equivalent to an Australian university criteria because there is so much variation in quality and approach between institutions. A provider does not have substantial credit if endorsed in one state and refused standing in another because of Acts that vary. Considerable work has gone into smoothing out irregularities in the system, and making the AQF genuinely national in scope. Other quality controls are imposed through the Commonwealth's Trade Practices Act 1974. State/Territory fair trading legislation helps protect the quality of higher education.

PREPRIMARY & PRIMARY EDUCATION

In most states and territories, except Queensland and Western Australia, there is one year of part-time preschool education followed by one year of full-time preprimary education. In Queensland, one year of part-time preschool is available. In Western Australia, one year of part-time preprimary education is accessible. As preprimary education is not compulsory in Australia, the teaching of preprimary teachers is not as regulated as the preparation of primary and postprimary teachers, though universities such as Curtin University and Macquarie University have flourishing early childhood teacher preparation schemes.

Primary education is largely the responsibility of the states: State governments are responsible for around 88 percent of the funding for government schools. They are also the major employer of primary principals. Federal funding tends to come back to state primary schools through general allocations such as the States Grants (Primary and Secondary Education Assistance) Act 1996; and Indigenous Education (Supplementary Assistance) Act 1989, and through the funding of particular programs (such as support for literacy and numeracy programs, book purchases, foreign language, special needs, among others).

Federal government expenditure exceeding $16 billion was spent on school-based education (1997-2000). From 1997, under a conservative government, any school recognized by a state education department (public or private) could access government funding from 12 categories of eligibility.

Shifts in funding are affected both for primary and secondary by government policy targets, and the Government School Recurrent Costs (AGSRC) and Building Price (BP) indices. An example of the former is the arrangement whereby the Australian government channels funds provided by the Italian government (through the organization Co.As.It) for the teaching of Italian (Australia's largest non-English language group) in Australian schools.

The progressive movement of federal agencies into primary education is marked by the fact that Commonwealth funding (worth $2.1 billion in 2000) is increasing at a faster rate than state funding. This remains a sensitive issue, however, as the constitution delineates states rights over these areas. The Federal government has proclaimed its interest to emerge out of:

> pursuing the Government's broad national, social and economic agenda and in improving the well-being of all Australians, promoting national consistency in the provision of schooling across Australia, the reporting of nationally comparable data on student achievement and other outcomes of school education, and improved accountability by education providers for schooling outcomes to parents and the wider Australian community. (DETYA 2000c)

The priorities driven through these funding and standards mechanisms are numerous and include the following: improve the literacy and numeracy skills of all young Australians in order to articulate into higher levels of education and serve the labor market; increase focus on vocational education and training in the senior secondary curriculum; enhance teacher and principal development and professionalism to meet the ever increasing demands of educational, social, economic and technological change; support educationally disadvantaged students; improve educational outcomes of schooling for Indigenous students; support the right of parents to choose the educational environment which best suits the needs of their child, whether the school is public or private; use new technologies and scientific principles; increase focus on civics and citizenship education; teach designated priority languages other than English; and aware students of and economically cooperate with the Asia-Pacific region, through the encouragement of Asian studies and languages. Despite priority 10, Asian languages have developed comparatively slowly, with Indonesian, Japanese (the largest at the HSC level), and Chinese among the favorites.

SECONDARY EDUCATION

Secondary Education is provided by a mix of private and public educational institutions, relationships between which have reflected larger class and social tensions in the country. As government budgets shrink relatively, competition for federal and state funding has intensified, leading to some remarkable public outbursts. The NSW Labor government, for example, has recently supported teacher trade union calls for a review of Commonwealth spending on private schools, shifting blame for its own allocations on the basis that Commonwealth priorities have provided for a 12 percent real increase in funding to private schools and no real increase to public schools. The case of private schooling has not been helped by bitter public debates over, for instance, the teaching of creationism in some Christian schools, and several celebrated student abuse cases in a number of large and prestigious private colleges. In the larger framework, these debates should probably be seen within the context of "new knowledge" professionals attempting to push the boundaries of secularization in an age when governments are more committed to retaining diversity across the educational system and support from subcultures within the multicultural mix of Australian society.

Increasing public provision in the context of an aging population is a large budget proposition in an age of decreasing budgets. In an attempt to quell the issues of class in the debate, on May 11, 1999, Dr. David Kemp (Commonwealth Minister for Education, Training and Youth Affairs), issued *Choice and Equity: Funding Arrangements for Non-Government Schools 2001-2004,* which abolished the *Education Resources Index* (ERI) and replaced it with a measure of socioeconomic status (SES) of school communities. The means-testing of aid, however, has not stopped the criticism, since the real issue is the shrinking hold public education has on the Australian imagination and the budgetary policies, which reflect a shift in attitude to education as a relative rather than an absolute good.

In 2000, some 81,000 students enrolled for the School Certificate (year 10 matriculation) in NSW, around a core of subjects relating to mathematics, English, and science. The next most common subjects were personal development/health, commerce, computing, geography studies, technics I, history, and visual arts. The movement towards the integration of VET subjects in secondary education is evident, even to the extent that students may opt for courses taught in technical and further education colleges rather than on the campuses of high schools. This process is even more advanced in Victoria. By contrast, there were some 66,000 students who sat for the Higher School certificate in NSW in 1999, of which 52 percent (slightly above population average) were female, and most of whom sat for the Board of Studies' developed courses rather than Board endorsed subjects. The status of public examinations for matriculation to universities, though criticized as elitist in some circles, still holds considerable attraction in the market place. Some 77 percent of students received a university admissions score, indicating an offer of a place in a higher education institution attached to the Universities Admissions Centre (NSW Board of Studies 1999).

HIGHER EDUCATION

Postsecondary education in Australia is divided by the Commonwealth Department of Education, Training, and Youth Affairs (DETYA) into nine categories, three of which are public (University, TAFE/Technical College, and Skillshare or other government training) and the remaining six of which are private (business college or adult/community education center; industry skills center; professional/industry association; equipment/product manufacturer or supplier; other private training organization; and other organization or institution) (DETYA 2000a). Of the nearly 900,000 enrollments in the award sector (1997) private providers represent about 11 percent of postsecondary award enrollments. Non-award enrollments were also offered. The niche role of private providers is demonstrated by the much larger percentage of private over public enrollments involved in part-time and external study (45 percent versus 32 percent in 1997), and in programs not leading to an award.

Most universities (following the models of the Universities of Sydney and Melbourne) are state-owned, statutory bodies established under their own acts of state parliament. The Australian National University is unique, being constituted by an Act of federal parliament in 1946 as Australia's only research university. Its position in the Australian Capital Territory drove it to seek a larger student base, and through amalgamations successively with Canberra University College and the Institute of The Arts, it has since 1960 been offering undergraduate education and since 1992 broadened to include creative arts.

The rash of new universities peaked in the late 1960s, and few new institutions were created until the 1990s. The pressure of new settlement areas has been the major reason for new institutions since then—the University of Western Sydney, for instance, which combined a number of pre-existing colleges (including the venerable Hawkesbury Agricultural College) under one masthead in 1990. The latest university in this category is the University of the Sunshine Coast (USC), formed from a private university formed in the 1980s, made a university College in 1994, and was claimed a university by the Labor Party government in Queensland in 1998. It finds itself at the heart of the major growth corridor of the Sunshine Coast, Australia's fastest growing region.

USC also represents the growth of higher education with an increasing number of private tertiary institutions. Few of these (Avondale College, Seventh Day Adventist;

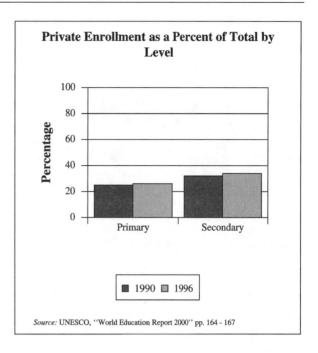

Private Enrollment as a Percent of Total by Level

Source: UNESCO, "World Education Report 2000" pp. 164 - 167

Australian Catholic University, Catholic; and Notre Dame University, Catholic being among the exceptions) obtain government funding. The most highly profiled of these (in media terms) was Bond University, begun by a corporate entrepreneur (Alan Bond) before facing financial stringencies and restructuring in the late 1980s. It has since gone on to considerable achievements, particularly in business, economics, and law. Growth is restrained largely by the absence of large pockets of private wealth in Australia, and the size of the population. The position of these institutions as private providers included within the government funding model was a major factor suggesting devolvement of government funding on a voucher basis that could be used at the registered institution of the student's choice. If this were to happen, the private sector would receive considerable impetus, and the small start-up agencies (for instance, those hoping to building on the base provided by the large number of theological colleges and Christian schools in Australia) in formation would emerge as further competition for a public sector which is itself quickly moving to broaden the number of privately funded places offered.

Most Australian universities admit students competitively on the basis of secondary matriculation and demand for courses. In New South Wales, for instance, this is handled through the Universities Admissions Centre (UAC), which mediates student applications via an index called the *Universities Admissions Index*, successor to many disputed and publicly debated systems. Essentially, the UAI uses weighted HSC results to mediate between student demand and university supply. Most students are offered places in particular institutions on the basis of

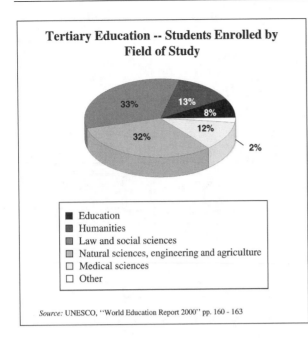

Tertiary Education -- Students Enrolled by Field of Study

33% 13% 8% 12% 32% 2%

- Education
- Humanities
- Law and social sciences
- Natural sciences, engineering and agriculture
- Medical sciences
- Other

Source: UNESCO, ''World Education Report 2000'' pp. 160 - 163

their UAI. Some institutions also add bonus points to applications if students live in a particular area, fulfill pre-enrollment interviews, or fit other desirable target criteria. ACT students obtain a score from the ACT Board of Senior Secondary Studies, and in most other states a *Tertiary Entrance Rank* is calculated on the basis of weighted matriculation examination scores. In Western Australia, the equivalent is a TER calculated by the Tertiary Institutions Service Centre (TISC). In Queensland, entry is determined by the Queensland Tertiary Admissions Centre (QTAC) on the basis of overall positions determined through moderated internal assessment and the Queensland Core Skills Test (QCS).

ADMINISTRATION, FINANCE, & EDUCATIONAL RESEARCH

With federation in 1901, the Australian states retained the obligation to fund education. A federal framework gave reason for them to seek standardized approaches across the country. The emphasis was not on content so much as on citizenship, character, and the underpinnings of social democracy, the development of intelligence, faculty, and character. In addition, practical courses ran alongside academic ones, with students effectively streamed into technical, superior, and academic streams by the end of primary Qualifying Certificate, through to the Continuation, and other Certificates.

As the aftershocks of the disastrous 1891 depression settled down, improved economic conditions allowed expansion of the systems. Committees like the Fink Commission in Victoria (through the Education Act of 1901, and the subsequent Teacher's Act) and the NSW Royal Commission on Education (through the Free Education Act 1906), guided the reform of technical education, eliminated pupil teachers, abolished fees in state schools, promoted the building of state high schools, provided for teacher education institutions and registration, extended the compulsory base of education, and the centralization of education under permanent heads.

Though technical education would have to await full implementation until World War II, the cyclic nature of the Australian economy encouraged pragmatism, and militated against a leisured liberal arts tradition. Two major depressions, recurrent recessions, and war made Australians a practical people. The influence of Scots and English thought, influenced by German idealism, was particularly strong in this period, though as the Ascham School in Sydney, and the introduction of Rudolph Steiner and Montessori schools showed variety was a local possibility in the period from 1914.

Montessori became mainstream in New South Wales, and from there influenced Tasmania and South Australia, but made less headway in other states. The Jena school in Germany was a regular stop on Australian tours abroad for educational ideas, those that also filtered into Australia through the medium of journals, and British domination of the book trade. The Kindergarten movement, also German in origin, had been introduced to keep young children off the streets in the 1890s depression, and began to spread in Australia after the return of prosperity in 1906. By 1914, however, due to the period of reform through 1901-1914, children entering Kindergarten could look forward to a complete K-Tertiary education provision in their own country. The growth of a specifically Australian (as opposed to Anglo-Australian) form of patriotism was one outcome of this, as the Australian intelligentsia could now be embraced within Australian institutions. Despite the lack of demand for local authors and other creative talents, it was a trend that reinforced the deliberate attempts of history and social studies curricula to engender concepts of citizenship.

Though education was a state issue, the Commonwealth became more vitally involved in state provision through the two world wars. After both wars, tens of thousands of ex-servicemen had to be retrained to enter into post-war reconstruction society. This was done through Commonwealth funding of technical and university places for returned servicemen. The cohort that emerged from Australian institutions in the early 1950s was, thus, more mature, worldly-wise, and destined to lead Australian social institutions into the 1980s. The new industries encouraged by war also demanded a flow of technically-educated men (and, increasingly, teachers were among the first semi-professionals to begin moving up), the first major step in which was the take over of teacher training by the universities that defined the field of education.

Similar processes were to occur through the 1970s and 1980s with regard to nursing, and through the 1990s with regard to policing, paramedics, business, and other social service areas. Meeting the demand for teachers in a democratic country meant maintaining or elevating the drawing power of the profession, either through social status or financial reward. As society became increasingly consumer-oriented, the two types of reward began to run into one another, relativizing the pseudo-religious roots of the so-called "honourable professions." The pluralization of society, on the other hand, was marked by rising crime rates and the decline of social security in precisely those areas where the state desired cohorts of new teachers to begin work. Increasing the leaving age just meant more uninterested students in school for a longer period of time. Fewer matriculants were offering for an occupation requiring higher levels of knowledge, ever improving teaching skills, for lower relative social and economic return. The phrase "the crisis in education" shown by rising teacher resignation rates, and global transfer of teachers to other parts of the world was to remain a key element of Australian public debate through to the end of the century. Professionalization was thus driven by the destabilization of a rapidly modernized and globalized society. The University of Tasmania took over teacher education as early as 1948 for rational economic reasons and struggled to fit teaching practicums into the academic timetable.

By the late 1950s, the prospect of the baby boom doubling the population of Australia's universities in a very short period of time was beginning to worry Commonwealth and state planners. In 1949, the New South Wales University of Technology was founded at Kensington, to articulate between the burgeoning number of Technical College students and the need for increased numbers of technical professionals to oversee post-War reconstruction. Eventually, renamed the University of NSW, it grew through a pattern of regional expansion and proliferation of degrees, as well as a marketable commodity for educational exports to the expanding economies of Asia, to become one of Australia's largest universities. But this was not enough. From 1954-1957, university enrollments in Australia rose by nearly 30 percent. From 1954, under pressure from the rural vote, the University of New England gained its independence from the University of Sydney, and entered the field of distance education. None of these universities were financially stable, and greater need again was emerging with the rising numbers of students, and academic union militancy over poor wages and conditions.

The Murray Report and the demographic bulge of the period opened a golden age of state funded university

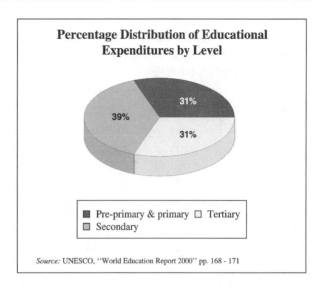

Percentage Distribution of Educational Expenditures by Level

31%
31%
39%

■ Pre-primary & primary □ Tertiary
■ Secondary

Source: UNESCO, "World Education Report 2000" pp. 168 - 171

expansion. New faculties were added at the newly named UNSW and the major metropolitan universities, and new Universities were founded (Monash, 1958; James Cook (University College of Townsville), 1960; Wollongong University (College), 1962; Macquarie, 1963; Newcastle University, 1965; Flinders University, 1961-1966; La Trobe University, 1964).

Dawkins *unified national scheme* regularized relationships between the states and the commonwealth with regard to federal leadership over national education policy, as did the "Common and Agreed National Goals for Schooling in Australia" (the Hobart Declaration), which emerged out of the 1989 conference of Education Ministers. The high point of this golden age of university expansion, and of education for democracy was under the Whitlam government, 1972-1975. The Whitlam revolution retained the last remnants of 1960s optimism before the oil shocks of the early 1970s, and the recession budgets of the Fraser government began to function. E. Gough Whitlam broke more than 20 years of conservative, minimalist government style in the Liberal tradition by appealing to the white collar middle classes who had been the most enthusiastic patrons of the university and education sector. While retaining labor union support, he reconceptualized Welfare as the means by which government enriched the life of every citizen. In this sense, government was in *loco parentis* for the dissolving local communities on which education had been built in earlier years. "Any function or activity," declared Whitlam, "which can be hitched to the star of the Commonwealth grows in quality and affluence. Any function or activity which is financially limited to the States will grow slowly or even decline" (Whitlam, ALP Policy Speech, 1972). The major areas were education, health care, urban planning and social services, with equality of opportunity in each the immediate aim and equality of outcomes as a recognized unreachable benchmark for different social groups. The bold vision was in the end torn down by recession and cultural reaction from a people for whom the social costs were too much too fast. Whitlam still divides the Australian opinion today, as the proponent of the last great cause.

Universities received greatly increased per capita funding for student places. Equal opportunity and affirmative action was entrenched in the public sector well beyond the federal sphere of influence. Official multiculturalism was promulgated and the rights of minorities, especially girls, Aborigines, rural children, migrant children and the physically and mentally handicapped were protected and advanced. Funding for childcare was made available to empower working mothers—a system that existed in moderated form until the early 1990s. At secondary level, the radical experience of South Australia was extended to the federal scene by Peter Karmel through the Australian Schools Commission. The system of government grants to schools was means tested, meaning that more resources flowed to the poorer Catholic schools than to the private grammar schools. More importantly, the beneficiaries of a student generation of free university education remained beholden to the vision of democratic education, a cohort that still fills many of education's senior positions, and resents the swing to a market economy that is transforming social activism into market awareness.

As the century ended, Australians awaited the federal government's final word on whether the recommendation of devolved educational funding, such as a voucher system would be put into place. Elements of devolved budgeting are in place, such as the Howard Liberal Government of Enrollment Benchmark Adjustment (EBA) which facilitates the establishment of non-government schools, and penalizes those public systems which lose market share. The use of the EBA has also provided a way of estimating the scale of movement towards the private system in Australia: in 2000, DETYA estimated that, "the gradual movement of students to the non-government school sector has saved the states some $3 billion since 1983" (DETYA, 2000c). The NSW government estimated in 2000 that its public system would be losing some $50 million per year by 2003 to EBA due to the shift towards private schools (NSWDET 2000). In the same year, most states were closing surplus public schools in older suburban areas due to declining numbers of school-aged children and the growth of the private sector. Some tensions, particularly as relates to hiring policies and such issues as corporal punishment, have arisen over the fact that receipt of federal funding requires private schools to comply.

NONFORMAL EDUCATION

The quality of the Australian education system is protected by prosecuting misleading or deceptive conduct, including the provision of misleading or deceptive information on courses or accreditation. Similar protection is extended to overseas students through the Education Services for Overseas Students (Registration of Providers and Financial Regulation) (ESOS) Act 1991, which requires that "all providers offering education and training services to overseas students must be accredited to provide specific courses (and approved to provide these courses to overseas students) by relevant State/Territory authorities, and be registered on the Commonwealth Register of International Courses for Overseas Students (CRICOS)." Quality controls were implemented in 2001-2 through the Multilateral Joint Planning Committee (MJPC) protocol formulated through joint discussions between Federal and State ministries (DETYA 2000e).

In 1997 private providers accounted for 49 percent of external courses not leading to an award and public providers accounted for the remaining 51 percent. With the formalization of state-based laws requiring the accreditation of most awards, the amalgamation of universities, and the search for community-based support for university programs, there has been a significant reduction in the percentage of non-award courses offered by private providers in the postsecondary sector (declining from 73 to 49 percent between 1993 and 1997) and a slight rise in the market share of private providers in enrolled award students (DETYA 2000a). There are 46 tertiary institutions presently obtaining government funding as recognized tertiary providers, in addition to a widespread state system for technical education, and a great number of smaller privately run business, professional, and vocational colleges.

TEACHING PROFESSION

In 2000, almost all Australian universities prepared teachers for primary education. Most covered education in both school and non-school settings and included such areas as early childhood education; primary and secondary education; vocational education and training; and special education, applied linguistics, language education, and technology Education. With a swing towards standards-based education, there was increasing pressure for preparation for tertiary teaching. The development of standards such as the AQF has been followed by national standards development for an increasing number of areas, for instance, the National Assessment Framework for Languages as Senior Secondary Level, which allows comparison between matriculation level language curricula across the various states.

Recognition of external teacher qualifications demonstrates the existence of a general consensus that, despite variation between the various teacher registration schemes in various states, basic teacher preparation requires four year trained status, the equivalent of an Australian Bachelor's degree, at least a year's of specific studies in education and methodology, and six weeks of supervised practical teaching. The competition for positions in the state systems has pushed teacher education even further up the road to professionalization, with it being very common for teachers to pursue professional advancement through Masters degrees, one of the proliferating professional doctorates (in Educational Administration, Education, or Management), or upskilling by horizontal expansion of skills into new areas, such as computer sciences.

In the end, it was the baby boom and the expansionist government's immigration policies aimed at filling up the empty spaces of Australia that democratized the system more effectively than progressive educational policy. On the one hand, progressivism in education, as with modernism in theology and the theory of progress generally, was a dying force. During war and depression, the world saw enough to blunt its belief in humanist utopias. On the other hand, more children staying in school longer stretched resources to the limit. Increasing numbers within the primary school encouraged regular promotion from class to class and reduced the significance of the examination or other system of assessment by which pupils at the end of the primary school were allocated to secondary schools. This wave, in turn, put pressure on the comprehensive secondary schools, which were increasingly built in drawing areas located on the edge of the metropolitan sprawl developing in Australian cities, and on the teachers' colleges, which needed to produce sufficient graduates for the new educational growth industry.

SUMMARY

In an age of rapid change, it is clear that educational standards, content, and means of delivery are under constant pressure. The challenge for Australian education is multi-leveled. At the K-6 level, the devolution of funding and organization, on the one hand, tied to increasing bureaucratic control through imposition of external standards raises serious questions about the role of the Australian Welfare state. The presupposition built up among most Australians since the middle of last century was that the State would provide the basic needs of life. That expectation has been impossible, despite government review of national taxation systems, that have led to public angst about hospitals, roads, social welfare and other elements of Australian life. One spin off of this is a declining faith in public education, as marked by steady growth in private provision at all levels of education. For those institutions in the public system, the gap created by the status of government needs to be overcome, in particular by a closer embedding of institutions in real constituencies. The sort of alumni support of institutions and culture of private philanthropy which underpins the American system of education is largely absent in Australia, a lack which will be of supreme importance as institutions are increasingly privatized and forced into competitive markets. The launching of devolution programs among primary schools was often destructive, as the communities in which they were meant to fish for support did not actually exist in sociological terms (Welch 1996).

Geographical placement of schools means little in suburban settings when most members of those suburbs are free to create private spheres unrelated to their actual location. The information age continues to exacerbate this problem, with the extension of communities into supranational virtual spaces. This is a major challenge to a public provision system based on principles of geographical saturation. While the re-orientation of the Australian tax system towards goods and services taxation has released new resources for public expenditure, it has also worsened the shift away from the states observable in financial arrangements since the 1950s. Primary and secondary education are likely to see an increase in federal supervision of their activities, despite the fact that the legal responsibility lies with the states.

This federal supervision creates significant problems in meeting local needs and in overcoming the welfare gap. As Peter Berger noted with regard to religious organizations, the vacuum created for mediating institutions by the overarching welfare state will no doubt continue to provide considerable impetus to the growth of private providers. The problem this creates is that private providers have historically been unable to unlock the sorts of resources needed to meet the huge range of social needs found in a multicultural, scattered, and geographically extensive Australian society. Public schools thus face the threat of becoming providers for special needs only.

A small player in a large international market, Australian education has much to teach the world about distance education, flexible delivery, and teaching in a first world, multicultural society. It is, however, facing significant issues in terms of retaining coherency between public policy and actual provision and social outcomes, issues which will remain with Australian education for years to come.

BIBLIOGRAPHY

Ashenden, Dean. *State Aid and the Division of Schooling in Australia.* Deakin University, 1989.

Barcan, A. *A History of Australian Education.* Melbourne: OUP, 1980.

Beazley, Hon. K. *International Education in Australia through the 1990s.* AGPS, Canberra.

Bell, Philip, and Roger Bell. *Implicated: the United States in Australia.* Melbourne; New York: Oxford University Press, 1993.

Cassin, Ray. "What's Left of the Tribe: Recollections of a Catholic Education." *Eureka Street,* v.4, no.4 (May 1994): 33.

Dawkins, J. *Higher Education: A Policy Statement.* Canberra: AGPS, 1988.

DETYA: Department of Education Training and Youth Affairs. *Selected Higher Education Statistics.* Department of Education, Training, and Youth Affairs, Canberra: AGPS, 1999.

———. "Public and Private Provision of Postsecondary Education and Training: 1993 and 1997 Compared." *IAED Occasional Papers Series.* Canberra: DETYA Research and Evaluation Branch, 2000a.

———. "Commonwealth Programmes for Schools Quadrennial Administrative Guidelines 1997 to 2000," 2000b.

———. "Commonwealth Programmes for Schools: Quadrennial Administrative Guidelines 1997 to 2000," revision. Canberra: DETYA, 2000c.

———. *SES Funding Arrangements for Non-Government Schools,* 2000d. Available from www.detya.gov.au/schools/ses/SES.htm.

———. *Higher Education Report for 2000-2002.* Triennium, Canberra: AGPS, 2000e.

Fletcher, J. *Documents in the History of Aboriginal Education in New South Wales.* Sydney: for the author, 1989.

Foster, L. E. *Australian Education: A Sociological Perspective.* New York: Prentice Hall, 1992.

Freudenberg, G. "The Program." In *The Whitlam Phenomenon (Fabian Papers).* McPhee Gribble, Melbourne, 1986.

Karmel, Peter (comp). *Schools in Australia.* Canberra: AGPS, 1973.

Keeves, J. and K. Marjoribanks. *Australian Education: Review of Research 1965-1998.* ACER, 1999.

Kitchenn, R. G. *State Aid for Non-state Schools,* Melbourne: *Australian Council of State School Organisations,* 1971.

Lippmann, L. *Aboriginal Education.* Clayton Vic: Monash University Centre for Research into Aboriginal Affairs, 1974.

Marginson, S. *Markets in Education, Sydney: Allen and Unwin,* 1997.

NSW Board of Studies. *1999 Higher School Certificate Statistics,* 2001. Available from http://www.boardofstudies.nsw.edu.au/.

Postman, Neil. *Technopoly: the Surrender of Culture to Technology.* New York: Vintage Books, 1993.

Rothblatt, Sheldon. *The Revolution of the Dons: Cambridge and Society in Victorian England.* Cambridge; New York: Cambridge University Press, 1981.

Roussel, S. "Factors Influencing Employees' Participation in Education & Training: Evidence from the ABS Surveys of Education & Training 1989, 1993, & 1997." Draft report. DETYA, August 1999.

Trudgen, R. *Why Warriors Lie Down and Die.* Darwin: Aboriginal Resource and Development Services, 2000.

Watson, L. *Survey of Private Providers in Australian Education.* Canberra: DETYA, 1998.

—Mark Hutchinson

AUSTRIA

BASIC DATA

Official Country Name:	Republic of Austria
Region:	Europe
Population:	8,131,111
Language(s):	German
Literacy Rate:	98%
Academic Year:	September-June
Number of Primary Schools:	3,703
Compulsory Schooling:	9 years
Public Expenditure on Education:	5.4%
Foreign Students in National Universities:	27,172
Libraries:	2,016
Educational Enrollment:	Primary: 381,927 Secondary: 793,485 Higher: 240,632
Educational Enrollment Rate:	Primary: 100% Secondary: 103% Higher: 48%
Teachers:	Primary: 31,251 Secondary: 79,806 Higher: 26,356

Student-Teacher Ratio:	Primary:	12:1
	Secondary:	9:1
Female Enrollment Rate:	Primary:	100%
	Secondary:	102%
	Higher:	49%

HISTORY & BACKGROUND

Austria has an area of 32,376 square miles and a population of 8.1 million inhabitants, of which 98 percent are German-speaking. Austria officially recognizes six ethnic minorities, primarily in the southern and eastern provinces: Croatian, Roma, Slovak, Slovenian, Czech, and Hungarian. Seventy-eight percent of the population is Roman-Catholic, 5 percent Protestant, and 4.5 percent other religions. Austria is therefore characterized by a relatively homogeneous population, which nevertheless seeks to accommodate diversity. This commitment to accommodation is to a considerable extent a product of the various stages of the nation's historical development. The history of this small, land-locked European republic has reflected and shaped the continent's turbulent history for the past three millennia. Several distinct stages of Austrian history have played a central role in the establishment of its national identity.

During the fifth century A.D., Austria found itself at the crossroads of major successive incursions and migrations, including the Germanic tribes from the north, as well as the Huns, Avars, and Magyars from the east. The threat from the eastern Magyars was finally ended in the decisive battle of Lechfeld in 955 A.D. Shortly thereafter, in 976 A.D., a period of stability and development was ushered in under the rule of the house of Babenberg. Of particular interest during this ascendency in Austria's medieval importance was the establishment of several monasteries and religious orders that greatly fostered a climate of scholarship and learning.

By the end of the thirteenth century, the house of Habsburg emerged as the dominant political force in Austria, a position it was to hold nearly uninterruptedly until 1918. The University of Vienna was founded in 1365. Following a period of territorial expansion during the fourteenth century, the Habsburgs, under Albert V, assumed the crown of the Holy Roman Empire in 1438 and retained a virtual monopoly over it until Emperor Franz renounced the title of Holy Roman Emperor in 1806 in favor of the hereditary title of Emperor of Austria.

A further period of expansion and alliances through marriage extended Austria's empire during the fifteenth and sixteenth centuries to include Flanders, Burgundy, Bohemia, and Hungary. The sixteenth and seventeenth centuries were characterized by Austria's position as easternmost line of defense against the expansionist Turks, and it was a decisive victory in 1683 by the Austrian forces under Prince Eugene of Savoy that finally ended the threat of Turkish expansion into Western Europe.

The Austrian eighteenth century stood largely under the aegis of the formidable figure of Empress Maria Theresia, who ruled from 1740 to 1780. She stands in many respects at the threshold of the modern age in Austrian affairs, particularly in the administrative reform of the educational system. The spirit of reform was fortuitously continued under her successor, Joseph II. Following the dissolution of the Holy Roman Empire, Austria emerged from the changing political landscape wrought by reaction to the Congress of Vienna and the Revolution of 1848 as a politically and economically advanced member of the European community of powers. With the establishment of the Vienna Polytechnic in 1815, Austria recognized the relationship between education, commerce, and industry that promoted dramatic growth during the Industrial Revolution. Austria's first constitution dates from shortly after 1848 and pays early tribute to the changing realities of the European nation state.

The Austro-Hungarian Empire: In 1866 Emperor Franz Joseph, who dominated nineteenth-century Austria as much as Empress Maria Theresia had dominated the eighteenth, was defeated by the armies of Prussia. The Austrian constitution was modified in 1867 and, in recognition of the more limited role that Austria was to play henceforth with its German neighbors, the Austro-Hungarian *Doppelmonarchie* (dual monarchy) was established. Although it was an Austrian, the heir-apparent Archduke Franz Ferdinand, whose assassination in Sarajevo triggered the cataclysm of World War I, Austria itself quickly ceded the field of battle to the greater powers of Europe, who continued the war until 1919.

The winds of change and disillusionment that had brought down the monarchy in Russia and Germany at the end of World War I also claimed the Austrian monarchy. The last Austrian emperor, Karl, abdicated in 1918, and on November 12, 1918, the Austrian Republic was proclaimed by the Provisional National Assembly. In several political and economic respects, the shock of the war's aftermath mirrored developments in neighboring Germany. During the first years of the First Republic, intense battling between increasingly radical forces challenged the credibility and sapped the authority of successive governments. Resurgent nationalism, in its extreme Fascist incarnations, seized the imaginations of Austria's German neighbors to the north and Italy in the south.

In March 1938, finally, German troops marched into Austria and a subsequent plebiscite in April 1938 confirmed Austria's de facto annexation to the German Empire. By the time World War II broke out in 1939, Austria's military, economy, and political infrastructure had been largely integrated into Germany's war efforts.

The Second Republic: When Germany collapsed in 1945, Austria experienced, along with other targets of Germany's aggressive expansionism, a sense of liberation. After U.S., Soviet, and British troops had entered Austria by March 1945, a Provisional Government was proclaimed under Karl Renner on April 27. Following a long series of negotiations with the occupying powers, Austria finally regained sovereignty through the Austrian State Treaty, signed by all parties on May 15, 1955. On October 26, 1955, the Austrian parliament affirmed the country's permanent neutrality. Austria's reintegration into the community of nations was acknowledged formally on December 15, 1955, when it was admitted into the United Nations.

According to its constitution, the democratic Republic of Austria consists of nine independent provinces. The constitution furthermore guarantees all civil rights commonly associated with a modern, democratic republic, including: equality before the law, individual liberty, freedom of opinion, and an independent judiciary. Legislative competence is vested in the parliament, which is divided into the *Nationalrat* (National Council) and the *Bundesrat* (Federal Council). The National Council is elected in equal, direct, and secret elections according to a proportional-representation system. The 183 delegates currently represent the Social Democratic Party, the People's Party, the Freedom Party, and the environmentalist Green Party.

The Federal Council consists of 54 delegates who are elected by the respective provincial legislatures. In general terms, the Federal Council acknowledges formally, and represents the interests of, the provinces. Executive competencies are divided between the federal president and the federal government. The president is elected by general, equal, and free ballot for a term of six years. The powers of the federal president include appointment of the federal chancellor and ministers, convocation and, under specific circumstances, dissolution of the National Council.

The federal government consists of the federal chancellor and federal ministers. While the federal chancellor and cabinet together enjoy broad competencies in governing the country, a vote of no confidence can be invoked to relieve members of the federal government from office. The interests of the provinces are represented by the provincial government, headed by the provincial governor. The competencies of the provincial governments are further delegated to subordinated district and municipal governments.

The Second Republic has enjoyed a remarkable stability and level of support. Domestic and international crises have not substantially challenged the legitimacy of Austria's political foundations. Two international crises have, however, suggested that Austria faces questions about its past association with anti-democratic forces. The first crisis involved Kurt Waldheim, Austrian president and former general secretary of the United Nations, whose tenure was overshadowed by international criticism of Waldheim's alleged role as officer during World War II. The second crisis involves Jörg Haider, Provincial Governor of Carinthia and one-time leader of the Freedom Party, whose anti-European and anti-immigration policies have given rise to concern, within Austria and abroad, about the rise to prominence of right-wing extremism in Austrian politics and society.

Until the eighteenth century, Austrian education was dominated by the Church. Since the introduction and promotion of monastic schools throughout the Carolingian empire in the late ninth and tenth centuries, education was the province of the clergy for most of the Middle Ages. The strict control of the Roman Catholic clergy became even more pervasive during the Counter-Reformation in the sixteenth and seventeenth centuries. The monastic schools not only oversaw the basic education of the nobility, but were also one of the few avenues out of their situation available to poor but talented sons of commoners, be it as members of the clergy, tutors to the gentry, or as administrative assistants.

The situation changed with the advent of the Enlightenment and a general European spirit of fostering education as a necessary means to a desirable end. The origin of systematic efforts on behalf of Austrian public education goes back to the educational reforms in 1774 under Empress Maria Theresia. Although economic constraints led to the establishment of fewer new schools than envisioned, the notion of mandatory and public education became a fundamental element of public policy.

Legislation to guarantee academic freedom in science and teaching was enacted in 1867. Two years later, in 1869, the entire compulsory-education system was unified under the Imperial Primary Schools Act. Compulsory education was raised from a period of six to eight years. The basic elements of the 1869 act established the foundation of Austrian educational policy, to assure the best possible education to students without regard to gender, status, national origin, or religion.

Reforms instituted in 1918 under the Viennese superintendent of instruction, Otto Glöckel, built upon the concept of generally accessible and optimal educational opportunities by advocating for the importance of considering the child's educational development and aptitude in matters of academic progress.

CONSTITUTIONAL & LEGAL FOUNDATIONS

The Federal Constitutional Law of 1920, and subsequent amendments, confirmed the authority of the federal government in educational legislation and policy implementation. The *Hauptschule* (general secondary school), a compulsory school for students 10- to 14-years-old, was introduced in 1927. With the exception of universities, amendments to federal legislation governing education require a 2/3 majority of the National Council.

In the interest of representing the broadest possible spectrum of parties, legislation is generally developed in cooperation with the so-called "social partners," which may include employers' and employees' associations, labor unions, agricultural representatives, and similar interested parties. Significant legislation has reaffirmed fundamental tenets of Austrian educational policy, while at the same time recognizing specific needs and changing circumstances. Since the inception of the Second Republic, the Austrian educational system was codified and revised comprehensively through the comprehensive 1962 School Organization Act. It included extending compulsory education from eight to nine years, reorganization of teacher training, and expanded educational training, as well as the promotion of a uniform educational system. The act also guaranteed free access to educational opportunities and made schools co-educational.

Likewise in 1962, Federal School Superintendency Act was enacted as an administrative complement to the School Organization Act. The act deals with issues of educational jurisdiction and governance, as well as school inspection and administration. In the same year, the complementary Private Schools Act was enacted.

Subsequent legislation further coordinated and clarified specific educational-policy issues. The 1974 School Education Act dealt comprehensively with the issue of tracking, student transfer and promotion, examinations, schools as learning communities, as well as the relationship between parents, students, and teachers. Given the historical context, the School Acts reflect a wide-spread desire to liberalize the educational process, a desire which was affected by the European protest movements, which had already sought, in many cases successfully, to reform the encrusted and exclusionary hierarchies of the universities. Co-determination was further codified in the 1990 Student Government Act.

In 1985, two items of legislation updated and codified specific issues of educational policy: The Compulsory Education Act, and The School Lessons Act, which regulates the number of weekly classroom hours for the various types of schools. Standardization of testing criteria for diplomas and certificates was addressed in the 1997 Professional Certification Act. The extent to which Austria seeks to establish clear and comprehensive guidelines for the implementation of educational policies is reflected in a number of specific laws, including the 1949 Religious Education Act, which deals with religious instruction in public schools.

Sensitivity to ethnic minorities in Austria is reflected in the 1959 Minority-Education Act for Carinthia and the more recent 1994 Minority-Education Act for Burgenland. In recognition of the need to accommodate nontraditional learners, Austria continues to promote fluid and permeable access to educational opportunities through the 1997 School Education Act for the Employed. Such legislative initiatives confirm Austria's continuing commitment to use the resources of the federal government to guide, promote, coordinate, and supervise educational policies.

EDUCATIONAL SYSTEM—OVERVIEW

The Austrian educational system reflects three distinct learning stages and educational philosophies. Compulsory education for all children who are permanent residents of Austria, regardless of national origin, ranges from ages of 6 to 15. Compulsory education is divided approximately between a uniform four-year primary school, a minimum of four years at a secondary school, and, depending on aptitude and interest, a minimum of one year in a pre-professional program.

The secondary schools reflect differences in aptitude and interests in their curricula, length of study, admission criteria, and diplomas. Secondary schools are generally divided into a lower and upper level. Given the different emphases of the various types of secondary schools, and the qualifications to which they lead, the issue of tracking students at a relatively young age into academic, technical, or vocational secondary schools requires that important decisions about a child's educational future must be made relatively early. In its attempt to provide a more permeable secondary educational system for children, Austria continues to develop alternative means securing the necessary qualifications to transfer among available types of secondary schools.

The postsecondary schools include universities, colleges, academies, and professional institutes, access to which is based upon successful completion of requirements for graduation from secondary school. Since the secondary school diploma is sufficient entitlement for most university study, there is in most cases no separate academic entrance requirement or admissions test. The

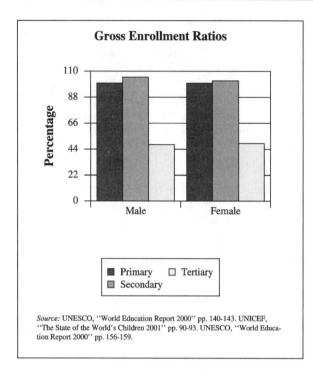

Gross Enrollment Ratios

Legend: ■ Primary □ Tertiary ■ Secondary

Source: UNESCO, "World Education Report 2000" pp. 140-143. UNICEF, "The State of the World's Children 2001" pp. 90-93. UNESCO, "World Education Report 2000" pp. 156-159.

postsecondary schools, like the secondary schools, have sought to liberalize access to university-level study by establishing equivalency criteria for alternative admission and providing greater access to non-traditional students.

Although Austrian schools are co-educational, traditional patterns of enrollment continue to reflect gender-based disparities. The number of females who complete no more than compulsory education, for example, is still considerably higher than males. Lack of apprenticeship opportunities for vocational qualification likewise affects females more than males. Finally, females continue to limit selection of vocational, professional, and academic programs of study to more traditional areas, thus avoiding educational and career opportunities in fields like mathematics, computer science, and engineering.

In response to such gender-based disparities, the government has developed special initiatives, the most comprehensive of which is the Federal Ministry of Education, Science and Cultural Affairs' Action Plan 2000, which includes "99 Steps for Promoting Equal Opportunity in School and Adult Education" and calls for such measures as targeted educational advising, increased school autonomy, and administrative decentralization, as well as a comprehensive survey of parents and students on specific issues of educational quality.

The school calendar varies somewhat from province to province, and with respect to certain specialized schools, but the academic year for primary and secondary schools lasts from September to July. The school week includes regular instruction on varying Saturdays. The school day generally ends in early afternoon and by noon on Saturdays. Not all classes are taught every day, and students must pay relatively close attention to their respective schedules. The calendar for Austrian universities is divided into two semesters, with the academic year beginning in October and ending in June.

The primary language of instruction is German, although there is emphasis at all educational levels on learning foreign languages. More than 90 percent of all 10- to 19-year-old students are trained in at least one foreign language. There are opportunities for learning subject matter in a foreign language at secondary schools, including general subjects like history, economics, and geography. In addition, there are opportunities for ethnic minorities to receive instruction in their native language. Bilingual education has been introduced through pilot projects such as the International Bilingual School in Graz. The grading system in Austrian primary and secondary schools is based upon a numeric scale ranging from 1 (very good) to 5 (failing), with 4 generally considered to be a passing grade. The reliance upon numerical grades as the principal assessment instrument contributes to a relatively high rate of repeaters. In the 1994-1995 school year, 2 percent of students in compulsory schools, approximately 8 percent of students in general academic secondary schools, and 13 percent of students in postsecondary vocational schools had to repeat a grade.

Certain optional courses, particularly at the primary level, are not graded. These include cultural enrichment courses like choir and drama. On the other hand, certain required courses, particularly at the academic secondary level, are weighted in terms of their importance. In addition, such weighted courses are important when students wish to transfer into a higher-achievement secondary school or pursue study at specific postsecondary institutions.

Private schools, which provide primary and secondary education, as well as some teacher training, are administered primarily under the auspices of the Roman Catholic Church. They account for roughly 10 percent of Austrian schools and teachers. Since there is no history of private universities in Austria, the federal government maintains a virtual monopoly over higher education.

Austria fosters a number of initiatives to integrate modern technology and practically oriented principles into the academic and training curriculum. In seeking to promote foreign-language education, general textbooks increasingly include material written in a foreign language. Multimedia and Internet-assisted language instruction is promoted to bridge the access gap between urban and rural schools. Austria also aggressively pursues opportunities for international exchange programs.

The integration of new technology into the classroom is furthermore aided by ancillary educational innovations like "training firms," in which schools provide a base for carefully supervised student business ventures. Business operations encourage the practical application of information technology on behalf of an optimal transition from school to career.

Although such initiatives are presently coordinated and initiated through the central authority of the federal and provincial governments, there is indication that the movement toward school autonomy is gaining more wide-spread acceptance. Such movement toward autonomy has already been largely accepted for technical and vocational schools, on which the pressure to adapt to rapidly changing conditions is particularly great. It is hoped that increased autonomy will not only allow the Austrian educational system to adapt more flexibly and efficiently to the demands of the future, but that an enlarged and diversified marketplace of ideas will promote the kind of healthy competition that will benefit Austria's economic and cultural position in the world.

Foreign influences on Austrian education have increased in recent years on the strength of several impulses, the most important of which has come with the admission of Austria into the European Union in 1995 and the EU's ongoing initiatives to coordinate key activities of member states' educational policies for optimal transferability within the EU.

PREPRIMARY & PRIMARY EDUCATION

Although preprimary education is not part of the Austrian compulsory education system, it plays an important role in two respects. First, the number of nursery schools and accredited day care facilities continues to increase as working parents seek supervised, structured, and high-quality care for children who are not old enough yet to enter primary school. Second, the demand for appropriately qualified staff in preprimary education has created additional educational and career-training opportunities for students. Of the 27,389 staff members employed during the 1999-2000 school year in 5,321 preprimary facilities, more than one-half (13,794) had some form of appropriate certification. The specific needs of preprimary education have also given an impulse to secondary and postsecondary vocational and professional schools to devise specifically targeted curriculum options and certification modes.

Compulsory education begins with enrollment in a primary school on September 1 of the year following a child's sixth birthday. Exceptions may be made for early enrollment in the case of children who are born between September 1 and December 31, provided that they possess the requisite physical and intellectual maturity to participate successfully in instruction.

Similarly, enrollment may be deferred in the case of students who are deemed not to be ready yet for regular instruction. Such children may receive instruction in a preschool group (*Vorschulgruppe*) or a preschool year (*Vorschule*), both located in primary schools, to acclimate them to regular classroom instruction and, thus, avoid potential failure in early schooling. Preschooling is also available to early-admission students who are not, in fact, ready yet for regular classroom instruction. Performance is not assessed or graded.

The principal educational objective of Austrian primary education is to provide all children with a basic and well-balanced general education that promotes social, emotional, intellectual, and physical development. Primary schooling is divided into two essential levels. The first two years are taken together as a unit. Students who have attended the first year may move to the second year without regard to assessment. In addition to required subjects, students may also pursue special interests in nongraded classes, such as singing in a school choir.

Beginning in the third year, or Elementary Level II, compulsory but non-graded foreign-language study begins. With the exception of English and French, the choice of languages clearly reflects Austria's ethnic diversity and geographic context, since they include Croatian, Czech, Hungarian, Italian, Slovak, and Slovenian.

Given sufficient demand, remedial classes may be offered to add an extra period of instruction per week in compulsory subjects like language and mathematics. In addition, tutors may be employed to assist special-needs students and students whose native language is not German. With the exception of religious education, classes are taught by classroom teachers.

Following completion of the last, or fourth, year of primary school, there is an assessment of the student's aptitude for one of several types of secondary schools. This preliminary "tracking" has important implications for the student's future educational and career options.

The premise of a comprehensive and uniform education in the primary school calls by law for the integration of normal and special-needs students. Special-needs schools are available to students whose parents or guardians choose such instruction instead of conventional schooling, but the emphasis is clearly on an integrative approach to education wherever feasible. The integration of normal and special-education schools has been aided by the establishment of Special Education Centers, which assists in developing and implementing integrative measures by working in cooperation with experts, regional compulsory schools, other special education centers, the district education board, the special education administrator, and community agencies. In addition to integrated

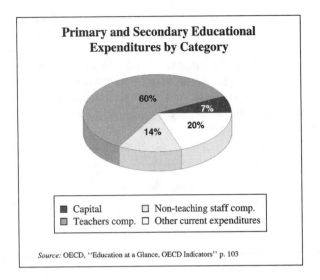

Primary and Secondary Educational Expenditures by Category

60%
7%
14%
20%

■ Capital   □ Non-teaching staff comp.
■ Teachers comp.   □ Other current expenditures

Source: OECD, "Education at a Glance, OECD Indicators" p. 103

classes, special tutors supplement normal classroom instruction within the context of the student's specific needs.

In certain cases students are mentally or physically disadvantaged to the point where they are unable to participate in normal classroom instruction. In other cases parents or guardians prefer to have disadvantaged children taught in special schools. For such students the special school provides an alternative to the integrative model. The curriculum of the special school varies to some degree from the normal primary school, since it includes grades that already fall into the range of normal secondary schools. The first level comprises grades 1 to 3, the second level grades 4 and 5, and the secondary level comprises grades 6 to 8. Special-needs schools are available for a variety of disabilities, including physically handicapped, speech impaired, hearing impaired, visually impaired, and emotionally disturbed children.

SECONDARY EDUCATION

The Austrian secondary-school system plays a key role in the preparation of students for further vocational, technical, and academic education. The fundamental philosophy is to provide a diverse spectrum of educational opportunities that accommodate the interests and aptitudes of all students. Since secondary schools are separated physically by academic type, each with distinctive academic programs, the issue of transfer from one type to another is an important one. Early tracking of students by aptitude and interest has historically limited opportunities for mobility through education. Moreover, such limitations tended to affect disproportionately children from rural and lower socio-economic backgrounds. Similarly, the children of educated parents were more likely to pursue academic courses of study. The two-track edu-

cational system, which fundamentally separated vocational and academic tracks in secondary education and which limited transferability, had the effect of perpetuating a student profile and placement, which was based more upon social and economic factors than assessment of student aptitude.

Fundamental reforms initiated by the 1962 School Organization Act, amended and revised though subsequent legislation, have sought to increase the permeability among types of secondary schools; expand the range of vocational, professional, and academic educational options available to students; refine student assessment instruments in the primary and lower secondary schools; and lengthen the period of observation and, hence, opportunities for optimal student assessment, before recommendations are made about student placement into vocational, technical/professional, or academic tracks. Postprimary education takes place in one of several types of secondary schools, which may in turn be grouped into two larger categories: general secondary school and the academic secondary school.

Students who have completed four years of primary school advance to the general secondary school. The four-year course of study at the GSS is similar to the primary school in the sense that it is designed to provide all students with a basic general education. Students are also prepared, however, for continuing education and training in vocations, or for further education. To that end, the GSS is divided into a largely uniform two-year lower level and a specialized upper level that includes further education or training ranging in length from one to five years. The upper-level secondary schools are distinguished not only by type, but also by name. In some cases the different names reflect traditional distinctions between vocational, technical/professional, and academic preparatory schools. In other cases, the names reflect particular courses of study that have been developed in response to changing economic and educational needs.

At the lower level, students are ability-streamed in German, mathematics, and foreign language. It is possible to transfer between ability groups at any time. Schools are free to modify certain aspects of their curriculum, within the context of legislated school autonomy, to emphasize particular strengths or specializations such as foreign languages, sports, fine arts, and computer science. Individual schools frequently profile an area of specialization on their web pages. During the third and fourth year of the lower general secondary school, increasing emphasis is placed on assessment of student aptitude and interest with respect to recommendations about the student's further education or training. To assist students in exploring appropriate vocational options, a number of programs are available, including career-guidance classes, on-site training internships, as well as regularly scheduled field trips to businesses and companies.

After completion of the four-year general secondary school, students have several options available for further training or education. The various types of upper-level secondary schools reflect differences in length of further study, as well as increasing specialization in the course of study offered. Moreover, the various types of upper-level secondary schools differ in the postsecondary higher education to which they provide access. The basic types of upper-level secondary schools include vocational track, technical/professional track, and academic track.

The prevocational year is designed to prepare students for apprenticeship programs in specific careers and for possible further education after apprenticeship or employment. German, mathematics, and English, the required modern foreign language for the prevocational year, continue to be taught in achievement groups. Students also have the opportunity to visit companies and businesses, vocational schools for apprentices, and to attend special vocational training workshops. The mixture of academic and practical learning is designed to prepare students for future careers, to nurture individual abilities, and to provide students with the necessary skills to pursue vocational certification.

In addition to required core courses, the prevocational year offers instruction in fields of specialization, which correspond to the major vocational employment sectors, including: metalworking, electronics, civil engineering, timber and woodworking, commerce, secretarial work, service-sector employment, and tourism. Given the emphasis on vocational preparation, all students have access to computers. While most graduates of the pre-vocational year continue their training by entering an apprenticeship program, students who meet admission requirements may apply for further formal education in various technical and vocational schools or colleges, or to transfer to a secondary academic school.

Various types of technical and vocational schools are designed to prepare students for careers which require more advanced qualifications and skills. Students who enter one of the Compulsory Vocational Schools, usually in conjunction with an apprenticeship program, receive an optimal blend of up-to-date theoretical and practical learning. This dual system also offers advantages to Austrian employers, since vocational schools can often provide the kind of training that is difficult to impart on the job or that companies cannot always afford to provide. The relationship between the educational and employment sector is, therefore, mutually beneficial.

The curriculum of the technical and vocational schools is designed under the auspices of the Vocational Training Act, the Commercial Code, and the accreditation of vocational qualifications rests with the Federal Ministry of Economic Affairs. The Vocational Training Act is the legal basis for business-based apprentice training. There are some 240 legally recognized, accredited, and protected skilled trades in which apprentices may be trained. Technical and vocational schools specialize in a variety of areas, including engineering, business, tourism, fashion and clothing, agriculture and forestry, and social service professions.

The most popular apprenticeship trades for females, who account for slightly more than 30 percent of all apprentices, are in retail merchandising, hair styling, and office staffing. Almost half of male apprentices are concentrated in the skilled-trade sector. The most popular career is auto mechanic, followed by electrician.

Approximately 40 percent of Austrian students enter apprenticeship programs after compulsory schooling. Some 120,000 apprentices are trained in approximately 40,000 companies. Slightly less than half of apprenticeship program graduates continue to work for the company in which they were apprenticed. At the end of the contracted apprenticeship period the apprentice may take the Apprenticeship Leaving Exam, which is divided into a written and oral practical and theoretical examination. The Apprenticeship Leaving Exam qualifies students for admission to the Master Craftsman Exam and subsequent certification, and it provides access to further education. Students who do not immediately pursue the dual system of apprenticeship training may continue their education in Medium and Higher Level Technical and Vocational Schools. Depending upon particular fields of study, technical and vocational schools offer three to five-year programs. They are organized variously as full-time secondary or postsecondary schools. Working students may participate in evening courses. Distance-learning opportunities further increase accessibility.

The most important fields of study in medium and higher-level technical and vocational schools are three-year programs in social work, family services, counseling, elderly and handicapped care, as well as one-year pre-nursing and forestry service programs. Programs available at Medium-Level Agricultural Colleges vary depending upon field of concentration and previous training.

Higher Level Technical and Vocational Schools offer both a broader general education and more in-depth theoretical preparation in certain professional fields. The five-year programs of study culminate in the Matriculation Exam, which is prerequisite for admission to higher-education courses of study.

The introduction of the Technical and Vocational Education Examination in 1997 has added a fundamentally new dimension to certification. It is recognized to be equivalent to the Matriculation Exam and consists of a four-part examination in German, mathematics, a modern foreign language, and a subject area of the candidate's choice. The subject area is one in which the candidate has professional experience. The importance of the Reifeprüfung and TVE as a broadly recognized diploma is underscored by the fact that, since 1995, the European Union has accepted the equivalency of these secondary-school diplomas to qualifications acquired through technical and vocational training in other EU member countries.

The third form of secondary school, Academic Secondary Schools (or AHS), has traditionally been the university-preparatory track. The AHS comprises an eight-year course of study beyond primary school and ends with the *Reifeprüfung* (Matriculation Exam). The AHS is divided equally into a lower and an upper level Admission to the AHS from primary school requires a grade of "very good" or "good" in the key subjects of German, reading, and mathematics. In the event of inadequate grades, a positive written referral by the primary school may be accepted. Students who wish to transfer into an AHS from a general secondary school must give evidence of excellent past achievement and likely placement in the highest general secondary school achievement group in German, mathematics, and a modern foreign language. The minimum grade in other subjects is "satisfactory." Consistent placement in the top general secondary school achievement group is prerequisite for transfer into the upper-level AHS. The AHS may require a placement or entrance exam in one or more subjects of students wishing to transfer from a general secondary or other school. Required core courses for AHS students include: German, two foreign languages, history and social studies, geography and economics, mathematics, physics, chemistry, biology and ecology, psychology and philosophy, music education, art, crafts, and computer science, beginning in the ninth grade.

The first two grades of the AHS are uniform. Thereafter, students continue for the next two grades in one of three basic types. The different designations for the AHS do not reflect qualitative differences, but rather differences in curricular emphases: *Gymnasium,* general comprehensive with Latin as one of the foreign languages; *Realgymnasium,* with greater emphasis on science and technology; and *Wirtschaftskundliches Realgymnasium,* with greater emphasis on economics. During the last four years of the AHS, students in the Gymnasium add Greek or a second modern foreign language. Students in the Realgymnasium add Latin or a second foreign language, along with more specialized courses in science and technology. Students in the *Wirtschaftskundliche Realgymnasium* add Latin or a second foreign language, along with

more specialized courses in domestic sciences, nutrition, and economics.

In addition to core courses, AHS students are required to take additional specialized courses ranging from 8 to 12 courses per week, depending on AHS type. Three special types of upper-level AHS are available for students with particular aptitudes or interests: upper-secondary academic school for science, upper-secondary academic school specializing in instrumental music, and upper-secondary academic school specializing in fine arts. Finally, evening courses and, under selected pilot projects, distance-learning opportunities are available to non-traditional students or working students to complete the requisite course work for attaining the all-important Matriculation Exam.

The Matriculation Exam is a school-leaving certificate that provides access to higher education. It emphasizes practically oriented learning, independent working, general command of subject matter, and foreign languages. The tests include both written and oral exams. The subjects in which the students are tested differ with respect to the type of secondary school attended. Each student, however, has to do a written exam in the core subjects of German, mathematics and foreign language. Students who opt for a fourth written exam only have to do three oral exams, all others have to do four. In addition, students' individual interests are accommodated by offering a choice among various types of written and oral exams. Instead of doing a fourth written exam, students may also choose to do a written project in the first semester of the eighth year. The written project becomes the basis for discussion during the oral exam and is designed to prepare students for independent university-level study. The oral exam, furthermore, comprises a combination of specialized subject matter and general knowledge in selected required and elective courses. The Matriculation Exam certifies that the student has acquired a broad general education and has thus met standard entry qualifications for university study. The student has also acquired specialized knowledge and skills for more specialized education or training in postsecondary courses, at a postsecondary college or on the job. Finally, the Matriculation Exam indicates that the student has learned a number of important life-learning skills, including study habits and the ability to work both cooperatively and independently.

In that context, the Matriculation Exam is not only the indispensable prerequisite for university study but is also a key qualification for entry into higher management, civil service, and technical careers. In recognition of the important role that the Matriculation Exam plays in the opportunities open to students, the Austrian educational authorities continue to explore options for making the process of attaining the Matriculation Exam more permeable without jeopardizing the traditional commitment to academic excellence which characterizes the AHS.

HIGHER EDUCATION

The organization and differentiation of Austrian higher education institutions reflect an educational philosophy that is, in many respects, similar to secondary education. The accent is on a variety of postsecondary options that meet specific professional needs, permit qualification at the highest level of one's career, and offer academic programs of study at a university. Most types of higher-education institutions combine research and teaching. This ensures that earned qualifications represent high intellectual standards and state-of-the-art research. Unless otherwise noted, admission requires the Matriculation Exam, TVE diploma, and/or a Higher Education Entrance Examination.

Several types of postsecondary colleges provide further education and certification in particular professional fields: Postsecondary Para-Medical College leading to certification in fields like physiotherapy, radiology, and dietetics; Postsecondary College for Social Work leading to advanced certification in fields like youth and family counseling and crisis intervention; Postsecondary Teacher Training College leading to certification of teachers in primary, lower secondary, special education, and the pre-vocational year; Postsecondary Vocational Education College, leading to certification for technical/vocational schools and colleges; and Postsecondary Religious Education College, leading to certification for religious-education teachers in primary and secondary schools.

An important innovation in the development of advanced courses of study came in 1993 with the enactment of the Advanced Professional Studies Act. It marked the establishment of a new type of postsecondary educational institution in Austria. Advanced postsecondary professional studies offer advanced professional and academic training in specific fields. The course of study differs from most other postsecondary courses of study in the fact that admission requires several years of professional experience in the field of study. Approval of particular advanced postsecondary professional courses of study rests with an independent Advanced Postsecondary Professional Studies Council, and specific courses of study may be offered under the auspices of state or public corporations.

Postsecondary programs comprise a minimum of six semesters of study and, where required, practical training. Graduates of advanced postsecondary professional courses of study earn the academic degree of Master's Degree or Certified Engineer with the designation FH.

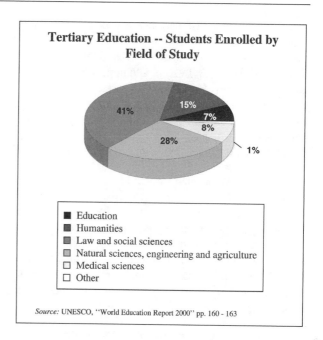

Tertiary Education -- Students Enrolled by Field of Study

- ■ Education
- ■ Humanities
- ■ Law and social sciences
- ☐ Natural sciences, engineering and agriculture
- ☐ Medical sciences
- ☐ Other

Source: UNESCO, "World Education Report 2000" pp. 160 - 163

These postsecondary degrees are internationally recognized. During the 1998-1999 academic year, 46 courses of advanced study were offered. Of the 7,869 students enrolled, some 2,202 were female (Statistisches Jahrbuch 2001). The most popular fields of advanced study include technology, business administration, and tourism.

There are 13 Austrian universities and 6 colleges for music and the arts, all of which are public. The number of private universities and colleges is very small, and they do not play a significant role in Austrian higher education. They include the IMADEC University (Vienna) and the International University (Vienna), both of which have a strong international business and law basis, and the Catholic Theological Private University (Linz).

The tradition of Austrian university education is long and internationally respected. The University of Vienna, founded in 1365, is the oldest university in the German-speaking countries. The most recent addition, the Danube University of Krems, was established in 1994. Its focus is on postgraduate professional and continuing-education courses of study. Although Austrian universities remain under the authority of the federal government and its various ministries, there have been significant initiatives to move Austrian universities toward greater autonomy. The 1993 University Organisation Act grants universities greater flexibility in matters of internal organization and statutes, while the federal government is responsible for strategic planning and funding. The 1997 University Studies Act coordinates policies on admissions requirements, degree programs, and academic degrees. The 1998 Universities of the Arts Organisation Act granted full university status to the former arts and music academies.

Prerequisite for admission to university study is the Matriculation Exam or its equivalent, which may include the Higher-Education Entrance Exam or the Technical/Vocational Exam, or TVE. In addition, some courses of study at university and admission to the arts and music universities require an aptitude or entrance examination. Information about admission requirements for foreign students is coordinated under NARIC, the Austrian National Academic Recognition Information Center.

Students pay a small student fee per semester. Austrian students, European Union citizens, and some groups of foreign students do not pay tuition for university education. All other foreign students pay a nominal tuition fee. All students are entitled to state-supported health insurance, and most Austrian students are entitled to some form of financial assistance. Foreign students may be eligible for need-based and merit-based public and private financial assistance, grants, or scholarships.

Austrian universities are organized on the principle of shared faculty and administrative governance. The most important administrative bodies are the *Rektor* (Chancellor), the *Dekan* (Dean), and the *Institutsvorstand* (Academic Program Chair). They are elected by various university committees, each of which represents, to a greater or lesser degree, tenured and non-tenured faculty members, other staff, and students. The university's overall curriculum is coordinated by a *Studienkommission* (Curriculum Committee).

Coordination among universities is promoted at the federal level through the Federal Ministry for Education, Science, and Cultural Affairs, at the administrative level through the *österreichische Rektorenkonferenz* (Standing Conference of Austrian Rectors), and at the curricular level through *Gesamtstudienkommissionen* (Joint Curricular Commissions).

During the 1998-1999 academic year, 228,936 students were enrolled in Austrian universities (*Statistisches Jahrbuch* 2001). Women made up 48 percent and foreign students 13 percent of total enrollment, respectively. Of the 15,789 graduates from Austrian universities during the same year, women made up 46 percent and foreign students 10 percent of the total. Despite increasing female enrollments during the past decade, women constituted only 7.7 percent of the 2,001 faculty members and slightly less than 30.0 percent of all instructional staff at Austrian universities.

The following three kinds of academic degrees are awarded by Austrian universities: *Diplom* (Diploma) degrees after the conclusion of a corresponding degree program, which lasts from eight to twelve and eight to sixteen semesters at university and art colleges, respectively. Graduates of regular degree programs are conferred with the title of *Magister/Magistra* (gender specific titles: men/women) abbreviated *Mag.,* for most degree programs or *Diplom-Ingenieur/Diplom-Ingenieurin,* (gender specific titles: men/women), abbreviated *Dipl.-Ing* or *DI* for specific degree programs in engineering and applied sciences. *Doktor* (Doctor) degrees come after the conclusion of a corresponding doctoral program. Graduates are conferred with the academic title of *Doktor/Doktorin,* (gender specific titles: men/women) abbreviated *Dr.* Special programs of study lead to Masters degrees after the conclusion of a corresponding university course program at the graduate level, consisting of a minimum of 70 semester credit hours: Master of Advanced Studies, abbreviated MAS, or Master of Business Administration, abbreviated MBA.

The most popular degree programs are social sciences and economic, liberal arts, law, and the natural sciences, which together represent more than half of the total number of degree-seeking students enrolled in the 24 general programs of study. Almost half of the 28,956 foreign students studying at Austrian universities during the 1998-1999 academic year came from Italy, Germany, Bulgaria, and Turkey. Foreign study is encouraged and supported. In addition to the federal funding that universities receive to cultivate international relations in the areas of research, cooperation with universities abroad is promoted through a variety of different initiatives, including subsidized university partnerships, bilateral governmental agreements with other countries in the form of scientific-technical or cultural exchanges, and multilateral agreements under the auspices of international organizations.

Federally-funded scholarships facilitate the exchange of students in both directions: for Austrians to study abroad at foreign universities and for students from abroad to study at Austrian universities. The Austrian Exchange Service provides information for foreign students wishing to study at Austrian universities. In addition, there are bilateral scholarship arrangements that exist under the auspices of cultural and other special agreements as well as a network of treaties on the academic recognition of secondary school leaving certificates, examinations and academic degrees. Austria is a signatory to the UNESCO Convention on the Recognition of Studies, Diplomas, and Degrees Concerning Higher Education in the States Belonging to the European Region and the European Convention on the Equivalence of Diplomas.

Austria's membership in the European Union has increased the country's integration into important common educational and research initiatives undertaken in the EU. In March 1995, the European Union launched the comprehensive pilot SOCRATES program for the promotion of educational cooperation of all kinds and at all levels. It consists of ERASMUS (for universities and university-level education), COMENIUS (for schools), and transfer measures (in particular LINGUA for the promotion of learning foreign-language learning, adult education, as well as open-and distance-learning). More than half of its large budget has been allocated for higher education.

In December 1994, the European Union's new program for vocational and professional education and training, LEONARDO DA VINCI, was launched. At least 25 percent of the total budget is allocated to promote cooperation between universities and the private sector. In particular, Austria acknowledges its geographic and ethnic proximity to eastern Europe by fostering direct exchange and equivalency agreements with countries like Poland, Hungary, Bulgaria, and Yugoslavia. In 1990, the Austrian Academic Exchange Service established the Office of Exchange Program with Central and Eastern Europe to coordinate targeted programs on a national level. CEEPUS, the Central European Program for University Studies is a multilateral treaty between Austria, Bulgaria, the Czech Republic, Hungary, Poland, Romania, Slovakia, and Slovenia. It coordinates collaboration in the areas of education and continuing education, especially with respect to transferability.

Austria has more than 50 research libraries open to the public. The Austrian National Library in Vienna, founded in 1526, is the largest. A further approximately 200 public research libraries have restricted access. There are also several hundred private libraries in Austria. The university libraries in Vienna, Graz, and Innsbruck are the largest. For historical records, the National Archives in Vienna remains an indispensable source. Together, libraries and archives play a crucial role as repositories of published research. Interlibrary loan arrangements and technology make holdings at specialized libraries and archives increasingly accessible to students and researchers.

ADMINISTRATION, FINANCE, & EDUCATIONAL RESEARCH

The administration of legislated educational affairs is vested at the federal level in the Federal Ministry for Education, Science, and Cultural Affairs. The Ministry's key departments responsible for education include General-education schools, Vocational training, Educational affairs, Adult Education, Teacher and Pedagogue training, and Universities and Postsecondary institutes. The ministry has wide-ranging authority regarding essential educational matters, including teacher training, including administrative staff, continuing teacher training, and professional development. There are a number of other jobs and departments it is responsible for as well.

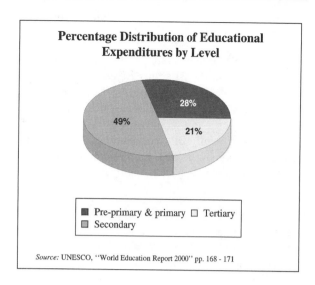

Percentage Distribution of Educational Expenditures by Level

28%
21%
49%

■ Pre-primary & primary □ Tertiary
■ Secondary

Source: UNESCO, "World Education Report 2000" pp. 168 - 171

The ministry has the authority to delegate certain administrative functions to provincial and local district educational boards. Standing and ad-hoc committees assist the ministry and its departments in developing and implementing policies that reflect a broad range of interests. Committees include, where appropriate, parent and teacher representatives as voting members appointed by the federal ministry. In addition, advisory bodies representing recognized churches, the superintendent of the provincial school boards, school inspectors, and other interest groups assist the ministry in formulating and implementing policy. While the federal ministry retains central administrative authority over much of the educational system, regional and district school boards have considerable control over key aspects of the educational system.

Individual provinces have specific legislation that vests educational authority either in the regional education board or in the provincial government. The regional education board, or the provincial government, has responsibility for appointments and is hence the official employer of teachers in compulsory public schools. With the exception of teacher training and postsecondary professional schools, the provincial education board also issues and enforces guidelines governing the structure, organization, and maintenance of general-education schools.

Responsibilities that are not delegated to the regional education boards or provincial governments remain under the control of the Federal Ministry for Education, Science, and Cultural Affairs, with the exception of universities, as well as schools of agriculture and forestry, for which special provisions and administrative authorities have been established.

University administration has been codified separately under the 1966 General University Education Act, the 1975 University Organisation Act, and more recently the 1993 University Organisation Act.

In the case of agriculture and forestry, considerable authority for educational affairs is vested in the Federal Ministry of Agriculture, Forestry, Environment and Water Management. Direct public expenditures in 1997 for all educational institutions in Austria accounted for 6.0 percent of total GDP. An additional 0.5 percent of total expenditures were covered through private sources (*Statistisches Jahrbuch* 2001).

In this respect, Austria lies somewhat above the OECD (Organization for Economic Co-Operation and Development) average with respect to public expenditures for education, but it lags behind the OECD average for private educational funding.

NONFORMAL EDUCATION

Nonformal educational opportunities in Austria are adult education and instructional-technology initiatives, including distance-learning. Adult education refers to learning opportunities that are pursued after the completion of formal education for various purposes, such as life-long learning for personal enrichment, attainment levels of certification after the completion of formal education and, in most cases, after substantial working experience. Updating skills and qualifications related directly to one's career, required for promotion, or maintaining certification. Unlike school and university education, adult education in Austria is not regulated by constitutional law. The 1973 Promotional Measures Act remains a key legislative foundation for adult education, since it provides for Federal Centers for the Promotion of Adult Education.

Adult-education courses are offered in schools for working individuals by various interest groups, private providers, and under the coordination of the Austrian Conference of Adult-Education Institutions. The most important providers of further career training are the quasi-private Vocational Training Institute and the Institute for Economic Development. Although adult-education initiatives are now further coordinated in a department of the Federal Ministry of Education, Science, and Cultural Affairs, the nature of adult education calls for the involvement of other managing and funding agencies, including the Federal Ministry of Labor and Social Affairs, the Federal Ministry of Science and Transport, the Ministry of Agriculture and Forestry, as well as the Federal Ministry of Economic Affairs.

Personal-enrichment courses and programs are offered under the auspices of the Austrian Adult-Education Centers. One of the key challenges confronting non-traditional learning in a centrally legislated and adminis-tered system is the development and integration of new learning technology opportunities, both in all levels of formal schooling and in adult education.

Distance-education programs have been offered in Austria since 1979 under the coordination of the Inter-University Research Institute for Distance-Education Programs. Courses including mathematics and teacher education have been developed. For other distance-learning courses and degree-level programs of study students may enroll through the Open University in Hagen, Germany, which offers normal degree courses in economics, law, social sciences, education, and management. Currently, some 2,000 Austrian students are enrolled in these programs. Other forms of non-traditional and outreach education include short-term courses), supplementary courses, specialization courses, study-abroad programs, senior-citizen access to courses, and complementary courses for graduates of foreign universities.

Austrian universities are entitled to develop distance-learning courses under the 1997 University Studies Act. Together with initiatives toward greater autonomy in schools and universities, distance education is likely to play an increasingly important role as a customized, site-independent, learning facilitator.

TEACHING PROFESSION

Principal and continuing, in-service teacher training in Austria reflects the different types of primary, secondary, and postsecondary schools, as well as the relative vocational, technical, and academic emphases which they pursue. In addition, teacher-education training includes preparation of preprimary educators and non-instructional educational staff. Admission to teacher-education programs requires the *Reifeprüfung,* or its equivalent, and special aptitude tests in some cases.

Preprimary teachers are prepared in Kindergarten Teacher-Training Colleges. The three-year course of study ends with a teaching certification.

Teachers in primary, lower secondary, special-needs schools, and the pre-vocational year are trained in Teacher Training Colleges. The teacher-training colleges are also centers for educational research and hence prepare non-instructional educational staff. Student teaching is supervised in schools that are affiliated with the colleges. Vocational teachers at the secondary and postsecondary level combine a high degree of pedagogical, subject-specific, and vocational expertise in their field. They are prepared in Vocational Teacher-Training Colleges.

Teachers in academic secondary schools are university-trained. The minimum course of study is nine semesters, which includes practice teaching. Candidates are required to earn a second diploma in a subject area and to complete a probationary teaching period. The qualifications for university teaching staff vary considerably, but generally require a minimum qualification of a first degree (*Diplom*) for instructors. Advancement to the rank of professor requires an earned doctorate and requires a further, advanced documentation of significant scholarly, scientific, or creative accomplishment (*Habilitation*). Candidates for professorships are called *berufen* by the university.

Austria recognizes tenure. Austrian teachers are civil servants. Salary and benefits issues are therefore negotiated between the government and the trade union that represents most teachers, the Public Service Union. In 1999 the average monthly salary for teachers was less than one percent higher than the average for civil servants in general. The salary for university teachers was approximately 30 percent above the average for civil servants, and the salary for school administrative staff was almost 80 percent higher. The Austrian Research Information Service (AURIS) offers comprehensive access to educational research.

SUMMARY

The Austrian educational system reflects a tradition of comprehensive learning in all areas of personal and professional life. Its highly stratified and hierarchical organization permits a degree of coordination among various principal participants in the vocational, academic, research, and economic sectors. The synergy between the various ''social partners'' and the availability of diverse avenues toward initial and further qualification provides a high degree of stability, which benefits both employers and employees. Employers contribute to the educational process by providing the vocational and professional infrastructure within which students can learn ''on the job.'' Employees bring a high degree of practical and theoretical preparation to the work place.

The hierarchical nature of Austrian education can also be an impediment to flexibility, however. The fact that matters of educational administration and policy implementation devolve from the federal level means that there is a potential delay in reacting to changing educational, vocational, or social circumstances. Developments in the employment sector, for example, materially affect the number of apprenticeships available. This fact, in turn, affects career guidance counseling, as well as development of new curricula and educational methodologies, for example in information technology.

The history of Austrian education during the past four decades has been characterized by an increasing shift toward a more open, accessible series of permeable educational options. Much has been done to make the rigid tracking system, particularly into the secondary schools, more flexible, to allow more opportunity for transfer between vocational, professional, and academic courses of study. In addition to greater permeability, federal legislation has sought to recognize the exigencies of regional, economic, and demographic differences by phasing in greater school autonomy, particularly in the upper secondary and postsecondary vocational and technical sector. The introduction of largely customized vocational-courses represents an important step in that direction.

Other initiatives have failed because of the constitutionally mandated two-thirds majority requirement for key changes in educational legislation. An example is the Social Democrats' attempt to replace the formal distinction between the *Hauptschule* (general secondary school) and the AHS (academic secondary school) with a more unified, comprehensive secondary school. In the area of higher education, the steady increase in student enrollments has strained the capacity and infrastructure of many universities. In addition, critics continue to point to the relatively high percentage of students who do not complete their degree programs ''on time,'' or not at all, to suggest that greater permeability in the secondary schools has led to a lowering of academic standards, which in turn affects the intellectual preparation of students for university study.

As the Austrian educational system becomes more integrated into the European Union's comprehensive transfer model, the question of reform will necessarily be debated in a broader context. Given the traditional strengths of the Austrian educational system at all levels, there is every reason to believe that Austrian will not only be a recipient of European Union directives, but that it will also have a voice in shaping them.

BIBLIOGRAPHY

Aigner, Helmut. *Secondary Education in Austria.* Strasbourg, France: Council of Europe Press, 1995.

Alheit, Peter, et al., eds. *The Biographical Approach in European Adult Education.* Wien: Verband Wiener Volksbildung, 1995.

Buchberger, Friedrich, and Irina Buchberger. ''Success for All? Description and Analysis of Measures to Combat Failure at School in Austria.'' *European Journal of Teacher Education,* 21, nos. 2 and 3 (1998): 143-60.

Egger, Rudolf, and Wolfgang Grilz, eds. *Bildung an der Grenze.* Graz: Leykam, 1999.

Kahr-Dill, Brigitte. *Austria: Development of Education, 1990-92.* Wien: Bundesministerium für Unterricht und Kunst, 1992.

Konrad, Helmut. "State and University—the Austrian Example." In *Higher Education in Europe*. New York: Garland, 1997.

Persy, Elisabeth, and Eva Tesar, eds. *Die Zukunft der Schulen der Vierzehn-bis Neunzehnjährigen*. Frankfurt am Main: P. Lang, 1997.

Plank, Friedrich H. *Education in Austria: a Concise Presentation*. Vienna, Federal Ministry of Education and the Arts, 1991.

Schmid, Eleanor, trans. *Education and Vocational Training: An Overview of the Austrian System*. Vienna: Federal Ministry of Education and Cultural Affairs, 1996.

Schratz, Michael, et al. "Changes in Postgraduate Research Training in Austria." *European Journal of Education* 33, 2 (1998), 183-97.

Steiner, Kurt, ed. *Modern Austria*. Palo Alto, CA: Society for the Promotion of Science and Scholarship, 1981.

Wissenschaftliche Hochschulen in Österreich. Wien: Bundesministerium für Wissenschaft und Forschung, 1974.

—*Siegfried Christoph*

AZERBAIJAN

BASIC DATA

Official Country Name:	Azerbaijani Republic
Region:	Middle East
Population:	7,748,163
Language(s):	Azeri, Russian, Armenian
Literacy Rate:	97%
Number of Primary Schools:	4,454
Compulsory Schooling:	11 years
Public Expenditure on Education:	3.0%
Foreign Students in National Universities:	3,986
Libraries:	4,700
Educational Enrollment:	Primary: 719,013 Secondary: 819,625 Higher: 115,116
Educational Enrollment Rate:	Primary: 106% Secondary: 77% Higher: 17%
Teachers:	Primary: 35,514 Higher: 15,929
Student-Teacher Ratio:	Primary: 20:1
Female Enrollment Rate:	Primary: 105% Secondary: 81% Higher: 18%

HISTORY & BACKGROUND

The Azerbaijan Republic (*Azarbaycan Respublikasi* or Azerbaijan) is the largest of the three Transcaucasian republics of the former Soviet Union, located in southwestern Asia. Bordered by the Caspian Sea to the east, Iran to the south, Armenia (and nine kilometers of Turkey) to the west, Georgia to the northwest, and Dagestan of the Russian Federation to the north, Azerbaijan measures 86,600 square kilometers. Slightly smaller than the U.S. state of Maine, Azerbaijan includes the noncontiguous autonomous enclave of Naxçivan to its southwest as well as 500 square kilometers of water. About 20 percent of the country, including the Nagorno-Karabakh region in the southwest, is occupied by Armenian forces who came into violent conflict with Azerbaijanis starting in 1988.

While a cease-fire was declared in May 1994, the final peace settlement with Armenia had not yet been reached by early 2001 and hundreds of thousands of Azerbaijani citizens were still displaced from their home communities. In 1998 the total number of Azerbaijani refugees and internally displaced persons (IDPs) living within Azerbaijan was about one million; the refugees included about 230,000 Azerbaijanis who fled Armenia when the armed conflict began and 50,000 Meshetian Turks who fled from Uzbekistan in 1989. The IDPs are primarily from Nagorno-Karabakh, an internationally recognized part of Azerbaijan occupied by Armenian troops and separatist fighters since the early 1990s. In 1998 13 major refugee camps existed in Azerbaijan; in addition, numerous, overcrowded public buildings, many of them in almost complete disrepair, housed Azerbaijani refugees. (About 300,000 Armenians who previously lived in Baku and other Azerbaijani cities are now living outside of Azerbaijan due to the unresolved conflict.) Certain European nations and international organizations, like the Organization for Security and Cooperation in Europe (OSCE), have worked steadily to help Azerbaijan settle its conflict with Armenia, but with incomplete success.

Azerbaijan has often been the battleground for contesting forces over the centuries. Three centuries before Christ the land now occupied by Azerbaijan was ruled by the Sassanid dynasty of the Persian Empire. During the Middle Ages the land was divided into several *khanates* that eventually were united by Shah Ismayil, the founder of the Safevid dynasty. Two-thirds of what used to be known as Azerbaijan in historic times is now in present-day Iran, and 20 million or more Azeris now live in Iran's northern region. Over the centuries Azerbaijan's territory was the object of fighting by the Persian, Arab, Seljuk, Mongol, Ottomon, and Russian empires. The territory that currently is Azerbaijan came from areas relinquished by Persia to Russia in 1828.

Annexed to the fledgling Soviet Union when the "Red Army" invaded the Caucasus region in April 1920, Azerbaijan remained under communist rule for 70 years as part of the Transcaucasian Soviet Federative Republic, which also included Georgia and Armenia. Azerbaijan declared its independence from the Soviet Union on 30 August 1991; soon after, it was recognized by the international community as an independent country. Azerbaijan joined the UN Organization and OSCE in 1992. It also became a member of NATO's "Partnership for Peace" programs, one of the first of the former Soviet republics to join.

A land consisting mainly of mountains and valleys due to the Caucasus Mountains passing through the north of the country, Azerbaijan has a wide range of climates, ranging from the cold weather of the mountainous north to the temperate weather of the Kura River's plain and the subtropical climate of the Lenkoran lowlands along the Caspian coast. The country's average temperature is 27 degrees Celsius in July and 1 degree Celsius in January. Baku, the capital city, has more days of fair weather than any other place in the Caucasus. It is moderately warm, subtropical, and dry but quite windy throughout the year. The highest elevation in Azerbaijan is Bazarduzu Dagi at 4,485 meters.

In 2000 the ethnic composition of Azerbaijan's population was about 90 percent Azeri, 3.2 percent Dagestani, 2.5 percent Russian, 2.3 percent Armenian, and 2 percent other, with most of the Armenians living in the Nagorno-Karabakh region. At that time about 93 percent of Azerbaijan's population was Muslim (mainly Shiite); the rest of the population was Russian Orthodox or Armenian Orthodox (each about 2.3 percent) or other. Approximately 57 percent of Azerbaijan's population lived in urban areas in 1999 when the country's population density was 92.2 persons per square kilometer. By the year 2000 approximately 99 percent of Azerbaijan's male population age 15 and older was literate, as well as 96 percent of the female population in that age range.

In 1999 the population of Azerbaijan was estimated to be 8 million and had a growth rate of only 0.9 percent, in part because difficult economic conditions in the 1990s caused many young Azerbaijanis to delay starting their own families. The total fertility rate in 1999 was 2.0 (i.e., a woman bearing children for her entire childbearing years at the current fertility rate would produce two children). Approximately 30 percent of Azerbaijanis in 2000 were 14 years old or younger while nearly two-thirds of the population was between 15 and 64 years of age and only about 7 percent were 65 or older. Azerbaijan had an infant mortality rate of 16.2 per thousand live births in 1999 and an under 5 years child mortality rate of 21.0 per thousand. The life expectancy at birth of Azerbaijanis in 2000 was 62.9 years, 58.5 years for men and 67.5 years for women.

World Bank analysts noted the degree of poverty in Azerbaijan in their November 2000 Country Assistance Report for the country and remarked on the changes that had occurred during the 1990s: "Azerbaijan had strong social indicators before independence. Basic food and consumer needs were met and access to health and education was universal. Since independence [in 1991], however, social indicators have deteriorated, partly because of the large number of displaced people. About 60 percent of Azerbaijan's population are considered poor, compared with around 40 percent in other Central Asian countries."

The Gross Domestic Product (GDP) at market prices in 1999 was four billion in current U.S. dollars. Widespread corruption and patronage had interfered with the transition to a well-functioning, free-market economy in Azerbaijan in the transition period of the 1990s. The Azerbaijani workforce in 1997 was composed as follows: 15 percent of the labor force was employed in industry, 53 percent in service jobs, and 32 percent in agriculture and forestry. (The comparable figures for the value added by each sector expressed as a percent of GDP were the following: industry, 35.4 percent; service, 41.3 percent; and agriculture, 23.3 percent.) By 1999 the Azerbaijani economy had an annual growth rate of roughly 7.4 percent, which further improved to an annual rate of about 8.5 percent by the first 6 months of 2000. However, Azerbaijan's annual per-capita income (measured as GNP per capita) in 2000 was about $550 in current U.S. dollars, representing a significant drop in per-capita income since the early 1990s. Azerbaijan's poverty rate of 60 percent at the turn of the millennium was due in large measure to the effects of the government's attempts to shift the economy from a centralized, state-controlled economy to a free-market economy; to falling oil revenues in the early 1990s; and to the war with Armenia, which had produced streams of refugees and thousands of displaced persons in the country. As the World Bank analysts noted in November 2000, about 75 percent of the IDPs were living below the poverty level. In 1999 about 20 percent of the population in Azerbaijan was classified as very poor. Sparked mainly by the richly promising oil opportunities in the country, foreign direct investment in Azerbaijan in 1999 was $510.3 million in U.S. dollars, while the country's debt value was $744.3 million. About 70 percent of the export commodities in the year 2000 were oil and gas. Other natural resources in Azerbaijan include iron ore, nonferrous metals, and alumina. The primary agricultural products are grains, wine, cotton, fruit, vegetables, tea, tobacco, crude sheepskin, and livestock (cattle, pigs, sheep, and goats), but only 18 percent of the land is arable.

Azerbaijan joined the World Bank and the International Development Association in 1992 and received its first loan from the Bank in 1995 for financing advisory services and setting up a framework to attract foreign private investment in Azerbaijan's burgeoning petroleum industry, in the amount of $21 million in U.S. dollars. A credit of the same amount also was provided that year to improve the water supply in the capital city of Baku, where about 25 percent of Azerbaijanis live. Other World Bank projects have followed, including an Educational Reform Project developed for Azerbaijan in 1999.

In 1997 Azerbaijanis had about 170,000 televisions and 175,000 radios. In 1998 10 AM radio stations, 17 FM stations, and 1 short-wave radio station broadcast programs in Azerbaijan. Computer and Internet access was growing by the end of the 1990s, when Azerbaijan had two Internet service providers.

CONSTITUTIONAL & LEGAL FOUNDATIONS

Azerbaijan is a parliamentary republic with a strong-presidential form of government. The governing structures were established by the Constitution of 1995, which was adopted by referendum. All Azerbaijanis, men and women alike, are allowed to vote beginning at age 18. Azerbaijan's elected chief executive and head of state, the president, serves a five-year term of office. Since 1993 Heydar Aliyev has been the President of Azerbaijan, having overthrown the previous democratically elected president in 1993. The executive branch of the national government also includes a prime minister as well as a Council of Ministers appointed by the president and confirmed by the National Assembly (the *Milli Mejlis*), Azerbaijan's national unicameral legislature of 125 members who are elected for five-year terms by popular vote. As of the November 2000 parliamentary elections, the legislature continued to be dominated by the New Azerbaijani Party whose chairman was incumbent President Aliyev. (In that election, substantial vote fraud was protested, and the competition of opposition parties initially was somewhat limited by the government, who eventually relented closer to the time of elections and

sought to correct some of its previous measures taken to discourage political competition). The Constitution accords the national legislature the power to approve the national budget and to impeach the President of the Republic. The third branch of Azerbaijan's national government is the judicial branch, consisting of a Supreme Court. While the judiciary supposedly is independent of the other two branches of the national government, in the year 2000 the judiciary continued to be influenced by the executive branch and was rife with corruption and inefficiency. Subnational governance is effected through a system of 59 rayons (*rayonlar*), 11 cities, and 1 autonomous republic (*Naxçivan Muxtar Respublikasi*) attached to Azerbaijan.

The police, together with the Ministries of International Affairs and of National Security, are responsible for the internal security of the country. However, in the year 2000 the police allegedly were committing numerous human-rights abuses against Azerbaijanis, such as conducting searches and seizures without warrants, arbitrarily arresting and detaining people, and torturing and beating persons in custody. In general, the government reportedly failed to intervene; though in a few cases, police accused of abusing the rights of others were prosecuted. Harsh prison conditions led to the deaths of some prisoners in 2000, pre-trial detention was sometimes illegally extended, and freedom of expression and of the press was actively limited by the government, despite the participation of opposition parties in the November elections.

Laws Affecting Education: Education in Azerbaijan has long been valued by many of the people, and before the economic and political problems of the late 1980s and early 1990s arose, the general level of education in the country and literacy rates among many segments of the population were relatively high. In 1992, shortly after independence was declared, legislation establishing a new educational system for Azerbaijan was passed: "The Law of the Republic of Azerbaijan on Education." Educational reforms were also proposed in the late 1990s by the World Bank in consultation with Azerbaijani educational authorities, researchers, and other experts. The World Bank's Education Reform Project was approved by the President of Azerbaijan in June 1999 and was being implemented in three phases: 1999, 2000-2003, and 2004. The decision was made to concentrate on improving the first several grades of general, compulsory education, although it was also clear that higher education institutions needed attention, too. However, because a number of private efforts already were being made by the late 1990s to increase quality educational offerings at higher levels in Azerbaijan, the Bank and the Azerbaijani government chose to focus the initial Education Reform

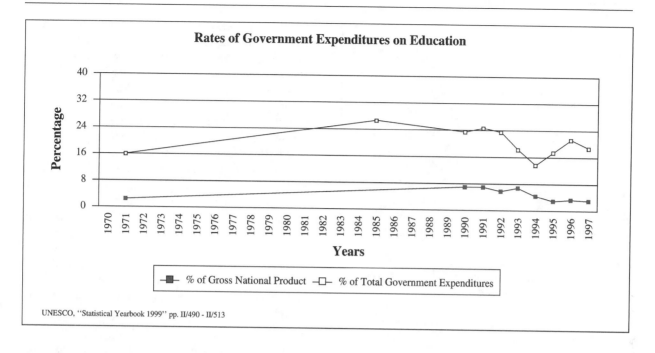

Rates of Government Expenditures on Education

UNESCO, "Statistical Yearbook 1999" pp. II/490 - II/513

Project on measures that would strengthen basic education.

To transform Azerbaijan's educational system from the inefficient, heavily burdened system of the Soviet era, the Education Reform Project had the following goals: 1) upgrading curricular content and developing improved processes for creating new curricula; 2) improving teacher education as well as teaching and learning methods by making teachers knowledgeable of modern teaching methods and making learning a more-active, engaging, and individualized experience for each student; 3) increasing financial resources for educational materials and programming and encouraging the state to dedicate more resources for education; 4) improving methods of education budgeting, creating a better balance between expenditures for educational staff salaries and other education-related expenditures, and allowing greater flexibility across line items within the same fiscal year; 5) providing support to build and repair educational facilities and to equip school programs with freshly developed textbooks that correlate well with current curricular needs; and 6) decreasing inequities in education—e.g. between rural and urban students and between impoverished students and those coming from better circumstances. To meet the goals of the Project, the Bank outlined several main areas of activity: 1) creating in-service teacher-education institutes (TEIs) in five pilot districts (Baku, Sumgayit, Lenkoran, Genje, and Nakhichevan) which would pilot the training of more-modern teaching methods involving active learning and projects, support new in-service teacher-education courses, increase linkages between schools and TEIs, train trainers who could replicate the training of other teachers in new teaching methods, and

develop small teacher resource centers as part of the pilot TEIs; 2) establish pilot schools (4 in each of the 5 pilot districts, for a total of 20 pilot schools) and involve local community members more actively in the schools; and 3) monitor and evaluate the effectiveness of the project interventions by answering specific questions related to the effectiveness of the measures taken in the Education Reform Project. In conjunction with working toward accomplishing the above-outlined goals, the Project was designed to bring about reforms in educational policy-making and in the performance of educational institutions.

Vocational education schools and programs already had received special attention from the Azerbaijani government in 1996, when the Cabinet of Ministers adopted Presidential Decision #16, "On the Measures for Improvement of the Vocational Education System in the Republic of Azerbaijan," on 23 August 1996. This Decision gave vocational education institutions newly recognized status as vocational schools and vocational lycées, and a list of specific professions for which vocational training would be provided was approved. According to the Ministry of Education, new vocational-education initiatives were being promoted by the President in the late 1990s that included developing vocational education according to strategic guidelines, creating new opportunities for the continuing education of workers (especially to manage new technology), and democratizing education.

EDUCATIONAL SYSTEM—OVERVIEW

Compulsory Education: In the 2000-2001 school year, 1,591,000 Azerbaijani students were enrolled in a

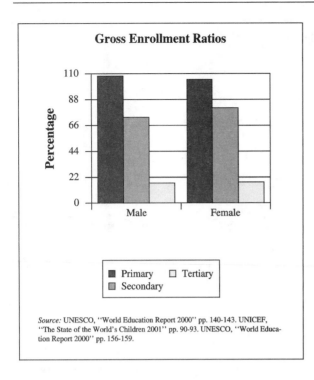

Gross Enrollment Ratios

Source: UNESCO, "World Education Report 2000" pp. 140-143. UNICEF, "The State of the World's Children 2001" pp. 90-93. UNESCO, "World Education Report 2000" pp. 156-159.

total of 4,486 general education schools operated by the Ministry of Education covering grades 1 through 11, the years of compulsory education where most fees are covered by the government. Gross enrollment in the primary classes (grades 1 through 4) and the main classes (grades 5 through 9) averaged 97 percent for boys and 96 percent for girls that year (with net enrollment rates of 89 percent for boys and 90 percent for girls). At the secondary level gross enrollment rates were 73 percent for boys and 81 percent for girls. General education in Azerbaijan is divided into three stages: 1) four years of primary education, where students in each class are taught by a teacher who progresses with them each year up through the four primary grades, 2) main education, consisting of five years of schooling, and 3) secondary education, where students receive their final two years of state-provided schooling.

The violent conflict in the late 1980s and early 1990s exacted a heavy toll on Azerbaijani students and the education system in Azerbaijan. 616 general education schools reportedly were captured and destroyed by Armenian forces. This led to the displacement of over 100,000 pupils and 10,000 educational staff members, according to the government of Azerbaijan, with 85,000 displaced children served by 707 schools established in the densest areas of refugee and IDP concentrations.

Although schooling at the secondary level is free in Azerbaijan, by the late 1990s parents of primary students were increasingly asked to pay a certain proportion of the school fees and to purchase textbooks for their children.

This is attributable apparently to the economic problems the country was experiencing at that time. With the educational support provided by the World Bank Education Reform Project begun in 1999 and other international donors to the education sector, as well as the gradually improving economic conditions in the country at the turn of the millennium, this trend toward parents' paying increasingly for their children's basic education hopefully would be turned around. It should be noted, however, that improvements began to be seen by the year 2000 in the national economy due to proceeds from a major oil-pipeline project in the country and the development of the petroleum industry through foreign investment. These are not anticipated to immediately change the bleak economic picture prevailing in the country in the 1990s. It is expected that an additional five to eight years of continuing economic improvements would be needed before oil revenues would have a positive impact on government funding in the education sector.

Private Schools: While government-supported schools were the norm for students in basic education at the turn of the millennium, increasing efforts were being made by international organizations and other private funders to create private educational opportunities in the country, especially at upper levels. Statistics on the number of private schools operating in Azerbaijan in 2001, however, are not readily available.

In the 2000-2001 school year, 17,000 pupils attended boarding schools and 10,000 very-talented students attended 39 new kinds of educational institutions—lycées and gymnasiums—some of which may have been privately funded. Special education was provided for about 6,000 mentally and physically handicapped students through 21 boarding schools, 3 "subsidiary schools," and 2 "home-schools," although again it is unknown to what extent these schools were publicly or privately funded.

Textbooks—Curriculum Development: With the World Bank's Education Reform Project begun in 1999, special attention was directed toward revising and improving Azerbaijani textbooks and the curricula used in Azerbaijani schools. As already indicated, significant problems existed with the textbook situation in the 1990s. Textbooks were neither sufficiently plentiful nor of adequate quality to provide students with the necessary instruction in subjects that would have direct applicability in their lives, nor were students given the type of instruction that would enable them to transfer school learning to everyday situations or to competently solve problems in the real world. For this reason, the World Bank education project concentrated heavily on developing new norms for the production and improvement of texts and curricula in the country. A leftover from the Soviet era, two state-sponsored publishing houses essentially had complete control over the production of texts, a situation that demanded reform so that teaching materials could be made more responsive to the needs of contemporary Azerbaijani students preparing for jobs in a globalizing labor market no longer dominated by the Soviet-style centralized economy of the past.

Curriculum—Development: The teaching style in Azerbaijan emphasizes passive learning and generally speaking is not adequately individualized to the needs of each student. Although in some schools, administrators and teachers were ready to implement a more student-focused and active-learning style of teaching by the late 1990s, a lack of appropriate resources on contemporary teaching methods hindered progress in updating teaching methodology in the country. Emphasis during the Soviet era had been placed on learning facts rather than the skills needed to solve problems and apply school-based learning to real-life situations. Consequently, one of the major reforms attempted by the Azerbaijani government in tandem with the World Bank starting in 1999 centered on training and retraining teachers in more child-focused, active styles of teaching involving student projects and activities.

Foreign Influences on Educational System: While Azeri, the main language spoken in Azerbaijan, is the country's official language, only 89 percent of the population spoke Azeri in 1995. Three percent of the population spoke Russian, 2 percent spoke Armenian, and 6 percent spoke other languages at that time. The Azerbaijani language, part of the south-Turkic group of languages, originally was written using the Arabic script, but the Latin alphabet was introduced in 1929. Cyrillic script became compulsory in 1939 when Azerbaijan was well enmeshed in the Soviet system. After independence in 1991, the Russian language was phased out by the Azerbaijani government, and Latin was reintroduced in 1992. Nonetheless, Russian is still commonly used in urban areas such as Baku and Sumgayit and understood in most parts of the country.

By the year 2000 Azerbaijan was cooperating on a regular basis with over 30 countries in the area of higher education and had been admitted to both the Asian and Pacific Basin Regional Committee of UNESCO on higher education and UNESCO's European Regional Committee on higher education. Azerbaijan also acceded to the Conventions on Mutual Recognition of Higher Education Institution Diplomas, Scientific Titles and Degrees and Educational Programs pertaining to the countries of those two regions. Azerbaijani educators were becoming increasingly involved with a growing number of international organizations such as the European Union, UNESCO, and the Soros Foundation, whose programs and projects provided necessary financial supports and technical assistance to Azerbaijani educators and the country's educational institutions.

About 5,000 Azerbaijani students were studying outside of Azerbaijan in about 40 countries in the second half of the 1990s. Key areas of specialization for these students were economics, international relations, business, tourism and the hotel industry, finance, the customs business, and banking. In the late 1990s students from about 50 countries were studying in Azerbaijani schools and universities, focusing in particular on law, medicine, construction, and the oil industry.

Role of Education in Development: Aware of the key role education plays in a country's socioeconomic development, Azerbaijan's government was actively collaborating with many international organizations and donors by the late 1990s to improve the country's education system and training institutions in order to develop the human resources necessary for the country's economic and social development. Unfortunately, problems of poverty and population displacements during the 1990s further exacerbated existing disparities in school attendance across the country. For 6- to 16-year-olds from very poor households in 1999, for example, 97 percent of those living in Baku and Apsheron were attending school but only 75 percent of children from very poor families in the near southwest were enrolled in school.

PREPRIMARY & PRIMARY EDUCATION

Kindergarten attendance in Azerbaijan during the 1990s had declined due to the economic and political problems the country was experiencing. In 1990 about 19 percent of children between the ages of 3 and 6 were enrolled in kindergarten, but in 1997 only 13 percent of this age group was enrolled (19.1 percent in cities and 7.1 percent in villages). In the 2000-2001 school year 1,854 preschools—1,659 of them operated by the Ministry of Education and the other 195 operated by other Ministries and organizations—educated 116,100 young children with 101,700 of the children attending Ministry of Education preschools. The preschoolers were taught by 16.1 thousand educational staff, three-quarters of whom were mid-level or higher professionals. Primary education and compulsory schooling in Azerbaijan begins at age six, and the primary grades (grades one through four, as noted above) represent the first of three stages of required general education.

SECONDARY EDUCATION

As previously noted, grades five through nine form the "main education" stage of general education in

Azerbaijan. Grades 10 and 11 are considered the upper-secondary grades in the country and represent the third stage of compulsory schooling. As with schooling overall in the country during the troubled times of the 1990s, the second and third stages of education suffered from the violence of the Armenia-Azerbaijan conflict and the economic problems that beset Azerbaijan as the country shifted from a centralized economy to a free-market economy and came to rely, perhaps too heavily and prematurely, on oil revenues to finance the national budget. Whereas 34 percent of the relevant age group of 15 to 18 year olds had attended upper-secondary school (the final 2 grades of compulsory schooling) in 1990, only 28 percent of the age-relevant group was enrolled in upper-secondary education in 1996. Many students had been displaced or had become refugees during the early part of the 1990s, and the difficult economic conditions led a larger share than normal of secondary school students to drop out of school or be absent for extended periods in order to find work to help support their families.

Vocational Education: Special importance came to be attached to improving the quality of vocational education in Azerbaijan in the transition years of the 1990s, and as already mentioned, the government had begun special initiatives to improve the quality of vocational training with new legislation in 1996. In 1999 over 23,000 Azerbaijani students were enrolled in a total of 108 vocational institutions (including 61 vocational schools and 47 vocational lycées) that provided training in 120 professions. The number of educational staff in these institutions was 5,136 of whom 1,990 were teachers and 1,806 were production training masters. In addition to the vocational schools and lycées already mentioned, 11 evening correspondence schools, plus correspondence groups and 2,137 evening classes given at day schools, provided continuing education opportunities for more than 40,000 youth in their late teens at the start of the new millennium.

HIGHER EDUCATION

Types of—Public & Private: In the mid-1990s about 17 percent of the age group appropriate for tertiary studies was enrolled in higher-education programming in Azerbaijan. Since 1993 Azerbaijan has been reshaping its college and university level training programs to match European multi-stage standards for Bachelor's and Master's level courses. By the late 1990s, higher education in Azerbaijan was provided through a network of 48 educational institutions (30 government-supported and 18 privately funded) that encompassed a total of twenty universities, 8 academies, and 20 other types of educational institutions (institutes, higher colleges, higher seminary, and higher-education institutions for professional im-

provement and retraining). Through this network of 48 institutions, training was provided in more than 90 fields (related to 390 professions) at the Bachelor's level and in 80 fields (related to 580 professions) at the Master's level. Over 110,000 students were enrolled in higher-education institutions in Azerbaijan, taught by about 15,000 professors and teachers (about 1,000 of them professors and over 8,000 assistant professors and senior lecturers). Over 15,000 additional staff members were employed as managers, logisticians, teaching assistants, service staff, and the like in institutions of higher education.

Admission Procedures: Admission to university-level training in Azerbaijan is through competitive examinations taken at the end of secondary education. More than 20,000 students—about 20 to 25 percent of secondary school graduates—were being admitted annually to higher-education institutions by the end of the 1990s. Professors or teachers of higher education were each responsible for 5.2 students at that time, when attendance at higher-education institutions cost about US$100 per student for the academic year.

Administration: Responsibility for higher education in Azerbaijan falls principally to the Ministry of Education, composed of a carefully structured array of departments, divisions, and offices. Higher education in the sciences and at the doctoral level is the responsibility of an entirely separate department in the Ministry of Education, the Science Department, which supervises training and research, including pedagogical training and research, and provides leadership and planning for doctoral programs and post-graduate training and credentialing in the sciences and the arts.

ADMINISTRATION, FINANCE, & EDUCATIONAL RESEARCH

Government Educational Agencies: Responsibility for developing and implementing educational policies and programs rests primarily with the Ministry of Education, which collaborates directly with the World Bank-funded Education Reform Project. Under the Minister of Education is the Central Administration, which includes the Ministry of Education's assistant, secretary, jurist, licensing office, press, and Refugee Affairs bureau. Also directly under the Minister are the Economy and Finance Department (which in turn supervises the Division of Planning and Finance, the Division of Accounts, the Payroll office, and the office of Capital Construction and Procurement), the Human Resources Department, and the Higher Education Department (which in turn supervises two other departments: one for higher education and one for vocational education). Three Deputy Ministers are also directly under the authority of the Minister of Education. One of the Deputy Ministers supervises the Preschool and General Education Department, the Division of Textbooks, Press and Publications, and the Education of Children with Special Needs, Social Care and Rehabilitation Programs Section. Another Deputy Minister oversees the Science Department, the Analysis and Prognosis Department, and the Vocational-Technical Education Department. The third supervises the International Relations, Information and Coordination Department (which oversees Study Abroad and Overseas Students' Affairs), Patriotic Education, and the Office Management Department (whose responsibility includes supervising the offices in charge of Protocol, Service Staff, Logistics, and Archive).

Education Budgets: In 1997 Azerbaijan spent less than 4 percent of its GDP on education, a sizable drop from the nearly 7 percent of GDP spent on education in 1992. In 1999 over 50 percent of all non-defense-related budgetary expenditures on employment went to salaries for educational staff. Educational staff accounted for more than 10 percent of all employment—rates that were considerably higher than other countries in the region. Due to the decline in government revenues during the 1990s, funding for education fell and in 1997 public expenditures on education were only one-third of what they had been in 1992.

SUMMARY

As oil revenues begin to be generated at an increasing rate and international donor agencies continue to provide significant aid for education, Azerbaijan's currently rather difficult economic situation in the education sector hopefully will be remedied. Through the World Bank-funded Education Reform Project, educational conditions in the country should improve, if only gradually at first. One of the most promising initiatives in the World Bank project appeared to be that of improving teacher-training institutes through a set of five pilot programs that include training of trainers who will be able to replicate the teaching of newer, more-appropriate methods of engaging students in the learning process. In addition, international nongovernmental donors, such as the Soros Foundation that is interested in promoting ethnic conflict resolution, democratization, and human rights in Azerbaijan, should have a very positive impact over time on the political and social climate in the country, as they work collaboratively with Azerbaijanis in schools and community programs to plan and implement programming meant to encourage the development of a strong civil society and greater democratic participation. As the culturally rich and historically experienced people of Azerbaijan continue to further their country's progress through imaginative solu-

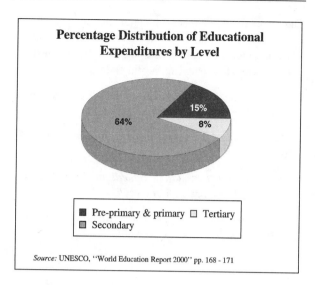

Percentage Distribution of Educational Expenditures by Level

64%   15%   8%

■ Pre-primary & primary   □ Tertiary
■ Secondary

Source: UNESCO, ''World Education Report 2000'' pp. 168 - 171

tions to educational problems and the dilemmas of sustainable development at the start of the new millennium, Azerbaijan should be able to return to its previously highly regarded status as a center of culture and learning where education is prized and made available to all segments of the population, regardless of their economic status.

BIBLIOGRAPHY

Bureau of Democracy, Human Rights, and Labor. *Country Reports on Human Rights Practices-2000.* U.S. Department of State, February 2001. Available from http://www.state.gov.

The Central Intelligence Agency (CIA). *The World Factbook 2000.* Directorate of Intelligence, 1 January 2001. Available from http://www.cia.gov/.

The European Commission. *The EU and Azerbaijan.* 2001. Available from http://europa.eu.int/.

Human Development Network. *Education Sector Strategy.* Washington, DC: The International Bank for Reconstruction and Development/The World Bank, 1999.

Human Development Sector, Europe and Central Asia Regional Office. *Project Appraisal Document on a Proposed Learning and Innovation Credit in an Amount of SDR 3,700,000 to the Azerbaijan Republic for an Education Reform Project.* The World Bank, 4 May 1999. Available from http://www-wds.worldbank.org.

Human Rights Watch. *World Report 2001.* Available from http://www.hrw.org/.

Ministry of Education of Azerbaijan Republic. 2000. Available from http://edu.gov.az/.

Operations Evaluation Department. *Azerbaijan Country Assistance Evaluation. Report No. 21459.* The World Bank, 30 November 2000. Available from http://www-wds.worldbank.org.

The Task Force on Higher Education and Society. *Higher Education in Developing Countries: Peril and Promise.* Washington, DC: The International Bank for Reconstruction and Development/The World Bank, 2000.

UNICEF. *Azerbaijan.* 26 December 2000. Available from http://www.unicef.org/.

United Nations. *Azerbaijan: Country Information.* 2000. Available from http://un-az.org.

World Bank. *Participation in Education.* Available from http://www.devdata.worldbank.org/.

World Bank. *World Development Report, 2000/2001.* Available from http://www.worldbank.org.

World Bank Group. *Azerbaijan.* 2001. Available from http://wbln0018.worldbank.org/.

World Bank Group. *Azerbaijan at a Glance.* September 2000. Available from http://wbln0018.worldbank.org/.

World Bank Group. *Azerbaijan Data Profile.* World Development Indicators database, July 2000. Available from http://devdata.worldbank.org/.

World Bank Group. *Country Brief: Azerbaijan.* September 2000. Available from http://wbln0018.worldbank.org/.

—*Barbara Lakeberg Dridi*

BAHAMAS

BASIC DATA

Official Country Name:	Commonwealth of the Bahamas
Region:	North & Central America
Population:	294,982
Language(s):	English, Creole
Literacy Rate:	98.2%

The independent Commonwealth of the Bahamas, a group of about 700 islands totaling 3,400 square miles, is headed by the Prime Minister; the British monarchy, represented by a local governor-general, is the honorary head of state. Literacy in the Bahamas is estimated as ranging from as low as 85 percent (functional literacy, as defined by the National Literacy Project) to as high as 98 percent.

Educational direction and oversight is centralized in the Bahamas under the Ministry of Education, as defined by the Education Act of 1962. This appointed minister directly controls all publicly funded education and supervises private education at the primary, secondary, and tertiary levels. Education, the largest single appropriation in the national budget, is compulsory from age 5 through 16 (attendance is 95 percent). In 2000 more than 64,000 students attended the 210 primary (ages 5 to 11) and secondary (ages 11 to 16) schools—three-fourths (158 schools) were public and free and one-fourth (52 schools) were private. Where the distance from home to school is burdensome—for example, in the Family Islands—students attend all-age schools.

The Bahamian school system is based on the British model. In the primary (the first six) grades, students ad-

vance depending on their performance on examinations administered at the end of each academic year. In the secondary grades, they take their first major external examination, the National Junior Certificate Examination. To graduate, they must pass the Bahamas General Certificate of Secondary Education (BGCSE).

In the mid-1980s, teacher shortages, substandard equipment and supplies, deteriorating school buildings, and deficient results on national tests led to dramatic educational reform in the 1990s. In 1993 a government-appointed National Task Force evaluated the entire educational system and formulated, in 1994, a Five-Year Plan that established interrelated goals for preschool, primary, secondary, and higher education. Curricula at all levels have undergone development with special reference to the focus of the Caribbean Community and Common Market (CARICOM) for emphasizing language arts and mathematics. In the Bahamas, social and academic education are inextricably intertwined—multicultural values and attitudes are taught across the curriculum.

The standards for high school graduation, normally verified externally by nationwide testing, changed in the 1990s. Before 1993 high school students had graduated with a General Certificate of Education (GCE) from the University of London. After 1993 they received a Bahamas General Certificate of Secondary Education (BGCSE), which reflected their standing on a seven-point scale of grades ranging from A to G. Educational reform has been controversial. Critics claimed that the new certificate watered down the higher standards of the GCE; supporters applauded the modifications for recognizing that students have a wider range of abilities than had been tested by the GCE. The Ministry of Education also focused on educational outreach by creating the National Literacy Project "Let's Read Bahamas" to improve functional literacy within the entire population. And, as part of a continuing effort to reduce widespread unemployment among the young, education at all levels includes vocational training.

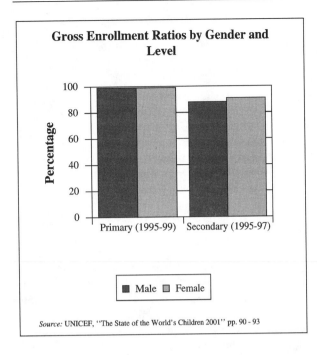

Gross Enrollment Ratios by Gender and Level

Source: UNICEF, "The State of the World's Children 2001" pp. 90 - 93

2000. Available from http://www.state.gov/www/background_notes/.

—*Stephen Curley*

Higher education is offered by the College of The Bahamas (formerly a two-year but now a four-year institution), the regional University of The West Indies, the Bahamas Hotel Training College, and the Bahamas Technical and Vocational Institute (formerly Industrial Training Centre). In addition students can take classes in the Bahamas offered by the University of Miami, Nova Southeastern University, and other universities in the United States.

BIBLIOGRAPHY

Bahamas Two Thousand, Co. Ltd. "TheBahamas-Guide.com," 1998. Available from http://www.thebahamasguide.com/.

International Bureau of Education, UNESCO. "Analysis of the Questionnaire of May 1999 on Curriculum Developments Needs at Primary and Secondary Education Levels in Caribbean Member States and Associate Member States of UNESCO," September 2000. Available from http://www.ibe.unesco.org/.

Lonergan, Patricia. "Other Side of Paradise: Patricia Lonergan Describes Life in a Bahamian Classroom." *The London Times Educational Supplement, 19* (September 1986): 18.

Miller, Errol. "The Last Word: UWI Professor Applauds Bahamas Education." *Jamaica Daily Gleaner,* 8 April 1999.

McCulla, Patricia E. *Places and People of the World: Bahamas.* New York: Chelsea House, 1987.

U.S. Department of State. *Background Notes: The Bahamas.* Washington, DC: Bureau of Inter-American Affairs,

BAHRAIN

BASIC DATA

Official Country Name:	State of Bahrain
Region:	Middle East
Population:	634,137
Language(s):	Arabic, English, Farsi, Urdu
Literacy Rate:	85.2%
Academic Year:	September-June
Compulsory Schooling:	9 years
Educational Enrollment:	Primary: 72,876 Secondary: 57,184 Higher: 7,676
Educational Enrollment Rate:	Primary: 106% Secondary: 94%
Teachers:	Higher: 655
Student-Teacher Ratio:	Primary: 18:1 Secondary: 15:1
Female Enrollment Rate:	Primary: 106% Secondary: 98%

HISTORY & BACKGROUND

The State of Bahrain is an archipelago consisting of 1 large island and about 35 smaller islands located in the shallow waters of the Arabian-Persian Gulf. Only four of these islands are actually inhabited. In Arabic "Bahrain" means "two seas." Ancient legends associate Bahrain with the Garden of Eden and the Tree of Life, and the name "The Pearl of the Gulf," gives an indication of the beauty found on this island-oasis amid generally barren desert. It has been listed as the second most attractive tourist location in the Middle East. Although located in a desert region, the country benefits from underground aquifers that provide life-sustaining water. The total land area of Bahrain is 706,550 square kilometers, and the main island, Bahrain Island, comprises 85 percent of the country's total land area. The capital city of Manama is situated on Bahrain Island, which is linked to the Saudi Arabian mainland by the King Fahd Causeway. Two of the smaller islands, Al Muharraq and Sitrah, are linked to Bahrain Island by causeways.

Most of the population of Bahrain lives in the northern part of Bahrain Island. The population in 1994 was an estimated 568,000, reaching 600,000 people in 1997, demonstrating a growth rate of 2.6 percent. Of these figures, approximately one-third of the population consisted of expatriate workers from Iran, Yemen, Oman, Pakistan, and India, as well as from other Asian countries and Europe. Shiite Muslims constitute the majority (about 60 percent), but the ruling Al Khalifa family is of the Sunni Islamic sect. Islam is the state religion, and Arabic is the official language, although English and Farsi are widely spoken. People descended from the original island inhabitants are known as the Baharna, those with origins in Saudi Arabia trace their ancestry to the Hassawis, and others, known as the Ajami, are descended from earlier migrants from Iran.

In ancient times Bahrain was known to the Sumerians as Dilmun, and as the Land of Eternal, mentioned in the *Epic of Gilgamesh* as a land abundantly supplied with the essentials of life: water and food. Thus, from earliest recorded history the island has been known as a trading center, famous for its pearls, agricultural produce, and fishermen. The Greeks referred to the island of Bahrain as Tylos, as depicted on the 200 A.D. map of Ptolemy.

Arab settlements on the island began around 300 B.C., and control was maintained by the Rabyah tribe, who converted to Islam in 630 A.D.. The island's strategic importance led to various occupations amid jostlings for power in the Gulf by the Portuguese and the Persians, while Britain later controlled the island well into the twentieth century. The Portuguese established their presence from 1521 onwards, until they were evicted in 1602 by a combined Bahraini-Persian force supported by Shah Abbas the Great. A Persian influence followed the eviction of the Portuguese until 1718, when Oman temporarily annexed Bahrain. But the Persians returned and renegotiated their control in 1719, effected through a local puppet ruler. In 1783 the Persians invaded the island of Zubara, the home of the Al Khalifa tribe, who with the help of the Al Sabah tribe of Kuwait repelled the Persian attack on Zubara, then defeated the occupying Persians on Bahrain Island. The ruler of the Al Khalifa, Sheikh Ahmed bin Mohammed Al Khalifa, became known through this conquest as Ahmed Al Fatih, or Ahmed the Conqueror. In 1861, Britain took over Bahrain as a protectorate to prevent further foreign encroachment. The Al Khalifa dynasty still controls the monarchial rule of the modern state of Bahrain, maintaining its rule for more than 200 years.

Bahrain was the first Arab Gulf state to discover oil, with the first oil well commencing production in 1932. As such, Bahrain's development began much earlier than the other Arab Gulf states, giving Bahrain the advantage of being the most socially advanced and developed of the Arab Gulf countries. But in comparison to the richer petroleum-exporting states of Saudi Arabia, Kuwait, and the United Arab Emirates, the Bahraini oil reserves are insignificant, currently meeting little more than domestic consumption requirements. Significant gas reserves, however, and Bahrain's petroleum refining industry, which processes Saudi crude petroleum, are likely to maintain a comfortable standard of living for Bahrainis well into the twenty-first century. As of 1996, oil and gas reserves totaled an estimated 65 percent of national revenues (Sick 1997) for Bahrain, the lowest percentage of all the Arab Gulf states, and an indicator of Bahrain's economic diversification. The early realization that Bahrain's oil reserves were relatively insignificant drove Bahrainis to embrace the diversification of their economy and to prepare for the time of oil-reserve depletion. As a result, the country has made a great investment in human resources development, including the development of educational and training programs.

This emphasis on human development in the 1990s was quite successful: Bahrainis are more involved than ever in the education sector as well as other sectors of the economy. Women have benefited greatly from the human resources development drive. Female employees work in one of the best labor environments in the world, where liberal maternity leave is strictly enforced. Women in Bahrain have moved beyond the traditionally acceptable role of teacher into such areas as banking, finance, engineering, the civil service, commerce, and administration. In 1996 through 1998, Bahrain came in first among Arabian countries on the Human Development Index as part of the United Nations Development Program's Human Development Report. At the dawn of the twenty-first century, Bahrain's status as one of the most—if not the most—socially developed Gulf Cooperation Council (GCC) countries was underscored by the progress made in education.

Shifts in the political climate have also been influential. In the late twentieth century, Bahrain began a process of rapid change under the leadership of His Highness Sheikh Hamad bin Issa Al Khalifa. From being one of the most oppressive and authoritarian Arab Gulf states, Bahrain appears to be moving toward becoming one of the most liberal and socially advanced. When Sheikh Hamad came to power in 1999, he did away with censorship, ordered the release of political prisoners, invited exiles

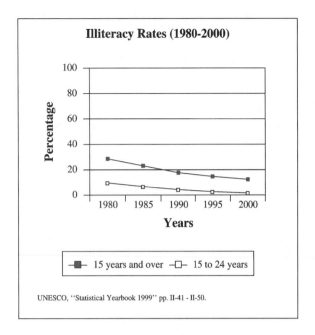

Illiteracy Rates (1980-2000)

Y-axis: Percentage (0, 20, 40, 60, 80, 100)
X-axis: Years (1980, 1985, 1990, 1995, 2000)

■ 15 years and over □ 15 to 24 years

UNESCO, "Statistical Yearbook 1999" pp. II-41 - II-50.

5 ensures the government's oversight of the "physical, mental, and moral growth of youth." Article 6 elucidates the Islamic orientation of Bahraini education:

> The State shall preserve the Arab and Islamic heritage, it shall participate in the furtherance of human civilization, and it shall strive to strengthen ties with the Muslim countries and to bring to fruition the aspirations of the Arab Nation for unity and advancement.

Finally, Article 7 sets forth the commitment to encouraging the arts and sciences, literature, and research, and to ensuring the provision of educational and cultural services to citizens. Primary education is made compulsory, and the government's plan to eliminate illiteracy is outlined. The article prescribes religious education (i.e., Islamic education) to foster an Islamic identity and pride in the Arab national heritage. The establishment of private schools is permitted "under the supervision of the State," and the inviolability of educational institutions is guaranteed.

In addition to the constitutional provisions, the government has enacted further legislation in support of education. The Education Law Project of 1989 specifically outlines the objectives underlying the regulation of education in Bahrain. These include opportunities for citizens to improve their standard of living through education; individual development along physical, mental, emotional, social, moral, and spiritual lines; the acquisition of critical thinking skills and sound judgment; and the inculcation of the Islamic faith and an Arab identity. Legislation has also addressed private educational and training institutions, training systems, student evaluation systems, equalization of GCC students in public education, school placement guidelines for new entrants, academic degree equivalence, and licensing of educational service providers. Such legislation has the general aim of promoting community-minded, socially active, educated citizens who are aware of their roles within local, regional, and international contexts.

Progress has not been easy. To meet the goal of placing more Bahraini nationals in the workforce, the government has supplemented education with laws assuring the employment of nationals. The "10,000 jobs" project and other initiatives have focused on training Bahrainis to replace foreign professionals. Even so, businesses have been reluctant to hire nationals—whose retention tend to require higher wages—and have instituted practices such as year-long internships prior to completing the hiring process. Moreover, the perception that the royal family, and not the other levels of society, is the sole beneficiary of national wealth and development, stifles motivation and productivity. Thus even in 1997 the estimated unemployment rate stood at 15 percent (Bromby 1997).

Changing political trends may help Bahrain meet its educational objectives. For much of the twentieth century

home, and most importantly, issued a charter calling for a national parliament and outlining a national vision of Bahrain as a European-style democratic monarchy. Bahrain's first experiment with democracy had ended in failure shortly after independence from Britain in 1971. By 1975 the parliament was suspended, and strong opposition movements, mainly Shiite majority factions opposing the Sunni Al Khalifa family, were brutally crushed. The 1999 referendum for the new national charter was approved by 98.4 percent of the voters with a 90 percent voter turnout rate. These changes in Bahrain's system of governance appear to be the beginning of a new era in the country's history, likely to increase domestic tranquillity and decrease monarchial control by the ruling Al Khalifa family.

CONSTITUTIONAL & LEGAL FOUNDATIONS

The constitutional foundations of Bahraini education are based upon two principles set forth by the Ministry of Education:

1. The provision of education for all school age children throughout the country.

2. The improvement of the quality of education to meet the needs both of the students and that of the country's social and economic development.

Adopted on May 26, 1973, and effective since December 6, 1973, the Constitution of the State of Bahrain guarantees education as a basic right of Bahraini citizens. Article 4 of the Constitution refers to education as one of the "pillars of society guaranteed by the State." Article and earlier, disagreements with the ruling family called for constitutional reform, and parliamentary restoration constituted treasonable acts punishable by imprisonment and exile. At the start of the twenty-first century, however, the state of Bahrain appeared to be moving toward less repressive state control. If this trend carries through, the greater freedom and involvement of Bahrainis in their system of governance will likely enable more significant progress toward Bahrain's educational goals.

EDUCATIONAL SYSTEM—OVERVIEW

Given its early start, Bahrain has been at least a generation ahead of its neighbors in modern educational development, but it has also upheld its traditions. From the beginning, Bahraini education has been non-coeducational, and there appear to be no plans to change this structure. In 1919 the first elementary school in Bahrain was established for boys, while the first girls' elementary school opened in 1928. In 1936 the first industrial school was established, and a secondary school for girls was opened in 1951. A religious school for Shari'a (Islamic law) scholars opened in 1943, which later became the Religious Institute of Bahrain in 1960. The Teachers College was inaugurated in 1966, and in 1968 Bahrain University opened its doors, after a reincorporation of Khaliji Technical College (also known as Gulf Polytechnic). The first private education endeavors began in 1952 with the opening of the Manama School, an in 1961 the Private Education Act was promulgated. As of 2001, private education accommodated an estimated 15 percent of school age students. In 1971 the Joint National Committee for Adult Education was organized, and in 1979 the Bahrain University's College of Arts, Sciences, and Education opened. In the same year the Arabian Gulf University was inaugurated with the institution of its Faculty of Medicine.

From 1990 to 2000 the number of government schools in operation steadily increased, as did student enrollment in these schools—and the percentage of Bahraini nationals working in the education sector. In the academic year 1990-1991 there were 158 government schools up to the secondary level. This number jumped to 193 by academic year 1999-2000. Total student enrollment in the government schools for 1990-1991 was 100,658, while by 1999-2000 this figure had reached 114,669. In 1999-2000, about 88 percent of the teachers in these schools were Bahraini, a dramatic increase of nearly 20 percent throughout the 1990s from only 68.5 percent of the teachers being Bahraini in 1990-1991. According to UNESCO, the literacy rate in 1997 was 85.2 percent, up from a 45 percent literacy rate in 1984. The improvements in adult literacy have allowed the Ministry of Education to shift its focus from general illiteracy to *computer* illiteracy.

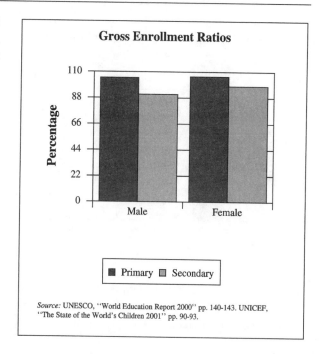

Gross Enrollment Ratios

Source: UNESCO, "World Education Report 2000" pp. 140-143. UNICEF, "The State of the World's Children 2001" pp. 90-93.

PREPRIMARY & PRIMARY EDUCATION

Nursery and preprimary schools, both private and public, provide care and instruction for preschool age children. Primary education in Bahraini government schools throughout the three cycles of basic education centers on compulsory core subjects including religious education (Islamic education), Arabic language, science and technology, social studies, art, physical education, and music. English language and family-life studies do not begin until the fourth grade in the second cycle, and practical studies do not begin until the seventh grade in the third cycle. The study plan for the third cycle allows for three additional periods per week in order to increase the subject range for students as well as the teacher-student contact hours.

In the academic year 1999-2000 there were a total of 165 government schools in the primary school category, including 115 schools (59 male, 56 female) classified by the government as primary schools, 18 (12 male, 6 female) classified as primary/intermediate, and 32 (14 male, 18 female) classified as intermediate. Enrollments in government primary schools totaled 90,938, with 62,289 students at the primary level (31,043 male, 31,246 female) and 28,649 at the intermediate level (14,094 male, 14,555 female) according to government classification.

SECONDARY EDUCATION

At the secondary level of education, students diverge along various educational tracks and vocational professional specializations, including science, literary studies,

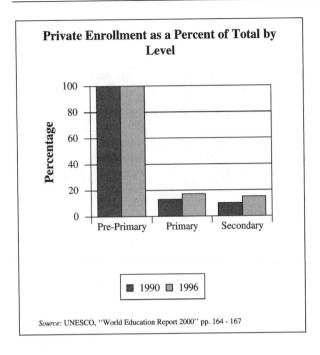

Private Enrollment as a Percent of Total by Level

1990 ■ 1996

Source: UNESCO, "World Education Report 2000" pp. 164 - 167

agriculture, printing, textiles, and advertising, among others. Most technical and vocational programs are limited to men, and textile and advertising are limited to women. Thus while male enrollment is split fairly evenly between the traditional arts and sciences tracks and the more vocationally oriented programs, female enrollment at the secondary level is predominantly in the science and literary programs, in some cases representing more than 60 percent of a given track's enrollment. The coursework at this level comprises core courses, courses in the area of the student's specialization, free elective courses, and programs designed to prepare students for either higher education or the labor market.

In 2000 there were 28 government schools at the secondary level, including 3 commercial secondary schools, 17 general secondary schools, 4 technical schools, a religious institute for men, and 3 schools classified by the Ministry of Education as intermediate/secondary institutions. There were a total of 1,879 teachers at the secondary level in 1999-2000, of whom 466 were non-Bahraini expatriate teachers, roughly a quarter of the total number of teachers at this level. Performance evaluation of secondary schools consists of both internal and external indicator review as well as cumulative and summative evaluations.

HIGHER EDUCATION

Bahrain has two universities for higher education: Bahrain University (BU), founded in 1968, and the Arabian Gulf University (AGU), which opened in 1979. In the late 1970s and 1980s higher education in Bahrain saw

rapid development. Within the university system, the College of Health Services graduated students for entry into the health profession, and Gulf Polytechnic expanded in the 1980s to meet the specialized technical needs of the Gulf region in such areas as computer science, engineering, and business management.

Arab Gulf countries, sharing a common heritage and common challenges, established AGU with the goals of calibrating programs and curricula according to the cultural, scientific, and occupational needs of the GCC member states. Education and research related to the Gulf region is the mandate of AGU carried out in the programs of study and research within its two colleges: the College of Medicine and Medical Sciences, and the College of Postgraduate Studies. Beyond AGU, promising students are funded for studies abroad in areas such as the medical sciences, information and communications sciences, energy sciences, desertification, biotechnology, astronomy, oceanography, educational planning, guidance and counseling, vocational education, and special education.

While institutions of higher learning in the Arab world and the Gulf region have proliferated, coordination among these institutions has been less than ideal. In 1995 Muain H. Jamlan, Chair of the Department of Educational Technology in BU's College of Education, proposed incorporating trends in distance learning and the concept of an Arab "open" university to deliver online instruction as a way of addressing the challenges of greater cooperation in educational planning.

ADMINISTRATION, FINANCE, & EDUCATIONAL RESEARCH

The Ministry of Education in Bahrain administers the government's educational institutions and supervises private educational institutions in the country. The organization consists of the Minister of Education, the Undersecretary, and the Assistant Undersecretaries, who oversee the following directorates: Educational Services and Private Education, General and Technical Education, Financial and Administrative Affairs, Curricula and Training, and Educational Planning and Information. The development of Bahrain's human resources potential is a high priority: the Ministry aims to develop Bahrain's services and industrial sectors to compensate for decreases in oil revenues. Under the Ministry of Labor and Social Affairs, the Training Promotions Office is working to establish an internationally accredited national vocational qualification system, modeled after the British system. Aligning the industrial and services sectors with the national education system is a key component of this strategy. The government is pursuing ambitious technological agendas, as exemplified by the introduction of Internet-based teaching and learning initiatives in government schools. In 1998 the government's investment in education totaled BD (Bahraini Dinars) 82 million (about US$21.8 million).

In 1999 Dr. Hamad Ali Al Sulayti, formerly Director of Bahrain's Educational Planning and Cultural Affairs under the Ministry of Education, and previously the Acting Secretary General of the Bahraini Center for Studies and Research, outlined in a cutting-edge report some of the common challenges faced by GCC countries in reforming and developing their educational systems. This report, delivered at an educational conference in Abu Dhabi, underlined the importance of aligning the education sectors of Gulf countries with actual labor market needs so as to ensure greater economic productivity, workforce efficiency, and social stability. Bahrain has taken the lead in meeting such challenges, and as an educational pioneer can draw on its own experience of facing the early necessity for economic diversification. Important requirements for GCC countries suggested by educational research include curriculum reform, employer involvement, and a higher level of quality assurance through systems of external accountability—areas in which Bahrain already has a head start.

NONFORMAL EDUCATION

Institutions in Bahrain offering special education include the Saudi-Bahraini Institute for the Welfare of the Blind, the Al-Amal Institute, the Social Rehabilitation Center (including a hearing defect unit and a vocational rehabilitation unit). The Ministry of Education's Directorate of Adult Education oversees illiteracy eradication programs and continuing education programs for adults. The continuing education programs offer language courses (English, Arabic, French, German, Japanese) and specialized courses in auto mechanics, electrical appliance maintenance, art, family life, and office/secretarial skills. The Youth and Sports Authority sponsors junior science clubs, science centers, and the Sulman Cultural Center for children. There are also a number of training centers, as part of Bahrain's plan to develop the country's training resources, and to promote Bahrain as the regional center for such programs. The Higher Council for Vocational Training is the main government body tasked with this agenda, and throughout the late 1980s and 1990s the council qualified 10,528 Bahraini workers in its training programs.

TEACHING PROFESSION

Throughout the 1990s the education sector saw the number of Bahraini teachers steadily increase. By academic year 1999-2000 approximately 88 percent of the teachers in government schools were Bahraini. Among female educators, nearly 97 percent were Bahraini na-

tionals, while among male educators, 79 percent were Bahraini. By contrast, in 1990 some 68 percent of teachers in government schools were Bahraini (79.6 percent of females and 57.8 percent of males).

Student-teacher ratios are comparatively low in the government schools. According to statistics from 1999-2000, the ratios decreased according to age and level of specialization. From a rate of 20:1 at the primary level, the ratio gradually decreases to 18:1 at the intermediate level, 13:1 at the intermediate/secondary level, 15:1 at the general secondary level, 14:1 at the commercial secondary level, 10:1 at the technical secondary level, and 11:1 at the Religious Institute of Bahrain. On average the student-teacher ratio is 17:1 in Bahraini government schools.

SUMMARY

The statistics and social indicators relevant to the education sector in Bahrain are relatively positive. Although petroleum revenues are important to the development of the physical facilities and technological capabilities of Bahrain's educational infrastructure, the priority of human resources development is even more crucial. Some of the social problems faced by other Arab Gulf states—high unemployment, lack of coordination between educational programs and the labor market, even apparent apathy—seem to have been tempered in Bahrain, a country with significantly less oil wealth than its richer neighbors. But it is an awareness of constraints brought on by resource depletion that has provided the motivation for Bahrain's human resources development and the establishment of its services and industrial sectors.

Bahrain has forged highly successful enterprises in the face of resource-depletion challenges. This spirit of entrepreneurialism has established the country as the leading financial center of the Middle East, a pioneer in education, an innovator in training services, and a model for other Arab Gulf states. Moreover, the ruling Al Khalifa family appears to be relinquishing some of its monarchical control, which bodes well for the greater freedom and motivated involvement of Bahrainis in developing their individual and collective potential.

BIBLIOGRAPHY

Al-Sulayti, Hamad. "Education and Training in GCC Countries: Some Issues of Concern." In *Education and the Arab World: Challenges of the Next Millennium*, 271-278. Abu Dhabi, United Arab Emirates: Emirates Center for Strategic Studies and Research, 1999.

"Bahrain." In *Arab Gulf Cooperation Council: The 19th GCC Summit*, 18-43. London: Trident Press, 1998.

"Bahrain: Your Kingdom for Our Rights." *The Economist*, 24 February 2001.

Bromby, Robin. "Bahrain and Qatar Have Big Import Appetites." In *Contemporary Women's Issues Database,* 2: 5-8. Farmington Hills, MI: Gale Group: 1997.

Government School Education Statistics, The Bahrain Ministry of Education. 15 March 2001. Available from http://www.education.gov.bh/.

Jamlan, Muain H. "Proposal for an Open University in the Arab World." *Technological Horizons in Education Journal 22,* January 1995: 53-55.

Sick, Gary. G. "The Coming Crisis in the Persian Gulf." In *The Persian Gulf at the Millennium: Essays in Politics, Economy, Security, and Religion,* eds. Gary G. Sick and Lawrence G. Potter, 11-30. New York: St. Martin's Press, 1997.

Yamani, Mai. "Health, Education, Gender, and the Security of the Gulf in the Twenty-first Century." In *Gulf Security in the Twenty-first Century,* eds. David E. Long and Christian Koch, 265-279. Abu Dhabi, United Arab Emirates: Emirates Center for Strategic Studies and Research, 1997.

—*John P. Lesko*

BANGLADESH

BASIC DATA

Official Country Name:	People's Republic of Bangladesh
Region:	East & South Asia
Population:	129,194,224
Language(s):	Bangla, English
Literacy Rate:	38.1%
Number of Primary Schools:	45,914
Compulsory Schooling:	5 years
Public Expenditure on Education:	2.2%
Educational Enrollment:	Primary: 11,939,949
	Secondary: 3,592,995
	Higher: 434,309
Teachers:	Primary: 189,508
	Secondary: 130,949
	Higher: 22,447
Student-Teacher Ratio:	Primary: 63:1

HISTORY & BACKGROUND

Bangladesh, officially called the People's Republic of Bangladesh, is a newly formed state that represents a very ancient culture. It was mentioned in Mahabharata, an ancient epic of India sometime during the ninth or tenth century B.C. During the two centuries of British rule in the Indian subcontinent, it was the first territory colonized by the empire.

When the British left India after a long struggle for political independence, the country was divided into two nations: a Hindu-majority, secular India; and a Moslem-majority, sectarian Pakistan. Pakistan, too, was divided into two parts, more than 1,500 miles distant from each other. Eastern Bengal became East Pakistan, but the capital and ruling government leaders stayed in West Pakistan. The people of East Pakistan became increasingly impatient when they realized that valuable resources were being transferred from their region to West Pakistan. They also became restless because of ill treatment by the militaristic-bureaucratic West Pakistan elite, which led to a demand for secession in 1970 and, subsequently, the formation of a separate, autonomous state in 1972.

Bangladesh, despite its natural resources, industrial potential, and agricultural growth, has been facing massive socio-economic problems, making it one of the least developed countries in the world. Sometimes referred to as "an international bread basket," it has been affected by great natural disasters such as rainstorms, floods, and famines.

Bangladesh is one of the most densely populated countries in the world with more than 128 million people living in an area of 147,000 square kilometers (868 people per square kilometer). It has been plagued by high population growth, very low levels of literacy (less than 20 percent in 1970), and widespread poverty (originally with the per capita income of $150, and estimated at $280 in 2001).

CONSTITUTIONAL & LEGAL FOUNDATIONS

During the first 15 years of its statehood, the two significant legacies of the British rule, namely English-centered public education and parliamentary democracy, were not as beneficial in Bangladesh as they were to its immediate neighbor, India. The debates on official language and medium of instruction have been costly and difficult to resolve. In the former East Pakistan, the state language was Urdu, and not Bangla, their own mother tongue. Despite British influence, the majority of Bangladesh students (approximately 70 percent) use Bangla as their medium. The parallel institutions of religiously based education, called *Madrashas* use Urdu, which is vastly different from Bangla.

The legacy of parliamentary democracy, while accepted in principle from the start, has been often negated during the period of military rules, unstable governments, and other national crises. Results from 1998 through 2001 show that the educational system seems to be gradually improving in Bangladesh.

EDUCATIONAL SYSTEM—OVERVIEW

The census figures from 1981 and 1991 indicate that the low level of literacy was even lower among females than males in Bangladesh's basically patriarchal society. With a strong Moslem influence, women have been traditionally passive and largely excluded from the schools and colleges in Bangladesh. The gender gap in education was even wider in the villages in the vastly rural population; these gaps have been shrinking gradually due to the influx of urban-industrial areas and the impact of mass media (newspaper, radio, television, and, recently, computers).

Since the liberation war in 1971, Bangladesh, as an independent and secular state, has been allowing many forms of educational institutions, various modes of instruction, and different languages as mediums of instruction to co-exist. Students are free to choose from three types of schools: English medium, Bangla medium, and religious schools. English medium schools and universities tend to be privately governed, tend to serve the needs of the wealthy and political elite, and tend to have a shortage of textbooks and adequately trained teachers in these schools; their exams in English were sent to England or to the British Council in Dhaka. Bangla medium schools are government-sponsored and are free, or less expensive, than their English-medium counterparts and are divided into 4 levels—primary from grades 1 to 5; secondary from grades 6 to 10; higher secondary for grades 11 to 12; and colleges, universities, and vocational institutes. Religious schools or *Madrashas* have millions of children, including many who come from lower socio-economic backgrounds (including the homeless), who have been sheltered, fed, and taught the ways of Islam by the Moslem priests meeting inside the mosques and studying the religious text, the Koran, in Arabic script and the Urdu language. The *Madrasha* graduates have been assuming the role of future teachers in the mosque-affiliated schools. Since 1985 these schools, which are traditional hallmarks of Bangladesh, have been going through innovations and modernizations. Some have been introducing secular, non-religious subjects in scientific and technological fields, and some have been attracting female students. These institutions, financed by public donations and serving the needs of vast populations, are likely to thrive through non-sectarian and non-sexist reforms. During 1997-1998, a generous amount of 2 billion takas (50 takas equals US$1.00) was sanctioned

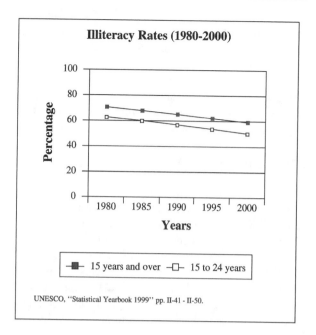

Illiteracy Rates (1980-2000)

Percentage / *Years*

15 years and over ─ 15 to 24 years

UNESCO, "Statistical Yearbook 1999" pp. II-41 - II-50.

by the government in order to educate more female students, to improve educational facilities, and to incorporate modern scientific curriculum within these traditionally defined schools.

Education Planning & Policies: During the last 20 years, education in Bangladesh has been gradually changing from its previous class-based system to the current mass-based system. Since 1971, the Ministry of Education and Culture has been responsible for planning, financing, and managing education at all levels. In 1972 a special Education Commission was appointed to investigate and report on all major aspects of education in Bangladesh. In 1987, another high-level Education Commission was instituted; it recommended a national policy for compulsory free education for all children, reforms in *Madrashas,* and the growth of scientific, medical, and technical education. The Commission's recommendations were incorporated in the fourth and fifth five-year plans covering the period up to the year 2002.

The 2001 female-headed government of Bangladesh has been emphasizing education for women who have traditionally kept away from schools. This objective is to be achieved by training additional female teachers, establishing women's colleges, and offering special scholarships. A recent government report in 1999 mentions that 7000 female teachers were being appointed. Between 1997 and 2002, 18 non-government women's colleges, as well as three polytechnic institutes, were established.

Bangladesh has been actively participating in various international organizations such as UNESCO and has declared a target of "Education for All." The government hopes to remove illiteracy from the country by the year 2005. The latest available figures indicate overall literacy went from 47 percent to 56 percent from 1997 to 2001. Various governmental and nongovernmental plans are being developed to spread formal, nonformal, general, and specialized education, with the help of international agencies and increases in the present budget plan.

PREPRIMARY & PRIMARY EDUCATION

The primary school age population in Bangladesh has been greatly handicapped by high dropout and low completion rates. Many reports mention that more than 50 percent of the students drop out during the primary level (ages 6 to 11) and only 4 percent complete the 12 years of general education. Other problems that affect the primary school attendance include lack of schools at accessible distances, lack of teaching aids and equipment, shortage of teachers, and poor community involvement.

Many needs have been identified to meet the objectives set forth for primary education. Additional classrooms will be provided depending on the increased enrollment, and the ultimate aim is to have minimum of five classrooms in each school. Additional teachers will also be recruited for the additional classes. Teacher training programs and the teaching of learning materials will be improved, and the training of teachers will be conducted and reviewed. Also, the Thana County Resource Centers will be established to conduct in-service and refresher training for teachers. To facilitate this teacher training, one primary school will be developed as a model school for teachers in localized school sub-clusters. The Primary and Mass Education Division will be strengthened, and the Directorate of Primary Education will be organized to facilitate the quality improvement of the management of the primary education system as well.

SECONDARY EDUCATION

In Bangladesh, school enrollment rates fall drastically from primary (grades 1 to 5) to secondary (grades 6 to 10). In 1998 about 78 percent of pupils completing grade 5 made a transition to the first year of secondary school. Gross enrollment in the secondary phase was only 7 million (38 percent of eligible children).

Due to special encouragement and financial assistance, the enrollment of girls at the secondary level has increased; it is now equal to that of boys in the secondary phases. However, at the next postsecondary level (grades 11 and 12), the girl/boy ratio changes to 34:66. Female students from rural areas and from lower economic strata have fewer chances of joining and completing secondary education.

The Bangladesh National Education Commission has laid down a number of aims and objectives to improve secondary education, especially in these areas:

- utilizing existing physical infrastructure and adding new facilities

- arranging double shifts in as many educational institutions as possible

- reducing the gender gap by encouraging and rewarding female students and their families

- reducing the rural-urban gap in a largely rural agricultural country

- reforming curricula by introducing and improving scientific, technical, and medical education at the secondary level, since the British-inherited system emphasizes liberal arts.

HIGHER EDUCATION

Although the number of government and private universities and colleges has been steadily increasing since Bangladesh gained statehood in 1972, the enrollment completion rates are still very low. The major factors related to the problems of low enrollment and high dropout rates at the college and university levels in Bangladesh seem to be a combination of factors, including poverty. In a country where the per capita income is still less than US$1.00 per day, higher education may cost as much as US$400 per year. Another factor is large-scale unemployment. This is a major source of frustration among the graduates, particularly among those majoring in the liberal arts. In addition, there are problems with English as a medium in higher education. It was recently noted that more than 70 percent of the university students in Bangladesh answer their examination questions in Bangla, although the texts are in English. A lack of resources and facilities also contributes to unhappiness. The colleges and universities are often understaffed and ill-equipped, leading to frequent cases of student unrest where politically misguided and academically unsuccessful students channel their frustrations into destructive activities.

Proposed Remedies: The problems hindering higher education appear to be emphasized in Bangladeshi media, and the present government seems to be well aware of them. Both the governmental and many nongovernmental agencies have been trying to address to these issues.

In the late 1990s, the government gave priority to human resource development and emphasized "Educational for All" as a target. Recent five year plans provide for a larger proportion of national budgets for opening additional colleges and universities, especially in the area of medicine, science, and information technology. The Bangladesh National University, to which many hundreds of colleges are affiliated, is being modernized and revamped.

ADMINISTRATION, FINANCE, & EDUCATIONAL RESEARCH

One of the best-known efforts to finance higher education is being made through rural banking and rural welfare agencies in Bangladesh. Grameen rural Bank programs have proposed a much-praised Higher Education Loan Program (HELP) to help needy and promising college students through an annual loan; this program has been inspired by a successful effort of granting micro credit to the rural poor in Bangladesh. Also developing is a parallel system to help loan recipients in finding and maintaining jobs after graduation. If these programs succeed, they can be emulated in other poverty-stricken, Third World countries where large scale education-related issues are common.

NONFORMAL EDUCATION

In order to reach the target of total literacy by the year 2005, Bangladesh is in the process of implementing many nonformal educational programs. Under the sponsorship of BRAC (Bangladesh Rural Advancement Committee), thousands of nonformal schools have recently been established. Literacy centers are utilizing courtyards, open spaces, and school premises at night. These programs are specifically aimed at out-of-school children (especially rural girls), illiterate adults, and neo-literates.

Since Bangladeshi women are greatly handicapped by their traditionally segregated status and unfavorable sex ratio, governmental, as well as nongovernmental, organizations have been offering special stipends and free transportation to them. The efforts to reduce the gender gap also included one condition for accepting the stipend, namely the student's commitment to remain unmarried at least until the legal age of 18, but preferably beyond it.

The country is facing another problem of education that is common among highly populated countries lacking adequate space and financial resources. Seven countries in the South Asia (Bangladesh, Bhutan, India, Maldives, Nepal, Pakistan, and Sri Lanka) are affiliated with an organization called SAARC (South Asian Association for Regional Cooperation). Many of these countries have been searching for the systems of distance education that can attract millions of students to their less expensive and tailor-made curricula and can enable adults can earn their academic credentials without abandoning their full-time jobs or domestic obligations.

Bangladesh, with its very high population density and problems of poverty, is an ideal candidate for such

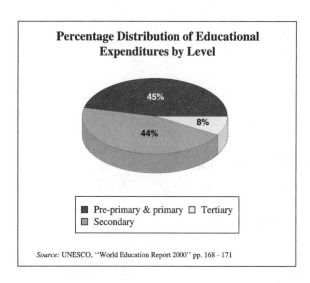

Percentage Distribution of Educational Expenditures by Level

45%
8%
44%

■ Pre-primary & primary □ Tertiary
■ Secondary

Source: UNESCO, "World Education Report 2000" pp. 168 - 171

a nonformal alternative to regular campus-based educational programs. It has already established an open university and, through Bangladesh Institute for Distance Education (BIDE), has been providing in-service training of teachers. Around 1990, as many as 7,000 students, selected from a pool of 20,000 applicants, were granted the degree of Bachelor of Education (BED) through BIDE. Such programs are likely to be very popular among future teachers as well as others interested in vocational and tertiary education. More formal degree and certificate programs and short-term courses are likely to be established under the open universities.

SUMMARY

With its huge population in search of socio-economic betterment and a rightful place in the global community, Bangladesh is likely to face many challenges and remains grateful for many success stories in the field of education. While its governmental and nongovernmental agencies are busily refining the methods for educating huge masses, outside help is also being increasingly available for these tasks. The issues of spreading literacy in the remote, rural areas and providing the newly demanded skills of information technology are at the forefront. If the cooperative links between the governmental agencies and nongovernmental efforts, especially the rural cooperatives, remain strong, most, if not all, educational goals may be successfully met in a gradual manner.

BIBLIOGRAPHY

Bornstein, David. *The Price of a Dream: The Story of the Grameen Book.* Dhaka: University Press, 1996.

UNESCO. *Education Indications in Asia and the Pacific and Basic Education in Asia the Pacific.* Bangkok: UNESCO, 1998.

—*Ashakant Nimbark*

BARBADOS

BASIC DATA

Official Country Name:	Barbados
Region:	South America
Population:	274,540
Language(s):	English
Literacy Rate:	97.4%
Academic Year:	September-July
Number of Primary Schools:	106
Compulsory Schooling:	11 years
Educational Enrollment:	Primary: 26,662
	Secondary: 28,818
Educational Enrollment Rate:	Higher: 29%
Teachers:	Primary: 1,553
	Secondary: 1,231
Student-Teacher Ratio:	Primary: 17:1
Female Enrollment Rate:	Higher: 35%

HISTORY & BACKGROUND

The nation of Barbados, the easternmost island of the West Indies, lies in the Atlantic Ocean, 100 miles (160 kilometers) east of the Windward Islands; a former British colony, it has a total of 166 square miles, about 2.5 times the size of Washington, D.C. The name Barbados comes from the Portuguese word for ''bearded'' and probably refers to the bearded fig trees that grow there.

Barbados, sometimes referred to as ''little England,'' was colonized by the British in the 1620s. However, Amerindian tribes were the first inhabitants of Barbados. Both the peaceful Arawaks and the more warrior-like Caribs claimed the island as their home. Barbados historians believe that the Caribs may have forced the Arawaks off the island. By the early 1600s, few Indians

remained on the island because the Caribs either migrated to the north or south or were taken by Spanish sailors as slaves. In 1625, Captain John Powell arrived in Barbados and claimed it for Britain. Later British colonists settled the island; it was officially made a Crown possession in 1663. The introduction of sugarcane as a principal crop prompted the importation of African slaves to work the plantations. This practice continued until Britain abolished slavery in 1834. Its economy remained heavily dependent on sugar, rum, and molasses production throughout most of the twentieth century. In the 1990s tourism and manufacturing surpassed the sugar industry in economic importance. Although Barbados had a relatively high per capita growth rate in the 1980s, unemployment, especially among the youth and women, has been a serious problem. Most of the employment is in service and distribution trades, the greater part of which has been unionized.

Barbados is one of the world's most densely populated countries. In 2000 the population was estimated to be 275,000, with 1,597 persons per square mile. Three quarters of its population is under age 44. Population projections put growth at less than 2 percent by the year 2010. Since the 1950s the rate of population growth has been slowed by a successful family planning program and by emigration, now mostly to the other parts of the Caribbean and to North America. During this same time, the death and infant mortality rates declined sharply, and life expectancy rose to 73 years. More than one third of the population is concentrated in Bridgetown, the capital and only seaport, and its surrounding area. About 80 percent of its residents are descendants of African slaves brought to the island 300 years ago. The remaining population includes whites (about 4 percent), East Indians, and persons of mixed African and European descent. English is the official language and is the language of instruction in the schools; a nonstandard English called Bajan is spoken.

CONSTITUTIONAL & LEGAL FOUNDATIONS

Barbados was established as an independent member of the Commonwealth of Nations on November 30, 1966. It has a parliamentary form of democracy based on the Westminster model. The British monarch is officially head of state and is represented by a governor general with limited power. Legislative power is vested in the Parliament, comprised of a 27-member elected House of Assembly, a 21-member appointed Upper House or Senate, and the Governor General. Executive power is vested in the Cabinet, comprised of the Prime Minister and other Ministers of Government. The general direction and control of the government rests with the Cabinet, which is collectively responsible to Parliament. The Barbados Parliament is the third oldest in the world with 358 years of an uninterrupted parliamentary system of government.

The government holds the view that the development of Barbados is dependent upon the quality of its educational system; in the Government of Barbados Development Plan, 1988-1993, is a statement of its commitment to "the development of an educational system that enables all persons to realize their talents to the fullest extent possible."

There are three political parties in Barbados, all of which place great emphasis on educational development. The Barbados Labour Party (BLP) is one of Barbados' oldest leading parties and currently the ruling party; it was in power in 1950 when universal adult suffrage became the law.

EDUCATIONAL SYSTEM—OVERVIEW

Formal education in Barbados can be traced back to 1680. The present system developed largely from the 1890 Education Act, which established rigid distinctions between and even within levels of education. In 1932, the Marriot-Mayhew Commission carried out a comprehensive investigation of the colony's educational service. It recommended additional educational programs to cater to specific groups, especially teachers, and to the wider community. As a result, a new Teachers' Training College was opened, new secondary schools were established, and a loan fund was created to assist individuals in obtaining higher education abroad. Technical and vocational training was also introduced. A new Education Act emerged in 1981 that sought to provide greater equality of opportunity. Once universal access to basic education was achieved, the country turned its attention toward reform of the education system to stay current with economic and technological change. The Planning Section of the Ministry of Education, Youth Affairs and Culture compiled a White Paper on Education Reform for Barbados in 1995.

The Barbados government pays the cost of educating its students through primary, secondary, and tertiary level, including provision of textbooks. This strong emphasis on education has resulted in a literacy rate of 98 percent, one of the highest in the world. Public education is compulsory for children, thus providing for 100 percent participation at the primary and secondary levels (children ages 5 to 16). Such an accomplishment was achieved at the primary level for most of the century and at the secondary level in more recent times. In order to ensure active participation by all students, programs include the provision of school meals at the primary level; a textbook loan scheme; transportation assistance; a uniform grant and bursaries at the secondary level; and a wide range of awards, grants, and scholarships at the tertiary level. These support systems reflect the underlying belief that "every person has a right to education opportunities to allow him/her to develop... abilities to the fullest and to contribute to the social and economic development of the country" (White Paper).

The challenge is to improve quality rather than access. The theme of the 1995 White Paper on Education Reform, "Each One Matters—Quality Education for All," shifts the focus of education to the needs of each individual and identifies those areas of the system that have to be fixed, hopefully leading to an overall improvement in the quality of graduates from Barbadian schools and educational institutions.

The school year includes three terms of 13 to 14 weeks and runs from September to July. The school day begins at 8:30 a.m. and ends at 3:00 p.m. The education system is multi-staged with some overlap at each stage.

PREPRIMARY & PRIMARY EDUCATION

Preprimary education is offered to all children between the ages of three to five; they are taught in the four nursery schools and/or in nursery classes in some primary and composite schools. At present about 66 percent of three- and four-year-old children in Barbados are receiving preprimary education. Because of the declining birth rate, the government has been promoting the use of available space at primary and composite schools to provide nursery education.

Primary education is required for children between the ages of 5 and 11 with the goal of preparing them to be able to read and write, to reason, to deal with normal and conflict situations, to be numerate, and to develop high self-esteem. They are taught in 110 primary schools, of which 86 (78 percent) are public. At age 11, students take the Common Entrance Examination, a measure of what children have learned at the end of primary schooling. Because each child develops at his or her own rate, the government proposed, effective May 1996, that children be allowed to take the examination when they are ready. The class teachers and principal of the primary school determine readiness. Children only take the examination once, must be exposed to the entire primary school curriculum, and must be at least 10 years of age to enter secondary school.

SECONDARY EDUCATION

Secondary education is provided for children ages 11 to 18. There are 34 secondary schools, of which 22 are government-run and 12 are assisted private secondary schools. These schools fall into three categories: nine government-owned former grammar or older secondary schools, four of which have sixth forms; 13 assisted private schools; and newer secondary schools. In between the primary and secondary schools are the composite and

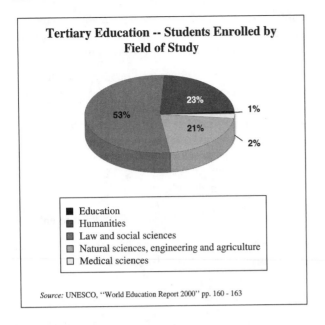

Tertiary Education -- Students Enrolled by Field of Study

- ■ Education
- ■ Humanities
- ■ Law and social sciences
- ▨ Natural sciences, engineering and agriculture
- ☐ Medical sciences

23%
53%
21%
1%
2%

Source: UNESCO, "World Education Report 2000" pp. 160 - 163

senior schools. The function of these schools is to ensure that all students acquire knowledge, skills, and attitudes that will lay the basic foundation for future jobs and careers. In addition this level of schooling will ensure high levels of literacy, numeracy, and oracy by building on the primary foundation.

Admission to government secondary schools is based on the score the child receives in the Barbados Secondary Schools Entrance Examination (BSSEE), familiarly known as the Common Entrance Examination (CEE). On completion of five years of secondary education, pupils are tested for the Caribbean Examinations Certificate. On completion of a further two-year sixth-form course, pupils take the General Certificate of Education (GCE) Advanced 'A' levels, which allows direct entry to university-level studies.

HIGHER EDUCATION

Four institutions provide higher education, or tertiary education:

1. Erdiston Teachers College, opened in 1948, provides training for nongraduate and graduate teachers.

2. Samuel Jackman Prescod Polytechnic was established in 1970 to provide day and night courses and programs in electrical, building and engineering trades, commerce, agriculture, and garments. Students can also prepare here for entry into the Division of Technology of the Barbados Community College.

3. Barbados Community College (BCC) provides a range of programs in academic, vocational, and tech-

nical areas. Divisions of the college include fine arts, liberal arts, science, technology, and health sciences. In addition students can pursue studies at the Barbados Hospitality Institute (BHI), a full service hospitality training facility operated by BCC, providing certificate, diploma, and associate training programs in all aspects of the hospitality industry. The institute comprises both educational and accommodation components and is the first training facility of its kind in Barbados and the eastern Caribbean.

4. University of the West Indies (UWI) (Cave Hill Campus) has faculties of arts and general studies, natural sciences, social sciences, medical sciences, law, and education. The UWI offers high educational standards and quality research and thus attracts the brightest students from the Caribbean and beyond, and maintains partnerships with the universities in the United Kingdom, United States of America, and Canada, including Oxford, Johns Hopkins, and McGill.

ADMINISTRATION, FINANCE, & EDUCATIONAL RESEARCH

Administration: Administrative control of the formal education system is fairly highly centralized. The Ministry of Education was first established in 1954 under the Premier while Barbados was still a British colony. In 1958, a separate ministry was created with its own staff of administrative and technical offices.

The Ministry is divided into two main sections, technical and administrative. The Chief Education Officer is in charge of the technical staff and is the chief professional advisor. The Permanent Secretary is the chief administrative officer with responsibility for finance. The primary schools are administered directly by the Ministry of Education; the secondary schools have Boards of Management that are appointed by and answer to the Minister of Education. All tertiary-level institutions have Boards of Management, except for UWI, which is a regional institution.

Finance: For more than three decades, Barbados has been committed to a policy of free education from primary schools to university. Between 1990 and 1999 an average of 20 percent of the public expenditure was devoted to education. This level of social investment led the United Nations Development Program (UNDP) to rank Barbados the top Caribbean country in human development. In its 1998 Human Development Report, the UNDP said Barbados ranks first overall in health, education, and average standard of living for the Caribbean region and 24th in the world rankings.

The education reform initiatives outlined in the 1995 White Paper were estimated to cost $35 million (Barbadian dollars) over a five-year period (1995-2000). In addition, the Ministry sought US$82 million in foreign and regional financing to fund a wide variety of projects. For example, in 1998 the Inter-American Development Bank approved a US$85 million loan to Barbados to support modernization of the education system and to prepare primary and secondary students for an information and technology-based economy of the twenty-first century. Primary and secondary schools began rehabilitation and re-equipment programs to make them computer and network ready, with computers gradually introduced in all classrooms. Teacher and student training to support the modernization process were included. Media centers created in each classroom include a TV set, videocassette recorder, and TV-OC converter. An additional joint venture by the Inter-American Development Bank and the Caribbean Development Bank resulted in a loan to Barbados of US$116.5 million to implement a computer-aided education program called EduTech 2000. The funds supported the purchase of about 10,000 computers for primary, secondary, and special education schools.

Educational Research: Educational research efforts called for in the 1995 White Paper included the adoption of a new teacher appraisal system; the establishment of a Teachers' Service Commission and a Curriculum Development Council; the provision of a national diagnostic assessment at the primary level; and new legislation establishing a council responsible for certification and articulation of programs at the secondary and tertiary levels.

NONFORMAL EDUCATION

The Ministry of Education, Youth Affairs, and Culture has established a system of adult and continuing education that provides opportunities for the adult population to broaden their general education and acquire specific skills through its nonformal and skills-training programs. Other government ministries and departments, such as the Ministries of Agriculture, Community Development, and Health, Employment, and Labor, also offer nonformal education (NFE) programs. The largest government provider of NFE programs is Barbados Community College through its Division of General and Continuing Studies. Several nongovernmental organizations (NGOs) are also involved in providing adult education, such as the School of Continuing Studies of UWI and the Barbados Institute of Management and Productivity, and various community groups such as the Young Men's Christian Association, the Young Women's Christian Association, and the Family Planning Association. The educational programs include skills training for hobbies and potential employment as well as personal development.

TEACHING PROFESSION

The 1995 White Paper on Education Reform highlighted teacher empowerment as one means for improving the overall educational experience for all students. The low morale of teachers has negatively impacted their effectiveness in the classroom. Additional problem areas include limited career paths, inadequate opportunities for training in technical and vocational areas, and limited opportunities for training and retraining to deal with the changing society—disciplinary problems and deviance, and social problems such as drugs, AIDS, and gender issues.

A strategic set of initiatives was created to enhance teacher satisfaction and improve student performance. Included was a broad-based committee to review terms and conditions of employment of teachers and principals.

SUMMARY

As Barbados enters the new millennium, numerous reforms of its educational system have focused on helping Barbados "compete in the global market economy on equal terms in the knowledge-based and skilled-intensive industries..." (White Paper). Although many improvements have already begun, certain areas of concern will continue to be addressed. Those areas of concern include:

- Teacher empowerment designed to raise morale through incentives, new appraisal systems, upgrading of training opportunities, and establishment of a Teachers' Commission

- Curriculum reform through the establishment of a Curriculum Development Council to consider key issues like composition of the curriculum, student performance, and the need to establish attainment targets at each level of the national curriculum

- Special education, including better identification of children in need of special education services, upgraded curriculum, additional teacher training, expansion of public awareness programs, and trying to secure grant financing to support special education programs in the private sector

- Early childhood education (ECE) expansion in existing public primary schools through an acceleration of teacher training in ECE, an increase in production and dissemination of ECE curriculum materials, and use of parents as teacher aides

- Primary education focus on the main factors that impact on student learning through initial screening of primary school children for physical impairments of sight, hearing and speech; teacher training to detect emotional problems; and diagnostic testing on a national scale at ages seven and nine

- Senior and composite schools curriculum reform to meet more appropriately the educational life preparation needs of students who obtain very low scores in the Barbados Secondary Schools' Entrance Examination (BSSEE)

- National certification to provide evidence that the holder of the certificate has satisfactorily completed an approved program of secondary education and attained an acceptable level of competency in a set of subjects

- Assisted private schools government support through financing of teachers of remedial education and a subvention for introduction of information technology, along with strengthened supervision from the Ministry of Education, Youth Affairs and Culture

- Children-at-risk problems to be met through appointment of two additional education psychologists to the Ministry, greater training for guidance counselors, and a new option in the out-of-school suspension program where students report to specified locations for remedial and counseling services

- Sixth form schools curriculum expansion to include technical-vocational education, business education, and aesthetics, and establishment of a committee to review all pupil applications to ensure equitable access

- Tertiary education initiatives to rationalize and accelerate the provision and quality of education that include establishing an advisory committee to the Minister on delivery of tertiary education and coordination and articulation of programs and management of postsecondary education; creating by statute a national accreditation and certification body to deal with accreditation matters at both the secondary and tertiary levels and for private and public sector bodies; specific measures to expand access to the various postsecondary institutions, including Barbados Community College (BCC), Samuel Jackman Prescod Polytechnic (SJPP), participation in the adult and continuing education programs, and the use of distance education as a relevant tool; an advisory committee to help government keep its word and not charge tuition fees at the aforementioned institutions

- Institutional strengthening through the launching of a Barbados/Inter-American Bank (IDB) Education Project designed to address organizational and management weaknesses

- Financing education by instituting fiscal incentives to encourage community groups and the private sector to participate in the general maintenance of schools in an "Adopt-a-School" program

Perhaps the most pressing concern for Barbados in the future will be the rising costs of providing education to its citizens in this competitive world. However, the government remains committed to maintaining excellence in its educational system and to the belief that placing a premium on the education of its citizens will result in social, economic, and political growth.

BIBLIOGRAPHY

Barbados Education and Educational Facilities. Available from http://barbados.org/educate.htm.

Barbados—Education System. *World Higher Education Database 2000* International Association of Universities/ UNESCO International Centre on Higher Education. Available from http://www.usc.edu/.

The Central Intelligence Agency (CIA). *The World Factbook 2000.* Available from http://www.cia.gov/.

Coward, Louis Antonia. "Graduates' Perceptions of Program Processes and Outcomes of Selected Postsecondary Technical and Vocational Education Programs in Barbados." Ph.D. diss., Ohio State University, 1996.

Ellis, Patricia. *Adult Education in Barbados.* Caribbean Network of Educational Innovation for Development (CARNEID): UNESCO, 1993.

———. "Non-Formal Education and Empowerment of Women: Report of A Study in the Caribbean." December 1994. ERIC, ED392960.

Executive Summary of Education Sector Enhancement Program (BA_0009) Loan Proposal. Government of Barbados Ministry of Education, Youth Affairs and Culture. 1998.

Government of Barbados 1988b Barbados Development Plan 1988-1993. Ministry of Finance and Economic Affairs, Bridgetown.

Hewitt, Guy. "The Political Significance of Working Class Youth Subculture in Barbados." *Studies in Caribbean Public Policy.* Vol. 2. ed. D. Brown. Kingston, Jamaica: Canoe Press University of the West Indies, 1998. 1-29.

Lundy, Christine. "Caribbean Conference on Early Childhood Education Summary Report (1997)." ERIC, ED419577.

Senior, Olive. *Working Miracles: Women's Lives in the English-Speaking Caribbean.* Cave Hill, Barbados: University of the West Indies Institute of Social and Economic Research, 1991.

Tree, Ronald. *A History of Barbados.* New York: Random House, 1972.

White Paper on Education Reform for Barbados. The Planning Section, Ministry of Education, Youth Affairs and Culture, Barbados. July 1995.

—*Bonnie W. Epstein*

BELARUS

BASIC DATA

Official Country Name:	Republic of Belarus
Region:	Europe
Population:	10,366,719
Language(s):	Byelorussian, Russian
Literacy Rate:	98%
Academic Year:	September-May
Compulsory Schooling:	9 years
Public Expenditure on Education:	5.9%
Foreign Students in National Universities:	3,714
Libraries:	11,329
Educational Enrollment:	Primary: 625,000 Secondary: 1,064,700 Higher: 328,746
Educational Enrollment Rate:	Primary: 98% Secondary: 93% Higher: 44%
Teachers:	Higher: 40,300
Student-Teacher Ratio:	Primary: 20:1
Female Enrollment Rate:	Primary: 96% Secondary: 95% Higher: 49%

HISTORY & BACKGROUND

The Republic of Belarus (the former Byelorussian Soviet Socialist Republic) became an independent state in 1991, after the disintegration of the Soviet Union. Situated on the crossroads between Russia, the Baltic states, Poland, and Ukraine, Belarus has an important geopolitical location and covers a territory of 80,134 square miles (207,546 square kilometers) with a population exceeding 10 million. The capital and the biggest city is Minsk (1.7 million people). Of 118 ethnic groups living on its territory, the major ones are Belarusians (77.9 percent), Russians (13.2 percent), Poles (4.1 percent), and Ukrainians (2.9 percent).

Belarusians are Eastern Slavic people with a language similar to Russian. They use the Cyrillic alphabet invented by the Byzantine monk, scholar, and philosopher Cyril (827-869 A.D.) and his brother Methodius (826-885 A.D.). In the tenth to twelfth centuries, the territory of modern Belarus was part of Ancient Russia. The main method of instruction was teaching children how to read religious books copied in Turov, Vitebsk, Slutsk, Pinsk, and other major cities. One of the first Belarusian educators was the bishop Cyril Turovsky (c. 1130-1182), who wrote numerous precepts on moral values. In the thirteenth century, Belarus became part of Lithuania. In spite of the national and religious contradictions, which were tearing the Lithuanian Principality apart, literacy gradually spread among townspeople, artisans, and merchants.

After the establishment of the Polish-Lithuanian state, called Rzecz Pospolita (1569), the development of Belarusian culture was strongly affected by the Reformation. The followers of the Orthodox Church were, consequently, in an underprivileged position. The curricula of confessional Protestant schools included religious dogmata, church singing, languages (Belarusian, Latin, Greek, and sometimes Ancient Russian), rhetoric, poetry, dialectics, history, and mathematics. The emergence of printing shops resulted in the publication of textbooks, some of them in the Belarusian language.

Brotherhood schools established in 1590 in Mogilev, Brest, and other large cities had a tremendous impact on the development of Slavic culture. These schools were affiliated with Orthodox monasteries and admitted children from different social groups. The educational process was divided into two stages. In the first stage, reading, writing and church singing were taught. In the second stage, Old Slavic, Greek, grammar, rhetoric, poetics, foundations of mathematics, and philosophy were covered. Orthodoxy played an important part in the curriculum. All the organizational problems, including the length of study, were negotiated by the parents and the teacher in the presence of neighbors. The children who excelled in studies were granted honorable seats in the classroom. Corporal punishment was limited, and the schools even had elements of student self-government.

The period from the late 1700s to early 1800s saw the growth of Catholic and Uniate schools, which were often attached to monasteries. Such schools prevailed until the abolition of Unia in 1839. Most of the teaching in Catholic and Uniate schools was done in Polish. Between 1773 and 1794, general secular education developed under the influence of the Education Commission, which opened twenty schools with curricula centering on natural sciences. The first establishment of higher learning in Belarus was the Grodno Medical Academy (1775-1781).

In the 1790s, after the breakup of Rzecz Pospolita, Belarus was reunited with Russia. This resulted in the formation of 20 new Russian schools. The first teacher training seminary opened in Vitebsk in 1834. The opening of the Gory-Goretsk Agricultural School in 1840 marked the beginning of secondary professional education. The democratic trends and reforms of the 1860s fostered the development of cultural life in Belarus. By 1865 there were 567 educational institutions, including 12 secondary, 45 incomplete secondary, 21 theological, and over 400 elementary schools. The progressive public movement for the education of female students initiated the establishment of almost 30 schools for women. In response to the 1863-1864 Polish resurrection, the Russian government issued Temporary Rules, which intensified the policy of Russification in Belarusian schools. In 1867, the czarist government prohibited publishing in the Belarusian language, its use in the school curricula, and as a language of instruction. Because of insufficient financing parents had to collect their own money in order to build primary schools. For the most part, secondary schools were unaffordable for common people. In 1894 Belarus and Lithuania, which constituted one educational district, had only 16 secondary schools. The literacy rate in the age group from 9- to 49-years-old was only 32 percent.

The Russian Revolution of 1905-1907 sparked the struggle of the Belarusians for their cultural identity and creation of national schools. About 25 preschools emerged in Minsk, Vitebsk, Mogilev, Grodno, and Bobruisk. In 1906 the first illegal teachers' convention in Belarus called for the establishment of general compulsory schooling and the use of the mother tongue as a language of instruction. The same year the czarist government lifted the prohibition against publishing in Belarusian. Another convention, which assembled in Vilna in 1907, instituted the Belarusian Teachers' Union. Its activities, including the publication of a newspaper for teachers, promoted the reconstruction of public education on democratic principles, introduction of self-government,and the use of the Belarusian language in schools. By 1917, Belarus had 7,682 general education institutions, including 7,492 primary, 119 incomplete secondary, and 71 secondary schools with a total number of 489,000 students, mostly from well-to-do families. On the professional level, there were 15 secondary professional schools with nearly 1,500,000 students, 10 agricultural and 3 obstetrical schools, 8 teacher's seminaries, and three teacher training institutes. Higher education was virtually nonexistent. Although progress was evident when the Mogilev and Vitebsk pedagogical institutes were opened in 1918.

In 1919 Belarus became part of the Soviet Union. The Statute on Unified Labor School of the Russian Federation was applied to the Belarusian educational network. Its primary aim was to reshape the educational system on the basis of free compulsory schooling. Labor education was deemed the basis for ''the Communist rebirth of society'' and the medium for promoting proletarian values. Major efforts were directed against illiteracy. Most of the big schools used Belarusian as the language of instruction. The main type of school was the labor general or polytechnical school with seven years of instruction for students aged 8 to 15. In 1920, *Narkompros* (Peoples Commissariat of Education) organized a preschool department, which supervised 25 nursery schools and kindergartens, as well as 10 preschool children's homes. The search for innovation initiated the development of experimental communal schools and other nontraditional forms, which were strongly encouraged by Lenin and his wife Krupskaya. Programs of Communist ideology were introduced on all educational levels, from preschools to universities, as well as through the network of workers' clubs, libraries, and publications. Active propagation of the ''foundations of Leninism'' began in 1924. The policy of promoting workers to higher education (at the expense of other social groups), in order to train intellectuals loyal to the Soviet government, was materialized in the form of *rabfaki* (workers' faculties). The first one was opened in 1921 at the Belarusian University in Minsk. By 1935 there were 28 workers' faculties with 11,000 students. The revised university curricula included historical materialism, history of the proletarian revolution, economic policy of the dictatorship of the proletariat, and other indoctrination subjects. In 1932, it was claimed that Belarus had attained universal primary education. That same year the Soviet of People's Commissars of the Belarusian Republic made a decision about universal education for illiterate adults aged 15 to 45. By 1939 the literacy rate was 78.9 percent. In 1940 the system of professional education included 40 FZUs (primary factory schools), 6 railway schools, 58 *technicums* (secondary technical schools), and 15 institutions of higher learning.

During the period of Stalinist political terror, almost 4 million Belarusians were executed, imprisoned, deported, or otherwise forcibly relocated, among them were numerous representatives of the intellectual community. In Western Belarus, which was annexed by Poland in 1919, the situation with schooling was drastic. By the late 1930s, about 400 Belarusian schools had been closed and almost 70 percent of the population was illiterate. After the reunification of Belarus in 1939, a unified school system started functioning in Belarus. By 1941 there were about 12,000 primary and secondary schools with 1,700,000 students; 128 professional secondary schools; and 25 higher educational institutions with 56,500 students.

The Nazi troops, which occupied Belarus in 1941, destroyed 9,000 school buildings (60 percent) with all the equipment and 20 million textbooks. The forest schools located within the zones controlled by 1,108 guerrilla groups (Brest, Minsk, Vitebsk, and others) continued to work throughout the war. Professional technical schools were evacuated to the Urals and Western Siberia. After the liberation of Belarus in 1944, the school network was restored and developed further. By 1945-1946, some 24 higher educational institutions with 12,600 students had resumed their work. From 1946 to 1956 the number of students increased by 511,000 in secondary schools, 22,700 in specialized professional schools, and 35,900 in higher education.

The Twentieth Communist Party Congress condemned Stalinism and began radical reforms in all spheres of life, including the educational system. The new curricula aimed at forging close links between general education and productive labor. The period after 1959 was marked by the emergence of complex facilities, such as nursery school kindergarten. By 1976 the Republic had attained universal secondary education. In 1981 there were 3,716 preschools, 12,294 general education primary and secondary schools, 220 vocational technical schools, 135 secondary professional schools, and 32 higher educational institutions. The educational crisis of the 1980s made it evident that the system did not adequately meet national and regional requirements or create favorable conditions for the use of the Belarusian language. The innovations of the perestroika (reconstruction) period of the late 1980s and early 1990s resulted in the establishment of new types of schools, as well as bilingualism based on close relations between the Belarusian and Russian languages. The Law on Languages of the Belarus Republic (1990) and other changes followed the declaration of independence of Belarus in 1991 and contributed to the democratization and diversification of the educational system.

CONSTITUTIONAL & LEGAL FOUNDATIONS

The legal foundations of the Belarusian educational system are in the Constitution adopted in 1994 and further revised in 1996. Article 49 guarantees every Belarusian citizen the right to a free general secondary education and vocational training. Secondary specialized and higher education can be obtained free of charge in state educational institutions on a competitive basis. The principles and functions of education are further defined in the laws: ''On Education in the Republic of Belarus,'' ''On Languages,'' ''On National and Cultural Minorities,'' ''On the Child's Rights,'' as well as a number of statutes and regulations.

According to Article 14 of the Law on Education, the system is composed of preprimary education, general secondary education, professional technical education, secondary specialized education, higher education, educational staff training, advanced training and retraining, and independent education. The Law spells out the main principles of the educational policy, which include:

- the priority of human values
- national and cultural basis of schooling
- scholarly character achieved through improvement of the content of education
- forms and methods of instruction
- cooperation of research institutions with educational establishments
- connection with social practice
- continuity and structural coherence
- secular character
- compulsory basic (nine-year) schooling

One of the principles emphasized by the Law is the ecological orientation of education. This issue is of special importance because of the disaster at the Chernobyl nuclear power plant, situated six miles from the southern border of Belarus. The disaster at Chernobyl occurred on April 26 to 28, 1986, and Belarus suffered 75 percent of the effects of the explosion. As a result, more than 20 percent of its land was contaminated by radiation, and more than 500,000 people had to be relocated. Schools in Belarus were expected to educate students about security and behavior under unfavorable ecological conditions. The law also prescribes educational establishments to take care of the children's health, especially in regard to those who live in the areas affected by the radiation.

The goals of education identified by the law are:

- to promote the harmonious development of personality and realize its creative potential
- to foster national identity and preserve and increase the intellectual wealth and national values of the Belarusian people and other ethnic groups of the republic
- to develop the scientific, technical, and cultural activities in accordance with the needs of the republic
- to develop a conscious attitude towards democracy as a form of administration and existence
- to cultivate respect for the world order, based on the acknowledgement of political, economic, and social rights of all peoples

EDUCATIONAL SYSTEM—OVERVIEW

The educational system of Belarus combines the structure inherited from the Soviet Union with a new content developed as an independent state. Preprimary education, which includes nursery schools and kindergartens, is optional. Primary education (three or four years of instruction), basic secondary education (five years of instruction), and upper secondary education (two years of instruction) usually coexist within one school. Initial or secondary vocational education requires from one to four years of training. Higher education is represented by institutes, academies, and universities.

In 1998-1999, Belarus had 4,500 preschool facilities; 4,783 general education schools; 249 vocational schools; 151 specialized secondary; and 57 higher educational institutions. The total number of students exceeded 2,100,000. The number of teachers employed in the educational sphere approached 200,000. There were more than 100 advanced training and retraining institutions.

In 1990, when Belarus was still part of the Soviet Union, the law ''On Languages in Belarus'' proclaimed Belarusian the state language of the republic and stipulated the right to use Russian as the medium of international communication. After the declaration of independence in 1991, language became a political issue. The Belarusian government authorized a state program aimed at the development of Belarusian and other languages in the territory of the republic. The Constitution of 1994 (amended in 1996) gave equal status to the Belarusian and Russian languages. Article 6 of the Law on Education states that the choice of the language of instruction is voluntary. The study of Belarusian, Russian, and one foreign language is obligatory. The decision of administrative organs, as well as the request of citizens can initiate the establishment of programs with full or partial instruction in the language of a national minority.

In the 1990s, more than 3,500 schools (66.7 percent) were using Belarusian as the language of instruction. There were 140 schools with intensive study of Belarusian. In 1,600 schools the teaching was done in Russian, and 140 schools (mostly in the Grodno region) introduced Polish into their curricula.

PREPRIMARY & PRIMARY EDUCATION

According to the Law on Education (1991), the main aim of preprimary education is the stimulation of a child's natural desire to learn about the surrounding world. While the leading role belongs to the family, preschools are expected to contribute to children's moral and physical development, and provide them with access to the Belarusian language, culture, and folk traditions.

Yasli (nursery schools), which constitute the initial stage of preschool education, cater to the needs of infants from six months to three-years-old. *Dzetsady* (kindergartens) take care of children from three to six years of age

and prepare them for entry to primary school. Traditional preschools include half-day (6 hours), full-day (12 hours), and 24-hour facilities. The law prescribes that state organs, enterprises, social organizations, and individuals give material, pedagogical, and psychological support to preschool institutions. In reality, in the 1990s the state financing of preprimary education was reduced, and the financial situation in preschools significantly deteriorated. The number of institutions decreased from 4,988 in 1992 (485,000 children) to 4,500 in 1997 (434,000 children), and this tendency continues.

The innovations of the post-*perestroika* period (the 1990s) initiated the establishment of preprimary institutions of new types: family-type and boarding-type preschools, facilities with short-term stay, flexible programs, and individual schedules. They are based on the best world experience and take into account the ideas of personality-oriented pedagogy. *Vykhavatseli* (teachers) for preschools are trained in 15 educational institutions: 3 pedagogical universities, 1 pedagogical institute, 3 colleges, and 8 pedagogical secondary schools situated in Borisov, Gomel, Grodno, Minsk, Mogilev, Brest, Vitebsk, and other cities.

SECONDARY EDUCATION

General secondary education is the main part of the system of continuous education in Belarus. It is represented on three levels:

- primary school (first to fourth grade, six or seven to nine years of age)

- basic secondary school (fifth to ninth grade, ten to fifteen years of age) leading to incomplete secondary education

- upper secondary school (tenth and eleventh grade, sixteen to seventeen years of age), which leads to complete secondary education

The primary and secondary level institutions sometimes function separately (predominantly in rural areas); in the city they are usually combined within one school. The academic year begins on September 1 and continues through the end of May, and they have an examination session in the ninth and eleventh grades. School operates on a quarterly schedule, with four vacations: a week in November, two weeks in early January, a week at the end of March, and two and a half or three months in the summer. Students go to school five or six days a week. The daily number of classes varies from four in primary school to six in the senior grades. Lessons last 40 or 45 minutes, with shorts breaks between classes.

Almost all the schools are coeducational. On the primary level, children are divided into classes of twenty-five to thirty students, who study as a permanent group until the end of secondary school. The program opens with a relatively simple curriculum, with new subjects added every year. In the eleventh grade, there can be as many as 17 or even 20 subjects. The grades used for evaluation are numerical: five is excellent, four is good, three is satisfactory, and two is failure. Students who fail in two or more subjects are required to repeat the year's program. Successful completion of secondary school is the main route into higher education. In 1998-1999 the system of general secondary education in Belarus included 4,783 secondary schools with 1,650,000 students.

Primary education begins at six or seven years of age and encompasses the first three or four grades of the general education school. The reform of the 1980s, when Belarus was still part of the Soviet Union, attempted at the transition to universal four-year primary education starting with the age of six. The reform was premature and schools could not cater to the needs of all the six-year-olds. As a result, the modern Belarusian primary school allows for two options: children can start school at the age of seven and study three years (old system), or enter the first grade at the age of six and study four years with a lighter schedule and more attention given to games. The choice depends on the child's medical state and the parents' wish. The program of the first grade can be also covered in kindergarten. In the future, all primary schools are planning to adopt a four-year program.

The curricula include basics of the Belarusian and Russian languages (reading and writing), mathematics, nature study, initial knowledge about society, and national history and culture, all of which are taught by the same teacher. Other subjects are labor, music, and physical training. Great attention is given to the development of the child's individuality, personal hygiene, and a healthy way of living. Students also engage in extracurricular activities: school concerts and holiday parties, trips, excursions to museums, theaters, and libraries. In 1997-1999 the Ministry of Education, in conjunction with the National Education Institute, developed new curricula and textbooks for primary schools.

Basic secondary school (fifth to ninth grade) is compulsory and leads to incomplete secondary education, which can be continued on the upper secondary level (tenth and eleventh grade). The content of education and forms of control are based on the curricula developed according to the state requirements, as well as regional and national peculiarities. The Communist indoctrination programs, which was a significant part of the curricula during the Soviet times, have been replaced by more diversified courses that allow room for alternative points of view and personal opinions. Yet, the state control of education is strong and reveals itself in the requirements

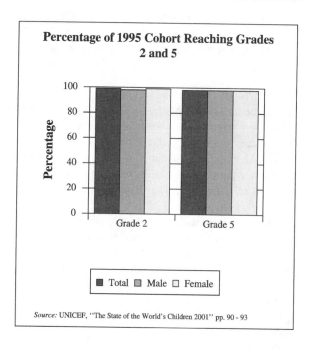

Percentage of 1995 Cohort Reaching Grades 2 and 5

Legend: ■ Total ■ Male □ Female

Source: UNICEF, ''The State of the World's Children 2001'' pp. 90 - 93

of the content of education, which are prescribed by the executive organs of the Republic. The state standards include an obligatory list of subjects and the minimum number of hours assigned for them. The major subjects are the Belarusian and Russian languages, literature, mathematics, sciences, Belarusian and world history, law, foundations of modern civilization, art, music, world culture, labor, and physical training. A foreign language (predominantly English, German, or French) is introduced in the fifth grade. Students get cumulative grades in every subject at the end of each quarter. After the ninth and eleventh grade they are required to take examinations. All students who successfully complete 11 years of study receive the Certificate of General Secondary Education. Those who get excellent marks for all the semesters of the tenth and eleventh grade, as well as the final exams, are awarded a gold medal. Students with no more than two good grades (all the others being excellent) receive a silver medal. The medals have a moral value, but they also give their owners privileges when they apply for entry to higher educational institutions. In 1998, gold medals were awarded to 6 percent and silver medals to 6.1 percent of secondary school graduates.

In addition to the traditional general education secondary schools, the 1990s saw the development of new types of institutions—gymnasiums and lyceums. Gymnasiums provide comprehensive humanitarian education, often centered on the study of foreign languages. They are expected to have a highly qualified teaching staff, use innovative textbooks, and to have modern methods of teaching. Lyceums offer professionally oriented education and are usually affiliated with higher educational or research institutions. In 1999 the Republic of Belarus had 73 gymnasiums (69,100 students) and 25 lyceums (13,600 students), which correspondingly made up 1.5 and 0.5 percent of all secondary daytime schools.

Due to the social and economic problems of the 1990s, the number of orphans and children left without proper parental care has significantly increased. In 1998 there were 27 ordinary and 22 family-type children's homes, 31 general secondary boarding schools, and 25 sanatorium-type institutions under the supervision of the Ministry of Education. The disturbing statistics of the same period showed that 10.9 percent of Belarusian children had problems with their psychic and physical development. These 21,500 students were accommodated at 80 boarding schools for mentally and physically handicapped children, 27 rehabilitation centers, and 707 special schools. There were 417 secondary school classes for students with learning disabilities. Two thousand children with health problems were tutored by visiting teachers at home.

The general secondary school reform of 1998 foresaw the development of culturally specific programs, restructuring of the curricula, and the introduction of new state standards and an innovative syllabi. One of the long-term goals was a gradual transition to 12-year secondary schooling, which would provide for a more even distribution of the study load across the curricula, and which would include 17 courses instead of 24 or 27. The new arrangement would also allow more time to students' individual needs, interests, and peculiarities, as well as a greater diversification of the educational process. An additional school year would help solve a number of demographic and social problems (e.g. insufficient, number of opportunities in the job market). Other innovative state programs dealt with the improvement of rural schools, intensification of the study of foreign languages, computerization of the education system, dissemination of 212 new textbooks, and other issues. An important step would be the development of a unified national test for admission to higher educational institutions. It would involve the creation of a national testing center, the development of assignments on all the subjects, entrance exams, and the replacement of separate exams by a universal test, which would be recognized by all higher educational institutions.

The Belarusian system of vocational training functions on two levels. The first level encompasses vocational technical schools (PTU) and apprenticeship programs for blue-collar jobs. Applicants may be accepted by PTU after 11 years of general secondary school and in this case take a year-long course to acquire a professional skill. Students with basic general education (nine grades) study three years to get both professional training and complete secondary education. The curriculum of PTU is distributed between theoretical (73 percent) and practical courses (27 percent). It includes general secondary, general professional, and special subjects, as well as electives and individual consultations.

Students are divided into groups of 12 to 25 people and are supervised by their main teacher called the "master of industrial training." Schools are usually attached to industrial enterprises, which provide students with on-the-job training. The modern tendency is to integrate several skills into the educational process in order to ensure the students' greater adaptability to the job market. In 1998, about 250 vocational technical schools with more than 130,700 students trained specialists in 400 professions. The number of PTU graduates totaled 54,400. There were 4,000 teachers and 7,363 masters of industrial education employed on the initial vocational level program.

The second level of vocational training is provided by technicums, colleges, and professional secondary schools called *vuchylishcha*. These institutions prepare middle-level technicians, assistants of higher-qualification specialists, independent qualified workers performing tasks that require both practical skills and theoretical knowledge, as well as specialists of non-production areas (librarians, obstetricians, nurses, preschool and primary school teachers). In 1999 this network comprised 151 state and 6 non-state secondary professional institutions, which provided training in 154 specialties. There were 16 professional technical colleges for students with physical disabilities, with training in 14 different specialties.

The course of study at the secondary professional level lasts from three to four years and is concluded by qualification exams and the defense of a diploma project. A number of former professional schools have been transformed into colleges. Professional schools are usually affiliated with higher educational institutions and work in close contact with them. Consequently, this arrangement can lead to a bachelor's degree at a college. Another option is for the college students to continue their studies at a higher educational institution, with the courses previously taken counting towards the university degree. Educational institutions are expected to reveal and develop the students' interests and abilities and to give them vocational guidance and advanced professional training. Integrated continuous education is provided by a study complexes' *lyceum* (college or higher educational institution) with a coordinated curricula. Faculty from higher educational institutions often lecture at colleges, assist instructors with curricula development and methodological work, participate in qualification exams, and prepare study materials. Partnerships of this kind prove to be highly effective.

Innovations in the system of vocational training are primarily defined by new trends in society. Educators have to review the inventory of professions with regard to the market demand; change the content of education by diversifying the curricula; give the students an opportunity to express their individuality and creativity; and introduce new subjects in response to the changing times. Schools must work in close contact with prospective employers, enterprises, and businesses.

HIGHER EDUCATION

The Belarusian system of higher education consists of universities, academies, and institutes. It comprises 42 state and 15 non-state higher educational institutions (VNU) with a total of 243,700 thousand students. Universities and academies offer graduate and post-graduate programs and are engaged in fundamental research. Whereas universities offer education in a wide variety of areas, academies have a narrower specialization (e.g., medical or management academies). Institutes are also highly specialized and usually have no post-graduate programs. They can function as separate entities or as part of a university. Higher educational institutions offer full-time (day) and part-time (night and correspondence) programs.

The degree that has been traditionally conferred by Belarusian higher educational institutions is Certified Specialist. It usually requires five years of training, success in final state examinations, and defense of a thesis. The study at medical institutions lasts longer and has a different set of requirements. The need to integrate into the world educational community has stimulated the introduction of two other degrees: Bachelor's, after four years of training, and Master's, after six years of instruction. The advanced scholarly degrees include *Kandydat navuk* (literally "Candidate of Sciences") and *Doktar navuk* (Doctor of Sciences). The degree of *Kandydat* is approximately equivalent to a Ph.D. and requires at least three years of post-graduate study, success in qualification examinations, and the defense of a dissertation. The *Doktar's* degree is highly prestigious and can be obtained after many years of teaching and independent research. A three-year sabbatical called *daktarantura* leads to the defense of a second dissertation of high theoretical and practical value. The defense is preceded by the publication of several dozen articles and at least one monograph. In 1999, about 54 percent of all faculty members in Belarus had advanced scholarly degrees. The total number of post-graduate students exceeded 2,500.

Teachers of higher educational institutions are promoted to faculty positions through the process of competition. Applicants submit documents, which are expected to prove their professional competence and ability to en-

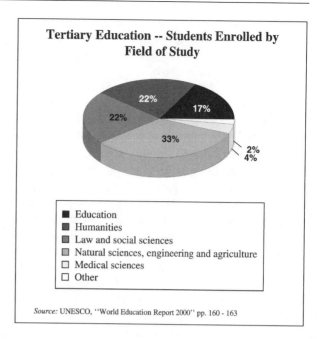

Tertiary Education -- Students Enrolled by Field of Study

22% 17% 22% 33% 2% 4%

- ■ Education
- ■ Humanities
- ■ Law and social sciences
- ▨ Natural sciences, engineering and agriculture
- □ Medical sciences
- □ Other

Source: UNESCO, "World Education Report 2000" pp. 160 - 163

gage in scholarly research. All the papers are reviewed by a special commission, which conducts an interview with the candidate. Since there is no tenure, all the faculty members have to go through this process every five years. The faculty positions are: Assistant, Senior Lecturer, *Datsent* (which usually requires a *Kandydat's* degree), and Professor (usually with a *Doktar's* degree). The scholarly ranks of *Datsent* and Professor are conferred to faculty members who have worked in the corresponding position for at least a year and have a number of post-defense publications.

A higher educational institution is headed by the Rector, elected by the Academic Council, which makes major decisions about educational policy, curricula, and staffing. The institution is divided into faculties, headed by Deans. All faculty members are organized according to their specialty into departments called *kafedry*.

Applicants to higher educational institutions must have completed secondary education. The admissions are highly selective: on the average, in 1996 there were 250 applications per 100 spots in full-time programs. Since some specialties are much more popular than others, the competition in the departments can be very intense. The prospective students have to take three to five entrance examinations. The obligatory subjects for all applicants are the Belarusian language and literature or the Russian language and literature. Other subjects, which have to be connected with the future specialty, are set up by the institution on the basis of the list, developed by the Ministry of Education, which includes: a foreign language, history of Belarus, new world history, humankind and society, geography, physics, information science, mathematics, chemistry, biology, art, music, technical drawing, and other subjects. The applicants who score the highest are admitted to free studies and are even paid a small monthly stipend. Those who have a gold or a silver medal take only one exam and are admitted if they get an excellent grade. Previously, higher education was free for all students. Now a certain percentage of students at state universities (those who passed the examinations but did not win the competition) pay tuition fees.

All the enrolled students are divided into permanent groups of 25 to 30 people. They stay together as a group throughout the period of their studies, which allows them to develop close friendships. The schedule is made for the whole group. The structure of the curricula largely depends on standards developed on the state level. This is done in order to ensure the quality of education in the whole Republic. The main categories included in the curricula are general, general professional, and specialized subjects. The share of electives is comparatively small. The academic year begins on September 1 and is divided into semesters.

Students are graded both for their current work and examinations taken at the end of each semester. The grades used for evaluation are "excellent, good, satisfactory, and unsatisfactory." In case of a failure, students are allowed to retake the examination three times, the last time before a panel of professors. If they fail, they are expelled from the university. Excellent students receive an increase to their stipend. The course of study culminates in a state profile exam and/or defense of a thesis. Students who graduate with honors are awarded a "red certificate."

Under the new socioeconomic conditions, higher education is increasingly charged with the task of restructuring the curricula, diversifying the educational process, and adapting it to the requirements of the market economy. The enrollment figures are steadily growing, mostly because of the emergence of private institutions, as well as paid programs within existing universities. The most popular and competitive programs are in management, economics, law, and foreign languages. The new specialties offered by higher educational institutions include:

- classical languages and literature

- Japanese and Chinese

- commercial activity in commodity and service markets

- standardization and certification

- printing industry technology

Among the most important tasks in higher education are:

- the preparation of a new law on higher education

- development of educational standards that would establish universal requirements for institutions of different types and provide a basis for their accreditation

- a gradual switch to multilevel higher education

- the integration of universities into the world educational community

ADMINISTRATION, FINANCE, & EDUCATIONAL RESEARCH

The Belarusian educational system is administered by the National Assembly of the Republic of Belarus (legislative function), the Council of Ministers (executive function), the Ministry of Education, and the local administrative organs. The state organs define the educational policy; formulate the requirements to educational institutions; authorize the order of their establishment, reorganization, and liquidation; allocate resources for their financing, and approve the curricula. In their turn, local organs are responsible for the development of education within the range of their control. They define the numbers and structure of personnel training, allocate funds and establish tax benefits for the educational institutions in their territory, and pay special attention to the national peculiarities of the region under their jurisdiction. Educational institutions are independent in their decisions about the organization of the educational process and their financial activities, as long as they observe the laws and respect the students' and teachers' rights.

Belarusian education is financed from state and non-state sources. The primary sources of financing are the state and local budgets. According to the law, the state funds must constitute at least 10 percent of the national revenue. Other sources include the profit from paid educational services, research activities, contract sums for personnel training, and contributions of enterprises, organizations, and individuals. In 1996 the respective share of state and non-state financing of education was 80 and 20 percent.

When Belarus was part of the Soviet Union, education in all kinds of institutions was free of charge. The new economic situation of the 1990s brought about the establishment of private institutions, as well as the development of paid programs within state institutions. In 1999, about 83.0 percent of students were studying at the expense of the state budget, whereas 16.7 percent were paying tuition fees. There were 15 non-state institutions with a total of 36.5 thousand students.

NONFORMAL EDUCATION

According to Article 17 of the Law on Education, state organs, enterprises and public organizations are encouraged to establish extra school cultural, aesthetic, scientific, technical, and sports facilities, in order to satisfy the individual requirements of children and youth. In 1996 Belarus had 3,318 different nonformal educational facilities. They provide an elaborate arrangement of instructional and recreational activities through a network of children centers (former Young Pioneer palaces), ecological, technical, and computer teenage clubs, part-time music, art, and sport schools, as well as centers of folk art and crafts. Independent education for adults is carried out through "people's universities," which organize a variety of courses on different subjects; national cultural centers; evening courses on foreign languages, accounting, and finance; and sports clubs, which are gaining more popularity. An important educational role belongs to libraries, information centers, social organizations, publishing houses, and mass media.

TEACHING PROFESSION

The Law on Education guarantees teachers adequate working conditions, protection of their honor and dignity, and salaries at least 1.5 times higher than average wages in industry. In the 1990s, though, the state of educational institutions was steadily deteriorating because of inadequate financing. Teachers' salaries were humiliatingly low, with long delays in their payment. In spite of all the difficulties, teachers still constitute one of the most enthusiastic and selfless groups of the Belarusian population.

Teachers are trained at professional secondary schools (*vuchilishcha*), teacher training institutes and universities, as well as classical universities and other higher educational institutions. In 1999 secondary schools were staffed by teachers of different ranks: 80 percent with higher education, 16 percent with specialized secondary, 3 percent with incomplete higher and 1 percent with general secondary education. Out of 17,100 faculty members of higher educational institutions, 54 percent had advanced post-graduate degrees (*Kandydat* and *Doktar*). Educators are concerned that the teaching profession on the preprimary, primary, and secondary levels has become a predominantly female profession. In 1999 there were 2,672 women and only 67 men teaching in primary schools. In higher educational institutions the figures are more evenly distributed between men and women (correspondingly 58.7 and 41.3 percent).

Every five years primary and secondary school teachers have to go through the process of attestation. As a result, they are assigned a category, which reflects the level of their professional efficiency and influences their salary. University teachers are promoted to faculty positions on a competitive basis. The upgrading of qualification is attained through faculties and institutes of advanced training, methodological seminars, and professional development courses, *spirantura* and *dactarantura*.

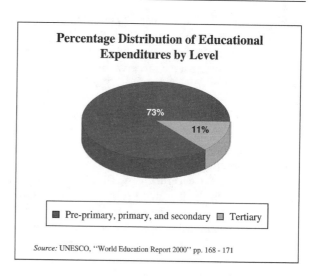

Percentage Distribution of Educational Expenditures by Level

73%
11%

■ Pre-primary, primary, and secondary ☐ Tertiary

Source: UNESCO, "World Education Report 2000" pp. 168 - 171

The research Institute of Pedagogy of the Ministry of Education, organized in 1928, is engaged in fundamental study of the history and theory of education, methods of teaching, as well as the development of state programs, curricula, and textbooks. Educational research is also conducted by the National Institute of Education, university departments of pedagogy and psychology, specialized research institutes, and laboratories. The Pedagogical Society founded in 1972 has a number of regional and city councils. Other organizations include the Teachers' Union, Council of School Directors, and the Association of Educational Researchers.

SUMMARY

Belarus' independence, the transitions to a market economy, and the quest for democratization have initiated important changes in Belarusian education. It was restructured and most of the educational institutions were subordinated to the Ministry of Education instead of to numerous ministries and agencies. Family and special education were included in the educational system. Courses indoctrinating Communist ideology were eliminated from the curricula. The content of education became more diverse, with more attention given to each student. The reform, which will continue until 2010, aims at providing equal educational opportunities for all citizens; reviving national and regional cultural peculiarities and reflecting them in the curricula; developing the legal basis of education; and working out new mechanisms of financing the educational system.

In order to integrate its educational system into the world community, Belarus is actively cooperating with Russia, the Commonwealth of Independent States (CIS), and a number of European countries. In 1999 Belarus and Russia signed a treaty on a two-state union envisioning their greater political and economic integration. The same year they adopted a joint program—The Formation and Development of a Unified Educational Community of the Belarusian-Russian Union. It is centered on a number of projects aimed at the preservation of the historical and cultural unity of the two states. The major ones are the coordination of educational standards and normative bases of the licensing; attestation and accreditation of educational institutions; the elaboration of a textbook on the history of Eastern Slavs for secondary schools; the unfolding of distance education programs; as well as the establishment of the department of Slavic Philology at Mogilev State University and the school of Slavic Studies at Smolensk State Pedagogical University. The CIS Council for Educational Cooperation was set up to ensure coordinated efforts directed towards the creation of a joint educational community, development of a mechanism of mutual equivalency of educational degrees and ranks, and generating a joint information system. In order to participate in European projects, the Republic of Belarus joined the European Cultural Convention. It also cooperates with UNESCO, the Council of Europe, TEMPUS/TACIS, the British Council, German Service of Academic Exchanges, and numerous United States organizations and agencies. Hopefully, all these efforts will stimulate an unprecedented expansion and diversification of the Belarusian educational system.

BIBLIOGRAPHY

Arlova, H.P. *Belaruskaya narodnaya pedahohika (Belarusian National Pedagogy)*. Minsk: Narodnaya Asveta, 1993.

Belarus at the Crossroads. Washington, DC: Carnegie Endowment for International Peace, 1999.

Drozd, L.N. *Razvitiye srednei obshcheobrazovatel'noi shkoly v Belorussii 1917-1941 (The Development of Secondary General Education School in Byelorussia in 1917-1941)*. Minsk, 1986.

Ermak, V.I. *Vysshie uchebnye zavedeniia Respubliki Belarus': Spravochnik abiturienta. 2000 (Higher Educational Establishments of the Republic of Belarus: Applicant's Handbook 2000)*. Minsk: TetraSistems, 2000.

Laptsionak, A.S., and V.A. Saleeu, eds. *Natsyianal'naia samasviadomasts' i vykhavanne moladzi (National Independence and the Upbringing of Young People)*. Minsk: Natsyianal'nyi institut adukatsyi, 1996.

Latyshina, D.I. *Istoriya pedagogiki. Vospitaniye I obrazovaniye v Rossii, X-nachalo XX veka. (The History of Pedagogy. Upbringing and Education in Russia, 10th-early 20th centuries)*. Moscow: Forum, 1998.

Obshcheye obrazovatel'noye prostranstvo-real'naya tsel' integratsii (Universal Educational Community-a Real Goal of Integration), 21 January 2001. Available from http://www.minedu.unibel.by/sb/2000/sb1/4.html.

Snapkouskaia, S.V. *Adukatsyinaia palityka i shkola na Belarusi u kantsy XIX-pachatku XX stst. (Educational Policy and School in Belarus in the late 19th-early 20th century)*. Minsk: Natsional'nyi in-t obrazovaniia Respubliki Belarus, 1998.

Sotsial'no-ekonomicheskie i organizatsionnye problemy obrazovaniia na etape ego transformatsii (Socioeconomic and Organizational Problems of Education at the Stage of its Transformation). Minsk: Natsional'nyi institut obrazovaniia Respubliki Belarus, 1998.

Struktura natsional'noi sistemy obrazovaniya Respubliki Belarus (Structure of the National Educational System of the Republic of Belarus), 28 January 2001. Available from http//cacedu.unibel.by/Education/BY.htm.

The System of Education in the Republic of Belarus: Basic Indicators and Tendencies of Development (Materials for National Report of the Republic of Belarus to UNESCO International Bureau of Education), 25 January 2001. Available from http://cacedu.unobel.by/Education/u2.htm.

—*Olga Leontovich*

BELGIUM

BASIC DATA

Official Country Name:	Kingdom of Belgium
Region:	Europe
Population:	10,241,506
Language(s):	Dutch, French, German
Literacy Rate:	98%
Academic Year:	September-August
Number of Primary Schools:	4,493
Public Expenditure on Education:	3.1%
Foreign Students in National Universities:	34,966
Libraries:	1,490
Educational Enrollment:	Primary: 736,782 Secondary: 1,053,445 Higher: 358,214
Educational Enrollment Rate:	Primary: 103% Secondary: 146% Higher: 56%

Teachers:	Primary: 60,738
	Secondary: 126,977
Student-Teacher Ratio:	Primary: 12:1
Female Enrollment Rate:	Primary: 102%
	Secondary: 151%
	Higher: 57%

HISTORY & BACKGROUND

Belgium covers a small geographic area of 32,547 square kilometers and has a population slightly greater than 10 million (10,239,085 in the year 2000). The country is often described as being situated at the "center" of Europe, since the exact geographic center of the 15 member countries of the European Union is located in the Belgian province of Namur and the political seat of the European Union is located in Brussels, the nation's capital.

Belgium's history of numerous conquests by neighboring powers has given rise to strong cultural pluralism. Celts populated the area until the Roman conquest under Julius Caesar in 57 B.C.E. The ensuing period of *Pax Romana* was characterized by a blending of Germanic and Latin cultural influences and economic progress in the form of improved trade and the rudiments of an education system.

Christianity entered Belgium in the fourth century A.D., but receded temporarily with the conquests of the Franks one century later. Linguistic and cultural pluralism characterized the northern part of what is now Belgium. The establishment of a proto-Dutch language, a Germanic and Latin influenced language, was evidence of the variety in culture and language. Under the powerful leadership of emperor Charlemagne of the Carolingian dynasty, school education received its second rudimentary movement.

The Middle Ages saw the development of textile and metallurgy industries, and the lower southern countries became the crossroads of trade. In the fifteenth century various parts of the lower southern countries were united by the Dukes of Burgundy. Under their rule Belgium became a center of intellectual and artistic endeavors. Austrian rule began in 1500, under Emperor Charles V, and was followed by Spanish rule and the imposition of Catholicism. Belgium became part of the French empire when Napoleon rose to power in 1794 and the *Code Napoléon* became the basis of the country's civil law. After Napoleon's defeat at Waterloo (in Belgium), the Congress of Vienna (1814-15) united the southern (Belgium) and northern (Holland) regions of the Netherlands, to establish a barrier against future French aggression. The

forced union led to protests by Catholics against the influence of a protestant Dutch King in clerical matters, and by Belgian liberals who demanded more political freedom.

Revolution against Dutch rule led to Belgium's independence in 1830 and the establishment of a constitutional monarchy, with an administrative division of the country into nine provinces (West Flanders, East Flanders, Antwerp, Brabant, Limburg, Hainaut, Namur, Liége, and Luxembourg) and more than 500 municipalities. Belgium's independence imposed its role as a buffer zone during the Congress of Vienna, and proved to be a political complication. The surrounding major national powers accordingly imposed neutrality on the newly independent state. Belgium nevertheless became involved in international conflict on several occasions, first as it established colonial rule in central Africa's Congo region under Leopold II, and subsequently during the two world wars.

CONSTITUTIONAL & LEGAL FOUNDATIONS

Education in Belgium is regulated by the first Constitution of 1831, by the constitutional reform establishing cultural and linguistic communities (completed in 1993), and by several school laws. Article 17 of the Constitution of 1831 set "freedom of education," prohibiting efforts to hinder said freedom, and that the state would legislate publicly funded education. Article 17 has been consistently interpreted as meaning that the state must fund education but could not hold a monopoly in it, and that free institutions—in particular the Catholic Church—may provide public education parallel to the state. Accordingly, Belgium has several education systems, and the understandably numerous disputes between these systems have been settled primarily by means of supplemental legislation.

Legislative action of May 1914 instituted compulsory education, to begin in the fall of the year during which the child reached age six. Initially, education was compulsory for eight years. The legislative action also stated that a Belgian could become a primary school teacher having completed only two years of education beyond primary school. In 1983, however, Belgium initiated 12 years of compulsory education, from age 6 to age 18. However, children as young as two and a half years old can attend preprimary education. Of the 12 required years, 9 must be full-time, and the last 3 years (ages 15 through 18) may be spent going to school part-time.

The School Pact of 1958 (made into law in 1959) recognized two basic types of schools in the provision of primary and secondary education, official schools organized by state bodies, and free schools, most of which are

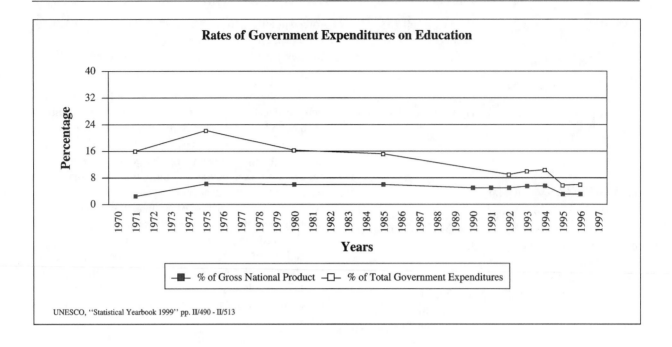

Rates of Government Expenditures on Education

UNESCO, "Statistical Yearbook 1999" pp. II/490 - II/513

Catholic. Parents were given complete freedom to select the type of school attended by their children. Moreover, the state was required to provide sufficient numbers of schools of both types within commuting distance, by direct provision of official schools, subsidies to free schools, or provision of school buses. Free schools that receive a state subsidy could not charge tuition or require fees for textbooks. The 1959 law also required official primary and secondary schools to provide two hours of instruction per week in religion or morals. While almost uniquely Catholic in 1959, religious instruction gradually came to be offered in other faiths, as well. Regardless of their religious beliefs, many parents elect to enroll their children in nondenominational moral instruction.

An immediate political problem generated by independence and affecting education policy was the selection of French as the national language, thereby essentially requiring bilingualism on the part of the Flemish population without parallel imposition on francophones. Throughout Belgium, all administrative offices, courts, hospitals, and other institutions functioned using French as their language. In the Flemish provinces, secondary and university education could only be obtained in French, while primary education was available in Flemish, taught in one of the dialects of the region. By the mid-nineteenth century, a Flemish political movement had developed under the leadership of Flemish intellectuals, who adopted the Dutch language spoken by their northern neighbor as a unifying language for the Flemish people, pushing the diverse multitude of local dialects into the background (a move that has come to be criticized by scholars who see in it the deepening marginalization and even disappearance of local culture and

folklore). Legislation passed in 1898 recognized Dutch alongside French as an official language. However, the Flemish population continued to be treated as second best. While a 1932 law required that the language of instruction in primary and secondary education be that of the region (Dutch in Flanders, French in Wallonia and German in the municipalities of the eastern part of Belgium), the law also provided too many loopholes for the Flemish to give up demands for cultural equality.

After the Second World War, relations between the language and cultural communities of Belgium became increasingly strained, as the Flemish northern part of the country realized more rapid economic growth and had a larger population than the French speaking southern part. By the beginning of the 1960s several radical political parties gained popular power, notably the *Volksunie* and the *Front des Francophones*. A number of new laws, passed in 1962 and 1963, attempted to settle the language wars by establishing a linguistic frontier that ran horizontally through the middle of the country and requiring the language of instruction for primary and secondary schools to be that of the region. In the bilingual area of Brussels, children were to receive instruction in their "mother tongue," which was determined on the basis of a written declaration by the head of the family. The 1963 law further allowed teaching of a second language to be initiated in third grade, in primary schools that were located in the Brussels region, while primary schools located in Flanders and Wallonia were required to do so only in fifth grade. As a result, "frenchification" of the Brussels capital region, geographically located to the north of the language border continued, fueling the frustration of the Flemish population.

Continued demands for cultural self-determination led to a revision of the constitution and Belgium was transformed into a federal state through four stages of constitutional reforms, which were effected in 1970, 1980, 1988-89, and 1993. Belgian education policies are intertwined with its political progress towards federalism. An important step towards constitutional reform was the passage of language laws from 1873 to 1963, which ultimately recognized French, Dutch, and German as the three official languages of the Belgian state. In response to continuing Flemish demands for cultural autonomy, constitutional reforms of 1970 and 1980 established three geographic regions: the Flemish Region (*Vlaams Gewest*), the Walloon Region (*Région Wallonne*) and the bilingual capital region of Brussels (*Région Capitale/Hoofstedelijk Gewest*), as well as three cultural/linguistic communities (Dutch, French, and German). Each cultural/linguistic community obtained its own parliamentary government. While the Flemish and Walloon geographic regions would also have their own government, the government of the Flemish region coincides with that of the Flemish community. The French language community does not coincide easily with the French region (Wallonia), since the French speaking population of the capital region of Brussels is large in comparison with that of Wallonia, while the Dutch speaking population of Brussels is small compared with that of the Flemish region. Complicating matters even more, the German cultural/linguistic community comprises the population living in the eastern portion of the Walloon geographic region.

The third phase of constitutional reform, initiated in 1989, operationalized the previously established Brussels capital region (*Région Capitale/Hoofstedelijk Gewest*). It, too, was endowed its own parliamentary government. On July 14, 1993, the new Constitution was voted into law, with as its first sentence ''Belgium is a federal state, constituted of several cultural/linguistic communities and geographic regions.'' Approximately 58 percent of the population lives in the Flemish region, 33 percent in Wallonia, and 9 percent in Brussels. Of those living in Wallonia, 70,000, or 2.1 percent are German and constitute the German community. Article 24 of the new Constitution decentralized educational authority and transferred it to the communities. Three types of schools coexist within each of the three communities: secular schools administered directly by the communities, grant-aided schools administered by provinces and local communes, and grant-aided free schools with or without religious denomination.

Education policy also is becoming more and more influenced by the needs imposed by Belgium's membership in the European Union (EU). The influence of the EU is especially evident in the teaching and utilization of technology in schools, provision of equal opportunity to children of immigrants, the equivalency ratings of diplomas obtained in other EU member countries, and access to educational exchange programs such as ERASMUS, LINGUA, and SOCRATES.

The linguistic configuration of Belgium is more intricate than evidenced by the three language communities, each of which oversees its own unilingual cultural institutions, since in each of these communities there are significant groups of ''foreign'' people whose mother tongue is different from that of the language community. These groups, constituting 11.3 percent of Wallonia, 4.2 percent of Flanders, and 27.2 percent of Brussels (Swing 1991/92), comprise educated European Community members as well as second and third generation immigrant workers whose origins are from Italy, Turkey, Morocco, and other countries. While direct immigration to Belgium has virtually come to a standstill, children and grandchildren of migrant workers continue to crowd Belgian schools and will comprise increasing percentages of the school age population. While close to 15 percent of the Belgian population is age 15 or younger, the percentages are the same, or are much higher among Belgians whose ethnicity is Italian (15 percent), Spanish (22 percent), Turkish (43 percent) or Moroccan (48 percent). While Dutch-language schools tend to attract relatively fewer ''foreign'' children, because children have been socialized in the French language, Belgian francophone children are increasing their participation in these schools owing to favorable student-teacher ratios, the recognition of the need for fluency in the Dutch language for economic advancement, and because of racist sentiments on the part of some parents. To deal with these realities of trilingualism, the European Community funded the experimental Foyer Project in 1981. The program recruited immigrant children into Dutch-language schools, where speaking and writing of both the native language and Dutch are stressed, and French is taught as a second language, even though many children are familiar with a street language version of French. The Dutch language is introduced gradually, for a few hours each week, until the child is literate in the home community language. Stressing the importance of the mother tongue is rooted in the belief that it provides the cognitive base for learning, together with Dutch, which eventually becomes the language of instruction for children enrolled in the program.

The approximately 850 square kilometer German-speaking area of eastern Belgium (Eupen-Malmédy) has seen substantial progress towards autonomy in the Belgian federal state. After the defeat of Napoleon at Waterloo in 1815, the two German regions became part of Prussia, remaining so until the end of World War I when the 1919 Treaty of Versailles granted it to the Belgian state. Education policy relating to the language of instruction has varied substantially in the schools of this region, including a period of German unilingualism during the annexation of the region by Germany, followed by a period of imposition of the French language in education and government between 1945 and 1963. The year 1963 was a turning point, marking a move toward decentralization and regionalization and emergence of a new generation of German-speaking intellectuals. The nation's constitutional changes, leading to the four-stage reform of Belgium into a federal state, provided important additional stepping stones in the region's move towards educational autonomy.

Linguistic legislation of 1963 provided that German would be the language of instruction in all classes. A survey of parents, teachers and school principals, conducted in 1976, showed that extreme positions relative to the use of French (no teaching in French or all teaching in French) were those of a minority. Schools in the region range from those in which all classes are taught in German to those where German and French languages exist side by side to schools in which all classes are taught in French. The third stage of the completion of the Belgian federal state, completed in 1989, gave near complete independence in education matters to the three language communities from the central government, including the small German-speaking language community. Today, the people of this region are no longer Walloons or even Germans-they have evolved into German-speaking Belgians.

EDUCATIONAL SYSTEM—OVERVIEW

Of the total population of 10.2 million, 2.4 million are 19 years or younger, roughly evenly divided by sex. The school population was 2,254,000 in the year 2000, with 399,000 children enrolled in preschool, 778,000 in primary school, 779,000 in secondary school, and 298,000 in higher education, of whom 128,000 were in universities and 170,000 in non-university institutions. The rapid aging of the Belgian population is evident in the numbers of school age children. In only five years, compared with the 1995-1996 school year, enrollments have declined from 428,000 to 399,000 in preschool, although higher education enrollments are still rising somewhat. In the following two decades, the pupil-teacher ratio will likely decrease in primary and secondary schools.

The education system is divided in four general parts: preschool education for ages 2½ to 6, primary education for ages 6 to 12, secondary education for ages 12 to 18, and tertiary education in both university and non-university format averaging four years. The general school year starts in September for preprimary through secondary education and in the second week of October at universities. School holidays and vacations include Christmas and Easter vacations, several single-day holidays, such as Armistice and Labor Days (November 11 and May 1, respectively), and summer vacation starting on July 1.

Owing originally to Article 17 of the Constitution of 1831 (which was retained as Article 24 in the new constitution), Belgium has more private than public schools, and almost all private schools are government subsidized. Federalization of education in 1989 gave the communities authority to organize education with federally provided financial resources and gave them very few areas of decision-making under federal control. The federal government determines the length of compulsory education, the minimum requirements for obtaining diplomas, and pensions and other benefits of teachers. Although at the community level the education authorities can set their own time tables, curriculum, and teaching methods, education has remained fairly comparable across the three communities. Belgian educators are well aware of the need to retain high standards in education, and to maintain its strong position among the world's 15 main trading nations.

PREPRIMARY & PRIMARY EDUCATION

Preprimary or preschool education (*Enseignement préscolaire/Voorschool onderwijs*) is separate and not compulsory and is provided free of charge at three levels, covering the age groups of two and a half to four years old, four to five years old, and five to six years old. Parents may have to provide assistance in the form of meals, transportation, and activities outside the classroom. More than 90 percent of Belgian children are enrolled in the first level. The number of pupils in preprimary education runs at roughly more than 120,000 for ages three, four, and five. At age five, the number is only half as much, since children who are six years old before September enter primary school. Primary education comprises six years of instruction, divided in three cycles of two years each. The school week has 28 periods of instruction, consisting of 50 minutes each. With five days of instruction per week and 182 school days per year, annual instruction is 849 hours.

Upon satisfactory completion of the sixth grade, pupils receive a Certificate of Primary Education, which guarantees acceptance into secondary education. Primary schools are generally coeducational, with the exception of some denominational private schools. Subjects taught include the mother tongue, a second language, history, mathematics, music, physical education, science, social education, artistic activities, and geography. While compulsory subjects are determined by the community governments, they are very similar. For children 10 years of age in the third cycle of primary education, the number of hours of compulsory subjects totals 848-850 hours for the school year, distributed in the three communities. The time table for the German community closely emulates that of the French community, with the main difference in its 90 hours of compulsory foreign language instruction instead of a flexible time table, which is explained by the fact that the German speaking part of Belgium lies within Wallonia and familiarity with French is emphasized as early as preschool.

SECONDARY EDUCATION

Secondary education in Belgium covers a six-year period, divided in three cycles of two years each, named the observation, orientation, and determination cycles. While a number of subjects are compulsory, students must make curricular choices beginning in the first year of study, ultimately leading to a variety of specializations that generally combine two lines of study. Compulsory subjects for students of ages 13 and 16, at the end of the observation and orientation cycles, generally include mathematics, natural sciences, human sciences, foreign languages, mother tongue, physical education, and artistic activities. The scheduling of compulsory subjects is identical in the French and German communities. While secondary schools in the Flemish community also require the same number of overall hours per year (849 at age 13 and 850 at age 16), they differ from secondary schools in the French and German communities by requiring fewer hours of instruction in the mother tongue, in physical education, and in the natural and human sciences, while requiring more hours in artistic activities, optional compulsory subjects, and other subjects.

A 1971 law drastically reformed the structure of secondary education that had been established during the school wars of the 1950s. It set up a Type I education track that paralleled the traditional education—called Type II—which provided students with very little curricular choice once they had entered lower secondary education in a particular subject area. The traditional education track was heavily influenced by classical languages (Greek and Latin), which could be pursued in their own right or in combination with sciences and mathematics. Type I is a modern education track, divided in three cycles of two years each (observation, orientation, and determination cycles), with a choice of orientation at the end of the first cycle. Although the allocation of school resources varies according to type of education, a single school may offer different orientations or streams. Type I coexists with Type II, and has become more common since its introduction. Of the 18 specialties that can be selected by pupils, eight are combinations with mathematics, six require Latin, and four require Greek. However, modern fields of study have been introduced, such as combinations involving physical education (tracks 7 and

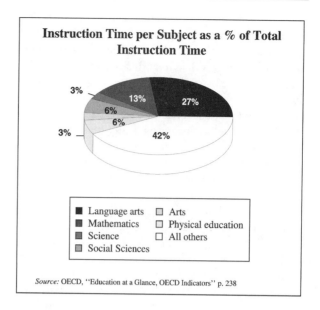

Instruction Time per Subject as a % of Total Instruction Time

3% 13% 27% 6% 6% 3% 42%

■ Language arts ☐ Arts
■ Mathematics ☐ Physical education
■ Science ☐ All others
■ Social Sciences

Source: OECD, ''Education at a Glance, OECD Indicators'' p. 238

8), economics (tracks 9, 16, and 17), modern languages (tracks 14, 15, 16, and 17), and tourism. Since the number of options and streams available to students has greatly increased with Type I education, so have public expenditures on education. Availability of the two types of secondary education has helped equalize opportunities for pupils from different cultural backgrounds and social classes, an important goal of education reform.

In lower secondary education, students follow a fairly common curriculum during the observation cycle, and then make a choice between general education leading to a university track, vocational education, technical, or artistic education. The option to transfer from one type of education to the other is used more frequently by students wishing to move from general to vocational education. Students in the vocational stream receive the same certificate as those in other streams, although they sometimes have to spend more than six years to obtain the secondary education certificate.

Students can obtain a general lower secondary education certificate after three years, a general upper secondary education diploma after six years in the general, technical, or artistic education streams, and after seven years in vocational education. There are no common examinations and inspectors are utilized to validate adherence to educational standards. The completion rate for the secondary education certificate is 65 percent and approximately one in three adolescents leave compulsory education without having obtained any qualifying certificate at the age of 18.

Education & Technology: Education authorities have begun to promote the inclusion of information and communication technology (ICT) in schools, especially within a national five-year initiative started in 1997-1998. Efforts are not equally aggressive at all levels of education, however. The French and Flemish communities have incorporated ICT in the primary education curriculum since 1997, but with a somewhat different perspective. In the French community, a 1997 decree on missions of the school system stipulated that ICT would be mainstreamed into education using skills platforms, which were introduced in 1999. The most common emphasis by the various education authorities in the French community is to promote ICT as a learning tool. Financing has focused on purchases of equipment, training by pupils and teachers, and use of the Internet. Computer hardware was distributed to all primary and secondary schools over a period of three years. Programming skills do not constitute a curricular objective at the primary level. In the Flemish community, the initiative focuses on acquisition and distribution of software by the Ministry of Education. The ministry also provides the planning framework and time schedule for introduction of ICT, and all pupils are expected to be proficient in the use of ICT and in data processing by the end of primary school.

The German community emphasizes introduction of ICT beginning at the lower secondary level and continuing through the upper level, giving attention to all areas except for computer programming. One hundred hours of compulsory instruction in ICT is incorporated in the curriculum of secondary schools in this community. In both the French and the German community, ICT subject competency must be demonstrated for students to progress to the next year. At the upper secondary level, the Flemish community is the only one of the three that has not yet included ICT in the curriculum, although it is in the process of formulating requirements that students should master by the end of the sixth year. In the German community, ICT is an optional subject at this level of study.

In the French and Flemish communities, basic ICT competency training is a compulsory component of the initial training of general class teachers and for those specialized in certain subjects such as mathematics. In the German community, in-service training is relied upon to achieve teacher ITC competency.

HIGHER EDUCATION

Tertiary or higher education is offered in universities, settings in which teaching and research are combined, and at other institutions of higher learning and training. The typical route into the university track is via the diploma of secondary high school education. Until 1965, higher education followed the traditional French system and was confined largely to four universities, of which two were run by the state (Gent and Liége), two used Dutch as the language of instruction (Gent and Brus-

sels), and two used French (Brussels and Liége). Laws of 1965 and 1970 made possible the creation of new universities and other institutions providing higher education, and divided higher education into long-type and short-type. As a result of these reforms, Belgium obtained a total of 17 university institutions and 407 institutions for higher education. These institutions reflect its multifaceted pluralism in culture, religion, language of instruction, philosophy, and political leanings.

There are six long-standing major universities, of which two (Liége and Gent) are state universities, two are catholic (Leuven and Louvain-la-Neuve), and two are free universities (the Université Libre de Bruxelles or ULB and the Vrije Universiteit van Brussel or VUB). The Catholic University of Leuven was founded in 1425 by papal decree and is one of the oldest in Europe. In 1968 the Flemish university elected to remain in the Flemish city of Leuven, banishing the university's French component to a new location at Louvain-la-Neuve, a town in the middle of the Walloon countryside. Thence, the Katholieke Universiteit and the Université Catholique became two separate institutions. The medical faculty moved to the Brussels suburb of Woluwe. About half of the universities offer comprehensive programs, including philosophy, letters, social sciences, economics, law, natural sciences, and medicine. Including the Royal Military School and the joint research institute of the Free University of Brussels, there are a total of 19 universities in Belgium.

All universities offer two levels (called cycles) of university education. Students obtain the *Candidature* (*Kandidaat*) after two years and the *Licence* (*Licentiaat*) after four years. Universities in the French community offer a third cycle leading to the diploma of specialized studies (*DES, diplôme d'études spécialisées*), the diploma of advanced studies (*DEA, diplôme d'études approfondies*), teaching qualification (*agrégation*), or the doctorate degree for which a thesis must be completed. The third cycle requires a minimum of one and up to three additional years of study. The university curriculum in the French community is organized in three sectors (human and social sciences; sciences; health sciences), containing 22 different fields of study overall. Professional and technical higher education pursued at non-university institutions of higher learning (*Hautes écoles*) comprises the long type (four to five years) or the short type (two to three years), and prepares students entering professions in industry, commerce, arts, and the fields of paramedical maritime studies.

In the Flemish community, non-university higher education in *hogescholen* and other institutions was reorganized in 1995-96 to make the curricular requirements similar to those in universities. Short-type and long-type tertiary education in those institutions was replaced by first-cycle and second-cycle coursework. The reforms caused the merger of 163 institutions of higher learning into 29 additional *hogescholen*. Students in *hogescholen* make up 60 percent of all higher education students in the community. Since Belgian universities have an open admissions policy, increasing numbers of Dutch students study at Flemish universities and other institutions of higher learning. Some observers believe that this open admissions policy contributes to the high dropout rate of nearly 50 percent in the Community. Flemish universities also have begun to collaborate with the universities of the Netherlands in the "open university" model, a distance education environment, serving a student body that includes many part-time and older students, and making use of modern technologies to deliver instruction. Multimedia technology is being widely applied to innovate and redesign curricula, to deliver instruction, and to enhance student learning. In the 1990s, cooperation between universities in the Flemish community with those in the Netherlands led to stringent quality control in the form of self-assessment by institutions and peer evaluation.

In June 1987 the council of the European Communities initiated the ERASMUS higher education program (European Community Action Scheme for the Mobility of University Students), designed to foster:

- students incorporating study in another member country, contributing to direct experience in social and economic life of members of the labor force;

- cooperation between universities and other institutions of higher learning of the member states;

- inter-university mobility of faculty;

- citizen interaction;

- development of a pool of university graduates experienced in inter-community cooperation.

Success of this ambitious program would require establishment of a European cooperative university network, thus far nonexistent, grant funding for both students and faculty, enhanced recognition of diplomas, length of study, and increased reliance on conferences and similar academic activities. The commission provides financial support to universities in the member states for the establishment of Inter-University Cooperation Programs (ICPs) that tie in with the five stated goals.

During the adoption of the second phase of ERASMUS, in the 1988-89 academic year, Belgian universities were involved in 191, or 17.5 percent, of the 1,091 funded ICPs from the twelve member countries, and Belgian ICPs provided grants to 219 university students, or 3.1 percent of the 7,031 total in the European Community. While European students entering the program in Bel-

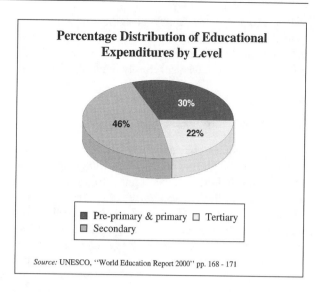

Percentage Distribution of Educational Expenditures by Level

30%

46%

22%

■ Pre-primary & primary □ Tertiary
▨ Secondary

Source: UNESCO, "World Education Report 2000" pp. 168 - 171

gium encountered a number of academic problems, particularly in relation to foreign language courses and examinations being administered in a foreign language, Belgian students experienced relatively few academic difficulties, with only 11 percent performing at a level below that of domestic students in the member countries' institutions of higher learning. Participation by Belgian students in ERASMUS had increased steadily from 1,385 students in 1989-1990, to a high of 8,111 in 1995-1996.

In the 1990s two new programs have been introduced in the European Union: SOCRATES and LEONARDO DA VINCI. While the latter supplants earlier vocational training programs, SOCRATES has replaced the community programs of ERASMUS and LINGUA (a community language teaching program) and is intended to provide a European dimension in education at all levels.

University Research: Basic research has been part of university activities and education since 1874, and several university institutes connected with Belgian universities have achieved international reputations in scientific research. The Center for Human Heredity at the Katholieke Universiteit Leuven has achieved international recognition in gene technology research, and the Inter-University Microelectronics Center in Leuven, established in 1984, is a leader in computer chip technology. The Rijksuniversiteit Gent maintains a very large bacteria bank and its Plant Genetic Systems, established in 1982, is renowned for its research in developing insect-resistant plants. Several scientific research projects at Belgian universities have also become part of larger EU and international programs. The AIDS epidemic in Africa was first documented by Belgian epidemiologists and the European network for AIDS treatment is coordinated by a faculty member from the Université Libre de Bruxelles. Moreover, the faculty of agronomic sciences at Gembloux is a participant in the European program Biotech, and the Université de Liége has a space research department that collaborates closely with the European Space Agency.

TEACHING PROFESSION

Formal education requirements for teachers increase according to the level of education in which they are expected to teach. Initial teacher training for the preprimary and primary levels (2½ to 12 years of age) requires three years of concurrent academic/teaching training and teaching observation at the *Institut Supérieur Pédagogique* (French) or the *Pedagogische Hogeschool* (Flemish). Prospective teachers graduate with a teaching diploma that details a specialty in either preschool or primary school. They are expected to teach all subjects. The initial training for teachers in lower secondary education (12 to 15 years of age) also takes place at the *Institut Supérieur Pédagogique* or the *Pedagogische Hogeschool*, where students pursue three years of course work in a specific and an optional subject and increasingly intensive training and practice in teaching, receiving a teaching diploma at the end of three years. Teaching in the upper secondary level (15 to 18 years of age) requires four to five years of university education. The requisite teacher training courses and practice can be taken alongside with the other courses during the last two years or the final year of university study. Alternatively, students may take a two-year part time course in teacher training upon graduation. Teachers at this level have the *Licence* or *Licentie* degree as well as a separate teaching diploma. A doctorate degree is generally required to teach in tertiary education, especially at the university level. It is not unusual for teachers with a doctorate degree in upper secondary education and who also are productive scholars to become university professors when they have matured. All teachers are employees of the respective community's administrative education authority and must go through a period of probation before obtaining a permanent appointment.

Belgian teachers have the right to pursue limited in-service training. Each of the communities make available noncompulsory continuing training for teachers, and certificates are awarded accordingly, making it possible to apply for higher level positions. In-service training covers a variety of subjects, including additional education in the sciences, development of communication skills, provision of pluralist education for immigrants and, above all, introduction of new computer technologies.

In the 25 years following the School Pact of 1958, the teaching profession was held in high regard, especially at the secondary and tertiary levels. Teachers in the upper secondary education level enjoyed an elite social status and enjoyed relatively high salaries. In the 1980s and 1990s, it had been suggested that the profession may be losing status, while at the same time demands on teachers were increasing due to curricular reform and the requirements of delivering pluralist education. However, surveys of teachers seemed to indicate continued high levels of job satisfaction. For example, a teacher survey on satisfaction levels in French-speaking Belgian schools in the Free Catholic System (Meuris 1993), revealed that teachers in nursery schools were more satisfied with their profession than were those in primary education, while those in the first cycle of secondary education conformed with the satisfaction levels of teachers in primary education. Generally, the experience of teachers was a positive one.

Belgian educators were faced with new challenges from the European Union. During the July through December period of the Dutch presidency of the European Community, teacher training received special attention. The Treaty on European Union (The Maastricht Treaty of 1992) made up for a shortcoming of the original Treaty of Rome (1957), which incorporated a specific provision for a common policy on vocational training (Article 128), but was silent on the overall area of formal education. The Maastricht Treaty began its Article 127 with the statement ''The Community shall contribute to the development of quality education by encouraging cooperation between Member States and, if necessary, by supporting and supplementing their action, while fully respecting the responsibility of the Member States for the content of teaching and the organization of education systems and their cultural and linguistic diversity'' (Rudden and Wyatt 1994). Teachers were mentioned in Articles 126 and 127. Article 126 aimed community action at ''encouraging mobility of students and teachers, . . . the development of youth exchanges and of exchanges of socio-educational instructors, . . . and development of distance education,'' while Article 127 aimed action at encouraging ''mobility of instructors and trainees.'' Educators were facing the challenge of providing access to the wealth of diversity of knowledge that comprised the people of the union.

SUMMARY

Following independence in 1830, provision of education in Belgium has gone through several phases. Nearly a century and a half of cultural and language strife has ended with constitutional reform and the formation of a federal state. The concomitant introduction of reforms in education have progressively decentralized decision making from the federal government and towards the communities. Throughout the reform, Belgium has maintained the spirit of Article 17 of the Constitution of 1930, now Article 24 of the new Constitution, which guarantees that parents can choose the type of school (secular or denominational) they wish their children to attend, and that education will be financed by government funding. Compulsory education has progressively been extended to 18 years of age, with students given the option of going to school part time after their fifteenth birthday. Traditional secondary education, modeled on the French system and basically providing a transition to universities, has been reformed into Type I (modern) and Type II (traditional) education, greatly increasing curricular specialties ranging from general to vocational and artistic education, and providing opportunity to students to change direction after the observation stage and even between Type I and Type II education. However, completion rates are still only around 65 percent, leaving many young people without a secondary education diploma.

In universities and other institutions of higher learning, curricula and study cycles are becoming increasingly comparable across institutions and across national boundaries. Belgian students show significant participation in the programs organized by the European Commission; the pluralist cultural background and extensive language skills acquired in diverse Belgium helps them succeed in such programs. Belgium must continue to meet the challenge of providing high quality education to its people, as they are the primary resource for a nation of this small size. Despite the fact that education is organized by many different authorities, quality has remained high, and the required courses in the different communities are not diverging drastically over time.

The future holds a number of challenges. Financing a pluralist education system as diverse as that of Belgium leads to high costs per pupil. Although the population is aging, it does not mean that education costs are predicted to decline in the future, since adult life long education is becoming more important and the demands of technology and multimedia education drive up costs. Teachers requiring in-service training also contribute to cost increases. Belgium must continue to facilitate the recognition of diplomas and credentials across its own internal community borders as well as vis-à-vis present and prospective members of the European Union.

BIBLIOGRAPHY

Brutsaert, Herman. "Home and School Influences on Academic Performance: State and Catholic Elementary Schools in Belgium compared." *Educational Review 50* (February 1998): 37-43.

Cahill, Helen et al. "Blind and Partially Sighted Students' Access to Mathematics and Computer Technology in Ireland and Belgium." *Journal of Visual Impairment and Blindness 90* (March/April 1996): 105-14.

Commission of the European Communities. "ERASMUS: European Community Program for the Development of Student Mobility in the European Community." *European Education 23* (Summer 1991): 5-27.

Driessen, Geert. "The Limits of Educational Policy and Practice? The Case of Ethnic Minorities in the Netherlands." *Comparative Education 36* (February 2000): 55-72.

European Commission Education Information Network (Eurydice). *Key Data on Education in the European Union*. 4th ed. Brussels, Belgium: Eurydice European Unit, 2000.

European Commission Education Information Network (Eurydice). "Belgium." In *Two Decades of Reform in Higher Education in Europe: 1980 Onwards*. 195-215. Brussels, Belgium: Eurydice European Unit, 2000.

Fletcher, Ann. *Belgium: A Study of the Educational System of Belgium and a Guide to the Academic Placement of Students in Educational Institutions of the United States*. American Association of Collegiate Registrars and Admissions Officers, 1985.

Kiefer, Rob. "University Everywhere." *European Education 26* (Winter 1994/95): 12-17.

Koninklijk Atheneum Etterbeek. *Studierichting*, 2001. Available from www.luon.be/.

Maiworm, Friedhelm and Ulrich Teichler. "ERASMUS Student Mobility Programs 1991-92 in the View of the Local Directors." *European Education 30* (Fall 1998): 27-55.

Massit-Folléa, Françoise. *L'Europe des Universités; L'Enseignement supérieur en Mutation*. Paris: La Documentation Française, 1992.

Meuris, Georges. "Satisfaction or Dissatisfaction of Teachers Surveys in French-Speaking Belgian Schools." *European Education 25* (Fall 1993): 70-80.

Nationaal Instituut voor de Statistiek. *Statistieken: Bevolking en Onderwijs*. Belgium: Ministerie van Ekonomische Zaken, 1998-2001.

Phillips, David, ed. "Introduction: Aspects of Education and the European Union." Special issue of *Oxford Studies in Comparative Education 5* (1995): 7-11.

Rudden, Bernard and Derrick Wyatt, eds. *Basic Community Laws*. 5th ed. Oxford: Clarendon Press, 1994.

Schifflers, Leonhard. "75 Years of Education in the German-Speaking Areas of Eastern Belgium." *European Education 26* (Fall 1994): 36-48.

Swing, Elizabeth Sherman. "Bilingual/Multilingual Education: Reaction and Reform in Belgium, Wales and England." *European Education 23* (Winter 1991/92): 32-44.

—*Brigitte H. Bechtold*

BELIZE

BASIC DATA

Official Country Name:	Belize
Region:	North & Central America
Population:	249,183
Language(s):	English, Spanish, Mayan, Garifuna (Carib), Creole
Literacy Rate:	75%

Belize, formerly British Honduras, is a central American country on the Caribbean Sea bordered by Mexico and Guatemala. A British colony for more than a century, Belize is now a parliamentary democracy and constitutional monarchy. The official head of state, Queen Elizabeth, is represented by a governor general. The head of government is a prime minister. Belize occupies 22,965 square kilometers (8867 square miles), 92 percent of which is forest and swampland. In 2000 the population was estimated at 249,183 people, making Belize the least densely populated nation in Central America. English is the official language of Belize, though approximately half the inhabitants also speak Spanish. Most of the population is of mixed mestizo, Creole, Maya, and African descent. Approximately 60 percent of the population is Roman Catholic. The literacy rate, variously estimated at 75 to 90 percent, is the highest in Latin America. Poverty and unemployment remain pervasive, though the economy has benefited from an increase in tourism and foreign investment in the 1980s and 1990s. The majority of the labor force work in the service sector. Belize has greater trade and cultural links with the United States and Europe than its Central American neighbors. In 1997 the United States purchased 45 percent of Belize's exports, while Mexico accounted for less than 4 percent. Belize receives American television broadcasts via satellite and relies greatly on American news sources.

In Belize education is provided by a loose confederation of school subsystems, most following the British model. The Belizean school system is divided into five sectors: preschool, primary school, secondary school, tertiary (junior colleges/sixth forms), and adult and continuing education. Higher education is available in colleges in Belize City and Corozal. The University College of Belize is the largest institution of higher education in the country. Belize contributes to the University of the West Indies, which operates a small extramural department in

Belize City. Other postsecondary institutions include the Belize School of Nursing, the Belize School of Agriculture, and the Belize Teachers' College. Only a small percentage of Belizeans receive any kind of postsecondary education.

Education is compulsory for children aged 5 to 14. Religious denominations operate the majority of primary schools, which enrolled 47,200 students in the early 1990s. Religious institutions managed the majority of secondary schools until the 1980s, when expanded public schools began to enroll more than 50 percent of the students. Approximately 8,900 students attended secondary schools in the 1990s.

The Ministry of Education and Sports is responsible for the school system in Belize. The Ministry cooperates with volunteer agencies and church schools to ensure that all Belizeans are given "the opportunity to acquire the knowledge, skills, and attitudes required for full and active participation in the development of the nation."

Educational philosophies and practices in Belize were greatly influenced by the British system and Jesuit institutions from the United States. Since the 1960s the Peace Corps and other U.S. volunteer programs have introduced American pedagogical methods.

Belizean nationalists long wished to decolonize the educational system and rely less on foreign academic institutions. In 1979 the ruling People's United Party (PUP) established the Belize College of Arts, Science, and Technology (BELCAST) as a state institution free of church involvement. The government secured funds from the European Economic community for construction, but the campus was never built. The rival United Democratic Party (UDP) assumed power in December 1984 and established an alternative college, created and maintained by Ferris State College of Big Rapids, Michigan. Nationalists were dismayed that the new University College of Belize would be administered by non-Belizeans. Intense political controversy arose in 1991 when it was discovered that the university had not been properly accredited, calling into question the value of its degrees. A new PUP government severed its agreement with Ferris State College, and the state of Belize assumed full control over the university.

In the 1980s studies conducted by Belizean government and outside observers revealed that up to one-third of primary school students dropped out before they turned 14. Dropout rates and absenteeism were notably higher in rural areas where the seasonal demand for agricultural labor led many students to opt for work rather than school. The studies indicated that many poor parents did not regard education as a priority for their children, seeing few benefits from secondary or tertiary schooling.

The children of illegal aliens, farm workers, and subsistence farmers are increasingly ill-equipped to find employment in an economy where secondary school credentials are considered minimum requirements for employment. In the late 1980s, only 60 percent of students completing primary school attended a secondary school.

Secondary schools in Belize are not free, and government attempts at providing financial aid have proven inadequate to assist the vast majority of low income families. It is estimated that 50 percent of secondary school students drop out before completing their studies. In some city schools, the drop out rate has reached 70 percent, caused mainly by lack of funds, poor discipline, and teenage pregnancy. Fewer than 15 percent of secondary school graduates continue their education by entering the sixth form, which would prepare them for university studies.

Higher education opportunities in Belize are extremely limited. Few scholarships to foreign universities are available, though in the 1980s a number of Belizeans were given scholarships to Cuban universities. In the mid-1980s Central American Peace Scholarships were awarded to Belizeans, giving them opportunities to enroll in U.S. colleges and universities.

In 2000 the Ministry of Education and Sports called for a series of school reforms. The ministry called for designing a national curriculum, administering national testing, devising criteria for teacher training and licensing, and establishing higher standards in all levels of education.

As a country increasingly dependent on international trade and tourism, Belize recognizes the importance of education to both improve its national prospects in a global economy and alleviate the chronic poverty of many of its citizens.

BIBLIOGRAPHY

Belize, February 2001. Available from http://www.countrywatch.altavista.com.

The Central Intelligence Agency (CIA). *The World Factbook 2000.* Directorate of Intelligence, 1 January 2000. Available from http://www.cia.gov.

—*Mark Connelly*

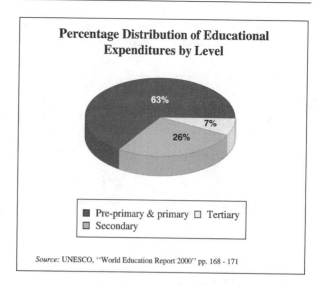

Percentage Distribution of Educational Expenditures by Level

63%

7%

26%

■ Pre-primary & primary ☐ Tertiary
■ Secondary

Source: UNESCO, "World Education Report 2000" pp. 168 - 171

BENIN

BASIC DATA

Official Country Name:	Republic of Benin
Region:	Africa
Population:	6,395,919
Language(s):	French, Fon, Yoruba
Literacy Rate:	37%

The Republic of Benin lies on the western coast of Africa, between Nigeria and Togo. The educational system was inherited from the French when the country achieved independence in August 1, 1960. It has since undergone many reforms to make it serve the country's needs. The system is public and secular, and consists of two years of preprimary education, six years of primary school, three years of junior secondary school, three years of senior secondary school, and a university. There are also three-year vocational or technical schools to attend in place of secondary schools.

Primary education begins at six years and is free and compulsory. But that does not guarantee that every child attends. In 1995 (the most recent statistics), primary enrollment was only 59 percent (males 74 percent, females 43 percent). Secondary education is not free, and enrollment is therefore considerably low. In 1994, enrollment in secondary school was only 16 percent (23 percent of males, 10 percent of females). Scholarships are available to girls from rural areas who want to attend secondary school.

A national exam is given at the end of each level of schooling to determine eligibility for further education.

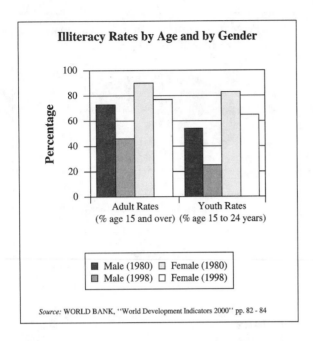

Illiteracy Rates by Age and by Gender

Male (1980) Female (1980)
Male (1998) Female (1998)

Source: WORLD BANK, "World Development Indicators 2000" pp. 82 - 84

ernment initiated massive programs to revamp the educational system, which had collapsed during the last years of the Marxist-Leninist regime. The central objectives of the reform were to restore efficiency and quality of instruction at the primary and secondary schools by providing better teacher training and facilities and updating school curricula; to increase access to and promote female participation in the school system; to reduce the cost of vocational schools; and to provide instruction that empowers students to function adequately in the Beninese economy.

With financial and technical support from many international organizations, Benin has made tremendous progress in its educational reform initiatives. The government consistently makes education a priority by allocating more funds towards the school system each fiscal year. In 1990, the budget allocation for education was 14,839 million francs FCA, representing 12.8 percent of the national budget. The 2001 budget allocated 22 percent of its funds to education.

BIBLIOGRAPHY

Djibril, M. Debourou. *The Process of Education Policy Formation in Africa, The Case of Benin.* Paris: Association for the Development of African Education, 1995.

Guezodje, Vincent. "Educational Reform in Benin." *Prospects 8* (1977): 455-471.

—*Salome C. Nnoromele*

Students graduating from primary, junior secondary, and senior secondary schools receive the Certificate of Primary School (*Certificat d'études primaires*), Lower Secondary School Certificate (*Brevet d'études du premier cycle*) and Secondary School Certificate (*Baccalauréat*), respectively.

The National University of Benin at Cotonou, founded in 1970, is the primary institute of higher learning in the country. Student enrollment for 1997, the most current statistics, was 8,890. The university awards undergraduate and graduate degrees as well as special certifications from its many colleges, including the colleges of Letters, Art, and Human Sciences; Law, Economics, and Political Science; Science and Technology; Agriculture; and Health Sciences. A course of study runs from two to seven years, depending on the student's area of specialization. A secondary school certificate or the equivalent is needed for admission to the university. All students seeking admission to the National University of Benin or funds to study abroad can obtain financial assistance and scholarships.

The language of instruction in all Beninese schools is French; native languages as well as English are taught as subjects in the secondary and university levels. The school year runs from October to July, in terms from October to January, January to March, and April to July. The Ministry of National Education (*Ministère de l'Education nationale*) oversees the educational system at all levels.

After the collapse in 1989 of the Marxist-Leninist oriented government, the new Beninese democratic gov-

BERMUDA

BASIC DATA

Official Country Name:	Bermuda
Region:	North & Central America
Population:	62,997
Language(s):	English, Portuguese
Literacy Rate:	98%

Discovered by Spanish explorer Juan de Bermudez in 1503, Bermuda, known as "the isle of devils," inspired the setting for Shakespeare's *The Tempest* because of its treacherous seas and reefs. Bermuda is the oldest English-speaking settlement in the Western Hemisphere; as a result of the slave trade, however, 60 percent of Bermudans have African ancestors. A self-governing, parliamentary British colony since 1620, Bermuda is ruled by executive and judicial branches and a legislature that was strengthened in 1968. The British monarch is Chief of State.

For children ages five to sixteen, education, conducted in English, is compulsory in only 1 of 24 free government schools or 6 tuition-based private schools, which are modeled on the British system. There are no local boarding schools in Bermuda. School uniforms are required in all public and private schools. The school year for Bermuda's 6,500 students lasts 10 months, starting in September. In the 1990s a major restructuring resulted in the creation of 18 primary schools (grades 1-6), 5 middle schools (7-9), and 2 senior schools (10-13). Bermuda High School for Girls (with 650 enrollees) is the island's only all-girls school.

The American Head Start program inspired Bermuda's preprimary education curriculum. In more than 40 daycare and preschool facilities, children develop social skills while learning and playing. The new middle school and senior secondary curricula include such vital enrichments as the visual and performing arts and business/technology instruction. Special needs children are mainstreamed. The average class size is 24 students, but the pupil-teacher ratio is 13:1 including all professional staff. Public school students take the Bermuda Secondary School Certificate exam (BSSC); private school students take the British General Certificate in Secondary Education exam (GCSE). Those who earn the GCSE are eligible to enter grade 11 or 12 at an American school or to matriculate for an associate degree at Bermuda College.

A 20 percent annual increase in the number of home schooled children reflects some families' desires to avoid traditional schoolroom distractions for their children. Before they leave public school, however, home schooled students are tested to determine their grade level. Because no alternative school exists, a program is planned for "at risk" adolescents since 435 high school students dropped out in 1994.

Due to import duties, customs fees, and licensing costs, Bermuda has the highest Internet fees in the Western Hemisphere. Nevertheless, in 1999 Bermuda's Education Ministry, in concert with the University of Virginia and Stanford University, initiated a Technology Infusion Project, the first phase of which was to train Bermuda's teachers through video-conferencing and collaborative learning. Middle school and primary school students were to receive their computer training in 2000 and 2001. So serious is Bermuda about integrating technology and education that faculty trained in technology education earn academic certification. Moreover, recognizing that business has a vital stake in education's future, Bermuda's Corporate Partnership Program infuses scholarship money and business expertise into schools.

As of 2001 Bermuda College had about 4,000 students and 75 full-time faculty; it offered 10 associate degree and fifteen certificate programs in arts and science, hotel/business management, technology, and continuing education. Since there is no degree-granting university in Bermuda (although plans are underway to expand Bermuda College to a four-year institution), students may transfer abroad to obtain a baccalaureate degree. Many secondary graduates attend higher education in the United States, Canada, and Europe. American universities usually require Bermudans to take the SAT; many who transfer to universities in the United Kingdom study law. The National Education Guarantee Scheme, begun in 1994, promises loans to any Bermuda-born student with university potential.

Bermuda's Ministry of Education is responsible for all school programs. Its structure includes a comptroller, permanent secretary, chief education officer, and personnel director, as well as directors of curriculum, schools, student services, and early childhood, each of whom reports to the minister of education.

Bermuda College and the Community Education Development Program offer extensive adult education—non-credit courses related to technology, recreation, and personal development. Such private sector initiatives as the Seniors' Learning Centre and the Bermuda Biological Station for Research deliver additional continuing education services.

The Bermuda Union of Teachers (BUT) represents all 713 public school teachers. In 1996 Bermuda's teachers were required to upgrade their education. Fitchburg State College offered the M.Ed. degree through distance learning. In 2000 Bermuda College began a Centre for Education to promote and ensure qualified professional development and adult education; two of the Centre's constituent entities, The Teacher Education Institute and Educational Outreach Initiative, support ongoing teacher training and assist local teachers with core subjects.

Although Bermuda has one of the highest per-capita incomes in the world, Bermuda College reported in 2000 that some 70 percent of its applicants did not meet academic standards due in part to social problems and lack of family discipline; poor workplace skills, dropouts, and lagging technical training were also concerns. To its credit, Bermuda began addressing its declining educational standards in the late 1990s by enacting stronger secondary graduation requirements, smaller primary class size, updated technology integration into the classroom, and more teacher training.

BIBLIOGRAPHY

Bermuda Online. ''Education in Bermuda at all schools.'' *Welcome to Bermuda,* 2001. Available from http://bermuda-online.org/educate.htm.

Boultbee, Paul G., and David F. Raine. *Bermuda.* Oxford, England: Clio Press, 1998.

Ziral, James, and Liz Jones. ''Education and Child Care.'' *Insider's Guide to Bermuda, 2nd Edition,* 2000. Available from http://www.insiders.com/bermuda/main-education.htm.

—*Howard A. Kerner*

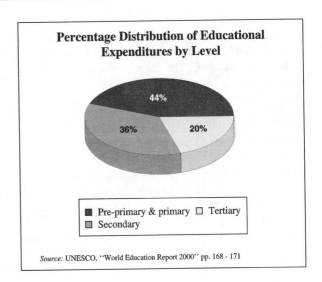

Percentage Distribution of Educational Expenditures by Level

- ■ Pre-primary & primary   □ Tertiary
- ▨ Secondary

Source: UNESCO, ''World Education Report 2000'' pp. 168 - 171

BHUTAN

BASIC DATA

Official Country Name:	Kingdom of Bhutan
Region:	East & South Asia
Population:	2,005,222
Language(s):	Dzongkha
Literacy Rate:	42.2%

Bhutan is a small, landlocked South Asian country of 47,000 square kilometers located in the eastern Himalayas between China and India. In the year 2000, Bhutan had a population of about 2 million people with 40 percent below the age of 14 years. (Official statistics do not include people of Nepalese origin, though, and place the population count at 600,000 people.) Nearly 90 percent of the population lives in rural areas in the 5,000 scattered villages and hamlets. The population growth rate is 2.2 percent with a life expectancy of 52 years. Agriculture, animal husbandry, and forestry employ 94 percent of the population and account for 40 percent of the Gross Domestic Product (GDP) in the world's smallest and least developed economy.

In 1616, for the first time, Bhutan became unified under the leadership of Ngawang Namgyel. The nineteenth century witnessed constant conflicts with the British that divided the country. The second unification occurred under the regimes of Ugyen Wangchuk and Jigme Dorji between 1873 and 1948. Jigme Dorji Wangchuk succeeded in 1952, and after his death in 1972, then Jigme Singye Wangchuk became the youngest king. He has paved way for slow modernization of this traditional country.

Bhutan is a monarchy. The country is divided into twenty *dzongkhags* (districts). The head of the state is the King with a unicameral *Tshogdu* (National Assembly). *Tshogdu* has 154 seats of which 105 are elected from village constituencies, 12 from religious bodies, and 37 nominated by the king. The supreme court of appeal is the king. The government is committed to universal education as a signatory to the policy of ''Education for All'' and the Convention of the Rights of the Child (in 1991 at New Delhi, India). In 2000, the literacy rate in Bhutan was 42 percent, with female literacy being only 28 percent.

Until the twentieth century the only schools that existed in Bhutan were the monasteries set up by the Drukpa subsect of Kargyupa sect of Mahayana Buddhism. The growing influence of the British in the late nineteenth century influenced Ugyen Wangchuk (1907-1926) toward Western style education, and he set up English-medium private schools for the elite in Ha, Bhumthang, and Thimphu (the national capital). In the 1950s, Jigme Dorje Wangchuk began government-supported primary schools for common people. In 1960, there were 29 public and 30 private schools that enrolled nearly 2,500 children. Secondary level schooling was available only in neighboring India. Systematic efforts toward developing the education sector began in 1961, with the introduction of the First Development Plan (1961-1966) that provided for free and universal primary education. By 1998, the government had established 400 schools, of which 150 were primary community schools in remote areas, 188 regular primary schools, 44 junior high schools, and 18 high schools. However, in the twenty-first century there is still a shortage of schools with adequate facilities.

The schooling begins with preschool (at age four) for one year, followed by five years of primary school, three years of junior high (grades six through eight), and then three years of high school (grades nine through eleven). The National Board of Secondary Education in the Department of Education conducts nationwide examinations at the end of the eleventh grade. Instruction is in English and the national language, Dzongkha. The Department of Education is responsible for producing textbooks, course syllabi, in-service teachers training, organizing inter-school tournaments, recruiting, testing and promoting teachers, and procuring foreign assistance. Curricula have been developed in assistance with UNESCO, the University of London, and the University of Delhi.

In 1998, gross primary school enrollment was 25 percent with a total enrollment of 77,300. The proportion of girls among primary students was 45 percent. In addition, in the remote areas, 12,600 students were enrolled in community schools. In 1998, the percentage of primary school entrants completing fifth grade was 82 percent. Also in 1998, gross secondary school enrollment ratio was 7 percent for males and 2 percent for females.

In 1998, there was only one four-year degree college, located in Kanglung, that offered undergraduate degrees in arts and commerce, as well as nine technical institutes. Under a national service plan and fellowships, many Bhutanese students receive higher education abroad.

Bhutan's government spends 22 percent of its budget on health and education. The Department of Education sets educational policies. In the 1990s, Asian Development Bank funding boosted the Department of Education and its Technical and Vocational Education Division.

Nonformal education (NFE) supported by UNICEF, UNESCO, and ESCAP has established 54 centers with an enrollment of about 4,000 participants, of which 70 percent are women. The course, in Dzongkha, is designed for completion within 6 to 12 months. The course materials deal with everyday situations and messages concerning health and hygiene, family planning, agriculture, forestry, and the environment.

In 1998, there were a total of 2,785 teachers in Bhutan. Each primary school teacher has an average of 37 students, but the class size goes up to 70 in some schools. Although the government offers special incentives to those who join the profession, it has not been able to train enough teachers. The National Institute of Education (NIE) does provide distance education courses to already-trained teachers.

Bhutan is a slowly modernizing, traditional country that had approximately 100,000 students in its educational system in 1998. The country is still grappling with the problem of illiteracy with more than half of its population being illiterate and more than two-thirds of its women

being without education. Since the 1960s, the country has been able to develop a basic educational infrastructure that is slowly expanding with foreign aid. The governmental commitment toward universal education is a healthy sign for its continued progress.

BIBLIOGRAPHY

The Central Intelligence Agency (CIA). *The World Factbook 2000*. Directorate of Intelligence, 1 January 2000. Available from http://www.cia.gov/.

Central Statistical Organization, Planning Commission. *Bhutan at a Glance 1999* Thimpu, Bhutan: Central Statistical Organization, 1999.

Cooper, Robert. *Bhutan*. New York: Marshall Cavendish, 2001.

Dompnier, Robert. *Bhutan: Kingdom of the Dragon*. Boston, MA: Shambhala Publications, Inc., 1999.

Karan, Pradyumana P. *Bhutan: Environment, Culture, and Development Strategy*. Columbia, MO: South Asia Books, 1990.

Planning Commission. *Eighth Five Year Plan 1997-2002*. Thimpu: Royal Government of Bhutan, 1998.

Savada, Andrea M. *Bhutan Country Study*. Washington, DC: Federal Research Division. Library of Congress, 1993.

—*Manoj Sharma*

BOLIVIA

BASIC DATA

Official Country Name:	Republic of Bolivia
Region:	South America
Population:	8,152,620
Language(s):	Spanish, Quechua, Aymara
Literacy Rate:	83.1%
Academic Year:	March-December
Compulsory Schooling:	8 years
Public Expenditure on Education:	4.9%
Libraries:	250
Educational Enrollment:	Primary: 1,278,775 Secondary: 219,232

Teachers: Primary: 51,763
                             Secondary: 12,434

Student-Teacher Ratio: Primary: 25:1

HISTORY & BACKGROUND

The Republic of Bolivia, in the center of South America, is land-locked and surrounded by 5 countries: Paraguay, Argentina, and Chile in the south; Brazil in the east; and Peru in the north. Because it is split by some of the highest mountains in the world, isolation plagues educational progress. La Paz is the government capital of Bolivia, but Sucre is the legal capital and the seat of the judiciary power of the country.

The geographic, political, and economic factors of Bolivia and its demography have long been an impediment to easy progress and development. The country covers 1,098,581 square kilometers (about 425,000 square miles) and, according to the National Institute of Statistics it has an average of about 7.58 inhabitants per square kilometer. The estimates of population range from 8,000,000 to 8,328,700 inhabitants in 2000, depending on the sources. By any estimate, Bolivia has one of the lowest demographic densities in the western hemisphere and a yearly population growth of only about 2.3 percent. Its inhospitable living conditions are reflected in the percentages of land types: 20 percent desert, 11 percent land with negligible irrigation, 40 percent rain forest, approximately 25 percent pasture and meadows, 2 percent inland water, and 2 percent Andean range, including an uninhabited area called the "Altiplano" with arctic weather at more than 5,500 meters high. Only two percent is arable land. As for the population, only 57 percent have access to potable water, and 76 percent have inadequate sanitary facilities. However, in the early 1990s this unfortunate state of affairs began to improve.

Like the rest of the Andean region, Bolivia is believed to have been permanently inhabited for about 21,000 years. Its history is usually divided into three broad historical periods: Pre-colonial (from the origins until 1525), Colonial (1525-1809), and Republican (from 1809 until now). Agriculture seems to have started around 3000 A.D., but not much is known of the period previous to the Tiwanakan culture that started about 600 B.C.E. Centered around Tiwanaku, south of Lake Titicaca, the Tiwanakan civilization developed through colonization rather than conquest. The ruins of Tiwanaku reveal advanced architectural techniques. The causes of the city's disappearance around 1200 A.D. are still a subject of speculation, but it signals the rise of the Aymara kingdom. The Aymara improved the food supply through a very sophisticated system of irrigation, the source of an agricultural prosperity that sustained a large population. The drying out of its system of canals seems a likely explanation for the decline of the region. The Aymara could not contain the expansion of the Quechua-speaking ethnic group. Around 1450, the latter added the highlands to the empire they already controlled. In the early fifteenth century they took the name of Incas after their rulers, and they remained in power until the arrival of the Spanish in 1525. Other ethnic cultures like the Moxos in the lowlands and the Mollos north of where La Paz stands also disappeared in the thirteenth century.

During the Colonial Period, the region became known as "Upper Peru" since it depended on the Viceroyalty of Lima, but it was also known as Charcas because the local government was centered in Chuquisaca (now Sucre). Due to the region's abundance of silver, the Spanish settled and prospered. The conquest brought with it the Roman Catholic Church. The church, led primarily by the Jesuits, became the prime provider of education and continues to deeply influence education, though a parallel private system has become a new feature of Bolivia since 1989. The take-over of education by the Jesuits deeply affected the indigenous populations. First, Spanish, the language of the oppressor, so dominated education that Quechua, Aymara, Guarani/ Chiriguano, Chiquitano, and the many other existing native languages were absolutely ignored in the very places where they were the languages of the majority. This change had a dramatic effect inasmuch as the indigenous populations, who still represented 56 percent of the population in 2001, were denied education unless they first became bilingual. Furthermore, since no provision existed for their learning Spanish, the indigenous populations became and remained second-class citizens within their own territories.

The representatives of the Roman Catholic Church privileged their own compatriots, the newly arrived Spaniards and Europeans, so that education, with the exception of a few Indian leaders, excluded Indians and women. Under the best of circumstances, education became the choice instrument of transculture, of subversion, and of the loss of the Amerindian cultural heritage and identity. The fact that 95 percent of the total population of Bolivia is now Catholic demonstrates the degree of the sweeping transcultural indoctrination that occurred in the country after the arrival of the Spanish. Although independence was declared in 1809, it was not until August 6, 1825, when, after a long struggle, Bolivia was established. Named in honor of Simon Bolivar, one of the heroes of Independence, the country, at the time of independence, was more than twice its present size. After the independence a series of brief, unstable constitutions were implemented. When the country engaged in the war of the Pacific against Chile and Peru (1879-1883) it was weak, due to a succession of coups. In 1884, Chile won the nitrate-rich Atacama desert, Bolivia's only seacoast access. This loss irremediably damaged the economy.

At the end of the nineteenth century, Bolivia's situation was somewhat improved by the world increase in the price of silver and later by the exploitation of tin. But bad capitalist policies left the majority of indigenous population living under the most primitive conditions in deplorable poverty, all for the benefit of a small elite.

Bolivia engaged in the Chaco war against Paraguay from 1932 until 1935, and was defeated, losing about 60,000 men, a large part of its territory, and its last strategic access to the sea through the Paraguay River. After the war, the Revolutionary Nationalist Movement, MNR, emerged as a popular party. The Amerindians, representing the majority in numbers, had gained political awareness while serving in the Bolivian military; nevertheless, they had no access to education, no economic opportunities, and no representation in politics. They grew tired of having no representation in the political arena, and their demands remained inadequately answered. The last straw came when the MNR, which had gained victory in the 1951 presidential elections, was denied its victory. Soon afterwards a rebellion erupted, culminating in the 1952 revolution. A civilian government was established under the presidency of MNR leader Victor Paz Estenssoro (1952-1964). A series of reforms improved the conditions of indigenous peoples: universal suffrage, the development of rural education, the spread of primary education, and the implementation of important land reforms. Most of the Altiplano taken from the Amerindians was returned to them. Tin mines were nationalized, as were both the Bolivian mining corporations.

In spite of such progress, human rights were not respected, and a military junta overthrew the presidency in 1964. One of its members, Rene Barrientos, was elected president in 1966 but died soon after in 1969. It was during his presidency in October 1967, that Che Guevara attempted to start a Cuban type revolution. The army later executed him. In response, a series of military coups occurred and weak governments succeeded until Colonel Hugo Banzer Suarez became president in 1971. In spite of an impressive growth of the economy during his presidency, the suspension of political activities that he enforced reduced his initial popularity. Fraudulent successive elections took place in 1978 and 1979. There was a short break of successions in 1979 and 1980 when Lidia Gueiler Tejada became the first female president, but in 1980, after coups and counter-coups, the ruthless General Luis Garcia Meza, a known human rights abuser and trafficker in narcotics, led a violent coup. He remained in office only until 1981. After leaving office,

General Luis Garcia Meza was convicted in absentia, extradited from Brazil, and began serving a 30-year sentence in 1995.

Several short-lived military governments and other weak leaders followed until 1985. Paz Estenssoro was then returned to power thanks to a coalition between the MIR (*Movimiento de Izquierda Revolucionario* or Revolutionary Left Movement) and the MNR, winning over General Hugo Banzer Suarez, representing the Nationalist Democratic Action Party (ADN). However, the situation he inherited was precarious. The economy was in crisis, annual inflation was at 24,000 percent, strikes and unrest were rampant, and drug trafficking was widespread. Paz Estenssoro managed to achieve stability in four years but at a high price. The 1985 collapse of tin prices forced his government to lay off more than 20,000 workers, leading to social unrest. In the 1989 elections, General Hugo Banzer Suarez, who had learned his lesson from the previous elections, formed the Patriotic Accord (AP) with the MIR and won. Paz Zamora became the president and continued the reforms begun by Estenssoro. He ordered the 1992 crackdown against the domestic terrorism of the Tupac Katari Guerrilla Army (EGTK). His integrity became questionable when he was later investigated for his personal ties to drug trafficker Isaac Chavarria.

In 1993, MNR's Gonzalo Sanchez de Lozada was selected as president by a coalition between the MBL (*Movimiento Bolivia Libre* or Free Bolivia Movement) and the UCS (*Unidad Civica Solidaridad* or Civic Solidarity Unit). Many reforms took place, including the Capitalization Program, which let investors acquire 50 percent ownership and management control in public enterprises. People opposed to these changes instigated frequent social disturbances until 1996. In the 1997 elections, General Hugo Banzer Suarez (ADN) again formed a coalition with the MIR, UCS, and CONDEPA (*Conciencia de Patria* or Patriotic Conscience) parties, and the Congress selected him as president. On August 6, 1997, he took office. Significant to the big picture is the fact that in the 176 years of its independence Bolivia had 189 governments.

Some facts about the poverty level of Bolivia are necessary to help understand the reforms in the educational system and to appreciate the country's current problems. According to the U.S. Department of State, the per capita income was officially in US$1,100 in 1997. In spite of an apparent large increase in income in 1999, the average purchasing power parity was estimated at $3,000 per capita, making Bolivia the poorest country in South America. The external debt was $5.7 billion, and 70 percent of the population lived below the poverty line and suffered from malnutrition. But this data shows only a part of the picture; the fact that the average income in Bolivia is the lowest of the continent is, of course, important, but the inequalities among Bolivians themselves are far worse. While 10 percent of the population receives 40 percent of the total national income of Bolivia, 40 percent of the population is in poverty, totaling only 10 percent of the same national income.

After the tin crash and the 1985 peak of inflation, unemployment rose to 20 percent in 1987; by 1999 it was estimated at 11.4 percent along with widespread underemployment. The rapid growth of the population, fostered by improved health, has made it difficult to increase the percentage of literacy. In 2000, the birth rate was 31.86 per 1000 versus a death rate of 8.36 per 1000. Infant mortality decreased by more than half, from 124.4 per thousand in 1989, to approximately 60.44 per 1000 in 2000. Life expectancy figures improved from 52 years in 1989 to an estimated 61.19 years in 2000 for males, and from 56 years to an estimated 66.34 years for females, though this life expectancy remains comparatively low. The overall population is young; 39.11 percent of the population is under 14-years-old (1,624,404 males and 1,564,057 females), 56.42 percent is between 15 and 64, and 4.47 percent is 65-years-old or above (164,473 males and 199,849 females). The literacy rate, rose from 75 percent in the mid-1980s, to 79.4 percent in 1998, with a large gap between genders: 90.5 percent for males against 76.0 percent for females. These literacy figures compare well to the ones given by the *State of the World's Children* data for 1995: 91 percent and 76 percent, respectively, for males and females.

The number of ethnic groups and languages complicates the picture of educational reform in Bolivia. The majority of the population is Amerindian. There are approximately 30 percent Quechua, 25 percent Aymara, nearly 30 smaller Amerindian subgroups, 30 percent mestizos, and 5 to 15 percent whites. These groups represent nine major linguistic groups with many subdivisions. As a rule very few Amerindians intermarry, and not all speak Spanish. Other factors that impact schooling are the distance from home to the nearest facility, and the lack of infrastructure and security. Inadequate means of transportation and communication still slow progress in Bolivia. Only 2,872 kilometers of the 52,216 kilometers of roads were paved in 1995, including 27 kilometers of expressways. However, recent community participation programs are accelerating the very slow process of modernization. In 1999 alone, for example, these efforts resulted in 791 kilometers of improved farm-to-market roads and 693 new hectares of land under irrigation. In 1999, 13 of the 32 official airports were paved; there were, in addition, some 1096 unofficial unpaved airstrips.

The first television set appeared in Bolivia in 1969. The 1999 *State of the World's Children* listed 672 radio sets per thousand people for the year 1995, and 115 television sets per thousand. In 1997 there were 5.25 million radio accesses, 900,000 televisions, 6 daily newspapers, and 400,000 telephones. The number of Internet providers rose from 5 in 1999 to 31 at the onset of 2001. At that time the country also had 7 cybercafés, 22 computer companies, 6 main television stations, 6 main radio stations, 7 daily newspapers, and 4 periodicals and weekly papers. Telephones had multiplied, and there were 10 telecommunication providers. The advance of technology constitutes a significant improvement for the prospect of education.

CONSTITUTIONAL & LEGAL FOUNDATIONS

The present constitution of Bolivia dates back to 1967 but was revised in 1994. There are three branches to the government: executive, legislative, and judicial. The executive branch is the president and vice-president, both elected for five years, and the cabinet, appointed by the president. Traditionally strong, the executive branch tends to initiate the legislation and, by doing so, it limits the power of Congress to debating and approving the laws. The last elections took place in 1997; the next ones are scheduled for June 2002. The National Congress is composed of two chambers, the Senate with 27 senators and the chamber of deputies with 130 seats. Both chambers are elected by popular vote for five years. The Supreme Court heads the judicial branch of five levels, which include a lower court and a departmental court. Though very corrupt in the past, the courts have been reformed by the present government. The National Congress appoints judges for 10 years. A recent governmental reform distributes a significant part of the national revenues to municipalities, which has allowed considerable improvements to take place in the traditionally neglected countryside. Another significant reform gives less power to the central government in the choice of officials and more to the nine departments' local governments. Each town elects its mayor and council. Every five years, general elections obligate all citizens of voting age to vote.

The Education Reform Law (Law 1565) of 1994 provides for free education, extends the primary school requirement and, above all, recognizes popular public participation in the planning of intercultural and bilingual education. Together, these three laws, among others, have proven to have made a positive impact on education in Bolivia.

In pre-colonial times, the great Inca Empire granted only the indigenous nobles and upper classes an education. The transmission of the Incan culture and social structure was thus assured. Inca monarchs lived in polygamy and usually left very large families of 100 or even 200 children. There were two types of nobility. The first were the male descendants of royal blood. Their privileges included the education they received, the way they dressed, and the language they spoke. They lived at court, belonged to counsels, had access to great offices and the priesthood, and commanded armies.

A second type of nobility, the Curacas, were chiefs of colonized nations. They were allowed to rule over their subjects but had to leave their descendants to be educated by the Incas as proof of their loyalty and as guarantee of their good will. The Incan schools taught the children of noblemen and of Curacas the dialect, religion, astronomy, agriculture, science, quipus (knotted threads that served as a means of communicating ideas and arithmetic), laws, government, geography, and history of the Empire. Students also listened to the chronicles compiled by the *amautas* (wisemen) and by the *haravecs* (poets). When the Spanish arrived in 1525, they deliberately ignored the Amerindians education and dramatically cut the transmission of tradition. The Amerindians' plight was then ignored until 1993 when President Gonzalo Sanchez de Lozada recognized the many native languages of Bolivia, in an act that changed a policy that had kept Indians uneducated. Together with world efforts to improve education in third world countries, this 1993 act helped trigger the attempt at a national education reform. However, the implementation of this act requires a better infrastructure, and the resolution of problems is slow.

EDUCATIONAL SYSTEM—OVERVIEW

Generally speaking, education in Bolivia is divided into three cycles—four if one counts the optional pre-scholar or preprimary years. There are 5 years of elementary education in the primary cycle for 6- to 10-year-olds; 3 years of intermediate education in the middle schools for 11- to 13-year-olds; and 4 years of secondary education for 14- to 17-year-olds. The four years of secondary school are themselves divided into two cycles lasting two years each. The first cycle is a common core, while the second allows for some degree of specialization, either in the humanities or in a variety of technical fields. A movement exists to integrate both intermediate and secondary levels of education into one single cycle of eight years.

Prior to the reforms of the 1980s, the educational system operated with a six-year primary cycle followed by four years of intermediate schools and two years of secondary school with the baccalaureate degree as the terminal exam. The country passed a law that claims an official 8 years of compulsory schooling between the ages of 7 and 14. Unfortunately, this law is not regularly enforced. A 1991 study of the Cochabamba rural area

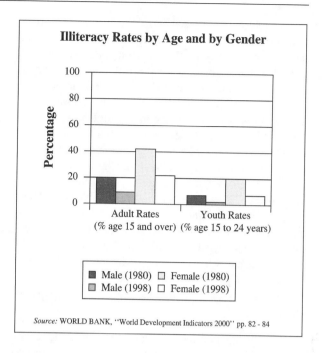

Illiteracy Rates by Age and by Gender

Source: WORLD BANK, "World Development Indicators 2000" pp. 82 - 84

showed that between the ages of 6 and 14 only 52.5 percent of males and 50.3 percent of females attended school exclusively. In other words, nearly half of the children worked. Nationwide, 83.4 percent of males and 70.4 percent of females attend school; also, 16.6 percent of males and 29.6 percent of females are not accounted for either in schools or at work. Additionally, 18.8 percent of males and 17.2 percent of females combine school with herding, and 12.1 percent of males and 2.9 percent of females combine school with agriculture.

A further cycle, higher education for 18- to 24-year-olds comprises different specialized schools, institutes below degree level, and universities. At the university level there are two avenues: the *pregrado* (undergraduate level) offers the *Superior Technician* and *License* degrees; the postgraduate programs deliver *doctorados* (doctorate degrees).

There are now both public and private institutions at all levels of education. At the intermediate level, the private sector represented approximately 25 percent of the national enrollments and 35 percent of the secondary levels in the early 1990s. Teacher training programs provide educators with opportunities to advance and develop skills in the classroom. One of the first of many institutions and associations created and called upon to implement the reform was the Reform Institute at the Ministry of Education, Culture, and Sports.

PREPRIMARY & PRIMARY EDUCATION

Before 1900, tutors (generally from the clergy) educated the sons of white elite families. The Indians were taught only enough to convert them to Catholicism. At that date only 17 percent of the adult population was literate. But, in the early 1900s, a teaching mission from Belgium laid the foundation for the Bolivian rural primary school, and in 1931 Elizardo Pérez founded a large nuclear school, teaching grades five to eight. Subsequently, this central school became the model for education in the rural Andes. By the 1952 Revolution, in spite of this effort, less than one third of adults were literate. By the mid-1980s when the overall adult literacy stood at 75 percent, 350 centers for adult literacy programs, with approximately 2,000 teachers, were established. These programs however were set up mainly in La Paz. The last ''Education For All'' (EFA) survey compiled by international agencies headed by UNESCO reports substantial improvements in the literacy rate by genders. For 1997 it quotes 78.4 percent for female adults and 91.6 percent for male adults, but the rates also show the pervasive gender gap.

The most recent statistics available reveal the results of efforts to equalize the standards between females and males. For example, the gross enrollment ratio for preprimary education shows that the percentages for girls rose from 30.2 percent to 36.6 percent and for boys from 30.3 percent to 36.2 percent during the 10-year period from 1989 to 1999, an improvement slightly higher for females. As for the actual enrollment in primary school, the results are far more spectacular; the numbers rose from 57,855 for females to 85,085; and from 64,728 for males to 90,986. Although this rise was encouraging, the increase seems to be due largely to an increase in population, and the survival rate to fifth grade actually declined from 60.5 percent to 47.1 percent in 1998. Despite the small net gain in actual numbers who make it to fifth grade, not many children make it through the supposedly compulsory period. In fact, although there were 87,180 girls of the age to start primary education in 1990, only 38,390 or 44 percent actually registered. By 1999, out of 109,360 girls, 52,800 enrolled, or 48.2 percent. As for boys, out of a total of 88,500 in 1990, some 44,885 (50.7 percent) enrolled in primary education. By 1999, out of 113,660 boys of the entry age, more than half (51.9 percent) or 58,989 enrolled. Although the percentages from 1990 to 1999 have changed very little, there has been a considerable gain in the actual number of students attending school. Clearly, the increase is doing little more than keeping up with the increased population.

In the mid-1980s, approximately 60 percent of the 59,000 Bolivian teachers were teaching in urban schools, and the educational expenditures had plunged to less than 40 percent of the total expenditure of 1980. The portion of the gross domestic product (GDP) represented by education dropped from 3 percent to less than 2 percent because of the economic crisis. The latest numbers recorded by the EFA show a steady improvement in educational investment from 1989 to 1999. The public current expenditure in primary education as a percentage of the GNP went from 1.615 percent in 1990 to 2.265 percent in 1999. (Numbers peak in 1993, 1996, and 1997, which should translate into improved statistics in the future.) The public current expenditure in primary education per pupil, as a percentage of the GNP per capita, went from 10.08 percent to 11.96 percent—though it represents a decline from the peak years between 1992 and 1997. As in other levels of education, the reform movement made its way into initial and primary education, but many problems persist.

In 1998 the Bolivian Center for Educational Research and Implementation (CEBIAE) published its findings and came up with an integral proposal for educational innovation at the Preschooler and Primary levels (PIIEN) in the Bolivian Andes, a region lagging behind the rest of the nation. This alternative project—to be implemented in the nuclei of La Paz, Oruro, and Potosi—is based on the cumulative experience of participating primary school educators. A remarkable project, it has one main objective: the improvement of the quality of learning. The project aims to improve the quality of teaching, to democratize the management of education, to improve the local curriculum by making it truly intercultural, to promote the development of educational research, to construct learning networks between teachers in the many establishments of the nuclei, and to construct educational projects in the various educational units and in each nucleus of every unit. Other aims are to increase autonomy, personal initiative, and responsibility and to make good use of whatever qualities individuals demonstrate. The project promotes participation at all levels among students, teachers, and parents from different communities. Their participation helps develop the curriculum, make decisions on methodology, raise the levels of citizenship and intercultural awareness, increase communication, improve research, and democratically manage the school and ultimately the nucleus itself, all within the reform framework. The project tries to respond to teachers' needs and to local necessities; it brings the community together, but above all, it implements measures to allow teachers to educate themselves to become better teachers.

In order to carry out the functions of the project, four different types of networks are organized: between same grade teachers, between cycles, within the educational unit, and with the educational nuclei. This project went through a period of increased awareness starting in 1998, then through the recreation and constructive phase in 1999-2000. In 2000-2001 the consolidation phase was under way.

Enrollments are still higher in urban areas than rural areas, but the gap between them has seriously diminished, despite the fact that the urban count reflects many once-rural students who migrated to the cities to obtain an education. Night classes, more frequent in urban areas, have helped improve literacy and education at all levels, especially with older students. A 1989-1992 study done by the Secretary of Education showed that the number of students in intermediate education was still very low; less than 50 percent of the students of the appropriate age group were enrolled. As expected, an apparent discrepancy existed between cities and rural areas. In cities, close to 70 percent of students within the corresponding age range were enrolled in intermediate education, as opposed to around 25 percent in rural areas.

The number of students enrolling at both intermediate and secondary levels seems to be directly affected by such factors as the age of students, the size of the family, the language spoken at home, and the migration patterns. Significant, too, are the family expenses and the level of education of both parents, especially the level of the mother's education as it influences the education of female students. A higher family income correlates with a higher enrollment of males, while the use of Spanish at home and the educational level of the head of the household correlate with the enrollment of females. Being a recent migrant has a negative influence on the enrollment of both genders.

One fact is clearly noticeable: the more educated the parents are, the more Spanish is spoken at home; the more Spanish is spoken, the more income the family has and the less the adult family members trust the public educational system and the more they rely on private education. The weakness of public education, and the consequent public distrust of it, explains the need for reform in public education and the increase in the creation of many private schools starting in 1989. They provide a welcome alternative to public education, although they exist primarily in urban areas. The ETARE study of 1992 shows that the private sector serves 19.5 percent of the total students in urban areas but only 0.038 percent of the total students in rural areas. Parents increasingly demand quality education, which explains the large migration of students towards cities, even at the intermediate stage of education. Parents believe that their children' chances of obtaining financial aid at the university level is directly related to how well they do at the intermediate and secondary levels. According to data published by UDAPSO, based on information gathered by ETARE, in 1992, 10,167 or 37.8 percent of the rural enrollment migrated to an urban area to study at the intermediate level; these migrants represented 12.1 percent of the urban enrollment.

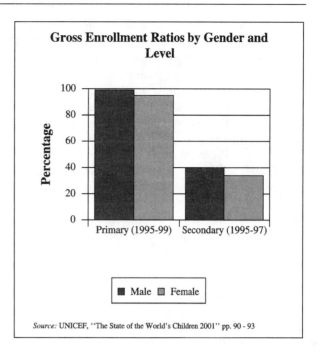

Gross Enrollment Ratios by Gender and Level

Source: UNICEF, ''The State of the World's Children 2001'' pp. 90 - 93

In another area of particular importance, sexual education is known to have a positive impact on fertility rates when female students attend school between the ages of 8 and 12 but, in 1992, more than half of the females (54 percent) in Bolivian urban areas and almost all the females (95 percent) in rural areas failed to complete the intermediate cycle during which they would have gained the necessary knowledge to make informed reproductive choices. Without the results of the latest study, it is difficult to do justice to Bolivia's progress in intermediate education, but there are reasons to believe that the situation has improved in the last decade. Gender parity was recently achieved in urban private schools at the intermediate level.

SECONDARY EDUCATION

The real lack of public educational infrastructure and the policy of Paz Estenssoro encouraged private educational investment in Bolivia. Since 1989, about 380 new private schools were created and attendance rose. Students who complete secondary school successfully earn the title of *bachiller* when they pass the exit *bachillerato* exam. This exam, along with a health certificate, is a requirement to enter the university, which also administers its own entrance examination.

To really understand the progress that education is making, it helps to look back to mid-November 1989 when education was in real distress. Less than 50 percent of the population spoke Spanish as their first language, though it was the only language used in education. Approximately 90 percent of the children attended primary school but often for a year or less, and the literacy rate was low in many rural areas. Eighty thousand state teachers, supported by the COB (*Central Obrera Boliviana* or Bolivian Workers Center), went on strike demanding a $100 special bonus to supplement their low $45 monthly wage. Paz Zamora, following the customary strategy, imposed a state of siege, banning strikes, public meetings, and demonstrations for 90 days. He imprisoned 850 union members, banished 150 of them to internal exile and, in order to bring the strike to an end, offered teachers a 17 percent pay increase on top of a negotiated annual spring bonus. At the same time, Zamora planned to sell off 100 of the 157 state-owned companies and use the $500 million revenue for health, education, and public works.

Furthermore, student enrollment in secondary schools in the 1970s and 1980s grew twice as fast as the increases in population for the age group, making all numbers more dismal. Only 33 percent of first graders completed the fifth grade, 20 percent started secondary education, 5 percent started postsecondary education, and only 1 percent graduated from universities. At all levels, dropout rates were much higher for rural students and higher still for girls. In the 1980s secondary education was still beyond the reach of most Bolivians; as a result only 35 percent of the total population in the appropriate age group attended, and numbers showed a large disparity between male and female enrollment rates. By 1996, 40 percent of males and 34 percent of females, regardless of age, enrolled in secondary schools. According to the 1989-1992 study done by the Secretary of Education, less than a third of the students of the appropriate age group were enrolled in secondary education.

The numbers at this level showed a terrible discrepancy between cities and rural areas. In cities, close to 65 percent of the age group were enrolled in secondary education, as opposed to only 11 percent in rural areas. According to the 1999 "State of the World's Children" study, 60 percent reached grade five. The ETARE study of 1992 also showed that in urban areas, 33.2 percent of the male students who started in the first year in 1980 reached the twelfth year in 1992, versus only 2.2 percent in rural areas. (Comparable figures for females were 29.4 percent for urban females and 1.1 percent for rural females.) In spite of all the evidence showing that a minimum of five to eight years of education is needed to bring noticeable results in agricultural production, 71 percent of rural students didn't reach the lower mark of five years of schooling. This study also showed that private schools enrolled 27.5 percent in urban areas, versus only 0.049 percent in rural areas.

It must be pointed out that the data was skewed since a variety of schools, which are technically private, were at this point integrated into the public sector and were counted as such. These schools included those operated by institutions, religious groups, or by ONGs. Many of these schools are suburban, serving the poor population; these schools are a strange mix. They receive public funding and, while their fees are the same as public establishments, they remain private as far as their operation and structure are concerned. They are, however, allowed to add lab and computer fees when appropriate. They also operate under different rules—they can dismiss teachers; supplement the state salary, plus give additional benefits; and are far more autonomous in respect to their curriculum. Thus, they can attract and keep better teachers and are in higher demand than ordinary public establishments.

HIGHER EDUCATION

The traditional history of Bolivian higher education starts with the foundation of the Royal and Pontifical University of San Francisco Xavier UMSFX, in La Plata (Sucre), in March 1624. In Colonial times and under Spanish rule, Saint Thomas Aquinas's *Summa Theologica* influenced education. As a result, higher education awarded degrees in theology and law only. Forensics was later added in 1776 in the Caroline Academy. In 1830 the Bolivian University of San Andrés UMSA, was started in La Paz as a college. Shortly after, in 1832, the Bolivian University of San Simón UMSS (Universidad Mayor de San Simón) was also started in Cochabamba. Medicine was added in 1863.

Several universities were established in the late 1800s. In 1880, the University of St Thomas Aquinas was created. The name of the latter, like most of the universities, underwent many changes. In 1911, it was known as the University Gabriel René Moreno; in 1938, the Autonomous University of Santa Cruz; and then back again to Gabriel René Moreno (UAGRM). In 1892 the University of St. Augustine was created. (In 1893 it became the University of Oruro, in 1937 the Bolivian Technical University, and it is now the Technical University of Oruro or UTO). In 1892 the University of Potosi was founded; it is now the Bolivian University of Tomás Frías (UATF).

In 1946 the Bolivian University of Juan Misael Saracho (UAJMS) opened. In 1966 the Catholic University of Bolivia (UCB) was started in La Paz. In 1967 another public university, the Bolivian University of General José Ballivián, also called the Beni Technical University (UTB), was established. The twentieth century National University (UNSXX) was founded in La Paz in 1984. The Amazonian University of Pando (UAP) opened in 1994; also in 1994, the Military School of Engineering (EMI) was founded.

After 1985, Paz Estenssoro's policies fostered the growth of private universities as a means of increasing new programs and reversing declining standards in public universities that had been brought on by open admissions. Universities grew so rapidly that the overall system of higher education consists of 48 universities in 2001. Thirty-five private universities were built after 1989, the date when the Ministry of Education demanded that universities be made accountable and apply a test of academic efficiency. The universities and faculty saw this demand as an intrusion on their prior autonomy. They believed the government was strangling them, and the students viewed this measure as elitist leading to a slow privatization of universities. No one was happy.

Public universities are increasingly inefficient; they only cater to a small percentage of Bolivian students at the rate of 30,000 new students a year and produce mediocre professionals without modern working skills. Private universities are able to compete by generally providing computer labs and better technology than traditional universities. They also try to address the needs of the country in more practical ways. One way is through the proliferation of some 639 higher technical institutes and 22 teacher training institutes.

Only universities can award degrees. Apart from the *Licenciatura,* giving the title of *Licenciado,* which corresponds roughly to the Bachelor's degree in sciences or arts and takes four or five years to complete, the advanced degrees of the *Maestria* and the *Doctorado* are awarded. They correspond roughly to the Masters and Ph.D. degrees, the latter carrying the title of Doctor. Other titles awarded include University Intermediate technicians (a two-year program), University Superior technicians (a three-year program) and Bachelor (a four-year program).

Ten universities are public and autonomous, running a total of 244 academic programs, distributed under 6 different knowledge areas: economics and judicial, social and humanities, natural sciences and biology, health sciences, engineering techniques, and agricultural. The 33 private universities run 221 academic programs, a good many in the same areas of knowledge as public universities.

The growth of private universities between 1990 and 1998 (the last year when the data were available) was remarkable. The enrollment in private universities alone, in the course of their short lives, went up from around 2,000 female students and slightly more than 2,000 male students to approximately 14,341 and 17,812, respectively. Despite the fact that females lag in pre-university education and in university admissions, women have recently outperformed men in completing their studies. In 1998, some 5,606 new male students registered, as did 4,046 females. Whereas the number of women in education went unnoticed in most statistics before 1996, in 1998, approximately 669 men and 759 women exited the university as *Egresados* and 347 males received the title against 411 females.

Students enroll in universities by an academic test of basic skills acquired in secondary education, together with a psychotechnical diagnostic, or a course for people who have not taken or passed the above test. Some students receive special admission, which is entrance granted to experienced professionals who finished high school, officers of the armed forces or the police, or students with foreign titles recognized through international agreements. In 1930 all universities became autonomous in academic and economic matters. In 1971 the universities were closed for restructuring to respond to economic and social necessities. The National Council of Higher Education of the Bolivian University was created, and all universities came under the umbrella of the University of Bolivia. In 1975 a law requiring departmentalization brought greater efficiency, reducing duplication and redistributing professors and units of research and service within the departments. For the first time, each university matched its courses with the national needs; its aim was to develop graduates who would participate in the nation's growth. To this end universities felt that training must be humanistic, scientific, and technological and that there must be collaboration among institutions to find common solutions to national problems.

ADMINISTRATION, FINANCE, & EDUCATIONAL RESEARCH

The ten universities that are public and autonomous are grouped in the National Coordination Organization, the Executive Committee of the Bolivian University (CEUB). Both the Catholic University and the Military School of Engineering are also affiliated with the CEUB. Altogether, they educate about 70 percent of the total university enrollees. As the private universities grew after 1985, they also formed their own group in 1992, the National Association of Private Universities (ANUP). This group functions under the auspices of the Ministry of Education, Culture, and Sports.

Ever since the beginning of the reform, the main concerns in the foreground of the Ministry's work show the ambition of its programs. Efforts include the improvement of standards through the accreditation of teachers; the subsequent combating of illiteracy; the integration of indigenous people through the creation of bilingual programs of education; the social participation by parents, teachers, and students in decision-making; and the integration of women to the educational system.

Another achievement is a teaching accreditation program for former students who had not graduated from UMSS. Launched in 1997, it consisted of refresher courses, updating of practices, workshops, and interdisci-

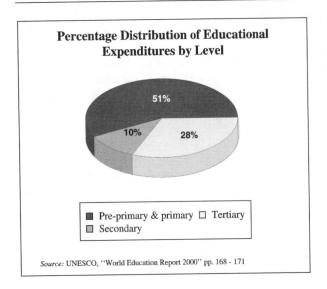

Percentage Distribution of Educational Expenditures by Level

51%

10%   28%

■ Pre-primary & primary   □ Tertiary
■ Secondary

Source: UNESCO, "World Education Report 2000" pp. 168 - 171

plinary and professional seminars lasting six months. Nearly 1,185 students registered for the program, 218 of these in the School of Humanities and Sciences of Education. These back-to-school teachers were organized in sub-modules.

Developed in 1994 as a result of the Reform Project Andes (PROEIB), the bilingual and intercultural educational training for countries in the Andes, the program directed a refreshers' sub-module in bilingual intercultural education. The first aim was to improve the quality of teachers, especially in the rural areas. The second aim was to improve the learning standards of the lower levels through better teaching. The third and ultimate aim remained the integration of indigenous people in education.

This training program is remarkable in many ways. Experience and evaluation are shared among five countries so that the program develops a true sense of collaborative work through interdisciplinary projects, workshops, material, and teachers in the organization. The countries are Colombia, Chile, Ecuador, Peru, and Bolivia. They share common challenges due to the need to integrate the languages of their indigenous populations into the educational systems. In some special PROEIB programs, more than five countries are involved. PROEIB and other educational projects in the five countries receive wide support from international organizations, including UNESCO, OREALC (Regional Education Office for Latin America and the Caribbean), and UNICEF. They work with the help of Germany, the United States, Denmark, Mexico, France, Belgium, Spain, Guatemala, Panama, Brazil, England, Holland, Nicaragua, Argentina, and Canada, among other nations.

PROEIB is a Bolivian-based organization located at the University Mayor of San Simón in Cochabamba. Its headquarters are in the School of Humanities & Sciences

of Education. The network the association created integrates 19 universities and 20 indigenous organizations in the different countries involved, together with the Ministries of Education of the five participating countries. Each of the other four countries has chosen one of its universities to serveas the focal point, or the PROEIB link institution, for the rest of the country's participating institutions. These universities are strategically placed to deal with indigenous matters, either because of their location or because of the special programs they offer. They are the University of the Amazon in Florencia, Colombia; the Institute of Indigenous Studies in the University of La Frontera in Temuco, Chile; The Cotopaxi Academic program in the Salesian Polytechnic University of Latacunga in Ecuador; and the Investigation Center of Applied Linguistics in the University Mayor de San Marcos in Lima.

The five countries organize workshops and accreditation programs, and they created a new Master's in Bilingual Intercultural Education (EIB) to efficiently help jumpstart their programs. The first group started with 50 students belonging to 9 different indigenous tribes native to the 5 countries. Students go through a strict selection program to enter this highly competitive EIB program. Investigators try to answer the questions that arise in the course of EIB programs to enrich the present vision and transform the programs as needed; they develop specific projects and study problems. The promotion of investigation is stimulated by competitions. An international jury evaluates the projects and awards three research grants valued between US$4,000 and US$8,000 depending on the project itself. The winners present their results in various workshops, thus enriching the program, and PROEIB publishes each study.

There is now a Regional Documentation Center in Cochabamba with a library specialized in EIB. It holds more than 8,000 books focusing on indigenous problems from the point of view of culture, language, and education. PROEIB wants to multiply the number of Regional Documentation Centers; several published titles are already available.

The creation of the Network of Bilingual Intercultural Education of countries in the Andes to encourage education among rural indigenous peoples helps to execute the actions promoted by the program. Within the whole program, the Beni Technical University of the Mariscal José Ballivián is in charge of the teaching and learning of Amazonian indigenous languages. This particular program started in the Beni region in 1994 with 60 students. In 1997, it already had 250 students, and 87 teachers from the teacher training programs defended their theses. By 1998, about 120 new students entered the program. These new teachers will have a strong impact in years to come.

Regardless of whether university students want to be teachers, nurses, veterinarians, economists, or agronomists, all students are required from the fourth semester on to take native languages and cultures; the hope is that this requirement will better prepare graduating students to work in the Beni region. They will have the option to learn the Trinitario language but also any of the 17 other languages of the region. Grants are available for indigenous students. These efforts represent a complete reversal of former politics in favor of the conservation of the very same languages that historically had been regularly ignored throughout the Bolivian educational system.

One of the latest indigenous events backed by the Education Ministry was the historical gathering in November 2000 of at least 200 *Guaranies Capitanes* from the 23 Guarani settlements in the city of Monteagudo-Chuquisaca. The aim was to integrate the indigenous educational demands with the municipal management of the region. This meeting validated the Guaranies' organization and recognized the importance of their demands. It marked the beginning of the Guaranies' participation in the future of their children's education through their involvement in the management and through the sharing of responsibility in local educational programs (PREMU).

To answer some of the shortcomings of the public school programs, the *Redes Educativas Urbanas en Marcha* (Urban Educational Network on the Go) was created as a means to diffuse information to the PEN (Nucleus Educational Projects) to improve infrastructures and teaching. Each network covered 8 or 12 educational units and around 6,000 or 7,000 school children. As of September 2000, some 33 network workshops had taken place in La Paz. In 2001, these networks will be organized and put to work, including 370 public schools responding directly to the seat of the government.

International conferences and workshops in the different programs established in the five countries (Bolivia, Colombia, Chile, Ecuador, and Peru) are organized regularly for feedback. Teachers share their experiences and exchange ideas with others. Bolivia has also participated in several important international conferences that helped create the climate to stimulate changes. Among these was the March 1990 World Conference on Education in Jomtiem, Thailand, a conference that helped foster the 1994 reform; conference participants pledged to combat illiteracy, to promote primary education, and to provide basic education for all. Another important conference was the Childhood World Summit in New York. Also, conferences like the Cairo, Egypt, 1994 Conference on Population and Development; the 1995 Conference on Social Development in Copenhagen, Denmark; and the Beijing, China, Conference on Women positively reinforced Bolivia's commitment to "Education for All."

In view of this worldwide concern for literacy, the 1993 Bolivian Law recognizing indigenous languages and the 1994 Education Reform Law didn't come a moment too soon. Other world conferences like the one in Amman, Jordan, in June 1996, certainly helped Bolivia keep track of progress and renew its commitment and accountability. The Dakar, Senegal, 2000 Education For All (EFA) Forum must have had the same consolidating effect.

After these reform laws were passed, the first major change was a shift of priority by the Bolivian government. The educational investment budget jumped from 9 million Bolivianos in 1994 to 143 million in 1999. As of 2000, about 71.5 percent of schools participated in the educational reform, and it is expected to be 100 percent by 2002. There are now 1,324 qualified pedagogical specialists helping teachers in their classes. By 1999, about 83 percent of primary teachers received pedagogical training, and the retention rate in schools increased 30 percent from 1997 to 1999. By the year 2000, precisely 13,069 out of 14,000 schools received sports equipment, and 13,695 schools received class libraries and teaching materials; however, the distribution of teaching materials remained a problem in many educational units.

Bolivia has approximately 758 pedagogical recourse centers open in the country, and they all received furniture, audiovisual equipment, libraries, and other materials. Altogether, in the year 2000, US$265,000 worth of teaching materials was distributed to *Institutos Normales Superiores* (training institutes); US$14,664,000 worth of material was distributed by the Education Reform, as well as a total of 2,879,963 kilos of sports and teaching materials. Thirteen thousand PTA-type organized school groups, called *juntas escolares,* already participate in a quality control program for children's education.

It is impossible to speak of education in Bolivia without going into the external help that Bolivia received, and still receives, from a variety of foreign states. This help, apart from debt relief help, always seems to come earmarked for education in one form or another. Even when it does not seem to be directly related to any schooling, it educates communities about health problems, the eradication of drugs, the substitution of crops, or environmental issues. The aid may fund a university research project, improve economics or agriculture, or teach development and management, but ultimately foreign help programs educate people, laying a foundation for a transition towards self-reliance.

Contributions from international donors have averaged US$500 million annually throughout the past decade; nevertheless, one must also credit Bolivia for taking an active role in its future. It was the first country of the hemisphere to create a Ministry of Sustainable Development, which collaborates economically with international aid programs. A leader in such help programs is USAID, which has helped bring issues to the front and has devised and promoted programs to remedy problems. This organization works in close collaboration with the Government of Bolivia (GOB). It has been very influential, not only in helping many of the poorest indigenous people through a variety of programs, and developing and expanding social marketing projects, but also in revamping the justice sector itself. Recently it has worked in association with other donors to avoid duplication or overlapping of programs and to become more efficient. In 1997 other donors included the Official Development Assistance (ODA), which contributed US$163 million; Japan, $65 million; the Netherlands, $59.8 million; Germany, $47.5 million; and Sweden $20.1 million. Since 1997, donations have almost doubled, probably due to the trust Bolivia gained with its positive results. By 1998, some 26 countries and international organizations at the Paris Consultative Group (PCG) committed about $940 million, representing a 45 percent increase in donations in only one year; of this, 44 percent was in the form of grants to support Bolivia's socio-economic reforms and investments program. The recognition of the success of these efforts is, in part, due to the development of indicators to measure progress. This constant feedback and self-evaluation process have helped the right recommendations go forward and have raised the confidence of other countries in the effectiveness of their investments.

In the Bolivian fiscal year 2000, USAID contributed $75.9 million to continue eradication of illicit coca, to strengthen the social base of democracy and governance, to help increase income and opportunities for the poor, to improve production technology and the health of many Bolivians, and to reduce the degradation of forest, water, and bio-diversity resources. All of these efforts showed dramatic results; goals have been met or will be met by 2003. For example, it is estimated that in the period 1996-2002, about 19 Bolivian municipalities will have been assisted. The USAID plan will be completed with the participation of at least 60 percent nongovernmental organizations (ONGs). In the period 1994-2002, co-participation funds (the 20 percent share of national revenue distributed to municipalities on a per-capita basis) will have been raised from 0 to 65 percent.

The number of clients involved in loans from microfinance institutions is expected to increase 200 percent between 1997 and 2002. In 1999 and 2000, two thousand rural families per year benefited from production, marketing services, and technical assistance, which represents a massive educational achievement in the limited areas that have been targeted. Production units receiving technology services are expected to rise from 1,430 in 1994 or 1995 to 9,200 in 2002. The number of production units receiving marketing services will rise from 230 to 5,290 during the same period, and the number of house-holds with access to credit will also rise from 130,877 to 320,000. The number of communities that will have seen infrastructure constraints resolved will also rise from 130 to 870.

Also encouraging is the fact that in 2001 some 100,000 children per year receive free school meals programs, helping reduce considerably the dropout rates and the grade repetition rate, especially for girls. This program, directed at the poorest primary students in rural areas, complements World Bank programs. In 1999 both the World Bank (WB) and the Inter-American Development Bank (IDB) initiated large health projects to improve infant and maternal health. The aim was to reduce infant mortality, which was 75 deaths per 1000 live births in 1994, to 52 in 2000 and 47 in 2002. Likewise, they aim to reduce maternal mortality, which was 390 per 1000 live births in 1994, to 220 in 2000 and 194 in 2002, by increasing the percentage of births attended by a trained provider and by reducing malnutrition.

Private universities are recognized by article 190 of the state Constitution and the Educational Reform Law number 1565 of July 7, 1994. A general director of university and postgraduate education, helped by a secretary office, manages them. The areas of knowledge taught in private universities all come under the following headings: humanities, healthcare, economy and finance, sciences and technology, arts and architecture, and social sciences. The educational research published in 1997 by Charles N. Myers and Miguel Urquiola analyzed the educational system as a market in which the state, the private sector, and some ONGs (especially the Catholic Church) compete to provide services. They based their analysis on works done by the National Statistics Institute (INE) in 1990 and 1992, work by the Technical Support Team of the Educational Reform (ETARE), and work by the Ministry of Education's Secretary for Human development. The strength of Urquiola and Myers' research resides in the fact that it links the levels of education completed with the improvement rates of agriculture, fertility, and child health, as well as with the industrial production and labor market.

NONFORMAL EDUCATION

Distance learning is still a very new concept in Bolivia; however, the possibilities the method offers are being studied. Bolivia has been looking at the long established models of distance education like that offered by the United Kingdom's Open University, which started in 1969, and like the National Technological University in the States. But for practical reasons, Bolivia is more interested in Spanish language-based programs such as Venezuelan's Open University, *Universidad Nacional Abierta,* in place since 1977, and the Mexican Virtual

University of Monterrey, among others. Although Bolivia can see and appreciate some of the advantages of distance learning and seems to be eager to adopt a proactive approach to distance learning, the cost of computer technology proves to be a problem for the widespread adoption of such programs and methodology for the near future.

TEACHING PROFESSION

According to the Education for All (EFA) study, the number of primary school teachers having the required academic qualifications went from 63.7 percent in 1990 to 67.0 percent in 1999 for females, and from 59 percent to 60 percent for males during the same period. The percentage of school teachers who were certified to teach according to national standards decreased very slightly between 1990 and 1999, remaining almost stagnant at 74.7 percent for females in 1990 and 73.8 percent in 1999; the same was true for males during the same periods at 68.6 percent and 67.5 percent, respectively. Considering the growth in the number of actual classes, this increase seems a fairly good result.

The pupil-teacher ratio in primary schools moved slowly upward from 1995 to 1999 and stood at 23.3:1 in 1999. From 1990 to 1998, the number of teachers within private universities went up from 393 to 2,519 men and from 131 to 984 women; this increase is very important to the future of education as is the soaring enrollment in teacher training programs.

The Educational Reform Law of 1994 states that, as a minimum, teachers must hold the *Licenciatura* to be eligible to teach in private universities. Further training must be provided for teachers of 40 hours per semester.

SUMMARY

Overall, Bolivia is showing an increase in total enrollments and a general improved parity between males and females, especially in urban private schools at the secondary level. Moreover there has been a beneficial increase in the private schools sector. An increased demand for quality education on the part of parents has meant a large migration of students towards cities. The citizens of Bolivia seem to be increasing their awareness of the importance of education, which, in turn, is beginning to produce higher quality labor skills in Bolivia.

Further, the government of Bolivia seems to have developed and fostered surprisingly clear and ambitious strategic educational objectives in the last decade. The long term effects of its multiple programs and of private programs on education overall, and in particular those applied to the indigenous population, remain to be seen. In the early years of the new millennium, Bolivia will depend on foreign funds for most new programs fostered by its reform. A large number of associations have been created with the ultimate goal of Bolivia's reaching self-reliance so that the negative impact that decreased foreign funding would have on the Bolivian education will hopefully be softened. The future of education in Bolivia seems to be heading in the right direction.

BIBLIOGRAPHY

Baker, Colin, and Sylvia Prys Jones. *Encyclopedia of Bilingualism and Bilingual Education.* Multilingual Matters, 1998.

Myers, Charles N., and Miguel Urquiola. *La Educación Intermedia y Media en Bolivia: Un análisis desde la perspectiva de la demanda.* La Paz: UDAPSO, 1997.

PROEIB Andes Bulletins. *Boletines,* 1997-2001.

Propuesta Integral de Innovación Educativa en Nucleuss-PIIEN. La Paz: CEBIAE (Centro Boliviano de Investigación y Acción Educativas), 1998.

The State of the World's Children. UNESCO, 1999.

World Education Report. Oxford: UNESCO Publishing, 1995.

—*Danielle Raquidel*

BOSNIA AND HERZEGOVINA

BASIC DATA

Official Country Name:	Republic of Bosnia and Herzegovina
Region:	Europe
Population:	3,835,777
Language(s):	Croatian, Serbian, Bosnian
Literacy Rate:	NA

HISTORY & BACKGROUND

Bosnia and Herzegovina (*Bosna i Hercegovina*, designated here as BiH), once a culturally rich jewel of the Balkan republics in the former Yugoslavia, suffered dramatically during the 1990s from a tragic civil war involving its three main ethnic groups—Serbs, Bosnian

Muslims ("Bosniacs"), and Croats. The war impacted all aspects of Bosnian society and dramatically reduced the material and social quality of life in the country. Similarly, the war reshaped the percentages and numbers of ethnic minorities living in the country as well as the personal and professional relationships between members of various ethnic groups. In 1991 approximately 31 percent of the Bosnian population was Serb, 17 percent was Croat, and 44 percent was Bosniac, with 5.5 percent of the population considering themselves "Yugoslav" and 2.5 percent belonging to other ethnic minorities such as Roma/Sinti and Jews. About 27 percent of marriages were "mixed" across ethnic lines in 1991, and Bosnia and Herzegovina was well known for the compatible ethnic blending of the inhabitants in many of its towns and villages. Following the radical social, economic, and political transformations that occurred throughout Eastern Europe in the late 1980s and early 1990s, the break-up of the Soviet Union in August of 1991, and a build-up of ethnic tensions in Yugoslavia (a six republic federation created by outside powers in 1918 at the end of the first World War), Bosnia and Herzegovina declared its independence from Yugoslavia in October 1991. By 1992 BiH was engulfed in a genocidal civil war, with significant outside military intervention from the Serbian army of the Federal Republic of Yugoslavia.

Heavy shelling and violent attacks by the three warring sides destroyed the people, land, and social infrastructure of BiH, including the education system, between March 1992 and October 1995. Violence subsided only with a ceasefire declared in October 1995 when representatives from the three warring sides (Bosnian Muslims, Croats, and Serbs) met in Dayton, Ohio to develop a peace accord. This peace agreement, known officially as the "General Framework Agreement for Peace in Bosnia and Herzegovina" (unofficially, as the "Comprehensive Peace Agreement" or "Dayton Accords") was signed in Paris in December 1995. A freshly written Constitution for BiH was annexed to the peace agreement.

The Constitution developed as part of the Dayton Accords detailed a complete restructuring of the government of BiH, with Bosnia and Herzegovina to be kept intact as a single country with internationally recognized exterior boundaries equivalent to those standing before the war and the internal boundaries significantly realigned. The Dayton agreement recognized 51 percent of the territory of BiH as belonging to the Federation of Bosnia and Herzegovina (*Federacija Bosna i Hercegovina*, designated here as FBH), whose population is mainly Bosnian Muslim or Croat, and 49 percent of BiH as belonging to the Serbian Republic (*Republika Srpska*, designated here as RS), where the majority of the population is Serbian. ("Herzegovina" refers to a region just south

of the country's border with Croatia in northern BiH where the majority of the population is Croat.) In addition to the two Entities, the northeastern Bosnian town of Brcko was demilitarized in March 2000 and is now recognized as a self-governing administrative unit under the jurisdiction of the national state, neither part of FBH nor of RS.

Each of the two sub-national territories, FBH and RS, is known as an "Entity," with Bosnia and Herzegovina itself considered a single, unified national state. In turn, the Federation (i.e., the Muslim/Croat majority Entity) is subdivided into ten Cantons where political power is relatively decentralized for many government functions. The Serb Republic is not subdivided. However, at both the national level and in both the FBH and the RS, much political control remains centralized with key policy decisions issuing from the national government organs and from each Entity's governing structures. At the national level, economic and foreign policy are decided by the national government organs of BiH. Based on the Dayton Accords, internal affairs, including education policies, are left to the Entities, and in the case of the Federation, in large measure to the ten Cantons. However, due to the problems arising from the operation of two entirely parallel educational systems and, in the case of FBH, ten subsystems, efforts were being made by the year 2000—with substantial encouragement and financial support from international organizations such as the World Bank, the European Union, the Council of Europe, the United Nations Educational, Scientific, and Cultural Organization, and the United Nations Development Programme—to redesign the country's education system and administrative structures, to upgrade and modernize teacher training, teaching methods, the curriculum, and textbooks, and generally to reform schools and improve the quality of instruction. (The World Bank loan of $10.6 million for the Education Development Project, for example, was designed to improve primary education and teacher training and, more specifically, was to be used to 1) finance grants for schools, teacher training (both pre-service and in-service), and scholarships; 2) define and assess performance standards in primary and secondary schools and to harmonize them with European standards; 3) provide technical assistance and training for academics to improve higher education; and 4) provide data for a Poverty Reduction Strategy and conduct a Living Standards Measurement Study.)

By early 2001, nearly 10 years after Bosnia and Herzegovina's declaration of independence from Yugoslavia, the ethnic make-up of BiH had changed rather significantly from the pre-war situation, along with the residential concentrations of the various ethnic groups living in different parts of the country. In 2001 approximately 40 percent of BiH's population was Serb, about

22 percent Croat, and about 38 percent Bosniac, the large number of war casualties and population displacements caused by the war having altered the ethnic mix. Regarding religion, the composition of BiH is approximately 40 percent Muslim, 31 percent Orthodox, 15 percent Roman Catholic, 4 percent Protestant, and 10 percent other (including some Jewish).

The population of BiH, estimated at about 3.8 to 4.2 million in 2000, had recovered in numbers almost to its pre-war size of 4.4 million, though the population had dropped dramatically in the 1990s due to the numbers of Bosnians who were killed in the war (about 250,000) or who fled the country (about 1.2 million). During the 1990s about two-thirds of the population in the 20- to 40-year-old range left the country. In 1999 only 3.5 million people were estimated to be living in Bosnia. In addition to those killed, more than 200,000 Bosnians were wounded in the war, and 13,000 were permanently disabled, including thousands of children. Within the country, about 850,000 people were still displaced (living outside their home communities) in 2001. (An official population census was to have been taken in 2001 but was postponed to 2003, making it very difficult to provide accurate statistics concerning the population and school enrollments or attainment, graduation, and literacy rates.) Approximately 60 percent of Bosnia's population lived in urban areas in 1999, at which time BiH had a population density of about 72 persons per square kilometer.

By 2000 BiH had a growth rate of about 3.1 percent, which was in part due to the increasing return of refugees who had been living abroad during the war. The fertility rate in BiH in 2000 was about 1.71 percent. Approximately 20 percent of Bosnians in the year 2000 were 14-years-old or younger while 71 percent of the population was between 15 and 64 years of age and about 9 percent was 65 or older. BiH had an infant-mortality rate of 15 per 1000 live births in 2000 and an under 5 years child-mortality rate of 18 per 1000. The average lifespan of Bosnians in the year 2000 was about 71.5 years (68.8 years for men and 74.4 for women).

Geographically speaking, BiH is an almost entirely land-locked country with only about 20 kilometers of coastline, though the country is situated close to the Adriatic Sea. BiH is bordered on the west and the north by Croatia, while Serbia (one of the two states remaining in the Federal Republic of Yugoslavia in 2001) is located on its eastern side and Montenegro (the other remaining Yugoslavian state) is to its southeast. Measuring 15,209 square kilometers, BiH is slightly smaller than the U.S. state of West Virginia. The terrain of BiH is primarily mountains and valleys with large forested areas, especially in the RS; the highest elevation is Maglic at 2.386 meters high.

For centuries the Bosnian economy was primarily agricultural. The primary agricultural products were wheat, corn, fruit, vegetables, and livestock. In the decades before the war of the 1990s BiH became increasingly industrialized, producing wood products, furniture, and military equipment for the Socialist Federal Republic of Yugoslavia due to the prevalence of forests and metallic ores in the country. In 1996 about 23 percent of the Bosnian workforce was employed in industry, 58 percent in services, and just 19 percent in agriculture. After the war, as international donors infused substantial financial support to restart BiH's economy and State and Entity officials and international actors collaboratively developed new plans to prepare BiH's population for employment, this balance was expected to shift even further toward the service sector, though the transformation was anticipated to be gradual. By 1999 the Bosnian economy was growing at an annual rate of roughly 5 percent of the gross domestic product (GDP). However, a sizable black market also was in operation, as well as a ''gray market'' of workers who were paid but did not receive job-related benefits. Furthermore, many of those legally employed waited long periods for delayed paychecks, a situation that may have discouraged many from seeking regular employment. The unemployment rate in the country was about 35 to 40 percent in 1999. BiH's annual per capita income (i.e., the gross domestic product per person in U.S. dollars) was only $1,030 in 1999—a substantial drop from the per capita income level of $2,400 in 1990, but a significant rise from the immediate post-war rate of $456 in late 1995. (Per capita income in the *Republika Srpska* for 1999 was significantly higher: US$1,934.) International donor aid accounted for about 30 percent of the GDP in BiH in 2000. Before the war Bosnia and Herzegovina was the second-poorest republic of the six member states in Yugoslavia. About 27 percent of Bosnians were living below the relative poverty line in 2001, while 11 percent were living in extreme poverty. Regional disparities are quite apparent in the standard of living in different parts of the country; about half the population of RS in 2001 was living below the poverty line whereas in Sarajevo (the Federation's capital city) and West Herzegovina (one of the Croat-majority areas) fewer people were living in poverty.

CONSTITUTIONAL & LEGAL FOUNDATIONS

Bosnia and Herzegovina is an emerging democracy governed by a complex array of structures at the State, Entity, and Cantonal levels. The basis for the educational structures at the State level, in each of the two Entities, and in the ten Cantons of the Federation is laid out in the Constitution prepared as part of the 1995 Dayton Accords. In addition to the governing organs whose members are selected and elected by Bosnians, the post-war government of BiH includes the non-Bosnian Office of the High Representative, designed to oversee the implementation of the Dayton Accords and to monitor progress toward ethnic reintegration and the just and peaceful resettlement of Bosnia's large population of refugees and internally displaced people. Whereas a sizable UN peacekeeping force was deployed throughout Bosnia after the war to ensure the country's stability and to prevent a return to ethnic violence, by the late 1990s a Stabilization Force (SFOR) led by NATO was in place in the country to implement the military side of the Dayton Accords and to protect the security of civilians as the country moved toward reconstruction and rehabilitation. In addition, an International Police Task Force (IPTF) was established by the United Nations in an Annex to the Dayton Accords to monitor local police and provide them with training and advice as well as to investigate alleged abuses of human rights. Human rights conditions in the country remained difficult in the late 1990s; as of 2001 security forces in the country—including the regular police, "special" or secret police, and the armies maintained by the two Entities—continued to provoke complaints from Bosnians of human rights abuses, largely involving police brutality.

A very helpful chart depicting the complex layout of BiH's principal governing structures at the national level and the Entity levels is provided by the Bosnian Embassy on their website (http://www.bosnianembassy.org/). As the chart graphically shows, the Bosnian people elect the three member rotating Presidency (consisting of one Bosniac, one Serb, and one Croat, where the President rotates every eight months) to a four year term. In turn, the Presidency appoints the members of the Council of Ministers for BiH, who are approved by the national, 42 member House of Representatives and who report to the national, 15 member House of People, the second national level legislative chamber (consisting of 5 Bosniacs, 5 Serbs, and 5 Croats elected for 2 year terms).

The voters of the Federation directly elect 28 members of the national House of Representatives (who serve 2 year terms) as well as the 140 members of the Federation's own House of Representatives (who also serve for 2 years). The Federation's House of Representatives and the Federation's House of Nations (consisting of 30 Bosniacs, 30 Croats, and 14 others) constitute the 2 chambers of the Federation's legislature. The Federation has its own Presidency for the Entity, a two member Presidency consisting of one Bosniac and one Croat elected for a two year term and rotating between President and Vice President every six months.

The Serbian Republic has its own unicameral legislature, the RS National Assembly, consisting of 83 members elected for 2 year terms by the voters of the RS. The members of this Assembly elect the RS's members of the national House of Representatives and also select the RS members for the national House of People. The RS has its own Entity President, one person elected for a two year term.

In addition to the executive and legislative branches of government, BiH has a judicial branch consisting of a Constitutional Court of nine members, four of them selected by the Federation's House of Representatives, two by the RS's National Assembly, and three non-Bosnians selected by the president of the European Court of Human Rights. The judiciary at the national level is supplemented by judicial organs in each of the Entities as well as by the International Criminal Tribunal for the Former Yugoslavia (ICTY) in The Hague, leading at times to confusion by Bosnian authorities as to which rules apply to which situations in terms of arrests and detention. According to the U.S. Department of State in early 2001, the judiciary in both the RS and the Federation was unduly influenced by the dominant political parties and by the executive branch. In addition to rather widespread problems of discrimination against women and violence against them, especially domestic violence, minorities were often subject to severe discrimination in Serb and Croat majority areas and to a lesser extent in Bosniac majority areas. This was especially the case for refugees and the internally displaced, many of whom had not yet returned to their home communities or who had returned to areas now controlled by a different ethnic group than lived there in pre-war days. Job discrimination and discrimination in education have plagued many people in BiH since the war and are not likely to be fully addressed until better arrangements are made by the nationalist parties in power to ensure the fair distribution of employment and education benefits to all people living in Bosnia—including those who belong to none of the three major ethnic groups.

Although Bosnia has made some progress in rebuilding schools and beginning education reforms since the war ended, progress has been slowed by the conflicts and contradictions existing between the two parallel education systems of RS and FBH; by the presence of ten separate educational systems across the Federation's ten Cantons; by the clashing co-existence of pre-war and more recent educational laws, teaching methods, and curricula; and perhaps most significantly, by the presence and resistance of ethnic nationalist individuals and political parties among the Serbs, Croats, and Bosniacs who wish to impose their own particularistic interpretations of history and of the war on their communities and the curricula in their schools. Especially problematic in terms of subject matter has been the teaching of recent history, notably the war period of the 1990s. Certain international organizations and experts have called for a moratorium on the teaching of the history of this period in the country until a combination of international historians and local experts can thoroughly revise the history texts and curricula used in Bosnian schools so that teaching is accurate and can impartially reflect what transpired before and during the war years. However, this recommendation for a moratorium has been met with heavy protests and resistance from ethnic nationalists interested in preserving their own interpretations of Bosnian history and war-related events and promulgating their biased views in Bosnia's schools.

In 2001 international education specialists and Bosnian educators, government officials, and pedagogical researchers continued to work collaboratively to revise offensive textbooks throughout Bosnia and to remove passages of inaccurate, inflammatory, and/or nationalist writing from the books and curricula used in schools. Rewriting texts and removing objectionable material from the teaching curricula was begun in August 1999 after the three education ministers in the country—the Minister and Deputy Minister of Education for the Federation and the Minister of Education for the RS—responded to international pressure and finally signed an agreement concerning the excision of objectionable passages and the identification of other passages as debatable. Based on an agreement made by the Minister of Education in May 2000, this work was to be completed by the end of June 2000 with substantial improvements in the quality of textbooks made by the end of the year 2000.

At the turn of the millennium, the focus of educational reforms in Bosnia and Herzegovina was on rebuilding schools, retraining teachers, improving the curriculum, reducing the number of subjects taught in the schools so as to increase educational quality and efficiency, and developing more functional vocational education systems at both secondary and higher levels of instruction, including at the level of adult education, so that workers with employable skills could be trained for the newly reviving Bosnian economy. In general, a major emphasis of educational reform work was being placed on unifying the school systems operating in the country and dismantling the often conflicting parallel systems that had developed between the two Entities and across the ten Cantons. The duplication and mismatching of educational programs and schools in the separately developed systems around Bosnia and Herzegovina were making the return and re-integration of refugees and internally displaced Bosnians especially problematic. Since the languages and subjects taught in one part of the country were not matched by those taught in other places, students seeking to transfer from one community and educational system to another often experienced rejection and/or confusion. Furthermore, since examinations, diplomas, and credentials were not uniformly established or awarded across the various educational systems, problems often have arisen for graduates seeking to work in another part of the country from where the original exams had been taken or diplomas and credentials had been awarded. In the year 2000 the RS developed three new laws concerning education in primary and secondary schools and at higher levels of education. A new strategy for vocational education in the RS had been defined and adopted by the Entity government in 1999. In turn, FBH had ten different laws pertaining to vocational education in secondary schools, one for each of its ten cantons. Major reforms were being planned by the World Bank and other international partners of Bosnian education officials through their collaborative work with Bosnian teachers and administrators by early 2001, when special efforts began to address in earnest the problem of harmonizing the various conflicting educational systems and the problems of ethnic segregation and discrimination that appeared to be widespread. Roma and Jews were especially marginalized in the education systems that had developed after the war.

EDUCATIONAL SYSTEM—OVERVIEW

During the period of post-war recovery in Bosnia and Herzegovina, education is viewed as a very crucial component in the reconstruction and rehabilitation process. As a potential means of helping children and youth of different ethnic backgrounds to practice tolerance and understanding and of helping adults to reconcile their differences, communities to stabilize, and ethnic minorities to live safely with the dominant majority in each part of the country, education—and especially "civic education"—is seen as essential. International observers and Bosnian educators attuned to the need to foster a multi-ethnic society have expressed the belief that carefully planned and implemented educational programs may promote democratization and facilitate the reintegration and resettlement of refugees and the internally displaced. Moreover, educational programs are viewed not only as important for the children and youth of BiH but also for Bosnian adults, many of whom must retrain for new labor market conditions and a less-industrially based economy.

Few international data sources on population and education-related issues contain statistics for Bosnia in the post-1995 period, making an accurate depiction of the status of education in the country extremely challenging. Nonetheless, it was apparent at the turn of the new millennium that the status of BiH's schools remained quite poor, judging from the reports of a number of international donor agencies and organizations working with national and local authorities in BiH to reconstruct and reinvigorate the educational system. The World Bank, the European Commission, the Council of Europe, several UN agencies, international organizations like the International Foundation for Election Systems, and private donors such as the Soros Foundation have been instrumental in fostering educational reform and reconstruction in the country, providing a combination of funding and technical advisors to improve education in BiH. In 1996 BiH became a member of the World Bank (with membership retroactive to 1993) and the country began receiving massive amounts of international assistance to recover from the war. The 26 initial reconstruction grants given to BiH by the World Bank to catalyze the rebuilding of social infrastructure included grants for educational programming. Additionally, the European Training Foundation (ETF) of the European Commission dedicated significant resources and expertise to promoting improved vocational training in the country at both secondary and higher levels. As part of the assistance from ETF, a National Bosnian Observatory was established in Mostar in the FBH in 1999 with a branch office in Banja Luka, the capital of the RS. The Observatory was charged with the following tasks in collaboration with national education authorities and international ''social partners'': 1) to gather, analyze, and distribute information about vocational training, the labor market, and the implementation and assessment of education reform; 2) to serve as a contact point for national and international actors concerning information on vocational training and the labor market; 3) to conduct studies and prepare evaluation papers and policy reports pertaining to vocational training that could be used by the Bosnian authorities to develop and improve programming; 4) to assess developments in vocational training and the labor market; 5) to link up educational institutions with labor market institutions; and 6) to store data concerning social partners and institutions.

Free and compulsory education is provided by both Entities in BiH for all children between the ages of 7 and 15 or for the 8 years of primary schooling. By 2000 approximately 98 percent of adult males and 89 percent of adult females were considered literate. School enrollments at the primary level were estimated to be about 100 percent for both boys and girls; general enrollment statistics at the secondary level were not available.

Language of Instruction: Three versions of the Serbo-Croat language (''Serbian,'' ''Croatian,'' and ''Bosniac'') are used in BiH's schools—essentially, variants of the same language that were developed in conjunction with the nationalistic campaigns that swept the country in the 1990s. Despite their differences, the three versions of Serbo-Croat are mutually comprehensible. The languages of instruction in specific geographical areas typify the ethnic composition of those areas, although according to BiH's new Constitution of 1995 all areas should provide educational opportunities to all minority groups. In

2001 both the Latin and Cyrillic alphabets were in use in Bosnian schools, with both scripts legally mandated for all students to learn.

Unfortunately, during the post-war years, Bosnian schools often have failed to provide instruction in the home language of some of their students, a defect that hopefully will be addressed and at least partially corrected in the reforms taking place at the State, Entity, and Cantonal levels from the year 2000 on as the educational systems are harmonized into one cohesive system. Linguistic and cultural rights had not yet been clarified in the context of education at the turn of the millennium due to situations of ethnic dominance and the continuing nationalistic influence of dominant majorities throughout the country. Lluís Maria de Puig of Spain, education rapporteur for the Council of Europe's Committee on Culture and Education, studied the country's educational system through in-depth interviews with education specialists, government administrators, and international experts working in BiH and wrote in the Committee's March 2000 report, ''Language, and more generally, education policies have become a vehicle for promoting 'national' separation. The political struggle within education manifests itself both in the context of 'national subjects'—history, language and literature and social studies—and in the desire for political control of the three separate education systems (created by the Serbs, Croats, and Bosniacs in the country).'' Educational programs serving the needs of all children, including ethnic minorities, thus had not been fully or adequately developed by the year 2000. This is likely to change, though perhaps gradually, as national and international partners in education continue to work together to improve the Bosnian education system.

PREPRIMARY & PRIMARY EDUCATION

While several conflicting education systems existed in BiH in the year 2000 and a campaign was beginning among national educators and administrators and international partners to harmonize the systems, the following description of the levels of education provided in Bosnian schools generally applied to schools throughout the country in the year 2000.

From ages one to three, children may attend daycare centers that emphasize physical care. Children ages three to six or seven may attend kindergarten. ''Special kindergartens'' also exist for children ages three to seven (or nine). In the RS 41 public kindergartens and 2 private ones were in operation in the 1999-2000 school year, educating 5,987 children; with 772 kindergarten teachers in the RS, the pupil to teacher ratio was 7.76.

Compulsory schooling begins at age 7, when children begin primary school, and lasts for 8 years to age

15. Primary schooling is typically divided into 2 tiers: a first tier for ages 7 to 11, with children taught in classes, and a second tier for pupils ages 11 to 15, where subjects become the focus of educational arrangements. Special primary education is provided from ages 7 (or 9) to 15. Alongside the regular public schools where the full range of academic subjects are taught, parallel schools exist for teaching music and ballet at the primary level. All together, approximately 21,000 primary teachers provided education to pupils between the ages of 7 and 15 in BiH in the year 2000. During the 1999-2000 school year in the RS, 7,059 teachers in 196 public primary schools provided education to 124,305 pupils (60,418 in the lower-primary grades, grades 1 to 4, and 63,887 in the upper-primary grades, grades 5 to 8).

SECONDARY EDUCATION

Between the ages of 15 and 18 or 19 (sometimes 20), students attend the third tier of schooling, 3V (vocational) or 3G (general or gymnasium). Again, special education is provided at the secondary level for students between the ages of 15 and 18. Students in the 3G tier take four years of instruction in academic subjects, after which they take examinations that lead to their admission to institutions of higher education. Students in the 3V tier take either three or four (sometimes five) years of training in vocational areas. In the Federation, attending Teacher school at the secondary level, which lasts four years, is one option for students. In both Entities secondary students can follow educational programs in Arts, Music, and Ballet schools (lasting four years), Religion schools (four or five years), Technical and related schools (lasting four years), and Crafts schools (lasting three years). Students in the Crafts schools take terminal exams that permit them to practice their craft commercially if they are qualified and/or to move on to higher education as Professional Craftsmen through a course and examination program lasting two years coupled with two more years of practical experience. Students in the four year technical-training programs at the secondary level take exams that allow them to go on to higher education training in their field. Other secondary students (e.g. those in the Gymnasium programs and the Teacher schools) take exams at the completion of their studies that permit them to enter appropriate institutions of higher education. Among the types of vocational education provided at the secondary level is religious education, which is offered through religion schools for students ages 15 to 19 in FBH and for students ages 15 up to 20 in RS.

In the year 2000, almost 9,000 secondary teachers were teaching students in BiH (both Entities). The number of teachers was about 3,400 in the RS, where 54,232 students were enrolled in a total of 92 public secondary schools in 1999-2000, yielding a student to teacher ratio of 16.1. Secondary level vocational students accounted for about 75 percent of all secondary students in the Federation in the 1998-1999 academic year and numbered 82,605 (for the Federation alone), with a pupil to teacher ratio of 21 to 1. As to vocational schools at the secondary level, the Federation had 37 types of technical and related schools covering 120 crafts and technical professions in the year 2000, while the RS had comparable programs in about 14 occupational areas for over 100 professions that year.

HIGHER EDUCATION

Higher education can take several forms in BiH. Students who have pursued an academic program or an art, music, or ballet-focused course of study at the secondary level are eligible for admission to Faculties of higher education or Art Academies after successfully passing their exams. These programs last three to six years in the Federation and four to six years in the RS. Pedagogical Academies and Senior Secondary Schools are another option for students graduating from the secondary education programs in BiH; programs in these institutions last two years. The final levels of higher education include Masters degree programs (lasting two years) or Specialization studies (lasting one year), with the Masters programs followed by doctoral studies for some students leading to the Ph.D. degree. In the RS 13,883 postsecondary students were enrolled in 2 public universities (including 28 faculties, schools, and academies) and 4 public non-university educational institutions during the 1999-2000 academic year.

Foreign Students: Before the war Yugoslavian universities and schools, including the renowned University of Sarajevo, attracted many foreign students, including students from developing countries who received academic grants from the formerly socialist government of Yugoslavia. However, because of the widespread destruction of schools, universities, and libraries during the war and the general degradation of economic and social conditions in the country, this picture of foreign enrollment in Bosnian educational institutions changed completely in the 1990s. In contrast, many Bosnia students found placements in colleges and universities abroad, often sponsored by international peace and development-related organizations such as the Fellowship of Reconciliation.

ADMINISTRATION, FINANCE, & EDUCATIONAL RESEARCH

Government Educational Agencies: The three Ministers of Education in charge of planning and implementing education policy in the country are the Minister and Deputy Minister of Education, Science, Culture and Sports of the Federation of Bosnia and Herzegovina and the Minister of Education of the *Republika Srpska.* According to the Constitution of 1995 attached to the Dayton Accords, administration of education in Bosnia and Herzegovina is the responsibility of the two Entities, and in the case of the Federation, the ten Cantons as well. In some parts of the country, Canton-level legislation specifies that educational authority further rests at the municipal level. This has led to a confusing array of responsibilities and government agencies in charge of various aspects of education in the country with often overlapping and contradictory responsibilities, visions, and priorities. In the March 2000 report of the Council of Europe's Committee on Culture and Education, de Puig wrote, "It is increasingly openly acknowledged that the current Bosnian Constitution, as annexed to the Dayton Agreements, is in practice an obstacle to the country's proper functioning." De Puig explained that since 1992, three separate educational systems had established themselves in the country: 1) in the *Republika Srpska* the education system had been "imported from Serbia and uses texts from Belgrade, the Cyrillic alphabet and the 'Serb language,'" 2) in the three Croat-majority Cantons of the Federation, in parts of two other Cantons, and in the Catholic schools set up by Croatians around the country, a Croatian system was in place, "using school books from Zagreb, the Latin alphabet, and the 'Croat language,'" and 3) a third system developed by Bosniacs in Sarajevo was also in place which used the "Bosniac language" and textbooks produced in Sarajevo while the city was under siege.

By May 2000 the three education ministers in BiH had met and agreed to the following measures aimed at eliminating ethnic segregation and harmonizing the disparate education systems into one integrated system: 1) revision of textbooks to remove objectionable material and improve their quality; 2) creation of a Curriculum Harmonisation Board consisting of one representative of the Ministry, one representative from a Pedagogical Institute for each community, and representatives of the international community to coordinate curricula, exchange information about the education systems, and recommend ways to streamline the teaching of subjects throughout the curricula; 3) development by each ethnic group of curricular modules reflecting the group's culture, language, and literature and the needs of the Roma/ Sinti minority and other minorities in BiH, with the modules to be integrated into the curricula of the other two major ethic groups; 4) teaching of both the Cyrillic and Latin alphabets, the shared linguistic, literary, and cultural heritage of the three main ethnic communities, and all major religions practiced in BiH; 5) introduction of "shared, core elements" into all curricula to foster "a sense of common identity and citizenship of Bosnia and Herzegovina" among all students in Bosnia, drawing upon European educational experience and practice, and replacement of the old civic defense/social studies courses with a new Human Rights and Civic Education course; 6) hiring of teachers from the different ethnic groups constituting the Bosnian population to teach in a multiethnic system where teachers are not segregated by ethnicity; 7) recognition of pupils' educational certificates and records and of teachers' and teacher-trainers' qualifications throughout the country, regardless of their place of origin within the country; 8) removal of national subjects textbooks that emphasize one ethnic group and do not refer to BiH as a whole or as the country in which instruction is being given; and 9) peaceful negotiation of all outstanding cases of school crises. This agreement was the product of meetings facilitated by the Office of the High Representative in Sarajevo and other representatives of the international community working to improve the quality of education in BiH and to smooth the way for the education system to be better integrated and more functional.

Educational Budgets: In 1998 BiH spent about 10.8 percent of the national budget on education. That same year, about 4.8 percent of the Federation's budget was spent on education. In the year 2000 about 17 percent of the budget of the RS was planned for educational expenditures, with 4 percent of the Entity's budget reserved for secondary education. In the RS about US$51.7 million was spent on education by the Entity government (including expenditures for the Ministry of Education itself and for primary, secondary, and tertiary education but not including expenditures for secondary-education material expenses, which are the responsibility of the municipalities); about 83 percent of this $51.7 million covered salaries. In general, greater expenditures have been made in the Federation of Bosnia and Herzegovina than in the *Republika Srpska* on education.

Financing education in BiH is accomplished through taxation and other public financing measures; contributions from private and international donors; legacies, gifts, and foundations; and the sales of school products and services, intellectual services, and material goods. As an indication of the scale of international support given to the reconstruction of schools and the education system in BiH in recent years, it can be noted that the World Bank loan approved in May 2000 for the Education Development Project in BiH was valued at US$10.6 million, with the total project expected to cost $14.6 million (and much of the additional $4 million expected to come from other international partners).

NONFORMAL EDUCATION

Adult Education: In addition to the vocational training efforts already mentioned above, some of them directed toward increasing the employability of adults, continuing education programs for adults were in the process of being developed in the year 2000 through the collaborative efforts of education authorities in BiH and international specialists in education. Besides these programs, civic education programs designed to promote ethnic tolerance, democratic participation, and human rights were developed and implemented throughout the country from the late 1990s on, receiving international funding support and technical assistance from international nongovernmental organizations like the Open Society Institute and the International Foundation for Election Systems.

Distance Education (TV, Radio, and Internet):   Distance education has been recommended in BiH as one possible means of addressing the educational needs of the refugees and internally displaced who have not yet returned to their home communities or been fully resettled and reintegrated. Thirty-three television stations and 292 "repeaters" broadcasted television programming in BiH just before the end of the war, in September 1995. About 940,000 radios were in use in 1997; one year later eight AM radio stations, 16 FM radio stations, and 1 shortwave radio station were transmitting broadcasts throughout the country. In 1999 two Internet service providers were operating in the country.

SUMMARY

In March 2000 the Council of Europe's Committee on Culture and Education recommended that the Committee of Ministers of the Council of Europe do the following to improve education in Bosnian schools: 1) provide funding for the Council to continue to offer key support to the education sector in BiH, 2) work with the High Representative and international organizations operating in BiH to reinterpret the Dayton Accords so education planning, implementation, and management responsibilities will be better distributed at the Canton, Entity, and State levels; 3) coordinate the work of the Council and other international organizations to link international funding with Bosnian compliance with prior conditions set by international donors concerning such issues as textbook improvements, ethnic desegregation, coordination, and language policies; 4) continue to encourage a moratorium on teaching about the 1990s war so that historians from all of BiH's ethnic communities can work together with international experts to develop a commonly agreed-upon approach to teaching recent history; 5) provide moral and material support for local educational initiatives, especially those that counteract ethnic segregation; 6) continue to support multiethnic pilot projects in education and consider expanding these in places where the greatest impact may be had, such as Brcko and Mostar; 7) make sure that all ethnic communities, including minorities besides the three major ethnic groups, can exercise their rights to education via a multiethnic perspective; 8) suggest administrative, financial, and legislative solutions to establish a cost-effective system of higher education capable of meeting current and future needs; and 9) "consider using distance learning to overcome ethnic segregation at university level."

As the international community progressively disengages itself from providing funding and technical assistance to Bosnia and Herzegovina in the coming years, and once the country becomes more economically secure and has overcome the fragmentation it suffered during the recent years of violent ethnic conflict, it is hoped that educational authorities will be able to envision a future for the children and youth of their country that includes multiethnic cooperation and the protection of human rights, regardless of the ethnic group to which a person belongs. To this end, the views of the Council of Europe's Committee on Culture and Education on the complexity and significance of educational reform in Bosnia and Herzegovina, expressed in their March 2000 report to the Council, come to mind: "Achieving the transition to a more integrated education system—or at least the more effective co-ordination of parallel systems—is an immensely difficult task which necessitates complex planning in stages and the restoration of confidence between the different communities. In the present post-war context, where most of the country's regions continue to be divided along ethnic lines, few issues can have a higher priority."

BIBLIOGRAPHY

Amnesty International. *Amnesty International Report 2001*. Available from http://web.amnesty.org/.

Borcanin, Natasa, Stephen H. Connolly, and Edgar Morgan. *Bosnia and Herzegovina: Civic Education Program for 1999-2000*, July 2000. Available from http://www.ifes.org/.

Bosnia@caltech.edu. *Culture, Academia and Daily Life*, 2001. Available from http://www.cco.caltech.edu/.

Bosnian Embassy, 2001. Available from http://www.bosnianembassy.org/.

Bureau of Democracy, Human Rights, and Labor. *Country Reports on Human Rights Practices—2000: Bosnia and Herzegovina*. U.S. Department of State, February 2001. Available from http://www.state.gov.

The Central Intelligence Agency (CIA). *The World Factbook 2000*. Directorate of Intelligence, 1 January 2001. Available from http://www.cia.gov/.

Committee on Culture and Education and Rapporteur Mr. Lluís Maria de Puig. ''Education in Bosnia and Herzegovina.'' Parliamentary Assembly, Council of Europe, 14 March 2000. Available from http://stars.coe.fr/.

The European Commission. *The EU and South Eastern Europe,* 2001. Available from http://europa.eu.int/.

European Training Foundation. *Bosnia and Herzegovina,* 2001. Available from http://www.etf.eu.int/.

European Training Foundation. *ETF Activities: Guide to the European Training Foundation's Support to Vocational Education and Training—Labour Market Reform Process in Bosnia and Herzegovina in 2001.* Available from http://www.etf.eu.int/.

European Training Foundation. *Vocational Education and Training in Bosnia and Herzegovina,* 2001. Available from http://www.etf.eu.int/.

European Union. *Bosnia and Herzegovina: A Major Post-War Reconstruction Programme,* 2001. Available from http://europa.eu.int.

Gakovic, Aleksandra. *Statistical data for background purposes of OECD review—Country: Bosnia and Herzegovina—Republic of Srpska.* Centre for Educational Policy of Studies, Faculty of Education, University of Ljubljana, December 2000. Available from http://www.see-educoop.net/.

Human Rights Watch. *World Report 2001.* Available from http://www.hrw.org/.

Office of the High Representative. *Meeting of the Conference of the Ministers of Education of Bosnia and Herzegovina.* Declaration and Agreement, 10 May 2000, Sarajevo. Available from http://www.ohr.int/.

Open Society Institute. *Step by Step Program in Bosnia—Hercegovina,* 2001. Available from http://www.see-educoop.net/.

South East European Educational Cooperation Network. *Educational Development in Post Crisis Situations,* 2001. Available from http://www.see-educoop.net/.

UNICEF. *Bosnia and Herzegovina,* December 2000. Available from http://www.unicef.org/.

United Nations Educational, Scientific and Cultural Organization. *Terminal Project Report: Conclusions and Recommendations,* 2001. Available from http://www.unesco.org/.

World Bank Group. *Bosnia and Herzegovina at a Glance,* September 2000. Available from http://wbln0018.worldbank.org/.

———. *Bosnia and Herzegovina Data Profile.* World Development Indicators Database, July 2000. Available from http://devdata.worldbank.org/.

———. *Country Brief: Bosnia and Herzegovina,* September 2000. Available from http://wbln0018.worldbank.org/.

———. *Education Development Project,* 2001. Available from http://www4.worldbank.org/.

—*Barbara Lakeberg Dridi*

BOTSWANA

BASIC DATA

Official Country Name:	Republic of Botswana
Region:	Africa
Population:	1,576,470
Language(s):	English, Setswana
Literacy Rate:	69.8%
Number of Primary Schools:	681
Public Expenditure on Education:	8.6%
Educational Enrollment:	Primary: 313,693 Secondary: 111,134 Higher: 8,850
Educational Enrollment Rate:	Primary: 108% Secondary: 65% Higher: 6%
Teachers:	Primary: 12,306 Secondary: 6,670 Higher: 765
Student-Teacher Ratio:	Primary: 25:1 Secondary: 18:1
Female Enrollment Rate:	Primary: 108% Secondary: 68% Higher: 6%

HISTORY & BACKGROUND

The Republic of Botswana was established in 1966 when Great Britain terminated its status as the colonial protector of Bechuanaland. Botswana is located in southern Africa, north of South Africa. It has a land area of 603,200 square kilometers. A landlocked nation, Botswana is completely dependent upon South Africa for access to ocean ports. Botswana is a member of the British Commonwealth and has a multiparty political system within a republican form of governance. In 1998 its economic growth rate was approximately 7 percent, with mineral resources being its principal exports.

The original inhabitants of Botswana were the Basarwa, more commonly known as the Bushmen. The Basarwa were nomadic hunters and gatherers who adapted well to harsh environments. Totally dependent upon the availability of water and game, the Basarwa were astutely cognizant of their environmental surroundings, and they developed ingenious techniques to extract what meager sustenance the land offered. They had no crops or domesticated animals and few possessions. Everything they owned was portable and necessary for sustaining daily existence. In 2000, approximately 60 percent of the 55,000 remaining Basarwa resided in Western Botswana. Their traditional way of life has been compromised by civilization, causing most to work on farms or cattle ranches; others live in settlements near water holes.

Sixty percent of Botswana's 1.4 million people claim Tswana heritage. The Tswana, a Bantu group, migrated into what is now Southeastern Botswana where environmental conditions were more hospitable to their sedentary way of life. They continued moving south and established village settlements in what is now the Transvaal Region of South Africa. Early in the nineteenth century, Zulu aggression pushed the Tswana towards the Western Kalahari where they regrouped and restructured their society around centralized towns surrounded by satellite villages. The Tswana are divided into eight principal groups governed by hereditary chiefs.

White Afrikaners, descendants of seventeenth century Dutch settlers, began colonizing the fertile lands of the Transvaal Region. British intervention protected the Tswana from Afrikaner domination. Towards the end of the nineteenth century, Britain extended its political control over the area from the coastal colony of Cape Town deeper into the higher plateau of the Transvaal region. In 1881 Britain subdued the Afrikaners and granted them independence in exchange for their allegiance to the crown, but opportunistic Afrikaners continued to migrate into traditional Tswana lands and captured the town of Mafikeneg.

Tswana leaders, Chiefs Sechele I and Mosielele, sent emissaries to petition Britain for protection. Britain was concerned because of Mafikeneg's strategic location as a planned rail link connecting mineral rich Zimbabwe with the port city of Cape Town. Therefore, in 1886 Britain established a protectorate over Bechuanaland. In return, the Tswana chiefs granted Cecil Rhodes' British South African Company (BSAC) a narrow strip of land for a railroad corridor that would run through the heart of Tswana settlements. The tribal chiefs reluctantly accepted that the railroad would bring Western technology and Christianity, which would change their traditional way of life.

Their concerns increased when Britain considered granting control over all of Bechuanaland to Rhodes' company in 1895. Tswana chiefs Bathoen Khama III and Sebele, accompanied by sympathetic missionaries, sailed to England to meet with Colonial Minister Joseph Chamberlain. They argued that BSAC would corrupt Tswana society by bringing in alcohol. The London Missionary Society (LMS) and other Christian groups forced the government to relent and maintain its protective status over Tswana lands.

Administration of the protectorate was headquartered in Mafikneg, the South African town in the Transvaal. The British resident commissioner was responsible to a High Commissioner of Basutoland, Bechuanaland and Swaziland who, in turn, was accountable to the colonial office in London. Three advisory councils were established with the Tswana chiefs and their counselors in one group, white businessmen and farmers in the second, and a joint council of delegates from the other two. The tribes actively participated in the commercial economy evolving in the protectorate. Each chief was granted a tribal reserve with jurisdiction over all black residents with the authority to collect taxes. They retained a 10 percent commission of all monies collected, including the sale of cattle, draft oxen, and grain to Europeans.

The Anglican Church has always been an influential factor in Botswana's politics. This was especially evident during the protectorate period. Not satisfied with the slow rate of progress, the resident commissioner, Sir Charles Ray, tried to compromise the autonomy of the Tswana chiefs by proclaiming them local government officials who were accountable to colonial magistrates. It was feared, in 1923, that such arbitrary action would eventually lead to annexation by South Africa. The Church was a strong advocate for the chiefs; their involvement caused Ray to be removed from his position and the proclamation to be annulled. Botswana remained a British protectorate until independence was granted in 1966.

In 1997, about 27 percent of Botswana's 1.6 million people lived in urban areas. Because of Botswana's harsh environment, population density averages 2.3 persons per square kilometer. The dominant urban centers exist in the east while smaller cities are dispersed in the outlands bordering the Okavango Delta and Kalahari Desert. Approximately 4,300,000 people live in the eastern rim of the country along the railroad corridor connecting Zimbabwe with South Africa. In the 1800s, before protective status was conferred over the Tswana tribes and the railroad corridor created, the largest and most important towns were located in the east.

Until Botswana was granted independence, the affairs of the protectorate were administered from the South African city of Mafikeng. In 1964, with independence pending, it was decided to create a capital at the village Gaberones. The capital city, renamed Gaborone, was planned to accommodate 20,000 people; however, in 2000 it had almost 250,000 residents and was one of the world's fastest growing cities. Gabrone functions as Botswana's administrative, commercial, and industrial center. Typical of most large cities in developing countries, wealthier neighborhoods exist close to the city's center while shanty communities belonging to the urban poor and recent migrants are located in the outer suburbs.

According to the 1994 census, Botswana's birth rate was 45.6 per 1,000 persons, and the death rate was 11.1 per 1,000 persons. Approximately 40.6 percent of the population was less than 15 years of age, while 4.1 percent was 65 and older. Thus, Botswana's population could double by 2030. The rate of literacy has increased in Botswana. Adult female literacy increased from 44 percent in 1970 to 70 percent in 1998, and adult male literacy increased from 37 percent in 1970 to 67 percent in 1998.

Botswana is the country whose population has been most afflicted with the AIDS virus. A United Nations Development Report estimates that 36 percent of the country's population carry the virus. More conservative estimates place the figure in the high twenties. Botswana is making headway in fighting the disease by providing drugs to pregnant mothers. The United Kingdom Institute of Actuaries is making a detailed projection of what the epidemic may mean for Botswana and identifying the best ways to fund long-term health and social security costs. In 1999, the annual death rate from AIDS was 24,000. In 2000, life expectancy was 40.2 years for women and 39.9 years for the entire population. In 1993, there was 1 hospital bed per 434 persons. In 1994, there was an average of 1 physician for each 4,395 persons.

Diamonds were discovered in 1967, one year after Botswana gained its independence. Rather than lease extraction rights, the government negotiated a partnership with De Beers that gives 75 percent of the profits to Botswana. In 1966 mining contributed only 1 percent of gross domestic product (GDP); in 1998 it comprised 36 percent of GDP. Mining has been largely responsible for Botswana's rate of economic growth, which averaged 7.3 percent between 1970 and 1995, the highest in the developing world. While mining should remain stable, diamond output is reaching its peak, and further production gains may be limited. Tourism is the second vital component of Botswana's economy, but it could decline in the twenty-first century because of political unrest in neighboring countries.

Economic planners are working to expand the manufacturing sector, but a disappointment occurred in 1999 when an automobile plant, Motor Company of Botswana, closed. Vehicles had been Botswana's second largest export earner and a flagship for industrial development. The Botswana Export Development and Investment Authority (BEDIA) was created in 1999 to expand exports by offering foreign companies attractive incentives to establish businesses in the country. Eleven new companies, mostly textile firms from India and Sri Lanka, created 3,000 new jobs, which helped alleviate the severe unemployment problem.

Botswana is a member of the Southern African Development Community (SADC). A Trade Protocol went into effect late in 2000. The protocol's goal is to remove tariff and non-tariff barriers to trade in the region by 2008. Tariff reduction could become a problem because South Africa and the European Union have their own trade agreements. There is concern that the SADC countries may be flooded with cheaper European imports.

In 2000 Botswana's rate of inflation was more than 10 percent for the first time since 1995. Because the bulk of Botswana's consumer goods are imported from South Africa, increased costs in consumer prices in South Africa have an adverse effect on Botswana. The rising cost of international oil has also generated inflationary pressure. The government is maintaining a tight monetary policy and resisting pressure to deflate its currency. Fiscal policy will focus on improving control over government expenditures while increasing receipts. Proposals have been made to replace a sales tax with a value added tax and to charge user fees for health services and education.

Fiscal discipline has enabled Botswana's independent central bank to accumulate substantial foreign exchange reserves and maintain a disciplined monetary policy. In 2000 Botswana was one of only five African states classified by the World Bank as a lower middle-income country. The key challenges faced by government and economic planners are the high levels of poverty and unemployment and the rapid increase in the prevalence of HIV and AIDS.

CONSTITUTIONAL & LEGAL FOUNDATIONS

Botswana is a unitary republic with a national legislature, the National Assembly, elected by universal suffrage. The national government consists of the president who is selected by the assembly, his appointed vice-president, and cabinet officials. The Minister of Educa-

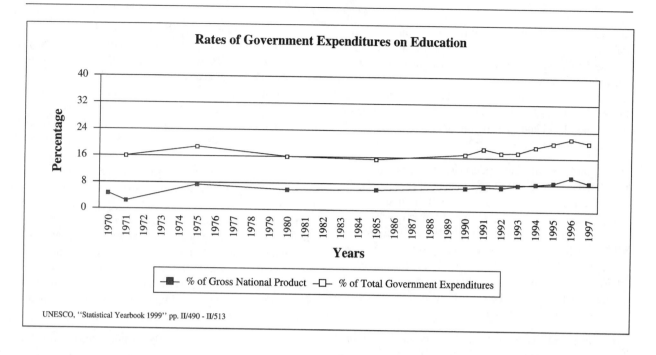

Rates of Government Expenditures on Education

Legend: ─■─ % of Gross National Product ─□─ % of Total Government Expenditures

UNESCO, "Statistical Yearbook 1999" pp. II/490 - II/513

tion is a member of the cabinet. There is also a House of Chiefs consisting of 15 hereditary leaders that advise on tribal matters separate from the assembly.

A multi-party system emerged soon after Botswana gained independence. The ruling party is the Botswana Democratic Party (BDP). The president in 2001, Festus Mogae, has been successful in calming factional politics within his party. Botswana's next national election is scheduled for October 2004. Mogae has confirmed that he plans to run for another presidential term, which has helped maintain unity within the BDP. Other political organizations include the Botswana Congress Party (BCP); Botswana Workers Front (BWF); Botswana People's Party (BPP); United Action Party (UAP); and the Botswana National Front (BNF), which is the main opposition group.

One problem that emerged immediately after Botswana became an independent country was financing the impoverished educational system left over from the protectorate. Primary education had been funded exclusively from tribal resources; some tribes had funded as much as 70 percent of educational costs. Government leaders were faced with two options: educating the majority of the population with the long-term goal of creating a literate society or providing limited educational facilities for a few that could occupy civil service jobs, which were then held primarily by expatriates. The second option was selected, and, as a result, income distribution became highly skewed. Critics argued that the educational policy was creating a small, privileged elitist educated group.

To address these social inequalities, the government commissioned a study in 1977. The National Commis-

sion on Education's recommendations received top priority, and Botswana began providing universal primary education and ensuring equality of educational opportunity at secondary and tertiary levels through the fair distribution of facilities, the provision of scholarships, and the use of an objective national selection system. However, the wide geographic dispersal of Botswana's population has made it difficult and costly to achieve universal education and expand the opportunities for economic development.

EDUCATIONAL SYSTEM—OVERVIEW

Education in Botswana is free, but it is not compulsory. The Ministry of Education has authority over all of Botswana's educational structure except the University of Botswana. The educational structure mirrors that of the United Kingdom: there is universal access to primary and junior secondary school, but a process of academic selectivity reduces entrance to the senior secondary school and the university. However, educational curricula incorporate prevocational preparation in the junior and senior secondary schools.

In 2001 Botswana's education system was comprised of seven years of primary education, three years of junior secondary education, and two years of senior secondary education. Each year at the primary level is a Standard, and each secondary level is a Form. This system was implemented in 1995 as a result of a 1993 National Education Commission study. Botswana's basic education program is comprised of the primary and junior secondary levels.

Primary education is the most important stage in the educational system, and the government strives to make this level of education accessible to everyone. One central objective of primary education is for children to be literate first in Setswana and then in English. Other goals are for children to become knowledgeable in mathematics and to have a command of science and social studies. From 1991 to 1997, the number of students completing the primary level and entering junior secondary increased from 65.0 percent to 98.5 percent.

Completing the Junior Certificate program may lead to admission to the senior secondary school program. Only those pupils whose grades are high enough on the Junior Certificate Examination are admitted to the senior secondary program. From 1991 to 1994, the number of students admitted to senior secondary schools increased from 28 to 34 percent. Botswana is in the process of building unified secondary schools, Form I to Form V, in the remote areas of the country to increase access to a senior secondary education.

Education has been given priority in the national budget. In the 1994-1995 financial year, the Ministry of Education received 10 percent of the national budget. The Department of Secondary Education and Teacher Training and Development shared 64 percent, and the ministry headquarters, which was responsible for four projects including the University of Botswana and Brigades development, received 25 percent. The 11 percent balance was spent on improving facilities and functions under the technical education, nonformal education, curriculum development, and evaluation and special education departments. The Ministry of Education expanded from a small unit of government in 1966 to one that looks after the educational needs of hundreds of thousands students from primary to tertiary levels. In addition, the ministry writes all required textbooks. The ministry's emphasis is on training qualified teachers, developing a diversified curriculum, and expanding facilities to meet the national commitment of universal education. The concern for achieving national literacy is underscored by the fact that 40.6 percent of the country's population is under the age of 15.

Botswana's first educational policy, called Education for *Kagisano* (Social Harmony), guided the country's educational development and administration from 1977 to 1993. In the early 1990s, the recognition that the country's socioeconomic situation had changed significantly resulted in a review of policies and strategies for Botswana's educational development. In March 1994, the Minister of Education presented Government Paper No. 2, The Revised National Policy on Education. Its recommendations will provide direction for Botswana's educational system until 2020.

The objectives of the new policy are to review the current education system and its relevance and to identify problems and strategies for its further development in the context of Botswana's changing and complex economy; to reexamine the structure of the education system to guarantee universal access to primary and junior secondary education, while consolidating and vocationalising the curriculum content at these levels; to advise on ways to ensure the education system is sensitive and responsive to the people's wishes and the country's manpower requirements; to study the various methods of streaming into vocational and academic groups at the senior secondary level; to study how the senior secondary structure relates to the University of Botswana degree programs and to determine how the two programs may best be reconciled; to advise on the organization and diversification of the secondary school curricula to prepare students who do not continue with higher education; and to make recommendations to the government on the best and most cost-effective methods of implementing the recommendations proposed by the Ministry of Education.

The education system makes minimal provisions for children with disabilities. Few disabled children are integrated in regular school classes, and there is a limited special education curriculum. Parents must pay fees to nongovernmental organizations if their special needs children are educated. However, the government has committed to intensify efforts to educate these children by paying the nongovernmental organizations' fees.

PREPRIMARY & PRIMARY EDUCATION

Preschool education is available only to those children whose parents can afford to send them to expensive private day care centers and preschools. The overwhelming majority of parents have no access to preschool programs. The University of Botswana's Primary Education Department and Home Economics Education Department offer courses for students seeking the Baccalaureate Degree in Education. Following a 1998 study reporting that the university lacked a comprehensive plan and policy on preschool education and that the Department of Primary Education did not offer a full-fledged program in preschool education, the Department of Home Economics Education opened a day care center. The center, managed by students as part of their curriculum, is for children of the university's employees who do not have the financial resources to send their children to other day care centers.

Children begin the seven-year primary education program at age six. Botswana's education system recognizes that primary education is the foundation upon which future learning is based. Setswana and English are the only two languages taught in the schools. Setswana is the language of instruction for the first four years of primary school, so those not speaking it, such as the Basarwa children, choose not to attend.

The primary curriculum is based on the country's principles and goals of democracy and is designed to prepare children for life after they have completed school. Teachers continually assess their students and provide remediation when needed. At the end of the primary program, Standard VII, students take the Primary School Leaving Examination. Those who pass this examination enter the junior secondary schools. The government increased the number of primary schools from 537 in 1986 to 669 in 1994 as part of their plan to achieve universal access to education, but there is a noticeable shortage of classrooms in the rural areas.

By 1994 primary school enrollment was 310,050, an increase of more than 30 percent from the 1986 enrollment of 235,941 students. In 1990 the Ministry of Education projected a primary school enrollment of 342,155 students by 1994; the 1994 enrollment figure was just 9.6 percent below this projected number. In 1986 there were 7,324 primary teachers, and the student-teacher ratio was 32:1. By 1994 the number of primary teachers had increased to 11,726, and the student-teacher ratio had dropped to 26:1.

SECONDARY EDUCATION

Botswana's secondary education program has two levels: the three-year junior secondary program and the two-year senior secondary program. Each year is a Form; Forms I to III are completed in junior secondary and Forms IV and V in senior secondary. In 1996 the junior secondary level was expanded from two years to three years so that it would align with the 1994 revision of the government's basic education policy to emphasize prevocational preparation. Prevocational preparation is implemented by including vocational applications in academic subjects; providing more practical elective courses for students; emphasizing skills relevant to work situations including problem solving, team work, self-identity, and computing; offering both curricular and co-curricular activities that focus on the organization and demands of working life; and offering career guidance and counseling.

In 1997, about 98 percent of students leaving primary school enrolled in junior secondary schools, which is a significant increase from 1991 when only 65 percent of those completing primary school entered a junior secondary school. One reason for this change is the increase in the number of junior secondary schools. In 1977 there were 32 junior secondary schools in Botswana; by 1990 the number had increased to 150. In 1977 only 35 percent of those completing primary school had access to a junior secondary school. In 1991, about 95 percent of the students completing primary school had access to a junior secondary school.

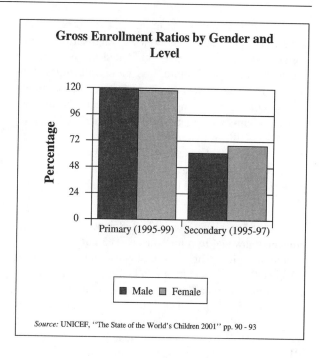

Gross Enrollment Ratios by Gender and Level

Source: UNICEF, "The State of the World's Children 2001" pp. 90 - 93

There is a nationwide network of community-based junior secondary schools. Each community elects a Board of Governors that oversees the school. Ex-officio members, mainly government workers, also serve as on these boards. The Botswana government supports community schools by providing assistance for capital projects and recurrent costs, providing teaching staff, supervising construction, and housing teachers. Communities are expected to employ ancillary staff and maintain school buildings.

The majority of students not completing the secondary level are boys who must herd cattle and girls who become pregnant. For every 100 girls dropping out due to pregnancy, only 10 return. There is a gap in academic performance between girls and boys, and the underachievement of girls impacts their opportunities for employment and thus exacerbates gender inequality.

Admission to senior secondary schools is determined by student performance in the junior secondary school. The number of students admitted to the senior secondary school has increased from 28 percent in 1994 to 34 percent in 1997. The government's goal is to increase access to senior secondary schools by 50 percent before the year 2003. To accomplish this, unified secondary schools for Forms I to V will be built in the remotest areas, and larger senior secondary schools will be constructed in the urban areas.

The Ministry of Education provides secondary school curricula guidelines. The headmaster of each school, in consultation with his staff, determines the actual options that will be offered. The junior level prescribes a minimum of 10 and a maximum of 11 subjects. All students must take eight core subjects: English, Setswana, social studies, mathematics, integrated science, design and technology, agriculture, and moral education. Students must also select a minimum of two and a maximum of three of the following optional subjects: home economics, commerce, principles of accounts/bookkeeping and office skills, religious education, third language, art, music, and physical education. The purpose of this broad curriculum is to meet the needs of students who enter the junior secondary school having a wide range of differing abilities.

In 1984 a science curriculum, Science by Investigation in Botswana, was introduced. The curriculum consists of 15 units inclusive of biological and earth science subjects. Pupils at both junior and senior secondary levels are encouraged to participate in science clubs so they can apply classroom knowledge to practical experiences. Supporting this curriculum is the Botswana Science Association (BOTSA), which has made it possible for students to exhibit their projects in annual science fairs.

There has always been an agricultural program in the junior secondary school, but it has been expanded since the junior secondary program was increased to three years. Vegetable production is a required topic; optional topics include bee keeping, ostrich farming, fish farming, and other forms of poultry husbandry. The agricultural program in the senior secondary school offers basic research and technical report writing skills through what is referred to as project methods of teaching. The Botswana Agriculture Teachers Association organizes fairs at both regional and national levels. These fairs enable schools to reach out to the public and demonstrate what students can produce if given adequate support. The agrarian program is not meant to be vocational. Its main objective is for students to have knowledge and skills they can apply on a daily basis that will have a positive impact on their environment.

HIGHER EDUCATION

The University of Botswana is located in Gaberone. Until 1975 the University College of Botswana was part of the Regional University of Botswana, Lesotho, and Swaziland. When Lesotho dropped out, Botswana and Swaziland developed as a joint university until 1982 when collective planning ceased and the two institutions separated. The University of Botswana admits approximately 3,000 new students annually. All those receiving first and second class in their final senior secondary examinations are eligible to be admitted. Enrollment for the 1999-2000 academic year was 9,500 students.

By act of Botswana's Parliament, the university was established as a separate corporation. The institution is in complete control of its funds and can govern itself without direct intervention from the State. The University of Botswana directly controls its staff salaries, promotions, employment, and staff expulsion. It can decide student policy and programs. The university's budget is primarily financed by a government endowment and through government scholarships that pay full fees and personal allowances to all secondary school graduates who qualify academically. In 1990-1991 government subvention provided 74 percent of the university's revenue.

The University of Botswana offers a broad range of educational programs. Most are on the undergraduate level. Students can earn certificates for professions and career studies or baccalaureate degrees in accounting and business studies, engineering, law, library science, nursing, social work, and most of the basic arts and sciences areas. Baccalaureate degrees are also offered in home economics, agricultural science, and engineering and technology. Graduate degrees at the master's level are offered in education, business administration, public administration, and in arts and sciences.

In 1996 Botswana Polytechnic was incorporated into the University of Botswana as the Faculty of Engineering and Technology. Various ministries cooperate with the university to support the technical programs. The Ministry of Education and the Ministry of Labor and Home Affairs share the responsibility of oversee the provision of craft training.

Non-university vocational training is provided at government Vocational Training Centers (VTCs). Enrollment is open to Botswana's employed and unemployed citizens. These centers are strategically located in development areas, which have diversified major industrial and commercial infrastructures. VTCs offer short courses during the day, evening, and weekends for fulltime trainees and apprentices. Courses include mechanical, automotive, textile, computing, construction, electrical, commercial trades, and hotel/catering. The VTCs emphasize the importance of practical training and experience. The programs require apprentices to spend three months at a VTC and nine months at job training supervised by the Ministry of Labor and Home Affairs.

Aided by the British Broadcasting Corporation, Botswana's national television channel opened in the summer of 2000; however, much of the country will have access only to radio for some time because it is expensive to run lines to sparsely populated remote areas. Botswana Telecommunications Authority provides Intersawana, radio-based Internet connectivity throughout Botswana and the University of Botswana. The service is funded by the United States through the Education Democracy and Development Initiative, which supports delivering teaching and learning programs through various communication technologies including distance learning. Secretary of State Madeline Albright signed the agreement on behalf of President Clinton in December 2000 at the University of Botswana.

ADMINISTRATION, FINANCE, & EDUCATIONAL RESEARCH

With the exception of the University of Botswana, the Ministry of Education has authority over Botswana's educational structure. The Department of Curriculum Development plans, develops, and evaluates school curricula for primary and for junior and senior secondary schools. Each of the department's five divisions has a specific responsibility. The Curriculum Development Division operates through subject panels and promotes consultation in the development of educational programs. This division is responsible for reviewing, revising, and developing syllabi; for creating instructional materials; and for adapting published materials for curriculum needs. The Educational Publications Division is the public relations division of the ministry. It also provides supplementary materials for teachers and pupils. The Guidance and Counseling Division provides programs for career guidance and teacher training and is involved in material development. The Teaching Aid Production Division develops teaching aids primarily for use at the primary levels. These aids may be print materials or other instructional items, such as those used in science and mathematics instruction. The Educational Broadcasting Division develops radio lessons to support the school curriculum and provides teachers with notes to help them use the radio lessons. Most of these lessons are developed for the primary level.

The Examinations, Research, and Testing Division was at one time a part of the Curriculum Development and Evaluation Division, but has since become a semiautonomous unit. This division designs and implements national examination programs for primary and secondary systems and ensures that the exams meet acceptable standards in operational procedures as well as in technical quality. The division is also responsible for training teachers to develop criterion-referenced tests for classroom assessments.

The National Examination Board of the Ministry of Education conducts the Junior Certificate examinations in October and November. The "O" level examinations are written twice a year in June and November and administered by the Examinations, Research, and Testing Division.

Since 1987 public education in Botswana has been free except for the cost of school uniforms and other incidentals. However, impoverished parents cannot buy school uniforms for their children. Although a uniform is not required, not wearing one subjects individuals to peer pressure so often these children do not attend school. Education has always been given priority in national budgets. In the 1991-1992 national recurrent budget, 22.6 percent was for education. This increased to 30.5 percent the following year. An estimated 27 percent of government expenditures in 1999-2000 were spent on education. In 2000 education minister George Kgoroba proposed partial school fees, but it was doubtful such charges would be approved because of the government's financial reserves and the low economic status of many citizens. There have been some changes in school management, however, such as the privatization of catering services.

In 1992 the president commissioned a study to prioritize manpower needs essential to the Botswana's development. The most critical manpower shortage areas were in science and technical fields: medicine, accounting, engineering, actuarial science, and teaching of mathematics, science, and Setswana. The next most critical area was for vocations that seem unattractive to students: paramedical, teaching, and sub-professionals. The category prioritized as the third most critical identified vocations where there were too few individuals to meet the country's needs: law, public administration, human resource management, psychology, hotel and tourism, and fashion design. The fourth category identified those areas seen as beneficial to society and the economy but of less priority: library information systems, sociology, and land board administration. The final category identified those occupations described as beneficial to an individual or a small section of the economy: cosmetology, performing arts, and interior design.

In 1995 a Grant/Loan Scheme administered by the Department of Student Placement and Welfare (DSPW) went into effect. The program is designed to attract more students into critical occupations and professions. Students entering high priority areas receive aid priorities over those in areas deemed less essential. Career guidance units disseminate career related information and offer more professional student counseling. The number of students administered by the DSPW grew from 3,000 in 1991 to more than 4,300 in 1995. The projected number for 2001 is 7,000.

Another function of the DSPW is administrating programs for students who travel to other countries, primarily the United Kingdom or the United States, as part of their education. When the DSPW became responsible for these students, there were approximately 100 students traveling abroad, all in either the United Kingdom or the United States. In 2000, there were approximately 500 students in the United Kingdom and 300 in the United States.

NONFORMAL EDUCATION

Botswana Extension College was founded in 1973 as part of the Ministry of Education. In 1978 the Department of Nonformal Education was created and incorporated into the Botswana Extension College. The department supplements secondary level education by offering Junior Certificate and Cambridge ''O'' Level courses via distance learning.

In 1980 literacy programs began for the then 250,000 men, women, and youths who were illiterate or unable to do simple computations. In the program's first year, 7,676 individuals enrolled in the four regional districts. The number of participants increased steadily until 1986 when enrollments leveled. One part of the literacy program is the *Ditiro tsa Ditlhabololo* (Home Economics Course); district adult education officers work with extension teams and village development committees to create locally-oriented activities.

Brigades Centers are autonomous, community-based, and predominately rural organizations that provide practical on the job training for Botswana youth. Their primary objective is to develop self-reliant individuals. Training is offered in automechanics, agriculture, construction, office studies, carpentry, electrical, drafting, general maintenance, machinery, plumbing, tannery, textiles, and welding. In 1999 there were 37 registered Brigades with 33 actively engaged in training.

Until 1999 graduates of the senior secondary school system were required to perform *Trelo Setshaba* (National Service) for one year. The government guaranteed places at the University of Botswana for those who completed the program. The service program began in 1980 as a pilot program with 28 participants; by 1991 there were more than 6,000 participants. The Ministry of Presidential Affairs and Public Administration managed the program; by the late 1990s, there were many logistical and budget problems that eventually led to the program's termination. National Service was designed to provide secondary graduates with opportunities to mature more and to explore possible career choices. They lived and worked in rural areas and remote places where more than 80 percent of Botswana's population reside. The program provided educated workers who assisted with government programs and bridged gaps between urban and rural dwellers, as well as between the educated and uneducated.

When National Service ended in 1999, the University of Botswana could not accommodate the unusually large freshman class comprised of those who had completed National Service and those who had just graduated from senior secondary schools. To accommodate everyone, the university switched some courses and sent some students to universities outside of Botswana but within the Southern African Development Community region. The national parliament appropriated additional funds for these expenses.

TEACHING PROFESSION

Two years after Botswana gained its independence, there were 1,791 primary level teachers, but 1,114 of these were not certified teachers. By 1985 the number of primary level teachers had increased to 6,980, and 74.3 percent were certified. The percentage of certified primary teachers has continued to increase. In 1993, about 83 percent of the 11,190 primary level teachers were certified. This trend is also found at the secondary level. In 1985 there were 1,368 secondary teachers; 72.3 percent of these were certified. In 1993 there were 4,391 secondary teachers; 81.9 percent of these were certified.

In 1985, about 77 percent of the primary level teachers were female. Of these, 21 percent were not certified. In 1993, about 76 percent of the primary teachers were female, but the percentage of uncertified female teachers decreased to 9.0 percent. That same year 8.0 percent of the male primary teachers were not certified. In 1985, about 43 percent of the 1,368 secondary teachers were female; 13.0 percent of these were not certified. That same year 14.0 percent of the male secondary teachers were not certified. In 1993, about 42 percent of the 4,391 secondary teachers were female. That year only 9.0 percent of male and female teachers were not certified.

Botswana has four primary level and two secondary level colleges of education. With the exception of the Botswana College of Agriculture, which has its own teacher-training program, all of the teacher training institutions (TEIs) are affiliated with the University of Botswana. The University has a mandate from the Ministry of Education to oversee the maintenance of academic and professional standards of diplomas and certificates for which students in the TEIs are prepared. Boards and committees systematically consult and participate in the decision-making process between the university and the ministry. The TEIs are provided with advice, guidance, technical, and qualitative capacities. Therefore, all teachers are trained in programs validated by the University. The University has the authority to implement whatever is necessary to achieve universal education; however, Botswana's government controls all funding.

African tradition dictates strict divisions of responsibility and positions of authority. Females have lower status than males. Males dominate the University of Botswana's Faculty of Education. It is only in the primary level colleges that the majority of lecturers and heads of departments are women. Male department heads lead in those areas traditionally seen as the responsibility of males, such as engineering and technology. Female department heads lead in areas such as primary, home economics, and nursing education.

Policy makers at the Ministry of Education are aware of hierarchies and gender inequities within the University and the TEIs. To address these problems, the University of Botswana established the Department of Primary Education, which, since 1980, has offered diploma courses to primary school teachers in order to replace expatriate lecturers in the TEIs. Enrollment in the University's Master's of Education program increases every year. In 1994 the government upgraded the primary level teachers colleges by phasing out the certificate program and replacing it with a diploma. In 1990 the Faculty of Education established the Gender and Education Committee (GEC), which is committed to encourage and support gender reform within the University as well as in schools and in the Ministry of Education. The University of Botswana is the only education establishment in the country with a gender policy.

SUMMARY

Botswana is a unique country in Africa because of its sustained economic growth and political stability. Education is free, but not compulsory. While Botswana's government strives for universal education, there are barriers that must be overcome. In addition to overcrowded school facilities, the efficiency and effectiveness of teacher education is constrained by the centralized and hierarchical nature of educational administration. The Department of Curriculum Development and Evaluation is in charge of basic educational curriculum development with only a minimal involvement of teachers, teacher training institutions, and the University of Botswana.

Many of Botswana's problems exist because of the republic's rapid transition from a rural to a technologically developing country. While the problems are great, they do not appear to be insurmountable. The motto on the University of Botswana's Coat of Arms, *Thuto Ke Thebe* (Education Is A Shield), underscores the important role education has in the country.

BIBLIOGRAPHY

"Botswana." *EIU Country Report,* (October 2000): 5-23.

Comely, Peter, and Salome Meyer. *Botswana.* Lincolnwood, IL: Passport Books, 1995.

Else, David, et al. *Africa-The South.* Hawthorn, Australia: Lonely Planet Publications, 1997.

Mannathoko, Changu. *The Role of the University Of Botswana as a Teacher Education Institution: Current Developments in Teacher Education.* The World Bank Group, March 1998. Available from http://wbln0018.worldbank.org.

Shales, Melissa, ed. *Touring Southern Africa.* Lincolnwood, IL: Passport Books, 1977.

Stamp, L. Dudley. *Africa: A Study in Tropical Development.* New York: John Wiley & Sons, Inc., 1961.

The Atlas of Africa. New York: The Free Press, 1973.

The 1997 Demographic Yearbook. New York: The United Nations, 1999.

The World Bank Group. *Countries: Botswana,* September 2000. Available from http://www.worldbank.org/afr/bw2.htm.

University of Botswana, December 2000. Available from http://www.ub.bw.

—*Sherman E. Silverman*

BRAZIL

BASIC DATA

Official Country Name:	Federative Republic of Brazil
Region:	South America
Population:	172,860,370
Language(s):	Portuguese, Spanish, English, French
Literacy Rate:	83.3%
Academic Year:	January-December
Number of Primary Schools:	196,479
Compulsory Schooling:	8 years
Public Expenditure on Education:	5.1%
Educational Enrollment:	Primary: 34,229,388 Secondary: 6,405,057 Higher: 1,716,263
Educational Enrollment Rate:	Primary: 125% Secondary: 56% Higher: 14%
Teachers:	Primary: 1,413,607 Secondary: 352,894 Higher: 141,482
Student-Teacher Ratio:	Primary: 24:1

HISTORY & BACKGROUND

The Federative Republic of Brazil is the only nation in South America whose language and culture derive from Portugal. The country was discovered by Pedro Álvares Cabral in 1500. As the fifth largest country in the world, its territory covers an area of 3,300,171 square miles, which represents almost half of South America. With a population of almost 172 million people, Brazil is also the fifth most populated country.

Brazil is considered one of the world's most productive countries because of its great number of natural and mineral resources, metropolitan cities, developed industrial and hydroelectric complexes, and fertile soil. At the same time, Brazil is a country that historically has had to face many internal problems, such as the lack of political and economic stability, long periods of high inflation, and an unplanned population growth. These factors led Brazil to major educational problems.

The history of education in Brazil begins in the second half of the sixteenth century, when the Jesuits from the *Companhia de Jesus* (Company of Jesus) arrived in 1549. The Jesuits founded the first Brazilian elementary school in Salvador, in the state of Bahia. They followed the educational principles established in the *Ratio Studiorum* (a regulatory educational document written and promoted by Friar Inácio de Loyola). The Jesuits' work was driven not only by educational goals, but by a religious purpose as well: to spread the Christian faith among the indigenous population. For 210 years, the Jesuits were responsible for the entire educational system in Brazil. Their primary and secondary schools were of good quality, and some of the secondary schools even offered higher-level studies. The Jesuits also created many missions in Brazil to educate and catechize the indigenous people. These missions would help the people escape from slavery.

The first rupture in the history of the Brazilian educational system occurred in 1759 when the Jesuits were expelled from Portugal and its colonies by the Marquis of Pombal, King José I's minister. Pombal was trying to restore the Portuguese power in Europe. The Jesuit's religious educational system implemented in the colony conflicted with the Marquis's commercial interests. Pombal's idea was that education should serve the state, not the church. As an alternative to the Jesuit's system, Pombal created the *subsídio literário* (literary subsidy), a tax to finance elementary and secondary education, as well as the *aulas régias,* the teaching of Latin, Greek, and rhetoric. However, Pombal's new educational measures had no effect, and by the beginning of the nineteenth century, Brazil's educational system was stagnated.

Brazilian education and culture started to move forward in 1808, when the Portuguese royal family, escaping from the invasion of Napoleon's troops, transferred the Kingdom of Portugal to the colony. Although tailored to the Portuguese Court's immediate needs, King João VI's educational work started a period of undeniable achievements for education. He created a considerable number of schools and scientific institutions, the first public library, a number of technical teaching schools for professional training, and the first university courses in Rio de Janeiro and Bahia. However, King João's educational policy, focusing on higher levels of education, neglected elementary schooling.

Brazil's educational policy was deeply affected by the country's independence in 1822. The Constitution of 1824 guaranteed free elementary education to all citizens, and the state created basic-level public schools in cities, towns, and villages. The state also decentralized the basic education system by promulgating the Additional Act in 1834. This act gave the provinces the power to determine legislation for elementary education, casting off the government's duty to grant free education for all.

In the first years of the newly formed Republic (1889), the decentralized educational policy was maintained, preventing the state from taking over the formulation and coordination of the elementary educational system. This lack of action by the government resulted in a greater social and educational gap between the popular classes and the elite. Since little attention was focused on public elementary education, only the favored members of the upper classes could afford to keep their children in private institutions.

The twentieth century was a period of transformation for education in Brazil. Influenced by European positivism, Brazilian educators adopted a series of reforms and laws that transferred the responsibility of administrating elementary schooling in the country back to the government. During the 1920s and 1930s, the first universities were created in Rio de Janeiro (1920), Minas Gerais (1927), Porto Alegre (1934), and São Paulo (1934). The first "real" Brazilian university was the University of São Paulo, created with the support and import of French and German scholars, following the French model for its structure.

A new constitution was promulgated in 1934, incorporating significant advances into the educational system. Both the government and the family were considered responsible for the elementary education of all citizens. In the 1940s, the educational system focused on the professional aspects of education. At this point, education in Brazil had the following structure: five years of elementary school, four years of secondary school, and three years of high school.

During the 1950s and the beginning of the 1960s, the educational system underwent some significant changes.

Some of the important achievements of this period include the creation of CAPES or *Coordenação de Aperfeiçoamento de Pessoal de Nível Superior* (Coordination of Improvement of Higher Learning Personnel) in 1951; the CFE or *Conselho Federal de Educação* (Federal Council of Education) in 1961; campaigns and movements for eradicating adult illiteracy; and the approval of National Law 4024 (*Lei de Diretrizes e Bases*) in 1961.

From 1964 to 1980, a military dictatorship ruled Brazil during this period of social and political upheaval. However, it was during this time that two of the most significant events of the history of Brazilian education took place: the creation of MOBRAL (*Movimento Brasileiro de Alfabetização*), or the Brazilian movement for eradication of adult illiteracy, in 1970, and the approval of Law 5,692 in 1971. This law significantly changed the structure of higher learning (students could choose between a general or professional curriculum) and of elementary and secondary education (basic mandatory education was extended from four to eight years).

Despite a number of updates and amendments, the basic text of Law 5,692/71 was still in force in the 1990s. Also during that decade, the government created the National Program of Literacy and Citizenship in an effort to reduce the number of illiterate people in Brazil by up to 70 percent. A new model of elementary school, the CIAC (*Centro Integrado de Educação Popular*), was also created. These CIACs were integrated centers to support children from low income families with education and food.

In 1995, the Brazilian government created an experimental program to evaluate the performance of university students called the *provão* (National Course Evaluation). The *provão* is an exam given the last semester prior to graduation. After a period of adaptation, it has become permanent. Eighteen subjects are included in this exam. In the year 2000, more than 2,700 university courses (around 203,000 students) were examined by the *provão*.

In 1997, the same program was extended to the high school level, creating the ENEN (*Exame Nacional do Ensino Médio*), or National Secondary Education Examination. ENEN has become an important instrument to evaluate the performance of secondary level students. It provides students the necessary credentials for either continuing their university studies or for entering the job market. At the elementary school level, the SAEB (*Sistema de Avaliação da Educação Básica*), or Evaluation System for Basic Education, is recognized worldwide as one of the most sophisticated procedures used in the evaluation of primary school performance. In testing the efficiency of schools and universities, the government aims to control and improve the quality of education throughout Brazil.

CONSTITUTIONAL & LEGAL FOUNDATIONS

The Constitution of 1824 established that basic education was a right of the citizen and an obligation of the state. Since then, all Brazilian constitutions have included free primary education as one of the basic needs the state must provide to the population. However, the Brazilian government became actively involved with educational constitutional rights only after the Revolution of 1930.

The Brazilian educational system was revolutionized by the promulgation of Law 5,692 on August 11, 1971. Unlike the preceding law (Law 4,024/61), Law 5,692/71 was very well received by the educational community for the amplitude of its articles and its promise of updating and expanding the teaching of primary and secondary education. The main changes implemented by Law 5,692/71 included: redefinition of the role of primary education (based on students' potentiality, citizenship consciousness, and working-skills development); free and mandatory primary education for children between the ages of 7 and 14; 8 years of schooling at the primary educational level; a national, unified primary level curriculum that would also take into consideration relevant individual and/or regional differences; *ensino supletivo* (primary and secondary educational opportunities for adult citizens), which is the equivalent of the GED in the United States; and rules for teaching and financing (on federal, state, and municipal levels).

Elementary education in Brazil is free in all state schools and compulsory for all citizens between the ages of 7 and 14. Secondary education is not compulsory, but it is still free. Nevertheless, the free and mandatory basic educational system has not prevented two serious educational problems derived from social and regional inequalities: illiteracy and child labor. Although the number of illiterate people has decreased over the last 20 years, the illiteracy rate in Brazil during the 1990s was still significant (approximately 16 percent in 1993). According to a U.S. Department of State report on human rights (February 2001), recent governmental figures from Brazil state that the number of children working has decreased since 1993, conversely increasing the number of children attending school. The Brazilian federal government administers 33 programs to combat child labor. The Ministry of Labor's program for the eradication of child labor provided supplemental income to 147,000 families in rural areas, who in return were required to send their children to school. Similar programs administered by municipalities benefit another 202,000 children living in the major urban cities.

The most recent educational objectives of the Brazilian educational system, started in the 1990s, are still based on the main changes established by Law 5,692/71.

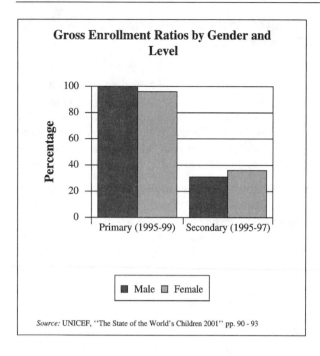

Gross Enrollment Ratios by Gender and Level

Source: UNICEF, "The State of the World's Children 2001" pp. 90 - 93

Nevertheless, there were some innovations and pledges included in the Constitution of 1988. Infantile education was seen as a preliminary step towards schooling. The state must provide day care for a variable number of hours and kindergarten (not mandatory) for the under-privileged. Public universities must offer free, high-level quality courses and promote research. The state must support poor students with food, books, transportation, and health care. Additionally, special attention must be paid to students who suffer any kind of physical or mental disability.

Other important legal tools for education are: Law 9,131 of 1995; constitutional amendment 14 of 1996; the National Educational Guidelines and Framework Law 9,393 of 1996 (*Lei de Diretrizes e Bases-LDB*); and the FUNDEF (National Education Fund), Law 9,424/1996. Other legal tools include decrees and administrative rulings that regulate the LDB; in addition, recommendations and resolutions issued by the National Council of Education contain important legal information.

EDUCATIONAL SYSTEM—OVERVIEW

Brazil has 26 states and the Federal District. The educational system is a collaborative organization between federal, state, and municipal government organizations. The federal government, through the Ministry of Education (also known as the MEC—*Ministério da Educação*—with the "C" appearing as an initial because the MEC was also previously in charge of Culture), is responsible for legislation and financial assistance. It is in charge of the federal universities, middle school techno-

logical education, and technical and agricultural high schools. Eight years of fundamental schooling is now compulsory.

PREPRIMARY & PRIMARY EDUCATION

Preschool Education: Preschool is designed to provide physical, psychological, and intellectual development for children under the age of six. It complements family education. There are day care nurseries for children who are up to three-years-old, and kindergartens for those age four to six. This system started with the Constitution of 1988 and is fostered by the municipalities. Although emphasized by the government, its implementation reaches only 17.5 percent of the population. The enrollment was 5.9 percent in 1980 and rose to 17.4 percent in 1989.

Special Education: Special education is offered from preschool to secondary level. Support for special education is provided by the Ministry of Education, by the state, by some municipal secretariats, and by nongovernmental organizations. Depending on the kind of program, an institution might include rehabilitation centers, clinics, hospitals, and more. According to 1989 statistics, 63 percent of the special education students were mentally retarded, 14.4 percent had hearing problems, 9.3 percent were physically handicapped, and 4.4 percent had visual deficiencies. There is much interest in aiding blind students or those with subnormal vision at an early stage to increase academic performance.

Elementary Education: Elementary education is called *escola de primeiro grau* (first degree schooling). It is constitutionally mandatory for students aged 7 to 14. Its main objectives are to develop reading, writing, and calculating; to understand natural laws and social relations in contemporary society; and to develop the capacity of thinking and creating. State Councils of Education structure the elementary school curricula. The curriculum includes: communication and expression (Portuguese language); social studies (geography, history, and social and political organization); and sciences (mathematics and biological). In 2001, about 91 percent of students from seven to fourteen had access to schooling. Recent data indicates that about half of first graders fail, which causes about 2.3 percent of them to abandon school. This index reaches 32 percent by the end of the fourth grade.

A public educational policy for indigenous schools exists to prepare teachers to teach the native people, to produce didactic material, and to disseminate indigenous themes in schools. Indigenous education is part of the Constitution of 1988. Children go to school half a day, either in the mornings or in the afternoons. In 1984, the state government of Rio de Janeiro created the *Centro Integrado de Educação Popular* or CIEP (integrated center for popular education) for the poorer population. The purpose was to keep the students busy eight hours every day with instruction, sports, medical assistance, food, and cultural activities. These schools were especially built with a uniform architectonic project and were easily recognizable. This idea was followed by the government of President Fernando Collor de Melo under the name *Centro Integrado de Atendimento à Criança* (CIAC). Although the idea was excellent, its costs were too high and there were not enough qualified teachers and staff. The project slowly faded, with pieces of it being picked up by other programs.

At the turn of the millennium, the government was placing major emphasis on elementary education. In 1996, the Constitutional Amendment 4 created *Fundo e Manutenção e Desenvolvimento do Ensino Fundamental e Valorização do Magistério* or FUNDEF (Fund for Maintenance and Development of Basic Teaching and Valuation). One of the purposes of this fund was to train teachers and raise their salaries. The average national salary increase was 13 percent, 50 percent in the municipal systems.

The *Programa Nacional do Livro Didático* or PNLD (National Textbook Program) was broadened and renovated, and in 1999, about 110 million books that had been selected by the teachers themselves were distributed to elementary schools from the first to the fourth grade. Throughout the country, there is an ongoing pedagogical evaluation, which started in 1996. The *Secretaria de Educação Fundamental* (SEF) prepares the *Guia de Livros Didáticos,* a guide to help choose the right books and to ease the teacher's task.

Adult Education: Adult education is remedial schooling. The minimum age is 18 for the elementary level and 21 for the secondary level. The Ministry of Education and the state secretariats provide support for this kind education through special courses, equivalent to the American GED, that can be taken in schools or online. Supervision is handled by state boards of education and inspection services. For the students who successfully complete the course, a diploma is granted.

Popular Education: Popular education is a new concept of teaching created by the educator Paulo Freire. His method was successful in teaching literacy in 40 hours of classes without any didactic material. He conceived education within the existential reality. For him, reading and writing is a social *praxis.* Dialogue is the key for interaction between teacher and students.

Freire's model revolutionalized traditional schoolroom teaching, transforming adult education into a healthy approach for those students who come to class already knowing what they want and need to learn. His model is reflected in the work of adult educators in the United States and in other countries, principally in Africa. Paulo Freire's main books are Cultural Action for Freedom (1970), Education as the Practice of Freedom (1976), and Pedagogy of the Oppressed (1993). This model is called "educación popular" in Latin America, "andragogy" by Malcolm Knowles, or "action learning" by learner-centered education proponents. Jane Vella, an educator who adapted Friere's model, explains the characteristics of popular education as:

> learner's participation in naming content via needs assessment, mutual respect, dialogue between learner and teacher and among learners, achievement-based learning objectives, small-group work to engage learners and to provide safety, visual support and psychomotor involvement, accountability of the teacher to do what he or she proposes, student participation in the evaluation of program results, a listening attitude on the part of teachers and resource people, and learning by doing. (Vella 1995)

Professional Education: Professional education treats the needs of local and regional markets. The curriculum is modular—that is, organized in units as short courses that can be taken by the student in between his or her working schedule at different times. The technical and professional schools issue diplomas are for the job market, mainly in industry and agriculture. The market has been giving clear signals that without a secondary diploma the candidate will not get a good job.

Across Brazil, 2.8 million students are enrolled in professional education; 24.1 percent are in industry courses, followed by agriculture, and commerce. There are 33,000 professional education courses, 83.5 percent are on the basic level. There are 5,000 technical and 433 technological courses. Computer science is the most requested course. In total, 3,948 institutions offer these courses, 2,216 of which are technical.

Professional education takes place on three different levels: Basic: courses for young and adult workers. They do not demand previous schooling and its goal is to qualify the student; Technical: for young and adult students who are taking or have already finished their secondary education. Receiving a diploma demands having finished 11 years of basic schooling; Technological: this provides higher education on the undergraduate and graduate level.

SECONDARY EDUCATION

According to Law 9,394 of December 20, 1996, secondary schooling is the final stage of basic education. From 1990 to 1998, the enrollment in secondary schools almost doubled, from 3.5 million to 6.9 million students. The yearly increase averaged 11.5 percent.

In 2001, a major reform was being undertaken by the government at the secondary level that focused on contextualization, curricular integration, and flexibility. The reform was established along three lines: it was based on the new federal law of *Diretrizes e Bases* (Directives and Bases); it focused on changing the curriculum in the secondary schools; and it placed an emphasis on the occupational content of the technical schools.

The basic secondary school's objectives are: to consolidate previous acquired knowledge; to prepare the student for high school or technical professions; and to teach the student how to relate theory to practice. The curriculum is organized by the *Conselho Federal de Educação* or CFE (Federal Council of Education) together with the *Conselho Estadual de Educação* or CEE (State Council of Education). Individual schools can select additional subjects.

The curriculum has the same basic subjects as in the elementary school: communication and expression, including a foreign language as well as Portuguese; social studies; and sciences. The curriculum includes five to six subjects, and Portuguese is obligatory. In addition, the curriculum has become more flexible over time—75 percent is established by the government on a national basis, and 25 percent is left to each school's discretion.

There is still a low rate of students attending secondary school—only 16 percent of the population between the ages of 15 and 19 participates. There is an age variation-many youngsters in this age span are still attending elementary school. Many students arrive at the secondary level when they are young adults because they have to work and complement the family's salary. Therefore, secondary schools have become in large part evening schools; 55 percent of the secondary level students enrolled in 1998 attended classes at night.

HIGHER EDUCATION

Compared to other Latin American countries, Brazil has not only a respectable number of universities, but they are also better equipped than other countries. In the 1960s it launched a major program to award graduate degrees.

The university system is made up of public (federal or state), Catholic, and private institutions. The structure comprises universities, *faculdades* (colleges), and isolated institutions. The purpose of higher education in Brazil is to implement teaching, research, and extension, although research is principally done in federal institutions. Universities also offer short training courses in many different subjects, serving the university population as well as the community. Private higher education has increased excessively in the last 20 years, creating 300,000 new vacancies for students. As a result, there has been a decrease of quality in these institutions, especially because they are profit-oriented.

The main objective of higher education is to professionalize students. This differs from the American system in which the student goes to college to acquire a general education then opts for professionalization. In Brazil the student immediately selects law school (a five-year course) or medicine (six years).

There are 127 universities in Brazil, 68 of which are public. Of the 894 institutions of higher education, 222 are public. Higher education careers are integrated in blocks (criteria used by CAPES) as follows: *Ciências Biológicas e Saúde* (Biological and Health Sciences), *Ciências Exatas da Terra* (Exact Sciences), *Ciências Humanas e Sociais* (Human and Social Sciences), *Ciências Sociais Aplicadas* (Applied Social Sciences), and *Engenharias e Tecnologias* (Engineering and Tecnologies).

In 1997, there were 1,945,000 students enrolled in higher education; in 2000 this number increased to 2,125,958. Women comprise 55 percent of the total number. It is estimated that 3 millions students will be enrolled by the year 2002. Once enrolled, 64.2 percent of the students who begin a course in higher education graduate. Most of these students study in private institutions, their average age is 25, and 53 percent of the students are 24 years old when they initiate their graduate studies.

As of 1998 the five largest universities in the country were: *Universidade Paulista* (state of São Paulo), 44,598 students; *Universidade de São Paulo* (city of São Paulo), 35.662; *Unisinos* (Rio Grande do Sul), 25,269; *Universidade Federal do Rio de Janeiro* (Rio de Janeiro), 24,971; and *Pontifícia Universidade Católica* (Minas Gerais), 22,434.

In order to be accepted in a university, students have to pass a competitive entrance exam called *vestibular*. As long as they have finished their secondary education and have a diploma, grades do not factor into university selection. This gives an advantage to socially privileged students who get extra help from private instruction or teachers and do not have to work while studying. This system actually creates a social discrepancy, because rich students end up in federal universities that are free, while lower-income students enter private universities that are paid. In 2001, governmental measures were being launched in order to transform the system. Some universities had started making their own individual *vestibular*, and others had begun taking grades into consideration.

The Federal Education Council (CFE) determines the minimum curriculum and time allotment for the different courses. Each institution has the freedom to include additional subjects. Under the presidency of

Fernando Henrique Cardoso, a new legislation to evaluate the performance of institutions was introduced that required students to take an examination at the end of their courses. Those exam results, together with the evaluation of committees of specialists designated by the Ministry of Education, were expected to show how well the institutions and courses were performing. That evaluation would provide the government with data that would help it know where and how to best allocate money and efforts. Additionally, undergraduate teaching was prioritized, as investments totaling 70 million dollars were made to upgrade libraries, computers, and information technology.

In the Constitution of 1988 it was determined that student loans, previously financed by the *Fundo de Assistência Social* (Social Assistance Fund), were to be allocated from the resources of the Ministry of Education and administered by the *Caixa Econômica Federal.* The loans are mainly used by students to pay for tuition through monthly installments.

A financing program called *Financiamento Estudantil* (FIES) was created in 1999. Approximately 700 higher education institutions throughout the country have participated. In 2001, some 102,000 students received aid from this program, with total resources approaching $225 million.

Graduate schools have always been the jewel of Brazilian education. In the 1950s, the Ford and Rockefeller Foundations gave grants to bring Brazilian students to the United States for their graduate studies. Since then, funds are given by several public agencies to finance graduate studies abroad and at home; these agencies include FINEP, FAPESP, CNPQ, and CAPES.

Many universities have their own master's and doctorate programs. Graduate programs are evaluated every two years and, according to their performance, receive public funds in larger or lesser amounts to promote research and pay fellowships for their students. In 1994, there were 18,900 students working on doctorate degrees; in 1999, that number jumped to 29,900—an increase of 58 percent.

ADMINISTRATION, FINANCE, & EDUCATIONAL RESEARCH

Administration: The Brazilian Constitution (1988) stated that education is the duty of the state and that its principle aim would be the total development of the individual, including his or her preparation to exercise citizenship and to qualify for work. The administration of the educational system by the federal government, the states, the Federal District, and the municipalities would follow a number of constitutional principles. For example, it is

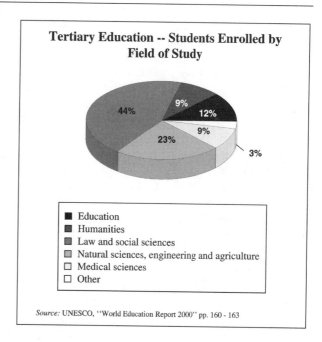

Tertiary Education -- Students Enrolled by Field of Study

- ■ Education
- ■ Humanities
- ■ Law and social sciences
- ■ Natural sciences, engineering and agriculture
- □ Medical sciences
- □ Other

Source: UNESCO, "World Education Report 2000" pp. 160 - 163

the responsibility of the Brazilian government to conduct a census of elementary school students, to publicize the enrollment process, and to be responsible, jointly with the parents or guardians, for students attending school.

Private teaching enterprise is allowed by the Brazilian constitution, provided it complies with the general rules of Brazilian education. The state must authorize and guarantee the quality of education provided by any private institution.

The different parts of the federal government—including the Ministry of Education, the states, the Federal District, and the municipalities—cooperate in the organization of the Brazilian educational system. The federal government organizes and finances the federal educational system of the states and of the territories. It grants technical and financial assistance to the states, the Federal District, and the municipalities for the development of their educational systems and provides compulsory schooling on a priority basis. Municipalities act on a priority basis in elementary and preschool education. It is the responsibility of the federal government to manage federal universities, public higher learning institutions, federal centers for secondary technological education, and a number of agricultural and technical high schools. The states direct most of the day cares, kindergarten schools, some elementary and secondary schools, and the state universities. The municipalities act on a more basic level, controlling most of the primary schools, some day cares, and kindergarten schools.

Each educational system is managed by an executive body. In the federal sphere, the *Conselho Nacional de Educação* (Nacional Council of Education) establishes the working rules. The Ministry of Education handles political issues, such as planning and administrative decisions. On the state level and in the Federal District, regulatory functions belong to the *Conselho Estadual de Educação* (CEE). Administrative functions, as well as the control of private education at the primary and secondary levels, are managed by the *Secretaria Estadual de Educação* or SEE (State Secretariats of Education). In the municipalities, the *Conselho Municipal de Educação* or CME (Municipal Council of Education) and the local secretariats or departments of education are responsible for regulatory and administrative functions. Each system is autonomous and hires personnel by means of competitive public examinations, and each manages their resources within certain rules and principles. The federal government, the state, the Federal District, and the municipalities must organize a yearly national plan to integrate actions aimed at the coordination and development of education on various levels.

Finance: Each year the federal government is mandated to apply no less than 18 percent of public expenditures on education. In reality, about 5 percent of the gross domestic product (GDP) is applied. The Federal District, states, and municipalities must apply at least 25 percent of their tax revenues, including those resulting from transfers from the federal government. The federal government contributes 20 percent, the state contributes 50 percent, and the municipalities, 30 percent. Supplementary food and health assistance programs must be financed with funds derived from social contributions and other budgetary funds. An additional contribution called *salário educação* (education salary) is made by companies and constitutes another source of funds for public elementary education. Companies that maintain an in-house educational program for their own employees and dependents may deduct from this fund the amount of money invested in elementary education.

Public funds are allocated to public schools. They may also be allocated to community, religious, or philanthropic schools as long as they prove that they do not seek profit and that they invest their funds in education. These institutions must ensure that their equity is assigned to another community, philanthropic, or religious school, or to the government in case they cease their activities. Funds can also be allocated to elementary and secondary school scholarships for those who are needy, or for whenever a student must attend a private school because there are no vacancies or regular courses at the appropriate level in the public school system nearest to the student's residence. In such cases, the government is required to invest, on a priority basis, in the expansion of its network in that area.

Research & Technology: Brazilian universities are autonomous. They enjoy didactic, scientific, administra-

tive, and financial autonomy, as well as fair management. However, they must follow the principles of coherent teaching, research, and advanced study, which makes them eligible to receive financial support from the government and/or private sponsors. In 2001, one of the problems that the federal universities faced—and which was in the process of being reformed—was the lack of freedom the administrators had to reassign resources. Changing this system would increase flexibility and provide greater autonomy to the universities. However, the matter required a constitutional change, so in the meantime, other legal instruments were being used to ease this problem.

Although educational research in Brazil is conducted by different institutions (universities, institutes, research centers, etc.), research activities are concentrated at public universities. In 1993, some 99 institutions were officially involved in all areas of research. That number more than doubled in 2000 to over 200, and 80 percent of the almost 12,000 groups involved in academic research belonged to public universities.

According to the results of a census organized by the *Conselho Nacional de Pesquisa* or CNPq (National Council of Research) that polled all of the groups involved with academic research in Brazil in the year 2000: 57.0 percent of those groups conducted their work in the southeast region of Brazil, 31.0 percent in São Paulo, and 16.0 percent in Rio de Janeiro; 11.5 percent were affiliated with the Universidade de São Paulo (University of São Paulo); 27 percent of the studies concentrated on the humanities; the most studied fields were health (31 percent) and education (30 percent); 79.5 percent of the groups started their research between 1995 and 2000.

In total, 10 percent of the research conducted by these groups resulted in high quality work, according to international standards. Considering the fact that most of these research groups (almost 60 percent) were still in the formative stages in 2001, the Brazilian government considered the results satisfactory. The most traditional research institutions in Brazil are the independent public agencies CAPES, CNPq, FINEP, FAPESP, and FAPERJ, and two private foundations—*Fundação Getúlio Vargas* (FGV) in Rio de Janeiro and São Paulo, and *Fundação Carlos Chagas* (FCC) in São Paulo.

Coordenação de Aperfeiçoamento de Pessoal de Nível Superior or CAPES (Coordination of Improvement of Higher Learning Personnel) is a public entity linked to the Ministry of Education. It was created in 1951 as a program (*campanha*) and transformed into a foundation (*fundação*) in 1992. CAPES is responsible for the graduate policies and the coordination of education and research on this level by granting scholarships and aid. It is responsible for the formation of highly qualified human resources to teach at the university level, to perform research, and to fulfill professional demands and needs in public and private sectors. CAPES has a system of course evaluation that is highly respected by other national institutions.

The *Instituto Nacional de Estudos Pedagógicos* or INEP (National Institute for Pedagogical Studies), a national institute for educational studies and research, is an independent entity responsible for obtaining, evaluating, and storing the country's education information. It created the *Sistema Nacional de Avaliação da Educação Básica* or SAEB (Evaluation System for Basic Education) to evaluate the performance of elementary and secondary schools. Another innovation is the *Exame Nacional do Ensino Médio* or ENEM (National Secondary Education Examination), which is used to evaluate, give credentials, and promote further studies on entry into the labor market. The exam for higher education (ENC) includes 18 higher-level subjects and 2,700 courses. In 1992, the state of Minas Gerais, took the initiative and created a comprehensive system, testing every school in the state.

INEP's major policies are designed to implement a new funding model for basic education (FUNDEF), to transfer funds directly to public schools (the "Money at School" Program), to expand and decentralize the National School Meal Program, to implement the Minimum Income Program (an education grant), to develop the Integrated System of Educational Information (SIEd), and to expand the *Nordeste* (Northeast) Project through the Basic Education and School Empowerment Fund (FUNDESCOLA).

NONFORMAL EDUCATION

The Brazilian educational system has faced many problems throughout its almost 500 years of existence. As a means of finding solutions in this crucial area, the government has developed a considerable number of nonformal and/or informal educational programs.

The federal government has industrial and agricultural technical schools throughout the country. Business associations operate other institutions, such as *Serviço Nacional de Aprendizagem Industrial* or SENAI (National Industrial Apprenticeship Service), and *Serviço Nacional de Aprendizagem Comercial* or SENAC (National Commercial Apprenticeship Service). They correspond to primary and secondary schools and are free of tuition. Training for managers and employers of small business is provided by *Serviço de Apoio às Micro e Pequenas Empresas* or SEBRAE (Service to Support Small Enterprises).

The international community considered the creation of SENAC and SENAI in the early 1940s as a pioneering

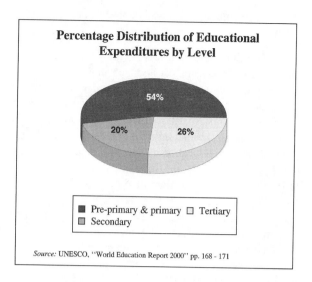

Percentage Distribution of Educational Expenditures by Level

54%
20% 26%

■ Pre-primary & primary □ Tertiary
■ Secondary

Source: UNESCO, "World Education Report 2000" pp. 168 - 171

model for Latin America's educational system. These successful Brazilian institutions offered commercial and industrial training programs, which were adopted by other countries due to their high quality.

Most of the nonformal systems of education in Brazil in the 1960s and 1970s were designed for adult education in an attempt to eradicate illiteracy. Paulo Freire's *Movimento de Cultura Popular* or MCP (Movement of Popular Culture), *Projeto Minerva* (a radio broadcast program), *Movimento Brasileiro de Alfabetização* or MOBRAL (Illiteracy Program), and *Programa Nacional de Teleducação* or PRONTEL (National Program of Television Education) are examples of programs developed during this period.

In the beginning of the 1990s, universities and technical schools started offering a number of short training courses on a diverse variety of subjects, from soccer to philosophy. Currently, in the major cities, both private and public institutions offer programs on secondary level administration and computer programming. There is also competition among private institutions to offer courses in foreign languages and preparation for international examinations like the GRE, the GMAT, and the TOEFL. Additional nonformal governmental projects held by the *Secretaria de Educação Fundamental* or SEF (Secretariat of Fundamental Education) include the establishment of a public educational policy for indigenous schools and the expansion of the curriculum of elementary and secondary schools to include environmental issues.

Contemporary technology has also affected the nonformal education sector in others ways. In the past decade, numerous online educational programs were launched in Brazil. These programs provide students with a demanding, creative, and interactive online learning environment. The UNB (University of Brasília) is one of the governmental institutions that offer a variety of online courses.

On an international level, the Ministry of Education maintains intense technical and financial cooperation to improve educational needs and human resources. It works in close contact with the *Ministério das Relações Exteriores* (Ministry of Foreign Affairs). Productive results have been attained through contact with UNESCO (United Nations Educational, Scientific and Cultural Organization), OEA (Organization of the American States), OEI (Organization of Iberian-American States), BID (Inter-American Development Bank), and BIRD (World Bank). The Ministry of Education also participates in the meetings of the Ministers of Education, in the meetings of Ministers of Education of the community of countries speaking the Portuguese language, in the meetings for Ministers of Education of the Inter-American Council of integral development of the OEA, and in the Conference of Iberian-American Education of OEI.

Distance Education: At the start of the twenty-first century, the Brazilian federal government created the *Secretaria de Educação a Distância* or SEED (Secretariat of Distance Education). This is an example of the government's commitment to modernizing education. SEED strategically applies new technologies and methodologies in order to diversify and raise the standard of education quality.

Television is a major vehicle for education. Distance learning is done with the help of the *TV Escola* (TV School), which reaches 60,000 schools. It is broadcast on a special channel by satellite and provides four hours of programs that are repeated four times a day. *TV Escola* is also a program designed for teachers and is updated by the *Reforma do Ensino Médio* or REM (Reform of Secondary Education). It was created in October of 1999 as an experimental program and proved to be one of the most efficient tools that the Ministry of Education had for updating the methods and resources of primary and secondary level teachers.

Both public and private TV stations offer courses and support programs for basic education. *Telecurso 2001,* for example, which is broadcast by TV Globo, is a program intended to prepare students for elementary and secondary school equivalency examinations.

The *Programa Nacional de Informática na Educação* or ProInfo (National Program for Information Technology in Education), created in 1977, was a program established to train teachers and improve learning through computer technology. Approximately 30,000 computers had been installed in more than 2,000 schools. In 2001, this program was expected to reach 6,000 schools, or 7.5 million students, with a total of 100,000 computers. The pedagogical use of technological equipment is assured by means of the proper training of the teachers of the benefited schools and by linking these computers to the *Núcleo de Tecnologia Educacional* or NTE (Nucleus of Educational Technology). Nearly 20,000 teachers have already been trained for this program and 223 NTEs have been created.

Recognizing the need for skilled educators, a national plan for the expansion of nonformal education was created in 2001 called *Proformação-Programa de Formação de Professores em Exercício.* It is an educational program designed for teachers. The program started in January of 2000 in the states of Amazonas and Bahia and provided training for teachers from the public network who did not meet the established minimum qualification standards required by law. The government plans to qualify 15,000 teachers from the public network.

Programa de Apoio à Pesquisa em Educação a Distância or PAPED (Program to Aid Research in Distance Education) is also an important program for the development of educational alternatives. It was created in 1997 to finance theses and dissertations on long-distance learning projects and/or on new information and communication technologies applied to education.

TEACHING PROFESSION

It was only in the second half of the nineteenth century that Brazilian federal legislation opened the first professional teaching schools (*Curso Normal*). Male teachers tended to concentrate their training at the secondary level, with an emphasis on subject area specialties. Female teachers tended to be relegated to the primary level. This situation lasted until the mid-1930s, when new legislation created the *Magistério,* a well-defined teaching certification course. Entrance into this program required the completion of all eight grades of primary school. At that time, a primary level education was the minimum requirement for teaching primary school. Subsequently, in the 1950s, secondary level teachers were required to have a college degree.

Census figures from the 1970s and 1980s revealed that teaching, particularly in the early primary levels of education, was an underpaid occupation, although educators were required to invest considerable time in their professional training and credentials. Wage figures for the 1990s are not very different from previous decades. In the state of São Paulo, for instance, the average salary was 5.3 times the national minimum salary for male secondary level teachers and 1.9 times the national minimum salary for females.

Eighteen percent of the Brazilian gross national product is spent on education, with the greater part of this expenditure going to federal universities that do not charge tuition or fees. In 1997, the average beginning primary school teacher earned an average monthly salary of less than US$200 (this figure was US$223 for teachers in the state of São Paulo).

In addition to widespread undercompensation, teaching conditions are also difficult. Despite the low wages earned, many teachers work two shifts per day, usually at two different schools. This tight schedule barely provides the minimum salary necessary for survival, and it does so at tremendous cost to teachers and classrooms. Teaching double shifts generally means that teachers have to be prepared for teaching almost 10 classes—or 350 students—a day. Teaching under such conditions has compromised the quality of instruction and led teachers to long term union strikes over the last few decades.

Brazil has powerful teacher's unions. During the 1980s and 1990s, they leaned politically to the left, creating monopolies in forums and conferences and also creating the so-called "ideological patrols." The most active teacher's unions are the regional *Sindicato dos Professores* (SINPROs), *Sindicato Nacional e Democrático dos Professores* (SINDEP), and *Associação Nacional de Docentes de Ensino Superior* (ANDES).

SUMMARY

In the 1960s, the so-called "Brazilian economic miracle" accelerated the development of the economy, but education was on a slow pace. This changed radically toward the end of the last century because government realized that growth and productivity are linked to education. Quality was a main concern due to regional disparities in the country. Technology and educational improvement needed to be made to meet the demands of the job market.

In 1999, the number of students in higher education in all of Latin America was 5.6 percent of the population. In Brazil, only half of the students finished elementary school, therefore only a small number of students went to middle and high school. Few students made it into higher education. In 1990, there was just over one vacancy in higher education for each student who finished high school.

Claudio de Moura Castro (2000) points out the advancements made in the 1990s and the necessary steps for the further development of the Brazilian educational system. Some of his considerations are as follows: of those aged seven to fourteen, 97 percent are enrolled in schools. This means that illiteracy is no longer a major issue; In 1998, 63 percent of the students finished elementary school; approximately eight million students attend secondary school, therefore, the number of students applying to higher education has risen at a considerable rate.

Brazil has advanced and has a balanced educational system. But, illiteracy must be reduced. Elementary school still has to improve in quality, consolidating universal access to primary education. Teachers have to be better prepared and paid to meet this challenge. The legislation of higher education has to meet contemporary needs: there have been only a few attempts to implement community colleges, and a country as large as Brazil needs to have more courses offered by distance education (*à distância*) using modern technology. New legislation and decentralization would ease the burden imposed by too many inflexible rules. More money has to be allocated by the federal, state, and municipal governments for the advancement of education. Nevertheless, in comparison to the past, Brazil has taken gigantic steps.

The government is working on current targets and future perspectives. It created a Ten-Year Plan (1993-2003) and redefined the Political Strategic Plan (1955-98) to improve the quality of teaching and to better institutional performance. As the Minister of Education, Paulo Renato Souza (April 11, 2000) states:

> Education today can no longer be carried out only in the stages of infancy and youth. Professional updating must be permanent, given the speed of technological evolution. As professional careers are less rigid and clear-cut, they require a very high degree of interdisciplinarity and flexibility in the curricular structure of courses. Incorporating the new technologies of information and communication is crucial and should stimulate the growing use of distance learning as a means of guaranteeing access to professional training and updating.

The Brazilian education system has made important advances since 1995. In educational terms, the government seems to be falling into step with the rest of the world. Since 1995, there has been an expansion in access to elementary education. The proportion of children enrolled in school considerably increased in 1999, as four million new students were added to the system.

Age and grade distortion rates continue to be high in Brazil—47 percent of students could be in higher grades. Nevertheless, Brazil is trying to improve its performance at the elementary education level. The promotion rate, which measures the number of students who are promoted to a higher grade, also increased from 65 percent in 1995 to 73 percent in 1997. During this same period, the number of students repeating a grade fell from 30 percent to 23 percent. The dropout rate also decreased, from 5.3 percent to 3.9 percent.

The expectation of finishing the first level of education has risen to 63 percent, and the average time taken to pass through the eight grades has fallen from 12 to 10 years. Secondary educational level enrollment rose to 57 percent between 1994 and 1999. In 1999 alone, the growth rate was of 11.5 percent. This increase in secondary school enrollments may be explained by the improvements in fundamental education and the increasing demand for better-educated people in the job market.

Regional inequalities are diminishing as well. In the northeast region, enrollment in elementary education has grown by about 27 percent, as compared to 13 percent countrywide. In secondary education, it has increased 62 percent compared to a previous national figure of 57 percent. In the last four years, higher education enrollment has grown in absolute terms more than in the previous 14 years. In 1998, the growth rate was 28 percent more than in 1994.

There has also been marked growth at the graduate level in Brazil. Between 1994 and 1999 the number of students at the master's level increased by 27 percent. The rate at the doctorate's level was even more impressive—around 60 percent. Brazil is producing 14,500 graduates at master's level and 4,600 doctorates per year.

Considering all enrollments at all levels of education, Brazil had approximately 54.3 million students in 2001. One third of Brazil's population was attending school. Public schools were meeting the learning needs of 45.8 million students at the basic educational level, which represents 87.8 percent of all students.

BIBLIOGRAPHY

Azevedo, Fernando de. *A Cultura Brasileira (Brazilian Culture).* 5th ed. New York: Macmillan Company, 1950; São Paulo: Melhoramentos, 1977.

Birdsall, Nancy, and Richard H. Sabot, eds. *Opportunity Foregone: Education in Brazil.* Washington, DC: Inter American Development Bank, 1996.

Brunner, Borgna, ed. *Time Almanac 2000.* Boston: Information Please, 2000.

Castro, Claudio de Moura. "A Educação é combustível do crescimento no Brasil." *Veja* (27 December 2000): 196-99.

———. *Myth, Reality and Reform, Higher Education Policy in Latin America.* Inter-American Development Bank: The John Hopkins University Press, 2000.

Castro, Maria Helena Guimarães de. "Education: From the Access Challenge to Increasing Quality Standards." IDB Brazil Seminar: "Brazil 500 Anos: Social Progress and Human Development." Washington DC, 11 April 2000.

Errant, Jenna. *Education in Brazil,* 10 March 2001. Available from http://www.tulane.edu/.

Fernandes, Florestan. *Universidade Brasileira: Reforma ou revolução?* São Paulo: Alfa-mega, 1975.

———. *Educação e Sociedade no Brasil.* São Paulo: Dominus Ed., 1966.

Freire, Paulo. *Educação como prática da liberdade (Education as Practice of Freedom).* 5th ed. Rio de Janeiro: Paz e Terra, 1975; London: Writers and Reader, 1976.

———. *Pedagogia do Oprimido (Pedagogy of the Oppressed).* 3th ed. Rio de Janeiro: Paz e Terra, 1975; New York: Continuum, 1993.

Goldenberg, José. *Relatório sobre a educação no Brasil.* São Paulo: Instituto de Estudos Avançados, 1993.

Haar, Jerry. *The Politics of Higher Education in Brazil.* New York: Praeger Publ., 1977.

Haussman, Fay, and Jerry Haar. *Education in Brazil.* Hamden, CT.: Archon Books, 1978.

Lima, Lauro de Oliveira. *Estórias da Educação no Brasil: de Pombal a Passarinho.* Rio de Janeiro: Brasília, 1969.

———. *Educar Para a Comunidade.* Petrópolis: Vozes, 1966.

———. *Tecnologia, Educação e Democracia, Educação no Processo de Superação do Subdesenvolvimento.* Rio de Janeiro: Civilização Brasileira, 1965.

McNeill, Malvina Rosat. *Guidelines to Problems of Education in Brazil: A Review and Selected Bibliography.* New York: Teachers College Press, Columbia University, 1970.

Niskier, Arnaldo. *Educação Brasileira: 500 Anos de História, 1500-2000.* São Paulo: Melhoramentos, 1989.

———. *A Nova Escola.* 10th ed. Rio de Janeiro: Nova Fronteira, 1987.

———. *Educação: Reflexão e Crítica.* Rio de Janeiro: Bloch Ed., 1983.

Piletti, Nelson. *História da Educação no Brasil.* São Paulo: ática, 1996.

Plank, David N. *The Means of Our Salvation: Public Education in Brazil, 1930-1995.* Boulder, CO: Westview Press, 1996.

Ribeiro, Maria Luisa Santos. *História da Educação Brasileira: a Organização Escolar.* São Paulo: Autores Associados, 1993.

Romanelli, Otaiza de Oliveira. *História da Educação no Brasil.* Petrópolis: Vozes, 1993.

Schwartzman, Simon, et al. *Educação no Brasil em Uma Perspectiva de Transformação,* 10 March 2001. Available from http://www.10minutos.com.

Souza, Paulo Renato de. *Education in Brazil: Reforms, Advances, and Perspectives.* "IDB Brazil Seminar: Brazil 500 Anos: Social Progress and Human Development." Washington DC, 11 April 2000.

Teixeira, Anísio. *Educação no Brasil.* 2nd ed. São Paulo: Companhia Ed. Nacional, 1976.

Tobias, José Antônio. *História da Educação Brasiliera.* São Paulo: Ed. Juriscredi, 1979.

Torres, Carlos A., ed. *Education and Social Change in Latin America.* Somerville, Australia: James Nicholas Publishers, 1995.

U.S. Department of State. *1999 Country Report on Human Rights Practices,* 10 March 2001. Available from http://www.state.gov/.

Vella, Jane.*Training through Dialogue, Promoting Effective Learning and Change with Adults.* San Francisco: Jossey-Bass, 1995.

Wanderley, Luís Eduardo. *Educar Para Transformar: Educação Popular, Igreja Católica e Política no Movimento de Educação de Base.* Petrópolis: Vozes, 1984.

—*Monica Rector and Marco Silva*

BRITISH VIRGIN ISLANDS

BASIC DATA

Official Country Name:	Virgin Islands (British)
Region:	Puerto Rico & Lesser Antilles
Population:	19,615
Language(s):	English
Literacy Rate:	97.8%

The territory of the British Virgin Islands (GBVI or BVI), an archipelago comprising 36 islands, lies east of Puerto Rico and immediately northwest of the U.S. Virgin Islands (USVI), its culturally dominant neighbor. Under British rule from the seventeenth century onward, the BVI has been a crown colony with a ministerial government since 1960. In 1990 its mainly black population was about 18,000 people, one-sixth that of the USVI.

Nominally, BVI schools still follow British models, with uneven results. Proposed reforms in 2001 aimed at improvements that would stress business and vocational-technical studies geared to the tourist economy. Development of native resources through better education is officially a priority in the territory in the new millennium.

Education is compulsory and free, and 97 percent of children stay in school through age sixteen. Instruction is in English—a British variety with the regional inflection. The published literacy rate is 98 percent, but in 1991, for example, more than 70 percent of all high school graduates in the BVI were immigrants, not natives.

In 1991, some 15 private (but no public) preprimary facilities enrolled 635 children. In 1998, some 16 public and 5 private primary schools enrolled nearly 3000 students aged five through twelve, with most students attending the free, public facilities. Seventy percent of the primary teachers had formal training, an improved record aided partly by a Hull University in-service program. (In 1988, when one in three primary students failed to pass the terminal Primary V assessment examination, just 35 percent of the teachers had training. Success rates on the test have remained disappointing, and some students persist at the primary level until age fifteen.) Expenditures per student for education in 1997 was $3584, almost tripled since 1985. A five-year program of reform was under way in 2001.

Of the three BVI high schools, one enrolls 80 percent of all students; among 85 BVI high school teachers in 1990, 80 percent had formal training. Form I of secondary school is unofficially "streamed." Examinations in Form II officially track students, beginning at age thirteen, into divergent academic and non-academic curricula, with some of the latter programs occurring off-campus. At the end of Form V, students can take the CXC proficiency test. Of the 180 BVI high school graduates in 1997, about 72 sat for the CXC; only two passed all subjects. Most students, upon completion of the CXC, received the basic (and not the general) proficiency diploma. Because achievements of BVI students are roughly on par with their Caribbean neighbors, studies in 2001 have questioned the testing system itself and the prevalent methods of teacher training and classroom delivery and have proposed remediation and intervention methods to improve student achievement.

With the founding of H. L. Stoutt Community College, the BVI inaugurated a modest tertiary education program in 1991. From 1994 to 1997, the college awarded 158 associate degrees and training certificates. The University of the Virgin Islands (in the U.S. Virgin Islands, which is contiguous) offers the nearest senior-college options.

BIBLIOGRAPHY

The British Virgin Islands Government, 18 January 2001. Available from http://www.bvigovernment.org./.

Development Planning Unit of the British Virgin Islands, 10 February 2001. Available from http://www.dpu.org.

Peterson's Register of Higher Education, 1995: The Sourcebook for Higher Education, 8th ed. Princeton, NJ: Peterson's, 1995.

—*Roy Neil Graves*

BRUNEI

BASIC DATA

Official Country Name:	Brunei Darussalam
Region:	Oceania
Population:	336,376
Language(s):	Malay, English, Chinese
Literacy Rate:	88.2%

The small (2,226 square miles) South-East Asian Sultanate of Brunei is located on the northwestern coast of the island of Borneo, sandwiched between two states belonging to neighboring Malaysia. The official name of this wealthy, oil-rich country that became independent of British control (although it was never an outright colony) in 1984 is *Brunei Darussalam* (Arabic for "Abode of Peace"). It has a predominantly Malay Muslim population with a substantial Chinese minority, many of whom are classified as non-citizens. One striking educational feature of this country, which due to its prosperity ranks third in the world in per capita income, is that citizens of Brunei enjoy the benefit of access to free schooling at all levels.

Historically, the first Malay language school began in what was then Brunei Town (now the capital and renamed Bandar Sri Begawan) in 1912. Similar schools in other towns followed it. A Chinese school was established in 1916, followed by an English medium one in 1931. The growth in schools, both government and private, continued through World War II and beyond. The first five-year plan for economic development, beginning in 1954, resulted in the creation of the Ministry of Education.

This Ministry, which was subsequently reorganized in 1974 on the basis of an official governmental commission report, continues to oversee educational policy and allocate resources to all schools under its control. All government and private schools are overseen by the Ministry of Education in conformity with the Education Act of 1984. All primary and secondary schools follow a common curriculum that is set by the Ministry. Although there have been both official and unofficial recommendations urging the adoption of Malay as the sole medium of instruction, currently *dwibahasa* (bilingualism, using both English and Malay for teaching purposes) is being practiced. Due to Brunei's small population, many teachers have historically been expatriates from neighboring countries in Asia or from Australia and Britain. One provision of the Education Act is the requirement for private school teachers to register with the Ministry.

Based on Brunei's Islamic heritage and government by monarchy, its official educational philosophy emphasizes Koranic elements, such as faith and piety, along with loyalty to the Sultan. At the same time, its past reliance on Britain has resulted in educational structures and curricula that draw from that nation's educational system. Brunei's educational policies, as stated by the Ministry of Education, aim to achieve the following. They wish to provide:

- greater scope for the use of Malay in education;
- a total of 12 years of education for all students;
- a system of integrated curricula and public examinations;
- Islamic religious education as part of the school curriculum;
- facilities for education in scientific and technological fields;
- appropriate co-curricular activities;
- access to higher education as appropriate; and
- educational structures that are in harmony with national needs.

In the year 2000, a total of 221 educational institutions were in Brunei. These consisted of 175 primary schools, 39 secondary schools, 2 vocational schools, and 1 each of the following: technical college, nursing college, mechanical training center, technological institute, and university, the Universiti Brunei Darussalam (or UBD). There were 32,316 students in government primary schools and 27,914 in government secondary schools. In addition 24,370 students attended private primary schools and 4,038 were in private secondary schools. There were 2,867 students at the University of Brunei while 2,500 students attended the other vocational and technical colleges. Clearly, a significant proportion of the country's population (more than one-third) consists of students at the primary, secondary, or tertiary levels. One additional feature worth noting is that, according to official statistics, while the enrollment numbers of males and females keep pace with each other at the primary and secondary levels, approximately 57 percent of students at the tertiary level are females.

Brunei follows a 7-3-2-2 pattern of education. This means that there are seven years of primary education (including one year of preschool), followed by a public examination known as the Primary Certificate of Education. Lower secondary education is for three years, followed by another public examination, the Lower Secondary Assessment examination. Based on the performance of an individual student and following the ninth year of schooling, he or she will be tracked into one of two streams. One stream leads to technical or vocational education that prepares the student for immediate skill-based employment after graduation; such education is provided at a number of technical and vocational institutes described below. The other ''academic'' stream leads to two or three years of upper secondary education culminating in the student's appearance in the Brunei-Cambridge General Certificate of Education (GCE) examination at either the O- (Ordinary, similar to its British secondary school counterpart) or N-Levels. The GCE examinations are conducted jointly by Cambridge University's Local Examinations Syndicate and Brunei's Ministry of Education. Those not immediately prepared to take the O-Level examinations are allowed to take the N-level examinations which, if passed, give them an additional year of schooling and preparation to tackle the O-Level examinations. Finally, students with adequate achievements at the O-Level examinations can go on to two years of pre-university education that prepares them for the Brunei-Cambridge A-Level (similar to the British GCE Advanced Level) examinations.

At the apex of Brunei's education system is its only university, the UBD. This relatively new institution of higher learning began operations in 1985 and offers undergraduate and a few graduate programs through its six *faculties* (colleges). These include faculties in the arts and social sciences; business, economics and policies studies; Islamic studies; Brunei studies; science; and education. The last named faculty originated as a separate institute of education that predates and was incorporated into the UBD in 1988. UBD's teaching staff numbers slightly more than 300 people. While most undergraduate programs of study are offered in the English medium, some are also offered separately in Malay.

Brunei's educational system will face two major future challenges. The first is to expand available educational resources and choices at all levels to match the demand both from its own population and the changing economy of Southeast Asia. The second is the continuing dilemma of integrating historical and traditional (religion, monarchy, and ''colonialism'') as well as modern (liberalization and globalization) elements into a coherent educational infrastructure.

—*N. Prabha Unnithan*

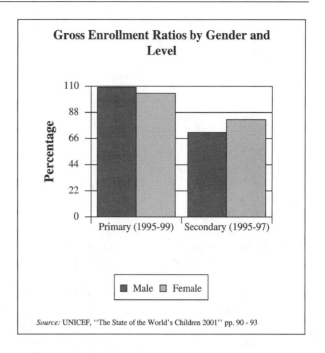

Gross Enrollment Ratios by Gender and Level

Source: UNICEF, ''The State of the World's Children 2001'' pp. 90 - 93

BULGARIA

BASIC DATA

Official Country Name:	Republic of Bulgaria
Region:	Europe
Population:	7,796,694
Language(s):	Bulgarian
Literacy Rate:	98%
Number of Primary Schools:	3,170
Compulsory Schooling:	8 years
Public Expenditure on Education:	3.2%
Foreign Students in National Universities:	8,496
Libraries:	4,237
Educational Enrollment:	Primary: 431,790 Secondary: 733,362 Higher: 262,757
Educational Enrollment Rate:	Primary: 99% Secondary: 77% Higher: 41%
Teachers:	Primary: 25,860 Secondary: 67,088 Higher: 26,303

Student-Teacher Ratio:	Primary: 17:1
	Secondary: 11:1
Female Enrollment Rate:	Primary: 98%
	Secondary: 76%
	Higher: 52%

HISTORY & BACKGROUND

Bulgaria is a South East European country situated in the heartland of the Balkan Peninsula. With a territory of 110,993 square kilometers, it ranks among the smaller states of Europe. Bulgaria borders Romania to the north, Yugoslavia and the Former Yugoslav Republic of Macedonia to the west, Greece to the south, Turkey to the southeast, and has a Black Sea coast line to the east. Demographic trends in the 1990s led to the decline of a population of roughly eight million. An estimated one million Bulgarians reside abroad, primarily in North America and Western Europe. Turks constitute the largest ethnic minority (about 10 percent), followed by the Roma or Gypsies, a group elusive to statistics. There are also Russian, Jewish, Armenian, Tatar, Pomak (Bulgarian Muslim), and Greek populations in Bulgaria. Bulgarian is the official language and the language of education, although most minority groups also use their mother tongues.

Bulgarian is written in the Cyrillic alphabet, a choice made in the ninth century at the time of conversion to Eastern Orthodox Christianity. Bulgarian is a Slavic language, akin to Macedonian, Serbo-Croatian, and Russian. Compulsory education was widespread for most of the twentieth century, causing literacy rates to be as high as ninety-nine percent and to be almost equal for both genders. The capital city Sofia is a major center of culture and education and boasts some of the nation's most prestigious schools of higher learning. Otherwise, educational facilities are evenly distributed throughout the country and available to both urban and rural citizens.

Bulgarian traditions in education go back to the Middle Ages when the First Bulgarian Kingdom (893-1018) provided the conditions for a blossoming of early Slavic literature and culture based on the Cyrillic alphabet. The Bulgarian Tsar Simeon The Great (893-927) welcomed the disciples of the "Apostles of the Slavs," St. Cyril and Methodius and furthered their effort. A court school was established in the Bulgarian capital of Preslav. St. Clement, founded a school on the shores of Lake Ohrid in Macedonia. Thus Bulgaria became the "cradle of Slavic civilization", where an estimated 3,500 priest-teachers were trained, large-scale translation of service books was carried out, and original works of theology, philosophy,

literature, and art were created. This legacy later enriched other Slavic Eastern Orthodox nations, including Serbia, Russia, and Ukraine. The Bulgarians celebrated May 24th, the day of the Slavic alphabet and culture, as one of the most cherished national holidays.

The Ottoman conquest (1396-1878) brought education and culture to a standstill. The nation had lost the institutions that previously sponsored it: the state was defeated and the autocephalous church submitted to the control of the Greek-dominated Orthodox millet in Constantinople. The only Bulgarian schools during this period were kiliini (cell) schools at monasteries which taught basic literacy. The Greek schools available at the time were not Bulgarian in spirit and were not trusted by the local population. The national revival was stirred by a "Slav-Bulgarian History," a book written in 1762 by the monk Paisii from the Hilendar Monastery in Mount Athos. It revived the memory of past glory and had enormous impact on the nation. Other books followed and generated a popular movement for secular education, which was at the mainstream of the Bulgarian national renaissance. In 1824, the distinguished Bulgarian scientist Dr. Peter Beron published the "Fish Primer," titled after the illustration on the front page. This textbook taught the essentials of arithmetic, geography, biology, and hygiene. In its forward, the author gave valuable pedagogical advice to teachers and promoted the concepts of secular education. The first fully secular Bulgarian school, known as the Aprilov Gymnasium, was established in the town of Gabrovo in 1835. Secular education quickly gathered momentum and by the middle of the nineteenth century, a real system of schools existed throughout the entire territory of the country.

State education dates back to 1878 when independence was restored with the decisive help of Russia. However, the first Ministry of Education did not have to start from nothing; a system of 1,479 primary schools, 50 secondary institutions, and 130 reading clubs was already in existence. The young modern nation-state pursued vigorous policies in the field of education. The legal foundations for these were laid out in the Turnovo Constitution of 1879, which sanctioned free and secular primary education, compulsory for all children regardless of gender, age, nationality, or faith. A law adopted in 1921, during the rule of the Bulgarian Agrarian National Union, extended the period of compulsory education to seven years. The establishment of the first institution of higher learning, St. Clement Ohridski University of Sofia, occurred in 1888. During the period 1878-1912 a fine arts and a music academy, teacher-training institutes, vocational schools, theological institutions, and the Bulgarian Academy of Sciences was established. Educational development was slowed down during the period of the Balkan Wars (1912-13) and the First and Second World Wars.

The advent of communism's rise to power, shortly after the end of the Second World War, had a decisive impact on education. During the period 1944-89, education in Bulgaria was heavily centralized and placed under the rigid control of the Communist Party. Religious influences, previously quite strong in the schools, were replaced by heavy obedience to the atheistic doctrine of Marxism-Leninism. Private schools were abolished. In the meantime, the education system was expanded and new schools were founded at all levels. A law passed in 1948 made education compulsory until the age of 16. The curriculum was rigorous and comprehensive, with very few elective subjects, and placed special emphasis on math and the sciences. Education was free at all levels, including higher education and post-graduate studies. Many new universities, mostly with technical profile, opened new opportunities for professional growth to previously underprivileged groups of society and to women. A typical characteristic of academia was the separation of higher teaching from research, institutionalized in the parallel existence of universities and research institutes. Under communism, education bred sophisticated urban elites, whose covert opposition to the system undermined its very foundations and facilitated its fall in the "tender" revolution of 1989. The freedom of travel after the fall of communism enabled many Bulgarian professionals to look for employment on the world labor market. Many found white-collar jobs in North America and Western Europe during the 1990s—a testimony to the quality of Bulgarian education in this period.

Since 1989, the nation has lived through a transition period, which has encompassed thorough changes of the economy, from command to market-oriented and the polity from totalitarianism to pluralist democracy. These changes affected education in a variety of ways. Some of the immediate positive effects included freeing of the education system from ideological constraints, its decentralization, and the restoration of private schools as an alternative in education. Nonetheless, the transition brought about an acute economic crisis. The state economy could no longer continue as the only source to fund education. The cuts in the state appropriations for science and education were extremely severe in the beginning of the 1990s. For example, in 1990 the resources provided by the Bulgarian government for higher education and research were reduced 2.5 times compared to the level of 1989, after corrections for inflation. This underscored the need for introducing paid tuition in higher schools. The economic crisis reached unprecedented official rates of 15 to 17 percent and families in which one or both parents were unemployed were struggling to keep their children in school or college. Despite the crisis, the best traditions in education were preserved and enrollment in higher schools increased. This fact underscores the value that Bulgarians placed on education.

CONSTITUTIONAL & LEGAL FOUNDATIONS

Education was in a state of reform and had been subject to intense legislative activity throughout the 1990s. The Bulgarian Constitution adopted by the Great National Assembly in 1991 and promulgated in The State Newspaper No. 56 on July 13, 1991 laid out the basic principles of education. Article 53 guaranteed the right to education for all citizens as well as the right to free primary and secondary education in state and municipal schools. Higher education was also free under conditions specified by law. Education was compulsory until the age of sixteen. The constitution placed all schools under the control of the state; however, it provided for the academic autonomy of institutions of higher learning.

The Public Education Act of 1991, amended and supplemented several times since, gave substance to the constitutional provisions and enhanced the democratic character of changes in the education system. It established the secular character of education; however, it also authorized the establishment of religious schools and the equality of religious education. The Act sanctioned the restoration of private schools as an alternative to state and municipal schools, and allowed the establishment of schools with foreign participation. The Act specified the compulsory age and the official language of instruction. The law guaranteed the right to choice of school and type of education based on personal preference and ability. It ruled out corporal punishment and guaranteed students the right to dignified treatment. The Act detailed the rights and obligations of both teachers and students. It further laid out the structure of the education system, comprising of basic, secondary, and higher education and outlined the system of administration and finance of education.

The Higher Education Act of 1995 describes the goal of higher education; the training of highly qualified specialists and promoting the progress of science and culture. The Act legalized many changes that were made in the sphere of higher education during the period of 1990-1995. The state allowed higher schools to initiate their reform and sanctioned the results, which included the introduction of new system of academic degrees—specialist, bachelor, master, doctor; the initiation of the process of accreditation; and the principle of academic autonomy. The latter gives expression to the intellectual freedom of the academic community and provides for academic freedoms, academic self-government, and the inviolability of the higher school's territory. The law also strictly lessens

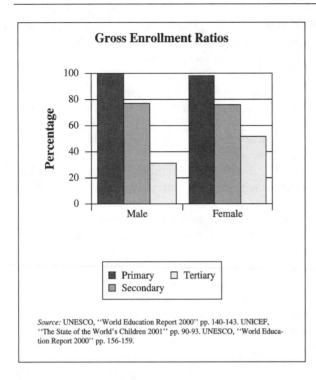

Gross Enrollment Ratios

Source: UNESCO, "World Education Report 2000" pp. 140-143. UNICEF, "The State of the World's Children 2001" pp. 90-93. UNESCO, "World Education Report 2000" pp. 156-159.

the functions of the state in the management of higher education, reducing considerably its role of supervisor and sponsor of higher learning. The Act has been amended several times since its adoption in 1995.

A Law on the Level of Schooling, the General Educational Minimum, and the Curriculum was adopted in 1999. It aimed at establishing uniform requirements for all schools in the country, guaranteeing equivalency of certificates issued for the completion of a particular grade and level of schooling. The law regulated the first two levels of schooling, basic and secondary. It provided the basis for curriculum development and grading.

The Vocational Education and Training Act of 1999 sanctioned a large variety of educational programs guaranteeing professional education to all citizens who were older than thirteen and had completed at least sixth grade of general education. It established uniform requirements for certification of the acquired professional skills, comprising six degrees of proficiency. The law also sanctioned the establishment of a network of centers for professional orientation.

EDUCATIONAL SYSTEM—OVERVIEW

Education in Bulgaria is compulsory between the ages of 7 and 16. Parents have legal responsibility to secure the school attendance of their child. All schools in the country are co-educational, admitting students of both genders. The official language of instruction is Bulgarian. Schoolchildren who have a different first language, be-

sides the compulsory study of the Bulgarian language may study their mother tongue in municipal schools under the protection and control of the state.

The educational system (prior to higher education) comprises 12 grades, organized in two major levels: basic and secondary. Basic education (grades first through eighth) is subdivided into two sub-levels: elementary (grades first through fourth) and presecondary (grades fifth through eighth). Secondary education normally encompasses grades eighth through twelfth, but can start earlier depending on the type of school. There are two major kinds of secondary schools: secondary comprehensive, usually called *gymnasia* (high school) and secondary vocational, most often referred to as *tehnikum* (vocational school.) Special schools at all educational levels accommodate students with impaired health. Private schools constitute a new element in the structure of the education system.

Special schools accommodate students in need of special care because of learning disabilities, health, or emotional problems. There is a wide variety of special schools, catering to children who are chronically ill, mentally retarded, blind or visually impaired, hearing and speech impaired, or who have behavioral problems bordering on juvenile delinquency. In 1999-2000, there were 146 special schools at all levels of the education system with 16,000 students enrolled. A significant number of the special schools function as internati (boarding schools).

Private schools are still relatively few in numbers. By January 1999, there were only 52 private schools. Six of the private schools were elementary, twenty-three basic, two presecondary, seventeen high schools, and four general comprehensive including all levels. There were 4,382 students enrolled in all private schools, or only 0.5 percent of the whole student population. Private schools are subject to social controversy because of widespread concerns that they undermine the nation's democratic traditions in education. Despite that, their numbers slowly increase: in comparison with 1998, there were eight more private schools and student enrollment enlarged by 389.

The curriculum is structured into three components: compulsory, elective, and optional; the correlation between those varies at different types of schools. Subjects fall into the following eight major areas of content: Bulgarian language and literature, foreign languages, mathematics, information technologies, social sciences and civics, natural sciences and ecology, music and art, physical culture and sports.

Schools operate on a five-day week schedule. September 15 or the workday closest to it marks the beginning of the school year. This is a festive occasion. Many students go to school carrying bouquets of flowers for their teachers and may be accompanied by their families. The duration of the school year varies by the school level and grade and depends on the quantity of material that needs to be covered. It ends on May 24 for grades 1 and 12 (in the latter case, the intention is to provide time for the matriculation examination). The school year continues until May 31 for grades 2 through 4, until June 15 for grades 5 through 8, June 30 for grades 9 through 11. The school year is divided into two *sroka* (terms, singular is *srok*); the first term begins on September 15 and ends on February 4, the second one starts on February 9. There is a Christmas break (December 24 through January 6), an inter-term break (February 7-8), a spring break (April 1-10), and a two-day break before Eastern Orthodox Easter. In addition, first graders only have a short break in the fall (November 11-13). Setting school vacations in relation to religious holidays is a departure from the practices of the communist regime, which did everything possible to discourage religion and banish it from the public sphere. The summer vacation spans from the end of the school year until September 15. If schools are to be closed due to inclement weather or fuel shortage, the days missed are compensated at the expense of vacation time.

Students from grades 1 through 12 normally spend half a day in school; the other half is dedicated to homework and independent study at home. In elementary school and sometimes in presecondary school there exists an option called *zanimalnya* (extended care) for students to spend the other half of the day in school working on their lessons under the control of a teacher. This is done upon the explicit request of the parents. Schools in big cities operate according to a two-shift scheme (morning and afternoon) because of shortage of school premises. In small cities and villages the one-shift scheme is prevalent.

The grading system is based on numerals, where 6 is *otlichen* (excellent), 5 is *mnogo dobar* (very good), 4 is *dobar* (good), 3 is *sreden* (satisfactory), and 2 is *slab* (poor). Passing grades are 3 through 6; 2 denotes a failure. Very rarely applied, 1 (very poor) is sometimes given for academic misconduct. This grading system is used at all levels of schooling. Grading is based on written and oral testing, homework, and in-class participation. Students do not pass automatically to a higher grade level. Students who have poor grades in more than three subjects repeat the year. In case of three or less poor grades the student has the right to take a supplementary examination, a failure in which also results in repeating the grade. There is no passing to a higher grade on probation. Students are not allowed to repeat grades more than twice in their school career.

Textbooks are subject to contest-based writing, publication, and distribution. All Bulgarian publishing houses that meet the criteria set by the Ministry of Education and Science can compete. The textbooks suitable for use in a particular subject are selected under conditions of real competition with respect to content, artistic layout, and price. On those terms, the Ministry works with more than thirty state and private publishing houses, which print and distribute over 480 textbooks for comprehensive and 800 textbooks for vocational instruction. The schools then place their orders directly with the publishers. The introduction of the contest principle in the publication of textbooks raised professional standards and resulted in improved quality of textbooks.

Bulgarian schools are well equipped with traditional audiovisual aids, such as maps, charts, and globes. Simple technical appliances (like overhead projectors, TV sets, cassette-recorders, and slide-projectors) are also widespread, but the instructional materials that go with them are often obsolete and not in compliance with the new content of study. Office equipment, copiers, and printers are generally lacking in classrooms. But schools face grave problems in securing contemporary computer hardware, software, and communications. The need to update information technologies is well recognized and guidelines have been developed for their introduction.

Bulgarian educators are generally quite open to new instructional techniques and methods. The problems stem from a poor material base. Relatively few computers are available, and those tend to be outdated models with inadequate performance. The existing computers in 1995 were IBM (about 30 percent), Macintosh (2 percent), and the archaic Bulgarian Pravets-8 (67 percent). Due to financial difficulties, very few funds have been allocated for purchase of new computers and any contributions in this field come primarily from donors. Despite all these difficulties, many Bulgarian schools are on-line and teachers and students partake in the information exchange.

Bulgaria has significant minority populations whose first language is not Bulgarian. Under the circumstances, it is very important that schools breed a public spirit of tolerance and dialogue. Traditionally, minorities have enjoyed all rights to education as Bulgarian citizens and have been well integrated in the education system. After the fall of communism in 1989, many former Eastern Bloc nations lived through a process of redefining of national identity, nation-states and citizenship that led to the eruption of conflicts and civil wars. Bulgaria constituted a fortunate exception from this pattern and the education system was entitled to some credit for preserving the national peace. Though, a significant deficiency is the lack of methods for teaching Bulgarian as a foreign language to schoolchildren who speak another language at home. An alarming symptom of alienation is the increasing dropout rate among Roma children who are of compulsory education age.

Education in Bulgaria, although fundamentally national in character, has significant foreign influences. Russian impact was most pronounced during the period of the national revival in the nineteenth century and stemmed the ideas of Slavophilism and pan-Orthodoxy. Many young Bulgarians went to pursue their education in St. Petersburg and Odessa. Immediately after the liberation from Ottoman domination in 1878, achieved with decisive help from Russia, Russian experts remained in Bulgaria to assist with the establishment of the administrative structure of the young nation-state. After the end of the World War II, Bulgaria became a satellite state of the Soviet Union and was heavily subjected to Russian influence in the sphere of culture and education. The model of the entire education system, and particularly that of higher education, was designed to emulate the Soviet education system. Russian language became a compulsory subject as early as fifth grade and intensified at every subsequent school level. The generations of Bulgarians educated under communist rule have command of Russian which provided immediate access to a much larger scope of publications. Russian was promoted as a *lingua franca* among professional circles of the Eastern Bloc nations. Many Bulgarians received their higher education in Soviet institutions of higher learning, particularly in the technical fields. Although, after 1989, Russian influences on Bulgarian education were on the decline.

Western European and American influences are also evident. German impact, channeled through the Bulgarian royal house which was of German dynastic descent and facilitated by German economic interests in the Balkans, was considerable during the two World Wars that Bulgaria entered as an ally of Germany. French cultural and educational influences infiltrated through the efforts of Jesuit priests in the nineteenth century and the francophone programs of the French government throughout the twentieth century. The first exposure to American educational influence began with the work of Protestant missionaries in the middle of the nineteenth century, remained in the country until the communist regime expelled them in 1945. Meanwhile, they opened some of the first nurseries in Bulgaria, as well as teacher training institutes, vocational schools, and a college in Sofia. The latter was restored in the early 1990s; despite its name, it is in fact one of the most prestigious high schools in the Bulgarian capital. The most significant embodiment of American presence in the Bulgarian education system is the American University in Blagoevgrad, which attracts students from all Balkan nations. Well-educated strata of the population normally speak at least one Western language. Until the 1970s, choices were almost evenly split between German, French and English; younger generations, especially after 1990, overwhelmingly opted for English.

A major goal of the reform of Bulgaria's education system was to bring standards in line with the European context and to harmonize the educational process with that of Western Europe. This was expected to assist the nation's accession to the European Union. In December 1999 Bulgaria was invited to begin negotiations to that effect with practical discussion that begun in March 2000 on six topics, the first two of which were "education and training" and "science and research." Of primary importance is the impact of educational programs and initiatives sponsored by international organizations: UNESCO, the Council of Europe, the European Union, the World Bank. Joint initiatives in education, such as the programs PHARE, TEMPUS, COPERNICUS in the 1990s vastly improved Bulgaria's structure and content of its education.

PREPRIMARY & PRIMARY EDUCATION

Preprimary and primary education in Bulgaria consists of two levels—*detski yasli* (nurseries) for children through the age of three and *detski gradini* (kindergartens) for children ages three to seven. These age limits are not absolute, since kindergartens often accept children who are two and a half years old, and elementary schools enroll six-year-olds. Attendance in both cases is voluntary and fees are charged. The nurseries are under the jurisdiction of the Ministry of Health and are not considered part of the education system.

Bulgaria's traditions in preprimary education go back 120 years. An education act in 1891 introduced compulsory kindergarten attendance in the cities. While preschool education is not a requirement, there exist impressive facilities, sufficient to enroll the entire children population in all-day kindergartens. However, attendance is on the decline. The major reason for that are the high unemployment rates and the economic difficulties encountered by many families. In 1990-1991, about 312,000 of 595,448 children ages two through seven attended kindergartens (52.4 percent). The percentages slightly differ between cities (53.13 percent), and villages (50.78 percent), and are lowest in Sofia (49.78 percent). The number of children in this age rapidly decreases as well, due to falling birth rates. This explains why relative numbers increased, and absolute enrollment in kindergartens fell. For instance, in 1998-1999 nearly 230,330, or 58 percent, of the children in this age group, attended kindergarten. In consequence to declining enrollment, preprimary education enhances the intellectual and social development of youngsters and prepares them for a smooth transition to grade school. Kindergarten attendance is socially desirable; most of the children who are not enrolled in preprimary education come from low-income families where one or both parents are unemployed.

Grades 1 through 4 comprise the first sub-level of basic education or *nachalno uchilishte* (elementary school). According to a 1998 amendment of the Public Education Act, children start school at the age of seven; they are supposed to have turned or are going to turn seven in the year they join first grade. Six-year-olds may be enrolled in case their physical and mental development allows for such a step, a decision left to the discretion of their parents or guardians. The curriculum for grades 1 through 4 includes eight compulsory subjects: Bulgarian language, mathematics, introductory Bulgarian history and geography, natural science, fine art, music, and physical education. Minimum comprehensive instruction includes 22-25 hours per week. The curriculum also provides for three to four hours of optional subjects per week. Primary education is completed without exam. *Svidetelstvo* (certificate) of primary education is issued on the basis of the grades earned in fourth grade. In 1999-2000, there were 385,000 students enrolled in elementary education.

The second sub-level of the basic school, called *progimnaziya* (pre-high school) covers grades 5 through 8. The curriculum at this level includes 12 compulsory subjects: Bulgarian language and literature, mathematics, history, geography, physics, chemistry, biology, fine arts, music, technical education, physical education, and one foreign language. A second foreign language may be included in the seventh grade. The minimum instruction time includes 27-30 hours per week; another four hours per week are allowed for optional subjects. A *Svidetelstvo* (certificate) for completed basic education is issued on the basis of the grades earned in eighth grade without a final exam. In 1999-2000, there were 357,000 students enrolled at this school level.

SECONDARY EDUCATION

Secondary education normally covers grades 8 through 12 and is regarded as a preparation for higher education. There exist several types of schools, usually called gymnaziya (high school). Most common is the secondary comprehensive school, which is the third and completing level of general comprehensive school, following the elementary and presecondary levels. In 1999-2000 there were 398 secondary schools. Socially more prestigious and widely preferred are the profile-oriented secondary schools, of which there are two kinds. The first one comprises secondary schools with intensive instruction in a foreign language (most often English, but also

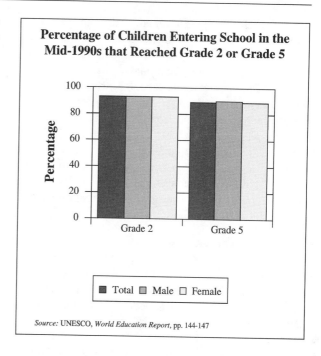

Percentage of Children Entering School in the Mid-1990s that Reached Grade 2 or Grade 5

Source: UNESCO, *World Education Report*, pp. 144-147

French, German, Spanish, and Italian). A peculiarity of this foreign-language *gymnaziya* is that admission takes place after the completion of seventh grade and is based on competitive entrance examination in mathematics and the Bulgarian language. The first year of instruction, called preparatory class, is dedicated to an in-depth study of a respective foreign language. This is followed by grades 8 through 12, which complete the general curriculum. The second kind of profile-oriented secondary schools, with entrance after eighth grade and competitive admission, are those specializing in math and science, the humanities, sports, and the arts. In 1999-2000, there were 69 foreign language, 14 sports, 15 humanities, and 34 math and science profile-oriented secondary schools.

The course of study ends with a compulsory matriculation examination, which comprises three exams: Bulgarian language and literature, social sciences and civics, and a subject corresponding to the profile of the school. Those who complete a secondary comprehensive school successfully are awarded a diploma, which qualifies them to apply to institutions of higher learning. In 1999-2000, there were 177,000 students enrolled in all secondary comprehensive schools.

Traditions in the secondary education field go more than 120 years back in history. In the 1990s, vocational education was given special attention resulting in the Vocational Education and Training Act of 1999. Secondary vocational education combines the goals of providing professional qualification with broadening the general comprehensive education of the students. There are several types of schools: *tehnikum* (technical school) with admission after completed eighth grade and a four-year course of instruction; technical schools with admission after completed seventh grade with intensive foreign language studies and a five-year course of instruction; secondary vocational-technical schools with admission after eighth grade and a three-year course of instruction; vocational schools with admission after sixth, seventh, and eighth grade; and vocational classes within the framework of the secondary comprehensive school. This is practiced in small settlements lacking a developed network of vocational schools. The fields and degrees of qualification are in accordance with standards established by the International Labor Organization.

Forms of instruction include daytime, evening, extramural, correspondence, individual, and self-instruction. This flexibility allows for the inclusion of adults in vocational education. Studies are completed after matriculation exams and result in a diploma, which entitles graduates to continue their education on a higher level or to enter the workforce. Statistics showed a trend towards increase in the percentage of students who pursue higher or semi-higher education after graduating from secondary vocational schools. In 1999-2000, there were 189,000 students enrolled in secondary vocational schools, six percent more than the students in secondary comprehensive schools.

HIGHER EDUCATION

Vische obrazovanie (higher education) is the sector of the education system that experienced most intensive growth during the 1990s, despite unfavorable economic conditions and diminishing state funds. This tendency indicates that Bulgarian society in times of economic duress and social crisis resorts to higher education as a reliable investment. The pace of reform and the changes introduced in higher education are also more considerable than those in preprimary, basic, and secondary education. Some major outcomes of this reform are the abolition of ideological subjects and content; the reshaping of study programs, curricula, and syllabi; the abolition of research institutes and ensuing unemployment among researchers; the introduction of tuition fees in public universities; the increase of the number of universities as a result of the transformation of many higher institutes into universities; and the establishment of private universities and colleges.

The total number of higher schools in Bulgaria is 88. There exist three types of higher schools: universities, specialized higher schools (academies and institutes), and independent colleges. There are 26 universities, belonging to one of the following two kinds: traditional universities with faculties of law, history, education, philosophy, economics, philology, chemistry, biology, physics, mathematics, and geography; and specialized universities of medicine, technology, agriculture, and economics. The number of specialized high schools is 15. Some of them are institutes (of technological sciences), others are academies (of fine arts, music, sport, theology, theater and cinema, and the military). Because universities and specialized high schools have an equal status, it is often said that there are altogether 41 universities. There are also 47 colleges specializing in technology, teacher-training, nursing, tourism, and telecommunications. Although, there are slightly more colleges than universities, the latter are more prestigious because of the quality of education offered and the employment possibilities after graduation. Despite the fact that most colleges exist within the structure of a university, the 'functional bridges' between them are not well constructed. Ten of the higher schools in Bulgaria are private: four of them are universities and specialized high schools and six are colleges.

Higher schools offer study programs that result in the following types of degrees: a specialist diploma awarded for completion of a three-year program; a bachelor's diploma awarded for completion of a four-year program; a master's diploma awarded for the completion of a five-year program, or one year after the bachelor's degree; doctoral degree awarded for completion of a three-year research program after the master's diploma. A necessary prerequisite for enrollment in a higher school is a diploma for completed secondary education. Otherwise, rules of admission are left to the discretion of the particular school and vary considerably, being lower in the newly established private institutions of higher learning. The most prestigious universities apply a formula, which combines results from written admission exams with grades from the high school diploma.

During the 1990s student enrollment in institutions of higher learning increased considerably. In 1988-1989, there were 160,000 students pursuing higher education. By way of comparison, the number for 1992-1993 was 192,000; in 1994-1995, about 221,000; in 1996-1997, about 263,000; and in 1999-2000, about 258,000. Taking into consideration that the country's population as a whole and the numbers of university-aged individuals is on the decline, this trend is even more pronounced. According to Popov, the main reasons for this lie in the expansion of public universities and the opening of private ones, the attraction of students from medium-sized towns to newly established university branches outside the major urban centers, the introduction of paid tuition and the subsequent lowering admission requirements for paid education, as well as the option for adult college graduates to obtain bachelor's and master's degrees in part-time, short-term university programs. This boom reached a peak in 1996-97, coinciding with the deepest financial, economic, and social crisis of the 1990s. The number of enrolled students is slightly declining, reflecting the decline of university In 1999-2000, there were 258,000 students of higher education, 57 percent of whom are women. Highest enrollment was in the economics and business programs, followed by the technological sciences. Some fields of the humanities and the social sciences, and particularly law, are also considered prestigious fields of study. An surprising fact is the large number of students enrolled in teacher training programs. Colleges experience a markedly low rate of enrollment: in 1999-2000, they had only 18,500 students. In the same year, the private higher schools had 27,500 students, or 10 percent of the total enrollment.

The faculty ranks consist of professor (full professor), docent (associate professor), assistant (assistant professor), and *prepodavatel* (lecturer). The total number of teaching faculty in 1999-2000 was 26,735, approximately 42 percent of which are women; there were 2,447 full professors, 19 percent of whom were women.

Higher education in Bulgaria is managed at two levels: national and institutional. The entities supervising higher education at the national level are the parliament (the National Assembly), the cabinet (Council of Ministers), and the Ministry of Education and Science. The parliament acts as the decision-making authority on the establishment, transformation, and the closing of public and private higher schools. It also annually allocates subsidies to public higher schools on the basis of the State Budget Act. The main actor in managing higher education on the national level is the Council of Ministers, which has wide-ranging prerogatives; the Ministry of Education and Science plays a more limited role. A National Evaluation and Accreditation Agency is established by the Council of Ministers as the specialized government authority for quality assessment and accreditation of higher school activities. The institutional level of management has acquired significant importance according to the principle of academic autonomy. The general assembly, the academic council, and the rector (president) are the main figures of importance.

Financing of higher education has been a most controversial issue of public discourse since 1989. Under communism, the general public was accustomed to the nearly egalitarian character of higher education, and grew to perceive it as a kind of social service. The popular expectation that the government should be the main source of funding higher education is still widespread and made it very difficult for those in power to renounce the government's function. The introduction of student paid education, parallel with the limited state funded enrollment, was met with considerable social and political resistance, despite the apparent need for additional sources of uni-

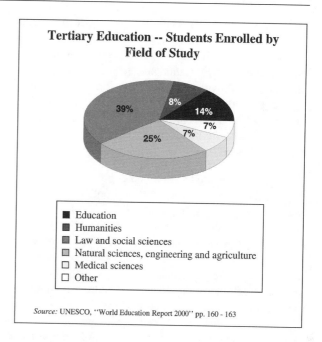

Tertiary Education -- Students Enrolled by Field of Study

- ■ Education
- ■ Humanities
- ■ Law and social sciences
- ◻ Natural sciences, engineering and agriculture
- ◻ Medical sciences
- ◻ Other

Source: UNESCO, "World Education Report 2000" pp. 160 - 163

versity revenue. The government continues to sponsor a limited number of students enrolled through the system of *darzhavna porachka* (state quota), a quantity of specialists perceived as necessary to sustain the continuity of manpower in every professional field. These spots are highly contested in the enrollment process and only the best candidates qualify for these positions. In addition, the schools of higher learning admit a great number of students who pay for their own tuition.

ADMINISTRATION, FINANCE, & EDUCATIONAL RESEARCH

Under the communist regime, education was strongly centralized and placed entirely under the control of the state and the communist party. Since the early 1990s, an on-going process of decentralization has brought about considerable changes in this respect. Administration of basic and secondary education is effected on four levels: national, regional, municipal and school level.

The Ministry of Education and Science is a specialized body of the Council of Ministers for the administration of education on the national level. It determines and carries out the government policy in the field of education. The ministry plans activities related to the development of education in long-term programs and operation plans, organizes and coordinates the work of all administrative units and education establishments, and exercises control over all levels and types of schools in the country, including kindergartens and private schools. It interacts with other ministries and state departments in connection with the administration of schools which train specialists in respective spheres (e.g., engineering, mining, agriculture) and also conducts international activities in the field of education. There are 28 school inspectorates set up on a regional level which act as specialized territorial bodies of the Ministry of Education and Science. They exercise planning, coordination, and control functions over the work of the schools on the territory of a particular region. The staff of a regional inspectorate comprises experts in school administration as well as specialists in various academic subjects.

The municipal education bodies have a broad range of prerogatives to further educational policies on the territory of a city. According to article 36 of the Public Education Act, municipalities are responsible for the compulsory school education of children up to the age of 16; the health care and safety of schools and kindergartens; the funds for maintenance, construction, furnishing, and repair of schools, kindergartens, and servicing units; the funds for meeting the annual cost per schoolchild, remuneration of teachers, as well as for financial back-up of all sections of the syllabus of municipal kindergartens, schools, and servicing units; the appropriate conditions in canteens, boarding houses, recreation and sports facilities; for transportation for preschoolers, schoolchildren, and teachers; and for scholarships and grants for students. This makes the municipal level a very important part of the system of the administration of education. The school is a legal entity. During the 1990s, its autonomy in pedagogical, organizational, methodological, administrative, and managerial matters had been considerably extended. Schools are headed by a director (principal), who continues to teach on a reduced workload and has the status of a head-teacher. They are not purely a manager. The director and the pedagogicheski savet (pedagogical council) are the administrative bodies of the school. Since 1995-1996, an old Bulgarian tradition of establishing boards of school trustees as a link with the community has been restored. The boards of trustees comprise the school principal, teachers, parents, public figures, businessmen, among others. The National Assembly discussed a special law to regulate the functions of the school boards of trustees. Most schools also have a parents council, a students council, and a class councils which act in accordance with the age of the student body and the administrative needs of the school.

Education is funded from two major sources: the state budget through the Ministry of Education and Science and the local budgets through the municipal administrations. Funding is appropriated according to the level of education and type of school. Other sources of funding, such as donations and contributions from private companies and government entities are permitted by law. The government does not subsidize private schools. The relative share of expenditures for education in the gross domestic project has been steadily on the decline since

the beginning of the 1990s. It reached 3.20 percent in 1998, which is half from the relative weight of educational expenses in 1992 (6.06 percent). Though, there was a modest increase of capital investment in education, for instance investment in repairs of existing school facilities and building new ones. The chronic deficit in the education budget made the practice of distributing free textbooks impossible to all students from first to eighth grade. Distribution of textbooks was then abandoned. Scientific research in the field of education is carried out at the Institute for Education as well as some other higher education institutions, universities, and the Bulgarian Academy of Sciences.

NONFORMAL EDUCATION

Under communism, formal classroom education was complemented by an extensive system of children and youth organizations and establishments. Since 1989, nonformal education has been gravely destabilized, owing this to ideological considerations, acute shortage of material and financial resources, and a lack of a strategy on the part of the education administration. There exists municipal children's centers, sports, art, and music schools, young technicians and agrobiologists labs, and centers for works with children, in Bulgaria. However, their number and capacity is considerably lower than the actual needs. There is an acute shortage of summer schools and activities for schoolchildren.

Legislation adopted in 1998 specified that distance education is a legitimate mode of study for obtaining a university degree. Approximately 85,000 students of higher education are enrolled in extra-mural courses. These students constitute a significant potential market for high quality distance education programs. Distance learning is institutionalized and operates within the framework of the National Center for Distance Education, established in 1994 by the Ministry of Education and Science. This is a consortium of 20 universities, with representatives of the Ministry of Education and Science, the Bulgarian National Television, and the Bulgarian National Radio. It is chaired by a representative of the PHARE program for Bulgaria. The role of the center includes development of distance learning strategy, research, development of materials, dissemination of information, promotion of contacts with external entities, and co-ordination of the implementation of the PHARE Multi-Country Program for Distance Learning.

TEACHING PROFESSION

A total of 68,482 teachers taught in all Bulgarian schools in 1999-2000: 23,820 in elementary schools (first through fourth grade); 32,479 in presecondary schools (fifth through eighth grade); and 12,283 in secondary schools (ninth through twelfth grade). Women constituted 82 percent of the overall number of teachers, which indicated a marked feminization of the teaching profession. The percentage of the teachers who possessed the necessary formal qualifications for teaching at a particular school level was higher than 98 percent. Elementary school teachers are required to have a specialist or a bachelor degree in the field *nachalna uchilishtna pedagodika* (elementary school pedagogy). There are six schools of higher learning in the country that train elementary school teachers.

There was a marked increase during the 1990s of the numbers of teachers at this level who hold advanced university degrees. In 1999-2000, some 14,948 (63 percent) of all elementary school teachers held higher than a specialist degree. The student-teacher ratio, which in the 1990s fluctuated between 14:1 and 18:1, is much higher in the cities. In the remote countryside it may drop as low as 6:1, but still the prevalent policy is to keep the schools open and hire teachers, thus preventing villages from depopulation.

Teachers at the presecondary and secondary level are required to have professional qualification in the subject(s) they teach accompanied by pedagogical qualification. A specialist, bachelor, or a master degree can establish these. There are specific demands for hiring teachers in vocation schools, including previous practice and specific training in the subject they teach. In 1999-2000, some 23,132 teachers (71 percent) at the pre-secondary school held bachelor and master degrees. The student-teacher ratio at this level is thirteen-fourteen. During the same year, the number of secondary school teachers holding bachelor and master degrees was 11,652 (94 percent) and the student-teacher ratio was 16:1 or 17:1. There is a well-established system of continuing education, and teachers are motivated to improve their qualifications by higher salaries.

Despite the fact that teachers' salaries had been relatively low for many years, the education system of Bulgaria managed under the stress of acute economic crisis to maintain professional integrity and prestige of the profession, and preserve the continuity of teaching. The overall number of teachers increased slightly in comparison with previous years and so did the numbers of students enrolled in teacher-training programs. There was a minimal decrease of the number of elementary school teachers, which corresponds to the demographic decline. There was a marked trend of improving teachers' qualifications.

SUMMARY

Bulgaria has established democratic traditions in modern secular education, which date back to the middle of the nineteenth century. During the 1990s, the education system was subject to a thorough transformation running parallel to the nation's post-communist transition. The success of the education reform will shape the future of the nation in profound ways. Schools are expected to be an agent of democratization, grooming generations with better skills for critical thinking and public discourse. Transformed and modernized education is regarded as a vehicle of Bulgaria's integration in the European context.

The educational reform is an on-going process and more changes are bound to occur in the foreseeable future, while some of those that have been introduced have not come to fruition. Private schools at all levels, which have a considerably lower enrollment than the public ones and often face unfavorable attitudes, are yet to prove themselves as a viable alternative in education. Higher education is disconnected from secondary education; there is no system of pre-university establishments. The education system does not correspond to the needs of the labor market. Because of the shrinking of the latter, the schools overproduce specialists. The worst problem is the general lack of facilities to meet the challenges of a technology-based society and foster the qualifications that the nation needs in a high-tech environment.

Despite all difficulties, in the 1990s Bulgaria sustained the integrity of its education system and introduced considerable improvements. This positive trend is bound to continue because Bulgarian national psyche relates education closely to the ideas of progress and personal betterment.

BIBLIOGRAPHY

Avramova, Bistra. *Education in Bulgaria.* Sofia: Sofia Press, 1971.

''The Balkans—Ethnic and Cultural Crossroads: Educational and Cultural Aspects: Sofia'' (Bulgaria), 27-30 May 1995. Strasbourg: Council of Europe Publishing, 1997.

Bulgaria. *Ministry of Education, Science and Technologies. Institute for Education and Science. Development of Education in 1994-1996: National Report of the Republic of Bulgaria.* Sofia: 1996.

Georgeoff, John P. *The Social Education of Bulgarian Youth.* Minneapolis: University of Minnesota Press, 1968.

Heath, Roy E. *The Establishment of the Bulgarian Ministry of Public Instruction and its Role in the Development of Modern Bulgaria, 1878-1885.* New York and London: Garland Publishing, 1978.

Kyuchkov, Hristo. *Romany Children and Their Preparation for Literacy: a Case Study.* Tilburg, the Netherlands: Tilburg University Press, 1995.

Makariev, Plamen. *Interkulturnoto obrazovanie v Bulgaria: ideali I realnost.* Sofia: AKSES/IPIS, 1999.

Ministry of Education and Science. Administration. Governments Priorities. Legislations. Educational Institutions. Networks and Projects. Publications. Statistics. Available from http://www.minedu.govern.bg/.

Ministry of Education and Science. Publications. National Education Strategy for Information and Communication Technologies (abstract), 1998. Available from http://www.minedu.govrn.bg/english.html.

Nikolov, Ivan P. "Tempus I in Bulgaria: Institutional Impact of the European Community assistance Program in Higher Education During 1990-1994." Ph.D. diss., Southern Illinois University at Carbondale, 1996.

Obshto I profesionalno obrazovanie: 1999/2000 uchebna godina. Sofia: Natsionalen statisticheski institut, 2000.

Obrazovanie za vsichki: natsionalna otsenka—2000 g. Sofia: Ministerstvo na obrazovanieto i naukata - Natsionalen institut po obrazovanie, 1999.

Popov, Nikolay. *A Review of the System of Higher Education in Bulgaria.* Budapest, Hungary; New Haven, CT: Civic Education Project, 2000.

Republic of Bulgaria: Laws for Education. Sofia: St. Kliment Ohridski University Press, 1999.

Russell, William F. *Schools in Bulgaria: With Special Reference to the Influence of the Agrarian Party on Elementary and Secondary Education.* New York City: Teachers' College, Columbia University, 1924.

Slantcheva, Snejana. "The introduction of the bachelor-master-doctor degree system in Bulgarian universities: a case study." Ph.D. diss., University of Massachusetts at Amherst, 2000.

Stefanov, Michael. *New Technologies, Labour Organization, Qualification, Structures and Vocational Training in Bulgaria.* Berlin: European Centre for the Development of Vocational Training, 1990.

Tzokova, Diana, and Zlatko Dobrev. "Bulgaria: Gypsy Children and Changing Social Concepts of Special Education." In *Inclusive Education,* edited by Harry Daniels and Philip Garner; series editor: Crispin Jones. London: Kogan Page; Sterling, VA: Stylus Publishing, 1999.

Vische obrazovanie: 1999/2000 uchebna godina. Sofia: Natsionalen statisticenski institut, 2000.

The World Bank Group. *World Development Series. Bulgaria—Education Modernization Project,* 7 August 2000. Available from http://www-wds.worldbank.org/.

—Petya Nitzova

BURKINA FASO

BASIC DATA

Official Country Name:	Burkina Faso
Region:	Africa
Population:	11,946,065
Language(s):	French, native African languages
Literacy Rate:	19.2%
Number of Primary Schools:	3,233
Compulsory Schooling:	7 years
Public Expenditure on Education:	1.5%
Foreign Students in National Universities:	755
Libraries:	21
Educational Enrollment:	Primary: 700,995 Higher: 8,911
Educational Enrollment Rate:	Primary: 40% Secondary: 7% Higher: 1%
Teachers:	Primary: 14,037 Higher: 352
Student-Teacher Ratio:	Primary: 50:1
Female Enrollment Rate:	Primary: 31% Secondary: 5% Higher: 0.4%

HISTORY & BACKGROUND

Similar to other French West African colonies, Burkina Faso (known as Upper Volta until 1983) based its educational system on that of France up until it achieved independence in 1960. Six years of primary education, beginning at age six, was followed by up to seven years of secondary instruction. Less than 1 percent of the population actually enrolled in secondary education; those who did graduate were forced to seek higher education in France as none existed at the time in Upper Volta. During the 1950s, the French government increased the percentage of the national budget spent on education from 13 percent to 23 percent. As a result, primary education enrollment jumped from 2 percent to

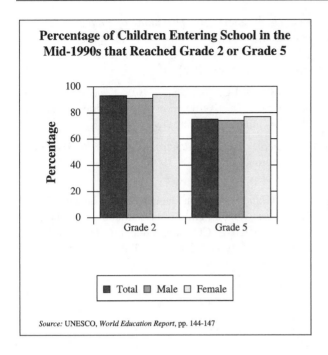

Percentage of Children Entering School in the Mid-1990s that Reached Grade 2 or Grade 5

■ Total   ▨ Male   ☐ Female

Source: UNESCO, *World Education Report*, pp. 144-147

6 percent. Concerned that such a sizable portion of the budget was needed to maintain such a meager enrollment rate, education officials began examining ways to make education more accessible—particularly to girls and to children living in rural areas—while at the same time increasing the economic efficiency of the system.

CONSTITUTIONAL & LEGAL FOUNDATIONS

The *Societe d'Etudes pour le Developpment Economique et Social* (SEDES) began examining the educational system of Upper Volta in 1959. Later that year the French agency put forth the Christol and Medard Report, which recommended a modest expansion of the current primary education efforts, along with the development of a system of rural nonformal education as a means in offering relevant education at a modest cost to larger segments of the population. According to the terms of the proposal, rural education centers (RECs) would be set up only in communities that requested such a facility and were also willing to fund it; enrollment would be restricted to children ages 12 to 14 years. Also, the three-year curriculum would consist of reading, writing, French language, arithmetic, humanities, physical fitness, and agriculture training. Local instructors, while not required to possess the qualifications of a formal educator, would receive training specific to the REC program. The Voltaic Legislative Assembly approved the recommendations of the Christol and Medard Report, seeing the rural system as a means of temporarily increasing access to some sort of education, particularly agricultural training, until the

nation—one of the poorest in the world—was better able sustain the cost of universal primary education.

Despite the Ministry of Agriculture's heavy promotion of rural education, enrollment in the RECs dropped by roughly 20 percent between 1970 and 1971, mainly because "conventional primary schooling was regarded by the population in general as a means of escaping traditional society and economy and gaining access to the modern and privileged sector. To close off this only option for a better life was unacceptable to those living in the rural areas, so they just refused to send their children. . ." (Haddad 204). The rural education system was dealt another blow by a successful populist revolt, led by Captain Tomas Sankara in the early 1980. Believing the two-tiered educational system was elitist, the new regime began examining more equitable solutions to the nation's education dilemma. It was not only the rural education segment of the system that needed reform, but also primary enrollment rates were only 19 percent in 1983, compared to 14 percent a decade earlier. Although most officials agreed that a reduction in primary education costs was essential for an increase in accessibility, how to go about doing this remained an issue for debate well into the 1990s.

EDUCATIONAL SYSTEM—OVERVIEW

School enrollment in Burkina Faso is among the lowest in Africa. In 1992 primary enrollment reached 28 percent; roughly 37 percent of these students were girls. Free primary education is not compulsory. French is the primary language of instruction at all educational levels, and the academic year runs from October to June.

PREPRIMARY & PRIMARY EDUCATION

Burkinabe children attend primary school between the ages of 7 and 13. After six years of study, students must pass a final examination to receive a primary school certificate of completion. The student-teacher ratio is 64:1, notably higher than the 40:1 student-teacher ratio average for all of Sub-Saharan Africa.

SECONDARY EDUCATION

Secondary education in Burkina Faso is divided into two tracks: lower and upper. Lower secondary school consists of four years of general study. Upon successful completion of a final exam, students are awarded the *Brevet d'Etudes du Premier Cycle.* Those who wish to continue their education may either continue at an upper secondary school for another three years of general study or seek entrance to a vocational school to pursue a two- or three-year program of training for teachers, nurses, midwives, police officers, customs officials, or public administrators. Those who successfully complete such a program are awarded the *Certificat d'Aptitude Profes-sionnelle,* while upper secondary graduates who pass their Baccalaureate exam earn a *Diplome de Bachelier de l'Enseignement du Second Degre.* The student-teacher ratio in secondary education is roughly 65:1.

HIGHER EDUCATION

Ouagadougou University (founded in 1974) was the only institution of higher education in Burkina Faso until 1995, when the Polytechnical University, in Bobo-Dioulasso, was established. The *Institut des Sciences de l'Education,* now known as *Ecole Normale Superieure de Koudougou,* moved to Koudougou in 1996. Most departments at the universities began offering doctoral programs in 1998, with the exception of the Faculty of Health Care Sciences of Ouagadougou University, which launched the first doctoral degree program in the country in 1994. Although enrollment at higher education institutions jumped nearly 62 percent in 1999—bringing the total number of higher education students in Burkina Faso to roughly 10,000—many Bukinabe students continue to seek higher education in France, Senegal, or Côte d'Ivoire.

ADMINISTRATION, FINANCE, & EDUCATIONAL RESEARCH

The Ministry of Basic Education and the Ministry of Secondary and Higher Education oversee all curricula-based decisions regarding scheduling, examinations, grading, and syllabi.

TEACHING PROFESSION

Primary school teachers are usually required to complete lower secondary school, as well as a two-year program at the *Ecole Nationale des Enseignants du Primaire,* (ENEP) which awards graduates the *Certificat de Fin d'Etudes des ENEP.* Secondary school teachers are required to attend either a university or a teacher-training institute to earn a teaching license. Higher education teachers must hold doctoral degrees.

SUMMARY

Despite improvements in school enrollment, mainly at the higher education level, literacy rates in Burkina Faso remain among the lowest in the world. Only 29.5 percent of males and 9.2 of females were considered literate in 1997. Education officials continue to examine methods of making education more accessible to all residents, particularly those in remote farming communities.

BIBLIOGRAPHY

Grabe, Sven. *Nonformal Education for Rural Development, Case Study No. 14: The Rural Education System in Upper Volta.* Essex, Canada: International Council for Educational Development, 1972.

Haddad, Wadi D. *The Dynamics of Education Policy-making: Case Studies of Burkina Faso, Jordan, Peru, and Thailand.* Washington, DC: Economic Development Institute of the World Bank, 1994.

OSEAS-ADCEC. *Burkina Faso: Education Profile.* Washington, DC: Association of International Educators, 2000. Available from http://www.oead.ac.at.

U.S. Dept. of State. *Background Notes: Burkina Faso.* Washington, DC: GPO, 1998. Available from http://www.state.gov.

World Higher Education Database 2000. *Burkina Faso—Education System.* Paris: International Association of Universities/UNESCO International Centre on Higher Education, 1998-1999. Available from http://www.usc.edu.

—*AnnaMarie L. Sheldon*

BURUNDI

BASIC DATA

Official Country Name:	Republic of Burundi
Region:	Africa
Population:	6,054,714
Language(s):	Kirundi, French, Swahili
Literacy Rate:	35.3%

The country of Burundi continues to go through fundamental changes that affect, like all its institutions, the educational system. Early in the twentieth century, what is now Burundi was part of Belgium's colony of Ruanda-Urundi (which also included what came to be known as Rwanda). From 1908 until 1948, many of the schools were operated by churches. These were mostly primary schools with some middle schools. The Catholic missions were given an official status and government funding. Protestant schools were also permitted and recognized, but they did not receive government funds. Some of this changed when the Belgium government created a new plan, the "Organization of Free Subsidized Instruction for the Indigenous with the Assistance of Christian Missionary Societies," which promoted greater diversity in curriculum and the establishment of more secondary schools. This set the foundation for education when Burundi became independent in 1962.

Since that time Burundi suffered through tribal wars, between the Hutu and Tutsi, that also involved neighbor-

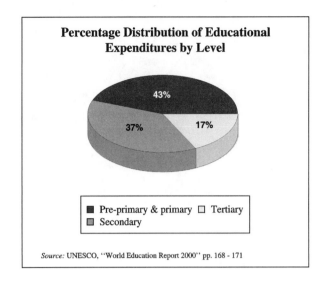

Percentage Distribution of Educational Expenditures by Level

- ■ Pre-primary & primary □ Tertiary
- ▨ Secondary

Source: UNESCO, "World Education Report 2000" pp. 168 - 171

ing Rwanda. At least 250,000 people are believed to have died in Burundi between 1993 and 1999. Besides the citizens' loss of life and, for many, their livelihoods, the country is also dealing with many refugees who are moving back and forth between other counties such as Tanzania and the Democratic Republic of Congo. The governmental infrastructure has been strained.

With a population estimated in 2000 at 6,054,714 people, the nation has been receiving some international assistance for humanitarian and educational programs from organizations like the United Nations. The need for a primary and secondary education system is substantial since 17 percent of the population was 14-years-old or younger (2000 estimate). The national literacy rate (those at least 15 years old who are able to read and write) is 35.3 percent, one of the lowest in the world. To break the figures down further, 49.3 percent of males and 22.5 percent of females were categorized as literate, according to a 1995 estimate. Kirundi and French are the country's official languages, and Swahili is also used is some of the districts.

Education is free in the country and taught mainly in Kirundi. Primary education, which is compulsory, begins at age seven and lasts for six years. Secondary education, which is not mandatory, consists of two programs, one of four years and another of three years. The University of Burundi, which uses French as a primary language, is located in the capital city of Bujumbura and is the country's only major university. The minority Tutsi students are often accused by the Hutu of having a disproportionate percentage of the enrollment in both the secondary and university levels. This is seen by some as an impediment to the Hutu majority assuming greater upward mobility in government and business.

BIBLIOGRAPHY

The Central Intelligence Agency (CIA). *The World Factbook 2000.* Directorate of Intelligence, 1 January 2000. Available from http://www.cia.gov/.

—Michael W. Young

CAMBODIA

BASIC DATA

Official Country Name:	Kingdom of Cambodia
Region:	Southeast Asia
Population:	12,212,306
Language(s):	Khmer, French, English
Literacy Rate:	35%
Number of Primary Schools:	5,026
Compulsory Schooling:	6 years
Public Expenditure on Education:	2.9%
Educational Enrollment:	Primary: 2,011,772
	Secondary: 312,934
	Higher: 8,901
Educational Enrollment Rate:	Primary: 110%
	Secondary: 24%
	Higher: 1%
Teachers:	Primary: 43,282
	Secondary: 19,135
	Higher: 1,001
Student-Teacher Ratio:	Primary: 46:1
	Secondary: 18:1
Female Enrollment Rate:	Primary: 100%
	Secondary: 17%
	Higher: 0.5%

Formal education in Cambodia was first provided solely to young boys by Buddhist monks, known as bonzes. During the second half of the nineteenth century, French leaders implemented a system based on their own model, with primary, secondary, and higher levels all overseen by the Ministry of Education. Although Cambodia maintained this system for several decades, it was not until the southeast Asian nation achieved independence from France in 1953 that educational efforts there became widespread.

Public and private schools in Cambodia offered six years of primary education, separated into two segments, each of which required successful completion of a national examination. Subjects included history, ethics, civics, mathematics, drafting, geography, language, science, and hygiene. Although Khmer was the language of instruction during the first three years of schooling, students were taught French, which became the language of instruction in the second three-year cycle of primary instruction. Secondary education consisted of four years at a *college* (lower secondary school) and an additional three years at a *lycée* (higher secondary school). Students who completed the first four-year cycle and passed a national examination received a secondary degree. Those who completed two years of the additional three-year cycle were required to pass a national examination to receive their first baccalaureate, and another examination after their final year, to receive their second baccalaureate.

Secondary education became increasingly focused on technology during the late 1960s and early 1970s; during this period, higher education institutions in Cambodia began to expand. Enrollment at the University of Phnom Penh grew to more than 4,500 men and 730 women. Three provincial universities opened in Batdambang, Kampong Cham, and Takev. However, the communist takeover of Cambodia in 1975 dealt the educational system there a nearly fatal blow. Schools were systematically closed, and of the 20,000 teachers living in Cambodia in the early 1970s, only 5,000 remained when the Vietnamese overthrew the Khmer Rouge regime and estab-

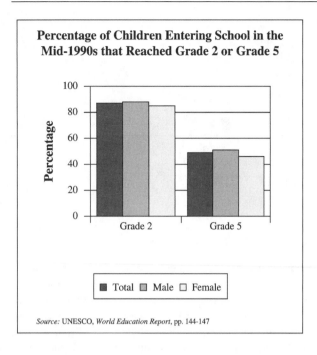

Percentage of Children Entering School in the Mid-1990s that Reached Grade 2 or Grade 5

Source: UNESCO, *World Education Report*, pp. 144-147

In 1998, more than 5,000 primary schools were in operation; enrollment was roughly 78.3 percent of children aged 6 to 11. However, nearly 50 percent of all primary schools, mainly ones in rural areas, were unable to offer a full range of grades one through six. Lower secondary schools in operation totaled 350, while upper secondary schools numbered 125. The mid-1990s launch of a new 12-year education system, which included six years of primary education and two three-year cycles of secondary education, increased the school year to 38 weeks. As prescribed by the new curriculum, each five-day week consists of six periods lasting 45 minutes each. To help fund the expanded educational system, the government increased the 8.1 percent of the national budget spent on education in 1997 to 10.3 percent in 1998.

Credentials for primary and lower secondary school teachers have also been upgraded. Once simply required to complete lower secondary school and then a two- or three-year teacher training program, primary and lower secondary teachers must now graduate from both lower and upper secondary school prior to completion of a two-year teacher training program. Upper secondary school teachers must complete five years of study at the University of Phnom Penh.

BIBLIOGRAPHY

Ayres, David M. *Anatomy of a Crisis: Education, Development, and the State in Cambodia 1953-1998.* Honolulu: University of Hawaii Press, 2000.

Kingdom of Cambodia Ministry of Education, Youth, and Sport. *Country Education Profile.* Phnom Penh, December 1999. Available from http://www.moeys.gov.kh.

U.S. Library of Congress. Federal Research Division. *Cambodia—A Country Study.* Washington, DC: August 1994. Available from http://rs6.loc.gov.

World Higher Education Database 2000. *Cambodia—Education System.* Paris: International Association of Universities/UNESCO International Centre on Higher Education, 1998-1999. Available from http://www.usc.edu.

—*AnnaMarie L. Sheldon*

lished the People's Republic of Kampuchea in 1979. Some teachers had fled, others died of malnutrition or illness, and others had been murdered. What education remained focused on Khmer doctrine.

In the early 1980s, Cambodia slowly began rebuilding its educational system under Vietnamese rule. The Ministry of Education, which later became known as the Ministry of Education, Youth, and Sport (MEYS), shortened the prior 13-year French-based program to 10 years. Primary and secondary education programs more closely resembled Vietnamese models, and students—limited to those who could afford tuition fees—were required to study the Vietnamese language. By 1986, several institutions of higher education had been founded or reopened, including the University of Fine Arts, the Faculty of Medicine and Pharmacy, the Chamkar Daung Agriculture Institute, the Kampuchea-USSR Friendship Technical Institute (now known as the Institute of Technology), the Institute of Commerce (now known as the Faculty of Business), the Faculty of Law and Economic Sciences, and the Center for Pedagogical Education. The Institute of Languages and the Normal Advanced School merged into the University of Phnom Penh in 1988.

The State of Cambodia (SOC) gained control of the country in 1989, followed by the United Nations Transitional Authority in Cambodia (UNTAC) in 1992. Public education was again made free to all residents, and the coalition governments in power since 1993 have, in general, supported efforts by the MEYS to bolster literacy rates—81.8 percent for males and 58.1 percent for females in 1998—and improve access to education, particularly in rural communities.

CAMEROON

BASIC DATA

Official Country Name:	Republic of Cameroon
Region:	Africa

Population:	15,421,937
Language(s):	African language groups, English, French
Literacy Rate:	63.4%
Academic Year:	September-June
Number of Primary Schools:	8,514
Compulsory Schooling:	6 years
Educational Enrollment:	Primary: 1,921,186 Secondary: 459,068 Higher: 33,177
Educational Enrollment Rate:	Primary: 88% Secondary: 27%
Teachers:	Primary: 39,384 Secondary: 14,917 Higher: 1,086
Student-Teacher Ratio:	Primary: 49:1 Secondary: 31:1
Female Enrollment Rate:	Primary: 84% Secondary: 22%

HISTORY & BACKGROUND

The Republic of Cameroon (*République de Cameroun*) is a unitary, constitutional democracy located in western Central Africa. Bordered by the Atlantic Ocean's Bight (bay) of Biafra to the southwest, Lake Chad to the northwest, Nigeria and Chad to the northeast, the Central African Republic to the east, and Equatorial Guinea, Gabon, and Congo (Brazzaville) to the south, Cameroon measures about 475,440 square kilometers in area, 6,000 square kilometers of which is water. Slightly larger than the U.S. state of California, Cameroon's terrain is composed of coastal and inland plains, mountains, and high plateaus. Cameroon's climate also is varied, ranging from hot and semi-arid in the north to tropical along the Atlantic coast. Sometimes referred to as "the hinge of Africa," the country sits between the first and thirteenth latitudes, just north of the equator.

Falling under colonial control in the second half of the nineteenth century during the Europeans' "scramble for Africa," Cameroon was governed by the Germans from 1884 until the end of World War I. When Germany lost the war in Europe, Cameroon was divided between the French and the British in 1918. On January 1, 1960 the French-speaking provinces of Cameroon declared their independence from the French-administered United Nations trusteeship, whereas the British-speaking prov-

inces became independent of the British-supervised United Nations trusteeship in October 1961. Northern Cameroons, the northernmost British province, voted to become part of Nigeria at independence while Southern Cameroons, the English-speaking southwestern highlands area, chose to follow a separate course of development before joining the French-speaking provinces in the Republic of Cameroon in 1972. Today, Cameroon is composed of eight Francophone and two Anglophone provinces.

By the year 2000 Cameroon's population had grown to about 15.4 million and comprised about 130 different ethnic groups, with most of the population belonging to a handful of groups. At the close of the twentieth century Cameroon's population was composed primarily of Cameroon Highlanders (31 percent of the population), Equatorial Bantu (19 percent), Kirdi (11 percent), Fulani (10 percent), Northwestern Bantu (8 percent), and Eastern Negritic (7 percent). Thirteen percent of the country's population belonged to other African ethnic groups, and less than one percent of the population was non-African in ethnic origin. Twenty-four indigenous African language groups are represented among the languages spoken in Cameroon, along with French and English. In terms of religious affiliation, Cameroon's population is similarly diverse, with about 40 percent of the people in Cameroon being Christian, 20 percent being Muslim, and another 40 percent practicing indigenous African religions.

Approximately half of Cameroonians lived in urban areas in 1999. Yaoundé itself, the national capital, had about 730,000 inhabitants in the 1990s, although Douala, the economic capital of the country, was the country's largest city. The population of Cameroon was growing at a rate of 2.47 percent in the year 2000. That year, the total fertility rate was measured as 4.88, with approximately 43 percent of Cameroon's population 14-years-old or younger, 54 percent 15 to 64 years of age, and only about 3 percent 65 or older, due to the low life expectancy in Cameroon (54.82 years at birth in the year 2000—54.01 for men and 55.64 for women). In 1999 Cameroon had an infant-mortality rate of 77.2 per thousand live births and an under-five-years child-mortality rate of 154 per thousand.

Cameroon's GDP was US$8.8 billion in 1999, with a real growth rate of 5.2 percent. GNP per capita that year was only about US$580; the country had recorded more than double that amount in earlier years when the economy was performing significantly better, before the January 1994 structural adjustment measures were taken. In 1997, about 42 percent of the GDP was derived from agriculture, 22 percent from industry, and 36 percent from services. Considering that the economy grew by about 3 to 5 percent of the GDP in each of the last three years of the 1990s, the potential for an economic upturn at the start of the new millennium was good. However, widespread corruption in the business and government sectors made it next to impossible to predict how the economy would fare as Cameroon entered the twenty-first century. Corruption interfered significantly with economic growth, since fraudulent business activity and bribes served to undercut the economic gains made. Cameroon's external debt was US$11.5 billion in 1999. With rich petroleum reserves and many natural resources, Cameroon has the potential to shine economically. However, continuing controversy over the placement of an oil pipeline running through Chad and Cameroon and contested parts of Nigeria due to the displacement of indigenous minorities living in the path of the pipeline and the possible environmental degradation to be caused by the offshore drilling and onshore transmission of petroleum resources were producing significant social and political upheaval in some parts of Cameroon around the year 2000 that was likely to impede the flow of petroleum through the region and into the national treasury.

About 13 percent of Cameroon was arable in 1993 and 38 percent of the country was covered by forests and woodlands in the late 1990s. About 60 to 75 percent of the population worked in the agricultural sector by the late 1990s, though most farmers practiced subsistence agriculture using traditional farming methods and their individual yields were relatively small. Unemployment in Cameroon measured about 30 percent in 1998. Cameroon received approximately US$606.1 million in international development assistance in 1995. In 1999, about US$14 million worth of active development projects coordinated by the World Bank were being implemented in the country, with US$12 million of these project funds coming from the International Development Association.

In 2001 Cameroon and several West-African countries came into the spotlight of international attention for the extensive use of slave laborers, including thousands of children, by large plantation owners growing cash crops such as coffee and cocoa for export. This problem of child abduction and forced child labor in this region of Africa had gone on for years but did not attract any serious outcries for reform until a few youths managed to escape from their captors early in 2001 and expressed their plight to a BBC news team. Only at this point did the international news media seemingly become aware of the massive scale of the interrelated problems of child abductions, the selling of children by impoverished parents, and forced child labor in the plantations regions of West and Central Africa.

CONSTITUTIONAL & LEGAL FOUNDATIONS

Cameroon is a republic with a strong presidency largely directing Cameroonian civil and political life. The country's current Constitution was approved by referendum on May 20, 1972, and adopted June 2 of that year. The Cameroonian legal system is a civil law system based on the French system of justice, with some influence from the common law system of the British. All Cameroonians, women and men alike, are eligible to vote at age 21; young men are eligible for military service at age 18. Cameroon's chief executive is a president, elected to seven-year terms of office, with a limit of two terms (since 1995, when a constitutional amendment modified the rules for electing presidents). It was unknown, however, whether President Paul Biya would relinquish his position after completing his term in 2004. (Biya had become president in 1982 when President Ahmadou Ahidjo, Cameroon's first president, resigned after twenty-two years in office.) The executive branch of Cameroon's national government also includes a prime minister and a cabinet of ministers, all appointed by the president. Since 1996 the Prime Minister of Cameroon has been Peter Mafany Musonge. The ruling party for all the years Cameroon has been independent has been the Union Cameronaise, a party that has jealously guarded its privileged position and put obstacles up to prevent an ascent to political supremacy by any other opposition party in the country.

At the national level the Cameroonian legislative branch in theory consists of a bicameral legislature composed of a House and a Senate. However, in practice, as of early 2001 the country had yet to see a Senate directly elected by the people and functioning in its constitutionally rightful place as part of the national government.

Despite its constitutional foundations, Cameroon operates essentially as an authoritarian state dominated by one political party, under the leadership of President Biya. Although the country has a national legislature, the National Assembly, the President of the Republic consistently rules by decree or by promoting his own agenda and bills in the legislature, which at the start of the new millennium had yet to enact a bill proposed by a member of an opposition party. The judicial system in Cameroon also is effectively shaped by the president and does not operate independently of the executive branch. Cameroon does not recognize the jurisdiction of the International Court of Justice (the ''World Court'') in The Hague.

International human rights organizations and agencies such as Amnesty International and the Bureau of Democracy, Human Rights, and Labor of the U.S. Department of State reported considerable problems with the abuse of human rights in Cameroon in 2000. Some

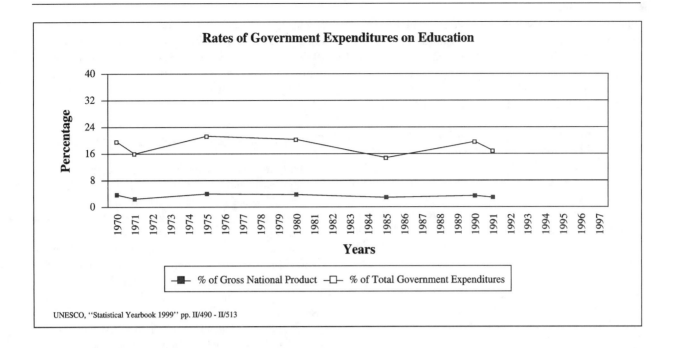

Rates of Government Expenditures on Education

UNESCO, "Statistical Yearbook 1999" pp. II/490 - II/513

of the most serious of these abuses were numerous extra-judicial killings and disappearances, and the unlawful detention and imprisonment of political opponents, members of the media, student protestors, and members of an opposition party labeled as secessionist for seeking greater independence for the formerly British parts of the country. Despite the widespread and egregious nature of the human rights abuses of which Cameroonian government officials, *gendarmes*, and "anti-gang" brigades were accused in the years since independence, Cameroon has been an active participant in many regional and international organizations and conferences. The country has received substantial social and economic development support from international agencies and intergovernmental and nongovernmental organizations aimed at supporting sustainable, democratic development in Africa and in reforming Cameroon's overly one-party system of government.

The legal basis for Cameroon's educational system rests in the Constitution of 1972 and particularly in various national laws, regulations, and executive decrees made in the 1990s and afterwards. For example, a series of decrees in 1993 paved the way for the substantial revision of the higher education system in the country. An additional presidential decree in April 2001 refined and restructured the plan for creating new institutions and improving higher education in the country. Decree No. 95/041 of March 7, 1995, set up the Ministry of National Education. A National Forum on Education held two months later, in May 1995, led to the passage of the Law of April 1998 on vocational and technical education in the country. Each year, the prime minister makes a speech in June to announce the Government's anticipated

program of actions to be taken in various sectors in the upcoming fiscal year. Through these speeches, policy goals are laid out before the members of the legislature, Government leaders, and the public, and the accomplishments of the previous year are reviewed. Much of the direction for national priorities in education can be ascertained through these speeches.

EDUCATIONAL SYSTEM—OVERVIEW

In 1999, approximately 81 percent of adult men fifteen years of age or older were estimated to be literate, as were almost 69 percent of adult women. This represented a significant improvement over conditions in 1995, when only about 63 percent of the Cameroonian population was estimated to be literate— approximately 75 percent of adult men and a little more than 52 percent women, based on UNESCO data. In 1995, Cameroon had had about 2.7 million adult illiterates, two-thirds of whom were women.

School enrollment rates for the late 1990s were not regularly recorded, making educational planning and evaluation considerably more difficult for government workers and educational specialists. The Government of the Republic of Cameroon estimated there were about two million students in primary and secondary schools in the year 2000, plus about thirty-five thousand tertiary students. Parallel English- and French-style school systems existed in the country, since national education plans for integrating students from the two main European language communities (the official languages of the country) were rather slow to be developed and implemented. Although school enrollment rates in Cameroon for basic education in the early 1980s had been among the highest in sub-Saharan Africa, attendance and graduation rates dropped markedly by the late 1990s. School enrollment rates decreased significantly as economic crises struck the country in 1985 and government funding was sharply cut for the education sector over the next few years.

School attendance for girls in Cameroon has been considerably lower, on average, than for boys, due to a variety of factors. The reasons for this gender disparity include the traditional undervaluing of formal education for girls among certain ethnic and religious groups and also sexual harassment of girls by male teachers and professors, a significant number of whom have demanded sexual favors of their female pupils and students, leading to a reluctance among many girls to attend school and an unwillingness of family members to send their daughters to school. In the 1990s significant World Bank support for education in Cameroon was directed toward increasing school participation rates for girls.

French and English are the official languages of instruction in Cameroonian public schools, although by fiscal year 2001-2002, efforts were being made to encourage the use of both French and English in the higher education institutes, to promote a sense of national unity and integration among university students, professors, and ultimately, the entire workforce trained through these institutions. The need to develop new textbooks, teaching approaches, educational programs, and course curricula relevant to Cameroon's diverse population was highlighted beginning in the 1990s in the World Bank's project reports. As of 1995, most textbooks used in Cameroon were produced outside the country. Cameroonians wrote just 28.6 percent of the 39 texts used in French-speaking primary schools. The picture was the same for English-speaking schools, where Cameroonians wrote 28.7 percent of the 51 texts listed for use in primary schools. Additionally, efforts to provide Cameroonian students, especially at the higher education level, with education on sexually transmitted diseases and HIV/AIDS increased after the turn of the millennium, with the June 2001 program report of Prime Minister Musonge to the National Assembly specifically referencing the need to reinforce medical training at the university level with assistance for information, educational, and communications activities related to these diseases, whose destructive effects were ravaging Cameroon, vastly increasing infant and child mortality rates, and diminishing the life expectancy of the general population in the country.

While training students in the use of computers, the Internet, and other high-technology learning tools, including distance learning, began to be prioritized in national educational planning by the end of the 1990s, the number of personal computers in Cameroon was quite small—only 27 computers per ten thousand persons in 1999. Significant economic resources will be needed to improve the level of computer training and the availability of high-technology-oriented courses in Cameroon's schools.

PREPRIMARY & PRIMARY EDUCATION

Participation rates declined dramatically in preprimary, primary, and secondary education programs in the second half of the 1980s and throughout the 1990s, with somewhat erratic ups and downs in school attendance from one year to the next. In his 1996 critique of schooling and democratic development (or lack of development) in Africa, Ambroise Kom wrote that *descolarisation* (de-schooling) had rapidly increased at the preprimary, primary, and secondary levels. Kom cited a September 1994 nationally televised speech of the Minister of National Education, who apparently had casually noted that due to a lack of funding about 300,000 pupils were forced to drop out of school in the 1993-94 academic year. Observing that government figures often are more optimistic than reality, Kom implied that school dropout rates that year actually might have been considerably higher. In 1997 the gross enrollment rate at the primary level was about 83 percent, although it had been 114 percent back in 1987. Because teacher-training institutes in Cameroon were closed between 1990 and 1995 and very few primary-level teachers were hired for the ten-year period of 1987-97, classes were overcrowded and some areas of the country did not receive the teachers they needed to conduct classes or run schools.

The first six grades of compulsory schooling, normally provided to 6- to 12-year-olds (though with high repetition rates, students up to age 14 are often included) are considered basic, or primary, education in Cameroon. In the two Anglophone provinces, pupils generally begin school at age five and attend preprimary and primary school for seven years. For those who completed their primary education, the *Certificat d'Etudes primaires élémentaires* or the *Concours d'Entrée en Sixieme* was awarded in French-speaking schools and the First School Leaving Certificate was awarded in English-speaking schools.

In general, primary school enrollment rates in rural areas have been considerably lower than in urban areas in Cameroon. In 1994, for example, the gross enrollment rate of 6- to 14-year-olds in a sampling of ten urban areas of Cameroon was 65.9 percent, while the corresponding rate for ten rural areas studied was only 36.9 percent. Of the 6- to 11-year-olds living in those urban areas, 109.8 percent of the age group was enrolled in school in 1994; in contrast, only 58.9 percent of 6- to 11-year-olds living in the rural areas studied was enrolled. In the 1994-95 academic year, about 79.2 percent of all children enrolled in school in Cameroon went to public schools, while 20 percent attended private institutions. Primary schools in 1995 had a gross enrollment rate averaging 88 percent—93 percent for boys and 84 percent for girls. The failure rate at the primary level in 1994 was 32.7 percent, and 4.9 percent of primary-level pupils dropped out of school in 1994. Repetition rates in 1997 averaged 29 percent at the primary level—only slightly better than three years earlier.

SECONDARY EDUCATION

In the French-speaking parts of Cameroon in 2000, students generally attended secondary schools between the ages of twelve and nineteen. Four years were spent at the lower-secondary level and three at the upper-secondary level, with the *Brevet d'Etudes du premier Cycle* awarded to students graduating after the four grades of General Secondary school in the Francophone system (*Collège d'Enseignement general* or *secondaire*) and the *Baccalauréat* awarded to successful completers of the last three years of secondary level (Lycées). In English-speaking secondary schools in the year 2000, students also usually attended education programs between the ages of twelve and nineteen, although typically the lower-secondary level entailed five years of study for 12- to 17-year-olds, culminated in the Cameroon GCE O Level, and was followed by a two-year, upper-secondary program for 17- to 19-year-olds, awarded the GCE A Level upon completion of their studies.

In both the Anglophone and the Francophone systems, technical secondary schools also exist where students can obtain an alternative education to the general, academically oriented course of studies described above. The technical programs also are normally seven years in length for students between the ages of twelve and nineteen. In the Anglophone system, Technical Secondary Schools lead to the end degree of City and Guilds Part III, which allows the graduate to go on to university or higher-level technical studies. In the French-speaking system, *Lycées techniques* (technical high schools) take the student through technical-training courses and qualify her or him for work or further study upon completion; the *Brevet de Technicien* and the *Baccalauréat* are the diplomas awarded, qualifying students to pursue careers or to study further at a higher-education institution. A government-sponsored conference held in April 1999, the National Forum on Technical and Vocational Secondary Education in Cameroon, followed up on the National Forum on Education of May 1995 by developing new thinking in how to modify technical and vocational training to better prepare students to meet the labor market's needs.

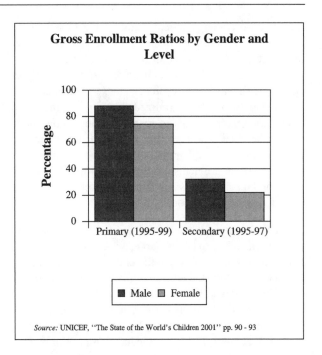

Gross Enrollment Ratios by Gender and Level

Source: UNICEF, "The State of the World's Children 2001" pp. 90 - 93

Gross enrollment ratios at the secondary level in 1994 were 32 percent for boys and 22 percent for girls, or 27 percent for secondary students as a whole. The net enrollment rate for secondary students was 22 percent. The failure rate at the secondary level in 1994 also was 22 percent. Twenty-four percent of secondary-level students in Cameroon dropped out of school that year.

HIGHER EDUCATION

In 1995 the gross enrollment rate for higher education in Cameroon was only 4 percent, with significant gender disparities: 7 percent of males and only 1 percent of females of higher-education age were enrolled in tertiary-level education and training programs. By 1998 enrollments had increased and were almost equivalent to what they had been before the higher education budget was trimmed in 1993. At the start of the new millennium Cameroon had six publicly supported universities—the Universities of Yaoundé I and Yaoundé II, plus the Universities of Buéa, Douala, Dschang, and Ngaoundéré. In addition, specialized institutions and schools of higher education offered students higher-level degrees and diplomas in various professions and occupations, with a gradually increasing emphasis on linking training opportunities to conditions in the labor market. The Catholic University Institute, established in 1990, was the main private university in the country.

World Bank analysts noted that a variety of factors led to significant flaws in many of the higher education institutes in Cameroon during the 1990s, the chief ones being that technical schools were "not providing meaningful job-oriented practical training due to a lack of teacher motivation, poor planning of the disciplines that are taught, resource constraints, and a complete separation between the colleges and the world of work'' (World Bank 1997). Furthermore, management deficiencies associated with overly centralized decision-making often made it hard for schools to respond to local conditions and to the needs and preferences of students or faculty. By the turn of the millennium attempts were being made to correct these problems; both the Government of Cameroon and outside actors appeared to be well aware of the need for significant reforms.

The demand for vocational and technical education carefully matched to labor-market needs increased appreciably during the 1990s. By the end of the decade, government ministers and educators placed greater attention on trying to develop a model that could be successfully replicated throughout the country to train youth for jobs and secure higher levels of employment for the graduates of both secondary and tertiary education programs. One model that appeared promising was an experimental university at Douala, started after the university-level reform decrees of 1993. This school, the *Institut Universitaire de Technologie de l'Université de Douala* (University Institute of Technology of the University of Douala, or *IUT Douala*), enjoyed close linkages with employers and entrepreneurs and was strikingly more successful at job-placing its graduates. Over eighty percent of *IUT Douala* graduates found jobs not long after graduating, compared with the graduates of most other university programs who rarely succeeded at finding employment directly after graduation. Based on the success of *IUT Douala,* the World Bank in June 1998 offered four years of credit totaling US$4.86 million from the International Development Association to supplement funds from the Government and self-generated monies derived from the institute itself to further support and test the development of *IUT Doula* so the successful elements of the model could be replicated throughout the country.

In their 1998 project-appraisal report reviewing the conditions in Cameroon that inspired this Higher Education Technical Training Project, World Bank analysts noted key problems in Cameroon's higher-education system which a public-private model of training might be able to address. According to the analysts:

> The higher education system in Cameroon has its roots in the traditional francophone African model, with almost all students in full degree courses, few links to the labor market, no involvement of the private sector in program selection and curriculum content, and virtually all financing (apart from small student fees introduced in 1993) provided and controlled by the *Ministère de l'enseignement Supérieur* (MINESUP) and the Ministry of Economy and Finance (MINEFI). This model, initial-

ly designed to produce personnel for the civil service, no longer conforms to the economy's needs in the era of shrinking public services, nor to international best practices. (World Bank HDN II)

Moreover, the analysts noted that the high number of Cameroonian students already enrolled in higher-education programs in 1998 precluded the Government's being able to find sufficient funds on its own to support more traditional university training. The Bank analysts spotted curious contradictions in the financial costs of traditional higher education in Cameroon, with potentially deadly, unanticipated, negative consequences:

> Few graduates from the ordinary universities find employment within a year of their graduation and the overall unemployment rate of university graduates is around 30 percent (unemployment rates rise with qualifications—only 6.5 percent of unschooled young people are unemployed, compared with 30 percent of university graduates). Such figures put in question the validity of the 24 years of schooling bestowed upon graduates. Furthermore, the defeated expectations of many of the youth introduce a dangerous element of instability into society. (Ibid.)

The Government of Cameroon and the Bank thus attempted to collaborate to introduce new forms of higher education where students could enter the job market directly after graduation with valuable, marketable skills attuned to the needs of the labor market and Cameroonian society. The differences between regular higher education programs in the late 1990s and the type of training programs the Bank intended to support were that institutes following the *IUT Doula* model would provide diploma-level courses instead of degree-oriented academic training, the institutes would limit course and program enrollments to the number of students the institutes could effectively teach, they would use private-sector internships to give students in training specific job skills directly transferable to paid employment after graduation, and the institutes themselves would generate income through courses offered on a part-time and ''à la carte'' basis where students could more easily pay for their own training. By April 2001 the National Assembly had passed a new law concerning higher education which reflected some of the same principles and understandings as the Higher Education Technological Training Project, including the key principle that private enterprise and public organs should be encouraged to work together to provide coordinated training opportunities for students beyond the secondary level of education.

ADMINISTRATION, FINANCE, & EDUCATIONAL RESEARCH

The Ministry of National Education has primary responsibility for overseeing the implementation of educational laws, decrees, and policy in Cameroon's primary and secondary schools and for developing administrative regulations pertaining to basic education. The Ministry of Higher Education is responsible for developing and monitoring training and educational program offerings past the secondary level. Besides the government actors and entities charged with planning, implementing, and evaluating educational policy in Cameroon, local, national, and international nongovernmental organizations and private schools increasingly have provided education to students in Cameroon. In particular, small technical-training institutes seemed to prosper and become more and more popular as public demand grew for training directly relevant to the job market. The government increasingly attempted to regulate private schools in the country in the 1990s so that private educational offerings would better coordinate with Cameroon's public education system, with financial audits ideally encouraging better performance as the number of private initiatives increased.

NONFORMAL EDUCATION

Cameroon lacked a well-developed system of adult education in the late 1990s. Nonetheless, at that time recommendations were being made to develop new educational opportunities for adults seeking to upgrade their skills, learn a new trade, or change jobs. Because computer training was seen as absolutely necessary to increase the marketability of graduates of training and education programs by the late 1990s, the government sought new ways to encourage the inclusion of distance learning and high technology in education initiatives. The opening address at the government conference on vocational and technical education in Cameroon held in April 1999 specifically referenced the need to better train students in the use of technology, to prepare them for the types of jobs that would increasingly support the growth of the Cameroonian economy. As Prime Minister Musonge observed, ''The prerequisite for the development of a country, the source of employment and prosperity, depends on the mastery of science and technology by its inhabitants, especially the youth.'' However, access to the Internet and to computers continued to be extremely limited in Cameroon at the start of the new millennium. Distance education arguably still was more readily accomplished through the media of television and radio in the late 1990s, as in 1997 there were 450 thousand televisions and 2.27 million radios in Cameroon. In 1998 only one government-sponsored television broadcasting station was operating while eleven AM radio stations, eight FM radio stations, and three short-wave radio stations transmitted broadcasts around the country. A law passed in 1990 which allowed for the privatization of radio was finally formally enacted in April 2000, leading to the multiplication of private and regional radio stations in the country.

SUMMARY

The people of the Republic of Cameroon have experienced a very erratic course of educational development in the last two decades of the twentieth century. Whereas school enrollments had reached admirable levels in comparison to many other sub-Saharan African countries by the early 1980s, economic crises in Cameroon in the middle of that decade spoiled the country's promising educational performance and led to severe disruptions in the provision of education and the training of teachers. Deliberate government efforts were made during the 1990s to turn the educational situation around and to correct many of the problems endemic in Cameroon's basic education and higher education systems. In tandem with educational specialists, administrators, nongovernmental organizations, and international donors, the Government of Cameroon held several conferences and promoted new legislation and decrees to correct systemic problems, with a certain measure of success by the turn of the new millennium. Plans were drawn to better coordinate public and private educational offerings and to gather support from the private sector to improve secondary and tertiary education so as to make education more responsive to labor-market needs. Continuing improvements in the educational system seemed to depend most heavily on the decentralization of government authority and the devolution of power in the educational sector, as well as the coupling of private industry with public education to better prepare secondary and tertiary students for employment. By once again making access to primary schooling free of charge in the 2000-2001 fiscal year, the Government of the Republic of Cameroon signified its intentions to support basic education and to help all Cameroonian children enter a future where their social and economic well being could be better assured.

BIBLIOGRAPHY

Amin, Martin E. *Trends in the Demand for Primary Education in Cameroon.* Lanham, MD: University Press of America, Inc. 1999.

British Council. ''Cameroon.'' 2000. Available from http://www.britishcouncil.org/.

Bureau of Democracy, Human Rights, and Labor. Country Reports on Human Rights Practices—2000. Washington, DC: U.S. Department of State, February 2001. Available from http://www.state.gov/.

International Association of Universities/UNESCO International Centre on Higher Education. *World Higher Education Database 2000.* Available from http://www.unesco.org/.

Kom, Ambroise. *Éducation et démocratie en Afrique: Le temps des illusions (Education and Democracy in Africa: Time of Illusions).* Yaoundé: CRAC and Paris: Éditions L'Harmattan, 1996.

Ministry of Higher Education, Government of the Republic of Cameroon. "Loi No. 005 du 16 Avril 2001 Portant Orientation de l'Enseignement Superieur" ("Law No. 005 of 16 April 2001 Regarding Direction of Higher Education"), 16 April 2001. Available from http://www.minesup.gov.cm/.

———. "Page du Ministre" ("Minister's Page"); "Le Ministère" ("The Ministry"), February 2001. Available from http://www.minesup.gov.cm/.

Musonge, Peter Mafany. Official Web Site of PM's Office (including news, speeches, and information about the Office of the Prime Minister of the Republic of Cameroon). Available from http://www.spm.gov.cm/.

———. "Opening of the National Forum on Technical and Vocational Secondary Education in Cameroon from 7 to 9 April 1999." Available at http://www.spm.gov.cm/.

———. "Programme économique, financier, social et culturel du Gouvernement pour l'exercice 2001-2002, Présenté à l'Assemblée Nationale par le Premier Ministre, Chef du Gouvernement" (Government's Economic, Financial, Social and Cultural Program for fiscal 2001-2002, Presented at the National Assembly by the Prime Minister, Head of the Government"). 15 June 2001. Available from http://www.spm.gov.cm/.

——— "Government's Economic, Financial, Social and Cultural Programme for fiscal 2000-2001, Presented at the National Assembly by the Prime Minister, Head of the Government." 14 June 2000. Available from http://www.spm.gov.cm/.

———. "Government's Economic, Financial, Social and Cultural Programme for fiscal 1999-2000, Presented at the National Assembly by the Prime Minister, Head of the Government." 1999. Available from http://www.spm.gov.cm/.

Sikounno, Hilaire. *Jeunesse et Éducation en Afrique Noire ("Youth and Education in Black Africa")*. Preface by Pierre Erny. Paris: É;ditions L'Harmattan, 1995.

Task Force on Higher Education and Society, The. *Higher Education in Developing Countries: Peril and Promise.* Washington, DC: The International Bank for Reconstruction and Development/The World Bank, 2000.

U.S. Department of State. "Cameroon—Consular Information Sheet." 6 June 2001. Available from http://www.travel.state.gov.

World Bank. "Cameroon—Basic Education Improvement Project." Report No. PID5206. 1 August 1997. Available from http://www-wds.worldbank.org/.

———. "Cameroon—Higher Education Technical Training Project" (Abstract and Profile). 4 June 1998. Available from http://www-wds.worldbank.org/.

World Bank Group. "Cameroon." 1999. Available from http://wbln0018.worldbank.org/.

———. "Cameroon at a Glance." August 2000. Available from http://wbln0018.worldbank.org/.

———. "Cameroon Data Profile." Source: World Development Indicators database, July 2000. Available from http://devdata.worldbank.org/.

———. "Country Brief: Cameroon." 1999 Available from http://wbln0018.worldbank.org/.

World Bank, Human Development Network. *Education Sector Strategy.* Washington, DC: The International Bank for Reconstruction and Development/The World Bank, 1999.

World Bank, Human Development Network II, Africa Region. "Project Appraisal Document on a Proposed Credit in an Amount of US$ 4.8 Million Equivalent to the Republic of Cameroon for a Higher Education Technical Training Project." Report No. 17375-CM. 4 June 1998. Available from http://www-wds.worldbank.org/.

—*Barbara Lakeberg Dridi*

CANADA

BASIC DATA

Official Country Name:	Canada
Region:	North & Central America
Population:	31,281,092
Language(s):	English, French
Literacy Rate:	97%
Academic Year:	September-June
Number of Primary Schools:	12,685
Compulsory Schooling:	10 years
Public Expenditure on Education:	6.9%
Libraries:	3,672
Educational Enrollment:	Primary: 2,448,144 Secondary: 2,505,389 Higher: 1,763,05
Educational Enrollment Rate:	Primary: 102% Secondary: 105% Higher: 87%

Teachers: Primary: 148,565
                             Secondary: 133,275

Student-Teacher Ratio: Primary: 16:1
                             Secondary: 19:1

Female Enrollment Rate: Primary: 101%
                             Secondary: 105%
                             Higher: 95%

HISTORY & BACKGROUND

Canada, the world's second largest country, stretches 4,000 kilometers from north to south and 3,500 miles from east to west. The nation is divided into smaller governing units known as provinces and territories. Located east of the U.S. state of Alaska and north of the northernmost boundaries of the lower 48 U.S. states, Canada has 10 provinces and 2 national territories. One of those latter units, the Northwest Territory, is itself politically broken into two separate territories. The provinces are divided into the Atlantic Provinces (Newfoundland and Labrador, New Brunswick, Prince Edward Island, and Nova Scotia); Quebec, Ontario, British Columbia, and the Prairie Provinces (Alberta, Manitoba, and Saskatchewan); and the territories of Yukon, Nunavut and the Northwest Territory. Nunavut (meaning "Our Land" in the Inuit language) became a separate territory from the Northwest Territory in 1999.

Canada's capital city is Ottawa, and each state and territory has a capital. Canada's legislative branch is an elected House of Commons and an appointed Senate. A prime minister serves as the government's leader. Since the Constitutional Act of 1982, Canada's constitution has been under the Canadian Parliament's own management. Previously, from 1867 to 1982, the dominion of Canada's constitution was subject to the control of Great Britain's Parliament (acting upon the request of Canada's bicameral Parliament). The roots of the Canadian educational system are found in the two countries most energetically involved in its colonial settlement and early exploitation: France and Great Britain. Though these influences were great, educators have long looked to the geography and climate of Canada as additional influences on educational development.

Since so many early schools were small—often a cabin or tiny schoolhouse—and isolated, some of the more elitist vestiges of French and British schools vanished. In their place, a school system evolved that was more attuned to life in a frontier society that trumpeted the ideals of equal educational opportunities for all. In that regard, early schoolhouses then housed both the children of poor trappers and rich merchants alike, and some

characteristics of that early social democracy still clung to Canadian schools even when the population shifted to urban centers and schools consolidated and grew large (Johnson 1968). Also, Canada's proximity to the United States, particularly since the majority of the population lives so close to the U.S. northern border, has been a factor in the evolution of the nation's educational system—a system that may indeed see additional changes because of an influx of immigrants to Canada's vast land mass.

While Canada has borrowed from the United States, it is in no way a mere U.S. clone since individual sections of the nation show strong adherence to British or French traditions. Canada's native Indian peoples have developed an educational tradition drawing from American, British, and/or French education, but also with their own cultural distinctions differing from these three. However, due to immigration, the uniting features of the Internet, and modern media outlets, even sprawling Canada has acquired in many areas the so-called "melting pot" characteristics that occurred in the United States when diverse populations underwent a process of integration.

According to 2000 figures, Canada's ethnic groups are broken down into British (28 percent); French (23 percent); miscellaneous European (15 percent); Asian, Arab, or African (six percent); aboriginal Indian and Eskimo (two percent); and mixed background (26 percent). The population of people of British and French origin in Canada has dropped since 1985 when 40 percent of the total population was British and 27 percent were French.

As early as A.D. 1000, explorers from Norway landed on the shores of what would become the eastern seaboard of Canada. Unheralded Basque and Norman sailors may have arrived in the fifteenth century. Great Britain's exploration of Canada began in 1497 when John Cabot, a Venetian representing and financed by British merchants, visited the eastern coast of (the land that would become) Canada in search of riches or a shorter route to the Indies. Cabot mistakenly thought he had located an unsettled section of Asia. His explorer son, Sebastian, also mistakenly boasted that he had located the Northwest Passage through the Americas. It is likely that he sailed instead to massive Hudson Bay. Because the Cabots found neither a passage to India nor the gold the Spaniards had looted from the Incas in the southern hemisphere, English backers in time lost whatever excitement they possessed for the exploration of the New World's far north. England's former interest, however, was taken over by France until the Hudson's Bay Company generated wealth from fur trading after 1670, and the English vied for this colonial land prize. Although disappointed no waterway linked the great Atlantic and Pacific oceans, French excitement was stirred by the founding of a settlement in 1605. In 1524, France had sent the Italian explorer Giovanni da Verrazano on a mission, and his ship traveled as far to the north as Newfoundland and as far south as North Carolina. The King of France claimed the land he explored in Canada.

The adventurer and explorer Jacques Cartier in 1524 went inland and explored the St. Lawrence River. Cartier and his men brought back furs and stories about the native aborigines they met in *Kanata,* a native term for "village." (Other theories as to how Canada got its name abound, but none are definitive.) The furs brought back to Europe raised hopes that other treasures might be found. The Indian tribes also inspired droves of black-robed missionaries to voyage to the New World in quest of religious conversions. Cartier's explorations brought him to sites that later would become the province of Quebec and the city of Montreal, which sprung up from an island village on the St. Lawrence River.

Since England and France saw Canada as a nation of conquest, hostilities in the late seventeenth and much of the eighteenth century erupted into numerous battles and all-out war. Hostilities ceased in 1632 when England and France signed a treaty that returned Acadia and Quebec to the French, but peace was short-lived. Throughout the seventeenth and eighteenth centuries, an intermittent series of battles occurred between the two great empires, England and France, for control of the northern empire. These frontier squabbles, massacres, and political wrangling culminated in the French and Indian War between 1754 and 1763. Some intellectuals in France questioned Canada's importance; the philosopher Voltaire, for example, dismissed the importance of "acres of snow."

Each nation put its generals to the test as France and Great Britain struggled for supremacy in Canada. In 1759, Quebec was wrested away from French control. Great Britain was ultimately the victor of the French and Indian War. The Treaty of Paris in 1763, among other things, ended France's claim to Canada and established Britain's supremacy. Jesuit lands and the schools on them were taken over by the British. Nonetheless, from the eighteenth through the twenty-first century, nationalistic fervor in Quebec has remained high as that province continued to embrace the customs and language of France.

In 1774, Britain passed the Quebec Act of 1774, which established Britain's Parliament as law in Canada, a political display of power much despised by the American colonies and cited as one of the causes of the American Revolution. Canada became a place of refuge for American colonists who remained loyal to King George, and these Loyalists continued to settle many years after the Revolution because they found themselves despised in America.

In an attempt to keep the peace in Canada after the successful American Revolution that drove Loyalists in great numbers to settle in Canada, the British created, out of Quebec, British-speaking Ontario (formerly Upper Canada) and French-speaking Quebec (formerly Lower Canada) in 1791. The two areas were reunited in 1841 as Canada Province, but in 1867 the British divided the newly named Dominion of Canada into the provinces of New Brunswick, Quebec, Ontario, and Nova Scotia. In 1869, following their purchase from the Hudson's Bay Company, the Northwest Territories were established (with Yukon splintering off as a territory in 1898). In time, separate provinces were founded as Manitoba (1870), British Columbia (1871), Price Edward Island (1873), Alberta (1905), Saskatchewan (1905), and Newfoundland (1949). Nunavut became a separate territory from the Northwest Territory in 1999, and some 85 percent of the population was located in a single city, Iqaluit.

Latter-day Canada is a land of geographic contrasts. It has great hot and frigid temperature extremes and an uneven distribution of natural resources and lands suitable for settlement or farming. A great disparity exists in wealth generated by some sections of the country as opposed to others, allowing the wealthier sections such as Ontario to provide educational services, up-to-date technology, and higher teacher salaries more readily. In July of 2000, Canada's population was 30,750,087. With fewer people in all Canada than residing in the single U.S. state of California, the nation ranks as one of the world's more sparsely settled countries. Its unemployment rate was 7 percent in April 2001.

Unlike the United States, Canada conducts a census twice a decade, sending questionnaires to citizens in years ending in a "1" or "6." Thus, unless otherwise specified, data contained here refers to information obtained in the 1996 census. The 1996 census provided a comprehensive look at the aggregate educational attainments of Canada's citizenry by highest degree. Of 22,628,925 citizens 15 years of age or older, 8,331,615 had neither degree nor diploma, 5,217,20 had a secondary school diploma, 525,560 had a community college degree or other certificate below bachelor level, 1,979,460 had a bachelor degree, 501,505 had a master's degree, and 103,855 had an earned doctorate in 1996. These numbers represented a significant gain in one decade. In 1986, of the 19,634,100 people 15 and older, 9,384,100 had neither degree nor diploma, 3,985,820 had a secondary school diploma, 381,580 had a community college degree or other certificate below bachelor level, 1,254,250 had a bachelor degree, 293,335 had a master's degree, and 66,955 had an earned doctorate degree.

CONSTITUTIONAL & LEGAL FOUNDATIONS

The British North America Act of 1867 was a statute providing for the unification of the country a few years

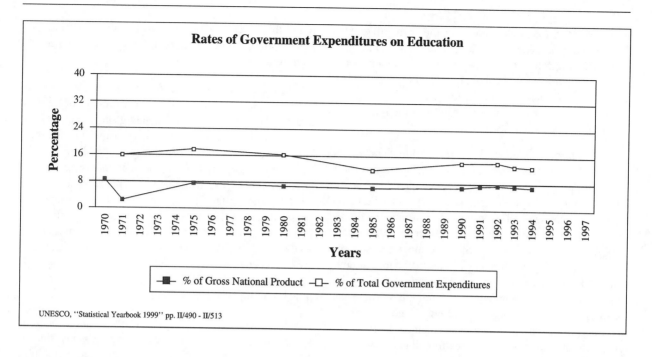

Rates of Government Expenditures on Education

Percentage / Years

Legend: —■— % of Gross National Product   —□— % of Total Government Expenditures

UNESCO, "Statistical Yearbook 1999" pp. II/490 - II/513

after the disastrous Civil War in America provided a valuable lesson in the dangers of secession, as French-speaking Quebec has often threatened to do from the rest of Canada. In addition, some of Canada's desire to unite its disparate provinces no doubt was incited by periodic U.S. political discussions about the possibility of annexing Canada; to be sure, a minority of Canadian leaders, mainly in Montreal, also touted what they claimed would be the economic benefits of annexation. In the end, Canadians, proud of their country and seeing the effect civil war had on the United States, expressed desire for a strong federal government. In 1866, at talks at an important conference in England, a confederation then called "The Dominion of Canada" was begun. The British North American Act became law on 1 July 1867. That date became Canada's Independence Day.

Of utmost importance, the constitution and bylaws offered citizens the assurance that the governing body of each province would be empowered to make laws related to education. This was particularly important in Canada where the primary language in a province or territory might be French, English, or even Inuit.

The Constitutional Act of 1982 reaffirmed many of the resolutions present in the 1867 BNA Act. Citizens in a province whose first language is French or English have the right to have their children given a primary and secondary school education in that same language. If enough children of a minority language are in the system, they have the right to an education taught in that language that is financed by public funds.

Rather than a federal educational system, the schooling of Canada's citizens is a responsibility assumed by provinces and territories. Such a system was the most practical way to permit the diverse cultures to address concerns and values different from those of other provinces. Each province has its own department of education under the administration of an elected minister. Each province mandates a curriculum and funnels grants to institutions under its jurisdiction.

EDUCATIONAL SYSTEM—OVERVIEW

Canadians historically have believed that formal education should turn out not scholars so much as educated citizens capable of achieving and sustaining useful, self-sufficient lives (Johnson 1968). The educated citizen is therefore ideally equipped to use his knowledge to benefit his community and nation.

The ideal of a unified school system is one that evolved over time, since originally the French and British cultures generally founded schools unlike each other's.

In what would become the province of Quebec, the growth of towns was very slow in the seventeenth and early eighteenth centuries. The missionaries who served the children of the merchants, traders, and farmers first began their work in 1616. In the next 15 years, Jesuit missionaries also turned their talents to the education of native Indian children. The Jesuit order also founded a small college in colonial Quebec, creating a campus on lands designated for that purpose by the French crown.

Perhaps the low-water mark in the education of Canada's citizenry occurred in the areas once known as New France after the French defeat by Britain in 1763. The driving out of the French governors ended years of financial support for church schools in the form of grants. Worse, many of the teaching clergy and French missionaries elected to return to Europe or take assignments outside Canada following the defeat. In Quebec, accounts of the day by travelers report an astounding number of Canadians unable to read or write well into the nineteenth century.

The alarming number of illiterate children and adults in Canada during the nineteenth century spurred reform attempts among educators that recommended the creation of nondenominational elementary and secondary schools open to the young of all religious sects. Around the fourth decade of the nineteenth century, many provinces arranged the construction of public, tax-supported schools to be overseen by government-connected boards or education departments. Decade after decade, province by province, these nondenominational schools became the primary institutions designated for public moneys. Some remnants of the past continue to be changed. In 1998, for example, the Government of Newfoundland and Labrador revamped some existing Pentecostal schools into a school system regulated by nondenominational guidelines.

Canada's prime minister and ruling government are involved tangentially in the running of schools. The government budgets grant moneys for postsecondary education, vocational training for the adult populace, and second language training to meet the goals of a nation committed to bilingualism. Government moneys assist with student loans, as well as meeting the needs of Indians pursuing an education, the education of those serving in the armed forces, and schooling and vocational training for those undergoing rehabilitation in federal prisons.

In May of 2001, in spite of strong objections from officials in the Ontario Department of Education, the provincial government recommended a measure that would give financial relief to parents of private school children in the form of a hefty tax credit (similar to vouchers in the United States) with a cap of $3,500. By June of 2001, public meetings between government officials and parents of public and private school children had deteriorated into name-calling sessions, making the educational issue one of the most controversial in Ontario's history of education.

The country of Canada also traditionally has differed province to province in the administration of rural schools, many single-room schoolhouses harboring several grade levels. A 1998 oral history report by education faculty member Barbara Mulcahy of Memorial University of Newfoundland reported that two-thirds of all Newfoundland and Labrador schools were classified as single-room schoolhouses. She cites the Report of the Royal Commission on Education and Youth in 1967 that found this percentage reduced to less than one-third. By 1998, there were but three such schools in existence, according to Mulcahy's research.

In the late 1940s and early 1950s, educators recognized a wide disparity in the greater amount of moneys that the United States was spending on its educational system as compared to what Canada spent. This was remedied in the late 1960s when Canada expenditures by the government surpassed even the amounts spent by the governments of the United States and Sweden. As occurred in the United States, Canadian provinces began to consolidate smaller schools into larger school districts. However, as Canada faced hard economic times in the 1970s through 1990s, many school districts struggled to meet expectations of the highest educational standards while facing budget cuts and the need for costly educational equipment such as computers.

Nonetheless, according to a 1999 United Nations survey, in spite of Canada's struggling economy, the nation devoted 7 percent of its gross national product (GNP) to education, which was second only to Norway with 7.5 percent of its GNP devoted to education. The United States trailed Canada at 5.4 percent of its GNP devoted to education. In the late 1990s, wide public attention was directed toward Canada's Fraser Institute as it collected data on Alberta and British Columbia kindergarten through twelfth grade private, public, and separate school systems, providing statistics that showed where schools are exceeding expectations and where they are failing. In 2000, Quebec schools were also given report cards, followed by Ontario in 2001. By 2001, the system also offered comparisons over a five year period to indicate where schools have made improvements or where conditions have deteriorated. Provincial ministries of education provided information. The report cards have received wide praise from the public and some condemnation from educators and government leaders, particularly in Ontario, that claim some data analyzed was flawed, leading to lower rankings by some schools. In general, however, school critics have insisted that test scores by Canadian students ought to be higher, a complaint frequently heard in other industrialized nations such as the United States.

Enrollment: Enrollment in elementary and secondary schools combined rose from 5,141,003 in 1990 to 1991 to 5,386,301 in 1997 to 1998. During the 1990s, the year of greatest enrollment was 1995 to 1996 when 5,430,836 children enrolled in elementary and secondary schools across Canada. By 1998-1999, the number had dropped to 5,369,716.

Of the 22,628,925 persons that are 15 years of age or older living in Canada, 2,801,280 attended school at one level or another full time, according to the 1996 census. Another 1,167,820 attended part time. This represented only a slight change from 1991 census figures. Of the 21,304,740 persons at least age 15 living in Canada, 2,537,715 attended school full time and 1,243,450 part time.

Technology in the Schools: Canadian politicians have long said that the Internet seemed made for Canada as an important way to link its outer provinces and territories. In 2001, a spokesperson for the Canadian government claimed that Canada boasted the highest percentage of population using the Internet in the world. Quickly putting emphasis on wiring the schools, Canada as a nation succeeded in linking every school and library to the Internet in the 1990s. Even in remote provinces, Canada's schools have vowed to have one computer for every five students by 2005. It has more computers in households than any other country. Canada's universities, though few in number, are the envy of most industrialized countries in quality of computer technology programs.

Compulsory Education: Canada's primary and secondary public school system is co-educational and paid for by the Canadian government. Canada is one of the many nations signing a United Nations resolution guaranteeing children the right to an education. Compulsory education laws, by province or territory, generally decree that children attend school from 6 or 7 years old until they are 15 or 16 years old.

About one-half of all Canadians have a high school graduation certificate. Individual provinces can also require certain classes to be taught. In Ontario, compulsory classes include Grade 7: History and Geography; Grade 8: Geography; and Grade 10: Canadian History in the Twentieth Century. In all provinces, physical education is mandatory from kindergarten through twelfth grade. Following lobbying attempts by Canadian war veterans who expressed shock at student ignorance about their country's participation in World War Two, the province of Nova Scotia made Canadian history mandatory in grade 11.

In 1871, Canada's first compulsory attendance statute was passed in Ontario. By 1890, nearly all provinces and territories followed Ontario's lead as many legislators were upset by an alarming increase in child labor in factories.

Because so much of Canada consists of remote outposts and homesteads, particularly in the nineteenth century, territories and provinces have recognized the right of parents to home school their children as an alternative to school-based classes. Generally, the parent applies to a provincial Department of Education officer to seek permission to home school and for an exemption from compulsory schooling in a classroom.

Minority Education: After the United States passed the Fugitive Slave Law of 1850, which allowed or even required police officers and citizen trackers to return escaped slaves to their "owners" after capture, many slaves and their children crossed the northern border to begin anew in Canada. Religious organizations, most prominently the Colonial Church and School Society, welcomed children—black or white—into its schools.

Canada took a little longer to provide for the educational needs of Indians and mixed culture peoples known as métis who were at loose ends in the nineteenth century with the reduction in buffalo herds and fur-bearing animals. Acting on the recommendation of Catholic religious leaders in the territories, the government began to establish residential schools in the 1880s.

In the twentieth century, Indian schools in the Northwest Territories came under the management of the Federal Department of Indian Affairs and Northern Development's Education Division under a superintendent. The Canadian government maintained these schools, open to other races under different budgetary line items.

As of 2001, the Department of Indian Affairs and Northern Development (DIAND) funnels educational grant moneys to First Nation education authorities. Moneys pay for the expenses needed to operate First Nation reserve schools run either by the federal government or First Nation tribal authorities. The government also pays for the tuition and many incidental costs of on-reserve students that choose to attend provincial schools.

In 1997, founding members of the First Nations Adult and Higher Education Consortium (FNAHEC) created a charter. Numerous Indian schools of higher learning were represented, among them Blue Quills First Nations College, Maskwachees Cultural College, Nakoda Nation Post-Secondary Education Center, Red Crow Community College, and Old Sun Community College. According to a FNAHEC position paper on the Internet, FNAHEC exists "to provide quality adult and higher education, controlled entirely by people of the First Nations'" tribes. FNAHEC was modeled after the American Indian Higher Education Consortium (AIHEC), but it contains its own distinguishing characteristics.

As the mission statement of the University of Saskatchewan Native Studies Department states, today's academic research involving aboriginal peoples strives to end a long-standing parasitical exploitation system between non-Indian researchers and their subjects. Instead of past "intellectual colonialism, today's researchers attempt to carry out studies and uncover data in a way that is both intellectually and ethically sound."

To meet the demand for more professionals in under-represented professions such as law, University of Victoria offered a cooperative law school program in 2001 that would allow up to 20 Inuit students to enter Akitsiraq Law School in Iqualuit to earn their professional degrees in law. The program was offered on a one-time basis and would not be repeated.

In 2000, after Canadian legislators received test scores demonstrating that minority student scores trailed drastically behind those of non-minority students, parents and legislators nationwide demanded reforms and an infusion of public moneys into the lower grades of the poorest performing schools to raise scores. However, the wide debate showed that the Canadian public differed widely as to what should be done to help raise minority test scores.

By 2001, the new government was debating plans for a new school in Iqaluit that would have classes taught only in Inuit. There also was adopted a cooperative program with the law school at the University of Victoria that would allow up to 20 Inuit students to enter Akitsiraq Law School in Iqaluit and earn their professional degrees in law.

PREPRIMARY & PRIMARY EDUCATION

Unlike some other countries such as France, which has a high preschool enrollment by age three, Canadian children generally wait until age four to enter preschool. According to 1992 figures, 46 percent of all 4 year olds and 69 percent of all 5 year olds attended public or primary schools of education. Canada's children average 1.2 years in preschool as of 1992, far below France (3.4 years) and the United States (1.8 years).

According to 1995-1996 figures, enrollment in Canadian preprimary schools had risen to 509,589 students. Of that total, 248,071 students were gender classified as female. While many 5 year olds in the United States enroll in kindergarten, Canada enrolls 30 percent of its 5 year olds in primary schools of education, according to 1992 statistics.

The first primary schools were French and related to the Catholic Church. Each parish priest was responsible for starting and maintaining a school where reading, writing, and arithmetic were taught. These most often were broken into separate schools for boys and girls by 1750. The most widely known school for French and Indian girls before 1750 was run by the Ursuline Order of nuns; it was opened in Quebec on a spacious campus in 1642. The Congregation of Notre Dame founded other schools in Montreal and other communities. Some convent schools founded by the latter order still exist. British forces destroyed one convent school in 1758, however.

Marguerite Bourgeoys, one of Canada's earliest and best known pioneering female personages in education, began the Congregation of Notre Dame. The Congregation of Notre Dame de Montreal was one of the first boarding schools in North America for girls. The reputation of the school and its foundress Bourgeoys led citizens in the American colonies to request similar missions. Additional missions were built in diverse Canadian locations such as Cape Breton Island and Trois Rivières, Quebec. The Congregation of Notre Dame de Montreal was literally built in a forest cleared by local supporters and farmers. In the territories, the Hudson's Bay Company encouraged the education of the Indians and the sons and daughters of settlers.

The seventeenth century also saw the establishment of Anglican and other Protestant schools in Canada, particularly where English was the primary tongue. However, other Protestant sects rebuffed Anglican leaders in their attempts to establish their church elementary and grammar schools to the extent that such schools found recognized acceptance in other British possessions such as Northern Ireland. Catholic church leaders in 1789-1790 also successfully objected to a proposal in lower Canada that would begin a system of free parish schools, but contained a proposal for the building of a college in which theology was noticeably absent from the curriculum. After the departure of France, the Royal Institution for the Advancement of Learning was instrumental in setting up nondenominational schools, not an easy or controversy-free task in many parts of Canada where French-Catholic settlers were in the majority.

One of the more progressive educational decisions was the 1790 publication of the Means for Promoting Education, which was the work of a special legislative council committee headed by Chief Justice William Smith. The committee recommended the establishment of free elementary schools in all parishes and villages, as well as schools for older, more advanced students roughly equivalent to secondary schools.

Primary education was conducted on a haphazard basis throughout Canada around 1800. That is, while all or nearly all cities and most towns of any size possessed such schools, their quality varied greatly, and neither provincial nor territory governments established standards. Under such conditions, the way was open for charlatans posing as itinerant scholars to set up shop in smaller schools and one-room schoolhouses; the situation was quite like the situation with frauds posing as dentists or preachers in North America in the nineteenth century. Finally, according to historian Edgar McInnis, legislatures in Upper Canada and Nova Scotia established schools in 1807 and 1811 respectively, but public funding of the schools lagged by a few years. The most important single piece of legislation for elementary schools in the nineteenth century was the Common School Act of 1816.

Not until the nineteenth century and in many provinces not until near mid-century did educational reformers obtain political support for nonsectarian primary, grammar, and secondary schools. Sociologists Wilfrid B.W. Martin and Allan J. Macdonell note that, until the nineteenth century, education was a right of the privileged and wealthy that was too often denied the common citizen. Local school boards under the watchful eyes of government education departments administered these early schools, depending upon the locale. Such schools grew rapidly in number and acceptance. In the late nineteenth and early twentieth centuries, nondenominational schools supported by public moneys were the norm in many parts of Canada such as Ontario. Nonetheless, Catholic, Anglican, and miscellaneous Protestant denominations fought for the recognition of tax-supported church-related schools, particularly in fiercely Catholic areas of Quebec. The influence of the church schools cannot be overestimated in contributing to high literacy rates in many Catholic and Christian strongholds in Canada prior to the departure of France.

By 1850, the Canadian West was a stirred pot with reformers clamoring to reduce the influence of churches on schools and political issues. The need for more diverse schools became clear between 1897 and 1912 when great numbers of immigrants from the United States and parts of Europe, neither British nor French, streamed into the country at the invitation of Canada, which then favored a policy of so-called "national expansion" (McInnis 1969). While standardized school systems and a common curriculum had elevated educational standards in Ontario and other settled provinces, the Northwest and Western provinces battled over such issues as restrictions on Catholic schools and parochial school instruction, administrative structure of schools, and unifying scattered schools into comprehensive school systems. In short, these squabbles focused on ways to serve the majority of citizens while taking into the account the needs of a minority of citizens, some of whom had established roots long before the newcomers built homes.

In modern Canada, elementary schools are overseen by locally elected school boards, which are sometimes known as school commissions. These boards are responsible for fiscal matters, the employment of teaching professionals, and the carrying out of the curriculums provided by the province's department of education.

In terms of enrollment, according to 1990-1991 government figures, 2,375,704 students were enrolled in Canada's primary grades. Of that total, 1,147,503 students were female. The student to teacher ratio was 15 to 1. During the 1995 to 1996 school year, according to government records, the total enrollment in primary grades rose slightly to 2,448,144. Of that total, 1,185,025 were female. The student to teacher ratio had changed slightly to a 16 to 1 ratio.

An attempt to begin elitist schools reminiscent of British schools in Eton and other grammar schools was doomed to failure in egalitarian Canada. A public corporation that administered many common schools in the nineteenth century, the aforementioned Royal Institution for the Advancement of Learning, in 1816 founded two such classical schools supervised by headmasters. These Royal Grammar Schools struggled for three decades, closing in 1846, according to educational scholar John Calam.

The early grammar schools were important for two reasons. They were created by legislation, the District Public Schools Act of 1807, and they showed the government's willingness to support the costs of education and even the salary of a schoolmaster. Second, the law involved the state in education, an important first step in the creation of nondenominational schools. These schools were much like today's private schools in that tuition and fees were required. The schools themselves proved highly unpopular. Canadians thought them too elite and too close to the class-conscious schools of England such as Eton.

SECONDARY EDUCATION

The Jesuits founded the first secondary institution in Canada. Its curriculum was closely based on Jesuit colleges in Europe.

High schools in Canada actually were modifications of grammar schools. They were late taking hold in Canada, not finding supportive voices among educators until the mid and late 1860s. By the 1870s, high schools in Ontario would prove to be the model for future secondary schools in Canada. Just as common schools became known as public schools in that era, so too were grammar schools known always as high schools in Canada. The high schools by then offered a sophisticated collegiate curriculum, although the percentage of students attending college would not increase substantially until the twentieth century.

Similar to elementary schools, Canada's secondary schools fall under the governance of elected school boards at the local level. Board members establish guidelines for budgets and teacher employment. They are responsible to the province's department of education regarding curriculum matters.

In Canada, students for the most part pursue one of two high school tracks. One track serves the interests of students intending to attend a university. The other track

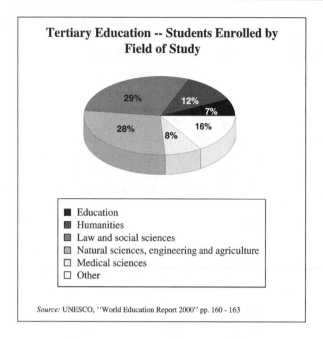

Tertiary Education -- Students Enrolled by Field of Study

29% 12% 7% 28% 8% 16%

- ■ Education
- ■ Humanities
- ■ Law and social sciences
- ▨ Natural sciences, engineering and agriculture
- □ Medical sciences
- □ Other

Source: UNESCO, "World Education Report 2000" pp. 160 - 163

is more geared to students that will enter the workforce after either education or who will do so after getting additional training in a vocational or technology school or from a community college. Remedial programs meet the needs of students having difficulty with their high school studies.

In enrollment at the secondary level in Canada, 2,292,497 pupils were enrolled during the 1990 to 1991 academic year. Of that total, by gender breakdown, 1,118,112 were female. During the 1995 to 1996 academic year, 2,505,389 pupils were enrolled for a slight increase. Female students represented 1,218,403 of that total.

HIGHER EDUCATION

With few exceptions, Canadian postsecondary schools break down into universities and colleges. In the twenty-first century, the term "colleges" usually refers to community colleges.

Because of bickering and cultural differences among the nation's disparate groups, it took hundreds of years before the people of Canada concentrated on their common beliefs and values to form a quality system of higher education. Canada's early schools of higher education were then called colleges. All these colleges possessed denominational affiliations, often instituted by ministers, dioceses, or colonists with strong religious ties. Consequently, their early offerings stressed religious studies or theology and a classical education such as was pursued in Europe at the University of Paris or Oxford or at Harvard College in the American colonies.

Canada's first "college," the Collège des Jésuites, established in 1635 by the Jesuit Order in Quebec, actually was a primary school (*petite école*) for children and young Indians. To give some idea of this accomplishment, Harvard College would not be established in Massachusetts until 1636. In short time, Latin was taught and eventually the school offered seminary studies. By the 1660s, a full college course and the opportunity for a classical education were also offered. The British closed this school in 1768 after the French defeat.

Until late in the eighteenth century, British authorities frowned upon French Catholic educational institutions, but eventually came to tolerate and even support them. However, the Petit Séminaire de Montréal (formerly the Collège St. Raphaël) was begun by Catholic religious in 1773, offering a partial classical course. Université Laval was founded in 1663 as the Séminaire de Québec; the school still exists today.

The aforementioned 1790 Means for Promoting Education, the special legislative council committee headed by Chief Justice Smith, recommended the formation of a college similar to the great universities of Europe, but theology-free, an attempt to suppress Catholic teachings. This was blocked.

Higher education was not absent from Canada through 1860, but colleges were in very short supply. Potential students had the choice of attending two major institutions at Quebec or Montreal that were similar to the classical universities of Europe or attending five smaller institutions, specifically Nicolet (1803), St. Hyacinthe (1811), Ste. Thérésé-de-Blaineville (1825), Ste. Anne-de-la-Pocatière (1827), and L'Assomption (1832) (Harris 1976). A number of short-lived institutions failed to outlast the nineteenth century. All these were propelled by the enthusiasm and entrepreneurial abilities of various parish priests and their bishops who, perhaps less nobly, were attempting to keep Catholic students from choosing to enter British, non-sectarian institutions such as McGill University.

Not surprisingly, one of the important reasons for the establishment of institutions of higher learning in English-occupied Canada was the training of missionaries and ministers. Until 1763, the British lagged behind the French in higher education, having established no colleges up to that time. Other institutions, particularly those large non-denominational schools such as McGill (first operating in 1821 with a medical faculty and then eventually expanding to include numerous professional and academic disciplines) and Dalhousie (1818) Universities, were founded to preserve British culture, traditions, and way of life. The King's Colleges at Frederickton, Windsor, and Toronto consciously and warily attempted to preserve Canadian traditions, lest Canadian schools become

"Americanized" culturally. The founders of the Windsor, Ontario, and Frederickton, New Brunswick institutions were United Empire Loyalists. Many of today's universities originally had different names at the time of their founding. The University of Toronto was King's College in Toronto when chartered in 1827. The Frederick institution begun in 1829 is now the University of New Brunswick.

Canada's colleges tended to have denominational roots. Four colleges were independent as of 1867, while the remaining 13 had denominational ties, according to the Association of Universities and Colleges of Canada. Rather than continue to work against one another, Canada's nondenominational and religious universities formed cooperative, if sometimes uneasy, alliances. For example, the nonsectarian University of Toronto collaborated with three religious colleges that were Anglican, Catholic, and Methodist by the early 1900s (McInnes 1969).

As of 2000, Canada possessed 92 universities ranging from small liberal arts institutions mainly or exclusively for undergraduates to extensive, heavily enrolled research communities of knowledge. A few offer specialties such as art and design; others contain every imaginable specialty study. (Some of the specialty schools are comparable to community colleges in the U.S.)

Some of the more noteworthy universities in Canada and the dates of their founding include the following: Carleton University (1957, formerly Carleton College with a 1942 founding), Lakehead University (1965, formerly Lakehead Technical Institute), Memorial University of Newfoundland (1949), University of Alberta (1906), University of Guelph (1965), University of Lethbridge (1967), and University of Saskatchewan (1907). Like U.S. state universities, many universities in Canada have a similar relationship to province governments.

In spite of attempts by the government and universities to minimize U.S. influences on higher education, sociologists and educators frequently note the tendency of institutions to form boards of governors similar to trustee boards in the United States. Like those of the U.S., these boards tend to be heavily populated with members outside the immediate university community. Other American influences can be seen in the methods of operation Canadian universities employ in their graduate and professional schools, according to sociologists Wilfrid B.W. Martin and Allan J. Macdonell. Finally, the four western provinces of Alberta, British Columbia, Manitoba, and Saskatchewan established universities that borrowed from the model of U.S. land grant colleges, according to the Association of Universities and Colleges of Canada.

In the twentieth century, Canada's government and people placed growing importance on higher education, requiring trained and educated employees and management for the knowledge-based industries. Approximately 8 percent of Canada's gross domestic product (GDP) goes toward education expenditures. A little over one quarter of Canadian citizens possess a university or college degree.

Not surprisingly, Canada's biggest boom in university enrollments came during the Baby Boom era. Enrollment in full-time studies more than tripled from 1960 to 1970, with more than 350,000 students enrolled during the 1970-1971 academic year. All told, student enrollment (including part time students) exploded to 493,000 students during the 1973-1974 academic year. By the 1998-1999 school year, attendance of full and part time students had increased to 580,376 full time students and 245,985 part time students. Of these totals, Ontario is the leader by province in student numbers with 229,985 full time students and 72,958 part time students. Quebec is second with 134,162 full time students and 98,116 part time students. Not all provinces have prospered equally in recent years. From 1994-1995 to 1998-1999, the provinces of Prince Edward Island, Newfoundland, New Brunswick, and Manitoba recorded slight drops in full time student enrollment.

Community Colleges & Technical Colleges: In Canada, in addition to the universities offering degreed programs, there are also in operation a wide number of community colleges, technical schools, agricultural colleges, schools of agriculture, two-year colleges of art, and schools of nursing.

Canada has built a significant number of these schools in a relatively short time. As late as the 1960s and 1970s, community colleges were struggling to find a niche in the country's educational system. Many of the educational offerings and vocational courses are designed to be completed in two years. Often students transfer to four year institutions after attending community colleges.

In 1996-1997, Canada awarded 85,908 degrees in career programs. These were broken down into business and commerce (23,327), engineering and applied sciences (18,279), social sciences and social services (16,779), health sciences (11,618), the arts (7,191), the natural sciences (4,819), humanities (1,235), arts and sciences (2,531), and miscellaneous unreported categories (129).

Vocational Training: The first trade school in Canada offered not only vocational courses but also training in the arts such as painting and sculpture. The school was founded in Quebec at St. Joachim around 1670. In the early 1700s, a similar institution opened in Montreal. The Jesuits ran both schools. These schools served mariners, artisans, and students aspiring to become farmers.

Primary and Secondary Educational Expenditures by Category

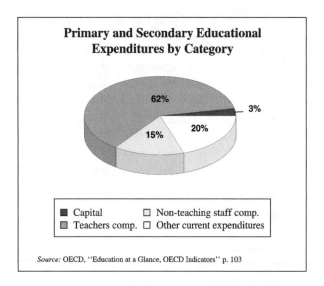

62%

3%

20%

15%

■ Capital   □ Non-teaching staff comp.
■ Teachers comp.   □ Other current expenditures

Source: OECD, "Education at a Glance, OECD Indicators" p. 103

In modern times, when the presence of a skilled work force increasingly demands that workers bring skills to a job instead of getting them on the job, trade and vocational training has become nearly mandatory for Canadians lacking a community college or college education. The types of vocational programs and the number of programs vary from province to province. Both community colleges and vocational centers advertise classes in advance. The applicant pays for most programs, although some are government-funded such as language skills for newcomers or courses for aboriginal peoples. Many trades require skills that increase as one advances. For example, an electrician may move from an apprentice to a journeyman.

ADMINISTRATION, FINANCE, & EDUCATIONAL RESEARCH

Both the provinces and federal government invest in Canada's attempt to cultivate an educated populace through aid programs benefiting students in need of some or all financial resources. The federal government, in addition to loan guarantees through the Canada Student Loans Program, works closely with provinces to provide student aid. In 1991-1992, the last year for which data was available, student aid totaled nearly $800 million combined from the federal government and province governments.

TEACHING PROFESSION

Canada takes pride in being a pioneer in teacher training in North America. The first teacher training institution, then referred to as a "normal school," operated in 1836 in Montreal. This was the first teacher training school in North America, opening three years before the United States began a normal school under the direction

of pioneer educator Horace Mann. However, normal schools were slow to catch on in Canada, unlike the United States where they proliferated. Nonetheless, a handful of schools for teachers did open in Upper Canada and New Brunswick (1847), Nova Scotia (1855), Prince Edward Island (1856), and Quebec (1857).

A failed experiment in the late nineteenth century was the opening of model schools for teachers that required the briefest of courses and very little practice teaching. They largely died out in the early years of the twentieth century, but hung on in remote provinces until 1924, according to author-educator F. Henry Johnson who refers to the model schools as a "travesty."

The more rigorous normal schools flourished in most urban centers in Canada, but critics frequently objected to relaxed admission standards and failure to require a high school diploma for entry in many cases. The Roman Catholics also established normal schools for the training of nuns and laity in the twentieth century. Even by 1940, many normal schools such as one in Prince Edward Island still failed to require a diploma from high school for admission to their programs. Others, however, were more demanding in entrance requirements and curriculum improvements included the offering of classes in educational psychology (Johnson 1968). Many reform efforts were internal, the work of professional teacher associations. These groups advocated curriculum standardization, formal textbook adoption procedures, and the inclusion of teacher training at respected Canadian universities.

In modern Canada, teacher education programs are now part of university course offerings at numerous institutions, nearly all offering a curriculum overseen by departments of education. Teacher training is typically a vigorous one year program (in some cases two years), and would-be teachers spend an additional three or four years to receive their university degree. Standardization has not fully occurred, and teacher certification programs vary, depending upon the province or territory. Teachers typically specialize in elementary, middle, or secondary school programs. Others specialize in subjects such as the teaching of English or French as a second language. Many focus on specialty subjects such as music, the arts, or physical education.

Teacher education programs stress the learning of not only educational theory and academic subjects, but also require mastery in the classroom before actual students during practice teaching stints called practicums. By the twenty-first century, in spite of abundant reforms from 1940 to 2001, it became clear that teacher reform was an unfinished business. In New Brunswick, reformers frequently mounted platforms for methods to ensure that teachers experienced continuous growth and improvement over the course of their careers. The Canadian

Association of Deans of Education (CADE) and the Association francophone des doyens, doyennes, directeurs, et directrices d'éducation (AFDEC) stress that good teachers need to continuously update their skills by reading, taking workshops, traveling, and participating in teacher exchange programs.

SUMMARY

Education in Canada has contributed to a remarkable era of prosperity in the nation during the late 1990s and first part of the twenty-first century. Reforms in the educational system have been apparent in primary and secondary education, colleges and universities, and vocational training. Although there has been recent dissatisfaction with the test scores of students in the primary and secondary grades, the rising number of Canadians with degrees and advanced degrees has offered some consolation. Conflicts between French and British interests in the far-flung provinces have been eased by the government's strong support of bilingual education. Likewise, the government has been supportive of attempts by the aboriginal peoples to better their lot in life through education, even as they preserve their customs and language.

While Canada's economy is expected to lose some of its luster as the United States and other industrialized nations experience economic downturns in 2001 and lower population rates will certainly lead to declines in university and college enrollments in certain provinces, the future of Canada overall looks brilliant in the twenty-first century as its ample resources and educated or trained workforce give the nation benefits many other nations only can envy.

BIBLIOGRAPHY

Calam, John. "The Royal Grammar Schools." *Educational Record 79(4)* (October-December 1963): 256ff.

Cochrane, J. *The One-Room School in Canada.* Toronto: Fitzhenry and Whiteside, 1981.

Fraser Institute, The. *Report Cards.* Available from http://www.fraserinstitute.ca.

Harris, Robin S. *A History of Higher Education in Canada: 1663-1960.* Toronto: University of Toronto Press, 1976.

Katz, Michael B. and Paul H. Mattingly. *Education and Social Change: Themes from Ontario's Past.* New York: New York University Press, 1975.

Johnson, F. Henry. *A Brief History of Canadian Education.* Toronto: McGraw-Hill of Canada, 1968.

Martin, Wilfred B.W. and Allan J. Macdonell. *Canadian Education: A Sociological Analysis.* Scarborough, Ontario: Prentice-Hall of Canada, 1978.

McInnis, Edgar. *Canada: A Political and Social History.* Toronto: Holt, Rinehart and Winston of Canada, 1969.

McNaught, Kenneth. *The Penguin History of Canada.* London: Penguin, 1988.

Mulcahy, Dennis. *Learning and Teaching in Multi-grade Classrooms.* St. John's: Faculty of Education Monograph, Memorial University, 1993.

———. *The One-Room School in Newfoundland and Labrador. An Oral History Project.* 19 January 1999. Available from http://www.ucs.mun.ca.

Robinson, Laura. *Crossing the Line.* Toronto: McClelland & Stewart, 1998.

Statistics Canada. *1996 and 2001 Census Information.* 2001. Available from http://www.statcan.ca.

UNESCO Statistical Overview: School Enrollment. *Canada.* 1999. Available from http://www.ibe.unesco.org.

University of Sakatchewan. *Native Studies Review.* 31 October 1999, Available from http://www.usask.ca.

U.S. Department of Education. *Condition of Education: 1995.* 2001. Available from http://www.ed.gov.

—*Hank Nuwer*

CAPE VERDE

BASIC DATA

Official Country Name:	Republic of Cape Verde
Region:	Africa
Population:	401,343
Language(s):	Portuguese, Crioulo
Literacy Rate:	71.6%

The Republic of Cape Verde, an archipelago of 10 islands and 5 islets located 385 miles off the northwest coast of Africa, is in the unenviable position of having to import approximately 80 to 90 percent of its foodstuff and of being prone to droughts leading to famines. These factors and others, including high unemployment, impact the educational system.

The independent (1975) Republic of Cape Verde inherited 75 percent illiteracy from the Portuguese. The official language is Portuguese; however, it is not the

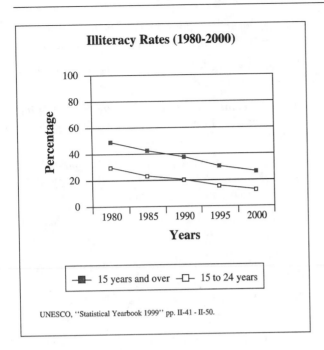

Illiteracy Rates (1980-2000)

Legend: ■ 15 years and over — □ 15 to 24 years

UNESCO, "Statistical Yearbook 1999" pp. II-41 - II-50.

language in common use. At the time of independence and regularly thereafter, it was proposed that students have lessons in Cape Verde Creole, a mixture of Portuguese and West African languages, which is the language most commonly spoken. The proposal has not yet been accepted because some officials feel that Cape Verde Creole is simply an offshoot or dialect of Portuguese and, therefore, not a valid language.

However, efforts in the late 1990s, including work at public schools in Boston and Brockton with a high proportion of Cape Verde immigrants, have led to a proposed alphabet for Cape Verde Creole that reflects actual pronunciation. This alphabet, ALUPEC, was introduced in Cape Verde for a provisional five-year trial. If the alphabet is successful and accepted, it will become the government-sanctioned standard for Cape Verde Creole, the first step in accepting Cape Verde Creole as the official language of government and, thus, instruction.

Since the majority of people do not actually speak and use Portuguese, literacy rates are difficult to assess. Literacy rates, defined as those over the age of 15 who can read and write (no standard specified), are reported by various agencies to be between 70 and 86 percent.

The Republic of Cape Verde has a Ministry of Education, Science, Youth and Sports. Like most sub-Saharan countries, it has difficulty in filling teaching positions though.

The school year runs from October to July. Schooling is free, universal, and compulsory for students aged 7 to 13; however, attendance is not enforced. Early schooling enrollment rates exceed 90 percent, but dropout rates are high and later schooling is not well attended.

School laws were revised in 1987. Prior to 1987, schooling consisted of the first six years of *instrução primária* (primary education) and a *escola preparatória* (middle school) of three years. After middle school, two tracks were possible: a three-year track leading to a *Curso Complementar do Ensino Tecnico* (Certificate of the Completion of General Technical Education) or a two year pre-university course leading to a *Curso Complementar dos Liceus* (Certificate of the Completion of a Lycee).

In 1987 the middle school was abolished and *instrução primária* (primary education) became a single six-year cycle. Secondary education became a single five-year stage with two cycles: a three-year general track followed by two-year pre-university preparation, successful completion of which leads to a *Curso Complementar do Ensíno Secondario* (Certificate of the Completion of Secondary Education).

Cape Verde has no university. Several teacher-training institutions and one industrial-commercial institution exist, but none of these institutions is considered postsecondary.

A law effective December 29, 1996, states that Cape Verde will provide equal access to educational success for special needs students. The law supports the integration of special education into regular classrooms in situations that support student learning.

Outside influences also impact Cape Verde education. For example, the World Bank and its arm, the International Development Association (IDA), were investing in educational and development programs (1999) to increase access to primary school, to improve classrooms, and to raise teacher and workforce skills to enable the workforce to respond to social and economic goals.

BIBLIOGRAPHY

Almeida, Raymond. "Chronological References." *Cabo Verde/Cape Verdean American,* 14 March 1997. Available from http://www.umassd.edu/specialprograms/caboverde/cvchrono.html.

Cape Verde Embassy Fact Sheet, 1999. Available from http://capeverdeusembassy.org/factmain.html.

Caswell, Linda J., and Isabel Pina-Britt. "The Importance of Using Cape Verdean Creole in the Classroom." *Cimboa: A Journal of Letters, Arts and Studies,* 31 July 1998. Available from http://www.softlink.web.

The Central Intelligence Agency (CIA). *The World Factbook 2000.* Directorate of Intelligence, 1 January 2000. Available from http://www.cia.gov/.

"Country Profile: Cape Verde." ABC News, 1998. Available from http://www.abcnews.go.com/reference/contries/CV.html.

Friere, Paulo. *Pedagogy in Process.* New York: Seabury Press, 1978.

Janet Matthews Information Services. "Cape Verde Country Profile." *Africa Review World of Information,* May 1996.

"Legislation Pertaining to Special Needs Education." UNESCO, February 1996. ERIC No: ED407777.

Macedo, Donaldo. "The Politics of an Emancipatory Literacy in Cape Verde." In *Rewriting Literary: Culture and the Discourse of the Other,* eds. Candace Mitchell and Kathleen Weiler, 147-59. *Critical Studies in Education and Culture Series.* Ed. Henry A. Giroux and Paulo Freire. New York: Bergin and Garvey, 1991.

Miller, Yawu. "Alphabet Is a Start for Cape Verdean Creole." *Bay State Banner,* 31 December 1998. Available from http://www.softlinkweb.com.

Sevigny, Joseph A. *Cape Verde: A Country Guide Series Report from the AACRAO-AID Project.* American Association of Collegiate Registrars and Admissions Officers, 1995. ERIC Document 388127.

"WB Approves $22.1 Million for the Republic of Cape Verde." *The Cape Verdean News,* 31 July 1999. Available from http://www.softlineweb.com.

—*Emily Dial-Driver*

CAYMAN ISLANDS

BASIC DATA

Official Country Name:	Cayman Islands
Region:	North & Central America
Population:	34,763
Language(s):	English
Literacy Rate:	98%

The Cayman Islands, a dependency of the United Kingdom, are located in the Caribbean Sea about 160 kilometers south of Cuba and 290 kilometers northwest of Jamaica. This British Crown Colony consists of three islands: Grand Cayman, Cayman Brac, and Little Cayman. The islands, discovered by Columbus in 1503 and taken over by the British in 1670, are a self-governing member of the Federation of the West Indies.

The literacy rate on the Cayman Islands was 98 percent in 2000. Free public education based on the United Kingdom model is available to all children beginning at age five. There are 17 government schools that include primary (K-6), middle school (7-9), and high school (10-12). There is one special education school. Additionally, there are several elementary and secondary private schools on Grand Cayman.

Government-funded postsecondary education began in 1975 when a part time community college was opened. During the next six years, three other postsecondary institutions were opened: the Trade School, the Hotel School, and the Marine School. In 1985 the administration of these institutions was centralized as the Community College of the Cayman Islands, located on Grand Cayman. In 1987, the college was established as a semi-autonomous institution granting an Associate Degree and offering continuing education and professional/vocational courses.

The International College of the Cayman Islands (ICCI), founded in 1970 and accredited by the Accrediting Council for Independent Colleges and Schools in Washington, DC, operates as a non-profit, privately controlled, American-style senior college. ICCI offers the following degrees: Associate of Science, Bachelor of Science, Master of Business Administration, and Master of Science in management. There are approximately 30 full-time and adjunct faculty members. Guest lecturers from around the world share their expertise with the students who come from every continent to study at ICCI.

The Cayman Islands is one of 15 non-campus countries contributing to the University of the West Indies, which offers outreach and distance education programs. Some universities in the United States also offer summer and short-term courses in the Cayman Islands; these courses are usually related to tropical biology or marine study. Other private organizations offer continuing education courses and certified instruction in underwater photography, snorkeling, and scuba diving.

BIBLIOGRAPHY

The Central Intelligence Agency (CIA). *The World Factbook 2000.* Directorate of Intelligence, 1 January 2000. Available from http://www.cia.gov.

Community College of the Cayman Islands, 2001. Available from http://www.ccci.edu.ky.

Eubanks, Edna S., and James Bovell. "Cayman Islands Information." *Dream Finders,* 1 January 2001. Available from http://www.dreamfinders.com.

George Hicks High School. "Education in the Cayman Islands," February 2001. Available from http://www.ghhs.edu.ky.

George, Shurlaud, and Andrew F. Clark. "Tourism Education and Training Policies in Developing Countries: A

Case Study of the Cayman Islands.'' *Journal of Third World Studies* 15 (Spring 1998): 205-220.

International College of the Cayman Islands, 1998. Available from http://www.cayman.com.ky.

Steen, Sarah, ed. *Vacation Study Abroad: The Complete Guide to Summer and Short-Term Study.* New York: Institute of International Education, 1999.

University of the West Indies, 5 March 2001. Available from http://www.uwichill.edu.

—Jo Anne R. Bryant

CENTRAL AFRICAN REPUBLIC

BASIC DATA

Official Country Name:	Central African Republic
Region:	Africa
Population:	3,512,751
Language(s):	French, Sangho, Arabic, Hunsa, Swahili
Literacy Rate:	60%

HISTORY & BACKGROUND

Upon gaining its independence from France on August 13, 1960, the former French colony known as Ubangi-Shari became the Central African Republic. The Central African Republic covers approximately 240,535 square miles (622,984 kilometers) and borders Cameroon, Chad, the Democratic Republic of the Congo, the Republic of the Congo, and Sudan in the central part of Africa. Its capital is Bangui. Although French is the official language of the Central African Republic, Arabic and Swahili are also spoken. Its national literacy rate is 60 percent.

The first formal schools began in the Central African Republic in about 1930. These schools were primarily extensions of the Catholic church, and the teachers were missionaries. After 1937, a government education system was established. Between the mid-1940s and 1960, the population grew at such a fast pace that both private and government schools were needed to meet the educational demands. In 1963 the government ordered the abolition of private schools; however, by 1975 another spurt in population growth made it necessary for private schools to resume their role in meeting the educational needs of the growing country.

PREPRIMARY & PRIMARY EDUCATION

The educational system of the Central African Republic has four levels: nursery, primary, secondary, and higher education. Education is compulsory for eight years between the ages of 6 and 14, and instruction is in French. Nursery schools take children between the ages of four and six and prepare them to enter primary education.

Primary education focuses on teaching children both practical and general educational skills and is divided into two levels: primary one and primary two. Primary one begins around the age of six and continues for five years. Upon completion of primary one, students are tested to see who will be promoted to primary level two and who will go on in the area of vocational education. Primary level two starts at the age of 11 and continues on for 4 years. Students who satisfactorily complete both primary levels are eligible for secondary education.

Primary education has traditionally had a larger enrollment than secondary. In 1991 an estimated 58 percent of children of primary-school age attended school; however, only 10 percent of children of secondary-school age attended school. At both the primary and secondary levels, more boys were enrolled in school than girls.

The pupil-teacher ratio in the primary schools was 77 pupils per teacher for 1990-1991, making it the highest pupil-teacher ratio for any country in the world. This high pupil-teacher ratio can be partly explained by the fact that during the 1990s state-funded education was greatly disrupted and handicapped overall as a result of insufficient government resources. Despite the lack of government resources, a national educational plan was launched in 1994 to help fund capital educational projects.

SECONDARY EDUCATION

Secondary education lasts for three years and is divided into two options: general secondary education, and technical and professional secondary education. Those who successfully complete general secondary education and pass their baccalaureate exams become eligible for higher education. Those who take technical and professional secondary education are trained and prepared to work in various trades and given a proficiency certificate upon the completion and passing of their exams.

HIGHER EDUCATION

The Central African Republic has one main university, the University of Bangui, which was founded in 1969.

The academic year starts in October and ends in June. In the 1995-1996 school year, the University of Bangui had 3,590 students and 140 academic staff. In addition to the university, there are also specialized colleges that focus primarily on agriculture and the arts.

The University of Bangui provides eight units of study. Four units are in the area of professional training, including health sciences and medicine, teacher training, rural and agricultural development, and business management. Three academic units are inclusive of a variety of academic fields of studies, and one unit is in the area of research. The minister of higher education functions as the chancellor of the university, but the Council of Administration officially governs the university, authorizing the use and disbursement of funds and establishing general academic policies.

SUMMARY

Overall, education in the Central African Republic has made progress in eradicating the illiteracy problem among its citizens. Nonetheless, the continued population growth creates a milieu in which added resources and attention must be given to ongoing teacher training, technological support, development of new school sites, and an instructional commitment to science and technical education.

BIBLIOGRAPHY

The Central Intelligence Agency. *The World Factbook 2000*. Directorate of Intelligence, 26 May 2001. Available from http://www.odci.gov/.

The Europa World Yearbook 2000. 41st ed. Vol.1. London: Europa Publications Limited, 2000.

Touba, Theophile. "Central African Republic." *Handbook of World Education: A Comparative Guide to Higher Education and Educational Systems of the World*, edited by Walter Wickremansinghe, 155-158. Houston, TX: American Collegiate Service, 1992.

Turner, Barry, ed. *The Statesman's Yearbook 2001*. New York: St. Martin's Press, 2000.

The World of Learning 1999. 49th ed. London: Europa Publications Limited, 1998.

—*Kimberly A. Battle-Walters*

Gross Enrollment Ratios by Gender and Level

Source: UNICEF, "The State of the World's Children 2001" pp. 90 - 93

CHAD

BASIC DATA

Official Country Name:	Republic of Chad
Region:	Africa
Population:	8,424,504
Language(s):	French, Arabic, Sara, Sango
Literacy Rate:	48.1%
Number of Primary Schools:	2,660
Compulsory Schooling:	6 years
Public Expenditure on Education:	1.7%
Educational Enrollment:	Primary: 591,493 Secondary: 99,789 Higher: 3,446
Educational Enrollment Rate:	Primary: 57% Secondary: 9% Higher: 1%
Teachers:	Primary: 9,395 Secondary: 2,792
Student-Teacher Ratio:	Primary: 67:1 Secondary: 37:1
Female Enrollment Rate:	Primary: 39%

Secondary: 4%
Higher: 0.2%

HISTORY & BACKGROUND

The Republic of Chad is a land-locked country located in central Africa. It is bordered by Libya on the North; Niger, Nigeria and Cameroon on the West; the Central African Republic on the South; and the Sudan on the East. Chad has an area of 495,624 square miles and a population of more than 8 million (2000 estimate). Both French and Chadian Arabic are the official languages. Chad is made up of more than 200 different tribes and more than 12 major ethnic groups, with the Saras (28 percent) and the Sudanic Arabs (12 percent) representing the two largest ones. The country is 50 percent Muslim, 25 percent Christian, and 25 percent Animist. For political and educational purposes, Chad is really two different countries melded into one. Linguistic, geographic, religious, and economic criteria sharply differentiate the two halves. Northern Chad is a barren land with desert-like features; it is inhabited by nomadic tribes who are, for the most part, Muslim. Southern Chad, on the other hand, is a fertile, rain-drenched valley where Christian farmers live a sedentary life.

Chad became a French protectorate in 1900, a colony in 1920, and one of the four constituent territories of French Equatorial Africa in 1946. It gained full independence in 1960 when it became an autonomous republic within the French Community of Nations. Civil war soon erupted between the Muslim north and the largely Christian-animist south. For almost 20 years, Libyan-backed troops vied for power with indigenous political factions supported by France and the United States. The 1990s ushered in some measure of political stability when self-proclaimed president Idriss Déby assumed power and the International Court of Justice finally recognized the long-standing Chadian claim to the Aozou territory, a mineral-rich strip of land occupied by Libyan soldiers. However, peace was slow in coming, as opposing factions continued to wage civil war throughout Chad, and human rights organizations accused the Chadian army of committing atrocities in the south. Déby was elected president in 1996, and parliamentary elections were held in 1997. Civil unrest continued sporadically as opposition groups pledged to overthrow Déby's government by force. A new pipeline was being built by a French-American and Dutch consortium to tap newly discovered oil reserves and bring, by 2001, much-needed revenues to this war-torn and impoverished nation. In 1998, European Union finance ministers agreed to allow France to continue to guarantee the CFA Franc (the Communauté Financière

Africaine franc)—the currency used in Chad and in 14 other African nations.

CONSTITUTIONAL & LEGAL FOUNDATIONS

A new constitution, adopted by referendum on March 31, 1997, guarantees a free and compulsory education for all Chadian citizens between the ages of 6 through 14. Civil war, however, has long prevented the full implementation of that goal, and school enrollments at all levels remain low.

EDUCATIONAL SYSTEM—OVERVIEW

The educational system has been essentially held back, and in parts, destroyed, by the incessant civil war that annihilated the country's civil service infrastructure between 1960 and 1985. The challenges facing the rebuilding and the reform of the educational system are all the more daunting because Chad is one of the poorest nations in Central Africa, with almost no paved roads or modern railroads. Burdened with unrest, terrorism, and a chronic lack of necessary funds, since nearly all resources were summarily allocated for the war effort, Chad has had to struggle since the mid-1980s to salvage its educational system. The available services in existence in 1960 did not constitute a solid basis upon which a new structure could be elaborated. After its independence, Chad lagged behind other francophone nations in central Africa. While Chad was one of its colonies, the French had decided not to build secondary schools and only instituted a rudimentary structure that relied heavily on Catholic and Protestant missionary efforts. After 1960, Chad attempted to build a credible educational system, only to see those efforts undermined by civil war, overcrowding, and a lack of qualified teachers and proper funding. Despite such unfavorable circumstances, several attempts at reform were made; one attempt was operation ''Mandoul,'' launched in 1962, which tried to reform primary and secondary curriculum by making it more practical. Farming and basic skills were integrated in the programs of a few experimental schools between 1962 and 1968. The experiment was limited in scope and, ultimately, proved to be a failure. The other reform attempt was in 1973. An effort was made to change the old colonial pedagogical structure left behind by the French. A new, gradually selective system would enable students to enter professional occupations if they proved to be unable to continue along the more academically oriented track of primary and secondary schools. Again, however, these efforts did not result in any lasting or concrete changes.

By 1980, an ever-spreading civil war had stopped most reform attempts and effectively closed down the majority of Chadian schools. When they reopened in

1982, they faced the arduous task of trying to rebuild, once again, on the ruins of inadequate programs and assets. It took 10 years to erect buildings and train a minimum number of teachers. By 1990, Chad was consolidating its primary and secondary school systems, while still facing a shortage of funds and qualified personnel.

PREPRIMARY & PRIMARY EDUCATION

Preschool is not yet a widely accepted concept in Chad, as most children tend to remain at home with their mothers until they enter kindergarten. Preschools exist only in large cities. They offer a basic curriculum centering on socialization skills, and their enrollment is limited.

Primary schools offer a six-year curriculum. Children enter at the age of six in larger cities, and around age seven in rural areas. In 2000, there were 913,541 children enrolled in 3,644 primary schools, taught by 11,641 teachers. Chad has a three-tier primary school system, which includes public, private, and community-centered schools. (The latter have been developed mostly in rural areas.) In 2000, there were 2,077 elementary public schools employing 8,318 teachers; 1,302 community-centered schools with 1,827 teachers; and 265 private schools with 1,496 teachers. The public and community-centered schools have a 1:68 teacher-student ratio.

Teachers are divided into several categories: *instituteurs* and *bacheliers contractuels* (full-time teachers), *moniteurs* (teaching assistants), and *suppléants* (substitutes and adjuncts). Despite vigorous efforts aimed at training new faculty, it is estimated that 30 percent of primary school teachers hold no professional qualifications. The teacher-student ratio is 1:65 in rural areas and can be as high as 1:100 in large agglomerations such as Moundou, Sarh, Bongor, Abéché, Dobra, and N'Djamena, the capital. The Chadian government has launched efforts to promote the teaching of the standard curriculum in many of the local tribal languages. However, many parents, working through the influential parents' associations, tend to resist this, as they insist that their children be taught in French, especially in southern Chad. At the end of the six-year curriculum, a national exam, the CEP, or *Certificat d'Etudes Primaires* (primary skills certification), is administered to all children. Those who successfully pass are admitted to secondary schools, while the others are directed to vocational and technical schools. They can enter a six-year program leading to the CAP, or *Certificat d'Aptitude Professionelle* (professional skills certification), in a variety of manual and technical fields. In 2000, the passing rate for the CEP was 59.84 percent. Those who were held back one more year accounted for 27.69 percent, while 12.47 percent abandoned their schooling at that point.

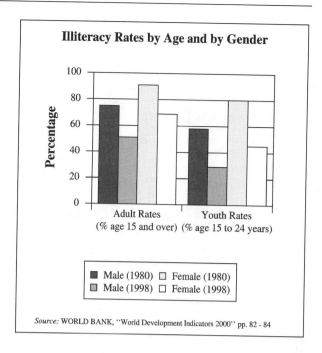

Illiteracy Rates by Age and by Gender

Adult Rates (% age 15 and over)   Youth Rates (% age 15 to 24 years)

Male (1980)   Female (1980)
Male (1998)   Female (1998)

Source: WORLD BANK, "World Development Indicators 2000" pp. 82 - 84

SECONDARY EDUCATION

Designed largely after the French system, secondary education in Chad lasts seven years, and its curriculum is divided into two parts. The first one is a four-year curriculum leading to a national exam called the *Brevet d'Etudes du Premier Cycle,* (Junior High School Diploma) or BEPC. Only the students who pass this exam are allowed to continue to the next level. The second part lasts three years, during which students can choose among four different sections that already define their future professional orientations: humanities, economics, math, or natural sciences. These three years are usually spent in a *lycée* (an academic-track high school), and they end with another national exam, the selective *Baccalauréat,* which is a prerequisite for admission to the university. At the secondary level, students are offered instruction in either French or Arabic, the emphasis depending on the geographical location of the school. The state-run Lycée National d'Abéché, in the Ouaddai prefecture, offers a completely bilingual program. Its graduates are often employed by state and governmental agencies. In 2000, there were 112,904 students in secondary education, taught by 3,238 teachers in 533 public schools and 809 private institutions. There were 83,980 students in the first part of the curriculum, and 26,565 in the second cycle (post BEPC).

Vocational Education: Chad has a two-tier system of vocational and technical education. Students who have completed the first year of the first cycle of the secondary school system (one year after the CEP), can enter a three-year curriculum in a *collège technique* leading to a *Certi-*

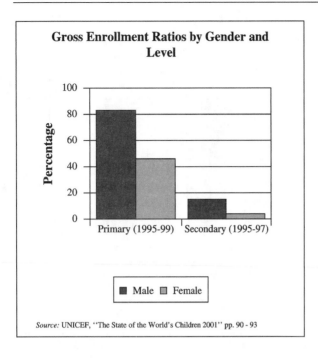

Gross Enrollment Ratios by Gender and Level

Percentage

Primary (1995-99)   Secondary (1995-97)

■ Male   □ Female

Source: UNICEF, "The State of the World's Children 2001" pp. 90 - 93

ficat d'Aptitude Professionelle. Those who have successfully passed the BEPC can enroll in a three-year program taught in a *lycée technique,* leading to the degree of *Baccalauréat de Technicien.* In 2000, there were 1,268 students enrolled in technical and vocational schools.

HIGHER EDUCATION

The only university in Chad is the Université de N'Djaména, located in the capital and founded in 1971 under the name of "Université du Tchad." Its academic year runs from October to June, and the two languages of instruction are French and Arabic. The university is divided into four schools: the *Faculté des Lettres et Sciences Humaines* (School of Humanities and Social Sciences); the *Faculté des Sciences Exactes et Appliquées* (School of Exact and Applied Sciences); the *Faculté de Droit et Sciences Economiques* (School of Law and Economics); and the *Faculté de Médecine* (Medical School). The School of Medicine is the most recent addition to the Université de N'Djaména. It opened in 1990 and had a six-year curriculum (as with the French medical model, medical studies in Chad include both premed and medical education in one continuing program) and graduated its charter class in 1997. In 2000, the medical school had a total enrollment of 251 students. In 2001, the Université de N'Djaména had 5,230 students and a faculty of 122, including only 5 women. The university offers a three-year curriculum. After the successful completion of the first two years, students are awarded the DEUG *Diplôme Universitaire d'Etudes Générales* (General Education University Certificate), and after one additional year the *Licence* (B.A., or B.S.). Since 1998, the

Université de N'Djaména offers programs leading to the Master's degree in jurisprudence, economics, biology, history, geography, and Arabic literature. The language of instruction in graduate and medical education is French, with a minority of programs offering dual instruction in Arabic (literature and history).

In the 1960s, the French government offered a large number of graduate scholarships to Chadian students, but this trend tapered off by the early 1980s. In the late 1970s, the Soviet government also began to offer scholarships for graduate education, but these almost disappeared after the collapse of the Soviet Union. Today, the majority of Chadian students continue their graduate education on the African continent, receiving scholarships from francophone countries such as Morocco and Tunisia, or Arab countries such as Egypt and Iraq. To Chadian students of the new millennium, the United States and Canada represent a popular and much-sought after destination, though a fair amount of students grow disillusioned at the materialism and racial tensions they encounter on the North American continent.

There are also other schools and institutes within the Chadian system of higher education:

- *The Ecole Normale Supérieure* (The National Normal School). Located in N'Djamena, it trains secondary school teachers.

- *The Ecoles Normales* (Normal Schools). These are located in N'Djamena, Moundou, Sahr, Abéché, and Bangor to train primary school teachers.

- *The Ecole Nationale d'Administration et de Magistrature* (The National Training Institute for Civil Servants) (ENAM). It is located in N'Djamena and was founded in 1965.

- *The Ecole Nationale des Télécommunications.* Located in Sahr, it trains telecommunication technicians.

- *The Institut de Recherches du Coton et des Textiles Exotiques* (IRCT). A research institute located in N'Djamena, it was founded in 1939.

- *The Laboratoire de Recherches Vétérinaires et Zootechniques de Farcha* (Veterinary and Zoological Research Institute). Founded in 1952, it researches and produces vaccines.

- *The Institut National des Sciences Humaines.* Founded in 1961 in D'Djamena, it conducts research in paleontology, ethno-sociology, and oral traditions.

ADMINISTRATION, FINANCE, & EDUCATIONAL RESEARCH

The Ministry for primary, secondary, and adult education in N'Djamena, the *Ministère de l'Enseignement de*

Base, oversees all education in Chad, except higher education and scientific research. For primary, secondary, and vocational education, the country is divided into 14 *préfectures* (regional administrative areas.) Each area is granted a certain amount of administrative independence and is responsible for school inspections. Parents' associations and various community and civic organizations also participate in this process. Curriculum and methodology are the responsibility of the *Institut Supérieur des Sciences de l'Education* (ISSED). The Université de N'Djaména is controlled by a rector, a vice-rector, and four deans.

Since 1992, the government has redistributed the financial burden of a free primary and secondary education among different constituencies. The government of Chad supplies 35 percent of the educational budget, foreign aid accounts for 60 percent, and 5 percent comes from parents' associations. By 1992, the government allocation of money for education represented 14 percent of the national budget; it rose to 17 percent in 1997, and 18 percent in 2001.

SUMMARY

The history of the educational system of Chad has been negatively impacted by the civil wars that have divided and impoverished the country for 20 years, following its independence from France. Since 1996, some degree of political and social stability has taken hold, and it has had a positive influence on education. There have been improvements, and the literacy rate has increased from 15 percent in 1960, to 20 percent in 1985, to 48 percent in 1996. The Université de N'Djaména has experienced continuous growth, with a budget for fiscal 2000 of 970 million CFA Francs. The educational budget should represent at least 20 percent of the national expenditures to fund education adequately at all levels.

In 2001 the percentage of children in full-time education was improving for boys (84.56 percent), but still remained very low for Chadian girls (50.02 percent). The economy of Chad has an immediate impact on its educational system and, in 1995, an inflation rate of 41 percent and a 50 percent devaluation of the currency had devastating effects on existing and developing programs. Civil unrest continued in Northern Chad and the U.S. Peace Corps decided to withdraw in 1998 since it could no longer guarantee the safety of its volunteers. Once political stability has been restored, the resources, which for so long have been appropriated by the military, can be reallocated to education. The training of a greater number of qualified teachers and adequate funding for school equipment remain a challenging task for Chadian education.

The World Bank is currently funding a new project for primary education: the addition of 1,000 qualified teachers each year until 2015. The successful implementation of this plan would enable Chad to build a pedagogical foundation on which its educational future could be firmly established.

BIBLIOGRAPHY

Ali, Mahamat Seïd, ed. *Données Statistiques sur l'Education.* N'Djaména: Services de Planification et de Statistiques Unifiés, 2000.

Annuaire Statistique de L'Enseignement Elémentaire. N'Djaména: Direction de la Planification, des Examens et Concours, Division des Statistiques, 1992.

Doréba, Téguidé Sig., Dijimtola Nelli, and Adoum Khamis. *Une Education Nationale pour l'An 2000! L'Indispensable Sursaut.* N'Djaména: CEFOD, 1995.

Esquieu, Paul, and Serge Peano. *L'Enseignement Privé et Spontané dans le Système Educatif Tchadien.* Paris: Institut International de Planification de l'Education (UNESCO), 1994.

Mbaïosso, Adoum. *L'Education au Tchad: Bilan, Problèmes et Perspectives.* Paris: Karthala, 1990.

Nomaye, Madana. *L'Education de Base au Tchad: Situation, Enjeux et Perspectives.* Paris: Harmattan, 1998.

Rapport National sur le Développement de L'Education. N'Djaména: Ministère de l'Education Nationale (Commission Nationale Tchadienne pour l'UNESCO), 1996.

—*Eric H. du Plessis*

CHILE

BASIC DATA

Official Country Name:	Republic of Chile
Region:	South America
Population:	15,153,797
Language(s):	Spanish
Literacy Rate:	95.2%
Academic Year:	March-December
Compulsory Schooling:	8 years
Public Expenditure on Education:	3.6%
Libraries:	289
Educational Enrollment:	Primary: 2,241,536 Secondary: 679,165 Higher: 380,603

Educational Enrollment

Rate:	Primary:	101%
	Secondary:	75%
Teachers:	Primary:	73,960
	Secondary:	51,042
Student-Teacher Ratio:	Primary:	30:1
Female Enrollment Rate:	Primary:	100%
	Secondary:	78%

HISTORY & BACKGROUND

The Republic of Chile is to the north of Peru, to the northeast with Bolivia, to the east with Argentina (separated by the Andes that forms a natural border), and to the west with the Pacific Ocean. Its geographical location offers a variety of climates. A small area of the extreme north of the country is semi-tropical, immediately followed to the south by a harsh desert extension (Atacama Desert), considered one of the most arid areas of the planet. Benjamin Subercaseaux, national writer and scholar, described the topographic territory as *Chile o una Loca Geografía* (Chile, a Geographic Extravaganza), in his book of the same title, referring to its vast variation of climates.

The country occupies an area of 756,950 square kilometers that includes island possessions (292,132 square miles) and 1,250,000 square kilometers (482,628 square miles) of claimed sovereignty of Chilean Antarctic territory, located between 53 and 90 longitudinal degrees West of Greenwich. The latter is mainly populated by military personnel and few civilian families, 1,200 individuals live year round in four permanent bases. Twelve summer bases open for a period of 4 months where national and international scientists, maintenance, and logistic support personnel triplicate its population. Additionally, two laboratories, one of cosmic radiation and one of marine sciences occupy the Chilean Antarctic zone.

Industry/manufacturing contributes 20.8 percent of the country's labor force. During the last twenty years, Chile has promoted exportations of non traditional products, processed and canned food, and manufactured goods, and has expanded the markets of its most traditional ones (wine and iron steel among others.) More recently, tourism has been stimulated as another income source to the country increasing the national gross domestic product.

Chile is a republic where the president is democratically elected by direct vote. The official language is Spanish; Chileans, though, refer to it as Castellano (Castilian.)

Chile's population in the year 2000 was 15,153,797 people. Its major population concentration is found in the capital city, Santiago (5,400,000 people). The national population density is 52 persons per square mile.

In terms of religion, Chileans who declare to be Roman Catholic are 76.6 percent, protestant 13.2, atheist 7 percent, and 4.2 percent other (including Jewish, Muslim, and Orthodox.)

According to the 1992 national census, Chileans who declared to be *mestizo* (European and native Indian mix) were 66 percent of the population, European descent 25 percent, Indigenous 7 percent, and other 2 percent. As compared to other regions in the Americas, slavery from Africa was scarce, particularly because plantations were not developed due to the climate and because importing slaves was not profitable considering the long distance to sail. For this reason, slavery was limited to few local natives and was abolished during the early years of the country's independence.

Currently, these are the main native ethnic groups that survived the Spanish conquest. The Aymara is a group that populates the northernmost geographical area of Chile, corresponding to the Altiplane, a highland territory shared by Chile, Argentina, Peru, Bolivia, and Ecuador located in the Andean zone. The Pascuense is a Polynesian group that inhabits the Rapa Nui/Isla de Pascua (Eastern Island), located across the Chilean coast that was annexed to Chile in 1888. The Mapuches, also called Araucanians, are the most numerous ethnic group with approximately 500,000 members who originally concentrated in the southern territory of the country.

Of all groups, the most racially intact is the Eastern Islanders, approximately 3,800 kilometers west away from the coast of Chile; foreign access is difficult so its mixture is rare. *Mapuches* (Men of land) are recognized as the most significant numeric minority of the country.

As in most territories in the Americas, Spanish exterminated natives in pursuit of land claimed in name of the crown. In a more contemporary context, assimilation, on the other hand, including formal education, military service, and other national activities have not permitted the maintenance of traditions acculturating aboriginal groups, in some cases to their extinction.

As the Chilean territory expanded to the south, few nationals demonstrated interest to inhabit the areas of hostile climate. Due to this reason, the Chilean government invited Italians and Germans to populate a vast region of the country. Germans created a number of prosperous cities, including Valdivia, Puerto Montt, and Puerto Varas, as a result of this colonization. Apart from developing agriculture, they also developed new industries in the area and incorporated their traditions to the national culture. They expanded the territory by settling with their families in inhospitable zones for Chileans, founding Osorno and Punta Arenas. Despite the government efforts, few immigrants came to Chile compared to other countries in the Americas such as Argentina, Peru, Mexico, and Brazil. The Spanish tradition and culture predominated up to after the independence when French enlightenment and encyclopedist philosophies captivated Chilean founder fathers.

CONSTITUTIONAL & LEGAL FOUNDATIONS

The *Primera Junta Nacional de Gobierno* (First National Government Junta), under the initiative of nine Creoles, organized the first government in 1810 by calling the people to join the first town council. The most important contributions that created the nation were to make economic decisions to develop commerce with adjacent territories and to call to form the first national congress in 1811.

Once the first congress was established, the Appealing and the Supreme Judiciary Tribunal were organized. However, the Congress' magnum contribution, in terms of justice and legislation, was to abolish slavery and to establish libertad de vientre (freedom of birth); this decision made Chile the third country in the world that eliminated such practice.

The first Provisional Constitution of 1812 was formed by 28 articles. Among them, the most important article declared the king of Spain a symbolic figure with no legal or political power over the Chilean territory.

A series of wars followed the political movement and kept the monarchic Spain rejecting the idea of losing the territory. The Constitution of 1818 broke the last ties with Spain, eliminating nobility titles that were granted by the monarchy to subjects born in Chile. This regulation was the first step towards a more egalitarian society.

The Constitution of 1828 contributed significantly to the separation of state from the church. The religious orders in the country lost their privileges, acquiring organizational status as many other secular ones, their extensive land properties were partially confiscated, and taxes were imposed by the government on the properties they conserved.

The most solid Chilean Constitution was that of 1833. It was in force for over ninety years. The authors of this constitution were a group of jurists, scholars, and intellectuals whose dedication organized the government of the country systematizing and articulating many aspects in detail.

The Constitution of 1925 was elaborated during a period of power struggle between civilians and the military.

This time, the *Comisión Consultiva* (Advisory Committee) represented by different political parties and institutions was in charge of writing the document. The separation of state from church and social protection and welfare to all citizens were stipulated among many other contributions to solidify a democratic nation.

The Constitution of 1980 was promulgated under the dictatorial government of General Pinochet. His reign was an era characterized by increasing the budget for defense while reducing it for social welfare and education. This regime has been well known for the interference with educators and educational institutions such as universities, and other centers. Public education suffered the most serious deterioration of the century. As a consequence of declaring secondary and higher education a ''situation of privilege'' and contrary to the precept of universal education, dropout rates dramatically raised, inversely, performance and retention dropped in the country.

The three elected presidents who succeeded the dictatorship have been experienced politicians who in an agreement with a coalition of parties advocated to recover education in all its aspects as well as social benefits for the constituents. Former presidents Aylwin and Frei Ruiz-Tagle represented Christian Democrats, while President Lagos became the second socialist elected president in the history of Chile. These three governments have exercised moderation in their missions and have recovered respect in the international context lost during the dictatorship.

EDUCATIONAL SYSTEM—OVERVIEW

Previous to the independence, Christian religious orders predominantly influenced Chilean education. In fact, Jesuits founded the first educational institutions in the country. Since the Primera Junta Nacional de Gobierno (First National Government Junta) in 1810 there was interest on developing educational systems in the new country manifested by the independentist movement members. This desire was concretized by an approved decree that specifically waived taxes for a year and a half on books, maps, printers, physics instruments and machinery that contributed to social and educational advancement. Based on this predisposition to facilitate education, during the year 1813 the National Library was created, freedom of press was instituted, and the first official government newspaper, *El Monitor Araucano*, was established.

These efforts though were consolidated only partially due to prioritization of needs. Solidifying Chilean independence, as well as continuous wars related to territorial limits with adjacent countries, delayed the establishment of public education at a national level that covered all social strata.

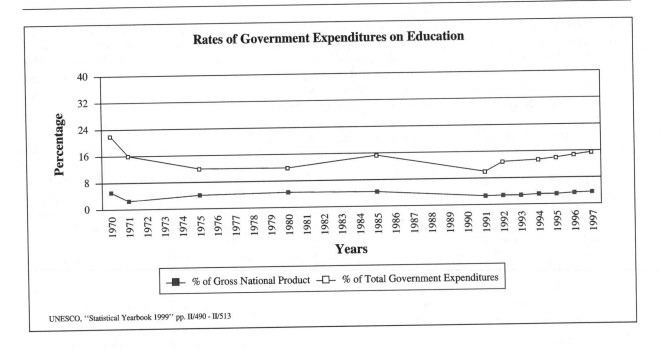

Rates of Government Expenditures on Education

UNESCO, "Statistical Yearbook 1999" pp. II/490 - II/513

From the conquest, late 1500s, to the early periods of the independence, the 1800s, education was in the hands of Catholic organizations. Churches, where reading and writing were taught, had as a main objective evangelizing and gaining new Christians raised in the faith. Additionally, education was highly stratified, it was intended for members of traditional Spanish families, and later, for aristocrats who formed the national elite. Equally, education was emphasized for men who were expected to hold political positions and play roles of leadership for the nation.

Following the Spanish colonial pattern at the time in the Americas, priests were predominantly scholars. The *Aurora de Chile*, (The Chilean Sunrise) the first Chilean newspaper was created and edited by Camilo Enriquez, a catholic priest, patriot, and man of letters who was deeply influenced by the ideas of Jean Jacques Rousseau. Other Europeans influenced Chilean early educational models. The German educator Friedrich Froebel, the father of kindergarten, and the Swiss educational reformer Johann Heinrich Pestalozzi, whose interest in creating schools for the poor and the new didactic for elementary education influenced the development of Chilean education that likewise was reflected on teaching training.

Tradition, on the other hand, predominated over law, educational institutions were created mainly for boys, as in the case of secondary education. Equally, from a professional point of view, girls' access to education was also limited. Only twelve years after the first normal school was opened for males, the first school for girls of this type was created.

It was not until the beginning of the 20th century when drastic and moderate educational reforms solidified public education in the country mainly motivated by political movements and social force led by labor unions.

In 1927, the Ministry of Education was created, having as a main role to plan, implement, and enforce educational laws and oversee the conditions of education at a national level. With the exception of some short periods of time, its administration was characterized by offering centralized policies that favored uniform curricula nationwide including content, providing text books, and basic school supplies free of charge for elementary education. This policy favored relocation of families along the country making education transition easy for children to readapt to new schools on different geographical areas of the nation for decades.

Curricular flexibility began to be attained at the end of the second decade of the 20th century, when advances in education were conducted and partially accomplished by radical laws. Nevertheless, due to political turns, a promising educational system was abruptly ended.

Chilean education adopted a great degree of rigidity reflected on social and geographical inequalities. The most disadvantaged children were those of poor stratum who lived in rural areas where authority did not enforce matriculation and access to schools was difficult due to distance. Emphasis on education for the economically disadvantaged and rural zones of the country was given by president's E. Frei M. Christian Democratic government during the last five years of the 1960s decade when more contemporary methodologies were applied to public education or re-adopted from previous projects carried out in the 1920s and 1930s.

The school dropout rate was also a concern among policy makers. Afterstudying the situation during the 1950s, social strategies were implemented to reduce this rate by offering free nutritionally balanced breakfast and lunch to assist school-age children who fell below the poverty level and had no other significant assets. The *Junta Nacional de Auxilio Escolar y Becas* or JNAEB National Council for School Aid and Scholarships) was created to assess social needs that could prevent children from abandoning school prematurely. Low-income children were also provided with regular access to health and dental care and treatments, if required, free of charge on a regular basis as referred by school authorities. Other services were developed to serve the stratum, *Colonias de Veraneo* (vacation summer camps) were offered to students during their summer vacations that liberated them from work and as a strategy to motivate elementary school attendance. This initiative was put in practice for the first time in 1929, but was discontinued due to political circumstances. Nevertheless, it was revived as a successful effective program in elementary education by the JNAEB. All these initiatives were implemented to reduce school inequalities and to provide equal opportunity of education.

Scholarships were offered on a competitive basis for those low-income students who demonstrated academic outstanding performance to continue their secondary education. Funds for postsecondary education were allocated in the form of scholarships that did not have to be repaid.

Until 1965, primary grades were 6 years of compulsory schooling and 6 years of optional secondary education called *bachillerato* or *humanidades* (baccalaureate/humanities). The reform of 1966 extended free elementary compulsory public education to eight years while reduced secondary grades to four, changing its name to *grados de enseñanza media* (high school).

Administrative decentralization began with the country geo-political regionalization in 1974. Later on, during the decade of 1980, the process of school municipalization provided more autonomy to educational institutions, while the government authorized subsidized private schools, known as *escuelas subvencionadas* for elementary and secondary education in the country. The Ministry of Education approved the Education Organic Constitutional Law of 1990 that authorized educational centers/institutions to develop their own curricula for elementary and secondary education.

A significant characteristic of the most recent national education reform is the extension of the school day transforming it into a single shift—whereas traditionally, most schools group children and teachers into two shifts: morning and afternoon. This new modality has been implemented since 1998. The two-shift school day supported the notion of better utilizing public school buildings by offering more courses while keeping a low student-teacher ratio. Students were given the option to attend school either in the morning or in the afternoon. The single shift schedule refers to the extension of the number of pedagogical hours students remain in school to solidify the learning process leading to expand curricular content areas: specifically, increasing weekly hours from 30 to 38 in elementary education and to 42 hours in high school.

The reform was questioned by school professionals arguing the need for more school buildings to contain all students and teachers to keep low teacher-student ratio. Existing facilities don't have the capacity to absorb the demand for education under these conditions. Aware of the magnitude of this change, gradual implementation was planned; for this purpose, the government allocated extra funds exclusively to build new school buildings as a first step. Another concern that afflicted educators and administrators was a shortage of teachers who previously worked two shifts to cope with low salaries, as compared to other professions. The new schedule load increase did not financially compensate the second shift teachers held in the previous system. This reform was not accepted by everyone in the educational system. Private school professionals argued that they lacked funds to hire teachers for longer hours, additionally, private educators argued that extending the number of hours in schools not necessarily would improve the quality of education, remarking that quality and quantity not necessarily correlated. Another argument posed by opponents was centered on traditionally under-funded zones, which ultimately led to displaced students.

Spanish has been the only language of instruction in public schools, however, one of the most recent attempts to improve education for the ethnically disadvantaged has been the incorporation of bilingual-bicultural programs. The *Unidad de Cultura y Educación de la Corporación Nacional de Desarrollo Indígena* or CONADI (Division of Culture and Education of the National Corporation for Indigenous Development), represented different tribes, presented in 1995 a proposal on Educación Intercultural Bilingüe in which they expressed their interest of preserving their native languages and cultures. Together with the recognition of Chilean indigenous groups by the government (Law 19.253 D of 5.10.1993) local universities where zones of high indigenous density existed had adhered to the initiative. In 1998-1999 a pilot project sponsored by the Ministry of Education, Division of Multicultural and Bilingual Education, made a national call to compile didactic material for 1st and 2nd grades on a competitive basis. This was the first initiative of this nature in the country conducive in solidifying the project.

All the reforms during the twentieth century were efforts addressed to improve education for all students. They were to establish high content and performance standards and redesign the various components of the educational system in a coordinated and coherent fashion to support and solidify students' learning and promote universal education in the country.

Examples of effective policies were reflected on the progressive literacy rate among Chileans 15 and older during the last century: from 50.0 percent in 1920, to 80.0 percent in 1952, to currently attaining 95.6 percent in 1998.

The enrollment of students in elementary education increased from 64.0 percent at the beginning of the 1960s, to 95.0 percent in the 1970s, and 98.3 percent in 1998. A mixed educational system, non-sectarian private and public, innovative in Latin America, provides parents with the option to send their children to the school of their choice, while funding is available to subsidize private schools. A national flexible free market economy has permitted Chile to allocate funds exclusively to subsidize private schools. In Chile, 93 percent of schools that serve children attending elementary and secondary education in the country are financed by the government. The central government uniformly distributes financial support paid per pupil attending school, being calculated per trimester in addition to the municipal budget assigned locally per institution.

In 1981, about 78 percent of Chilean students were registered in municipal schools as compared to 56 percent in 1996; and 15 percent of students in 1981 registered in private subsidized schools as compared to 35 percent in 1996. Private institutions have captured a stable rate (during the same periods) of approximately 10 percent of the total students nationally.

The drop out rate of 21 percent in elementary education during the 1970s was dramatically reduced to 1.5 percent in 1998 and to 5 percent in secondary education the same year.

Average schooling among Chileans in 1992 was 7.2 years, increasing to 9.9 in 1998. The average among men was 9.6 years, and was 10.6 among women. In 1998, the Ministry of Education allocated 82.7 percent of its financial resources to preschools, elementary and secondary educational systems, 16.1 percent to higher education, and 1.2 percent to cultural programs. Since 1992, The Education Quality and Equity Improvement Program of the National Ministry of Education has advocated to systematically focus on the quality of education in the country.

This project has been financed with the support of the World Bank loans.

General Characteristics of the Chilean Public Education: The school calendar starts in March and ends in December. In Chile, students in elementary and secondary schools wear uniforms showing a badge that identifies the institution. The national public transportation provides reduced fares to students attending elementary, secondary, and higher education, who are properly identified with cards granted by their institutions, who need transportation at the local level. The grading system has a 1 to 7 scale, 1 being the lowest, requiring 4.0 as minimum passing grade. Repetition of grade has been the practice in the country when minimum levels of competence have not been attained by students in order to ensure assimilation of curricular content. The repetition rate in 1993 was 8 percent at municipal schools, 6 percent at subsidized schools, and 2 percent at private schools in elementary education.

The distribution of educational institutions as of 1998 was: 59.6 percent municipal schools, 28.8 percent private subsidized schools, 10.9 percent private schools, and 0.7 percent to others. The maximum teacher-student ratio of 1:45 per class has been established by the Ministry of Education.

PREPRIMARY & PRIMARY EDUCATION

Preschool Education: The *Educación Parvularia* (preschool) was developed and organized by German teachers according to their traditional model in 1911, and was known as kindergarten. However, the first program offered in the country for preschool teachers was in 1905 graduating the following year the first *kindergaterianas*. Later on, the Decree no. 4.156 of 1928 incorporated preschools into elementary education, as optional schooling. During this period, Chilean preschool was deeply influenced by the Montessori method. Unfortunately, due to political turnouts, this innovation was implemented for a short period of time.

In 1945 the *Escuela de Educadora de Párvulos* was authorized and incorporated to the University of Chile's educational programs.

Three years later, in 1948, the notion of kindergarten was readopted and authorized, nevertheless, it still remained optionally added to the elementary school curriculum. Though some were aware of the benefits this level could offer to students, economic and social conditions did not support this type of schooling as a need. Extended family (elders and siblings) had traditionally preserved culture, and had been in charge of taking care of minors as parents were away for work. At the time, additionally, women had not massively participated in the labor force, and there was reticence from the part of mothers to separate their children at early ages from home. The aim at creating habits of independence and readiness for curricular elementary education has been more fully understood by the population in contemporary times, yet preschool is not part of the national compulsory education.

The objective of preschools in Chile concentrates on cognitive, language, psychomotor and affective development pertinent to educate well balanced citizens.

Educación parvularia or *educación preíescolar* assists pupils from 84-days-old up to 5-years-old. This type of education is supervised by *Junta Nacional de Jardines Infantiles* (National Council of Child Care Centers), an organization of the Ministry of Education, and the *Fundación Nacional para el Desarrollo Integral del Menor* referred to as INTEGRA (National Foundation for the Integral Child Development), an organization depending from the Ministry of Interior. It has been observed that as women integrate into the national labor force and the composition of the family changes, preschools have become a necessity. To 1990, about 20 percent of children up to 6-years-old attended preschool, eight years later the percentage raised to 30 percent (1998.)

Elementary Education: The first attempt for the creation of a national educational system in Chile took place in 1813, when the Junta de Gobierno decreed the creation of *escuelas de primeras letras* (schools of first letters) in cities and towns having a population of 50 or more individuals. These schools had to be administered by the correspondent local municipalities and the education had to be offered free of charge. This initiative turned the country into the education pioneer in the Latin American context. Nevertheless, this resolution was only partially carried out due to the lack of infrastructure, government supervision, and political instability in the country. At the time, most free education was in the hands of the Catholic church. Conflicts with the church dealing with the freedom of teaching prolonged for decades, getting intensified during 1870s. In 1882, Monsignor Celestino del Frate was sent by the Vatican on special assignment to solve the conflict, but agreement between the two parties was never fruitful, the Papal dignitary was declared persona non grata, and subsequently, expelled from the country by the Chilean government. This situation precipitated the approval of *Leyes Laicas* (lay laws) between 1883-1984 and the expansion of non-sectarian schools.

Elementary education began expanding vigorously to rural zones during the first decade of the twentiethth century (1906) gaining solidification in 1920 when the *Ley de Instrucción Primaria Obligatoria* (compulsory

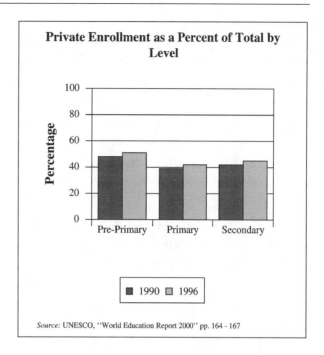

Private Enrollment as a Percent of Total by Level

Source: UNESCO, "World Education Report 2000" pp. 164 - 167

primary instruction law) was promulgated, put in effect, and enforced.

Historical Framework: During the decades of 1920 and 1930 varied innovations were carried out in public education in the country. Collaborative projects with foreign education experts and political leaders introduced significant new pedagogical models and methodologies to public education.

The Supreme Decree of December 1927 introduced revolutionary changes in the national educational school system's exemplary for the other nations in Latin America. Educators opened themselves up to new psycho-pedagogical models recognizing the integral development of children as a function proper and inherent to the Ministry of Public Education.

Highly influenced by Decroly, Montessori, and Parkhurst, the passive lecture school was transformed into an active laboratory where children could freely express their innate interests. This movement known as *la escuela nueva* (new school), was characterized by the how focusing on the methodological processes and comprehension rather than on the how much or memorization of facts. Whole language was introduced in the language arts as parallel to phonics.

Though educational change was greatly influenced by Europeans, the purpose was to integrate new theories in a framework that recognized characteristics that were unique to the Chilean fabric by incorporating German postulates known as *Heimatkunde*. To implement this principle, schools were divided into rural (coeducational), urban, farm, and boarding schools (having a family regime created for orphan students and pupils who lived at a distance inappropriate to attend school daily.)

Though emphasis was centered on elementary education based on the promulgation of Primary Education General Regulations, secondary schools and adult education benefited and dramatically improved.

Provincial Education Councils oversaw the participation of land owners who agreed to donate land to create schools in the regions, while industrial zones' participation was requested to implement adult and regular public education. In both cases when mandates were violated the government fined the responsible party.

In 1928, two new educational systems were adopted in the country: *escuelas experimentales* (experimental schools) and *escuelas modelo* (model schools). Innovative experimental schools were instituted in Chile in 1928, the second country in the world where they were adopted, after Italy where they were created in 1923.

Two types of experimental schools were incorporated: the limited schools where a foreign specific plan or program had to be tested in a Chilean context; and broad schools where a variety of methods had to be tested previous to their adoption. Model schools, on the other hand, had to adopt methods and plans that were already tested by experimental schools. Rural schools were envisioned as temporary, which objective was to be turned into regular schools after certain standards were achieved.

The coeducational system was introduced partially for preschoolers, first and second graders, and rural schools.

Binet, Simon, and Dearburn Psychological tests were incorporated into schools to offer schooling appropriate to the pupils' needs. Unfortunately, and due to political conflict, the ideal school system that had begun to be implemented so successfully was abruptly ended by Ibañez's government, 1929-1930, declaring teachers revolutionaries. Chilean education suffered deterioration, offering minimum opportunities to students by reinstating archaic systems. Nevertheless, extensive systematic documentation on the adoption and assessment of these innovative programs was collected that not only became historical documentation, but educational material for the coming generations.

The creation of the *Junta Nacional de Auxilio Escolar y Becas* (national council for school aid and scholarships) in 1953, started programs in public schools that were two folded: to indirectly contribute to poor family income and to motivate students to remain in school and reduce dropout rate.

A more populist movement began during the decade of 1960, governments that concentrated on educating agrarian workers. The reform was influenced by the Christian Democrat party guided by a religious doctrine that reconciled church and state as participant forces with a common objective—education for the poor. Though elementary education continued having adequate support, the objective was to expand what had been accomplished searching for an articulation of elementary and secondary levels. The idea of experimental schools was retaken, nevertheless, it was applied to secondary education, that had remained traditional for almost a century requiring modernization to expand serving the national population.

The influence of Paolo Freire's teaching methodology contributed to the emphasis given to adult education during the presidencies of E. Frei, (1964-1970) and particularly S. Allende (1970-1973). Previous to this time, adult education had had no notable advancement for half a century.

The Pinochet era, in terms of education, is known for its reduction of educational funds from the national budget and its increase to defense. The development of subsidized non-sectarian schools imposed a new conception of schooling, which at the same time contributed to reduce the government expenditures opening to school privatization. The reduction of educational expenditures was systematic between the years 1975 and 1990. It was a phenomenon opposed to what was happening in democratic countries where priority to education predominated. The financial framework contributed to the deterioration of education in Chile.

Since 1988, the *Sistema de Medición de la Calidad de la Educación* or SIMCE, (Education Quality Measurement System) has been applied to all elementary schools in the country. Tests are given to fourth and eighth graders alternatively every other year to assess academic performance of students in the areas of Spanish and mathematics. It has been argued that variables such as family income, geographical residence, and the system to which students attend (private versus public schools) have an impact on the results. Due to these circumstances, and based on scores revealed by the instrument, the Ministry of Education has developed a number of projects to cover the needs of the populations who traditionally score low.

Since 1990, a special program known as P-900 offers extra infrastructure and economic support to 900 schools that show the lowest scores at the national level, has been implemented. Simultaneously, *Talleres de Aprendizaje* or TAPs (learning workshops), have been developed to offer remedial education to at-risk students at the elementary education level. These workshops meet twice a week beyond the regular school schedule, and are monitored by high school graduates trained for the purpose.

Additionally, Rural Programs in the *Escuelas Multigrado Incompletas* (multigrade incomplete schools) that house children of varied ages at different school levels, offer from preschool to secondary education according to the zone demand, have been created.

Special Education: Special education schools were created by European expert educators who were hired by the public education ministry to incorporate the most advanced techniques for the different needs during the decade of 1920. The school for the deaf located in Santiago, for example, was developed by Belgians whose global method of demutation was the most advanced in the world; at the time, Chile became the first foreign country to adopt the method.

Special education was an active part of the Compulsory Primary Instruction Law and the 1928 educational reform that incorporated new methodological practices. Besides, the deaf schools, schools for the blind, and for the mental deficient were expanded. Psychology clinics articulated their functions with the new pedagogy, training teachers to understand and apply psychological testing that was newly adopted (Meyers, Gooddeaugh, and Binet-Simon.)

Special education offers study programs to students between 2- and 24-years-old, at three levels: preschool, elementary, and vocational. The curricula of studies are directly approved by the Ministry of Education.

Two modalities of special education are offered in Chile: Educación Especial in special schools and Differential Groups to students who attend traditional schools. The former is imparted by highly specialized professionals in schools offering programs designed for particular purposes attending the needs of children who suffer from: mental deficiencies, visual, hearing or language deficit, motor skills and relation, and communication impediments as diagnosed by professionals through certified organisms. The latter is offered as parallel programs in regular schools assisted by psycho-pedagogues to students who have learning deficiencies related to reading and writing affecting literacy and/or numeracy. Normal intelligence should be demonstrated through testing in order to be included in this category.

Private Education: Two types of private schools offer education in Chile. Non-sectarian schools, which demonstrate special interests such as bi-national schools where the primary language of instruction is not Spanish are offered. These schools were originally created in Chile to keep tradition and language alive among immigrants. Later on, these schools became popular among students whose interest is to fluently learn another language and culture. The main method of instruction is bilingual education where total immersion is applied. A second type of private education is imparted by religious schools run

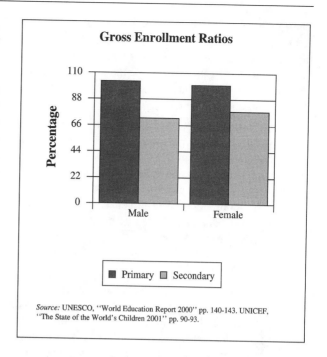

Gross Enrollment Ratios

Source: UNESCO, "World Education Report 2000" pp. 140-143. UNICEF, "The State of the World's Children 2001" pp. 90-93.

by religious congregations. A percentage of these schools also offer international education and bilingual instruction. Private religious schools are viewed by people as rigid systems, where respect and classic traditional education is maintained.

Reforms have not negatively affected private enrollment, to the contrary, during the last fifty years private education has raised its relatively high stable enrollments. The current percentage of Chilean children aged 4 to 18 registered in private education is of 10 percent.

Secondary Education: Chilean history recognizes Seminario de Santiago as the first secondary institution funded in 1608 in the territory. However, this religious institution graduated priests exclusively.

The first secondary school not having the sole purpose of graduating priests was the Convictorio de San Francisco Javier, a religious Jesuit institution intended for the upper class of Spanish lineage during the early colonial period. This school was closed when the Jesuit order was expelled by the Spanish king from his territories in 1767. While colonial education was scarce, the kingdom authorized a second secondary institution during the same year, the Convictorio Carolino, recognizing the need for educating Spaniards who lived out of the Iberian Peninsula. All these institutions were boarding schools. Other secondary schools were created during the last two decades of the century and early 1800s, though all of them were regented by the clergy.

The first secondary public institution was created by the Junta de Gobierno of 1813, August 10, in Santiago.

The initiative unified four previously private secondary schools, Convictorio Carolino, Academia de San Luis, the Seminar, and the division of education of the Real Universidad de San Felipe to create the Instituto Nacional. The newly created institution turned into the most prestigious national secondary school for males.

The creation of secondary education in the country was originally aimed at attending universities. Based on the rigid encyclopedist model, secondary education was predominantly authoritarian offering a rigid curriculum reflecting the European models, particularly the French one. Reflecting this European influence, secondary education has been referred to as *liceo* (lyceum) in the country. The first private secondary school for girls was created in 1823, and the first public institution in 1891 in the city of Valparaíso.

The new century brought national political radical *movimientos gremiales* (labor unions), urbanization, and industrialization leading towards democratization and influencing the adoption and modification of new pedagogical theories predominant in Europe. These conditions offered the ideal framework to create experimental secondary schools where theoretical models could be applied and tested, and at the same time, to serve as professional development for pre-service teachers. Experimental schools were administered by pedagogical institutes that were well known at the time as professional innovators.

The year when the Ministry of Education was created, 1927, the government transferred the administration of secondary education from the university to the officially recently created Ministry. During this period, for the first time the concept of technical-professional education was incorporated in a modality proposed as liceo integral in 1928, where humanistic tradition was viewed as different from the productive reality of the country in a first effort to implement it.

The last two years of general Carlos Ibáñez del Campo reign in power (1930-31) were particularly repressive against unionized educators who had played a preponderant role in the national pedagogical advancement. Schools were closed, the systems partially abolished, and teachers incarcerated—accused of provoking civil disobedience.

In 1940, the *escuelas consolidadas* were specifically developed in rural areas or urban poor neighborhoods to attend the needs of a growing population to continue their education. The post war movement influenced Chilean education creating technical-professional training as an alternative to the traditionally humanistic secondary education that to the time predominated as a model. Unfortunately, the nitrite crisis impacted greatly Chilean economy, obligating the government to reduce public expenditures.

New economical stability in the country during the 1960s permitted the government to expand education to certain sectors. The population growth demanded a system that required new facilities, hence the instauration of *escuelas completas* provided the possibility to continue education for 12 or 13 years at the same public institution.

Upgrading elementary education to 8 years required restructuring the secondary educational system. As secondary education was reduced to four years, it was strictly necessary to reallocate funds to optimize its infrastructure.

Preparatory Secondary Education: Secondary education remains characterized by a tracking system based on abilities and goals that prepare students to continue studies in higher education. Core classes are offered as common plan for the first two years; while the last two years emphasize either scientific or humanistic content to better prepare students for higher education within the disciplines they have chosen.

The Academic Aptitude Test is a standardized exam offered nationally and simultaneously to all students during the last semester of the twelfth grade. The Prueba de Aptitud Académica (PAA) was administered for the first time in 1970. This is the culmination of secondary education requirements.

Private school students obtain better scores than public school attendees. This fact has been observed as discriminatory from the part of some sectors conducive to fill vacancies to register in higher education institutions reserved for the best students. On the other hand, those who support this process of selection claim that due to the limited resources of the country, authorities cannot afford to open universities for everyone, hence, higher education institutions have to search for predictors reliable to ensure graduating students who respond to more rigorous curricular demands than those expected in secondary education.

The process of pre-selecting students to attend higher education begins with the publication of *Listas de Selección* (score lists), which are of public domain. The PAA's scores (verbal, math, and specific knowledge in the areas of history and geography of Chile, biology, social sciences, physics, mathematics, and chemistry) are currently published by the newspaper *La Nación*, the third Sunday of January every year.

Higher education institutions have the right to preestablish a cap, which limits the number of students admitted to a competitive selection. Grades, and/or additional tests of pre-selection including, in some cases personal characteristics established as compatible with the profession, are additional requirements to apply to some professions.

In 1970, about 49.0 percent of Chilean adolescents attended secondary schools as compared to 75.0 percent in 1989, and 81.8 in 1998. As of 1998, the retention rate was 87.1 percent, the repetition rate 7.9 percent, and the dropout rate was 5.0 percent. By 1995, about 58 percent of secondary students attended the scientific-humanistic modality in the country.

Secondary Technical-Professional Schools: The first secondary technical institution recognized in the territory was the Academia de San Luis, founded in 1797. This modality though scarce, as most institutions during the colonial times, was also regented by religious organizations.

Between 1939 and 1941, there was strong support from the part of the government as well as from the part of Chileans en general to promote and establish *Educación Técnico-Profesional*, an educational modality directed at inserting secondary graduates into the labor force having specific skills received systematically though a well articulated curriculum, activities and assessment. People perceived this modality, from the beginning, as practical, particularly by those sectors where apprenticeship had been a tradition, and who had not contemplated higher education. This new education was accepted as a way of stepping up in socioeconomic terms.

Focusing on different specific purposes, the most common types were commercial schools, industrial, agricultural, and vocational for girls.

This modality, that had gained many adepts until Allende's government, attained 36 percent of secondary students in the country. Matriculation in secondary technical-professional schools was dramatically reduced to 19 percent as a result of the policies applied by the military educational reform directly affecting popular classes. The educational reform of 1980, changed their traditional names to *Liceos técnico-profesional*. During the period, more than 50 percent of these schools were transferred to private companies for their administration to reduce government's expenditures in education in addition to their municipalization. Privatization was adjudicated by means of contracts regulated by the Ministry of Education.

As a result of allocating extra funds from the part of the democratic government, matriculation in secondary technical-professional recovered to 35 percent in 1990 to reach 42 percent in 1995. The repetition and dropout rates in this modality have been higher than in scientific-humanistic schools during the 1990s, reaching an average of 12 and 7.5 percent. In 1999, industrial and commercial schools have been the most frequented by students, 43 and 36 percent, respectively.

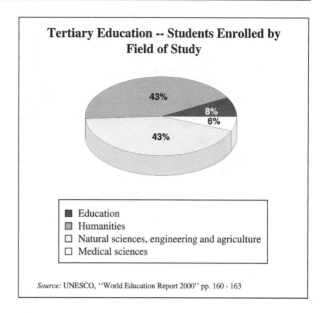

Tertiary Education -- Students Enrolled by Field of Study

43%
8%
6%
43%

■ Education
■ Humanities
□ Natural sciences, engineering and agriculture
□ Medical sciences

Source: UNESCO, "World Education Report 2000" pp. 160 - 163

Adult Elementary & Secondary Education: The reform of 1928 incorporated evening and night schools for adults. They were organized in two categories: *de alfabetización* (for literacy) and *escuelas complementarias* (complementary schools) designed for adults of both sexes to give them the opportunity to begin or continue their studies while working. The main innovation introduced by this reform was turning the school into a center that bridged students and the labor market. This objective included looking for contracts that satisfied students' interests while matching their training.

From 1965, the Christian Democrat government centered its interest on agrarian reforms. The government created centers to organize peasantry to receive land that was confiscated from owners who did not work it. As an extension, the government adopted the responsibility to educate new farm workers to become autonomous. Organizations such as *Corporación de la Reforma Agraria,* (Corporation for the Agrarian Reform), *Instituto Nacional de Capacitación* (Training National Institute), *Consejo Nacional de Promoción Popular* (National Popular Promotion Council), and *Servicio de Cooperación Técnica* (Service for Technical Cooperation) among many others promoted cooperativism, peers support and mainly education, from literacy courses to technical agrarian training.

Some sectors adopted for adult literacy education in the country a new method developed by Brazilian educator Paolo Freire that focused on social participation known as education for liberation. The Church adhered to the cause, though separated from the political forces that involved ideology, contributed to educating disenfranchised classes. These innovations were implemented during the complete Christian Democratic presidential period (6 years.) Legislation on adult education systematized, articulated (between elementary and secondary adult education) and organized schools into *educación vespertina* (evening education) and *nocturna* (night school) utilizing public infra structure destined originally for elementary and secondary children education. For the first time, public buildings were used to their maximum capacity.

To the year 2000, public Adult Education serves persons of all ages from 15 years and over free of charge at a national level. These students obtain the same benefit school children have regarding reduce fares on public transportation to facilitate attending schools. In addition, the *Centros de Educación Integrada de Adultos* or CEIA (Adult Integrated Education Centers) offer classes to stop-outs, of the ages established by the law, also during the day.

The first Chilean University was founded August 19, 1622. Governed by Dominican priests, the Santo Tom s de Aquino University's curriculum was mainly directed, as most universities at the time, at theological studies conducive to clergy and sacerdotal professions, including the arts, at the levels of baccalaureate, master, and doctoral degrees. The curriculum was organized as trivium or cuadrivium, according to the conservative scholastic tradition. The former incorporated grammar, logic and rhetoric, while the latter included geometry, music, mathematics, and astronomy.

After a century, and due to political circumstances, Phillip V, king of Spain, authorized on July 28, 1738, a teaching and cloister university, named in his honor Real Universidad de San Felipe. As compared to the first higher education institution, the new one expanded its studies to law, medicine, and mathematics, as its counterparts located in other viceroyalties in the Americas (Peru and Mexico) and Salamanca, Spain.

The foundation of the Universidad de Chile took place in 1842. This institution partially incorporated the disciplines offered by the Universidad de San Felipe when by law the nobility titles were banned in the republic, adding disciplines that had developed to supply contemporary academic needs. This university has been historically considered a blending between the academic European tradition and the national Chilean character. The Universidad de Chile developed campuses at different national geographical locations, making it until 1988 the largest national university in the country.

The Pontificia Universidad Católica de Chile, the first private institution, was founded in 1888, governed by the Catholic Church. As well as its public counterpart, it expanded to other locations beyond the capital city where it was originally established.

The second public higher education institution was created in 1952, Universidad Técnica del Estado (UTE), offering a shorter curriculum on technical professions as compared to other universities to supply the country's needs for specialized highly trained technicians.

The Christian Democrat government of 1965 reformed the most traditional system to survive the strictness of the previous century in the country: university education. For the first time in the history of Chilean education, students and academicians could participate in the process of decision-making within the higher education system. This reform was known as the democratization movement.

Until 1980, there were eight universities in the country that had multiple campuses in different geographical areas of the national territory. Two were public, Universidad de Chile and Universidad Técnica del Estado, while all others were private. The authoritarian reform of 1981 stratified and segmented the Chilean university system. Regional branches of the two public institutions became separated independent universities (17); additionally, the government authorized the creation of private new universities (42 during the first year). The original higher education institution central offices conserved their names, with the exception of the Universidad Técnica del Estado that changed its name to Universidad de Santiago, and are currently known as traditional universities. Chilean higher education gained prestige in the Latin American context, the University of Chile and Pontificia Universidad Católica de Chile currently offer international programs in areas as varied as engineering, medicine, commerce, and education.

In 1999, there were 66 universities in Chile, and 200 other higher education institutions had been authorized. Nevertheless, during the 1990s the Ministry of Education did not accredit the 5 universities and 6 professional institutes.

Chilean Higher Education is defined as postsecondary education and is offered at three types of institutions: Universities, Professional Institutes, and Centers for Technical Formation. Traditional universities created before 1981 are subsidized by the government while those private institutions created after the reform are financed by tuitions and fees, including Professional Institutes and Centers for Technical Formation.

Alternative Higher Education: *Establecimientos de Educación Superior de las Fuerzas Armadas y de Orden* (Armed Forces Educational Institutions) grant technical and academic degrees adequate to their specific military functions that are equivalent to those similarly granted by regular higher education institutions offered to civilians. *Institutos militares* are educational institutions offering alternative higher education restricted exclusively to Chilean citizens. In Chile, even though these institutions are not affiliated to universities, but to the Ministry of Defense, they fall under the category of educational institutions granting postsecondary degrees. Therefore, they are also governed by the *Ley Orgánica Constitucional de Enseñanza* (Constitutional Educational Organic Law) of 1980 that establishes institutional autonomy, academic freedom, and political independence for higher education institutions.

Administration: Higher education is overseen by the *Consejo Superior de Educación* (Higher Education Council): an autonomous body where all areas of higher education are represented. The main functions of this council are to supervise the official accreditation of higher education institutions as established by the law, to accept or reject curricular programs proposed by the Ministry of Education, and to decide on appealing cases by elementary and secondary schools on study programs rejected by the Ministry of Education. This council is presided by the Minister of Education; three members represent the three types of higher education institutions; three members of the national scientific community are nominated by the two other national councils; one judge from the Supreme Court; and one representative of the Armed Forces Commanders. Additionally, a technical secretary is elected by the members of the council. The Rectors' Council, on the other hand, oversees the traditional eight universities and those created from their regional branches.

Budget & Finance: Historically, higher education had received stable financial government support, that had been increased according to its needs. Nevertheless, between 1970 and 1989 this budget was reduced dramatically to almost half of its original total of 30 percent assigned from a fiscal national budget to 17 percent. By privatizing institutions, the reform liberated the government from assigning financial support to practically half of these institutions. Since the political system returned to be a constitutional system, the three democratic elected governments put emphasis on increasing the fiscal budget to restore the quality of higher education. Currently, the government resources are assigned in two forms, direct and indirectly. Both are granted to traditional universities, in addition to the Institutional Development Fund, University Credit, fee scholarships, and the National Commission on Technological and Scientific Research (*Comisión Nacional de Investigación Científica y Tecnológica* or CONICYT). Private universities on the other hand, are limited to apply for the indirect government budget and CONICYT's. Finally, the Centros de Formación Técnica (Centers for Technical Formation) and the Institutos Profesionales (Professional Institutes) can only apply for the Indirect government budget. Of the total national budget for education, 18.1 percent is allocated to higher education.

Admission Process: Until 1966, all traditional eight universities selected their students based on a set of tests known as *bachillerato*. Examination commissions assigned by the Ministry of Education visited the places where students had to be tested on areas chosen by the candidates consisting of written and oral tests in humanities and sciences.

The Prueba de Aptitud Académica verbal (Spanish), mathematics, and Chilean history and geography are administered once a year. This is a standardized test required by all universities and institutions of higher education in the country. Minimum scores are set, nevertheless, other standards apply in addition to this score. Grades from secondary education, Specific Standardized tests in one or more of five disciplines offered: biology, chemistry, physics, social sciences, and math, and in some cases, internal testing (psychology tests, spatial orientation, vision and auditory, etc.) after pre-admittance to some professions and careers are also required so as to complete the application process. The process is highly competitive, as well as the retention rate based on performance of higher order skills. Traditionally, during the last century, it has been observed that two are perceived as the most prestigious universities in the country capturing students whose academic performance has been exceptional: the Universidad de Chile and the Pontificia Universidad Católica de Chile.

The length of professional studies vary according to specific curricula between 5 and 7 years. A new proposal presented to higher education in Chile suggests the incorporation of core curriculum for all university careers, increasing an additional academic year of education is currently in the process of analysis.

Cátedras (classes offered at the higher education level) are taught by *catedráticos,* (faculties/professor) also known as *docentes* (faculties), individuals whose professional preparation, advanced degree and experience, qualify them to teach classes at a higher education institution. Twelve percent of faculties hold doctoral degrees at universities in the country, which is proportional to the pyramidal educational stratification of the nation.

In addition to the core curriculum, and after approving all courses, the *memoria de titulación* (thesis) and a *práctica profesional* (practicum or supervised internship) are the last requirements for graduation for all careers, undergraduate as well as graduate degrees. The memoria is a scholarly research work relevant to the curricular specialty, within a higher educational institution, students have to write during their last year of studies. Students carry out the *práctica profesional* as an activity with the purpose of demonstrating articulation between relevant curricular aspects in their major and the incorporation of theory to concrete situations. These two activities vary in length from a semester to a year as established by the institutions.

Licenciaturas, magisters, and doctoral degrees are offered in the country, nevertheless, they are limited to some professions and careers, and they are limited to a reduced number of participants. Higher degrees (particularly doctorates) are limited to professionals who have demonstrated solid advancement in their careers, leadership, and commitment. These degrees are well known for their curricular demand. Magister and doctoral degrees are considered postígrado and demand to hold a baccalaureate degree; nevertheless other alternatives are offered to higher education graduates such as: postítulos, especializaciones, and actualizaciones that consist of official studies directly related to the degree held shorter in time as compared to postígrados.

In 1989, about 10.0 percent of the population between 18 and 24 years old enrolled in higher education. In 1998, from the total students enrolled in higher education, 71.2 percent attended universities, 15.3 percent attended Professional Institutes, while 13.5 percent attended Centers for Technical Formation. The higher education graduation rate in the country is of 9.1 percent, one of the lowest in Latin America.

Nominal fees according to family income are charged to students nationally. However, scholarships have increased during the democratic governments, for instance, scholarships have been offered to sons/daughters of teachers who are accepted into the teaching profession and who have demonstrated high academic performance. Low interest loans, on the other hand, have contributed to support students of low income families to attend higher education.

Educational Research: Research was very limited in Chile until 1960, when a number of programs of international cooperation were implemented. During the period previous to the military regime, research had increased in the country. The political military coupe episode of 1973 and subsequent dictatorship provoked a recess in this activity, international cooperation from all countries were discontinued, and the limited funds allocated by the government for the purpose were suspended.

As higher education was declared a "privileged situation" by the military regime, the system was intervened by the government provoking the rupture of the articulatory process of education. In the scientific areas, the phenomenon of brain drain, or exodus of scientists to foreign countries was accentuated due to the lack of resources.

On the other hand, social scientists who were viewed as leftists, were prosecuted ending up on exile.

Due to repressive practices such as rectors assigned by the government, military personnel (who hadn't experienced university systems) were perceived as vigilant to the systems while researchers were perceived by non-academician military representatives as suspiciously attempting for freedom of expression. Private organizations, some under the umbrella of private higher education institutions, were able to continue conducting research particularly in the humanities and social sciences during the dictatorship. Additionally, the church and international organizations supported research dealing with controversial aspects the government did not approve sometimes acting underground.

To the year 2000, the National Commission on Technological and Scientific Research (CONICYT) administers the National Scientific and Technological Development Fund (FONDECYT) and the National Science and Technology Promotion Fund (*Fondo Nacional de Fomento de Ciencia y Tecnología* or FONDEF) that finance research projects on a competitive basis. Since the constitutional state was restored in the country, international cooperation has increasingly funded research at the national and international levels.

NONFORMAL EDUCATION

Nongovernmental organizations (ONGs) are nonprofit organizations of a wide range of categories. In general terms they are services, that cover populations that are not reached by government traditional organizations. They concentrate on development, and social activism contributing to improve life quality transforming passive sectors into responsible self-supportive subjects. In Chile, most ONGs focus on poverty and disenfranchised groups. These organizations are mostly financed by private sectors, donations and volunteerism. Community projects and workshops, are directed to homemakers, young mothers, country leaders, and in general to individuals who are marginal to institutions. Religious organizations, on the other hand, have also offered informal education.

TEACHING PROFESSION

Previous to the foundation of the *magisterio* (educationist circle) education for the non-privileged was scarce and was the clergy domain, private schools and upper class count with individuals who were highly educated, mostly in European countries who served as tutors.

In 1842, the *Escuela Normal de Preceptores* (Normal Teacher School) became the first institution intended for elementary school male teachers. Normal schools at the time began as secondary education when students apart from receiving traditional education corresponding to the level, a curricular parallel pedagogical program was incorporated for five years. Those individuals who held regular secondary school diplomas could attend normal schools for two additional years to obtain the adequate training to become teachers.

The first counterpart for females, *Escuela Normal de Preceptoras,* was founded in 1854, replicating the standard model for normal schools already established. The foundation of the *Instituto Pedagógico* (Pedagogical Institute) for secondary educators in 1889 in Santiago was the corner stone for the professionalization of teachers. The institute was incorporated as part of the University of Chile known as Facultad the Filosofía, acquiring the status other professions received.

The Compulsory Primary Instruction Law of 1920 simultaneously incorporated development courses for teachers required to implement innovative pedagogical practices. To 1927, the Ministry of Education offered educational teacher exchange programs to Europe, mainly to Germany, Switzerland, Belgium, and the United States to study the most advanced teaching techniques. The educational progressive movement that incorporated into school pedagogy influenced by Dalton, Montessori, and others led by Chilean teachers became a model and the object of study for other nations that later on adopted these methodologies in Latin America.

Normal schools and tertiary teacher education institutions coexisted for decades. In fact, normal schools were supervised by universities. Since the beginning of the twentieth century, common interests between normal schools preparing elementary school teachers and universities were evident. For example, since 1929, the maximum authority of elementary education, the primary education general director was member of the national University Council.

Beginning in 1928, elementary teachers who worked for a year in public schools and satisfactorily passed an exam offered by a committee assigned by universities were granted a university diploma accrediting their profession. The teaching profession at the university level was not a mere transfer of normal programs, a modality adopted by many countries in Latin America, once students graduated from secondary schools, they continued higher education studies that added years of innovative theory pedagogical models and further foundations to the field.

The professionalization of elementary and secondary teachers was developed early nationally as compared to other countries in the region where until recently normal schools graduate students.

Normal schools were eradicated as educational institutions in 1988 by the military regime. Those who wanted to become teachers had to attend universities that were transformed into the only organisms authorized to graduate such professionals. Due to privatization, other institutions grant teaching degrees, however, on a limited basis. To 1999, some 29 institutions were accredited nationwide (18 universities & 11 professional institutes) in teacher education offering programs that vary between 9 and 10 semesters.

Due to the fact that historically salaries have jeopardized the teaching profession, objectives of the democratic governments and the Ministry of Education in order to overcome the issue have included: developing projects that provide promotions, modifying salaries on a fixed scale nationwide offering incentives for the most rural areas, where school professionals resist to go, and allocating financial resources for further professional development.

Teachers who work in elementary and secondary public schools are under the Statute of Education's Professionals (*Estatuto de los Profesionales de la Educación*) approved in July 1991. According to this law, those educators who work for municipal institutions have the character of public service professionals.

Degrees offered by the universities are licenciatura, magister, and doctor in education, directed mainly to administrative positions and the continuation of higher education to those who already hold the title in pedagogy. The professional title obtained in Chile is Profesor de Estado.

Professional educators are distributed as 85 percent working in subsidized institutions whereas 15 percent work in private schools. Chilean teachers are categorized according to their areas of specialization: preschool education 7 percent, special education 3 percent, elementary education 52 percent, and secondary education 39 percent.

In-service Resources: The Center for In-service Pedagogical Training, Experimentation and Investigation was created in 1967 (*Centro de Perfeccionamiento, Experimentación e Investigaciones Pedagógicas* or CPEIP) to provide permanent professional development and support, test programs, and develop curricular agendas. *Programas de Perfeccionamiento* (development programs) are offered by the Ministry of Education or university institutions non conducive to degrees to in-service educators. These programs are equivalent to continuing education, development or formal refresher classes having the objective to update studies within the profession or discipline. When these programs are not offered at the regional level, leaders are sent to the centers representing different zones holding the responsibility to disseminate the knowledge at their local levels.

The Microcentros de Programación Pedagógica were created to provide in-service training to teachers who work in isolated areas of the country. Meeting once a month, teachers discuss school problematics related to curriculum decisions and receive technical support from techno-pedagogical supervisors from the Ministry of Education. These centers are autonomous and are organized cooperatively by their members according to their needs.

The Basic Rural Program, a sub-division of the P-900 program, has provided professional development to those teachers who are marginal from urban centers due to geographical distances. Special emphasis has been given to benefit teachers who work at multi-grade incomplete schools with a maximum of three teachers. Particular attention has been put into content areas, functionality of performance, and technology education coping with the demands of contemporary society.

One of the four components incorporated by the government into the reform of 1996 includes the *fortalecimiento de la profesión docente* (strengthening the teaching profession) directed to in-service teachers' development. This initiative includes: curricular up-dating; financial support for prospective teachers; pasantías, and *diplomados* (scholarships) to study abroad (pasantías include short exposure to professional experiences, while diplomados combine theoretical and practical studies conducive to a specialization); professional individual excellence awards; and institutional excellence awards. Additionally, the Centro de Recursos Educativos is a Web site created for teachers organized to offer curricular support.

Professional Organizations: The first educators' labor union, *Asociación de Educación Nacional*, was founded in 1904 joining all individuals who had interest in teaching which focus of attention was intellectual development.

The *Asociación General de Profesores de Chile* was created in 1923 after a strike that took place as a consequence of not receiving their salaries. This organization influenced the progressive *Reforma Integral de la Enseñanza* (Integral Teaching Reform) during the 1920s gaining power over educational decision makings for a decade.

Chilean teachers were well known through history as political left wing activists who represented a threat to some authoritarian governments. For this reason, labor unions were in particular historical instances suspended to be considered powerful leader organizations.

It was not until the 1950s when the *Asociación de Profesores de Estado* was organized by secondary educa-

tors graduated from the universities excluding those from normal schools.

The *Sindicato Unico de Trabajadores de la Educación* was created in 1970, grouping all sort of educators for the first time. Two years later, the organization was recognized by the state revoking a law that prohibited state workers to unionize. This union joined the Central Unica de Trabajadores, becoming one of the most powerful organizations in the history of the country. The Military junta suspended all association rights to be only recovered eighteen years later. To 2001, the *Colegio de Profesores de Chile Asociación Gremial* (Labor Union) is the official organization that negotiate teachers contracts and oversees professional conditions adequate to social demands for its members.

Technology in Public Education: Technology has expanded greatly during the last decade in the country, a concept that has successfully been introduced in public education. However, as resources are limited, so is technology. One of the most ambitious projects of the Ministry of Education has been the creation of the *Red Educaciónal Enlaces* (Links National Network) an interactive service to support students at the elementary and secondary levels. This consists of computers installed in public school facilities subscribed to the Internet that connects public schools emphasizing rural areas to reduce isolation. Fifty percent of elementary schools in the country and one hundred percent of secondary schools will participate in this project. This project is one of the components the Ministry has implemented known as *Programa de Mejoramiento de la Calidad y Equidad de la Educación* or MECE (Quality and Equity Education Improvement Program.)

The first distance courses offered in the country were designed for educators sponsored by universities. One of these examples is Teleduc. This service was created in 1977 by the Pontific Catholic University to develop and coordinate resources optimized by the Corporación de Televisión, channel 13, to be offered to their university and the community focusing on elementary and secondary education. The successful programs expanded rapidly, extending the service to other areas. Up to 1999, an average of 25,000 students per year register in their courses offering 32 percent in teaching development, 32 percent in general education, 10 percent in languages, 9 percent to educate women, and 17 percent in other areas. Lately, this service has expanded into international cooperation projects. Tele y Videoconferences are offered by a number of private institutions (governmental and nongovernmental) that benefit citizens at the national level.

SUMMARY

The history of education in Latin America has revealed a high degree of vulnerability associated to political turns, to which Chile has not escaped. Nevertheless, the relative stability of democratic governments in this country has permitted to approach the solidification of elementary universal education, that has led to the expansion of a well-structured vertical education among citizens.

National experiences, radical, superficial, and profound, have shaped up current democratic governments, guiding them to exercise moderate political decisions for the implementation of new educational programs and reforms leading toward a more egalitarian society that can provide opportunities for all to reach their full potential.

In the international context, Chile has proved to be a pioneer in education among peer nations demonstrating capability to optimize limited resources. Efforts of a different nature are still to be seen: to cope with contemporary rapidly changing technology education demands and globalization without losing its identity are two arduous educational challenges for this nation.

BIBLIOGRAPHY

Aedo, Cristian. ''Aporte Municipal en Educación.'' *Persona y Sociedad, Instituto Latinoamericano de Doctrina y Estudios Sociales (ILADES)* 11, 2, 1997.

Aedo, Cristian, y Jaime Vargas. ''Economía de la Educación, un Futuro Plagado de Desafíos.'' Persona y Sociedad, Instituto Latinoamericano de Doctrina y Estudios Sociales (ILADES) 11, 2, 1997.

Aldunate, Carlos, et al. *Nueva Historia de Chile Desde los Orígenes Hasta Nuestros Días.* Santiago de Chile: Instituto de Historia de la Pontificia Universidad Católica de Chile, 1996.

Alvarez, Francisco, and Giaconi, Enriqueta. *El Primer Día de Clases en Primer Año.* Básico: Análisis del Ingreso de los Niños y Niñas a la Escuela. Santiago, CIDE, 07.272-00, 1994. Available from http://www.reduc.cl/.

———. *Tendencias, Criterios, y Orientaciones en la Formación de Maestros.* Santiago de Chile, CIDE, 08.433-00, 1999. Available from http://www.reduc.cl/.

Beca, Carlos Eugenio. ''La Gestión de Políticas Educativas y las Políticas de Capacitación Docente.'' *Ponencias Congreso Nacional Red Latinoamericana de Información y Documentación en Educación: Investigación Educativa e Información.* Santiago de Chile, 16-17 October 2000. Available from http://www.reduc.cl/.

Bravo, David, Dante Contreras, and Claudia Sanhueza. ''Rendimiento Educacional, Desigualdad, y Brecha de Desempeño Privado/Pú: Chile 1982-1997.'' Documentos de Trabajo, Serie Investigaciones, No. 163, Santiago: Departamento de Economía, Universidad de Chile, 1999.

Brunner, José Joaquín. *La Educación Superior en Chile.* Caracas: Centro Regional Para la Educación Superior en America Latina y el Caribe, 1987.

Cañulef Martinez, Eliseo. *Introducción a la Educación Intercultural Bilingü en Chile.* Instituto de Estudios Indígenas, Universidad de la Frontera, 1998.

Cuadra, Ernesto, and Birger Fredriksen. *Scope of Efficiency Gains Resulting from Reduction in Repetition and Dropout.* Washington, Banco Mundial, 07.336-00, 1992. Available from http://www.reduc.cl/.

Diaz Román, William, ed. *Educación en Chile: Un Desafío de Calidad.* Santiago, Chile: Enersis, 1996.

Donoso, Sebastián, and Gustavo Hawes. ''El Sistema de Selección de Alumnos de las Universidades Chilenas: Discusión de sus Fundamentos, Resultados y Perspectivas.'' *Education Policy Analysis Archives,* 1 May 2000.

Gilbert, Gastón. ''Evaluación y Proyecciones en Educación Parvularia en los Sectores Subvencionados.'' *Segundo Simposio Nacional: Educación Parvularia en Chile: del Diagnóstico a la Acción.* Santiago, Junta Nacional de Jardines Infantiles, 1991.

Hanson, Mark. *La Descentralización Educacional: Problemas y Desafios.* Santiago, Preal, 08.141-00, 1997.

Instituto Antártico Chileno. *Áreas Protegidas en el TACH,* 2001. Available from http://www.inach.cl/.

Kellaghan, Thomas. *Seguimiento de los Resultados Educativos Nacionales.* Santiago, Preal, 08.241-00, 1997. Available from http://www.reduc.cl/.

Latorre, Carmen Luz. *El Financiamiento de la Educación en Chile: Evolución Histórica y Alternativas Futuras.* Santiago de Chile: PIIE, 1987.

Lemaitre, María José. ''Políticas de Mejoramiento de la Educación 1990-1997. Orientaciones Generales y Cambios en el Sistema.'' *Persona y Sociedad, Instituto Latinoamericano de Doctrina y Estudios Sociales (ILADES),* Vol xi, no. 2, 1997.

Mellafe, Rolando y otros. *Historia de la Universidad de Chile.* Santiago de Chile: Ediciones de la Universidad de Chile, 1992.

Ministerio de Educación de Chile. *Compendio de Información Estadística 1995.* Santiago: Ministerio de Educación. Available from http://www.mineduc.cl/.

———. *Compendio de Información Estadística 1998.* Santiago: Ministerio de Educación. Available from http://www.mineduc.cl/.

———. *Educación para Todos: Evaluación en el Año 2000.* Informe Nacional, Chile 1999. Available from http://www.unesco.cl/pdf/actyeven/EPT/chile.pdf.

Núñez, Iván. *Historia del Trabajo Docente y Formación de Profesores de Chile.* Santiago, Chile: Programa Interdisciplinario de Investigaciones en Educación, 1989.

Subercaseaux, Benjamín. *Chile o una Loca Geografia.* Santiago de Chile: Editorial Universitaria, 1973.

Universidad de Chile. *Síntesis Histórica de la Universidad de Chile*, 2001. Available from http://www.uchile.cl/historia/historia.html.

Vargas, Jaime. ''Mercado, Competencia y Equidad en la Educación Subvencionada.'' *Persona y Sociedad, Instituto Latinoamericano de Doctrina y Estudios Sociales (ILADES)* Vol. xi, no. 2, 1997.

—*Angela M. Arrey-Wastavino*

CHINA

BASIC DATA

Official Country Name:	People's Republic of China
Region:	East & South Asia
Population:	1,261,832,482
Language(s):	Chinese (Mandarin), Yue (Cantonese), Wu (Shanghaiese), Minbei (Fuzhou), Minnan (Hokkien-Taiwanese), Xiang, Gan, Hakka dialects
Literacy Rate:	81.5%
Academic Year:	September-June
Number of Primary Schools:	628,840
Compulsory Schooling:	9 years
Public Expenditure on Education:	2.3%
Libraries:	2,600
Educational Enrollment:	Primary: 139,954,000 Secondary: 71,883,000 Higher: 6,075,215
Educational Enrollment Rate:	Primary: 123% Secondary: 70% Higher: 6%
Teachers:	Primary: 5,794,000 Secondary: 4,437,000 Higher: 516,400
Student-Teacher Ratio:	Primary: 24:1 Secondary: 17:1
Female Enrollment Rate:	Primary: 123% Secondary: 66% Higher: 4%

HISTORY & BACKGROUND

By 2000 B.C., Chinese education had developed to the level of institutions specifically established for the purpose of learning. From 800 to 400 B.C. China had both *guoxue* (government schools) and *xiangxue* (local schools). Education in traditional China was dominated by the *keju* (civil service examination system), which began developing around 400 A.D. and reached its height during the Tang Dynasty (618-896). Essentially, the *keju* was a search program based on the Confucian notion of meritocracy. This civil service examination system remained almost the exclusive avenue to government positions for China's educated elite for more than 1,000 years.

Historically, formal education was a privilege of the rich. Mastering classical Chinese, which consisted of different written and spoken versions and lacked an alphabet, required time and resources most Chinese could not afford. As a result, for much of its history, China had an extremely high rate of illiteracy (80 percent). The result was a nation of mass illiteracy dominated by a bureaucratic elite highly educated in the Confucian classical tradition. The earliest modern government schools were created to provide education in subjects of Western strength such as the sciences, engineering, and military development to address Western incursion and to maintain the integrity of China's own culture and polity. The aim of these schools was to modernize technologically by imitating the West, while maintaining all traditional aspects of Chinese culture. These schools were never integrated into the civil service examination system.

In 1898, Emperor Guang Xu, supported by Kang Youwei and Liang Qichao, well-known reformers, issued a series of decrees to initiate sweeping reforms in Chinese education. The measures included the establishment of a system of modern schools accessible to a greater majority of the population, abolition of the rigid examination system for the selection of government officials, and the introduction of short and practical essay examinations.

Between 1901 and 1905, the Qing court issued a new series of education reform decrees. The old academies that had supported the civil service examinations were reorganized. A modern school system was built on their foundations with primary, secondary, and college levels reflective of Western models. Schools throughout China were organized into three major stages and seven levels. Elementary education was composed of kindergarten, lower elementary, and higher elementary; secondary education consisted of middle school; and higher education was divided into preparatory school, specialized college, and university. The Qing Court also instructed provincial, prefectural, and county governments to open new schools and start a compulsory education program. The civil examination system (*keju*) was officially abolished in 1905, marking the end of the trademark of traditional Chinese education.

Six years later, China's dynastic tradition also came to an end when the new Nationalist Republic replaced it. With this political metamorphosis, China's educational system experienced further transformations. The search for modern nationhood and economic prosperity created the first golden age of education in modern China. Education in China enjoyed a rare interval of uninterrupted growth as the Beijing government enthusiastically pursued educational development in both the public and private sectors as an essential component of the Nationalists' nation-building program. In 1912 and 1913 the Republican government issued *Regulations Concerning Public and Private Schools* and *Regulations Concerning Private Universities;* these documents laid out the criteria for private schools and stipulated proper application and registration procedures, while calling for financial investment in education nationwide.

The eruption of the Sino-Japanese War in 1937 and rapid Japanese conquest of coastal areas in the months immediately following changed the educational situation dramatically. As a result of military operations, 70 percent of Chinese cultural institutions were destroyed. By November 1, 1937, no less than 24 institutions of higher learning had been bombed or demolished by the Japanese. Seventy-seven of China's institutions of higher learning were either closed down or literally uprooted and moved many hundreds of miles into the interior. Not all the students could follow their respective universities. As a result, the retaining rate of their original student bodies for these institutions ranged from 25 to 75 percent. The subsequent civil war (1946-1949) between the Nationalists and the Communists continued to subject China to a state of political turmoil in which education suffered drastically as a result.

After the founding of the People's Republic of China (PRC), the new Communist government pursued the movement to "learn from the Soviet Union" with all the enthusiasm that had characterized the Western imitation process in earlier decades. The entire national educational system was first reorganized to conform to the Soviet model in 1952-53. American-style liberal arts colleges were abolished, with arts and science facilities separated from the larger universities to form the core of Soviet style *zonghexing* (comprehensive) universities; about 12 of these were formed, in more or less even distribution around the country. The remaining disciplines of the old universities were reorganized into separate technical colleges or merged with existing specialized institutes. Also following the Soviet example, nationally unified teaching plans, syllabi, materials, and textbooks were introduced for every academic specialty or major.

The Great Leap Forward of 1958 introduced educational reforms as part of a comprehensive new strategy of mass mobilization for economic development. To end the continuing influence of such pre-revolutionary ideas as "education can only be led by experts" and "the separation of mental and manual labor," as well as to strengthen party leadership, the Ministry of Education (MOE) issued a directive on September 19, 1958, launching the educational reforms. It called universities to fill both academic and administrative leadership positions with party members. Productive labor became part of the curriculum in all schools at all levels. More specifically, the half-work/half-study schools were founded to meet the task of rapidly universalizing education for the masses, since these schools could be run on a self-supporting basis without financial aid from the state. The party directives also stipulated that no professional educational staff was necessary; anyone who could teach would suffice.

The Cultural Revolution further broke the power of the existing educational bureaucracy, the professional academics, and any party leaders who supported them. This represented a final abolition of the obstacles the Chinese intellectual establishment had always imposed against radical reform of the educational system as a whole. It ended the authority of education professionals, which led to a general lowering of academic standards, particularly in higher education. As a result of the experimentation in that area, the content of college curricula on the average was reduced by half. The policy of sending city youth to rural areas to be "re-educated by peasants" also produced many millions of dissatisfied young people who failed to adapt to the rural lifestyle.

After the death of Mao Zedong, Deng Xiaoping's reform period began with a major national education conference in April 1978, which abandoned the Cultural Revolution's goals of class struggle and adopted modernization as the main goal for educational development. The nation witnessed a remarkable new era of rapid reconstruction and expansion of all levels of education, especially higher education. In both the formal and nonformal sectors, one of the goals of the reforms was that a college-level education was to be a prerequisite for all officials, including county-level leaders. This is a goal yet to be accomplished in the twenty-first century, but it is already underway in the political reintegration of China's intellectuals within the ruling class.

The scene in higher education in the PRC has changed rapidly since the 1990s. With the increasing drive to modernize China by integrating free-market forces, the government has introduced radical new reforms to privatize education. The most recent reforms include introduction of student fees, abolition of guaranteed job assignment after graduation, localization of institutions, and the development of private educational institutions.

CONSTITUTIONAL & LEGAL FOUNDATIONS

The Chinese have always regarded education as a tool for strengthening the country instead of cultivating individuals, which dictates that learning for the sake of knowledge is not enough. Students are expected to develop, first, as patriotic Chinese with strong morals, then as individuals with the necessary skills to serve the country and people. Throughout the educational system, the ideal of a well-rounded, cultured person with a strong socialist consciousness is deeply embedded. Article 46 of the Constitution, adopted on December 4, 1982, stipulates that ''citizens of the People's Republic of China have the duty as well as the right to receive education.'' It also states that minorities ''have the freedom to use and develop their own spoken and written languages'' (Article 4), and the blind, deaf-mute, and other handicapped citizens should receive help from the state to improve their education (Article 45). The most important provision of the 1982 Constitution on education is Article 19. It states that ''the state develops socialist educational undertakings and works to raise the scientific and cultural level of the whole nation.'' It sets the nation's educational goal as ''to wipe out illiteracy and provide political, cultural, scientific, technical, and professional education'' for China's citizens, and ''encourages people to become educated through self-study.'' These principles set the keynote for subsequent legislation in the 1980s and 1990s.

The document that led to the rehabilitation and expansion of education in post-Mao China was the 1985 *Decision on the Reform of China's Educational Structure*. It stated that the major goal of the reform was to develop education as a significant tool of socialist construction, economic expansion, and modernization. To this end, the reform document specifically called for a commitment to a compulsory nine-year cycle of primary and middle school education, diversifying high school education, expanding vocational education, improving teaching quality, granting more autonomy to higher educational institutions, reforming the job assignment system, and allocating more responsibility to education professionals over party officials.

In February 1993 the Central Committee of the Communist Party, together with the State Council, officially distributed the *Outline for Reform and Development of Education in China*. This document details strategic tasks to guide education reform in the 1990s and into the next century. The *Outline* calls the nation to make education a strategic priority because of its fundamental importance to China's modernization drive to raise the ideological and ethical standards of the entire population, as well as to raise its scientific and educational levels. The main tasks include gearing education to the needs of the future modernization efforts, improving the quality of the workforce, and establishing an educational system suited to a socialist market economy (Ashmore & Cao 1997).

EDUCATIONAL SYSTEM—OVERVIEW

China has one of the world's largest (in terms of numbers of students) educational systems: a total of approximately 289,859,000 students were enrolled in 1998. Sixty-seven percent of the students were in primary and junior secondary schools, grades one through nine (*China Statistical Yearbook*). (Unfortunately though, statistics issued by the Chinese government should be used with caution; they best represent trends or the general picture.) These nine grades constitute China's formal basic education. Compulsory education has been very successful at the primary level (first through sixth grades), but not as impressive at the junior secondary level (seventh through ninth grades).

Although the quality of schools varies widely in China, there are standard textbooks and curricula for all subjects at all levels. The textbooks convey a strong nationalist message in content. Teaching style emphasizes the authority of the teacher and demands great amounts of memorization and recitation.

Higher education is merit-based and extremely competitive in China. The overall enrollment in 1998 was 3,409,000 in the formal higher education sector (*China Statistical Yearbook* 1999) and 74,967,300 in the nonformal sector (*China Statistical Yearbook* 1999). On average, formal higher education institutions admit about 50 percent of the graduates of general senior secondary schools (Agelasto & Adamson 1998).

Foreign influences on Chinese education manifested themselves through two main channels: foreign missionary schools and the Western-educated Chinese. Missionary education in China dates back to 1818 when British missionaries opened schools in Malacca for the children of overseas Chinese. Starting in the 1840s, missionary schools came under the protection of a series of ''unequal treaties'' between the Chinese government and the Western powers. The second half of the nineteenth century witnessed a steady rise in the number of mission schools due to missionaries' growing interests in education and a general advancement of Western powers in China. In many ways, mission schools were a catalyst for the educational reform in modern China.

The reform was initiated in the 1860s as a component of the Self-Strengthening Movement and sponsored by a few high-ranking officials involved in *yiwu,* (barbarian affairs). From the point of view of the Chinese court in Beijing, there was an urgent need to understand Western culture and Westerners. In 1903 the imperial government issued the *Guidelines for Educational Affairs,* which established an educational system modeled after that of the Japanese, who had successfully replicated the Western system.

During the Nationalist decade (1928-1937), Chinese education experienced a transition from the earlier Japanese model to the American model, partly because of the return of students from the West, especially the United States, and partly because of China's deteriorating relationship with Japan. China started a public school system patterned after that of the United States and adopted American textbooks in its 1922 educational system.

In addition to help from universities and colleges in the United States, American missionary colleges in China also played an important role in the Americanization of the Chinese educational system. By the 1930s there were 16 Christian colleges and universities in China. Three of them were sponsored by Catholic missions and 13 of them were by Protestants. Academically, they were the first to introduce relatively comprehensive programs in science, technology, and medicine. However, in spite of all their positive attributes and efforts to communicate with the Chinese populace, a huge gap always existed between mission schools and Chinese society at large. The factors that contributed to the distance included the unwillingness of the missionaries to learn Chinese and the unwillingness to address Chinese concerns about national sovereignty and China's cultural heritage.

Missionary institutions not only transformed the life of Chinese youth who enrolled in them, but also smoothed the way for those who desired to study abroad. For students who planned to go abroad to pursue graduate studies, a degree from a western missionary school was invaluable. The pro-Western attitude manifested itself most in universities and colleges in the 1920s and 1930s. By 1927, Western-educated men monopolized nearly all important posts in higher education. Returnees, especially those from the United States, also dominated the diplomatic corps, military forces, and top government positions. After the founding of the People's Republic of China in 1949, the Communist Party expelled all missionary schools from China and forbade Chinese from going to the West to study, except for a very few who were allowed to study Western languages for diplomatic purposes. These measures were intended to end all Western influences on Chinese education. Since 1949 there has not been any private school operated exclusively by foreigners in China.

According to the *China Statistical Yearbook,* by 1998, China had a total population of 1,248,100,000 peo-

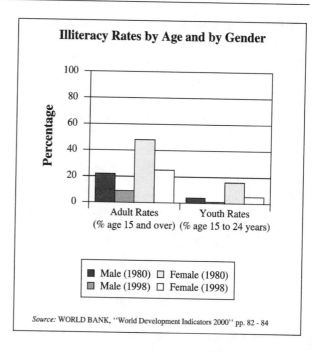

Illiteracy Rates by Age and by Gender

Source: WORLD BANK, "World Development Indicators 2000" pp. 82 - 84

ple. Among those over age 15, an estimated 83.22 percent were literate (*China Statistical Yearbook* 1999). In 1998, about 139,538,000 Chinese were enrolled in primary school; 63,010,000 were in middle school, among them 9,380,000 were high school students; 3,409,000 were students attending a university; and 198,885 were graduate students (*China Statistical Yearbook* 1999).

Illiteracy in China still poses a big challenge. Of those age 15 and older, 16.78 percent of Chinese know fewer than the 1,500 characters needed for basic literacy. Illiterate male Chinese make up 9.01 percent of the total male population over age 15, while illiterate female Chinese account for 22.61 percent of the total female population over age 15 (*China Statistical Yearbook* 1999).

Another problem of educational attainment is the huge discrepancy between urban and rural areas. Generally, almost all urban residents are literate due to better funding of schools and the prohibition of child labor. The majority of Chinese illiterates live in rural area. The lack of teachers and schools, poor funding, and the necessity for children to participate in farm-work contributes to the long-term problem.

The Compulsory Education Law of 1986 mandates six years for primary education and three years of middle school. Compulsory education serves two purposes: to prepare students for employment and to enable them to lay a solid foundation for entering schools of higher level. Although the law says the nine-year compulsory education should be free for all children, schools, often driven by economic necessity, ask parents to pay many fees, such as examination paper fees, school construction fees, water fees, and after-school coaching fees. Sometimes due to the high fees charged by schools, rural parents have to pull their children out of school (Lin 1999).

In order to develop compulsory education nationwide, the Chinese government is assisting economically deprived areas. To further increase state education appropriations, the government established the Hope Project, a back-to-school fund for children in impoverished areas who had discontinued schooling. By the end of 1994, the government had collected more than 350 million *yuan* (US$42.7 million) in donations, and 1,000,000 children who had been forced to leave school because of their impoverished situation were able to resume their education (Ashmore & Cao 1997).

The academic year in China is comprised of a fall semester and a spring semester. Students have classes five days a week with much homework assigned over the weekend. The school year extends from September to July. The teaching language is *Putonghua,* (Mandarin Chinese). Occasionally, local dialects are used as the teaching language in remote minority areas; however, the teaching of Mandarin Chinese is strictly enforced and is mostly used alongside local minority languages.

The new orientation of the Chinese economy in the 1980s required many skilled and trained laborers. Private education proved to be a pragmatic solution to meet the challenges of China's burgeoning market economy. Various nongovernmental schools became established in urban areas. They emphasized vocational training and offered courses such as foreign languages, accounting, bookkeeping, home economics, architecture, tailoring, and industrial management. By 1998, the total enrollment in nonformal institutions had reached 74,967,300 students (*China Statistical Yearbook* 1999).

In 1987 and 1988, the State Education Commission issued a series of documents, including the *Provisional Regulations Concerning Educational Institutions Run by Social Forces* and *Provisional Regulations on the Finance of Educational Institutions Run by Social Forces.* With these documents, the government allowed state-owned enterprises and institutions, the democratic parties, popular organizations, economic collectives, and learned societies to set up educational institutions. Private citizens were also allowed to do so with special permission from the educational office at various levels of the government. Foreigners, overseas Chinese, educators, and businessmen from Hong Kong and Taiwan were invited as well.

The first pre-college private school since the economic reforms was Guangya school in Dujiangyan, Sichuan Province. It opened in June 1992 by Qing Guangya. Three years later there were 20,780 private kindergartens,

3,159 private primary and secondary schools, and 672 private vocational and technical schools. In addition, there were 12,230 private colleges with an average enrollment of 2,400 students. Generally, there have been three types of private schools developed since the 1980s in terms of their funding and operation. The first type was founded and controlled by private investors, including former educators and businessmen. The second type of private schools was set up by Chinese individuals or business firms in collaboration with foreign investors. The third type included those founded and operated by Chinese enterprises and institutions in the tradition of the *minban* school, which are popularly-run schools supported by village funds in rural areas. Although the majority of *minban* schools are primary schools, there may be a few middle schools. Many private schools involved government officials or agencies in their administration or boards. In the 1990s, with strong financial support, private schools became much better equipped than most public schools. Computer labs, language labs, indoor gyms, swimming pools, and piano studios have enabled these schools to implement programs that prepared their students for the challenge of the market economy.

Although the future of private institutions remains uncertain, it seems that it is improving. More than ever before, the People's Republic of China is committed to economic reforms. Given the benefits of private universities, they are very likely to prosper in China's drive for modernization.

Although the philosophy of Communism dictates that women should enjoy equal rights with men, in educational life there have been consistently fewer females than males both overall and at each level of education throughout the history of the People's Republic of China (PRC). Females have consistently constituted a declining proportion of total students as one moves up the educational ladder. The obstacles of gender discrepancies at all levels of education stems in part from deeply embedded cultural sentiments. Female inferiority was enshrined in the Confucian ethic *nan zun nu bei* (male honorable, female inferior). This concept of female inferiority remains firmly entrenched in the basic social structure of modern Chinese society. Overt institutional discrimination occurs in the admission of females to both secondary and higher education. In the post-Mao Era, technical schools have been particularly active in this area, imposing quotas on the proportion of females enrolled. They argue that while girls mature faster intellectually than boys, they begin to fall behind at the later stage of junior middle school or in senior high school. More importantly, they use employment demands to justify gender discrimination. Since potential employers prefer male recruits, female graduates would have a hard time finding jobs. In addition women are considered less committed and are viewed as having less energy for their work because of their domestic responsibilities. Family attitudes and behavior also present obstacles to female education. Throughout the history of post-1949 China, the family has continued to favor the education of sons over daughters, especially in rural areas where both traditional attitudes and the virilocal family structure have persisted. Girls are often withdrawn from junior high school and even primary school to assist with domestic chores, accounting for their lower participation rates in education (Epstein 1991).

Despite the continuous disproportion of enrollment, female participation in education has increased over the period as a whole. Up to the mid-1980s, women's participation in formal higher education improved rapidly, from 23.4 percent in 1980 to 38.3 percent in 1998 (*China Statistical Yearbook* 1999). It is important to note, however, that free-market reforms have not always benefited women. Since the mid-1980s, female graduates have faced increasing discrimination in employment, as the centralized job allocation system has been modified to allow for greater autonomy on the part of employers. Because employers now have a choice, many choose to hire males over females to avoid paying maternity benefits. A new law protecting women's rights was passed by the national People's Congress in 1992, specifying that "schools and pertinent departments should ensure that females and males are treated equally when it comes to starting school, progressing from a lower-level school to a higher one, assigning jobs on graduation, awarding academic degrees, and selecting people for overseas study." But this is increasingly difficult to implement since educational institutions have less and less control over the employment of their graduates.

At the end of 1998, China had 55 minority groups with a population of 75,774,500. Although they constitute 6.07 percent of the total population, they are very unequally distributed among the 31 province-level territories. In 10 territories, their share of the total population is less than 1 percent. In 2 other territories, their share is between 10 and 20 percent (*China Statistical Yearbook* 1999). Because the Communist Party wanted to promote a unified country, it maintained that non-Han populations had the right to preserve their own languages, customs, and religions over a long period of time until all minorities would ultimately "melt together." In the meantime, the government also insisted that minorities were backward in their customs, economy, and political consciousness. Therefore, they needed assistance from the Han people to achieve a developed socialist country.

As a result of these contradictory policies, China has developed one of the oldest and largest programs of state-sponsored affirmative action for ethnic minorities. By 1950 the government had established 45 special minority primary schools and 8 provincial minority secondary schools. The minority students in these schools were provided free education, books, and school supplies and were subsidized for food and housing (Hansen 1990). For the long-term political goal, the government also focused on the education of minority cadres. An important institution to accomplish this goal is *minzu xueyuan* (special minority institutes), which trained minority cadres to work in minority regions as representatives of the Communist party and government. In college entrance examinations, minorities are given additional points to give them greater access to higher education—20 points are automatically added to their scores if they apply to minority institutes, or 5 points are added if they apply to other schools. Also, in many cases, minority students are allowed to take the examinations in their indigenous languages and later enroll in classes taught in Mandarin. Many prominent universities now have *minzu ban* (ethnic classes or cohorts). Since the early 1980s, there have also been one-year *yuke ban* (preparatory courses) for minorities at key universities and minority institutes. These classes, which may be arranged by agreement between minority areas and universities, can serve students who failed to enter a university through the national enrollment system. Minority students also benefit from quotas that set aside a certain percentage of the spaces in classes for them. Furthermore, governments at different levels tried to strengthen the training of local teachers and re-establish bilingual education, particularly among Tibetans, Mongols, and Uygurs. The autonomous governments of minorities are allowed to decide which kinds of schools to establish, the length of schooling, whether a special curriculum is needed, which languages to teach in addition to Chinese, and how to recruit students. The central government also decided that minority students studying in cities should be allocated jobs in their home-counties after graduation in order to ensure that poor and underdeveloped rural minority areas would benefit from minority higher education. In exchange for the preferential policies, minorities are expected to support China's construction by providing more natural resources.

In spite of governmental preferential policies, many minority areas are still characterized by low levels of school enrollment and educational attainment. In 1990, the level of illiteracy of the national minorities as a whole (30.8 percent) is markedly higher than that of all Han combined at 21.5 percent. While minority students continue to do relatively well in terms of opportunities to enter higher education, they are increasingly disadvantaged in their access to the job market upon graduation. Furthermore, both minority men and women are highly disadvantaged in applying to enter graduate school, due to the foreign language requirement. It is not easy for them to reach an adequate level in a foreign language when they must master Chinese in addition to their own language and then learn the foreign language through the medium of Chinese. Nor is there much evidence of affirmative action for minority students at the graduate level. Also, the fact that many minority undergraduates intend to become cadres, rather than academics, contributes to the scarcity of minority graduate students. In 1993, only 3 percent of graduate students were minorities.

The use of instructional technology in China's classrooms remains inadequate. Many schools, particularly in rural area, still rely on blackboard and chalk as their major instructional media. Since the economic reforms in the 1980s, some schools in the cities have acquired limited audio-visual resources. Both key high schools and universities have the advantage of being equipped first due to funding priority from the state. Private schools are better equipped than most public schools due to their generous donors, usually overseas Chinese or the newly rich entrepreneurs. As for Internet access in classrooms, Chinese schools are behind most advanced Western countries. Only very few researchers at key universities, supported by outside funding, have unlimited access to Internet resources. Due to both high cost and the fear of influx of undesired information, the Chinese government hesitates to make the Internet a valuable teaching tool on campuses.

In using both radio and television as instructional media to provide educational opportunities for Chinese mass, however, China is ahead of many countries in the world. Even during the Cultural Revolution (1966-1976) when all schools were closed, Chinese Central People's Broadcast Station started to offer English lessons through radio broadcast in the 1970s. In February 1979 a television university was formed to offer different courses to Chinese citizens. In 1998 there were 45 radio and television universities with a enrollment of 484,400 students (*China Statistical Yearbook* 1999). Upon passing all required tests in a particular field, students can receive diplomas from the universities. The well-developed network presents lectures and classes in all major cities and regions throughout China. By presenting lectures of top experts in a given field, these radio and television universities provide educational opportunities to a large viewing audience who cannot attend formal college.

PREPRIMARY & PRIMARY EDUCATION

Unlike primary education in Chinese cities, kindergarten education is not offered on a universal basis. Nationwide, in 1998, approximately 24,030,000 children attended 181,368 kindergartens (*China Statistical Yearbook* 1999). The proportion of children who attend kindergartens in cities is higher, with more children

spending at least some time in kindergarten between the ages of three and six when they enter primary school. It is a general principle that children who have attended a reputable kindergarten will more easily attain a spot in a good primary school. Consequently, despite the higher fees charged at the best kindergartens, places are often difficult to secure. Sometimes there are entrance examinations designed to test coordination, verbal development, simple counting, and the recognition of shapes. Despite the existence of formal selection procedures, access to *guanxi* (connections), or a "back door" may help with entry into a good kindergarten.

Factories, companies, universities, and government offices all operate nurseries for their own employees. Their quality varies, depending in part on the nature of the unit to which they are attached. Usually, the elite kindergartens are operated by local education bureaus. University kindergartens are renowned for their standards, and the admission criteria are very stringent. When choosing kindergartens for their children, however, closeness to the work place and opening hours coordinated with the working day make enterprise kindergartens a convenient choice. The majority of urban kindergartens are run by the residents' committees. These provide day care only. The equipment is simpler and their staff less highly trained than in the elite establishments.

Kindergarten activities have undergone significant changes in the 1990s. The popularization of a national kindergarten syllabus has produced a surprising degree of similarity in the children's day and in teaching methods used in kindergartens all over the country. The subjects taught include language, arithmetic, social studies, music, art, and physical education. The learning through play approach is much better established than in the past.

The status of kindergarten teachers has not risen very much since the days when the majority of staff were kindly but uneducated elderly women. Today, the qualified teachers are graduates from normal schools for kindergartens. They are called *laoshi* (teacher) as a mark of respect, rather than the familiar address form *ayi* (auntie) used in the past. However, their wages are poor, and kindergarten training tends to be taken by less competitive students whose grades are not good enough to get into any other college.

Moral and ideological education in kindergarten has changed a great deal in the years since Mao's death (1976). In the past, words like "revolution," "socialism," "communism," and "Chairman Mao's thought" were common in the kindergarten classroom. Today, although the government still requires kindergartens to instill a strong ideology and children are still taught to "love China and the communist Party," kindergartens also teach children to be modest, unselfish, tidy, and polite. Children also need to learn to distinguish between good and bad, care for their environment, and help one another. These values are important considering the fact that today's Chinese children are from one-child families, and most of them are spoiled by their parents and grandparents.

The most important document regarding primary education policy was *The Government Administration Council Directive Concerning the Reorganization and Improvement of Primary School Education* signed by Premier Zhou Enlai in 1953. It asked primary schools throughout China to have the same pedagogical plan and to develop the same systems of governing attendance, leave, and certification of attainment. Children begin primary school when they are seven-years-old or often six-years-old in urban areas. Primary education includes six-year programs, although in the past there were some five-year programs. There are three types of schools: full-time elementary, rural elementary, and simple elementary (Ashmore & Cao 1997). In 1998, about 139,538,000 students were enrolled in 609,626 primary schools (*China Statistical Yearbook* 1999).

Primary classes are large, the atmosphere is formal, and discipline is quite strict. Children are no longer required to sit with their hands clasped behind their backs as they were before the Cultural Revolution (1966-1976), but they sit in straight rows, stand up to answer the teacher, and recite much of what they are required to learn in unison.

Two programs were developed to satisfy the need for education in less developed areas. One is the half-and-half agricultural secondary school. Students in this kind of school spend a half-day in study and a half-day in labor to support themselves. Their facilities are often primitive: a hastily erected shack or the floor of a barn. Another program is the part-time primary school, often called ''simplified primary school.'' It usually offers a few daily classes taught by locally recruited teachers, usually themselves only primary school graduates. The classrooms are often located in old temples and the facilities are ill-suited for students. These are known as *minban* (popularly-run) schools, which are run communally by villages; they are solely supported by village funds and do not receive any financial support from the national government. *Minban* schools do not intend to prepare students for further education or for vocations different from those of their parents. The number of *minban* schools is unreported by Chinese authorities. Theoretically, every primary school teacher should be paid by the government. In reality, sometimes it is hard to find a teacher in rural areas. Villagers need to recruit teachers themselves, and the salary of the teacher is drawn from village funds.

The curriculum for primary schools is very much standardized in China. There are standard textbooks for

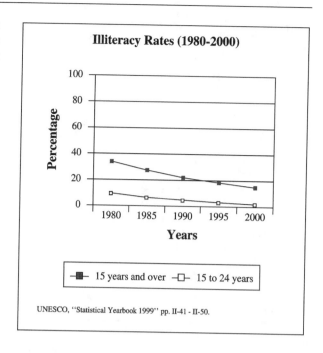

Illiteracy Rates (1980-2000)

Legend: ■ 15 years and over □ 15 to 24 years

UNESCO, ''Statistical Yearbook 1999'' pp. II-41 - II-50.

curricula at all levels. The central theme of these uniformly written textbooks is that China is a unified, glorious country with a great past and a bright future. Despite considerable variation in geography, agriculture, climate, language, and local customs, nearly the same subjects are taught with the same materials throughout the country. The standardized curriculum dictates that 40 percent of class hours should be devoted to the study of Chinese (including reading, writing, composition, and speaking). A further 24 percent of class hours is devoted to arithmetic. The remaining class hours are absorbed by physical education, music, art, natural science, politics, geography, and history. Increasingly, foreign languages, particularly English, have become optional courses. The government planned to make English a mandatory course starting at the third year of primary school at the beginning of the twenty-first century.

SECONDARY EDUCATION

The First National Conference on Secondary Education was held in Beijing in March 1951. Based on the conference, the Ministry of Education issued the ''Temporary Rules for Middle Schools'' in the next year. According to this directive, the task of middle schools was to educate a generation of young people for the new China, which meant to combine the theory of Marxism-Leninism with a concrete appreciation for Chinese society and to cultivate proletarian successors who loved the party, the people, and the country. In the early 1950s, a unified system of middle schools was set up in China. All private middle schools were eliminated, and all curriculum and textbooks were standardized.

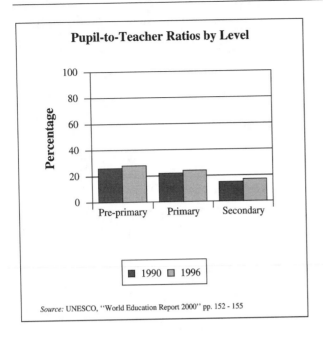

Pupil-to-Teacher Ratios by Level

1990 1996

Source: UNESCO, "World Education Report 2000" pp. 152 - 155

leges in China and abroad, perpetuating a syndrome of ever-increasing pressure on children to gain admission to the best secondary schools. Although the State Education Commission and local bureaus of education have attempted to reduce student work loads by banning excessive examinations, stipulating the number of hours secondary school pupils must sleep each night, restricting homework during semester breaks and holidays, and preventing merit pay for instructors who teach solely the top students, there is not much improvement.

Besides inequality between key and ordinary schools, there has been a huge discrepancy between urban areas and less-developed rural areas since the 1980s. Historically, the Chinese government's investment on education for peasants has always been meager. In rural areas 90 percent of secondary schools fail to meet national standards for such basic facilities as chairs, desks, and safe drinking water.

In 1998, among 13,948 regular senior secondary schools in China, only 20 percent (2,721) were in rural areas, serving 70 percent of Chinese population, not to mention the huge discrepancy in their equipment, government funding, and the quantity and quality of the teachers. In terms of student enrollment, rural pupils only constitute 14 percent (1,310,436) of senior secondary school students (*China Statistical Yearbook* 1999). Besides inadequate resources, the fact that many peasants believe that formal schooling is useless and irrelevant to their agrarian life is also responsible for the high illiteracy rate in rural areas. The poorest of China's counties are so behind in secondary school provision that the government implemented a prairie fire program to push rural educational efforts (Epstein 1991).

The academic year for junior secondary school consists of two 20-week terms, 11 to 12 holiday weeks, and one or two weeks for flexible use. Six classes are offered each day, Monday through Friday. Classroom instruction involves 28 to 30 hours each week. The core curriculum of secondary schools includes three fundamental subjects: Chinese, mathematics, and English. Each is taught for six years and together account for more than 50 percent of the total hours students spend in the classroom. Political study is required in each year of secondary school. It consists of political ideology and morality, the history of social development and dialectical materialism, political and legal knowledge, political philosophy, political economy, and review during the senior year. In addition, students study five years of physics, four years of chemistry and biology, three years of geography and history, and one year of computer science, which includes basic computer literacy and programming. Pupils also participate in physical education in each year of secondary school and two or three years of art and music.

General secondary schools include a 3-year junior secondary school and a 3-year senior secondary school. Some systems have a 4-year junior/3-year senior plan; a few others have a 2-year senior school structure. Secondary schools in China are divided into "key" and "ordinary" schools. Designated key schools are schools distinguished from ordinary schools by their academic reputation and are generally allocated more resources by the state. Their original purpose was to quicken the training of highly needed talent for China's modernization, but another purpose was to set up exemplary schools to improve teaching in all schools. This stratified structure has given key schools numerous privileges. They can select the best students through city-wide or region-wide examination and transfer the best teachers in the area to teach in their school. They receive much more funding from the government, and in getting funds for upgrading equipment or the purchase of expensive items such as computers, they always have priority. Because of these advantages, key schools often boast 90 to 99 percent admission rates to universities (Lin 1999).

In addition, key schools dominate the creation and distribution of secondary school education materials. Their best teachers are not only called upon to write and grade national examination test papers, but they are also publishing researchers who authoritatively resolve secondary school disputes through their domination of district education bureau publications. Some key schools are even affiliated with overseas alumni associations that are a source of prestige and hard currency. Such schools embody China's modernization goal of defining success in relationship to international standards. Admission into key schools often paves the way for entering elite col-

Many schools now teach typing in the second year of junior secondary school.

Besides the senior secondary schools that prepare students for going on to college, there are vocational and technical senior secondary schools (VTE) that train pupils in specialized fields and prepare them to enter the workforce immediately after graduation from secondary school. Full-time senior secondary school programs are commonly classified into specialized technical and teacher-training schools, technical and pre-service skilled worker schools, and, the largest sector, vocational and agricultural schools. The most prestigious VTE programs are offered by more than 4,109 specialized schools that train middle-level technical personnel and kindergarten and primary school teachers. These institutions, developed in the mid-1950s and directed by technical ministries as well as the State Education Commission, are managed directly by education, technical, and labor bureaus at the local, district, county, and provincial levels. Entering students are junior secondary school graduates who are selected through competitive state examinations administered by bureaus of higher education. The four-year study program includes nine broad specializations in technical fields (agriculture, art, economics, engineering, forestry, medicine, physical culture, politics and law, and a miscellaneous category that includes everything from the training of Buddhist monks and nuns to flight attendants) and one type in teacher training for secondary schools.

Less prestigious than specialized schools, technical schools are run by education bureaus and industrial units. They train technicians in steel, textile, petroleum, pharmaceutical, agricultural, and botanical enterprises, as well as middle-level workers in law, finance, health, art, and physical culture. These primarily three-year institutions recruit junior middle school graduates who are assigned to them by labor and personnel bureaus on the basis of entrance examination results and preferred choice of specialty. They are more successful than specialized schools in forging close and flexible ties with specific enterprises because their enrollment and curriculum are not controlled by national ministries. Like specialized schools, they have the advantage of high demand since students receive employment upon graduation.

Key and non-key vocational and agricultural schools, normally managed at the district and county level, have offered the least prestigious VTE programs because their graduates have not enjoyed secure employment opportunities and because graduates from these three-year programs are classified as skilled workers rather than technicians. Therefore, they provide the last chance for students hoping to pursue senior secondary schooling and have the highest level of dropouts. Howev-

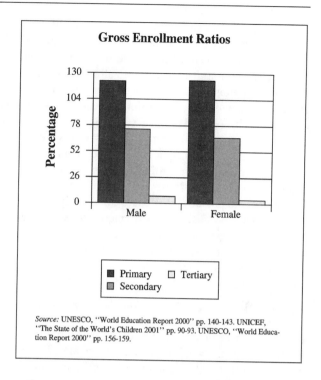

Gross Enrollment Ratios

Source: UNESCO, "World Education Report 2000" pp. 140-143. UNICEF, "The State of the World's Children 2001" pp. 90-93. UNESCO, "World Education Report 2000" pp. 156-159.

er, vocational and agricultural schools in relatively developed regions of China have managed to compensate for the lack of formal employment mechanisms by powerful local contacts with surrounding enterprises and capitalizing on economic demand for skilled labor. Job security, in turn, has raised the confidence of the public in such schools, which are attracting increasingly qualified junior high school graduates.

There are two kinds of examinations conducted in secondary schools. One kind is the graduation test. Every student is required to pass examinations for the following ten subjects in order to graduate from secondary school: Chinese, mathematics, foreign language, physics, chemistry, political study, history, geography, computer science, and biology. The examination for each subject is conducted in different years of secondary school. Each examination is graded on a 100-point scale and students receive grades curved from "A" to "E." All students take each test at the same time, and results become a matter of public record. Students who pass all classes receive a graduation certificate and are eligible for applying to take the college entrance examinations.

The second kind of test is college entrance examinations. All students who wish to enter college are also required to take a unified national examination in their last year of high school. The score on this examination is the main criteria for college, and almost the entirety of the last year of high school is devoted to preparation for this examination. It takes place from July 7 to July 9 annually and covers seven different subjects. During senior year all high school students need to declare whether they are on the humanities track or the science track, in accordance with the two specialties tested by the college entrance examination. This early specialization has been blamed for a premature narrowing of intellectual pursuit. In the college entrance examination, humanities students are tested in history and political study. Science students are tested in physics and chemistry. All students are also required to take examinations in Chinese, mathematics, and a foreign language regardless of their future majors. Nationally, only about 25 percent of high school graduates are able to pursue higher education directly through public support because of the extremely competitive nature of the college entrance examination. Those students whose examination scores are not high enough or who lack the resources to pursue higher education privately go straight into the workforce without further education.

While the establishment of schools for the physically disabled dates to the late nineteenth century, institutional expansion proceeded moderately until the Cultural Revolution and has increased substantially since the 1980s. In general, however, education for the disabled in China remains in its infancy, and serious improvement remains to be done to promote the social integration of disabled Chinese youth.

The first Chinese school for the blind and deaf was established in 1927 in Nanjing. After the founding of the PRC in 1949, the Chinese government reaffirmed its commitments to educate the disabled in a 1951 document published by the Ministry of Education. By 1998, there were 1,062 schools for the blind, hearing impaired, and mute, with a total student enrollment of 97,649. There were 21,415 full-time teachers out of a total staff of 30,868. Schools for retarded children date from as late as 1979 and numbered 90 by 1987. The best estimates indicate that 504 schools employ 14,400 special education teachers and staff, who served 52,800 children at the beginning of the 1990. But only six percent of China's 6,000,000 children and youth who suffer from disability are enrolled in any type of educational programs.

Basically, Chinese special schools only offer a primary-school level education, which emphasizes mastery of survival skills along with those manual skills traditionally performed by adults with specific disabilities. The curriculum follows a work-study structure. The goal of the work experience in these schools is to teach socialization and survival skills. The textbooks used in these schools are the ones used in primary schools with the translations of Braille. Recently, some colleges started to admit disabled students and even established special education majors and teacher training programs devoted to teaching disabled students.

China established reformatories and work-study schools since the late 1950s and early 1960s when urban and rural theft, fighting, and poor school discipline became noticeable problems. They are under the supervision of the public security apparatus. Based on early Chinese Communist practice in Yanan, reformatories were conceived as production units, and inmate labor would be used to make them self-sufficient and to make them contribute to the socialist economy. Work-study schools for delinquents, on the other hand, were founded for those guilty of less serious delinquent activity. They also emphasized the importance of offenders participating in productive labor. During the Cultural Revolution, the work of both reformatories and work-study schools was disrupted, as reformatories were viewed as overly coercive, and work-study schools were dismissed as ineffective and were shut down completely. During the 1980s when reformatories resumed, the Chinese government still emphasized the use of productive labor as a character-reforming device. Furthermore, the removal of youth from normal family environments, the use of drill and militaristic ritual within the institutional settings, and the display of offenders completing production tasks in public view reinforced the strong negative social labeling that is associated with reformatories and work-study schools. The quality of education provided at both reformatories and work-study schools is often substandard. In addition, they have no systematic counseling system; offenders are put together regardless of their specific offence and few preparations are made to facilitate their readjustment after their release.

HIGHER EDUCATION

The 1952 reorganization of higher education resulted in three types of government-controlled institutions. First, there were a small number of comprehensive universities with departments in the classical arts and science disciplines of the European tradition, as well as six national normal universities that had departments of education, fine arts, and music, which were established with the intention of training academic teachers for the secondary and tertiary level. Second, based on the Marxian concept of polytechnical education and a broad exposure to the applied sciences, several great polytechnical universities such as *Qinghua* and *Jiaotong* were reorganized with the broad range of engineering sciences included in their curricula. Finally, since some sectors of the society need special kinds of knowledge, some colleges were designed to train advanced personnel to meet these special demands. Thus, medical colleges and institutions of finance, economics, political science, and law were created for this purpose. At the head of the system was a new revolutionary university, People's University, which had the task of developing an authoritative Marxist, Leninist, and Maoist canon for the social sciences. By the end of 1953, all private institutions of higher learning had been taken over by the government.

The educational reform document of 1985 dictates that Chinese higher educational institutions are responsible for two main tasks: "training advanced personnel" and "developing science, technology, and culture." Abolishing the excessive government control of past policies, the State Education Commission promised new autonomy to universities, including freedom to develop "ties with productive units, scientific research institutions," and greater jurisdiction over the institution's curriculum and the use of state funds. As part of the scheme to make China a modernized country in the twenty-first century, a few private institutions have also been established either by social organizations or individuals. All universities are required to abide by the principles set forth in the Chinese Constitution. In 1998, approximately 3,409,000 students were enrolled in 1,020 higher education institutions.

Since 1949, owing to the different political and economic situations in China, the weighing of admissions criteria constantly shifted, depending on the political climate. Immediately following the Communists' rise to power, admissions criteria focused heavily on the background of a student's family: the "good" (red) classes included the workers, peasants, the former poor, Revolutionary cadres, and revolutionary martyrs; the "bad" (black) consisted of former capitalists, landlords, rich peasants, Nationalists, reactionaries, and criminals. Later, however, because China was in desperate need of professionals and engineers for socialist construction, academic achievement became more important than class background in admissions criteria. Deng Xiaoping's reforms abolished class background as a factor of consideration altogether. Instead, he instituted the national unified college entrance examinations taken by high school graduates in their last school year. Students are admitted to colleges according to two factors: their scores in the *gaokao* (unified college entrance examination) and the quotas of enrollment in specific institutions and specific majors. The quotas are assigned to an institution according to a national plan. Students obtain an average score in the *gaokao,* in a range that permits choices of specialties in institutions. Each major within a college sets up a *fenshuxian* (score mark), meaning cut-off score. Students whose score is below the cut-off point cannot be accepted by that institution. A prestigious university, usually a key institution, may require a score of 850 out of 900 for entrance. A second-rate institution may require only 600. Economic reforms have motivated institutions to admit *zifeisheng* (self-supported students) since 1995 in order to increase income. *Zifeisheng* are candidates below the cut-off point and hence outside the state plan.

Meanwhile, there is a direct entrance system that allows a tiny number of superior students who achieve outstanding examination results or win prizes in important

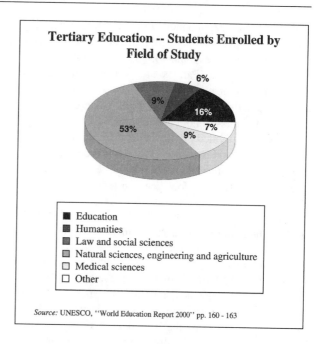

Tertiary Education -- Students Enrolled by Field of Study

6%
9%
16%
7%
53%
9%

- ■ Education
- ■ Humanities
- ■ Law and social sciences
- Natural sciences, engineering and agriculture
- □ Medical sciences
- □ Other

Source: UNESCO, "World Education Report 2000" pp. 160 - 163

academic contests to enroll directly in a designated postsecondary institution without sitting for the college entrance examination. Key universities allot several *minge* (positions) to appropriate key secondary schools, and students to fill them are normally selected by a school administrator and the student's homeroom teacher in consultation with the student and his or her parents. This process is extremely competitive except for students who choose to enter institutions, such as normal colleges and universities, which have trouble attracting highly qualified students.

The structure of Chinese higher education is still based on the Soviet pattern in which the arts and sciences are taught at comprehensive universities with separate institutions responsible for other fields. Academic departments within each institution still follow the Soviet example by offering a host of narrow specialties or majors, conforming to specific job requirements. Since the late 1980s, most Chinese universities have adopted the credit system, aiming to grant all undergraduates the opportunity to select courses in areas outside their own specialization. These courses are often in interesting new areas of the humanities and are offered as frequently in specialist engineering and agricultural universities as in comprehensive universities. However, students still have little freedom of choice among courses, and they choose not to study at their own pace because to graduate out of turn would disrupt the predetermined enrollment and job assignment plans.

A student's major is decided before entering college. After the college entrance examination, students, teachers, and parents meet based on the estimates of each student's entrance examination scores to choose a college and a major. Every college publicizes their standard cut-off point after the examination. The main purpose is to get into a college. Parents and students are realistic enough not to pick a good school whose cut-off point is above the estimated student's score. Once entering the college, students cannot change their majors. Each academic year is divided into spring and fall semesters. The former lasts from February to July while the latter is from September to January. University degree programs are usually either three or four years in length.

The degree system in China is still in quite an early stage in its development. Despite attempts to set up a degree system during the 1950s and 1960s, it was successfully established only after the Cultural Revolution (1966-76) and first implemented on January 1, 1981. A complete undergraduate education consists of four years of study, at which time the student is granted a diploma, which is separate from the B.A. degree. Only those students who have successfully completed a senior thesis along with their four years of study are granted a B.A. degree. In the late 1980s, double major programs have been introduced to outstanding students, and major/minor programs have been arranged for students wishing to develop a second area of professional expertise.

Since the establishment of the Academics Degrees Committee under the State Council, graduate programs have been rapidly developed. Master's studies last for three years (full-time) with heavy coursework in the first two years and a thesis to follow. Doctoral studies are also normally full-time over three years, again with substantial coursework. It was only in the 1990s that institutions began to accept postgraduate studies in a part-time mode. Strict academic control has been maintained through a system whereby academic departments must be approved by the academic degree committee before they can enroll masters students, and only individual professors of high academic standing are accredited to supervise doctoral students. While expansion has been extremely rapid at the master's level, there has been much greater caution at the doctoral level. Graduate enrollments have grown from 21,604 students in 1980 to 198,885 students in 1998.

Until the 1980s college graduates' jobs were guaranteed. Under the old job assignment system, central and provincial authorities drew up the employment plans each year. The Communist Party of China (CPC) organization within each school then assigned their graduates to fill the slots. Since the mid-1990s the system has been in transition from centralized job assignment to allowing market mechanisms to determine job placement. In early 1988, the State Education Commission asked higher learning institutions in Guangdong Province to start ex-

perimenting on a new package of enrollment, tuition, and job assignment reforms. As a part of the design to institute aspects of the free market into China's centralized socialist system, the aims of this package of reforms are to abolish free higher education, to change the centralized system of enrollment (student enrollment quota to each school and each major from each province), and to abolish job assignment plans. This same set of reforms was extended in the autumn of 1989 to 36 institutions administered directly by the State Education Commission. The freshmen class in 1997 was the first to pay for their own college education and find jobs for themselves upon graduation through a "two-way selection," meaning both employers and college graduates can decide with whom they want to work without the interfering of the process from the party officials. At provincial and local levels, graduates were almost always expected to return to the place they had come from, though they were sometimes able to move to a slightly better location or situation. But for students who fail to find a work unit within the choices given them by the plan, the school must make the assignment as before. The state employment plan is used to place only a minority of China's college students as necessary for the hard-to-fill occupational quotas.

The main argument against the free-market approach to job placement was that only when the government can guarantee fair competition in the job market should the job assignment system be abandoned. Without a legal guarantee, the best opportunities are reserved for male students from big cities whose parents have many well-connected friends and relations. Other concerns include that the employers in remote and backward regions do not receive much needed graduates and that there are not enough opportunities waiting each year for all the graduates. The lack of attractive job openings generated a low student morale that became increasingly evident on many campuses. There even arose the feeling that "study is useless."

Deng Xiaoping's Open Door policy has brought an unprecedented exodus of both faculty and students to Western countries. The resulting increase in educational, scientific, and commercial contacts with the outside world brought China closer to its long-held goal of acquiring world-wide scientific and technical knowledge through Western educational institutions. From 1978 to 1998, some 147,000 students went abroad to study in Western institutions. China's "going abroad fever" is likely to continue. In academic year 1999-2000, there were 54,466 Chinese students in the United States, topping the number of any nationality of foreign students in that country.

On the other hand, with the unparalleled number of China's brightest students leaving the country, the government soon faced a ''brain-drain'' dilemma. Only 53,040 students, or less than 36 percent of those who left, eventually returned. To counter the ''brain-drain'' problem, Chinese officials have introduced specific regulations since the mid-1980s. First, Chinese students are supposed to work for a specified period at home before going abroad for further study. Any violators of the rule are punished financially. For example, a college graduate must work in China for five years before going abroad. Anybody who wants to leave China earlier must turn in money to the state, about 5,000 *yuan* for a year. A graduate student (MA degree holder) must serve three years before leaving China. For every unfulfilled year, the student needs to pay 6,000 to 7,000 *yuan* to the state. Second, in terms of visa restrictions, all state-sponsored students went to the United States on the more restrictive ''J'' visas. Upon completion of their studies, U.S. rules require such visa holders to return to their home countries for at least two years before being eligible to work in the United States. Third, all visa-extension requests must be forwarded to the State Education Commission; the U.S. Embassy in Beijing will not grant an extension without the Commission's approval. Finally, all students are required to sign contractual agreements with their Chinese employers before leaving China. These agreements should specify obligations on both sides, including what the employer needs and what the student will study, the posting of bonds, the guarantor's signature, and compensation if the student failed to return on schedule.

Visiting scholars, on the other hand, differ greatly in background from students that study abroad. In terms of their backgrounds, the vast majority of visiting scholars have been teaching at universities, although a significant percentage have been from government institutions. Visiting scholars make up the largest percentage of Chinese exchange visitors. They do not go abroad to enroll in specific degree programs but rather to conduct research and study on their own. In general, they must have an established reputation in China or a relatively long and successful academic career or research experience when selected for the program. Since the mid-1990s, the Chinese government has implemented a new policy to ensure the return of visiting scholars; basically, before leaving China they need to turn in a huge amount of money, about 100,000 yuan, to the government as a deposit. Upon their return to China, the money will be returned to them in full plus the interest earned during the period. Also, visiting scholars' decisions are linked to their colleagues' chances of going abroad. If one does not return, one's colleagues cannot go abroad. Besides the strict government policy and the pressures from colleagues, the possibilities for further professional development and for putting to use the new areas of knowledge acquired abroad motivate visiting scholars to go back to China. Usually, visiting scholars tend to be much older than students and, unlike students, have a high returning rate. Visiting scholars have been funded by both Western and Chinese sources. Studying abroad can be a significant turning point in Chinese professionals' lives, and it has opened up areas of research and teaching that would otherwise have been impossible.

With the crackdown of the student movement in June 1989, many graduate students abroad decided not to return. The outrage in the West over Chinese government action in the violent suppression of the students has led to several countries granting permanent residency to Chinese citizens. Even though it is more difficult for older visiting scholars to establish professional careers abroad, some of them have also decided not to return.

ADMINISTRATION, FINANCE, & EDUCATIONAL RESEARCH

The educational system is almost entirely centralized in China. The first National Ministry of Education (MOE) was founded in 1952 and patterned closely on its Soviet counterpart. It experienced reorganization three times before 1966. When the Cultural Revolution broke out in 1966, the Red Guards, with the support of Mao Zedong, abolished the entire educational administration in China.

A single Ministry of Education was re-established in 1975. As the political situation in China became more stable, the MOE was consolidated by the State Council. On June 18, 1985, a major reorganization of central educational administration took place in China. The 11th Plenary of the Standing Committee of the People's Congress in China passed a resolution that called for the abolition of the Ministry of Education and the establishment of the State Education Commission (SEC), a multi-functional executive branch of the State Council. The SEC is the supreme administrative authority for the education system in China and is responsible for turning out personnel well-educated and well-trained in various subjects and fields for China. For the first time in China's history, those who have assumed direct command of the country's educational system have high positions in the State Council. The SEC formulates major educational policies, designs overall strategies for promoting education, coordinates educational undertakings supervised by various ministries, and directs education reform.

In terms of accountability, institutes of higher education in the PRC are divided into four categories:

1. Those under the direct administration of the SEC

2. Those under the non-educational central ministries

3. Those under provincial and other local authorities

4. Private institutions

Usually, those under the direct administration of the SEC are considered as *zhongdian daxue* (key universities). The concept of key universities was first introduced in 1954. It has never been abandoned by the Chinese government except from 1972 to 1977 when students were not selected by college entrance examinations. Since the economic reforms in the 1980s, Beijing has more than ever before emphasized the importance of key schools. In 2000, eleven universities were designated as key institutions nationwide, following the example of American-style comprehensive universities to become leading higher educational institutions in the world.

Besides the universities under the SEC, there are some universities under the non-educational central ministries. Those universities tend to specialize in certain areas. For example, the Beijing Institute of Forest is under the Ministry of Forest; the Beijing University of Agriculture is run by the Ministry of Agriculture. Another type of university is managed by provincial and other local education bureaus. The proliferation of provincial and city universities has been encouraged both in order to meet rising social demand and in order to produce the mid-level technical personnel greatly needed in China's modernization drive.

Before the reform, financing of higher education was characterized by a number of features. First, since the early 1950s when the enrollment and job assignment plans went into effect, the majority of Chinese universities have been funded by both national and provincial governments. Second, the central government was in absolute control of the education budget. Funds were channeled through the Ministry of Finance to various ministries and local governments, with the endorsement of the then Ministry of Education. Third, funds were calculated by "basic number plus development." The "basic number" referred to the student enrollment and staff size as dictated by the national plan. "Development" referred to the incremental changes, again as required by the national plan. Unspent funds were returned to the government. Fourth, the national student-stipend scheme was designed to help students from low-income families. However, the government's overall education budget is not enough and is mostly spent in urban areas. As a result of poor facilities and lack of qualified teachers, students in the countryside have little access to adequate education.

The application of the *Guangdong* experiment in 1988 drastically altered China's highly centralized, socialist education system by introducing tuition payments and abolishing strict enrollment quotas. In the meantime the national student-stipend scheme began to be phased out at the end of the 1980s, and the student loan program was introduced in 1986-1987 by state-financed loans.

Among those exempt are students at teacher training and national minorities institutes, who continue to receive a monthly cost-of-living allowance.

The *Guangdong* experiment immediately was perceived as changing the egalitarian distribution system and adding to the burdens of poor students. Also, as a result of this reform, "out-of-province" students were reluctant to attend colleges in Guangdong. To address these concerns, the State Education Commission has directed that college students should be divided into two basic enrollment categories. One is *zhilingxing jihua* (directed or state-assigned plan), while the other is the more flexible *zhiddaoxing jihua* (guided plan). Students enrolled under the state-guided plan will generally be exempt from paying tuition, and their other expenses will be largely state-subsidized. In return, they must agree to major in one of several unpopular specialties, enrollment quotas for which are typically difficult to fill. They must also accept a state-assigned job in the area for which they have been trained. Other students, under the guided plan, will be responsible for their own tuition and living expenses and for repaying any loans incurred, but they will be free to apply for enrollment in more popular specialties that train for better-paying and more prestigious careers, and they will find employment on their own after graduation. The two functions of the division are allowing students from poorer families to attend college and guaranteeing enrollments in essential specialties that are unpopular. Usually, those fields include teacher training, agriculture, water conservancy, geology, petroleum engineering, and mining. In addition, a small number of *dingxiang peiyang* students (under contractual arrangements between the school and the locality) who are enrolled from border and mountain regions must return after graduation. They also belong to the category of directed plan.

The Outline of Reform (1993) and the Education Law of 1995 stipulated that the two major sources of income that an institution receives are state appropriation and other non-state income. The former is known as *yusuannei* (budgeted), the latter, *yusuanwai* (unbudgeted). Budgeted refers to those that are appropriated by the state. Basically, the state provides funding for salaries and the general operation of the institutions. The state also provides partial funding for capital investments. The principle for the management of government appropriation is "one-line budget, retention of surplus." This is to provide incentive for institutions to economize on the resources available. Unbudgeted income is not recorded in government accounts. The five main sources of unbudgeted income are: university-run enterprises; research services and consulting sponsored mainly by individual academic departments; selling teaching services (correspondence courses, refresher courses, adult evening classes, technical training programs); endowment/

donations; and student fees. The proceeds are used to supplement faculty salaries.

Since 1953, all college students received tuition-waiver scholarship and free dormitory. The food subsidies depend on the student's family income. Usually 80 percent of the students receive food subsidies from the national government. From 1997, all higher education institutions started charging student fees. Those students whose admission to college is based on their score have been required to pay 4,000 to 6,000 *yuan* per academic year while those *zifeisheng* are asked to pay 20,000 to 30,000 *yuan* per year.

Total World Bank loans to Chinese education have amounted to about US$1.2 billion since the 1980s. It has been managed in a bureaucratic way, with the Ministry of Finance having overall supervision, a loan office in the State Education Commission overseeing the disbursement of loans to all institutions at the national level, and similar offices in provincial education commissions responsible for the oversight of projects at the provincial level. In contrast to World Bank projects, cooperative projects funded by agencies such as UNESCO, UNDP, UNFPA, and UNICEF in China have been small in scale and focused on particular developmental goals related to their area of responsibility. These agencies have a fairly diffuse presence within many different governmental offices and provide a wide range of opportunities for university scholars to participate in regional or international projects of mutual learning and enhancement.

The restrictive policies of the Chinese government in the past have posed a major obstacle to qualitative and quantitative research regarding many aspects of Chinese society, including education. Since the institution of the Four Modernizations and the subsequent Open Door Policy, the leadership has been more lenient in permitting education research by both domestic and foreign scholars. Nevertheless, much of the material published on Chinese education immediately following the reform period are empirically and theoretically weak. Often, the only source for the assertions made are the writers' own impressions, and any data originates from state-arranged interviews with designated educational professionals and policy-makers. Since the 1980s, there has been steadily growing interest in domestic issues among Chinese intellectuals, fostered by the reform era and growing international interest in China. As a result, the increase in dissertation research, as well as the growing number of social science research institutes, indicates a promising future for education research in general.

Main research institutes in China include the Chinese Academy of Sciences and the Chinese Academy of Social Sciences, and eleven key universities. They may apply on an equal basis for research funding, with all applications judged by a peer review process. For applied research, institutes and universities are officially encouraged to seek support through contracts with productive ministries and enterprises in addition to traditional allocations available within the national plan. This enhanced flexibility and opportunity for the exercise of initiative has made possible a more significant research role for higher level institutions.

NONFORMAL EDUCATION

From 1949 to 1981 the Chinese term for nonformal education was worker-peasant education. After the founding of the People's Republic of China, the Chinese Communist Party (CCP) launched a campaign to improve worker-peasant literacy for the sake of economic reconstruction. Formal classroom instruction, distance instruction through correspondence, and radio instruction were utilized at factories, production brigades, and government agencies. By 1956, about 62,000,000 peasants had attended different types of literacy classes, representing about 30 percent of the age group of 14 years and older from the country's rural population. To prepare students for college and quickly produce a new kind of intellectual drawn directly from working-class ranks, the CCP also initiated the *gongnong sucheng zhongxue* (worker-peasant accelerated middle school) experiment in 1950. However, because these schools could not compete with formal educational institutions, and students did not produce good academic records, the experiment was declared a failure and abandoned in 1955.

The term "adult education" was introduced to China by a study team from the International Council for Adult Education. After the Cultural Revolution, the Chinese government issued its first document regarding adult education on November 6, 1978, titled "Directives on the Issues of Literacy." It set up the standard to eradicate illiteracy among workers and peasants throughout the country; the ability of peasants to master 1,500 Chinese characters and of workers to master 2,000 characters; the capacity to read a newspaper; the ability to write simple letters and complete applications and appropriate forms; and the ability to complete a simple test measuring the above mentioned skills.

Adult education during the post-Mao period can be characterized by the restoration and re-establishment of institutions abolished during the Cultural Revolution. The 1980s witnessed a radical expansion of higher adult education institutions. Promotion and employment were more directly linked to one's academic rather than political background, increasing the demand for a college diploma. Because of the restrictive admissions policies of formal higher education institutions, the vast majority of high school graduates sought nonformal higher education training. By the end of 1998, approximately 661,705 schools of varied types of nonformal education produced 94,841,000 graduates.

Nonformal higher education is largely three years in length. It follows the curriculum for formal higher education in corresponding disciplines. Entrance to such programs usually requires passing the Adult Higher Education Entrance Examination, which is a national public examination. The State Education Commission now includes an adult educational department as do provincial, autonomous regional, municipal, and county-level education commissions, departments, and bureaus.

In addition to institutional nonformal higher education, open learning through the Self-Study Examination has attracted many candidates. Candidates may enroll in individual subjects and may accumulate their credentials over time. There is no entrance requirement for the self-study examination. The approach was first piloted in three major cities and one province in 1981 and was extended nationwide in 1983. This system was designed to expand the benefits of higher education with minimal investment. It appeals to many adults who do not want to sacrifice their jobs and family life to obtain a college diploma. With no limitation on age and formal education, it opens up higher education to an enormous number of Chinese citizens who would not have had a chance in regular colleges, and inspires great enthusiasm in higher learning.

The Self-Study Examination is offered twice each year. The National Examination Committee creates the tests, which are administered by local committees. Citizens can apply to take these examinations without having acquired previous course credit. Students who pass the examinations for four-year degree courses receive a bachelor's degree; those who pass three-year courses or single courses are issued certificates. At present, most of the provinces, municipalities, and autonomous regions have set up their own local committees for self-study examinations, whose specializations include the liberal arts, science, engineering, agriculture, finance, economics, politics, and law. In the first examination in April 1995, enrollment reached 3.65 million. Of these candidates, 50 percent were students of adult education institutions in one form or another; the other 50 percent had undertaken private study.

TEACHING PROFESSION

The scope of the teacher education system in the People's Republic of China is extensive. In numerical terms, teachers in China form the largest teaching force in the world. In 1998, there were 229 training institutions at various levels with 138,745 education majors enrolled. Yet this massive training system has barely met the de-

mand for the number of teachers required to sustain the even larger school system in terms of both quantity and quality. A range of serious policy problems, organizational barriers, and socioeconomic factors undermine the ability of the teacher education system to make adequate contributions to the nation.

There are two main categories of teachers in China, distinguished according to the source and structure of their pay. The first category is the *gongban* (state-paid) teachers who are regarded as state employees and earn a regular monthly salary comparable to other civil servants or workers in state-owned enterprises. The second category is the *minban* (community-paid) teachers who are paid by the local community. Their monthly income depends on the economic conditions of the local community.

The education of teachers is directly supervised by the State Education Commission. The Teacher Education Bureau is one of the 23 bureaus in the SEC and is immediately responsible for formulating policies on teacher education and supervising the development of the teacher training system, including the goals of teacher education, curriculum structure, recruitment of teacher trainees, and accreditation criteria. It also directly administers six key normal universities, namely those in Beijing, East China, Central China, Northeast China, Southwest China, and Shanxi. Provincial education commissions and education bureaus in the prefectures and counties are responsible for teacher education under their purview, and they are expected to implement the policies formulated by the central government.

The system of teacher education comprises two distinct subsystems: pre-service and in-service. Pre-service education is housed in monotechnic colleges or *shifan xueyuan* (specialized teacher education institutions), which enjoy a unique status within the overall education system. The lowest level of the pre-service subsystem recruits trainees from among junior secondary school graduates who are trained to be kindergarten and primary school teachers. This structure originated from the teacher education system that was first established in 1897 and heavily influenced by Japanese and German models. Because of the need for large numbers of teachers at various levels of schooling, the Chinese government, in different periods, still favored the hierarchical, monotechnic, and specialized teacher education system. In 1953, the Ministry of Education stipulated a three-tier system of pre-service teacher education: normal universities for the large administrative zones, teachers colleges in provinces and metropolitan cities, and junior colleges and secondary normal schools of various types at township and county levels.

The in-service teacher education is designed to provide unqualified teachers with appropriate training and education credentials. It is organized into four levels: provincial college of education; county or city college or teachers' advancement college; county teachers' school; and town and village teachers' supervisory center. Every level has specific target trainees. Provincial colleges are responsible for training senior high school teachers; county or city colleges for junior high school teachers; county teachers' school for primary and kindergarten teachers; and town and village teachers' center for teachers for their own geographic areas. The in-service courses are offered on a part-time basis and are more flexible in length and format. They also tend to accommodate the needs of individual groups of teachers. Sometimes, in-service institutions also organize research to address local problems.

The government maintains strict control over the teacher education curriculum and the SEC outlines the curriculum framework for all normal institutions, as well as specifies basic teaching hours and promotes the standardization of instructional materials by producing national course books for teacher trainees. The normal education curriculum is comprised of five major components: foundation courses, including politics, moral education, second languages and physical education; professional education courses, consisting of pedagogy, psychology, philosophy, history of education, sociology and so forth; subject matter specialization that replicates the major academic subjects in the secondary school curriculum; optional courses, such as art appreciation, computer literacy, counseling and extracurricular activities; and the teaching practicum, which is divided into a two-week and six-week block in the third and fourth year respectively. Besides setting development targets for the teaching training system, the Chinese Communist Party seeks to reaffirm the political and ideological orientation of teacher education, which is "to cultivate cultured persons as teachers with lofty ideals, high morality, strong discipline, and a sense of mission as educators, the engineers of the human soul and the gardeners of the nation's flowers" (Leung and Hui 2000).

Unlike the United States and many other countries, China traditionally has had no system of teacher certification. It was assumed, rather, that teachers were qualified by the professional training they received in their teacher education program. However, due to dramatic influx of untrained teachers in the Cultural Revolution decade, many teachers have not received pre-service preparation and have no claim to technical qualifications. Thus, in the mid-and-late 1980s, the government tried to directly reshape the teaching force through a system of teacher examinations and credentials.

The examinations are standardized for secondary teachers by the central government, while examinations for elementary teachers are the responsibility of each province. The system has a potentially powerful impact as it was designed to be coordinated with teacher ranking and salaries from 1989 on. Generally speaking, primary teachers should have at least graduated from the secondary normal schools or senior secondary schools; junior secondary schoolteachers should at least have a teaching diploma from the junior teachers colleges, while senior secondary teachers should be graduates of the normal universities and teachers colleges or degree holders from other tertiary institutions (Epstein 1991).

The state-paid teachers are categorized into grades according to their years of service and their standard of performance. In 1980, the Chinese government introduced a five-grade system. The highest grade is the super-grade teachers, who occupy 5 percent of the teaching force. The other grades, in descending order, are the senior, first, second, and third grade teachers. In 1990, only 6 percent of secondary teachers belonged to the senior grade, while the majority of secondary teachers were in the second grade. Most primary teachers were in the senior grade and first grade. This pattern of distribution of grades of teachers illustrates that the teaching force at the primary level is more experienced and older than that of secondary school teachers.

The lack of qualified teachers has been a serious problem in China since economic reforms started in the 1980s. Although the in-service teacher education system has contributed significantly to alleviating the problem, the national situation is far from satisfactory. There are two major factors accounting for the inconsistency in the demand for and supply of teachers. First, there is a general reluctance on the part of secondary school graduates to become teacher trainees since the reform of the Chinese economy opened up better paying opportunities for young people. Teacher remuneration became relatively unappealing in comparison with other state-paid occupations, not to mention the more lucrative jobs in the private sectors or foreign-invested enterprises. In 1991, the average annual income of state-paid occupations was 2,563 *yuan,* but the annual salary of the teaching profession averaged only 2,257 *yuan* and it ranked among the bottom third of the twelve major categories of occupations. Furthermore, it was not uncommon to see the delayed payment of teachers in the countryside and poor areas. Some villages and townships even paid teachers various factory or farm products instead of cash. Moreover, teachers were seriously deprived of fringe welfare benefits, such as good housing quarters, traveling, and medical care allowances that are critical in Chinese society.

The second factor accounting for the shortage of teachers is the internal efficiency of the school system and the teacher training system in general. The training capacity of the existing normal universities and teachers colleges has reached a maximum level, with an average of 28,000 trainees per institution. Most of these institutions are suffering from overcrowding and large class sizes, yet a proportion of the expansion in enrollment is taken up by non-normal specialties, as schools desperately try to attract more able students by offering more popular specialties such as finance, international trade, law, business management, accounting, and marketing.

The unique aspect of China's teacher training system is the rigid regulation of teacher education by the state and the Communist Party within the context of an economy and labor market that is experiencing a rapid reduction in the degree of state control. Because education remains a state-run business there has been a subtle change in terms of people's perception of teaching profession since the end of the twentieth century. Some young people started to view teaching as a guaranteed job with a stable income (although not very high), and it is better than facing uncertainties in private sectors. The teaching profession is gradually climbing up the occupational ladder. In the twenty-first century, China plans to implement system of teacher certification. After having their diploma and teaching experiences reviewed, current teachers should obtain their certificates quickly. For those who plan to choose teaching as their career, they will need to pass examinations on several education-related courses, such as education, psychology, and Mandarin.

Teacher education suffered severe setback during the Cultural Revolution from 1966 to 1976 when anti-intellectualism reached its climax. With the death of Mao Zedong, Chinese leaders once again emphasized the importance of teacher education in order to achieve nine-year compulsory education and the nation's grand modernization scheme. In 1987 the Chinese government established a national Teachers' Day on September 10 to honor the teaching profession. Despite the fact that teachers experience the ups and downs and receive low pay for their job, they enjoy unquestionable authority when they deliver knowledge to their students. The universal assumption in Chinese society is that the teacher tells the single and absolute truth, and the job of the students is to absorb the knowledge conveyed by the teacher without question. While some subjects (such as English, geometry, or algebra) provide more opportunities for students to practice or to drill, the structure of the lessons, their pace, and the nature of questioning are all determined by the teachers, who control the nature of classroom interactions. The most common experience for students is to go through the forty-five minute period without talking once, without being called on individually, or without asking a question. Students are taught that important knowledge comes from teachers and textbooks; that learning involves listening, thinking, and silent practice; and that the knowledge espoused by teachers and textbooks is not to be challenged, despite the lack of connection between course material and the immediate lives of the students.

SUMMARY

Since the founding of the People's Republic of China in 1949, education has been valued for the improvement of Chinese society rather than as a basic human right. Although the fundamental purpose or function of education has not changed, there have been some structural changes. Qualified personnel have been trained, and school conditions have improved. Education reform has progressed steadily—the nine-year compulsory education program has been implemented, primary education is becoming universal, and technical and vocational education has developed. Higher education also has developed quickly. Enrollments have increased, and a comprehensive system featuring a variety of disciplines is in place. Education for adults and minorities has been funded, and international exchange and studying abroad opportunities are also available. Most types of educational reforms in China since the 1980s have led to decentralization and the granting of semi-autonomy to lower administrative levels. In addition, college education has become a prerequisite for official bureaucratic positions.

However, much remains to be done in order to provide education to most Chinese citizens. Overall, education is insufficiently and unevenly developed. The discrepancy in the quality of education between rural areas and urban areas is overwhelming. There are no reliable sources of rural school financing. Investment in education also is inadequate. Teachers' salaries and benefits remain low, and working conditions often are poor. The elitist nature of key schools and the early determination of students' majors prevent students from discovering and developing their talents and imagination freely. The "brain-drain" problem goes beyond accommodating returned students from the West. Educational philosophy, teaching concepts, and methodologies are divorced from reality to varying degrees; practical and personal applications need to be emphasized over ideological and political work in the curriculum. Furthermore, the educational system and its management mechanism cannot meet the needs of the continual restructuring of the economy, politics, science, and technology. These problems are caused by variable combinations of politics, economics, and professional assumptions about how to develop modern education in China. As the economy expands and the reform deepens, serious efforts must be made to solve these educational problems.

BIBLIOGRAPY

Agelasto, Michael, and Bob Adamson, eds. *Higher Education in Post-Mao China.* Hong Kong: Hong Kong University, 1998.

Ashmore, Rhea A., and Zhen Cao. *Teacher Education in the People's Republic of China.* Bloomington: Phi Delta Kappa Educational Foundation, 1997.

Ayers, William. *Chang Chih-tung and Educational Reform in China.* Cambridge, MA: Harvard University Press, 1971.

Deng, Peng. *Private Education in Modern China.* Westport, CN: Praeger Publishers, 1997.

Epstein, Irving, ed. *Chinese Education: Problems, Policies, and Prospects.* New York: Garland Publishing, Inc., 1991.

Gardner, Howard. *To Open Minds: Chinese Clues to the Dilemma of Contemporary Education.* New York: Basic Books, Inc., Publishers, 1989.

Hansen, Mette Halskov. *Lessons in Being Chinese: Minority Education and Ethnic Identity in Southwest China.* Seattle: University of Washington, 1990.

Hayhoe, Ruth. *China's Universities, 1895-1995: A Century of Cultural Conflict.* New York: Garland Publishing, Inc., 1996.

Hu, Chang-Tu, ed. *Chinese Education Under Communism.* New York: Teachers College, Columbia University, 1962.

Leung, Julian Y. M., and Xu Hui. "People's Republic of China." In *Teacher Education in the Asia-Pacific Region: A Comparative Study,* eds. Paul Morris and John Williamson, 175-197. New York: Falmer Press, 2000.

Lin, Jing. *Social Transformation and Private Education in China.* Westport, CN: Praeger, 1999.

Liu, Hai-chen, et al. *Voices from Unoccupied China.* Chicago: The University of Chicago Press, 1944.

Liu, Judith, Heidi A. Ross, and Donald P. Kelly, eds. *The Ethnographic Eye: An Interpretative Study of Education in China.* New York: Falmer Press, 2000.

Lutz, Jessie Gregory. *China and the Christian Colleges, 1850-1950.* Ithaca, NY: Cornell University Press, 1971.

National Bureau of Statistics. *China Statistical Yearbook,* 1999. Available from http://www.stats.gov.

Ni, Ting. *Stones from Other Hills: A History of the Chinese Who Studied in 1930s/40s America.* Ph.D. diss., Indiana University, 1996.

Niu, Xiaodong. *Policy Education and Inequalities in Communist China since 1949.* Lanham, MD: University Press of America, Inc., 1992.

Orleans, Leo A. *Chinese Students in America: Policies, Issues, and Numbers.* Washington, DC: National Academy Press, 1988.

———. *Professional Manpower and Education in Communist China.* Washington DC: National Science Foundation, 1960.

Peake, Cyrus H. *Nationalism and Education in Modern China.* New York: Howard Fertig, 1970.

Pepper, Suzanne. *China's Universities.* Ann Arbor, Michigan: University of Michigan, 1984.

———. *China's Education Reform in the 1980s: Policies, Issues, and Historical Perspectives.* Berkeley, CA: University of California, 1990.

———. *Radicalism and Education Reform in 20th-Century China.* New York: Cambridge University Press, 1996.

Postiglione, Gerard A., ed. *China's National Minority Education: Culture, Schooling, and Development.* New York: Falmer Press, 1999.

Prybbyla, Jan S. "Hsia-Fang: The Economics and Politics of Rustication in China." *Pacific Affairs,* vol. 48 (summer 1975).

Trueba, Henry T., and Yali Zou. *Power in Education: The Case of Miao University Students and Its Significance for American Culture.* Bristol, PA: The Falmer Press, 1994.

Walton, Linda. *Academies and Society in Southern Sung China.* Honolulu: University of Hawaii Press, 1999.

Wheeler, David. "More Students Study Abroad, But Their Stays Are Shorter." *Chronicle of Higher Education,* 17 November 2000.

Yeh, Wen-hsin. *The Alienated Academy: Culture and Politics in Republican China, 1919-1937.* Cambridge: Harvard University Press, 1990.

—*Ting Ni*

CHRISTMAS ISLAND

BASIC DATA

Official Country Name:	Christmas Island
Region:	Oceania
Population:	2,564
Language(s):	English, Chinese, Malay

Literacy Rate: NA

The territory of Christmas Island is 870 miles northwest of Australia. Seventy-three percent of the population is Chinese; however, English is the primary language taught in school. The rest of the population is Malaysian, European, or Australian. The educational system recognizes and celebrates the various multicultural holidays and ceremonies.

Children between the ages of 6 and 15 must attend school or some other government program. The Christmas Island High School provides education through tenth grade only; students must transfer to the mainland or elsewhere to complete the last two years of high school or university. Home schooling is a common trend, but parents must apply for approval. As of September 2000, there were a total of 450 students: 64 students enrolled in preprimary school, 271 in primary school, and 115 in secondary school.

The educational system is based on the Australian curriculum. Teachers on the Island come from Western Australia. Since 1990, more money has been allocated to ensure that students receive a comparable education to the mainland, despite the remote location. Recent improvements include the acquisition of computers and a technology laboratory for students, a new science laboratory, and a new library.

BIBLIOGRAPHY

Australian State Department of Education, 1997. Available from http://www.eddept.wa.edu.au.

—*LeAnna DeAngelo*

COLOMBIA

BASIC DATA

Official Country Name:	Republic of Colombia
Region:	South America
Population:	39,685,655
Language(s):	Spanish
Literacy Rate:	91.3%
Number of Primary Schools:	47,663
Compulsory Schooling:	5 years
Public Expenditure on Education:	4.1%

Educational Enrollment:	Primary: 4,692,614
	Secondary: 3,317,782
	Higher: 644,188
Educational Enrollment Rate:	Primary: 113%
	Secondary: 61%
	Higher: 17%
Teachers:	Primary: 189,123
	Secondary: 169,816
	Higher: 66,538
Student-Teacher Ratio:	Primary: 25:1
	Secondary: 20:1
Female Enrollment Rate:	Primary: 112%
	Secondary: 66%
	Higher: 18%

HISTORY & BACKGROUND

Located in the northwestern part of South America, Columbia touches both the Atlantic and Pacific Oceans, bordering Ecuador and Peru on the south and Brazil and Venezuela on the east. In July 2000, the census reported the population to be 39,685,655, with the majority of people living in large cities in the center and the northern part of the country. The census reported that the population was divided into six ethnic groups: 58 percent *mestizo* or of Native American and Spanish ancestry; 20 percent white; 14 percent mulatto; 4 percent black; 3 percent were both black and Native American; and 1 percent Native American. Spanish is the official language, and over 90 percent of the people indicated that they were Catholic.

Since 1886, the official name of the country has been the República de Colombia. Administratively, the country is divided into 32 departments and one capital district. Geographically, three mountain ranges and two major rivers divide the country into four regions. Although the central executive branch dominates the government structure, Colombia has a long history of regionalism. The early constitutions reinforced the notion that Colombia was a loose federation of different regions, which allowed each region to develop its own government. While countries such as Mexico, Argentina, and Brazil built railways and systems of roads to unify their peoples, Colombia resisted such innovations. In 2000, although the country had a land mass of 1,038,700 square kilometers, there were only 3,380 kilometers of railways. There were a total 115,564 kilometers of roadways; however, only 13,864 kilometers of which were paved (Williams and Guerrieri; Central Intelligence Agency).

Columbia is a country of contrasts. There are large cities facing the common problems of industrialization such as air pollution from vehicle emissions. There are rural sections where underdevelopment is a problem. Only about 4 percent of the land is arable, and about 48 percent of it remains forests and woodlands. Despite these large natural areas in Colombia, deforestation and soil abuse persist as serious problems. The population suffers from extreme income inequality. In 1995, 10.0 percent of the population consumed 46.9 percent of the available income, while the lowest 10.0 percent of the population consumed only 1.0 percent. In 1999, this disparity of wealth and poverty was reflected in Colombia's per capita purchasing power of $6,200. An unemployment rate of 20 percent intensified the economic problems (Central Intelligence Agency).

Before the arrival of the Spanish, several Native American groups occupied the region. However, none of these people had developed the ability to write. Some groups, such as the Taironas constructed impressive roads, bridges, systems of platforms for large buildings, and mountainside terraces for agriculture. The Taironas also produced stone statuary, gold objects, and fine ceramics. The largest group was the Muisca, who lived in the intermountain basins of the Cordillera Oriental. Depending mostly on agriculture for survival, the Muisca made cotton textiles, worked gold, and made some stone sculptures. Although there is reason to believe the Muisca were unifying their society when the Spanish arrived, the group never demonstrated the engineering abilities of the Taironas. Within 100 years after the first Spanish settlement, nearly 95 percent of all Native Americans in Colombia had died. Many were killed during armed conflicts with European settlers, but the majority of deaths were caused by diseases such as smallpox and measles, which were imported by Spanish settlers (Bushnell).

The era of Spanish colonization began in 1510 with the founding of San Sebastian near Panama. In 1526, settlers founded Santa Marta, the oldest Spanish city still in existence in Colombia. For most of the colonial period, New Granada, which included the areas that became Columbia, Panama, Venezuela, and Ecuador, fell within the Viceroyalty of Peru as part of the Spanish empire. In 1739, New Granada retained independent status as a Viceroyalty separate from Peru. Administrative divisions such as these influenced the boundaries of the countries when they sought independence (Bushnell).

Although many Spaniards began their explorations searching for gold, other colonists took advantage of the sedentary lifestyle of Native American groups such as the Muisca. The Spanish established themselves as the leaders and ruled through the existing native social organizations. The Spanish crown outlawed this system of exploiting Native American labor, called *encomienda*.

However, the practice did continue for some time because it served as a type of educational institution through which the European leaders were able to teach the Native Americans the Christian faith and the ways of civilization.

Most Spanish colonists avoided the tropical grasslands of the interior. Jesuit priests went into those regions and established missions that gathered together the communities of semi-settled Native American groups who lived there. Depending on Native American labor, these missionaries created cattle ranches and plantations that passed into the hands of other religious orders in 1767 when the Jesuits were expelled from the Spanish empire. Through these mission communities, Catholic priests served as mediators between the settled Native Americans and the Spanish state, and they provided education for the Native Americans that otherwise was unavailable. However, critics complain that the education Native Americans received in the missions actually was nothing more than an indoctrination into the Christian faith and instruction in Spanish. In spite of existing historical documents that show that the clergy was urged to teach the Native Americans, little education actually took place (Bushnell; Londoño).

The earliest missionary schools date to the mid-sixteenth century. In 1533, Fray Juan Luis de los Barrios founded a school, while Archbishop Luis de Zapata de Cárdenas established the Seminary San Luis. Although the seminary closed in 1586 due to student dissatisfaction, it later reopened. In 1580, the first university, Universidad de Estudios Generales, was opened in Bogotá by Orden de los Predicadores. This university later merged with the Santo Tomás School and taught religion under the new name Colegio-Universidad Santo Tomás. In 1622, the Jesuits opened Javeriana University, offering grammatical studies, and in 1635, Archbishop Fray Cristóóbal de Torres created the Colegio Mayor de Nuestra Señora del Rosario. All of these schools were in Bogotá, and each had a curriculum that was theoretical and focused on subjects such as law, logic, grammar, theology, and oratory (Londoño).

In 1783, José Celestino Mutis, Barón de Humbolt, and Francisco José de Caldas came to New Granada, the area now known as Colombia, to start the Expedición Botánica. Their goal was to record all of the botanical species found in South America. Although this task was too great for the expedition to fulfill, group members spread scientific thinking through the colony and Mutis won honorary membership in the Swedish Academy of Science (Londoño; Bushnell).

Nonetheless, the educational efforts in New Grenada were extensive. By the end of the colonial period in 1819, the number of Catholic clerics—whose calling essentially required spiritual and educational endeavors—rose to nearly 1,850. With a population of 1.4 million during the early 1800s, the ratio of priests to citizens reached 750 to 1. This ration exceeds the ratio found in any Latin American country in the 1990s (Bushnell; Low-Maus).

In 1819, when the famous leader Simón Bolívar addressed the Congress of Angostura, he called for the establishment of universal popular education, claiming that the Catholic religious orders had not created anything that resembled a proper system. The clerics could not provide education for children from rural areas or from lower classes, despite the large number of priests in colonial New Grenada. To some extent, Bolívar's request went unheeded. The members of the congress had not come together to improve education. Having broken with Spain, they sought to define the country's political organization. Thus, they unified the regions of the former New Granada, Venezuela, and Ecuador into what they named *Gran Colombia*. The members of the congress appointed Bolívar president and Francisco de Paula Santander vice president.

In 1821, the Congress of Cúcuta devised a constitution for this new country. However, before the regular Congress of Gran Colombia could form, the Congress of Cúcuta abolished all monasteries with fewer than eight members, confiscated their assets, and placed the money in an endowment for the development of secondary schools. Although these actions were driven more by anticlerical feelings than by educational concerns, Santander did open several new secondary schools. Despite opposition from the Catholic Church, Santander urged that works by unorthodox authors, such as Jeremy Bentham, be included in the school's curriculums. In the meantime, Bolívar continued as the head of the Colombian armies that were battling Spain for control of the country (Low-Maus; Bushnell).

According to the congressional delegates in 1821, Spanish indifference had caused widespread illiteracy, a condition they pledged to correct. Thus, in the constitution of 1821, the delegates chose 1840 as the date by which all voters would have to pass a literacy test. Unfortunately, for the next 10 years, educational reform moved slowly. In 1832, delegates met in a national convention to draft a new constitution. However, acknowledging that literacy had not spread throughout the new republic, the delegates postponed the date for voter literacy tests until 1850 (Bushnell).

A civil war called the War of the Supremes (1839-42) interrupted educational reform. After the war, because of the tendency of local leaders to inflate their positions, Colombian president Pedro Alcántara Herrán and his secretary of the interior, Mariano Ospina Rodríguez, introduced new methods and pedagogical principles. For example, they removed the controversial authors from the secondary curriculum, reduced the extent of theoretical studies, and increased studies that had more practical applications, such as natural science. In addition, Herrán invited the Jesuits back to become teachers and to continue their work in frontier missions (Bushnell; Low-Maus).

In 1849, after a close and controversial election, José Hilario López, a Liberal Party candidate, became president. In 1850, fulfilling the Liberals' desire to reverse many of the Conservative policies, the Congress enacted various policies that were intended to increase the freedom of education. The Congress disbanded all universities, placing those programs of higher education into *colegios* (secondary schools), and ended all academic requirements for people to practice any profession, with the exception of pharmacy. The citizens had the freedom to decide what training they needed, or if they needed any education at all, before entering a profession. In the same year, López reversed Herrán's invitation to the Jesuits. He argued that the sanction of 1697, which originally expelled the Jesuits from the Spanish empire, was still valid in New Granada. According to the anticlerical views held by some of López's associates, the Jesuits had to be expelled because their schools converted citizens to conservative Catholicism (Bushnell).

To consolidate their victories, the liberals adopted a new constitution in 1853. They offered universal male suffrage, removed the electoral college system, and increased the number of officials who were elected rather than appointed. The provincial legislature of Vélez extended suffrage to women. In addition, the new constitution guaranteed freedom of worship for all citizens and introduced civil marriage and divorce. In 1863, the liberals framed another constitution that changed the name of the state to *Estados Unidos de Colombia* (United States of Colombia) and advanced the regionalism of the country. The new constitution gave extensive authority to the then nine states, allowing them to determine their own suffrage laws and maintain their own services, such as postal delivery. To further limit the authority of the federal government, the constitution of 1863 reduced the president's term to two years and prohibited anyone from serving consecutive terms (Bushnell).

By 1867 the liberal government had started to undo the educational reforms of 1850. It established the Universidad Nacional de Colombia in Bogatá. Emphasizing the traditional disciplines of law, medicine, and philosophy, the university offered technical studies to help Colombia enter the mechanical age. Three years later, the Congress made primary education in Colombia free and compulsory and established several teacher training institutions—called normal schools—to meet the sudden need for teachers. To assist in the process, German experts were brought in to serve as instructors at the normal schools. Fearing this represented the beginning of a godless education, church leaders called on parents to ignore the public schools. Some Catholics complained that the German educators imported to staff in the schools belonged to the Protestant faith. To alleviate the controversy, the government allowed church representatives to offer religious instruction in the public primary schools during specific hours to pupils whose parents requested it. Some states required religious teaching in the primary schools. These controversies continued to grow and became part of the civil war that erupted in 1876 (Bushnell; Londoño).

CONSTITUTIONAL & LEGAL FOUNDATIONS

The Conservative Party ended the Liberal Party's domination of the federal government in 1882 with the election of Rafael Nuñez. After sitting out two years as required by the Constitution of 1863, Nuñez regained the presidency and called a convention to draft a new constitution. Adopted in 1886, this constitution, which remained in effect until 1991, offered free elementary education to any child who wanted it. However, the constitution reversed the 1870 law that made such elementary education compulsory. At the same time, the constitution declared Colombia a republic and recognized the Catholic Church as the national church. The following year, the government entered the Concordat of 1887, requiring that all public education be done in accordance with the Roman Catholic religion. As result, clergy could approve school texts, determine the curriculum, and appoint teachers (Bushnell, Hanson).

In 1903, the central government took responsibility for establishing a national system of education with the passage of the Organic Law of Public Education, which made education free but not compulsory. Together with its regulating decree of 1904, the Organic Law set up a system of national inspection, divided schools into elementary and secondary levels, and established professional, industrial, and artistic branches. Although the law of 1903 placed education under the control of the states, it gave the power to set policy for all public, private, state, and national schools to the Ministry of Education. Other levels of government took different responsibilities. For example, states had to pay teacher salaries while municipalities had to construct and furnish the schools. Unfortunately, the law perpetuated discrepancies between urban and rural education by ordering cities to provide six years of schooling and requiring rural areas to provide only three (Hanson).

In 1927, the Conservative government of Colombia made education compulsory, but did not provide funds to make this possible. Consequently, public education remained unavailable for most Colombians even though it was supposed to be free and compulsory. As a result, in 1930, most Colombians lacked basic literacy skills (Hanson; Bushnell).

With the Great Depression of the 1930s, the Conservative Party lost control of national politics. The Liberal candidate, Alfonso López Pumarejo, became president in 1934, and he increased spending on schools and rural roadways. To increase the status of teachers, López Pumarejo's Liberal government established registries, required high school teachers to have university degrees, and set up national salary scales for teachers. In 1936, the Liberal government adopted a law stating that neither race nor religion was an adequate reason to deny students admission to schools (Bushnell; Hanson).

In his most controversial act, López Pumarejo changed the constitution to remove the Catholic Church as the final authority on permissible practices in schools. Enacted in 1936, these amendments enabled the Colombian Ministry of Education to encourage coed education, even though Pope Pius XI urged Catholics to avoid this practice. At the same time, the Ministry of Education invited liberal humanist scholars from Europe to come to Colombia. In addition, while the Conservative government had mandated religious training in the public schools, the Liberal Party turned schools toward patriotic education. As a result, instructional materials and programs emphasized the patriotic duties of citizens, the accomplishments of traditional heroes, and the value of national goals instead of spiritual development. In reaction, Conservatives complained that the Liberal administration assaulted moral and religious values (Bushnell; Hanson).

The controversy over religion and education grew into the struggles known as the *Violencia* (The Violence). During the election of 1946, dissension split the Liberal Party. Marino Ospina Pérez, a Conservative Party member, won the presidential election. Two years later, a leader of the Liberal party was shot and killed. Liberals blamed Conservatives for the assassination and riots broke out. According to some estimates, the fighting claimed the lives of 300,000 people. Ironically, as the death rate rose, so did the economy—the rate of industrial output increased 9 percent per year from 1945 to 1955 (Bushnell; Hanson).

In 1957, a military junta took control of the federal government. To bring peace, they adopted a set of mathematical guidelines to the Constitution that required the Liberal Party and the Conservative Party to share all elective and appointive offices. According to this agreement, the two parties alternated control of the presidency. Although criticized for being undemocratic, these rules created a coalition known as the National Front that ended the *Violencia*. Other violent outbreaks would occur in Colombia, such as the drug war of the 1980s, but the killings did not reach the levels of the 1940s and 1950s (Bushnell).

During the 1980s, the governor of each of the country's departments (equivalent to a U.S. state) served as the chief administrative officer of his or her department and controlled all the educational matters in that department. Each governor appointed a secretary of education, who directed the schools in his or her department and reported to the governor. In 1986, there were about 32,000 such schools in the different departments, which at the time numbered 22. On the national level, the president appointed a minister of education to oversee national schools, of which there were about 500, and private schools, of which there were about 8,000. At the same time, the president appointed the governors (Hanson).

In 1991, Colombia approved a new constitution. Although the constitution declared Colombia to be a unitary republic, it added that it was decentralized, with territorial entities remaining autonomous, democratic, participatory, and pluralist. In accord with the goal of making the country more open to popular participation in local affairs, the new constitution introduced the popular election of departmental governors. Under the previous constitution, the national president appointed the governors. The constitution of 1991 required proportional representation when electing members of upper house of the Congress. Among the other provisions, the constitution of 1991 made education compulsory for children between the ages of 5 and 15 years and recommended one year of prekindergarten training. It recommended other changes, such as bilingual education for communities where the population spoke an indigenous language, and it repeated the requirement that all teachers had to be professionally trained (Hanson; Bushnell).

Reinforcing the growing secular influences in Colombia, the new constitution eliminated any reference to Catholicism as the national religion. It specifically placed all religious denominations on equal legal footing, and it made divorce subject to civil law, thereby making civil divorce legal (Bushnell). Unfortunately, it is unclear what effect this change in religious policy will have on educational matters. For example, in 1936, the government amended the constitution by removing the authority of the Catholic Church in educational matters. However, as late as 1971, critics had complained that, although the Ministry of Education was most responsible for education in the country's departments, the ministry could not regulate such things as private school tuition because these schools were Catholic. In the church dioceses bishops ensured that the Catholic faith was taught in public

schools and that lessons did not contradict the Church's magesterium. The bishops approved religion textbooks adopted by elementary and high schools, and the archbishop of Bogotá decided what religion texts the universities used. If a religion teacher ignored a bishop's requirements the bishop could remove the teacher from his or her position (Londoño).

The practice of religious control of the schools continues despite constitutional changes because the Catholic Church has more influence in Colombia than in any other country in the Western Hemisphere. In Colombia, clerics wield their power informally through interpersonal relations. Consequently, though the constitution of 1991 sought to establish distance between the government and the church, church officials continued to appear in public forums offering their blessings to official acts. Thus, while private schools may have had to adjust to government regulations and conform to courses of study prescribed by the Ministry of Education, Catholic bishops unofficially retained authority over such matters in the public school (Williams and Guerrieri).

EDUCATIONAL SYSTEM—OVERVIEW

As a result of increased school enrollment, nearly 92 percent of the adults in Colombia over age 15 had at least the basic ability to read and to write in the year 2000. The increases in education were significant. In 1935, enrollment at the elementary school level reached about 550,000, while in 1980, that number had risen to nearly 4,200,000. A dramatic increase took place at the secondary level as well, although it was not as far reaching as the elementary increase. In 1935, enrollment in high schools totaled 45,670 students; by 1980, the number had grown to 1,824,000 (Hanson).

In 1999, the preschool enrollment for private and public schools in urban and rural areas totaled 1,034,182 students. This included 522,209 boys and 511,973 girls. In elementary schools, total enrollment reached 5,162,260 students, including 2,632,187 boys and 2,530,073 girls. The total high school enrollment reached 3,594,083 students, including 1,734,012 boys and 1,860,071 girls. These figures imply that females were somewhat more likely to attend high school than boys.

Academic Year: In general, the academic structure of the educational system in Colombia remains relatively constant. Preschool or kindergarten is usually in private hands. A child may enter at age four and continue through age six. Primary schooling in Columbia begins with five years of elementary education followed by four years of secondary education. After this basic cycle, students proceed to a second level of secondary education, lasting two years. Generally, these six years of secondary education appear together. Upon finishing that level, the students may pass on to some kind of technical training or commercial studies, or they can attend university and eventually pursue graduate studies (Low-Maus; Wellington).

The National Ministry of Education offers two options for the school calendar. One option begins in February, offers a four-week vacation in June and July, and finishes in November. The second option begins in September, offers a four-week vacation in December, and finishes in June. Both systems offer 198 days of school attendance (Wellington).

Language of Instruction: Some schools offer bilingual opportunities and employ languages like French, German, or English for instruction. However, these are expensive, private academies serving the students of prosperous families. In general, Spanish is used in most schools, especially those in those rural areas where Spanish is the dominant language. In areas of the country where an indigenous language dominates, the law requires that schools offer bilingual programs using the native languages (Parra).

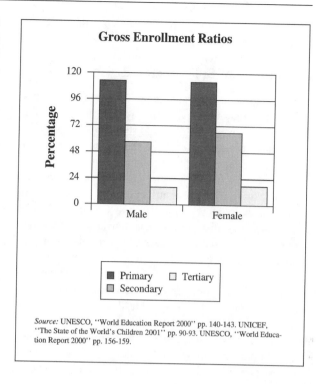

Source: UNESCO, "World Education Report 2000" pp. 140-143. UNICEF, "The State of the World's Children 2001" pp. 90-93. UNESCO, "World Education Report 2000" pp. 156-159.

Grading System: In most high schools, grades are awarded on a scale extending from 1 to 10. This system was adopted in 1973, replacing a system that used a scale of one to five. However, universities retained the shorter system. In university courses, students take final exams that count for twenty percent of the grade. These tests are two hours long and the students take one per day for five days (Wellington).

Religious Schools: The distribution of enrollment between public schools and private schools, most of which are Catholic, illustrates that, while private elementary schools have become more popular, public high schools have also increased in popularity. In 1935, about 93 percent of the elementary age students attended public schools. However, at the high school level, about 46 percent attended public schools. In 1980, the proportion of students attending public elementary schools dropped to 85 percent, while the proportion of high school students attending public schools increased to about 56 percent (Hanson).

In general, schools do not buy textbooks. Instead, the parents must purchase school supplies after schoolteachers or administrators indicate which books they should buy from local sources. These books may come from publishers in Colombia or from foreign firms. Usually, when a school adopts a textbook, it uses the book for three years. For many years, the Instituto Colombiano de Pedagogía (ICOLPE) of the Ministry of Education developed primers, called *cartillas,* and used five of the prim-

ers per subject to enhance elementary school teachers' pedagogical skills and to provide materials and suggestions to facilitate their daily work. Distributed without charge, the cartillas were well received. A less successful effort was the Ministry's attempt to develop and publish textbooks that followed appropriate educational objectives for each subject (Londoño).

Curriculum—Development: Colombia has long sought to turn the secondary curriculum toward practical or vocational education. After the civil war of 1839, President Pedro Alcántara Herrán, and his secretary of the interior, Mariano Ospina Rodríguez, introduced new methods of instruction and pedagogical principles into the secondary schools. For example, they removed the controversial authors from the secondary curriculum that Santander had introduced in the 1830s, reduced the extent of theoretical studies, and increased studies that had more practical applications, such as natural science (Bushnell; Low-Maus).

From 1948 to 1970, the Ministry tried to spread vocational, technical, and agricultural schools throughout the country. Despite these efforts, in 1977, more than 70 percent of the high school students enrolled in academic programs. Unfortunately, very few of these students went on to any higher education, often leaving school unprepared to earn a living (Hanson 1986). Efforts were made to increase vocational education, but most secondary school students enrolled in academic programs. When colleges and universities opened new programs to meet the growing number of academic students, the programs were often poor quality.

PREPRIMARY & PRIMARY EDUCATION

In Colombia, the available pre-kindergarten and kindergarten programs vary from day care programs that simply watch over the children to sophisticated programs employing specialized teachers and advanced technology. Almost 92 percent of the pre-kindergarten and kindergarten centers are Catholic, privately owned and operated, and are located in urban centers. In 1970, to increase educational opportunities, the Congress allowed universities to offer pre-kindergarten and kindergarten programs. Thus, public universities currently offer programs to train early childhood teachers. While most of these require four or five years of study, the Universidad Pedagógica de Bogotá offers a three-year early childhood teaching program. However, this did not increase the number of public kindergartens because the graduates of these training programs chose to work in private kindergarten centers that offered better salaries and more opportunities for teachers than did the public schools (Londoño).

According to 1999 statistics (from the National Administrative Department of Statistics), about 56 percent of preschool students enroll in public institutions. Although the public preschools enjoy a higher percentage of the total preschool enrollment, there are fewer public preschools because, public preschool centers are usually larger than the private ones.

Unlike preschools, most primary schools are free public institutions operated by the department government with the assistance of the National Ministry of Education. Although children may enter these public primary schools at six years of age, most children enter at age seven. Usually, the classrooms are self-contained and the instructional day lasts for six hours, divided into two sessions. Each day contains three 45-minute class periods and a 45-minute break. Instruction includes the following subjects, in order of their importance: Spanish, arithmetic, social studies, aesthetic and manual training, natural science, physical education, and religious and moral training (Wellington).

Early efforts to establish primary education did not enjoy great success. In the 1830s, under the direction of President Francisco de Paula Santander, public primary school enrollment rose from 17,000 children to 20, 000. Combined with private school attendance, this still meant that less than 15 percent of the primary school population was attending school. In 1870, when the Congress made primary education in Colombia free and compulsory, the national government offered 4 percent of its budget (200,000 pesos) to education, with 20 percent of that sum

going to universities. Nonetheless, primary schools spread. In 1870, 60,155 students were enrolled, and by 1874, the number had grown to more than 84,000 (Bushnell).

In 1957, in an effort to stabilize public schooling, the Congress sought to dedicate 10 percent of the national budget to education. However, those efforts were inadequate, as the system needed more extensive funding. In 1970, for example, about 70 percent of rural school age children did not attend school. Nearly 77 percent of the rural schools had one classroom, and 80 percent of the rural schools had one teacher. Few students attended school for very long. As a result, of the students enrolled, 55 percent attended the first grade. Facilities were poor—21 percent of the students lacked desks. Of the rural teachers, 68 percent lacked normal school preparation, and 52 percent had not registered as teachers (Hanson).

In fairness, the problems of rural education were complex. In 1970, when the majority of rural children received less than three years of formal education, a teacher could expect to meet only about one-third of the students enrolled. However, this did not signify a lack of interest. In some cases, the school calendar conflicted with the labor needs of the family, which depended on agriculture to survive. In other cases, the lack of paved roads made travel to school difficult during periods of heavy rain (Havens and Flinn).

In rural areas, schools tended to stress practical subjects. In the 1970s, educators repeatedly said that the rural schools should teach students about the problems that existed in the country. Unfortunately, this meant that current technology was little-used in classrooms. Worse, the department secretaries expected teachers to present problems at the central office. Consequently, the teachers closed their classrooms and rode buses to the reach the city where the office was located. In 1977, to solve this problem, the secretaries tried to divide each state into planning, administrative, and instructional systems. Since most rural primary schools offered programs that were shorter than five years, the plan tried to include one five-year school in each district, which were about 10 kilometers in length. Secondary schools almost never appeared in rural areas (Hanson).

In the 1980s, Colombian educators introduced an innovation called the New School Movement that spread throughout Latin America. It was an effort to encourage self-instruction. Specially written guides took the place of textbooks. These guides covered such subjects as math, social science, and language. They offered detailed instructions allowing students to proceed on their own. In addition, the guides suggested activities and exercises the students could pursue in school or at home. Such flexible programming allowed students to leave school to help the family during harvest time, for example, and to resume studies at the same point when they returned to school.

Teachers asked parents and community members to form school councils, tend school gardens, and help teachers during lessons. Some critics complained that the New School Movement reduced teacher involvement, and other critics complained that many teachers misused the guides by making the students work through them as they marched through textbooks. Although the new schools emphasized self-instruction, they cost about 10 percent more than traditional ones. Nonetheless, about 12,500 new schools spread throughout Colombia, and, in 1989, the World Bank recommended that other developing nations adopt the New School Movement. As a result, Guatemala, Chile, Argentina, Nicaragua, and the Philippines adopted the movement (Lopez).

Unfortunately, elementary education remained in poor condition. In the 1991 four-year plan, the government acknowledged that studies on primary education revealed the quality was low, the rate of school failure was high, and the curriculum was of little relevance to students (Hanson).

SECONDARY EDUCATION

In Colombia, secondary education is concentrated in urban areas. As a result, a disproportionate number of high school students come from wealthy families. This bias toward the wealthy children remains true even though about 60 percent of the students enroll in public schools. (Hanratty and Meditz).

Secondary education grew rapidly in Colombia. In 1970, 20 percent of children in the appropriate age group enrolled in some form of secondary education. However, by 1980, this number had doubled to 40 percent (Psacharopoulos and Loxley). In 1990, secondary school enrollments reached 1,849,243, which was about 46 percent of the school-age population (Hanson 1995).

In Colombia, secondary education is divided into two parts, middle school training (*educación media*), and secondary school training (*educación secundaria.*) Both terms refer to level 6 through 11 and are often offered together. The sole requirement to enter a public secondary school is to satisfactorily complete a primary school course. Generally, private schools require the students to pass an entrance examination. As a result, public secondary schools tend to serve the lower income groups and offer more diversified educational programs leading to employment as well as higher education. Most private secondary schools offer a *Bachillerato Académico o Clásico*. However, since 1974, the secondary schools have had to offer at least one other curriculum besides those leading to an academic diploma (Wellington).

In 1974, the Ministry of Education mandated that the curriculums operate on two cycles. The *Ciclo Básico* (Basic Cycle) occupies the first four years of instruction and all students receive the same fundamental academic instruction. In addition, they spend five hours per week in what might be called vocational exploration. The advanced secondary cycle takes up two years. It may be called *Ciclo Vocacional* (vocational cycle) or the *Ensen nza Media Diversificada* (diversified courses). In these programs, students may complete programs leading to different degrees, such as *Bachillerato Acádemico o Clásico, Bachillerato Pedagógico,* or *Bachillerato Agropecuario* (Wellington).

In general, there are three types of secondary schools. The bulk of the institutions include public and private schools that prepare the students for university training and teach humanities and science courses. In 1981, the enrollment in these schools included about 72 percent of overall secondary enrollment. The second type of secondary school includes vocational or teacher training institutes. Although students in these schools take the basic academic subjects, the schools emphasize vocational subjects through all six years. In 1981, about 25 percent of the students were enrolled in this type of school. Finally, a small percentage of students enroll in *Institutos Nacionales de Enseñanza Media Diversificada,* or comprehensive high schools (Psacharopoulos and Loxley).

In 1969, the Ministry of Education began the *Institutos Nacionales de Enseñanza Media Diversificada* to encourage vocational education. Offering academic courses and various vocational programs, these schools operate on the same four-year Basic Cycle and two-year Vocational Cycle pattern found in other schools. However, instead of different schools offering different specialties, many options are grouped together in the same building. These schools spread rapidly, in part because international organizations such as the International Bank of Reconstruction and Development and the United States Agency for International Development contributed to their establishment and support (Wellington 1984).

Another highly regarded vocational program in Colombia operates from the Ministry of Labor. Called *Servicio Nacional de Aprendizaje* (SENA), this program provides on-the-job training to people who have completed a primary school education. It began in 1957 and is supported by a payroll tax. Shortly after the ministry introduced SENA programs, all the departments began offering them, enrolling more than 23,000 trainees annually. By 1987, more than 15 percent of the urban workforce had attended SENA training sessions (Renner; Hanratty and Meditz).

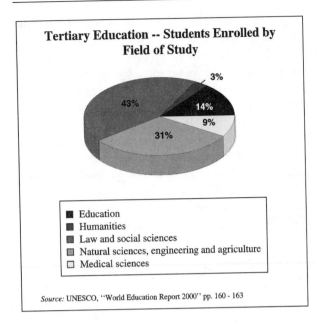

Tertiary Education -- Students Enrolled by Field of Study

- Education
- Humanities
- Law and social sciences
- Natural sciences, engineering and agriculture
- Medical sciences

Source: UNESCO, "World Education Report 2000" pp. 160 - 163

HIGHER EDUCATION

After completing secondary education, students wishing to attend a university must pass the official entrance examination, *El Examen de Estado* (The State Examination). For many years, students applying for higher education had to possess a Bachiller (secondary school) diploma and pass an exam. In 1980, the Ministry of National Education issued a decree that made this common practice a legal requirement. Although the state examination is administered through the *Servicio Nacional de Pruebas,* each institution weighs the results in accordance with its own academic requirements. Thus, universities and colleges determine what level of performance they can demand of students in order to fill their own enrollment quotas. Although admission is based on academic performance, the students in institutions of higher learning come disproportionately from high-income families (Wellington; Hanratty and Meditz).

In 1940, there were fewer than 3,000 students enrolled in universities studying to enter medicine, law, and engineering. The main objective of this system was to transmit information that students had to memorize. However, university programs changed as a result of the growth of national industries. Called "*modernización*" (moderization), these economic changes required more specialized technicians, workers, engineers, accountants, managers, and economists. Consequently, universities have diversified their programs and opened them to many social groups (Parra).

In 1980, the Ministry of National Education officially established four levels of higher education: intermediate professional studies, technological studies, university

studies, and graduate studies. Within these categories, the number of institutions grew rapidly. In 1970, the Colombian Association of Universities recognized 25 public and private universities. However, the National University Fund identified 65 more institutions of higher learning. By the late 1980s, there were more than 235 institutions of higher learning, and in 1999, university enrollment exceeded 807,000 students. (Wellington).

The number of applications to public universities exceeded the schools' capacity to accept students. Facing such demand, public universities raised their admission requirements. One reason for the large number of applications was that tuition in a public university was based on the parents' declared income. This made education affordable. Furthermore, since 1950, completion of higher education has been the avenue for social mobility. To meet the increased demand for higher education, more private universities and technical institutes were opened (Parra).

In 1993, a study demonstrated the importance of finishing college in Colombia. After surveying 4,027 workers in Bogotá, the researchers found that students who dropped out of an institution of higher learning held jobs of lower status with less pay than students who successfully completed the programs. However, students who failed exams and had to repeat them, or who repeated some grades in any school, did not earn less or work at some lower level (Psacharopoulos and Velez).

When universities grew to meet the demand for higher education, the institutions could not find faculty to teach the classes. In 1970, for example, the University of Antioquia ranked as one of the best schools, with a well-planned new campus and above average financial support. Although it had eight basic departments, the staff in those departments was underqualified. In the department of mathematics, one professor had a master's degree. The other instructors included six civil engineers, one chemical engineer, an economist, eight teachers with bachelor's degrees in education, and two people without degrees in higher education (Waggoner).

At any rate, in the 1990s, higher education in Colombia expanded more than the other, lower levels of education. Private institutions grew faster than public ones. Unfortunately, most observers agreed that the institutions grew at the expense of quality. They offered courses in areas that did not meet the developmental needs of the country. Since the faculty members were often untrained, they did not engage in scientific or technical research (Hanratty and Meditz).

ADMINISTRATION, FINANCE, & EDUCATIONAL RESEARCH

Until 1989, the major administrative problem was providing continual improvement in the face of tradition-

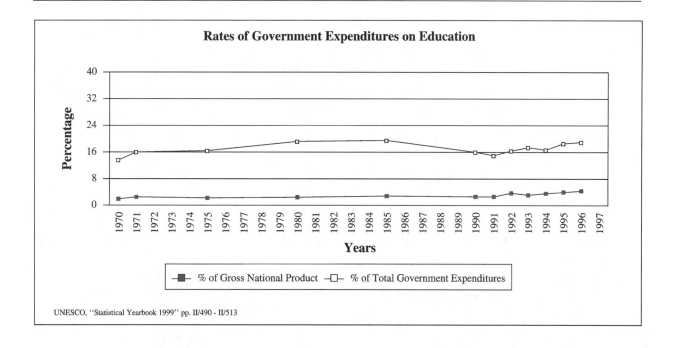

Rates of Government Expenditures on Education

UNESCO, "Statistical Yearbook 1999" pp. II/490 - II/513

al regionalism and the lack of resources in Colombia. The Ministry of Education, representing the national government, exerted control over the governors and departmental secretaries of education through a corps of inspectors who accredited individual schools. One way this control took place was for students to send their diplomas to the central ministry upon graduation. The ministry checked each diploma against university records of the student's progress, validated the diploma, and entered it in a registry. Such a process protected against fraud and allowed graduates to prove they were qualified for further education or to practice an appropriate profession (Londoño).

In 1957, in an effort to bring continuity to the process of educational development, organizations such as the United Nations Educational, Scientific, and Cultural Organizations (UNESCO) persuaded the national government to add a planning office to the Ministry of Education. The planning office recommended, and the Congress adopted, the first five-year educational plan, which became a model for other Latin American countries. In the following years, the national government of Colombia adopted a series of four- and five-year educational plans. Frequently, the presidential platforms of the political parties included a four-year plan.

Although the Ministry of Education sought to offer nationwide planning to control the expansion that took place from 1945 to 1970, these plans were rarely implemented. Instead the educational system expanded rapidly, and local administrators hired people who belonged to the correct political party to become teachers, even though these new teachers lacked proper training. Administrators erected buildings that were not needed and

spent money on schools that did not exist. Such abuses happened because the members of each community could obtain education for their children by pressuring local politicians. Unfortunately, the politicians could arrange the construction of a building, but they lacked the authority to find real teachers to staff the building. Worse, communities without political influence didn't get the buildings or even the teachers (Hanson).

Until 1968, the only way the Ministry of Education could influence department governors to conform to central policies was through the use of inspectors. To increase the authority of the central ministry, the national government adopted the Regional Funds Program (FER). This sent money from the national government to the departments to pay teacher salaries, providing the state education secretary followed established criteria, such as hiring qualified teachers, replacing unqualified teachers within two years, and allowing the ministry to supervise state budgetary expenditures.

The benefit of this model was that it allowed the national government to respect the division of authority among the regions while encouraging uniform national improvement. Delegates from the national Ministry of Education lived in the capital city of each department and devoted their attention to the schools in that area. This program increased the central government's control by making the Minister of Education responsible for paying teachers' salaries. Payments were made only if each department's Secretaries of Education met certain conditions, such as annually increasing state appropriations for education, hiring qualified teachers, and replacing unqualified teachers within two years. Although the program began with some difficulty, by 1975, bureaucracies developed within bureaucracies to try to ensure that the department secretaries followed the minister's expectations. In addition, governors were prohibited from hiring more teachers than the state budgets could pay (Hanson).

In 1975, the national government augmented the FER with a nationalization law. This law was intended to create a financial system that would standardize teachers' salaries and benefits, terminate the practice of hiring of teachers without authorization from the federal ministry, and eliminate the uncoordinated construction of school buildings. Unfortunately, education costs increased so rapidly that the central government could not maintain the system it sought to establish (Hanson).

Local officials resented the intrusion of delegates from the national ministry, and political leaders continued to appoint teachers whose only qualification was that they had been faithful campaign workers. Further, although the Regional Funds Program gave the ministry authority to direct changes in the departments, the ministry's recommendations sometimes contradicted local needs (Hanratty and Meditz).

In 1989, two years before the adoption of the new constitution, the Congress shifted school administration functions from the Ministry of Education and each department's secretaries of education to the 1,024 municipal mayors in Colombia. With this change in responsibilities, the Ministry of Education released more than 1,300 school inspectors. Officials in the different regional departments took over the responsibilities formerly handled by inspectors (Hanson).

This transition was uneven. In 1992, a report by the Ministry of Education noted that there was no way to coordinate the efforts of the central ministry members, department officials, and municipal mayors. In part, this happened because the average tenure of the ministers of education and of the department secretaries was often less than 18 months. No one could create the necessary bureaucratic structures because the leadership changed too rapidly (Hanson).

Worse, the decentralization reinforced unequal educational development. According to the policy, the mayor of a municipality oversaw the schools in his or her area. However, the mayor also had to supervise work in other areas of life, such as transportation, water, agriculture, and public health. The mayor and the city council members were elected officials who attained office because they won votes—not because they demonstrated the ability to manage daily affairs.

Colombia does not have a tradition of employing professional city managers. Most municipalities have their own secretary of education. Some cities employ *nu-cleo* directors—employees who administer 8 to 20 schools that form a school district. Often, these secretaries and directors lack administrative training and leave their jobs quickly. While large cities have an advantage, the vast majority of municipalities have only a few thousand occupants. Further, a mayor can hold office for no more than three years, which means new people must be trained for these positions frequently (Hanson).

The rationale behind the decentralization was that it would force the citizens to learn how to participate in civic life intelligently. Political education might grow slowly, but it seemed the best way to encourage people to become involved in their own government. Such decentralization and increased citizen involvement offered a way to reduce the political violence that racked the country. Thus, in the early 1990s, Colombians chose to reverse the program of central planning and enforcement that the external agencies and the Ministry of Education had encouraged since the late 1960s. To stem a growing rate of assassinations and kidnappings, they chose to emphasize participatory democracy instead of efficiency in educational planning (Hanson).

Through the 1970s and 1980s, the total public expenditure for schools remained approximately 3 percent of the gross national product (GNP). Private expenditures for schools during the same period represented approximately 2 percent of the GNP. Thus, total education expenditures in Colombia through the 1970s and 1980s somewhat exceeded 5 percent. By comparison, other Latin American countries made an average public expenditure of 4.3 percent of their GNPs. On the other hand, Colombia's private expenditures for education exceeded those of other similar countries (Hanson).

Within the Ministry of Education, various agencies direct funds to education. For higher education, the Colombian Institute for the Development of Higher Education (*Instituto Colombiano para el Fomento de la Educación Superior*) is responsible for the coordination and distribution of central government funds to public and private universities. The Colombian Institute for School Construction (*Instituto Colombiano de Construcción Escolar*) is responsible for carrying out Ministry of Education plans for school construction and for providing school equipment and teaching materials to primary and secondary schools. Further, the departments—through the secretaries of education—play a key role in financing primary and secondary education. They are responsible for building and maintaining schools and paying teachers and departmental university faculties. The municipalities provide the land for school buildings and they maintain the school buildings. Throughout the 1960s, however, many small, poor municipalities could not meet their educational obligations. As a result, the three biggest municipalities—Bogotá, Medellín, and Cali—consumed about 70 percent of the total amount of expenditures (Jallade).

In the 1960s, the industrialized cities had a much wider tax base from which to support schools than did rural areas. Consequently, the Ministry of Education allocated more funds for public education in less advantaged areas such as Boyacá and Cauca than in wealthy areas such as Antioquia and Valle. In 1971, the Congress passed the *Situado Fiscal* (financial security legislation) to require that the ministry follow a formula in deciding how to allocate these funds. According to this statute, the ministry was to divide 30 percent of its funds equally among the departments. It would divide the remaining 70 percent according to the size of the population in each region. In considering population size, the ministry used 1963 census figures that were out of date. The resulting bias helped rural areas, however, because those regions had been losing population (Hanson).

In 1975, the Congress passed the nationalization law that stipulated the central government would assume financial responsibility for all educational expenditures. In doing this, the Ministry of Education would set expense limits for each department. The departments and the municipalities would pay for any expenses beyond those limits. Although department governors would appoint teachers, the ministry determined how many appointments the governor could make. In addition, the ministry had to approve any new school construction (Hanson).

According to the nationalization law, the central government would gradually assume these responsibilities. Thus, from 1970 to 1978, the central government increased its share of the total educational expenditures from 65.5 percent to 83.7 percent. Departments reduced their expenditures from 34.5 percent of the total to 16.3 percent. Unfortunately, in 1980, the ministry realized it would never be able to pay for all school expenses and required the departments to continue making contributions to education (Hanson).

In 1989, when the Congress required that municipalities control education rather than the Ministry of Education, it adopted a strategy to finance those schools. Before decentralization, the national government provided about 84 percent of the needed funds. Departments offered approximately 13 percent, and municipalities contributed 2 percent. The national government froze its level of contributions and required that any needed expansions would have to come from the other contributors (Hanson).

Many mayors feared they could not adequately finance or administer the schools in their municipalities. Even in wealthy cities, the schools were understaffed, the buildings were in disrepair, and many classrooms were overcrowded. Consequently, by 1992, only 70 percent of

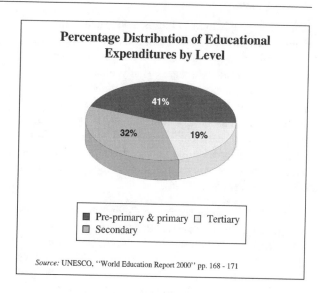

Percentage Distribution of Educational Expenditures by Level

41%
19%
32%

■ Pre-primary & primary □ Tertiary
■ Secondary

Source: UNESCO, "World Education Report 2000" pp. 168 - 171

the municipalities had accepted responsibility for the local schools. Twenty percent of the schools passed into the control of the departments, and 10 percent remained with the Ministry of Education (Hanson).

In 1993, to increase public financial expenditures, all branches of the government dedicated a sum equal to about 5 percent of the gross internal product (*Producto Interno Bruto-PIB*) to education (Trujillo). The 10-year plan of 1996 called on those same parts of government to raise contributions to match 8.5 percent of the PIB.

NONFORMAL EDUCATION

During the early twentieth century, small towns and cities had local newspapers that produced issues of less than 10 pages to a small circle of readers. Not until the 1930s did a major newspaper achieve national circulation. In 1929, Elías Pellet Buitrago made the first radio broadcast in Colombia. However, there were only about 250 receivers in the country. By 1935, radio's popularity grew. Although news programs of that time consisted of nothing more than commentators reading stories from journals, politicians recognized radio's potential as a campaign tool and sought to use it to mobilize crowds of voters. As a result, in 1941 there were 70 stations in Colombia, most of which played a various forms of music. Occasionally, literature and theater found their ways on to the airways. In the 1950s, transistor radios became popular and appeared everywhere (Williams and Guerrieri).

To some extent, radio offered a means to help rural education. In 1947, Father José Joaquin Solcedo initiated a church-sponsored program named *Acción Cultural Popular* (ACPO), or Popular Culture Action. The idea was to use a radio relay system to transmit classes in reading and writing to all parts of the country. The classes concentrated on basic literacy but included such items as agricultural extension programs and sanitation suggestions. ACPO offered paperback texts at a nominal cost that the parish priest could distribute. Usually, an assistant helped the students follow the instructions. Financed entirely by the church, ACPO claimed to have 16,000 radio schools in the rural areas of Colombia in 1970. Despite these claims, some researchers found that many priests did not invest the necessary time in the program and that the broadcasts rarely reached the more remote areas of the country (Havens and Flinn).

In 1954, television came to Colombia, where it was initially controlled by the state bureau of information and news (*Oficina de Información y Prensa del Estado*). In 1955, the authority passed to the national office of television (*Televisora Nacional*). Not long after that, the state monopoly passed to the *Instituto Nacional de Radion y Televisíon* (National Institute of Radio and Television), also known as Inravisíon. As a result of such governmental control, politicians used the television to campaign, and they cancelled programs that were critical of their policies. Nonetheless, television spread rapidly, covering 80 percent of the territory by 1960 and reaching almost two million viewers. Although most of the programming consisted of soap operas and sporting events, in 1961, television channels began carrying educational programs for children and agricultural information for farmers in rural areas. By 1970, there were two national television channels dedicated to educational programming (Williams and Guerrieri).

In 1972, more than 12,000,000 radios were in use in Colombia. In the 1970s, the number of member radio stations held by the major networks increased. However, the three principal networks—CARACOL, RCN, and TODELAR—established ties with television and print media. Similarly, newspapers consolidated. In the late 1970s, there were 42 papers in 16 Colombian cities. Each had circulations of approximately 200,000 readers. Finally, in 1985, the national television network, Inravisíon, broke into three branches, and channels appeared in the different regions of Colombia (Williams and Guerrieri).

TEACHING PROFESSION

In 1979, The Congress of Colombia passed the Teacher's Law (*Estatuo Docente*), which specified the rights and benefits of teachers throughout the nation. This statute established a salary scale for teachers with 14 levels and benefits. At the same time, the teachers were expected to enter a registry. The lowest level at which a person could enter this registry required completion of a teacher training program offered at a high school. The highest level demanded a post-graduate degree in education, or a university degree in education and the publication of a work in the field. To draw teachers to rural areas, the statute offered incentives, such as rapid advancement. Despite the incentives, many teachers transferred to urban areas, which led to a surplus of qualified teachers in urban areas and a lack of adequate personnel in rural areas (Hanson).

In Colombia, teacher training takes place at two levels. Some secondary schools offer a teaching diploma (*Bachillerato Pedagógico*), or an identical program called normal school training (*Formación Normalista*). These programs offer a basic cycle of academic courses and a second cycle of specialization. After receiving their diplomas, students may teach in primary schools or apply for admission into an institution of higher learning. To qualify to teach at a secondary school, the candidates have to graduate from a postsecondary institution or a university school of education. Critics complain that the normal schools are inflexible and offer poor quality specialized training. In 1980, to address these criticisms, the national Ministry of Education adopted Decree 80, which promised to promote the scientific and pedagogical training of teachers in universities (Hanratty and Meditz; Wellington; Hanson).

Despite the criticisms, the level of teacher preparation rose significantly. In the 1960s, 11 percent of primary school teachers had only a primary school education or less. At the same time, only 2 percent of primary school teachers had any postsecondary training. In the 1980s, the percentage of primary school teachers with primary school training or less dropped to about 1 percent. However, only 13 percent of the primary school teachers had postsecondary training. Among secondary school teachers, the level of preparation is higher. During the 1980s, about 55 percent of secondary school teachers had completed university studies (Hanratty and Meditz).

SUMMARY

Since the inception of Colombia, the government has formulated laws to improve schools. These have included such efforts as standardizing educational programs, raising teacher qualifications, and making buildings more sanitary. Unfortunately, for several reasons, the different governments that held power could not implement the measures they mandated. One important reason was that the tradition of regionalism impeded the development of national plans to improve education. A second reason is the historical lack of financial resources and the extreme inequality among the people, which made educational reform difficult.

Unfortunately, educational development in Colombia has not been consistently successful in overcoming political obstacles and finding resources to support reform. For example, during the 1960s and 1970s, the central government took steps to increase its authority. However, in the 1980s and 1990s, maintaining a desire for local control, Colombians adopted measures that prevented central authorities from garnering the control needed to enact widespread improvements.

At the same time, economic improvement was inconsistent. In the 1970s, industry surpassed agriculture as the major contributor to the nation's economy. Bogotá, Medellín, and Cali became the manufacturing centers. Although coffee remained Colombia's most important crop, in areas such as Medellín, cocaine and heroin contributed billions of dollars to an underground economy and stimulated such legal trades such as construction. Thus, although most Colombians had no connection to the drug trade, a large part of the relative economic health of Colombia during the 1980s came from that trade (Williams and Guerrieri).

Colombia enjoys many natural resources and agricultural advantages. Thus, some citizens have achieved worldwide fame, but many other citizens languish in poverty. During the 1990s, Colombia enjoyed the prestige associated with being the home of novelist and 1982 Nobel Prize winner, Gabriel García Márquez. In addition, Colombia supported such world-class painters as Alejandro Obregón, Fernando Botero, and Enrique Grau. Unfortunately, in rural areas especially, children faced inadequate educational opportunities, and a high percentage left school early (Williams and Guerrieri).

Fortunately, opportunities to increase the level of popular learning exist within the culture. In Colombian cities, urban design and architecture is varied and interesting. Distinct regional traditions that have been preserved nurture a rich and varied body of Colombian music. Such cultural resources may sustain dramatic increases in all levels of education that will overcome the political and economic problems afflicting the nation (Williams and Guerrieri).

BIBLIOGRAPHY

Bushnell, David. *The Making of Modern Colombia*. Berkeley: University of California Press, 1993.

The Central Intelligence Agency (CIA). *The World Factbook 2000*. Directorate of Intelligence, 1 January 2000. Available from http://www.cia.gov/.

Chiappe, Clemencia. "Problemas del Método y de la Enseñanza de la Metodología." *Revista Colombiana de Educación* 6(1980): 75-85.

DANE Departamento Administrativo Nacional de Estadística (Colombian Statistical Office) Web Site, 2001. Available from http://www.colombia.gov/educación/htm.

Hanratty, Diane, and Sandra Meditz, eds. *Colombia: A Country Study*. Washington: Government Printing Office, Federal Research Division, 1990.

Hanson, E. Mark. *Educational Reform and Administrative Development: The Cases of Colombia and Venezuela*. Stanford: Hoover Institution Press, 1986.

———. "Democratization and Decentralization in Colombian Education." *Comparative Education Review 39(1)* (1995): 101-119.

Havens, A. Eugene, and William Flinn. "Structural Blocks to Higher Educational Attainment." In *Internal Colonialism and Structural Change in Colombia*. New York: Praeger, 1970.

Helg, Aline. "La Educación Primaria y Secundaria Durante el Primer Gobierno de Alfonso López Pumarejo (1934-1938)." *Revista Colombiana de Educación, 6* (1980): 4-36.

Jallade, Jean-Pierre. *Public Expenditures and Income Distribution in Colombia*. Washington: John Hopkins University Press, 1974.

Londoño, Felipe. *Situación de la Educación en Colombia 1971*. Bogotá: Centro de Investigación y Acción Social, 1971.

Lopez, Asbel. "Colombia Exports Its 'New School' Blueprint." *UNESCO Courie 52(6)* (1999): 14-16.

Low-Maus, Rudolfo. *Compendium of the Columbian Educational System*. Bogotá: N.P., 1971.

Moreno, Heladio. *Ensayos Sobre la Educación Colombiana*. Bogotá: Colombia Nueva Limitada, 1984.

Parra, Rodrigo. *Escuela y Modernidad en Colombia: La Universidad*, Tomo IV. Santafe de Bogotá: Tercer Mundo Editores, 1996.

Psacharopoulos, George, and Eduardo Velez. "Educational Quality and Labor Market Outcomes: Evidence from Bogotá, Colombia." *Sociology of Education 2* (April 1993): 130-145.

Psacharopoulos, George, and William Loxley. Diversified Secondary Education and Development: Evidence from Colombia and Tanzania. Baltimore: John Hopkins University Press, 1985.

Restrepo, Gabriel. "Antonio Vargas Vega, Informe Relativo a las Enseñanzas Universitarias (1878)." *Revista Colombiana de Educación 6* (1980): 105-108.

Renner, Richard R. "Colombia." *The Encyclopedia of Education*. New York: Macmillan Co, 1971.

Tezanos, Araceli. "La Escuela Primaria en Colombia." *Revista Colombiana de Educación 6* (1980): 136-144.

Trujillo, Juan Pablo. "Educación Para la Interncacionalición." In *Colombia ante de la Economía Mundial*. Bogata, Colombia: T/M Editores, 1993.

Vivas, Jorge. "Ciencia, Tecnología y Estilos." *Revista Colombiana de Educación 6* (1980): 87-101.

Waggoner, George R. "Latin American Universities." *Journal of Higher Education 41(9)* (1970): 739-741.

Wellington, Stanley. *Colombia: A Study of the Educational System of Colombia and a Guide to Academic Placement of Students from Colombia in Educational Institutions of the United States.* N.P.: World Education Series, 1984.

Williams, Raymond Leslie, and Kevin G. Guerrieri. *Culture and Customs of Colombia.* Westport, CN: Greenwood Press, 1999.

— *Joseph Watras and Isabel Cavour*

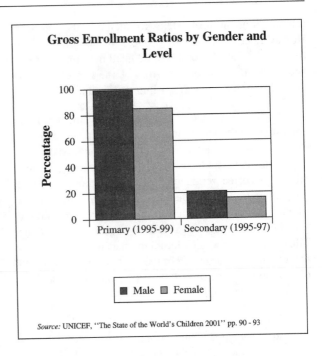

Gross Enrollment Ratios by Gender and Level

Source: UNICEF, "The State of the World's Children 2001" pp. 90 - 93

COMOROS

BASIC DATA

Official Country Name:	Islamic Federal Republic of the Comoros
Region:	Africa
Population:	578,400
Language(s):	Arabic, French, Comoran
Literacy Rate:	57.3%

One of the poorest countries in the world, Comoros is an archipelago, or group of islands, in the western Indian Ocean. It is located between eastern Africa and the island of Madagascar. Under French ownership from 1843 until 1975, Comoros modeled its educational system after that of France. Education, which is free, is mandatory for children between the ages of 7 and 16.

Primary education lasts for five years. Primary school enrollment rates were roughly 75 percent in 1993. Secondary enrollment rates that year were 21 percent for males and 17 percent for females. Some postsecondary training is available on the islands, but students pursuing university degrees must go elsewhere. In the mid-1990s, there were 1,508 primary school teachers, 591 secondary school teachers, and 198 higher education instructors in Comoros. The overall student-teacher ratio is 52 to 1, and the primary language of instruction is French.

The percentage of illiterate adults over the age of 15 in the nation decreased slightly from 52.1 percent in 1980 to 42.7 percent in 1995. During that time period, the percentage of illiterate adult males decreased from 44 percent to 35.8 percent, and the percentage of illiterate adult females decreased from 60 percent to 49.6 percent.

The Ministry of National Education, Culture, Youth, and Sports oversees the educational system of Comoros. The government spent 21.6 percent of its budget on education in 1994. Increased violence towards teachers throughout the late 1990s and early in the twenty-first century became a concern for Education Minister Sultan Chouzour and the Comoran teachers' union.

BIBLIOGRAPHY

Eastern Africa Sub-Regional Resource Facility. *Health and Education.* 26 May 2001. Available from http://www.easurf.org/.

NUPSA. *Comoros and Congo.* 26 May 2001. Available from http://www.nupsa.org.za/.

Panafrican News Agency. *Teachers Protest Harassment.* AllAfrical Global Media, 13 January 2001. Available from http://allafrica.com/.

United Nations Division for Social Policy and Development. *Comoros.* United Nations Youth Information Network, 26 May 2001. Available from http://www.un.org/esa/socdev/unyin/.

—*AnnaMarie L. Sheldon*

CONGO

BASIC DATA

Official Country Name:	Republic of the Congo
Region:	Africa
Population:	2,830,961
Language(s):	French, Lingala, Monokutuba, Kikongo
Literacy Rate:	74.9%

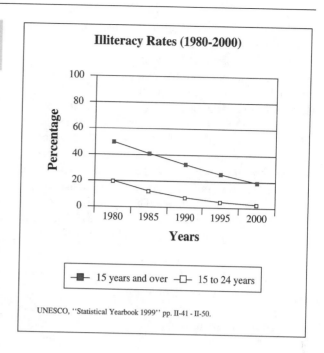

Illiteracy Rates (1980-2000)

UNESCO, "Statistical Yearbook 1999" pp. II-41 - II-50.

Congo is commonly called Congo-Brazzaville to distinguish it from its neighbor, Zaire, which recently renamed itself as The Democratic Republic of Congo (informally called Democratic Congo). Congo has a landmass of 342,000 square kilometers and a population of about 2.5 to 3 million. Its capital is Brazzaville, which is located on the Congo River directly across from Kinshasa, the capital of Democratic Congo. The population of Brazzaville is about 1 million. Congo is situated on the Atlantic Ocean of equatorial Africa and is bounded by Democratic Congo in the east and south. It is also bounded in the south by Cabinda, a small oil-rich territory that belongs to Angola. It is bounded by the Central African Republic (CAR) and Cameroon in the north and Gabon in the west.

The boundary between Congo and Democratic Congo is the Congo River, starting at about 80 kilometers south of Mindouli all the way north to Liranga. At that point the Congo River turns east into Democratic Congo. North of Liranga the river is called Oubangui. It continues to be a boundary between the two Congos until the Oubangui also turns east to become a boundary between CAR and Democratic Congo.

Congo formed part of French Equatorial Africa (FEA) until its independence from France in 1960; FEA included what are now known as Congo, Gabon, Cameroon, CAR, and Chad. It broke apart into five independent Francophone states after 1960. Brazzaville was also the capital of FEA. In its longstanding history as capital, first of FEA and then of Congo, Brazzaville has been privileged in every respect. It is the center of industry, commerce, and education in Congo. Its medical facilities and infrastructure are the best in the country. The World Health Organization (WHO) has one of its African headquarters in Brazzaville. The national university, known as Université Marien Ngouabi, is situated right in its center.

Congo's population could reasonably be divided into three groups: the Bakongo, the Bateke, and the rest. The Bakongo are the largest ethnic group. They constitute about 40 to 50 percent of the total population and inhabit the southern quarter of the country. The Bateke are the second largest group. They occupy the territory directly north of the Bakongo, stretching quite far to the north and northwest. Their numbers are greatest towards the south. The northern two-thirds of the country are very sparsely populated. The territory north of the Bateke is even more sparsely inhabited. It is made up of small groups and several speech communities that have larger numbers of speakers in Gabon, Cameroon, CAR, and Democratic Congo.

Congo must contend with five major languages—Kikongo and its various dialects, Kituba, Kiteke, Lingala, and French. Of these, Kituba, Lingala, and French are the major competitors as languages spoken across ethnic lines within broad-based speech communities. Of these three, French is the official language in government and education at all levels. Kituba, Lingala, and Kiteke have a strong presence at the unofficial levels of government and education, including informal discussions between teachers and students. The educational system is based on the French system inherited from precolonial days. Only a small number of Congolese, however, are fluent enough in French to satisfy all aspects of their lives. A Congolese citizen must of necessity be quadrilingual in Kiteke or a dialect of Kikongo, Kituba, Lingala, and French to negotiate successfully through Congolese life.

The government of Congo is acutely aware of these circumstances. The university, Université Marien Ngouabi, has dynamic and substantive departments of foreign languages, Langues Vivantes Etrangères (LVE) and linguistics, Département de Linguistique et Litérature Orale, where intensive research is carried out in Congolese languages, particularly Kituba and Lingala. In addition the government funds two research institutes, Institut National de Recherches et d'Action Pédagogique (INRAP) and Institut Supérieur des Sciences de l'Education (INSSED), where intensive efforts are under way to develop Kituba and Lingala textbooks for the primary and secondary levels of education. There is no effort to supplant French. Congolese society seems to have reconciled itself to becoming at least a trilingual society in French, Kituba, and Lingala. The greater hope, certainly the government's hope, is for Congolese society to evolve into a bilingual society in French and Kituba.

Informal education at the very age when children would attend primary schools progresses as it has from time immemorial. Cultural information and first language fluency is passed down from generation to generation quite effectively. In the case of Congo, this kind of ethnocentric education does not pose a problem. The presence of two African languages—Kituba and Lingala—and a Western language of colonial legacy, French, provides means of communication that do not compete with Congolese society's own Afro-ethnic languages. Indeed the Congolese feel particularly free to exercise their knowledge and education in French concurrently with Kituba or Lingala.

BIBLIOGRAPHY

Abshire, David M., and Michael A. Samuels. *Portuguese Africa, A Handbook.* London: Pall Mall Press, 1969.

ACCT, CERDOTOLA, Equipe Nationale du Congo. *Atlas Linguistique de L'Afrique Centrale, Atlas Linguistique du Congo.* Brazzaville: Centre pour l'Etude des Langues Congolaises, Université Marien Ngouabi, 1987.

Loutard, J. B. Tati. *Le Récit de la Mort.* Paris: Présence Africaine, 1987.

Ngoie-Ngalla, Dominique. *Lettre d'un Pygmée à un Bantou.* Brazzaville: C. R. P., 1988.

Pinto, Françoise Latour da Veiga. *Le Portugal et le Congo au XIX Siècle.* Paris: Presses Universitaires de France, 1972.

Tchicaya, U Tam'Si. *Les Phalènes.* Paris: Albin Michel S. A., 1984.

UNESCO. *African Community Languages and Their Use in Literacy and Education.* Dakar, Senegal: 1985.

———. *Statistical Yearbook.* Lanham, MD: Berman Press, 1999.

—*Haig Der-Houssikian*

COOK ISLANDS

BASIC DATA

Official Country Name:	Cook Islands
Region:	Oceania
Population:	20,407
Language(s):	English, Maori
Literacy Rate:	NA

The Cook Islands, located in the South Pacific, maintains public education that is free and compulsory for all children between 5 and 15 years of age. Although governed by the Ministry of Education, the administration of the system is divided among three regions: Rarotonga Island, the Southern group, and the Northern Group. The use of Maori is encouraged in all the schools, although English is also widely used.

Primary education in the Cook Islands covers the first five years with an emphasis on agriculture, mathematics, and science. In 1996, 90 percent of Cook Islanders reported having completed primary school. As with the primary system, secondary education in the Cook Islands is modeled after the system adopted in New Zealand and is available through seven colleges, all of which follow the national syllabus for forms one to five. Studies in the secondary curriculum include specific technical courses, commercial studies, environmental studies, social science, health, and Maori culture and heritage. Forms six and seven are also available for individuals interested in continuing their education at the college level.

In addition to public education, a number of church-based programs have been established throughout the islands, and they account for approximately 12 percent of the student enrollment. Two other private, non-religious schools account for an additional 3 percent of the total enrollment.

Individuals seeking postsecondary education may attend the teacher training institute at Nikao or attend college in New Zealand. Although there is still some concern about unlicensed teachers, this situation is rapidly improving, and the Ministry of Education hopes to insure that all teachers will be certified.

Distance education includes vocational and cultural education, with special concern for the Maori culture. The Ministry of Education also intends to utilize the two radio stations, the daily newspaper, the telephone system with Internet access, and the two libraries and museums. There has also been a recent increase in the use of correspondence courses emanating from New Zealand.

Major future concerns articulated by the Ministry of Education include developing further opportunities for female students, encouraging the developments of trade and technical education, increasing budget allotments, attracting qualified teachers, and decentralizing the education system as a whole.

BIBLIOGRAPHY

Crocombe, Ron, and Marjorie Tuainekore Crocombe. "Scale, Sovereignty, Wealth, and Enterprise: Comparisons Between the Cook Islands and the Solomon Islands." *Comparative Education 29.3*, 1993.

Educational Characteristics of the Cook Islands, 1986. Rarotonga, Cook Islands: Statistics Office, 1991.

Suva, Fiji: *Institute of Pacific Studies, University of the South Pacific in association with United Nationals Educational, Scientific, and Cultural Organization,* 1992.

—*Matts G. Djos*

COSTA RICA

BASIC DATA

Official Country Name:	Republic of Costa Rica
Region:	North & Central America
Population:	3,710,558
Language(s):	Spanish, English
Literacy Rate:	94.8%
Number of Primary Schools:	3,711
Compulsory Schooling:	10 years
Public Expenditure on Education:	5.4%
Educational Enrollment:	Primary: 529,637 Secondary: 202,415 Higher: 88,324
Educational Enrollment Rate:	Primary: 104% Secondary: 47%
Teachers:	Primary: 19,235 Secondary: 10,943
Student-Teacher Ratio:	Primary: 29:1 Secondary: 20:1
Female Enrollment Rate:	Primary: 103% Secondary: 49%

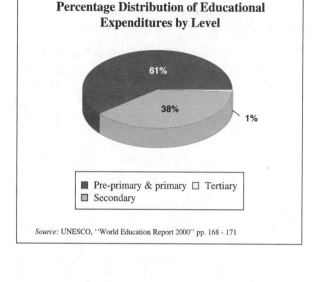

Percentage Distribution of Educational Expenditures by Level

61%
38%
1%

■ Pre-primary & primary □ Tertiary
■ Secondary

Source: UNESCO, "World Education Report 2000" pp. 168 - 171

HISTORY & BACKGROUND

Costa Rica has the highest standard of living in Central America, the highest level of education, and the most stable political structure. The 1948 revolution eliminated the national army and established national health care and education systems with funds that were no longer needed for the army. As a result, Costa Rica has the most highly developed welfare state in Central America, and, consequently, the largest middle class in Central America.

The Costa Rican population is one of the most schooled and literate in Latin America. Approximately one-third of the national budget is directed towards education. Of 192 countries in the world, Costa Rica ranks 89th on the schooling index, 62nd on the education index, and 28th on the human development index. Adult literacy is 93 percent. Primary and secondary education is free. Primary education is compulsory from the ages of 6 to 15. Study of a foreign language, usually English or French, is mandatory. Costa Rica achieved universal primary education in 1980. Twenty-five students per 1000 attend universities, which is double the rate of university enrollment in Mexico. Economic difficulties, nonetheless, may create challenges in the future, since Costa Rica was ranked among the top thirty debtors in the world in the 1990s. Families with money increasingly place their children in private educational institutions.

Costa Rica is 51,000 square kilometers, approximately the same size as West Virginia. Nicaragua borders Costa Rica to the north and Panama to the south. It remains the only country in Central and South America without an army. Political and economic refugees from El Salvador, Guatemala, and Nicaragua moved to Costa Rica in the 1980s. The U.S. financing of the Contra war in Nicaragua and of military regimes in Central America contributed to the growth in refugees. Costa Rica has more teachers than soldiers and spends more of its federal budget for education than for its military. It spends about one-third of the national budget on education.

About 50 percent of the population lives in urban areas, including the capital of San Jose, which is located in the Central Valley. The population is approximately 3.4 million people, with 52 percent residing in urban areas and 48 percent in rural locations. Spanish is the official language.

The Costa Rican population is estimated to be 80 percent white, primarily of Spanish, Italian, German, and other European ancestry; 17 percent Mestizo; 2 percent English-speaking Afro-Caribbean, and less than 1 percent indigenous Indians. At 0.6 percent, Costa Rica has the lowest percentage of indigenous population of any nation in Central America. Somewhere between 10,000 and 70,000 Afro-Caribbeans speak an English Creole language. The indigenous population of Amerindians, estimated at 27,200 people in 1522 when the Spanish arrived in the area, was reduced by 1800 to 8,281 people. Meanwhile the Spanish, Mestizo, and Afro-Caribbean population increased from 0 to 44,310 people in the same period. In rural areas, 8 different indigenous groups inhabit 22 reservations with a total population around 21,200 people. The primary Amerindian group is the Talamanquenos, with three subgroups: the Bribri, Cabecar, and Teribe. All subgroups have similar culture and language patterns. The Bribri find the Cabecar language difficult to understand, but the Cabecars are bilingual in Bribri and Cabecar. The Bribri population is approximately 7,500 people at Talamancca and 3,650 people at other locations.

Costa Rica maintains strong ties to the United States, its principal trading partner. The current economy is based on agriculture and tourism. The most important commodity exports are coffee, bananas, and sugar. Tourism is a large industry constituting about 21 percent of the national income.

Costa Rica industrialized more slowly than other Central American nations. Approximately 16 percent of its workforce is employed in manufacturing, a greater number than in the rest of Central America. The agricultural sector, 29 percent, employs fewer numbers than the rest of Central America.

Costa Rica encounters many of the same socioeconomic difficulties of other Central American countries but experiences them less severely. Costa Rica had a severe recession in the 1980s, but it remains more economically viable than the rest of Central America. Its GDP per capita of $2,283 in 1994 was 55 percent higher than the next highest in the region, which was in Guatemala. Costa Rica experienced a recession in the 1980s with a 9 percent decline in GDP from 1981 to 1987, but again this was the least severe in the region, which averaged a 17 percent GDP decline during the same period. From 1990 to 1994 Costa Rica's GDP per capita recovered 10 percent, double the regional average.

Income distribution is more equitable in Costa Rica than the rest of Central America. The average income of the poorest fifth of Costa Ricans is $177 per year, which is 85 percent above the regional average. The average income for the poorest fifth of U.S. citizens is 12 to 15 times greater than that in Costa Rica.

Costa Rica's literacy rate of 90 percent is 23 percent higher than the regional average, and university enrollment per capita is four times higher than the Central American average. The patterns of mortality and morbidity are similar to developed countries. Infant mortality per 1,000 births in 1993 was 14; the mean for the region is 55. The rest of Central America has more than three times this rate of infant mortality, with 62 per 1000 on average. Thirty-eight percent of children ages 0 to 4 suffer from malnutrition, compared to an average of 58.5 percent for Central America in general. Life expectancy of Costa Ricans is 76 years, which is 9 years longer than the regional average.

The higher life expectancy is based in part on public policy. Costa Rica's ratio of spending for human services to defense ranges around 20:1 in favor of human services; in other Central American countries, ratios between spending for human services and defense range from 1:1 to no higher than 4:1.

Costa Rica self-describes itself as the Switzerland of the Americas. Unlike other Latin American countries, Costa Rica has a long established history of democracy. Equality of land distribution, racial homogeneity, and a tradition of nonviolence characterize Costa Rica. During its first 300 years, inhabitants of Costa Rica embraced an agrarian democracy. Costa Rican history is comprised of three periods: the colonial era until independence in 1821, independence to the revolution in 1948, and 1948 to the present.

Christopher Columbus landed in Costa Rica in 1502 at Puerto Limon. The indigenous population at the time consisted of the Grin Nicolas of northwestern Costa Rica and smaller tribes of Chichi origin in the southern and Atlantic regions. When they saw Indians wearing gold jewelry, they named the territory Costa Rica, meaning Rich Coast. Costa Rica had no gold of its own. The gold jewelry had been acquired through trade. This lack of gold meant that few conquistadors were drawn to the area. Around 1560, the first Spanish settlements were made in the central mountains. In 1564, the capital city of Cartago was founded. San Jose, the eventual capital and largest city, was not founded until 1755.

Unlike the rest of Central America, Costa Rica developed a democracy based on agrarian farmers, not a feudal hacienda system controlled by a European aristocracy with large tracts of land supported by the army and police. The economy was based on farming. Catholic priests first arrived with the Spanish in 1522. There were about 38 priests in Costa Rica by the close of the sixteenth century.

During the period of early national life, from 1821 to 1905, Costa Rica had a weak military and an economy based on coffee cultivation. Their colonial status ended without any local combat in 1821 when Mexico won independence. The farmers of Costa Rica declared their independence from Spain in 1821. The first constitution of Costa Rica was drafted on December 1, 1821. In 1882, anticlerical polices were enacted to counter the growing strength of the Catholic Church. The Liberal Laws of 1884 provided for secular, compulsory, and free education. The Jesuits were expelled. Marriages and cemeteries were secularized at this time and divorce was legalized.

CONSTITUTIONAL & LEGAL FOUNDATIONS

Private donations and separate municipalities provided the first support for primary schools. The first public school was established in 1807. The Franciscans were the most numerous clergy in Costa Rica; they ran a number of private parochial schools in and around the capital of San Jose, and they converted the indigenous population.

Higher education was developed in Costa Rica just 23 years after independence from Spain. The Casa de Ensenanza de Santo Tomas (School of St. Thomas) opened in April 1814. Its basis was religious education, but the curriculum included mathematics and writing. Ten years later, the government assumed funding of this institution. The school of Santo Tomas was the first primary through higher education school in Costa Rica. The school opened in San Jose to provide an alternative to foreign education. Santo Tomas initially focused on primary education: reading, writing, grammar, and theology. After independence, the emphasis was on secondary education, and three departments were added: theology, jurisprudence, and medicine. In 1843, the school became a university.

The 1823 Declaration of the Supreme Juanta claimed, ''the provision of education is the essential foundation of individual happiness and the prosperity of all.'' Many early government leaders, including the first president of Costa Rica, Jose Maria Castro, were former teachers.

During the administration of Juan Mora Fernandez from 1824 to 1833, the government affirmed the munici-

pal character of primary schooling and assumed the operating responsibilities for the Casa de Ensenanza de Santo Tomas. Additionally, the Escuela de Primeras Lecturas School of literature was located in Cartago, the colonial capital of Costa Rica.

The Law of Bases legislation passed in 1841 placed the control of schools under the state and established five regional departments. This was the first time education in Costa Rica became centralized. In 1843, the University of St. Thomas was created by an executive decree. Legislative Decree Number 11 in 1843 made Casa de Ensenanza the official University of Santo Tomas. The chief of State, Don Jose Afar, and the Minister of State Don Jose Castro Madras, directed it. The University began granting degrees in literature and studies in medicine. In 1843, liberals created the Universidad de Santo Tomas to train future leaders of the country and to stop dependence on the Universidad de San Ramon in Leon, Nicaragua. The Universidad de Santo Tomas was closed 14 years later in 1888 by the congress of Costa Rica because the higher education system had been under the influence of foreign educators who came from Europe. In 1888, the university in Costa Rica was closed by order of President Bernardo Soto, so students now pursued higher education outside the country.

The constitutions of 1844 and 1847 provided specifics for the development of the education system. In 1849, legislation was passed to support the building of schools and to guarantee the right of all Costa Ricans, including females, to receive free primary education. A unified school system was created. The law of 1852 repealed the exclusive role that the Catholic Church had played in education. It made education independent of the church and expelled Jesuits from Costa Rica.

In 1853, a conservative government transformed the Universidad de Santo Tomas into a Pontifical University under the direction of Pope Pius IX. The Universidad de San Carlos in Guatemala then took the place of the Universidad de San Ramon for professional education. In the 1860s, most students seeking higher education attended European universities. The constitution of 1869 established free compulsory public education.

After the closing of the University of St. Thomas in 1888, there were no opportunities for university education within Costa Rica until the University of Costa Rica was established in 1940. During this period, Costa Rican students attended universities in Nicaragua, Guatemala, South America, and Europe.

Santo Tomas University closed in 1888, just 45 years after opening when Fernandez decided to focus on secondary school education. Students who earned a *bachillerato* at the end of their secondary schooling had a degree that was comparable to two years of college. The law school continued, however, and during the next 50 years, schools were also established for the fine arts, pharmacy, education, and agriculture. Another university was not established in Costa Rica until 1940 when the University of Costa Rica was founded. Despite these achievements, 70 percent of the population remained illiterate at the end of the nineteenth century.

Reforms from 1882 to 1888, called the "Liberal Laws," prohibited priests from attacking public education because it was secular in nature. The General Law of Common Education passed in February 1886 supported the creation of an army of teachers to meet educational needs. Laws were drafted in 1899 to define the teacher's role in Costa Rica.

An 1890 decree to dissolve the university was nullified. The legislative assembly decided instead to reestablish the university, but steps to reopen it were not taken. In 1895, a school of pharmacy was opened, then a school of fine arts in 1897, and a normal school in 1914.

The influence of Latin American Marxist thinkers called for higher public education that was free. The Reform of Cordoba in 1918 sought to open universities to an emerging middle class. Until Cordoba, the Napoleonic University model, a collection of independent professional schools, had dominated higher education in Costa Rica.

A national school of agriculture opened in the suburbs of San Jose in 1926. This site would become the main campus of the University of Costa Rica. In 1940, President Calderon's administration created the University of Costa Rica. The normal school, or teacher-training college, became the school of education. In 1942, a school of dentistry was added, and in 1960, a school of medicine opened. The constitution of 1949, as well as recent amendments, guaranteed university autonomy and state funding for state educational institutions.

The new University of Costa Rica opened in March 1941 with schools of law, engineering, and pharmacology. It later incorporated the school of education and became the University of Costa Rica (UCR). UCR was the only institution of its kind in the country for 32 years until the Technology Institute was created in 1972. The Technological Institute, Universidad Nacional (UNNA), and the Universidad Estatal a Distancia (UNED) were founded in 1971, 1973, and 1977, respectively.

In the 1970s, reform movements in education worked to transform the University of Costa Rica from an elite institution to an open one. The purpose of this reform was to offer all people equal opportunity to access higher education. Within 10 years, the percentage of students pursuing higher education increased from 8 percent of the population to 27 percent. In the interests of democratizing higher education in Costa Rica, three community colleges were also founded in the 1970s.

Law established the University of Costa Rica in 1940. The social Christian and social democratic governments of the 1940s sought to extend social benefits to all Costa Ricans. Social benefits included a public university, national health insurance program, and abolition of the army. When UCR opened in 1941, it consisted of the professional schools of agriculture, fine arts, law, and pharmacology, as well as a normal school. New academic units of philosophy, letters, and engineering were added within a few years. In the constitution of 1949, approved after the revolution of 1948, article 77 made primary and secondary education free and primary education compulsory. A peaceful coup in 1948 by Jose Figueres abolished the army and gave women the right to vote. In the 1970s, student-led, anti-imperialist protests began.

EDUCATIONAL SYSTEM—OVERVIEW

The 1869 constitution made education free, mandatory, and tax supported. Costa Rica was one of the first nations in the world to make this provision. The education system of Costa Rica is similar to systems in other parts of Latin America. Typically, preschool consists of two years; primary school, six years; secondary school, five or six years. The academic year begins on the first Monday in March and concludes on the last Saturday in November. Classes meet six days a week for a total of 36 weeks or 210 days of instruction, and Spanish is the language of instruction.

Dr. Angel Calderon Guardia, an education reformer, was president of Costa Rica in 1940 when the University of Costa Rica was created under Law number 362. The constitution of 1949 had 13 sections pertaining to Education, including that a primary education of six years is mandatory, both primary and secondary education is free and funded by the government, and university education is supported by scholarships for needy students. The constitution also mandates that the government is responsible for providing needy students at all levels in the education system with food and clothing. The government is also mandated to provide adult education in order to eliminate illiteracy.

The Universidad Nacional was created by the General Assembly in January 1973 through the issuance of plan 5182 during the administration of President Jose Figueres Ferrer. This law mandated that the Escuela Normal de Costa Rica and the Escuela Normal Superior merge to form a new university.

PREPRIMARY & PRIMARY EDUCATION

The government placed a priority on primary education, so few preprimary programs are available. The largest number of preprimary programs are found in the capital city of San Jose. Children from the ages of two through six are enrolled in instructional programs, and two meals a day are provided. Preprimary educational curriculum consists of instruction in arts, crafts, music, and language development.

Children enter school at the age of six years and six months. The academic year begins in March. Based on special testing or attendance at preschool programs, age requirements may be waived by three months. Currently, 525,273 children attend kindergarten to sixth grade in 3,671 primary schools. Current figures indicate that 96 percent of school-age children are enrolled in primary schools. In rural schools, only 50 percent of enrolled students might attend on any given day because attendance depends on whether or not the students are needed at home to work for their families.

Students receive a certificate called a "Conclusion of Cycle" after grades three and six. The grading scale for the standardized tests is based on a scale from 0 to 100 percent. Students must score at least 65 percent for a minimum, passing grade. The *Ministeriod de Educacion* (Ministry of Education), establishes the contents of the exam. Students must pass standardized Ministry of Education tests in fifth, ninth, and eleventh grades to receive a high school diploma.

The number of students enrolled in elementary schooling increased dramatically within the two decades after the 1948 revolution. In 1950, 66.5 percent of school age children were enrolled in primary education. That number rose to 92.6 percent by 1960, and 100 percent by 1970.

Although the primary language in Costa Rica is Spanish, daily English lessons are offered to most students beginning in preschool. By high school, most students take English language lessons for 80 minutes a day. School classes, however, are taught in Spanish.

Since 1972, under executive directive 3333E of the National Plan for Educational Development, students are given mandatory education for nine years, consisting of three cycles of three years each. This education is compulsory and funded by the government. The first two cycles correspond to primary education in the United States, and a certificate is awarded on completion. The third cycle corresponds to the junior high school years of secondary education in the United States.

Classes are half a day with some grades attending in the mornings, while others attend only in the afternoons. Grades are combined in some schools. Taking into account recess and lunchtime, students spend as little as three hours a day in the classroom. Costa Rica has one of the shortest school years in the world: 180 days.

Teachers teach different classes and different grades in the morning and in the afternoon. The curriculum is developed by the Ministry of Education and is identical throughout the country.

Because of cutbacks in government funding in the 1980s, parents now contribute an average of 1000 *colones* annually for each child. By the 1990s, the total family contribution to send a child to public primary school was about 7000 *colones* annually. Parents directly bear about 30 percent of the public primary school costs. Urban schools often have 50 students in a classroom. Rural schools have the fewest computers, libraries, and supplies. Though children are required to wear school uniforms, many come to school without the uniform, often an indication of lower socio-economic status.

Costs for attending school include uniforms, notebooks, pencils, pens, rulers, and transportation. Additionally, students in primary schools provide their own lunches and/or snack. Students in high school pay for all their food and bus transportation. Unfortunately, most schools do not have enough textbooks for all their students. Schools lack books, notebooks, audiovisual equipment, libraries, gymnasiums, and workshops.

Costa Rica has excellent primary education in most areas. At the secondary level, the coverage is lower than some other Latin American countries. Only two of every three enrolled students in first grade complete sixth grade, and only one in every three students complete secondary education. These enrollment percentages drop with declining family incomes in all age groups. The grading scale in Costa Rica consists of: S—*Sobreasaliente* (outstanding); N—*Notable*; Suf—*Suficiente* (sufficient); and I—*Insuficiente* (insufficient).

The qualifications for primary teachers are higher in Costa Rica than in many other Latin American countries. In Costa Rica, teacher education takes place in universities rather than secondary schools. Primary-teacher candidates must earn a high school diploma before gaining admission to the two-year normal school teacher education program or to the School of Education at the University of Costa Rica.

The first special education school was established in 1939, the Centro Nacional de Enzenanza Especial Fernando Centeno Guell. In 1968 a special education department opened in the Ministry of Public education. By 1986, there were 19 special education schools and more than 200 regular schools developed special education classes. In 2001 more than 400 regular schools integrate special education classes, and 15 special education schools exist. Two main universities, the University of Costa Rica and UNI, offer bachelor degrees in special education. The University of Costa Rica also offers masters

Gross Enrollment Ratios

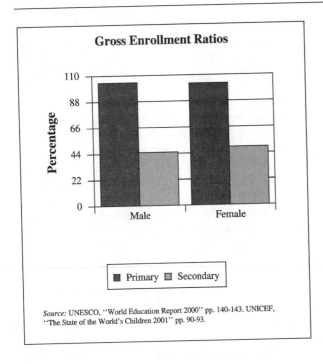

Source: UNESCO, "World Education Report 2000" pp. 140-143. UNICEF, "The State of the World's Children 2001" pp. 90-93.

degrees in integral rehabilitation. While most teachers average 14.1 years of experience, special education teachers average 3.5 years of experience.

SECONDARY EDUCATION

The first modern secondary school was opened in San Jose in 1887. Those pursuing university educations before the end of World War II had, on the whole, achieved a secondary education. The secondary education program was restructured into two cycles by 1964. During the first three years, all students take course work in Spanish, social studies, mathematics, science, music, and religion. The next cycle is comprised of two or three years of study. Students can take two additional years of courses in the humanities or sciences, or they can take a three-year professional program in agriculture, industrial arts, or office skills.

Education through eleventh grade is mandatory, but only 47 percent of age-appropriate children attend. Currently, 220,151 secondary students attend 342 high schools. The percentage of students at the secondary level in 1970 was 23.7 percent, which increased to 40 percent by 1980, far above the average for Latin America.

The exams had been discontinued for 15 years, but Minister Francisco Pacheco reinstated them in 1988. The cost to administer the exams was a big part of the total educational budget. In 1991, 33.7 percent of students taking secondary school exams failed the math exams; 4.4 percent failed science; 5.9 percent failed Spanish; and 4.5 percent failed social studies. Since students must pass all parts of the exam, 48.3 percent of the students failed the

exam and could not go to college. In remote regions like Guapiles and Liberia, 62.3 percent do not pass the exams and 56.4 percent do not graduate.

The cost of sending two children to attend *colegion* is about 1000 *colones* or US$5.00 a day, which is 25 percent of the average family income. There are more boys than girls in the upper grades. Education for girls is not considered necessary. Many girls take care of younger children in their families, especially in rural areas. Even if they do not drop out of school, girls have many household and childcare responsibilities that interfere with their studies.

Teachers rely on rote learning methods. Generally, teachers write on blackboards and students copy from the board or from a textbook. Textbooks are limited, so children generally work in groups, with one child reading from the text while others copy from it. Books are scarce, and school libraries are either non-existent or filled with very old books. Few extra materials are available and books are never taken home for study. Additionally, most schools do not have paper for children to use, and teachers must buy their own chalk and other teaching tools.

After nine years of basic education, students enter specialized education that lasts three years in the technical track and two years in the academic track. In 1988, provisions were passed that now require students to take an examination to obtain their diploma in secondary education, a prerequisite for university admission. The diploma is similar to a high school diploma in the United States. Admission tests are also required at some institutions like the University of Costa Rica and the Technological Institute of Costa Rica. There is no restriction on foreign student enrollment and many foreign students in Costa Rica come from Central American countries.

In 1990, approximately 97 percent of graduating secondary students planned to continue with higher education. The University of Costa Rica was their first choice. Finances were the number one problem for 58 percent of public students and 34 percent of private secondary students who planned to pursue higher education. For male graduates, their choices for higher education were 84 percent for public universities, 9 percent for private universities, and 7 percent for foreign universities. Female students' choices were 78 percent for public universities, 17 percent for private universities, and 5 percent for foreign universities. Graduates from private secondary schools earn the *bachillerato* and gain admission to universities at higher rates.

In 1968, a normal school of secondary-teacher training was opened due to a shortage of teachers that the University of Costa Rica program could not combat. Only 10 percent of students attend private schools; most private schooling is available at the secondary and higher education levels. At the highest quintile, 40 percent of students attend private institutions. The percentage of students who fail exams is higher at public schools than at private schools. By 1989, there were 4,089 primary and secondary schools; 49 semi-private, publicly supported private schools; and 316 private schools.

Students who attend vocational school during their last two secondary years of school have a reduced academic load and increased vocational instruction. In 1956, two previously private vocational schools became public schools. Commercial vocational schools have the highest student enrollments, followed by industrial, agricultural, and technical programs. The first school of agriculture was not opened until 1962. Many agricultural schools are located in rural areas and offer a five-year course of study. Students who complete the technical track in school obtain the *tecnico medio* (mid-level technician diploma), which allows them to practice particular trades.

HIGHER EDUCATION

Higher educational institutions in Costa Rica fall into several categories: state universities, private universities, and parauniversities, both state and private. In the category of state institutions there are four primary universities: the University of Costa Rica, established in 1940, with its central campus in San Jose and regional campuses in Guanacaste, San Ramon, Turrialba, and Limon; the National University, established in 1973, with a central campus in Heredia and regional campuses in Perez, Zeledon, and Liberia; and the State University at Distance, distance education established in 1977 with a central campus in San Jose and 31 satellite branches. There is also the Technical Institute of San Jose, established in 1973.

Public universities were expanded in the 1970s, and private universities were increased in the 1980s. Public universities traditionally defined their role as offering liberal arts education to future professionals, while private universities emphasized technical training. The public higher education system began in 1940 with the founding of the University of Costa Rica (UCR). This marked a shift away from a monopoly by a small oligarchy of elites in higher education. The remaining three public universities were founded in the 1970s: the Instituto Tecnologico de Costa Rica in 1973, the Universidad Nacional in 1973, and the Universidad Estatal de Distancia in 1977.

The University of Costa Rica started in 1941 with 8 small schools, a few professors, and 700 students. The first public alternative to the University of Costa Rica, the Instituto Tecnologico de Costa Rica (ITCR), was opened in 1973 with an orientation in science and technology.

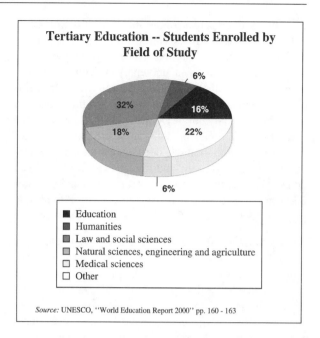

Tertiary Education -- Students Enrolled by Field of Study

- ■ Education
- ■ Humanities
- ■ Law and social sciences
- ▨ Natural sciences, engineering and agriculture
- □ Medical sciences
- □ Other

Source: UNESCO, "World Education Report 2000" pp. 160 - 163

Applicants to the University of Costa Rica and the Technological Institute of Costa Rica are required to pass an entrance exam. Some fields have additional special requirements. The National University and the State University at Distance have an open admissions policy. The University of Costa Rica, created by law in 1940, had increases in enrollments by 58 percent from 1960 to 1966. Enrollments increased again by 109 percent from 1966 to 1969. The university system grew from a population of 12,913 students in 1970 to 44,818 students in 1979. In the 1970s, the expansion of higher education in Costa Rica increased student populations from 9 out of 100 age-appropriate students in 1970 to 25 out of 100 by 1980. The student population grew three times as rapidly as the total population.

More than 50 percent of high school graduates, particularly from rural areas, cannot enter the university. The University of Costa Rica limited its student population to 18,000. Only 8 percent of the students at the University of Costa Rica come from working class and peasant backgrounds. The University of Costa Rica has more upper-class students than the university system as a whole. The University of Costa Rica is 29 percent upper class, 54 percent middle class, and 17 percent lower class. At the ITCR, 8 percent of students are higher class, 63 percent middle class, and 29 percent lower class.

The University of Costa Rica went from a single campus in San Jose to a multi-campus system. Distance learning, using the British Open University model, was instituted. The teacher-training college, normal superior located in Heredia, was upgraded to the Universidad Nacional. The National Library was established in 1888.

Ninety-three percent of the students at the University of Costa Rica come from Central America and 77 percent of university students are male. The University of Costa Rica is the newest national university in Central America. It opened with eight schools: agriculture, fine arts, sciences, law, pharmacology, philosophy, engineering, and education. The School of Dentistry opened in 1942, the School of Economics in 1943, and the School of Medicine in 1960. In the last two decades, a school of sciences and letters, a laboratory, and library facilities have been added. The central campus is located in San Jose. Students are graded on a scale of 0 to 10 with a minimum of 7 on the scale being the requirement to pass a course.

A rector presides over the university. Rectors are elected every three years and may be reelected by the University Assembly, which is comprised of directors of departments, as well as professors and members of national professional and student associations. The governing board of the university is the University Council, which consists of the rector and vice rectors, the minister of education, the deans, and two student representatives. This group approves curriculum, budgets, and university policies. Professors within the school, as well as the student representatives, elect the deans.

Academic rank is divided into five categories. The lowest rank is instructor, followed by assistant professors (*profesor adjunto*), associate professors (*profesor asociade*), and full professors (*catedratico*). Promotion through the ranks is based on degrees, publications, and length of service. Tenure can be earned after three years; fifteen years of employment are required to meet the rank of full professor. Not all faculty members have earned doctoral or terminal degrees and hiring part-time faculty is common. Most faculty research is conducted only when funds are acquired from international organizations.

Many students leave the university before acquiring their degrees, most often citing the need to gain employment. Only 5 percent of the students earn their degrees after the required five or six years of study. Current student enrollment exceeds 30,000 enrollees. Some students have trouble registering for required classes. In 1967, the university student association demonstrated for a larger school budget in front of the presidential palace and the legislative assembly.

The *bachillerato* (bachelor's degree) takes four years of study. The school semester lasts 16 weeks. Oral public defense of studies is required for graduation. Graduate studies leading to master and doctoral degrees are available at the University of Costa Rica in a variety of fields, including biology, microbiology, philosophy, law, medicine, public administration, and education. Required standards are comparable to those in North American universities regarding requisite credits, length of study, and other requirements for graduation. Higher education is free for nearly 50 percent of the enrolled students.

The University of Costa Rica's Carolost Monge Alfare Library is the best university library in Central America. The University of Costa Rica also has the best teaching conditions, followed by the Technological Institute and the Open University.

The Universidad Nacional (UNA) was created in 1973 with a curriculum similar to the University of Costa Rica but a normal school legacy. In 1977, the Universidad Estatal a Distancia was established, a university without walls. Parauniversity colleges, legalized in 1980, offered short programs. Three parauniversties were created in Cartago, Alajuela, and Puntarenas. Until the end of the 1960s, the University of Costa Rica was the only university and remained the premier university of the country. Today it offers 72 programs and has the largest enrollment of any institution of higher education.

In 1973, a new university, Universidad Nacional Autonoma was established in Heredia, which is about 15 minutes from San Jose. The University of Costa Rica is still considered a most prestigious college and the first choice for secondary school graduates. Degrees earned at foreign universities have more prestige, as well.

The Federation of Costa Rican Students (FECR) is the largest student organization. After two additional years of schooling beyond the *bachillerato*, students write a thesis and can then write "Lic" (*licenciade*) before their names. The general studies programs (*estudios generales*) of public universities have been criticized in light of the shorter period in which private universities, which forgo liberal arts education, are able to train managers for industry.

In the 1990s, a requirement of *trabajo comunal universitario* (TCU) was implemented. TCU required students to complete 150 to 300 hours of community service. This program gave students an opportunity to apply professional knowledge to national problems. In 1987, an Interdisciplinary Gender Studies Program (*Programa Interdisiplinario de Estudios de Genero* (PRIEG) was created in the Division of Social Sciences. In 1987, Cora Fiero, dean of the school of philosophy, founded *El programa Interdisiplinario de Estudios de la Mujer* (The Interdisciplinary Women Studies Program) at La Universidad Autonoma de Costa Rica. It has focused, thus far, on training human service providers for marginalized women. The program used visiting Fulbright scholars on several occasions. The program was an immediate success and each course had more than 40 students enrolled with a waiting lists of many more interested students. The program now includes three full-time faculty members and other related faculty throughout the university.

The first private university, the Universidad Autonoma de Centro America, was founded in 1975. A few international universities, established by governments or businesses outside Costa Rica, have been established as well. Executive decree number 5622-EO202 called for the opening of the first private university, the Universidad Autonoma de Centro America, in December 1975. By 1990, seven private universities existed and, by 1992, seven more had been opened.

In 2001, about 10 private universities and 14 parauniversities (technical schools) existed. Private and parauniversities enroll approximately 35,000 students—about half the number of the four public universities. Thirty-one parauniversities, similar to community and junior colleges in the United States, exist in Costa Rica. Today Costa Rica has 22 private universities, but most of them have small enrollments. As the family income level rises, students are more likely to seek private educations. In 2001, 13 private noninternational universities exist. The Universidad InterAmericana de Costa Rica, which began offering an MBA program in 1985, enrolls around 90 students. The institution appeals to working people who want to upgrade their skills.

The Costa Rican private sector of higher education lacks prestige. It was created primarily to meet higher education needs at lower costs. The parauniversity offers short study courses that take two or three years. This course of study, which is public or private, prepares students for a technical or administrative position. It grants diplomas but not university level degrees. The total public sector enrollments consisted of 28,336 students in 1974, or 100 percent of total enrollments. By 1992, this share had dropped to 68 percent of total enrollments or 60,892 students.

Private Universities include the Universidad Autonoma de Centro America, established in 1975; Universidad Internacional de Las Americas, established in 1985; the Universidad Adventista de Centro America, established in 1986; the Universidad Latin Americana de Ciencia y Technologia, established in 1987; the Universidad PanaAmericana, established in 1988; Universidad Latina de Costa Rica, established in 1990; the Universidad InterAmericana de Costa Rica, established in 1990; the Universidad Central Costarricense, established in 1990; the Universidad Hispano Americana, established in 1992; the Universidad de San Jose, established in 1992; Universidad Nazarena, established in 1992; Universidad Libre de Costa Rica, established in 1993; Universidad Anselmo Llorente y Lafuente, established in 1993; and the Universidad del Diseno, established in 1993.

Private sector enrollments were first measured in 1977 when they constituted 1 percent of total enrollments. By 1992, that percentage had risen to 32 percent of total enrollments.

ADMINISTRATION, FINANCE, & EDUCATIONAL RESEARCH

The Organization of the Ministry of Primary and Secondary Education and the Organization of the Ministry of Higher Education are the two administrative sections of the educational system in Costa Rica.

About one-fourth of the national government budget is devoted to education with two-thirds of this allotted to primary education. About 4 percent of Costa Rica's Gross National Product (GNP) is spent on education, a rate comparable to many industrialized nations. The traditionally strong anti-militarist policy allows more money to be spent on education in Costa Rica than in other Latin American countries.

In 1995, government spending by the ministry department listed 20.0 percent of the money spent on education, 39.0 percent on finance, 6.0 percent on works, 3.5 percent on public health, 9.9 percent on public labor, and 2.2 percent on public housing.

The Ministry of Education regulates the school system and heads the national school board. The educational system is directed by the National Education council presided over by the minister of education. Each school district has a board of education appointed by the municipality. Employees of the ministry of education and all school employees have civil service status. Of all the government ministries, the ministry of education has the largest number of employees—28,000. The ministry of education has separate departments of finance, teacher preparation, personnel, and the national library. Seven provinces in Costa Rica each have their own local administrator and school boards.

The Officinal de Educacion Indigena is the institutional counterpart of community groups that concern themselves with educating Amerindians. The Commision Nacional Indigenista works to preserve culture and maintain indigenous languages through the public school system. The school system is broken down administratively by regions and subdivided by districts. A community needs 25 eligible children to establish a school. Public spending on education is financed from Costa Rica's general budget, which is primarily generated by indirect taxes. Increasingly, the cost of higher education is borne by the Costa Rican people. Schools are funded at the national level, not at the local level.

Ninety percent of Costa Rican educational funds are spent on salaries. Under Costa Rican law, the country changes the president and presidential administration every four years, as well as high and medium level officials. The percentage of the national budget devoted to public education dropped from 30 percent to 18 percent from the mid-1970s to the 1980s. A special tax levy al-

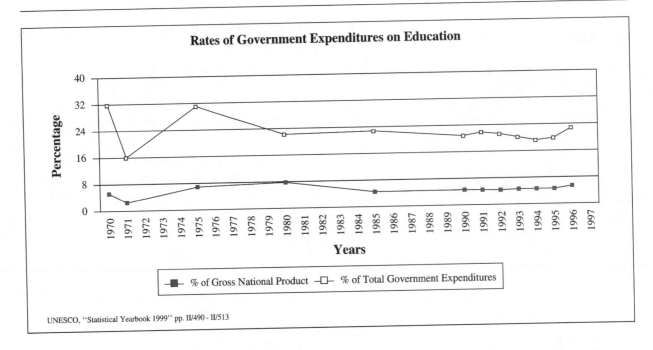

Rates of Government Expenditures on Education

UNESCO, "Statistical Yearbook 1999" pp. II/490 - II/513

lowed vocational education to expand in the mid-1970s to mid-1980s. The National Liberation Party (PLN) social democratic governments of Luis Monge from 1982 to 1986 and Oscar Arias from 1986 to 1990 limited the development of higher education to the private sector due to economic pressures the country faced. During the Arias Sanchez administration in 1990, more resources were devoted to education (approximately 25 percent of the national budget in 1990).

Fees are charged at higher educational institutions, but all institutions have a system of scholarships. The National Commission for Educational Assistance offers financing for study in priority subject areas. In 1974, the public university set up the council of coordinating bodies for state universities.

The constitution of 1949 established state financing of university education with no less than 10 percent of the annual national budget diverted to this purpose. In 1982, the national, higher-education, planning office was created to provide technical support to the council of state universities. In 1990, 33.4 percent of students in the University of Costa Rica and 63.8 percent in the UNA paid no tuition.

A coordinating commission consists of the ministers of home affairs, education, and planning, as well as representatives from the Office of Higher Education Planning, and the rectors of the four state universities oversee the funding for higher education. The rectors of state universities also form the National Council of Rectors, which is attached to the Office of Planning. This group coordinates decision-making regarding state university policies in the country.

The National Council of Higher Education, which oversees coordination related to private institutions, governs private universities. Parauniversity institutions of higher education (*colegios universitarios* and *institutos*) are organized under the provisions of Law number 9541, which was passed in 1980.

Direct payment by students is less than 10 percent of the university budget. The government, as dictated in the constitution, funds the University of Costa Rica. In order to finance educational reforms, Costa Rica has gotten loans from the Inter-American Development Bank. From 1962 to 1966 the university also received funds from the United States and from the Ford, Kellogg, and Rockefeller Foundations.

Transfers from the Ministry of Public Education finance university and parauniversity higher education. Direct payments by university students account for less than 10 percent of total expenditures. In 1995, the total public expenditure on education was 5.0 percent of the national budget. Basic education accounted for 2.8 percent of the national budget, with 1.9 percent being spent on primary education and 15.0 on secondary education. Public expenditures on higher education accounted for 1.7 percent of the national budget, with 1.6 percent directed to universities, and .1 percent to parauniversities.

The minister of education serves as chair of the Higher Council of Education. The budget of the University of Costa Rica is to be no less than 10 percent of the budget of the minister of education. The Higher Council of Education makes decisions concerning curriculum, budget, textbook selection, teacher certification, supervision, and other policy decisions.

NONFORMAL EDUCATION

The Higher Council of Education oversees state and private training institutes aimed at increasing technical skills. These private institutes offer shorter programs, and their graduation requirements are less stringent than universities. In addition to the National Apprentice Institution, a special cultural and educational channel focuses on informal education. A State Distance University was established in 1977 to allow adult and rural populations to continue their educations after completion of their secondary diplomas. Courses are offered for credit through the medium of radio and television. Most courses offered are in management.

TEACHING PROFESSION

Dr. Jose Castro Madriza established the normal school in the capital of San Jose in May 1887 to train teachers. The program was five and a half years in length with five years mandatory teaching after graduation for students who had received financial aid. In 1968, a new normal school was founded in Heredia next to a previously existing one, but the new school had the purpose of educating teachers specifically for secondary schools. This Escuela Normal Superior lasted until 1973 when the Universidad Nacional was created and absorbed the program.

Reductions in teacher salaries caused many to leave the profession. Many teachers had to work at second jobs. Some worked at markets on weekends. When teacher's salaries were cut in the 1980s, teachers went on strike to bring their salaries back to 1970 levels. They were successful, but little progress has been made since then. The Ministry of Education has been forced to hire aspirants, probationary teachers who are recent secondary school graduates. This has affected the quality of education, especially in rural areas. Books, supplies, maps, and libraries are scarce in many rural and inner-city schools.

State universities in Costa Rica are also responsible for training teachers, and three state universities offer this course of study. Students can obtain the title of professor or teacher after two years of training at the university. Two more years lead to the *bachiller* degree in education. The *licenciatura* degree education can be obtained after a further period of two years of study with specialization in educational administration, preschool education, primary education, and teaching curriculum development.

Ninety percent of primary school teachers are female. The low salaries for primary teachers draw few males to the profession. More males teach at the secondary level and occupy administrative positions. Teacher salaries account for more than 50 percent of the education budget, but the salaries are low when compared to those of other public employees. Additionally, many teachers must buy supplies and pay for school repairs out of their own salaries.

Teachers are classified by their level of preparation. *Profesores titulados* (teachers with titles) occupy the highest rank and posses university degrees. *Profesores autorizados* (authorized teachers) do not posses a degree for teaching, but have other education or qualifications beyond secondary schooling. *Profesores aspirantes* (aspiring teachers) have only a secondary school degree.

The largest teacher association, the National Association of Educators (ANDE) was founded in 1941. Two additional professional organizations, the Association of Professors of Secondary Education founded in 1955, and the Syndicate of Costa Rican Educators, exist as well. In the mid-1970s, the government supported the construction of housing for teachers in order to draw more qualified candidates into the field. Local communities were asked to donate land and lay the foundation for a home. The national government then erected prefabricated houses large enough for a family of six.

SUMMARY

Inadequate efforts to provide higher education in Limon, with its large Afro-Caribbean population, is still not close to parity with the schooling available in the central valley. An increased emphasis on privatization has led to an increase in the number of private institutions in recent years. Expenditures declined during the 1980s and 1990s. The affects of this reduced funding could result in increased illiteracy or lower graduation rates. The school system experiences a high number of dropouts, which contributes to an increase in illiteracy.

Private spending on education in 1995 differed significantly in terms of income. Of those in the top quintile, 49 percent were spending funds on private education; in the next to the top quintile, 24 percent; in the middle quintile, 13 percent; in the next to lowest quintile, 7.5 percent; at the lowest quintile, only 5 percent spent funds on private education. Attendance at public and private educational institutions differs significantly depending on income. At the top quintile, 60 percent attend public institutions and 40 percent private; at the second highest quintile, 82 percent attend public institutions and 19 percent private; at the middle quintile, 90 percent attend public institutions, and 10 percent attend private; at the second to lowest quintile, 98 percent attend public and 2 percent private; at the lowest quintile, 99 percent attend public and 1 percent attend private.

When data on students who are passed, held back, or failed in basic education is compared between public and private institutions, stratification is apparent. At the primary levels, 87 percent of public school students pass exams, compared to 95 percent of private students. Students who fail at the primary level comprise 8 percent in public schools and 2 percent in private schools. At the secondary level, 56 percent of public school students pass exams compared to 72 percent of private school students. Failure rates at the secondary level are 12 percent for public school students compared to 6 percent at the private schools.

Differences appear regarding school attendance by age group and income level. In the top quintile, 68 percent attend preschool; 52 percent at the second highest quintile; 41 percent at the middle quintile; 34 percent at the second lowest quintile; 29 percent at the lowest quintile. In primary education, 99 percent attend at the highest quintile; 98 percent at the second quintile; 96 percent at the middle quintile; 92 percent at the second to lowest quintile; 39 percent at the lowest quintile. At the secondary level, the numbers range from 85 percent attending at the highest quintile to 50 percent attending at the lowest quintile. With regard to university education, 52 percent of those at the highest quintile attend universities; 32 percent at the second highest; 22 percent at the middle level; 17 percent at the second lowest quintile; 13 percent at the lowest quintile.

School attendance by age group and geographical setting indicates that, at the preschool level, an average of 39 percent attends school—55 percent in urban areas and 25 percent in rural areas. At the primary level, an average of 94 percent attends school—95 percent in urban areas and 92 percent in rural areas. At the secondary level, a clear difference emerges with an average of 60 percent attending school, translating as 75 percent in urban areas and 45 percent in rural areas. At the university level, an average of 27 percent attends school, meaning 39 percent in urban areas and only 14 percent from rural areas. Schooling is obviously not adequate to meet the needs in rural areas.

BIBLIOGRAPHY

Castillo-Serrano, Deyanira. *Afro-Caribbean Schools in Costa Rica, 1934-1948*. Ph.D. diss., University of Texas, Austin, 1998.

Cravath, Jay. "Elementary Education." *Social Education 64* (2000): 297.

Frost, Lynda Elizabeth. *Policy development and the implementation of educational reform: A study in human rights education*. Ph.D. diss., University of Iowa, 1996.

Funkhouser, Edward. "Changes In The Returns To Education In Costa Rica." *Journal of Development Economics 57* (1998): 289.

Funkhouse, Edward. "Cyclical Economic Conditions and School Attendance in Costa Rica." *Economics of Education Review*, 18:31 (1999).

Gutierrez, Miguel. *Evaluation and the change process in higher education: A case study in Costa Rica*. Ed.D. diss., East Carolina University, 1998.

Heffington, Douglas. "Sustainable Development in Costa Rican." *Social Education 63* (1999): 80.

Leitinger, Ilse Abshagen, ed., *The Costa Rican's Women's Movement*. Pittsburgh, PA: University of Pittsburgh Press, 1997.

Potter, Elsa. *The primary education of bilingual indigenous children on the Talamanca Bribri Reservation in Limon Province of Costa Rica*. Ph.D. diss., Texas A & M University, Kingsville, 1998.

Rodino, Ana Maria. *Determinants of Writing Performance and Performance Difficultures in Costa Rican Adults with High Levels of Schooling*, 1997.

Thompson, Julie Ann. *The politics of educational policymaking in Costa Rica*. Ph.D. diss., University Of California, Los Angeles, 1998.

Twombly, Susan. "Curricular Reform And The Changing Social Role Of Public Higher Education In Costa Rica." *Higher Education 33* (1997): 1.

—*Donna Langston*

CÔTE D'IVOIRE

BASIC DATA

Official Country Name:	Republic of Côte d'Ivoire
Region:	Africa
Population:	15,980,950
Language(s):	French, Dioula
Literacy Rate:	48.5%

HISTORY & BACKGROUND

The Republic of Côte d'Ivoire is located on the southern coast of West Africa and is one of the richest nations in the country. It is bordered by Liberia and Guinea on the west, Mali and Burkina-Faso to the north, Ghana to the east, and the Atlantic ocean to the south. Its area is 124,501 square miles, and its population in 2001 was 15,900,000 people. The population of Côte d'Ivoire is diverse, with more than 60 different ethnic and tribal groups, among them Baoulé (23 percent of the population), Bété (18 percent), Sénoufou (15 percent), and large

Krou, Malinke, and Mandingo tribes. Côte d'Ivoire's prosperous economy has also attracted a large number of foreign African workers, mostly from Guinea, Ghana, and Burkina-Faso (estimated at 2.6 million in 2000), as well as a contingent of 200,000 Lebanese expatriates. Together, these workers represent nearly 20 percent of the country's population. Abidjan is the economic capital of Côte d'Ivoire, with an estimated 2001 population of 3,305,000 people. Yamoussoukro (population 125,000) is the official capital and the site of the world's largest Christian church: the basilica of Notre-Dame de la Paix, erected at a cost of $200 million and dedicated by Pope John-Paul II in 1990. The population is 60 percent Muslim and 22 percent Christian, with another 18 percent representing animist and indigenous religions. French is the official language, though the Dioula dialect is also widely used.

French settlers first appeared in 1687, but France did not exercise political control over Côte d'Ivoire until the late nineteenth century. Côte d'Ivoire became a French protectorate in 1883, a colony in 1889, and a territory of French West Africa in 1904. It gained full independence from France in 1960. For 33 years, between 1960 and 1993, Côte d'Ivoire was ruled by a single man: president Félix Houphouet-Boigny, a benign dictator who led the country from independence to economic prosperity. He chose to keep close cultural, political, and economic ties with France (the French still maintain a modest military presence), and in 1985 changed the nation's official name from Ivory Coast to Côte d'Ivoire. Côte d'Ivoire is a member of the "Zone Franc," and its currency is backed by the French treasury. True democratic institutions were slow to arrive, but Houphouet-Boigny's single-handed rule (no opposition parties were allowed until 1990) was not marred by the sort of terror and torture that characterized many of the dictatorial governments that emerged from the former colonies of West Africa after 1960. From the late 1950s through the start of the twenty-first century, Côte d'Ivoire enjoyed a prosperity and a political stability unmatched in neighboring countries. When Houphouet-Boigny died in 1993, president Bédié became the country's leader until he was ousted in a coup in 1999. In October of 2000, Laurent Gbagbo was democratically elected to a five-year term as Côte d'Ivoire's president.

CONSTITUTIONAL & LEGAL FOUNDATIONS

The constitution of Côte d'Ivoire, originally adopted in 1960 and modified between 1971 and 1985, was abrogated in 1999. The new constitution, adopted by a vast majority of voters in a referendum in July of 2000, stipulates that education is free and compulsory for all between the ages of 7 and 13. Prior to that, in 1995, the government adopted the *Loi de Réforme* No. 696. This

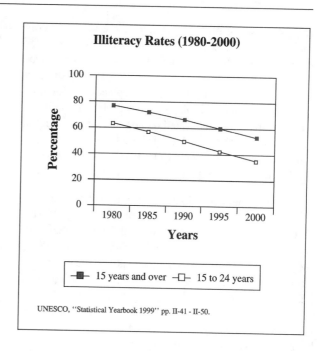

Illiteracy Rates (1980-2000)

UNESCO, "Statistical Yearbook 1999" pp. II-41 - II-50.

document spelled out the fundamental principles behind the government's educational policies and outlined strategic planning and curricular developments for all educational levels.

EDUCATIONAL SYSTEM—OVERVIEW

The early history of Côte d'Ivoire's educational system is rooted in French colonial policy in Africa at the end of the nineteenth century. Originally, African colonies were considered a new frontier for missionary work, as well as a source of raw materials and ores. The French government, though officially unattached to religious organizations, welcomed the outreach efforts of Catholic and Protestant missionaries. These groups effectively laid the foundations of primary and secondary education in Côte d'Ivoire and the other colonies that made up the *Afrique Equatoriale Française* (French West Africa). Today's religious private schools, which still educate the children of the elite, are the direct descendants of these colonial institutions.

As the French intensified their political influence, they also began coordinated efforts to create an official public school system. By 1923, Côte d'Ivoire had a rudimentary network of primary schools in place, The first secondary school opened in 1928. French authorities, however, faced a pedagogical and sociocultural dilemma. They intended the primary school system to educate young Ivoirians in the three Rs(reading, writing, and arithmetics) with the intent of encouraging their entry into the lower echelons of the workforce. Secondary education, by contrast, represented a potential long-term threat: officials worried that further education might nurture a climate of resistance against the established colonial order. Because of such misgivings, secondary education was never developed to its full potential between 1928 and the end of World War II. But since the French also planned gradually to replace their own administrators and officials with native Ivoirians, it was vital to establish an educated demographic base. Accordingly, only the sons of local tribal chiefs were selected for secondary education in Côte d'Ivoire and later sent to France on scholarships for postgraduate training.

The formal education of former president Houphouet-Boigny is itself an illustration of that policy. Born in Yamassoukro, the son of a powerful Baoulé tribal chief, he was educated in private elementary schools and then sent to Dakar, in French Senegal, to attend the prestigious *Ecole Normale William Ponty*. Later he studied at the *Ecole de Médecine et de Pharmacie de Dakar*, the first medical school established by the French in their West African colonies. After graduation in 1925, Houphouet-Boigny returned to Côte d'Ivoire, where he practiced medicine while running a coffee plantation. He became mayor of Abidjan, was elected a congressman to the French National Assembly, and was ultimately appointed to a cabinet minister post in Paris.

When Houphouet-Boigny became Côte d'Ivoire's first president in 1960, he favored the elaboration of an educational system that would both democratize and retain most of the elitist characteristics of his own schooling. He chose not to follow the path of radical Africanization favored by Guinea and Ghana, and against the criticism of neighboring African nations decided instead to continue a close alliance with France. Politically, economically, and educationally, that controversial decision handsomely paid off as Côte d'Ivoire became the wealthiest and most literate nation of the sub-Sahara. Since the death of Houphouet-Boigny in 1993, a new generation of Ivoirians has initiated some distancing from French influence and has been more assertive in the affirmation of its African heritage. In a like manner, the educational system of Côte d'Ivoire is gradually adopting an identity of its own, while still solidly resting on its French foundations.

PREPRIMARY & PRIMARY EDUCATION

Preprimary education is still a new concept in most developing African nations. In rural areas, women tend to remain at home and care for their own children until they enter elementary schools. In large urban centers like Abidjan, Bouaké, Divo, and Daloa, the increasing integration of women into the workforce has encouraged the growth of childcare centers and preschools. In 2000, there were 35,553 preschoolers (17,381 girls) enrolled in 276 schools. Of these, 19,075 were enrolled in 230 public

institutions. They were taught by a total of 1580 teachers (96 percent women)—870 of them working in public schools.

Ivoirian children attend primary schools between the ages of 6 and 11. Classes are divided into three two-year cycles: preparatory stages I and II (CP1 and CP2, or *Cours préparatoires de première et deuxième année*), elementary levels I and II (CE1 and CE2 or *cours élémentaires de première et deuxième année*), and intermediary levels I and II (CM1 and CM2 or *cours moyens de première et deuxième année*). In 2000, there were 1,910,820 children enrolled in primary schools in Côte d'Ivoire: 1,688,503 in public schools and 222,317 in private institutions, with a gender distribution of 58 percent boys and 42 percent girls. There were 8,082 primary schools (including 781 private institutions) offering a total of 43,406 classes and a teacher-student ratio of 1:44. There were 44,731 primary school teachers (including 5,791 in the private sector) and 23 percent of them were women.

The six-year primary school program ends with a selective national examination known as the CEP (*certificat d'études primaires* or elementary school proficiency examination). Only the children who pass this exam are allowed to continue into the secondary education cycle. In 2000, there were 285,391 candidates for the CEP, and a total of 155,246 succeeded—a 54 percent passing rate. It is a measure of both the selectivity and the pedagogical difficulties of primary education in Côte d'Ivoire that, after six years of schooling, only 15 percent of the children who originally entered the system at the age of six qualified as candidates for the national examination, reflecting a dropout rate of 85 percent over six years. In 2000, out of the 253,293 children enrolled in CM2 (the grade preparing the children for the CEP), 107,827 were also repeating the entire year.

SECONDARY EDUCATION

Secondary education in Côte d'Ivoire consists of a seven-year curriculum divided into two cycles. The lower level, lasting four years, prepares the students for a selective, national exam known as the BEPC (*brevet d'études du premier cycle*, or junior high school national proficiency exam). Only those students who succeed are allowed into the next cycle of secondary education, which lasts another three years. It leads to the Baccalauréat, a highly selective national examination and a prerequisite for admission to the university or other levels of higher education in Côte d'Ivoire. The last three years of the secondary school curriculum are sub-divided into different sections that allow students to concentrate on a future major: section A for the humanities, B for economics and law, C for exact sciences, D for biological sciences and pre-medicine, and so forth.

In 2000, there were 565,850 students enrolled in secondary education (365,795 in public schools), and 193,742 were female. There were 508 secondary schools (194 public and 314 private) offering 10,667 classes. The total number of teachers was 18,033 (10,905 in public schools and 7,128 in private institutions.) In 2000, at the end of the first cycle of secondary education, there were 137,779 candidates for the BEPC and 36,122 passed (26.2 percent). At the conclusion of the second cycle of secondary education, there were 72,627 candidates for the baccalauréat examination and 26,590 passed (36.1 percent).

Vocational & Technical Education: After relegating vocational education to a lesser level of importance for decades, Côte d'Ivoire decided in 1985 to create a cabinet-level post that would invigorate and supervise technical and vocational education at the national level: the *Ministère de l'Enseignement Technique et de la Formation Professionelle.*

Students enter vocational training at two different stages. At the secondary level, once they have successfully passed the BEPC, they can gain admission to the National Institute for Technical and Professional Training (the INFTP) or the National Office for Professional Training (the ONFP). The students who pass the baccalauréat have access to numerous public and private institutes that award the BTS (*Brevet de Technicien Supérieur*) after a three-year curriculum, such as the Institute for Higher Technical Training (the INSET). They can also enter university-run programs that award the DUT (*Diplôme Universitaire de Technologie*). In 1999, there were over 27,000 students enrolled in technical and vocational schools, taught by 2850 instructors (19 percent women). Côte d'Ivoire's largest vocational school is the *Institut National Polytechnique Félix Houphouet-Boigny* founded in 1975 in Houphouet-Boigny's native town of Yamassoukro. In 2000, it enrolled over 3,500 students and employed 350 teachers.

HIGHER EDUCATION

Higher education is well-developed in Côte d'Ivoire, with a university system and research centers that are highly respected in Africa. The system is organized after the French national model: holders of the selective baccalauréat follow a two-year curriculum leading to the DUEL (*Diplôme Universitaire d'Etudes Littéraires*), the DUES (*Diplôme Universitaire d'Etudes Scientifiques*), or the DEUG (*Diplôme Universitaire d'Etudes Générales*). One more year of study leads to the *Licence* (the level of an American bachelor's degree), and an additional year leads to the *Maîtrise* (the equivalent of a master's degree). Further studies lead to the DEA (*Diplôme d'Etudes Approfondies*), a post-graduate specialized de-

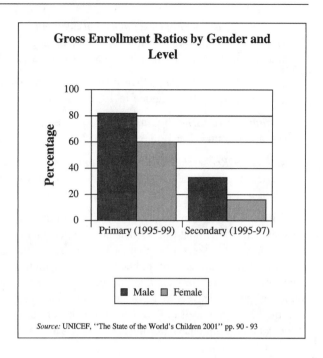

Gross Enrollment Ratios by Gender and Level

Source: UNICEF, "The State of the World's Children 2001" pp. 90 - 93

gree, and after the successful defense of a doctoral dissertation, to the *Doctorat de Spécialité de Troisième Cycle* (the Ph.D.). The university also awards the M.D. and the degree of Doctor of Engineering. The university system in Côte d'Ivoire has grown at such a rate that, following student-led demonstrations against crowded facilities in the early 1990s, the government opened two additional campuses. The universities of Côte d'Ivoire have also acquired their own distinct identities. Until 1985, the majority of professors were expatriates from France or French-speaking countries, but by 2000 their number had dwindled to less than 5 percent of the faculty.

The *Université de Cocody* is the main university in Côte d'Ivoire. Founded in 1958 in Abidjan as the *Centre d'Enseignement Supérieur*, it became the *Université Nationale de Côte d'Ivoire* in 1964 and adopted its present name in 1995. It is comprised of 12 different schools, including Law, Medicine, Pharmacy, Economics, Liberal Arts, and Engineering. In 2000, there were over 45,000 students enrolled at Cocody, with a faculty of 990. In 1992, a new university opened in Bouaké, to alleviate the crowding problems of Cocody (which had been built to accommodate 7,000 students.) The *Université de Bouaké* started with 2,800 students and 45 professors. In 2001, it enrolled 15,700 students and employed 145 faculty members. To continue to decentralize the main campus, the government also opened the *Université d'Abobo-Adjamé* in Abidjan in 1995.

Côte d'Ivoire also runs numerous research institutes, including:

- *Institut Africain pour le Développement Economique et Social* (economics, sociology, and ethnology), founded in 1962 in Abidjan by the Society of Jesus

- *Institut Pasteur de Côte d'Ivoire* (research on viral diseases and AIDS), founded in 1972 in Abidjan

- *Institut Pierre Richet* (research on tropical endemic diseases), founded in Bouaké in 1973

- *Centre de Recherches Océanographiques* (research on oceanography and hydrobiology), founded in Abidjan in 1958.

Higher education in Côte d'Ivoire is not limited to the university system and its associated research facilities. In 2000, there were more than 50,000 Ivoirians students enrolled in private and public institutes of higher education and in the *Grandes Ecoles*. The latter are prestigious, highly selective post-graduate schools (patterned after their French models in Paris) that train the very best of the country's diplomats, politicians, civil servants and engineers:

- *Ecole Nationale d'Administration,* founded in Abidjan in 1960. In 2000, it enrolled more than 1000 students.

- *Ecole Supérieure d'Agronomie,* founded in 1996 in Yamoussoukro. In 2000 it enrolled 600 students and employed 75 teachers.

- *Ecole Nationale Supérieure des Travaux Publics (civil engineering),* founded in 1963 in Yamoussoukro. In 2000, it employed 97 professors for a student population of 597.

ADMINISTRATION, FINANCE, & EDUCATIONAL RESEARCH

The Ministry of National Education in Abidjan supervises the educational system of Côte d'Ivoire, while delegating administrative and curricular authority to three other cabinet-level ministries: the Ministry of Primary Education, the Ministry of Technical and Vocational Training, and the Ministry of Higher Education and Scientific Research. The Ministry of National Education is the only agency in Côte d'Ivoire that accredits schools and validates diplomas and degrees. It delegates authority to ministries in matters of specific curricular development, faculty evaluation, and school inspections. In 2000, the educational budget of Côte d'Ivoire represented 26 percent of national expenditures. The government has pledged to increase this figure to at least 30 percent of the national budget by fiscal 2003.

TEACHER TRAINING

Primary school teachers are trained in several *écoles normales* and *centres d'animation et de formation péda-*gogiques. They are open to those who have passed the BEPC. After completion of the program, students are awarded the *Certificat d'Aptitude Professionelle des Instituteurs.* Teachers for the first cycle of secondary schools must hold the baccalauréat degree and follow a three-year program of study at the *Ecole Normale Supérieure,* leading to the *Certificat d'Aptitude au Professorat des Collèges d'Enseignement Secondaires.* Those wishing to teach in the second cycle of the secondary school system must study for an additional year and pass the CAPES (the *Certificat d'Aptitude au Professorat de l'Enseignement Secondaire*). The national teacher training program has been quite successful: whereas in 1985 up to 80 percent of Ivoirian secondary school teachers were not in possession of proper teaching credentials, within 15 years that number fell below 5 percent. In 1999, there were 15 teacher training colleges in Côte d'Ivoire, with 538 professors and 2,821 students.

SUMMARY

Côte d'Ivoire enjoys an educational system the quality of which is unparalleled in other sub-Saharan nations. This success, however, has been achieved primarily at the tertiary level, with universities and research centers that have become a benchmark of quality for other developing African nations. Though substantial progress has been made at the primary and secondary levels, especially in the area of teacher training, problems and weaknesses remain. After 1960, Côte d'Ivoire inherited an educational system that was a carbon copy of the French national model. President Houphouet-Boigny retained a pedagogical philosophy that many Ivoirian educators consider excessively elitist and out of touch with the country's needs. An illustration of the educational system of Côte d'Ivoire is a pyramid in which the base represents 85 percent of the eligible population, while the top consists of a 1.3 percent minority that alone shapes the destiny of the country. Thus while Côte d'Ivoire is one of the richest and most stable countries of West Africa, it still has an illiteracy rate of 58 percent.

Secondary education in Côte d'Ivoire has set an impressive example in enrollment growth, developing from 12,000 students in 1960, 70,000 in 1970, 238,000 in 1980, to nearly 566,000 in 2000. Nonetheless its rewards remain limited to a privileged few: after nine years of schooling, only 26.2 percent of qualified candidates pass the national proficiency examination (BEPC) at the end of junior high school. Ivoirian educators are well aware of this disproportion. The Educational Reform Law of 1995 has laid down the theoretical principles that will allow a larger segment of the population to gain access to higher levels of academic opportunities. The government also faces a dilemma if it attempts to rectify the apportionment of its educational resources: selectivity is

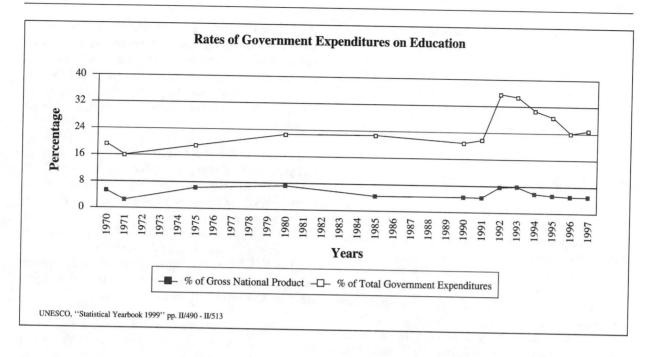

Rates of Government Expenditures on Education

UNESCO, "Statistical Yearbook 1999" pp. II/490 - II/513

viewed as a necessary evil, since the Ivoirian economy cannot absorb a larger number of qualified personnel, and the nation's universities are already being used to maximum capacity. The primary and secondary educational systems need to be reshaped from their rather obsolete French model and adapted to the future needs of Côte d'Ivoire.

BIBLIOGRAPHY

Annuaire Statistique de l'Enseignement Pré-Scolaire, Primaire et Secondaire. 2 vols. Abidjan: Ministère de l'Education Nationale, 1999.

Bretherick, Dona. *Côte d'Ivoire.* Washington, DC: American Association of Collegiate Registrars, 1995.

Kompass: Côte d'Ivoire. Abidjan: Kompass Côte d'Ivoire, S.A., 1999.

Kouadio, Aska. *Enseignement Technique et Professionnel en Côte d'Ivoire: Evolution et Eléments pour une Pédagogie Rénovée.* Villeneuve d'Ascq: Presses Universitaires du Septentrion, 1998.

Ogbu, S.M. "On Public Expenditures and Delivery of Education in sub-Saharan Africa." *Comparative Educational Review 36* (1991): 295-318.

—*Eric H. du Plessis*

CROATIA

BASIC DATA

Official Country Name:	Republic of Croatia
Region:	Europe
Population:	4,282,216
Language(s):	Croatian, Italian, Hungarian, Czech, Slovak, German
Literacy Rate:	97%
Academic Year:	October-September
Number of Primary Schools:	1,094
Compulsory Schooling:	8 years
Public Expenditure on Education:	5.3%
Foreign Students in National Universities:	725
Libraries:	232
Educational Enrollment:	Primary: 203,933 Secondary: 416,829 Higher: 85,752
Educational Enrollment Rate:	Primary: 87% Secondary: 82% Higher: 28%
Teachers:	Primary: 10,762 Secondary: 31,070 Higher: 6,038

Student-Teacher Ratio:	Primary: 19:1
	Secondary: 14:1
Female Enrollment Rate:	Primary: 87%
	Secondary: 83%
	Higher: 29%

HISTORY & BACKGROUND

The Republic of Croatia (in Croatian, *Republika Hrvatska* or *Hrvatska* for short) is a constitutional parliamentary democracy in the Balkan region of southeastern Europe. Bordered by the Adriatic Sea to the west, Slovenia and Hungary to the north, and Serbia to the east, Croatia forms the northern and western borders of Bosnia and Herzegovina. At its extreme southern-most tip, Croatia is contiguous with Montenegro for 25 kilometers. Croatia measures 56,538 square kilometers and is slightly smaller than the U.S. state of West Virginia. The country has a diverse terrain, with flat plains along its northern border with Hungary and low mountains and highlands forming its western coastline and islands in the Adriatic. Croatia also has a varied climate, ranging from continental, with hot summers and dry winters in the inland portions of the country, to Mediterranean, with mild winters and dry summers along the coast.

Croatia had a population of about 4.3 million people in July 2000. Croatia's ethnic composition was 78.1 percent Croat, 12.2 percent Serb, 0.9 percent Muslim, 0.5 percent Hungarian, and 0.5 percent Slovene, and less than half a percent Czech, Albanian, Montenegrin, and Roma each in 1991 (the last year estimates were taken before the war that enveloped Croatia from 1991 until 1995). About 6.6 percent of the population in 1991 belonged to other ethnic groups, considered themselves ''Yugoslavs,'' or were of unidentified ethnicity. Croatia's population was 76.5 percent Roman Catholic, 11.1 percent Orthodox, 1.2 percent Muslim, and 0.4 percent Protestant. The religious affiliation of 10.8 percent of the population was other, none, or unidentified.

Approximately 57 percent of Croats lived in urban areas in 1999. The rural population density was 132.9 persons per square kilometer in 1998. In 1999, approximately 99 percent of adult men 15 years of age or older and approximately 97 percent of adult women were literate (i.e., able to read and write). The population of Croatia was growing at a rate of only 0.93 percent in the year 2000. The total fertility rate was 1.94 in 2000, with approximately 18 percent of Croatia's population was 14 years old or younger, two-thirds of the population was between 15 and 64 years of age, and about 15 percent was 65 or older. In 2000 Croatia had an infant-mortality rate of 7.35 per 1000 live births, significantly lower than the rate for the European/Central Asian region as a whole; the under five years child mortality rate was 9 per 1000. The life expectancy at birth for Croatians in 2000 was 73.67 years (70.04 years for men and 77.51 years for women—a considerable gender disparity in favor of women).

Croatia's GDP was US$20.4 million in 1999 with a real growth rate of zero percent. For the first half of 2000, the economic growth rate was more promising, with the rate of growth estimated as 2.5 percent of the GDP. Croatia's annual per capita income that year was about US$4,490, which was more than twice the per-capita income for the European/Central Asian region and just a few hundred dollars lower than the upper middle income average. However, unemployment in Croatia was measured at 22.4 percent at the end of 2000.

Croatia required an infusion of US$87 million in international development disbursements from the World Bank in 1999 to help the country recover from four years of war (1991-1995) and to assist in transforming Croatia's state-controlled, centralized economy of pre-independence days to a liberal market-based economy. In the 1990s the World Bank committed US$762 million to Croatia for at least 15 development and reconstruction projects. During the 1990s Croatia received US$99 million from the United States through SEED Act funding, not including significant amounts of humanitarian assistance provided through other programs and nearly US$1,566 million from the European Union. The economic situation of the late 1990s stood in stark contrast to Croatia's previous economic prosperity before the Balkans wars of the 1990s.

Just before its independence from the Socialist Federal Republic of Yugoslavia on June 25, 1991, Croatia was the second richest country in the former Yugoslavia. It was second only to Slovenia, which declared independence from Yugoslavia at the same time. One of the six republics that together constituted Yugoslavia for most of the twentieth century, Croatia held a referendum in May 1991 during which 94 percent of the voters opted for independence. The official separation from Yugoslavia on 25 June 1991 was quickly followed by Serb aggression to attempt to bring the country back under Serbian control. This resulted in four years of brutal war from 1991 until 1995, during which ethnic Serbs, and to a lesser extent Croats and Bosnian Muslims (Bosniacs), waged genocidal war on each other. Early into the war Croatia formed a pact with Bosnia-Herzegovina to try to halt the crushing blows of the Serb army as Serbia, the most-powerful state in the former Yugoslavia, attempted to subdue Croatia and in the process wiped out thousands of ethnic Croats and created enormous refugee flows.

With the Dayton Accords of 1995 and the end of the war in Bosnia-Herzegovina, Croatia was able to slowly rebuild its economic and social structures. Its political system dramatically transformed. By the mid-1990s Croatia had become a fledgling democracy, joining the ranks of Eastern and Central Europe's "transitional countries."

CONSTITUTIONAL & LEGAL FOUNDATIONS

The Republic of Croatia is a parliamentary democracy with a strong presidency. The Croatian government's basic purposes and structures were established by the Constitution of December 22, 1990. The Croatian legal system is a civil law system. All Croatians, women and men alike, are eligible to vote at age 18; 16- and 17- year-olds are also eligible to vote if they are employed. Croatia's democratically elected chief executive and head of state, the president, is elected to a five year term of office. The executive branch of the Croatian government also includes the prime minister, who is appointed by the president and must be confirmed by the House of Representatives. The prime minister also recommends other ministers to the president for appointment to the executive branch. Early in the year 2000, Ivica Racan was chosen as Prime Minister. Since February 2000 the President of the Republic of Croatia has been Stjepan Mesic, a member of the Croatian People's party (HNS).

At the national level the Croatian legislative branch consists of a bicameral Assembly, or *Sabor,* composed of the House of Counties (*Zupanijski Dom*) with 68 members (63 elected by popular vote and 5 appointed by the president) who serve 4 year terms and the House of Representatives (*Zastupnicki Dom*) with 151 members also elected to 4 year terms. The third branch of Croatia's national government is the judicial branch, consisting of the Supreme Court whose judges are appointed to eight year terms by the Judicial Council of the Republic and the Constitutional Court with eight judges similarly appointed. The Judicial Council of the Republic is elected by Croatia's House of Representatives. Croatian regional affairs are administered through a system involving 20 counties (*Zupanijski*), though the national government continued to operate in a fairly centralized fashion and to exert significant control over administrative affairs throughout the country in the year 2000.

International human rights organizations and agencies such as Human Rights Watch and the Bureau of Democracy, Human Rights, and Labor of the U.S. Department of State praised many of the steps Croatia took in 2000 to promote human rights and further democratize the country. For example, in February 2000 at the start of the new national administration under President Mesic and Prime Minister Racan, the government announced its intentions to make US$55 million available to assist in the resettlement and reintegration of 16,500 Croatian Serb refugees who had fled their homes in 1995 when Croatian government troops attacked rebel Serbs— an operation later subjected to consideration by the International War Crimes Tribunal for the former Yugoslavia (ICTY) in the Hague. Croatia also announced its support of the ICTY in 2000 and made significant legislative reforms to strengthen the country's protection of minorities and the privacy and free expression of its citizens. A new government body was appointed in 2000 to oversee the return of refugees, replacing the previous problematic Commission on Return, to enable the more effective return of Croatian Serbs who had taken refuge in *Republika Srpska.*

However, continuing problems in Croatia during the year 2000 of discrimination against ethnic Serbs, particularly regarding property rights, had not yet been effectively addressed by the end of the year; crimes of ethnic violence against Serbs also occurred in 2000. Croatia's Roma population of 30,000 to 40,000 people also faced continuing problems with the general population and Croatian authorities. Many Roma lacked access to education and employment opportunities, unfairly prevented from receiving state assistance and housing, met obstacles as they sought Croatian citizenship, and found themselves the targets of racist abuse with inadequate government protection. Discrimination and violence against women continued to be prevalent in Croatia in 2000.

Concerning its participation in regional and international organizations and conferences, Croatia has a better record. Croatia became a member of the World Bank and the International Development Association in 1993 but received no loans until 1995 when the security situation in the country had improved. Croatia is well linked to many international bodies and activities such as those associated with the United Nations, the European Union, the Organisation for Security and Co-operation in Europe, the Council of Europe, and NATO's Partnership-for-Peace program and has received development aid and post-war recovery assistance from numerous nongovernmental, international organizations. Croatia's chief trading partners are Germany, Italy, Slovenia, Bosnia and Herzegovina, and Austria.

The legal basis for Croatia's education system rests in the Constitution of 1990 and various laws and measures passed since the country declared independence in 1991. Higher education is organized according to the principles laid out in the Higher Education Act of 1996 and through the recommendations of the Council of Europe's Legislative Reform Program. The transformation of the general education system in Croatia has been slower in coming. Although several attempts were made in the 1990s by government commissions and public actors to assess and reform the overly rigid, bureaucratic, authoritarian education system left over from when Croatia was part of Yugoslavia, by the end of the decade none of the proposals discussed had crystallized into an approved action plan. By June 2000 the Education Council of the Croatian government's Ministry of Education and Sports had drawn upon some of the proposed reforms made since 1985 and prepared a comprehensive set of recommendations for the country's entire education system at all levels and was inviting the public to formally review and comment on their proposal. The anticipated timetable for reviewing the proposal, making further recommendations to the Ministry and to the government as a whole, and advancing the proposal to the national Assembly went as follows: 1) Between mid-June and mid-September 2000 the proposal was to be reviewed by a full range of civil-society actors—schools, teachers' associations, professional nongovernmental organizations, employers' associations, business organizations, political parties, religious communities, and individuals—who would be invited to develop their own proposals and comments in writing for submission to the Council for consideration; 2) From mid-September until the end of October a working group appointed by the Education Council was to gather and review the above submissions and pass them along with their own comments to the Council as a whole, which by October 30, 2000, was to have completed discussions on what it had received; and 3) After the Education Council had adopted and passed along its recommendations on proposed education reforms to the government of the Republic of Croatia, the government was to decide whether to forward the material to the National Assembly for debate. Along the way, various government commissions would be engaged to review and prepare documentation and plans related to the proposed reforms.

The reform efforts begun in the year 2000 to accomplish the above evaluation of the entire school system and to propose a new, comprehensive package of recommendations in line with European standards was both nationally essential and strategically wise from an international perspective. Croatia was well aware that reforming its education system would bring better economic, political, and social relations with other European states and simultaneously facilitate transfers of students, professors, researchers, and funds between Croatia and the wealthier countries of Europe. European educational standards have become ever more important to the transitional countries in Eastern and Central Europe as they sought to improve their antiquated, often overly bureaucratic systems inherited from political predecessors of the socialist era. Not only would reforms in Croatia bring the

education system up to the par with the European countries with which Croatia was doing business, but the reforms would also improve the likelihood that Croatia one day could be integrated into the European Union or at least made a more-valuable trading partner whose educated citizens would be welcomed as qualified employees for European jobs.

The essence of Croatia's official stance toward education is captured in a simple statement included in the government's program for 2000-2004 and cited by Minister of Education and Sports Vladimir Strugar in his presentation to the public of a Ministry proposal to fully transform the country's educational system: ''Upbringing and education are development priorities of strategic importance for the overall development of Croatian society. . . .'' Croatia's underlying philosophy of education is reflected in a speech presented by Bozidan Pugelnik, Minister of Education and Sports in 1998, at a UN-sponsored conference for government ministers in charge of youth-related issues held in August 1998. As Pugelnik remarked:

> We believe that for the development of policy for young people, the active participation of young people is a condition sine qua non, based upon the following:

- Strengthening democratic societies,

- Peaceful resolution of problems within each individual country and among the nations of the world,

- Strengthening democratic societies,

- Peaceful resolution of problems within each individual country and among the nations of the world,

- Strengthening awareness of the equality among nations, sexes, races, religions, i.e., the strengthening of multiculturalism,

- Strengthening awareness of environmental protection,

- Facilitating access to education, health care, employment and a general improvement of living conditions for young people, especially for the neglected groups,

> in order to begin the attempt to provide young people with an opportunity for a better future.

EDUCATIONAL SYSTEM—OVERVIEW

The educational experience of most students in Croatia was severely disrupted by war in the early 1990s. As of 2001, thousands of refugees who had left Croatia during the warfare of the 1990s had yet to be resettled, and those who had returned often were housed in temporary quarters away from their original home communities. Regular school attendance was thus especially hard for some children and youth even where schools had been rebuilt and classes restarted shortly after the Dayton Accords were signed in 1995. Consequently, some measures of educational enrollments, attainment levels, literacy rates, and other school-related statistics for the 1990s are fairly imprecise or nonexistent. Certain knowledge gaps exist regarding the status of education in Croatia in the 1990s, making a full evaluation of the country's educational situation at the start of the new millennium somewhat difficult to achieve.

Nonetheless, in June 2000 a number of solid recommendations were being advanced to reform the education system in Croatia. However, they had not yet been acted upon, due to the need for public debate in the policy-formulation process. In the proposal drafted by the Government Ministry's Council of Education, the Council had identified several major flaws in the education system, the remedy of which could vastly improve the country's schools. The partial catalogue of deficiencies included the following: 1) a lack of democratic relations and procedures in the schools; 2) an atmosphere predominantly authoritarian and conservative; 3) overly rigid scheduling of the school day; 4) inflexible rules for placing and promoting students; 5) dualistic secondary education uncharacteristic of European systems; 6) denying opportunities to higher education to about half the secondary-school population; 7) an inconsistent and formalistic grading system; 8) over-centralization in educational administration; 9) lack of recognition of parents' rights and obligations; 10) poor-quality and inadequate physical facilities and equipment; 11) few private schooling alternatives; 12) little entrepreneurial activity supporting education; 13) fragmentation among the parts of the education system; 14) arts schools poorly coordinated with other schools; 15) formalistic and unmotivating methods of evaluating teachers; 16) a lack of professional teaching publications and pedagogical literature understandable by or useful to most teachers; 17) and poor management of the education system, schools, and classes. Interestingly, the evaluation contained in the June 2000 proposal underscored that the above problems had little to do with the fault of the teachers in the system. The Education Council carefully noted that teachers in Croatia "for some incomprehensible reason, have been systematically belittled, financially discriminated against and professionally thwarted and restricted, while the entire education system was run in a manner totally out of synch with European tradition and experience" (Council 7). The rampant problems in Croatia's education system were especially surprising considering that Croatian schools and culture are centuries old, including at the university level. The first university in the country was established by Dominican priests in Zadar in 1396 as the *Universitas Jadertina,* the General University. According

to the Ministry of Science and Technology, the government arm formally in charge of higher education in Croatia in 2001, *Universitas Jadertina* had conferred the "degrees of Master of Science and Doctor of Science and was thus equal in status to the other eminent European universities of the time."

In 1991, approximately 29 percent of Croatia's population was of school age or between the ages of 3 and 24. The gross enrollment rate for basic education, the first 8 years of free, compulsory schooling for students generally between the ages of 6 and 14, was 89 percent in 1996. Twelve years of public schooling was the expected norm in Croatia in 1995, although attendance was compulsory for only eight years. Croat was the first language of instruction used in Croatian public schools in the year 2000.

In June 2000 the Education Council of the Ministry of Education and Sports made several recommendations to bring the country's education system into better alignment with European and UNESCO-approved international standards. The Council suggested adding a year of compulsory preschool education for all children between the ages of five and six beginning in 2010. Additionally, the Council recommended making nine years of basic education compulsory and divided into three phases: a Junior phase where students would be taught in forms (classes); an Intermediary phase where students would be taught in a combination of forms and subjects; and a Senior phase where students would be taught subjects by specialized teachers. Two, three, four, or five years of secondary schooling, depending on the course of study chosen by the student, would follow this nine-year pattern of elementary schooling. The overall goal of the reforms recommended by the Council was to make schools in Croatia capable of delivering education that would fulfill one basic requirement: making high-quality education available to all. As the Council noted, "A fundamental human right and a democratic prerequisite for equality among the young generation is the same educational (pedagogic) standard and quality of upbringing as the most important condition for social promotion and professional success" (Council 40).

The need to develop new textbooks, teaching approaches, educational programs, and course curricula sensitive to the needs of all of Croatia's people, including ethnic minorities, was highlighted in the Education Council's proposal for school reforms in June 2000. Similarly, providing students with the means to develop knowledge and skills in information and communications technology (ICT) has been a goal of education reformers in recent years. With the strengthening of the economy in the first few years of the 2000 decade and the improvement of education likely to come about through reforms initiated by the Croatian government in the year 2000, new programs in ICT were likely to be added to schools to qualify students for high-technology employment. In 1999 the number of personal computers in Croatia was 67 per 10,000 persons. This was more than triple the number of computers just two years earlier (22 per 10,000 in 1997). The new reforms for Croatia's schools in the 2000 decade surely would upgrade student knowledge and functionality in educational technology. This was evidenced by the Education Council's recommendation of a compulsory "national curriculum" that would develop in each student 18 areas of literacy, with "information technology" the third literacy area in the Council's proposed list, just after "alphabetical" literacy and literacy identified as "mathematical, suited to the use of technical aids."

Croatia's government clearly recognizes the important role education plays in the country's socioeconomic and political development. In the June 2000 education reforms proposal, the Education Council pointed out, "Any country in today's day and age desirous of achieving high economic growth must ensure that a high percentage of its population acquires secondary education." Two key international donors collaborating with the Croatian government and Croatian educators from the mid-1990s on were the European Training Foundation of the European Union, which supported vocational education and training, including staff development, organizational strengthening, and curricular reform, and the Soros funded Open Society Institute, which implemented the Network Step by Step Program to encourage more child-centered teaching in preprimary and primary schools, ensure greater cooperation among parents, teachers, and educational faculty, and promote the equitable integration of Roma children and children with disabilities in the schools.

PREPRIMARY & PRIMARY EDUCATION

Although kindergarten in Croatia was still optional at the turn of the millennium, approximately 31 percent of children of preschool age in Croatia were enrolled in preschool education programs in 1996. In the year 2000 primary school gross enrollment rates were 94 percent for boys and 97 percent for girls; the corresponding net enrollment rates were 93 percent for boys and 96 percent for girls. Girls had represented 49 percent of total enrollments in primary education in 1995. That same year, only 1 percent of primary students were enrolled in private education programs. In the mid-1990s about 98 percent of primary students (measured as percent of cohort) reached grade 5.

SECONDARY EDUCATION

In 1995, approximately 51 percent of students enrolled at the secondary level were girls. The student to teacher ratio was 15:1 for secondary level education in 1995. Only 1 percent of secondary enrollments that year were in private schools. In 1996 only 18.7 percent of Croatia's 15- to 18-year-olds were enrolled in general upper secondary education; 57.1 percent of that age group was enrolled in vocational and technical upper secondary education. Consequently, the overall upper secondary enrollment rate in 1996 was 75.8 percent. Thus, three-fourths of all upper secondary students were taking vocational and technical courses of study while one-fourth were enrolled in general education programming. Gross enrollment ratios at the secondary level were 81 percent for boys and 83 percent for girls at the end of the millennium.

HIGHER EDUCATION

In 2001 Croatia had four universities—the Universities of Zagreb, Rijeka, Split, and Osijek—which together encompassed 55 faculties, four arts academies, three university departments, and one additional university-operated course of study. Professional education was provided through seven polytechnics, six independent schools of professional higher education, one teachers' academy, and eight teachers' schools of professional higher education. Higher education institutions in the 2000-2001 academic year employed 1,133 full professors and 801 associate professors.

The Zagreb area had the highest number of students in tertiary education in 2001: 33,889 students in university programs and 14,640 students in professional studies, which was 58 percent of all tertiary students in Croatia. In the mid-1990s about 28 percent of the age-relevant population in Croatia was enrolled in higher education. Just 8 percent of Croatia's population over age 25 held a higher education diploma in 1995, but by 1996 approximately 17 percent of 18- to 22-year-olds were enrolled in tertiary studies.

Of the 84,088 students enrolled in higher education institutions in the country in the 2000-2001 academic year, 59,230 were following university courses of study at least 4 years in length that led to a Bachelor's degree while 24,858 students were enrolled in professional studies programs of at least 2 years that led to an Associate's degree. Of the students enrolled in Croatian universities in 1997, approximately 25 percent concentrated in the humanities, approximately 42 percent in the social and behavioral sciences, a little more than 2 percent in the natural sciences, about 9 percent in medicine, approximately 47 percent in engineering, and more than 10 percent in other fields. The Ministry of Science and Technology, whose responsibilities have included administrative oversight of the universities and professional training in Croatia, anticipated implementing the European credit transfer system early in the 2000 decade to facilitate transfers of Croatian students and other European students between each other's higher education programs.

ADMINISTRATION, FINANCE, & EDUCATIONAL RESEARCH

As already noted, the Ministry of Education and Sports has had primary responsibility for making and implementing educational policy in Croatia's preschools, primary, and secondary schools, with the Ministry of Science and Technology administering Croatia's higher education system. Attached to these ministries are a number of councils and commissions charged with specific tasks in administrative oversight, policy direction, or program implementation and management. For example, the National Council for Higher Education is an independent body of 18 members nominated by the Rectors' Conference and higher education institutions and appointed by the national parliament to carry out quality assessments and evaluations of the higher education system. The National Scientific Research Council also is an independent body whose tasks include preparing the National Scientific Research Program for Croatia. The country's educational system was still highly centralized in the year 2000, though proposals were under discussion to bring administrative authority closer to the local level. In 1997 Croatia's total public expenditures on education amounted to about 3 percent of the GDP.

Besides the government ministries and other formal bodies charged with planning, implementing, and evaluating educational policy in Croatia, nongovernmental associations, community organizations, and private individuals became increasingly involved in the development of educational policy and the provision of learning opportunities to students in the years after the Balkans wars. The National Federation of the Young People in Croatia, for example, was an umbrella organization of 20 associations in 1998 and had observer status in the European Youth Forum. Teachers' associations also provided their input. Likewise, local community organizations and more informal groupings of parents and community members became more involved in developing and implementing school programs in Croatia from the mid-1990s on. For example, the Step by Step Program, begun by the international nongovernmental Open Society Institute in 1994 with funding from the Soros Foundation, has encouraged individuals and groups in local communities to come together to plan programs fostering the development of children's problem-solving skills, more democratic decision-making in schools, and greater respect for ethnic minorities. As Croatians continue to decentralize their government and participate more in public decision-making, additional opportunities undoubtedly will emerge where students and their parents, along with edu-

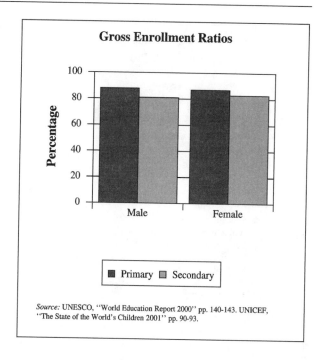

Source: UNESCO, ''World Education Report 2000'' pp. 140-143. UNICEF, ''The State of the World's Children 2001'' pp. 90-93.

cators and other interested members of local communities, will work more closely together to develop the education programs that suit them best.

NONFORMAL EDUCATION

A well-developed system of adult education appeared to be lacking in Croatia in the year 2000. At the same time, recommendations were being considered to tie professional training, including training at the secondary level, more closely to the labor market. Reforming secondary schools so that a full range of education and training programs, including continuing education, could be provided for students was one practical solution suggested by the Council on Education. The possibility of using distance education as a means of teaching more of Croatia's young learners, university students, and adults also was indicated in the Council's June 2000 proposal, which included the suggestion that ''correspondence courses through the Internet'' could be a viable option for training skilled professionals. Croatia had 4 Internet service providers in 1999 and approximately 26 Internet hosts for every 10,000 people. In 1997 there were 1.2 million televisions and 1.5 million radios, all of which also could be used for educational purposes.

SUMMARY

The people of the Republic of Croatia have faced many challenges in the years since the Dayton Accords of 1995 brought the war involving Croatia to a halt. Significant progress had been made by the year 2000 in planning for the thorough transformation of an educational

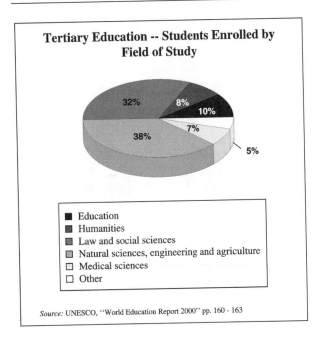

Tertiary Education -- Students Enrolled by Field of Study

- ■ Education
- ■ Humanities
- ■ Law and social sciences
- ▨ Natural sciences, engineering and agriculture
- □ Medical sciences
- □ Other

Source: UNESCO, ''World Education Report 2000'' pp. 160 - 163

system long outdated and ripe for improvement. With an upturn in the national economy by early 2000 and the political shift that occurred in February 2000, Croatia seemed ready to begin the formidable task of restructuring its education system and improving its methods of training not only students but also teachers, administrators, and other adults. Most government officials closely involved with the plans for education reform realized the magnitude of the work that lay before them, but Croatia's Minister of Education and Sports in June 2000 may have best summed up the broad significance and basic requirements of the changes to be made. In his foreword to the proposal of education reforms prepared by the Ministry's Council of Education for public discussion and official debate, Minister Vladimir Strugar astutely observed:

> The building of a multi-party, pluralistic and democratic society, a return to re-embracement of authentic moral and cultural values, values of work and entrepreneurship, respect for private property, respect of laws and recognition of personal differences, as well as a whole range of other characteristics within the contemporary European school—while at the same time retaining all those elements specific to Croatia—is an ambitious task which can be realized only through good organization and with well motivated teachers.

BIBLIOGRAPHY

Berryman, Sue E. *Hidden Challenges to Education Systems in Transition Economies.* Washington, DC: The World Bank, Europe and Central Asia Region, Human Development Sector, 2000.

Bureau of Democracy, Human Rights, and Labor. *Country Reports on Human Rights Practices—2000.* Washington, DC: U.S. Department of State, February 2001. Available from http://www.state.gov/.

CARNet. *Croatian Homepage.* Available from http://www.hr/.

The Central Intelligence Agency (CIA). *The World Factbook 2000.* Directorate of Intelligence, 1 January 2001. Available from http://www.cia.gov/.

Council of Education, Ministry of Education and Sports. *The Basis for the Education System in the Republic of Croatia (Proposal for discussion).* Zagreb: Ministry of Education and Sports, June 2000. Available from http://www.mips.hr/

European Training Foundation. *Croatia.* European Union. Available from http://www.etf.eu.int/.

Government of the Republic of Croatia. Available from http://www.vlada.hr/.

Human Rights Watch. *World Report 2001.* Available from http://www.hrw.org/.

Independent Task Force with Steven Rattner and Michael B.G. Froman. *Promoting Sustainable Economies in the Balkans.* New York: Council on Foreign Relations, Inc., 2000.

Jeffries, Ian, ed. *Problems of Economic and Political Transformation in the Balkans.* New York: Pinter, 1996.

Ministry of Foreign Affairs of the Republic of Croatia. *About Croatia.* Available from http://www.mvp.hr/.

Ministry of Science and Technology, Government of the Republic of Croatia. *Higher Education.* Available from http://www.mzt.hr/.

Pugelnik, Bozidar. ''Address by the Minister of Education and Sports of the Republic of Croatia, His Excellency Bozidar Pugelnik.'' Speech presented at UN-sponsored World Conference of Ministers Responsible for Youth, 10 August 1998. Available from http://www.un.org/.

Ramet, Sabrina Petra, and Ljubiša S. Adamovich. *Beyond Yugoslavia: Politics, Economics, and Culture in a Shattered Community.* Boulder, CO: Westview Press, 1995.

South East European Educational Cooperation Network. *Step by Step in Croatia.* Available from http://www.see-educoop.net/.

UNICEF. *Croatia.* Available from http://www.unicef.org/.

World Bank, Human Development Network. *Education Sector Strategy.* Washington, DC: The International Bank for Reconstruction and Development/The World Bank, 1999.

World Bank Group. *Country Brief: Croatia.* Available from http://wbln0018.worldbank.org/.

———. *Croatia.* Available from http://wbln0018. worldbank.org/.

———. *Croatia at a Glance.* Available from http:// wbln0018.worldbank.org/.

———. *Croatia Data Profile.* World Development Indicators database. Available from http://devdata. worldbank.org/.

—Barbara Lakeberg Dridi

CUBA

BASIC DATA

Official Country Name:	Republic of Cuba
Region:	North & Central America
Population:	11,141,997
Language(s):	Spanish
Literacy Rate:	95.7%
Academic Year:	September-June
Number of Primary Schools:	9,926
Compulsory Schooling:	9 years
Public Expenditure on Education:	6.7%
Foreign Students in National Universities:	4,243
Educational Enrollment:	Primary: 1,094,868 Secondary: 712,897 Higher: 111,587
Educational Enrollment Rate:	Primary: 106% Secondary: 81% Higher: 12%
Teachers:	Primary: 92,820 Secondary: 70,628 Higher: 22,574
Student-Teacher Ratio:	Primary: 12:1 Secondary: 11:1
Female Enrollment Rate:	Primary: 104% Secondary: 85% Higher: 15%

HISTORY & BACKGROUND

From the first Spanish settlements in 1511 through 1898, Cuban education was typical of Spanish-speaking Latin America: a combination of parochial and secular institutions supporting and supported by the affluent Roman Catholic Spanish colonial elite. The first institution of higher education, the University of Havana, was established in 1728. However, as the Royal Economic Society reported in 1793, learning was confined to private tutoring (for elite families) and church-based schools with limited curriculum and poorly-trained teachers (de Varona 1993). The Society called for a secondary education curriculum that included mathematics, physics, chemistry, natural science, botany, anatomy, and drawing; this sparked the founding of the first secular schools in Havana.

Nineteenth Century Government & Colonial Church: In 1816 the government created an agency that introduced new methods, selected texts, created standards, and employed school inspectors. More than 90 secular schools existed in 1820, but these elite institutions relied on student fees and patron donations. By 1833, Cuba had 210 schools for whites with 8,460 students but only 12 schools for 486 black students. Few poor or minority students received free instruction in public or religious schools. An 1842 law required the construction of public primary and secondary schools on the same site, mandatory attendance for children aged 7 to 10, and control by provincial committees, a seeming democratization of learning (de Verona 1993). However, home-tutored students of the affluent were exempted from sharing facilities and conditions with the children of small business owners, workers, and peasants.

An 1863 law enabled the government to operate public schools and to oversee private schools, obligated attendance by children aged 6 to 9, and specified fines to be paid by parents who failed to comply (de Varona 1993). Major upheavals of this period—freeing of slaves in 1868 and the Ten Years War, the first War for Independence—rendered these decrees moot. These conditions ripped social life asunder, impoverished the nation, and left minimal funding for education. For example, only $1800 was budgeted for all school inspectors in 1880 to travel throughout the country to enforce compulsory attendance. Also, schools averaged only about 1 teacher per school and approximately 34 and 40 students per class in private and public schools, respectively (Perez 1945).

During the 1890s, calls for reform of the corrupt education system and for "educational emphasis on practical, utilitarian instruction instead of classical studies" became major issues for Cuban nationalists (Paulston and

Kaufman 1992). As a result, dissent was especially strong on university campuses and support for educational investment was minimal.

Equally as important was the Roman Catholic Church. It controlled about 46 percent of Cuba's schools, but its influence and the larger imprint of colonial domination extended to the public schools. Local priests held seats on school boards, were legally entitled to review and approve the hire of teachers, and were legally entitled to provide weekly religious instruction in the public schools. They used this ''second pulpit'' to promote religious orthodoxy, stereotypical gender and racial hierarchies, and to sanctify the dominant means and relations of production. Thus, poor and minority students had a curriculum that stressed morality and religion, but were not provided with a means to rise above their economic status (Paulston and Kaufman 1992). As a result, few students remained in public school beyond age 10. In sum, the segregated system established by locally unaccountable colonial elites was reflective and supportive of the slave and hacienda system of Cuba's sugar economy.

U.S. Intervention: The ostensible motive for U.S. intervention on the side of the dissidents in 1898 was to free Cuba from Spain and to create democratic, locally controlled institutions. However, the U.S. government established military control in 1899, followed by a pseudo-independence that veiled U.S. control. The Platt Amendment, creating a permanent U.S. military presence in Cuba, solidified that control in 1901. While the rationale for intervention was a facade, the United States did succeed in transforming a marginal education system.

Cuba's educational system included 541 primary and 400 private schools. About 60 percent of the population was illiterate, and only one percent of the literate population had attained higher levels of education. Only about 90,000 out of 550,000 Cuban children attended school. In the five largest cities, about 30 percent of children attended school—elsewhere, only 11 percent attended (Thomas 1998).

An overarching administrative structure was established when U.S. military governor John Brooke issued Order No. 297, series 1900, and modified Order No. 368 in 1900. It included a Commissioner of Education, a Board of Superintendents (comprised of a general and provincial superintendents for each province), and local education districts with separate school boards (Turosienski 1943). The law also mandated schooling for children aged 6 to 14.

Governor General Leonard Wood, who succeeded Brooke, initiated programmatic reform. Wood augmented Brooke's efforts by giving substance to the Spanish reforms—creating a nationwide system of primary schools, training teachers, and instituting changes identified by dissidents. He reorganized secondary and vocational schools and promoted practical knowledge in universities by introducing engineering and architecture. Seeking to infuse attributes of the American educational system into Cuba, Wood hired Cuban educators and administrators versed in the U.S. model of education. Access to education increased across racial and class lines, and attendance rose—a seeming realization of the dissidents' goals.

Despite these educational advances, general dissatisfaction with the government led to instability and, in 1906, the United States dispatched additional personnel to establish order. Among those dispatched was Judge Charles Magoon who directed efforts in Cuba until 1909. Magoon's educational accomplishments were ''less sensational than Wood's, but in some ways more effective'' (Thomas 1998). Sharp penalties were established for violations of mandatory education; school-age children found in the street during school hours were arrested, and factory owners employing child laborers were fined. In 1908, the school enrollment was reported to be 200,000 pupils in the public system and 15,000 pupils in the private system. However, problems remained as Magoon ignored complaints of corruption and nepotism in the educational system.

Batista Period: Under dictator Fulgencio Batista in the 1950s, roughly 50 percent of the school-aged population did not attend school, and expenditures were concentrated in urban areas to the exclusion of rural provinces (MacDonald 1985). The average child progressed only to the second grade, and only 17 percent of students attended high school. More than 1,000,000 people—half the adult population—were illiterate. The curriculum had regressed to a ''classic Hispanic education with a great emphasis on memorization'' while ignoring practical issues and modern conditions (Padula and Smith 1988). As Arthur Gillette discussed in his book *Cuba's Educational Revolution,* reaction against the inadequacies of pre-Revolutionary education (a dynamic of class inequity and reproduction, a labor force unsuited to the modern economy, and societal alienation) shaped the revolution's educational goals.

Castro Period: Educational reform in Cuba took root following the Cuban Revolution of 1959, though Castro had called for educational reform as early as 1953. As Castro's supporters won control of various regions of the country, they taught peasants to read as part of the revolutionary strategy. After the 1959 Revolution, two major education-related goals emerged: making education available to all and connecting this new educational system to socioeconomic development (Gillette 1972).

Achieving these goals required a new national educational system that could educate a largely illiterate population.

The Great Literacy Campaign of 1961 sought to instill basic literacy skills to citizens in the poorest and most remote regions of the country. Junior and senior high schools were closed for an entire year as the campaign mobilized an unprecedented 274,000 volunteer literacy workers, including students, workers, women not in the workforce, and trained teachers, who taught an identified 979,000 illiterate people. Of the 979,000 illiterate individuals, 707,200 gained basic skills of reading and writing (MacDonald 1985). Tutors used manuals designed to teach subjects related to the Revolution; *Alfabeticemos,* the instructor's manual, was composed of lessons dealing with ''such subjects as the revolution, Castro, land reform, nationalization of foreign property, industrialization, and imperialism'' (Padula and Smith 1988). Similar topics were included in the student text, providing both a point of departure for literacy instruction and educating the masses about the foundations of the new social order. Volunteers worked individually with learners using progressively more challenging reading and writing exercises. This campaign brought a new sense of unity to the country.

Following the 1961 campaign, illiteracy fell from 25 percent to 4 percent and, unlike other Third World efforts that rendered short-term benefits before reversing, have remained low. While curriculum and methodology are set nationally, local councils, teachers, administrators, and parents contribute to policies within particular schools. Many parents support the school by volunteering at extracurricular events.

Cuba remains an outpost of socialism in a ''nonsocialist world'' (Lutjens 1998). The nature of its socialism has changed, but the commitment to universal education remains a point of national pride. With a literacy rate of approximately 99 percent, Cuba is unique within Latin America and the Third World in general (UNESCO 1995).

CONSTITUTIONAL & LEGAL FOUNDATIONS

Beginning in 1842, education policy emerged as a paradox between the poles of legal mandates and a policy of benign neglect. While compulsory schooling, free instruction, and integration laws were passed, they languished, unenforced by colonial officials. Much of the formal education occurred outside the purview of public officials, overseen only by parents and religious leaders. After 1898 the United States imposed its own model of system structure, methodology, and governance starting with Military Orders No. 297 and Order No. 368 in 1900.

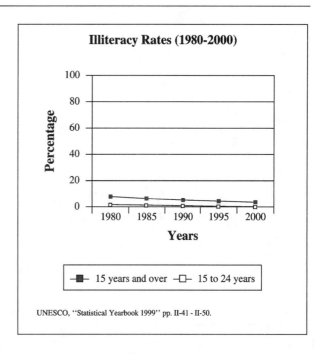

Illiteracy Rates (1980-2000)

UNESCO, ''Statistical Yearbook 1999'' pp. II-41 - II-50.

When this system was later transferred to Cuban bureaucrats, funding and enforcement backslid and became increasingly corrupt through 1958.

Education in post-Revolutionary Cuba is guaranteed and obligatory as noted in Article 39B of the Constitution. Laws number 76 and number 367, combined with decree number 2099, decentralized schools, and number 680 revised the structure of education itself. The Declaration of Havana in September 1960 declared that every child had the right to a free education; the Law of General Nationalization and Free instruction, passed in June 1961, suspended private education and made the state officially responsible for all education (Epstein 1988).

EDUCATIONAL SYSTEM—OVERVIEW

Hallmarks of Cuban education have been reorganization and adaptation to changing social needs and social conditions. There have been three major periods of Cuban education: mass education (1959-1962), education for economic development (1962-1968), and ''creating the new man'' (1965-1990). To this we might add a fourth period—the ''special period,'' an era of post-Soviet adaptation after 1990 (Gillette 1972).

The goals of this changing system have been constant: to provide improved educational opportunities for all persons, to develop skills necessary to improve the industrial and agricultural output, and to promote collective responsibility. Education is compulsory for students through the ninth grade. The school year is roughly 200 days per year, organized in four 10-week terms. The language of instruction is Spanish. Schools place heavy em-

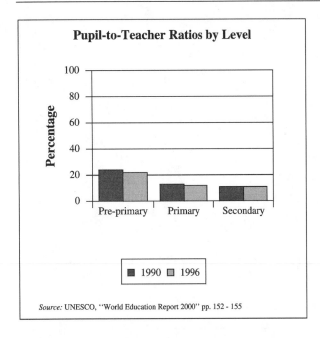

Pupil-to-Teacher Ratios by Level

Percentage

Pre-primary   Primary   Secondary

■ 1990   □ 1996

Source: UNESCO, "World Education Report 2000" pp. 152 - 155

the second cycle grades five and six. Most schools are located in the students' community, and attendance is mandatory. The number of teachers has fluctuated during the last 40 years, but the pupil-teacher ratio has continually decreased during the period. From grades one through four, classes are 30 minutes in duration. The curriculum focuses on Spanish language (reading, writing, and oral expression) and mathematics. These two subjects together account for 57 percent of classroom time. Scientific approach, life training, economics, labor, artistic topics, and physical education are other subjects. A new topic was introduced in the mid-1990s, the "World in Which We Live"—a blend of natural and social ecology, health, and morality (Ministry of Education 1996). The curriculum emphasizes basic education, productive activity, and social benefit and responsibility. Classroom learning is often integrated with basic skills, such as gardening, pruning, wood and metal crafts, and handicrafts. The boundary between classroom and practical learning is blurred into a holistic learning environment.

Evaluation is a continuous process. Tests are administered at the end of the second and fourth grades, with results categorized as excellent, very well, good, regular, and poor, instead of numerical grades. Testing, like instruction, combines formal learning and practical application, and students advance when they receive a satisfactory grade.

In grades five and six, classes include Cuban history, natural science, geography, aesthetics, civil education (to convey political, ideological, moral, and judicial information), economics, and labor education, which is an initial linkage of classroom learning to productive work. The behavioral goal is to encourage independent working habits and cooperative learning skills. The students are again expected to demonstrate competence in each discipline. All students must complete the sixth grade, and those who fail may retake examinations. Less than 1.0 percent of students drop out of primary education, and 98.2 percent continue their studies after the sixth grade (Ministry of Education 1996).

Special education is a sub-system of the primary schools designed to provide appropriate training and instruction to develop the intellectual and vocational abilities of "special needs" children. These children are initially evaluated by specialists in one of Cuba's Diagnosis and Guidance Centers that refer them to an appropriate school. There are schools providing specialized instruction for students with mental disabilities, blindness, visual handicaps, amblyopia, physical disabilities, deafness, speech impediments, behavioral disorders, learning disabilities, and language disorders. Often these schools have relationships with local schools, which allows for mainstreaming of students where appropriate (Ministry of Education 1996).

phasis on Cuban history, mathematics, practical and applied knowledge, community service, and problem solving. A close relationship exists between education, daily life, and work.

Following the literacy campaign, Cuba created a two-pronged, multi-faceted, but complex educational structure. However, in the last 15 years, they have streamlined the structure while allowing a small series of highly specialized institutions with very limited foci for students with special abilities, interests, or needs.

PREPRIMARY & PRIMARY EDUCATION

Cuba's preschool educational structure enrolls about 145,000 students from age 6 months to 5 years, more than twice the number before the revolution. The curriculum is based on the child's age; it emphasizes group play; seeks to assure the physical, intellectual, moral, and aesthetic development of the child; and establishes the basis for future learning.

The academic year extends from September to June, with July and August devoted to recreation. Preprimary education grew after the Revolution as women entered the workforce. The Federation of Cuban Women initially directed preschools, which later fell under Ministry of Education control. Attendance is optional and home education is common. Home-educated preschoolers often attend nonformal groups that meet in parks and neighborhood centers twice a week. A kindergarten year offered for children aged 5 to 6 may either be taken in a daycare or a primary school.

The primary education sequence consists of two levels. The first cycle includes grades one through four, and

SECONDARY EDUCATION

Cuba's secondary education system generally has two components: compulsory and non-compulsory. The compulsory basic secondary education system includes grades 7 through 9. There are two different forms of secondary schools: urban and rural. Urban schools have 35 weeks of class and require 7 weeks of work in the countryside. Rural schools have 37 weeks of class and require 5 weeks of work in the countryside. Each has approximately three weeks of testing.

In 1966, the "Schools to the Countryside Program" started when 20,000 basic secondary education students and their teachers moved to the country to work with farmers and agricultural workers. In 1971, this practice was institutionalized as the "schools in the countryside," which are boarding schools that operate during the workweek on a year round basis. Boarding schools divide their students; while half tend crops in the morning, the remainder learns in the classroom, and in the afternoon the groups exchange tasks. Again, practical knowledge and classroom materials are integrated into a single curriculum focused on observation and problem solving. During the summers, the schools are vacation centers where students are joined by their families. Families receive free room and board and participate in various recreational programs, including trips to beaches and parks, but they are expected to work two hours per day (Carnoy and Werthein 1983).

Only 3.3 percent of students drop out of basic secondary, and 92.8 percent continue their studies after the 9th grade. Following completion of the basic secondary curriculum, students seeking additional education can pursue one of several options: pre-university, poly-technical training, or vocational/trade school education. The attendance at this level is free, but is not compulsory.

The course content in pre-university education is more evenly distributed across the curriculum. Mathematics and Spanish comprise only 42 percent of the course contact hours; natural science is about 20 percent. History, geography, art, and physical education constitute about 18 percent. Labor education, civics, military preparation, and fundamentals of Marxist-Leninism constitute about 10 percent of the curriculum and occur in a patterned manner—labor and civics in the seventh through ninth grades and military and Marxist-Leninist studies in the tenth through twelfth grades (Ministry of Education 1996).

Pre-universities are divided between urban and rural locations. They operate in a fashion similar to basic secondary education. Significant emphasis is placed on study of the environment, especially the interplay between ecological and social problems. Classes last 41

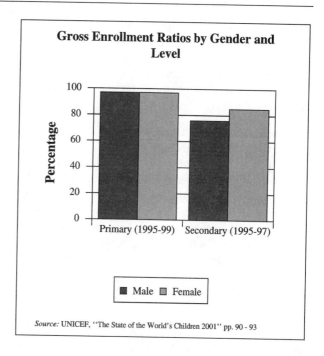

Gross Enrollment Ratios by Gender and Level

Source: UNICEF, "The State of the World's Children 2001" pp. 90 - 93

weeks. The twelfth and final year has two main goals: completing the pre-university courses and strengthening knowledge to prepare for university entry.

The other two options following basic secondary are poly-technical institutes, where students can delve deeper into scientific and technical subjects while gaining vocational and professional guidance, and vocational/trade schools, which offer specialized technical curriculum for students and for workers seeking skill enhancement.

Universities: Between 1962 and 1964, following a period of upheaval, efforts to reorganize the university system were initiated by the government, students, faculty, and party officials. By 1964, a multi-tiered system had been created with campus-based participation by the above noted groups, answering to the Centralized National Council of Universities and responsible to the Ministry of Education.

For a decade after the Revolution, higher education was not a major concern, as emphasis was placed on literacy and basic education. Equally as important, the pre-Revolutionary professorate had been hired by, and had trained, the children of the privileged elite. Many retained their positions. For many years, university faculty were a source of anti-Revolutionary ideas and mobilization, a condition that discouraged social investment in these institutions.

By 1970, a shift in curricular focus from humanities to medicine and applied sciences was implemented at three universities: Universidad de la Habana, Universidad Central de Las Villas (Santa Clara), and Universidad de Oriente (Santiago). Problems within universities, including poor pay and resource shortages, were addressed in 1975 as part of a renewed emphasis on university learning; also the University of Camaguey was established and the Ministry of Higher Education was created (MacDonald 1996).

Since 1982, the Ministry of Higher Education has overseen diplomas and degrees granted by the 47 Cuban institutions of higher education. Administratively some are subordinate to other Ministries, including Public Health, Center State, and Education proper (Ministry of Education 1996). Cuba has four universities, each of which has departments of engineering, sciences, agriculture, humanities (including law), medicine, education, and economics. These four universities, three university branch campuses, and 40 specialized institutes collectively constitute the higher education system of Cuba (MacDonald 1996).

By 1975 "New Man" graduates of post-Revolutionary institutions of higher education populated industrial, cultural, social, and governmental institutions as employees and managers. Yet with the humanities-focused training still in place within universities, product development, technical innovation, and bureaucratic efficiency lagged. With pressing social and economic needs, Cuban officials started emphasizing the importance of higher education as a revolutionary tool in transforming the economy. The end result of this effort was the coordination of universities with national economic agencies, better aligning the needs of society with the expertise of university graduates.

In the immediate post-Revolutionary era, Cuba placed emphasis on agricultural self-sufficiency. By 1980 a shift in the focus, composition, clientele, and outcomes of higher education emerged as part of a larger social transformation (MacDonald 1996). This shift toward increased education and technology, evident from 1970 to 1995, resulted in a tight coordination of national need and educational preparation. The emphasis on mass participation in higher education increased university attendance by farmers and workers. Additionally, a strong indicator of the importance of higher education was its expansion. Student attendance changed from 24,300 pupils (per 100,000 population) in 1958; to 20,600 by 1965; and to 26,300 by 1975.

From 1980 through 1992, higher education flourished in Cuba. In 1980 Cuba had 151,700 students enrolled in higher education. Enrollment declined during the crisis of the mid-1990s, as total enrollment fell from 165,891 in 1993-1994; to 140,815 in 1994-1995; to 134,100 in 1995-1996. Despite these declines, Cuba's rate of higher education enrollment per 100,000 population has, since 1978, exceeded the Latin American and world average (Epstein 1988; Ministry of Education 1996). There were approximately 23,000 faculty members in higher education in 1995, which resulted in an extremely low faculty to student ratio, a condition conducive to effective pedagogy.

Requirements for university attendance include graduation from high school, passage of a specialty examination, a personal interview, and letters from a local "people's organization" or other indicators of revolutionary attitude. Education is free and available to all interested and qualified individuals. There are three kinds of programs available: daytime, worker in-service, and distance learning courses, with the latter two providing courses for non-traditional students—farmers and workers seeking to pursue interests and/or upgrade their skills. This student base differs greatly from the pre-Revolutionary days of students from privileged upper class status. Clearly, universities will move the Revolution to its next stage.

ADMINISTRATION, FINANCE, & EDUCATIONAL RESEARCH

The Ministry of Education oversaw the operation of 13,340 schools and 270,100 teachers (including daycare) in 1995-1996. Consistent with Article 39B of the Constitution of the Republic, responsibility for education rests with the state. The Ministry guides, performs, and implements state and government policy in education, except for higher education. The National Education System is composed of a central authority, provincial and municipal organs, and several administrative bodies that answer only to the National Assembly of People's Power, the legislative structure of the Republic of Cuba.

The Ministry of Education, provincial and local educational officials, and teachers and professors periodically propose changes that are consistent with their charge to conduct, organize, and manage educational services in their respective territories. The local education authorities are subject to the principle of double subordination: to the Ministry and to local councils. A total of 2,173,000 students were in the formal education system (excluding universities), and an additional 145,000 children were in daycare centers in 1995-1996. The Ministry of Higher Education is charged with overseeing universities and various institutes and is distinct from the Ministry of Education.

Following the "Nationalization of Education" in July 1961, all educational expenses are covered by public funds from the state budget. The Ministry of Finances controls expenditures and auditing, and the Ministry of Education is accountable for spending. Cuba's support for education is remarkable, rising from about 3.4 percent of GNP before the Revolution, to 7.0 percent by 1965, to 7.2 percent in 1980, to 11.0 percent in 1994. Yet, the impacts of the "Special Period" are such that actual expenditures have fallen from 1853.9 million pesos in 1990 to 1430 million pesos in 1995-1996 (Ministry of Education 1996).

NONFORMAL EDUCATION

Nonformal education is an integral part of Cuban society at the national, provincial, and municipal levels and is strongly linked to the education system. Contributing sectors include Public Health, Culture, and Sports, as well as organizations such as the Federation of Cuban Women, neighborhood watch Committees for the Defense of the Revolution, People's Councils, Pioneer Youth groups (similar to Boy and Girl Scouts), and the National Commission for Prevention and Social Care (Ministry of Education 1996).

Another nonformal sphere is adult education, which provides learning opportunities for workers, farmers, housewives, and undereducated adults at three levels: *Educacion Obrera y Campesina* or EOC (a four-semester basic instruction course sequence); *Secundaria Obrera y Campesina* or SOC (a four-semester mid-level course); and *Facultad Obrera y Campesina* or FOC (a six-semester higher level instruction) (Ministry of Education 1999). The matriculation rate of these programs has remained high, and course materials are frequently refined. From 1962 to 1974 about 650,000 adults graduated from these adult education programs, with a record number of 95,000 matriculating in 1974 (Paulston 1976). Participation remains high (Ministry of Education 1999).

The Cuban government has been a leader in the use of media for nonformal education. Starting in the 1960s, radio has served an important function in making education available to all citizens. As of 1996, eleven of the fourteen provinces offered local radio instruction at important work centers. Increased use of television has also offered opportunities for distance learning. For example, in 2000, "University for All" was introduced on state television, offering telecourses in English, Spanish, and other topics. Distance learning is offered through institutions of higher education, with periodic meetings held between students and professors; approximately 25,000 participants were involved as of 1996. The use of computers and Internet technology is limited, although Cuba is working to increase this resource for its populace.

TEACHING PROFESSION

Education of teachers is a strong priority in Cuba, and teacher preparation programs are invariably joined with the political and cultural transitions of the country. Teachers are trained in one of 13 teaching (pedagogical) universities and programs in several methods of instruc-

tion. Entry is based upon test scores and analysis of one's aptitude and interpersonal qualities specific to teaching. The training program lasts for five years, with students beginning their studies in their pre-university year of school. During the first two years of the program, emphasis is placed on general studies, emphasizing political and cultural topics. During the third year of instruction, educational psychology is introduced, while in the fourth and fifth year of study, practice teaching is emphasized under the direction of experienced teachers. Practicing teachers can also attain advanced degrees from these institutions.

Teachers are evaluated for performance effectiveness based on qualitative evaluations by peers and administrators, as well as comparison to National Education Quality Control criteria. Salaries are paid on a wage scale initially established in 1975, and professors are paid wages similar to that of doctors and engineers. Teachers are encouraged to continue their education and are given leave from their positions to attend classes.

SUMMARY

Cuba's position in the world has changed dramatically in the years since the Revolution, and its educational system has continually met the needs of its people. Change has been so constant that one might argue paradoxically that Cuba's future emerges as its past. Cuba has a highly literate population and a technologically trained workforce, yet it has limited venues for utilizing the talent of its populace because of its difficult economic circumstances.

Cuba remains on the edge of the digital divide. While it is gradually increasing its ability to provide computer technology for its people, information technology resources are limited. For Cuba to enter the twenty-first century, those resources must increase; there is little doubt that Cuba's educational system will embrace the changes that technology brings.

One of Cuba's strengths is its integration of culture, social order, and education. Especially noteworthy has been its integration of formal education, practical arts, and problem-solving applications outside of the classroom. Ironically, that same path is now being promoted worldwide by major corporations and conservative education policy experts who seek to promote problem solving and teamwork. The developed nations have much to learn from Cuba's ability to integrate education into all aspects of its culture. It is also clear that this innovative synthesis of learning activities is not exclusively socialist or liberal.

Another irony involves Cuba's preparation to deal with change. The rigid structure and technology for learning has created for its people a framework for self-discovery and an intrinsic application of knowledge. Times are changing in Cuba, especially with its increased reliance on a tourist economy. Educators are leaving the profession to work in tourism, and this is yet another challenge to be faced. Cuba is again required to create new innovations to maintain its revolutionary vision but, with change as its strength, Cuban education is well positioned to further its transformation and to meet its people's needs.

BIBLIOGRAPHY

Berube, Maurice. *Education and Poverty: Effective Schooling in the United States and Canada.* Westport, CT: Greenwood, 1984.

Carnoy, Martin, and Jorge Werthein. "Cuba: Training and Mobilization." In *Better Schools: International Lessons for Reform.* Praeger Special Studies Series in Comparative Education, 1983.

Castro, Fidel. *History Will Absolve Me.* Havana: Radio Havana Cuba, 1953.

de Varona, Frank. "Perspectiva Historica de la Educacion en Cuba." In *el Comite de Estudios para la Reforma Educacional en Cuba, La Educacion en Cuba: Pasado, Presente y Futuro.* The Endowment for Cuban American Studies of the Cuban American National Foundation, 1993.

Gillette, Arthur. *Cuba's Educational Revolution,* London: Fabian Society, 1972.

Lutjens, Sheryl. "Education and the Cuban Revolution: A Selected Bibliography." *Comparative Education Review* 42, 1998: 197-224.

————. *The State, Bureaucracy, and Cuban Schools: Power and Participation.* Boulder, CO: Westview Press, 1996.

MacDonald, Theodore. *Schooling the Revolution: An Analysis of Developments in Cuban Education Since 1959.* London: Carlyon Printers, 1996.

————. *Making a New People: Education in Revolutionary Cuba.* Vancouver, BC: New Star Books, 1985.

Ministry of Education, Republic of Cuba, Organization of Education 1994-1996. *Report of the Republic to Cuba to the 45th International Conference on Public Education.* Havana: Ministry of Education, 1996.

Ministry of Education, Republic of Cuba, Pedagogia 1999. "Encuentro por la Unidad de los Educadores Latinoamericanos." *Report of the Republic of Cuba to the Congreso Internacional Pedagogia 1999.* Havana: Ministry of Education, 1999.

Padula, Alfred, and Lois M. Smith. "The Revolutionary Transformation of Cuban Education, 1959-1987." In *Making the Future: Politics and Educational Reform in the United States, England, the Soviet Union, and Cuba.* Atlanta: Center for Cross Cultural Education, College of Education, Georgia State University, 1988.

Paulston, Rolland. *The Educational System of Cuba.* Washington, DC: U.S. Department of Health, Education, and Welfare, 1976.

Paulston, R., and C.C. Kaufman. "Cuba." In *International Handbook of Educational Reform.* Westport, CT: Westview, 1992.

Perez, Emma. *Historia de la Pedagogia en Cuba: Desde los Origenes Hasta la Guerra de Independencia Havana,* 1945.

Thomas, Hugh. *Cuba: The Pursuit of Freedom.* New York: Da Capo Press, 1998.

UNESCO. *Compendium of Statistics on Illiteracy.* Paris: UNESCO, 1995.

—*Patrick McGuire and Karen Vocke*

CYPRUS

BASIC DATA

Official Country Name:	Republic of Cyprus
Region:	Middle East
Population:	758,363
Language(s):	Greek, Turkish, English
Literacy Rate:	94%
Number of Primary Schools:	376
Compulsory Schooling:	9 years
Foreign Students in National Universities:	1,675
Libraries:	117
Educational Enrollment:	Primary: 64,761 Secondary: 61,266 Higher: 9,982
Educational Enrollment Rate:	Primary: 100% Secondary: 97% Higher: 23%
Teachers:	Primary: 4,202 Secondary: 4,934 Higher: 1,061

Student-Teacher Ratio: Primary: 15:1
                                   Secondary: 13:1

Female Enrollment Rate: Primary: 100%
                                   Secondary: 99%
                                   Higher: 25%

HISTORY & BACKGROUND

Cyprus is the third largest island in the Mediterranean Sea, after Sicily and Sardinia, and is situated at the eastern end of the sea. The island has an area of 9,251 square kilometers (3,572 square miles), measuring 226 kilometers long and 98 kilometers wide. The 755,000 inhabitants create a population density of 82 persons per square kilometer. The Greek Cypriots (including Armenians, Maronites, and Latins) comprise more then 85 percent of the population, the Turkish Cypriots make up 12 percent, and foreign residents the remaining amount. These population figures do not reflect the more than 115,000 Turkish settlers residing in the northern Turkish-occupied part of the island.

The strategic position of the island has earned Cyprus the designation of ''crossroads of the world.'' The prehistory and history of the island document this title. The earliest signs of life in Cyprus date back to the pre-neolithic period, 10,000 to 8500 B.C. During the Bronze Age (2500 to 1050 B.C.), copper was extensively exploited and a metal work industry developed on the island. During the Late Bronze Age (1650 to 1050 B.C.), commercial contacts with the Aegean world were established, and Myceneans (ancient Greeks) settled on the coasts of Cyprus. The Mediterranean indigenous people gradually assimilated, creating a peripheral center of Greek culture in Cyprus.

The years 1050 to 333 B.C. witnessed waves of immigrants from mainland Greece (Arcadia), invasions by the Phoenicians, and successive submission to the Assyrian, Egyptian, and Persian states. King Evagoras of Salamis, who ruled from 411 to 374 B.C., unified Cyprus and it became a leading political and cultural center of the Greek world. In 323 B.C., Cyprus came under the rule of the Viceroys of Ptolemy I of Egypt and his successors. The capital transferred from Salamis to Paphos.

In 45 A.D., the Apostles Paul and Barnabas arrived in Cyprus to spread the Christian doctrine and succeeded in converting the Proconsul, Sergius Paulus, to Christianity at Paphos. Cyprus thereby became the first country to be governed by a Christian.

Constantine the Great, became sole ruler of the Roman Empire in 324, and proclaimed his mother Helena as Augusta soon after. Legend reports that Helena established the Stavrovouni Monastery in Cyprus, where she stayed during a return journey from Jerusalem. The monastery occupies the easternmost summit of the Troodos mountain range, at a height of 2,260 feet.

The seventh to tenth centuries A.D. are chiefly notable for continuous Arab raids on the island that caused great destruction, especially to churches and ecclesiastic art. In 965 A.D., the Arabs were expelled from Asia Minor and neighboring coastal areas by Byzantine Emperor, Nikiforos Focas, ending the raids. Nicosia became the capital of Cyprus in the tenth century.

From 1192 until 1489, the time known as the Frankish (Lusignan) Period, Cyprus was ruled under the feudal system. While the Catholic Church officially replaced the orthodox, the latter managed to survive.

A period of rule by the Venetians began in 1489 that would continue until 1571. The Venetians used Cyprus as a fortified base against the Turks. Trade and culture languished under the heavy taxes imposed to pay for the fortifications. Even so, Turkey successfully attacked Cyprus, eventually gaining control of the island.

Under Turkish rule, which lasted for 300 years (1571 to 1878), the Greek Orthodox Church was re-established and the Latin Church expelled. Turkish rule ended in 1878, under the Cyprus Convention, when Turkey transferred the administration of Cyprus to Great Britain in exchange for assistance in the event of Russian hostility. In 1923, under the Treaty of Lausanne, Turkey relinquished all rights to Cyprus. In 1925, Cyprus was declared a Crown colony.

A national liberation struggle launched in 1955 against colonial rule was finally resolved in February 1959 when Cyprus became an independent republic under the Zurich-London Treaty, with a Greek Cypriot president and a Turkish Cypriot vice president. In 1960, following the treaty agreement, and with Greece and Turkey guaranteeing its independence, territorial integrity, and constitution, Cyprus was proclaimed an independent state and became the 99th member-state of the United Nations. It became a member in the same year of the Commonwealth and was the sixteenth member-state of the Council of Europe in 1961 (Panteli 1990).

Evidence of an emerging social demand for education is the fact that in 1960, when the British left Cyprus, 90 percent of the 6 to 12 year old population attended primary schools, although compulsory education had not been implemented (Persianis 1996a). This is in stark contrast to school attendance just two decades earlier. In 1938 and 1939, of the 77,000 children of elementary school age, only 46,926 (61 percent) were attending school. Of the 60,000 children of secondary school age, only 4,784 (8 percent) were attending school. Through the postwar years (1945-1950), ''the Cypriot youngster, as in the England of Dickens' Oliver Twist had to find work and receive next to nothing or toil in the field for ten to fifteen hours a day to supplement the meager family income'' (Panteli 1990).

In 1963 the president of Cyprus, Archbishop Makarios, suggested amendments to the constitution, with which the Turkish Cypriot leaders disagreed. The Turkish leaders then engineered an intercommunal crisis, withdrew from the Cyprus government and House of Representatives, and set up Turkish military enclaves in Nicosia and other parts of the island, with the help of military personnel from Turkey. This event marks the separation and division of Greek Cypriots and Turkish Cypriots, although in many villages and towns the people of Cyprus continued to live together in peace and friendship. However, the first riots between the two communities in 1963-1964 and later in 1967 created an atmosphere of fear and mutual distrust, which gradually poisoned the friendly relations of the past.

On 15 July 1974 the Greek military junta organized a coup against Archbishop Makarios, who escaped to England. The coup and the constitutional provisions for the guarantor powers, provided Turkey the opportunity to invade Cyprus. On 20 July 1974, alleging they were coming in peace to protect the Turkish Cypriots and restore the constitutional order, 40,000 Turkish troops landed on the island assisted by Turkish air and naval forces. This maneuver violated the Charter of the United Nations, the fundamental human rights of thousands of Greek Cypriots, and all principles governing international relations. Three days later the coup was overthrown and constitutional order was reestablished.

If Turkey wanted to maintain any claim to be acting as a guarantor power, it would have withdrawn its forces on 23 July. Instead, in August it mounted a second attack against Cyprus. As a result, the Turkish Army occupied the northern third of the island, including 204 of 626 Greek Cypriot villages and 51.5 percent of the island's coasts and shores (Katsonis & Huber 1998). Thousands of people were killed or disappeared, and 200,000 people became refugees in their own country. A truce arranged by the United Nations (UN) mandated that the island be partitioned. Currently the Greek Cypriots occupy the southern two-thirds of the island and the Turkish Cypriots, with the aid of Turkish military and budgetary support, occupy the northern third. A United Nations peacekeeping force maintains a buffer zone between the two sectors.

The area under Turkish occupation unilaterally declared independence in 1983, fanning emotions in the south about previously owned property, family burial sites, and the loss of famous historical sites (Bradshaw 1993). The continued division and occupation of Cyprus serves as a major factor in understanding educational policy. One of the major problems that education in Cyprus continues to face is the occupation by Turkish troops of a number of primary and secondary schools (Papanastasiou 1995). The political division, rather than political pluralism, impacts every aspect of the culture, including education.

CONSTITUTIONAL & LEGAL FOUNDATIONS

Cyprus is an independent, sovereign republic of a presidential type. Under the 1960 Constitution, the executive power is entrusted to the president of the republic who is elected for a five-year term of office. A transitional body governed education until the Proclamation of Independence on 16 August 1960. Thereafter, the administration of Greek Cypriot education was undertaken by the Greek Communal Chamber consisting of 26 members elected from the Greek community and the administration of the Turkish minority by the Turkish Communal Chamber. The Armenian and Maronite populations were given the option to choose the Communal Chamber by which they wished to be governed; both chose the Greek Communal Chamber. Within the framework of the Constitution, the Greek Communal Chamber has legislative power over all religious matters; all educational, cultural, and teaching matters; all staff matters; and the composition and instance of courts dealing with civil disputes relating to personal status and to religious matters. The Greek Communal Chamber was dissolved on 31 March 1965, with legislative powers passing to the House of Representatives and the administrative power to the Ministry of Education.

EDUCATIONAL SYSTEM—OVERVIEW

Knowledge Traditions: Unique to Cyprus may be the influence of the ancient Greek civilization, where the knowledge of theory was considered superior to the knowledge of practical skills (Persianis 1996b). Cypriot Greeks have historically related the concept of the ''educated Cypriot'' to the knowledge traditions of Greece. Cypriots traveled to Constantinople, Alexandria, Salamanca, Venice, Rome, and Paris for higher education during the years following the fall of Constantinople to the Ottomans in 1453 (Persianis in Koyzis 1997). The tradition accelerated with the creation of modern Greece in 1830, particularly following the founding of the University of Athens in 1837.

''Teachers in Cyprus before 1830 (during Turkish rule), were mainly priests, or others, with some reading and writing skills. After 1830, and the establishment of teacher training institutes in Greece, the first educated teachers started returning to Cyprus'' (Persianis and Polyviou 1992). The first teacher training institution to be established in Cyprus was in 1893 (Maratheftis 1992), when Cyprus was under British rule. The Pancyprian Teacher Training School commenced as a branch of the Pancyprian Gymnasium in Nicosia. It consisted of four years of primary education, three years of postprimary and four years gymnasium. After 1893, the Pancyprian Teacher Training School was upgraded to six years primary education and six years gymnasium.

In 1903 the first female teacher training institution was established in Nicosia, and in 1910 a priest training institution was established in Larnaca. In 1915 gymnasium education for teachers was increased to seven years. In the 1930s all the teacher training institutions were abolished by the British after political disturbances, the governor taking full control over elementary education.

In 1937 the Morphou Teacher Training College was established as a two-year institution by the ruling British, offering teacher training in English both for Greeks and Turks, with graduates qualifying as primary teachers. This action of the colonial government was not popular with the church and other educationalists. In 1943 a similar institution opened for females, admitting only Greeks until 1948. In 1958 the Morphou Teacher Training College was transferred to a large area of land in Nicosia replacing the Morphou and Larnaca colleges.

In 1959, after the Zurich-London agreements for the independence of Cyprus, the Teacher Training College became the Pedagogical Academy, providing education for the training of primary school teachers, its programs being offered in Greek. Graduates of public high schools were admitted for a two-year teacher training program. The Pedagogical Academy followed the system offered in Greece. The program became of three year duration in 1965, while in 1975, a nursery department was established for the training of nursery school teachers (Anastasiou 1995).

Greece has remained the model for Cypriot knowledge traditions, education, and culture with a relatively steady number of Cypriot Greeks studying in Greece (35 to 40 percent of the students studying abroad as reported by Koyzis 1997). The majority of all secondary school teachers in the Greek secondary schools are graduates of Greek universities (Koyzis 1997).

Perhaps the greatest impact of the Greek higher education tradition was the favored area of study, philology. The term has been interpreted to mean an education combining classical Greek literature, philosophy, and history with a uniquely Greek version of educational humanism—Greek Orthodoxy, classical Hellenism, and an em-

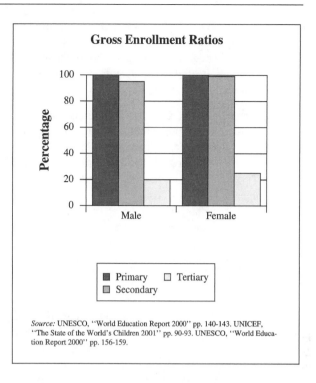

Gross Enrollment Ratios

Source: UNESCO, "World Education Report 2000" pp. 140-143. UNICEF, "The State of the World's Children 2001" pp. 90-93. UNESCO, "World Education Report 2000" pp. 156-159.

phasis on literary humane studies (Koyzis 1997; McClelland 1980). According to Koyzis (1997), over 60 percent of all secondary teachers are philologists, along with 70 percent of the personnel in the Ministry of Education. The philologist-humanist knowledge tradition is a dominant factor in the state's conception of what is worth knowing. The philologist-humanist ideal recognizes the university as an extension of the state with the institution serving to produce the "disciplined, cultured, and moral Christian-Greek" (Koyzis 1997).

The School of Philosophy at the University of Athens in Greece (where languages, literature, and history are taught as well as philosophy) has been the center for the preservation of the humanist tradition. It has maintained links with the secondary school teachers' union, whose members have been trained largely in this university school. There is also a wider consumer for humanist education. The School of Philosophy at Athens retains the highest prestige (Koyzis 1997).

Another knowledge tradition which has influenced Cypriot intellectual life and invariably the development of higher education has been English essentialism. A third knowledge tradition which influenced the development of higher education in Cyprus is North American educational utilitarianism (Koyzis 1997).

Contemporary Context: The main political goal of the government—survival of Cyprus as a unified, independent, and sovereign country—has contributed to the educational philosophy of "I do not forget" (Papanastasiou 1995; Katsonis & Huber 1998). Greek Cypriots do not forget the people, churches, schools, homes, and lands in the Turkish occupied territory. School materials, programs, and publications keep the invasion of 1974 and subsequent events in contemporary focus.

The Greek Cypriot community (which comprises about 85 percent of the population of about 1 million inhabitants) uses the Greek language as the language of instruction in schools, and the Turkish Cypriot community uses the Turkish language. Each community encourages the teaching and learning of foreign languages, especially English, but not each other's language. The minority population of other non-Greek, non-Turkish ethnic groups are normally trilingual, having a native command of their own ethnic language, a near-native command of Greek, and, in most cases, a mastery of English (Papapaviou 1999).

Since the 1974 invasion and the subsequent division of the island, the languages of instruction have remained divided with little interaction. Numerous overseas Cypriots, mainly from Australia, the United Kingdom, and the United States, have returned to their homelands. Immigrants to Cyprus, primarily for employment, have added their languages to the linguistic situation, mainly Arabic, Filipino, Rumanian, and Russian. The majority of children attend Greek-speaking monolingual state primary schools. These schools do not provide auxiliary classes in Greek as a second language, nor do they provide instruction in the children's native ethnic language (Papapaviou 1999). The linguistic situation of the early twenty-first century finds many bilingual children in monolingual public schools. Private instruction, relatively expensive, is available for those seeking an English-speaking educational experience.

The formal education system of Cyprus is highly centralized and controlled by the state. School curricula and textbooks are determined by governmental agencies, along with guidelines on how to implement the national curriculum. Schools at all levels are visited by the state inspectorate, which is responsible for evaluating schools. Private schools are owned and administered by individuals or committees, but are liable to supervision and inspection by the Ministry of Education.

Education is free at all levels and compulsory from the age of five years and six months to the age of 15. All public schools use the same curriculum and textbooks, though teachers are free to adapt the material to their local environment. The 205-day school year is based on a nationwide core curriculum. According to 1999 figures on education published by the Department of Statistics of Education, there were 163,800 full-time students at 1,208 educational institutions of the island with more than 80 percent enrolled in public institutions.

Curriculum Development: The centralized system of educational administration, a centre-periphery model (Schon 1971), impacts the management of curriculum improvement in Cyprus (Kyriakides 1999) along the following five dimensions:

1. The design of the curriculum of 1981 and the new curriculum were almost completely controlled by the government inspectors and did not establish any mechanism for consulting teachers.... Inspectors control the design of the curriculum, the implementation through provision of guidelines and advice to teachers for problems with implementing the curriculum policy, and teacher evaluation.

2. School Based Curriculum Development (SBCD) is weak in Cyprus and is also a consequence of high central control that does not allow for much differentiation among the schools. Cypriot teachers struggle with their problems and anxieties privately, spending most of their time apart from their colleagues. There is very rarely interaction concerned with professional issues among the staff of schools (Kyriakides 1994).

3. The difficulties of the centre-periphery model of the curriculum change also has to do with the fact that the quality of teachers determines to some extent the implementation of curriculum policy. The need for a strong link between curriculum reform and teacher development is also reflected in theories of curriculum change (Fullan & Hargreaves 1992). This raises questions on links between teachers' professional development and curriculum reform in Cyprus. It is argued that there is no link between curriculum reform and teacher development, which is attributed to the process of curriculum change followed in Cyprus that implies a limited role for teachers (Kyriakides 1994). The underlying model of change management is based on contractual rather than professional accountability.

4. The aims of the education service in Cyprus are set out in various government publications and policy documents. By analyzing these aims one can identify an attempt to link education to the historical, social, moral, cultural, economic, and political context of Cyprus (Kyriakides 1994; UNESCO 1997). However, the aims say little about the concept of partnership that is now given high priority in many countries. It can be argued that policy documents do not encourage the idea that schools should take account not only of policy decisions of government inspectors, but also of the expectations of parents, employers, and the community at large. Neither official policy documents nor any nonstatutory guidance suggest that the development of the curriculum at the local

level should be seen in terms of the pupils' and parents' role (Kyriakides 1994).

5. Systematic information about the conditions of schooling, educational processes, and educational outcomes for all grades and subjects appears to be lacking (Kyriakides 1999). In addition, innovation, evaluations, and curricular changes need to be designed for the specific conditions in Cyprus.

Examinations, Promotions, & Certifications: The Cypriot system requires no entrance examinations for primary and secondary schools. Almost all primary school students are promoted to the next grade. Only in the first grade is there a failure rate of about 1.5 percent of the students. Primary school students earn a leaving certificate at the end of the sixth year after evaluation through continuous assessment. All primary graduates proceed to secondary school without any examination. In secondary education, every student receives a school report three times a year at the end of each school term. At the end of grades 9 and 12, all students take common final exams prepared by the Ministry of Education.

Beginning in 1991, students in Grade 12 also take an externally prepared final exam. The following year, 1992, Grade 9 students were required to take compulsory common exams in four subjects.

Special Education: In 1995, the United Nations Educational, Scientific, and Cultural Organization (UNESCO) conducted an update of the initial ''1988 Review of the Present Situation of Special Education.'' The division in the Ministry of Education in Cyprus provided information by means of questionnaire responses. The forms of special education available were reported as emotional and behavioral disturbance, mental retardation/severe learning difficulties, physical/motor disabilities, visual impairment, hearing impairment, language disorder, and learning disabilities (UNESCO 1995).

The aim of special education policy in Cyprus is to encourage and support the integration of children with special needs into the ordinary education system and give them an opportunity to grow and learn together with their peers. Special provision is made for physically handicapped children (e.g., deaf, blind) and the mentally retarded, who attend special schools.

Children who are profoundly handicapped, mainly characterized by physical disabilities and mental retardation, are cared for in residential institutions operated by the Ministry of Labour, the Ministry of Social Welfare, or voluntary agencies. The full range of facilities employed in meeting the needs of students in special education includes boarding special schools, day special schools, special classes in regular schools, resource rooms in regular schools, and the support of teaching in regular classes. The provision of these special education facilities is mainly the responsibility of the Director of Primary Education. The Inspector of Special Education has primary operational responsibility.

For secondary school students with special needs, the responsibility lies with the Department of Secondary Education and the Department of Technical Education within the Ministry of Education. Administrative decisions are made at the national level. In settings where special education is provided by voluntary bodies (estimated to be about 4 percent of the expenditure on special education), the Ministry of Education provides teaching staff to cover some of the needs of the institutions (UNESCO 1995).

Legislation specific to special educational needs is concerned principally with primary education. The basic law, Special Education Law 1979, describes the kind of special needs that should be met in special schools and special classes, the procedures for multiprofessional assessment and placement of these children, the roles of the psycho-pedagogical committees, the obligations of parents, and the roles of governing bodies of special schools. A further law in 1993 governs the integration of hearing-impaired children. More recent legislative consideration has been given to meeting students' needs in the least restrictive environment (UNESCO 1995).

PREPRIMARY & PRIMARY EDUCATION

Since Cyprus has been at the crossroads of world travel through the centuries, the country's educational system has been influenced by many different civilizations. During the Ottoman Period (1571-1878), children attended school as early as age four in sibyan classes of elementary schools. Classes were mixed-age and included both genders. The children were confided to the teacher in a special religious ceremony called Amin Alayi, and this trust required certain religious qualifications of the teachers, both male and female. In 1878, when the British took over administration of education in Cyprus, there were 65 Turkish elementary schools (Mertan 1995).

During the British Period (1878-1960), the Elementary Education Committees conducted meetings between Ottoman and British educators that continued until 1929. During this time, the education of children between the ages of four to six was an issue. In 1926, for instance, only four schools existed on the island to educate children in this nursery age group, one in Famagusta and three in Nicosia. Weir explained in 1952 that nursery schools were completely lacking in Cyprus. The few schools that had been in operation were closed due to economic issues. Both the need for teacher training and the subsequent availability of trained teachers were lacking.

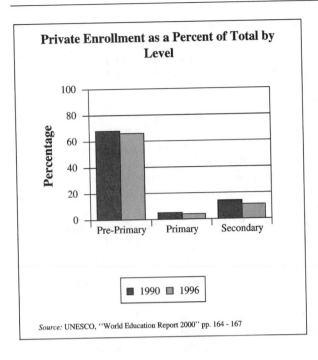

Private Enrollment as a Percent of Total by Level

Source: UNESCO, ''World Education Report 2000'' pp. 164 - 167

most significantly, the inherent, inalienable right of every child to receive care and education with attention to physical, cognitive, social, and emotional development. In Cyprus, about 0.06 percent of the population is under the age of five with virtually none of the population living below the absolute poverty level. Equally positive is the life expectancy average age of 77, the highest in the Mediterranean region (with the same life expectancy reported for Israel and Malta). The under-five mortality rate (U5MR) of 11 percent, as an indicator of the crucial components that indicate early childhood development, places Cyprus in an enviable position in contrast to other countries of the Mediterranean region—Israel was rated the only country with a better rate at 9 percent, while Turkey's rate was 50 percent and Morocco's, 75 percent (van Oudenhoven & Wazir 1997). Cyprus ranks comparatively healthy in the consideration of malnourished children as well, with 8 percent.

School enrollment and dropout rates can be considered as indicators of the psycho-social development of children. In Cyprus, school enrollment for all boys and girls in the late twentieth century stood at 99 percent, with virtually no dropout rate. That these rates are equal for boys and girls accounts for Cyprus having the highest female literacy rate in the region (91 percent), compared to only 31 percent in Morocco, 49 percent in Algeria, and 72 percent in Turkey.

Most of the primary schools in urban areas and larger communities are divided into two cycles: cycle A, catering to grades I through III, and cycle B, comprised of grades IV through VI. The pupil-teacher ratio at the national level is 19:1 with a ceiling set at 34 pupils for the largest classes.

Experiential, meaningful learning is promoted through an emphasis on environment, science and social subjects, language development, music, art, physical education, home economics, design and technology, and information technology. The acquisition of the basic skills of reading, writing, and mathematics is given an important place in all grades of primary schooling. Primary school graduates receive a leaving certificate at the end of the sixth year after evaluation through continuous assessment.

State preprimary education is a particular priority since the Turkish invasion of 1974 in order to support refugee families, equalize educational opportunities across economic groups, and enable more mothers to secure gainful employment. Preprimary institutions include public, private, and community-based nursery schools, day care centers, and kindergartens. The nursery schools are certified and supervised by the Ministry of Education, the day care centers by the Department of Social Welfare and Services. A uniform curriculum is provided for the nursery school experience, promoting integrated development and preparation for citizenship. The Pancyprian School for Parents serves as a primary agency for parental education in Cyprus.

Since 1962, primary education has been free and compulsory for children between the ages of 6 to 12. Schools operate in every community of at least 15 children. Area schools serve neighboring communities with fewer than 15 pupils. Parental choice is not an option, and children must attend the school in their area.

Cyprus is a signatory to the Convention of the Rights of the Child and the action plan developed at the Summit for Children organized by UNICEF in 1991. In a paper prepared for the 1997 Health and Social Welfare Conference, van Oudenhoven and Wazir (of International Child Development Initiatives, the Netherlands) provided an extensive overview of the Mediterranean experience regarding early childhood development and social integration, including the issue of social inclusion/exclusion in early childhood education. They describe critical factors to consider in early childhood preprimary education—

Northern Cyprus: The northern region of Cyprus under Turkish occupation provides preschool education in kindergartens for children between the ages of four and six. Primary education is provided at two stages: elementary school for the 7 to 12 age group, which lasts for five years, and secondary-junior school for the 13 to 15 age group, which lasts for three years. Both preschool and primary education is free and compulsory.

SECONDARY EDUCATION

Public general secondary education is divided into two cycles, the Gymnasium and the Lyceum, which provide a six-year course to children in the 11 to 17 age group. Secondary education has become compulsory up to the third year of gymnasium, and has been free for both cycles since 1985. The U.S. reader should be mindful that gymnasium has a different meaning in Europe. A student who attends a gymnasium will be studying at a level equivalent to the U.S. high school junior and senior (Bradshaw 1993).

The lower cycle comprises the first three years of secondary education, during which all pupils follow a common course of general education. The second cycle, which comprises the last three years of secondary education, is offered either in the Lyceum of Elective Subjects or in the technical/vocational schools. Pupils are assisted in making their choice by the vocational guidance services. At the Lyceum of Elective Subjects there are three categories of subjects: the subjects of the main core, which have to be attended by all pupils, specialization subjects, and supplementary subjects, which are elective. Although pupils are in principle free to choose any of the elective subjects, in practice there are five main combinations. These are combinations with emphasis on classical studies, sciences, economics, commercial subjects and subjects related to skills for office professions, or foreign languages.

In September 1995 the Department of Secondary Education introduced educational system reform on an experimental basis in three Lycea in Nicosia. This step was taken in connection with the change from the Lyceum of elective subjects to the unified Lyceum, in order to combine secondary general with secondary technical education. The goal is that the unification cost will not be unbearable for the public sector and will not prejudice technical education.

Northern Cyprus: In Northern Cyprus secondary education is designed for the 16 to 18 age group at high schools known as lycees and vocational schools. The technical and vocational schools are comprised of commercial lycees, technical training schools, agricultural vocational school, the school of nursing and midwifery, and the tourism and hotel management and catering school.

Vocational & Technical Education: Since independence from Britain in 1960, the establishment and organization of technical education in Cyprus has been one of the primary concerns of the Cyprus government (Bradshaw 1993). Seen as a contributing factor in the economic progress of the island, technical education was implemented to meet the needs of the newly independent country. During the first 30 years, 11 technical schools were established. The A Technical Schools in Nicosia and Limassol began under British administration in 1956. The Agriculture School opened in 1959 at Morphou. The Technical School at Xeros was begun in 1961. The B Technical School and Dianellos Technical School in Larnaca started in 1962, as did the Morphou and Kyrenia Commercial Schools. The Technical School in Polis and The Famagusta Technical School began in 1963. The Technical School in Paphos began in 1969. The next school, opened in 1976, was the B Technical School in Limmasol. Lazaros Technical School opened in 1980 in Larnaca, followed in 1981 by Makarios in Nicosia. The Hotel and Catering School at Paralimni opened in 1984, and, finally, the Hotel and Catering School at Limmasol opened in 1987. Before 1959 the British colonial government operated four bicommunal technical schools: apprentice schools in Nicosia, Limassol, and Lefka, and a junior preparatory school in Nicosia (Bradshaw 1993).

According to Bradshaw (1993), who worked with the Fulbright-Hayes Commission in Cyprus from January to July 1991, technical education program development has passed through a number of developmental stages. An overview of each of the six stages follows.

During the initial stage, which immediately followed independence in 1960 to 1961, the basic aims of technical education were the continuation of the traditional humanistic and cultural scope of education, and the training of suitably skilled manpower for the emerging Cyprus industries (Bradshaw 1993). This education was offered at two levels, or sections—a four-year and a six-year program. During the initial years, general education was offered in both programs—two years of general education in the four-year program and three years of general education in the six-year program. Basic technical subjects were introduced in addition to the general education classes. During the second phase of the programs, emphasis was given to the technical subjects, while the percentage of time focused on general education was reduced (Bradshaw 1993).

The second developmental stage evolved in 1964, based on assessment of the implementation of the two types of programs of technical education for four years. More general education was assigned to the first two-year cycle in the four-year program, thus reducing the percentage of time for technical subjects.

The third developmental stage, initiated in 1967, was based on the prevailing trends in Europe and on the demands of the industries and the people of Cyprus. These pressures necessitated partial revision of the first cycle of the four-year program, increasing it to three years, thereby making the program a five-year program. The first three years became identical to the first three years of the six-year program, and identical to the gymnasia curricula (secondary schools). This development meant that students could choose the type of school they wanted to attend after completing the first cycle (Bradshaw 1993).

The political division of Cyprus in 1974 interrupted the fourth developmental stage that was introduced in 1972 and interfered with the evaluation of the reforms of 1972 and the assessment of the programs, as well as the functioning of the programs. The fourth stage was not implemented until 1976, and was based on the expansion of technical education; study of problems and functions of the technical schools; and the consideration of worldwide trends in education (i.e., equal opportunity). The following pattern was developed for implementation:

1. Technical education was promoted as one unit, the second cycle having a three-year program (with the exception of hotel and catering curricula and the dressmaking curricula, which remained two-year programs).

2. Broad, basic training in groups of related specializations during Class IV, followed by greater depth in the specialty for the following two years.

3. The education and training offered to the students of classes IV, V, and VI were aimed at achieving a predetermined level of competence. (Bradshaw 1993)

After the division, the technical schools at Xeros (1961) and Famagusta were no longer available to Greek Cypriots because they were in the areas secured by the Turkish Army. "The loss of these two schools was especially severe... as they were large, well-equipped, modern facilities" (Bradshaw 1993). Following the division, the refugee students were distributed to the remaining technical schools. Overcapacity necessitated that all technical schools except those at Paphos and Polis operate both mornings and afternoons, which continued for four years, with Limassol continuing the two-shift basis until 1982. Enrollment continued to rise during this stage at a higher percentage than increases before the division of Cyprus.

Based in part on the determination that the unification of the vocational and technical sections had been made at the expense of the strengths of each, modifications were made and the fifth developmental stage was implemented as follows. After completing gymnasium, pupils could enroll in class IV in the technical and the vocational schools. Class IV was common to all students, but they were divided according to their interests into mechanical, electrical, or building and construction. During this year, the students were each provided with opportunities to gain extensive technical knowledge and training in their area of interest so they could discover their inclination and capabilities. At the end of class IV, students could choose either the vocational or technical section according to their test results in math, physics, chemistry, and technology. Special emphasis was given (technician level) to theory for the technical section, whereas the vocational program (craft level) had an emphasis on workshop training. The course duration was three years, the first common year followed by two years of technical, specialized education. The vocational students could leave school after one year of specialization. However, the vocational students who completed three years of specialization could sit for the technical section certificate exam.

Students who had completed two years could choose to attend afternoon or evening class to prepare for the certificate exam (Bradshaw 1993). The sixth developmental stage, determined by the Education Council at the Ministry of Education in 1976 and implemented in 1978, focused on allowing more flexibility in technical education and making that education available to all interested students. "The curriculum would allow those leaving school to continue their education and professional development, and to stay current in their specialization . . . [and] satisfy the needs of industry" (Bradshaw 1993).

The new structure provided for vocational and technical sections in all the Cyprus technical schools and required each course syllabus to be based on behavioral objectives. The technical section offered a three-year curriculum with an emphasis on mathematics, the sciences, and a technology of specialization. Graduates could be employed as technicians in industry or pursue further studies (for which they met the qualifications) in colleges and universities. The technical section had five branches, each with one or more specialization: mechanical engineering, with a specialization as a machinist-fitter or in automobile mechanics; electrical engineering, with specializations in electrical installations, electronics, and computers; building, with a specialization as a technical assistant; graphic arts, with a specialization in graphic design and interior decoration; and fashion design, with a specialization in garment design and construction (Bradshaw 1993).

The vocational section offered a two-year curriculum with an emphasis on acquiring skills by increasing the percentage of time spent in workshop practice. An optional sixth year offered on-the-job-training, with either one-third or twp-thirds industry/school attendance. Graduates could be employed as craftspersons in industry. In addition, the vocational student could move to the technical curriculum after passing prescribed examinations. By 1982, there were six vocational branches: mechanical engineering, electrical engineering, building and construction, hotel and catering, dressmaking, and pottery (Bradshaw 1993).

Since gaining independence from Britain, Cyprus has stressed the college preparatory course in both the gymnasium and vocational/technical curriculum, with the latter making a transition toward a comprehensive education curriculum (Bradshaw 1993). Since 1976, fewer changes have been made in technical education. Additional coursework has been offered in foundry, agriculture machinery, joinery, carpentry, graphic design technology, fashion design, garment construction, drafting, goldsmithing and silversmithing, building science and technology, shoemaking, and vocational catering and waiting, with increased space for hotel catering and graphic arts curricula. The pottery and ceramics program was dropped due to low enrollment.

An issue regarding technical education should be noted. All males are required to spend two years in the national military service after completion of secondary school. Given how quickly technical education changes and advances, this is problematic for the students who achieve a technical education and then are forced to postpone work to complete their two years of military service.

HIGHER EDUCATION

Postsecondary education was established in Cyprus when two teacher training colleges were opened by the then British Colonial Office of Education, one for male students in 1937 and one for female students in 1946 (Koyzis 1989). In January 1958, both of these institutions were combined in the coeducational pedagogical Academy of Cyprus, and by 1959 the institution was turned over to the Greek community of Cyprus, which was preparing for the following year's independence from Britain. In 1960, an equivalent Turkish teacher's college also began. In 1958 the Pedagogical Academy had adopted the two-year curriculum used by pedagogical academies in Greece. A third year was added to the curriculum in the early 1960s. At that time, mandatory teaching of English was added to the curriculum.

By the 1992-1993 school year, the Republic of Cyprus was providing postsecondary education to 33 percent of all Cypriot students. These students comprised 58 percent of all secondary school graduates who continued beyond that level. Of the students enrolled in postsecondary education, 25 percent were studying abroad. There was a significant decline in the percentage of students studying abroad in the mid-1980s, primarily due to the founding of the public university in 1992 and an expansion of the private sector of higher education (Koyzis 1997).

While the Ministry of Education was established in 1965, a separate Department of Tertiary Education was not established until 1984, with the first law regulating tertiary education enacted in 1987. Thus, the history of higher education in Cyprus is fairly recent.

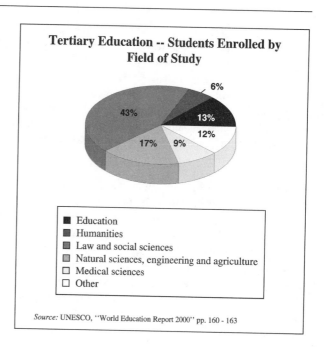

Tertiary Education -- Students Enrolled by Field of Study

- ■ Education
- ■ Humanities
- ■ Law and social sciences
- ▨ Natural sciences, engineering and agriculture
- □ Medical sciences
- □ Other

Source: UNESCO, "World Education Report 2000" pp. 160 - 163

Despite being a young republic, Cyprus compares favorably with older nations in terms of enrollment ratios. In 1990, approximately 36 percent of students continued to tertiary education, a percentage that compares positively with the most developed countries of the world (Anastasiou 1995).

Higher education includes: private tertiary institutions, of which the major ones are Cyprus College (founded in 1961), Frederick Institute of Technology (1975), Intercollege (1980), and Philips College (1978); public tertiary institutions, of which the largest ones are The Higher Technical Institute (established in 1968) and the School of Nursing (1964); and the first public university, the state University of Cyprus (1992). "The University of Cyprus' official languages of instruction are Greek and Turkish as primary languages, and English as the secondary language. But due to the political situation on the island, Turkish is only used in Turkish Studies Program. Since 1992 Greek has become the de facto language of the University of Cyprus. However all programs require some English instruction as well"(Koyzis 1997). The University of Cyprus includes schools of humanities and social sciences, a school of pure and applied sciences, and the school of economics and administration. Other public sector institutions include a school of nursing and midwifery, the Hotel and Catering Institute, the Higher Technical Institute, the Forestry College, and two management institutes. Other institutions function as Cyprus campuses for U.S. institutions, such as the Intercollege's connection with the University of Indianapolis (Koyzis 1989).

A significant feature of higher education in Cyprus is the large private sector developed since the mid-1970s.

The private sector provides higher education to Cypriots in English and models its curricula and courses of study on British and North American institutions. These private sector institutions rely exclusively on British or North American accreditation and degree validation, offering programs in business studies, computers and information sciences, hotel management, engineering and technology, secretarial studies, and social sciences (Koyzis 1989, 1997).

Like other developing countries, the demand for higher education has risen in Cyprus over the last three decades, with 60 percent of all secondary school graduates continuing their studies beyond that level (Department of Statistics and Research 1995, as reported by Menon 1997). Unlike other developing countries, Cyprus has not yet recorded high graduate unemployment rates, with fewer than three percent of recent higher education graduates reporting unemployment, according to the Planning Bureau (Menon 1997).

A development in tertiary education at the close of the twentieth century was the announcement by the Cyprus government that it would promote the development of private colleges into private universities. The International Committee for the Establishment of an Independent University of Cyprus (Coufoudakis 2000) proposed a plan for accomplishing the goal at the Intercollege institutions. Intercollege, the largest private institution in Cyprus, enrolled more than 2,500 students during the academic 1999-2000 year, of which 25 percent were international. For the 2000-2001 academic year, the number of students enrolled at Intercollege's three campuses reached 3,500 students, making it the largest tertiary educational institution in Cyprus.

School curricula have focused on theory as preparation for postcompulsory education, rather than on the practical aspects of life and employment. In Menon's 1997 study of the forces impacting secondary school students' motivation to pursue higher studies, strong parental encouragement for the continuation of studies beyond the secondary level ranked at the top of the list.

Over 10,000 Cypriots were studying abroad in the 1997-1998 academic year. Of those, 45.2 percent were studying in Greece, 27.3 percent in the United Kingdom, 17.8 percent in the United States, and 9.7 percent in other countries.

Northern Cyprus: In Northern Cyprus, university education is provided by Teachers Training College, Eastern Mediterranean University, Near East University, Girne American University, and International American University, with distance education opportunities from Turkey's Anadolu University.

ADMINISTRATION, FINANCE, & EDUCATIONAL RESEARCH

According to Law 12/1965, the highest authority for making and shaping educational policy is the Council of Ministers. The Ministry of Education is responsible for the administration of education, policy, curricula, personnel preparation, hiring and promotions, enforcement of laws and regulations, and resource allocation and budget. Preprimary, primary, and secondary education are under the authority of the Ministry of Education. The Ministry of Education is advised in its policies by the Educational Council.

The president appoints the Educational Service Commission, an independent five-member committee with a six-year term. The commission has authority over appointments, promotions, transfers, disciplinary measures, and dismissal of teacher and instructors.

Construction, maintenance, and the equipping of school buildings are the responsibility of local school committees under the supervision of the technical services of the Ministry of Education. Committees may be appointed by the Council of Ministers, or, in rural areas, may be selected by community members. The committees have regional functions concerning the educational budget, which they submit to the Ministry of Education of the upcoming school year; they also submit a detailed financial statement at the end of each year for a state audit.

The most recently available figures show that government expenditures on education at all levels have reached 217.5 million Cyprus pounds, which accounts for 13.8 percent of the state budget and 5.0 percent of the island's GDP. There were 163,800 full-time students at 1,208 educational institutions on the island, with more than 80 percent enrolled in public institutions. The total number of teaching staff reached 10,984.

Public education is mainly financed by the government through school committees. In addition, elected members of the central committee of the Parents' Association (PA) assist schools financially by raising money through various events to support particular needs and school programs. The national assembly of the PA is a powerful pressure group and policymakers take the PA into account at all times.

The process followed for the design and diffusion of curriculum change in Cyprus has been a centre-periphery model (Schon 1971), operating in a highly centralized system (Kyriakides 1999). Inspectors control the design of the curriculum, the implementation through the provision of guidelines and advice to teachers, and the evaluation by being responsible for teachers' appraisal. No mechanism exists for consulting teachers.

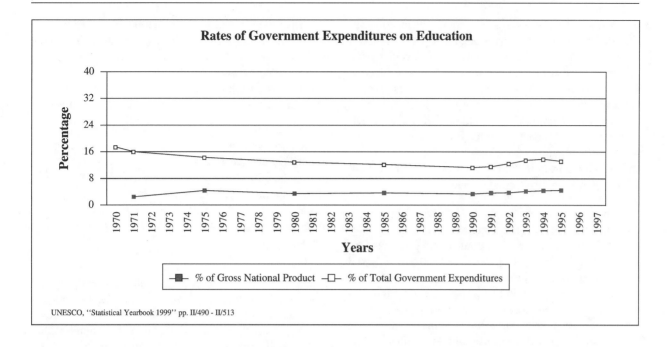

Rates of Government Expenditures on Education

Percentage / Years

—■— % of Gross National Product —□— % of Total Government Expenditures

UNESCO, "Statistical Yearbook 1999" pp. II/490 - II/513

A lack of systematic research in the field of research in Cyprus has been noted (Kyriakides 1999). The research studies that are undertaken are mainly small-scale and uncoordinated (UNESCO 1997). An important implication from the lack of any research for the evaluation of curriculum change is that no innovation has been designed for the specific conditions of Cyprus (Kyriakides 1999). It is important for the Ministry of Education to establish a national educational research unit (UNESCO 1997) to conduct research into curriculum policy and to inform pedagogical debate.

Despite 35 years of existence, the Ministry of Education has yet to pursue a complete analysis of all of Cyprus's tertiary education needs, costs, and benefits (Biggs 1992). A strategic plan to encompass private and public tertiary education, the Cyprus University, students traveling abroad, students coming from abroad, and a serious analysis on how to proceed is very much needed (Orphanides 1995).

NONFORMAL EDUCATION

The post-World War II era witnessed the development of adult and continuing education in Cyprus. Persianis (1996) has identified the following six features of adult and continuing education in Cyprus: the great impact of political developments; the great dependency on foreign know-how, models, and institutions; the low socio-economic origin of its target groups; a different educational and cultural tradition from that of mainstream education; an increased emphasis on social advancement courses rather than on cultural and community advancement courses; and its use as both a spearhead for modern-

ization and a shield for protecting the integrity of mainstream education from foreign dependency.

The political independence of 1960 created a need for adult education owing to new administrative posts in the expanded political structure, government emphasis on economic and social advancement, the requirement of higher qualifications for civil service, and minimum educational qualifications required for "ex-fighters... who had established the new state with their sacrifices" (Persianis 1996).

The case of the ex-fighters was a real revelation and a blessing to many capable people who had not had an opportunity in their youth to acquire high educational qualifications. In fact it officially established the way towards adult education. It showed that the acquisition of academic qualifications by people who had passed the normal school age was possible, and it established completely new educational routes. At the same time it pointed out the need for additional routes, and it created pressure on the government to provide the necessary means (Persianis 1996).

One additional educational route the government established provided for evening gymnasia (seven-year, part-time secondary schools) for working young people, as well as evening technical classes leading to external examinations and evening foreign language institutes.

The political division of 1974 had tremendous impact on the value of adult education as well, as wealthy, landed people became destitute refugees. Only academic qualifications seemed to afford hope of gainful work in divided Cyprus or abroad.

A third wave of adult and continuing education appeal has started since Cyprus applied to join the European Union in 1990. The four freedoms envisioned by the Maastrict Treaty of 1992 have stressed the importance of the qualitative improvement of Cyprus products and services and the efficiency of its labor force in order to cope with the globalization of competition. The existing evidence is that the country seems to depend more on its adult and continuing education rather than on its mainstream schooling in its efforts to meet the challenges of the European Union (Persianis 1996).

The second feature of adult and continuing education, dependency on foreign models, was a logical outgrowth of four centuries of Ottoman occupation and 84 years of British rule. Independence in 1960 was followed by the immediate need for quick development to traverse the technological and industrial divide. As high-tech equipment was imported, the need for high-tech training created a dependency on foreign trainers, examining boards, and accreditation institutions. A number of Cyprus private schools of higher education have established dependent relationships with primarily British and U.S. institutions of higher learning that are characterized in one or more of the following ways: as a kind of foreign college offering foreign courses; as the initial source of coursework leading to completion of degrees abroad; as sites subject to external examiners; and as the site for course offerings identical to those of their foreign affiliates.

The third feature of adult education is that it targets people from the lower socioeconomic strata. An exception to this is "in the case of the foreign language institutes (now called State Further Education Institutes). The majority of their students are higher secondary schools students who need coaching either for the University of Cyprus and the Universities of Greece entrance examinations or for the external examinations (mainly GCE)" (Persianis 1996).

The fourth feature distinguishes the cultural tradition of adult education from the knowledge tradition of the mainstream educational system. The majority of the courses, mainly those offered by the Industrial Training Authority, constitute a different educational and cultural entity from the traditional one. The courses are mostly technological, managerial, and professionally oriented, and they are short and accelerated, built on different epistemological assumptions from those that are dominant in the formal education courses. The educators in the adult courses are usually professionals with a long history of hands-on experience, but without formal teaching qualifications. Some of them are foreigners (for 96 out of the 1,519 programs the educators were foreigners; 89 programs were held abroad).

The modes of teaching and learning in the adult education courses differ tremendously from those of formal teaching. This is considered an advantage both because it is regarded as more appropriate for adult learning and also because it alleviates the cultural embarrassment of adults having to become students at an advanced age.

Parallel to these courses, however, are the courses offered by the Ministry of Education (i.e., evening gymnasium, in-service training courses for teachers at the Pedagogical Institute), which follow the traditional mode of teaching and learning. So, in fact, with regard to this characteristic, there is a division of courses on the lines of the individual ministry offering the courses (Persianis 1996).

The fifth feature distinguishing adult education from mainstream general education is that, with the exception of the adult education centers and the state further education institutes (which offer cultural and advancement courses), all other institutes of adult and continuing education offer professional advancement courses (i.e., courses leading to qualifications necessary for appointment or promotion). For instance, in 1993, approximately 883 adults attended cultural courses, while 20,008 adults attended social advancement courses (Persianis 1996).

The final, and most important, feature of adult and continuing education has been its role as the source for meeting the needs of modernization, thus protecting the education system's tradition of Greek educational humanism. The goals of nonformal education are to help early school graduates to supplement their basic education, secondary school graduates to enter the world of work, and working people to acquire professional knowledge. The government covers the expenditure for public nonformal institutions.

Other public and private institutions offer courses as well, but may charge fees. It is estimated that 9.5 percent of people above the age of 18 attend nonformal education provided through various agencies and institutions, including evening gymnasia, part-time institutes, adult education centers, the Industrial Training Authority, and the Cyprus Productivity Center (Papanastasiou 1995).

Distance Learning: Cyprus was first introduced to cyberspace in 1990 (Miltiadou 1996). The Ministry of Education and Culture (MEC) recognized the significant academic uses of computers for a small country like Cyprus, and in the late 1990s, it was the first government department to connect with the European Academic and Research Network (EARN). The Trans-European Research and Education Networking Association (TERENA) was formed in 1994 by the merger of RARE (Réseaux Associés pour la Recherche Européenne) and EARN, "to promote and participate in the development of a high quality international information and telecommunications infrastructure for the benefit of research and education.''

In October 1996 the Ministry of Education and Culture was invited to attend the Web for Schools (WfS)conference in Dublin, Ireland. The WfS program, funded by the European Union, is designed to produce a self-sustaining group of secondary school teachers who have the skills, knowledge, and understanding necessary to collaborate in order to use the World Wide Web to produce learning materials.

The Cyprus Fullbright Commission has created a web page that provides information about its grants to Cypriot and U.S. residents, educational advice concerning studies in the United States, and information on special bicommunal projects between the Republic of Cyprus and the Turkish-Cypriot side. Hypertext links provide U.S. education resources and other interesting links to students and teachers in Cyprus (Miltiadou 1996).

TEACHING PROFESSION

Preservice Teacher Training: Admission standards to the elementary education major at the University of Cyprus have been compared to those at U.S. institutions and were determined to be higher (Papanastasiou & Papanastasiou 1997). In order to be admitted to the Department of Education at the University of Cyprus, students have to compete with approximately 2,000 other candidates in the fiercely competitive University Entrance Examinations. Among those 2,000 candidates, only 150 are admitted to the elementary education program every year.

Since these examinations are highly competitive, the students that eventually get these positions are the best candidates. These students rank among the top 10 percent of the candidates that want to enter the elementary education major (Papanastasiou 1989).

At least one study of the factors influencing students' decisions to major in elementary education suggested that the external, extrinsic factors were the most compelling: high salaries, variety of benefits, guaranteed employment after graduation, job security, multiple job possibilities, and long vacations (Papanastasiou & Papanastasiou 1997). Intrinsic factors were reported to be the most compelling for a U.S. sample of elementary education majors who focused on the love of working with and teaching children. Certainly the national context for these disparate groups would need to be considered in applying the findings.

Cypriot preprimary and primary student teachers are trained through courses equivalent to a four-year bache-

lor's degree in education. However, neither the Pedagogical Academy of Cyprus nor the Department of Education at the University of Cyprus requires any compulsory course on curriculum development (Kyriakides 1999). The lack of emphasis on pedagogy is echoed at the secondary level, as well. To become a secondary teacher, the candidate must obtain a university degree related to the specific subject to be taught. Initial teacher training is not required.

Initial teacher training has an optional element on special needs, and teachers in regular schools can attend various in-service training courses about different aspects of special needs. Teachers specializing in special education may need to travel abroad for extended training in special education but have in-service training opportunities within Cyprus (UNESCO 1995).

In-Service Teacher Training: The in-service teacher training (INSET) of primary and secondary school teachers is the task of the Pedagogical Institute. There is no school-based INSET, though the argument for such has been provided for some time. Optional courses provided by the Pedagogical Institute are the main kind offered by INSET. The seminars are primarily held in the afternoon and may be difficult for teachers to attend. Moreover, the decision to attend these courses seems to be purely individual, rather than as part of an educational plan or building team outcome. This seems to support the interpretation that there is a lack of coherent educational planning in each school (Kyriakides 1999).

All secondary teachers must undergo in-service training during the first year of their probationary period. This compulsory training is provided by the Pedagogical Institute. Reduced teaching hours accommodate the weekly training. While the 1997 UNESCO report, ''Appraisal Study on the Cyprus Education System,'' reported that INSET offered a balance between pedagogical considerations and subject teaching, Kyriakides's 1999 review of the model contested this claim because curriculum change and curriculum reform were not included. In addition, topics like school effectiveness and school improvement were not offered. Kyriakides called for professional development that linked teachers to the process of curriculum change.

In November 1999 the Ministry of Education and Culture, committed to the upgrading of educational provisions in public schools in Cyprus, organized an international workshop called The Teaching of Modern Languages to Mixed Ability Classes. The workshop, organized in collaboration with the European Center of Modern Languages of the Council of Europe (in Graz, Austria), with the assistance of the British Council, Goethe Institute, and other organizations, was held in November 1999 in Nicosia. It was attended by 25 delegates from European countries with 15 local participants, mainly foreign language teachers at the secondary level. The aims of the workshop were to provide participants with input regarding the nature of mixed ability teaching and the key elements involved; examine the complex interaction of pupils, teachers, and materials in instruction so as to promote effective learning and teaching strategies; explore ways of assessing learners' performance in mixed ability classes; and encourage the exchange of relevant ideas and successful practices among foreign language teachers (Christodoulou 1999).

The Minister of Education and Culture, Ouranios Loannides, addressed the 30th session of the UNESCO General Conference (October to November 1999) in Paris. Cyprus has been a member of this organization since 1961 and has participated actively in its programs in the fields of education, science, and culture. In his address, the minister referred to Major Areas of the Proposed Program for the period 1999-2001. Concerning Major Program I, which deals with education for all throughout life, Loannides pointed out that illiteracy on the island has been eradicated, with attendance in primary and secondary education at 100 percent while approximately 60 percent of school graduates continue their studies beyond secondary level. Measures have been adopted for enhancing adult education, such as evening schools, institutes for further education, and an open university. Concerning Major Program II, which deals with the sciences in the service of development, the minister reported that a new type of school will be introduced where time allocated to science education is increased and more emphasis is placed on experimental and practical work (Christodoulou 1999).

SUMMARY

Cyprus entered the twenty-first century as a divided nation state. Nearly three decades of ethnic conflict are symbolized in its divided capitol city, Nicosia. The United Nations peacekeeping forces stationed in Cyprus are a daily reminder to a generation that has suffered the pain of the Cyprus conflict. The effect of this ethnic conflict on students and the educational process is hard to understand or measure. The necessity for further research into the psychological effects of ethnic and political conflicts on children in general, and in Cyprus in particular, has been emphasized (Charalambous 2001; Erduran 1996; Ladd and Cairns 1996). The situation of the children of some 200,000 refugees is particularly vulnerable.

Though Cyprus cannot be characterized as a multilingual society, it has many small ethnic communities living permanently on the island, less permanent groups who live on the island for economic reasons but do not

have their own language schools, and repatriated Cypriots who rely on state schools for their children's education. The monolingual Greek Cypriot educational system needs to be considered in the evaluation of the academic success of these students, particularly those who are bilingual and multilingual.

The division of Cyprus has impacted the languages of instruction. The political decision to offer foreign languages but not the language of the other major ethnic group on the island provides a stumbling block for dialogue between the Greek Cypriot and Turkish Cypriot communities. The increase in mixed-ethnic marriages and the addition of other ethnic groups and respective ethnic languages heightens the need for additional study and consideration of the official languages of instruction and the offering of foreign languages in Cypriot schools.

Representatives from the educational system could be sending teachers and sharing ideas with developing countries. As Bradshaw noted (1993), the educational system in Cyprus has distinguished itself in the following areas: highly qualified and sought after graduates of both gymnasium and technical/vocational programs, with top students continuing to study abroad after completion of secondary programs; well-established, ongoing curriculum development; and foremost skills in the translation of technical manuscripts, textbooks, and materials into the modern Greek language.

Based on the Bradshaw's (1993) experiences in Cyprus, the following suggestions were made to reduce tension between the two Cypriot communities and to enhance the quality of technical education: use a neutral language for instruction, perhaps English; free the technical school curriculum from religious education and allocate time for religious education for each student while having it taught within the religious communities of the family's choice by qualified religion teachers; free the technical school curriculum from ethnic history with provisions for historical background to be delivered outside the technical school curriculum and facilities; and develop a counseling program specifically designed to identify individual student weaknesses, prepare individual educational plans to address these deficiencies, and place students in classes where each has the opportunity to maximize his or her educational experience.

Regarding Bradshaw's first recommendation, Coufoudakis (2001) cautioned that Bradshaw's recommendations do not recognize either the educational traditions of the island or the political realities as they exist. Similar recommendations have been made for other divided ethnic societies, and were even made for countries like Germany during the Cold War. How could a bicommunal country like Cyprus abandon its traditional languages and opt for English? Recommendations of this type reflect a lack of understanding of the cultural foundations of societies (personal communication, March 15, 2001).

Curriculum change should be based on a two-way relationship of pressure and support and continuous negotiation between the center and the periphery which will amount to both top-down and bottom-up influences (Fullan 1993; Turnbull 1985). Both educational theory and teachers' perceptions should be taken into account by policymakers when they attempt to design and/or evaluate the national curriculum. The new model of curriculum change should also advocate the need for both national and local curricula. The new role of teachers will encourage both professional autonomy and self-motivated development that have been seen as significant sources of curriculum change (Kyriakides 1999). Finally, a close relationship between initial and in-service training with curriculum policy does not exist in Cyprus, but is required (Kyriakides 1999).

Koyzis (1997) has highlighted several poignant questions that require ongoing consideration as Cyprus evolves its educational policy: "What is the nature of Cypriot society? Should this be perceived as an extension of Greek society? Or rather is it unique and pluralistic enough to be able to be considered as a separate entity?" In addition to these questions should be added the challenge highlighted by Anastasiou (1995): the needs and future of tertiary education in Cyprus so that a planned development of Cyprus can occur.

The creation around the world of nation-states as political entities has relied greatly on the institutional socialization of the masses; state-controlled education has provided the major means of accomplishing the goal. Through homogenization, or the perception of sameness, a uniform account of history, culture, and national identity can be promoted. The division in Cyprus has made such homogenization difficult, as participants in and observers of the process explain that the focus has been on the differences rather than the similarities that have bound the communities of Cyprus together (Charalambous 2001; Gellner 1983; Hobsbawm 1990; Spyrou 2000).

"Teaching students in separate Greek and Turkish schools was perhaps one of the greatest errors in the recent history of the island" (Loizos 1974; Spyrou 2000). Furthermore, "the continuing division of the island is a testament to the thorough success of these curricula" (Charalambous 2001). Yet another scholar adds that, "if present difficulties are to be overcome—and the key to their solution probably lies far from Cyprus, as far away as Washington and Moscow—it will once again play its historic role as a bridge between east and west" (Browning 1990). Discourse regarding education in Cyprus needs to be founded on the awareness of curriculum as

"a political document 'that reflects the struggles of opposing groups to have their interests, values, histories, and politics dominate the school curriculum' fully applies in the case of Cyprus" (Koutselini-Ioannidou 1997).

The challenge for educators in the twenty-first century is to provide an education system that facilitates overcoming these difficulties—to promote tolerance, understanding, and respect as educators prepare future generations of citizens to lead meaningful lives in a globally interconnected, interdependent universe.

BIBLIOGRAPHY

Anastasiou, Nicholas. "Cyprus Tertiary Education: Continuity and Innovation." *Journal of Business and Society 8(1)* (1995): 28-46.

Bradshaw, Larry L. "Technical Education in Cyprus." *International Journal of Educational Reform 2* (July 1993): 279-285.

Browning, Robert. In *The Making of Modern Cyprus, from Obscurity to Statehood.* Stavros Panteli, ed. Herts, England: Interworld Publications, 1990.

Charalambous, Andreas. "Foreword...Bridging the Gap: Inclusion, Representation, and Communication in School Curricula." *Journal of Critical Inquiry Into Curriculum and Instruction 2* (2001): 4-5.

Christodoulou, Christina. *Cyprus Today.* Nicosia, Cyprus: Press and Information Office, July-December, 1999.

Creemers, Bert T., and N. Osinga. *International Congress for School Effectiveness and Improvement (ICSEI) Country Reports.* Leeuwarden, the Netherlands: GCO, 1995.

Cuttance, Peter. *Frameworks for Research on the Effects of Schooling.* In *Studying School Effectiveness.* D. Reynolds, ed. Lewes: Falmer Press, 1985.

Cyprus. *About Cyprus: Education,* 2001. Available from http://www.pio.gov.cy/.

Department of Statistics and Research. *Statistics of Education, 1994-1995.* Nicosia, Cyprus, 1995.

Elefteriades, Andreas. "Academic Accreditation in Cyprus: Myth and Reality." *Journal of Business and Society 8(1995).*

Georgiou, S. N. "Parental Involvement in Cyprus." *International Journal of Educational Research 25(1): 33-43.*

Hadjikyriacou, Ritsa Maria. "Science Education in Cyprus: The Primary School Curriculum." *Science Education International 10 (4 1999): 11-12.*

Holmes, B., and M. McLean. *The Curriculum: A comparative perspective.* London: Unwin Hymen.

Huber, Tonya. "Saint Helena." In *The Ancient World: Dictionary of World Biography* (1998): 375-377.

Katsonis, Costas, and Tonya Huber. "Cyprus: A Small Suffering Island." *Multicultural Education 5* (Summer, 1998): 20-22.

Koutselini-Ioannidou, Mary. "Curriculum as Political Text: The Case of Cyprus (1935-90)." *History of Education 26*(4 1997): 395-407.

Koyzis, Anthony A. "Private Higher Education in Cyprus: In Search of Legitimacy." *Higher Education Policy 2* (1989): 13-19.

———. "The University of Cyprus: Questions and Future Implications." *International Review of Education 39*(5 1993): 435-438.

———. "State, Society, and Higher Education in Cyprus: A Study in Conflict and Compromise." *Mediterranean Journal of Educational Studies 2* (1997): 103-117.

Kyriakides, Leonidas. "The Management of Curriculum Improvement in Cyprus: A Critique of a 'Centre-periphery' Model in a Centralized System." In *Third Millenium Schools: A World of Difference in Effectiveness and Improvement.* Tony Townsend, Paul Clarke, and Mel Ainscow, eds., 107-124. Lisse, the Netherlands: Swets and Zeitlinger, 1999.

Loizos, Peter. "The progress of Greek nationalism in Cyprus, 1878-1970." In *Choice and Change: Essays in Honour of Lucy Mair, London School of Economics Monographs on Social Anthropology.* No. 50. John Davis, ed., 114-133. London: London School of Economics, 1974.

Maratheftis, M. I. *The Cypriot Educational System.* Nicosia, Cyprus, 1992.

Marcou, Costas. *Secondary Education in Cyprus: Guide to Secondary Education in Europe.* English ed. Croton-on-Hudson, NY: Manhattan Publishing Company, 1997. (ERIC Document Reproduction Service No. ED 417 468).

McClelland, Charles. *State, Society and University in Germany 1700-1914.* New York: Cambridge University Press, 1980.

Menon, Maria. "The Demand for Higher Education in Northern Cyprus: An Educational Policy Perspective." *Higher Education in Cyprus 10*(1 1997): 31-39.

Network Information Center. *The University of Cyprus,* 1996. Available from http://www.ucy.ac.cy/.

Orphanides, A. G. "A Need for Reforms in Tertiary Education." *Philelephtheros* 5 March 1995.

———. "Cyprus." In *International Encyclopedia of National Systems of Education.* 2nd. ed. T. Neville Postelwaite, ed., 250-57. Oxford, UK: Oxford Press, 1995.

Papanastasiou, Constantinos and Elena Papanastasiou. "Factors that Influence Students to Become Teachers." *Educational Research and Evaluation 3* (1997): 305-16.

Papapaviou, Andreas N. "Academic Achievement, Language Proficiency and Socialisation of Bilingual Children in a Monolingual Greek Cypriot-speaking School Evironment." *International Journal of Bilingual Education and Bilingualism 2* (1999): 252-67.

Persianis, Panayiotis. *The Political and Economic Factors as the Main Determinants of Educational Policy in Independent Cyprus (1960-1970).* Nicosia, Cyprus: The Pedagogical Institute, 1981.

———. "The British Colonial Education 'Lending' Policy in Cyprus (1878-1960): An Intriguing Example of an Elusive 'Adapted Education.' Policy." *Comparative Education 32*(1 1996a): 45-68.

———. "Higher Education and State Legitimation in Cyprus." *Mediterranean Journal of Educational Studies 4* (2 1999): 51-68.

Persianis, Panayiotis, ed. "The Epistemological Traditions of Cyprus and the European Challenge." In *The Education of Cyprus Before the European Challenge.* Nicosia, Cyprus, 1996b.

Persianis, Panayiotis and G. Polyviou. *History of Education in Cyprus.* Nicosia, Cyprus: The Pedagogical Institute, 1992.

Phtiaka, H. "Each to His Own? Home-School Relations." *Cyprus Forum of Education 51*(1 1996): 47-59.

Reilly, David H. "Rural Education in the Republic of Cyprus." *Journal of Rural and Small Schools 4* (1 1989): 44-51.

TERENA. *Activity Plan 2001.* 2001. Available from http://www.terena.nl/.

———. *Information Index.* 2001. Available from http://www.terena.nl/.

Townsend, Tony, Paul Clarke, and Mel Ainscow, eds. *Third Millenium Schools: A World of Difference in Effectiveness and Improvement.* Lisse, the Netherlands: Swets and Zeitlinger, 1999.

UNESCO. *Appraisal Study on the Cyprus Education System.* Paris, France: IIEP, 1997.

———. *Review of the Present Situation in Special Needs Education.* Paris, France: Author, 1995.

Weir, William W. *Education in Cyprus, Some Theories and Practices in Education in the Island of Cyprus Since 1878.* Nicosia, Cyprus: Cosmos Press, 1952.

—*Tonya Huber*

CZECH REPUBLIC

BASIC DATA

Official Country Name:	Czech Republic
Region:	Europe
Population:	10,272,179
Language(s):	Czech
Literacy Rate:	99.9%
Academic Year:	September-June
Number of Primary Schools:	4,889
Compulsory Schooling:	9 years
Public Expenditure on Education:	5.1%
Foreign Students in National Universities:	3,901
Libraries:	7,435
Educational Enrollment:	Primary: 541,671
	Secondary: 1,190,725
	Higher: 191,604
Educational Enrollment Rate:	Primary: 104%
	Secondary: 99%
	Higher: 24%
Teachers:	Primary: 28,356
	Secondary: 114,373
	Higher: 19,769
Student-Teacher Ratio:	Primary: 19:1
	Secondary: 12:1
Female Enrollment Rate:	Primary: 103%
	Secondary: 100%
	Higher: 23%

HISTORY & BACKGROUND

Geography: The Czech Republic (*Ceska Republika*) is a constitutional parliamentary democracy established in 1993 when the Czech and Slovak Federation ("Czechoslovakia") peacefully separated into two independent states, the Czech Republic and Slovakia. The country sits in Central Europe to the southeast of Germany. Measuring 78,866 square kilometers—slightly smaller than the U.S. state of South Carolina—the landlocked Czech Republic is bordered by Germany to the northwest and west,

Poland to the northeast, Slovakia to the southeast, and Austria to the south. With cool summers and cold, cloudy, humid winters, the Czech Republic has an average summer temperature of 20 degrees Celsius and an average winter temperature of 5 degrees Celsius. Bohemia, the western part of the Czech Republic, has a terrain of plains, hills, and plateaus bordered by low-lying mountains; Moravia, the eastern part of the country, has a very hilly landscape. The point of highest elevation in the Czech Republic is Mt. Snezka, measuring 1,602 meters above sea level; the lowest point is at Hoensko on the Elbe River (*Labe*), where the elevation is just 117 meters. Forty-one percent of the land in the country is arable, about 2 percent is planted with permanent crops, about one-third of the country is covered with forests and woodlands, and the remaining area includes significant pastureland.

Cultural Background & History: With a population of about 10.3 million in the year 2000, the Czech Republic is composed of diverse peoples from the lands of Central Europe and elsewhere. In March 1991 estimates of the ethnic background of the country's population yielded the following: 81.2 percent Czech, 13.2 percent Moravian, 3.1 percent Slovak, and less than 1 percent each of the Roma, Polish, German, Silesian, Hungarian, and other minorities. Since these estimates the size and proportion of ethnic groups has changed to some extent, with some Slovaks choosing to relocate to Slovakia after the 1993 split and a number of Roma ("Gypsies") leaving the country due to widespread segregation, discrimination, and racist actions directed against them. In the year 2000 about 200,000 to 250,000 Roma were living in the Czech Republic, some 10,000 having left the country between 1997 and 2000. Concerning the religious affiliation of the Czech Republic's population in the 1990s, the estimated breakdown of the population was about 39.8 percent atheist, 39.2 percent Roman Catholic, 4.6 percent Protestant, 3.0 percent Orthodox, and 13.4 percent other.

The Czech Republic emerged as an independent state only in 1993, but the Czech people and most of the ethnic minority groups composing the country's current population have lived in the territory now known as the Czech Republic for centuries. Strategically poised as an historical gateway for traders and military campaigners crossing Europe and Asia, the Czech Republic dates its earliest recorded history with the arrival of the Celts around the fourth century B.C., nearly two and a half millennia ago. The country's Latin name, *Boiohaemum*, or Bohemia, came from the name the Celtic Boii tribe gave the area. The Celts were later pushed out by Germanic tribes, the Marcomanni and Quidi.

In the late-fifth and early-sixth centuries, the Slavs arrived in what is now Moravia and Slovakia during a time known as the "Migration of Peoples." Slavonic tribes were united in the first half of the seventh century under "Samo's kingdom" of Slavs, who successfully protected themselves from advances by the Avar empire of the Hungarian lowlands and partly defended themselves from attacks by the Franks from the west. In 863 Byzantine Christian missionaries came to the region, by then known as the Great Moravian Empire. It was attacked and destroyed by the Magyars from 903 to 907.

The Roman Catholic Church, becoming more influential in Europe, spread into the region over the next few centuries. However, the growing Czech state, centered in Bohemia and governed by the native Premyslid Dynasty from the ninth century until 1306, preserved its sovereignty while developing feudal ties to the Holy Roman Empire. In 1212 the Bohemian sovereign, Premysl Otakar I, received the Golden Bull of Sicily, a decree announcing Bohemia's status as a kingdom and the Bohemian princes as hereditary kings. One of the Holy Roman Empire's most important states, Bohemia was governed by the Luxembourg Dynasty from 1310 until 1437 and reached the zenith of its power under Charles IV, who reigned from 1346 to 1378.

Prompted by political, economic, and religious crises in the late-fourteenth and early-fifteenth centuries, a religious movement known as the Hussite reform movement emerged, inspired by Master Jan Hus, a preacher later executed in 1415 for his allegedly heretical preaching. From 1420 until 1431 the Roman Emperor Sigismund, heir to the Bohemian crown, attempted to subdue the religious reformers by force. The Hussite revolution ended in 1434 with the victory of religious moderates and an agreement between Hussite Bohemia and Catholic Europe in 1436 known as the "Compacts of Basle," which paved the way for the Protestant Reformation of the sixteenth century by establishing the validity of an alternative form of Christian practice.

In the second half of the fifteenth century Bohemia grew increasingly politically unsettled. With the emergence of George of Podebrady, a Czech noble whose diplomatic skills enabled the European sovereigns to form a peaceful confederation and who was elected King of Bohemia in 1458, the Czech nation and culture exerted significant influence on European cultural and political life. From 1471 until 1526 Bohemia was ruled by the Jagellon Dynasty. By 1526 the Habsburgs had taken the throne of Bohemia, reintroduced Roman Catholicism to the region, and formed a multinational empire that included the Crownlands of Bohemia. The Habsburg Dynasty would last for nearly three centuries, until the end of the First World War in 1918.

Despite the long reign of the Habsburgs, a Czech national revival movement gradually emerged over time.

Beginning with an attempt to revive the Czech language and culture, the movement gradually gained strength in the nineteenth century and looked toward the political freedom of the Czechs. The movement gained momentum during Europe's revolutionary year of 1848, when much of Europe was in political turmoil as capitalism dramatically reshaped social and economic relations and the protests of workers unwilling to tolerate their miserable conditions echoed around the industrial world. By the end of the nineteenth century, Bohemia, quick to industrialize, had become the most economically developed country of the Habsburg Dynasty.

During the First World War, Czech politics became more radical under the leadership of T.G. Masaryk and E. Genes, each of them later becoming president of the Czechoslovak Republic, which was founded in 1918 after the defeat of Austria-Hungary in World War I. As an independent state, the Czechoslovak Republic became one of the ten most highly developed countries in the world. For 20 years the country prospered, until Hitler's invasion in March 1939, the German occupation, the Holocaust, and the Second World War. The Jews of Czechoslovakia, once among the most active intellectuals, political figures, business people, and supporters of the arts in Bohemia, were essentially erased from the country during Hitler's murderous rampage. In October 1941, just two and a half years after the March 1939 Nazi take-over of Czechoslovakia, the Jews of Czechoslovakia numbered about 80,000. By April 1945, after the genocide that specifically targeted Jews, Roma, and other minority peoples, fewer than 8,000 Jews remained.

After the Second World War, Czechoslovakia came under the Soviet sphere of influence, and the brief period of "limited democracy" the country enjoyed after the war ended in February 1948 with a Communist takeover. Private property was confiscated and nationalized, and human rights were widely abused, particularly with the Soviet Army's invasion in 1968 and the reassertion of Soviet control following a brief respite known as the "Prague Spring." During the 1980s, with decaying economic conditions in the Soviet Union and the weakening of Soviet power, advocates of democracy and human rights in Czechoslovakia and other Soviet satellite countries directed their efforts towards the political and economic transformation of their countries. The efforts of the peoples of the Czech and Slovak Federation culminated in their freeing themselves from Communist rule in 1989, followed soon after by the smooth creation of two independent countries on 1 January 1993: the Czech Republic and Slovakia. After gaining independence, the Czech Republic moved rapidly to liberalize its centralized economy and to decentralize its public bureaucracy.

Social Conditions: Approximately 75 percent of the Czech Republic's population of 10.3 million in 1999 lived in urban areas, the largest of which is Prague (*Praha*), the capital city, which alone had a population of 1.2 million inhabitants by the year 2000. With an average population density of 133 persons per square kilometer, the Czech Republic had a rural population density of just 84 persons per square kilometer in 1998. During the 1990s the country's population decreased slightly, and by 1999 the population growth rate was zero percent. In 1990 about 10,330,000 people lived in the Czech Republic; by 1997 the population had declined to about 10,304,000. About 31.3 percent of the population in 1997 was of school age (between 3 and 24 years old). The total fertility rate in the Czech Republic in 1999 was one—that is, a woman bearing children for her entire child-bearing years at the current fertility rate would produce only one child. Approximately 16 percent of the population in the year 2000 was 14 years old or younger while 70 percent was between 15 and 64 years of age and about 14 percent of the population was 65 or older. The Czech Republic had an infant-mortality rate of 4.6 per 1000 live births in 1999 and an under 5 years child-mortality rate of 5 per 1000 that year. The life expectancy at birth of the population in the year 2000 was about 74.5 years (71.0 for men and 78.2 for women). In 1995 the adult literacy rate was estimated to be about 95 percent. Specific literacy rates for adult men and women were not available as of early 2001, but the adult population was said to be almost completely literate in 1999.

Economic Status: For centuries the territory now known as the Czech Republic had a primarily agricultural economy based on forestry, livestock-rearing, and family farms. With the arrival of the industrial age in Europe, Czechoslovakia's economy shifted to a more industrial base, and the country became one of the most industrialized countries in Europe by the first decades of the twentieth century. In the 1930s private agricultural enterprise still contributed strongly to the national economy, but Czechoslovakia was a net importer of agricultural products. The Communist-dominated era lasted from 1948 to 1989, except for the short hiatus of the "Prague Spring" in 1968 when liberal Czech reformers temporarily succeeded at freeing up the country's economic and political life before the Soviets reasserted their control through a military invasion. Under the Communists the economy was centrally controlled and depended on the outputs of large, nationalized heavy industry and engineering firms. Nonetheless, under Communist control, Czechoslovakia's collectivized farms produced higher agricultural yields than did any of the other socialist countries. Agricultural yields in Czechoslovakia were lower, however, than in Western European countries where more modern agricultural methods were used.

In 1989 the Communists lost power in what has been termed the country's "Velvet Revolution." During the

transition from Communism to democratic independence between 1989 and 1993, the country's agricultural sector continued to diminish in importance. Agriculture's contribution to the GDP declined from 6 to 4.7 percent between 1990 and 1994, and the percent of the civilian workforce employed in agriculture shrank from 10 to 6.9 percent during that period. The Czech Republic also witnessed a gradual shift in the agricultural sector during the 1990s from animal to crop production. By 1998 only 5.5 percent of the civil labor force was employed in agriculture or about 267,000 persons. Because many agricultural workers shifted to non-agricultural jobs during the transition period, the agricultural sector came to operate more efficiently and its productivity increased, exceeding that of over two-thirds of the European Union's 15 member states.

With the change from a state-controlled, centrally planned economy to a more-liberalized production and marketing regime, the Czech Republic in the 1990s dismantled its large-scale, state-owned industrial enterprises and enacted legislation enabling small and medium scale private industries and enterprises to flourish. This change came about rather gradually, however, with the privatization of national assets taking place at a slower pace than initially had been anticipated and the economic gains of the early 1990s slowing significantly by the middle of the decade. In 1997 the national currency was devalued in an attempt to halt significant economic setbacks, though the deliberate measures taken by the World Bank and the national government made these setbacks relatively temporary. During the 1990s foreign investors and firms entered the newly liberalized Czech marketplace and introduced significant investments into the industrial sector. Business people in the Czech Republic developed many joint venture and contractual agreements with foreign investors, mainly the EU partners—especially Austria and Germany. At the same time, rapid growth in the tourist industry contributed to a shift towards greater employment in the service sector where the number of persons employed increased from 39.4 percent to 53.5 percent of the active civil labor force between 1990 and 1997. In 1997 about 32 percent of the labor force was employed in industry, 8.7 percent in construction, 46.8 percent in service jobs (excluding communications), 6.9 percent in communications, and 5.6 percent in agriculture.

The GDP at market prices in U.S. dollars was about $53.1 billion in 1999, with about 5 percent of the GDP derived from agriculture, 42 percent from industry, and 53 percent from services. The national economy became relatively stagnant by the late 1990s, despite a promising start in the nation's transition to a liberalized economy at the beginning of the 1990s. Whereas the economic growth rate was 6 percent of the GDP in 1995, by 1999 the growth rate was a negative half percent of GDP; annual per-capita income in 1999 was only US$5,020, a drop of $250 from the 1997 figure of $5,270. Much of the economic decline was related to the currency crisis that precipitated in May 1997 and the government's inability to spur economic growth despite two austerity packages introduced in the spring of 1997. In the late 1990s persistent and excessive government controls on the newly privatized national economy continued to negatively impact the country's economic situation. In 1999 the net inflow of foreign direct investment was US$5.1 trillion but the debt value was US$22.5 trillion. Imported goods and services that year were equivalent to 65 percent of the GDP, exceeding the value of exported goods and services by 1 percent of the GDP.

A special government economic revitalization program was begun in 1999 that involved the restructuring of enterprises and the improvement of management styles, and at the close of the 1990s, the economy of the Czech Republic had begun a slow recovery. The unemployment rate in the Czech Republic in 1999 was roughly 9 percent with the highest unemployment rates seen among persons with only a primary school education (13.4 percent of the unemployed in 1997). This rate was significantly higher than the country's unemployment rate in the mid-1990s when the general economic situation was considerably rosier and many optimistic analysts of transitional economies looked to the Czech Republic as a role model for other former-Communist states undergoing the transition from state-controlled to liberal market economies. However, unemployment was lower than in a number of other European countries at the time.

CONSTITUTIONAL & LEGAL FOUNDATIONS

The Czech Republic is a parliamentary democracy established by the Constitution ratified on 16 December 1992 that became effective 1 January 1993 with the country's formal separation from Slovakia. The Czech Republic has a legal system based on Austro-Hungarian civil codes dating from the years when the country was ruled by the Habsburg monarchy.

Political Participation: All citizens of the Czech Republic 18 years and older are eligible to vote; men are also eligible for military service at that age. At the national level of government, the chief of state is the president, who is democratically elected to a five-year term of office by the Parliament and is eligible for reelection just once consecutively. The executive branch of the national government also includes a prime minister, deputy ministers, and a cabinet of ministers, appointed by the president upon the prime minister's recommendation. Since 2 February 1993 the president of the Czech Republic has been

Václav Havel, an ardent supporter of democracy and human rights during the Communist era and one of the country's key campaigners for a more liberal, democratic state. Havel was re-elected as president in 1998 for a second five-year term. Any citizen of the country who has attained the age of 40 and is an active voter is eligible to run for election as president.

At the national level the legislative branch consists of a bicameral Parliament (*Parlament*) consisting of a Senate (*Senat*) of 81 members elected by popular vote for 6 year terms in office and a Chamber of Deputies (*Poslanicka Snemovna*) of 200 seats whose members are popularly elected for 4 year terms. Any citizen of the Czech Republic who is at least 21 years old is eligible to run for election to the Chamber of Deputies; the minimum age for Senators is 40 years. The third branch of the national government, the judicial branch, consists of the Supreme Court, which is the highest court of appeal, and the Constitutional Court, which has final decision-making authority regarding the constitutionality of legislation. Courts exist at district, regional, and higher levels. Since 1998 with the implementation of a new regional administrative system, sub-national affairs have been administered through a network of 14 regions, 86 districts (*okresi*), and 6,200 municipalities.

Despite the progress made in the Czech Republic during the 1990s in popular participation in government and the vastly improved climate for the free expression of secular and religious beliefs, international human rights organizations and agencies such as Human Rights Watch, Amnesty International, and the U.S. Department of State's Bureau of Democracy, Human Rights, and Labor identified significant human-rights problems in the Czech Republic in the year 2000. For the most part, these problems centered around the trafficking of women and children, gender discrimination and violence, ethnic discrimination and racist violence (especially against the Roma), and infringements on the rights of employees (particularly senior-level executives) who often were required to produce "lustration" or vetting certificates to prove their non-collaboration with the former Communist regime. Although the legal system guarantees women equal rights with men, in practice many women (reportedly almost half the female workforce, including female soldiers) frequently face sexual harassment in the workplace and about one in ten women is subject to domestic abuse. A 1998 study found that about 13 percent of women had been forced to have sex against their will; 51 percent of the abusers were the women's husbands or partners and another 37 percent were persons known to the women who were raped. Legal protection from spousal abuse is inadequate, although the Police Academy and secondary police schools in 1998 introduced training for their students and officers designed to help officers better identify victims of abuse and treat victims more appropriately. Additionally, women typically earn wages lower than those of men because women often are channeled into lower-paying, gender-stereotyped jobs. Few women in the Czech Republic hold high-level management positions in business, and women are significantly underrepresented in the Ministries and in Parliament. In December 2000, for example, none of the 16 government ministers was a woman and of the 200 members of the Chamber of Deputies and the 81 members of the Senate, only 30 deputies were women and only 10 senators were female.

The problems of the Roma minority are equally serious. Long an ethnic minority traveling through and residing in Central Europe, the Roma continued to face very serious human rights abuses in the Czech Republic in the year 2000 in the form of education and employment discrimination, racist attacks, residential segregation, rampant prejudice, and discriminatory treatment, sometimes condoned by government officials and the police. Human Rights Watch declared in their World Report 2001, concerning the problem of racial violence in the Czech Republic, that despite certain encouraging steps taken by the government in the year 2000 to confront these abuses, "increasing racial violence against the ethnic Roma minority demonstrated an alarming pattern of neglect on the part of police and legal authorities to investigate and prosecute hate crime. This pattern included lenient sentences for perpetrators of hate crimes, incompetent and protracted investigations, and little recourse for victims who in many cases feared reprisals."

As in many other European countries, violence against the Romani people and other minorities has increased since the break-up of the Communist system, and in the Czech Republic, prejudice against the Roma is held by many groups. As the U.S. State Department's Bureau of Democracy, Human Rights, and Labor reported in early 2001, "Roma suffer disproportionately from poverty, unemployment, interethnic violence, discrimination, illiteracy, and disease. They are subject to popular prejudice, as is affirmed repeatedly by public opinion polls. Nearly 65 percent of the respondents in a September [2000] opinion poll admitted to an unfavorable opinion of Roma and to racial intolerance, with more than 50 percent saying that there were too many non-Czechs living in the country."

By the start of the new millennium, the Czech Republic's government was attempting to address these problems more actively by establishing a Human Rights Council headed by a Commissioner for Human Rights. The Council was set up in January 2000 to provide the government with advice on human-rights issues and to develop proposals for legislation oriented toward protecting human rights in the country. In December 2000 former Justice Minister Otakar Motejl was named Ombudsman for Human Rights by the Parliament.

Developments concerning interethnic and international relations of a more-positive sort also have taken place from the 1990s on. The Czech Republic now participates in numerous regional and international organizations, including NATO. The country is expected to become one of the first former-Communist states of Eastern and Central Europe to accede to membership in the European Union (although a setback occurred when a majority of the Irish people voted in June 2001 not to extend EU membership to states beyond the EU's current 15 members). To a significant extent the Czech Republic served as a model in the early 1990s for other post-communist states, setting precedents for economic reforms where unemployment was kept low and inflation did not skyrocket. The country became one of the first in the region to free up government assets by selling off nationalized industries to foreign investors and to move toward decentralizing its economy. Receiving international assistance in the form of grants, loans, and technical advisors to assist in the transition from a state-controlled, centralized economy to a free-market-based economy and to make further democratic reforms, the Czech Republic officially became a member of the World Bank in 1993 when it separated from Slovakia (already having received a sizable Structural Adjustment Loan from the Bank amounting to US$300 million in 1991). Additional World Bank loans have helped the Czech Republic restructure its economy, privatize industries, and provide greater management training and support to executives seeking to manage enterprises in a dramatically transformed, privatized environment.

Educational Philosophy & Policy: With the split from the Soviet system in 1989 and again shortly after the break with Slovakia in 1993, the Czech Republic's government leaders began efforts to upgrade the quality of the country's education system and to ensure that education and training programs would be more responsive to labor market demands. Under the centralized Communist system, the goal of education had been to produce a uniform workforce narrowly trained in the specific skills needed for particular trades and occupations. The goal of the teacher remuneration system was to maintain a roughly similar wage structure for all those employed in the teaching field. Budgeting and management in education also were to be uniformly performed. As the country has shifted to a free-market-based economy and more democratic functioning, the Czech Republic has sought to develop better programs for preparing a more broadly trained workforce with flexible capabilities applicable across occupations and industries, including newly developing fields. Furthermore, developing a skillful set of teachers able to implement modern teaching methodology has become a priority, and new recruits to the teaching field are very much needed. The country may succeed at training sufficient numbers of new teachers only if the wages for jobs in the education field can be increased, which may be accomplished more easily through private investments in education. Attracting support from the business community—for example, from enterprises wishing to sponsor particular training and retraining or continuing education programs for current or future employees—has been seen as a necessary means to developing a more-skilled labor force in the teaching area that is ready to meet the needs of incoming classes of students.

Additionally, a major goal of educational administrators and school managers in the Czech Republic starting in the 1990s and becoming even more sharply accentuated around the year 2000 has been to harmonize educational standards, examinations, and certificates— and to a certain extent, the training programs themselves—with European standards. As the Czech Republic prepared itself for membership in the European Union, increased attention was given to promoting exchanges of students, teachers, and professors across the EU and EU-affiliated countries and to fostering international cooperation among researchers. The Czech Republic participated actively in planning and implementing policies and legislative initiatives aimed at harmonizing training methods and education systems so the country would fit better into the EU system and could benefit from the information and personnel exchanges facilitated by membership in the EU.

Laws Affecting Education: The Constitution of 1993, the 1993 List of Basic Rights and Freedoms, and a series of education laws enacted in the decades leading up to independence and since independence provide the basic principles for the national education system's mission, structure, and operation. According to the List of Basic Rights and Freedoms, for example, everyone has the right to an education and school attendance is required for a certain legally stipulated period; citizens are allowed a free elementary and secondary education, and, based on individual abilities and societal resources, a higher education as well; non-state schools charging fees for educational services are permitted to operate only according to the conditions provided by law; and legislation specifies how citizens can receive educational assistance.

An education law passed in 1995 introduced a new method for managing education by sectors or professional fields and also established the responsibilities of the Ministry of Education, Youth, and Sports and other ministries with education-related functions. Previously, the Ministry of the Interior and the Communist Party had managed the country's education system. The 1995 law amended the Act on State Administration and Self-administration in the Education Sector and established the basis for an official "school network" (registry of schools) administered by the Ministry of Education in order to better determine school functions and manage school principals in a more-active way. Key laws pertaining to higher education before independence included the Acts Concerning Institutions of Higher Education of 1950, 1966, and 1980. However, with the democratic revision of governance after the break with the Soviets in 1989, Czechoslovakia passed a new Act on Institutions of Higher Education in 1990 to reestablish academic freedom (substantially denied under Communist rule) and to limit state influence on higher education. Another Higher Education Act was passed in 1998 to authorize the creation of private institutions of higher education while keeping higher education a state monopoly and the national budget the principal source of financial support. The 1998 act also clarified the role of the bachelor's degree as one culminating a course of study that could lead directly to a career as well as to more-advanced studies. In addition, it enabled schools to generate education funds from other sources, such as the charging of tuition fees.

EDUCATIONAL SYSTEM—OVERVIEW

In the Czech Republic the education system is divided into several levels and types of schools according to age and the kind of training provided. Preprimary education for children between the ages of 3 and 6 is optional, although there were about 6,400 kindergartens in the country in 1998. Compulsory, basic education is provided to pupils between the ages of 6 and 15, with pupils ages 6 to 11, 12, or 13 enrolled in primary schools and pupils 11, 12, or 13 to 15 enrolled in lower secondary schools or gymnasiums. Basic education schools numbered about 5,000 in 1998. Upper-secondary schools include vocational and technical schools as well as general-education schools (gymnasiums) for students extending to age 19, although some shorter programs in vocational education for students ages 15 to 17 also exist. Higher-education institutions of various types provide education and training opportunities for students between the ages of 19 and 22, 23, 24, 25, or 26, depending on the type of training course followed.

In the 1996-1997 school year about 2.2 million children and youth, out of the country's total population of about 10 million, were enrolled in educational institutions. Of these students, about 325,000 were preprimary children, 661,000 were primary pupils, 539,000 were lower secondary students, 513,000 were upper secondary students, and 196,000 were tertiary students. Fifty-two percent of all pupils and students of school age were of compulsory school age (that is, between 6 and 15 years old) or nearly 1.2 million people. About 1,627,500 primary and secondary students were enrolled in public schools and approximately 85,400 additional students went to private schools, which also received government subsidies for education. The total number of primary and secondary students, public and private, was therefore about 1,712,900.

The gross enrollment rate in 1995 for basic compulsory education (the first 9 grades of school) was 95 percent. In 1996 the student to teacher ratio for basic education was 14.5:1. Net enrollment rates were 86.9 percent at the primary level and 87.1 percent at the secondary level. Net enrollment rates for girls, 86.8 percent at the primary level and 88.6 percent at the secondary level, were almost the same as for boys, a tribute to efforts made during the Soviet era as well as in recent years to provide equal educational opportunities for both girls and boys. In fact, the enrollment rate at the secondary level is even a bit higher for girls than for boys.

During the 1990s the level of education of the general population increased, though by early 2001 a breakdown of the adult population in the country by educational attainment levels was not readily available. In 1990 the composition of the economically active adult population (i.e., those working, seeking jobs, or temporarily unemployed) was as follows: 18.7 percent had a primary education; 43.1 percent had a lower-secondary education, mostly through apprenticeship training and some of which had been acquired through technical-training programs; 27.7 percent had received higher-secondary education; and just 9.6 percent held university degrees. Through the improvements made in upper-secondary and postsecondary education and training programs by the turn of the millennium, these proportions were expected to gradually shift in favor of a more highly educated workforce.

International Influences & Foreign Languages: During the years the country belonged to the Soviet-controlled Communist satellite system where Moscow was the center of political affairs, the Czech Republic's government was structured as a centralized administrative system. For this reason the public education system in the Czech Republic at the time of independence was infused with many of the principles and structures of centralized, state-controlled socialist education systems. Since the early 1990s, however, education officials, specialists, and practitioners have taken significant steps toward molding the education system into a more responsive, democratic, decentralized system. By the year 2000 the European Union had a far more significant influence on the course of educational thought and structuring than any leftover influence from the Soviet era, at

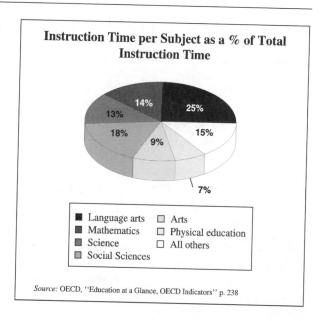

Instruction Time per Subject as a % of Total Instruction Time

Language arts — 25%
Mathematics — 15%
Science — 9%
Social Sciences — 7%
Arts — 18%
Physical education — 13%
All others — 14%

Source: OECD, "Education at a Glance, OECD Indicators" p. 238

least as far as the top-level educational officials were concerned. However, because about half of the teaching staff was middle-aged and had been trained before the 1989 break with the Soviet socialist system, Russian and socialist influence on the day-to-day practice of teaching undoubtedly was much stronger than ministry officials would have cared to admit. Nonetheless, educational reforms during the 1990s were substantial enough for the European Commission to write in an abstract of their October 1999 report on education in the Czech Republic that "the Czech Republic had achieved progress in this area by adopting legislation and participating in Community programmes." Their corresponding November 2000 report noted that the country "is continuing to make progress in implementing the legislation adopted in this field, particularly in education, training and participation in Community programmes. It has also made progress in the education of children from socially and culturally disadvantaged backgrounds, although the situation concerning the education of the children of migrant workers has not changed."

Since independence in 1993 Czech has been the only official language of the Czech Republic. However, more than a third of pupils in the primary grades learn a second language and more than half the students in the secondary grades learn second languages. Some primary and secondary students learn a third language, and some secondary students learn a fourth language as well. English and German appear to be far more commonly taught as second and/or third languages than any other non-Czech language at the primary and secondary levels.

Examinations: Students must pass an entrance exam before entering upper secondary-level education in the

Czech Republic. Those who fail to pass the entrance exam are allowed to continue their studies in vocational schools where one or two years of training are provided for basic manual occupations. Students in secondary general schools and secondary technical schools are permitted to take the *Maturita* exam at the conclusion of their secondary studies. However, because the individual schools administering the exams determine the content of the *Maturita* exams, it is difficult for institutions of higher education to compare students based on their performance on the *Maturita*. For this reason, students who pass the *Maturita* must take university entrance exams before they can enter the universities.

Private Schools: Private schools are a relatively new phenomenon in the Czech Republic, considering that all schools prior to the break with the Soviet system in 1989 were state-supported and state-controlled. Between 1990 and 1994 many non-state schools were started, particularly at the upper-secondary level, due to the unwillingness of a number of teachers to make schools reliant on market forces. By the end of the 1990s, private educational institutions included both parochial and non-sectarian schools, all of them eligible for state subsidies provided on a normative (per-pupil) basis, provided that the schools were registered with the government as private companies. In addition, private schools are allowed to request financial contributions from students and their parents for capital investments, since government funding to private schools only covers teacher salaries and operational costs. Competition among private schools has been encouraged, since the amount of subsidy a private school receives is based on the number of students it attracts; this in turn has improved the quality of private educational initiatives.

In terms of training programs available to adults, private initiatives have grown exponentially. By the year 2000 about 2,000 private training organizations were teaching adults new skills or upgrading existing practical and theoretical knowledge. Private training centers need only to be registered as companies to receive government funding, although accreditation by the Ministry of Education is required if educational certificates are to be awarded. With the shift to privatization in the economy and decentralization in schooling during the 1990s, businesses lost their apprentice and training centers attached to the state-supported system as well as certain financing they once received from the state to provide vocational and technical training. Consequently, private industry largely withdrew from financing vocational and technical education. However, by the year 2000, some companies once again had started to fund training programs, particularly those designed to prepare workers with specialized skills such as those needed in the automobile industry and in mining.

Instructional Technology: By the end of the 1990s, the Czech Republic was preparing to support new educational initiatives in computer technology to prepare a workforce better equipped for jobs in the high-technology sector. Although a national policy on the use of information and communications technology (ICT) in education was not yet in place by the 1997-98 school year, ICT courses were included at the lower-secondary level by that time, with ICT taught as a separate subject. ICT classes were taught as a compulsory separate subject in the first year of general upper-secondary education. At lower and upper secondary levels, specialists in ICT were employed to teach these classes. Objectives for ICT classes in secondary schools included developing programming skills in students; teaching them to use word processors, spreadsheets, and other computer software; teaching them to gather information using such tools as CDs and the Internet; and teaching students how to communicate via a network. The curriculum at the lower-secondary level also stressed the importance of information and the place of ICT in society.

Curriculum Development: Curricular innovations in the late 1990s were focused in particular on improving the quality of course offerings and training programs at the secondary level, especially in vocational education. Schools were given a certain measure of freedom to develop their own curricula in the directions they saw fit, with about 10 percent of the curriculum adaptable to local circumstances and about 30 percent of the syllabus changeable by the schools. In addition, schools could propose methods for modernizing curricula with regard to occupations and new sectors of employment. Before 1989 about 500 different curricula were developed by school initiatives and approved by the state for vocational instruction, whereas in the year 2000 over 800 different curricula developed by schools had been approved by the Ministry of Education. As private schools have entered the educational marketplace with the country's privatization efforts, competition for students has increased, resulting in competitive improvements in course offerings across the various schools providing vocational education. On the other hand, one obstacle to the smooth functioning and coordination of vocational programs that has emerged ironically is the ease with which new curricula can be approved by the Ministry, which has resulted in a proliferation of courses highly similar to existing courses and sometimes differing only in name from previous courses. The direct relevance of certain courses to specific occupations also is sometimes questionable, since the government no longer provides a generally accepted list of occupations for which training should be provided as was done in the days of socialist schooling.

Role of Education in Development: Clearly, education at all levels in the Czech Republic—for preprimary students through adults—can lead to an improved climate for economic development and democratic participation in civil society, which in turn engenders a higher quality of life and greater political stability. To this end, the World Bank, the European Union, the Soros Foundation, and other international nongovernmental organizations have provided substantial financial and technical assistance since the Czech Republic attained independence so that schools will become more responsive to the needs of children, youth, and adults in a greatly transformed society. As Peter Grootings, the author of a World Bank report on vocational education in the Czech Republic, wrote in March 2000, the educational experience of the Czech Republic presents several lessons with special relevance for transitional countries: 1) By encouraging private investment in education and limiting the labor supply through early retirements and the extension of schooling opportunities for youth, a better adjustment can be made in the national economy to a liberalized market regime; 2) Making vocational education more general and less terminal increases the appeal of vocational education institutions to students and draws more into this form of training, leading to a better-prepared workforce; 3) Maintaining low registered unemployment by tightening eligibility requirements for unemployment benefits controls public-training program budgets and prevents rampant spending from the national treasury to support workforce training initiatives; and 4) Setting favorable laws to encourage industrial growth encourages private industry to provide training opportunities for vocational students and adults without draining the public treasury.

PREPRIMARY & PRIMARY EDUCATION

While preprimary schooling was optional for young children below age six in the Czech Republic in 2001, primary education for children was, beginning at age six, compulsory. Nonetheless, many children of preprimary age were enrolled in education-oriented institutions, both privately supported and public. At the primary level most schools were supported by the state and under the Ministry of Education's jurisdiction. Primary schooling covered the first several grades of school, from ages 6 to 11, 12 or 13, depending on the age at which students entering gymnasiums chose to move on to the lower-secondary level.

In 1997 nearly 83 percent of three to five year olds were enrolled in preschools, a noticeable drop from the enrollment rate of 89.8 percent in 1989, the year Czechoslovakia broke from the Soviet system. In 1997 83 percent of 4 year olds and 90 percent of 5 year olds were enrolled in preprimary education. According to a 1999 World Bank report on the status of the Czech Republic

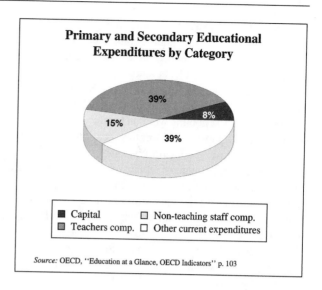

Primary and Secondary Educational Expenditures by Category

- ■ Capital
- □ Non-teaching staff comp.
- ▨ Teachers comp.
- □ Other current expenditures

Source: OECD, ''Education at a Glance, OECD Indicators'' p. 103

in various sectors as the country prepared for accession to the EU, preschool enrollments by 1996 were equivalent to those in most OECD countries and slightly higher than the preschool enrollment rate in any other Central European country.

About 104 percent of the school-age population in the year 2000 was enrolled in primary education, with gross enrollment rates at the primary level 105 percent for boys and 103 percent for girls. Classes generally ranged in size from 10 to 30 pupils each (sometimes more under exceptional circumstances). Most of the primary schools in the country by 2001 were created by and under the jurisdiction of the municipalities, which financed the schools primarily with subsidies received from the Ministry of Finance and from shares of centrally collected taxes.

SECONDARY EDUCATION

In 1995 nearly 87.1 percent of secondary age students were enrolled in lower and upper secondary school programs; 88.6 percent of secondary age girls were enrolled in secondary level educational programs. About 18.8 percent of the 15 to 18 year old age group was enrolled in general upper-secondary education in 1996, while two-thirds of students in this age group were enrolled in vocational or technical training programs. In 1996 approximately 22.1 percent of all students in the upper secondary grades (i.e., ages 15 and higher) were enrolled in general education, while 77.9 percent were enrolled in vocational and technical programs. In 1996-1997 about 538,900 students were enrolled in general education programs at the lower secondary level and only about 300 students were in lower secondary vocational education. For upper secondary students that year, about 31,000 male and 44,900 female students were enrolled in general education programs, and about 9,500 male students and 14,500 female students completed their general upper secondary education. Approximately 223,400 male and 213,200 female students studied in vocational programs in the 1996-1997 school year. As of 1998 at least 98 percent of all secondary level students who completed their compulsory schooling went on to study at the upper-secondary level, most of them in the vocational and technical streams. However, the proportion of students enrolling in the general stream of upper-secondary education (i.e., gymnasiums) gradually increased from 1989 to 1998, from 10 to 20 percent of all upper secondary students. Over the same period technical school enrollments at the upper secondary level increased from 30 to 45 percent, primarily because of the addition of new private schools during this time. Vocational enrollments declined substantially between 1989 and 1998, from 60 percent down to 35 percent of all upper secondary students enrolled in educational institutions.

During the Communist era in Czechoslovakia, enterprises and cooperatives had arranged practical vocational training in apprentice schools attached to specific enterprises. The Ministry of Education had developed the curricula and course syllabi for secondary level professional and technical schools and for the theory taught in apprentice schools with input from enterprise specialists and sector research institutes. A government-controlled central planning body determined how many students should be enrolled in each of the individual study fields. With the split from the Communist-controlled system in 1989, Czechoslovakia experienced a significant transformation in its vocational training system.

The Communist model of vocational education and training had made it difficult for students to change occupational tracks and specialties by transferring across training programs. With the transformation of the vocational education system at the secondary level that began in the 1990s, switching tracks has become much easier for students, particularly as new ''integrated'' schools, established with funding and technical assistance provided by the EU's PHARE program, have been introduced. The integrated schools offer training courses at the same level as secondary vocational and secondary technical schools. Additionally, some economic and technical secondary schools have been created with PHARE support that cross the lines between secondary general and secondary technical training, offering practical education with more theory than technical schools customarily provide and preparing students for university-level studies after graduation. Since the 1996 parliamentary elections, the Ministry of Education has been responsible for all secondary level vocational schools in the Czech Republic. Although the future direction of vocational training in the country had not yet been fully decided as of March

2000 when World Bank analysts prepared a study report on vocational education in the Czech Republic, it appeared that the national government was interested in continuing to support vocational training at the secondary level that would combine theory and practice and draw support from potential employers and the private sector. The Czech government had not yet fully determined how to overcome the hazard of training students along overly narrow lines, a problem fostered by the traditional style of vocational education in the country.

Apprenticeships: After 1989, state enterprises went bankrupt or were privatized and the directorates of enterprises folded, along with many of the apprenticeship schools. The remaining apprentice schools were consolidated, and the ministries took responsibility for vocational training. State apprenticeships were introduced in which students received state-funded training unattached to specific future employers. After attempts to establish central advisory bodies through government intervention failed to materialize in the first years after the break from the Soviet system, the Ministries of Economy, Agriculture, and Health assumed responsibility for supervising most of the apprenticeship programs, with some responsibilities falling to the Ministry of Education, Youth, and Sports. Beginning in 1992 the Ministry of Economy became primarily responsible for determining policies and regulations in the area of vocational education, setting the curricula, and providing financing. Professional groups were established to act as advisors as new vocational-training curricula were prepared.

Overall, the apprenticeship schools developed separately from the secondary-level professional and technical schools. Nonetheless, as curricula were revised and schools became increasingly competitive with each other for a declining school-age population, apprenticeship schools competed with the other secondary level educational institutions for students. Additionally, numerous private schools emerged to fill the gaps in the privatizing labor market and to attract and absorb students unable to find suitable or appealing training at other facilities. By 2001 private apprenticeship schools constituted about 13 percent of the Czech Republic's total number of schools and were educating about 24,000 apprentices, not quite one-tenth of the total. In the late 1990s because businesses were contributing to state-funded, continuing-education programs designed to train or retrain adults, many private enterprises were unwilling to dedicate additional financial resources to setting up private training initiatives at the secondary level for apprentices. This was expected to change over the next several years as business associations continued to form and assumed greater responsibility for professional preparation.

HIGHER EDUCATION

In the year 2000 nearly two-thirds of the secondary-school graduates who chose to pursue higher education in the Czech Republic had studied in secondary general schools, while about 30 percent of those going on to higher education had graduated from secondary technical schools and just 4 or 5 percent came from secondary vocational schools. Most students leaving secondary vocational schools entered the job market without further training, although during the 1990s vocational school graduates increasingly were opting to take a two-year course that allowed them to take the *Maturita* upon completion of their studies.

During the 1990s increasing numbers of students chose to study in institutions of higher learning. The gross enrollment rate of 18 to 20 year olds enrolled in higher education programs in 1997 was 17.3 percent. Of all students enrolled in universities in the Czech Republic that year, 28.1 percent specialized in the humanities, 22.7 percent in the social and behavioral sciences, 7.0 percent in the natural sciences, 6.7 percent in medicine, 29.5 percent in engineering, and 6.0 percent in other fields of study. In 1997 about 13,500 male students and 16,600 female students received degrees from tertiary educational institutions in the Czech Republic, with the ratio of female to male students graduating from higher-education institutions 120 to 100.

Teaching Styles & Techniques: By the year 2000 government officials were recognizing that significant efforts needed to be made to upgrade the teaching methodology in many of the Czech Republic's schools where about half the teachers were middle-aged and had been trained before 1989 under the Soviet socialist style of education. Many of the older teachers were overly rigid in their teaching style and lacked knowledge of more modern teaching methods, a result of the lack of in-service training opportunities provided to teachers during the years under the Communist regime. As the Czech Republic prepared for accession to the EU in the late 1990s and afterward, the need to upgrade teacher training became readily apparent. Reforms supported by the EU and other international education specialists were being planned in order to address this problem and to help teachers promoted to management positions in school administration receive specialized management training. With the lustration certificates required by the post-Communist government to certify that executives had not been part of the Communist system, virtually all the top ministerial level officials in the education system had lost their positions and experienced teachers who had never served in management-level positions were being promoted to take on management tasks. The demand for special management training for these teachers was thus very real.

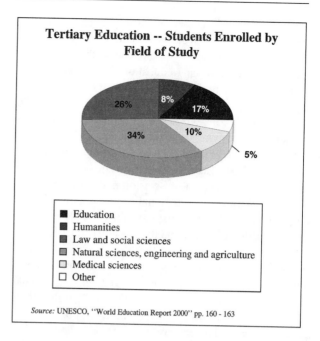

Tertiary Education -- Students Enrolled by Field of Study

8% | 17% | 10% | 5% | 26% | 34%

- ■ Education
- ■ Humanities
- ■ Law and social sciences
- ▨ Natural sciences, engineering and agriculture
- ▢ Medical sciences
- ▢ Other

Source: UNESCO, "World Education Report 2000" pp. 160 - 163

Professional Education: In the 1990s higher professional education became the fastest-growing sector of the Czech educational system. Started in 1992, this form of training was introduced to remedy the shortage of university level seats. Provided as three- or four-year courses enabling students to gain the practical qualifications needed for middle or high level jobs in professional fields, higher professional education has rapidly grown in popularity. Most courses are delivered at technical secondary school facilities, making better use of what are otherwise often-underutilized educational institutions. In just 2 years, from the 1995-1996 academic year to the 1997-1998 academic year, enrollments increased from 6,300 to 23,500 in higher professional schools.

ADMINISTRATION, FINANCE, & EDUCATIONAL RESEARCH

Government Education Organizations & Agencies: Education policy during the 1990s and at the start of the new millennium was set by the Ministry of Education, Youth and Sports, the government arm primarily responsible for preprimary, primary, secondary, and tertiary school facilities and programs as of the late 1990s, except for certain matters falling under the jurisdiction of the Ministry of Economy (and in the case of vocational training, of select other ministries such as the Ministry of Agriculture). The Ministry of Education also oversaw teacher training, scientific policy-making and technological development, advanced research (including educational and other social-science research), international cooperation in research and teaching, state-sponsored care of children and youth, physical education and sports, and tourism. The semi-autonomous Czech School Inspectorship, a subordinate, semi-autonomous entity attached to the Ministry, was charged with the tasks of improving education and educational management, ensuring the efficient utilization of educational resources, and supporting school compliance with education regulations. Beginning in 2001 new regional administrative arrangements involving the 14 regions established in 1998 were to be set in place to oversee educational administration in the Czech Republic, a significant step toward the greater decentralization of decision-making authority in the state. With the new regional administrations assuming their administrative responsibilities, the previously created school offices at the district level attached to the Ministry of Education were to be gradually eliminated. Ideally, this new arrangement would facilitate a more-coordinated network of entities charged with educational administrative tasks, since at the turn of the millennium educational administration in the Czech Republic had become increasingly complex and convoluted, involving arms and offices attached to the ministries, the 6,200 self-governing municipalities, school councils established by some schools after the 1995 Education Act to indirectly assist in school decision-making at the local level, school-based principals, and other educational administrators.

Educational Budgets & Expenditures: In 1997 the Czech Republic spent about 4.7 percent of the national budget on education. Financial responsibility for education mainly fell to the Ministry of Education, Youth, and Sports, which in 2001 was in charge of distributing most of the 80 billion Czech crowns allocated by the national government for education. The Ministry of Finance in 2001 distributed about 1 billion Czech crowns to the municipalities for education costs. The municipalities were responsible for covering 34 percent of investment and operating costs of kindergartens and 37 percent of primary-school expenditures, drawing upon the subsidies received from the Ministry of Finance and on tax shares. Local revenues cover only a very small percentage of expenditures on education. Municipal contributions for education constitute about 20 percent of the entire budget for education. During the 1990s the municipal share of funding for schools decreased as direct funding from the state has increased. In 1997 about 82.5 percent of the expenditures on education came from the state budget while 17.5 percent came from municipal budgets. Municipalities are rarely responsible for funding secondary schools, which for the most part are established by and receive funding from the Ministry of Education, Youth, and Sports.

As already noted, the public budget also provides a certain measure of funding for non-state schools established by private or denominational legal entities. The national state pays private and denominational schools about 60 to 90 percent of the per-pupil subsidies received by state schools, based on the level of education provided, the type of school established, and other formal criteria. Owners of non-state schools must provide the full capital investment needed to establish their schools but are free to set the wage scales for their educational staff, including teachers. In public schools salaries are determined according to a state salary table. Non-state schools also are permitted to collect tuition fees, something public schools are not allowed to do.

In the late 1990s the need for greater funds for capital expenditures on schools was readily apparent. Although the school-age population was declining in size and no major need existed for new-school construction, many of the existing facilities needed renovations and repairs. As Grootings observed in 1999, in the Czech Republic's vocational education and training system approximately three-quarters of non-investment expenditures went to salaries and social insurance for teachers and other educational staff, leaving little for building renovations or the purchase of equipment and teaching materials. The 1998 state budget for education allocated about 5 percent for capital expenditures, 55 percent for personnel expenses (including about 3 percent for staff subsidies for non-state schools), and 40 percent for per-pupil expenditures to pay for textbooks, educational supplies, school meals, boarding fees, utilities and heating costs, and building maintenance. As a World Bank study published in 1999 pointed out, "These figures are more a consequence of the low share of salaries, because of low remuneration levels of teachers, than an over-generous provision of services to schools. The low salary level, especially at the entry point, is a deterrent to the recruitment and retention of young teachers. The teaching force, which is about 75 percent female, is predominantly middle-aged, with a majority trained in the pre-1989 system."

Research Centers & Institutes: Between 1953 and 1992 the Czechoslovak Academy of Sciences was responsible for research and post-graduate (i.e., beyond the Bachelor's level) education. Additionally, research institutes belonging to various ministries and state-owned enterprises offered training opportunities as well as locations for professional research. In 1989 some 140 industrial research institutes were in existence in Czechoslovakia and the Czech part of the national budget spent 2.2 percent of the GDP on research and developing, providing jobs for 140,000 people. At the same time, research facilities were often overstaffed and poorly equipped, making research an expensive state enterprise.

Over the 10-year period between 1989 and 1999, substantial efforts were made to improve the research environment in the Czech Republic. Twenty-two research institutes were closed, and the new Academy of Sciences of the Czech Republic, begun in 1992, oversaw about 60 research institutes but assumed a lesser role in post-graduate education. Universities became increasingly involved in the provision of research training at the post-graduate level, employing instructional staff who could fulfill the roles of both professors and researchers. About 100 laboratories formerly attached to institutes were shifted to the universities, where research became more financially productive. A government-sponsored Research and Development Council was established in 1992 to provide oversight for the funding of activities in the areas of research and development, providing grants for specific research projects and programs as well as capital support and operating support for the institutions where research and development functions were carried out.

NONFORMAL EDUCATION

Adult Education: A Public Employment Service established by the state in 1990 under the Ministry of Labor and Social Affairs implements the labor policies of the Czech government, including adult retraining for the labor market. As of the year 2000, secondary vocational education and training schools were receiving state contracts to provide retraining opportunities to adults, since the Public Employment Service had no training centers of its own. Because of the Service's dissatisfaction with the quality and teaching approaches of many of the programs that had been developed, the Service was cooperating increasingly with education authorities by 2000 to find alternative methods for retraining workers. Private training programs for adults became increasingly common during the 1990s, and by the end of the decade, about 2,000 private training organizations were in operation. To a limited extent, private industries such as automobile factories, also had begun to offer training programs to prepare workers with new skills or to fill labor shortages in particular occupational areas needed by the industry.

Distance Education: As noted already, the Czech Republic resembles other European states in that during the 1990s increasing efforts were made to incorporate training in information and communications technology into the school curricula. By 1999 the Czech Republic had 86 Internet hosts for every 10,000 persons with 35 Internet service providers operating in the country. There were 107.2 personal computers for every 1,000 persons in the country in 1999, almost double the rate for 1995, which was 53.4 per 1,000. Televisions and radios, in use since the Communist era, have proliferated with the shift to a more-democratic government and a free-market, consumer-oriented economy, as have radio and television broadcasting stations. In 1999 some 21 AM radio stations

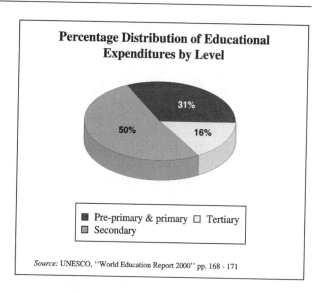

Percentage Distribution of Educational Expenditures by Level

31%
50%
16%

■ Pre-primary & primary □ Tertiary
■ Secondary

Source: UNESCO, "World Education Report 2000" pp. 168 - 171

were operating in the Czech Republic, 199 FM radio stations, and one short-wave radio station while 102 television broadcast stations (35 of them low-power stations) and about 500 repeaters transmitted television programming around the country. In December 1999 there were about 3.4 million televisions and 3.2 million radios in the Czech Republic—roughly 1 television and 1 radio for every 3 people.

TEACHING PROFESSION

Training & Qualifications: In 1996 approximately 138,500 full and part time teachers provided educational services to 16.6 percent of the country's population or the 1,712,900 students enrolled in primary and secondary schools. During the 1996-1997 school year about 36,000 teachers (approximately 33,000 women and 3,000 men) taught primary students, 46,000 teachers (approximately 35,000 women and 12,000 men) taught at the lower-secondary level, and 57,000 teachers (approximately 31,000 women and 26,000 men) provided instruction in upper-secondary schools.

Although kindergarten teachers in the Czech Republic receive their training in secondary schools and higher pedagogical schools, teachers of primary and secondary school students are initially trained at institutions of higher education. In-service training is provided by schools and paid for by subsidies received from the government for special programming determined at the discretion of the schools themselves. Special pedagogical centers and the pedagogical faculties in institutions of higher education also provide in-service training to teachers. Schools also have the option of sending their teaching staffs to courses in management, languages, and other subject areas. Subnational educational administrative offices or in the year 2000, the district-level school offices attached to the Ministry of Education also have provided and financed a certain number of teacher-education courses.

Because the majority of teachers and educational staff in the Czech Republic are government employees, most teachers are paid salaries relatively lower than those received by other professionals and persons employed in the business sector. This has been a formidable obstacle to attracting new teachers in the years since the Communist system was dismantled, as many young people find the pay levels in the education sector to be unappealing and therefore opt for careers where the wages are higher.

SUMMARY

As the Czech Republic prepares to become a member of the European Union sometime in the first few years of the new millennium, the country has been reshaping and improving its education system at all levels by giving consideration to some of the thorniest problems yet to be tackled and making solid progress at transforming a once heavily state-directed system into a more fluid, responsive publicly owned system. Significant problems remain to be overcome as the national economy begins to improve and the country regains some of the economic shine enjoyed in the first few years after independence when so many leaders of other transitional countries marveled at the economic accomplishments of this Central European state that once stood like a gem in the crown of the Holy Roman Emperor. As a 1999 World Bank-sponsored report concluded:

> The educational environment in the Czech Republic is dynamic in several respects: (i) overall enrollments are tending to decline as a function of the declining population; (ii) within this broad trend, university and other postsecondary enrollments have increased, along with technical secondary and to some extent gymnasia, whereas vocational secondary education has substantially decreased and kindergarten is slowly declining; (iii) private education has been introduced, especially at the technical secondary level; (iv) extensive decentralization took place, with district education authorities playing a key role, but even municipalities becoming involved in kindergarten and basic education; and (v) normative financing has become the dominant method of allocating educational expenditures.

All of the above seemed to bode well for the positive transformation of a previously state-controlled system relatively unresponsive to the needs or interests of the Czech people into a vibrant and invigorating system ready to deliver educational services to all the population, no matter the age, educational level, or economic circumstances of the individual student. However, at the same time, the World Bank authors identified certain challenges to progress apparent in the education system of the Czech Republic at the end of the 1990s. These were namely, overly numerous public schools, shrinking teaching loads in kindergartens and vocational schools but not a correspondingly shrinking teaching force, a generally conservative teaching force unversed in more-modern and appropriate teaching methods, the failure to recruit sufficient numbers of young people as teachers who could revitalize the system, and significant administrative fragmentation as the educational system attempted to decentralize, which was likely to impede improvements being made system-wide. The upper secondary level in particular appeared to have some rather serious problems in need of correction that were not being adequately addressed, in the eyes of the World Bank analysts.

The European Commission reported in November 2000 that the Czech Republic was making steady progress in implementing legislation related to education, training, and youth as well as legislation concerning participation in European Community-sponsored programs. While continuing problems were noted with the provision of education to migrant workers' children, the Czech Republic was seen as having made improvements in educating children from socially and culturally disadvantaged backgrounds. Undoubtedly, the groups referred to here included the Roma, who had been subjected to substantial educational discrimination in the years after the break with the Soviet system. In the year 2000 the parents of 18 Romani children in Ostrava, one of the largest cities in Moravia in the east of the country, had lodged a formal complaint with the European Court of Human Rights in Strasbourg claiming that the Czech state had regularly practiced discrimination and segregation by placing inordinate and disproportionate numbers of Romani children into special schools for children with mental disabilities. While Romani children constitute only 5 percent of the primary-school population in Ostrava, more than half of the students placed in special schools in Ostrava are Romani. In the nation as a whole, three-quarters of Romani children are taught in special schools, and more than half of students in special schools are Roma. Although many of the Roma decidedly have special language needs and have been reluctant to integrate among other ethnic minority groups and the ethnic majority Czechs, the practice of placing students in schools for the mentally deficient or disabled clearly should raise eyebrows and calls into question the validity of the educational philosophy underlying the Czech educational system. One of the greatest challenges for post-Communist states in Europe and elsewhere appears to be confronting racial and ethnic prejudice and ensuring the equitable distribution of social goods among the people in the society—no matter how small their numbers or how different their cultural traditions. An aspect of democratization that has created trauma in a number of countries around Europe in the late twentieth and early twenty-first centuries is the allowing of popular participation in governance that ensures everyone the right to express his or her views and preferences without infringing on the rights of the others in their midst. More troubling than the shortage of young teachers interested in entering the field of education and more likely to affect the larger society in terms of how peoples differing from the majority are accepted and treated, this problem of widespread ethnic prejudice and mistreatment of some people by others in the post-Soviet Czech society must be confronted and directly addressed. Admirably, some school administrators, education officials, and teachers, often with internal assistance, were developing educational programs designed to foster tolerance and better ethnic relations in their communities at the start of the new millennium. Such initiatives would be wise to replicate throughout the country with government support and the involvement of civil society groups interested in developing a more respectful civil discourse richly colored with the ethnic contributions of all the members of the Czech Republic.

In terms of the future for the Czech education system, perhaps the greatest need is to find a way to cope with the great administrative bureaucracy that has developed over time through the Communist era and again as the country has sought to reform its political system. Unless a greater streamlining of administrative functions and the clearer delegation of educational responsibilities is accomplished over the next few years, the long-term consequences for the education of the Czech Republic's children and youth are likely to be dismal indeed. By addressing the problems identified not only by school experts within the country but also by international specialists working to facilitate the Czech Republic's integration with the European Union in the coming years, Czech educators can improve their system and provide the means by which future generations may prepare themselves for life in a healthily functioning, politically stable, economically prosperous society. To this end, several recommendations developed by educational specialists in the Czech Republic and presented to World Bank analysts studying the decentralization of education in Europe's transitional countries are worth holding in mind. To address the problems arising in connection with efforts to decentralize the education system and to make it more responsive both to the needs of the people and the labor-market, the specialists suggest that appropriate ''support structures and processes'' be developed and put in place ''to ensure efficient management: management training, ongoing teacher education and room for personal initiative, improved information and evaluation mechanisms, and so forth'' (Hendrichova et al.). Additionally, the authors believe ''the Ministry of Education must strengthen its analytical, coordinative, conceptual, and strategic functions.'' Greater public participation in developing and implementing a more-responsive education system is recommended by these educational specialists, who state, ''Schools, teachers, parents, municipalities or other levels of regional administration and self-governance, employers, trade unions, and politicians—in a word, all stakeholders—should participate in consultative bodies at all levels and should create them where they do not yet exist. The school system and issues concerning education should become public matters.''

Assuredly, Václav Havel, first president of the Czech Republic, would agree that every member of the Czech Republic must help create a society where the government responds to the needs of the people and education serves the public. As Havel reminds us, ''Responsibility cannot be preached but only borne, and the only possible place to begin is with oneself.''

BIBLIOGRAPHY

Bacik, Frantisek. *Decision-making Processes in the Education System of the Czech Republic.* Prague: The Education Policy Center, Institute of Education Research and Development, 1995.

Berryman, Sue E. *Hidden Challenges to Education Systems in Transition Economies.* Washington, DC: The World Bank, Europe and Central Asia Region, Human Development Sector, 2000.

Bureau of Democracy, Human Rights, and Labor. *Country Reports on Human Rights Practices—2000.* U.S. Department of State, February 2001. Available from http://www.state.gov/.

The Central Intelligence Agency (CIA). *The World Factbook 2000.* Directorate of Intelligence, 1 January 2001. Available from http://www.cia.gov/.

Coulby, David. *Beyond the National Curriculum: Curricular Centralism and Cultural Diversity in Europe and the USA.* London: RoutledgeFalmer, 2000.

Dagan, Avigdor. ''The Czechoslovak Government in Exile and the Jews.'' *In The Jews of Czechoslovakia: Historical Studies and Surveys 3,* ed. Avigdor Dagan et al. Philadelphia: Jewish Publication Society of America, 1984.

Euro Info Centres. *Country Profile Fact Sheet: Czech Republic.* The European Commission, October 2000. Available from http://europa.eu.int/.

The European Commission. *Education, Training and Youth: Applicant countries and the Community acquis—The Czech Republic.* 2000. Available from http://europa.eu.int/.

————. *Key data on education in Europe.* Luxembourg: Office for Official Publications of the European Communities, 2000.

Glass, N. "Ministry in Dock over Racism Against Gypsies." *Times Educational Supplement*(24 June 1999): 24.

Grootings, Peter. "Czech Republic." In *Vocational Education and Training Reform: Matching Skills to Markets and Budgets,* ed. Indermit S. Gill, Fred Fluitman, and Amit Dar. Oxford: Oxford University Press, March 2000. Available from http://www.wds-worldbank.org/.

Havel, Václav. *Prayers for a Thousand Years,* ed. Elizabeth Roberts and Elias Amidon. New York: Harper Collins Publishers, 1999.

Hendrichova, Jana, et al. "Czech Republic." In *Decentralizing Education in Transition Societies: Case Studies from Central and Eastern Europe,* ed. Ariel Fiszbein. Washington, DC: The World Bank Institute, International Bank for Reconstruction and Development/The World Bank, March 2001. Available from http://www.wds-worldbank.org/.

Human Rights Watch. *World Report 2001.* Available from http://www.hrw.org/.

In't Veld, Roel, Hans-Peter Füssel, and Guy Neave, eds. "Relations between State and Higher Education." In *Legislating for Higher Education in Europe 1.* The Hague: Kluwer Law International, 1996.

Kieval, Hillel J. *Languages of Community: The Jewish Experience in the Czech Lands.* Berkeley: University of California Press, 2000.

Ministry of Education, Youth and Physical Training of the Czech Republic. Available from http://www.msmt.cz/.

Ministry of Foreign Affairs of the Czech Republic. Available from http://www.radio.cz/gov-cr/.

Organisation for Economic Co-operation and Development (OECD). *Reviews of National Policies for Education, Czech Republic.* Paris: OECD, 1996.

Potuček, Martin. *Not Only the Market: The Role of the Market, Government and Civic Sector in the Development of Postcommunist Societies.* Budapest: Central European University Press, 1999.

Task Force on Higher Education and Society, The World Bank. *Higher Education in Developing Countries: Peril and Promise.* Washington, DC: The International Bank for Reconstruction and Development/The World Bank, 2000.

World Bank. *Czech Republic-Toward EU Accession: Main Report.* Washington, DC: The International Bank for Reconstruction and Development/The World Bank, 1999.

World Bank, Human Development Network. *Education Sector Strategy.* Washington, DC: The International Bank for Reconstruction and Development/The World Bank, 1999.

World Bank Group. *Country Brief: Czech Republic.* September 2000. Available from http://wbln0018.worldbank.org/.

———. *Czech Republic.* 2001. Available from http://wbln0018.worldbank.org/.

———. *The Czech Republic at a Glance.* September 2000. Available from http://wbln0018.worldbank.org/.

———. *Czech Republic Data Profile.* World Development Indicators database, July 2000. Available from http://devdata.worldbank.org/.

—Barbara Lakeberg Dridi

D

DEMOCRATIC CONGO

BASIC DATA

Official Country Name:	Democratic Republic of the Congo
Region:	Africa
Population:	51,964,999
Language(s):	French, Lingala, Kingwana, Kikongo, Tshiluba
Literacy Rate:	77.3%

HISTORY & BACKGROUND

The Democratic Republic of the Congo, or DRC, covers 905,063 miles—making it one quarter the size of the United States. Its capital, Kinshasa, has approximately 4.2 million inhabitants, making it twice the size of St. Louis, Missouri, and almost as large as Chicago. Some 52 million people live in the DRC. People can vote once they reach the age of 18. The population is growing at 3.19 percent per year, which is very fast, and young people are the vast majority. Many people are age 15 years or younger. The rural population is dominant as 71 percent of the total. Only 29 percent of the population live in cities. The major languages spoken are French and Lingala in the capital as well as equator region and Upper-DRC, followed by Kingwana and Swahili in Kivu, Shaba, and the Eastern provinces, Kikongo in Lower DRC and Bandundu, and Tshiluba spoken in Kasai. Despite the fact that Arab slave traders from Zanzibar and Dar es Salaam, Tanzania on the east coast of Africa introduced Swahili as the language of the slave trade, most people in the eastern DRC speak Swahili. Swahili is the lingua franca of the eastern one-third of the DRC, despite the bitter memories of slavery associated with it and the Nyamwezi and Arab slave traders who brought the language to the DRC. Swahili is a Bantu language, and most of the DRC's 200 ethnic groups are Bantu speaking people. An estimated 70 percent of the population is Christian, 20 percent follow indigenous faiths, and 10 percent are Muslims.

Life expectancy for males is 47 years and for females it is 51 years. Malaria, AIDS, and other diseases are common and keep the population from experiencing explosive growth. The infant mortality rate is 101.6 per 1,000, and there is one doctor for every 15,584 people. Most health care is concentrated in a few large cities. The adult literacy rate is 77.3 percent. This is a result of Joseph Desire Mobutu's dictatorship of the late twentieth century in which the needs of the people and country were neglected. Education is compulsory between the ages of 6 and 12. There is 1 internet provider, 21,000 telephones, and 3 daily newspapers per 1,000 people, so information is difficult to acquire for many people in the DRC. The DRC has 97,340 miles of roads, but many are in such poor condition that people prefer to fly between destinations. There are 3,206 miles of railroad lines, 232 airfields, and 530,000 cars and trucks on DRC's roads. Despite the nation's vast mineral wealth the per capita income is a mere $710 per year. The GDP is growing at a rate of 1 percent per year, and there are approximately 14.5 million laborers in the workforce. The DRC has cobalt, copper, cadmium, petroleum, zinc, diamonds, manganese, tin, gold, silver, bauxite, iron ore, hydroelectric power, timber, coffee, palm oil, rubber, tea, manioc, bananas, corn, fruits, sugarcane, and much more. There are cement, mining, diamond, and light industries that process consumer products.

Political History: Europe has brought many new ways of doing things to the DRC, but historically its influence has been negative as well. When kings of the ancient Kongo kingdom asked Portuguese rulers for metal nails so that they could build modern homes and ships, they were denied access to this technology and encouraged to trade their own people as slaves instead. Portugal paid for each slave in guns, which set off a destructive arms race still seen in the Civil War that occurred in the 1990s. Belgium's King Leopold was notoriously cruel toward the population of the DRC after declaring the country a colony of Belgium. He brutally coerced the population of the DRC into hunting elephants to provide him with ivory to sell. He encouraged the growth of rubber plants. Those who either did not grow rubber or did not work fast enough to please Leopold's agents had their right hand or foot cut off. He destroyed whole villages to intimidate regions into working for him without pay. Some experts estimate that Leopold killed more than 10 million Africans over a period of 20 years. The people of Belgium eventually forced the King to abdicate his throne and started a series of reforms which ended Leopold's outrageous atrocities.

Belgium ruled the DRC from 1908 until its independence in 1960. Labor was recruited by corvee or force through local chiefs who collaborated with European authorities. Concessionaire companies forced laborers to work on plantations and in mines. Health and education were offered to African families that collaborated and withheld from those who resisted European rule. Few high schools were built and there was no local university in the DRC under Belgium colonial rule. At independence only 16 people from the DRC had earned any type of university degree. This elite was called *evolues* (developed or civilized ones) and worked with Belgium to rule the DRC. Union leaders and urban residents caught independence fever during the 1950s. Political change was sweeping across Africa, and the DRC was caught up in it as well.

A political crisis erupted culminating in independence on 30 June 1960. Joseph Kasavubu became President and Patrice Lumumba became the first Prime Minister of the DRC. The army mutinied and soon chaos ensued during which hatred of their white former colonial masters led to atrocities being committed against whites, many of whom were killed in the violence that broke out. Those who weren't killed fled the country. The wealthy Katanga province seceded, as did Kasai. Lumumba asked the UN for help and requested aid in the form of troops from the Soviet Union. The head of the army, Joseph Desire Mobutu, eventually eliminated Lumumba, and after a power struggle between Moise Tshombe and President Kasavubu, Mobutu assumed power. Mobutu was completely ruthless and very energetic in crushing rebellion after rebellion. Mobutu banned party politics and established a one-party state in which all power was concentrated in the hands of the "Founding Father." Every citizen of the DRC was expected to join Mobutu's Popular Revolutionary Movement (MPR), which was neither popular nor revolutionary. Mobutu was known as "the Guide," and his words, deeds, and decrees became law. Everyone was required to sing his praises at work, in school, and even in churches. He coined the term "authenticity," which meant rejection of European values and norms. He encouraged, for example, women to traditionally braid their hair, and the abandonment of European names for authentic African ones. At the same time he helped Europe rape the DRC of her mineral wealth. Mobutu changed the name of the country from the Belgium Congo to Zaire, a Kikongo word for "river." Mobutu briefly nationalized a few companies to give his program some teeth. This was in essence a sham to cover up the massive enrichment of a small African elite, which included Mobutu. They colluded with external business interests for profit while ignoring the nation's needs. By the mid-1970s Mobutu had amassed a personal fortune of over $5 billion which made him the "richest man in Africa." He owned villas and mansions worldwide and, it is alleged, even bought one entire city block in both New York city and Paris.

With Mobutu stealing billions and his cronies stealing millions, the country operated on a system of bribery and corruption. Common people suffered the most under this system. By 1990 real wages in cities had fallen to 2 percent of what they were at independence in 1960. Rural incomes fell to one fifth of what they were under an exploitative Belgium colonial government. People looked back at the colonial era nostalgically as hyper inflation eroded their meager earning further each day. Internal trade ground to a virtual halt and farmers uprooted cash crops and planted food to live on. Roads deteriorated so badly that trade was discouraged and people reverted to subsistence living. More than 30 percent of the national budget went to service IMF and debts on loans that allowed the rich to steal and forced the poor to pay the tab. Thus, despite U.S. support that propped up Mobutu, internal opposition continued to grow.

Mobutu's opponents were legendary, but he hunted down and killed most, often with help from Moroccan, French, or US military personnel. A few of Lumumba's left-leaning colleagues continued to try to establish a socialist state, despite Mobutu's depredations. These men were romantic figures, some of whom had been trained by the charismatic Cuban companion of Fidel Castro, Che Guevera. Laurent Kabila, was one of these shadowy figures. He created a base in eastern DRC and looked forward to the day when he could inspire the people of the DRC to rise up and overthrow Mobutu and establish a regime responsive to the common person's needs and aspirations. The 1994 Hutu genocide in Rwanda against the

Tutsi and moderate Hutu provided Kabila with the opportunity that he had been waiting for. When the Tutsi living in exile in Uganda attacked Rwanda and captured the country to stop the genocidal killings, the Hutu extremists fled Rwanda and sought asylum in the DRC. From refugee camps in the DRC, the perpetrators of the genocide plotted their return to power in Rwanda. They ordered and received weapons from France, which they then used to stage attacks on the Tutsi in Rwanda. The Tutsi feared that the Hutu would use the refugee camps in DRC to rearm, retrain, and invade Rwanda to finish killing the Tutsi. The Hutu in the DRC did begin to attack Tutsi who were citizens of the DRC, and the Rwandan Tutsi came to their defense. Once inside the DRC, Tutsi soldiers began closing refugee camps for Hutus who had escaped. Tutsi soldiers tried to locate the Hutu who were involved in the genocide in Rwanda in order to bring them to justice. The Tutsi hoped to prevent Hutu extremists from recapturing Rwanda and completing the massacre of Tutsi people. Tutsi fear of Hutu assassins was what eventually initiated the war in the DRC. Once Tutsi soldiers were inside the DRC, they looked for allies and found one in Laurent Kabila. Mobutu supported the Hutu extremists thus the Tutsi felt that it was in their best interests to topple his regime. In their minds he was aiding and abetting those bent on genocide in Rwanda. Together with Kabila's forces they defeated the Hutu extremists and closed the refugee camps. They then defeated Mobutu's troops and marched toward the DRC's capital, Kinshasa, to capture the country. Because Mobutu had oppressed the citizens of the DRC for so long, they welcomed Kabila and his Tutsi allies as liberators.

Immediately, after Kabila came to power, he changed the country's name to the "Democratic Republic of the Congo" or DRC. Kabila also immediately announced short term plans to create jobs and build roads, hospitals, schools, and a national fuel supply line. All of these measures resonated well with the common people and in the beginning enhanced Kabila's popularity. Unfortunately Mobutu and his supporters had moved most of the DRC's wealth into banks in Europe and America, and Kabila inherited a treasury that was bankrupt.

Kabila unfortunately turned out not to be the hero that he had been welcomed as when he invaded Kinshasa in 1997. The leader of a nonviolent movement that had struggled to overthrow Mobutu peacefully, Etienne Tshisekedi wa Mulumba was, for example, assaulted by Kabila's men soon after Kabila assumed the office of head of state. From that point on the people of the DRC began to worry that they had simply replaced one brutal dictator with another. Kabila allowed the country's decaying infrastructure to disintegrate even further. Mineral rich Katanga was inundated with 2 million refugees from Rwanda, as was the mineral rich province of Kasai. Ka-

bila's Popular Movement of the Revolution ruled the DRC with an iron fist. His Rwandan and Ugandan backers opposed his type of leadership and eventually asked him to step down. Kabila immediately called both the Rwandans and the Ugandans foreigners who were trying to manipulate the DRC and turned the nation against them. Internal war erupted. Uganda and Rwanda backed rebel groups, and Angola, Namibia, and Zimbabwe backed Kabila and his government forces. A member of Kabila's presidential guard eventually assassinated him, and his son, Joseph Kabila, took over. Joseph asked former Botswana President Sir Ketumile Masire, who had previously attempted to start peace talks but has been thrown out by Kabila, to return, invited UN troops to broker a withdrawal of all foreign troops, and opened talks with the rebel groups. Joseph's flexibility may make peace possible. Whether he can rule the DRC is a different matter. Joseph was raised in Tanzania and is not fluent in either French or Lingala. He is learning French fast but still gives all public speeches in English, which many people in the DRC cannot understand. The future of the DRC is thus still very uncertain.

Educational History: Although the Portuguese took a few Kongolese to Europe to teach them to speak Portuguese and to learn European culture, real Western education did not begin in the DRC until 1906 when the Roman Catholic Church established schools in return for government grants and land concessions. Belgium made the Catholic Church responsible for education under the terms of the 1906 agreement between the Vatican and the government of Belgium. These schools or *Ecoles Libres Subsidiees* formed the backbone of the educational system until 1948. The Catholics monopolized education throughout this early period.

Catholic schools taught religion and won converts, while also teaching utilitarian subjects that made Congo's population more useful to Belgium. First level primary schools were known as *ecole primaire du degre ordinaire*. Students began at age six and went to school for five years. Students who successfully completed only the first level of primary school were not considered candidates for secondary school. However, they were eligible to go on to second level primary schools known as, *ecole primaire du degre selectionne*.

This level took an additional six years to complete. Very few students went on to secondary school. Most were enrolled in the first level primary schools where reading, writing, mathematics, and French were stressed. Upon completion most went immediately into the labor force.

Secondary schools were specialized, somewhat like "A" levels in the British system and comparable to junior colleges. After finishing secondary school, many students spent an additional year taking college preparatory courses to help to qualify to enter universities. During the colonial era, the number of Africans who reached this level was so negligible that for all intents and purposes it was as if none did. Church schools, which received government subsidies were called *regime congolaise*. Schools that were for Europeans only were known as *regime metropolitain*. The curriculum in the African schools was far less rigorous than in the European schools where it was assumed that most students would go on to the university. In this two-tiered system equity did not exist. In 1954, the Belgium colonial government tried to remedy this problem by creating secular secondary schools called *ecoles laiques* or *ecoles officelles*, which were separate but allegedly equal to the *regime metropolitain* for whites. This was an apartheid-styled educational system. The aim was to provide minimal or basic education, not complete education. It was an education for servitude, rather than an education that made independent thinkers of learners who became problem solvers. Those who were allowed to receive secondary education concentrated on agriculture and industry, rather than academic preparation for leadership.

Two Catholic universities were created in 1954; the Lovanium and the Universite Officielle du Congo. They planned to prepare a well-educated African elite who would eventually assume power in a peaceful transfer of authority. They were overtaken by events before this could happen, so at independence the African population did not have enough educated individuals to efficiently run a modern government. The world blamed Belgium for failing to prepare them in time. Consequently the world judged the Belgium Colonial educational system a failure, compared to the British and French systems of colonial education.

The newly independent government abolished the *regime congolaise* in 1960 and adopted the *regime metropolitain* for all. This was seen as fair and non-discriminatory. Primary education was reduced to one six year course, which fed into secondary schools without a second level of primary education. Educational opportunities at all levels expanded rapidly for Africans. This created a teacher shortage and the Peace Corps, Belgium, and France sent volunteer teachers to the DRC to fill the void. Primary enrollment increased from approximately 1.6 million students in 1960 to approximately 3.2 million in 1970. By 1990, primary enrollment had skyrocketed to almost 4.6 million students, of whom 43 percent were females. Numbers released in 1996 show that enrollment climbed again to more than 5.4 million (a record number) primary students, but female enrollment declined to 41 percent. Similarly, secondary enrollment steadily climbed after independence from 25,000 students in 1960

to 266,000 secondary school pupils in 1970, a huge increase of 18 percent per year. By 1990, secondary enrollment had reached almost 1.1 million, of whom 32 percent were females. It topped out in 1996 at a little more than 1.5 million students, despite the turmoil gripping the DRC at that time. Female secondary school enrollment increased to 38 percent in 1996.

In 1971, Protestants added a third university known as Universite Libre du Congo. Other institutes of higher learning known as *institutes superieurs* or institutes of higher education helped train a modernizing workforce. There were 27 of these and together with *instituts techniques* or technical institutes they tried to add vocational skills to the labor pool. There were 12 such technical institutes. These schools taught technical and vocational subjects as well as humanities, arts, and social science courses. In 1990, some 40,000 students were enrolled in the DRC's universities. By 1996, there were more than 93,000 university students.

CONSTITUTIONAL & LEGAL FOUNDATIONS

In 1960, the Fundamental Law declared that all children had a right to an education. Each province assumed this responsibility for its children. University education was the domain of the central government. The Ministry of Education administered and oversaw all aspects of education, including school inspections. The 1964 Constitution restated that education was a right, not a privilege, as it had been during colonial times. Mobutu's 1965 coup erased this constitutional provision, thus the energy and will to enforce compulsory, universal primary education experienced a set-back.

Education between ages 6 and 12 is currently compulsory, but there are no mechanisms for enforcing this policy. Only the utilitarian desire to get an education in order to open the doors that allow you to get ahead drives pupils into the DRC's schools.

EDUCATIONAL SYSTEM—OVERVIEW

From its inception the educational system has favored primary schools. During the colonial period, this was deemed the most appropriate type of education required to produce useful Africans who were skilled but did not have the self-confidence to challenge the colonial system. By 1960, nearly 70 percent of primary school aged children were enrolled in school, which made Belgium a leader in providing primary education for its subjects. More than half of all of these students, however, were enrolled in Standard I and II. Many never went further. About 40 percent of those enrolled in primary school in 1960 completed this level of education. For boys the completion rate was 50 percent and for girls it was 30 percent. By 1978 gross enrollment rates were 90 percent and by 1980 it reached 96 percent and leveled off. Of these pupils, 99 percent of males were enrolled, while 93 percent of females of the appropriate age were enrolled. In 1990, there were approximately 4.6 million students enrolled in primary schools in the DRC, this climbed to more than 5.4 million by 1996. Roughly 42 percent of these students were females. Clearly most people in the DRC feel that having a primary education is essential. At the secondary school level, 24 percent of eligible students were enrolled in 1980. This percentage increased only slightly to 26 percent by 1996. Of these students, 32 percent of eligible males were in secondary school compared to 19 percent of eligible females.

Vernacular languages were used as the language of instruction for primary schools during the colonial era. Just prior to independence, access to opportunities to attend secondary school meant that French became the language of instruction and eventually primary schools adopted French as the language of instruction as well. Because it is difficult to find qualified primary teachers fluent in French, schools have reverted to local vernaculars as the medium of instruction, even though French is the official language of instruction.

School years begin in September and end in June. However, universities begin their academic year in October and end it in July. For universities each course lasts one full academic year.

Nonacademic courses traditionally receive priority over academic courses in primary school. Secondary school curriculums are more academically oriented and follow the *regime metropolitain* model. Limited effort is being made to Africanize the curriculum by teaching more local history and culture, as well as to promote the study of African languages. Students, however, are still eager to learn French and English for self-advancement. The curriculum is heavily influenced by the Belgium and French school models.

Secondary school students must take a national *examen d'etat* and pass with a minimum score of 50 percent to be admitted to a university. Once admitted to a university, students must pass an end of the year essay examination in each subject taken, as well as an oral examination. If they fail, they can repeat it by sitting through the entire course again for an additional year. To earn a *licence,* a college student must write and defend a thesis.

The government has worked on improving access to formal education, but informal education lags far behind. Private organizations, rather than the state apparatus, dominate informal education in the DRC. The Interdisciplinary Center for Development and Lifelong Education (CIDEP) is the main NGO in this sector. It retrains civil

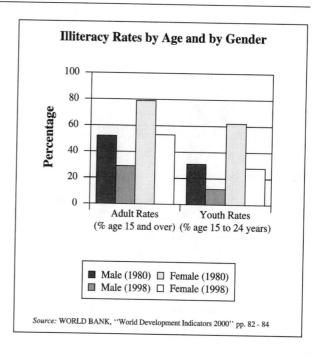

Illiteracy Rates by Age and by Gender

Male (1980)   Female (1980)
Male (1998)   Female (1998)

Source: WORLD BANK, "World Development Indicators 2000" pp. 82 - 84

servants and offers career development training in technical subjects. The CIDEP has the formal status of a division within the National University of the DRC. It is a link between the National University and civil society. The University has gradually taken over many of its functions since 1981.

PREPRIMARY & PRIMARY EDUCATION

In 1995, there were 429 preprimary schools in the DRC. They employed 768 preprimary schoolteachers who taught 33,233 students. Of these 15,956 were males and 17,279 were females. Most of these schools were in the capital and large cities. During the colonial era, only 3 percent of Africans enrolled their children in such schools. Today more people realize the value of such schools for their children's development and support them.

By 1995, the DRC had 1,885 primary schools and 121,054 primary school teachers. They taught some 5.4 million students of whom approximately 3.2 million were males and approximately 2.2 million were females. There was a pupil to teacher ratio of 40 students per teacher in 1990, but the explosive growth in enrollment pushed this ratio up considerably by 1996. Fast growth forced the DRC to hire many unqualified teachers and try to upgrade them on the job. Provinces now require that primary school students pass a provincial primary graduates examination to certify that they are prepared to succeed to secondary school.

Primary schools offer courses on religion, arithmetic, drawing, handiarts, singing, farming, penmanship,

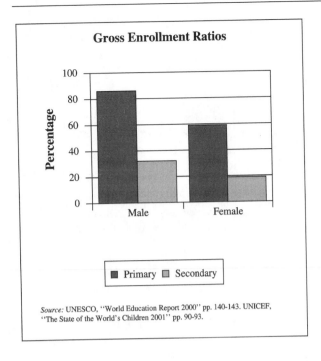

Gross Enrollment Ratios

Percentage

■ Primary   □ Secondary

Source: UNESCO, ''World Education Report 2000'' pp. 140-143. UNICEF, ''The State of the World's Children 2001'' pp. 90-93.

The system after independence offered a two year *cycle d'orientation* (CO) taken by all secondary school students. The CO offered intensive classes in mathematics, French, and the hard sciences. Successful students could advance to a short cycle offering two-year and three- year technical diploma programs or to long cycle, which took four years to complete and were more challenging. Short cycle students took classes in domestic sciences (usually recommended for females), textile production, auto mechanics, electrical work, woodwork, or construction. Long cycle students studied either the humanities or *humanites scientifques,* including mathematics, physics, chemistry or biology, and *humanties litteraires,* which taught Latin, Greek, and African literature. Teacher training was also available under *humanities pedagogiques* or *humanities techniques* for students wanting to study agricultural sciences, electrical engineering, commerce, construction, chemistry, or mechanics. All secondary school students received moral education warning them of the evils of idolatry and traditional religion, which missionaries considered devil worship, and teaching them the virtue of marrying only one wife at a time in a country where polygamy was accepted practice and most men had a *dusiem bureau* or second wife. Most students also took mathematics, science, physical education, geography, history, sociology, and English classes before graduating.

Before 1981, all students sat the CO exam. Those passing this hurdle entered the advanced secondary schools. Such students earned a *brevet du cycle d'orientation.* When short cycle programs were finished, students were awarded a *brevet d'aptitudes professionelles.* Those finishing long cycle programs earned the *diplome d'humanities.* The Ministry of Education oversaw examinations leading to the diploma *d'humanites* and guaranteed the quality of training represented by this diploma. The Ministry of Education also administered the *examen d'etat.* Scoring in the upper 50 percent on this examination granted students entrance into universities. Scores below 50 percent meant that students were awarded certificates indicating that they completed secondary school, most of these students immediately went to work.

Expatriate teachers were common in secondary schools. As more DRC citizens earned degrees, expatriate teacher numbers tend to decline. Throughout the 1960s over 65 percent of qualified secondary teachers with university degrees were expatriates. An estimated 74 percent of unqualified teachers who just had secondary school diplomas were from the DRC. Throughout the 1960s, because of the very limited enrollment of Africans and few opportunities for self-advancement, the pupil to teacher ratio was 4:1. This rose dramatically as Africans gained vastly expanded opportunities to enroll in secondary schools. Vocational courses were reduced following independence in part due to a change in educational phi-

trades, and French. For those tracked to attend secondary school, intensive French and geography are encouraged.

SECONDARY EDUCATION

There were two types of colonial secondary schools prior to 1960 in the DRC. Lower level secondary schools offered three- and four-year vocational education courses. A second type of secondary school offered six year vocational programs, as well as academic courses. Most programs ended in terminal diplomas, while a few were stepping-stones into universities and institutions of higher education. Type one secondary schools included *ecoles de monitrices* for women exclusively; *ecoles de moniteurs* were for students who wanted to train to become teachers; *ecoles d'assistants agricoles* prepared agricultural extension officers; *ecoles d'assistant medical* trained male nurses; *ecoles moyennes* taught clerical workers; and *ecoles professionnelles* taught a variety of industrial and commercial trades to students.

The second or more advanced type of secondary schools, which offered six-year programs could be divided into two three-year programs each. One set of courses was general education or academic classes. Schools offering these programs were known as colleges. They usually were Catholic schools. Other schools offered both the academic programs in the initial programs and vocational classes in the advanced programs. The vocations included administration and business, veterinary science and farming, surveying, and teaching. After the DRC won its independence, the first type of secondary school was either upgraded to a type two school or eliminated.

losophy from vocational toward more academic training, and in part because it became increasing difficult to get qualified teachers to offer such courses inside of the DRC under deteriorating social and economic conditions.

HIGHER EDUCATION

A high pass on the *examen d'etat* secures university admission for a student. They must also pass the *epreuve d'orientation* which is an aptitude rather than an achievement test. Each region is allocated a quota of students who can enter universities to keep from creating one ethnic group that dominates the country. This is a quota system such as India, Tanzania, and other developing nations employ to ensure equal access and opportunity for all ethnic groups. Students meeting all requirements for admission to the university receive full scholarships from the government. Failing to meet all requirements denies a student scholarship aid, but if space is available they can pay to attend as long as they are qualified. It cost $70.00 a year in 1971.

All institutions of higher education fell under the supervision of one institution, the Universite Nationale du Democratic Republic de Congo, during the period between 1971 and 1981. Following 1981, each constituent institution within the university became autonomous. Two types of institutes resulted. Universities on the one hand and higher education institutes on the other hand. Each type of institution is defined by law. They have their own boards from business, government, and faculty senates. The Commissaire d'Etat a l'Enseignement Superior et Universitaire et a la Recherche Scientifique controls higher education in the DRC. Each university is headed by a rector, while institutes are headed by a director-general. Both have secretaries-general for academic and administrative affairs. Universities are divided into faculties and institutes into so-called sections. Faculties are headed by deans, while sections have section heads. Admissions standards are set by law, as are programs leading to academic degrees.

The Universite de Kinshasa has faculties of law, medicine, dentistry, pharmacy, science (including mathematics, physics, chemistry, and biology), and economics. A polytechnic faculty teaches civil, mechanical, and electrical engineering. The Universite de Lubumbasi has faculties of law, medicine, arts and humanities, science, veterinary medicine, metallurgy, industrial chemistry, and mining. The Institut Facultaire des Sciences Agronomiques at Yangumbi trains agricultural engineers. Nineteen other institutes of higher education offer applied technology, building and public works, medical technology, commerce, information technology, statistics, agricultural technology, arts and crafts, rural development, social studies, and more. Fourteen institutes

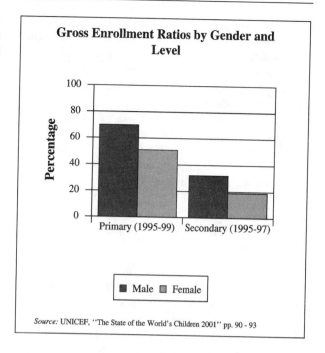

Gross Enrollment Ratios by Gender and Level

Source: UNICEF, "The State of the World's Children 2001" pp. 90 - 93

offer teacher training courses. Ten of these teacher training institutes offer two year training cycles. One teacher training institute is located in each region of the DRC. All of this began with a private Catholic university, the Universite Lovanium, and a public university, the Universite Officielle du Congo.

Before 1971 universities functioned independently, even though 80 percent of their funding was from the central government. Overseas organizations completely controlled these institutions. For example, the University of Louvain in Belgium controlled Lovanium. Belgian professors established the curriculum. Institutes of higher education on the other hand were locally controlled. Fear of foreign dominance ended this arrangement, and in 1971 all universities were nationalized. The Universite Nationale du Zaire was given control of all higher education for the next ten years. Following this period, universities were reorganized into specialized faculties with autonomy.

The *conseil adminstrtif* or administrative council, which is appointed by the president, controls the university on a day-to-day basis. The Ministry of Education retains the power to veto decisions that it disapproves of. The president appoints the rector, while heads of former university campuses, which are now autonomous, are headed by vice rectors. Chairpersons head institutes and can sit on administrative councils at their schools. The overall head is known as the director.

Instruction is based on the *cours magistraux* or lecture method, or by seminars in the upper or *licence* classes. Professors prepare lectures and seminars, while discussion sessions or *travaux practiques* are taught by graduate assistants who have their first degrees only. Due to shortages of funds, professors' notes are sold in lieu of books and assistants teach discussion sessions from such notes. Homework is also assigned based on these notes. In 1985, there were 40,878 university students in the DRC. By 1996, this number more than doubled to 93,266 students. Between 1971 and 1976 the number of professors increased from 1,335 to 2,010. The student to faculty ratio was 13:1, but if only qualified faculty are considered the ratio is 50:1. Only a tiny fraction of the population of the DRC has ever earned the privilege of a university education. The issue of providing high quality public service to a deserving public needs to be addressed squarely.

The *licence* or first university degree consists of two two-year programs. The first cycle is called the *candidature*. Successful completion enables a candidate to advance and compete for a *licence*, which takes two more years to earn. In the candidate's last year they prepare and defend a *memoire de licence* or senior thesis. After successful defense of this paper, they earn their *licence*.

In most universities, during the first stage of teacher training or *graduat*, students spend three years earning a *gradue* degree. Secretarial studies offered by the Institut Superieur de Commerce in Kinshasa leads to a *capacitariat* degree after a two-year course, plus practical work. All of these students write a thesis on the purpose of their studies as a culminating activity.

The second stage or *licence* lasts normally two years and leads to professional qualification in *pharmacien, dentiste, ingenieur civil, ingenieur agronome, architecte,* and so on. For medicine and veterinary medicine the course takes three years and leads to a degree of *docteur en medicine* or *docteur en medecine veterinaire*. To culminate studies at this stage, students write a dissertation which demonstrates their capacity for scientific research. The Universite de Kinshasa awards second stage *diplome special en bibliotheconomie* and *diplome special en gestion de l'environnement.*

The third stage is offered only through select faculties. It has two distinct levels: a two-year scientific and pedagogical course with a dissertation leading to a *diplome d'etudes superieurs* (DES); and a *doctorat* studies program for which a candidate must first earn a DES with distinction to enter. *Doctorat* candidates write an original high-level thesis, based upon unpublished research, which takes three to five years to complete. The faculty of veterinary medicine awards a *agrege de l'enseigenement superieur en medicine veterinaire* upon submission of an excellent thesis. Medical doctors earn a *diplome de specialiste*. If they wish to teach medicine, they prepare an *agregation* thesis. To do this they must first earn with distinction their *diplome de specialise*. There is then five more years of intensive study to earn a degree known as *agrege de l'enseignement superieur en medicine*.

Foreign students who want to come to the DRC must meet all entry requirements and have an excellent command of French. Most come with scholarships from their home governments or from the United Nations.

NONFORMAL EDUCATION

Many adults prefer to take *cours du soir* or night classes after work. Convenience is the key. Such classes are organized by NGOs, such as churches, clubs, and associations. A jury central allows qualified candidates to earn a degree, certificate, or diploma through guided self-learning. The Institut Nationale d'Etude Politiques offers political training to help build the DRC's civil society and its capacity to sustain democracy. Homemakers clubs or *foyers sociaux* teach homemaking, hygiene, health, childcare, and other skills that urban women request. Such groups do double duty as literacy centers.

University degrees can be earned at night through the Centre Interdisciplinaire pour le Development de l'Education Permanente (CIDEP) as discussed earlier. This institution offers in-service courses for civil servants, correspondence courses via mail, and a host of other services to the public. More than 40 employer organizations find theses services so useful that they back them financially. Distance learning is offered primarily through correspondence courses for rural students in isolated remote areas.

TEACHING PROFESSION

Higher technical and pedagogical institutes, which were established to train teachers, in theory train all teachers. In reality, specialists often fail to find jobs for which they are trained and teach other subjects. The rapid expansion of schools continues to force the DRC to staff many teaching positions with unqualified teachers. Teaching is not considered prestigious by youth, and this contributes to recruitment problems. Yet teaching is one area that offers hundreds of secure jobs yearly so people continue to train. Some view these jobs as ''stopgap'' employment that will temporarily tide them over until they can do better. High personnel mobility makes teaching in the DRC very unstable, and the turnover of teachers is a big issue.

Primary school teachers are trained at the secondary school level in teacher training colleges. Instruction in primary schools is in the local language. Science and mathematics are only taught up to, but not beyond the primary school level. Certified and trained teachers are supplemented by a legion of unqualified teachers who require on the job training on a massive scale. Graduates of *ecoles normales secondaires* provide education to students in upper primary schools, as well as lower secondary schools. The problem is that there are very few of these teachers in the system, and, due to the ''brain drain'' that siphons many of the most talented teachers off into industry to earn more money, the problem may grow worse in the future. Secondary school teachers are trained at the university and teacher training institutes. Three universities have departments that prepare future teachers for the *agregation de l'enseignement secondaire* through one year teacher training courses for students who already hold a final degree from a faculty. This course leads to the *agregation de l'enseignement secondaire du degre superior.* Teacher training institutes train *gradues* and *licences* in applied education. They teach lower and upper secondary classes as well. All instruction is in French. Upper secondary level teachers are provided by the 12 Instituts Superieurs Pedagogiques.

Before independence Africans had limited opportunities, and teaching was considered a high paying prestigious profession. Opportunities in private industry and government service since independence has reduced teaching to a low paying, non-prestigious ''stopgap'' form of employment. Deteriorating social and economic conditions and run-away inflation have severely eroded salaries paid to teachers. Many can barely get by and experience hardships that would have been unimaginable in former eras. This causes many teachers to leave the profession. Teachers unions, such as the Syndicat Nationale des Enseignants Congolais and the Centrales des Enseignants Congolais, fought for reform in the past. Today teachers unions are illegal. This also hurts recruitment and retention efforts.

SUMMARY

Massive increase in the number of students being educated is good in the sense that it expands opportunities for self-advancement for millions who were formerly denied such chances, but bad because it puts almost unmanageable strains on the entire education system. Projected growth in demand suggests that this problem will grow worse in the future and needs immediate attention. The desire and hunger for education can not and should not be halted, rather massive investment in teacher-training is needed to improve the quality of education and massive construction of new schools is needed to house the growing army of future leaders and productive citizens of the DRC. Where possible this should be internally financed, but if necessary low interest loans from friendly bilateral donors should be sought out to underwrite improvements in the system. At the very least, the people who benefit from such loans will feel that it is fair that they repay them rather than in the past where only a small elite benefited from foreign loans that the masses were forced to repay.

There is still too much of an imbalance between primary, secondary, and university enrollment. This needs correction to ensure a growing and prosperous middle class that has a stake in the system and will stabilize it. Teachers' education must be upgraded, and retention and recruitment must become top priorities, even if signing bonuses, housing allowances, and other devices are employed to meet projected needs. The curriculum also needs to be rethought in light of the DRC's current manpower needs. Teaching methods should be overhauled as well. Urban schools are currently favored and efforts need to be made to correct this and shift more resources to neglected rural schools, while not allowing the quality of urban schools to decline as a result.

The future health of education in the DRC will necessitate massive investment. Well-trained teachers who stay on the job because they are well-treated, valued, and well-paid will not come easily to the DRC. This, however, is necessary to reach and maintain high educational standards. Under these conditions the DRC will be poised to reach its true potential as a regional giant, assuming that political stability occurs and war ends, ushering in a period of peace and prosperity and an end to kleptocracy.

BIBLIOGRAPHY

Bienen, Henry. *Armies and Parties in Africa.* New York: Africana Publishing Company, 1978.

Chazan, Naomi. *Politics and Society in Contemporary Africa.* Boulder: Lynne Rienner Publishers, 1992.

Gingrich, Newton Leroy. ''Belgian Educational Policy in the Congo, 1948-1960.'' (Ph.D. diss., Tulane University, 1980.)

Griffin, W.E.B. *Special Ops.* New York: Putnam's, 2001.

Hennesy, Maurice. *Congo: A Brief History and Appraisal.* London: Paul Mall Press, 1961.

Hilton, Anne. *The Kingdom of Kongo.* Oxford: Claredon Press, 1985.

Inongo, Sakombi. *Les combats de Kabila.* Kinshasa: Editions la voie de dieu, 1998.

Kambere Muhindo, Leonard. *Regard sur les conflits des nationalites au Congo: cas des Hutu et Tutsi (Banyamulenge). Aux Kivu.* Kinshasa: Editions Yira, 1998.

Lofchie, Michael, ed. *The State of the Nations: Constraints on Development in Independent Africa.* Berkeley: University of California Press, 1971.

Madsen, Wayne. *Genocide and Covert Operations In Africa.* New York: Edwin Mellon Press, 1999.

Mapinga, Emmanuel. *Guerre en Republique Democratique du Congo.* Basel: Basler Afrika Bibliographen, 1999.

Omombo Omana, Adrieu. *Pour une croissance economique durable de la Republique democratique du Congo.* Kinshasa: Centre protestant de editions et de diffusion, 2001.

Risquet, Jorge. *El Segundo frente del Che en el Congo: historia del Batalion Patricio Lumumba.* Habana: Casa Editora Abril, 2000.

Vangu, Mambweni. *Guerres premeditees en region des Grande Lacs africains: roles et tentacules du Tutsi International Power en Republique du Congo.* Kinshasa: Medias pour la paix, 2000.

Weeks, John. *Among Congo Cannibals: Experiences, Impressions, and Adventures During a Thirty Years Sojourn Amongst the Boloki and other Congo Tribes with a Description of their Curious Habits, Customs, Religion and Laws.* London: Seeley, Service and Company Limited, 1913.

Weiss, Herbert. *War and Peace in the Democratic Republic of the Congo.* Uppsala: Afrikaninstitutel, 2000.

—*Dallas L. Browne*

DENMARK

BASIC DATA

Official Country Name:	Kingdom of Denmark
Region:	Europe
Population:	5,336,394
Language(s):	Danish, Faroese, Greenlandic, German, English
Literacy Rate:	100%

HISTORY & BACKGROUND

Education is and has been regarded as one of the essential pillars of the Danish welfare state and has contributed to a relatively homogenous population and work force in Denmark. By international comparison, the Danish educational system today appears relatively coherent, comprehensive, and egalitarian. It is mainly controlled and financed by the State. School leaving, as well as the recognition of competences in further and higher education, is almost entirely regulated by the State through the Ministry of Education. However, the educational system includes a range of private institutions under public regulation and funding, and the participation of social interest groups and organizations in governing education is important for the function of the system. The core of education is a comprehensive primary school, which is, though locally governed, quite homogenous, and comprises a system of pathways into further and higher education. Furthermore, a wide range of education and training is available, particularly in adult and continuing education. The aim is for the system to be open and flexible; however, removing dead ends and detours caused by traditional admission criteria and lack of institutional coordination is still being attempted.

Until the sixteenth century, the Roman Catholic Church was responsible for education. After the Protestant Reformation, Denmark was one of the first European countries to establish a national Lutheran Church, and the Church had a huge historical influence on Danish education. The foundations of the system, stemming from Reformation statutes of the 1530s, survived until the end of the nineteenth century. In 1536, the State took over the grammar schools from the Catholic Church, and the history of the Danish national education system may be said to have begun from this date. State supremacy was accepted and even promoted by the Lutherans, with the result that the Church and the State were never in conflict.

The later development has been motivated by the national State and has been strongly influenced by the fact that Denmark was an agricultural society until World War II. Since then, a rapid development of the industrial and service sectors has taken place, and the development of the educational system may be regarded as a specific consequence of modernization.

The impact of modernization and novel philosophies of education was felt in three different directions, all related to social class. The most famous direction was the growing class of independent farmers, liberated from landlords and influenced by the revolutionary democratic trends in the rest of Europe. The result was a Free School Movement, which owes its origin to the ideas of N. F. S. Grundtvig—poet, clergyman and philosopher. Grundtvig criticized the grammar schools for being too academic and elitist, and was opposed to the rigid style of the Church. He defended a more joyous and lively religious practice. He believed in the ''necessity of the living word for the awakening of life and the transmission of the spirit,'' as well as in the development of basic skills.

This rather romantic idea of a Nordic popular culture was to be promoted by folk high schools outside the control of the State. In 1852, Kristen Kold founded the first of many Scandinavian folk high schools. These schools had no entrance or leaving examinations, and instruction was confined to lectures. Students were generally adults from 18 to 30 years of age. The teaching included—with local variations— history, religion, Danish language and literature, mathematics, science, gymnastics, and practical farm work. The terms were five residential winter months and three residential summer months. This tradition of schooling based on an agricultural rural class endured until after World War II and has remained a part of nonformal Danish education, influencing the state school system and offering alternative schools of liberal as well as practical education.

During the nineteenth century, the rise of urban merchant classes needing a more practical type of schooling led to a secularization of the State school system, with the inclusion of modern languages and science in the curriculum. At the beginning of the twentieth century, a modern system of general education had thus already taken shape in the cities and towns, comprising the *folkeskole* (''school of the people'') at the elementary level and the *mellemskole* (''middle school'') at the middle level. The former Latin grammar schools were replaced by *realskoler* (lower secondary schools). A three-year upper secondary school, or *gymnasium*, prepared students for university education of the German Humboldt'ian type. For another half century, however, the modernization mainly affected secondary education in urban communities. It was a very selective education system with a strong class bias, the streaming (or channeling) taking place at the *mellemskole* level.

The influence of the growing working class led to a demand for a more egalitarian school system. The labor movement secured public funding of primary schools and evening classes. The selectivity in admission to secondary education, however, remained unchallenged. Urban and rural communities had different types of school systems until the 1950s.

CONSTITUTIONAL & LEGAL FOUNDATIONS

The Danish Constitution from 1849 (section 76) states that education shall be compulsory (whether provided by the family or school) and free in public institutions. It defines the goal of education to be the development of the pupil's personality, aptitudes, and needs, and the promotion of academic achievement and practical skills on the one hand and spiritual values and community consciousness on the other. Danish education has further been shaped by a small number of historic statutes and regulations such as the Grammar Schools Act of 1809, the Act of 1857 abolishing the control of

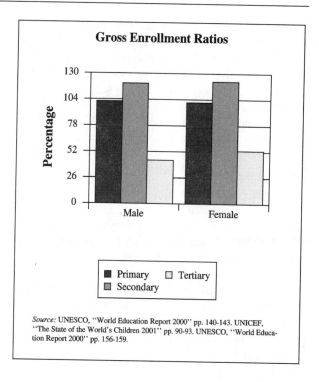

Gross Enrollment Ratios

Source: UNESCO, ''World Education Report 2000'' pp. 140-143. UNICEF, ''The State of the World's Children 2001'' pp. 90-93. UNESCO, ''World Education Report 2000'' pp. 156-159.

crafts training by the guilds, the Apprenticeship Act of 1889, and the Act of 1814 introducing seven years of compulsory education, as well as a number of pieces of legislation in the second half of the 1900s.

EDUCATIONAL SYSTEM—OVERVIEW

Denmark is generally considered a progressive country. Several factors, however—the late modernization, the parallel existence of very different lifestyles, the decisive political influence of a self-conscious class of independent farmers with its own educational ideas—help to explain the contradictory trends in educational development and the comparative absence of planning. Legislation has most often taken the form of national ratifications of existing developments and compromises.

After World War II, a whole range of educational reforms was passed for political, economic, and social reasons. The Act of 1958 unified urban and rural school systems and established the 10-year *folkeskole* with its two components: the elementary *hovedskole* (main school) and the optional lower secondary school, the *realafdeling*. The *gymnasium* (upper secondary school) was reformed by the Act of 1961. The first legislation on vocational education and training were the Act on Technical Schools and the Act on Labor Market Training in 1960.

In 1976, a new Education Act reshaped the school system as it exists today. It introduced nine years of comprehensive primary and lower secondary education for all, and an optional 10th year and an optional preschool year. The act permits local authorities to abolish the previous division between language and science in the eighth and ninth grades, and encourages individualized teaching in foreign languages, mathematics, physics, and chemistry. This is regarded as the last step towards abolishing streaming of children during their schooling. However, in upper secondary schools, children are still channeled into either an academic branch giving access to higher education or a less academic and more practical vocational branch.

The free school tradition remains alive and visible: Besides alternative primary schools, there are still about a hundred residential folk high schools that embody the ideas of Bishop Grundtvig. Rather than primarily rural, today's students come from a broad range of young people, as well as senior citizens. Group work and seminars dominate the instructional calendar. Furthermore, there are choices of free schools for 14- to 18-year-olds: *Efterskoler* (continuation schools) offer an alternative to tenth grade of the *folkeskole*, and *ungdomsskoler* (youth schools) are designed for school-leavers who lack particular skills.

PRIMARY & PREPRIMARY EDUCATION

In Denmark, education is compulsory for nine years and usually commences in August in the calendar year of the child's seventh birthday. While preschool is optional, the majority of children attend one or more of the three types: the *vuggestuer*, which are day nurseries for children younger than three; the *børnehave*, which are kindergartens for children between three and seven; and the *børnehaveklasser* or preschool classes for children between five and seven.

The municipal *folkeskole* and private schools offer optional preschool classes (i.e., *børnehaveklasser*) for the year preceding compulsory education; 97 percent of families accept this offer for their children. Since 1986, preschool classes have been an integrated part of primary education as it has been made possible for schools to combine some of the teaching in preschool classes with that of the first and second forms of primary school.

Primary & Lower Secondary Education: In Denmark, education—and not schooling—is compulsory for nine years, which means that education can take place in the public *folkeskole*, in private schools, or at home, providing that national standards are met and that an adequate range of subjects is offered to the pupil. Primary and lower secondary schooling is not separated in Denmark, and pupils thus attend the same school from the first form through to the ninth. Approximately 89 percent of children go to public schools (*folkeskolen*) free of charge, while approximately 11 percent attend private schools.

Folkeskolen: The Danish *folkeskole* provides nine years of compulsory education free of charge. It also offers optional preschool classes and an optional 10th form. The aim is to contribute to the all-round academic, social, and personal development of the individual child by providing subject-specific qualifications and preparing pupils for living in a democratic society. The latter requires that the school and its daily life be based on intellectual freedom, equality, and democracy. As the schools are required to emphasize the personal and social development of each pupil, an intimate collaboration between the school and the pupil's home is considered vital. Pupils and parents or guardians must accordingly receive information about the child's academic and social performance at school at least twice a year.

The school year starts in August and ends in June, and comprises two hundred school days. The *folkeskole* has virtually abandoned streaming of children, and all pupils therefore automatically proceed to the next level. Pupils remain together in the same class for all nine years. While class sizes must not exceed 28, the average is 19 children; the pupil-teacher ratio is 10:4.

The Danish *folkeskole* employs a unique "class-teacher" system, whereby one teacher is responsible for a class for nine years. The class-teacher supervises the academic, social, and personal development of all pupils in the class and is the principal link between the children's homes and the school. The class-teacher is allocated one weekly hour called "*Klassens* time" ("the lesson of the class") for discussion of issues concerning the well being of the class. Moreover, the class-teacher may spend some teaching time on camps, outings, or work experience.

Curriculum: The Minister of Education is responsible for setting the targets of achievement for each subject taught in the *folkeskole*; however, local authorities and schools are free to decide on how to reach these. The Ministry of Education provides curriculum guidelines for each subject; the guidelines are merely recommendations, and the schools are allowed to formulate their own curricula as long as they are in accordance with the overall target levels. Most schools appear to employ the guidelines articulated by the Ministry.

Danish, mathematics, physical education/sport, and Christian studies are compulsory all nine years. Art must be taught from the first to the fifth forms, science and music from the first to the sixth forms, and history from the third to the eighth forms. Textile design, woodwork and metal work, and home economics should be taught at one or more levels within the fourth to the seventh forms. English is compulsory from the fourth to the ninth forms, geography and biology at the seventh and eighth forms. Physics and chemistry must be taught from the seventh to the ninth forms, and social studies should be offered in the ninth form. Pupils are offered instruction in German from the seventh to the ninth forms, but may be offered French instead.

There are certain compulsory topics to be included in the educational program. These consist of traffic safety, health and sex education, and educational, vocational, and labor-market orientation. Furthermore, a wide range of optional subjects may be offered from the eighth to the 10th form, including, for instance, word processing, technology, drama, Spanish, and common immigrant languages.

Pupils in the ninth and tenth forms are required to complete and present an interdisciplinary project. The project is assessed in a written statement, and if the pupil so wishes, a mark may be given and indicated on the school-leaving certificate.

School Leaving Examinations: There are two levels of school-leaving examinations in the Danish *folkeskole*: The *Folkeskolens Afgangsprøve* (the Leaving Examination) and the *Folkeskolens Udvidede Afgangsprøve* (the Advanced Leaving Examination). Both comprise a mixture of written and oral exams. The former may be taken in 11 subjects after the ninth and tenth forms, while the latter may be taken in five subjects after the tenth form only. Marks are awarded on a scale from zero to 13. The Ministry of Education provides standard rules for the examinations; the questions in written exams are set and marked centrally.

Neither of the leaving examinations is compulsory, and the pupil, along with parents or guardians—and following consultations with the school—are free to decide whether to take them. School-leavers receive a leaving certificate with marks for the performance in classes during the final year and their examination results. Furthermore, the pupil may wish to include the mark for the ninth or 10th form interdisciplinary project.

Alternatives to the Public *Folkeskole*: There are 421 private schools distributed throughout Denmark. Rather than having been founded for academic reasons, these schools are generally based on denominational preferences, pedagogic theories, or political and social ideologies. Eleven percent of children attend private schools for the compulsory nine years of education.

The State subsidizes approximately 80 percent of private schools costs, while parents pay the remaining 20 percent, which in average amounts to 700 DKK per month, with substantial variation. The combination of non-academic reasons for founding private schools and the relatively low tuition fees means that, in contrast to other countries, Danish private schools are not generally

considered "elitist," and they do not necessarily provide pupils with higher social status or advantages in terms of entry to higher education. Private schools are free to articulate the content of their curricula, but they are required to meet national standards in their providing school-leaving examinations.

Education of Teachers for the *Folkeskolen*: Denmark has a unified training system, training a group of teachers who cover the whole period of compulsory schooling with a minimal specialization of subjects, clearly distinguishing primary and lower secondary school teachers from other categories of teachers. The training takes approximately four years and consists of a mixture of theoretical studies and practical training in the form of practice teaching. The curriculum includes common core subjects such as Danish, psychology, pedagogy, social studies, arithmetic, and religion, as well as the in-depth study of two optional subjects. The course contains 16 weeks of practice teaching, divided into four periods of four weeks each, in four different schools. There are currently 18 colleges offering teacher-training courses.

SECONDARY EDUCATION

Efterskoler & Ungdomsskoler: *Efterskoler* (continuation schools) are boarding schools for the eighth to the tenth forms, and are completed with either the Leaving Examination or the Advanced Leaving Examination. Previously, these schools catered to pupils who had encountered academic, social, or personal problems in the formal school system; however, this image has changed dramatically, and the continuation schools are now attended by an increasing number of young people who desire a year or more away from home.

Ungdomsskoler (youth schools) are designed for school-leavers who lack particular skills; they may be residential as well as non-residential.

Nearly all school-leavers continue in some type of secondary education; 53 percent continue in upper secondary schools, which are academically oriented, whereas 41 percent attend colleges emphasizing a vocational content (either technically or commercially oriented).

Gymnasium & Højere Forberedelseseksamen (HF): The Danish *gymnasium* and HF (Higher Preparatory Examination) are two forms of academically oriented upper secondary education and are attended by as many as 53 percent of all school-leavers. These programs contain a general education in its own right that also prepares students for higher education. Denmark has approximately 295 *gymnasiums* and HFs, of which 85 percent are publicly owned; the State covers the cost of these. The remaining 15 percent are private institutions; the State subsidizes 80 to 85 percent of the costs of these.

The *gymnasium* is the most traditional type of upper secondary school; it consists of a three-year course directed to students who have recently completed nine years of compulsory education. The HF was introduced in 1967 and is parallel to the *gymnasium*, but directed at those who have left the education system and wish to return to study. HF can be taken as a two-year full-time course or a single subject at a time.

Full-time students at the *gymnasium* or HF receive instruction in approximately 13 subjects. The courses contain a core of compulsory subjects such as Danish, English, mathematics, basic science, and history; students are further required to choose a number of electives from a wide range of subjects such as music, art, philosophy, and social studies. Students must also complete a major written assignment in their final year of study.

The *gymnasium* is completed with the *studentereksamen* (upper secondary school leaving examination) comprising 10 parts, three written and seven oral. Students are also assessed continuously in terms of their oral and written performance in classes. The HF is completed with the HF *eksamen* (higher preparatory examination). In contrast to the *gymnasium*, no marks are given for oral and written performance during the year; instead, students are required to take examinations in every subject studied. Marks are given on a scale from zero to 13, and students must have an average of six to pass their upper secondary education. The national examination system is administered by the Ministry of Education.

Højere Handels Eksamen (HHX) & Højere Tekniske Eksamen (HTX): The HHX (higher commercial examination) and HTX (higher technical examination) comprise a vocationally oriented upper secondary education, which qualifies students for admission to higher education as well as for employment in trade and industry, usually in training positions. The two programs take three years each and are offered at most business and technical colleges. Admission requires completion of nine years of compulsory education.

The HHX and HTX consist of a core of compulsory subjects such as Danish, English and a second foreign language, as well as subjects specifically related to either commerce (e.g., business studies, economics, and sales) or technology (e.g., technology studies, vocational studies, and natural sciences). Students are further required to choose five or six electives from subjects relevant to their course. In their final year, all students must complete a major written assignment.

Some commercial colleges also offer the *højere handelseksamen*, or HH (higher commercial examination),

which comprises a one-year course available to students who have completed an upper secondary school leaving examination. The HH consists of compulsory subjects and electives.

Examinations: Students at the HHX, HTX, and HH are required to take examinations in all subjects studied; students are also assessed continuously in terms of oral and written performance in classes. Marks are awarded on a scale of zero to 13, and students must obtain an average of six to pass their upper secondary education. The Ministry of Education is responsible for administering the examinations.

Teacher Qualifications & Teaching Structure: Teachers must have completed a master of arts or master of science degree, as well as an additional course in educational theory and practice to teach at the *gymnasium*, HF, HHX, or HTX. Unlike teaching in the *folkeskole*, upper secondary teaching is specialized—that is, each teacher teaches only one or two subjects.

Vocational Education & Training: An alternative direction of upper secondary education consists of vocational educations. Through the 1950s, vocational education took the form of apprenticeship in a specific craft. Through several reforms it has now become organized in the form of a number of vocational education programs, each oriented to a set of related technical, commercial, or service functions and consisting of schooling as well as practical training or apprenticeship. Since the nineteenth century, employers' branch associations and skilled workers' unions—rather than classical guilds—controlled the craft education. The intervention of the State resulted in a trilateral governing system, which remains today. The State, employers, and the trade unions share control of the quality of practical training and examinations, as well as the curriculum.

Today, vocational education offers dual programs with intermittent schooling and practical training (*vekseluddannelse*). Technical schools (*tekniske skoler*) provide a range of vocational programs based on traditional crafts, leading to recognized skilled professions. But the schools also offer training in advanced technical domains. Commercial schools, or *handelsskoler*, offer two-year day or evening classesleading to an examination (*handelseksamen*) in general subjects, languages, accounting, or retail trade. There have been no apprenticeships in agriculture, but the residential agricultural schools (*landbrugsskoler*) accepted students in this field without examinations for a professional education; recently this education has been included in the umbrella legislation of the traditional crafts' education. Banks and some public services have their own basic training programs. There is a tendency towards merging these particular programs with those provided and regulated by the State.

It appears that an increasing number of companies employ young people with no specific vocational skills or experience and train them. Meanwhile, the general level of vocational education is increasing. The commercial and technical schools also provide a general upper secondary education intended to be equivalent to the *gymnasium* as a path to higher education, but it puts less emphasis on classical education, arts, and sports, and more on vocationally relevant skills. Obviously these provisions of *erhvervsgymnasiale* programs (vocational education and training) attract different groups of young people with somewhat different class backgrounds and motivations, and they probably counteract a general trend of students moving into the *gymnasium* and academic higher education.

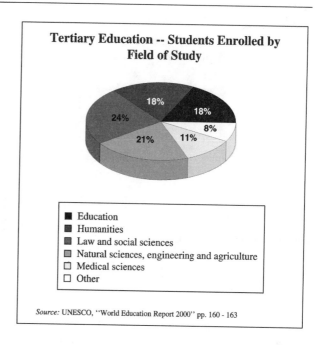

Tertiary Education -- Students Enrolled by Field of Study

- ■ Education
- ■ Humanities
- ■ Law and social sciences
- ▨ Natural sciences, engineering and agriculture
- □ Medical sciences
- □ Other

Source: UNESCO, ''World Education Report 2000'' pp. 160 - 163

HIGHER EDUCATION

Denmark has five universities and a number of professional colleges that have gradually achieved university status (e.g., engineering and commerce). Mass university education has developed without overhauling the fundamental structure of institutions and programs. However, two of the universities are relatively new ones: Roskilde and Aalborg. These differ from the others in that the courses are organized around project work, and research and teaching are regarded as interdisciplinary. They were established as reforms in the 1970s and have had some impact on teaching in other universities, but not generally on structure. During the 1970s, a democratic governing system replaced the faculty collegial government. An unusual democratic culture has developed and still prevails, although it is on the decline. Universities in general have not been able to meet the demands for general reforms and for more openness and sensitivity to problems of society. Universities have resisted political pressure to adapt directly to the needs of industry and the labor market, and thus fueled a political process of applying criteria of the labor market and reorganizing the governing system of universities by centralizing and delegating substantial executive powers to rectors, deans and department heads. The views on the possible impact on the quality of education and research and on academic independence vary substantially, as do views on the need to reform universities.

Besides institutions at university level, there is a range of professional colleges that train primary school teachers, kindergarten and preschool pedagogues, nurses, and social workers, among other professionals. These have grown separately from other educational institutions, but have gradually become essential parts of the ed-

ucation system. In 2000, these colleges began to establish direct links to university institutions and research to strengthen professional education and direct research to issues related to these fields. They are part of a more open system for continuing education (see below), which may create new and flexible educational pathways. A ''professional bachelor degree'' is being introduced, giving access to master's degree programs at universities, which could trigger major changes in the traditional universities as well.

ADMINISTRATION, FINANCE & EDUCATIONAL RESEARCH

Almost all types of education are legally regulated, in most cases placing the responsibility for the direction and quality on the Ministry of Education. The Ministry of Labor has developed training and general education for the least educated and skilled members of the labor force, sometimes in competition with the Ministry of Education. In the new millennium, the trend is to bring all education and training into one comprehensive system. Most education is provided in public institutions; in most private institutions, there is public recognition and a legal framework as well as substantial public funding. Within this standardized framework, there is, guided by relative political consensus, a strong tradition for delegating responsibility to local authorities for primary school administration. While the State had a more direct influence on universities and vocational education from the 1950s to the 1970s, since then there has been a political struggle between a market-oriented management style and a local democracy based on self-administration.

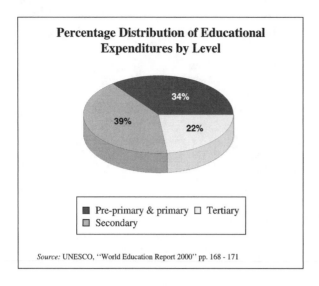

Percentage Distribution of Educational Expenditures by Level

34%

39%

22%

■ Pre-primary & primary   □ Tertiary
■ Secondary

Source: UNESCO, "World Education Report 2000" pp. 168 - 171

The executive governing is, however, quite different in the various educational domains. Primary schools and the academic secondary schools (*gymnasiums*) are state-regulated but run by local authorities—municipalities for primary schools, counties for upper secondary. Likewise, municipalities and counties are responsible for general adult education in community colleges and evening classes within the legal regulation of their minimum provision. Fundamentally, these schools have been controlled and developed by teachers. Today, we see new relations: The school management is strengthened in relation to teachers while held responsible to school boards in which parents have direct executive influence. Furthermore, the pupils' council is, in general, entitled to influence all matters deemed to concern them.

Though formally State-owned, vocational schools and labor-market training centers are governed by boards with a strong representation from local and national employers' associations and trade unions. On a national level, advisory councils also play a role in the development as well as in setting priorities. The State control has been strengthened, but is now being delegated while school management is strengthened.

Universities and folk high schools are both characteristic—although very different—sectors of self-managing institutions funded by the state. They both feel the indirect but persistent pressure to adapt to societal trends and government concerns.

NONFORMAL EDUCATION

Adult & Continuing Education: Adult education comprises at least three major sectors. One is the liberal adult education in folk high schools, in evening classes, and at university extensions. Today, the variety of forms

in this sector consist of compromises and has been influenced by the traditions of the rural free school movement in the nineteenth century and the working class in the first half of the twentieth century. During the second half of the twentieth century, a generous and liberal State support enabled this sector to become an educational leisure culture of substantial size. The formats vary from evening classes once a week through the winter season, to block courses, to residential courses of a few days, to the 14-week residential course of folk high schools. Approximately three-fourths participants are women), and all age groups are represented. During the 1980s, an interesting innovation took place in the form of day folk high schools; inspired by the classical folk high schools, these schools provide day courses mainly for unemployed adults—predominantly unskilled women. The courses are usually full-time for at least eight weeks and comprise general subjects, arts, language, personal development, and citizenship training.

A second sector, begun in the 1950s, provides general schooling for adults in community colleges (*voksenuddannelsescentre, or VUC*—literally, "adult education centers"). The VUC attract people with very different backgrounds and goals; women make up approximately two-thirds of attendees. Students may attend full time or take only a single subject with a few lessons per week, which can be accumulated for a full examination diploma. The community colleges are still largely concerned with general adult education; however, there is a clear trend towards including these in a wider market of continuing education that embraces and partly merges with vocational and general education.

A third sector consists of training and education related to the labor market. In 1960, the State introduced a program to retrain workers for industry and construction to facilitate labor market mobility (*arbejdsmarkedsuddannelserne, or AMU*—literally, "labor market educations"). This has developed into programs that provide both complete professional education and supplementary upgrading programs converting unskilled workers into skilled workers. This education and training covers a wide range of branches of industry and services, including business services such as cleaning and catering, and new branches such as waste handling and personal services. In most branches, there is a strong male dominance; a few domains, however, are dominated by females, which reflects the gender division of the labor market at large. The courses consist of basic and specific skills, whereas the comprehensive programs comprise technical skills as well as basic technology and social and general knowledge. The AMU centers have provided additional training services for young unemployed people and disadvantaged groups with the specific purpose of enabling access to the labor market, at times including general and vocational education.

Since 1990, an enormous expansion has taken place in continuing education, not only among workers, but to a larger extent among professionals, managers, middle managers, and specialists. Well-researched information about the extent of this activity is sparse, but it can be assumed to engage 2 percent or more of the work force in terms of work time spent. Much of it is provided *ad hoc* in the form of private courses for a specific group, or for employees of a specific company. Recently, State and communal employees have taken up continuing education and training as part of their employment, from part-time evening classes to concentrated courses, often two to three days in residence. The cost is usually higher than similar courses provided by the State, and such market-based activity carries no formal recognition to the participants outside their workplace.

Reform of Continuing Education: In 2000, the Danish government launched a major reform of adult and continuing education, which contained three pivotal aims:

- To re-orient the entire education system and its institutions to a more direct collaboration with industry and business enterprises, and to provide continuing education more extensively.

- To create a coherent system of continuing education—parallel to the present basic system—that enables people to accumulate competencies throughout their lives through a sequence of programs, admission to each of which requires practical professional experience after successfully completing the previous program.

- To reconstruct the funding of continuing education so that users (participants as well as their employers) pay more of the costs, and so that training and funding are offered in response to market needs.

For this purpose, a new "parallel system of competencies" has been established, comprising a sequence of programs at four levels: general adult education, advanced adult education, diploma, and master's degree. Part of the philosophy of this system is to allow for different ways of attaining these levels, including recognizing nonformal competencies. However, programs of study at each step are assumed to correspond to the level of teaching in the "ordinary" education system. They should largely cover the same content. In most cases, however, one step amounts to only one year of full-time ("ordinary") study; it is assumed that professional experience contributes to learning. Access to each level is defined by the completion of the previous level, plus at least two years of active relevant work based on the previous level of competence. The system is thus intended to enable a full "ladder climbing"—in principle even enabling someone to study at the Ph.D. level after the completing the master's level. This latter step is still controversial, however; bridging between the two ladders is possible, but not an ordinary path.

The system gives credit to relevant vocational and professional experience; it is also assumed, however—for better or worse—that the quality of the new levels is likely to be different from that of ordinary education.

The details of the system are still in the making, and it is, therefore, difficult to assess its future impact. Much will depend on funding mechanisms. The intention is to leave the burden to individual users and employers, depending on the type of education and training. In some domains, this may imply a substantial shift away from a system of public funding, and this is therefore subject to political discussion and organizational bargaining. However, there seems to be no doubt that the model represents a trend in the overall educational system in three ways: recognition of real competencies; modular programs and lifelong access routes; and more flexible and multiple uses of educational institutions and programs. There is thus no doubt that this trend will persist, with potentially great impact.

BIBLIOGRAPHY

Andrésen, A. *The Danish Folkehøjskole Today: A Description of Residential Adult Education in Denmark, Copenhagen*: Copenhagen: Folkehøjskole Association of Denmark, 1991.

Bjerg, J. "Reflections on Danish Comprehensive Education 1903-1990." *European Journal of Education*, vol. 26 (2), 1991.

Dixon, W. *Education in Denmark*. Copenhagen: Centraltrykkeriet, 1958.

The Danish Gymnasium: General Rules. Copenhagen: The Danish Ministry of Education, 1991.

The Danish Higher Preparatory Examination: General Rules. Copenhagen: The Danish Ministry of Education, 1991.

Danish Youth Education: Problems and Achievements, Report to the OECD. Copenhagen: The Danish Ministry of Education, 1994.

The Education System. Copenhagen: The Danish Ministry of Education, 1998.

Jensen, Jens Højgaard, and Henning Salling Olesen (eds.). *Project Studies—A Late Modern University Reform*. Copenhagen: Roskilde University Press, 1996.

Nordenbo, S. E. "Concepts of Freedom in Danish School Legislation," in *Education for the 21st Century—*

Commonalities and Diversities. Copenhagen: Waxmann, 1998.

Rørdam, T. *The Danish Folk High Schools*. Copenhagen, 1965.

Salling Olesen, H. *Adult Education and Everyday Life*. Copenhagen: Roskilde University Press, 1989.

Salling Olesen, H., and P. Rasmussen. *Theoretical Issues in Adult Education: Danish Research and Experiences*. Copenhagen: Roskilde University Press, 1996.

The Transition from Initial Education to Working Life in Denmark. Copenhagen: The Danish Ministry of Education, 1998.

Thodberg, C., and A. Pontoppidan. *N. F. S. Grundtvig— Tradition and Renewal: Grundtvig's Vision of Man and People, Education and the Church, in Relation to World Issues Today*, Copenhagen: The Danish Institute, 1983.

Webb, T. W., and L. Lerche Nielsen. *Higher Education in Denmark*. Roskilde: Institute VII and the Information Section, 1991.

—*Henning Salling Olesen and Thomas W. Webb*

DJIBOUTI

BASIC DATA

Official Country Name:	Republic of Djibouti
Region:	Africa
Population:	451,442
Language(s):	French, Arabic, Somali, Afar
Literacy Rate:	46.2%
Academic Year:	September-June
Compulsory Schooling:	9 years
Public Expenditure on Education:	8.1%
Foreign Students in National Universities:	8,982
Libraries:	892
Educational Enrollment:	Primary: 328,875 Secondary: 444,682 Higher: 174,975
Educational Enrollment Rate:	Primary: 101% Secondary: 121% Higher: 48%
Teachers:	Primary: 33,100 Secondary: 50,100
Student-Teacher Ratio:	Primary: 10:1 Secondary: 9:1
Female Enrollment Rate:	Primary: 101% Secondary: 122% Higher: 53%

The Republic of Djibouti, a country of about 500,000 people, is situated on the northeastern coast of Africa, bordered by Somalia in the south, Ethiopia in the west, and Eritrea in the north. Until 1967 it was called French Somaliland by France, the colonial power that owned this small piece of land since the late 1800s when the European nations divided up the map of Africa between them. An extremely poor, hot, desert territory, its main significance lies in its strategic location on the western shore of the Gulf of Aden at the entrance to the Red Sea and the Suez Canal, linking the Indian Ocean and the Mediterranean Sea. After 1967 the territory was renamed the French Territory of the *Afars* and *Issas,* after the Ethiopian *Afars* and the Somali *Issas,* the two largely nomadic ethnic groups that make up the majority of the population. On June 27, 1977, the country gained independence from France and became the nation of Djibouti. The capital is also called Djibouti.

In 2001, the country's economy was based almost entirely on the port and on the railroad that links it with Addis Ababa in neighboring Ethiopia, making it a major source of Ethiopian trade. The official languages of Djibouti are Arabic and French; most of the people speak Afar or Somali though. Radio and television stations broadcast in French, Arabic, Somali, and Afar. Because of a defense agreement with the former colonial power, Djibouti hosts more than 3,000 French military personnel, including the Foreign Legion.

Traditionally, education in Djibouti, a largely Islamic country and the first in Africa to adopt this religion, is the domain of the Koranic schools where tuition is in Arabic. Koranic, community-based preschools are especially abundant; here children learn the Holy Koran, reading, writing, religious instruction, Islam, and how to perform prayers. These preschools, usually run by a *sheikh* and staffed by preschool teachers characterized by good memory, honesty, modesty and total dedication to their mission, do not necessarily emphasize skill-oriented activities. Private preschools serve less than 500 children, or 0.3 percent of the population (0 to 6 years of age). Tuition fees of about $1,000 a year are out of the reach of any but the most affluent parents.

Western education first arrived in Djibouti when Roman Catholic missionaries opened a school in 1884.

After World War II, state schools became increasingly popular. In 1964 Koranic instruction became part of the curriculum even in state schools and, by the end of the 1970s, enrollment in primary schools rose from approximately 1,100 pupils shortly after World War II to 13,740. Primary school attendance is compulsory and free; however, Djibouti struggles, as do many other African countries, with impossible demands made by the international banking community that the foreign debt be serviced even if this means the disintegration of health and education services and the consequent destruction of the futures of millions of children. Thus, the government does not monitor compliance with compulsory school attendance policy, and many of the schools are in poor condition and need upgrading. Most secondary schools are in the larger centers and the number of classrooms for secondary students is inadequate. Approximately 20 percent of children who start secondary school complete their education. Less than 50 percent of the population can read and write. Approximately 32 percent of girls are literate, as compared with 60 percent of boys; 62 percent of girls attend primary school compared with 73 percent of boys; and 23 percent of girls attend secondary school compared with 33 percent of boys. Overall, girls make up 36 percent of all secondary students. In 1998 the government committed itself to increasing the number of female students in the educational system to 50 percent. Significant progress has been made toward this goal in the primary grades.

At the end of 1999, the Ministry of Education held a national week-long symposium on education policy. Representatives of the education profession, parents, students, and other parties interested in revitalizing education attended this meeting. The people's and the government's obvious will and commitment to education will only be successful if the international community accepts co-responsibility.

The proud and free nomadic people who live in the interior of Djibouti are not yet fully integrated into the country's educational system. Ways are being sought to provide a basic education to these people, who are totally unimpressed with modern ways. Some, in fact, regard someone who "goes to town" as a person who doesn't want to take responsibility for his/her community. One of the possibilities suggested is that teachers would be found, perhaps from their midst, who would travel with the community and so provide an education that would give the children a wider choice in the future.

The school year runs from September to June and the language of instruction is French in public and Catholic schools and Arabic in Koranic schools. A Teachers' Training College offers two-year training programs. Since 1990 the British Council English Language Project

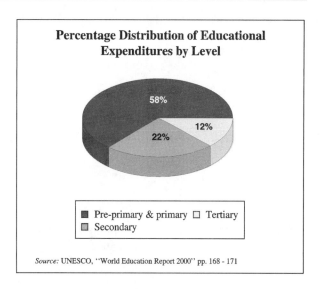

Percentage Distribution of Educational Expenditures by Level

58%

12%

22%

■ Pre-primary & primary □ Tertiary
■ Secondary

Source: UNESCO, "World Education Report 2000" pp. 168 - 171

for Teachers has conducted a program to help indigenous teachers of English in secondary schools become more competent in the teaching of English. Through independent study units, set texts, and face-to-face workshops, courses in teaching English language methods are conducted.

On October 14, 2000, in time for the beginning of the 2000-2001 academic year, *Pôle Universitaire de Djibouti,* Djibouti's new university, opened its doors to its first students. Initially, courses in the arts will be offered, but there were plans to expand the academic curriculum in the near future. The language of instruction is French.

Djibouti's education expenditure is 2.5 percent of the Gross National Product. Newspapers, books, and magazines, mainly in French, are expensive and not readily available except to those affiliated with the international embassies.

Djibouti hosts approximately 100,000 refugees, illegal immigrants, and displaced persons, about one-fifth of the population, from Ethiopia and Somalia, the two countries on its borders wracked by civil war, drought, and famine. As members of the larger community, they share in the health and education services of the country. However, the sheer number of people moving into Djibouti places a heavy burden on the already fragile economy. Several agencies, including the United Nations High Commission for Refugees and the International Labor Office based in Geneva, Switzerland, have started educational programs to help especially refugee women who, often without their men to help them take care of their children, need to see to the daily needs of their families. Vocational training centers that provide auto-mechanics and electrical installation for males and handicraft and tailoring for females attempt to ease dependence on outside aid and offer limited opportunities for gainful employment.

—*Karin I. Paasche*

DOMINICA

BASIC DATA

Official Country Name:	Commonwealth of Dominica
Region:	Puerto Rico & Lesser Antilles
Population:	71,540
Language(s):	English, French patois
Literacy Rate:	94%

HISTORY & BACKGROUND

The island of Dominica is part of the Lesser Antilles, located between the islands of Martinique and Guadeloupe in the Caribbean Sea, with a population of 74,900 people (1996). The island is approximately 754 square kilometers (290 square miles). The capital city of Dominica is Roseau.

EDUCATIONAL SYSTEM—OVERVIEW

Education is free and is provided by both government and denominational schools. Attendance is compulsory between the ages of 5 and 15 years. The educational system is divided into four main categories: preprimary, primary, secondary, and tertiary and is governed by the Ministry of Education. The system is modeled after the British (levels) and North American (grade) structures. Primary education begins at the age of five and lasts for seven years. Secondary education begins at the age of twelve and lasts for five years. Gross enrollment in 1999 at the preschool and primary level for children aged 5 to 11 was 15,982. Gross enrollment at the secondary level was 7,356 in 1999. Females accounted for 47.1 percent of enrollment in 2000 at the primary level and 57.0 percent of enrollment at the secondary level. The grading system (1997) for both primary and secondary schools is as follows: Excellent (85 percent to 100 percent); Very Good (70 percent to 84 percent); Good (55 percent to 69 percent); Improvement Needed (40 percent to 54 percent); Poor (26 percent to 39 percent); Ungraded (0 percent to 25 percent).

The educational system of Dominica consists of:

- 83 preprimary schools—all privately owned, managed, and funded;

- 63 primary schools—53 are government-owned, 5 are government-assisted, and 5 are private;

- 15 secondary schools—6 are government-owned, 8 are government-assisted, and 1 private-grant aided;

- 1 school for the hearing impaired (government-funded);

- 1 school for the mentally challenged (privately and government-funded); and

- Clifton Dupigny Community College; Dominica Teachers Training College; and Princess Margaret Hospital School of Nursing.

PREPRIMARY & PRIMARY EDUCATION

Preprimary and primary education is free and compulsory and is provided in public, assisted, and private (independent) schools. Enrollment of eligible students between the ages of 5 to 11 years was 98 percent in 1999. At the preprimary level, the student-teacher ratio was 18:1. At the primary level, the ratio was 22:1. The highest student-teacher ratio was in the government-assisted schools (25:1), with the lowest being at the private schools (20:1). The student-teacher ratio was lower in rural areas (21:1) than in urban areas (24:1). At the end of grade 6, primary students sit for the Common Entrance Examination (CEE), which determines entrance into secondary education. Transition rates from the primary to the secondary level are among the lowest in the Caribbean, with only 60 percent of the 12- to 16-year-olds enrolled in secondary education. The Junior Secondary Program is available for those students who were not selected by the CEE to enroll in secondary school. This is a three-year program that leads to a select number of students being able to enter formal secondary school. A review of the CEE shows that, at the primary level of education, girls consistently outperform boys in all subjects, leading to a higher level of representation at the secondary level. The overall repetition rate for primary school students in 1998 was 3.3 percent, with males having a slightly higher repetition rate of 3.5 percent. The overall dropout rate at the primary level was 0.16 percent in 1999, again, with males having a higher average rate of 0.25 percent.

SECONDARY EDUCATION

The main objective of the 15 secondary schools is to prepare students for the successful completion of the Caribbean Examination Council (CXC) examination, which determines entry into college. The secondary school system is divided into two cycles: a junior division for students normally between the ages of 12 to 14; and a senior division of secondary education for students older than the age of 14. To enter secondary school, all students are required to pass the CEE exam. The teacher-student ratio at the secondary level in 1999 was 18:1. The overall repetition rate was 9.9 percent in 2000, with males having a higher degree of repetition of 13 percent. The overall dropout rate at the secondary level was 2.8 percent in 1998, with males leaving school at a rate of 3.8 percent.

HIGHER EDUCATION

Secondary students who perform well (passing in five or more of their classes) on the examination(s) qualify for entry into postsecondary institutions. Postsecondary students have four options for enrollment: Clifton Dupigny Community College; The Teacher's Training College; Princess Margaret Hospital School of Nursing; and The University of West Indies.

Clifton Dupigny Community College (CDCC) was created in 1983 and consists of two "branches" or strands of instruction: the Academic Studies Division and the Technical Studies Division. The Academic Studies Division grants levels of certification and offers courses/majors in mathematics, chemistry, biology, physics, computer sciences, geography, accounts, economics, sociology, history, Spanish, French, and English composition. Of the 460 students enrolled in 1998, approximately 70 percent were female.

The Technical Studies Division offers full-time, two-year diploma courses as well as one- and two-year certificate courses. Courses are offered in engineering as well as building and technical trades. Females accounted for only 20 percent of enrollment at this level in 1998.

Dominica Teachers Training College (DTTC) is a two-year, full-time program leading to certification accredited by the University of the West Indies. The DTTC offers certification in both primary and secondary education. The DTTC graduates roughly 30 teachers annually.

The University of the West Indies (UWI) is available to students who have successfully completed all levels of their secondary studies and have passed the Caribbean Examination Council exam. On Dominica, UWI offers several part-time distance education courses that lead to certificates in public administration, business administration, and education.

Special Needs Education: The School for the Hearing Impaired and the Alpha Center are the two facilities that provide educational services for special needs students. The main objective of the Alpha Center is to educate students to be able to function independently in society to the highest degree possible. The Alpha Center also runs an early intervention program where young children, with their parents, learn to socialize and are taught rudimentary reading/writing skills.

ADMINISTRATION, FINANCE, & EDUCATIONAL RESEARCH

The educational affairs of Dominica are overseen by the Ministry of Education, Science, and Technology. The Ministry of Education, Science, and Technology is administered by a chief education officer, an assistant chief education officer, and several district education and specialist education officers. The Ministry also houses specialized units such as the Curriculum Development Unit, the Textbook Distribution Unit, the Education Planning Unit, the Measurement and Evaluation Unit, the Learning Support/Secretariat Unit, and the Materials Production Unit.

The total expenditure for education in 2000 was roughly $42 million, with primary education consuming the largest share of resources at 51.7 percent, followed by secondary education at 24.8 percent, postsecondary education at 7.0 percent, and contributions to the University of the West Indies at 5.0 percent. Total annual per-pupil expenditures in 1999 were as follows: preprimary ($60.07); primary ($1,405.45); secondary ($1,542.87); and postsecondary ($4,311.10).

TEACHING PROFESSION

To become a certified teacher, candidates must have attained four subject-passes on the Caribbean Examination Council (CXC), including both English and mathematics. Teacher training is completed at Dominica Teachers Training College. The teacher-training program and subsequent courses are administered under the auspices of the Faculty of Education of the University of West Indies.

There is a lack of certified teachers particularly at the primary level. In 1999 only 64 percent of the primary teachers were certified. The majority (41 percent) of trained primary school teachers in 1998 were located in the western portion of the island, and 77 percent of the teachers taught at public institutions in 2000. The student-teacher ratio for qualified primary teachers in 1999 varied between 31:1 and 50:1, dependent upon the district. At the secondary level, only 31 percent of the teachers were trained to teach the content appropriate for their individual grade levels. The student-teacher ratio for qualified secondary teachers in 1999 averaged 53:1 yet could be as low as 21:1, based on individual districts. The vast majority of secondary school teachers were employed at either public schools (53 percent) or assisted schools (44 percent).

Women dominate the education profession at both the primary and secondary levels. At the primary level, roughly 80 percent of the staff were women in 2000. And at the secondary level, women accounted for 66 percent of school personnel.

SUMMARY

Arguably, the facet of Dominican education needing the most attention is the area of teacher training. The majority of teachers are not certified. At the secondary level, there is no policy of continuous teacher training. Male teachers, particularly at the primary level, are scarce (representing only 20 percent of all primary teachers). Attrition rates among unqualified and temporary teachers, who form the bulk of the teaching force, are high. It is felt that the needs of Dominica's educational system is as follows: all teachers be certified to teach in their content areas; a continuing education program for all teachers be implemented; and male teachers should be actively recruited.

In an effort to increase professional development opportunities and to offer training to unqualified teachers, the Ministry of Education implemented the Teacher Training Project. This project trained unqualified teachers through select coursework. Also, professional development courses were offered for 50 principals and senior teachers. Though this project is surely a step in the right direction, it needs to be expanded to include supplemental training and professional development opportunities for all teachers.

Most promising and ambitious is the Long Term Education Development Plan. The Education Development Plan offers a philosophical and pedagogical blueprint for the education of Dominica for six years (1999-2005). The primary purpose is to raise student achievement with the premise that education leads to increased national and regional development. The Plan has six major components (Andrew 1999):

- strengthening the capacity of the Ministry of Education, improving the qualifications and professional development of the teaching staff, and strengthening the capacity of institutions through improved management and performance review

- establishing a Preprimary Council and increasing accessibility to quality preprimary provision through a partnership with the private sector

- introducing a National Curriculum and National Testing for primary and secondary schools and minimizing grade repetition and achieving Universal Secondary Education by 2003-2005

- establishing new levels of staffing and employment and conducting a review of small schools so as to consolidate them either through linking or closure where these are ineffective and inefficient

- improving reaching and learning materials and the provision of free textbooks for core subjects as well as new levels of professional development

- expanding access to tertiary education and the range of course provision, improving the management of tertiary provision by amalgamating current colleges and raising finances to enhance operations.

BIBLIOGRAPHY

Andrew, Max. *The Education System of Dominica: An Overview.* Roseau: Education Planning Unit, 1999.

Ministry of Education, Science, & Technology. *Indicators 2000.* Roseau: Education Planning Unit, 2000.

—Tim Lintner

DOMINICAN REPUBLIC

BASIC DATA

Official Country Name:	Dominican Republic
Region:	North & Central America
Population:	8,442,533
Language(s):	Spanish
Literacy Rate:	82.1%
Compulsory Schooling:	10 years
Public Expenditure on Education:	2.3%
Educational Enrollment:	Primary: 1,360,044 Secondary: 263,236 Higher: 176,995
Educational Enrollment Rate:	Primary: 94% Secondary: 54% Higher: 23%
Teachers:	Secondary: 12,504 Higher: 9,041
Female Enrollment Rate:	Primary: 94% Secondary: 61% Higher: 27%

HISTORY & BACKGROUND

Geography & Population: The Dominican Republic occupies the eastern two-thirds of the Caribbean island of Hispaniola, which is located west of Puerto Rico. Its only border is with Haiti. The Dominican Republic has an area of 48,400 kilometers, and its population was estimated at 8.4 million in 1999. For political and administrative purposes, the country is divided into three regions and seven subregions, which together contain the 29 provinces and the National District.

It was originally occupied by Tainos, an Arawak-speaking people. The Tainos welcomed Columbus in his first voyage in 1492, but subsequent colonizers were brutal, reducing the Tainos population from about 1 million to about 500 in 50 years. To ensure adequate labor for plantations, the Spanish brought African slaves to the island beginning in 1503.

In the next century, French settlers occupied the western end of the island, which Spain ceded to France in 1697, and which, in 1804, became the Republic of Haiti. The Haitians conquered the whole island in 1822 and held it until 1844, when forces led by Juan Pablo Duarte, the hero of Dominican independence, drove them out and established the Dominican Republic as an independent state. In 1861, the Dominicans voluntarily returned to the Spanish Empire; in 1865, independence was restored.

Political, Social, & Cultural Bases: Economic difficulties, the threat of European intervention, and ongoing internal disorders led to a U.S. occupation in 1916 and the establishment of a military government in the Dominican Republic. The occupation ended in 1924 with a democratically elected Dominican government.

In 1930, Rafael L. Trujillo, a prominent army commander, established absolute political control. Trujillo promoted economic development and severe repression of domestic human rights. Mismanagement and corruption resulted in major economic problems. In August 1960, the Organization of American States (OAS) imposed diplomatic sanctions against the Dominican Republic as a result of Trujillo's complicity in an attempt to assassinate President Romulo Betancourt of Venezuela. These sanctions remained in force after Trujillo's death by assassination in May 1961. In November 1961, the Trujillo family was forced into exile.

The Trujillo administration initiated a campaign to increase the literacy rate, which was no higher than 30 percent in the early 1950s. These efforts resulted in a number of primary schools being established in rural areas. Urban needs were also met, to the extent that at the end of the regime, at least one primary school had been established in each town. These schools, however, were overcrowded, and many of them had to operate on double shifts, problems that have persisted into the twenty-first century.

Trujillo had also signed a *concordato* (agreement) with the Catholic church that included all Catholic schools under the auspices of public support. The Catholic church initiated several institutes for technical instruction that raised the level of professional training within the country. During President Joaquin Balaguer's terms of governance (1966-1978, 1986-1996) the Catholic church played a key role as a recipient of international aid for running educational and social programs.

The period of 1967 to 1971 saw the intervention of the World Bank and other international agencies to create many of the most recent initiatives in the educational system. These years saw the creation of organizations to teach American English to Dominicans and the use of scholarships to create a professional elite formed in American university systems. The San Jose Reform of 1967-1969 emphasized vocational training to improve industrial capacity.

The Dominican economy has undergone profound changes since the 1980s. Until the mid-1970s, traditional export products, mainly from agriculture, represented 60 percent of the total value of the country's exports. Over the last two decades, the service sector has led the economy, particularly economic and financial services related to tourism and industrial free trade zones, which by 1995 accounted for more than 70 percent of exports.

In 1992 the gross domestic product (GDP) began to recover, and by 1996 it was maintaining an average annual growth rate of more than 5 percent. In 1999, the country was singled out as the best economic performer in Latin America after having sustained a growth rate of more than 6 percent for several consecutive years.

This stability and macroeconomic growth have improved the purchasing power of the working population, and absolute poverty appears to have diminished. Despite this, reduced public spending for education and health has affected family budgets, unemployment rates (which stood at 15 percent in 1996-1997), and the percentage of the population linked to the informal economy and non-wage-earning activities. There has therefore been a considerable increase in relative poverty and the number of people who are in need. The public domestic debt, estimated at about US$400 million in mid-1997, has been burgeoning, and this has tended to inhibit private domestic investment. A particularly vulnerable factor is economic dependence on the 43 free trade zones.

After a long history of authoritarian regimes, the Dominican Republic is entering a new era of democracy and

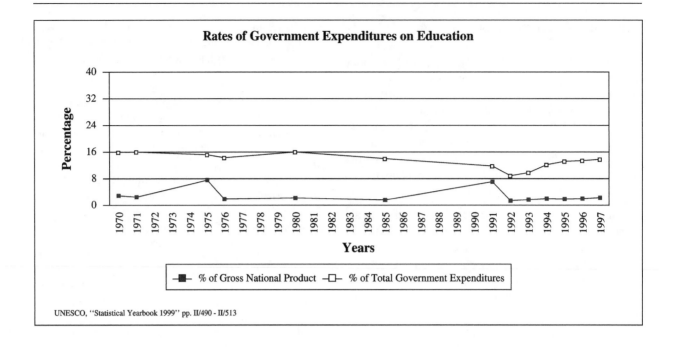

Rates of Government Expenditures on Education

UNESCO, "Statistical Yearbook 1999" pp. II/490 - II/513

social participation, including education. At the same time, the proportion of children in the overall population is shrinking. The vast majority of the population is of working age (15- to 64-years-old).

Although the Dominican Republic has one of the fastest growing economies in the world (average growth of 7.5 percent from 1997 to 2000), it has one of the lowest investments in education in the hemisphere. Public investment in education has increased since the 1990s, but it is still very low in comparison with other Latin American countries.

Nonetheless, the Dominican Republic shows enormous advances in education. The country developed its planning capacity and implemented some key programs. According to the Deputy Secretary of Education, Josefina Pimentel, there were developments in several areas: new education laws to replace the obsolete legislation of 1951; new curricula developed for Basic Education; new textbooks published and distributed throughout rural and urban schools; and an increase in the amount of compulsory education to nine years of basic education, including a preschool year.

CONSITITUTIONAL & LEGAL FOUNDATIONS

General Survey: Although there are a number of programs and rights granted in educational legislation, generally these rights are not enforced by the courts in the way that they are in countries such as the United States. This is largely because the Dominican legal system, which is based on the French Code, is not oriented to the

enforcement of the "minor" rights of educational entitlement.

Until shortly after independence in 1865, education in the Dominican Republic was not legally regulated, and most schools were run by Catholic groups. In 1857, the national budget provided for no more than five schools for the entire country. In 1884, Puerto Rican political activist and educator Eugenio Ma. de Hostos enacted the first educational law, making local authorities responsible for providing and financing primary schools and the newly created normal schools, but entrusting the central government with secondary education.

The real base for the educational system was created in 1918 as a direct result of the American occupation, with *orden ejecutiva 145* (executive order 145), which reformed the existing system along American lines. Though widely condemned at the time as anti-Dominican in intent, this system was further developed by the Trujillo dictatorship (1930-1961) with law 418, the General Law of Education (1938), and the Organic Law of Education (law 2909; 1951).

The reforms of middle secondary school (*educacion media*) in 1967 were created by *Resolucion 56-66*, for the development of the *Liceo Laboral* (Labor High Schools) and the *Laboral Especializado* (Specialized Labor High Schools), training schools for work in industry that put special emphasis on the training of women.

Another reform measure for high school level development, *Ordenanza 2-69* (Ordinance 2-69), emphasized a humanistic view of individual development and treated those aspects relating to technical and labor development as the means by which the individual could contribute to society. The goals of higher education were also based on integral humanistic development, where those who wished to retrain for a second career could acquire a technical degree and as such create the means by which they could be gainfully employed while furthering their education. These schools were termed *Liceos Diversificados*.

Institutions of higher education are established by law and their right to award degrees is sanctioned by the government. The *Universidad Autonoma de Santo Domingo* (UASD), the only public university in the Dominican Republic, was granted autonomous status and continuous state support in Law 5778 (1962). All private institutions of higher education are regulated by Law 236 (1967), which regulates both their structure and their right to award degrees.

In 1970, the objectives of the *Ciclo Comun* in middle school education emphasized human development as a goal for the first time. Within the reforms initiated by UNESCO in 1973 were two main efforts: the creation of a network of integrated centers of educational development with the goal of answering to the needs of both school-age and adult education, and technical schools dedicated to training individuals in rural education and agricultural work and health services. Literacy and vocational education scheduled at night for adults began in 1968, and the use of a radio-based program of primary school classes for *campesinos* began in 1974.

The 10-Year Plan: Between 1988 and 1990, the World Bank, the United Nations Development Program (UNDP), and UNESCO, working in tandem, began to quietly reinvest in Dominican education. As early as 1985, UNESCO began the formulation of what was to be the *Plan Decenal* (10-year plan), fostering interest among leaders of the education and business sectors in participating in an overall restructuring of the Dominican educational system. It took some five years from the first legal documents created in 1992 until the final version of the General Law of Education 66/97 was approved in 1997 for the different elements of the *Plan Decenal* to begin fully functioning. The more important acts are as follows:

- *Ordenanzas 1'92, 2'92* established the legal base for the *Pruebas Nacionales*, the national standardized tests administered at the end of 4th, 8th, and 12th grades.
- *Ordenanza 1'95* established the curricula for the Initial, Basic, and Middle schools and also for special and adult education.
- *Ordenanza 1'96* established the evaluation model for all academic levels.

The combined law 66/97 integrates all other acts and gives the final version of the general law of education,

the organization of its administration, and the relationship of all parts to the whole. Major foundations of the law are:

- that the universal right to education is "appropriate and free of cost, including those who are gifted, physically impaired, learning disabled and who, as such, must receive special education" (II.4.m);
- that nutrition and health in general are determining primary factors in scholastic achievement (II.4.ll); and
- that the goal of Dominican education is to form "people, men, and women, free-thinking, critical, and creative, able to participate in and construct a free society... that they can combine profitable work, community service, and humanistic, scientific, and technological training... to contribute to both national growth and their own personal development" (II.5.a).

The 12 major articles of the law address the principles and objectives of the Dominican educational system; the structuring of the educational system into preschool (*inicial*), basic, middle (*medio*), and higher (*superior*) education; safeguards for quality within the system; the executive structuring of the educational system; the decentralization of the educational system and the rights and responsibilities of the regions, districts, and local centers; professional requirements for teachers and academic staff and their training, rights, and duties; the social benefits due to teachers, including insurance, pensions, and retirement; student welfare; participation within the educational system; the financing of education; the accreditation of studies; and those bodies responsible for the carrying out of the provisions of the educational law and concerning equity within the system.

EDUCATIONAL SYSTEM—OVERVIEW

Structure & Degrees: In 1985 the structure of the educational pyramid consisted of three years of noncompulsory preschool education; six years in primary school; and six years in middle school, divided into two years of intermediate education and four years of secondary school, or into four years and two years (*Plan de Reforma*). Students who continued to that point received their high school degree (*bachillerato*) and might continue to the tertiary education provided by the Dominican universities, which conferred either licentiates (*licenciaturas*), *ingenerias,* or *doctorados* (doctorates—for law and medicine only), depending on the field of study.

The revised structure is no longer a simple pyramid. Of the three years of preschool education, one year became compulsory, as did nine years of basic primary school, effectively extending compulsory schooling by four years. Middle school (to receive the *bachillerato* degree) has been reduced to only three years and is noncompulsory, as is higher education. Middle school students are separated into academic and technical-professional tracks, receiving high school diplomas that specify their tracks. Education provided by the Dominican universities continues to confer *licenciaturas, ingenerias,* and *doctorados,* but with extended programs, especially in the areas of medicine and law, whose programs have been effectively doubled in both material and time. Also of note is the inclusion of *maestrias* and nonmedical *doctorados* as the higher education system expands its postgraduate degree systems.

Special Groups: Like many other countries the Dominican Republic must deal with the children of temporary migrant workers, primarily from Haiti. There appear to be no barriers to attendance within the school system, but many Haitian parents want their children to work in the fields and earn money rather than attend school. Some schools have been constructed in those zones where large populations of Haitians reside (the *bateys*).

In both secondary school and tertiary institutions, women predominated at the beginning of the millennium. The increase in women's employment, particularly in industrial free zones, has increased the pressure for wide availability of preschool. Some employers have begun a pilot program of four days working, four days off to allow women to go to school.

Education Reforms: In 1988, a "private" initiative combining interested business sectors and *Pontificia Universidad Madre y Maestra* (PUCMM, the major private Catholic university, a recipient of international money dedicated to research), with funding from the World Bank, began to work on a reconstruction of Dominican educational policy. This reconstruction plan was termed the *Plan Decenal,* or the 10-year Educational Plan. The unique participatory process that led to the formulation of the *Plan Decenal* produced three general outcomes: an identification of the main problems of education in the country; an understanding of research conducted about those problems, and the development of a series of proposals and innovations to solve them. More importantly, such a process increased the social capital of the nation for collective action around common goals. The initial success of the reform suggests that there is motivation and basic capacity in the country for undertaking national debates on social issues and developing general plans. The national government enthusiastically adopted the plans, which also garnered support throughout the international community.

Plan Decenal outlined the following goals:

1. Raising the Educational Level of the General Population: increasing school attendance, reducing illiteracy, expanding adult education, and developing programs for informal learning.

2. Increasing the Quality of Education: promoting innovation in education, compensating for the low socioeconomic level of students, bettering the living conditions of teachers, bettering the physical and pedagogical environment of the classroom, and raising the quality of the educational process.

3. Strengthening Educational Technology: promoting scientific and technological innovation, introducing the use of computers, expanding and bettering educational techniques, creating new technical careers, and establishing new technical schools.

4. Decentralizing the Educational System: modernizing the administrative system, encouraging the use of administrative meetings, and institutionalizing and standardizing the decision-making process.

5. Strengthening Community Ties to the School System: encouraging reciprocity between school and community, strengthening parent-teacher associations, and bringing the secular world into the classroom.

6. Increase the Investment in Education: by 1998, have use of 16 percent of the national budget for education; by 2001, have use of 25 percent of the national budget.

Organizational work continued throughout 1989 to 1990, when the commission *Nacional del Plan Decenal* (National 10-Year Plan) was formed through an alliance of SEEBAC (the Dominican Department of Education, later renamed SEEC), EDUCA, ADP (the teachers' union), the regional UNDP, and *Plan Educativo,* a Santo Domingo-based group of educators and industrialists. These groups worked both at the executive level of planning through use of chosen representatives and more extensively in the national *consultas* (consulting groups) that were to be developed for expanding and promoting the plan.

The system of *consultas* incorporated more than 100 institutions and involved more than 50,000 individuals. They were organized at five levels: open advising, institutional advising, national advising, internal advising, and regional advising. By 1993, through the process of the *consultas,* more than 100 organizations were officially listed as participants in the formulation of the *Plan Decenal.*

PREPRIMARY & PRIMARY EDUCATION

The Pre-Kinder and Kinder programs of the Dominican Republic were initiated by Rene Klang de Guzman, the wife of Antonio Guzman, in 1981. While this program never developed much beyond a pilot program, the organization for the welfare of children and their rights, CONANI, has lasted for over 20 years.

At the time of the midway assessment of the *Plan Decenal* in August 2000, approximately 23 percent of eligible children were in preschool (including those in mandatory kindergarten). The education department's goal is to increase that figure to 50 percent.

While the Kinder program is already mandated by law, very few schools have begun to create these levels due to a lack of classroom space and qualified personnel. While some universities have responded by opening training for this level, it will take years before an adequate number of people can be trained to fill the national demand.

Beyond the revamping of the curriculum for basic and middle schools, the most significant innovations of the *Plan Decenal* were likely the standardization of the school calendar to 42 weeks of five-hour days and the addition of national standardized tests for the fourth, eighth, and twelfth grade levels. These tests provide the system some means of comparison between school districts and allow for some quality control. A program was also designed to retain students, including free books, prizes, computer labs, and free breakfasts.

Additions to the curriculum include English and French (beginning in fourth grade), art and music, computer science, and a greater emphasis on math and science. These subjects add approximately 15 more teaching hours per week.

SECONDARY EDUCATION

Once past the sixth grade, two tracks are established for continuing students: the academic track that continues on through the twelfth grade with academic studies for those students who wish to pursue a university education, and the technical-professional tracks, for those who wish to enter any of the technical schools. Actual differentiation into tracks occurs at entry into secondary level at tenth grade. The simplest degree is that of the *tecnico basico,* wherein the student is prepared just one year past basic schooling. The two- and three-year technical track schools are mainly for business training (for the *bachillerato commercial* certification), agricultural training (for the *Perito agronomo,* or 13th grade agricultural diploma), and industrial training certifications. These schools offer a curriculum distribution of 30 percent academic subjects and 70 percent specialized subjects. Individuals in the technical-professional track number 62,286.

Participation in secondary education can still be characterized as weak. For each 1,000 students that enter

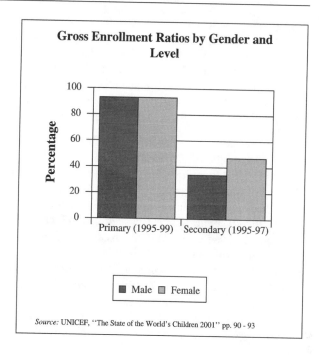

Gross Enrollment Ratios by Gender and Level

Source: UNICEF, "The State of the World's Children 2001" pp. 90 - 93

first grade, only 219 enter ninth grade. Of those, 62 percent of secondary students complete their studies and receive their certification. There was a total of 432,793 students in secondary level in 2000, showing an increase of almost 100 percent from the 1993 total of 232,383 students. This makes it the fastest growing sector of the education system, compared to preschool (48.6 percent growth) and elementary school (24 percent). Eighty-one percent of all secondary students are in public schools, compared to 62 percent of preschool students and 87 percent of elementary school students.

The projected unit cost per secondary student was estimated at US$177 for the academic tracks and US$360 for the technical-professional tracks, as of 2001. The total number of secondary school teachers stands at 13,698, approximately 59 percent of whom work in the public school system. This yields a student-teacher ratio of 43:1 in public schools and 51:1 in private schools.

Updates to the curriculum include an increased emphasis on literature, art and music, and computer science, as well as stronger programs in math and science, adding approximately 15 more teaching hours per week. Problems in secondary education include over-age students (over one-fourth of students are more than 19 years old), overcrowding, and the dropout rate.

HIGHER EDUCATION

Public & Private Universities: The present university system, both public and private, owes much of its standards and administrative policy to the influence of the

Universidad Autonoma de Santo Domingo (UASD). This university, the oldest in Latin America, was created by Pope Paul II in 1538 by Papal Bull and has a long academic tradition and influence in local politics. Awarded autonomous status in 1961, it remains the largest university system. Admission into the public university is very cheap and admission standards are low.

Private universities began with the 1962 formation of Roman Catholic *Universidad Madre y Maestra* (UCMM), later *Pontificia Universidad Madre y Maestra* (PUCMM), following a name change by Pope John Paul II in 1987. Precedent for awarding government subsidy to private universities was established in 1965 when the government awarded UCMM a subsidy of 1.2 million pesos. Following the establishment of UCMM, a multitude of universities were incorporated, including the *Universidad Nacional Pedro Henriquez Urena* (UNPHU, 1966), *Universidad Central del Este* (UCE, 1971), *Instituto Technologico de Santo Domingo* (INTEC, 1972), and *Universidad Technologica de Santiago* (UTESA, 1972).

Certification: The rapid expansion of the university system created problems of certification validity. These came to a head in the early 1980s with the closing of *El Centro de Estudios Tecnicos* (CETEC) in 1982. Of most concern for certification validity is the position of the English-language medical programs, which accept applications from many international students from such diverse areas as Pakistan, India, Saudi Arabia, Singapore, Canada, and the United States.

In response to such concerns, the Dominican Council for Higher Education (CONES) was created through *Decreto 1255* in 1983 to legislate, regulate, certify, and give consulting support to universities. In 1998 CONES recognized 29 universities with a combined total enrollment of 213,200. Not all universities, however, meet international agency standards for ''full'' university status, such as professional training with research-based departments. The *Britannica Yearbook* of 2000, for example, lists only seven universities and 73,461 students, numbers much lower than other sources. The state of California recognizes six of the medical programs. Much progress, however, was made during the 1990s to update curricula and improve the quality of academic professionals working within the university system. The study of medicine and law have been scrutinized heavily, and both programs have been substantially expanded and updated to meet system standards.

Enrollments & Courses: In 1997, according to the *Consejo Nacional de Educacion Superior* (National Council on Higher Education), the government department in charge of overseeing universities, there were 176,935 university students in the country. The UASD had 81,753 student. The largest private university, UTESA, had 21,353 students, followed by O&M with 17,504 students. CONES recognized 36 higher education institutions, including 29 universities and 7 institutes. Of the 29 universities recognized by CONES, 17 are located in Santo Domingo.

The 1997 study showed that most students opted to study accounting. From 1992 to 1997, some 10,376 students graduated in accounting, and 22,413 accounting students were enrolled. Education placed second, a turnaround from past years. There were 20,786 students enrolled in education, a marked increase from the 9,777 graduates of the previous five years. Marketing was another popular major, with some 17,672 students enrolled. Some 17,697 students chose computer sciences. Law maintained a steady enrollment of 19,100, but few Dominicans chose medicine, with only 2,224 enrolled.

The director of the CONES, Alejandrina German, said that her department is carrying out a study to determine the real demand for professionals in the country in order to make recommendations to high schools orienting their students in their choice of a university career.

ADMINISTRATION, FINANCE, & EDUCATIONAL RESEARCH

Administrative Structure: Apart from CONES, the supervisory board that oversees the entire system, the administrative system is comprised of the Secretariat, headed by the Secretary of Education, a position that is decidedly political. The auditing, insurance, international and public relations, judicial concerns, and project implementation departments all rely on the Secretariat. The subsecretariats of Education, Administration, and Culture form a second administrative level, with its regional and subregional offices forming the educational framework. The regional system is broken down into regional directives and subdivided into districts. The districts themselves are comprised of the individual schools.

The director of each district, apart from three consultants—one external, one internal, and a computer systems expert—has a staff divided into three sections: academic, special services, and operations. Each separate staff is comprised of eight individuals in charge of specific areas of focus, for example, the math coordinator or the national coordinator.

Each district has an administrative board and an internal consultant. Beyond this, the district has a staff of five, one each in charge of national exams, community participation, physical education, supervision, and administrative support. Each district also has direct control of the individual schools.

Each school director has a Board of Regents, a Parent-Teachers Association, a Student Association, and two consultants to which to respond. Under his control is a staff of eight, one each in charge of registration, health and nutrition, medical aid, social work, student services, curriculum development, maintenance, and administrative assistance. Each director also has direct control of the teachers and students.

The highly participatory educational reform process of the *Plan Decenal* was not able to effect much change in the persistently centralized and slow decision-making mechanisms of the Secretary of Education. Neither national consensus nor the formulation of new legal rules have been able to substantially change the patterns of interaction among the actors in education.

Expenditures: Dominican educational reform has been financed by money from international organizations and the legal provision requiring that a percentage of the national budget be devoted to education. Although the full amount was not appropriated in the first years of the plan, appropriations by 1998 neared the required percentage of 16 percent. By contrast, annual per capita expenditures on education from 1987 to 1990, adjusted for inflation, were just 40 percent of the total expenditures in 1980.

The needs for financing the *Plan Decenal* were laid out for investors and contributors following meetings held in early 1993. The plan was to be developed in three phases: a four-year emergency program to jumpstart the improvement of primary schools, a consolidation program to evaluate gains and "consolidate" achievement of objectives, and a support program to fund administration and infrastructure.

Projected costs of these programs for 1993 alone were US$244.8 million, of which only 15 percent would be covered by foreign aid. It was believed that if the government lived up to its funding commitments and could maintain a gross national product (GNP) increase of 3.5 percent, the plan would be effectively funded. The General Law of Education 66/97, which mandates that 16 percent of the national budget be paid into the educational system, also requires the equivalent of 4 percent of the GNP.

Other provisions of Chapter 1, Title 9, call for 80 percent of the budget be dedicated to operating costs and less than 20 percent to capital expenses. Tax-deduction incentives for private business funding nonprofit education, research, or technical innovation endeavors can be applied for up to 5 percent, and educational materials are exempt from customs duties. Funds generated from the confiscation of unclaimed inheritances, 5 percent of inheritance taxes, 5 percent of any property sold by the

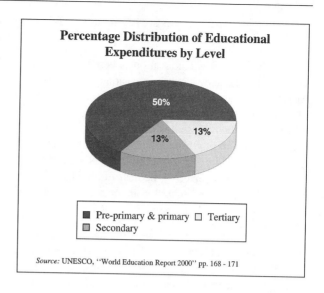

Percentage Distribution of Educational Expenditures by Level

50%

13%   13%

■ Pre-primary & primary □ Tertiary
■ Secondary

Source: UNESCO, "World Education Report 2000" pp. 168 - 171

state, 20 percent of unclaimed bank accounts, and all sale of property confiscated by police due to criminal activity are also earmarked for the National Fund for Educational Development. Apart from direct mandated financing from the national government, local schools and school districts can further depend on support supplied by the Parents and Friends Associations and patronage by private businesses.

In the 1998 fiscal year, the amount of funds budgeted for education represented 15.51 percent of the total budget. Given the growing state of the Dominican economy, increasing resources are becoming available. More importantly, the gap between the mandated rate of money earmarked for education and the amount spent in actuality is slowly narrowing. Between 1993 and 1996, for example, only 66 percent was paid into education, compared to 90 percent corresponding to 1998. Of the total educational budget of 1998, approximately 48 percent went to basic education, 813.4 million of which went into construction and infrastructure improvements. Of the personnel budget, approximately 66 percent went to payment of teachers, almost 24 percent went to administrative technicians, and about 9 percent went to management.

NONFORMAL EDUCATION

The *Plan Decenal* addresses inclusion of the nonformal programs and informal branches of the educational scheme (e.g., adult education, literacy, and vocational training). Special education is no longer isolated from traditional school programs, and there are interphasing links between the nonformal education network and the normal academic program. Total enrollment in adult education is 129,132, with literacy programs consisting of 42,132 students taught by 14,557 professionals in 669 night school centers. These classes are based on the ABCD Espanol Program.

Literacy and basic education is being expanded by use of radio and television transmissions to more isolated rural areas. Educational radio programs are offered in classes for grades one through eight. A new educational TV system is being installed for use in rural zones. This project, with funding from UNESCO, will transmit programs via a satellite signal from Mexico. New technology that will be implemented in the near future also includes establishing 500 new school computer centers and the creation of virtual classrooms.

All artistic institutions and training centers are financed and regulated from the *Direccion de Bellas Artes* (Direction of Fine Arts), a division of SEEC. Art and performing arts academies include *Escuela de Bellas Artes* (School of Fine Arts) in the San Francisco de Macoris; *Escuela de Artes Plasticas* (School of Plastic Arts) and the *Instituto de Cultura y Artes* (Institute of Culture and Art) in Santiago; *Acadimia Dominicana de Musica* (Music Academy), the *Conservatorio Nacional de Musica* (National Conservatory of Music), the *Escuela Nacional de Bellas Artes* (National School of Fine Arts), and the *Escuela de Arte Dramatico* (School of Drama) in Santo Domingo. The *Altos de Chavsn* School of Design, a Dominican institution located in La Romana and run by a U.S. foundation, has been affiliated with the Parsons School of Design, a division of New School University in New York City, for 20 years. By graduating more than 800 students, largely Dominican, the school has added a significant Dominican presence to the international design world. More than 200 of the graduates have gone on to study at the Parsons School of Design in New York. Another school of design exists in San Juan de la Maguana.

At present there are two open universities in the Dominican Republic, both of which base their curriculum on andragogical teaching methodology: the *Universidad para la Tercera Edad* (UTE) and the *Universidad Abierta para Adultos* (UAPA). Neither university offers online classes at this time.

TEACHING PROFESSION

Qualifications: In the past it was considered ordinary for a public school teacher to be a graduate only of one of the normal schools that trained high school graduates for two years in teaching techniques. Reforms have mandated that each teacher must have a *licenciatura* or a university five-year degree to be able to teach in the public school system. Under the *Plan Decenal* funds were made available for teachers to return to school to upgrade their credentials.

Given that this was a tremendous jump from the previous system, the emergency program has designated funds for retraining teachers. Most teachers have the opportunity to return to the university to complete their education with funds provided by the government. Between 1994 and 2000, approximately 11,000 teachers returned to school to upgrade their knowledge.

A related issue is the lack of qualified language teachers. Most language teachers are accustomed to receiving higher pay than the public school system can offer and are in high demand. Rural areas simply do not have them. While this problem may be balanced in the future, it creates uncomfortable conditions for the present.

Compensation: A significant development for the teaching profession has been the tripling of teachers' salaries since 1995, which has begun to attract teachers back into education. Because their insurance programs and retirement plans are mandated by law, while the private school system's is not, the public school system is now at an advantage in attracting well-qualified teachers. The 10-year plan also encouraged teacher housing projects.

SUMMARY

Five-Year Evaluation: The five-year evaluation of the *Plan Decenal* in August 2000 addressed the relative successes and failures in solving chronic problems within the Dominican educational system. Issues assessed for progress included illiteracy and enrollment, school calendar, standardized testing, curriculum reform, teacher shortages and professionalism, support associations, and health care and nutrition.

Illiteracy & Enrollment: The plan set a goal of eliminating illiteracy in the under-30 age group and ensuring that 9 out of every 10 children attend school. As of August 2000, the rate of illiteracy in the 15 to 24 age group had fallen to 9.5 percent, 11.2 percent of which is represented by males and 7.8 percent by females. School attendance in the 6 to 14 age group rose from 70.6 percent in 1990 to 85.6 percent in 1999, with an average growth rate per year of 2 to 4 percent. Current rates of promotion stand at 80 percent, repetition at 5.2 percent, and dropout at 15 percent, creating a 85.1 percent retention rate in basic education. Longitudinal cohort studies show that of 1,000 students that enter ninth grade, only 559 graduate.

Enrollments by gender demonstrate high numbers of females, with a 58 percent enrollment in secondary education and a 70 percent enrollment in postsecondary education. Total enrollment in education in 2001 stands at 229,161 for preschool, 1,713,783 for elementary school, 398,702 for secondary school, and 215,000 for university levels. Private schools now account for only 20 percent of total school enrollment.

School Calendar: Longer school calendars and school days were another aim of the plan, which specified expansion of the school calendar and daily schedule to 42 five-day weeks, with each day five-hours, from early September through the end of June. By 1995, the school calendar had been divided into 186 teaching days, 13 days dedicated to testing, and 18 days excluded for Christmas and Holy Week. Compliance with the new calendar is still not complete. In 1998, elementary and secondary schools reported an 82 percent compliance with the mandated schedule. Particularly problematic is compliance in the afternoon shifts that are the most likely to limit time.

Standardized Tests: The use of standardized tests has diverged somewhat from a diagnostic function and has focused solely on their promotional function. Still, the tests have provided a means by which nationwide standards may be set. By 2001, testing was being done annually in fourth, eighth, and twelfth grades, assessing students in language (Spanish, the language of instruction), math, natural sciences, and social sciences. Major problems still exist in the mechanics of test creation and scoring, and in reporting grades. Political opposition to testing from many quarters is said to be one reason for the slow implementation of the *Plan Decenal.*

Curriculum Reform: The creation and implementation of a new curriculum has had its greatest success in the design and publication of objectives, modalities, and specifications. Foci of the curriculum include computer science, compulsory English and French from fourth grade, ecology, and sports, as well as strengthening the traditional studies of language and math. Most areas now have government-issued books for 100 percent of basic education and 60 percent of secondary, together with their teachers' guides. These books are supplied for at least a minimal fee, however, and availability is not universal. Many schools, especially private schools, still opt for commercial texts approved by the Secretariat that are sold at prices that are almost prohibitive for the average breadwinner. Much training has been done to orient public teachers in the use of audiovisual equipment, yet most public schools lack both equipment and electrical supply for their use. Language and math programs, however are broadcast by means of contracted radio stations, especially to the border zones.

Teaching: In 1990, the salary paid to full-time teachers was RD$607.75 (US$50.00) per month, an amount that could only supply one-third of a typical family's cost of living. By the year 2000, this amount had been raised by 400 percent to a minimum of RD$3,200 (US$200.00). In 1992, the total number of education students in normal schools and university programs was only 1,463; by 1997, that number had risen to 26,240, equivalent to almost half of the public teaching population in 1990.

Support Associations: As part of the broad community support for the *Plan Decenal,* Parent/Friends Associations were to be created to aid schools. Most success has been seen at the individual school level, where 6,422 schools have active co-ops. These associations have initiated fundraising activities to boost income for supplies and maintenance needs, as well as activities to orient the community to responsibility in the educative process.

Health Care & Nutrition: School breakfasts are now served to one million children in kinder and elementary schools, compared to 45,000 in 1993. Of that one million, 70 percent come from 25 provinces and marginal urban zones of Santo Domingo. In the frontier zones, where poverty levels are more severe, 120,000 children receive more complete nutrition, including meat, through the United Nations Food Aid Program. This program is considered key in reducing the school desertion and repetition rate. Programs for visual screening had reached 40,950 children by 2000, and deparisitization programs had reached 190,000.

Second 10-Year Plan: Since the first 10-year plan did not complete all the desired educational reforms, a second 10-year plan is being formulated. The Secretariat states that while the first 10-year plan stressed quantity, the second 10-year plan will stress quality.

BIBLIOGRAPHY

Alvarez, Benjamin. *Autonomia escolar y reforma educativa.* Santiago: Programa de Promocion de la Reforma Educativa en America Latina y el Caribe, 2000.

Alvarez, Benjamin, Joan Dassin, Larry Rosenberg, and David Bloom. *Education in Central America.* Cambridge: Harvard Institute for International Development (in press).

Arrien, Juan. *La educacion y la reforma de la educacion en cinco paises centroamericanos.* Nicaragua: PREAL/Fundacion Ford/Universidad Centroamericana, 1998.

Berbaum, Marcia, and Uli Locher. *EDUCA: Business Leaders Promote Basis Education and Education Reform in the Dominican Republic.* Washington, DC: Creative Associates International, 1998.

Burki and Perri, eds. *Beyond the Washington Consensus: Institutions Matter.* Washington, DC: The World Bank, 1998.

Centro Cultural Poveda. Propuesta para el dialogo nacional. Unpublished document, 1998.

Comision Centroamericana para la Reforma Educative. *Manana es muy tarde.* Santiago: Programa de Promocion de la Reforma Educativa en America Latina y el Caribe, 2000.

Fernandez, Leonel. *La vision del futuro. Parques technologicos y fondos de becas tecnologicos.* Power Point presentation, n.d.

Filmer, Deon, Lant Pritchett, and Yee-Peng-Tes. "Educational Attainment Profile of the Poor. DHS Evidence from Around the Globe." Mimeo, Washington, DC: The World Bank, 1998.

Flores, Ramon.. "Ciencia, tecnologia, globalizacion y educacion." Presentado al Simposio Educativo Internacional, Magisterio 2000. Republica Dominicana, August 1999.

Fullan, Michael. "Managing Change." (Restructuring Brief). North Coast Professional Development Consortium, 1993.

Fundacion Economia y Desarrollo. 1998. *Analisis del gasto en programas de la ecretaria de Estado de Educacion y Cultura.* Fundacion Economia y Desarrollo, 1998.

Gajardo, Marcela. Reformas educativas en America Latina. Documenos, Programa de Promocion de la Reforma Educativa en America Latina y el Caribe, 1998.

IDB/USAID/HIID. Juan Carlos Navarro et al., eds. *Perspectivas sobre la reforma educative.* Washington, DC: USAID/IDB, 2000.

Inter-American Development Bank. *Dominican Republic Graphs: Social Indicators.* 15 May 2001. Available from http://www.iadb.org/.

———. *Economic and Social Progress in Latin America. 1996 Report. Making Social Services Work.* Washington, DC: IDB, 1996.

Navarro, Luisa. "El papel del maestro en el nuevo milenio." Presentado al Simposio Educativo Nacional Magisterio 2000. Republica Dominicana, August, 1999.

Oficina Nacional de Estadistica. *Estadisticas seleccionadas de la Republica Dominicana.* Santo Domingo: Oficina Nacional de Estdistica, 1999.

Pimentel, Josefina. *Reflexiones y perspectivas sobre la educacion dominicana.* Santo Domingo: FLACSO/PREAL, 1998.

Prats, Ibelisse. "El paradigma de una educacion de calidad social para todos." Presentado al Simposio Educativo Nacional Magisterio 2000. Republica Dominicana, August 1999.

Programa de Naciones Unidad para el Desarrollo. H. Gomez G., ed. *Educacion la agenda del siglo XXI. Hacia un desarrollo humano.* Bogota: Tercer Mundo, 1998.

Puryear, J. "El sector privado y la educacion: la experiencia en paises desarrollados de la OCDE." In USAID/IDB, *Perspectivas sobre la reforma educative.*

———. *Socios para el progreso.* Santiago: PREAL, 1998.

Revista Foro Comercio e inversion Caribe-Estados Unidos. Edicion unica, 1999.

Shaffer, James D. *Institutions, Behavior, and Economic Performance: Comments and Institutional Analysis.* September 1995. Available from http://msu.edu/.

UNESCO. *UNESCO Database.* Available from http://www.unesco.org/.

United States Agency for International Development. Competitiveness Program of the Dominican Republic. Unpublished paper, 2000.

———. *Evaluation of Education Private Initiatives in Primary Education Projects (PIPE).* USAID, 1994.

World Bank, The. Power Point Presentation on Dominican Education, 2000.

———. *World Bank Database.* Available from http://www.worldbank.org.

World Economic Forum. *Global Competitiveness Report 2000.* Available from http://www.weforum.org/.

Zaiter, J. "La busqueda de un consenso nacional para la reforma de la educacion dominicana." In B. Alvarez y M. Ruiz-Casarea, Senderos de cambio. *Genesis y ejecucion de las reformas educativas en America Latina y el Caribe. Politica educativa en America Latina y el Caribe, Informe tecnico 1.* Washington, DC: Academic para el Desrrollo Educativo/Agencia para el Desarrollo Internacional de los Estados Unidos, 1997.

Zaiter, J., et al. *La escuela dominicana y la reforma educativa.* Santo Domingo: FLACSO/UNICEF/PREAL, 2000.

—Virginia Nordin

EAST TIMOR

BASIC DATA

Official Country Name:	East Timor
Region:	East & South Asia
Population:	827,727
Language(s):	Indonesian, Portuguese, Tetum
Literacy Rate:	55%

Timor, an island north of Australia, gained its independence from Portugal in 1975 but was annexed by Indonesia in July 1976. At that time, 93 percent of the population was illiterate. A small percentage of the Timorese had access to education, and only 39 students attended universities.

Indonesia required schooling between the ages of 7 and 13 and implemented an assimilation policy through its educational system. This involved the imposition of the Indonesian language and the Pancasila ideology, which is the respect for Indonesian patriotic symbols and the dissemination of a new version of history. Most teachers in the Timorese schools were Indonesian.

The Timorese resisted this policy. In 1994 the Departments of Education and Culture published all the textbooks in their Tetum language and allowed 20 percent of the curriculum to be of local content. However, the resistance movement intensified upon the resignation of Indonesian President Suharto in 1998. In the following year, the Timorese voted for independence under a United Nations-supervised referendum.

In the struggle for independence, most of the school infrastructure was destroyed, and most teachers and headmasters left permanently. However, grants from the World Bank made possible school repairs and training and hiring of teachers. Japan also donated scholarship money for students to attend Indonesian universities.

Meanwhile, the control of the education system was placed under a coalition of the National Council of Timorese Resistance, the United Nations Transition Administration, and UNICEF until local elections in 2002. In late 2000 the Timorese government approved the opening of the University of East Timor.

BIBLIOGRAPHY

Arenas, Alberto. "Education and Nationalism in East Timor." *Social Justice 25,* summer 1988.

Cohen, David. "East Timor May Have Its Own University Soon." *The Chronicle of Higher Education 46,* 21 July 2000.

———. "Invasion of Timor," 2001. Available from http://www.educationunlimited.co.uk/.

UNICEF. "Appeal 2000 East Timor," 2001. Available from http://www.unicef.org/emerg/CAPetimor.htm.

—*Bill T. Manikas*

ECUADOR

BASIC DATA

Official Country Name:	Republic of Ecuador
Region:	South America
Population:	12,920,092
Language(s):	Spanish, Quechua
Literacy Rate:	90.1%

Number of Primary Schools:	17,367
Compulsory Schooling:	10 years
Public Expenditure on Education:	3.5%
Educational Enrollment:	Primary: 1,888,172
	Secondary: 814,359
	Higher: 206,541
Educational Enrollment Rate:	Primary: 127%
	Secondary: 50%
Teachers:	Primary: 74,601
	Higher: 12,856
Student-Teacher Ratio:	Primary: 28:1
	Secondary: 13:1
Female Enrollment Rate:	Primary: 119%
	Secondary: 50%

HISTORY & BACKGROUND

In the fifteenth century, Incan invaders, having conquered the indigenous peoples of Ecuador, incorporated the land and its people as *Tawantinsuyu,* under then Incan ruler Huayna Capac who a quarter of a century later divided his empire between two of his sons. One of the sons, Atahualpa, received the northern portion that included Ecuador, and a civil war erupted. While the Incan brothers were fighting for control of the empire, Bartolome Ruiz, a Spanish explorer under the command of Francisco Pizarro, landed in Ecuador in 1526. By 1533 Pizarro's forces were in command of the country and had executed Atahualpa. In 1548, Gonzalo Pizarro was defeated by the forces of a subsequent royal emissary and executed for treason. This ended the era of the conquistador and started two and a half centuries of colonial rule. Colonial Ecuador was first considered a territory within the vice-royalty of Peru, but in 1563 Quito became a presidency or a judicial district of the vice-royalty with its own courts and president. In 1822, at the Battle of Pichincha, Spanish royalists were defeated by Antonio Jose de Sucre Alcala, and Quito became known as the Department of the South, which was part of the confederacy known as the Republic of Colombia, a confederation with Venezuela and Colombia. Simon Bolivar had liberated the area by the same year. Some church control of education was loosened and Bolivar attended to the establishment of schools, libraries and other educational institutions. Church run schools continued to dominate the education culture of Ecuador. 1830 saw the breakup of the confederation, and Quito became an independent state adopting the name of Ecuador. By 1861 Garcia Moreno, the father of Ecuador's Conservative party, had organized the elementary school system. The next two decades witnessed growth in the number of schools in Ecuador, the budget for education, and the number of universities. Compulsory education was also introduced.

Today Ecuador is the smallest of the Andean countries, but it has the highest average population density in South America, the highest annual rate of natural population increase (2.8 percent) over the last decade of any country in South America, and the highest percentage of Native Americans. Extending over both sides of the equator, it is bordered in the north by Colombia and in the east and south by Peru. The Galapagos Islands are a province of Ecuador. Native Americans make up 40 to 60 percent of the population. Approximately 52 percent of the population live in the coastal lowlands with an average population density of 80 persons per square kilometer. The most densely populated region is Guayas, which includes Guayaquil with 130 persons per square kilometer. The development of oilfields and agriculture over the last 25 years has resulted in a significant increase in the population of the eastern region without sufficient educational support for this new population.

The period since the late 1980s when Ecuador moved beyond the debt crisis has witnessed a number of significant improvements in macroeconomic performance, some wise decisions as to what to do with society's surpluses and stabilized inflation. The 1980s were dominated by efforts to reverse the declining GDP, to limit inflation, and to shore up the currency, although the GDP fell by .3 percent per year from 1980 to 1992, and inflation averaged 39.5 percent. Increased capital flow into Ecuador combined with some stability in the early 1990s allowed Duran Ballen's administration (1992-1994) to stabilize inflation at around 25 percent. For the next two years after his administration, positive growth of 3.3 percent occurred. Part of Ecuador's economic and political instabilities arose from the fluctuations in world market prices of its main products, oil, bananas, and shrimp. Having joined the World Trade Organization in 1996, it has failed to comply with many of its policies. Growth has been uneven due to ill-conceived and unsuccessful fiscal stabilization methods. While it had recently recovered some stability with the increase in oil prices, the aftermath of El Niño and the depressed oil market of 1997-1998 drove Ecuador's economy into a free-fall in 1999 beginning with the decline of the banking sector in the early part of that year. A 70 percent depreciation of the currency with a desperate government dolarizing it in 2000 caused that government to collapse. With the highest 10 percent of the population possessing a household income or consumption percentage share of 37.6 percent (1994) of the purchasing power parity of $54.5 billion

(1999 estimate), inequalities in the education system are as inevitable as finance-driven reforms.

On 5 February 1997, between 2.5 and 3.0 million Ecuadorians, about one-quarter of the population, demonstrated in the streets against the president they had elected the previous July. While attempting systemic change, the uprising actually strengthened the military. In September 1998, President Mahuad announced the cancellation of subsidies on electricity, cooking gas, and fuel while at the same time beginning a new system of cash assistance to poor mothers. Added to these economic problems, in January and February 1995 the old border dispute with Peru flamed into open conflict in the upper Cenepa valley, although subsequent peace talks have proved successful. In August 1998, a flare-up of tension occurred again and was resolved in 1999.

The last decade of Ecuadorian politics has been filled with problems. In 1996, Abdala Bucaram, from the Guayaquil-based Roldosista Party (PRE), won the presidency on a platform that promised populist economic and social reforms and the breaking of what Bucaram termed the power of the nation's oligarchy. During his short term of office, Bucaram's administration drew criticism for corruption and Bucaram was deposed by the Congress in February 1997 on grounds of alleged mental incompetence. In his place the Congress named Interim President Fabian Alarcon, who had been President of Congress and head of the small Radical Alfarist Front party. Alarcon's interim presidency was endorsed by a May 1997 popular referendum. With the 1996 election, the indigenous population began to abandon its traditional policy of shunning the official political system and has entered the political arena as a force which will inevitably grow more powerful.

The new government leaders have attempted to deal with some of Ecuador's problems and to develop the country's potential. Ecuador passed comprehensive legislation setting forth protections for intellectual property rights in May 1998. The government has suggested plans to partially privatize some of the major state enterprises and has obtained legal authority to privatize 35 percent of the telephone service. However, two auctions of the telephone company scheduled for late 1997 and early 1998 had to be canceled due to a lack of bidders. There is substantial political opposition to privatization proposals. Since 22 January 2000, the chief of state has been President Gustavo Noboa, following a military indigenous coup that deposed President Mahuad. The last presidential election was held 31 May 1998 with a run-off election on 12 July 1998. The next officially scheduled election is 2002.

Servicing the national debt continues to be a drain on Ecuador, absorbing large portions of its foreign ex-

change earnings and fiscal receipts (14 percent and 45 percent). Ecuador's public foreign debt burden rose 0.25 percent to $11.2 billion in February compared with the month before. This debt is equivalent to 66.1 percent of the Andean nation's gross domestic product. Ecuador alarmed international investors in 1999 when it defaulted on part of its foreign debt. The government restructured Brady and Euro bond debt in August 2000, issuing new global bonds to reduce this debt by 40.6 percent. The Paris Club of creditor nations suspended negotiations with Ecuador over more than $300 million in debt and also over $800 million in debt agreed to in September 2000 if Ecuador does not reach a deal with the International Monetary Fund. In April 2000, Ecuador's Congress failed to approve an International Monetary Fund required tax increase. Ecuador is facing a grave economic crisis that greatly influences its plans to improve its education system.

Ecuador's diverse middle class has concentrated itself in cities and larger towns. A minute, ill-defined group during most of the country's history, its numbers grew in the twentieth century. In the late 1970s, estimates based on income indicated that roughly 20 percent of the population was middle class. Economic expansion and increase in government employment contributed both to the size of the middle class in absolute numbers and to the group's political awareness. The rise of a middle class whose interest was not like that of the rural oligarchy transformed national politics. The upper echelons of this middle class frequently identified with and emulated the elite while the lower levels often made common cause with the more prosperous segments of the working class.

The public education system is tuition free and attendance is mandatory from ages 6 to 14. In practice, however, many children drop out before age 14, and in rural areas only about one-third complete sixth grade. The government is striving to create better programs for the rural and urban poor, especially in technical and occupational training. In recent years, it has also been successful in reducing illiteracy. Literacy, according to age structure, is as follows: 0-14 years, 36.23 percent (male 2,379,541 and female 2,301,543); 15-64 years, 59.4 percent (male 3,794,515 and female 3,880,367); and 65 years and over, 4.37 percent (male 262,701 and female 301,425) (2000 estimate). Enrollment in primary schools has been increasing at an annual rate of 4.4 percent, which is faster than the population rate growth. According to the 1979 constitution, the central government must allocate at least 30 percent of its revenue to education, but in practice it allots education a much smaller percentage.

Public universities have an open admissions policy. In recent years, however, large increases in the student population, budget difficulties, and extreme politicization

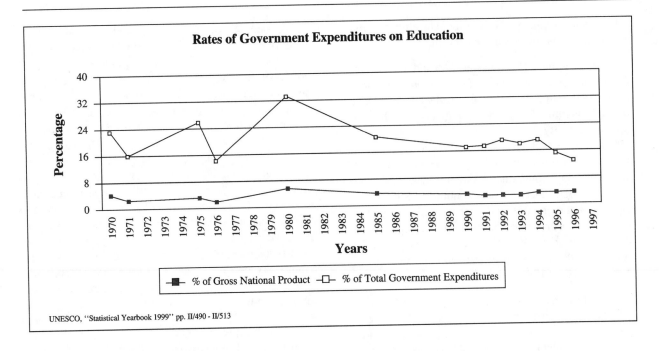

Rates of Government Expenditures on Education

UNESCO, "Statistical Yearbook 1999" pp. II/490 - II/513

of the university system have led to a decline in academic standards in some areas. The central, provincial, and municipal government all contribute to the financing of education. The provincial role is generally limited primarily to the construction and furnishing of schools. The municipal government has been required to give 15 percent of their budgets to education while the central government increasingly contributed to education until the 1980s.

CONSTITUTIONAL & LEGAL FOUNDATIONS

The law-making process in Ecuador begins when a bill is initiated by legislators or Plenary of Legislative Commissions (PCL), the president of the republic, judicial organs, or popular initiatives. A test is provided to each piece of legislation 15 days prior to debate in Congress. The proposed bill is discussed in two debates on different days. After the first debate, it may be returned to the originating commissions, which must report on new observations to modify, alter, or change it.

On 10 August 1998, Ecuador's new constitution came into effect. These constitutional changes enacted by a specially elected National Constitutional Assembly in 1998 strengthened the executive branch by eliminating midterm congressional elections and by circumscribing Congress' power to challenge cabinet ministers. To demonstrate his commitment to learning, President Mahuad chose Gustavo Noboa, Rector of the Catholic University in Guayaquil, as his Vice President. He also chose Ministers of Education who were committed to open and frank dialogue and to fixing a system that provides good education coverage, but poor and declining educational quality.

He submitted a comprehensive educational reform bill to Congress and gave them 30 days to approve it into law. Although literacy is high, Ecuador is still concerned about upgrading the quality of technical training and teaching teachers and professor modern practices of teaching. Dr. Vladimiro Alvarez Grau, former minister of Education, suggested that there is too much focus on memorization and repetition and insufficient work on critical thought and analysis.

The president serves for four years and can be re-elected after sitting out a term. The legislative branch is a unicameral National Congress with 121 seats. Seventy-nine members are popularly elected nationally to serve four-year terms. Forty-two members are popularly elected by province for four-year terms. Two are elected from each province. The constitution provides for concurrent four-year terms of office for the president, vice-president, and members of Congress. Presidents may be re-elected after an intervening term, while legislators may be re-elected immediately. The executive branch includes 17 ministries and several cabinet-level secretariats headed by presidential appointees. The president also appoints Ecuador's provincial governors who represent the central government at the local level. Provincial prefects and councilors, like municipal mayors and aldermen, are directly elected.

Each two years legislators elect from among themselves a president and vice president of the Congress. Congress meets for two months of the year. For the remainder of the year, unless an extraordinary plenary session is called, all legislative business is transacted by the 35 members of Congress who serve on 5 permanent committees. Ecuador has a three-tiered court system. The Congress appoints justices of the Supreme Court for six year terms. The Supreme Court names the members of the superior or provincial courts, who, in turn, choose ordinary civil and penal judges.

Throughout the years, Ecuador has faced some serious reforms in education. In 1930, the National Congress of Elementary and Normal School Education generated recommendations for a curriculum that still makes the educational programs today. The Congress produced the first detailed outline of curricular content and achievement expectations at each level. By 1938, the Organic Education Law put all schools under state control, focused on education at all levels, and made way for the current administrative organization of Ecuador's educational system. The education system in Ecuador still has developing to do, particularly in the areas of teacher education, textbook writing, and the addressing of ethnic, gender, and social bias. Some say that there has already been an educational revolution in Ecuador since in the 1990s when a process of updating and rewriting textbooks, workbooks, teacher guides, and other tools to begin to eliminate ethnic, gender, and social bias began. Only time will tell if this educational reform is successful. The Ministry of Education has an educational reform in mind that would introduce new courses and train thousands of adults in crafts, agriculture, small-business management, industry, trades, and services, as well as information management systems.

Literacy is defined as those age 15 and over who can read and write. A total of 90.1 percent of the population qualified (92.0 percent male and 88.2 percent female) in 1995. With 10 internet providers in 2001 and 30,000 internet users, 15 television stations, 392 AM stations, 27 FM stations, and 29 short wave radios (1998), getting news is easier than using the telephone system, which is inadequate and unreliable. One Intelsat (Atlantic Ocean) satellite earth station does make international telephone service possible though. There are approximately 748,000 telephones (1998) and 497,765 mobile cellular phones (1995).

According to the last census (1995), the following tabulation was made concerning the level of functional literacy, years of school, and consumption. Those who live in the countryside have 4.4 average years of schooling and an illiteracy rate of 17.9 while those who live in the city have an average 8.8 number of years of schooling and an illiteracy rate of 6.0. In the city 42.4 percent of the people are at or below the poverty rate, as compared to 75.9 percent in the countryside.

According to the 1979 constitution, the central government must allocate at least 30 percent of its revenue to education, although a much smaller percentage was ac-

tually allocated. The teacher's union claims that there has been a permanent reduction of the budget for education and although teachers, parents, and students successfully fought to have the new Constitution require 30 percent of the State budget be earmarked for education, currently only 2.3 percent of the budget is actually dedicated to education. The union also claims that there has been delayed payment of teachers' salaries and an elimination of benefits held in the past. Calling for an optimization of educational services, efficiency, effectiveness, and productivity, the government had one form of educational reform platform and the teacher's union had another. The 1982 law, still in effect in the university sector, was developed and passed to change the educational system and to restore democracy. The administration also developed a National Plan at this time, which privileged education in state expenditures.

Education in Ecuador has not always responded to the challenges posed by new development models because of international, economic, political, and social instability. While education is repetitively made a new priority by the newest leaders replacing failed administrations, the expertise required to adapt or create technological innovations with the ability to reason and to learn independently has not occurred in sufficiently large numbers either in the urban or rural communities of Ecuadorian citizens. Initiatives to overcome extreme poverty, child labor, urban and rural violence, and eliminate extreme social inequalities while establishing a community of informed and responsible citizens have not been completely successful. Inequitable education does not foster political tolerance or reduce violence.

EDUCATIONAL SYSTEM—OVERVIEW

In the nineteenth century, Ecuador's education structure was under the control of the Catholic Church. During this century various political leaders had a tremendous effect on the education system. Ecuador has had a strong history of educators. As early as 1835, Vicente Rocafuerte began to change the education system of Ecuador. A strong believer in education, he was known to say ''to govern is to educate.'' He stated that any government that holds power as a result of elections must have an education system that provides intellectual development and training for positions in industry and commerce. The National Assembly granted Rocafuerte the power to execute his educational objectives but they also required that he do the same for the Indian masses. Rocafuerte requested the creation of Colegio Santa Maria del Socorro, an all girl school in Quito. In 1836 he furthered his cause by attempting to establish a directorate to supervise curriculum and instruction throughout Ecuador. The purpose of this agency was to deal with university and secondary education. This agency, for example, developed the University of Quito's curriculum. Since it did not cover primary education, a slow educational development resulted at that level. In 1838 Rocafuerte established educational agencies to provide regional supervision in Guayaquil, Cuenca, Marabi, Loja, Chimborazo, and Imbabura. At this time primary education consisted only of religious and moral education, reading, writing, Spanish, and weights and measurements. The secondary school program differed from school to school and its curriculum was based on a variety of subject matters.

Arguably, the most significant education reform that Ecuador has ever experienced was that of Juan Leon Mera' in the 1850s. It based educational reform on the restoration of and emphasis on Ecuadorian themes in the entire educational system. Mera showed how "national education could encourage the integration of the country and define its cultural identity" (Paladines 1997). Gabriel Garcia Moreno took over the presidency of Ecuador in 1861. He made education the Church's responsibility. Secular educators were prohibited from teaching anything that would be considered different from church doctrine. Moreno wanted to create a system of primary schools. The Christian Brothers and the Sisters of the Sacred Heart took over the primary schools for boys and girls respectively.

The secondary schools, which prepared students for the university, were to be run by the Jesuits. At this time, primary education was free and mandatory. This increased the school population to 14,731 in 1871. In 1904, the structure of secondary schools was reorganized by reducing the program from seven to six years. The liberal arts program was reduced to the first three years of the program. In the last three years of secondary school a student must either specialize in philosophy, math, or natural science. The secondary school program required students to complete the following courses: moral and religious instruction, civics, hygiene, Spanish grammar, geography of Ecuador, world geography, history of Ecuador, world history, English or French, mathematics, literature, natural sciences, cosmography, physics, chemistry, philosophy, drafting, and penmanship.

There is no doubt that the governments of Ecuador have made good efforts to extend universal education through primary school. The Ministry of Education's 1970 plan addressed retention problems at the primary level and proposed workable solutions, a restructured curriculum, and increased practicality. Truly compulsory since the constitution of 1945, primary school has had a couple of serious leaps in the number of students attending. Perhaps the greatest leap was in the 1960s when primary enrollment almost doubled, secondary enrollment almost tripled, and those attending colleges and universities grew by 500 percent.

If the constitution of 1945 made primary school attendance mandatory by law, subsequent legislation required school attendance by all youth between the ages of 6 and 12. Before the 1960s primary schools in rural areas did not necessarily have a building nor did they uniformly offer education in grades one through six. In many areas no school existed within a reasonable radius until organizations like the Peace Corps stepped in. In other areas, only grades one through three or four were taught. The tuition free public educational system is mandatory from ages 6 to 14. In practice, however, many children drop out before age 15, and, in rural areas, only about one-third complete sixth grade. The government is striving to create better programs for the rural and urban poor, especially in technical and occupational training. In recent years, it has also been successful in reducing illiteracy. Enrollment in primary school has been increasing at an annual rate of 4.4 percent, faster than the population growth rate.

Primary education begins at age 6 with the first grade and ends at age 12 with sixth grade. Secondary education consists of two three-year cycles, a basic cycle, and a diversified cycle. This latter cycle may lead to higher education. University studies last from four to seven years, depending on specialization. The age limits for compulsory education are from 6 to 14. The minimum age for entry into preprimary education is four for kindergarten and six for the first grade of primary school. Preprimary education, which is noncompulsory, is two years. Primary school is six years. The primary years are divided into two cycles of three years each, and exams are given at the conclusion of each cycle.

Based on information from Banco Central del Ecuador, enrollment levels in 1979, 1983, 1984, and 1985 were respectively as follows: In primary school, 1,427,627; 1,677,364; 1,672,068; and 1,741,967. In the secondary school first cycle for the same years, 345,569; 405,445; 438,718; and 452,262. For the secondary school second cycle for the same years, 189,876; 244,833; 267,058; and 277,368. In higher education the total in 1979 was 225,343.

In 1989 the Confederation of Indigenous Nationalities of Ecuador (CONAIE) signed a historic agreement with the Ministry of Education that established a national program of bilingual, bicultural education designed and managed by CONAIE and its member organizations. It claims that 45 percent of Ecuador is indigenous, yet there is only 1 indigenous member of Congress (1995). It also claims that 80 percent of the rural, mostly indigenous population lives in poverty; that indigenous farmers produce 75 percent of Ecuador's basic foods while only having 35.5 percent of the arable land; and that these people are endangered by Ecuador having the highest rate of deforestation in the Americas.

Literacy rates have changed somewhat in terms of urban males and females. In 1950, approximately 89 percent of urban males were literate while in 1982 at least 96 percent were literate. In 1950, approximately 79 percent of urban females were literate while in 1982 about 94 percent were literate. In 1962, approximately 92 percent of urban males were literate while in 1974, about 94 percent of urban males were literate. In 1962, approximately 86 percent of urban females were literate while in 1974 that percentage had risen to 89 percent. In 1950 only 51 percent of rural males were literate but by 1982 that number had climbed to 80 percent. In 1950 only 38 percent of rural females were literate but by 1982 that number had climbed to 71 percent.

Traditionally, the school year is different in the *sierra* and *costa* regions. In the *sierra,* schools have operated from October to July; in the *costa,* they operate from April or May to December or January. This arrangement has been based on both climatic and economic considerations and has led to nationwide coordination problems as well as perpetuating a divisive regionalism. A proposal for a unified school year has not only been discussed but also enacted.

One problem, particularly in rural areas, is that even though education is compulsory, all classes were in Spanish even though, in many areas, indigenous Indian groups knew only their native languages. In the 1980s there were efforts to target literacy programs to the needs of the rural population and non-Spanish speakers, but Spanish is the official language of Ecuador. Quencha, the original language of the Incas, is widely spoken in the *sierra* and is being pushed for recognition as an official language. It is recognized by the Ecuadorian Constitution as an important part of Ecuadorian culture, but is not yet classified as an official language. Many Quechua words have been adopted into the colloquial language, oftentimes used to describe something that does not have a Spanish translation. Many of the indigenous people are bilingual using both their native languages and Spanish.

Examinations are given in the primary years at the end of each of two cycles of three years. Secondary education consists of two three-year cycles as well and exams are given at the end of each cycle. University studies last from four to seven years, and exams are given for entrance into university programs. Historically, since teachers relied on the lecture method, students were required to take notes and memorize massive amounts of material in the classics and humanities. Each level saw as its goal the preparation of students for the next level. Therefore students who did not complete a course of study found much of the material irrelevant memorization, and the attrition rate was high. In the last few years, serious attempts to change this have occurred both at the university and government levels.

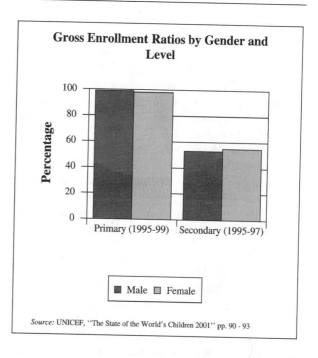

Gross Enrollment Ratios by Gender and Level

Source: UNICEF, "The State of the World's Children 2001" pp. 90 - 93

In 1946, Belasco Ibarra authorized private universities to be established in Ecuador. This permitted the founding of the *Universidad Catolica del Ecuador.* The Constitution of 1946 also granted public schools the right to operate freely. The Ministry of Education was instructed to make its social services available to private schools. Although less than 18 percent of the primary enrollment in Ecuador is in private schools, the percentage of enrollment in private schools increases in secondary education. The Catholic Church runs more than 88 schools. Protestant schools are increasing but still are few. Private schools are largely urban phenomena, making up less than 6 percent of the rural schools private. Over 20 private secondary schools or normal schools offer teacher-training programs to prepare students to be elementary teachers. With the economic problems of the government, much of the new growth in colleges in Ecuador has lately been in private schools. The enrollment in private schools increases with grade level; slightly less than 20 percent of primary students and more than 40 percent of secondary students attend private schools. Private education was predominantly an urban phenomenon. Approximately one-third of urban primary and secondary schools were private. With the worsening of the governmental economic emergencies, new growth of the population able to take advantage of higher education has provided opportunities for private schools and fee-based development. In the 1960s the government established a strong, centralized control over both the public and private system and allotted a high proportion of the national budget to education in an attempt to gain this control over its own school system and that of religious schools.

Another organization dedicated to helping improve education in the science and technology arena is Fundacyt. This is a private foundation, whose president is also the National Secretary of Science and Technology under the vice president of the republic. Fundacyt has very ambitious goals including funding science and technology research and sending university graduates to get their Masters and Ph.D. degrees. Only 2000 Ecuadorians living in Ecuador have Ph.D.s, as compared to 14,000 in Venezuela. Santiago Carrasco, President of Fundacyt in 1999, sees a future in areas such as biotechnology, biological engineering, and health and genetic research. As part of the arrangement, students who receive scholarships must come back to Ecuador and work in the country.

Through the 1980s textbooks and teaching aids were limited so learning had to consist mostly of memorization and rote work since the entire class would not have textbooks. Memorization, board work, and note taking often took the place of reading. Often rural children would be forced to read urban oriented books when they had them. One of several textbook-rewriting programs began in the 1960s, but it made little headway. The more recent textbook updating is clearly already more successful. In the 1990s the Ministry of Education began the gargantuan task of updating textbooks to rid them of ethnic, gender, racial, and class prejudice. One of the most successful textbook publications was a collection of articles entitled *Escuela Para Todos,* which in 1972 were placed in adult education centers throughout the country. Government efforts to increase access to education have been connected to textbook publication and adoption.

Both UNESCO and OEA have played major roles in offering technical advice and help to Ecuador. USAID plays an important role in Ecuador, but the World Bank, with its studies of the educational system and its great influence as an international agency, plays an even greater role. Some deterioration in the higher education system can be expected with the strains of democratization if not accompanied by governmental expenditure increases or international funding. The Flemish Association for Development Cooperation and Technical Assistance (VVOB) has during the last few years sent a group of GIS professionals to different Ecuadorian universities. The idea of this cooperation is primarily to improve the academic standard regarding GIS related subjects. A complementary benefit, however, is the implementation of GIS in both private and public projects. Experience was gained in the field of GIS applications in collaboration with academic staff and students within the faculties of agriculture and/or computer engineering of the National Polytechnic School (Quito), the University of Cuenca, and the National University of Loja. These universities were chosen because of their interest as well as for the

likelihood of reaching their desired goal. Collaboration with the faculties of civil, agricultural, and/or computer engineering within these universities was considered most likely to achieve success. Local collaboration and support varied due to political and financial differences.

From these experiences some conclusions can be drawn regarding the situation of GIS at university level in Ecuador. The general and preliminary knowledge of computers among agricultural engineers, the availability of hardware and software at universities, the introduction and acceptance of new technologies, the ability of the infra-system to handle the technologies, and the career perspective of GIS-trained professionals are all areas of concern. Wealthy Ecuadorians and fortunate outstanding students have often had access to external studies, and various scholarship programs, such as the Fulbright, have provided selective access to post-graduate education. This is compounded by the newly created business class, which has a stabilizing influence on the middle class in Ecuador but is also dependent on its links with foreign firms, products, and partners.

In the 1980s and to an extent even earlier, the burgeoning school populations led to students graduating from institutions of higher learning without being able to get a job because the number of new jobs remained smaller than the number of increasingly higher educated students. This caused many well-educated Ecuadorians to leave the country for opportunities abroad. However, education has been tied to the banking system in Ecuador and a good deal of development has occurred through this joint venture with the Bank of Ecuador, the World Bank, and the Inter-American Development Bank. The Inter-American Development Bank reviews the economic reforms in Ecuador in relation to earlier efforts, sequencing, structural reform and stabilization, sustainability, and priority. A new understanding of the role of higher education in development has brought the beginnings of systemic reform and a new conceptualization of the potential roles in development education can play. The Inter-American Development Bank optimistically believes that while economic stabilization has been difficult to achieve some meaningful structural reform and development have emerged through the chaos. The economy-driven nature of reform has caused a systemic approach to moving forward at a much slower rate than might otherwise have occurred. Jameson suggests that education has not played a more successful role in development because ''fundamental reform awaits a movement away from the current neo-liberal understanding of development'' (Jameson 124). However, it seems that, despite the crisis, development is going on right now in Ecuador. Pragmatism, efficiency, and international competitiveness have caused both government and development sectors to look to education to function well in training all

Ecuadorians. Forced upon Ecuador in part by its international lenders, systemic reform is occurring despite the defeat of plans to organize it. Higher education reforms are going on, and there is reason for optimism about the current economic reforms, actual outcomes, and at least initial assessments. Time will tell if the extended outcomes match the hopes and expectations of those involved with Ecuadorian higher education. Equity-driven reforms from the 1970s have taken another step in the 1990s. While the earlier reform extended education to disadvantaged groups such as women and indigenous people, the more recent reforms have extended the same educational opportunities to the disabled and those with learning problems so that society is maximizing human capital development or the human resources of its competent citizens. This is one of the rewards of inclusionary democracy in education.

As late as 1970, over 70 percent of the primary and secondary schools were run by the states, 10 percent by municipalities, and 20 percent or fewer by private organizations. The extreme increase in university enrollment and the expansion of enrollments at all levels, including higher education, are natural outgrowths of the expansion of primary and secondary education in earlier years and of the 1982 law guarantee of access to free university education without a national entrance examination. It originated from the need to create the education populace necessary for post-military democracy. Equity-driven reform fundamentally changed the nature of the educational system.

The Duran Ballen administration changed the mechanisms of access to economic and social services away from entitlements and government provision to market determination and the ability to pay. Higher education reform became private university and economic reform. In the 1960s the rural curriculum was upgraded to better compare with that of urban institutions, and the curriculum was revised to be more relevant to students' lives and to reflect the modern world. The government, after April 1998, promoted school autonomy in the rural centers and pushed municipalities to take charge of the educational establishments. The city of Loja, for instance, has turned over 10 schools to municipal control. It is also developing a new legal structure that includes the restructuring of teacher pay scales, the creating of new mechanisms for disciplining teachers through the Network Councils, and the transferring responsibility for teacher training to NGOs. On 11 November 1998, the Inter-American Development Bank announced the approval of a $45 million loan to Ecuador to support improvement in rural education by organizing school systems with greater autonomy and parent participation. A pioneering component of the program is projected to be results-based incentives for teachers that will improve quality and innovation in in-struction. The project was expected to benefit around 1,800 schools or 20 percent of the rural schools in Ecuador and is focused on improvements in grades one through nine. Investments were planned in school infrastructure and educational materials, and technical assistance was to be provided to assist the development of stronger, more autonomous systems. Non-profit organizations, universities, and other civil society organizations were to be enlisted to assist in the strengthening of rural school networks to reduce the isolation of individual schools and offer greater possibilities of educational improvement. One result of the great growth in enrollment of schools in Ecuador was that almost all funds went to the salaries of the teachers and little was left for building and maintenance costs. This worked to the disadvantage of rural areas. According to the 1983 UNESCO Statistical Yearbook, in 1980 approximately 33 percent of total government expenditures went to education, but only 6 percent of this was used for capital construction. A training component of the program was to increase management skills of local school officials, thereby enhancing their capacity for management in a more autonomous setting. Investments were planned in bilingual programs to benefit indigenous communities. The project, planned to be carried out by the Education Ministry, is designed to serve as a model to improve basic rural education throughout Ecuador. The total cost of the program is 50 million dollars. The IDB loan is for 25 years with a four year grace period at the variable annual interest rate. Local counterpart funds total $5 million.

PREPRIMARY & PRIMARY EDUCATION

In the late 1980s formal education was divided into four cycles: a preprimary two-year cycle; six years of primary school; secondary school, which was divided into two three-year cycles; and higher education. Children could begin attending preprimary school at four and primary school began at age six. Attendance theoretically was compulsory for children from 6 to 14 years of age. The first three-year cycle of secondary school dealt with general curriculum that elaborated on that of the primary school. In the second cycle, students could specialize in one of several different curriculums. An academic liberal arts course led to university admission. Other specialized courses prepared students for technical schools or teacher training. Roughly 20 percent of primary and secondary schools were privately run.

SECONDARY EDUCATION

In the 1960s the secondary curriculum was made up of general studies, Spanish, foreign languages, mathematics, natural sciences, physical sciences, history, geography, physical education, and applied electives such as agriculture, business, artisan skills, and music. Military

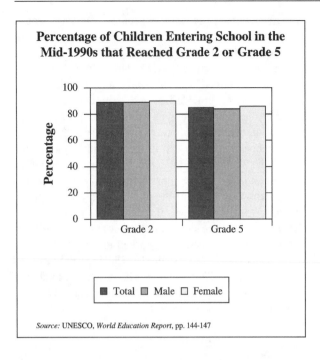

Percentage of Children Entering School in the Mid-1990s that Reached Grade 2 or Grade 5

Source: UNESCO, *World Education Report*, pp. 144-147

training was included in some schools in the sixth year. In the 1970s there were nine types of secondary schools in Ecuador. There were the traditional, university preparatory schools, such as Colegio de Humanidades Modernas and Colegio de Huanidades Clasicas. There were also business or commercial schools, normal schools, fine arts schools, music schools, manual arts schools for boys, manual arts schools for girls, and agricultural and animal husbandry schools. The large number of subjects as well as the long class day prevented most students from fulfilling any portion of the disciplines of the program. The rampant child labor abuse among the poor also caused students to drop out. Students began their day no later than 8:00 a.m. They were dismissed at noon and returned home for lunch. The lunchtime usually lasted from two to two and a half hours. Most schools followed lunch with an afternoon session that lasted two to three hours.

HIGHER EDUCATION

Much can be explained about Ecuadorian higher education by an understanding of arguably the most important historical reform in universities throughout Latin America, the Cordoba Reform of 1918. This reform provided universities the autonomy which they are still attempting to hold onto today. Because of that reform, universities have challenged the authoritarian excesses of civil and military regimes, provided presidents and vice-presidents of Ecuador, and generally been highly politicized organizations. Ecuador has 33 universities and technical colleges with 202,683 students. It has 12 state universities, equally divided between the *costa* and the *sierra*, and an additional 5 private universities, 3 in the *si-*

erra and 2 in the *costa*. A number of polytechnic schools and teachers' colleges offer specialized postsecondary studies. The number of university students per 100,000 members of the population grew fivefold from 1960 to 1980; the number of professors grew ten times. About two-thirds of those enrolled in higher education attended public institutions, especially the Central University in Quito. The postsecondary population of 208,000 students represents a 33 percent increase since 1982. Since 1985, some 12 new universities have been founded bringing the total to 29, and the number of faculty increased from 6,884 in 1980 to over 12,000 by 1993. Since providing high quality education, which will actually prepare university students for the technological and economic future, requires a heavy investment in human, technological, and physical resources, Ecuador faced a difficult challenge. Public universities generally have an open admissions policy. In recent years, large increases in the student population, budget difficulties, and the extreme politicization of the university system have led to a decline in some academic standards. The progress of higher education in Ecuador seems, in many ways, to be out of control because external forces such as economic and political conditions have changed the characteristics, emphasis, curriculum, and student populations of most public institutions. Certainly, during the past two decades, the chronic sifting of the educational, political, and economic agendas has resulted in new goals, priorities, and missions for public universities. New academic and economic models had to become important to the higher education equation. Extreme financial constraints have challenged the traditional vested rights of public higher education. Reforms have been difficult and are not likely to further equalize university entrance. Some university and student leadership has appeared that has attempted to solve some of the many problems faced by changes in the higher education in Ecuador. The *Consejo Nacional de Educacion Superior* or National Council of Higher Education is the coordinating body for institutions of higher education. Universities and colleges are members. Since higher education's share of the national government's budget fell from 26 percent in 1981 to 19 percent in 1994, and from 4.6 percent of the GDP in 1981 to 2.7 percent in 1993, it is understandable that much of the growth in recent years has been in the private sector.

Ecuador's universities are changing to meet the challenges of the technological age. During the colonial period, the authorizations for universities were by papal authority, royal decree, or authority of the Council of the Indies. All the universities established during the colonial era emulated the University of Salamanca model, which emphasized theology, law, arts, and medical studies. The Universidad de San Fulgencio de Quito was Ecuador's first university. It was authorized by papal bull in 1586.

Originally places to train priests, the universities of Ecuador have gone through changing missions. While more recently they have trained students in the law, arts, and philosophy, they now prepare to train students in engineering, technology, and CIS. Perhaps the greatest problem is one that is seen in many countries: budgets were not compensated when enrollment increases occurred. Thus the growing demand for admittance to universities and access to academia through public universities overcame the delivery abilities of those schools. University budgets, which needed room for the physical plant and operating costs, were almost entirely consumed by faculty and staff salaries. In the face of the growing student population, particularly with the population growth of Guayaquil, university administrations were faced with delayed maintenance, deteriorating physical plants, antiquated technologies, anachronistic curricula, and a professorate without the means of updating their knowledge-base or credentials. That is not to say that Ecuador's public universities do not have many well trained academics with terminal degrees from major international universities. Its universities have highly trained faculty, some of whom earned graduate degrees abroad and are themselves successful researchers and authors, but their numbers are inadequate for the job of educating the bulging population of university-bound students.

The government, attempting to finance the onslaught of students, embraced international economic ideologies, but was unable to create the massive public subsidies necessary for the growing student populations. One of the answers to this problem is to diversify funding resources through funding initiatives of different kinds. Since the traditional source of financial resources, the central government, of necessity has withdrawn much of its resources for the public university, academic administrations have had to develop new budget sources. Diversification of funding sources includes the volatile issue of student fees. University education had been a ticket out of poverty for many talented young people who were not likely to be able to pay anywhere near the real cost of their education. The problem that public institutions are facing is one of growing elitism. With rising student fees, increasing technological costs, and a government less willing and able to continue to pay the traditional percentage of the cost of educating a student, an economic crisis of sorts has occurred in major Ecuadorian universities. Free higher education is a longstanding tradition in Latin America and often constitutionally guaranteed. The administrations of the *Escuele Superior Politecnica de Litoral* (ESPOL) in Guayaquil, perhaps the hardest hit with this population explosion, and the *Escuele Politecnica Nacional* in Quito, the two leading public technical universities, have tried to face this issue. Variables such as family income and academic standing were considered in

designing the fee schedules. In Guayaquil students, frustrated by the outdated technical equipment, proposed a laboratory fee schedule that would repair old and buy new equipment. The university approved the student plan. The predominant sentiment sometimes seems to be in favor of improving the conditions and equipment for learning even if it means costs billed directly to the student, but this does not mean that there have not been student protests. There were brief demonstrations at ESPOL and at Politecnico. In both cases some concessions were made to student demands, such as the lengthening of implementation schedules, but income was still generated through student fees.

Student fees gathered insufficient funds to take the place of withdrawn government assistance. Other initiatives had to be implemented, many of them familiar to not only to Latin American university administrators, but to North American administrators as well. President Nelson Cevallos of ESPOL removed services such as maintenance, security, the bookstore, and bus service from the university budget and contracted them to providers in the private sector as part of a large privatization policy. The self-financing degree program was also considered. Reduction of the dependency of the university on the government could occur with self-generated income so Cevallos created 27 new self-financing degree programs, introduced a structure of reward for departments and faculty members who rent university faculties to outside groups, expanded continuing education, and sold consulting services. In 1992, approximately 26 percent of EXPOL's budget was self-generated. By 1996, approximately 56 percent of the operating budget was self-generated.

Another increasingly used technique to limit bulging enrollment is the admissions aptitude test. Limiting admissions to certain programs on the basis of who is likely to be able to be successful in that program contributed to the strike at the Politecnica. Denying the concept of open access and implementing the concept of limited access through admissions testing are still seen as threats to the older system and traditional students rights and entitlements.

Another concern in higher education is the knowledge of computer information systems. A study at the University of Cuena in 1996 found knowledge of computer sciences very low among the agricultural faculty, more acceptable among the civil engineers, and very application oriented in the faculty of computer engineers. Even the knowledge of geography is limited among both the agricultural and civil engineers and nonexistent amongst the computer engineers. Hydrology, soil sciences, topography, and computer science are all taught by different members of different faculties without any organized interrelationships or strategic partnering among them. In 1996 computers were not available in faculties other than computer science. The Program for Land and Water Management of the University of Cuenca is being executed by an interdisciplinary team of local engineers, economists, sociologists, and three foreign experts. This strategic partnership is active in research projects, teaching, and consulting.

In Loja, the Center for Agricultural Computer Science was created in 1994 at the Faculty of Agricultural Engineering of the National University of Loja with the goal of introducing computer science in the fields of agronomy, irrigation and forestry at university level as well as in local private and public organizations. In Quito, at the *Escuela Politenica Nacional*, the department of *Inteligencia Artificial y Sistemas de Informacion Geografica* was founded in 1993. The goal of the department was to organize courses in the field of artificial intelligence, GIS, and remote sensing. Most of the graduate students are doing their theses in computer engineering though. Database management applications in areas such as hydrology, irrigation, tourism, city planning, and natural resources management are only some of the GIS related projects. Funding is hard to find though. Interdisciplinary contact is also part of the training for the workgroup. The *Escuela Politecnica del Ejercity*, probably the best-equipped institute in Ecuador for both hardware and software, is the only university where a faculty of geographical engineers exists.

University faculty is selected for four-year terms by each institution's university council from lists suggested by the faculty. The 1970 Law of Higher Education requires that faculty appointments be based on merit. In 1995, the entire governance structure of higher education was to be changed to more closely resemble a corporate model. Two presidents of "Production Associations" would be added to the governing assembly of universities or the National Council of Universities and Polytechnical Schools (CONUEP). An executive committee of CONUEP was formed to centralize decision-making and create a series of new powers such as being able to audit universities, close inefficient programs, distribute funds according to a systematic formula based on production, create a national student admissions system, and run the university. The internal governance of the university would include traditional outsiders and concentrate power and authority in the University Council for each university. This council is composed of a businessperson, three ex-rectors, a representative of the President of Ecuador, and two alumnae. The University Council would designate the rector through a national search, set internal policy, evaluate the functioning of the academic units, and approve strategic plan (Jameson 129). If this is accomplished, it destroys the old system, which was based on university autonomy from national governmental control. Authority to create universities might be removed from Congress and given to CONUEP, which would also play a greater role in planning and programming if certain reforms suggested for higher education occur.

The National Council for Modernatization Reform (CONAM) was proposed as a process for removing faculty members and required scholarships for students unable to afford university education. Had this proposal been enacted, it would have formalized the de facto changes being imposed on the public university system. CONAM was proposed by an ad hoc committee, supported by Vice-President Alberty Dahik and two-day President Rosalia Arteaga. Dahik's resignation and flight from the country ended the possibility of enacting the CONAM proposal. Several of the new universities, such as the Universidad San Francisco de Quito, operate under a different set of rules since they refused to adopt governance systems mandated by the national law.

ADMINISTRATION, FINANCE, & EDUCATIONAL RESEARCH

A program of institutional diversity and of acquisition and differentiation according to market trends is part of the desired reform in the present decade. The market route to mass higher education, higher education markets and public policy, government strategy toward education, and the role of the university in promoting and developing technology are all part of the necessary strategic planning that must come from the Ministry of Education with the cost sharing mechanism already in play. Curricular changes based on these are certainly part of every rector's concern in Ecuador. Many have already started to create pools, internally or with other universities, to offer more training facilities and to develop educational packages that will be at the disposal of students in remote areas and other places or regions. Some are also developing a "flexible delivery" mode, meaning that parts of the courses are delivered traditionally, while others are based on the internet or other formats. Distance learning programs and modules, virtual courses, and virtual universities are already issues of higher education. The roles of international organizations such as UNESCO are being looked at in regard to them.

The successful expansion of the Ecuadorian educational system created its own set of problems. Construction of schools failed to keep up with the increase in students. A significant proportion of teachers lacked full accreditation, especially at the levels of secondary and higher education. These deficiencies were most evident in the countryside where the percentage of uncertified primary teachers was estimated to be double that of the cities. Finally, despite enrollment increases by the 1980s, the percentage of school-aged children attending school lagged. Rates were particularly low for rural primary school aged children. Relatively few children continued beyond the first cycle of secondary school. At this time, about 20 percent of primary and secondary schools were privately operated. Ecuador had about 12 state universities and 5 private universities throughout the *sierra* and the *costa*. There were a number of polytechnic schools and teachers' colleges that offered specialized postsecondary studies. Ten percent of the country was illiterate, and there were reading and writing centers and schools for adults. The official discourse of the recent governments of Ecuador has centered on blaming the teachers and their representative organization, the UNE, for the current education crises. Promotion of individual school autonomy and greater involvement by parents and the community are popular with the Education Ministry.

President Jamil Mahuad and his minister of education, in compliance with international institutions, implemented a project called the "Immediate and Long Term Plan for the Ministry of Education and Culture" that synthesizes its agenda for the education sector. To apply its educational proposals, the government used legal instruments that included the new Constitution of the Republic and various projects financed with international resources, such as the EBPRODEC (which attends to the main marginalized urban educational centers), PROMECER (which administers the main rural education centers), and PROMET 1 and 2 (which attend to technical education). These instruments are linked with putting legal parameters on teacher collective bargaining and training. The imposition of legal controls through regulations on the National Teachers Qualification Scale, collective bargaining, demonstrating, assembling, and striking.

In 1994, the Ministry of Education proposed new curricula reforms that contemplated three steams of education: basic education for the majority, technical or career education, and special education aimed at forming the new educated elite. This proposal met widespread disapproval from the teacher's union and was suspended due to activities of the National Educators Union. The National Congress approved the Ecuador Family Freedoms Act, which would require two hours of religious instruction. A large national movement spearheaded by the teachers claims to have prevented this law from entering into effect.

In April 1998, the National Constituent Assembly incorporated the decentralization of financial, pedagogical, and administrative aspects of the educational system into the new Constitution. It also revised the basis of payment of teacher salaries on measured performance. The teacher's union blamed the World Bank for special reference to the savings that can be made to the educational budget through increasing the number of students per class and noted that the World Bank argued that since they have measured no substantive increase in academic performance when class sizes are reduced from 45 to 35, these reductions are therefore costly and unnecessary. The teacher's union has claimed that while decentralization would appear a positive measure, it is really a policy whose primary purpose is to reduce the central government's financial and administrative responsibility for education and move even further away from an equitable national teacher pay scale. Local authorities supplement these funds when they can and teachers are badly paid when they cannot. Thus there is a reduction of educational resources for the poorest schools, a municipalization which becomes a kind of privatization since it is from local resources that the best schools are largely supported. The teacher union has argued that this "privitization" in the area of education is not a total privatization of the service but a privatization of the management of education. There are diverse formulas, such as cost recovery, the suppression of obstacles to the creation of private schools and universities, study vouchers, and "free choice" of school selection through public subsidies for private teaching. The teacher's union argues that while central government money is saved, according to World Bank planning, studies indicate that students from the upper classes showed a slight improvement, while those from lower income families showed a sharp drop in their performance. In 1994, the Chilean Ministry of Education, who had enacted a plan like this one, recognized that these policies had had negative effects on the quality of education. Part of larger economic austerity measures, they were to have helped to drop the inflation rate of 50 percent in the early 1990s to a more reasonable amount by the new millennium. The Ecuadorian reforms of the late 1970s, increasing the democratization of the primary and secondary systems, has put great pressure on higher education. This pressure brings greater efficiency and reform policies. Reform at the institutional level will not replace a larger reform policy in bringing change. Among the rather piecemeal changes is an increase in the number of universities, implementation of student fees in state universities, development of a program of voluntary accreditation, and creation of private universities. These reforms have come largely from external demands of a tactical rather than strategic nature. Several attempts have been made to organize a systematic and centralized process of development.

While the Ministry of Education is training teachers to teach better, Fundacyt is teaching students and professors how to conduct research. Part of the plan is to establish a world network for research and technology. Thirty universities in Ecuador are currently tied to the network.

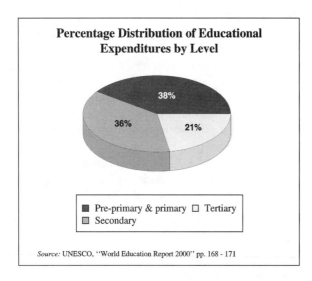

Percentage Distribution of Educational Expenditures by Level

38%

36%

21%

■ Pre-primary & primary □ Tertiary
□ Secondary

Source: UNESCO, "World Education Report 2000" pp. 168 - 171

Universities receive computers, get connected to the world, and develop their own databases in their primary fields, which are then used to support science and technology research. UNESCO supports the centrality of educational research, saying: "It is evident that no higher education system can fulfill its function and be a viable ally for society in general, if part of its teaching staff and its departments do not carry out any research work, in accordance with particular institutional goals, the academic potential and material resources" (Tunnermann 1996).

All schools are run by the Ministry of Public Education, which has control over the curricula it prescribes for schools, public and private. All schools are recognized only when a representative of the ministry has supervised final exams. State preprimary and primary schools are administered through provincial directorates of education, which employ more than 200 inspectors and a small group of inspectors that are attached to the ministry. At the secondary level, inspection is the responsibility of centrally based officials who specialize in a particular type of secondary school, such as academic, vocational, and normal. Because the Ministry of Education is in charge of all public and private schools in Ecuador, all schools must follow ministry approved instructional programs. The Ministry of Education is divided into five major agencies, all of which report back to the Minister of Education. The first agency is the Department of Educational Planning, which is responsible for the augmentation of all educational programs. The second agency is the Office of the Technical Director of Education, which administers and supervises activities such as adult and music education. The third agency is the Division of Internal Affairs. The fourth agency is Internal Administration. The final agency is the Department of School Construction.

NONFORMAL EDUCATION

To evaluate the level of effective literacy in a region or country, the presence in a household of a literate person who generates a positive public good for illiterate members as well as a considerable rise in nonagricultural employment and literacy is taken into account. Although the largest numbers of adults are trained by the military, in 1962 the Ministry of Public Education established a department of adult education in response to a law which required literacy training for all illiterates between the ages of 15 and 50 years. This program has been extremely successful. During the first year, 50,000 people participated.

The military acts in some ways as a nonformula educational institution. According to the Constitution, all Ecuadorians are subject to military service obligations, but in practice conscription applies only to those who are liable for call-up at age 19 for 1 year of service. As of 1988, about 80,000 of approximately 1.8 million males in the 18 to 49 age bracket were in the military. In a country of chronic underemployment, many poorer youths improve their education, housing, and dietary situations by joining the armed forces. Ambitious young men with few opportunities in the civilian labor market might be successful candidates for further service and training, thereby learning valuable skills and finding an avenue for upward mobility. Students in good academic standing receive deferments, and only sons, breadwinners, or heads of household are excused from service. All officers graduate from one of three military academies. Those of working class or middle class origins, whose fathers were artisans, military NCO, or workers, constituted approximately 20 percent. John Samuel Fitch's study found a striking pattern of recruitment to the officer corps from the interior highlands, which has persisted in spite of the shift of population toward coastal provinces. Fitch also notes a definitive trend towards the democratization of the officer corps.

Naval cadets attend the Advanced Naval Academy at Salinas in a four year program that stresses the humanities, scientific subjects, naval science, and physical training. Located in Guayaquil, the Naval War College was the senior instructional institution and prepared officers, generally at the level of commander, for higher ranks and general staff duty. The two year course of study covered such topics as strategy and tactics, logistics, geopolitics, operational planning, intelligence, and international maritime law, with sociology, economics, and other nonmilitary subjects. The marines operated their own instructional program, including a basic school for recruits and more advanced courses in amphibious operations, communications, intelligence, and weaponry, plus special courses in frogman and paratrooper skills. The navy also administered the Merchant Marine School whose cadets received some military training and formed part of the naval reserve after graduation as merchant marine officers.

In an effort to standardize army training, the Department of Instruction was created in 1988. Upon attaining the rank of corporal, conscripts accepted for enlistment for further service could apply to one of several NCO schools. Each school included a core curriculum accompanied by training in a military occupational specialty at such facilities as the armor school at Riobamba or the engineers' school at Esmeraldas. The intense competition and difficulty of courses produced a high dropout rate among NCO candidates. Cadets preparing for commissioning as army second lieutenants studied at the Eloy Alfaro Advanced Military School in Parcayacu. The Army War Academy, the Army Polytechnic Institute, and the Institute of Higher National Studies complete the training schools comparable to the National Defense University in Washington.

Distance Education is represented in Ecuador through Globatel, a company dedicated to interactive distance learning (IDL) that has come up with a way to open higher education to larger numbers of people. Kurt Freud, a founding member of Globatel and of the University of the Pacific in Ecuador, a university dedicated to finance and business, suggests that it is possible to develop an IDL system with fluid, interactive capabilities that will allow governments to popularize education in a way that is cost effective and feasible. Globatel has developed an IDL system that uses combined satellite and computer mediated communication. In the system, users can communicate simultaneously and interact freely and effectively, including sharing graphical and textual data via computers. Students can also interact with the instructor using regular telephones connected to the system via satellite. The phone keypads act as a keyboard for data communication, while voice communication is handled through regular headsets. Obviously, for this kind of system to work optimally, Ecuador needs a more reliable telephone system, and this has not gone unnoticed. Ecuador has been developing its computer and satellite capabilities for many years. Ecuanet was one of the first Internet providers in Latin America. It is also a non-profit organization under the auspices of the Banco de Pacific. A decade ago, Ecuanet came to life as a scientific network and today Ecuanet works with the University of Miami to provide access to schools, businesses, and individuals.

TEACHING PROFESSION

Traditionally, a large percentage of teacher-training institutions have been run by private secondary schools which cater to females, but both private and public school teachers must meet the same requirements. Primary school personnel must be 18 years old or older; must have graduated from normal schools, although this is not always the case; must be in good standing in their communities; and must be in good health. In addition to these requirements, secondary and normal school teachers must have completed a four year course of study in a faculty of philosophy, letters, or education at an accredited university. Teachers who meet these requirements are *titulado* or accredited by the Ministry of Public Education. Because of the requirement of a university education, a high proportion of secondary school teachers are not accredited, while a large percentage of primary school teachers are accredited or *titulado*. Many primary teachers are recruited largely from the lower classes in the urban areas, but they are often community leaders in the rural areas even though they are likely to be less educated there. Secondary teachers are appointed directly by the Ministry of Public Education and more often male.

The low wages for university professors hampers knowledge gathering in new "high-tech" fields and is the reason in some cases for why the transfer of knowledge to colleagues or students is limited. Employment opportunities in universities are often not very attractive because of low salaries and limited resources for research. A university professor earns about US$400 a month.

SUMMARY

There is remarkably little research done on higher education in Ecuador, but the World Bank financial support of $400,000 will create an information bank. The goal of the project was to develop reforms based on an empirical study of the system. The information gathered was primarily on organization, inputs, and activity levels. It resulted in a series of 10 volumes (CONUEP 1992). The rationale for reform was that there was a crisis due to the democratization of education and the expansion of access to higher education. The growing interest from both foreign development aid organizations and local institutions to apply scientific principles to problem solving has brought foreign professionals to support and organize courses. Existing faculties will need to take over again in the coming years. Perhaps it is too much to hope for a system-wide, top-down reform, as equity-driven reforms have been largely minimal. Ecuador is in a revolution in terms of broad-based education, but its serious economic problems and lack of funding will force it to face terrible challenges and make draconian decisions in the coming years as it attempts to fund new universities. Greater research and support of its best students ought to be a goal, as well as the broadening of the base for the democratization of education. Ideally, the most capable of even the most marginalized and threatened groups could take advantage of the best that education has to offer. Their capacities could be utilized as human resources to enrich the larger society.

BIBLIOGRAPHY

Auzpuru, P. "La educacion y la intergracion nacional del indigena en la Revolu ecuatoriana, 1895-1912." *Educacion rural indigena en Iberoamerica,* 65-86. Mexico/Madrid: Universidad Nacional de Distancia.

Arellano Escobar, E. *Pensamiento Universitario Ecuatoria Part.* Quito: Banco Central del Ecuador/Corporacion Editora Nacional, 1988.

CONADE. "The Reorientation of the Educational System of Ecuador." In *Section V of report on Ecuador.* Quito: 1991.

CONUEP. *Ecuadorian Universities: Their Mission for the Twenty-First Century.* Quito:1994.

———. *Evaluations of the Actual System and Perspectives of the Short and Medium-range Plans of the Universities and Politechnic Schools.* Quito: 1992.

IDB (Inter-American Development Bank). *Development Policy.* Washington, DC: 1996.

Jameson, Kenneth P. "Reform and Stress in a Vacuum: Higher Education in Ecuador." *Higher Education 33(3)* (1997): 1-17.

———. "Moving Social Reform to Center Stage: Lessons from Higher Education in Ecuador Higher Education Policy." 12. (1999): 123-140.

Ministerio de Educacion Nacional de Ecuador. *Sist Educativos Nacionales.* Madrid: OEI, 1994.

Tunnermann, C. "A New Vision of Higher Education." *Higher Education Policy 9(11)* 127.

Yanez, Cossio, C. "Algunos aspectos de la educacion bilingue inter Ecuador." *Revista de la Universidad Catolica del Ecuador 42* 6.

—*Merrilee A. Cunningham*

EGYPT

BASIC DATA

Official Country Name:	Arab Republic of Egypt
Region:	Africa
Population:	68,359,979
Language(s):	Arabic, English, French
Literacy Rate:	51.4%
Number of Primary Schools:	18,522
Compulsory Schooling:	8 years
Public Expenditure on Education:	4.8%
Foreign Students in National Universities:	6,726
Libraries:	187
Educational Enrollment:	Primary: 7,499,303 Secondary: 6,726,738
Educational Enrollment Rate:	Primary: 101% Secondary: 75% Higher: 20%
Teachers:	Primary: 310,116 Secondary: 424,586
Student-Teacher Ratio:	Primary: 23:1 Secondary: 17:1
Female Enrollment Rate:	Primary: 94% Secondary: 70% Higher: 16%

HISTORY & BACKGROUND

The Arab Republic of Egypt is situated at the crossroads between Europe and the Orient and between North Africa and southwest Asia. Egypt controls both the Sinai Peninsula, the only land bridge between Africa and the remainder of the Eastern Hemisphere, and the Suez Canal, the shortest sea link between the Indian Ocean and the Mediterranean Sea. The Mediterranean forms the northern boundary, on the east is Israel and the Gaza strip, on the south is Sudan, and on the west is Libya.

Approximately the size of Texas and New Mexico combined, Egypt occupies 1,001,494 square kilometers with 995,450 square kilometers of land area and 6,000 square kilometers of water. The land is mostly a vast desert plateau interrupted by the narrow green ribbon of the Nile Valley and delta. The longest river in the world, the Nile, flows 1600 kilometers through Egypt northward from the Egypt-Sudanese border to the Mediterranean Sea.

Egyptian economy is based on its natural resources: petroleum, natural gas, and several minerals. There are no permanent pastures, forests, or woodlands. Dependence on food imports is heavy. Almost all large-scale industry is in the public domain. Manufacturing produces mainly consumer goods, but also some iron, steel, aluminum, and cement. Economic diversity began in 1960 with industrialization efforts, development of oil revenues, tourism, Suez Canal income, and remittances from expatriates working in various Arab countries.

The private sector, dominated by food processing and textiles, is comprised of 150,000 small and medium businesses. Most Egyptians work for mini-firms; nearly 100 percent of the non-agricultural private enterprises have fewer than 50 employees, most have fewer than 10 and many have fewer than 4. Egypt ranks fourth in the world on the list of countries implementing privatization programs. In 1999, the economic picture turned rosy with a sustained growth rate of five percent, inflation below four percent, a budget deficit of approximately one percent of GDP, and foreign revenues of 18 billion, covering about 14 months worth of imports.

Egypt is a (limited) multiparty socialist state based on Islamic law. Suffrage is universal and compulsory. Politically, Egypt is divided into governorates (provinces) each subdivided into districts, which are further subdivided into communes. The governors heading each governate administer the plans and operation of the schools. The Eastern Hamitic stock (Egyptians, Bedouins, and Berbers) comprises 99 percent of the population with Greeks, Nubians, Armenians, and other Europeans (primarily Italians and French) at less than one percent. The Hamitic people are descendents of the ancient Egyptians. Islam is the religion of 94 percent of Egyptians with Sunni Muslims in the majority; Coptic Christians and others make up the remaining six percent.

The population is concentrated in the Nile Valley and delta, an area roughly the size of Vermont, where approximately 95 percent of the population is packed into 5 percent of the country. Some 45.1 percent of Egyptians live in urban areas; approximately 2.3 million were living abroad in 1997. In 1995, the workforce numbered 16.9 million; in 1999, it had grown to 19.0 million. Approximately 40 percent of the labor force is engaged in agriculture, 38 percent in services, and 22 percent in industry. Unemployment is high; in 1999, the unemployment rate was estimated to be 11.8 percent. The population explosion is staggering. The population of 49 million in 1985 expanded beyond 68 million in 2000, an increase of more than 105,000 people per month. More than one-third of the population was under the age of 15 in 2000. The population growth rate has slowly declined from 2.8 percent in 1986 to 2.1 percent in 1999.

In 1992, an estimated 9 percent of the children under the age of five were malnourished. Estimates in the late 1990s reported that 52 percent of school children suffered from anemia and 20 percent from vitamin and protein de-

ficiency. Poverty estimates vary; government statistics show 23 percent of Egyptian households to be below (the very low) poverty line in 1999. The consensus of independent observers is that the rate is closer to 35 percent. Arabic is the official language. Many variations of vernacular Arabic are spoken and the people in the Aswan region speak Nubian. The Coptic language spoken in the middle regions is the last stage of ancient Egyptian—no longer spoken but still used in the Bohairic dialect for liturgical purposes.

Egyptian history dates back more than 7,000 years. In the period between 6000 and 2686 B.C., hunters and gatherers settled along the banks of the Nile and evolved into settled, subsistence agriculturists. Written language, religion, and institutions developed. The unification of Upper (Red Land) Egypt and Lower (Black Land) Egypt in the third millennium B.C. is considered by Egyptians to be the "First Time" or the creation of the universe. Unification marked the beginning of the Pharaonic Age. The monuments that remain give testimony to the administrative and religious structures developed in that era. Higher education in ancient Egypt took place in the temples where sciences such as physics, astronomy, solid geometry, geography, mathematics, measurements, and medicine were taught as well as ethics, music, painting, drawing, sculpture, etc. Plato attended the University of "Eon" in Cairo.

The Pyramid Age lasted for five centuries and was followed by a long history of invasions. A Persian invasion overthrew the last Pharaoh in 525 B.C., and Persians ruled intermittently until 333 B.C. when Alexander the Great arrived, became the "king" of Egypt and founded Alexandria. Direct and exploitive Roman rule began in 30 B.C. upon the death of Cleopatra, lasting six centuries until 640 A.D. The Arab conquest of Egypt (639-641) eventually transformed a predominately Christian society into a Muslim country in which the Arabic language and culture were widely adopted. A number of dynasties ruled Egypt between 868 and 1260. In 1250, Turkish tribes crossed the borders eventually converting to Islam and controlling Egypt until 1517 when the Ottomans added Egypt to their empire. A dim period followed, lasting more than five centuries under the Mamluk and Turkish rules (1250 to 1798) and education, as with all aspects of life, stagnated and diminished. Napoleon's brief invasion (1798-1801) was accompanied by a commission of scholars and scientists sent to investigate every aspect of life in Egypt. Their report was later to become a valuable historic record. Ottoman pasha Muhammad Ali governed Egypt between 1805 and 1848 and initiated a dual system of education; one for children of the masses who attended traditional Islamic schools and the other for the elite civil servants and technicians who studied a broader range of subjects, generally of western origin.

Muhammad Ali established higher education military schools, a marine school, schools of medicine, pharmacology, veterinary medicine, engineering metallurgy, arts, irrigation, agriculture, industrial chemistry, gynecology and obstetrics, languages, accountancy, and administration during the first three decades of the 1800s. Turkey and other European countries forced Egypt to scale back education and military forces in 1841. The opening of the Suez Canal in 1869 highlighted Egypt's strategic geographic importance and paved the way for foreign intervention and domination. A 40-year British ''protectorate,'' beginning in 1882 and lasting until 1922, continued the social and economic stratification of the society and the dual education system. Colonization brought with it the imposition of non-Egyptian models of schooling including education elitism. Education for the masses (''education for serfdom'') was either nonexistent or limited to low-level subsistence activities. In the 25 years between 1882 and 1907, the Egyptian population grew from 7 to 11 million, but few new schools were founded. When independence came in 1922, more than 95 percent of the Egyptian population was illiterate.

Independence brought a monarchy with a multiparty parliamentary government system, but real power remained with the British and education remained elitist. It wasn't until Gamal Abdel Nasser came to power in 1954 that serious efforts to expand Egyptian education began. Islamic values were a cornerstone of this education. The government began appointing the functionaries of mosques and Islamic religious schools while simultaneously expanding secular education. Five-year plans for 1961-1965 and 1966-1970 included as goals the education of the masses and guaranteed government employment for all higher education graduates. Hampered by three wars in 15 years, only modest educational gains were made. Nasser's era was one of socialism, planning, Arab nationalism, and the rise of Islamic radicalism. Upon Nasser's death, Anwar Sadat (1970-1981) moved to open and liberalize economic and political participation. His economic Open Door policy (*infitah*) ended (*de facto*) the college graduate hiring requirement and, by the mid-1980s, unemployment among university graduates was estimated to be as high as 30 percent. Sadat continued Nasser's educational patterns. Comprehensive national planning lapsed, but higher education was flooded with students, and more than a dozen universities or branches opened in the 1970s accompanied by mass migration of professors to higher salaries in other Arab countries.

Hosni Mubarak revived national planning. The developmental strategies of the first (1982-1987) plan included increasing manpower productivity through training and educational programs. Under this plan, student enrollments increased 27 percent; university enrollments, 6 percent; and the number of schools, 14 percent. A major goal of a 1988-1992 National Plan was to promote education, especially technical education, to produce the manpower resources needed for the expanding economy. The 1989 Educational Development Plan was designed to ''equip the populace to value human rights, to grow mentally, physically, and spiritually, and to develop higher rational abilities; create a productive society by providing highly skilled and educated citizens; achieve the total development of individuals—economically, socially, and culturally—by integrating knowledge with attitudes and aspiration; and prepare a generation of scientists.'' The comprehensive plan proposed expansion of all educational levels, life-long education, and self education; educational reform, including coordination among educational sectors; eradication of illiteracy; continuous educational planning; educational research; variety in educational delivery systems; family participation in the education process; the separation of wages from college degrees; and improved dissemination of educational information and practices.

The succession of post-revolution leaders: Nasser (Arab Socialism), Sadat (Open Door), and Mubarak (Grand Revival) each established new national social and economic development goals, thereby requiring shifts in the direction of the educational system. The educational policies of the three national leaders, however, shared important common themes—they all supported universal education and the introduction of technological skills into society through the educational system.

The 1980s and 1990s saw Islamic acts of violence with assassinations of top government officials and security officers, members of the Coptic Christian minority, writers, and foreign tourists ''in a relentless murderous cycle.'' The Society of the Muslim Brotherhood, established in 1928, became the major Islamic fundamentalist movement and has remained so. Essentially, the Brotherhood is an Islamic protest movement against change and modernity, government corruption, social and economic injustice, and foreign influence. With branches in other Arab countries, it comes close to being a transnational, pan-Islamic movement. In the mid-1990s, the government attempted to rid the educational system of Islamic influences by transferring hundreds of teachers to administrative posts, removing Islamic tracts from library shelves, and banning the imposition of veiling on young schoolgirls. The costs of three wars in fifteen years (1956 Suez War, 1967 Arab-Israeli Six Day War, and the 1969-1970 war of attrition) followed by world recession, drops in oil prices, and an exploding population strained resources for Egypt's massive educational efforts. The picture is reversing in the new millennium due to the rise of oil prices in 1999 and improved fiscal management.

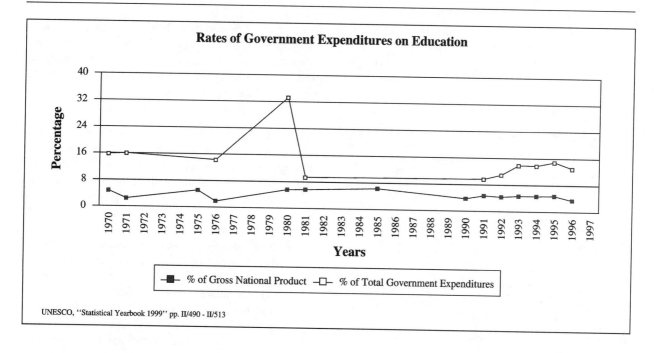

Rates of Government Expenditures on Education

UNESCO, "Statistical Yearbook 1999" pp. II/490 - II/513

CONSTITUTIONAL & LEGAL FOUNDATIONS

Egyptian constitutions date back to 1923, 1956, 1958 (provisional), 1964 (provisional), and 1971 (significantly amended in 1980). The current constitution declares Egypt to be a democratic, socialist state and the Egyptian people to be part of the Arab nation. Islam is the state religion and Arabic the official language. Islamic jurisprudence is the principal source of legislation, and sovereignty is for the people alone. Political parties are regulated by law. Education, cultural, social, and health services are guaranteed. Every citizen has a constitutional guarantee to "choose the level and type of education that suit and agree with her/his talents, abilities and attitudes." Religious education is to be a principal subject in general education. Free education in the state educational institutions is guaranteed, and combating illiteracy is declared a national duty. Education Act No. 146/1981 grants educational authorities the power to require payments for "additional services" and for "insurance on the use of school equipment." A Ministry of Education decree in 1992 (No. 187) imposes such an annual fee (9 Egyptian pounds in primary school and 13.2 in elementary school). Still another decree (149/1986) imposes private group tuition of 2 Egyptian pounds monthly in primary school (3 pounds in preparatory school) for each course attended. Parent and teacher councils can double these fees.

The ambitious provisions of the 1989 Educational Development Plan were implemented by laws and decrees in the 1990s that:

- changed the nine year compulsory education to eight years

- increased the academic year from 30 to 38 weeks

- established the General Organization for School Buildings to plan for school building needs

- established a ten-year plan to eradicate illiteracy with emphasis on the education of women, the elderly, and rural populations

- developed new training programs for teachers of learning-impaired children

- allocated funds to establish one- or two-classroom schools

- upgraded school quality at all levels with new curricula

- coordinated university admission with secondary school diploma requirements

- standardized teacher preparation

- created a central division for educational planning within the Ministry of Education.

The 1990s were declared the National Decade of the Child and the National Decade for the Eradication of Illiteracy. The next educational plan, which covered the period from 1992 to 1997, contained corresponding programs for education. Program I, the promotion of education, planned for expanding and upgrading schools and universities and for expanding outside-of-school projects for dropouts and primary school non-enrollers. Program II planned for the eradication of illiteracy by the year 2000.

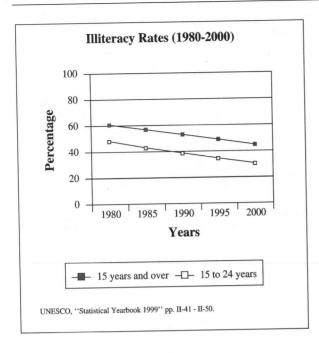

Illiteracy Rates (1980-2000)

Legend: ■ 15 years and over □ 15 to 24 years

UNESCO, "Statistical Yearbook 1999" pp. II-41 - II-50.

The plan set in motion the establishment of one-room rural schools for girls and community schools; upgrading the preparation of primary and preparatory teachers to the university level; initiation of a national program of in-service teacher training with in-county and overseas training; revision of primary and preparatory school curricula, textbooks, and teacher-guide books; expansion of modern technologies with laboratories, computer acquisition, remote teaching systems, video conferences for teacher training, and multimedia teaching materials; establishment of the National Center for Examinations and Educational Evaluation; transfer of kindergartens to the Ministry of Education; establishment of training for kindergarten teachers; and a center for developing kindergarten materials.

EDUCATIONAL SYSTEM—OVERVIEW

Current educational philosophy in Egypt is the product of three cultural heritages: British, secular (westernized) Egyptian, and Islamic (traditional) Egyptian. The British protectorate in Egypt left an exclusionary, state-controlled education system structured to serve elite (British) interests with little concern for the masses. The heritage was one of restricted opportunity, unenforced limited education (generally of poor quality), and higher education reserved mostly for the elite. Egyptians and non-English foreigners were left few options but to expand private and religious education.

Muhammad Ali, regarded as the father of modern Egypt and its education system, introduced a secular, modern, western educational philosophy complete with sciences. Egyptian leaders since the bloodless revolution

that ended the monarchy in 1952 have espoused this approach, viewing it as essential to Egyptian development. Islamic education remained in place and, eventually, the traditional Islamic and the western educational tracks, with their differing orientations, created a dichotomized educational culture that persists to the present.

The Islamic heritage is an educational system, parallel to public education, that is basically a system of transmitting culture. From its founding in 972 until the modern period in the nineteenth century, Al-Azhar University mosque played a central role in shaping the country's religious, educational, and cultural life. At the bottom of the Islamic educational system were *kuttabs* (mosque or Quranic schools), the *madrasas* (religious schools), and the *Sufi* (mystical orders). Resting on memorization and recitation, the traditional methods for learning the Quran, this educational system does not stress experimentation, problem-solving analysis, or learning-by-doing. Education is conceived as a process that involves the complete person, including rational, spiritual, and social dimensions. The Arab/Muslim heritage carries an orientation that transcends national boundaries to include all Arabs and Muslims. From 1922 on, Nasser offered free education, not only for Egyptians, but also for students from other Muslim countries. At the same time, Egypt sent teachers and administrators out to the rest of the Arab world where they set up and staffed schools and universities on a large scale.

Egypt's educational system both reflects and augments the socio-economic status of its own people. Historic conflicts between religious and secular leaders, between tradition and innovation, and between foreign and national interests all influence contemporary Egyptian education. Education in Egypt has political, social, and economic objectives, namely: education for strengthening democracy and comprehensive development as a continuous process, within the framework of Arab culture.

Political tides in Egypt are reflected in educational philosophy. In the early decades following independence, the political system was in a state of transformation and experimentation that resulted in confusing educational policies with fragmented development plans. In the era of economic concerns in the early 1960s, education became a tool to promote economic change. The social focus dominant in the later 1960s led schools to instruct strong Islamic values and democratic ideals. During the 1970s, which was a time of institutionalization, the educational system was bureaucratized.

The Egyptian government recognizes the tensions between Islam and western-generated science and attempts to develop educational goals facilitating both. Throughout the past 40 years, the strong autocratic government, rooted in the Islamic tradition of the protective father, sometimes conflicted with the democratization efforts in schools; nevertheless, the number of schools and technical schools increased even in times of economic downturns.

There is an abiding belief in education. It is viewed as vital to the transmission of cultural values and as a critical force in individual development and in national Egyptian development. Pre-university education reflects the dual secular and religious philosophies as it aims to develop the learner culturally, scientifically, and nationally at successive levels "with the aim of developing the Egyptian individual who is faithful to his God, his homeland, and to the values of good, truth, and humanity."

The public education system consists of three stages: the basic education stage for 4- to 14-year-olds (kindergarten for two years followed by primary school for five years and preparatory school for three years); the secondary school stage for three years, generally for ages 14 to 17; and the tertiary (university) stage. Education is compulsory for 8 years between the ages of 6 and 14. All levels of education are tuition-free at all government schools and institutions. In 1993, more than 13.8 million people were enrolled in state education at all levels. In five years, that figure grew by 5 million. Ninety-one percent of all school-age children were enrolled in school in 1991. When this figure is adjusted for school dropouts and students repeating grades, the enrollment figures drop to 84 percent. (Unofficial estimates place this figure at 70 percent). In 1996, the total official enrollment in primary, preparatory, and secondary schools topped 14 million, the equivalent of 88 percent of the school-age population (boys, 94 percent; girls, 82 percent). In 1998-1999, some 17 million students were enrolled.

Rural-urban inequities continue to persist; in 1991-1992, rural enrollments often did not exceed 50 percent of the appropriate age group and were as low as 10 percent in some regions. Gender inequities also persist; fewer female than male students are enrolled. Many girls drop out of school at the end of their basic compulsory program either to work or to marry. A law prohibiting girls from marrying prior to age 16 has slowly begun to affect the female dropout rates. The law is frequently ignored, however.

The planning process, especially at the basic education level, begins at the bottom as governate officials submit new project proposals (schools, classrooms, equipment, and teachers) and budget requests every year to the Ministry of Education.

Preprimary & Primary Education: Within the Ministry of Education, a Higher Council for Childhood supervises and coordinates preschool education with other

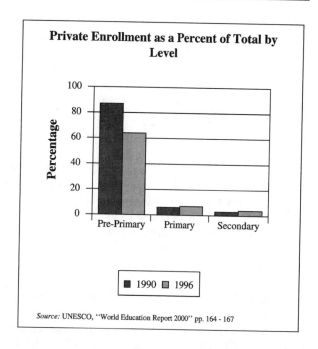

Private Enrollment as a Percent of Total by Level

Source: UNESCO, "World Education Report 2000" pp. 164 - 167

concerned authorities. By ministerial decree, preschool education is intended to aid mental, physical, social, moral, and emotional development; develop language skills and numerical and technical abilities, especially creativity and imagination; raise children in a better environment; help children develop good personalities; and help children gradually accept formal school life and discipline.

In 1995-1996 there were 2,060 preschools staffed by 10,913 teachers, enrolling 266,502 students. Preschool enrollment included 80 percent of the children in the relevant age group (boys, 86 percent, and girls, 74 percent). There are no periods in the preschool day; days are filled with activities and experiences to help children develop their spiritual, moral, physical, social, and emotional domains. Homework or outside duties are strongly discouraged.

All preschool institutions, whether state run or privately operated, are under the Ministry of Education, educationally, technically, and administratively. The Ministry selects and distributes textbooks; the use of any additional textbooks is forbidden. Guidelines state that each class is to have two teachers and a helper in addition to a music teacher. The maximum class size is 45 students. No child less than 4-years-old is allowed in state preschool classes or schools. The private sector can accept children younger than 4, but not less than 3 years and 9 months.

Primary school is also concerned with physical, social, moral, and emotional development, as well as with giving children the knowledge and technical skills needed for a successful practical life. Students may attend non-government private schools, religious schools, or government schools. Primary schools enroll 60 percent of the total school population for all levels of schooling in Egypt. Approximately 45 percent of the primary students are girls, and the majority of primary teachers are women. English and French private schools are growing in popularity as bilingualism gives children social and academic privileges and later lucrative employment. Primary enrollments continue to climb. Primary schools served more than 1.0 million more students (7.5 million) in 1995-1996 (in more than 22,000 additional classrooms) than in 1990-1991. In 1995-1996, the Al-Azhar Moslem system served 704,446 students in 1,912 primary schools with another 147,762 students enrolled in 1,030 preparation (grades 6 through 8) schools.

Secondary Education: The second tier of compulsory education (grades 6 through 8) lasts for three years. Students completing the primary tier of basic education can complete the second tier in general preparation schools, in vocational training centers or schools, or in vocational preparatory classes. Completion of this tier earns the Basic Education Completion Certificate or the Certificate in Vocational Basic Education. An important function of preparatory education is to provide a safeguard against illiteracy as early school dropouts tend to lapse back into illiteracy. The enrollments in preparatory schools in the 1990s totaled 3,679,325, less than half that of the primary schools. Preparatory schools reflect the attrition occurring in the final primary year.

There are two types of public secondary education: general secondary education and technical secondary education. To enter general secondary education, students must pass a national exam given at the end of their preparatory stage. Secondary schools conduct examinations every month for the first two years, and students take a national exam in the final year. Those who pass receive the Certificate of General Secondary Education, a requirement for admission to the universities (accompanied by a strong academic record). A wide range of social, cultural, athletic, scientific, and artistic extra-curricular activities are available in secondary schools, usually sponsored by the teachers. Enrollment expanded significantly between 1990-1991 and 1994-1995 in secondary school (47 percent in general secondary and 85 percent in technical-vocational secondary). In 1994-1995, general secondary enrollment reached 894,400 students, while technical-vocational enrollment was more than twice as high at 1,893.800 students. In 1996 secondary school enrollment included 68 percent of the appropriate age group (boys, 71 percent; girls, 64 percent). In 1995-1996 there were 2,753 secondary schools with 6,142,651 students and 369,107 teachers.

The parallel Islamic educational system, also known as the Al-Azhar system, has a four-year primary stage, a three-year preparatory stage, and a four-year secondary stage. Girls and boys attend separate schools. In 1995-1996, the Al-Azhar Moslem system operated 57 secondary schools with 165,829 students. The curriculum is identical to the normal public curriculum with additional study of the Quran and Islamic sciences. Graduates are automatically accepted into Al-Azhar University.

Special Education: In 2000 approximately 10 to 12 percent of pre-university students were special education students. Responsibility for the physically challenged is shared by the Ministry of Education (concerned with the education of the blind and partially sighted, deaf and partially deaf, and mentally retarded), the Ministry of Social Affairs (provides rehabilitation services to all disabled persons), the Ministry of Health, and the Ministry of Manpower. By 1994-1995, a total of 25 schools for the blind, 95 schools for the hearing-impaired, and 107 schools for the mentally impaired students were operating. Special schools and classes are provided at all levels, serving a total of 22,043 students in 1996-1997.

English language study is part of the curricula in the preparatory stage of basic special education (seventh and eight grades for the deaf and fourth grade for the blind). Changes in the 1990s include a library class added to primary education for the blind and the deaf as well as a class in Arabic handwriting as a separate subject from the Arabic language. A kindergarten for deaf children, starting from age 4, was planned for 1995-1996. Special government departments are authorized for multi-handicapped children and for learning disabled children. Government-sponsored special education schools serve the gifted and talented and the mentally retarded, as well as the physically challenged. Plans to identify gifted students in the kindergarten stage and then to provide special learning experiences for them were developed in 1996. In 1994-1995, some 699 new classrooms were established for 20,790 gifted secondary students. The Ein Shams University School for the gifted was developed with 12 classes serving 261 children.

Other special schools include private schools in villages attached to mosques and private foreign schools where the language of instruction is often not Arabic. At the end of each month, all children in each grade are tested on the same monthly educational unit. In January, they are tested on all three units. The process is repeated in May. The examinations at grades three and five and in preparatory school are prepared and administered locally and considered to be uneven and poor in quality. Children scoring badly on the Grade 5 exam are placed in the least desirable preparatory schools; those scoring badly on the Grade 8 exam may only enter technical secondary schools. An extensive nationally-constructed testing system devised in the 1990s was never implemented. Regional authorities resented national intrusion and refused to cooperate; however, gentler means of improving testing have been introduced.

Higher Education: In the 27 years between 1951-1952 and 1978-1979, student enrollment in public universities grew nearly 1,400 percent. In 1989-1990, there were 14 public universities with a total enrollment of 700,000 students. Four private universities opened in 1996, and there were 612,844 students (231,065 women) and 33,100 academic staff by 1993-1994. By 2000, the universities generated 150,000 graduates a year.

A two-semester system for the school year was instituted in all universities in 1992. The university academic year is 30 working weeks. Arabic is the medium of instruction in humanities, social studies, education, law, commerce, economics and political sciences, information, social service, tourism and hotels. English is widely used in the faculties of medicine, pharmacology, dentistry science, and engineering.

Higher education includes non-university training in Egypt in engineering and technological education institutes, education institutes, private institutes, technical industrial institutes, and commercial and hotel institutes. Since the late 1970s, the government initiated policies to reorient postsecondary education toward technical training programs in agriculture, commerce, and a variety of other fields. Student subsidies were partially responsible for a 15 percent annual increase in enrollments in the country's five-year technical institutes. In 1993-1994, 49,703 students were enrolled in commerce institutes (24,906 women) and 31,259 in technical institutes (9,401 women). Universities, however, permitted graduates of secondary schools and technical institutes to enroll as "external students;" they could not attend classes, but could sit for examinations and earn degrees. The policy resulted in a flourishing clandestine trade in class notes and professors overburdened with additional examinations.

Literacy education began in the 1930s when the Ministry of Social Affairs opened a number of rural welfare centers in the governates offering limited health services and literacy education. Progress through the next decades was slow, and rural illiteracy remained high. President Mubarak launched a massive campaign for the eradication of illiteracy from 1993 to 2002. The General Agency for the Eradication of Illiteracy and Adult Education oversees the schedule for the literacy plan, which targets the 9,792,800 illiterates between the ages of 15 and 35. The literacy plan includes evaluation and rewriting of literacy curricula and educational materials, a collaborative effort between the Agency, UNICEF, and the Center for Curriculum Development and Educational Materials (three integrated books on Arabic, mathematics and general culture plus teachers guides were Completed by 2001), and training programs for leaders and supervisors (more than 13,389 teachers and supervisors have been trained). In addition, the plan includes training unemployed institute and university graduates for teaching literacy (in 1996 about 30,000 of these graduates were trained); using 10,000 military-enlisted personnel to identify learners and equip classrooms with materials; a publicity campaign; conferences and workshops on literacy; the development of a database and information system; and bilateral agreements with UNICEF, UNESCO, Arab organizations, and NGOs (nongovernmental organizations). Special literacy classes are provided for those with special needs.

Female literacy in 1927 was only 5 percent; fifty years later it was 38 percent (male literacy was 62 percent). The combined adult literacy rate was estimated at 44 percent in 1980, the lowest of 10 comparable lower-middle income countries. In 1995, UNESCO estimated the literacy rate to be 51.4 percent (males, 63.6; females, 38.8 percent). As of June 1996, more than 956,000 adult learners completed the literacy program, with more than 596,000 other students attending 27,225 classes. By 1998, adult literacy is believed to have increased to 62.2 percent as a direct result of the government initiatives. Government financial support for literacy education increased from slightly less than 6 million Egyptian pounds in 1992-1993 to nearly 79 million Egyptian pounds three years later. In addition, the Social Fund allocated 105 million Egyptian pounds to mobilize college and institute graduates to work in the project.

Technology & Instructional Materials: In the early 1990s, The Center for Educational Technology was established within the Ministry of Education. Technology equipment is considered "as a medium for developing scientific thinking, problem solving, new modes of learning, and training and communication." New technology planned for pre-university schools includes computers, projectors, television and video sets, and CDI sets. A five-year plan to equip 10,000 schools with this new technology was completed, and 2,000 computer instructors were appointed to secondary schools. Advanced science laboratories were developed in secondary schools (1,500 laboratories with 16,500 new computers). By the mid-1990s, about 200 pre-university schools were linked to the Internet with one pre-university school working on the Globe Project, which gathers environmentally-related global data for sharing with other schools. The Center, in collaboration with the General Department for Educational Aids, is implementing an integrated plan to enhance educational aids such as transparencies, colored slides, still films, models, and microscopic and biological samples; to produce laser CDs for various topics in the curriculum starting with the very early years; and to produce videotapes and audio tapes—especially in the language areas (Arabic, English, and French).

Training on the new equipment has been introduced in Cairo and will eventually take place in educational technology centers closer to schools. In collaboration with Egyptian Radio and Television, distance-training programs are being developed to assist teachers. Six training centers throughout the country are being connected through a fiber optic network to facilitate exchange of information and maximize the use of the technology. Multi-media laboratories, the Internet, and language and computer laboratories are being introduced in the colleges of education. The Egyptian University's Network (EUN) links university computer centers and research institutes throughout Egypt and is the Egyptian gateway to the Internet and Terena. Internet use is available to all universities, faculty members, and graduate students (with about 1300 users in the mid-1990s). More than 80 organizations throughout Egypt can also access it.

Foreign Influences: Extensive foreign influence is apparent throughout Egyptian education. Examples include UNESCO and Fulbright support of overseas teacher training, World Bank engagement in distance education and educational reform as part of loan programs, and technical and scientific education aid using expertise, facilities, and equipment from Americans, French, Germans, Italians, and Japanese. UNICEF aids in development of educational materials. Teachers are sent overseas to the United States, the United Kingdom, and France for training. The Egyptian-Swiss Fund for Development works to improve primary education. Pan Arabic conferences set the aims and goals of education in Egypt and other nations.

PREPRIMARY & PRIMARY EDUCATION

Early childhood education is rooted in Arabic culture. Egyptian nursery schools and kindergartens date back to the turn of the twentieth century. In the 1930s, the Child Guidance Clinic attached to the Higher Institute of Education (now Faculty of Education, Ain Shams University) was founded. The movement for out-of-home education grew as more women entered the workforce and as they formed Women's Associations. Childcare centers and homes accept infants as young as two months. These are primarily "child keepers," lacking educationally oriented services or intervention programs. Day care centers are regulated by the Ministry of Social Affairs. Nursery schools accept children as young as two years, but three

is the most common minimum. Some nursery schools are attached to private regular schools (language schools and foreign schools) but are considered high cost. Others, sponsored by the Ministry of Social Affairs, are widespread and inexpensive, but lack resources and personnel. Some are sponsored by private organizations, especially women's societies, and some by mosques, churches, industrial factories and recreational clubs.

Kindergartens are primarily concerned with pre-academic orientation. Activities are designed for children to learn sound values of religion, social cooperation, and physical being. In 1977, a presidential decree bolstered the development of kindergartens through the establishment of a National Committee on the Welfare of Children. In the 1990s, the educational structure was revised to gradually include kindergarten into the basic education stage, although attendance is not compulsory. Enrollment doubled in the six-year period from 1990-1991 to 1996-1997. Kindergartens have many of the same sponsors as nursery schools. "Private for Profit" kindergartens have primarily middle class clientele because parents must pay. "Private Least Profit" kindergartens are frequently affiliated with educational institutions, humanitarian service organizations, or social associations. "Public Least Profit" kindergartens deliver services at very reduced costs to low-income families. The main objective is preparation for formal training with pre-reading, pre-writing, and pre-arithmetic activities. A secondary objective is sensory-motor development and emotional-social development. Approximately 60 to 70 percent of the time is spent in pre-academic and 30 to 40 percent in language-based activities (poetry, story listening and telling, environment, music, singing and rhythmic activities, and arts and crafts). Most activities are play-based.

The National Conference for the Development of Primary Education Curricula in 1993, maintained the dual aims of Islamic religious concerns and secular modern concerns when it identified as major goals for basic education:

- "Preparing and developing Egyptian citizens in a manner that will assist them to adjust to the demands of a modern changing society and to face the renewable challenges, besides enabling them to comprehend the religious, national, and cultural dimensions of their identity."

- "Providing the society with citizens who have mastered basic scientific skills, with special emphasis on skills of reading, writing, arithmetic, and the disciplines of future sciences (science, mathematics, and languages)."

- "Providing citizens with the essential fundamental knowledge on health, nutrition, the environment, and the development-related issues."

• ''Preparing and assisting citizens to develop transferable skills, including analytical skills, critical thinking, scientific skills, and problem-solving skills that can enable them to respond to ongoing demands and adjust to scientific and technological progress.''

The Ministry revised primary school curricula and teaching methods and increased the number of teachers in the 1990s. Primary education was redesigned into two levels. The first level includes grades 1 to 3 where the basic skills of reading, writing, and mathematics should be mastered (in addition to religious education). At the end of the second level, grades 4 and 5, children should be able to utilize these skills in everyday activities. Children are tested at the end of grades 3 and 5 in mathematics and Arabic, plus science and social studies at grade 5. Up to 70 percent of the curriculum is spent in acquiring skill in Arabic, although classes in English (for fourth grade) were introduced in 1994, as were French classes in 1995. In the 1990s, an experimental language school was established to teach French, and science clubs were established. Special classes and/or schools for the gifted and handicapped are also provided.

Recognizing the malnutrition of many children, the Ministry of Education has initiated a nutrition program of fortified snacks for students in full-day schools. In 1995-1996, some 5,814,067 children benefited from the nutrition program. In addition, health insurance is provided for all pre-university children.

There are three types of primary schools: public schools, subsidized private schools, and unsubsidized private schools. Public schools and subsidized private schools are, for all practical purposes, indistinguishable. Neither charges any tuition, and both types of schools follow the same centrally prescribed curriculum. Private (unsubsidized) schools account for less than 5 percent of all primary school enrollments in Egypt and are found almost entirely in urban areas. Private schools include language schools, ''service classes,'' or ''private schools with fees.'' The language schools are often the remnants of foreign and missionary schools. They are under the control of the Ministry of Education, although they do have some independence. They offer training in foreign language, primarily English and French, starting in early grades. ''Service classes'' are remedial classes for sixth graders who fail the primary certificate examination. Until 1968, promotional exams and repetition in primary schools were not allowed and the only criterion for promotion was 75 percent attendance in each school year. In 1968, the policy changed—one repetition was permitted at the end of the fourth grade with automatic promotion to the fifth grade after the repetition. In 1972, a similar policy of repetition was extended to the second grade. Rural schools are plagued by high dropout rates and gen-

der-related disparities in enrollment. To address these problems, three alternative school models attuned to the traditions of the local community were expanding in rural areas: elementary occupational schools, community schools, and one-room schools for girls.

Elementary occupational schools were designed for students who complete the five years of primary school but don't wish to enter preparatory school or who are dropouts or push-outs from primary school. They cannot enroll in occupational training centers before the age of 16. Completion of the Elementary Occupational program earns a certificate of occupational basic education and permits enrollment in occupational secondary schools.

Community Schools in Upper Egypt are developed through partnerships involving UNICEF, local NGOs, and the Ministry of Education. The communities select teachers and provide school buildings and general coordination. Learning is emphasized rather than teaching, and teachers are referred to as facilitators. In each ''corner'' of the classroom, a group of children is helped by a facilitator (and assistants) to plan their own learning. School hours are flexible. Facilitators train for several months in programs modeling the learning environments that they can create for the children. The syllabus is the equivalent of primary school's and includes basic elements of occupational training. Student achievement equals or betters that of government schools. In 1995, approximately 34 percent of girls in areas with community schools were attending them, 23 percent attended government schools, and 43 percent were not in school. By the end of 1996, some 112 schools had been established with 40 more added during 1997. Girls comprised 70 percent of the enrollment in 1995.

One-room schools grew out of the age-old *Quranic kuttab* schools. The lack of sufficient rural schools, absence of actual legal sanctions against parents not sending their children to primary school, child labor practices, and the distance to schools are countered by these schools with rural locations, flexible schedules, and mostly female teachers from the same rural area. The curriculum is confined to religion, Arabic, arithmetic, social studies, science, and English. There is no physical education, art, or music. One teacher teaches school subjects for the first three grades, another for the fourth and fifth grades, and one does the vocational practices and production projects for the five grades. Teaching is provided for three and a half hours daily, five days a week. Fridays and market days are excluded. The plan is to establish 3,000 schools in hamlets, villages, and isolated places. By 1996-1997, a total of 1,594 schools serving 24,144 girls were in operation.

The Ministry of Education reported in 1994 that approximately 25 percent of the students do not complete the five-year cycle of primary school. Due to grade repetition, the average child takes more than six years to complete primary school. Repetition is concentrated in grades 4 and 5 (approximately 20 percent for each grade). The majority of primary school non-attendees lived in rural areas where resource constraints are most severe. Dropouts generally occur after four and a half years. Dropouts, even in primary school, have real earnings possibilities, particularly in the agrarian part of the economy. Many children, however, do not enter the formal labor market after leaving school; instead, they tend to work in the home or on the family farm. Egyptian research indicates that children with greater ability and achievement are the most likely to stay in school, students of lesser ability tend to leave school early, and higher quality schools tend to retain more students than those of lesser quality.

The second tier (preparation cycle) of basic general education consists of a compulsory core curriculum of general study for the first two years with specialization occurring in the third year. The student selects a specialization in the arts, sciences, or mathematics. The curriculum centers around environmental, social, economic, and health topics considered relevant to the lives of the young. Admission to some preparatory schools, like language schools or sportive schools, requires preliminary exams. Vocational preparatory schools accept repeated failures from the fifth grade (as well as those who passed.) They also accept repeated failures of any grade of the preparatory schools when the child's abilities hinder his or her progress in such education. Children passing medical and ability tests are admitted in preparatory sportive schools, as are Egyptian students returning homeland and foreign students. Preparatory enrollment increased significantly in the late 1990s. The National Conference for the Development of Preparatory Education (1994) designated that the objectives of preparatory education are to:

- eliminate the main sources of illiteracy

- emphasize the components of values

- foster social cooperation

- equip the student with principles, values, and skills needed to work, adjust, and interact within a technological society

- provide the student with essential fundamentals of knowledge

- develop self-learning skills.

The curriculum for the second stage of basic (preparatory) education was revised in the 1990s. Textbooks and teaching materials were correspondingly revised. The last year exam is a major hurdle. Those failing this exam are essentially cut off from the remaining educa-

tional ladder, since schools are crowded and the chances for repeating the grade are limited by available space. As part of the educational reform of the 1990s, a 1993 conference laid the groundwork for undertaking comprehensive assessment, not limited to written examinations but including oral and scientific exams plus performance measures. The introduction of exams and repetitions led to the rise of private tutoring. In 1997, two-thirds of primary students and nearly all secondary students hired tutors.

SECONDARY EDUCATION

From the Ptolemaic Age (323-200 B.C.) through the rule of Mohamed Ali in the first half of the nineteenth century, secondary education in Egypt was intended to prepare students for higher education or for work in governmental departments. The three-year general secondary curriculum continues to prepare students for higher education.

Educational opportunities vary widely in Egypt, and many students engage private tutors during their third year in order to prepare for the national test (*Thanawiyya Aama*). The exam is extremely difficult, covering all content areas throughout the secondary curriculum. Students are ranked for possible college application on the basis of their exam scores. The ranking is very important because exam scores determine if university admission is possible and to which major (faculty) the student will be assigned. Universities cannot accommodate all secondary level graduates, and poor scores remand students to applying to technical institutes.

Traditionally, failing in one subject in the national exam meant retaking all subjects. After studying secondary school certification in the United States, United Kingdom, and France, the system was changed in the 1990s by extending the examination, requiring testing in some compulsory subjects, providing a choice from different sets of subjects, and providing unlimited chances for retaking the examinations. The new system was phased in during the late 1990s; the new exam, however, was not upgraded to assess higher-order skills.

Technical education comprises industrial, agricultural, and commercial schools. Advanced technical schools offer a five-year program to train "Senior Technicians." Technical secondary schools provide a three-year program to train "Technicians," and vocational secondary schools offer a three-year program to train "Craftsmen." In the 1990s, the curriculum and texts were revised in industrial schools and new specializations were added, including: mechanical, marine, vehicles, architecture and building, decorative, textiles, metal work, medical aids, railways, printing, and electrical. The curriculum is intended to provide students with knowledge and skills required in practical work situations as well as a basic academic core of courses. Technical education saw the introduction of application-oriented courses, new specializations, new equipment, new secondary schools, and improvements in technical teacher training.

Different organizations, companies, philanthropic societies, and ministries also offer training with study programs below university level that extend for three years. Vocational schools award a technical diploma equivalent to that of the industrial secondary schools. Their curriculum and training methods differ from those of the Ministry of Education. Fields of study include health education, nursing and first aid, transportation, mining, industrial education, communication, electrical power, and construction and building. In 1994-1995, enrollments in technical secondary programs totaled about 1.75 million, more than twice the enrollments in general secondary education. In 1992, approximately 67 percent of all secondary students were enrolled in a technical program. Only one percent of these students advanced to university study. The labor market cannot absorb all those graduating from the technical schools, and many remain unemployed for four to six years after graduation. School dropouts reaching labor force age in 1989-1990 numbered 162,000. In 2000, it was reported that 500,000 students leave the Ministry of Education's commercial, industrial, and agricultural secondary schools every year—400,000 as graduates and 100,00 as dropouts.

HIGHER EDUCATION

There are essentially three types of universities: those offering preparation for the world of work; those concerned with development of scientific research serving the community and contributing to the development of various fields; and those offering general cultural and intellectual activities. In 1994-1995 and 1995-1996, presidential decrees authorized 35 new institutions to be located in different areas of the country and to include new disciplines such as genetic engineering and new branches of existing disciplines such as colleges of education. In 1996 a presidential decree authorized the development of four new private universities: Egypt's International University, Egypt's Science and Technology University, October Six University, and The October University for the Arts and Contemporary Sciences. Higher education institutions expanded from 144 institutes and colleges in 1981 to 208 in 1996. Tuition is free at public universities for Egyptians; foreign students pay modest tuition fees. Tuition at the American University in Cairo was $10,000 in 1997. It differs from Egyptian universities in that it is based on the departmental and credit-hour system. In September 2000, plans were announced for a new British not-for-profit university to open as early as October 2002. The initial curriculum will focus on areas crucial to

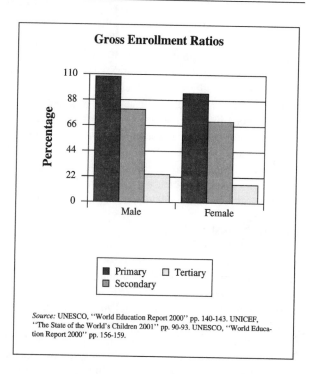

Gross Enrollment Ratios

Source: UNESCO, "World Education Report 2000" pp. 140-143. UNICEF, "The State of the World's Children 2001" pp. 90-93. UNESCO, "World Education Report 2000" pp. 156-159.

Egypt's long-term growth: engineering, management, and information technology.

A Central Orientation Bureau controls admission to undergraduate studies. The bureau matches student preferences with the availability of places and programs at the institutions. Admission requires a General Secondary Education Certificate. Some departments also require oral and/or written entrance exams and/or interviews or high grades in qualifying subjects. In 1991-1992, universities admitted 74,310 students. By 1996, admissions more than tripled, totaling 237,873. In 1991-1992, 11,899 students earned undergraduate degrees; by 1995-1996, this number had risen to 14,587. In 1991-1992, a total of 4,495 Masters degrees were awarded; in 1995-1996 this number was 6,097. In 1991-1992, some 2,128 doctorates were granted; the total rose to 2,818 in 1995-1996. In all, a total of 23,502 university degrees (at all levels) were awarded in 1995-1996 compared to 18,522 in 1991-1992.

While higher education is free for all Egyptians; foreign students pay modest tuition fees. Hostels are provided for Egyptian students from distant rural regions who need financial assistance. Separate hostels are available for males and females. Meals, medical care, and social services are also provided. Board and lodging are heavily subsidized. Fifty million Egyptian pounds have been allocated to upgrade university laboratories and relevant equipment. Ten million pounds have also been allocated for upgrading computer laboratories and computer instruction. An additional 50 million pounds are earmarked for upgrading university libraries. New undergraduate studies using English and French as the languages of instruction have been introduced in the colleges of commerce, economics, political science, and management. Plans for the ''science of the future'' specialized centers focusing on specialized disciplines such as genetic engineering, space, and analysis of new global trends, are to be introduced in all universities. The Genetic Engineering Center for Biological Technology was established at Menoufia and the Center for Futuristic studies at Assiut University. Computer education has been introduced, and colleges for computer science and information will be established at Cairo, Ein Shams, Mansoura, and Helwan Universities.

Several non-university advanced educational opportunities also exist. The National Institute for Higher Administration in Cairo provides training in administration for various levels of in-service personnel from all ministries and organizations. The English for Specific Purposes Center in Alexandria provides postgraduate study in linguistics and translation. Full-time students study for one year, while part-time students study for two years. Successful completion results in a diploma in linguistics or translation. The Higher Institute of Technology in Banha provides university-level education in various specializations in technological fields. The International Center for Inspection and Control Studies in Alexandria conducts training for university graduates from Egypt and Arab and African countries in a program lasting one year.

Schools of art and music include the Academy of Arts (Giza), Higher Institute of Ballet (Cairo with branches in Alexandria and Ismailia), Higher Institute of Cinema (Cairo), Higher Institute of Theatre Arts (Cairo), Higher Institute of Arab Music (Cairo), Higher Institute of Music (Cairo), Higher Institute of Folklore (Cairo), Higher Institute of Art Criticism (Cairo), and the Higher Institute of Child Arts (Cairo). The French University in Egypt (Cairo) offers a wide range of courses and hosts study-abroad students.

Postsecondary colleges and institutes were created to offer non-traditional disciplines and to respond rapidly to societal needs. Engineering and Technological Education Institutes, established in the 1990s, produce engineers who combine both theoretical and applied expertise. In 1995-1996, five institutes enrolled 3,854 students. Specialized Education Institutes offer training in music education, technical education, kindergarten education, home economics, educational technology, educational media, physical education, one-room school teaching, special education, and English. In 1995-1996, enrollment was 14,019 students. Private institutes offer training in areas such as computer technology, social work, tourism, hotel management, agricultural and management cooper-

atives, economics media, and language. Private junior institutes train in social work, secretarial skills and computers. In 1995-1996, some 43,766 students wereregistered. Technical Industrial Institutes produce graduates to fill the gap between expert engineers and technical laborers. In 1995-1996, some 22 institutes enrolled 56,491 students. Commercial and hotel institutes provide further education for graduates of commercial secondary high schools. In 1995-1996, some 65,721 students were registered. Health care, nutrition, housing and social care are heavily subsidized for students at institutes.

In 1995-1996, Egyptian universities and higher institutes hosted 3,493 foreign undergraduates and 1,299 postgraduate students. An additional 104 foreign students attended training centers. The Educational Center for Arabic language Instruction teaches Arabic to international students and has various clubs provide enriching experiences. Egypt participates in the American Project Hope (for nursing institutes), Fulbright educational exchanges, the German Corporation for Academic Exchange, and international university linkages for doctoral candidate supervision. Egyptian professors are sent to universities and organizations in other countries.

The university and college libraries are said to be very poor and, in many cases, outdated. They suffer from lack of funds; from poorly trained, poorly paid, uninterested librarians with limited English facility; and in some cases, from deteriorating facilities. The main gaps in holdings are in periodicals, reference books, bibliographies, abstracts, and indexes. Reasonable quantities of Arabic books and journals are available, as are audiocassettes and quantities of microfilmed journals from the 1960s and 1970s, donated by USAID. Even 1992 reports indicate that the typical Egyptian student is unlikely to have used a library before arriving at college and is even unlikely to use one during college, given the emphasis on rote learning and the unfamiliarity with independent learning. University libraries include Alexandria University Central Library (45,000 books, 1,000,000 microfiches and films, 1200 periodicals, 2,500 manuscripts, and 17,500 dissertations); Assiut University (250,000 volumes); Al-Azhar University (60,000 volumes and 20,000 manuscripts); the American University in Cairo (275,000 volumes); and Cairo University (1,407,000 volumes and 10,000 periodicals). Other libraries in Cairo include the Arab League Information Center (30,000 volumes and 250 periodicals); Central Library of the Agricultural Research Center (25,000 volumes); and the Center of Documentation and Studies on Ancient Egypt (scientific and documentary reference center for all Egyptian Pharaonic monuments with 4,500 volumes and 33,000 photographs). National libraries include the Library of the National Research Institute of Astronomy and Geophysics; National Archives of Central Administration, National Assembly Library; and the National Information and Documentation Center. Many of the higher institutes of art and music also contain specialized libraries. School libraries, when they exist, even in the 1990s are likely to be a locked cupboard in the headmaster's office.

In the 1990s, Mrs. Suzanne Mubarak, the wife of the President, led a national campaign to build libraries for young people in Cairo and other major cities with children's areas, multimedia, trained librarians, children's programs, and locations in attractive surroundings in public parks or near recreational activities. The Ministry of Education developed plans for upgrading school libraries in 1993, and space for libraries is part of new school designs. Basic school library lists were prepared in the 1990s, and 2,975 tapes were provided for schools.

ADMINISTRATION, FINANCE, & EDUCATIONAL RESEARCH

Government Agencies: Educational administration in Egypt is structured into four main levels. At the top is the Ministry of Education (MOE), headquartered in Cairo and headed by the Minister. The ministry contains nine functional areas of administrative support: finance, administrative development, statistics, education (technical, general, and basic), and service (extracurricular, instructional materials, and general). The MOE is charged with establishing plans, programs, procedures, and administrative support systems for carrying out national education policies established by the Higher Council for Pre-University Education, the highest educational policy body in the country. The MOE also oversees the Supreme Council of Universities. The Ministry of Islamic Affairs administers Al-Azhar University and associated schools.

The Supreme Council of Universities defines the general policies of university education and scientific research and determines admission numbers, fields of specialization, and equivalencies. The Supreme Council is comprised of the Minister of Education (Chair), presidents of various universities, experts, and the Secretary of the Supreme Council of Universities. In 1994, new councils were created to assist the Supreme Council: a Council for University Education and Student Affairs, A Council for Graduate Studies and Research, and a Council for Community Service and Environmental Development. The second main structural level is found in each of the regional governates. Since the 1970s, an incremental approach to decentralized decision-making has been taking place. An undersecretary or director general heads the educational system of each governate. Most of the regional planning, teacher appointments, evaluation, and training occur at this level. The third level is the district headed by a district director general. Finally, the fourth

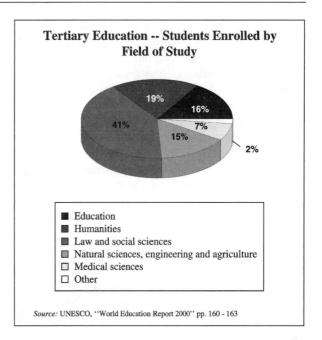

Tertiary Education -- Students Enrolled by Field of Study

- ■ Education
- ■ Humanities
- ■ Law and social sciences
- ▨ Natural sciences, engineering and agriculture
- □ Medical sciences
- □ Other

Source: UNESCO, ''World Education Report 2000'' pp. 160 - 163

level is the director of the individual school, called a headmaster. The headmaster has minimal decision-making authority and functions basically as a teacher coordinator and identifier of problems that are sent up the hierarchy for others to solve. Except for the Minister, all administrators begin their careers in the classroom and work their way up a rigidly maintained seniority ladder.

The Ministry of Education supplies capital and operating expenses for public education through taxes, customs, and other general and local revenues. Additional revenue derives from examination fees, local levies, and donations. In some cases, local jurisdictions construct new schools and turn them over to the Ministry. Significant external funding has been provided by USAID, extensively supporting basic education, and UNESCO, supporting literacy and adult education. Teachers are allocated to schools on the basis of official enrollment levels and are paid out of the central budgets allocated to each educational zone. Books and most other student supplies are centrally purchased and distributed to the schools according to enrollments. The budgeting process provides a degree of regional participation in resource allocation: the governates propose their financial requirements based on formula-driven teacher/student/school ratios. The rigid formulas, however, limit flexibility. The Ministry of Education prioritizes the budget requests before sending the entire package to the Ministry of Finance where final decisions are made.

UNESCO reported that from 1975 to 1983, the percentage of GNP spent on education declined from 5 percent to 4.1 percent. In 1988, education in Egypt received 10.6 percent of the national budget. Of 23 comparable middle and lower middle-income nations reporting, only Turkey spent less on education (10 percent). Expenditures on education increased during the 1990s largely as a result of an extensive school building program and in 1998, reached 19 percent of total spending (between 6 and 7 percent of GDP). In the 1980s, public universities—accounting for roughly seven percent of total student enrollment—received more than one-fourth of the education budget. In 1984, budget and personnel figures painted a "top heavy" picture as they reported as much as 25 percent of personnel salaries earmarked for administration, an unusually high figure. For each primary school (grades 1 through 6), there were 2.2 headmasters and 1.9 vice-principals.

Educational Research: The National Center for Educational Research in the Central Ministry of Education coordinates educational policy with that of the National Specialized Councils, exchanges information with the institutions throughout the world, provides local and foreign documents on education, and publishes various works on education in Egypt and the Arab world. Critics complain that research at the Center is rarely directed toward guiding the future of education with analyses of economic and social trends in terms of occupational needs.

Most research occurs in isolated sectors of schools of education housed in Egypt's main universities. Egyptian educational research was originally designed according to statistical models and focused on answering questions relative to the effects of student and environmental characteristics on rates of learning. The research largely resulted in teacher education programs characterized by study of psychology, environmental factors, cultural values, experiential education, and the "Egyptianization of the Stanford Binet IQ test." In the 1990s, university-sponsored research projects within masters and doctoral programs aimed at increasing effective planning in the areas of educational economics, adult education, special education, and educational administration. Little coordination occurs however, between the university and government research to inform national policy.

NONFORMAL EDUCATION

Nontraditional Learning Environments: Science clubs are developing at the governorate level. By the mid-1990s, 12 such clubs had been established to provide activities in the field of electronics, environmental studies, computers, and science. A new interactive, hands-on science museum (The Exploratory Science and Technology Center) is developing at Nokrashi Secondary School. Technologically equipped trucks (mobile laboratories) provide a form of "Exploratory Education Center" to reach distant villages and towns. Also under development are Culture Museums using multimedia (a collaborative project between the Ministry of Education and the Supreme Council of Antiquities) and model schools of the future and schools for the gifted.

Adult education in rural areas is of vital importance in Egypt where in recent years, agricultural performance has seriously declined. Self-sufficiency in food production once at 94.5 percent declined by 1995 to only 52 percent. Illiteracy is high. Skill training in the agricultural sector is provided by extension educators as part of a Training and Visit system (T&V) linking farmers and agricultural research centers. Extension educators train farmers as adopter-leaders. The Agricultural Research Centers (ARC) operates eight research stations in different regions, each specializing in the main commodity of regional importance. In addition, agricultural faculties exist at 10 universities. Primary educational concerns center on how best to deliver educational and training programs.

Open university education assists with the process of Continuing Education to provide education for those who might have missed it or provide an opportunity for those who are already employed. In 1996, a total of 20,000 students participated in open education programs at the universities at Cairo, Alexandria, and Assiut. In addition "directed affiliation" programs, available at the colleges of Art, Law, Commerce, Social Work, Arabic Studies, and Colleges of Arts at the Women's colleges, expand opportunities for students. One hundred twenty-nine thousand students, representing about 17 percent of all university students, participated in these programs in 1996. Egypt's distance education initiatives include a regional communications network (RITSENE) implemented in 1995 and a Regional IT Institute, established in 1992. Current IT use is centered within a small, well-educated elite. The state-sponsored Regional Information Technology and Software Engineering Center (RITSEC) promotes networking, software development, and education of computer professionals through conferences, training programs and its web-accessible Information Technology Service (IDSC). Internet services are available through Cairo University and the American university. Egyptian specialists, students abroad, and the expatriate community supply more online information from outside the country than is provided within Egypt.

Nonformal education is also offered by NGOs registered with Egypt's Ministry of Social Affairs. Egypt's NGO sector, today numbering 14,000 to 15,000 private non-profit organizations, offers training, sewing classes, religious instruction, and tutoring for the middle and lower-middle classes, but rarely for the poor. Most rural areas have no NGOs, as geographic outreach is concentrated around the provincial cities. The Community Development Associations (CDAs) category of NGOs offer sewing classes for girls and women, and skills training for youth as well as health clinics. Private (NGO) and governmental (rural welfare) societies have joined forces to deal with the accelerating out-migration from villages to the cities. Coordination of all services became codified into law in 1945. Religious-based (Muslim and Christian) welfare associations offering general education and religious instruction for youth. Although public education is free, the cost of supplementary tutoring so essential for success on all-important examinations, is a heavy burden on middle and low-income families.

Muslim NGOs and rural CDAs are establishing religious (Al-Azhar) institutes with government funding in response to the critical shortage of public schools and classrooms. ''Religious'' projects are frequently an effective NGO strategy for circumventing bureaucratic obstacles and garnering private donations for multipurpose facilities. There are 1 to 24 international NGOs (e.g., CARE, Save the Children, Project Hope, Near East Foundation) in Egypt that provide training and technical assistance to local NGOs, but little information on their educational activities is available. The MOE reports in 2000 that Egypt has about 90 postsecondary educational agreements with other countries including faculty exchange, joint research, delegations, symposia, and periodical and book exchange programs. Egypt and Qatar, for example, have an agreement for 2000-2003 on educational and scientific research cooperation. Egypt's international programs involve both Arabic and western countries. The international programs primarily benefit the educated elite.

TEACHING PROFESSION

A conference on teacher preparation in 1996 proposed a new plan to upgrade the skills of teachers and expose them to alternative methods of education, new trends, and new technologies. One result was in-country and international training opportunities for teachers. President Mubarak in 1995-1996 authorized overseas training for 1,000 teachers per year. They are sent to U.S., U.K., and French universities for four months. By June 1996, 1,939 teachers had completed overseas training.

Preprimary teachers traditionally were women with little formal university training. Plans call for gradually replacing unqualified teachers with qualified ones. Preschool teachers in 2000 must be university graduates, preferably with specialization in child development who study child development, development of disabled children and development of the gifted and talented. Candidates at universities are encouraged to choose an area of

childhood such as media, children's theater/library, early child psychology, or children's literature and museum study.

In the case of a shortage of properly qualified teachers, the Ministry may accept university graduates with other majors after giving them an extra year to earn a Special diploma in Childhood Education. Kindergarten headmasters must hold a higher degree in Childhood Education plus five years experience, or preferably a higher degree such as an M.A. or Ph.D. in this field.

The preparation of both primary and preparatory teachers was upgraded to university levels in the early 1990s. Preparation now takes place at universities in 15 colleges of education. Enrollment in 1996-1997 was approximately 10,000 teachers. The position of the special education teacher is viewed as a less than desirable position, socially and economically, and many low-achieving students are urged to enter the field.

Teaching positions at public secondary schools require a university degree and the postgraduate General Diploma in Education. Teachers are educated at one of the university schools of education. Teacher candidates can also take specialized courses in skill areas offered by the technical institutes. University education programs are of two types: integrated preparation and continuing preparation. The integrated teacher preparation begins with two years of courses that include principles of education and psychology, principles of teaching, social and historical foundations of education, and basic culture courses. If students successfully pass an exam at the end of the second year, they can advance to the third and fourth years of the program. In these years, they take courses in methodology, educational psychology and technology, educational philosophy, comparative education, curriculum, and social psychology as well as specialized and cultural courses. After student teaching, candidates are qualified for a Bachelor of Arts or Bachelor of Science degree.

The continuing teacher preparation is for graduates of non-education faculties who wish to become teachers. These candidates enroll in education courses full time for one year or part time for two years. Successful completion earns a General Diploma in Education. Technical schoolteachers are trained in special institutes. Teaching staff at the university level are generally required to hold the doctorate. Departments select faculty candidates subject to the approval of both a faculty board and a university council. An additional requirement is attendance in an educational training program on educational and psychological principles of teaching held annually for three weeks in the Faculty of Education. The teaching staff consists of lecturers, associate professors, and professors. Promotion to the rank above depends upon the originality and quality of research work and a minimum of five years in rank. The Permanent Scientific Committee affiliated with the Supreme Council of Universities administers university promotions.

Teacher-quality has been sacrificed by granting the General Diploma Program to non-education graduates, by requiring that university graduates performing poorly in technical fields become teachers, and by the lack of standard methods for qualifying teachers or standardizing their preparation. Additionally, pre-service teachers willingly work as expatriates in neighboring countries rather than assume Egyptian teaching jobs with lower salaries. In 1997, the average teacher's salary was less than $100 a month. Thus, some of the best teachers, those most able to handle content and develop a diverse repertoire of skills, are lost to Egyptian education programs. Further, few of the teachers received preparation in pedagogy. Their coursework is comprised of subject area classes and classes on teaching basic literacy. "They are products of the lecture-mode and don't adapt easily to the role of teacher-as-guide or instructional-manager"—roles stipulated in the national curricula. To upgrade primary school teaching quality, the Ministry of Education in 1981 recommended that primary teachers be unilaterally enrolled in an ongoing education program sponsored by a university faculty of education. The courses are given after school hours and are part of a university degree program.

In the mid-1990s, 75 million Egyptian pounds, allocated to address the problem of occupational stagnation, resulted in the promotion of 53,422 teachers. Additional incentive awards totaled 27 million pounds. By the end of 1991-1992, allocations for additional awards reached 46.5 million pounds, a practice continued for the next five years. Other compensations of various types are given and headmaster remuneration increased in 1991-1992 to almost 100 percent over that of 1990-1991. In 1992, resources and pension funds increased for the teachers union (Teachers' Syndicate) including those for retired teachers. The Teachers' Collegial Fund increased by 5 million Egyptian pounds, resources for local teachers' hospitals by 500,000 Egyptian pounds, and Teachers' Cultural and Social Welfare Resources by 500,000 Egyptian pounds. The Teachers' Syndicate is the largest syndicate of teachers with the largest financial resources in Egypt and the Arab world. All teachers belong to the syndicate. The syndicate does not deal with national educational causes; the government excludes it from participating in decisions on national educational policies and in decisions made by advisory educational councils for technical training institutes.

A member of the Ministry of Education traditionally directs the syndicate and so does not represent the ideas or values of the rank-and-file teachers. After the revolution of the 1950s, political blocs were abolished to prevent organized workers in any field from striking or organizing opposition to the government. The Teachers' Syndicate remains however, but government intelligence personnel are assigned to keep an eye on syndicate meetings and activities.

Parents who want their children to have the best chance at national exams take advantage of the low pay and status accorded teachers and hire them as private tutors. Most citizens accept this arrangement as a means of having some control over their children's education. Tutoring grew to a $2 billion industry by 1997. Aside from the financial burden on parents and the increased income for teachers, tutoring impacts the educational system per se. Students begin to disregard ministry-designed curricula and replace them with tutor-recommended materials and lessons that have been successfully used as exam preparation tools. Too, abuses are not uncommon. Some teachers pressure students into private tutoring and for some, tutoring becomes a more important part of their workday than their official classroom duties and occupies after school time rather than in-service training.

SUMMARY

The dawn of the 1990s found Egypt facing serious problems in education—problems compounded by low literacy rates and an exploding population. Educational quality, particularly in basic education and in technical and vocational education, had seriously declined. Increasing numbers of graduates were unemployable and virtually untrainable. The curriculum was generally irrelevant to the students. School quality was uneven, with better quality schools in urban areas where the wealthy could pay for tutoring. Teachers lacked training in pedagogy. Learning, conducted with martial drills and physical punishment, encouraged rote memorization rather than critical thinking. For many Egyptian children, the result was fragmented information, "never to be ground into knowledge." In-service training, encumbered in bureaucracy and inconsistent funding, was shunned by many teachers in favor of tutoring for extra income. Preschool assessment procedures did not exist. Required exams in primary and preparatory schools were often poorly designed. The national secondary final exam was fact-recall. Free education coupled with the population explosion led to burgeoning enrollments at all stages; an expansion beyond the capacities of the schools. Chronic teacher shortages, especially in rural primary schools, resulted from low prestige, low pay, and migration of teachers to better jobs in other countries.

In 1985-1986, nearly 155,000 primary and secondary teachers served 9.6 million people, a ratio of about

62 students per teacher. An over-abundance of administrators depleted salary budgets. Serious underfunding was reflected in deteriorating buildings, overcrowded schools and classrooms, poor or absent libraries, and lack of technology. Some city schools operated two and even three shifts daily. Crowded public classrooms held as many as 100 students in some Cairo schools, which was not the case in private schools. Only 31 percent of primary children attended a full-day school system. Most secondary schools lacked scientific laboratory and computer equipment.

Comprehensive educational planning tying educational programs and output to national needs was lacking. A serious mismatch between supply and demand produced incompetent degree-holders in unwanted subjects. Unemployment was high. Almost half of the students did not complete the basic school. Attendance was often poor and laws requiring primary school attendance were not enforced. Significant regional differences existed with nearly 90 percent of the urban children attending school, but that percentage was often far less than 50 percent for rural children. Dropout and grade repetition rates were high. Against this backdrop, massive changes began in the 1990s.

Egypt is in the midst of these changes as it implements a sweeping revision of its educational system; a revision aimed at upgrading and modernizing and transforming it into a coherent, continuous educational process. The primary and preparatory curricula were redesigned to be more relevant and more scientific with emphasis on experimentation and critical thinking. Texts and teaching manuals were revised. Kindergarten was designated as a part of the formal system and included in the comprehensive planning. Gender and rural/urban inequities and illiteracy are being addressed with special rural programs targeting girls, programs designed to be flexible and relevant to local needs.

To improve the quality and quantity of the teaching staff, pre-service and in-service training was revised and performance-related (merit) pay and changes in the technical standards of supervisors and inspectors instituted. Curriculum and texts are under revision in industrial schools with new specializations.

Medical insurance is provided for students in kindergarten and basic education, financed by charging the children four Egyptian pounds annually. (Private school students pay more.) These fees, plus fees for ''additional services'' and for taking primary and preparatory school exams, and the price of uniforms and tutoring costs (averaging 10 percent of family income per child in 1997) effectively removed the ''free'' from free education placing it out of reach for Egypt's poorest. No fees are charged however, in the rural community and one-classroom schools or to orphans whose fathers died in military or government service.

Education in Egypt will continue to face shortages of teachers, schools, and equipment unless the state makes a far greater financial commitment. Two decades of dropping birth rates means that the school-age population peaked in 1997 that should help to prevent shortages from worsening, but there is still a tremendous shortfall. The mechanistic learning of concepts and textbook-dependent learning and teaching are ingrained in the system. As long as testing is fact-dominated and doesn't cover higher order skills such as critical thinking and analysis of problems, teachers and tutors will continue to teach to the test and the lecture-rote system will persevere. In-service teacher training, distance learning, and technology may help, but so far they reach relatively few teachers. The rigid centralized bureaucracy clogged with excess seniority-promoted staff is cumbersome and slow moving and the highly centralized educational planning and policy-making tend to disenfranchise the very people at the local level who are entrusted with achieving its goals. Local districts need to be able to make adjustments suited to local needs.

Mindful of the lessons of Iran and Algeria, Egypt has so far curbed the violence and intrusion of the militant Islamic movement, something that is a concern for the future. Islamic militancy is the response to the grinding poverty, unemployment, and under-privilege of the masses and will continue so long as these conditions exist. The undercurrent of Islamic opposition to foreign ideas and western secular education still lurks however, and could ignite in the face of the sweeping educational changes aimed in that direction. Illiteracy is still extremely high, and eradication must continue to be a priority. The state's multi-pronged initiatives of the 1990s appear to be working and need to continue, as does the development of the rural alternative schools. Quality has not kept pace with quantity at the university level and there still appears to be a mismatch between university graduates and the fields of manpower needs and skill levels needs. Communication among agencies at the top educational levels is reported to be good. Vertical communication is poor however, as vividly illustrated by the attempt to impose national tests on the governates. Communication between policy-makers in national offices and regional and local implementers needs to be vastly improved.

Egypt recognizes the weaknesses and problems in its educational system and has gone to great lengths to address them, but there is a vast difference between idealized plans and implementation. A system short on resources, stifled by bureaucracy, and lacking in local expertise moves slowly. Only time will tell how well the comprehensive efforts of the 1990s to make education more relevant to national needs are working. Egypt has a long expensive road to travel given the enormity of illiteracy and vast educational shortages. The financial improvement at the millennium, stemming from rising oil revenues and better fiscal management, gives the education future a rosier glow than a decade ago.

BIBLIOGRAPHY

Razik, Taher, and Diaa El-Din A. Zaher. ''Egypt.'' In *Issues and Problems in Teacher Education: An International Handbook*, edited by Howard B. Leavitt, 91-108. New York: Greenwood Press, 1992.

Richards. Alan. ''Higher Education in Egypt.'' *Education and Employment Working Papers* (WPS), no. 862. Washington, DC: World Bank, 1992.

Shaw-Smith, Peter. ''Egyptians Welcome British Initiative.'' Times (London) *Higher Education Supplement,* 27 October 2000.

Soliman, Azza Abdel-Aziz. *The Current Status of Pre-University Education and Its Regional Disparity in Egypt.* Cairo Demographic Center, 1994.

Swan, Michael K., and Ismail Abd El-Fattah Aly. ''Rural Education and Training in Egypt.'' *Agricultural Education Magazine* 68, no. 4 (1995): 11-13.

Wise, Michael, and Anthony Olden, ed. *Information and Libraries in the Arab World.* London: Library Association, 1994.

The World of Learning 2001. 51st ed. London: Europa Publications, 2000.

—*M. June Allard and Pamela R. McKay*

EL SALVADOR

BASIC DATA

Official Country Name:	Republic of El Salvador
Region:	North & Central America
Population:	6,122,515
Language(s):	Spanish, Nahua
Literacy Rate:	71.5%
Academic Year:	February-October
Compulsory Schooling:	9 years
Public Expenditure on Education:	2.5%

Foreign Students in National Universities:	473
Educational Enrollment:	Primary: 1,191,052
	Secondary: 143,588
	Higher: 112,266
Educational Enrollment Rate:	Primary: 97%
	Secondary: 34%
	Higher: 18%
Teachers:	Secondary: 9,255
	Higher: 5,910
Female Enrollment Rate:	Primary: 96%
	Secondary: 36%
	Higher: 18%

HISTORY & BACKGROUND

The republic of El Salvador is the smallest country in Central America, with a total area of 21,041 square kilometers (8,124.59 mi.). It is bounded on the northwest by Guatemala, on the north and east by Honduras, and on the south by the Pacific Ocean. The local government is divided into 14 departments and 262 municipalities including cities, towns, and villages. The capital is San Salvador. The median age in the country declined from nineteen in 1950 to seventeen in 1975, and 41.3 percent were projected to be under the age of fifteen by 2001. The population for the year 2000 was 5.5 million. El Salvador is not only Central America's smallest country, but it is also the most densely populated country in the Western Hemisphere, with an average population of approximately 298 people per square kilometer. Most of the land is devoted to agriculture and the population is concentrated in industrial and agricultural areas centered on San Salvador, which attracts people on account of better job opportunities and higher salaries. The population is divided into: Mestizo 90 percent; Indigenous 50 percent; and European descendants 5 percent.

Spanish is the national language. The daily use of Indigenous languages has faded out. There has been some academic interest in preserving the old Nahua language of the Pipils, but Nahua is not spoken in the street, except in a few Indian villages in Morazán and Chalatenango. El Salvador is predominantly Roman Catholic, but a number of other churches are also represented.

Cuscatlán, the original name of El Salvador, dates to as early as 2000 B.C. The Spanish arrived in the sixteenth century. El Salvador was dominated by the Pipils, who were descendants of Nahua and Aztec (two Mexican tribes). The Pipils came to central El Salvador in the eleventh century. In 1540, Pedro de Alvarado conquered Cuscatlán and the region came under Spanish control. It was designated a province of Nueva España and placed under the direct control of the Capitanía General de Guatemala.

The Dominican order arrived first to the Provincia de San Salvador, later the Franciscans, and later still the Mercenary Orders. Churches and convents created by faith and the commitment of the religious orders were founded in the sixteenth century. Their prosperity was concentrated on agricultural labor and the teaching of arts and informal skills. It was during this period that the first public library, school, and university were created.

Education during this period began with the convent schools. The convents in the Provincia de San Salvador were more modest than those in the Capitanía General de Guatemala, but they used the same methods and educational tendencies. The *frailes* received from the Indigenous people a series of histories, chronicles, and historical narratives that have disappeared because of fires or earthquakes. During the Colonial period the schools were only for the Spanish children. The Indigenous received instruction, but this was limited to the teaching of Catholicism in their native languages. Later this instruction was improved, but in the classroom they were never recognized as being in the same category as the white students.

The first school was founded in 1548 by Lic. Francisco Marroquín. From the beginning, the education of the male was more important than that of the female; her instruction was considered not only less important, but dangerous. Although many women from privileged families enjoyed better conditions, colonial women's lives were mainly committed to difficult and inferior jobs. The convents began the liberation of women. For the first time in their history, women received instruction in reading, writing, and in improving their minds along Christian precepts. An example of women educated during this period are: Juana de Maldonado, Juana de Arévalo, Ana Guerra de Jesus, Catarina de Jesus, Isabel de Bustamante y Naba, María Ana de León, Lucía Villacorta de Cañas, Josefa de Barahona, Antonia Fagoaga y Aguilar, Felipa de Aranzamendi, and Manuela Antonia de Arce.

Independence from Spain came on September 15, 1821. On July 1, 1823, El Salvador joined Honduras, Guatemala, Nicaragua, and Costa Rica to form the *Provincias Unidas de Centro América*. However, regional and ideological conflicts beset the union, which was finally dissolved in 1840. In the following year, El Salvador adopted a constitution as a sovereign independent nation. The republic was formally proclaimed on January 25, 1859.

Turbulence, political instability, and frequent presidential changes characterized Salvadoran history during the second half of the nineteenth century. The land had been settled in large landholdings. The Indigenous were pushed off their land or *ejidos* (community land) and were forced to work on the Spanish plantations for miserable wages or no wages at all. Anastasio Aquino, chief of Nonualcos, led an unsuccessful Indigenous rebellion in 1833 with the idea that "Land is for those who work it." A hundred years later, Feliciano Ama, the last chief of Nonualcos, led another rebellion called La Matanza (The Massacre).

Relative stability was evident in the area of education from 1900 to 1942, but so was turmoil. The dictatorship of Gral. Maximiliano Hernández Martínez brought a period of constant military rule for almost 13 years. During this period, 95 percent of El Salvador's income came from coffee exports. Union activity in the industrial sector during the 1920s brought strikes and demands for better wages, but when coffee prices plummeted following the stock market crash of 1929 the situation between union workers and the landowners became unbearable. Landowners, no longer tolerating union activities, incited the government to take action. In January 1932, Agustin Farabundo Marti, the founder of the Central American Socialist Party, led an uprising of peasants and the Indigenous people. Under Hernández Martínez, the military responded by systematically killing 30,000 people. Farabundo Martí and other leaders were arrested and executed by firing squad. Martí's name is preserved in the Farabundo Martí National Liberation Front (FMLN).

In the 1960s, Colonel Julio Adalberto Rivera became president, creating a favorable political environment for constitutional reform, the creation of the Common Central American Market, improved civil rights organizations for workers (including teachers), and a new educational system. The minister of education was Walter Beneke, who was responsible for the Educational Reform. For the first time, televised instruction was used in the classroom. Students throughout the country were able to obtain the same instruction for the entire curriculum. Originally, this system was overseen by experts in this pedagogical technology, but by 1972 this system was increasingly run by native personnel. General student ability and reading scores increased, although there was little difference between television and non-television classes. Behavioral objectives were introduced and students showed increased skills in analysis, synthesis, and evaluation.

The students under this program were enthusiastic, but teacher enthusiasm waned somewhat after the initial uncritical acceptance. Teacher attitudes toward their profession as a whole and its attendant problems remained poor. Student aspirations became increasingly high, perhaps unrealistically so, but educational reform was working, as evidenced by the percentage of students going on to higher education. At the same time, Liberation Theology created an environment for preference to the poor. The social conflicts of the 1970s and 1980s cannot be explained plausibly just by population density and the socio-political balance between town and country, since the education of the masses played a significant role. Rural unions, which often originated from the cooperatives and communal associations sponsored by the church, posed little ostensible threat to the established order. That is, until the rural unions' support of the Preferential Option for the Poor brought about a rise in violence.

The era of Popular Education occurred in 1980-1992. The Civil War affected the mental health of children who were born and raised during the twelve years of the war, and exposed them to different levels of violence. Children from industrial neighborhoods who came from displaced villages reported higher war experiences and lower mental health, while children who experienced the highest personal-social effects of the war showed the poorest mental health and they were most likely to have difficulty in imagining the future. Popular education focused on children and women and their potential for societal change, and proved to be particularly relevant for women. By using popular education, the insurgent movement sought to fill the education gap created because most combatants and civilians were peasants, few of who had much opportunity for schooling in the communities where they grew up. The most sustained experiences of popular education occurred in FMLN-controlled zones of the country. Popular education was as much a political and organizational process as an educational process. The focus of the Christian-based communities was to work toward their conception of social justice and political change. Its work can be summarized as: Christian-based communities in the 1970s; refugee camps on the Honduran border in the 1980s; and repopulated communities in FMLN-controlled zones from 1980 to 1992.

CONSTITUTIONAL & LEGAL FOUNDATIONS

The Constitution adopted in 1983 rested in the executive power of the president, who appointed a cabinet to help run the country. The minister of education was responsible for all matters related to education. The Constitution of El Salvador declared that elementary education was free and compulsory for all children between the ages of seven and fifteen. In 1960, the compulsory education was extended three years more than had been the case under the old educational system, with students having to complete nine years of schooling. The public school system was controlled by the government. The curriculum for elementary and secondary levels was uni-

form throughout the country. The provision of education, however, suffered from rural-urban dichotomy. A number of national education plans developed by the ministry of education have recognized the inequality between the rural and urban education systems, but none have succeeded in bringing rural education up to the urban level.

EDUCATIONAL SYSTEM—OVERVIEW

The aims of the educational program designed in the 1960s differed significantly from the previous educational system; the objectives were democratization, introduction of technology into the classroom, and the preparation of students for achieving social and economic development. Democratization led to the rapid expansion of schools. During the 1960s, the government was able to open as many schools as possible under the program *Una escuela por día* (One school per day). This expansion was based on the idea that education is not a privilege, but a right of every Salvadoran. As a result, there were significant increases in enrollments at the elementary level, which reduced illiteracy rates from 72.0 percent in 1930 to 49.0 percent by 1988, and 28.5 percent by 1995.

PREPRIMARY & PRIMARY EDUCATION

The educational system begins with the preschool or "kindergarten," most of which are located in cities rather than rural areas. The children, ranging in age from five to six years old, receive instruction for two years, three hours per day, and five days per week. Most of these schools are under government supervision, although there are private preschools. The main objectives are to prepare the children for entry into elementary school, to inculcate in them good work habits, and to develop oral and listening comprehension skills.

The school calendar runs from February to the end of October, five hours per day, Monday through Friday. Graduation takes place on November 5th. Elementary education begins at the age of seven and last for nine years. From the seventh grade, students receive classes in English as a second language as a part of the curriculum; it remains a requirement throughout the rest of their elementary school years. Curriculum stresses the teaching of formal Spanish grammar as well the fundamentals of science and mathematics, and six hours are devoted to sports and cultural activities.

Most primary schools are not coeducational. However, the majority of classes in grades seven to nine are mixed. Both men and women are teachers at this level. Student-teacher ratios are high in public schools. With an insufficient number of teachers, classrooms are overcrowded. In 1993, there were 3,961 primary schools with an enrollment of 1,042,256 primary students. In order to best utilize the buildings, there are two groups of stu-

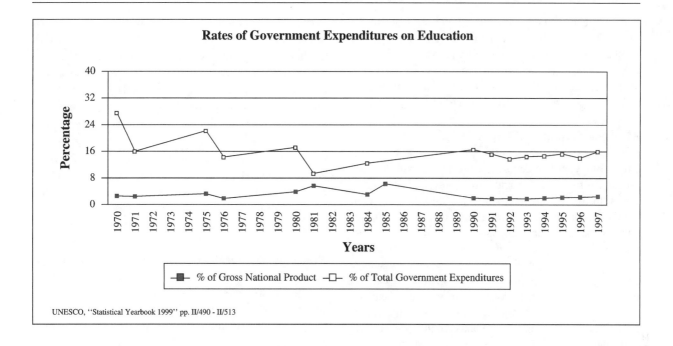

Rates of Government Expenditures on Education

UNESCO, "Statistical Yearbook 1999" pp. II/490 - II/513

dents: one group attends in the morning from 7:00 a.m.-12:00 p.m.; the other attends from 1:00-5:00 p.m. Some schools have adult evening classes from 7:00-9:00 p.m. Among school-age children, the total student enrollment in 1980 was 65 percent; in 1993, 70 percent; and by 1995 it had risen to 79 percent in public primary schools.

Only about 8 percent of the country's total enrollment in middle secondary education was rural children; the majority of the illiterate population reside in rural areas. The high degree of rural illiteracy reflects several factors, at the most basic level, the number of teachers and schools provided for rural areas. In the 1980s, only 15 percent of the nation's teachers served in rural areas, although these areas accounted for 64 percent of the primary schools. Of the primary schools available to rural children, approximately 70 percent offered education only below grade four or five. By contrast, 90 percent of the urban primary schools offered grade five and above.

There was a high attrition rate in school attendance in rural areas as students left school to earn wages or work at home. Although school attendance generally began at about the age of eight or nine, approximately 70 percent of all male workers began employment before the age of fifteen, many by age ten or earlier, thus permitting only one or two years of schooling. Many girls also dropped out of school at an early age in order to assume domestic responsibilities, such as caring for younger siblings, working in the fields, or tending animals. Therefore, only 20 percent of the rural school-age children reached grade six, and only a few percent reached grade nine. Efforts to improve this situation in the rural agricultural areas were somewhat discouraging, in part because

of the political tension during the Civil War and post-war period. In some situations, teachers, mainly women, faced threats if they supported political change. Many rural landowners seemed to prefer an uneducated rural population on the grounds that better-educated workers would expect better wages and be more likely to organize and lobby the government for reform, particularly land reform.

In the 1960s, Educational Reform integrated the middle school into elementary education. Aimed at preparing students for the secondary level, the curriculum, different from grades seven to nine, consists of history, geography, mathematics or algebra, science, English, physics, computer programming (available only at private schools), sports and cultural activities. Students who pass gain the primary school certificate and are allowed to progress to secondary educational institutions.

SECONDARY EDUCATION

Secondary education, for children from the age of sixteen, lasts for three years. Of children in the relevant age group, only 21 percent were enrolled in secondary schools in 1996. The curriculum at the secondary level was developed by the government to be uniform throughout the country. The provision of the secondary level suffers from the same rural-urban dichotomy as the public school system. Only a small percentage of students reach grade twelve and receive their *bachillerato* (equivalent to a high school diploma). Secondary-level enrollment among the rural population is about 8 percent of the country's total enrollment in secondary education; in grades ten through twelve it drops to about 1 percent. Although both men and women teach at this level, the majority are men. The school year runs from February through November. In general, the curriculum prepares students for either employment or further study. At the secondary level there are different programs: academic or general, technical, pedagogical, and commercial.

Academic Secondary Study: The academic secondary study has two programs, physics/mathematics and chemistry/biology. All students are expected to take the same courses in the first year and carry about 30 instructional hours. In the second year, students start taking different courses according to their program. For example, the science/mathematics program students would take the same classes as other students, and later add specialty classes such as vocational physics/mathematics, and, for science students, the instructional classes include vocational chemistry and advanced biology. In the third year, the number of courses is reduced, but the vocational classes are increased. For example, seventeen hours per week are dedicated to the specialty. Also, all students in the third year take the following common courses: letters, demography, English, and physics/mathematics. After completion of the three-year cycle of secondary education, students sit an examination administered by the government; those who pass are awarded a high school certificate. These programs are offered specially in private schools or Catholic colleges for upper class students. Most of the students continue to the university level.

Commercial Secondary Study: This program consists of three years of instruction. The curriculum at this level is vocational and is aimed at preparing students for employment or further vocational training programs. The program focuses on three areas of study: economics, business administration, and accounting. The certificate is earned after three years upon passing the final examination. The students either enter the labor market or a postsecondary institution. The curriculum of the commercial secondary studies is computer science, economics, accounting, typing and shorthand, among others. The total instruction hours per week are 30.

Technical Secondary Study: Technical secondary study is only offered to low income students at the National Institutes. There are three programs: general mechanics, general electrics, and auto mechanic. All these programs are based on three years of attendance, from Monday to Friday, 40 hours per week. In the first year, all students are expected to take the same courses. There are no electives until the second year, when each program introduces special courses according to each specialty. After completing the three years cycle of secondary education, the students take the government-administered examination.

Pedagogic Secondary Study: This program is offered for students who want to be preschool or elementary teachers. If they want to specialize in secondary education they need to attend the university level. The curriculum in this program is focused on pedagogy, children's literature, psychology, sociology, philosophy, methodology, and teaching techniques. After the second year, students spend a great of deal of time working on the practical, supervised by teachers. At the end of the third year, students take two examinations, on science and pedagogical material, administered by the government. Those who pass are awarded the diploma of education. Those who fail may take the examinations again.

Transitional Education: The aim of the Technological Institute is to make the transition from study to work simple and to make education relevant to the social and economic needs of the country. It also targets students who cannot afford tuition at the university level. Study at this institute, located in Santa Tecla, lasts for two years, 40 hours per week. The program offers technical industry, civil engineering, architecture, mechanics, and decoration courses.

HIGHER EDUCATION

There are three public and twelve private universities. The most important universities are the University of El Salvador authorized in 1841 and The Central America University (UCA) in San Salvador. After the war, the participation of women became very significant. In 1993, some 77,369 students were enrolled at universities and other higher-level institutions; approximately 51 percent of these students were female. Attaining a university education is still the key to status in Salvadoran society. For students from low-income families, the University of El Salvador, with its enrollment averaging 30,000 students, offers them the best opportunity. The enrollment age is between 19 and 23. The National University requires an admission examination, and offers all fields of study; the Central America University specializes in the humanities. Between 1950 and 1980, the country's urban population grew from 18 percent to 44 percent of the total, an average increase by regional standards; that of the city of San Salvador increased from 116,000 to 700,000 (this, too, by no means exceptional in Central America). Both men and women teach at this level, and there is strong competition between their numbers. The school year is divided in two semesters (circles) and runs from January to December. After completing the requirement for their specialty, students write and defend a dissertation. Successful completion enables them to earn the Licenciatura (Master's degree).

TEACHING PROFESSION

Traditionally, teachers were recruited from the high school level, but, after 1930, they were recruited from the graduating classes of the Escuelas Normales (teacher training schools). After 1965, under Educational Reform, the Escuelas Normales developed into part of the secondary educational system. Most of the teachers for universities and higher levels hold a Master's degree or doctorate.

SUMMARY

By the late 1990s, El Salvador was financially stable and had recovered from the economic crisis of the 1980s. However, there are many challenges to be met in the future. For example, for the vast majority of rural residents, unemployment, under-employment, and extremely low wages combine to keep the standard of living low and the quality of life barely tolerable. The educational system has emphasized elementary and secondary education in urban areas. Even the ministers of education have recognized the inequality between rural and urban education, but none have succeeded in bringing rural education up to the urban level. The earthquakes of January 13 and February 13, 2001 destroyed many rural schools. It is imperative that the government builds more schools and improves the lack of adequate facilities, equipment, and personnel in rural areas. According to the *Opicina de Referencia de Población* (PRB), the population in El Salvador is estimated to reach twelve million by the year 2030. The departments with the most population are: San Salvador with 2,240 people per square kilometer, La Libertad with 413 people per square kilometer, and Sonsonate with 367 people per square kilometer; compared with 97 people per square kilometer in Chalatenango. El Salvador needs to create a politically aware population in order to reorganize. High levels of poverty, agricultural stagnation, environmental damage, and increasing social crime and violence are all issues that the country urgently needs to confront.

BIBLIOGRAPHY

Berthell, Leslie, ed. *Mexico, Central America, and the Caribbean since 1930*, 251-282. New York: Cambridge University Press, 1990.

Browning, David. "History of El Salvador." *Worldmark Encyclopedia of the Nations Americas.* Detroit-New York: Worldmark Press, Ltd., 1997.

Cagan, Beth, and María Juli. "Maintaining Wartime Gains for Women: Lessons from El Salvador." Institutional Social Work 4 (October 1998): 405-415.

Gunson, Phil, and Greg Chamberlain, eds. *The Dictionary of Contemporary Politics of Central America and the Caribbean,* 132-133. London: T.J. Press Ltd. Cornwall, 1991.

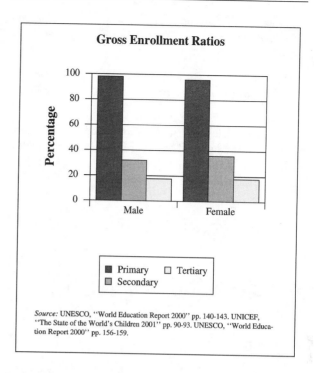

Gross Enrollment Ratios

Legend: ■ Primary □ Tertiary ■ Secondary

Source: UNESCO, "World Education Report 2000" pp. 140-143. UNICEF, "The State of the World's Children 2001" pp. 90-93. UNESCO, "World Education Report 2000" pp. 156-159.

Freire, Paulo. "Liberation and Pedagogic Empowerment: Identities and Localities: Social Analyses on Gendered Terrain. Symposium." *Latin American Perspectives* 26.4 (July 1999): 3-106.

Funkhouser, Edward. "Mobility and Labor Market Segmentation: The Urban Labor Market in El Salvador." *Economic Development and Cultural Change* 46.1 (October 1997): 123-153.

Haggerty, Richard A., ed. *El Salvador: A Country Study, Area Handbook Series.* Washington, DC: Library of Congress, 1990.

Hammond, John L., ed. *Fighting to Learn: Popular Education and Guerrilla War in El Salvador.* New Brunswick, NJ: Rutgers University Press, 1998.

————. "Popular Education as Community Organizing in El Salvador." *Latin American Perspectives* 26.4 (July 1999): 69-94.

————. *Popular Education in the Salvadoran Guerrilla Army—Human Organization* 55 (Winter 1996): 436-445.

Kincaid, A. Douglas. "Peasants into Rebels: Community and Class in Rural El Salvador." *Comparative Studies in Society and History* 3 (July 1987): 466-494.

Mayo, John K. *Educational Reform with Television: the El Salvador Experience.* Stanford, CA.: Stanford University Press, 1976.

Pan American Health Organization. *Health Condition in the Americas, 1981-1984.* Washington: Scientific Publication No. 500, 1986.

Sol, Ricardo. *El Salvador: Medios Masivos y Comunicación Popular*. San José, Costa Rica: Editorial Porvenir, 1984.

Waggoner, George R., and Barbara Ashton Waggoner. *Education in Central America*. Kansas: University Press of Kansas, 1971.

Walton, Joan Riley, Ronald L. Nuttall, and Ena Vazquez Nuttall. ''The Impact of the War on the Mental Health of Children: A Salvadoran Study.'' *Child Abuse & Neglect* 21 (August 1997): 737-749.

—*Marta A. Umanzor*

EQUATORIAL GUINEA

BASIC DATA

Official Country Name:	Republic of Equatorial Guinea
Region:	Africa
Population:	474,214
Language(s):	Spanish, French, pidgin English, Fang, Bubi, Ibo
Literacy Rate:	78.5%

HISTORY & BACKGROUND

The Republic of Equatorial Guinea is a small West African country that consists of Rio Muni and the five small islands of Bioko, Corisco, Great Elobey, Little Elobey, and Annobon. Its total area is approximately 10,831 square miles (28,052 square kilometers). Equatorial Guinea is a very fragmented country that suffers from internal differences and an unstable economy, both of which are in part attributable to its geographic separation from the other countries of Africa.

The Portuguese first explored Equatorial Guinea some time between 1472 and 1475. Because of the Treaty of Tordesillas (June 7, 1494) the Portuguese maintained control over Equatorial Guinea until 1778, when Spain took control of the colony. Spanish control of Equatorial Guinea was intended to give Spain a direct source of slave labor to use as needed in Spanish America. No occupation of mainland Equatorial Guinea took place at this time, however, as the Spanish left the island of Bioko (then Fernando Po) after a widespread yellow fever epidemic.

From 1827 to 1843 the British leased spaces at Port Clarence (later Santa Isabel, now Malabo) on Fernando Po to use as a base to regulate the abolition of the slave trade. In 1839 the first known school was established in Clarence City with 120 children. Because there was no Spanish administration in the area, the British administered the island and made Spain several offers to buy the island from them. All of these offers were denied, and the British left Fernando Po in 1843 after selling their buildings to a Baptist mission. A second school was established on Santa Isabel by Baptist missionaries some time between 1840 and 1858 (Liniger-Goumaz 2000).

The Baptist missionaries were forced off of the island of Fernando Po in 1858, and a group of Jesuits established themselves there. The Jesuits also opened a school in Santa Isabel, but the revolution in Spain of 1858 put an end to these efforts. In 1870 Primitive Methodists also opened a school, and between 1876 to 1877 an additional school was established and later directed by a Cuban, following the Spanish decision of 1879 to use the island as a penal settlement for Cubans (Liniger-Goumaz 2000). This school, along with the school established by the Methodists, was suppressed following the arrival of many Claretians, members of the Congregation of the Missionary Sons of the Immaculate Heart of Mary, which was founded in Spain in 1849. In addition, the American Presbytery Missionary operated schools in Corisco and Rio Benito from the nineteenth century. At the beginning of the twentieth century a school was opened in Bata for 180 boys and girls by the French Fathers of the Holy Spirit (Liniger-Goumaz 2000).

CONSTITUTIONAL & LEGAL FOUNDATIONS

After the Spanish-American War, which ended in 1898, Spanish Guinea became Spain's only significant tropical colony. It was around this period that the economic development of Spanish Guinea began, although for the most part it was concentrated on the richer island of Fernando Po. The Spanish budget law of 1902 provided for the creation of undenominational schools. This project lasted until 1909 and was restarted in 1922. In 1914 the *Escuela Externa* (secondary school for day students only) was founded in Santa Isabel, and in 1927 a school was opened in Evinayong. Vocational schools were also begun in 1931, the first of which was in Santa Isabel (Liniger-Goumaz 2000).

Despite this progress in the field of education, it was only following the Spanish Civil War, from 1936 to 1939, that mainland Spanish Guinea began to receive broad educational consideration from Spain. In August of 1943 the Guinean school system was organized and provided for the following stages: elementary and preparatory education, primary education, lower secondary education, higher vocational education for schoolteachers and administrators, technical and agricultural education, and complementary schooling for male and female natives (Liniger-Goumaz 2000).

In 1959 the status of Spanish Guinea was changed when it was divided into two overseas provinces of Spain. Each province was placed under the control of a civil governor. Under this new system, all citizens, including the Africans, were granted the same rights as those exercised by citizens of Spain. The free elementary education established under Spanish rule was designed to teach the Spanish language and to guarantee patriotic and moral education (Liniger-Goumaz 2000). Even under this system, however, most children did not go beyond elementary school and most teachers were vastly underqualified.

In 1963 the two provinces came to be known as Equatorial Guinea after a measure that agreed on economic and administrative autonomy was adopted by plebiscite (common vote). Then, on October 12, 1968, Equatorial Guinea gained independence from Spain, after ratifying a constitution on August 11, 1968. At the time of independence, 185 primary and elementary schools existed, with approximately 48,000 students (Liniger-Goumaz 2000).

The first president of Equatorial Guinea following independence was Francisco Macias Nguema. He was elected in 1971 and, following the election, was successful in passing through a constitution that named him president for life. His rule was marked by many arrests and executions, and during his rule the economy in Equatorial Guinea experienced rapid decline.

Macias maintained power until 1976, when he was overthrown by his nephew, Colonel Teodoro Obiang Nguema Mbasogo. In 1982, a new, more liberal constitution was approved. Presidential elections were held in early 1996 and President Obiang was re-elected to a seven-year term, winning over 97 percent of the vote. The president's party also won the legislative election held in March 1999, although most international observers agree that the elections were fraudulent.

EDUCATIONAL SYSTEM—OVERVIEW

In 1971, UNESCO inaugurated the *Centro de Desarrollo de la Education* (CDE) with the mandate to train high school teachers. The project was halted after just a few years by President Macias, however, who was anxious to put an end to anything that threatened his power and that he deemed ''intellectual.'' During President Macias' term in office, the educational system in Equatorial Guinea experienced severe setbacks. Teachers, students,

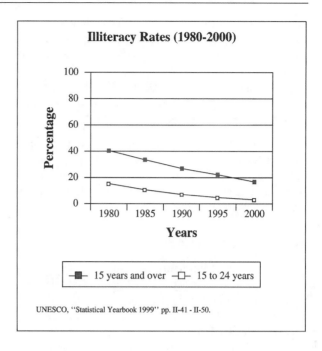

Illiteracy Rates (1980-2000)

UNESCO, ''Statistical Yearbook 1999'' pp. II-41 - II-50.

and parents were arrested and, in some cases, several ministers of education and other education officials were executed, arrested, or detained. Beginning in April of 1972 military education became a requirement in all schools, and in April of 1975 political instruction also became mandatory. By 1972 there were 360 primary schools with 578 teachers for 35,902 students. At that time, the teacher-student ratio was 1 to 62 (Liniger-Goumaz 2000).

Following the palace revolution of 1979, the educational system in Equatorial Guinea slowly recommenced operation. Despite assistance from Spain, France, the United Nations, and the World Bank in the forms of textbooks, teachers, and training, the educational system in Equatorial Guinea remains severely hampered by a lack of trained and qualified staff.

Compulsory Education: Education is compulsory for all children between the ages of 6 and 18, although it is widely accepted that the government does not enforce the laws concerning compulsory education. It is estimated that only about 79 percent of children actually attend primary school and that only 69 percent of children progress to receive secondary education. Both the primary and secondary levels consist of six years of schooling. The dropout level is very in high in Equatorial Guinea. Illiteracy rates (for 1999) for adult males age 15 and above are estimated at 8 percent while the rate of illiteracy for women age 15 and above is 27 percent (World Bank 1999).

There is rampant discrimination again women in the education system of Equatorial Guinea, as women tend to be constrained by traditional customs reinforcing their secondary social status. It is estimated that the average woman receives only one-fifth the amount of schooling that the average male receives. In addition, there is no national legislation for the protection of children's rights, so discrimination and truancy are overlooked by the state (U.S. Department of State 1999).

Because of the relatively poor conditions of most public schools in Equatorial Guinea, private schools are becoming increasingly more common, although problems still persist with resources and with adequate funding (Liniger-Goumaz 2000).

HIGHER EDUCATION

Higher education facilities are provided mainly through Spanish assistance via the Spanish National University of Distant Education; locations are in the principal cities of Bata and Malabo. Some students who reach the university level also go abroad to study, primarily in Spain and France. In addition, there are five institutions of higher learning in Equatorial Guinea: the National Institute for Health (Bata), the National Institute for Public Administration (ENAP), the National Institute for Agriculture (ENAM), the Santa Isabel and Bata Institutes for Teachers' Training, and the National Centre for Proficiency in Teaching (CENAFOD), financed by UNESCO (Liniger-Goumaz 2000).

TEACHING PROFESSION

Teachers in Equatorial Guinea face many challenges, especially their own lack of qualifications. In addition, they are faced with crumbling school buildings, very high student-teacher ratios, and a lack of blackboards, books, and materials. Teachers also face political constraints imposed on them by the Obiang regime and are subject to arrests should they act in ways that are perceived as threats to the regime (Liniger-Goumaz 2000).

SUMMARY

The educational system in Equatorial Guinea faces many challenges: the lack of facilities and textbooks, the lack of adequate training for teachers, the centralist control of the curriculum by the state and the bureaucracy, the inability of officials to devise effective long-term educational policies, and an overall lack of funding (Liniger-Goumaz 2000). These problems are all very severe in Equatorial Guinea and must be addressed comprehensively in order to combat educational deficiencies.

Oil was discovered in 1996 off the shores of Equatorial Guinea. Mobil Corporation is the principal oil company involved in Equatorial Guinea, producing 90 percent of the country's oil wealth. Since this discovery of oil, Mobil Corporation has given aid to the government, particularly to be used to improve the educational system. Corruption is a problem in Equatorial Guinea, however; it is very uncertain to what extent profits from the oil reserves will ever reach the population for improving living conditions and the educational system. Because of the lack of transparency within the public finance sectors of the government, it is difficult for the citizens of Equatorial Guinea to hold their government accountable for changes in incomes and expenditures (World Bank 2000). Now that the country has oil wealth, however, Equatorial Guinea also has the potential to choose a developmental strategy that will allow it to grow and prosper.

BIBLIOGRAPHY

The Central Intelligence Agency. *World Factbook 2000.* Directorate of Intelligence, 2 March 2001. Available from http://www.odci.gov/cia/publications/factbook/.

Liniger-Goumaz, Max. *Historical Dictionary of Equatorial Guinea,* 3rd ed. Lanham, MD: The Scarecrow Press, 2000.

Strieker, Gary. *Oil Brings Promise of Change to Troubled Equatorial Guinea.* CNN World News, 29 May 1997. Available from http://www.cnn.com/.

U.S. Department of State. *Equatorial Guinea Country Report on Human Rights Practices for 1998.* Bureau of Democracy, Human Rights, and Labor, 26 February 1999. Available from http://www.state.gov/www/global/human_rights/.

World Bank. *World Development Indicators,* 3 March 2001. Available from http://devdata.worldbank.org/.

———. *Equatorial Guinea,* September 2000. Available from http://www.worldbank.org/afr/gq2.htm/.

—Eleanor G. Morris

ERITREA

BASIC DATA

Official Country Name:	Eritrea
Region:	Africa
Population:	4,135,933
Language(s):	Afar, Amharic, Arabic, Tigre, Kunama, Tigrinya
Literacy Rate:	25%

Number of Primary Schools:	549
Compulsory Schooling:	7 years
Public Expenditure on Education:	1.8%
Foreign Students in National Universities:	117
Educational Enrollment:	Primary: 240,737 Secondary: 89,087 Higher: 3,096
Educational Enrollment Rate:	Primary: 53% Secondary: 20% Higher: 1%
Teachers:	Primary: 5,476 Secondary: 2,071 Higher: 198
Student-Teacher Ratio:	Primary: 44:1 Secondary: 45:1
Female Enrollment Rate:	Primary: 48% Secondary: 17% Higher: 0.3%

HISTORY & BACKGROUND

Eritrea, Africa's newest nation, celebrated its tenth year of independence in 2001. In May 1991, Eritrean liberation fighters swept the besieged remnants of Ethiopia's occupying army out of Asmara, the Eritrean capital, ending four decades of Ethiopian control and Africa's longest continuous modern war. In April 1993, Eritreans overwhelmingly endorsed independence in a UN-monitored referendum. On May 24, 1993, Eritrea declared itself an independent nation and four days later joined the United Nations.

The armed struggle for Eritrea's independence began in 1962, after a decade of Ethiopian violations of a UN-imposed Ethiopia-Eritrea federation, and following Ethiopia's annexation of Eritrea as its fourteenth province. In the early 1970s, the Eritrean People's Liberation Front (EPLF), was organized and, throughout the next decade, emerged as the dominant liberation force. The Eritrean independence struggle became synonymous with ''self-reliance''—a 30-year war fought from wholly within the country by a politically mobilized population supporting a large, well-trained army using captured weapons. The historical and political necessity of Eritrean self-reliance forced Eritreans to plan and test—while fighting for—the kind of society they wanted, with education a vital factor in the liberation movement's success and a key element in the Eritrean model of development.

Country & People: Eritrea is a torch-shaped wedge of land, about the size of Britain, along the Red Sea coast in northeast Africa. Sudan is to the north and west, Djibouti to the southeast, and the Ethiopian province of Tigray to the south. As a former province of Ethiopia, Eritrea formed that country's entire, 750-mile Red Sea coast. A highland plateau divides the northern half of the country, with lowlands to the west and east. The south is desert. Asmara and major towns are sited in the highlands. Massawa and Assab are significant Red Sea ports.

About 20 percent of Eritreans are urbanized, forming a significant working class. Of the rural population, more than 60 percent are farmers; the rest combine farming and herding, except for the less than 5 percent who lead purely nomadic lives in the far northern mountains and southern coastal desert. Eritreans comprise nine ethnolinguistic groups. The total population of about 3.5 million is approximately equally divided between Muslims and Christians, the religious division cutting across some ethnic lines. The predominant language is Tigrinya, spoken by the group of that name. Arabic is widely spoken among Muslims. English—the language of instruction in post-elementary schools—is increasingly common, especially in the cities.

Early History: Archeological sites in Eritrea have yielded hominid fossils judged to be two million years old. Tools from about 8000 B.C., unearthed in western Eritrea, provide the earliest concrete evidence of human settlement. Rock paintings found throughout the country, dating to at least 2000 B.C., have been assigned to a nomadic cattle-raising people. Between 1000 and 400 B.C., the Sabeans, a Semitic group, crossed the Red Sea into Eritrea and intermingled with the Pygmy, Nilotic, and Kushitic inhabitants known to have earlier migrated from Central Africa and the middle Nile. In the sixth century B.C., Arabs occupied the Eritrean coast, establishing trade with India and Persia, as well as with the pharaonic Egyptians. The ports of Eritrea enjoyed continuous contact with Red Sea traffic and Middle East cultures that fostered a cosmopolitanism unique to the coast.

The powerful Axumite kingdom, centered in the present-day Ethiopian province of Tigray, prospered on trade through Eritrea from the first to sixth century A.D., adopting Christianity in the fourth century, then declined as Beja tribes migrated from Sudan and Arabs gained dominance of the Red Sea. The Ottoman Turks ruled Massawa and its coastal plains from 1517 to 1848, when they were displaced by Egypt. With the opening of the Suez canal in 1869, the Red Sea coast gained strategic and commercial importance. In that year the Italian government purchased the port of Assab from the local sultan. The Italians occupied Massawa in 1885. In 1889 the Ethiopian King Menelik ceded Eritrea to the Italians in exchange for military support against his Tigrayan rivals.

Prior to Italian domination, education fell into two broad categories, religious and local. Christian and Muslim clerical hierarchies replenished themselves by educating—essentially raising—small numbers of children in the tenets of the faith. Local education, as in any society, consisted of training children in practical, productive skills: home construction, traditional medicine, music-making, storytelling, and decorative arts. These practices persist in all of Eritrea's cultures and can be detected in general in the force of authority, especially generational authority, and the educative functioning of exemplary behavior, demonstration, and imitation.

Italian Eritrea: Despite Menelik's treaty with Italy, Italian legions invaded Tigray in 1895. The Italian generals, however, blundered fatally at Adwa on March 1, 1896, losing nearly half of their forces. In the ensuing Treaty of Addis Ababa, Italy renounced claims to Ethiopia, while Menelik affirmed Italian control of Eritrea.

The Italians ruled Eritrea until their defeat in Africa by the British in 1941. Education in Italian Eritrea prior to fascism was in the hands of Protestant and Roman Catholic missionaries. Swedish missionaries had established the first school, in Massawa, in the 1860s, and by the 1920s had schools in eight centers, serving 1,100 students. An early center of Roman Catholic missionary education was the highland city of Keren, where a seminary, day school, and orphanage served a few hundred children. In 1909, the first colonial educational policy was declared, based on separate schools for Italians and Eritreans. Schooling was compulsory for Italians to age 16; the curriculum of Italy was used. Education for Eritreans, however, limited to the Italian language and basic skills, was designed to produce menials for the Italians.

After Mussolini's rise to power, strict racial laws enforced segregation and wage differentials based on color. Benefiting from low wages and extensive use of child labor, the Italians built diverse manufacturing concerns, increasing the drift to the towns; by the end of Italian colonial rule, about 20 percent of the population was living in urban centers, where they were restricted by law to native quarters. In 1932, the first central office for primary education was established, the purpose of which as defined by its director, Andrea Festa, was to ensure that education accorded with the principles of the Italian regime. In 1938 Festa wrote to headmasters: "The Eritrean student should be able to speak our language moderately well; he should know the four arithmetical operations within normal limits...and of history he should know only the names of those who have made Italy great." But education was never widely available to Eritreans, and fourth grade was the highest level an Eritrean was allowed to reach. There were only 20 schools for Eritreans in 1938-39, with 4,177 students.

British Administration: Italian colonialism was an early casualty of World War II. British forces entered Eritrea in January 1941. British administration continued to 1952. The British gradually removed the color bar, began an "Eritreanization" of lower administrative positions, and allowed the formation of political parties and trade unions. At the beginning of British rule, there were no Eritrean teachers but, in 1942, nineteen were recruited. Over the next ten years, the British increased the number of elementary schools to 100 and opened 14 middle and 2 secondary schools. The curriculum introduced in 1943 covered agriculture, woodworking, clay-modeling, carpet-making, shoe-making, reading, writing, and hygiene for boys, and reading, writing, hygiene, weaving, sewing, basket work, and domestic science for girls. Textbooks in Tigrinya were locally printed, books in Arabic and English were provided, and entrance to the middle schools required students to be able to read and write English. In 1946 a teacher training college was established; by 1950, fifty-three men and seven women were in training to be teachers.

Through school committees organized in the villages, Eritreans actively supported education, funding school construction, and paying teachers. But the demand for education far exceeded budgeted funds, a 1950 British government report admitted, leaving many children unserved because of a lack of buildings, equipment, and staff.

Federation & Annexation: In 1952, after lengthy debate, and with Cold War politics a factor, the UN General Assembly voted to federate Eritrea with Ethiopia. Eritrea was to be an autonomous unit under the sovereignty of Ethiopia's monarch, Haile Selassie. The contradictions of federation were immediately apparent. Ethiopia's feudal economy and imperial political system clashed with the capitalist development of Eritrea and the democratic constitution approved by the elected Eritrean Assembly in 1952. Eritrean political parties and trade unions were banned, newspapers censored, and protests attacked by police. Finally, in November 1962, Selassie terminated Eritrea's federal status, making Eritrea a province of Ethiopia.

Eritrea had passed from British control to the federal arrangement with better educational facilities than Ethiopia, but Ethiopia's imperial government soon began to undermine Eritrean education, along with other institutions. In 1956, Eritrean languages were banned and replaced by Amharic, an Ethiopian language virtually unknown in Eritrea. Ethiopian teachers brought in to teach Amharic were paid 30 percent more than their Eritrean counterparts. The first of many student strikes occurred in 1957 at the Haile Selassie Secondary School in Asmara, the first school at which Amharic was made compulsory; in response, 300 students were jailed for a month.

Following annexation in 1962, all education decisions were made in Addis Ababa. The policies of "Ethiopianization" and "Amharization" intensified and became factors that awakened Eritreans' national consciousness and united diverse ethnic groups against the imperial regime.

In 1962 the Santa Familia University, founded in Asmara by the Comboni Sisters in 1958, obtained recognition from the Ethiopian government, changing its name to the University of Asmara. But Eritrean students resented entrance policies they viewed as favoring Ethiopians.

The Independence War: In 1963, elementary and secondary teachers went on strike, ostensibly over the pay differential between Eritrean and Ethiopian teachers. Underlying the strike, however, were sympathies for the Eritrean Liberation Front (ELF), which had begun a guerrilla war for independence a year before. Teachers were active in clandestine nationalist organizations, and many were arrested, jailed without trial, or transferred to Ethiopia. Starting in 1967 when large-scale military confrontations broke out between the Ethiopian army and ELF, young nationalists began joining the guerrillas outright. In 1970, members of ELF had a falling out, some of the dissidents eventually forming the Eritrean People's Liberation Front (EPLF). The ELF was organized along religious and regional lines; the EPLF called for nonsectarian unity and social revolution, a stance that attracted even more students and intellectuals.

The Dergue: Ethiopia's monarchy was replaced by a military dictatorship, called the Dergue (committee) in 1974. Under Haile Mengistu Mariam, the Dergue pressed for a military victory over the Eritrean independence movement. Ethiopian forces steadily lost ground. By 1977 the EPLF was poised to drive the Ethiopians out of Eritrea. That year, however, a massive airlift of Soviet arms to Ethiopia enabled the Ethiopian Army to regain the initiative and forced the EPLF, largely intact, to retreat to the mountainous north of the country.

Educated Eritreans were a particular target of Dergue harassment and violence. Thousands were detained and many killed. Amharic remained compulsory, and the number of Ethiopian teachers increased—up to 2,000 by 1980. The Dergue had declared Ethiopia a Marxist state, and all teachers were required to attend weekly classes in Marxism-Leninism, where their allegiance to the official doctrine was scrutinized. Eritrean teachers were further demoralized by the lack of professional development afforded them. In this climate, school officials feared widespread desertion of students to the guerrillas, and

teachers were susceptible to accusations of political deviance; both factors led to a precipitous drop in educational quality and standards. In 1990 the Dergue disbanded the University of Asmara, taking its staff and movable property to Ethiopia.

The EPLF: Between 1978 and 1986, the Dergue launched eight major offensives against the EPLF; all failed. In 1988, the EPLF captured Afabet, headquarters of the Ethiopian Army in northeastern Eritrea. At the end of the 1980s, the Soviet Union withdrew support, the Ethiopian Army's morale plummeted, and the EPLF began to advance on remaining Ethiopian positions. Meanwhile, other dissident movements were making headway throughout Ethiopia. In May 1991, the EPLF entered Asmara without firing a shot. Simultaneously, Mengistu fled before the advance of the Tigrayan People's Liberation Front, which formed a new government in Ethiopia.

During the war the EPLF established healthcare and education programs and facilities in the regions under its control. Education was seen by EPLF leaders as integral to the national liberation struggle. An early EPLF slogan was "Illiteracy is our main enemy." EPLF-sponsored education was marked by the integration of theory and practice. In the 1970s, efforts focused on the combatants themselves with all new recruits—men and women (women made up a third of the fighters) with less than seven years of schooling required to complete their education in the EPLF, attending classes for up to six hours a day. Many rural villagers and farmers encountered education for the first time in the front.

In the mid-1970s liberated areas began to expand. In essaying the beginnings of a national school system, the EPLF began the Zero School, a boarding school for orphans, refugees, children of fighters, and those who had run away to join the front but were too young to fight. The Zero School, started with about 150 students and a handful of teachers, was designed as a teaching laboratory and workshop for the expanding education system. The Zero School eventually offered five years of elementary education and two years of middle school, adding grades as students continued. By 1983, the school had more than 3,000 students.

In addition to the Zero School, the EPLF maintained regular schools in liberated, predominantly rural areas. At many sites, students sat on stones in the shade of trees. Schools had to be camouflaged against air attack, and students had to be prepared to take cover.

In 1983 a national adult literacy campaign was begun with the dispatch of 451 teenage Zero School students to serve as teachers behind enemy lines. The literacy campaign reached 56,000 adults, 60 percent of them women.

The campaigners taught reading, writing, numeration, hygiene, sanitation, and health, and participated in agriculture in the rural communities.

Drought and Ethiopian military offensives after 1985 disrupted the literacy campaign, and the EPLF abandoned the campaign form altogether when it began its own offensives in 1988, continuing adult education only for civilian health, agricultural, and political workers brought in groups to protected areas for one to two months at a time. By 1990, with the war intensifying to its climax, adult education was available only to combatants. Nevertheless, in the vast areas of liberated countryside, education continued. In 1990, a year before liberation, there were 165 schools administered by the EPLF, with 1,782 teachers serving about 27,000 students.

Independent Eritrea: In May 1991, the EPLF established the Provisional Government of Eritrea (PGE) to administer Eritrean affairs until a referendum on independence could be held and a permanent government established. EPLF leader Isaias Afwerki became the head of the PGE, and the EPLF Central Committee served as its legislative body. On April 23-25, 1993, Eritreans voted overwhelmingly for independence from Ethiopia in a UN-monitored referendum. The government was reorganized and after a national, freely contested election, the National Assembly, which chose Afwerki as President of the State of Eritrea, was expanded to include both EPLF and non-EPLF members. Expressing the government's commitment to working towards gender equality, 30 percent of the Assembly seats were reserved for women, while the remaining seats were open to men and women. The EPLF established itself as a political party, the People's Front for Democracy and Justice (PFDJ) in February 1994. A new constitution establishing a tripartite government and guaranteeing human and civil rights for all Eritreans was ratified in 1997 but was not implemented, as pending parliamentary elections were postponed indefinitely following the start of a border conflict with Ethiopia in May 1998. The National Assembly—with 150 seats, half elected by the people, half installed by the PFDJ—continued to govern the country, and Afwerki remained president, but new elections were scheduled for the end of 2001.

After the long independence war, Eritrea faced an enormous task of reconstruction. The economy and infrastructure had collapsed, and social services had disintegrated, the result of war damage, population displacement, and prolonged, severe neglect. Education was seen as a key to overall development of the country, and an immediate priority: Five months after the May 1991 victory, the EPLF reopened schools country-wide. A 1994 policy document outlined these educational objectives:

- to produce a population equipped with the necessary skills, knowledge, and culture for a self-reliant and modern economy

- to develop self-consciousness and self-motivation in the population

- to fight poverty, disease, and all the attendant causes of backwardness and ignorance

- to make basic education available to all.

In meeting these goals, the government from 1991 to 2000 constructed 365 new schools, mostly in the severely disadvantaged lowland areas. An additional 323 existing schools were rehabilitated, in many cases old schools made of twigs and sacks being replaced by entirely new buildings. From 1991 to 2000, total school enrollment (government and non-government elementary, middle, and secondary schools) increased by 255 percent, from 168,783 pupils to 429,884 pupils. The number of teachers also increased, from 5,188 in 1991 to 8,588 in 2000. A sharp increase in the number of qualified elementary teachers, from 42.7 to 72.4 percent from 1992 to 1996, was the result of three consecutive summers of inservice training at the Asmara Teachers Training Institute.

In the ten years after independence, the existing curriculum was extensively reviewed, and weaknesses were identified. English curriculum, grades 2-10, was completely revised and new textbooks were created, but few other reforms had been implemented by 2001. Additionally during this period, a score of research projects looked into such areas as girls' participation at the elementary level, education of nomads, the structure of technical and vocational education, community response to mother-tongue teaching, and preschool education needs. Beginning in 1994, secondary school students were sent during summer vacation to various regions to engage in development work: environmental protection, road construction and maintenance, production and repair of school furniture, laying power lines, and improving community sanitation. Each summer, approximately 30,000 students (38 percent of them female) participated. The program's goals include strengthening students' cultural experience, work ethic, and ecological awareness.

In 1999 a border dispute with Ethiopia devolved into large-scale war. During the fighting, as many as a million Eritreans were internally displaced and 67,000 were expelled from Ethiopia, most arriving destitute in Eritrea, severely straining the nation's social services. Among those still displaced at the end of fighting in mid-2000 were 139,000 school-age children. The government responded with makeshift schools, enlarged class sizes, and emergency shipments of school supplies to the affected areas.

CONSTITUTIONAL & LEGAL FOUNDATIONS

A new constitution guaranteeing the right to education to all citizens was ratified in 1997 but was not implemented following the start of the border war with Ethiopia in 1998. Education is administered in the Ministry of Education, one of 17 ministries with cabinet status in the executive branch of the government, under President Isaias Afwerki. The government of Eritrea views education as a key factor in political transformation, economic growth, social justice, and the alleviation of poverty, and education for all Eritreans is the government's goal.

EDUCATIONAL SYSTEM—OVERVIEW

The government offers education at elementary (for five years), middle (two years), and secondary (four years) levels, and provides one special school for blind and two schools for deaf students. The University of Asmara, offering 17 bachelor degree programs, enrolled about 4,000 students in 1999. Nongovernmental Coptic, Catholic, Protestant, and Islamic schools (a total of 110) are found throughout the country. So-called public schools (a total of ten) are administered by municipalities or village committees. Five schools are administered by foreign communities in Asmara for their children.

The government also offers technical and vocational programs for middle and secondary graduates, as well as literacy, continuing education, and skill development training programs for adults. Additionally, the Ministry of Education is responsible for school sports programs at national and international levels.

In government schools, enrollment grew an average of 7.4 percent (6.1 percent primary, 14.9 middle, 7.0 secondary) each year from independence to 1999. However, the number of children not enrolled, at all levels and particularly in rural regions, was still high in 2000: about 320,000 at elementary age and 172,000 at middle school age. Literacy for the country is estimated to be 30 percent—for women just 10 percent. Despite the EPLF's and the government's longstanding commitment to women's equal participation in all areas of national life, female enrollment in schools, in numbers or growth, has not kept pace with male participation.

Government policy is for the local language, or the language locally chosen, to be the language of instruction at the elementary level and in literacy programs. To implement this policy, alphabetic forms have been created for six previously nonwritten languages. As of 2000, elementary education and literacy programs were being conducted in eight of the nine Eritrean languages.

Objectives of the educational system, as outlined in the Government's 1994 Macro-Policy, are to create a united, prosperous, peaceful, and democratic nation by educating women and men to:

- have the skills and commitment to work together to reconstruct the economic, environmental, and social fabric

- love and respect their nation and all people within it, regardless of sex, ethnic group, religion, or profession; this includes producing citizens who are fully literate in their mother tongue and who know and wish to preserve the best aspects of their culture while changing the negative aspects, including working toward the achievement of gender and ethnic equality

- respect democratic institutions and to fully and effectively participate in the democratic process, including developing and defending basic human rights, and to be guided by and adhere to the highest ethical principles

- have a deep knowledge of and respect for the environment and the need for its restoration and protection

- wisely use scientific processes and developments so as to achieve self-sufficiency in food, modern services, and industries, based on the principle of environmental sustainability

- develop to the fullest their creative potential in all aspects.

These principles are largely inherited from the liberation struggle, which included tremendous efforts to consolidate national identity and unity, promote social progress, and inculcate tolerance and democratic ideals.

PREPRIMARY & PRIMARY EDUCATION

Preschool education begins at age five. Early childhood education is largely a community responsibility, with the government giving functional support by developing policies, programs, and teacher training activities. The government considers early childhood education as the first component of the basic education strategy and envisages expansion of preprimary schools but not supplanting the role and responsibility of parents and the community in early childhood upbringing and education. In addition, the overall tendency is to encourage nongovernmental organizations and nonformal activities in this field. The policy gives much attention to the need and importance of early and extensive investment in health care, cognitive development, and socialization. The number of preschools—90 in 2000, almost all in urban areas—has not significantly increased since independence, but enrollment rose by 50 percent, from 7,747 children in 1993 to 11,885 children (or about 5 percent of eligible chil-

Pupil-to-Teacher Ratios by Level

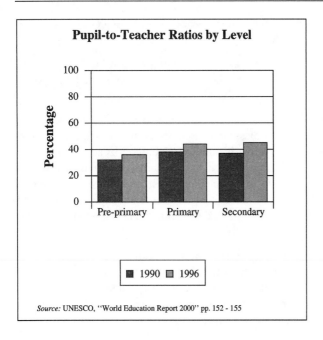

Source: UNESCO, "World Education Report 2000" pp. 152 - 155

dren) in 2000. In 1996, many preschools run by the municipalities were transferred to private institutions and communities, and some were closed for lack of funds. Most surviving preschools are situated in Asmara and are controlled by religious institutions. The learning environment in most centers suffers from lack of basic resources and play materials. More than 50 percent of preschool teachers were untrained, but in 1996 a summer training program was organized; approximately 90 teachers had completed this training by 1999. In 2000 there were 223 trained and 97 untrained preschool teachers.

Elementary, or primary, education lasts five years. The official starting age is seven, but due to the previous lack of access to school, the majority of students are older.

The academic year runs from September to June and consists of approximately 200 school days divided into two semesters. Schools in lowland areas operate six days a week in order to finish before the hottest season. At the primary level, school exams are given four times per year at the end of every half semester, and reports are given at the end of each semester. Total gross primary enrollment in 2000 was 295,941 students. The gross enrollment percentage (enrolled students to eligible children in the population) went from 36.3 percent in 1992 to 57.5 percent in 2000; within this, the female student enrollment percentage increased from 33.8 to 52.4 percent. Elementary teachers numbered 6,229 in 2000.

The elementary curriculum includes reading and writing in the mother tongue, mathematics, science, art and music, and physical education. Starting at the second grade, English (plus Arabic where teachers are available) and civics and moral education are added. Geography is added during fourth grade.

SECONDARY EDUCATION

Elementary education is followed by two years of middle level (completing what is called basic formal primary education) and four years of secondary education, at the end of which students take the Eritrean Secondary Education Certificate Examination. Instruction in middle and secondary classes is in English. In middle schools, overall enrollment grew by 266 percent from 1992 to 2000, from 27,917 to 74,317 students. This represented a doubling of the ratio of enrolled students to middle-school-age children in the population, from 20.1 to 43.2 percent. Female middle students totaled 33,284 in 2000. Secondary enrollment increased from 27,627 in 1992 to 59,626, of which 37 percent were female, in 2000. The gross enrollment rate grew from 12.2 to 26.0 percent for males in this period, but from 12.1 to only 16.2 for females. In 2000 there were 1,312 middle and 1,047 secondary teachers.

The middle curriculum includes general science; mathematics; English; Arabic; geography; Eritrean, African and world history; civics and moral education; physical education; and music and art at some schools.

Secondary subjects are biology, physics, chemistry, mathematics, English, Arabic, geography, history, civics, physical education, and music and art.

Instructional Technology: In 2001 computers were available in only a few secondary schools in Asmara; these schools had piloted computer education classes for selected students. In some cases, Parent-Teacher Associations had raised money to buy computers for a school. Adding more computers, as it becomes financially feasible, is slated to take place first at the secondary level, and then expand downwards. In preparation for these developments, a computer lab was set up at the Asmara Teacher Training Institute in order to have teacher-trainees computer-literate by the time they begin or return to teaching.

HIGHER EDUCATION

Eritrea faces a serious shortage of skilled professionals in all fields. The only institute of higher education in the country, the University of Asmara, since its reopening in October 1991, has been engaged in restructuring and revitalization and is still establishing new colleges. Since 1997, there have been eight—Agriculture and Aquatic Sciences; Arts and Language Studies; Business and Economics; Education; Engineering; Health Sciences; Law; Science—that offer a total of 17 bachelor degree programs, as well as diploma and certificate programs. The

College of Business and Economics offers evening programs for working adults. A degree program requires four years' attendance. All students follow a general freshman program during the first year, then enter the college of their choice. After their second year, students are obliged to serve one year of national service; this means that it will take them a minimum of five years to earn a bachelor's degree. In 2000, the university graduated 371 students with bachelor's degrees, 170 with diplomas, and 106 with certificates. Enrollment in Fall 2000 was 4,642 (about 13 percent women). Total faculty was 230. The university foresees steady growth, with enrollment reaching 6,000 students in 2005 and stabilizing at around 8,000 by 2010.

The university aspires to become a regional center of higher education, but first to primarily serve national needs, and has developed linkages both to national programs and initiatives and to international donor organizations and foreign universities. In 2001, the university was still suffering from a lack of basic equipment, computers, laboratories, library facilities, and a shortage of qualified academic staff.

ADMINISTRATION, FINANCE, & EDUCATIONAL RESEARCH

The Ministry of Education, the body responsible for administering the schools and setting and implementing the national curriculum, consists of three departments: General Education, responsible for early childhood through secondary education; Technical and Vocational Education, which includes adult literacy; and Research and Human Resource Development, whose responsibilities include teacher and staff training. At the regional level are six regional offices, which have autonomy to manage educational matters within their geographical area. Sub-regional offices are responsible for direct management of schools within each sub-region.

At the end of 1999, the Ministry of Education installed its first computer network, making information on all aspects of school administration available to all departments. The network extends to most district offices in all regions of the country, but in 2001 was still too slow in functioning to be of much use outside of the Asmara offices of the Ministry. When it is functioning efficiently, the network will aid decentralized decision-making in regions and sub-regions.

Education expenditures as a percent of the government's total expenditures grew from 4 percent in 1993 to more than 9 percent in 1997 (education accounted for an average of 38 percent of yearly social service expenditures in that period). As a percentage of GNP, education increased from 2 to 4 percent over those five years, a significant investment compared to many sub-Saharan Afri-

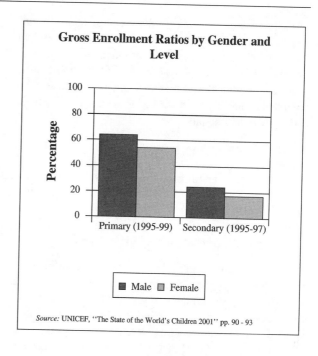

Gross Enrollment Ratios by Gender and Level

Source: UNICEF, "The State of the World's Children 2001" pp. 90 - 93

can nations and a testament to the government's commitment to education. In 2000, salaries, nonsalary recurrent expenditures, and capital cost totaled 115 million, 38 million, and 77 million *nakfa* respectively; international donors provided 66 million *nakfa* applied to capital expenditures.

NONFORMAL EDUCATION

Through the Department of Technical and Vocational Education, the Ministry of Education runs technical and vocational programs, adult literacy programs, continuing basic education classes, and adult skills development programs. Technical and vocational education is offered at basic, intermediate, and advanced levels. Seven basic level training centers provide employment skills courses, four to nine months in length, for elementary completers. The centers graduated 296 students (78 female) in 1999 and 157 students (0 female) in 2000. At the intermediate level, three technical institutes (Asmara, Wina, and Mai Habar) provide training programs, lasting two to three years, for middle-school completers. Total enrollment of the three schools was 908 (15 percent female) in 2000. At the advanced level for secondary graduates, two schools are available: the Asmara Business and Commerce Training School, providing courses in accounting, banking and finance, secretarial science, and management; and the nongovernmental Pavoni Technical Institute, which offers machine shop training. Enrollment in the Business School was 190 (30.5 percent female) in 2000; Pavoni had 67 students, including 5 women.

A school of fine arts and a school of music were pioneered by the EPLF during the independence war. The arts school trains secondary school completers in sculpture, painting, and printmaking. In 2000, the school had 29 beginning (8 female) and 39 intermediate (12 female) students. The Asmara Music School offers one to two years of theoretical and practical training to those who complete grade eight. In 2000, the school had 22 male and 34 female students.

In 2000, a literacy program was operating in 796 centers, serving more than 49,000 adults, 94 percent of them women. Four-fifths of these adults were new students in the first year of the three-year program; the border war with Ethiopia had reduced the number of continuing students. The literacy program was conducted, and primers printed, in seven languages.

Evening classes in basic education are conducted at the elementary, middle, and secondary levels, with 4,872 adults (3,461 female) attending in 2000, the majority at the secondary level. Since independence, many adult skills development programs were begun in cooperation with NGOs, but the Ministry of Education has largely taken over responsibility for the programs. From 1993 to 1997, some 6,000 to 7,000 adults were trained in building trades, metal fabrication, agricultural technology, secretarial skills, and other job skills.

Various professional training programs are run by other ministries, most importantly the Ministry of Health (nurses, pharmacists, village health workers, and technicians), and the Ministry of Agriculture (farmers and its own staff of technicians). The Institute of Management Studies has been established to upgrade the skills of existing civil servants. Quasi-governmental organizations such as the National Union of Eritrean Woman and the National Union of Eritrean Youth and Students offer a variety of vocational and some academic courses across the nation. The National Union of Eritrean Women has been especially active in mounting women's literacy projects in small towns and rural villages.

TEACHING PROFESSION

There is one Teachers Training Institute (TTI), located in Asmara; graduates are qualified for elementary teaching. Teacher training was given a high priority following independence, with TTI graduating about 1,600 students per year (using intensive short courses) from 1992 to 1995; however, from 1996 to 1999 enrollments averaged 350 a year. In 2000, TTI had 606 trainees enrolled. In 2000, 72 percent of the nation's elementary teachers were qualified.

The Faculty of Education at the University of Asmara trains middle and secondary school teachers, offering a diploma in middle school teaching and a bachelor's degree in secondary teaching, as well as bachelor's degrees in educational administration and educational psychology. In 2001, approximately 800 students were enrolled in all programs. The teaching staff totaled 21, the largest in the university. The school has strong links to the Ministry of Education, and its programs are keyed to national needs. Students are prepared to meet the challenges of teaching in rural schools, to innovate, and to rely on local resources and materials.

In 2000, about 32.0 percent of middle teachers and 71.2 percent of secondary teachers were qualified. To make up for a shortage of qualified teachers, and to allow Eritrean teachers to spend time abroad pursuing advanced degrees, the Eritrean government, in a program partially financed by the World Bank, has recruited expatriate teachers, mainly from India, since 1997. In 2000, approximately 250 such teachers were bolstering the teaching staff at secondary and technical schools. At the same time, 64 Eritrean teachers were studying in postgraduate programs outside Eritrea.

SUMMARY

Eritrean education has suffered from the disregard, and even malice, of colonial occupiers and the devastation of a long independence war—and benefited from the experience of the liberation movement that developed an educational system with some modern and progressive features years before coming to power.

From the liberation movement, the national education system inherited a respect for all the languages and cultures of the country, now seen in policies that primary and literacy education be conducted in students' mother tongue; that priority for educational expansion be given to disadvantaged and marginalized areas and ethnic groups; that communities be involved in the establishment and running of schools; and that women be accorded full educational equality with men. Additionally, Eritrean education has inherited from the independence struggle a self-reliant attitude. As a nation, Eritrea has sought to keep development firmly in the hands of Eritreans and is known for refusing international aid that would compromise that ideal. Nevertheless, the Ministry of Education has maintained and sought international aid and assistance to build its capacity and improve teaching and learning.

As an independent nation since 1991, Eritrea has managed to build or rehabilitate more than 600 schools, add 3,400 teachers, and more than double enrollments—a creditable achievement for a young, poor, and war-ravaged country. The government has stated its intention to provide basic education for all and considers education a key to development. For a country that is one of the world's poorest, Eritrea has devoted significant financial resources to education.

Still, in 2000 more than 716,000 school-age children remained unenrolled, curriculum reform was stalled, illiteracy for the population as a whole stood at 70 percent, and the planned-for widespread adult education had barely begun. At the turn of the millennium, improving educational quality was seen as the Ministry of Education's major priority. Plans were under way to fully implement curriculum reform in the coming five years; to improve and expand teacher training, including opening a second Teacher Training Institute, enlarging the Faculty of Education at the University of Asmara, and creating more opportunities for teachers to increase their skills and pursue higher education both in and out of the country; to establish new and strengthen existing Parent-Teacher Associations; provide more vocational training options to students; to create a unit to address the needs of children with learning difficulties; to systematize preschool education; to increase adult literacy; to expand computer technology at all administrative levels and in academic programs beginning with secondary schools; to better coordinate the educational activities of various government ministries; and to correct inefficiencies within the Ministry of Education itself.

BIBLIOGRAPHY

Connell, Dan. *Against All Odds: A Chronicle of the Eritrean Revolution.* Lawrenceville, NJ: Red Sea Press, 1997.

Davidson, Basil, Lionel Cliffe, and Bereket Habte Selassie, eds. *Behind the War in Eritrea.* Nottingham, England: Spokesman, 1980.

Doornbos, Martin, and Alemseged Tesfai, eds. *Postconflict Eritrea: Prospects for Reconstruction and Development.* Lawrenceville, NJ: Red Sea Press, 1999.

"Eritrea-Freedom of Expression and Ethnic Discrimination in the Educational System: Past and Future." *Africa Watch V,* 1 (1993).

Firebrace, James, and Stuart Holland. *Never Kneel Down: Drought, Development and Liberation in Eritrea.* Trenton, NJ: Red Sea Press, 1986.

Gottesman, Les. *To Fight and Learn: The Praxis and Promise of Literacy in Eritrea's Independence War.* Lawrenceville, NJ: Red Sea Press, 1998.

Iyob, Ruth. *The Eritrean Struggle for Independence: Domination, Resistance, Nationalism 1941-1993.* Cambridge, England: Cambridge University Press, 1995.

Killion, Tom. *Historical Dictionary of Eritrea. African Historical Dictionaries,* No. 75. Lanham, MD, and London: Scarecrow Press, 1998.

Ministry of Education. *Basic Education Statistics 1998/99.* Asmara, November 1999.

———. *Basic Education Statistics 1999/2000.* Asmara, in press.

———. *Education Brief 1999.* Asmara, March 1999.

———. *Essential Education Indicators 1998/99.* Asmara, November 1999.

Papstein, Robert. *Eritrea: Revolution at Dusk.* Trenton, NJ: Red Sea Press, 1991.

Pateman, Roy. *Eritrea: Even the Stones are Burning.* Lawrenceville, NJ: Red Sea Press, 1998.

Sherman, Richard. *Eritrea: The Unfinished Revolution.* New York: Praeger, 1980.

Stefanos, Asgedet. "Women and Education in Eritrea: A Historical and Contemporary Analysis," *Harvard Educational Review* 67, 4 (1997): 658-688.

Teklehaimanot, Berhane. "Education in Eritrea During the European Colonial Period," *Eritrean Studies Review* 1, no. 1 (1996): 1-22.

Wilson, Amrit. *Women and the Eritrean Revolution: The Challenge Road.* Trenton, NJ: Red Sea Press, 1991.

—Leslie D. Gottesman

ESTONIA

BASIC DATA

Official Country Name:	Republic of Estonia
Region:	Europe
Population:	1,431,471
Language(s):	Estonian, Russian, Ukrainian, English, Finnish
Literacy Rate:	100%
Academic Year:	September-June
Number of Primary Schools:	727
Compulsory Schooling:	9 years
Public Expenditure on Education:	7.2%
Libraries:	743
Educational Enrollment:	Primary: 125,718 Secondary: 112,288 Higher: 43,468
Educational Enrollment Rate:	Primary: 94% Secondary: 104% Higher: 42%

Teachers:	Primary: 7,276
	Secondary: 11,098
	Higher: 4,435
Student-Teacher Ratio:	Primary: 17:1
Female Enrollment Rate:	Primary: 93%
	Secondary: 109%
	Higher: 46%

HISTORY & BACKGROUND

Estonia is located in Eastern Europe, bordering the Baltic Sea and Gulf of Finland, between Latvia and Russia. The total land area is 43,211 square kilometers, of which 44 percent is forest and woodland. It is slightly smaller than New Hampshire and Vermont combined. The estimated population in July 2000 was nearly 1.5 million, with the two largest ethnic groups being Estonian (65.1 percent) and Russian (28.1 percent).

The Russians first mentioned Estonia in the eleventh century, but the first signs of human life in Estonia are 10,000 years old. Chronicled history began with the conquest of Estonian territory by German and Danish feudal landlords in the thirteenth century; it may also be regarded as the starting point of schooling in Estonia because the first schools were established in the larger towns. As a result of the Protestant Reformation, the first books in Estonia (the Lutheran Catechism-1535) were published. After the Livonian War, which began in 1558 and lasted 25 years, Estonia was divided between Poland and Sweden. After all of Estonia came under Swedish rule in the seventeenth century, a time of peace and prosperity ensued. In 1632, Tartu Grammar School was reorganized and given the name Academia Gustaviana, which is regarded as the establishment of the first university in Estonia, Tartu University. However, only students of Baltic German, Swedish, or Finnish origin could attend; Estonians were excluded. Public schools were established and, as a result, a majority of Estonians became literate. As a result of the Great Northern War, Tartu University was forced to close in 1710. Estonia became a part of the Russian empire.

The nineteenth century was a period of economic development and urbanization. Estonians were freed from serfdom, and, in the 1860s, they acquired the right to buy farmland. Not only was there an increase in wealth, but there was also a period of national awakening that was interrupted by a resurgence of Russification in the 1880s. In 1802, the University of Tartu reopened with the first native Estonians among its scholars. By the end of the century, 96 percent of Estonians were literate.

Independence came with the declaration of the Republic of Estonia on February 24, 1918. The independence period (1920-1940) resulted in the formation of the Estonian language national culture. The economic improvements during that period resulted in a living standard similar to Estonia's Scandinavian neighbors. As a result of the desire for a well-educated population, new upper-secondary schools and seminaries opened. In 1919, instruction in the Estonian language was introduced at the University of Tartu. In addition, Tallinn Technical University and the Estonian Academy of Music were established in Tallinn.

Estonia was occupied by the Soviet Union in 1940. During the first year of occupation, Estonian political and social leaders were either killed or deported to Siberia. A second deportation took place on June 14, 1941, when a large number of ordinary citizens, including women and children, were sent to Siberia. On June 26, 1941, Nazi Germany attacked the Soviet Union and also conquered Estonia; however, the Soviet Union reoccupied Estonia in 1944. Rather than live again under Soviet domination, approximately 80,000 Estonians fled to the West. Furthermore, Estonia lost one-third of its population as a result of World War II. The Soviets began a process of forced collectivization of the farms in the late 1940s, which included another deportation in March 1949. The rural life that had been the basis of the economy was destroyed. During the process of industrialization, a migratory labor force was imported from other regions of the Soviet Union with the purpose of inhabiting Estonia with a Russian-speaking population. By the end of the Soviet period, large regions of Estonia were populated almost entirely with Russian-speaking people. It was difficult to have an independent education policy because of the pressure to adopt the Soviet educational structure and curricula. However, the Estonian educational system was permitted to maintain instruction in the Estonian language.

At the beginning of the 1980s, student demonstrations began in Tallinn. Forty members of the Estonian Intelligentsia composed the "letter of the forty," which condemned Soviet policy and demanded cultural autonomy. The period of *perestroika* and *glasnost* permitted even more criticism of Soviet policy. The Heritage Protection Movement, the goal of which was to teach the correct history of politics and culture in Estonia, initiated a new wave of national awakening often termed "the singing revolution." On August 21, 1991, independence was restored, and, in 1992, Estonia implemented a new democratic constitution. In 1989, the Education Committee was reorganized to create a new Ministry of Education to administer general, vocational, and higher education. Reorganization in 1993 led to the establishment of the Ministry of Culture and Education, which had control over education policy, higher education, and science. A separate Ministry of Education was reestablished in 1996. Since 1991, extensive reforms have been instituted with the aim of integrating Estonia into the structures of the European Union (EU).

CONSTITUTIONAL & LEGAL FOUNDATIONS

Estonia is a democratic republic, and the supreme power of the state is vested in the people. The powers of the state are exercised solely pursuant to the constitution and specific laws that are in conformity therewith. The activities of the *Riigikogu* (Parliament), President of the Republic, Government of the Republic, and the courts are organized on the principle of separation and balance of powers.

The Constitution of the Republic of Estonia determines the right of every citizen to an education. Education is compulsory for school-age children to the extent specified by law and is free in state and local government general education schools. Other education institutions, such as private schools, may also be established pursuant to law. Parents have the final choice of education for their children. The 1992 Estonian Law on Education established the following general goals of education: to promote the development of personality, family, and the Estonian nation, as well as of national minorities; to promote Estonian economic, political, and cultural life and of nature preservation in the global economic and cultural context; to educate loyal citizens; and to set up prerequisites of continuing education for citizens. In addition, the Law on Education established a compulsory nine-year basic education (grades 1-9).

EDUCATIONAL SYSTEM—OVERVIEW

The Estonian educational structure is divided into four levels. Preschool education is provided at kindergartens and other childcare institutions. Primary education (grades 1-6), as well as basic education (grades 7-9), is compulsory in Estonia. Secondary education (grades 10-12) may be completed at a gymnasium in general secondary education school or at a secondary vocational school. Students have three options at the higher education level: vocational higher education, diploma level (applied) higher education, or academic higher education.

In Estonia basic education (grades 1-9) is compulsory. A child that is seven years old on October 1 of the current year must attend school and remain in school until the completion of grade 9 or age 17. Children of foreign citizens or stateless people who are residents of Estonia must fulfill the requirement of compulsory school attendance.

The duration of a school year is from the start of study in one calendar year until the start of study in the

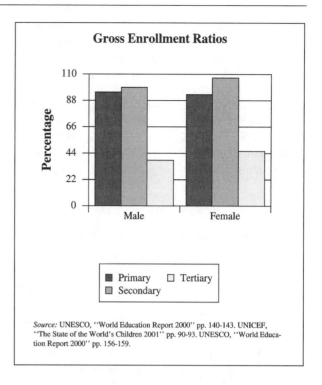

Gross Enrollment Ratios

Legend: ■ Primary □ Tertiary ■ Secondary

Source: UNESCO, "World Education Report 2000" pp. 140-143. UNICEF, "The State of the World's Children 2001" pp. 90-93. UNESCO, "World Education Report 2000" pp. 156-159.

next calendar year. A school year consists of a period of study, an examination session, and school holidays. The school year starts on September 1. A study period must include no less than 175 days of study. School holidays are determined in an ordinance issued by the Minister of Education.

The official language of instruction is Estonian; however, instruction in a basic school may be in another language. In a municipal school, the local government decides the language of instruction, and in a state school, the Ministry of Education decides. Since Russians are the largest minority group in Estonia, the Russian language is the second most common language of instruction behind Estonian. In the 2000/2001 academic year, Estonia had 566 Estonian schools, 100 Russian schools, 19 Estonian/Russian schools, 2 English schools, and 2 Finnish schools. By the year 2007, the level of competence in the Estonian language must allow students to continue studying all subjects in the tenth grade in Estonian, regardless of the basic school attended.

One week of study includes five days of study. The weekly study load and the number of lessons for students is determined by the curriculum of the school. The length of each lesson is 45 minutes, with a break of not less than 10 minutes. Usually, there is one meal break of 15 minutes. The school director determines the number of lessons and their sequence.

In planning the location of schools throughout the country, government officials keep in mind that basic education is compulsory; however, secondary schools for general education and vocational education must also be available. Primary schools are located as close to the homes of the children as possible. An upper-secondary school must have a large enough student population that will enable the school to provide elective courses in the curriculum and employ a teaching staff with excellent qualifications. The establishment of a school requires that the following number of children of an appropriate age must reside permanently within the district area of the school:

- 30 students to establish a three-grade primary school

- 60 students to establish a six-grade primary school

- 90 students to establish a basic school

- 60 students to establish an upper-secondary school (grades 10-12)

A local government also may establish a municipal school in a district area with a number of children at an appropriate age smaller than the number specified. In this case, the deficit in the salaries must be covered from the local governmental budget.

The network of vocational schools must take into consideration regional needs. At least one vocational school must be located in every county.

The list of children subject to the compulsory attendance law is composed by local authorities according to the children's places of residence. A school is required to ensure study opportunities for each child who resides in the district area of the school. Parents may freely choose a school for a child if there are vacancies in the school they wish their child to attend.

The obligation to attend school may also be fulfilled by studying at home. The procedures for home schooling have been established in an ordinance issued by the Minister of Education.

Local governments must allow children with special needs to attend a local school under the conditions established by the Minister of Education. If suitable conditions are not found, disabled children and children who need special support may attend the nearest school that meets their requirements. The conditions for admission to a private school are established by the school.

Religious education is offered, but it is non-confessional and attendance is voluntary. The teaching of religious studies is compulsory for a school if at least 15 students in a specific age group desire such a course. The school director approves the curriculum.

PREPRIMARY & PRIMARY EDUCATION

Preschool education is available at kindergartens and other childcare institutions. The role of preschool educa-

tion is to support and complement families by promoting the growth, development, and individuality of children. Several practices have emerged including family care, the setting up of integration groups, family counseling services, and the establishment of private kindergartens and centers for children. The childcare institutions offer primary education until the age of seven.

The 1992 Law on Education replaced compulsory secondary education with compulsory nine-year basic education (grades 1-9). The government of the Republic approves the state curriculum for basic and general secondary education; the simplified state curriculum for basic education and the state curriculum for students with moderate and severe learning disabilities have been established in an ordinance issued by the Minister of Education.

The state-approved curriculum for grades 1 through 3 consists of the following subjects: mother tongue, Estonian (non-Estonian schools), nature study, civics, mathematics, music, art and handicraft, physical education, and foreign language. For grades 4 through 6 the subjects are mother tongue, Estonian (non-Estonian school), foreign language A (Estonian school), foreign language B, mathematics, nature study, history, civics, music, art, physical education, and manual training/handicraft/domestic studies. For grades 7 through 9 the subjects are mother tongue, Estonian (non-Estonian school), foreign language A (Estonian school), foreign language B, mathematics, natural sciences, geography, biology, chemistry, physics, history, civics, music, art, manual training/handicraft/domestic studies, physical education, and elective subjects.

SECONDARY EDUCATION

Students have two options after completing basic education; they may attend either the gymnasium or a vocational education institution. The 1993 Law on Basic Schools and Gymnasiums established the gymnasium as the main structural unit of secondary education replacing the former secondary school. Educational standards are established in the national curriculum. This curriculum determines the objectives; duration of studies; relationship of the national curriculum to the school curriculum; list of compulsory subjects together with the number of lessons and their content, options, and conditions for selection of subjects; and graduation requirements.

Study in the gymnasium lasts for three years (grades 10-12). The maximum weekly course load is 35 hours. The national curriculum accounts for 75 percent of the total load, and the remaining 25 percent includes subjects selected jointly by the students and the school. The compulsory courses are mother tongue, Estonian (non-Estonian schools), foreign language A (Estonian schools), foreign language B, mathematics, geography, biology, chemistry, physics, history, civics, philosophy, art, music, and physical education. Certain subjects can be taught in more depth, and schools can develop their own instructional approach or course content. In 2001, schools exist with special focus on language, mathematics, natural sciences, and other subjects. State examinations at the secondary level were introduced in 1997.

Vocational Education: The 1998 Law on Vocational Education Institutions established two levels of vocational education in Estonia: secondary vocational education and vocational higher education. Secondary vocational education (length of study at least three years) has the prerequisites of basic education and one year of general secondary education. Vocational higher education (length of study three to four years) has the prerequisite of secondary education (gymnasium or secondary vocational education). In the 1999-2000 academic year, there were 87 different vocational education institutions in Estonia enrolling 34,312 students, with 3,165 students on the vocational higher education level. Vocational education institutions offer programs in 35 fields of study. The following fields of study are a priority of development—services: catering, tourism, hotel management, and trading; logistics (transportation and communications); information technology; electronics; and telecommunications.

HIGHER EDUCATION

Administration of higher education is the responsibility of the Ministry of Education; the institutions may be state, public, or private. Two types of higher education institutions exist in Estonia. The first type is the university, which provides academic higher education and applied, professionally oriented study programs. The second type is applied higher education institutions, which offer applied, professionally oriented diploma-study and vocational higher education programs. The tendency has been to merge applied higher education institutions into the universities as colleges.

Universities: A university is an institution of learning and research in which a student may acquire the academic qualifications of higher education. It is also possible to complete applied diploma-study at the universities. However, the broader objective of a university is to foster research and academic practices and to develop opportunities for obtaining higher education according to the standard of higher education.

Public universities are autonomous under the administrative jurisdiction of the Ministry of Education. Universities have the right to independently determine academic and organizational structure, develop academic content of courses, organize research, employ staff, and select candidates.

Private higher education institutions provide at least one baccalaureate-level study program. These institutions provide their own financing, but the state may participate in some programs if the public demand is apparent.

In the 2000-2001 academic year, six public universities and six private universities (with at least one study program accredited or conditionally accredited) operated in Estonia. The remainder of the 40 institutions and universities operating in Estonia during this period had non-accredited programs.

Applied Higher Education Institutions: Applied higher education institutions offer non-academic higher education (diploma-study) with an emphasis on professional skills and abilities. These institutions may also offer vocational higher education programs. State supported applied higher education institutions are funded by the state budget. Private higher education institutions provide study programs mainly in the field of social sciences, business administration, or theology.

Admission to Higher Education: The general requirement for admission to higher education is the gymnasium certificate. However, secondary education may also be obtained at a secondary vocational school in which secondary education is combined with vocational education.

Since 1997, secondary school students have been required to pass state exams. These exams are conducted mainly in written form. However, examinations in foreign languages include an oral section. These state exams serve as entrance examinations to higher education institutions. Although some higher education institutions may conduct interviews, the state exams serve as the most important selection criteria.

Administration: The collegial decision-making body of a higher education institution is the council, whose function is determined in the statutes of the higher education institution. All higher education institutions operate primarily under the direction of the rector who acts under the council. The rector is responsible for the daily operation and development of the higher education institution, as well as for the legal and effective use of financial resources.

Academic Staff: The academic staff of a university is comprised of professors, associate professors, lecturers, assistants, and teachers. Senior researchers and researchers conduct the research work at the universities. All tenured education staff are selected from public applications of staff who have completed at least five years at a public university.

Students & Courses of Study: Higher education institutions offer diploma-study, baccalaureate study, master's degrees, doctoral degrees, and vocational higher education study. In the 1999-2000 academic year, approximately 49,574 students, of which 956 were foreign students, were enrolled in Estonia's higher education institutions. The language of instruction is usually Estonian, but an increasing number of courses are taught in English. In addition, some courses are taught in Russian.

ADMINISTRATION, FINANCE, & EDUCATIONAL RESEARCH

Administration at the National Level: The Parliament passes laws and resolutions including those that impact education. Three tasks regarding education are assigned to Parliament only. One is the establishing of principles regarding the formation, operation, and development of the education system. Another is setting the fees for studies in public institutions of education and in public universities. The final task is determining the foundation, merging, splitting, and termination of a public university.

Since independence in 1991, the Parliament has passed several acts regarding education. The Child Protection Act establishes the right of a child to an education, freedom of study, and the principles of instruction. The Education Act defines the different types of education, including basic education, the principles of organization and management of the educational system, the forms of study, and compulsory school attendance, and also determines the types of institutions. The Basic and Upper-Secondary Schools Act determines the legal status and organization of a basic school under state or municipal ownership, as well as the organization of instruction and education at a school. The Private School Act regulates the same issues in a private school.

The Government of the Republic implements these acts, and all the state programs of education, through the Ministry of Education.

Administration at the Regional Level: The Preschool Institutions Act and the Basic and Upper-Secondary Schools Act mandate that the governor of each county act as the manager of the educational system on a regional level. The task of the county is to compose regional development plans on the same basis as the county development plans of education are composed.

Administration at the Local Level: The Education Act determines the authority of local governments in the general administration of education at the local level. The local authorities:

- Administer and implement education programs at the local level
- Establish, reorganize, and terminate municipal educational institutions within the limits established by

legal acts and keep the register of the educational institutions in the area of administration

- Provide the economic and financial oversight of the educational institutions
- Appoint and dismiss the heads of the educational institutions
- Keep the register of children of the age of compulsory school attendance and support children in fulfilling the obligation of compulsory school attendance by providing financial aid, transportation, medical services, or meals at school
- Provide vocational counseling for students
- Keep the register of people with special needs and provide instruction for them.

The executive body of the local government establishes a structural unit or appoints a person who is responsible for the implementation of the education development plans of the local authorities.

SUMMARY

One of the serious problems in the Estonian educational system is that the smaller towns are not able to provide the same quality of education as the larger cities. In addition, the teaching profession is not attractive to students. Almost half the teachers in Estonia are at retirement age or will reach that age by 2005. This older staff is very resistant to changes in educational philosophy and teaching strategies. The low teacher salaries are not attracting high-achieving students into the profession. Yet, the majority of students in Estonia meet the compulsory education requirement. In the 2000-2001 academic year, only 2 percent of 8- to 14-year-olds were not in school.

Estonia's low birth rate presents serious problems for the country. In the 1980s, an average of 22,000 babies were born each year. However, in the late 1990s the average birth rate dropped to between 14,000 and 15,000 births each year. The result has been fewer jobs for students who want to be primary teachers because 15 to 20 primary schools in rural areas are closing each year.

The required State Curriculum of 2000 is more student-centered than it was 10 years ago. A new revision, started in 2000, will be completed in 2007. The priorities of this new curriculum are student-centered instruction, Information Communication Technology (ICT), team work, skill development, and technology integration. In order to implement this new curriculum, more emphasis must be placed on initial and in-service teacher training.

The vocational educational track must be improved because, in the 1990s, it was often viewed as the place for students who failed in the academic track. A clear and successful job placement program must follow completion of the vocational track.

One of the most successful educational programs has been the integration of technology into the classroom. In the 1990s the government initiated the "Tiger Leap Project" with the goal of integrating computer technology into the educational system. In the 2000-2001 academic year, close to 100 percent of the schools had Internet connections, and computer science was the most popular elective. Schools had homepages with study materials accessible through the Internet. Since most of the instructional technology equipment was purchased since 1996, the equipment in the classrooms during the 2000-2001 academic year was modern and fast. It is common for students to use computer technology to make presentations even at the primary level. This emphasis on the integration of technology into the classroom at all levels should ensure that the Estonian educational system will graduate students who understand international issues and will be able to compete in the global economy.

BIBLIOGRAPHY

Eurydice Database on Education Systems in Europe. *The Education System in Estonia,* 2 March 2001. Available from http://www.eurydice.org/Eurybase/Application/eurybase.htm.

Vaht, Gunnar, ed. *Higher Education System in Estonia.* Tallinn: Academic Recognition Information Center, 1997.

Vaht, Gunner, Maiki Udam, and Kadri Këutt, eds. *Higher Education in Estonia.* 2nd ed. Tallinn: Academic Recognition Information Center, 2000.

—*Terry L. Simpson and Hasso Kukemelk*

ETHIOPIA

BASIC DATA

Official Country Name:	Ethiopia
Region:	Africa
Population:	64,117,452
Language(s):	Amharic, Tigrinya, Orominga, Guaraginga, Somali, Arabic, English
Literacy Rate:	35.5%
Number of Primary Schools:	10,256
Compulsory Schooling:	6 years
Public Expenditure on Education:	4.0%

Educational Enrollment:	Primary:	4,007,694
	Secondary:	819,242
	Higher:	42,226
Educational Enrollment Rate:	Primary:	43%
	Secondary:	12%
	Higher:	1%
Teachers:	Primary:	92,775
	Secondary:	25,984
Student-Teacher Ratio:	Primary:	43:1
	Secondary:	35:1
Female Enrollment Rate:	Primary:	30%
	Secondary:	10%
	Higher:	0.3%

HISTORY & BACKGROUND

Ethiopia is the oldest independent nation in Africa. The current Federal Democratic Republic of Ethiopia is located on a massive rugged mountainous plateau in Eastern Africa. Ethiopia is a large country, twice the size of Texas or about the size of Spain and France combined. It covers 435,071 kilometers or 1,127,127 square miles in area and is the tenth largest of Africa's 53 countries. Ethiopia's mountainous terrain discouraged many foreign invaders; however, this natural fortress posed difficulties for communication and travel, thus contributing to the slow spread of education.

Ethiopia has Africa's fourth largest population at 58,733,000. This number is despite millions who die periodically from some of the world's most devastating famines caused by prolonged cycles of drought. Millions of Ethiopians have fled natural and man-made disasters and live as refugees in Sudan, Kenya, Italy, Great Britain, and the United States. The population is increasing at an annual rate of about 3 percent, and is expected to double in the next 14 years. Almost 73 percent of the population is under 18 years of age. Addis Ababa, Ethiopia's capital city, has 2,431,000 inhabitants and is growing rapidly. The need for new schools increases with the rising youthful population. Ethiopia has a high infant mortality rate of approximately 121 infant deaths per 1,000 births. There is only 1 doctor for every 36,000 Ethiopians. Access to modern medicine outside of the major cities is a problem. Consequently, many people depend upon traditional ethnic medicine. The life expectancy for males is only 45, and for females it is 48 years. High death rates have moderated a massive population explosion. Because they depend on their children to support them in their old age, and, because there is no social security system, Ethiopians typically have large families.

Ethiopia has an ethnically diverse population. Some 40 percent of its population is Oromo, the Christian Amhara and their Tigre allies are 35 percent of the population, 9 percent are of Sidamo descent, and the remaining 19 percent come from small indigenous groups, such as the Mursi, Hamar, Konso, Karo, Surma, and Bumi. A wide variety of physical types are evident, along with many very different languages, religious affiliations, and beliefs. Some observers believe that this diversity holds back modernization and threatens to plunge the nation into divisive conflict. Other observers believe that this diversity is Ethiopia's strength and has enabled it to resist onslaughts from Europe and Asia. For millennia, the monarchy united Ethiopians in loyalty to the emperor, just as it has held Great Britain together.

Amharic (Amarigna) is the language of the dominant Amhara ethnic group. It was the language of the imperial rulers for many centuries and is still widely spoken throughout Ethiopia. This is the principal language of instruction in most Ethiopian schools today. Millions of Ethiopians also speak Tigrinya, Oromo, Somali, Arabic, Italian, or English. The English language is growing in importance as the main language of instruction, especially in universities. Arabic is widely spoken in the north and east, and 40 to 45 percent of the Ethiopian population is Muslim. These people must learn Arabic to read their holy book, the Koran, which is written in ancient Arabic. The latter is very different from modern spoken Arabic, thus many Ethiopians cannot speak modern Arabic fluently. Approximately 35 to 40 percent of Ethiopia's population is Coptic Christian.

For many centuries Muslims refused to attack or invade Christian Ethiopia. Today Muslims are converting four new converts for every one converted to Christianity. They are zealous in their pursuit of converts all over Africa. By contrast, Christians seem to have lost their missionary zeal. Muslims traditionally attend Koran school, rather than state sponsored schools. This puts them at a disadvantage on national examinations for civil service jobs, as well as exams used to select government workers. These national examinations are often written in either English or Amharic. Christian schools use either Amharic or English as the language of instruction. This gives Christians a decisive advantage and helps explain their continued domination of Ethiopia's institutions, despite their minority status. Emperor Yohannes IV (1871-89) sought national unity through religious conformity, while Menelik II (1889-1913) sought centralization of government functions, creation of government health centers, financing of small industries, and spreading education as a means of creating that unity for Ethiopia. Both used church schools to educate Ethiopians.

For several thousand years religion controlled education in Ethiopia. The ancient Axumites created a system of writing that evolved from a Sabean script believed to have been introduced from Arabia. Similar to written Hebrew and related to Phoenician, the system is phonetic. The ancient Ge'ez language descended from such origins. Stone monoliths record the daring feats of ancient kings in Ge'ez, which has been the liturgical language of Ethiopia's Jews for 3,000 years and the Ethiopian Coptic Christian church since A.D. 400. This language was developed by a sophisticated ancient civilization and used not only by priests, but also by rulers who created impressive stone palaces, temples, and tombs, like the obelisks found at Aksum. Writings in Ge'ez, as well as Greek and Sabean, inscribed on these monuments describe military campaigns, the victories of Ethiopian kings, and trade with Arabia, Egypt, Syria, Greece, and India. Gold and silver coins were minted to facilitate commerce and trade.

Judaism, Christianity, Islam, and indigenous African religions have long peacefully co-existed in Ethiopia, but tensions have occasionally erupted in violence. Each major religion created schools for children of its adherents. Christianity is dominant in the north, northwest, and central states. Judaism is limited to the Lake Tana region. Islam is strong in the east, south, and west. Indigenous religions are strong in the southern, eastern, and western regions.

By far, the greatest traditional schools were constructed and managed by the Ethiopian Orthodox Coptic Church. King Erzana started church schools to perpetuate Christianity, but church schools achieved their "golden age" of expansion between A.D. 1200 and 1500. Church education has changed little since that time. Its primary mission has been to train individuals for the priesthood, but the secondary mission has been to spread the faith through Christian culture. Church schools trained not only priests, but monks and *debtera* (cantors), who were often better educated than the priests they served. The *debteras* were church scholars, custodians of education, and a privileged elite who helped decide who held power. Many were children of the elite and sought to keep the elite in power. Teachers were also trained in church schools, along with civil servants, such as judges, governors, scribes, treasurers, and administrators of all sorts. Religious schools were the only source of trained personnel.

Prompted by Italy, which militarily occupied Eritrea between 1885 and 1892, Emperor Menelik II began the modernization and secularization of Ethiopian education. The church did not challenge his opening of competing secular schools from 1905 onward. The government was modernized by creating 10 ministries, and the administration of education was left in the hands of the church, which satisfied its leaders. Secular curriculums included the study of French, English, Arabic, Italian, Amharic, Ge'ez, mathematics, physical training, and sports. Tuition, as well as room and board, were paid for by the emperor. From 1905 on, Ethiopians began to associate secular education with national progress. The elite began to discuss the need for universal education and literacy.

Empress Zewditu Menelik declared in 1921:

Every parent is hereby required to teach his child reading and writing through which the child may learn the difference between good and evil. . . . Any parent refusing to do so will be fined 50 dollars. . . . Those of you who are leaders of parishes in rural as well as urban areas, in addition to your regular responsibilities in the churches, teach the children of your respective communities how to read and write. . . . If you fail to teach, you will be deprived of your positions entrusted to you. . . . Every parent, after you have taught your child how to read and write, make him attend your choice of any of the local trade schools, lest your child will be faced with difficulty earning a livelihood. If you fail to do so, you will be considered as one who has deprived another of limbs, and accordingly you will be fined 50 dollars, which money will be used for the education of the poor. This proclamation applies to those between the ages of 7 and 21 years. A parent will not be held responsible for any child of his who is over 21 years old.

In effect, Ethiopia declared war against ignorance and illiteracy with the aim of transforming the country into a literate industrial society.

The evolution of education in Ethiopia can be logically divided into five periods. The first is the Pre-European traditional educational system, which was followed by the initial period of Secular education from 1900-1936, during which Ethiopian monarchs attempted to modernize education. The Italian Colonial educational system began in 1936 and lasted until 1941. The Independence era, which lasted from 1941 to 1974, was characterized by the efforts of a restored Emperor, Haile Selassie, to revive and develop Ethiopia's educational system. Finally, there was the post-Selassie Afro-Marxist and post-Marxist modern educational reform period which continues into 2001.

EDUCATIONAL SYSTEM—OVERVIEW

Education between the ages of 7 to 13 is free and compulsory. Jobs in Ethiopia's growing industrial sector require command of English in many cases, especially in the computer-related high-tech sector. Illiteracy rates are very high in farming communities where farming techniques have changed little over the centuries. Agriculture employs most Ethiopians, but industrial employment is increasing rapidly as emerging industries create new jobs.

Calligraphy was at one time a valued skill. It took one year to copy a book by hand. Books were treasured.

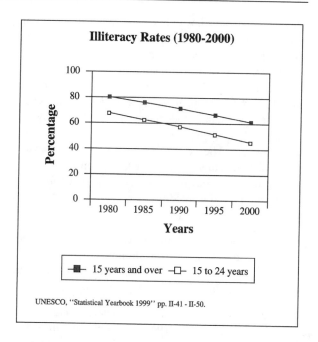

Illiteracy Rates (1980-2000)

Legend: 15 years and over; 15 to 24 years

UNESCO, "Statistical Yearbook 1999" pp. II-41 - II-50.

A good scribe could support himself reproducing books. Scribes learned to illustrate their books with beautiful art depicting selected topics. They made leather covers and bound their books. Each page was made from either goat or sheep skin. Because of the time involved, and materials needed, the cost of book production was high. Great artists were granted the title *Aleqa.* Carried in special leather cases on the back under one's shawl, these priceless treasures were read each morning after rising and each night before sleeping. The art of making reed pens, ink, and parchment were also learned skills, and a master scribe was a valued member of a community. Ethiopian calligraphy reached its peak of perfection between A.D. 1400 and 1500.

The adviser to the Ministry of Education, Ernest Work, argued for the creation of a uniquely Ethiopian system of education. Work recommended that Amharic be the language of instruction. He argued that, "Ethiopian boys and girls should be educated in their own languages, learn about their own country and men and interesting things, as well as the world in general." He drew up a plan that mandated six years of elementary education for all. Industrial and trade school, agricultural schools, and homemaking courses followed elementary school. Five or six years of additional education was recommended for students who wanted to go into business. The final piece of Work's plan called for an Ethiopian university. He felt it should be established with foreign, private aid. It should foster a college of education for teacher training as well. A resident of Addis Abba commented on general literacy in 1935, saying, "It was remarkable to the resident of many year's standing that whereas in 1920 the boy of his household staff who could read and write was notable, in 1935 among the same society there were few young men and boys who had not mastered the elementary processes of reading and writing the Amharic script.'' Some teachers still teach Amharic using the *fidel* (Ethiopian alphabet) with 231 characters, but rather than make students memorize these they use *Laubach,* which are representations that are easier for students to grasp. They call this their ''global approach.'' After mastering this, many students go on to learn the *derse* (how to write) or 12 types of essays. *Sawasiw* (grammar), is also learned by these *leed* (scholars). This honor is no longer restricted to the privileged.

There were 21 government schools and many more religious schools in 1935. The enrollment in just the government schools was 4,200 students, which excluded students studying abroad and in religious schools.

The language of instruction officially changed from Amharic to English after 1944. All books and materials were printed in English. This placed a heavy burden on learners for whom this was a second or third language. The British Council helped to ease the burden of this change by setting up libraries with books, pamphlets, and periodicals in English for Ethiopians. After 1954, Amharic was used from kindergarten to second grade, with English studied as a foreign language. English was the medium of instruction for third grade through the university.

The first evidence of radical educational reform was the post-revolution (1975-76) literacy campaign or *Zemecha.* More than half a million students with some high school education or more, as well as their teachers and professors, were pressed into service in an effort at development through cooperation. Their goal was to teach peasants to read and write in a year and a half. Each literate teacher was assigned 40 illiterate students. This army of literacy teachers was trained for 5 to 10 days in psychology, teaching methods, techniques for creating order in class, and the use of educational materials and teaching aids. The books they used also taught practical skills such as how to count money in a market place when selling crops, hygiene, childcare, and terracing land to prevent soil erosion.

The Empress Menen Girls' School originally opened in 1931 to educate Ethiopian girls and played an important role in educating Ethiopian women in the first decade following restored independence. By the early 1950s it had become one of the top four general secondary schools. The school sought to give girls a technical education, but it also tried to preserve traditional female occupations. Gradually, the school expanded to include a one-year teacher training course and a three-year diploma course.

Girls participated in traditional education far less than boys. Ethiopians believe that a woman's place is in the home or working in the farm fields with her husband. The art of homemaking was paramount. Attention was given to learning to bow low when greeting elders and strangers, as well as the custom of women receiving articles with both hands. These were the hallmarks of well-trained, traditional Ethiopian women. However, post-war Ethiopia declared that both boys and girls should be afforded equal opportunities. The number of female students between 1944 and 1951 averaged 19.5 percent. This was a problem. Many girls either stayed home or dropped out.

In addition to traditional classes and schooling, there were other educational opportunities as well. Technical schools were rebuilt and expanded. The language of instruction changed from French to English. Mechanics, electrical engineering, carpentry, and other practical subjects were offered along with mathematics, chemistry, physics, and history. The aim was to produce technicians, technical supervisors, and foremen.

Agricultural schools, such as the Ambo Agricultural School, were created to teach scientific commercial farming. The idea was to develop such schools into colleges of agricultural science. They were located near fertile farmland with ample rainfall and possible irrigation and hydroelectric sources. The United States provided a complete agricultural laboratory. Schools were well equipped with farm tools and machines. Graduates earned certificates that allowed them to work as agricultural technicians or to teach agricultural science in elementary schools. Some worked as farm managers, agricultural advisers, or as assistants on experimental stations. Modern farming techniques and practices thus entered Ethiopian society.

Traditional Ethiopian education was private and stressed the centrality of religion, the needs of the soul over those of the human body, modesty, humility, and dedication to persistent pursuit of thoroughness. Nobles prided themselves on being patrons of education, the arts, and literature. Many sponsored the creation of books and works of art. Elite parents hired resident scholars to teach their children. They gave generously to church sponsored schools, and the Orthodox Coptic Church jealously guarded its dominant role in education. Isolated cases of Roman Catholic, Lutheran, Greek Orthodox, Swedish Evangelical, and Hebrew schools could be found, and some noble children studied abroad at great expense. Students returning from overseas study often met with cool or even hostile receptions. Suspicion of things foreign was understandable given Ethiopia's history of defending itself against foreign forces that attempted to destroy it.

Decades ago, in principle, schools were open to girls and boys, but in practice, only boys whose parents were members of Orthodox churches were admitted. Traditional church schools were not impartial, nor were they democratic. No pretense of serving all citizens of Ethiopia was claimed or practiced. Most students lived at school, and the teacher served also as a parental figure. There were no classes on holidays or Sundays. Senior students assisted the priest in church services as a form of in-service training.

Preprimary schools remain the monopoly of church schools that teach writing and reading skills before children enter public, government-run schools. For tradition-bound conservative Ethiopians, such education is still important. Ethiopia has more than a quarter of a million trained priests educated within this traditional system. More than 20,000 churches and monasteries have schools attached which offer traditional education. In areas where the Ethiopian Orthodox Coptic Monophysite faith is practiced, other religions can set up schools, but they cannot recruit converts to their religion. Despite revolutionary change, such schools provide one type of literacy and training to large numbers of Ethiopians.

Curriculum under the Italians changed from how it was conducted under Ethiopian control; invading Italian forces changed the Ethiopian educational system in 1936. In the process of this change, thousands of educated Ethiopians were killed, and the survivors became exiles in England, France, and the United States. Italy created a dual system of education. European children were given sound academic training and prepared to lead, whereas Ethiopian children were educated for servitude. Their education was inferior in quality, thus preventing them from ever competing against Italians or challenging their authority or right to rule. Missionary schools complied with Italian educational regulations. Coptic, Catholic, Protestant, Muslim, and state schools were encouraged as a form of divide and rule tactic.

Beyond basic literacy, Italian colonial education for Ethiopians was designed merely to buy their loyalty. African schools were limited to teaching in Ge'ez, Tigranya, and Amharic. Religion, not science, was stressed for Africans, while just the reverse was true for Italian children. Italian scholars felt that ancient Rome made a mistake when it educated the native chiefs of Britain. Therefore, the Italians were advised not to educate Ethiopians beyond elementary school and not to teach them the Italian language.

Before the Italian invasion Ethiopia had over 4,000 students in schools, but after the invasion that number dropped sharply to 1,400 students. Inferior instruction for Ethiopians magnified the tragedy. Textbook printers were ordered to exclude all reference to Italy in 1848 and to the Italian revolution.

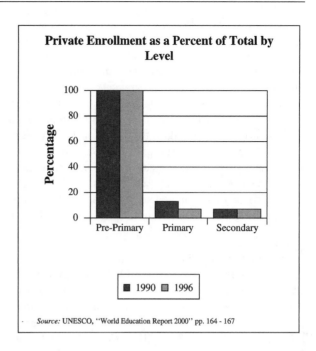

Private Enrollment as a Percent of Total by Level

Source: UNESCO, "World Education Report 2000" pp. 164 - 167

PREPRIMARY & PRIMARY EDUCATION

In the pre-European traditional educational system, children in primary schools, learned to read and write Ge'ez's 265 characters. Emphasis was placed on rote memorization. Admitted between the ages of 7 and 12, the time required for graduation depended on intelligence, health, and motivation. Elementary pupils had to learn to read, write, and recite the *Dawit Medgem* (Psalms of David). There are 15 sections, called *negus* (kings), which normally took two years to master. Next they learned to sing *kum zema* (church hymns), which took four years, and *msaewait zema* (advanced singing), which took an additional year to learn. Liturgical dancing and systrum holding required three years. *Qine* (poetry) and law required five years to learn. The interpretation of the Old and New Testaments, as well as the Apostles' Creed, took four years on average, while the interpretation of the works of learned monks and priests took three years. When a student knew the psalms by heart, he had mastered the "house of reading" and was now considered an elementary school graduate. His family gave a lavish feast to celebrate this achievement. If they could afford it, they gave his teacher property, money, clothes, or other gifts. Many subjects were learned simultaneously as in middle school.

Orthodox Coptic Church schools provided much needed training in reading and writing in preprimary schools. Thus, many children already had basic literacy skills by age six upon starting primary school. The first postwar formal curriculum was a 6-6 structure: six years of elementary school followed by six years of secondary school.

During the early 1930s, 18 percent of primary school age children were in school. By contrast, beginning in the early 1970s and continuing on into 2001, more than 50 percent of primary school age children attended school. The absolute number of primary school students increased from 859,000 to over 2 million. The number of primary school teachers rose from 18,642 to more than 35,000 during this period, but the teacher student ratio rose to 1 teacher for every 90 students. Overcrowding has also led the government to create a three-shift system, to extend the academic year by two months, and to stagger starting dates to accommodate rising demand. Nevertheless, the gains in education are impressive and substantial.

Revolutionaries increased primary schools from 2,754 to 5,800 between 1974 and 1984. They concentrated on building new primary schools in rural areas to end the placement of schools in privileged urban communities. Most new schools were built in under-privileged urban and rural areas. Formally neglected students had opportunities to learn, which were reinforced by quota systems that guaranteed them seats in secondary schools and universities as an additional incentive to learn. Revolutionary curriculums stress vocational studies over academic subjects. Gardening is introduced in the fourth grade. Polytechnic training begins in fifth grade, along with political education and history. The teacher pupil ratio increased from 1 teacher for every 44 students in 1974, to 1 teacher for every 64 students after the revolution because access to educational opportunities expanded.

SECONDARY EDUCATION

Middle school involved learning the *Merha Euoor* (Book of the Blind), which took six months, and history, which took one year. Mathematics, astronomy, canon and civil law, Christian ethics, world history, and the Amharic language were also studied in middle school. Amharic is considered the language of national unification and literature. Many subjects could be learned simultaneously if the student had the aptitude. Completion of middle school qualified a student to serve as a deacon in the Ethiopian Orthodox Coptic Church.

Many schools were boarding schools to accommodate the large number of war orphans who were homeless. This led to marked attrition at the secondary school level, except for bright students. Secondary school students who wanted to attend universities had to take the London Matriculation Examination, the General Certificate Examination, or the Ethiopian Secondary School Certificate Examination. Students headed for the United States took the College Entrance Examination set by the Board of Regents of New York State. These examinations measured Ethiopian secondary school graduates against international competitors for university seats globally.

In 1948 two years of junior high school were added, and secondary education was reduced to a four year curriculum. From 1954 on, primary school consisted of the first four grades, and junior high school started at the fifth grade and ended with the eighth grade. Efforts were made to create a uniform curriculum to facilitate transfers between schools. By 1943 the Haile Selassie Secondary School opened its doors and began training students. This school offered a full four-year secondary program. Most of the teachers were foreign. The school had two tracks. The first track prepared students for university entrance, while the second track prepared students for further technical training in vocations. The British assisted by opening the General Wingate Secondary School. This school had science laboratories, and offered classes in science, art, music, and handicrafts. Both secondary schools were boarding schools.

Competitive examination at the end of sixth grade determines which students can advance to junior high, high school, vocational training, and ultimately, the university. Elementary school students who fail the tests set by the Ministry of Education are not allowed to repeat a class. Failed students are not prepared for jobs, but neither can they go on to high school.

Junior high schools increased from 420 in 1973 to over 800 in 2001. Students attending junior high school rose from 101,800 to more than 215,000. The number of junior high school teachers rose from 3,226 to over 4,800. Polytechnic education is being expanded to include all children between the ages of 7 to 14 years of age. The goal is to stream junior high graduates into vocational training and productive work in line with Ethiopia's demands for industrial, health care, and service industry workers.

High school construction rose from 113 to an excess of 190 and is still rising rapidly. The secondary school population expanded from 82,300 to over 220,000 students. The high school teacher population rose from 2,955 to more than 5,500. The teacher pupil ratio rose from 1 teacher for every 10 students in 1962 to 1 teacher for every 30 students in 1970 and 1 teacher for every 44 students in 1984. In one sense this illustrates more open access to education; however, quality of education becomes a concern. Before 1974 approximately 91 percent of high school students entered the academic stream, 7 percent went into vocational subjects, and 2 percent studied education as part of teacher training.

HIGHER EDUCATION

Originally, the equivalent of higher education was reserved for students who intended to become *debtera* or *leed* themselves. This was a very small elite group of scholars. Advanced courses were only offered at special centers located in Gondar, Gojam, Tigre, and Wollo. Students had to memorize each lesson without flaw to advance. Three areas of specialization were studied. A student attended academies of music, poetry, and written texts. Life in the academy was severe, simple, and demanding. Students awoke at dawn each morning to prepare for the religious service. The master sat on an elevated platform, surrounded by admiring students. They recited the previous day's lesson and then began memorizing the new lesson for that day. Classes ended by late afternoon. They ate a modest dinner and then went out collecting firewood. The day's lessons were reinforced until midnight when they slept.

Advanced students began their training at the academy of music. These academies were attached to designated churches or monasteries. Works composed by Yared, a great composer and lyricist of the sixth century, were studied. He created a system of musical notation still widely used. Written in Ge'ez, it has dots, lines, and directional signs that tell the student how to sing a verse. Academy graduates can read these symbols and sing correctly. *Ezel* (low-voiced and dignified singing) was reserved for funerals, fasts, and vigils. *Arary* (light and happy singing) was reserved for great festivals and weddings. The *Degwa* (essential collection of ecclesiastical music) was mastered. Liturgical chants were accompanied by religious dancing, *kabaro* (drumming), and *tsentsil* (systrum) playing. It typically took eight years to complete the advanced courses in Ethiopian Church music. Ethiopian secular music, known as *azmari* (wandering minstrel), could also be studied. This music dealt with love, death, marriage, harvesting, and the like. An *azmari*, or minstrel, traveled widely, performing at weddings and joyous celebrations. He flattered, cajoled, and goaded people into dancing, laughing, and giving away money. He could use poetry and songs to insult anyone, even nobles.

The academy of poetry was the next challenge for advanced students. Students learned to translate Amharic into Ge'ez and enlarged their vocabularies in both languages. They studied Ethiopian culture, its traditions, folkways, values, and customs, as well as its rules and regulations. Comprehension of texts in Ge'ez was essential for students. They spent time in isolated solitude to compose original poems in Ge'ez. Though critiqued by the professors, originality was encouraged. Ge'ez grammar and philology and 12 styles of poetic composition form the curriculum of the poetry academy, which took 13 years to complete. Passages from famous philosophers, such as Plato, Aristotle, Zara Yacob, and Wolde Hiywet, were also studied.

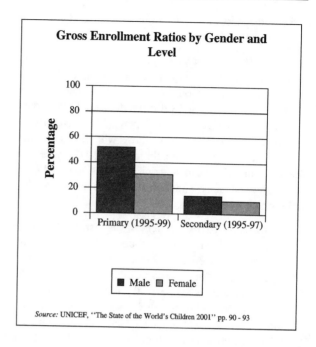

Gross Enrollment Ratios by Gender and Level

Source: UNICEF, ''The State of the World's Children 2001'' pp. 90 - 93

The literary academy was the third academy of higher education. This school of literary texts required scholars to properly interpret stories and passages from the Old and New Testaments, together with literature, fiction, and books on the monastic life. Texts such as the *Laws of Kings,* the foundation of Ethiopian law for centuries, were also studied. Global history was taught from an Ethiopian perspective. Ten years were required to graduate from the literary academy.

The development of local schools in each province that sent their better students for education in the capital or abroad was encouraged. These local schools stressed knowledge of Ethiopia. Ethiopia's most promising scholars were given scholarships to study in Europe, the Middle East, other African nations, and North America. The largest number went to France, where most studied law, politics, economics, and science. French was Ethiopia's leading foreign language, thus many students felt comfortable in French universities.

A university college in Ethiopia was created in 1931 to reduce the expense and training of administrators. In 1941, old blueprints for this college were reactivated, and the emperor approved a plan. A Canadian Jesuit priest, Dr. Lucien Matte, was selected to head the college. By 1954 a civil charter was granted, and Haile Selassie University became a reality in 1961. Thus, following World War II, Ethiopia had built an educational system that covered a wide range of learning needs from kindergarten to the university level.

In 1965 the Ethiopian University Service was created (EUS). This program required university students to serve as teachers in rural Ethiopia for one academic year, between their third and forth years of study.

Entrance examinations to universities have been extremely competitive. They were inequitable and favored children of the elite from the best schools, usually from major urban areas. The twelfth grade school leaving examination alone screened out 80 percent of university applicants. From 1940 to 1960 those who failed to enter college were given government jobs. By 1970, there were few government jobs to dole out. Even the Armed Forces were full to capacity with high school graduates who had failed the university entrance exam.

In the early 1970s, a program was instituted to make a quota system for university student selection. Students from each region were assigned seats based upon the percentage of their ethnic group in Ethiopia's total population. The idea was to be fair to all groups. To achieve this goal, admission standards were lowered. Many students admitted had never seen a science laboratory in their rural homeland schools. They often knew neither English nor Amharic and found it difficult to follow lectures. The urban terrain was unfamiliar and frightening, and many dropped out and retreated to their mountain homes. Quotas proved a failure and the old selection system was quietly put back in place. Another program also tried to shorten the time needed to complete a degree from four years to three. Given the low quality of education in the high schools, this experiment also failed and had to be phased out. Students simply needed more time to master English and gain scientific knowledge.

A small number of students who complete high school enter universities, despite the explosion of education at the primary and secondary levels. In 1981, approximately 75,000 students took the university entrance examination (ESLCE), but only 3,000 were admitted to four-year colleges, while another 2,000 were admitted into institutes of technology and training schools. The number of students seeking university education is increasing rapidly, but Ethiopia's institutions of higher education do not yet have the capacity to absorb them.

ADMINISTRATION, FINANCE, & EDUCATIONAL RESEARCH

Originally, the Ethiopian government alone could not finance universal education, so missionaries of all denominations were allowed to build schools. This further broadened the base of education, but Ethiopians viewed non-Coptic religious education as unpatriotic. To them, learning from Catholics was a betrayal of the nation. Any education outside of Orthodox Coptic Church schools was tantamount to being anti-Ethiopian. They felt that learning in a Catholic school amounted to accepting Catholicism and represented a betrayal of national honor

and the native religion. Such persons were willing instruments in the hands of alien powers. The Ethiopian Orthodox Coptic Church encouraged such attitudes toward both secular and non-Coptic schools, which hampered the spread of education nationally. Despite this, French Catholics opened the Ecole Francaise, which by 1921 had graduated 1,400 students. Education was free. The old Coptic Church monopoly on education was giving way to a diverse array of other schools, which complimented traditional religious education, which continues to flourish. To meet the rising cost of education a special education tax of 6 percent was levied on all imports and exports.

After his official coronation as emperor in 1930, Haile Selassie put all education under the control of the Ministry of Education and Fine Arts. The education tax generated revenue, and the new emperor added 2 percent of the treasury's national revenue to support education.

Finance for postwar secular education came from two sources. Approximately 3 percent of export taxes financed education. This was supplemented by dedicating 30 percent of the land tax to education. After 1948, elementary schools in rural areas were financed by a special rural land tax. Only church land was exempt. All other education was financed by the national treasury, which devoted 20 percent of its total income to education. This set a pattern followed later by Kenya's Jomo Kenyatta, who dedicated 30 percent of Kenya's budget to education.

Afro-Marxists have mobilized ordinary citizens in rural and urban areas to form associations. These committees furnish labor and building materials, and the government furnishes blueprints for school buildings. These citizen brigades are expected to build 16,000 learning centers throughout Ethiopia. Materials and tools are donated by the government if a community can not afford them. During the same period, the government committed itself to building 1,800 new primary schools. The new regime is promoting the idea of self-help and self-taxation to meet its educational targets.

NONFORMAL EDUCATION

Restoration of Ethiopia's education system was an impressive feat which included adult education. As early as 1948, the emperor opened *the Berhanih Zare New* (Your Light Is Today), a school and cultural institute whose ultimate purpose was to branch out into the field of mass education so that every person in the Empire would become literate in a prescribed period. Plans were made to adopt a simplification of the Amharic alphabet as a vehicle for achieving this end. Nevertheless, the goal of universal literacy remained elusive.

The adult literacy rate in 2001 remains at 35 percent. The main beneficiaries of adult literacy have been

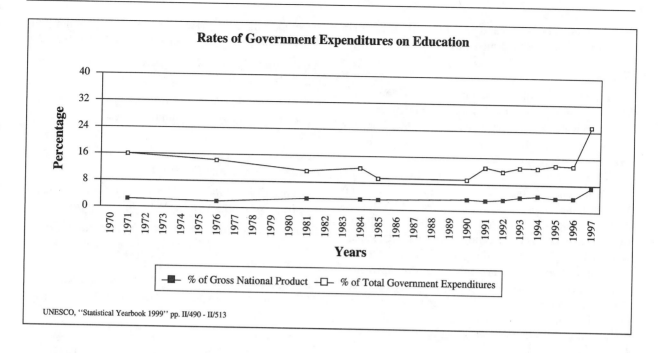

Rates of Government Expenditures on Education

UNESCO, "Statistical Yearbook 1999" pp. II/490 - II/513

women who traditionally were less likely to be educated then men. Female enrollment in most schools is less than 34 percent, but in adult literacy classes it exceeds 50 percent in rural areas and 74 percent in cities.

Distance learning, via radio and television, beams 1,200 lessons per year in 10 languages to millions of Ethiopians in remote regions. Impressive gains by the *Zemecha* suggest that if they could agree to stop fighting one another, Ethiopia could eliminate illiteracy.

TEACHING PROFESSION

With few educated Ethiopians to teach the children and educated foreigners still fully committed to successfully defeating the Axis Powers and ending World War II, it was difficult for Ethiopia to rebuild its education system. Few Ethiopians remained who were either qualified to teach or had teaching experience. At all levels Ethiopians had to rely on foreign teachers to reopen their schools. For this reason, the courses taught and the methods of instruction were not uniform. These varied from one school to the next. The English, Swedes, Americans, and other nationalities conducted classes as they would at home. In 1962, after several decades of rebuilding and training teachers, the Bureau of Educational Research and Statistics reported that 62 percent of Ethiopia's teachers had only elementary education or lower, 13 percent had 3 to 4 years, 16 percent had 1 year of teacher training, and 9 percent had some teacher training at the community level. Under colonial rule, the best teachers taught at the university level and the worst at the primary school level. Primary school teacher salaries were so low that it was difficult to recruit and retain teachers with

even a modest primary education. Ethiopia put the most money into the lower grades because it was believed that only a broadly educated mass could earn enough disposable income to support a small elite of doctors, lawyers, bureaucrats, artists, and administrators. Without such a semi-educated mass, the elite could not flourish. Ethiopia needed many teachers to reach this goal and to train them required constructing teachers' colleges.

A joint UNESCO- and USAID-funded and equipped teacher training program at Debre Berhan Community Teacher Training School failed because it required students to learn how to operate brick making equipment, build milking sheds for dairy cattle, make butter and cheese, and grow the vegetables that they ate at school. Parents objected that they wanted students to study academic subjects because the parents could teach them how to farm at home. Their attitude toward manual labor was negative. Many graduates were not accepted as agricultural experts when they returned home because elders culturally refused to accept orders or instruction from youth. Mothers pulled daughters out of the school complaining that they could learn hygiene, child-care, cooking, and handicrafts at home. They argued that their daughters did not have to go to school to learn such subjects. More than 42 percent of graduates dropped out of teaching after 5 years of service. More than money or materials, the limited number of teachers slowed the expansion of mass education. This teacher training college was abandoned after many parents transferred their children to other schools more academically oriented. Attitudes and culture held education back in postwar Ethiopia. Social Impact Assessments that predict the social response to development became mandatory by the 1970s to help avoid such costly cultural mistakes.

SUMMARY

Ethiopia is an old and proud African nation with a long tradition of education. With each era new forms of education were added to previous forms, which continue to function and provide literacy in Ge'ez, Amharic, and Arabic. The old religious schools still can be relied on to provide basic literacy in remote regions. Secular schools now build on this foundation and extend it. Emperors Menelik II and Haile Selassie added a secular layer of educational institutions on top of the existing religious schools. Literacy and education were offered to many who could not have dreamed of this privilege in the past. Prosecuting two costly wars led to the slow growth of secondary education and the virtual stagnation of university level opportunities, despite tremendous pent-up demand. This may lead to social volatility, tensions, and turmoil in the future unless it is resolved.

BIBLIOGRAPHY

Balsvik, Randi Ronning. *Haile Selassie's Students: The Intellectual and Social Background to Revolution, 1952-1977.* Lansing: Michigan State University Press, 1985.

Bartels, Lambert. *Oromo Religion.* Berlin: Dietrich Reimer Verlag, 1983.

Dalin, Per, et al. *How Schools Improve: An International Report.* London: Cassell Publishers, 1994.

Feurer, L.S. *The Conflict of Generations.* New York: Delacorte Press, 1968.

Hallpike, C.R. *The Konso of Ethiopia: A Study of the Values of a Cushitic People.* Oxford: Claredon Press, 1972.

Hansberry, William Leo. *Pillars of Ethiopian History, Volumes 1 and 2.* Washington: Howard University Press, 1981.

Heldman, Marilyn E. and Getatchew Haile. "Who is Who in Ethiopia's Past, Part III: Founders of Ethiopia's Solomonic Dynasty." *Northeast African Studies 9(1)*(1987): 1-11.

Hoben, Susan J. "Literacy Campaigns in Ethiopia and Somalia: A Comparison." *Northeast African Studies 10(2)*(1988):111-125.

Kalewold, I. *Traditional Ethiopian Church Education.* New York: Columbia Teachers College Press, 1970.

Kapeliuk, Olga. "A New Generation of Ethiopian Students." *Northeast African Studies 10(2)*(1988): 105-110.

Kapuscinski, Ryszard. *The Emperor: Downfall of an Autocrat.* New York: Vintage Books, 1984.

Keller, Edmund J. *Revolutionary Ethiopia: From Empire to People's Republic.* Bloomington: Indiana University Press, 1988.

Kessler, David. *The Falashas: The Forgotten Jews of Ethiopia.* New York: Shocken Books, 1985.

Legume, Colin. *Ethiopia: The Fall of Haile Selassie's Empire.* New York: Africana Publishing Company, 1975.

Levine, Donald. *Wax and Gold: Tradition and Innovation in Ethiopian Culture.* Chicago: University of Chicago Press, 1965.

Levine, Donald N. *Greater Ethiopia: The Evolution of a Multiethnic Society.* Chicago: The University of Chicago Press, 1974.

Pankhurst, Richard. "'Fear God, Honor the King': The Use of Biblical Allusion in Ethiopian Historical Literature, Part II." *Northeast African Studies 9(1)*(1987): 25-88.

——*The Ethiopians.* London: Blackwell Publishers, 1998.

Prouty, Chris. *Empress Taytu and Menelik II: Ethiopia 1883-1910.* Trenton: Red Sea Press, 1986.

Quirin, James. "The Beta Esrael (Falasha) and Ayhud in Fifteenth-Century Ethiopia: Oral and Written Traditions." *Northeast African Studies 10(2)*(1988): 89-103.

Rose, Pauline and Mercy Tembon. "Girls and Schooling in Ethiopia." In *Gender, Education and Development: Beyond Access to Empower Men,* ed. Christine Heward and Sheil Bunwaree. London: Zed Books, 1999.

Shack, William A. *The Gurage: A People of the Ensete Culture.* Oxford: International African Institute, 1966.

Vella, Jane. *Learning to Listen, Learning to Teach: The Power of Dialogue in Educating Adults.* San Francisco: Jossey-Bass Publishers, 1994.

Wagaw, Teshome G. *The Development of Higher Education and Social Change: An Ethiopian Experience.* East Lansing: Michigan University Press, 1990.

——*Education in Ethiopia: Prospect and Retrospect.* Ann Arbor: The University of Michigan Press, 1979.

—*Dallas L. Browne*

FAEROE ISLANDS

BASIC DATA

Official Country Name:	Faroe Islands
Region:	Europe
Population:	45,296
Language(s):	Faroese, Danish
Literacy Rate:	similar to Denmark proper

The Faeroe Islands comprise 18 rather small islands in the North Atlantic with less than 50,000 inhabitants. Once a colony of Denmark, they have been self-governing since 1948; however, the Faeroe Islands remain under Danish sovereignty. The local government (*landstyri*) receives a block grant to supplement tax income within the country, which covers one-third of public expenditures; the country is otherwise entirely dependent on the fishing industry.

There is an ongoing process towards economic independence and the forming of an independent sovereign state. In many international contexts, such as sporting events, the region is already recognized as a nation. The language of instruction in Faeroe Islands is the Faeroan language, which is a full specific language stemming from common West Nordic roots. All children also learn Danish in school and generally hold a full command of it.

The education system is entirely under the control of the local government, although it was only nationalized in 1979, and is historically and culturally influenced strongly by the Danish education system. There is a full general school system including upper secondary education and vocational education, the latter strongly oriented towards fishing and related marine business.

The options for higher education and specialized professional education in the Faeroe Islands are limited. The Faeroe Islands have a small university in the capital city of Thorshavn, with a focus on teaching and researching in the national language and literature as well as in science, and a teacher-training college and other professional schools, but the need to go abroad is still substantial. The colonial pattern of traveling to Denmark for advanced education is gradually being modified, however; advanced technological and other education may sometimes be more relevant in Atlantic fishing countries such as Norway or Iceland.

—*Henning Salling Olesen*

FALKLAND ISLANDS

BASIC DATA

Official Country Name:	Falkland Islands (Malvinas)
Region:	South America
Population:	2,826
Language(s):	English
Literacy Rate:	NA

The Falkland Islands (also known as Malvinas) are a United Kingdom's Overseas Territory that the British have continuously controlled since 1833. Largely a rural-agricultural economy produced an urban-rural dichotomy in the provision of education. Isolated rural areas compared to the capital, Stanley, made it difficult to recruit and retain teachers. In addition, costs were high in making opportunities for rural pupils comparable with those in Stanley, especially in the transportation of travelling teachers, the maintenance of sufficient itinerant staff to ensure visits to pupils at educationally desirable intervals, and the subsidy of the hostel in the capital.

Historically, low expectations on the part of pupils and parents in the rural areas, and a continuous outflow of pastoral revenues, have contributed to this dichotomy. The provision of universal suffrage in 1948 prompted increases in public funding and private contributions. The Falkland Islands Government provides staff, equipment, and supplies throughout the islands. Education is free and compulsory for all children between the ages of 5 and 16. The school year in Stanley, which begins in mid-January, is divided into three terms. Elsewhere, it varies due to local requirements. The English language, English methods, and English examination systems are standard.

The primary school, Stanley/Junior School, caters to preschool youth to 10-year-olds. It was built in 1955 with modern additions made in 1990, 1996, and 2001. Each classroom has two multi-media computers and printers, and some are equipped with TV and video facilities. Additionally, there is a well-stocked library and spacious hall used for physical education, music, drama, and other activities.

In 1992 Stanley opened its secondary school, the Falkland Islands Community School, which caters to the 11- through 16-year-olds, as well as providing an educational and recreational resource for the whole community. It offers 16 subjects at the General Certificate of Secondary Education (GCSE) level. In addition to general classrooms, there are two science laboratories, a music room, and rooms for art, information technology, business studies, design technology, home economics, and needle craft. Students receiving a grade of ''C'' or better are funded for A Level/GNVQ courses at Peter Symonds' Sixth Forum College or at alternate schools. There is funding, too, for vocational and higher education courses in Britain.

In the rural areas, known as Camp, younger children live in isolated settlements or on farms. Since the 1970s, parental attitudes have been favorable for more formal education. The majority of the children are taught by a combination of travelling teacher and radio/telephone lessons. A few are taught in the three settlement schools at Fox Bay, Port Howard, and North Arm. A team of six travelling teachers visit the more isolated pupils for two out of every six weeks; they work closely with the radio/telephone teachers provided by the Stanley based Camp Education Unit.

The changing parental attitudes of the older Camp children, between the ages of 10 and 16, have favored attendance at more distant schools. The children then live in a boarding hostel.

BIBLIOGRAPHY

''Education: Information for Teaching Staff and Other Interested Persons.'' Falkland Islands Government, 2000. Available from http://www.falklands.gov.fk/education.htm.

Falkland Islands Government, Education Department. ''Stanley Infant/Junior School,'' 2000. Available from http://www.falklands.gov.fk/ed1.htm.

Smith, David B. ''Scale, Isolation and Dependency in the Educational System in the Educational System of the Falkland Islands.'' *Educational Review* 43 (1991): 335-342.

———. ''Schooling in the Falkland Islands.'' Ph.D. diss., University of Hull, 1988.

—Bill T. Manikas

FIJI

BASIC DATA

Official Country Name:	Republic of Fiji
Region:	Oceania
Population:	832,494
Language(s):	English, Fijian, Hindustani
Literacy Rate:	91.6%

Fiji, officially the Republic of Fiji, is a nation and archipelago in the South Pacific Ocean that is part of the Melanesian Island group. It is comprised of 540 islets and 300 islands of which about 100 are inhabited. All the islands are volcanic in origin, and the largest of these are Vanua Levu and Viti Levu where the capital city of Suva is located.

Formerly a British colony, Fiji became independent in 1970. According to a July 2000 estimate, the total population of the islands is 832,494. The population consists of: Fijian (51 percent), the indigenous group whose heritage is a mixed Melanesian-Polynesian stock; Asian Indians (44 percent), descendants of laborers brought to the islands by the British in the nineteenth century to work on the sugar plantations; and European, Chinese, and other Pacific Islanders (5 percent).

The Indian population outnumbered the Fijians in the early 1980s and dominated both government and politics. However, this changed in 1987 after a coup and the creation of a new constitution that favored the Fijian ethnic group. This change in the power structure resulted in a large Indian emigration, which in turn shifted the population to a Fijian majority. However, the constitution was amended in 1997—granting access to political power to all groups.

Fiji has a high literacy rate (91.6 percent) and, although there is no compulsory education, more than 85 percent of the children between the ages of 6 to 13 attend primary school. Schooling is free and provided by both public and church-run schools. Generally, the Fijian and Hindu children attend separate schools, reflecting the political split that exists in the nation.

The structure of the Fijian educational system is divided into primary school, secondary school, and higher education. The language of instruction is English.

The primary school system consists of 8 years of schooling and is attended by children from the ages of 6 to 14 years. Upon completion of primary school, a certificate is awarded and the student is eligible to take the Secondary School Examination.

Entry into the secondary school system, which is a total of five years, is determined by a competitive examination. Students passing the exam then follow a three-year course that leads to the Fiji School Leaving Certificate and the opportunity to attend senior secondary school. At the end of this level, they may take the Form VII examination, which covers four or five subjects. Successful completion of this process gains students access to higher education.

The University of the South Pacific, called the crossroads of the South Pacific because it serves ten English speaking territories in the South Pacific, is the major provider of higher education. Admission to the university requires a secondary school diploma, and all students must take a one-year foundation course at the university regardless of their major. Financing for the university is derived from school fees, funds from the Fiji government and other territories, and aid from Australia, New Zealand, Canada, and the United Kingdom. The Ministry of Education, Women, and Culture is the administering body.

In addition to the university, the Fiji also has teacher-training colleges, as well as medical, technological, and agricultural schools. Primary school teachers are trained for two years, whereas secondary school teachers train for three years; they then have the option to receive a diploma in education or read for a bachelor's degree in arts or science and continue for an additional year to earn a postgraduate certificate of education.

The Fiji Polytechnic School offers training in various trades, apprenticeship courses, and other courses that lead to diplomas in engineering, hotel catering, and business studies. Some of the course offerings can also lead to several City and Guilds of London Institute Examinations.

In addition to the traditional educational system, Fiji also offers the opportunity to obtain an education through distance learning. The University Extension Service provides centers and a network of terminals in most regional areas. For students taking non-credit courses, no formal qualifications are necessary. However, students who enroll in the credit courses may be awarded the appropriate degree or certificate upon successful completion of their studies through the extension services.

BIBLIOGRAPHY

The Central Intelligence Agency (CIA). *The World Factbook 2000*. Directorate of Intelligence, 1 January 2000. Available from http://www.cia.gov/.

International Association of Universities (IAU). "Educational System-Fiji," 1996. Available from http://ftp.unesco.org/.

—*Jean Boris Wynn*

FINLAND

BASIC DATA

Official Country Name:	Republic of Finland
Region:	Europe
Population:	5,167,486
Language(s):	Finnish, Swedish, Lapp, Russian
Literacy Rate:	100%
Academic Year:	September-May
Number of Primary Schools:	3,766
Compulsory Schooling:	9 years
Public Expenditure on Education:	7.5%
Foreign Students in National Universities:	3,829
Libraries:	1,202
Educational Enrollment:	Primary: 380,932 Secondary: 469,933 Higher: 226,458

Educational Enrollment Rate:	Primary: 99%
	Secondary: 118%
	Higher: 74%
Teachers:	Primary: 21,459
Student-Teacher Ratio:	Primary: 18:1
Female Enrollment Rate:	Primary: 99%
	Secondary: 125%
	Higher: 80%

HISTORY & BACKGROUND

Until the early twentieth century, Finland was part of Sweden or Russia. In 1155, the first missionaries arrived in Finland from Sweden. Sweden ruled Finland from the twelfth to the nineteenth centuries. Russia ruled Finland from 1809 to 1917, when Finland finally won its independence.

The political and social character of the Finnish people has been shaped by their relationships with Sweden, Russia, and, in the twentieth century, the Soviet Union and the West. Under Swedish rule, the Swedish language was the official language, and much of the administration of the country was directed from Sweden and carried out by Swedes. Finland moved from Swedish to Russian control as a part of a deal struck between Napoleon of France and Czar Alexander I of Russia in an effort to complete Napoleon's blockage of England (1809). In the process, Russian troops occupied Finland (Jakobson 1998).

In an important way, this was the beginning of Finnish independence. As a Grand Duchy of the Czar, Finland was given its own administration headed by a senate. "As grand duke of Finland, the Russian Czar, an autocrat with absolute power in the rest of his empire, accepted the role of constitutional monarch" in Finland (Jakobson 1998). Thus began Finnish self-rule.

Along with self-rule, the Finnish language became the language of the government, furthering a sense of Finish identity. In 1835, *Kalevala,* the Finnish national epic, was published. This collection of Finnish folk poems, compiled and edited by Elias Lönnrot, played an important role in the development of the Finnish language and, more generally, of Finnish culture. This epic poem brought a small, unknown people to the attention of other Europeans. Within the Grand Duchy of Finland, the *Kalevala* bolstered self-confidence. These factors furthered faith in the possibility of an independent Finland, complete with a Finnish language and culture.

Finland declared its independence from Russia on December 6, 1917, though there were Russian troops in Finland. At the end of December 1917, Lenin recognized Finnish independence. The new state was also recognized by France, Germany, and Sweden. Thus began a long period of a complex and sometimes stormy relationship with the USSR.

With the encouragement of the Bolsheviks, a group of Finns broke from the "Red Guard" and engaged the "White Army" led by General Mannerhein. About 30,000 Finns lost their lives on both sides of the civil war that lasted from January to May 1918. The White Army forces won the day. In 1919 the present constitution was adopted, and Finland became a republic with a president as head of state. The legislative branch of government has a unicameral parliament or *Eduskunta* of 200 seats; members are elected by popular vote on a proportional basis to serve 4 year terms. A supreme court or *Korkein Oikeus* heads the judicial branch. The president appoints the *Korkein Oikeus* judges.

In the winter of 1939-1940, the Soviet Union attacked Finland, and the Winter War was fought. While the Finns did not defeat the USSR, they managed to hold them off and won wide respect in Europe and the world for their efforts. It is not exactly correct to say that Finland was the only country to fight on both sides during the Second World War. Finland was a co-belligerent with Germany against the USSR. Finland signed a peace agreement with the Soviet Union in the summer of 1944, and ceded some territory to the Soviet Union, but was never occupied by Soviet troops. Finnish independence and sovereignty were preserved.

After the war, the government of Finland walked a fine line between the two camps of the "Cold War." On the one hand, Finland refused to accept an American offer to participate in the Marshall plan, developed a trade relationship with the Soviet Union, and paid off its war debt to the USSR. On the other hand, Finland worked towards becoming a member of the European Union, succeeding in 1995.

Political, Social, & Cultural Bases: Finland's official name is Republic of Finland (*Suomen Tasavalta*). Its short local form is *Suomi.* The population of Finland is approximately 5.2 million. It is the sixth largest country in Europe in area, with a low population density of 17 persons per square kilometer. Most Finns, some 65 percent of the population, now live in urban areas, while 35 percent of Finns live in a rural environment. Metropolitan Helsinki is composed of three cities: Helsinki, the capital, with a population 551,000; Espoo, with a population of 210,000; and Vantaa, with a population of 176,000. These urban centers are home to roughly one-sixth of the country's total population. Other important cities include Tampere (193,000), Turku (172,000), and Oulu (118,000).

The Finnish language is a member of the Finno-Ugric linguistic family that includes, in one branch, Finnish, Estonian, and a number of other Finnic tongues; and, in the other, Hungarian, by far the biggest language of the Ugric group. An indigenous minority language is Sami, spoken by the Sami people (also known as Lapps) of Lapland.

The number of foreign citizens living permanently in Finland was about 85,000 in 1999. The biggest groups were from the neighboring countries of Russia, Estonia, and Sweden. The Finnish currency is the *markka.*

Lutherans constitute 86 percent of the population, with 1 percent of the population professing the Finnish Orthodox religion. Sweden, Norway, and Russia border Finland. Forests cover 68 percent of Finland, while 10 percent is water (188,000 lakes). Cultivated land constitutes 8 percent of Finnish territory with 14 percent listed as ''other.'' The official languages of the country are Finnish (92.6 percent), Swedish (5.7 percent), and other (1.7 percent). This latter figure is consistent with the percentage of foreign residents in Finland (1.7 percent in 1999). There are 2.5 million workers in the labor force (53 percent male and 47 percent female). The service industry comprises 64 percent of the labor force, with industry and construction making up 28 percent, and agriculture and farming making up the final 8 percent. Finnish exports are led by metal and engineering (43 percent), followed by paper (39 percent), with chemical, textiles, and clothing making up the final 18 percent. Finland's main trading partners are Germany, Sweden, and the United Kingdom. (Havén 1999)

Since 1917 Finland has been a sovereign parliamentary republic with a separately elected president. The president's term is six years. Two hundred members of parliament are elected for four-year terms. The voting age is 18 and is universal. The major political parties in Finland are the Social Democrats, Center Party of Finland, National Coalition Party, Left Alliance, Green League, Swedish People's Party of Finland, and Christian League of Finland. As of the March 1999 election, women held 37 percent of the seats in parliament, the largest female percentage in the European Union. For administrative purposes the country is divided into six provinces (*laanit*): Aland, Etela-Suomen Laani, Ita-Suomen Laani, Lansi-Suomen Laani, Lappi, and Oulun Laani.

Geographically, Finland is in the far north of Europe. This means that the southern tip of Finland has 19 hours of sun in the summer and 6 hours of sun in the winter. In the northernmost parts of the country, on the other hand, the sun does not rise for about six weeks in winter and does not set for about two months in summer. Despite its northern location, the Baltic Sea warms the south of the country so that both summer and winter temperatures are moderate.

Health care in Finland is under the guidance of the Ministry of Social Affairs and Health. While the ministry sets board guidelines and supervises the implementation of programs, the delivery of health services lies with the approximately 450 local municipal authorities. These authorities provide services independently or in cooperation with neighboring municipalities in joint municipal boards set up in a joint health center. Health services are funded with national and local taxes with around 10 percent of costs covered by the patient. Life expectancy at birth is 77.41 years for the total population. For males it is 73.74 years, while females have a life expectancy of 81.2 years.

There are 56 weekly newspapers (published 4 to 7 times a week) and 158 weekly newspapers (published from 1 to 3 times a week). The total circulation of all newspapers is 3.3 million. The Finnish Broadcasting Company, *Oy Yleiradio Ab* (YLE), is the biggest national radio and television provider. YLE is a noncommercial public service broadcaster that operates two television channels with full national coverage. There are 2 privately owned TV channels with national coverage and some 30 local TV stations. The only radio broadcaster with full nationwide coverage is YLE. The importance of electronic media is growing fast. Internet connections per capita in Finland were the highest in the world in 1999 with 25 Internet users per 100 inhabitants.

CONSTITUTIONAL & LEGAL FOUNDATIONS

The overall responsibility for educational, scientific, and cultural policies lies with the Ministry of Education. The ministry has responsibilities beyond schools and universities, promoting education, science, culture, sports, and youth work in the country, and emphasizing their significance for the citizens and society at large.

There are two ministers at the Ministry of Education: the Minister of Education and Science is in charge of education and research and the Minister of Culture is responsible for matters relating to culture, sports, youth, copyright, student financial aid, and church affairs.

In 1922, the Ministry of Education took its current name, though many of its functions date back to the beginning of autonomy in 1809 (the Grand Duchy of Russia), when the ministry started as the Senate Department of Ecclesiastical Affairs. This name is significant as education in Finland has traditionally included religious instruction (predominately, the Evangelical Lutheran of Finland or the Orthodox Church of Finland). When Finland gained independence in 1917, the name was first changed to the Department of Ecclesiastical Affairs and Education; in 1918, the senate became the Council of State and the departments became ministries. In 1922, the name of the Ministry of Education and Ecclesiastical Affairs was shortened to the Ministry of Education.

The relationship between the state and the church needs further explanation. While the Finnish state takes a neutral role with regard to religion and churches, it takes a hands-on approach with regard to the funding of the education of clergy in university faculties of theology and with denominational instruction in elementary and secondary school. The Ministry of Education also provides for ethics education for school children that have no denominational affiliation.

The majority of education is publicly funded using a two-tiered system: the national government and the local authorities. The national government funds 57 percent of the operating expenses of the schools based on a per pupil/per lesson or unit ratio. The municipal portion of the funding follows the student, rather than staying with the school district where the student began instruction.

Educational Philosophies: The overall educational philosophy in Finland is the promotion of citizen's "well-being, cultural wealth, sustainable development and economic success" (Ministry of Education 1999). Each of the four areas for educational development have an important part in the philosophy of education. The individual well-being is listed first. The developmental plan states that all citizens have a right to appropriate education according to their level of development. Equally important is the context for individual instruction; instruction occurs for the enhancement of cultural wealth, sustainable development, and economic success. In other words, the education of the individual is seen within a social-cultural-economic context. Efforts to raise general educational standards and to promote equality should be understood within that context.

The following statement from the Basic Education Act underscores the situating of education within an individual-cultural-social-economic matrix:

> The objective of basic education is to support pupils' growth toward humanity and ethical responsible membership of society, and to provide them with the knowledge and skills necessary in life. The instruction shall promote equality in society and the pupils' abilities to participate in education and to otherwise develop themselves during their lives (626/1998).

While this objective applies to compulsory basic education or comprehensive school education, it sets the tone for the philosophy of all Finnish education and is very consistent with educational objectives for upper secondary, vocational, university, and polytechnic education. For example, the objective for upper secondary schools has phrases like "balancing and civilizing individuals and members of society" and "furthering . . . the versatile development of their personal interests." The vocational objective is intended to foster "students' development into good and balanced individuals and members of society."

A statement by Jukka Sarjala, Director General of the National Board of Education, called "the school of civilization in the information society," adds another element to the overall philosophy of education in Finland. Sarjala places education in Finland within the context of ancient and Enlightenment philosophy that put goodness, beauty, and truth at the center of the civilizing function of culture and schools within the culture. Finnish education begins with the assumption drawn from the Enlightenment that we are born ignorant and become civilized through education.

The information age must be accompanied with a citizenry equipped to access and evaluate the great increase of data now available. This task requires a view of the person, the pupil, and the citizen as an active and not a passive learner (Sarjala 2001). From an administrative perspective, the national government sets the overall standards for educational outcomes, while local school authorities establish the methods and approaches to reaching those standards.

EDUCATIONAL SYSTEM—OVERVIEW

The Ministry of Education oversees education as schooling and as culture. Within education, the Minister of Education and Sciences oversees the schools and universities including the divisions of general education, vocational education, polytechnic, university, adult education and training, and science policy.

Compulsory Education: Basic education is required of all pupils between the ages of 7 and 16. It is free, and students can chose the school they wish to attend, including several private schools. However, most students attend a public school in their local community. If it is not possible for pupils to attend school for medical or other reasons, the municipality in which the pupil resides must provide alternate instruction that is equivalent to that of the regular school. Free transportation is provided for students who live five kilometers or more from school.

Teaching groups in basic education are organized according to forms or years. A teacher stays with one group of pupils for the year during the first six years of basic education. In the highest three forms, pupils are taught by subject area (i.e., mathematics, history, language).

Age Limits: Comprehensive, compulsory education is nine years in duration. Pupils begin school during the year that they turn 7 and end when they turn 17 or when they complete their comprehensive school syllabus, whichever comes first.

Enrollment: There were 591,700 pupils enrolled in 4,203 schools in 1998. These pupils were taught by 39,751 teachers (about a 15 to 1 pupil to teacher ratio). School sizes range from fewer than 10 to over 900 pupils. The male/female population in the comprehensive schools approximately parallels the population of the country with 48.8 percent of the school population being girls.

Academic Year: The academic year begins in late August and ends in late June. The school year is divided into autumn and spring terms, totaling 190 school days.

Language of Instruction: There are three languages of instruction in Finland: Finnish (Suomea), Swedish (Sverge), and Lapp (Sámi). Each school has its own language of instruction, and native speakers attend the school consistent with their language. The national matriculation examinations are also set up to honor the three language groups within Finland.

Examination: National matriculation examinations take place twice a year in the spring and autumn and are held in all upper secondary schools. The first national matriculation examination took place in 1852 under the Grand Duchy of Russia. Today it is a school leaving examination intended to test what was taught in the upper secondary schools. There are no national examinations required to get into basic education schools or lower secondary schools.

Candidates must take four compulsory tests: the mother tongue test, the second official language test, the foreign language test, and either the mathematics test or the general studies test. Each test is arranged at two different levels according to difficulty. While the tests are organized according to the curriculum the pupil takes, the student may chose either level of the examination regardless of their preparation. The head of the upper secondary school will check to see whether the candidate fulfills the requirements laid down to participate in the examination and tests that are part of it. Three of the four required subject tests can be taken at the lower level and passed, but at least one must be taken and passed at an upper level. Students who do not pass a test may retake it in the examination period immediately following the compulsory examination that he or she failed.

The original purpose of the examination was to determine admission to the University of Helsinki. Today, the purpose of the examination is to determine if pupils have the knowledge and skills of the upper secondary school curriculum. If a student passes the examination, they may continue to university studies. The test is in two parts, compulsory and optional. The grades and points for the examinations are as follows: *laudatur* (7), *eximia cum*

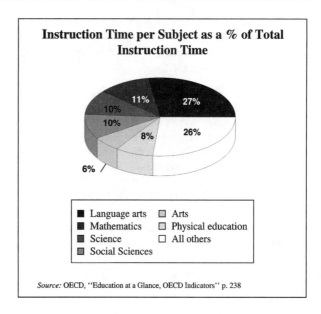

Instruction Time per Subject as a % of Total Instruction Time

11% 10% 10% 27% 8% 26% 6%

■ Language arts   □ Arts
■ Mathematics   □ Physical education
■ Science   □ All others
■ Social Sciences

Source: OECD, "Education at a Glance, OECD Indicators" p. 238

laude approbatur (6), *magna cum laude approbatur* (5), *cum laude approbatur* (4), *lubenter approbatur* (3), *approbatur* (2), and *improbatur* (0).

Private Schools: The only private schools in Finland are preprimary (for children between three and six years of age). There were 12,000 private preprimary schools and 105,200 municipal preprimary schools in 1998. Another 7,400 preprimary schools are located within comprehensive schools.

Religious Schools: Religion is a part of the curriculum in Finnish schools. All students take classes in Lutheran or Orthodox studies with the exception of those students who are not affiliated with those two major religious groups. Those students who practice other religions or who profess no religion are required to take a life philosophy course to replace religious instruction.

Instructional Technology (Computers): In 1995 the government issued a plan called Education, Training, and Research in an Information Society. The purpose of this effort was to promote national competitiveness and employment and to explore ways to provide wide access to these technologies by identifying the means for giving citizens basic skills in using information and communication technologies (Ministry of Education 1999). The Ministry of Education funded this project, which was monitored and evaluated by the Information Strategies Group of the ministry and the Finnish National Fund for Research and Development. Most of the grants in this project went to equipment acquisition and network building in educational establishments, universities, libraries, and archives.

The goal for Finnish education with regards to technology and development are ambitious. "Education, Training and Research in Information Society: A National Strategy for 2000-2004" states:

> By the year 2004, Finland will be a leading interactive knowledge society. Success will be based on citizens' equal opportunities to study and develop their own intellectual capacity and extensively utilize information resources and educational services. A high-quality, ethically and economically sustainable mode of operation in network-based teaching and research will have been established (Ministry of Education 2001).

Textbooks—Publication & Adoption: Textbooks are adopted on a national basis through the National Board of Education with consultation with experts and classroom and subject matter teachers.

Audiovisuals: Finnish schools are very current in terms of the use of audiovisual material and have a major project underway to make Finland among the leaders in Internet use in classrooms and in the larger society.

Curriculum—Development: Curriculum development is overseen and directed by the National Board of Education within the Ministry of Education. Curriculum development for comprehensive schools is usually a part of a national strategy. Curriculum formulation and implementation is based on long-term commitments and comprehensive planning, often including more that one ministry. The curriculum is locally implemented based on teacher training and supported by research and evaluation.

Foreign Influences on Educational System: Sweden and Russia have traditionally influenced Finnish education. Since about the middle of the twentieth century, Finnish education has looked to best practices all around the world with special attention paid to the Baltic states (especially after the demise of the Soviet Union). There are various Baltic country efforts concerning education including a project of environmental education. In the information society national strategy, specific references are made to policies and initiatives in the United States, Japan, and the European Union, with special reference to Denmark and Sweden. In many matters relating to research and education, Finland has been very active in learning from and providing leadership within the European Union.

Role of Education in Development: Finland has a developmental plan for education and university research set up in five year cycles. "Education and research form a vital part of the Finnish strategy for promoting citizens' well-being, cultural wealth, sustainable development,

and economic success" (Ministry of Education 2001). Finnish education is guided by a commitment to high quality equal opportunities for school and university-based education as well as a commitment to lifelong learning. Educational research is guided by a commitment to research ethics and a balance between basic and applied research. The education ministry sees this approach as leading to economic development. The development plan looks to provide basic security in education, lifelong learning, a mutual relationship between education and employment, the globalization of everyday life, diverse language programs, information accessing strategies, and quality through evaluation.

PREPRIMARY & PRIMARY EDUCATION

General Survey: Preprimary and primary education has two major divisions, preprimary and comprehensive schools. In 1998, there were 124,600 preprimary pupils attending programs in municipal and private schools, as well as preprimary education programs held at comprehensive school. These programs are not officially a part of the Finnish education system, but plans are underway to reform preprimary education.

The classification of schooling into primary and secondary schools does not fit the Finnish model. Finns distinguish between compulsory schooling and upper secondary schooling. The compulsory schooling is divided into two parts: primary school and lower secondary school. Primary schooling begins the year the student turns seven years old and is provided at no cost to the pupil. There are no admission requirements for primary school. Instruction is arranged in schools near the pupil's home. There are about 4,200 comprehensive schools throughout the country with about 380,000 pupils. The comprehensive schools are organized in forms or total class instruction units. Primary school goes from form one through form six.

There are three additional years of comprehensive education but this part of the child's education is completed in what the Finns call lower secondary school (grades seven to nine). Lower secondary pupils study in subject area classrooms rather than in forms or age-based classes. Students in lower secondary school can take an extra tenth year of schooling to satisfactorily complete their curriculum. Pupils are required to complete the curriculum in order to complete their compulsory education.

Curriculum—Examinations: The government determines broad national objectives and the allocation of teaching time. The National Board of Education decides on the objectives and core content of instruction. Within these parameters, the local educational authorities and individual teachers prepare the basic local curriculum. Pupils in the primary schools and lower secondary schools study their mother tongue and literature (Finnish or other national language), foreign language (beginning at the third form), environmental studies, civics, religion or ethics, history, social studies, mathematics, physics, chemistry, biology, geography, physical education, music visual arts, crafts, and home economics. Language instruction accounts for about one-third of instructional time in comprehensive schools. Science and mathematics makes up another third of instructional time. Instruction in the social sciences and the humanities comprise about 12 percent of instructional time. The remaining instructional time is divided among art, physical education, and other courses, including religion or ethics.

Local schools and teachers determine the granting of the final certificate upon acceptable completion of the syllabus for the comprehensive school. There is no national testing for completion of compulsory education. Pupils rarely interrupt or repeat a form. Almost all Finnish children complete comprehensive school. In 1996, some 99.7 percent of pupils finished comprehensive school. Finland has the highest percentage of pupils completing compulsory education in the world.

Urban & Rural Schools: Accessibility of schools is, on the average, good even though Finland has a low population density. More than 80 percent of comprehensive school pupils live less than five kilometers from their school. In northern Finland, the distance pupils have to travel to comprehensive school increases to between 50 and 75 kilometers. Pupils may have to travel as far as 100 kilometers to lower and upper secondary schools. Only a fifth of all pupils live in rural areas so the number of students who travel any distance to school is limited. Transportation is provided for all pupils living over five kilometers from their school.

Teachers: Comprehensive schoolteachers are required to obtain a master's of education degree. Only 10 percent of applications to teaching positions in the comprehensive schools are accepted because of the stringent selection criteria. Teachers salaries range from US$15,000 to US$25,600 (Nelson 1994).

SECONDARY EDUCATION

General Survey: Finnish education has two tracks for secondary education: general upper secondary education and vocational education and training. Both tracks are for students from 16 to 19 years of age. The number of students enrolled in upper secondary schools in 1999 was 111,328.

The general upper secondary education schools are for students who plan to attend university. The vocational

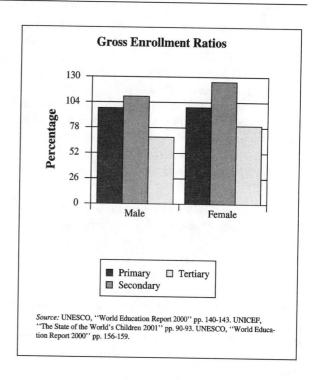

Gross Enrollment Ratios

Source: UNESCO, ''World Education Report 2000'' pp. 140-143. UNICEF, ''The State of the World's Children 2001'' pp. 90-93. UNESCO, ''World Education Report 2000'' pp. 156-159.

education and training schools are for students who are transitioning to the workplace upon completion of their secondary education. Students in both tracks may take the national matriculation examination and attend university if their scores are competitive.

The objective of general upper secondary education is to promote the development of students into good, balanced and civilized individuals and members of society and to provide students with the knowledge and skills necessary in further studies, working life, personal interests and the versatile development of their personality. Moreover, the education shall support the students' opportunity for lifelong learning and self-development during their lives. (Upper Secondary Schools Act 629/1998)

There are about 250 students in the average upper secondary school. Admission is based on completion of comprehensive school with students selected based on their previous study record. Students progress through their studies at their own pace within the context of a three-year curriculum. About half of the students complete upper secondary school.

Curriculum—Examinations & Diplomas: The curriculum is divided into compulsory, specialized, and applied courses. The curriculum in the upper secondary schools consists of 38 lessons organized around the following subjects: mother tongue and literature (Finnish or other national language), foreign language, a second foreign language, environmental studies, civics, religion or ethics, history, social studies, mathematics, physics, chemistry, biology, geography, physical education, music, visual arts, crafts, and home economics. Language instruction accounts for less than one-third of instructional time in comprehensive schools. Science and mathematics in the upper secondary schools constitute somewhat more than one-third of instructional time. This is a slight modification of instructional time in comprehensive schools. Instruction in the social sciences and humanities comprises about 18 percent of instructional time. The remaining 16 percent of instructional time is divided among art, physical education, and other courses, including religion or ethics.

The National Board of Education is responsible for the core objectives and the overall curriculum. Within these guidelines, the schools prepare a local curriculum. The matriculation examination is developed nationally with a centralized body to check examinations according to uniform criteria. Students are tested in four compulsory areas: Mother tongue, the other national language, a foreign language, and either mathematics or general studies. Students may chose to complete the examinations in three separate or one continuous examination period.

Teachers: Teachers in secondary schools are required to obtain a master's degree in the subject matter in which they will be teaching. There are 6,491 teachers in 447 secondary schools.

Vocational Education: Vocational training is largely conducted within vocational schools but efforts are underway to increase the number of apprenticeships to 10 percent of all enrollees. By law, local authorities have to maintain one place in vocational education for every 1,000 inhabitants. Around 45 percent of students between 16 and 19 years of age attend vocational schools. Local and national governments mutually fund the vocational institutes.

The training programs for vocational education are built on the comprehensive school curriculum. The curriculum consists of 120 credits: 20 credits of on the job learning, 90 credits of core subjects, and 10 credits chosen by the student. The core subjects are Finnish, Swedish, mathematics, physics and chemistry, social, business and labor-market subjects, physical and health education, and art and culture. Graduates from these programs may apply for admission to polytechnics or universities. Teachers in the vocational program usually have a master's degree or a polytechnic degree, three years of work experience in the field, and 35 credits in pedagogy.

The objective of initial vocational education is to provide students with the knowledge and skills necessary for acquiring vocational expertise and with capabilities for self-employment. The further objectives of the education are to promote the students' development into good and balanced individuals and members of society, to provide students with the knowledge and skills necessary in further studies, personal interests and the versatile development of personality, and to promote lifelong learning. (Vocational Education Act 630 1998)

In order to attend vocation schools, one must have completed the comprehensive school syllabus. Admission is generally based on comprehensive school performance, but students may arrange to take aptitude tests, and the applicants' work experience may also be considered. The program is generally three years long. On completion of the program, students may take the national matriculation examination and pursue their education at either a university or polytechnic. There were about 122,000 students enrolled in vocational schools in 2000.

Adult Education: More than 1 million Finns participate in some type of adult education, accounting for about 10 million classroom hours. This education is arranged by universities, polytechnics, vocational institutions, adult education centers and summer universities, adult upper secondary schools, study centers, sports institutes, and music institutes. There are also options for online courses and distance learning. Generally, adults engage in further education that is related to their employment. Courses allow adults to upgrade and update their employment-related knowledge and skills; however, this is not the only type of course adults take. Many adults are also interested in self-improvement and take courses in social studies and civic education.

HIGHER EDUCATION

There are two types of higher education institutions in Finland: universities and polytechnics (AMK institutions or *ammattkorkeakoulut*). There were 29 polytechnics as of fall 2000. There are 20 universities in Finland.

Polytechnics: Polytechnics provide instruction for expert functioning in the following areas: national resources, technology and communication, business and administration, tourism, catering and institutional management, health care, and social services among others. Lecturers are required to have a master's degree and principle lecturers need an academic postgraduate degree. Local and national governments fund the polytechnics (43 percent and 57 percent, respectively).

There are 3,118 full-time teachers and 1,261 part-time teachers in the polytechnics. Tourism, catering and institutional management, culture, natural resources, humanities, education in technology and communications, business and administration, health care, and social services follow the three largest enrollments. All degree programs have 20 credits (half of an academic year) in on-the-job training.

Universities: Universities offer bachelor's, master's, licentiate, and doctorates. Students generally complete a bachelor's degree in three years and a master's degree in five years. In cooperation with the Ministry of Education, each university conducts a three-year assessment to target outcomes for its overall operating principles.

> The purpose of universities is to promote independent research and scientific and artistic education, to provide instruction of the highest level based on research, and to raise the young to serve the fatherland and humankind. Universities shall arrange their operations in order for research, education and instruction to achieve high international standards, by observing ethical principles and good scientific practices. (University Act 645 1997)

Here is a list of universities in Finland: Abo Akademi University, HSme Polytechnic, Helsinki Business Polytechnic, Helsinki School of Economics, Helsinki University of Technology, Lahti Polytechnic, Lappeenranta University of Technology, Oulu Institute of Technology, Satakunta Polytechnic, Sibelius Academy, Swedish School of Economics and Business Administration (Finland), Tampere Institute of Technology, Tampere University of Technology, University of Art and Design Helsinki, University of Helsinki, University of Joensuu, University of JyvSskylS, University of Kuopio, University of Oulu, University of Tampere, University of Turku, and University of Vaasa.

The University of Helsinki is the oldest and largest university in the country. By a strange quirk of history, the University of Helsinki began as the "Academy of Turku." Turku was the former capital of Finland but when Finland was annexed to the Russian Empire in 1809, Helsinki became the capital, and in 1827, the university was transferred to Helsinki and then named Imperial Alexander University. There are about 33,000 students at the University of Helsinki. There are 3,063 teachers and researchers and 2,204 docents.

All universities in Finland are public. Ten of the universities are multidisciplinary, four are arts academies, three are schools of economics and business, and three are universities of technology. There is also a military academy, the National Defense College, that offers a degree in the military field.

Admission Procedures: Each university sets admission criteria and student selection procedures. University admission is highly competitive and annual intake quotas limit enrollment. Students must have completed and passed their matriculation examination. Additionally, various entrance examinations are included in the selection process.

The number of openings in all universities is limited to about one-third of the students of university age. The number of applications each year is around 66,000 and about 23,000 students are admitted.

Administration: University administration is independently organized under the University Act and Statute, 1997, 1998. Universities enjoy legal autonomy and can decide their own research and teaching policies. The highest official at the university is the chancellor. Decision-making is under the guidance of the senate made up of the rector, the first vice rector, one professor from each faculty, three other teachers and researchers, and seven students, one of whom must be a postgraduate. The dean and faculty councils are in charge of the faculties. The faculty elects both the dean and the vice-dean.

Enrollment: The number of undergraduates is about 128,000. Additionally there are approximately 19,000 post-baccalaureate students. In 1998, the universities graduated 16,500 students.

Teaching Styles & Techniques: There has been a move in recent years to shift instruction towards a more student-oriented direction by developing interactive, discussion friendly learning environments. There are large lecture classes and smaller discussion classes and seminars. University teaching aims at developing a critical mind, gaining and contributing to knowledge within a bilingual and multicultural perspective.

Finance (Tuition Costs): All education in Finland is tax supported. Students pay no tuition and receive free teaching material. Universities receive 1,131,000 Euros annually from the national government.

Courses, Semesters, & Diplomas: One hundred twenty credits are required for a bachelor's degree, while 160-180 credits are required for a master's degree. It takes an additional 6.5 years to complete a master's degree, with 4 additional years required for a doctorate. The academic year consists of two terms: the fall term running from August 1 to December 31 and the spring term running from January 1 to July 31. Christmas vacation lasts 20 days, 10 before and 10 after Christmas.

Degrees are awarded in natural sciences, humanities, industrial arts, sports sciences, theology, social sciences, business administration, psychology education, agriculture and forestry, health care, musicology, theatre, and dance. A bachelor's thesis is required. No lower degrees in medicine, engineering, or defense are offered. There is both a lower and upper degree in law.

Professional Education: Professional education is offered in medicine, dentistry, and veterinary medicine. The universities of Helsinki, Kuopio, Oulu, Tampere, and Turku have medical faculties. Basic medical education takes at least six years and leads to the degree of licentiate in medicine. In these fields, one first earns a practice degree or licentiate (between 200 and 250 credits) and then may continue to a doctorate that involves more coursework and the writing of a dissertation. Eighteen percent of physicians in Finland have taken the degree of doctor of medicine.

Postgraduate Training: After completing a bachelor's degree, students may pursue a master's degree, then a licentiate, and then a doctorate. All of the 10 multidisciplinary universities offer advanced degrees. In 1997, a total of 1,790 advanced research degree were awarded: 860 licentiates and 930 doctorates. About 40 percent of doctorates in Finland are awarded to women, while over half of all degrees go to women.

Foreign Students: There are about 8,000 international students studying at universities in Finland. The Finnish government does not assist foreign students. Admission to university by foreign students is the same as that for Finnish students with the individual universities establishing the selection criteria for admission. National health services are available to foreign students who also receive special concession for travel by air, road, and rail.

Students Abroad: Finnish students who study abroad are given a stipend to support themselves. The tuition of the host institution is paid for by the national government. Students (usually postgraduate students) submit applications to study abroad. Trying to receive these grants is highly competitive, and successful applications depend both on national priorities and student abilities.

Role of Libraries: The role of both university and individual faculty libraries is at the heart of education. University libraries in Finland work towards integrated and electronically-assessable collections. While printed material remains central to libraries, the integration of print and electronic materials is essential to keeping current in the various disciplines. This process will require increased cooperation within a single university as well as between universities.

ADMINISTRATION, FINANCE, & EDUCATIONAL RESEARCH

The Finnish parliament sets the broad educational agenda, fixes the general principles of educational policies, and frames educational legislation. The government, Ministry of Education, and National Board of Education are responsible for the implementation of policy at the central administrative level. The Ministry of Education takes a big picture approach to education. Its areas of responsibility include education, research, culture, youth affairs, ecclesiastical affairs, and sports, as well as copyright issues.

The National Board of Education (NBE) is the educational action arm of the Ministry of Education with re-

sponsibility for the development of educational objectives, content, and methods used in basic, general upper secondary, vocational, and adult education and training. It is also the board's responsibility to prepare and adapt the core curriculum for the schools and to the Finnish education system (not including universities and polytechnics).

The NBE has three main areas of operation: development of education, evaluation of education, and support services. The board has about 300 experts in different fields with a budget of approximately US$20 million, of which 10 percent is covered by sales activities. In addition, NBE uses national and international development funding of about US$200 million.

NBE supplies development, evaluation, and information services regarding education to managers of schools, teachers, policymakers, and employers. NBE works to support national education policy, to cooperate internationally, and to interact broadly and extensively with national interest groups in a client-oriented way. Its goal is to positively affect education and the Finnish economy.

Educational Budgets: The budget for the year 2000 for all areas of education was 4,696 million Euros. This includes expenditures for both the Ministry of Education (3,583 million Euros) and the Ministry of Culture (1,079 million Euros). The education budget makes up 14 percent of all public expenditures: early childhood education is 9.2 percent, primary education is 22.7 percent, secondary education is 36.9 percent, and tertiary education is 26.2 percent. This expenditure was 6.4 percent of the gross national product in 1996.

National Education Organizations: Among the national educational organizations in Finland are teachers' organizations, student associations, research institutions, developmental centers, and national boards. The teachers' organizations include the Trade Union of Education, Association of Kindergarten Teachers, Trade Union of Adult Educators, Federation of Adult Educators, Federation of Physical Education Teachers, and Science Teachers' Association. There is one national upper secondary school organization, the national school students' organization.

There are 22 research institutions, development centers, and national boards. The Academy of Finland is one of the key national educational organizations. It is an expert organization for research funding. The academy seeks to enhance the quality and reputation of Finnish basic research by funding projects on a competitive basis, by systematic evaluation, and by influencing scientific policy. The academy's operations cover all scientific disciplines, from archaeology to space research and from cell biology and psychology to electronics and environmental research. It operates within the administrative sector of the Ministry of Education.

Educational Research: One of the major research efforts underway was established by the National Strategy for Education, Training and Research in the Information Society (1995). An expert committee was set up to develop a strategy accessing effective utilization of information technology by the society as a whole. It was believed national competitiveness and employment would increase if these strategies were effective. To this end, proposals were made to increase the availability and use of information and to assess the needs and identify the means for giving citizens basic skills in using information and communication technologies. This research agenda falls within the national vision that states "Finnish society will develop and utilize the opportunities inherent in the information society to improve quality of life, knowledge, international competitiveness and interaction in an exemplary versatile and sustainable way" (Ministry of Education 2001).

An action research agenda has been established as a part of the information society efforts for 2001 to 2004. The following amounts have been set aside to research this goal: 7.5 million Euros for information skills for all, 6 million Euros for network as a learning environment, 3.3 million Euros for accumulating digital information capital, and 9 million Eros for strengthening information society structures in education, training, and research.

Additional research goes on in universities and polytechnics that are largely under the direction of university internal strategies. Other smaller projects are also funded and supported by the Ministry of Education and the National Board of Education.

NONFORMAL EDUCATION

Adult Education: Adult education is available through universities and polytechnics, public and private institutions, adult education centers, and summer universities. Adult upper secondary schools, study centers and institutes, sports centers, and music institutes also offer adult education programs. In-service training, outside the normal educational institutions, provided by employers, is the most common form of adult education.

Continuing adult education is a response to the changing economic situation that includes increased competition, information technology, and internationalization. To remain competitive, the Finnish government recognized a need for lifelong learning among all its citizens. About 10 million classroom hours are devoted to adult education each year for about 1 million adults.

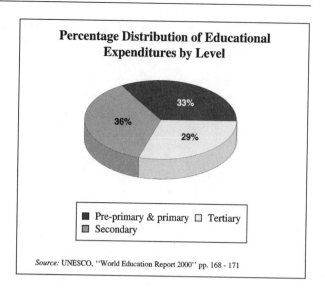

Percentage Distribution of Educational Expenditures by Level

- ■ Pre-primary & primary □ Tertiary
- ▨ Secondary

33%
36%
29%

Source: UNESCO, "World Education Report 2000" pp. 168 - 171

Face-to-face education is generally provided in the evenings and on weekends. Online courses are also available for adult education, often making use of workplace resources, but are also available in the evenings at home via personal computers.

Open Universities: Open university courses, as opposed to adult education, are generally for credit and may apply to the completion of an upper secondary school degree or to a university degree. Admission is dependent on the student—in other words, there are no admission standards to begin the program. However, the same standards apply to course evaluation and program completion as for courses taken at regular upper secondary schools, universities, or polytechnics.

Universities and polytechnics offer programs for non-degree and degree-seeking students through the open university. The open university system is widespread and easily accessible to all potential students. Students do not receive support in terms of transportation allowances or other student subsidies but part time open university students may continue eligibility for unemployment.

The open university allows students to complete their upper secondary school education by taking evening and weekend classes. Students may also work toward a university degree through open university or just take classes in their areas of interest. Some open university classes are offered over the Internet.

TEACHING PROFESSION

Training & Qualifications: Universities provide teacher education. Classroom teachers (*loukanopettaja*) who teach most of the subjects at the lower stages of comprehensive schools must have a master's degree in education, which is called *maisteri*. The degree amounts to 160 credits and studies take 5 years including practical training.

The education for subject teachers (who teach different subjects at the higher stages, beginning with lower elementary schools and including upper secondary schools) occurs at universities in respective faculties. These teachers must obtain a master's degree in a given field. It takes 5 years of study and amounts to 160-180 credits, including practical training. Teachers at vocational institutions have either a vocational diploma or a university degree. They complete their pedagogical training and teaching practice at vocational training colleges.

Salaries: Teachers' salaries start at US$16,500. The maximum salary is US$25,500. These salaries are for teachers who were prepared after legislation was passed requiring all teachers to have a master's degree before they can teach.

SUMMARY

General Assessment: Finland has a strong, inclusive, and in many ways "cutting edge" educational system. The compulsory education (ages 7 to 16) has the highest completion rate in the world. The upper secondary and vocational programs for 16 to 19 year old students provides education and access to over 75 percent of children this age. Finnish universities are internationally recognized for their quality.

Finland has a high percentage of citizens, including compulsory school pupils and secondary students, with access to computers and the Internet. The government, under the Ministry of Education, has initiated a research project to insure equitable access to technology for all Finns. This is one strong indication of the government's commitment to an equitable quality education.

International Programs: Finland is very involved with the European Community, the Baltic states, and the Nordic countries. Among other projects, the Baltic states are involved in an environmental project involving primary school pupils working to improve environmental conditions of the waters that connect the Baltic states. Individual Finnish schools are involved in many international educational programs, one of which is "Philosophy for Children."

Needs for Changes—Future: Most Finns see themselves not only as citizens of Finland and of Europe, but also as citizens of the world. This outward looking view is expressed in educational goal statements at all levels of education. Finland will continue to improve its educational policies and practices within that local and international perspective.

One of the hallmarks of Finnish education is its willingness to state its values clearly and boldly. The objectives developed by the National Board of Education list the goals of citizenship, full personal development, participation in culture, and involvement in Finnish, European, and world affairs as essential for an educated person. This approach to full human development and internationalism sets a high standard for citizens and educational institutions.

Finns also value equality of access to national resources, especially education. As the Internet is seen as one of the tools that will enhance education in the near future, access to it is now actively under study. The Finnish government and educational establishments are very concerned about the potential disparity of access to the World Wide Web. A three-year research program was underway in 2000 to assess the extent of that disparity and figure out possible solutions to narrow that gap. This project is a strong indicator of the way that the Finnish educational establishment works at self-improvement and towards the goal of an educated citizenry who will be able to function effectively in the twenty-first century.

BIBLIOGRAPHY

Havén, Heikki (ed.), *Education in Finland. Statistics and Indicators. SVT Education 1999: 4.* Helsinki: Statistics Finland, 1999.

Jakobson, M. *Finland in the New Europe.* Westport, CT: Greenwood Publishing Group, 1998.

Ministry of Education. *Education: Development Plan for Education and University Research for 1995—2000.* Helsinki: Ministry of Education, 1996.

———. *Education, Training, and Research in the Information Society: A National Strategy.* Ministry of Education, 1995.

———. *Higher Education Policy in Finland.* Helsinki: Ministry of Education, 1998.

National Board of Education. *Framework Curriculum for the Comprehensive School 1994.* Helsinki: National Board of Education, 1994.

———. *Framework Curriculum for the Senior Secondary School 1994.* Helsinki: National Board of Education, 1994.

———. *The Education System of Finland 1998.* National Board of Education, Helsinki 1999 and Database of Eurydice Network, Eurybase 1999.

Nelson, H. *Development on School Finance.* National Center for Educational Statistics, 1994.

Sarjala, J. *The School of Civilisation in the Information Society.* Helsinki: National Board of Education, 2001.

Statistics Finland. *Statistics on Educational Institutions 1998. SVT Koulutus 1998:5.* Helsinki: Statistics Finland, 1998.

Vocational Education and Training in Finland. CEDE-FOP, Office for Official Publications of the European Communities, 1997.

—*Richard Morehouse*

FRANCE

BASIC DATA

Official Country Name:	French Republic
Region:	Europe
Population:	59,329,691
Language(s):	French, Provencal, Breton, Alsatian, Corsican, Catalan, Basque, Flemish
Literacy Rate:	99%
Academic Year:	September-June
Number of Primary Schools:	41,000
Compulsory Schooling:	10 years
Public Expenditure on Education:	6.0%
Foreign Students in National Universities:	138,191
Libraries:	2,577
Educational Enrollment:	Primary: 4,004,704 Secondary: 5,979,690 Higher: 2,062,495
Educational Enrollment Rate:	Primary: 105% Secondary: 111% Higher: 51%
Teachers:	Primary: 211,192 Secondary: 483,493 Higher: 141,410
Student-Teacher Ratio:	Primary: 19:1
Female Enrollment Rate:	Primary: 104% Secondary: 111% Higher: 57%

HISTORY & BACKGROUND

The great cathedral schools of the eleventh century in Paris, Chartres, Laon, Orléans, and Tours first saw the light of day in France; over the twelfth century these schools would transform themselves into the prototype of the modern university. *Universitas* was the term used then to designate guilds (like that of butchers, vintners, and other trades) and came also to mean groupings of masters. From the eleventh through the fifteenth centuries, the Paris schools attracted teachers and students from all over Roman Catholic Europe.

Around 1050 the cathedral schools came into their own with a curriculum that focused on the language-based *trivium* (the liberal arts), identified as grammar, rhetoric, and dialectic (logic). Young pupils were taught to read, write, and speak in Latin, as well as selections from a corpus of pagan and Christian writers. They were shown how to imitate these models in order that they too might become models for posterity.

From today's standpoint, twelfth-century education in the cathedral schools and monasteries was as anarchic as it was exuberant and, all in all, foundational. The proliferation of schools and masters soon rendered it practically impossible for many local bishops to fully control and organize in a systematic way the schools and teachers present within their jurisdictions. The awarding of degrees, the career choices, and the life of most students were all rather chaotic. For the most part, students were destitute and obliged to find ways to keep alive. Their ways of doing so were often illegal.

As the century wore on a new system was introduced: a pupil who had completed his secondary education in the *trivium* was awarded the diploma of bachelor by the director of studies of his school; his qualification was based on his successfully passing an examination, usually oral in nature. The tripartite *trivium* led to advanced work in the four part *quadrivium*, the then called mathematical sciences composed of arithmetic, geometry, astronomy, and harmony (music).

The student who mastered this curriculum and who successfully participated in exercises known as disputations, was judged worthy of being awarded a license to teach (*licencia docendi*). He became a "master of arts" and could be admitted to the ranks of those who lectured, wrote, and formed younger students within what would become in the thirteenth century the Faculty of Arts.

By no means did all successful students go on to ecclesiastical careers. A significant number of school trained clerics served noble lay patrons, often as part of the royal or other noble bureaucracy that was burgeoning in French-speaking territories throughout the twelfth and early thirteenth centuries. Diplomacy, civil and legal administration, finances, and record-keeping, as well as written entertainment, all required well-schooled personnel.

If the eleventh and twelfth centuries sowed the seeds, they came to fruition principally in the thirteenth century with the founding of the university. In Medieval Latin *universitas* meant merely a corporation, usually of tradesmen, who exercised the same profession (shoemakers, barbers, etc.) or more or less what is understood today as a "guild." By definition and custom, the new university was international (its masters and students hailed from all over Christian Europe) and its purposes were to place human reason and intelligence at the service of the faith.

Since the ultimate ambition of Paris was to prepare for, undertake, and develop studies in theology, other more specialized university institutions were founded elsewhere in France. This was not done though in response to a centralized plan. A former center of literary study, Orléans, was chosen for the study of law; Montpellier dedicated itself to the study of medicine; and, as a result of the combat against the Cathar heresy, the University of Toulouse was founded as a kind of copy of Paris. Each of these institutions was granted a charter directly by the Pope.

For all intents and purposes, university governance was vested in its faculty (or faculties). In Paris, by midcentury, the chancellor had been forced to give up his former power. Power was transferred to a rector who, at the start, was merely the head of the Faculty of Arts and was elected as such by the professors of that faculty. He was aided by elected representatives (procurators) of each of the Four Nations into which students and masters were classified. Deans, or heads of the other faculties, were also directly elected by the masters. Considerable power was also enjoyed by a General Assembly of the faculties in which votes were taken not on an individual basis, but according to the seven "orders" constituting it. The interests of minorities were thus defended against the superior numbers of the more populous orders. Thus, the freedoms of individual teachers and groups of teachers were protected from outside interference as well as interference from the inside. Neither the bishop nor the king could force policies on the university as a whole or on parts of it; groups within the university could not force their views on other groups.

In this pragmatic manner a set of governing principles emerged that, by and large, still constitute the foundations of the institution known throughout the world as the university. International in scope from its very beginnings, the university was very much France's gift to education.

The day to day life of masters and students was hardly idyllic, at least not materially. Generally speaking, masters received no salary; they subsisted on what they could charge for administering examinations, although at times students gave them what they could. Only late in the century were there buildings designed for lecturing and giving examinations to students; before then masters rented out cheap halls that were usually miserably equipped. Costs for students varied greatly. The baccalaureate cost but a few pounds (under 100 gold francs or 20 gold dollars in pre-1913 money), while a doctorate in theology cost around 4,000 gold francs. Payment for taking examinations was calculated as follows: the basic living costs of a student (minus his rent and domestic servant) for one week were determined, and according to varying circumstances, the examination cost charged to him was several times the sum reached. Students varied in age from post-puberty to much older. The minimum age for taking the baccalaureate examinations in arts was 14, whereas 35 appears to have been the minimum age for a master of theology (who was required to spend some dozen years in specialized readings and courses). After receiving the licentiate in theology, the candidate was further required to sustain two lengthy argumentations before the entire faculty to which, along with all the bachelors of theology, all were invited to participate. It was only then that he could be officially received as a master.

The thirteenth century also saw the founding of many colleges within the university. A large number of these came into being through the initiative of individuals, often members of the royal family, churchmen, and provincial nobles desirous of establishing locales for study on behalf of students from their part of the kingdom. At the beginning, these colleges were essentially student residences; however, over time, masters were appointed to them.

The overwhelming majority of primary schools were run by the local parish priest who, in addition to the catechism, taught the bare rudiments of reading and writing. By no means were such schools freely open to all boys, let alone girls. Usually enrollments were open only to the sons of wealthy burghers and tradesmen and, from time to time, to especially gifted and motivated candidates for priesthood.

The peasant class in France remained largely illiterate until well into the nineteenth century. At times, a local convent or monastery sponsored a school; these were usually better equipped for serious primary/secondary learning than that of the poor parish priest. Girls were sometimes taught, though rarely, at nunneries, especially if they were of the aristocracy and/or seen as possibly having a religious vocation. Until the Revolution of 1789 the kings of France regularly sent their daughters to be educated at the feminine Abbey of Fontevrault in the Loire valley. It is consequently impossible to generalize about the state of primary education in medieval France; much depended on the circumstances of location and the conditions at given times. Thus, in 1324, the cathedral chapter at Chartres required every parish priest to maintain a school, but elsewhere, in poorer areas, such was not the case. During the bad times of the Black Death and Hundred Years War, primary education surely suffered as much as the universities did.

The disasters befalling France during the years 1340-1450 were reflected by a general decline of excellence in university education. The English and Burgundian wars of the period embroiled everyone, including the universities, in conflicts of interest and political turmoil. The university lost its marked international character as its leaders sought protection and support from new secular masters.

Indeed, the very organization of schools that came to be during the sixteenth century remains substantially the same as the kind of organization that still prevails in 2001: one building, housing pupils of different ages and consequently at different stages of preparation; the required breakdown of pupils into class years; six years of primary classes followed by another four to six years of more advanced preparation; and the whole leading to the pupil's earning a bachelor's diploma (more or less the equivalent of the modern French *baccalauréat*). Much pedagogical experimentation took place in these Renaissance schools, such as the elaboration of a direct method designed to teach the young pupils to speak Latin fluently. These innovations did not invariably meet with the unqualified approval of the traditional institutions of learning, particularly the Sorbonne and its Faculty of Theology, which remained faithful to ''tried and true'' disputation and dialectic. Consequently, the new breed of Humanists sought to create a brand new institution of higher learning, a kind of anti-Sorbonne that would be partial to their interests.

The Collège Royal was the first effort in France at putting into effect a truly ''public,'' State-recognized educational institution. Administratively, the Collège Royal was highly innovative. No degree was required in order to lecture there. A generally recognized distinction was the sole criterion of a professor's suitability for election to one of its chairs. Nor were students selected on the basis of any prior preparation. Anyone could attend lectures there. No examinations were given, nor were diplomas awarded. Attendance required no payment of tuition since the college's professors received (theoretically at least) a salary paid from the State treasury. Academic freedom characterized the teaching that went on there. A professor could, and did, lecture on the Psalms without possessing a degree from the Sorbonne and with no Faculty of Theology oversight or control. This state of affairs

infuriated the men of the Sorbonne who sought to close the college, but the king himself intervened and their suit was dismissed.

Little by little new disciplines and professors were added to the curriculum and the staff, such as mathematics, botany, astronomy, and Latin poetry. One professor, the influential Ramus, wrote a treatise demanding the systematic revision of the entire French system of education. Among the recommendations he made in his *Avertissement* was for a clearer distinction to be made between secondary and higher education (not achieved until the nineteenth century): secondary collèges would focus on grammar, rhetoric, and logic, while higher education would offer a more encyclopedic range of studies (including French grammar and literature). All education would be free and be paid for by the State. Indeed, the sixteenth century witnessed the rise of lay education. Schools founded and run by non-Churchmen proliferated as of this time. Many were paid for by local municipalities, as in the modern United States.

Generally speaking, however, despite individual successes here and there, the old universities underwent during the seventeenth century a process of decline whereas, especially during the second half of the century, the educational institutions founded and maintained by the Jesuit Order grew by leaps and bounds in size and influence. Their Paris college, the Collège de Clermont, became the Collège Royal in 1682 when it received the honor of being called Louis le Grand. The practicality of the Jesuits appealed to the bourgeoisie of the time who, as a class, were steadily gaining in wealth and power, just as the power of the potentially rebellious nobility was, as a matter of royal policy, declining. In many respects the Jesuits offered a kind of finishing school for the sons of the wealthy and socially conservative bourgeoisie. Teachings consisted of proper manners, geography and history, morality and religious formation, and proper and correct speech—in short, whatever it took to open up the world of affairs and officialdom to their clients. The education they offered, with its emphasis on good speaking and rhetoric, constituted an especially effective preparation for the Bar. What now is called the *haute bourgeoisie* in France is largely a seventeenth-century Jesuit creation.

Primary education was in far worse a situation. It remained totally under the control of the Church, local diocesan bishops, and parish priests. For the most part, teachers were miserably paid, especially in rural areas. They often doubled as assistants to the priest. Conditions varied a great deal from place to place. Reading and writing were taught, as was religion, but arithmetic was not always pursued. In some places an enterprising teacher would initiate his pupils in beginning Latin, but this was rare.

As the time of the great Revolution drew nearer, one notes a steady growth in the number of primary schools throughout the country: by 1776 the Haute-Marne region counted 473 schools in its 550 towns and villages; in 1750 the city of La Rochelle had about the same number of primary school pupils as it would in 1873. Yet, the diocese of Rieux counted a mere 41 schools for boys and 10 for girls out of 139 parishes. Illiteracy remained high. Though not entirely amenable to reliable interpretation, statistical studies have noted that on marriage acts about 47 percent of the men could sign their name while only 27 percent of the women could do so.

The consequences for public schooling in France were dreadful during the time separating 1914-1918 from 1939-1945, as can be imagined. Since the typical French infantry platoon was composed of about 40 men, mostly peasants, and a couple of non-commissioned officers, all led by a reservist second lieutenant who very frequently was a village or town school teacher (*instituteur*), the country's younger male teachers were almost wiped out as a class. Casualties among infantry lieutenants are generally the highest suffered by any Army rank.

The Revolution and the Napoleonic period that followed brought about massive change in the theory and practice of education. Despite some discontent with the inadequacies of public primary and secondary education, systematic reform of the *ancien régime* procedures was not at first a high Revolutionary priority. Increased funding was needed so that education might be offered to both rich and poor; the creation of a new centralized governmental agency was seen by some as needed to remedy inequities in educational opportunity throughout the nation. The old system remained in place until 1793. But with the passage of a bill in 1789 confiscating the property of ecclesiastic establishments and providing for their sale, decline set in due to lack of financial resources. Secondary education institutions had about 72,000 pupils in the country as a whole (with a population of approximately 20 million). The parish priest's approbation also remained necessary to the founding of a primary school.

At the end of the Second Empire, the university was in a lamentable state: the law and medicine faculties were bogged down in a repetitive kind of professional training, and arts and sciences had degenerated into a purely rhetorical lecture system. The Third Republic undertook important reforms. The university budget went from FF5,800,000 ($1.1 million gold dollars) to FF16,350,000, making a vast building program possible. The administrative structure was redesigned in such a way as to accord each faculty, led by a dean selected by the Education Minister upon proposal of its faculty, a substantial degree of faculty-controlled autonomy. The government, meanwhile, was represented by a rector nominated by the Ministry. Scholarship funding was provided, as were laboratory facilities for scientists and medical faculties. Student enrollments went from 9,000 in 1870, to 24,000 in 1892, to 41,000 in 1913. The basic post-*baccalauréat* degree remained in letters and sciences, the licentiate (*licence*), followed by the *diplôme d'études supérieures* (a kind of M.A. research degree requiring the writing of a thesis-like *mémoir*) and the thesis-based doctorate (the *doctorat d'université* and/or, in conjunction with the State competitive examination named the *aggregation*, the very prestigious *doctorat d'Éta* necessary for a university full professorship). This basic structure prevailed until well after 1945 and, indeed, remains the reference point for the many adjustments and reforms initiated subsequently to that date up to the present time.

It must be said, however, that quite unlike the situation prevailing in Great Britain, Germany, and the United States, the French university system, like its primary and secondary schooling (and *grandes écoles*), inherited the virtues and defects of Paris-focused centralization. Unlike the U.S. Department of Education, the Ministry of National Education exercised, and still exercises, virtual day to day control over teacher and faculty appointments, budgetary allocations, and other areas of policy. The minister himself is a political appointee, but aiding him is a tenured bureaucracy of civil servants (*fonctionnaires*) whose role in implementing policy is very powerful. *Tout passe par Paris* (Everything has to go through Paris) is no idle saying. Until the 1960s the monolithic and huge University of Paris enjoyed a prestige matched in no respect by any other institution. Many faculty members in provincial universities continued, and continue, to reside in Paris. Most of the grandest *grandes écoles* are located in the Paris area. The immensely rich Bibliothèque Nationale de France, the nation's incomparable research library has traditionally drawn to its collections the major part of the country's bibliographic resources.

In imitation of what its leaders believed the Revolution of 1789 had stood for, the Third Republic, almost immediately after its establishment, attempted to design and implement a unified and nation-wide educational system including all levels and types of school—the primary, the secondary, and the higher (both university and *grande école*). The system would be essentially free of tuition costs, open to all pupils, and students would be judged exclusively on merit.

In reality, the Republic built on what the July Monarchy law of 1833 had come to pass, especially on the primary level. In 1872 there existed some 50,000 community primary schools in France of which somewhat less than a third were Church-run (12,000 for girls and 3,000 for boys). Over 4 million pupils were enrolled in these schools (out of a primary school population of some 5 million). However, the country's illiteracy rate stood at about 20 percent. There existed some 70 *écoles normales* ("normal schools") for the training of male teachers, but only 12 for females. Work conditions for female primary teachers were miserable. Their annual salary averaged as little as 340 to 400 gold francs ($70 to $80 per year). It was up to the State to correct these imbalances. As of 1879 a law required each *département* to fund and equip decently an *école normale*. Only two years later, all tuition fees were abolished by law, and, in 1882, primary school attendance become obligatory. Moreover, each school teacher, whether public or religious, was required to hold the *Brevet de capacité* (a government-approved teaching certificate). Finally, in 1886, yet another law was passed providing for the obligatory replacement of religious teaching personnel in the school by state-certified laymen and women.

By law in 1886 the principal task of the non-ecclesiastical primary school teacher (*instituteur/ institutrice*) was to inculcate Republican morale in his or her pupils by stressing the latters' duty toward the family, the school itself, the *patrie*, the personal dignity of persons, charitable one's fellow man and community, and animals. In addition, the six-year core curriculum also focused on reading and writing, elements of mathematics (addition, subtraction, division, multiplication, fractions and abstract reasoning), French history and geography, and drawing and music. The pedagogical methods used involved much pupil-teacher interaction and classroom discussion. Each class in all the schools was visited periodically by an official known as the *Inspecteur de l'académie* who made sure that the instructional programs centrally drawn up by the national ministry were properly carried out. Schools were democratic in the sense that pupils came from all social classes and represented all economic levels.

The general excellence of these public schools produced striking results. From 1885 to 1912 public primary instruction gained some 400,000 boys and 800,000 girls, while their confessional competitors lost about 1 million pupils. To these figures should be added the population of "maternal schools" (*écoles maternelles*), which were a kind of national preschooling scheme, and those who attended adult schools. By 1910 the French illiteracy rate had dropped to 4.2 percent.

Secondary education programs led to the national and standardized baccalaureate examinations, which, if successfully passed by the *collégien* or *lycéen*, gave him access to further study either at one of the universities or one of the many other higher educational facilities available. (A highly competitive entrance examination was generally required in addition to the *baccalauréat* for acceptance into one of the prestigious *grandes écoles*.) In

short, the *colleges* and *lycées* of France were designed to identify what was socially regarded as the nation's pool of intellectually *elite* young men. This was seen by many critics as socially unjust, all the more so in that practically speaking the young men concerned were almost invariably drawn from the well-to-do bourgeoisie and traditionally intellectual classes represented by the liberal professions (doctors, lawyers, and teachers).

Girls and women offer an illustrative case in point. At about the same time as colleges like Bryn Mawr in the United States, and Girton in England, were being founded, several Third Republic politicians displayed enough far-sightedness to fight for women's educational opportunities in France. Already in 1880, Camille Sée sponsored a law widening these opportunities. However, as seen from today's perspective, the law was discriminatory in that it focused on teaching subjects "appropriate to women," which meant not exposing them to Latin or Greek, advanced mathematics, and so forth. But over the years various decrees of application concerning the law simply ignored these strictures, and, little by little, young women achieved parity with young men in their own *lycées* (only much later would these schools become coeducational in France.) A feminine *École Normale Supérieure* was founded in counterpart to each of the two major male schools and its pupils received the same education and training as their masculine coevals. However, the social and economic class to which these young women belonged was much the same as that of their male peers.

CONSTITUTIONAL & LEGAL FOUNDATIONS

Under the Constitution of the French Fifth Republic (1958), responsibility for nation-wide education lies with the government. That is with the office of the prime minister who in turn is responsible to the National Assembly and who forms a government composed of cabinet ministers, one of whom bears the title "Minister of National Education;" "Research and Technology" have spun off into ministries of their own. As it deems fit, the National Assembly passes laws relative to educational matters, and these laws are administered by the government which issues decrees of application. Thus, in July 1975, the Assembly passed a law known generally as the *Loi Haby* which established the present day system of single *colleges* (*le collège unique*), an institution occupying the intermediate space between the primary school and the more advanced secondary school known as the *lycée*. The aim of this law was to provide a secondary schooling context for all pupils of a given age cohort (roughly ages 11 to 12 to 14 to 15) so as to avoid both the social and the educational constraints of the former system's requirement that all pupils of that age group be irrevocably shunted as of age 11 or 12 into a specific educational directions. These choices have been set forward to a later date, when the pupil has completed the *college* curriculum, of about age 15 or 16. Over the quarter of a century or so since this reform was promulgated, various governments have introduced by decree a number of practices designed so as to make the reform work better. These decrees have ranged from major practical modifications to attempts at fine-tuning. No need has been felt to replace the *Loi Haby* by another comprehensive law, although it looks likely that such a major change lies soon in the offing.

It can be said that the considerable powers inherent in the national Ministry of Education of the Fifth Republic extend those enjoyed by the Ministry's counterparts under the Third and Fourth Republics (1944-1958). The Minister of Education and his delegates are in charge of all schooling in France, as well as in overseas territories and *départements*. He is assisted by a fair number of Secretaries of State and other political appointees, as well as by junior ministers and a huge bureaucracy. Although there do exist a substantial number of private and religious schools (primary, secondary, and university-level), they are very closely watched, indeed supervised, by the Ministry of Education as to programs of study and the qualifications of their teaching personnel.

Although the various regional, departmental, and municipal administrations in France contribute in various ways to defray local expenses relative to schools and universities, by far the majority of the educational budgetary burden is borne by the national Ministry. This includes teachers' and professors' salaries, administrative salaries and costs, equipment, and building and maintenance. Public education also constitutes the largest item by considerable measure of the French national budget.

EDUCATIONAL SYSTEM—OVERVIEW

Increased immigration, new emphases on innovative technology and popular consumerism, a desire of many for more democracy, the building of a new Europe (one of the truly significant French politico-economic ideas of post-war times), the eroding of erstwhile fixed class distinctions, the relative decline of agriculture with respect to manufacturing, services, and commerce, decolonization, international cooperation to a degree never before witnessed have all exerted tremendous influence on the French school and higher education systems.

Private Education: What in France is called *enseignement libre* (free teaching) corresponds to the British "public" school and to the American "private" school; however, private primary and secondary education in France is usually sectarian, indeed overwhelmingly

Roman Catholic (95 percent). Though run and traditionally staffed by the religious teaching orders, these schools are increasingly staffed by lay people. As stated above, they are closely monitored by the state's Ministry of Education as to their teaching programs and the qualifications of their teaching staffs. Their pupils take the usual national state examinations (*brevet* and *baccalauréat*). They charge tuition and fees, although a growing number of them attempt to provide financial aid to the disadvantaged. Programs of study follow closely those mandated by the Ministry for the public schools, although it is fair to say that, in addition to required classes in religion, these Church-run institutions tend to emphasize the traditional pre-university *baccalauréat* curriculum, perhaps somewhat at the expense of technology and professional training more than their public counterparts. Their *clientele* is largely, but not as exclusively as many would have one believe, drawn from the middle classes and indeed from the upper crust of French society. Many, but not all, of these schools are now coeducational. Each school is run, often by a religious director, who exercises a great deal of discretionary power in his or her establishment. The director is frequently called upon to perform a kind of balancing act involving the directives issued by his or her Order, the local bishop, and the State. The school's traditions are held dear by both its *clientele* and by those who teach in it. Usually the pupils are asked to observe a dress code. The kind of school violence increasingly present in urban public schools is virtually unheard of in this setting. A good number of the schools have living and boarding facilities. School morale is generally high.

The good reputation and morale of the majority of private schools is due to the personal care lavished upon the pupils by the teachers and their institution. Some schools even specialize in boys and girls handicapped by learning and psychological difficulties, and their success rate is remarkably high. Discipline and order are maintained, but affection is also. Certain private institutions have received the Ministry's designation "ZEP" (*Zone d'éducation prioritaire* or "Educational Priority Zone"), qualifying them for extra financial help because they have shown signal success in coping with pupils from disadvantaged backgrounds. Finally, Catholic schools have a long tradition of involving parents and the family in the educational process. Until very recently this has not been true of public schools. The *école républicaine* has traditionally been understood as a State institution, not as a State service responsible to its *clientele*; in fact, the Revolutionary ideology from which it stems historically mistrusted parents and family. It consequently tended to uproot the child from his affective milieu of origin in order to turn him into a "citizen." Many parents find this aspect of *enseignement libre* to be quite attractive, as do, very often, their children.

Some of the richer and more famous of the Church-run secondary schools are well equipped with modern amenities: computers, up-to-date laboratories, sports facilities, and even good libraries, although a good many are not so well favored. However, most succeed in promoting a good *esprit de corps*, and, given the class homogeneity prevailing in their student bodies, the pupils' degree of motivation, as well as smaller, more intimate classroom groupings, the scholastic results tend to be very good. The latest publication of the scores and percentages of candidates passing the national *baccalauréat* examination includes a large number of Roman Catholic *colleges* and *lycées* among the list of institutions with a passing rate of 90 percent or better.

Approximately one in six French primary and secondary school boys and girls attends a private (almost invariably religiously-affiliated) school, according to recent Ministry of Education statistics. Nevertheless, there remains a residue of anti-*enseignement libre* animus in certain French Republican circles. In 1984, when the then Socialist government was perceived as about to pass legislation severely damaging private Catholic schools, a huge mass demonstration involving thousands of people descended in protest on Paris. The government gave way and since then peace has prevailed. Slowly but surely the bitter quarrels of the 1880-1910 period are being laid to rest. Frenchmen who are rightly proud of the achievements of the public education system nevertheless do not, on the whole, wish to see the private sector abolished or even seriously tampered with.

Private school teachers number about 130,000 in France; by far most of these are lay people who take qualifying examinations virtually the same as their public school colleagues. Their pay scales are quite close to those enjoyed by public school faculty; however, since they are not tenured government functionaries (*fonctionnaires titularisés*), their retirement pay is much lower.

During the Fourth Republic, certain right-wing and centrist parties joined forces in order to vote State subventions to private schools; however, these were stopgap measures. In 1959, after the proclamation of the Fifth Republic, the Gaullist prime minister, Michel Debré, instituted a new *régime* of "permanent association" between public and private schools with the State financing much of the costs of the latter. The annual subvention today comes to 40 billion francs, approximately the sum required to pay teachers' salaries. The money goes to private schools willing to work "under contract" with the government. Few private schools have refused this contractual arrangement.

Very few graduates of the religiously-affiliated secondary schools choose to go on to Catholic institutions of higher education. The Catholic school system thus finds itself firmly embedded in the secular world.

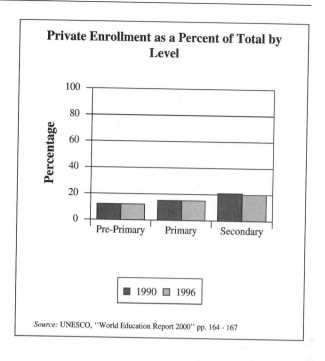

Private Enrollment as a Percent of Total by Level

Source: UNESCO, "World Education Report 2000" pp. 164 - 167

Private Higher Education: The Ministry of National Education classifies private higher education into two types: *les établissements privés d'enseignement libre* (a code word for Roman Catholic universities); and private establishments of technical education. The "establishments of 'free' higher education" are regulated by the July 1875 Law on Higher Education; no linkage between them and the State are allowed. Nevertheless, these establishments may agree to conventions signed between them and individual State-run institutions with a view toward offering joint preparations for State diplomas.

Apart from seminary-type establishments, two major Catholic institutions of higher learning stand out. One is called the *Institut catholique* and is located in Paris; the other is the *Université catholique de l'Ouest* (Catholic University of the West) in Angers. Both offer full-fledged programs of study on the university level, and in the case of the *Institut catholique*, the following faculties are notable: the Faculty of Theology and Religious Studies (which are essentially lacking in the State-run schools), the Faculty of Canon Law, the Faculty of Philosophy, the Faculty of Social and Economic Studies, the Faculty of Arts (Classics, French, History/Geography, and English-German-Spanish), preparatory classes for entrance into French Institutes of Political Studies, and the Faculty of Education (largely teacher-training). Close ties are maintained with a number of private technological and specialized schools, both Catholic-run and non-denominational. The *Institut catholique* enrolls some 12,000 full and part time students.

Private establishments of higher technological education are legion in France. Most are either engineering

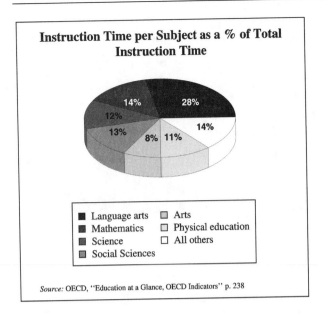

Instruction Time per Subject as a % of Total Instruction Time

- 28%
- 14%
- 14%
- 12%
- 13%
- 8%
- 11%

- ■ Language arts
- ■ Mathematics
- ■ Science
- □ Social Sciences
- □ Arts
- □ Physical education
- □ All others

Source: OECD, "Education at a Glance, OECD Indicators" p. 238

or business schools and must adhere to the national codes of technical education. They may benefit from State recognition and so award official state diplomas. Whether or not a private engineering school may award a State-type diploma is decided by the State Commission on Engineering Degrees.

PREPRIMARY & PRIMARY EDUCATION

Preprimary: During 2000-2001 over 6.5 million pupils were enrolled in the public preprimary and primary schools of France (about 2.5 million in the *écoles maternelles* and approximately 4.2 million in the *écoles élémentaires*). Previously organized by yearly "grades," present day primary programs fall into pluri-annual cycles: first apprenticeships (*apprentissages premiers*) cover the preprimary cycle; fundamental apprenticeships begin in the final year of preprimary and last over the first two years of primary; and deeper explorations (*approfondissments*) occupy the final three years of primary school.

Briefly summarized, the areas dealt with in the *école maternelle* (cycle I) include: Living Together; Speaking and Building Up Your Own Language (an initiation into the study of French); Acting in the World (interacting physically and imaginatively with objects; other people-games; and sports); Discovering the World (natural and human spaces; materials like wood, metals, etc.; hygiene; and the environment); Imagining, Feeling, and Creating (singing; drawing and painting; dance; theater; some writing; recognition of forms; and counting).

Primary (Cycle II): The goals to be achieved by the time this cycle is completed are as follows (in relation to the subjects dealt with):

- French: The pupils have learned to speak in public, to listen to others, to tell and invent stories; to read both out loud and silently; and to write in clearly formed characters.

- Mathematics: The pupils have mastered the numbers from 1 to 1000 and understand decimal numerals; they know how to compare numbers; they are in a position to practice addition, multiplication, and subtraction and can reckon mentally; they are able to resolve simple problems using these resources; they can recognize a few geometric shapes (circle, square, rectangle, etc.) and can reproduce them; they both know and can use common units of measure (meter and centimeter; gram and kilogram; and liter, hecto-liter and milliliter).

- Discovering the World (History, Geography, Sciences, and Technology): The pupils know their way around more or less proximate spaces and historical periods, and begin to put the latter into chronological order as they learn also to use maps, the globe, and certain major elements of the universe; they have some precise knowledge of how their bodies work, of rules of hygiene, and of animal and vegetable life; and they have learned to use simple technical tools, such as a camera.

- Civics: Basing themselves on their classroom experience, the pupils have learned fundamental rules of social interaction: respect for self and others and rules for living in common with others; they know that France is a republic; and are familiar with several of its symbols.

- The Creative Arts: The pupils interpret simple songs and do drawings, paintings, collages, and sculptures with various techniques and materials; they undergo some basic initiation to theater, dance, and imaging.

- Physical Education and Sports: The pupils develop their motor skills and learn to run, jump, throw, and swim better; learn to respect game rules; and learn team ship.

Primary (Cycle III): This final cycle explores more deeply the above-mentioned subjects and activities, taking into account the strengths and weaknesses of the class members. When required, special counseling and help will be made available to individual students. Every effort will be made in order to see to it that each pupil advances regularly alongside his or her classmates.

Some daily foreign language instruction will be introduced during this cycle. The time given over to this activity will rarely go beyond a quarter of an hour; video and audio cassettes will be made available to teachers that want them. Goals of this level are:

- French: The pupils learn to recite from memory a poetic text; they are capable of reading a 10-page piece of prose without excessive fatigue; they learn to correctly take down a dictated text of about 10 lines; and they are able to compose a short text respecting spelling and grammatical rules.

- Mathematics: The pupils can perform decimal calculations; they are familiar with the usual geometric shapes; they have mastered the four arithmetical operations and can calculate in their heads; they know how to use such tools as the ruler, the square, and the compass; and they can solve problems using the above operations and measuring instruments.

- History and Geography: The pupils are able to identify the major prehistorical and historical periods of French history; they know a number of important dates; and they can locate on a map the following elements of French geography: major rivers, mountain ranges, various regions, the basic French administrative units, and large cities.

- Science and Technology: The pupils have learned how to simply analyze the relationship between living beings and their habitat; they can perform simple experiments; and they understand the concept of assembly, such as how to set up an electric circuit.

- Civics: The pupils prove themselves capable of respecting the rules governing their school and of understanding each individual's responsibility with respect to society at large; and they can describe the political institutions of France, such as universal suffrage and the workings of the National Assembly.

- The Creative Arts (Music and the Plastic Arts): The pupils are capable of observing, listening, producing, and inventing in ways that develop their creative imagination and form their sense of culture by relating and comparing works drawn from different periods and styles; and they further develop their abilities with respect to theater, dance, and imaging.

- Physical Education and Sports: The pupils become increasingly aware of the rhythms of living beings; and through the practice of sports they acquire greater ease and try to attain a certain performance level in the activities, which they practice.

- Foreign Language: Initiation into foreign language study will continue as the pupils go on to middle school-level work.

The first year of *college* or the beginning of intermediate schooling, *la sixième*, will consist largely of consolidating what the primary school has taught the pupil with a view toward his acquiring new notions and developing more sophisticated intellectual tools and work methods.

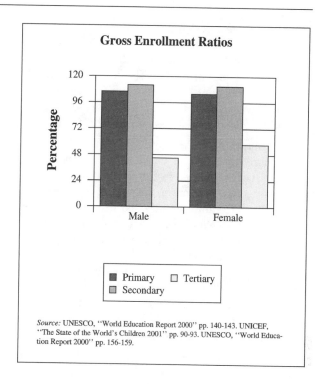

Gross Enrollment Ratios

Source: UNESCO, "World Education Report 2000" pp. 140-143. UNICEF, "The State of the World's Children 2001" pp. 90-93. UNESCO, "World Education Report 2000" pp. 156-159.

SECONDARY EDUCATION

Founded by the *Loi Haby* of 1975, the *college unique* is designed to follow through on the primary school principal of housing all pupils, whatever their talents and tastes, together under one roof. Specialization into university preparation, pre-professional, and technical training is thus put off until the pupil attains the age of 15 or 16. (Formerly, this specialization occurred when the pupil entered the class known as *sixième,* that is when he was 11 or 12 and it was largely based on an entrance examination now regarded as socially discriminatory.) Thus, the four years spent at the *college* are essentially transitional and given over to orientation. The *college* is structured largely in order to "fit" the pupil into one of the many orientations open to him at the *lycée* level. Consequently, in certain respects the *college* is "intermediate," and in other respects it is part of the secondary school cycle. It is characterized by flexible scheduling, the availability of many new programs, and by the careful monitoring of all pupils. Those who display difficulties in adjustment and in class work are provided with counseling and help. Serious attempts are made also to involve parents in the functioning of the school.

The goals and ideals of the new *college unique,* which in many respects resembles the American Middle School (or Junior High), have not always been successful in practice. The four years of the French *college unique* break down into three main periods: (1) the initial year called *sixième*; (2) the two years of *cinquième* and *quatrième*; and (3) the final year called *troisième*.

The *sixième* is designed to solidify what was learned in primary school; to introduce boys and girls to new subject-matters; and to help them develop good work habits and methods. Pupils have 23 or 24 hours of class weekly, undergo two hours of ''directed study'' aimed at all pupils, and have what is called an arrangement for ''consolidation'' aimed at pupils who encounter difficulties.

Not surprisingly, the curriculum of the *sixième* follows closely upon that of the final year of elementary school, yet it differs also in that it emphasizes practice and creativity on the part of the pupil. For example, in French, after reading carefully and discussing a given text, the pupils might be asked to rewrite part of it, retelling an episode from the perspective of a character other than the protagonist. Or they might be assigned to write a letter to a foreign pen-pal describing life in their school. After returning the corrected papers to the class, the teacher will focus on their grammatical and spelling errors to the entire group, ask the schoolchildren to rewrite their work, and have the other pupils correct them.

In mathematics the focus is on geometry, numeric works, and functions. Pupils describe and trace simple plane figures, and they measure, compare, and calculate areas and perimeters. They also deepen their knowledge of the four arithmetical operations by applying them to whole numbers and decimals, and they are introduced to relative numbers. During the later part of the course, they work with handling data and dealing with functions. Tables, diagrams, and graphics are studied and related to other disciplines, such as geography and technology.

History and geography are a combined focus. History deals mainly with the ancient world: the beginnings of agriculture, Egypt, the Hebrews, Greece, Rome, and early Christianity. Facts are learned, but pupils are also taught to examine critically the documents from historical knowledge: treatises, maps, photos, etc. Geography examines the relationship between mankind and his diverse habitats—the diversity of terrains, climates, urban and rural settings, and population densities.

Civics, now incorporated into the history-geography section, deals principally with the pupils and their fellow peers in the *college* itself. The establishment's structure is examined, as are the people who make it run (the student body, the faculty, the principal, and the social worker). Also, the principles of rights and obligations are closely studied, as is the text of The Declaration of the Rights of Man.

Life and Earth Sciences capitalize on the young adolescents' fascination with nature and its manipulation, as well as on their love of experimentation. In this class they study the classification of plants and animals, the cell, animal and vegetable reproduction, and the food chain. They also examine various types of tissue under the microscope, graft plant cuttings, and dissect a flower.

Technological study examines how objects are produced, manufactured, and placed for sale by different kinds of enterprise. Each pupil works on a specific project and is taught computer technology word-processing, searching, and how to use the Internet in order better to do so.

Physical education and sports focus on the latter during the *sixième*: pupils are introduced to gymnastics, swimming, combative and racket sports, and team sports. Motor capacities are developed, and special attention is given to a sense of effort and responsibility.

The plastic arts emphasize creativity in two and three dimensions and use various techniques and materials (clay, paper, collages, paint, and ink). Meetings are arranged with local artists and field trips are taken to museums.

In music, special attention is given over to the ''education of the ear.'' Six major compositions from various periods and genres are listened to and studied. In addition, six vocal works are sung by groups of pupils, and they are also initiated into playing instruments of percussion and the recorder. Some attention is paid to electronically generated music.

Thus, the above describes how the *sixième* builds on the advanced primary school program. Its major curricular innovation lies in the pupil's serious undertaking of study of a modern foreign language. Most *colleges* offer English, Spanish, German and Italian, although some also provide for Portuguese, Russian, Arabic, Chinese, and the local regional language. Latin is offered in *cinquième* where a full quarter of *collegians* opt for it; it has the reputation of being the place where the ''better pupils'' are. The first year of foreign language study is largely ''cultural.'' Pupils are introduced to how people relate to each other in Britain and the U.S. and how they express their tastes and dislikes. Some effort is made to have the young French boys and girls speak the language with a suitable pronunciation and a vocabulary that stresses the individual (size, clothing, and age) and his or her activities (games, holidays, and travels), as well as family relations. Some historical and geographical information concerning the country, or countries, in which the language is spoken are given.

The *cinquième* and *quatrième* years constitute the focal point of the four *collège unique* years. Essentially the program of study follows through on the subjects taught in sixième (including a modern foreign language—a second of which must be added as part of the *quatrième*), but the sciences are broken down into Earth and Life Sciences and Physics and Chemistry. It is here that many children, especially those from recent immigrant and disadvantaged families, find their studies to be fairly difficult. This is especially the case in mathematics and the sciences. Numerous pupils require remedial help. By and large the program does not differ radically from the older, traditional *collège* and *lycée* curricula that led to the "classical" *baccalauréat* and from there to the university. Moreover, in addition to the weekly 23 or 24 hours spent in the classroom, the pupils find themselves with homework assignments amounting to between 20 and 30 hours a week. Work in all the curricular subjects takes place on an ever higher level of abstraction (for which not all pupils are yet quite ready), and, of course, the work requires well-organized and critical consultation of manuals, dictionaries, and other reference works. Frustration and a sense of failure consequently affect many *collegians* at this level, particularly among males it seems. Of course, without the establishment of the *collège unique* a quarter-century ago, many of its present pupil clients would simply not be in a *college* at all, and this, of course, has no doubt prompted many conservative critics to question the validity of its establishment.

The subject-matter covered in the two-year course curriculum includes French, mathematics, foreign languages, history and geography, civics, life and earth sciences, physics and chemistry, and technology. More advanced classes in the plastic arts and music, as well as in physical education and sports, continue throughout these two years.

The *troisième* is the terminal middle-secondary school year constituting arguably the single most important school experience in the lives of French schoolchildren. It comprises three elements: the continuation and "perfection" of the studies undertaken so far; an endeavor to all the studies accomplished to date; and a way to determine the orientation to be followed by each individual pupil in his or her three year subsequent *lycée* level higher secondary schoolwork. Furthermore, at the close of *troisième*, or each pupil takes his first national examination: the *Brevet d'études*. This diploma is awarded, or not awarded, on the basis of each child's course grades in all classes taken during *quatrième* and *troisième* (these grades are counted with a coefficient of 1), as well as in combination with a timed written examination in French, Mathematics, and History-Geography (with a coefficient of 2). The *brevet* and access to the *lycée* is awarded to pupils attaining a global average of 10 through 20 (it should be added that grades exceeding 17 are very rare). The success rate for the *brevet* usually hovers around 75 percent. Enrollments in the state-run *colleges* in recent years have averaged about 3 million pupils.

Upper Secondary Education: Three main, and quite different, specialized options are open to *brevet* holders at the *lycée* level: the General Baccalaureate (*baccalauréat general*), which leads to the university, and to spe-

cialized schools of higher education (e.g., the *grandes écoles*, with their highly competitive entrance examinations); two types of Technological Baccalaureate (*baccalauréat technologique*), which opens to various specialized schools of a technological, professional or artistic sort; and the Professional Baccalaureate (*baccalauréat professionnel*), leading directly to insertion into the job market and on the job training (this last program involves two years of study, the previous two comprise three). Of these three options, the General Baccalaureate is the simplest; it also comes closest to the older, more traditional *lycée*; the Technological Baccalaureate structurally resembles the first. The "professional" curriculum is much more complex in that all its options (including a Baccalaureate-less path) recognize many diverse goals and levels. It is highly recommended that each pupil make as solidly based a decision as possible concerning his or her eventual path, and that both parents and school counseling staff be closely involved in this process which, it is urged, should begin no later than the year of the *cinquième*.

The Technology option, as well as the Professional curriculum, can lead to a Technological (or Professional) *brevet*, as well as, in the first case, a *baccalauréat* and, in the second, a *Certificat d'aptitude professionnel*, (Certificate of Professional Aptitude or CAP). Those youth who choose either the *brevet* or the CAP path usually go directly on to a job, with or without a formal program of on the job training. The *lycée* programs attempt to provide a basis for as many types of jobs as there exist in the country's job market; some programs combine school programs with apprentice-type internships in various firms. In the case of those who successfully pass the Technological *baccalauréat*, many specialized institutions, both public and private, are available.

Lycée enrollments have totaled on average over the past five years of about 1 million; slightly more than half of enrolled students have chosen the Professional option. The various apprenticeship programs attract an average of 350,000 students each year, while the special secondary level programs (e.g., agriculture, health services) enroll about 250,000 boys and girls. Thus, most *collegians* go on to some *lycée* level work; however, the programmatic unity imposed on pre-*brevet* pupils is followed up by an extreme diversity in the *lycée*.

Grosso modo, the French secondary educational system, seems both to promote and to respond to a division apparently built into French society. One large segment of its *clientele* uses the secondary school to prepare for advanced higher educational training and therefore postpones its insertion into the productive economic life of the country. An equally large segment either drops out of the educational system as such altogether or uses it as an

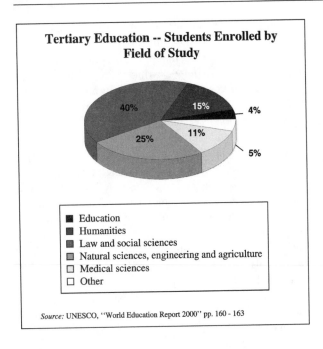

Tertiary Education -- Students Enrolled by Field of Study

- ■ Education
- ■ Humanities
- ■ Law and social sciences
- ▨ Natural sciences, engineering and agriculture
- □ Medical sciences
- □ Other

Source: UNESCO, ''World Education Report 2000'' pp. 160 - 163

(e.g., Letters, Sciences, Medicine, Law), it now boasts 14, none of which groups all faculties or branches of learning under a single administration. Expansion has been truly exponential.

Even in 2001, a large and fairly old provincial university will usually possess a library much smaller in size than that of a good American liberal arts college whose student body is less than 2,000, although in recent times research undertaken by university faculty has been more strongly encouraged. The Centre National de Recherche Scientifique (National Center for Scientific Research), founded after World War II, has had global responsibility for research and publication in all academic disciplines, sponsoring both ''laboratories'' of its own and the research of individual faculty members at the universities and grandes écoles, and subsidizing ''centers of technical competence'' involving one or more institutions. However, the movement away from the university as a purely teaching establishment has been, and remains (though less and less) a very slow one.

Each university is headed by a president responsible to the rector of the Academy in which it is located; academies often contain two or more universities. The university president is supported by vice-presidents and academic deans that correspond to the diverse disciplines. Faculty recruitment on the *maître de conferences* (assistant/associate professor) and *professeur* levels is lengthy and complex.

Cities in which two or more universities are located will usually witness a grouping of kindred disciplines at each of the institutions. This does little to foment interdisciplinary intellectual contact and cooperation.

Although each discipline introduces variations into its own teaching program, this is done in reference to a nation-wide model that corresponds to three cycles. The student spends his or her first year (cycle) preparing a diploma suitable to his field of major interest, the *Diplôme d'études universsitaires générales* or DEUG; this is followed by his or her registration in a second cycle, i.e., two or three year *licence* preparation immediately leading to study at the *maîtrise* (masters) level. At this point most students leave the university for the job market. Those who stay on, who tend to be the most highly qualified, will undertake the third cycle, which is the preparation of a research project leading to a kind of thesis, or mémoir, called the *Diplôme d'études approfondies* (DEA). The best of these students will be encouraged to pursue a doctoral degree. Once the doctorate is obtained, the student may sign up for an examination proving his or her capacity to do a high level research project and to supervise individual, as well as teams, of young researchers (*l'habilation à diriger des recherches*). At any time after the *maîtrise* a student may choose to sit for one of

immediate springboard to a wage-earning career. It is very much an either/or situation. Unlike the United States and Canada, France has no community college-type alternative, nor does it possess a truly varied gamut of institutions of higher learning. Also, theoretically at least, the state-recognized masters degree delivered by a remote provincial university or ''university institute'' in no way differs from the one earned at an older, established provincial institution or, for that matter, at the Université de Paris IV (Sorbonne).

HIGHER EDUCATION

The needs of a new, modernized post-industrial economy required an overhaul of higher education. Scholarship aid (*bourses*) was vastly increased, making it possible for larger numbers of less well-to-do young men and women to attend universities. The advent of the post-war Welfare State had important repercussions on university structures.

Reform of higher education, consequently, became a matter of urgency, and the 1970s saw its beginnings; this reform has become on-going. In fact, it appears more and more likely that reform will remain a permanent feature of French higher education for many years to come.

Universities: The Ministry of Education lists 91 institutions in its repertory of universities (including ''technological'' universities, certain ''institutes,'' and other entities) located in France and its overseas territories and *départments*; this is well over four times as many universities as existed in 1960. Whereas before the 1960s, Paris had 1 university, albeit broken up into various faculties the various competitive examinations, such as the *Certificat d'aprtitude à l'enseignement secondaire*, for a *lycée* teacher's certificate, the *aggregation*, or still other examinations. The success rate in these examinations is not encouraging: it averages about 14 percent for the CAPES and *aggregation*, though CAPES examinations have a higher rate of success than *agrégatifs*; the rate also depends on the discipline.

Alongside the DEA doctoral program there exists a one-year professional program, involving an obligatory internship within an enterprise or business called the *Diplôme d'études supérieures spécialisées* (DESS). Upon its completion the student leaves the university for a job.

One and two year university-level programs in technology are offered by the various *Instituts universitaires de technologie* attached to universities. These institutes offer a two-year *diplôme universitaire de technologie* (DUT) which leads directly to the job market. Access to the institute is selective. A cycle 1 one-year technological program is also available; it leads to the *diplôme d'études universitaires scientifiques et techniques* or DEUST, the technological equivalent of the DEUG.

Some *lycées* also offer very specialized and goal-directed *brevets de technicien supérieur* (BTS); some 85 fields are covered. About 220,000 students are enrolled in these *lycée* based programs.

The following ministerial list of average diploma awards (rounded off) over the past five years will provide an idea of the attrition rate among students at the various steps of their university careers: DEUG or the terminal DEUST - 132,000; *licence* - 133,500; *maîtrise* - 86,000; DESS - 24,500; DEA- 24,250; and doctorate - 10,000. These figures are to be compared to the total enrollment of students in the French university system: 1 million out of a total of some 2 million post-*baccalauréat* students altogether. The dropout rate appears to be quite high.

Tuition and fees are set each year by the Ministry of Education; these are very low by North American standards. Financial aid in the form of scholarships is made available on the basis of family need at all levels of university study. Scholarly criteria are used for third-cycle university work. Students are eligible for subsidized housing, provided there is dormitory space, and for inexpensive student restaurant meals.

Entrance to the university is non-selective. The only requirement is the *baccalauréat* or its equivalent, except in the case of medicine and certain other health-related fields. Students registered in these fields are also subject to individual review at the close of their first year of study.

State-sponsored post-*baccalauréat* schooling outside of the universities may be subdivided into three main

types: public engineering schools, the *grandes écoles*, and health service/social work-related institutions. In addition, one must also count the system of *lycée*-based preparatory classes, which are two-year programs designed to prepare students for the *grandes écoles* and engineering school competitive entrance examinations.

Whereas the great majority of the *grandes écoles* are administered by the Ministry of National Education, several depend on other ministries or administrations. Thus, the very prestigious *École Nationale d'Administration*, founded in 1945 in order to prepare upper-level civil servants.

Foreign Students: The Ministry of National Education and many cooperating universities and other institutions of higher learning (including certain *grandes écoles*) have established a variety of programs aimed at foreign students. The majority of these involve the French language (beginning, intermediate, and advanced) and diverse subjects (literature, art, and history) grouped together as "culture." Certificates and diplomas are awarded appropriately. There has been, and continues to be, considerable demand for these programs. A fair number of summer programs of the above type are also offered, some in collaboration with American colleges and universities, as are year or semester long collaborative programs that involve a variety of French institutions.

ADMINISTRATION, FINANCE, & EDUCATIONAL RESEARCH

The French Republic is headed by a popularly elected president who represents and serves the Nation and State. He is responsible for the country's territorial integrity and appoints the governing prime minister (following the political majority controlling the legislative National Assembly). In turn, the prime minister appoints his cabinet, who are the ministers responsible for governing the country, among whom one of the most important is the Minister of National Education. This Minister's official title is Minister of National Education, Research, and Technology. It is he who proposes policies, enjoys budgetary oversight, and directs numerous sub-ministerial political appointees (as well as myriad civil servants) subject only to the prime minister.

Constitutionally, the Minister operates within the parameters of certain fundamental laws, such as the 1875 laws governing education and Church and State. He also has the task of proposing new laws as the situation may require them. He is assisted by a large bureaucracy and permanent advisory committees whose decisions he normally accepts.

Each of the three main components of the system—primary, secondary, and higher education—has, under the Minister, its own area of competence and organizational traditions. In addition, the division of France into geographic areas known as "academies" provides input into decision-making from the diverse regions of the country.

A kind of executive chain-of-command descends from the Minister through a number of echelons down to the director of a primary school. Although each director, principal, *proviseur* (or *lycée* director), dean, university president, and academy rector heads his own bailiwick, his area of responsibility is fully integrated into a system of responsibilities headed by the Minister.

According to the latest figures publicly available (1998), the total costs of education (public and private) come globally to about FF607.3 billion (92.6 billion euros) of which FF343.3 (52.5 billion euros) are spent by the Ministry of National Education. The global figure represented 7.2 percent of the 1998 French gross national product. The difference between the global cost figure and the costs paid by the Ministry can be accounted for as follows: FF48.4 billion (7.4 billion euros) from other state ministries; FF124.3 billion (18.9 billion euros) regional, local, and territorial contributions; FF35 billion (5.3 billion euros) from business-operated training programs; FF13.5 billion (2.1 billion euros) other national administrations; and FF41.8 billion (6.4 billion euros) from family contributions. An additional FF25.1 billion (4.1 billion euros) were paid out to overseas territories and *départments*. The grand total was thus: FF634.4 billion (92.6 billion euros) at 1998 exchange rates. Of these sums 77.7 percent went for personnel salaries, benefits and pensions; 14.8 percent to upkeep and physical plant; and 7.5 percent to investment in future capital needs.

Further breakdowns show (in 2000-2001) a total of 528,000 persons employed in the *écoles maternelles* and elementary schools. Teaching staff in these schools amounted to 358,000 persons and cost per pupil amounted to FF24,700 (3,765 euros). In secondary education some 786,000 were employed, of which 508,000 were teachers; cost per pupil came to an average of FF25,000 (8300 euros). In post-*baccalauréat* classes the cost was FF68,900 (10,504 euros).

The Ministry of National Education provides financial aid to schoolchildren (both *collège* and *lycée* level) from families of demonstrably modest means; such aid can total as much as FF5000 per annum.

In recent years enrollments in higher education have been approximately 2 million students with a public sector teaching corps of about 75,500 professors. Yearly costs per student have ranged very widely depending on the diverse programs in which students are enrolled. Thus, the average university student in the humanities

and social sciences costs approximately FF40,000 (6000 euros), whereas an engineering student costs about FF78,000 (12,000 euros).

TEACHING PROFESSION

Pedagogical research is rather scattered in France. There are no schools of education as such, although pedagogy is treated as a research subject in various institutions like the *ÉNS de Cachan*; the *Institut catholique* maintains a Faculty of Education for the training, largely, of Catholic school teachers. Courses in "professional formation" are offered at many universities for future teachers, as well as at the *écoles normales* that train primary school teachers. C.N.R.S.-sponsored "research laboratories" in such subjects as educational psychology and counseling do exist, as do various offices of pedagogical services within the Ministry of National Education itself. Teaching methodologies, as in foreign language-teaching methods or the laboratory sciences, are variously studied and evaluated. Matters pertaining to proposed institutional restructuring are entrusted to the expertise of specially appointed commissions and boards of research before changes are introduced and implemented.

A final word must be said concerning the role of professional societies and teachers' unions (*syndicates*) within the general educational picture in France. Membership in unions is usually determined according to the members' various professional levels (primary, secondary, and higher education) and interests, as well as their political affiliations and tastes (left-wing, right-wing, and centrist). There are also a number of students' unions similarly affiliated. All of these unions are legally recognized as such, and they enjoy the right to strike, although their rôle in collective bargaining is not easily determined. In addition, university and research faculty, as well as some secondary school teachers, are members of the many various disciplinary professional associations. From time to time they speak out publically on matters pertaining to their discipline and, more often than not, what they say is taken seriously.

SUMMARY

The American example in business study, technology, and perhaps even in the pure sciences has provided a counter to native French institutions. In fact, some of the newer of these institutions directly copy and Gallicize American models, both physically and programmatically. Much of what has been genuinely innovative in post-war France has not been generated from within the native French system, except for such institutions as the ÉNA and Sciences Po, which were designed specifically to serve the ends of the French State. This raises the serious question as to whether, as presently constituted, the State is in fact capable of engendering educational innovation in such a way as to foment original intellectual, scientific, and artistic creativity.

There are four problem areas that appear at present to require urgent thinking and planning. The first of these and perhaps the most symptomatic of the four concerns the status, ideology, and purpose of the *collège unique*. Most Frenchmen agree that in its present form it simply does not work; it fails even in its intended purpose to further democratize the secondary school system. Apparently, the present Minister of Education thinks that the solution to the *collège unique's* difficulties lies in rendering it more flexible, financially independent, autonomous, and less rigidly programmatic. Furthermore, the Minister promises that, along with this flexibility, his office will provide a firm piloting of the institution and the numerous establishments constituting it: "*la souplesse avec la norme*" (flexibility within the norm). The norm, presumably, will involve a greater integration with the primary level (the *college* will become more authentically a "middle school"); entrance evaluations to the *sixième* will emphasize French and Mathematics less than at present; and curricula will be "more imaginative." A number of national evaluations will take place over the four year course of studies; these will culminate in a national examination awarding a *Brevet d'études fondamentales*. These evaluations and *brevet* will also constitute part of the norm and promised ministerial piloting.

The second and third major concerns have to do with foreign languages and foreign study/educational travel. The two are closely related. The first of these involves the entire educational system, and it also is designed to counteract the overwhelming choice of English as the major foreign language studied. It seems likely that the study of two modern foreign languages will soon be required of all secondary level schoolchildren. All university level students will be required to pass a competency test in at least one foreign language in order to graduate. The university requirement will go beyond the level of mere colloquy; it will involve the ability to function linguistically in the student's area of academic specialization. Thus, a French university student should be linguistically equipped to read work in his or her field written in an appropriate modern foreign language, as well as to follow lectures in his or her subject in that language. These new requirements constitute, along with much increased foreign travel and study on both the secondary and higher education levels, part of the "Europeanization" of French education, rendering the French system more like that of many of the smaller European countries. The policy, although not designed with these implications in mind, may eventually have some re-

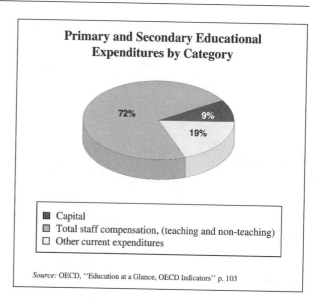

Primary and Secondary Educational Expenditures by Category

72% 9% 19%

■ Capital
▨ Total staff compensation, (teaching and non-teaching)
☐ Other current expenditures

Source: OECD, "Education at a Glance, OECD Indicators" p. 103

percussions on the nature of the French State-controlled educational system.

The last concern relates to the above quoted statement of Sylvain Auroux, director of the ÉNS-LHS. It is namely the urgency and importance of a new and informed humanistic reflection in the first century of the new millennium. Advances in science and technology, a commercially and monetarily driven world, and the lack of attention paid by the élites in the developed countries of the world have made such reflection indispensable. Given the largely materialist and careerist agendas of present day interest groups, however, the bright and the beautiful do not seem to have the time to give over to such reflection. Auroux appears to believe that France is blessed with educational establishments like the one he directs that are particularly well placed to form the highly articulate thinkers needed.

BIBLIOGRAPHY

Buisson, Ferdinand. *Dictionnaire de Pédagogie*. Paris: 1882.

Chervel, Antoine. *L'Enseignement du Français à l'école Primaire*. Paris: INRP, 1995.

Georgel, Jacques. *L'Enseignement Privé en France*. Paris: Dalloz, 1995.

The French Ministry of National Education, 2001. Available from http://www.education.gouv.fr.

Glatigny, Michel. *Histoire de l'enseignement en France. Que sais-je?* Paris: Presses Universitaires de France, 1949.

Le Monde, 2001. Available from http://lemonde.fr/education.

Office national d'information sur les enseignements et les professions. Ministère de l'Éducation nationale, de la Recherche et de la Technologie. *Onisep: de la ème au bac,* September 2000.

—*Karl D. Uitti*

FRENCH GUIANA

BASIC DATA

Official Country Name:	Department of Guiana
Region:	South America
Population:	172,605
Language(s):	French
Literacy Rate:	83%

French Guiana, an overseas department of France governed by the French Constitution, is located on the northeast coast of South America, adjacent to Brazil and Suriname. The educational system there is modeled after that of France.

Between 1980 and 1993, enrollment increased by 70 percent at the primary level and by 87 percent at the secondary level. Education, which is free, is mandatory for children between the ages of 6 and 16. Primary education lasts for five years; school enrollment at that level is nearly 100 percent, with the exception of the more remote areas of the country, such as the settlements of the Amerindians and Maroons, where resources are much more limited.

Secondary education is broken up into two cycles: a four-year program that concludes with the *Brevet de College* examination and an additional three-year program that culminates with the *Baccalaureat* examination, successful completion of which is required for entrance into tertiary institutions.

Higher education in the country is limited to teacher training and agricultural colleges and the University Antilles-Guyane, which offers postsecondary studies in administration, French language and literature, and law. Many students seeking higher education attend universities in France or the French Antilles.

The primary language of instruction at all levels is French, an issue that has been the subject of much debate given that many indigenous groups speak other languages. Also, the Guyane Educational Authority for Primary, Secondary, and Higher Education, based in Cayenne, is a decentralized government department that oversees the educational system in French Guiana.

BIBLIOGRAPHY

Crant, Phillip A. "La Guyane: Past and Present." Paper presented at the Annual Meeting of the Pacific Northwest Council on Foreign Languages, Portland, April 1975.

"French Guiana." In *Europa World Yearbook.* Pittsburgh: Europa Publications, 1999.

Reno, Fred, and Richard D. Burton, eds. *French & West Indian: Martinique, Guadeloupe, and French Guiana Today.* University Press of Virginia, 1995.

—*AnnaMarie L. Sheldon*

FRENCH POLYNESIA

BASIC DATA

Official Country Name:	French Polynesia
Region:	Oceania
Population:	249,110
Language(s):	French, Tahitian
Literacy Rate:	98%

French Polynesia is an overseas territory of France that includes Tahiti and 118 smaller islands in the eastern South Pacific. There are 5 major islands (archipelagos): Society Islands, which include Tahiti and Moorea; the Marquesas Islands; the Austral Islands; the Tuamotu Archipelago; and the Gambier Islands.

Children generally start school at age 5 and complete primary education by age 12. The ages of compulsory education are 6 through 16. Tahiti has a literacy rate of 98 percent. On some of the smaller islands though, the dropout rate is extremely high, with only 20 percent or fewer students even finishing elementary school.

All school instruction is in French. French Polynesia has the same educational system as France, but it is altered slightly to conform with needs specific to the territories. Additionally, public education is financed through the government, which also subsidizes some private schools that are operated by churches.

Higher education can be attained in French Polynesia. In 1987, the French University of the Pacific was founded in Papeete, Tahiti, to encourage citizens to attain higher education more frequently and to develop scientific and cultural relationships with other countries.

BIBLIOGRAPHY

The Central Intelligence Agency (CIA). *The World Fact-book 2000.* Directorate of Intelligence, 1 January 2000. Available from http://www.cia.gov/.

Tahiti Friendship Society. *The Friendship Society,* 1997. Available from www.tahitinet.com/presence.html.

—*LeAnna DeAngelo*

GABON

BASIC DATA

Official Country Name:	Gabonese Republic
Region:	Africa
Population:	1,208,436
Language(s):	French, Fang, Myene, Bateke, Bapounou/ Eschira, Bandjabi
Literacy Rate:	63.2%

HISTORY & BACKGROUND

Gabon gained its independence from France in 1960. It was ruled by autocratic presidents from then until the early 1990s when a new constitution provided institutional reform and a better electoral process. Oil was discovered in the early 1970s and now represents 50 percent of the economy; consequently, Gabon is one of the more prosperous countries in Africa with a GDP per capita estimated at $6,500 in 1999. The illiteracy rate was estimated to be 29.2 percent (males 20.2 percent, females 37.8 percent) in the year 2000. Also in 2000, the population was estimated at 1,208,436 people.

The first elementary schools in Gabon were established by American and French missionaries in the 1840s. To this day, Catholic and Protestant schools remain an important part of the educational system.

France applied the same educational policies in Gabon as elsewhere in Francophone Africa. Consequently, the institutions were similar and had a similar purpose: to assimilate the people and make them good French men and women who would spread French civilization and defend France's interests in the colony. Starting in 1883, France required that only French be used for instruction in the schools and that 50 percent of class time be devoted to teaching French language and culture. In the twenty-first century, French is still the official language.

Furthermore, opportunities for education were minimal and very few pupils were enrolled in schools. In 1931, Gabon, a country of about 400,000 people, had 3237 pupils in elementary school, most of them in the first three grades. After World War II, secondary schools were finally opened so students could receive the same diplomas as those awarded in France. At independence, however, Gabon still did not have enough educated citizens to meet its needs. The government, therefore, organized schools to train secondary school graduates for careers in government, forestry, and teaching in the lower secondary grades.

EDUCATIONAL SYSTEM—OVERVIEW

In present-day Gabon, education is compulsory for 10 years from the ages of 6 to 16. The system is modeled on education in France and French is the language of instruction. However, primary education lasts six years rather than the five it does in France because students need an extra year to begin learning French.

PREPRIMARY & PRIMARY EDUCATION

Gabon offers minimal preprimary education. Primary education starts at six and lasts for six years. In 1995-1996, there were 1,147 schools with 4,943 teachers teaching 250,693 students, 50 percent of whom were female. The student-teacher ratio is a very high: 51 students for every teacher. In 1994, approximately 38 percent of the elementary school students were repeating a grade and only 61 percent of the students who began first grade together reached the fifth grade.

SECONDARY EDUCATION

Secondary education lasts 7 years from the ages of 12 to 18. It is divided into two cycles: the first lasts four years and the second three years. In 1995-1996, there were 80,552 secondary students, of whom 47 percent were female, taught by 3,094 teachers, of whom only 18 percent were female. Most of the students were in general secondary education; only 7,588 students were enrolled in vocational education and 76 in teacher training.

HIGHER EDUCATION

Founded in 1970 and renamed in 1978, the Université Omar Bongo in Libreville has faculties of law, of letters and human sciences, and of medicine and health sciences, as well as schools of education, forestry and hydraulics, technical teacher training, and management studies. The academic year runs from October to June. The *baccalauréat* (secondary school certificate) is required for admission. French is the language of instruction. Students obtain a *Licence-ès-Lettres* in three years and a *Maîtrise-ès-Lettres* in four. The university also awards medical and engineering degrees. In 1998, the university had about 2400 students with an academic staff of about 300.

Gabon also has an *Ecole Normale Supérieure* (Higher School of Teacher Training), an *Institut National des Sciences de Gestion* (National Institut of Management), the *Ecole Nationale D'Etudes Forestières at Cap Estérias* (National School of Forestry), an *Ecole Nationale de Secrétariat* (National School of Secretarial Studies), and an *Ecole Normale Supérieure de l'Enseignement Technique* (Technical Teacher Training School).

The Université des Sciences et Techniques in Masuku, founded in 1986, has a faculty of sciences and an engineering school. In 1998, it enrolled about 550 students with an academic staff of about 110. In 1994-1995, there were 4,655 students in higher education institutions, of whom only 1,785 were women. From a different perspective, women represented 22.3 percent of the education students, 32.6 percent of the humanities students, 35.9 percent of the social science students, and 58.5 percent of the medical sciences students.

ADMINISTRATION, FINANCE, & EDUCATIONAL RESEARCH

France has had a great influence on the nature and organization of the institutions in Gabon. As in France, the Ministry of Education is responsible for both public and private education throughout the country.

NONFORMAL EDUCATION

The *Campus Numérique Francophone de Libreville* (The Francophone Digital Campus of Libreville) was being developed in 2001. One of its goals is to help university professors locally produce modules, seminars, publications, databases, and archives to support distance education courses as well as supplementary materials for local courses on the Internet in French. It also provides assistance to professors in the production of programs. It will bring together faculty from different parts of the university and help in the creation of university Intranets and in the development of tools to navigate the Web intelligently.

TEACHING PROFESSION

Students who have completed the *maîtrise-ès-arts* (Master of Arts) degree may take the entrance exam for the Ecole Normale Supérieure to prepare the C.A.P.E.S. exam to be certified as a teacher in the *lycée* or upper-secondary grades or for the C.A.P.C. exam to be certified as a teacher in the *collège* or lower-secondary grades. Students who want to teach in the *Lycées Techniques* (Technical Secondary Schools) study for five years after the baccalauréat in the Ecole Normale Supérieure d'Enseignement Technique.

SUMMARY

There is a tradition of student activism in Gabon. In spring 2000, students at the Université Omar Bongo boycotted classes for three months and participated in street demonstrations to protest the lack of computers and Internet access. During the demonstrations, some of the few existing computers were damaged. Students decided to end the boycott so as not to have to repeat the academic year, but they promised to renew the boycott in the future if computer access did not improve. One student leader declared that students wanted to enter the third millenium computer literate.

A more fundamental issue of course is the high grade repetition rate and the significant numbers of students who do not complete their education beyond the lower elementary grades. Both of these problems are related, and instruction in French, a language most of the students do not speak at home, may be one of the causes.

BIBLIOGRAPHY

Campus Numérique Francophone de Libreville, 20 January 2001. Available from http://ww.ga.refer.org.

Fatunde, Tunde. ''Computer-deprived students end boycott but remain defiant.'' *The Times Higher Education Supplement*, 30 April 1999.

Europa. *The Europa World Yearbook 2000*, Vol. 1. London: Europa Publications, 1999.

International Association of Universities. *International Handbook of Universities*, Fifteenth Ed. New York: Grove's Dictionaries Inc, 1998.

Gardiner, David E. "Gabon Republic." In *The International Encyclopedia of Education,* vol. 5. San Franciso: Jossey-Bass, 1977.

UNESCO. *Statistical Yearbook/Annuaire Statistique 1999.* Paris and Lanham, MD: UNESCO Publishing and Bernan Press, 2000.

The Central Intelligence Agency (CIA). *The World Factbook 2000.* Directorate of Intelligence, 1 January 2000. Available from http://www.cia.gov.

Université Omar Bongo, 15 January 2001. Available from http://membres.spree.com/education/uobsite.

—*Gilles Labrie*

GAMBIA

BASIC DATA

Official Country Name:	Republic of the Gambia
Region:	Africa
Population:	1,367,124
Language(s):	English, Mandinka, Wolof, Fula
Literacy Rate:	38.6%

HISTORY & BACKGROUND

Gambia, officially Republique of the Gambia, is an independent republic of western Africa and one of the smallest independent countries on the continent. It achieved its independence from Great Britain in 1965. Geographically, it is a narrow enclave that extends about 15 to 30 miles along the Gambia River and is almost completely surrounded by Senegal, a fact that forced a short-lived merger between the two nations between 1982 and 1989. There was a military coup in 1994, but a new constitution created in 1996 followed by parliamentary balloting in 1997 helped the nation to return nominally to civilian rule. The Gambia accepted a seat on the UN Security Council during 1998 to 1999, effectively ending their period of isolation.

The population (based on a July 2000 estimate) is 1,367,124 people and includes diverse ethnic groups that are 99 percent African heritage and 1 percent non-African. The most populous group is the Mandinka (42 percent), followed by the Fula (18 percent), Wolof (16 percent), Jola (10 percent), and others (14 percent). The official language is English, but each of the diverse ethnic groups also speaks their own language. The most popular are Mandinka, Wolof, and Fulu.

EDUCATIONAL SYSTEM—OVERVIEW

Gambia has a state educational structure inherited from its colonial power and continues to use English as the language of instruction. Schooling is not compulsory and the system remains under-developed as noted by the lack of adequate funding from the government and the insufficient number of schools to accommodate all of the potential students. Children under the age of 15 account for 45 percent of the country's population. Existing schools may actually operate as two distinct schools with one group of students attending a morning session and another attending an afternoon session. Some classes, even with the split shift, may still have an enrollment of 100 students or more with 3 or 4 students sharing a single desk, book, or other supplies. A lack of teachers and low salaries further demoralize educators, causing a downward cycle in education. This downward cycle is noted in the nation's low literacy rate (38.6 percent).

Educational accessibility to school also varies greatly. Although schooling is theoretically available to all children at the primary level, secondary schooling is competitive and available only to those who pass their examinations. However, failure to attend secondary school is due less to poor performance on the exam and more as a result of low income. Children from poorer families cannot afford school fees, books, or uniforms and thus are prevented from furthering their education. Children may also be needed to contribute to the family income by working in the fields or seeking other forms of employment. This further prevents them from progressing to the next level.

There are instances at the grass roots level where communities are striving to become more involved in the problem of education. For example, villagers from Kanuma built a bamboo classroom to accommodate the children of that village. Still, the basic structure of the educational system includes a Primary School, Secondary Middle School, Higher Secondary School, and Sixth Form.

PREPRIMARY & PRIMARY EDUCATION

Children attend primary school for 6 years from the ages of 7 through 13. Although schooling is not compulsory, almost all of the children living around Banjul (capital) attend school; only a third of those in other parts of the country go to school. At the completion of six years, students are awarded the Primary School Leaving Certificate.

SECONDARY EDUCATION

Secondary education is divided into Middle School (three years), Higher Secondary, and Sixth Form (2years); students attend from the ages of 13 through 21. At the successful completion of each level, a certificate is awarded. If students finish the sixth form and have completed all 13 to 14 previous years of education, they may earn the West African Examinations Council A Level Certificate.

HIGHER EDUCATION

Gambia has no university level institution, so students who wish to pursue a university degree must go abroad to study. Gambia College, located in the capital of Banjul, is the only institution of higher learning in the nation and is divided into schools of agriculture, education, nursing, and public health.

Primary school teachers are trained at the Gambia College School of Education for two years and earn a primary teachers' certificate. There is also a three-year, in-service course available to unqualified teachers to earn a basic teachers' certificate. Admission to the program is based on the middle school leaving certificate.

Secondary school teachers are also trained at Gambia College for two years and earn the higher teachers' certificate. Admission is based on earning the West African Examinations Council school certificate.

Studies at the higher technical and vocational institutes lead to certificates, diplomas, or examinations of the City and Guilds of London Institute and the Royal Society of Arts.

BIBLIOGRAPHY

The Central Intelligence Agency (CIA). *The World Factbook 2000.* Directorate of Intelligence, 1 January 2000. Available from http://www.cia.gov/.

"Education System in Gambia." newafrica.com, 2000. Available from http://www.newafrica.com/education/.

International Association of Universities (IAU). "Educational System-Gambia," 1996. Available from http://ftp.unesco.org/.

—*Jean Boris Wynn*

GAZA STRIP AND WEST BANK

BASIC DATA

Official Country Name:	Gaza Strip and West Bank
Region:	Middle East
Population:	1,132,063(GS); 2,020,298(WB)
Language(s):	Arabic, Hebrew, English
Literacy Rate:	NA

HISTORY & BACKGROUND

The West Bank and Gaza Strip lie on the western edge of Asia; both are territories of Israel. The West Bank is 130 kilometers long and ranges from 40 to 65 kilometers in width, and the Gaza Strip is 45 kilometers long and ranges from 5 to 12 kilometers in width. In 1997 the Palestinian population of the West Bank and Gaza Strip was 1,873,476 and 1,022,207, respectively.

About 50 percent of Palestinians in both areas are under 15 years of age, and this percentage is likely to increase; the fertility rates in both are among the highest in the world. Projections of population growth suggest that there will be over 4 million Palestinians in the West Bank and Gaza Strip in the year 2010, over 5 million in 2015, and over 7 million in 2025, presenting a significant challenge to the maintenance of a high quality educational system. Palestinians value education highly: literacy rates for males and females (approximately 92 percent and 77 percent respectively) are among the highest in the Arab world.

Education in these Palestinian territories during the nineteenth and early part of the twentieth century was controlled by the Ottoman Empire. There were two kinds of schools for Arabs: government and private. The private schools were Christian or Moslem institutions that had been established by missionaries or landowners. By 1917, the end of the Ottoman Era, there were 379 private schools and 95 government schools.

Between the end of the Ottoman Era and the founding of Israel in 1948, education in Palestine was controlled by Great Britain. The demand for education grew in both urban and rural areas, and by 1946 there was a total of 795 schools available to Arabs in Palestine (with 118,335 Arab students), of which 478 were government schools, 134 were private Moslem schools, and 183 were private Christian schools.

Following the 1948 war, Jordan assumed responsibility for education in the West Bank and Egypt for the Gaza Strip for children who didn't reside in refugee camps. Both created a government school system with elementary (grades 1-6), preparatory (grades 7-9), and secondary (grades 10-12) levels. Both governments instituted a matriculation examination at the end of the twelfth grade, commonly known as the *Tawjihi*, which was used to assess applicants for postsecondary education. The majority of the children of registered Palestinian refugees in the West Bank and Gaza Strip who resided in refugee camps received their first six to nine years of education at schools maintained by the United Nations Relief and Works Agency (UNRWA) and the rest in government schools. There continued during this period to be private Moslem and Christian schools in both the West Bank and Gaza Strip.

The basics of the Egyptian-Jordanian curriculum for the government schools in the West Bank and Gaza Strip remained intact after Israel occupied both in 1967. The Israeli occupation authorities (first military, then civil administration within the Ministry of Defense) took over the functions of the education ministries of Egypt and Jordan. They exercised control over curricula in the UNRWA and private schools as well as the government ones and, according to the Palestinian National Authority, attempted to suppress the teaching of Palestinian culture and history. The attempt to do so was at least partially successful: a group of 33 Palestinian students from the Gaza Strip taught by the author in 1994 had received almost no information about the history of the Gaza Strip during their previous education.

EDUCATIONAL SYSTEM—OVERVIEW

The Ministry of Education of the Palestinian National Authority (PNA) assumed responsibility for the education of the Palestinian populations of the West Bank and Gaza Strip in October 1994. Because the educational systems in both of these territories had been controlled by a foreign power for hundreds of years, this was the Palestinians first real opportunity to define and control their educational system. According to the PNA, the system was in poor condition in almost every possible way when they assumed control.

There are three supervisory authorities for the schools in the Palestinian territories: the government (PNA), UNRWA, and the private sector. The total number of schools in 1995-1996 was 1,474. Of these, 1,074 were government schools, 253 were UNRWA schools, and 147 were private schools. Total enrollment was 661,610 students, with the government schools enrolling approximately two-thirds of them. This number, however, does not include all Palestinians who are in school.

Many families from the West Bank and Gaza Strip send their children elsewhere for at least part of their education. The number of teachers was 24,342, of which approximately 60 percent were in government schools. Finally, there were 17,962 classrooms, yielding an average class size of approximately 37 students.

The educational system in the West Bank and Gaza Strip has five cycles. The first is preprimary (kindergarten) education for four and five year olds, which lasts for two years. It is provided by local or international nongovernment agencies and organizations (NGOs). The second, or basic, cycle consists of 10 years of education for 6 to 15 year olds. The third, or secondary, cycle lasts for 2 years and caters to 16 and 17 year olds. The fourth, or postsecondary, cycle consists of two years in a technical or vocational college. And the fifth, or higher education, cycle consists of four or more years of schooling.

PRIMARY & SECONDARY EDUCATION

The 10-year basic education cycle is compulsory and free of charge in government and UNRWA schools. UNRWA schools cover only nine grades, so students from these schools transfer to government or private schools to complete their education. Students who successfully complete the 10-year basic education cycle are promoted to a 2-year secondary cycle.

There are two types of secondary schools: academic and vocational. Each is two years in duration. The academic secondary school program is divided into two streams: scientific and literary. The vocational secondary school program is divided into four streams: commerce, industrial, agriculture, and nursing. At the end of this cycle, students take the General Secondary School Examination (*Tawjihi*). Their performance on this examination affects their likelihood of being admitted to a college or university in these Palestinian territories or elsewhere in the Arab world.

HIGHER EDUCATION

There are 16 community colleges in the West Bank and Gaza Strip, 5 of which are government sponsored. Study duration is two years after the *Tawhiji* examinations, leading to a diploma. They are one of three types: technical community colleges that prepare technicians, academic community colleges that prepare teachers, or hybrid community colleges that prepare both technicians and teachers. The total number of community college students in 1999-2000 was 5,286, distributed among 44 disciplines.

The higher education sector consists of 10 universities and a polytech. The universities, as a group, contain the following faculties: arts, sciences, commerce and economics, engineering, agriculture, law, pharmacy, medicine, medical professions, nursing, education, and hotel management. All were established during the 1970s or later. Their total enrollment for 1999-2000 was about 60,000 students, all but about 2,400 of which were undergraduates.

Two universities are located in the Gaza Strip: Al-Azhar University and Islamic University. The remaining eight are in the West Bank: An-Najah University, Birzeit University, Bethlehem University, Hebron University, Arab-American University, Jerusalem School for Economy and Diplomacy, Al-Quds University, and Al-Quads Open University. The polytech is in Hebron on the West Bank. The offerings of these universities are supplemented occasionally by those of foreign schools. Marquette University (United States) and the University of Calgary (Canada), for example, have conducted degree programs in the Gaza Strip in several rehabilitation and special education fields for which local training was unavailable.

SUMMARY

Palestinians have traditionally had a reputation for maintaining a high-quality educational system. According to the PNA, the system deteriorated significantly after 1967 for a number of reasons, including frequent school closures, curfews, and other restrictions resulting from the Intifada (civil uprising); a lack of financial resources for the maintenance and construction of school buildings; and insufficient preservice and in-service training for teachers. Spokespersons for the PNA's Ministry of Education have stated that they hope to restore the educational system to at least its previous level as quickly as available funding permits. The pace of such restoration is likely to be affected both by their ability to get grant funding from international governmental and private entities (e.g., NGOs) and by the Arab-Israeli peace process.

BIBLIOGRAPHY

Palestinian National Authority. *Education in Palestine,* December 2000. Available from http://www.pna.net/reports/edu_in_pal.htm/.

—*Franklin H. Silverman*

GEORGIA

BASIC DATA

Official Country Name:	Republic of Georgia
Region:	East & South Asia
Population:	5,019,538
Language(s):	Georgian, Russian, Armenian, Azeri, Abkhaz
Literacy Rate:	99%
Number of Primary Schools:	3,201
Compulsory Schooling:	9 years
Public Expenditure on Education:	5.2%
Foreign Students in National Universities:	69
Libraries:	3,929
Educational Enrollment:	Primary: 293,325 Secondary: 444,058 Higher: 163,345
Educational Enrollment Rate:	Primary: 88% Secondary: 77% Higher: 42%
Teachers:	Primary: 16,542 Secondary: 57,963 Higher: 25,549
Student-Teacher Ratio:	Primary: 18:1 Secondary: 8:1
Female Enrollment Rate:	Primary: 88% Secondary: 76% Higher: 44%

HISTORY & BACKGROUND

The Republic of Georgia has a long and difficult history that began in the Middle Ages. Georgia was an independent nation before and after its incorporation into the Russian sphere of influence, which has occurred twice in its history. It is once again a sovereign nation, a highly independent country that did not choose to join the Council of Independent States after the breakup of the Soviet Union.

Like many nations that were incorporated into the Soviet Union in the twentieth century, for much of its recent history, Georgia was considered simply a region of the USSR. Before it became associated with the Soviet Union, it was taken into the Russian Empire in the nineteenth century. In 1918, at the time of the Russian Revolution, Georgia became an independent nation, and remained so until 1921. In that year, the Republic of

Georgia was forced to become a part of the USSR. In the 1990s, the era of *perestroika* in Russia and the nations that were once called its satellites, the Republic of Georgia was one of the first countries to break away from the Soviet Union and declare its independence. It became a sovereign nation once again in 1991.

Despite its tense and complex relations with Russia, several of Russia's most important twentieth-century leaders were Georgians. Joseph Stalin, the Russian premier before, during, and after World War II, was from Georgia. So was Eduard Shevardnadze, the foreign minister of the USSR during its breakup, who later became President of Georgia shortly after it gained its independence. Lavrenty Beria, who lived from 1899 to 1953, was Stalin's head of the secret police (or KGB), and was also a Georgian. Despite his origins, he was especially brutal against Georgian dissidents. Beria was assassinated by the Russian administration that succeeded Stalin after his death.

Geography & Population: Although not well known to foreigners, Georgia has a distinctive character and significant national unity. It has its own primary language as well as several other languages that are used in special regions and by minority groups. Its culture, including its dance, music, and art, is significantly different from other formerly Soviet nations.

Georgia is a truly Caucasian nation—a nation that is located in the Caucasus region of the European and Asian continents. The Caucasus mountain range is located between the Caspian and Black seas; its northern parts are in Europe and its southern regions, which border Turkey and Iran, are in Asia. The Republic of Georgia's location is in southwestern Asia, bordering the Black Sea. Geographically, it falls between Turkey and Russia and is therefore influenced by both Europe and Asia. Georgia covers 69,700 square kilometers (26,911 square miles), which is about the size of South Carolina. The climate is warm and pleasant, similar to the Mediterranean region.

There are many natural resources, including forests, iron and copper, some coal and oil, and soil that can be used to grow tea and citrus. A good portion of the nation is woodlands and permanent pastures. Air and water pollution, lack of sufficient amounts of potable water, and some soil pollution from toxic chemicals are among the environmental problems the country faces.

The people of Georgia are many and are diverse: the total population is 5.4 million. About 70 percent of the people are Georgian, but 80 other nationalities and groups make up the balance. Some 6.3 percent are Russian, 5.7 percent are Azeris, 3 percent are Ossetes, 1.9 percent are Greek, 1.8 percent are Abkhazians, and 0.5 percent are Jewish. Two of these minority groups, Azeris

and Abkhazians, have their own republics within the Georgian Republic. The urban population stands at 56 percent, while 44 percent live in rural areas. Life expectancy for men is 69.43 years and 76.95 for women, with an average for the whole population of 73.1 years. About half the population, or 2.76 million people, are in the labor force. Industry and construction employ 31 percent of workers, while 25 percent are in agriculture and forestry. The unemployment rate is about 14.5 percent.

Although there are other religions, the great majority of the people of Georgia, over 80 percent, are Christians. Most of them (65 percent) are Georgian Orthodox, 10 percent are Russian Orthodox, and 8 percent Armenian Orthodox. Eleven percent are Muslim, and the nations that surround the Republic of Georgia are generally majority Muslim. This predominant Christianity is one of the bases for the close relations between the Republic of Georgia and Western nations, including the United States.

Language: Language is a central issue in any educational system and the languages of Georgia are different from those of the rest of the world. The Caucasus region is also the source of the Caucasian languages, of which there are some 40. Only Georgian, however, is considered a modern language. There is some dispute about the nature of the language. Some sources call it part of the Indo-European language group. Others, however, say that Georgian is not a part of that group or of the Finno-Ugric or Semitic language families, arguing that it is part of the Ibero-Caucasian or Kartvelian language group.

The Georgian language probably evolved around the fifth century B.C. It has 33 characters, distinctive word formations, and complex rules governing its use of verbs. Many of the Georgian words place several consonants together with few intervening vowels. The name of the capital city, Tbilisi, is an example. Although the official language of the nation is Georgian, in some regions people also use Megruli and Chanuri. All three languages derived from Old Kartvelian. Several other regional languages are also in modern use.

Georgia's multiplicity of languages dates to ancient times, when there were so many languages used in the nation that Romans needed 130 interpreters to do business there. Because of its long association with Russia, a modern visitor can typically navigate in the nation by using Russian. But those who speak neither Russian nor Georgian need to engage interpreters: few in the population speak other languages, except for specific ethnic languages.

Political, Social, & Cultural Context: Georgia is a member of the United Nations and many international compacts. It has close ties to the World Bank and the International Monetary Fund, both of which help the nation more fully develop its economy and, in the case of the World Bank, its educational system, as explained more fully in the summary.

Although Georgia is no longer subservient to Russia and has its own democratic government, there are Russian troops at military bases in Georgia. They serve as peacekeepers in two regions, Abkhazia and South Ossetia, which are separatist and sometimes threaten to break with the Republic of Georgia.

The United States and the Republic of Georgia have strong diplomatic relations and work closely together. Georgia receives the second largest amount of per capita assistance, among all the world's nations, from the United States. According to former Secretary of State James Baker, Georgia became important to the United States because it provided an opportunity to influence the institutions formed in the wake of the fall of the Communist Soviet Union. Moreover, Georgia was important because of Eduard Shevardnadze, Georgia's president, who was thought to be heavily involved in ending the Cold War. According to Baker, that era in world history would not have ended in a peaceful way without Shevardnadze, whom Baker considered a hero.

Post-Soviet Georgia is attempting to move the economy and the people toward a market economy that could be connected with Western institutions. Recent developments include an efficient telephone system, including cell phones, and delivery from Federal Express. Georgian food remains popular, but French, Chinese, and other national cuisines are also available in the Republic.

The Georgian economy has demonstrated annual growth rates of about 3.5 percent in recent years, although 60 percent of the population lives below the poverty line. A key problem is the inflation rate for consumer prices, which stands at 19 percent. Another problem has been the inability to collect all the taxes that they levy, and there are continuing problems with tax evasion and corruption. Moreover, the nation lacks sufficient energy, despite extensive hydroelectric power and the exportation of some electricity. Because they lack adequate oil and coal, they must import energy sources. Nonetheless, some hopeful projections anticipate that economic growth could nearly double in the twenty-first century.

Historical Development: With free and compulsory schooling a part of Georgia's educational tradition, the nation's population is generally well educated. The nation of Georgia has a long history of attention to higher education; according to one authority, the Georgian population was the most highly educated of all the peoples under the USSR. One indication of the careful attention

and expenditure of resources on education in Georgia is the number of physicians: there are 53.7 physicians for every 10,000 people in the nation. Moreover, a third of the working population of Georgia has some form of higher education or specialized middle education. This compares favorably to the United Kingdom, in which 11.2 percent of the population have some form of specialized education, and also to Japan, where 14.2 percent of the population have higher or other specialized education.

The history of education in Georgia dates from as early as the Middle Ages. Monasteries and academies functioned as vital centers of learning, which was important to the people of the nation because they assisted in preserving their national heritage when they were occupied by other cultures. By 1915, just prior to the Russian Revolution, there were 1,648 schools of all types in Georgia. In spite of that, most Georgians were illiterate. However, the era of Soviet connection increased the quantity of mass education and illiteracy was basically eliminated. The definition of literacy used by Georgia is the proportion of the population age 15 and over who can read and write. The total population is, therefore, 99 percent literate. One hundred percent of the men, according to Georgian government estimates, are literate, and 98 percent of females are literate.

Because of changes in the government in the 1990s, the education system of Georgia also changed dramatically. For example, in the era of the Soviet Union, the government provided for free education at all stages for all people. In post-Soviet Georgia, only nine years of primary education are compulsory and free for all; higher levels of secondary schools and the universities are free only for 30 percent of students, while others pay tuition. Perhaps the most significant change has been the granting of autonomous status to higher education institutions, which occurred in 1992.

CONSTITUTIONAL & LEGAL FOUNDATIONS

The first president of the Republic after the Soviet era was Zviad Gamsakhurdia. After a period of disorder in which Gamsakhurdia was forced to flee and ultimately died, President Shevardnadze was elected by popular vote for a five-year term and was re-elected in 2000.

The country has a legislature, referred to as Parliament, which is unicameral—that is, it has only one house—and the members serve four-year terms. There are 235 members. The judicial branch is a supreme court, which is elected by Parliament on the recommendation of the president.

With regard to education, Article 35 of the Constitution of the Republic of Georgia states:

- Each citizen has the right to education and freedom of choice in education is recognized.

- The state guarantees that educational programs conform to international standards and rights.

- The state guarantees preschool education. Primary education is mandatory for all, and the state provides free primary education. Citizens also have the right to free secondary, professional, and tertiary education at state institute, within the framework and by the rules established in law.

- The state supports educational institutions by the right established in law.

EDUCATIONAL SYSTEM—OVERVIEW

Public education in Georgia is comprised of the following categories: kindergarten, ages 2-5; elementary school, grades 1-4; secondary school, grades 5-9; and upper secondary school, grades 10-11. The system of kindergarten has largely collapsed, however, and has become increasingly privatized. Attendance is now a sign of prestige and, according to a World Bank report (Perkins 1998), only 20 percent of eligible children attend. There are plans to introduce a grade 12, but financial constraints have prevented any progress thus far.

Education is not limited to general day schools; there are also boarding schools for children with disabilities and ''Youth Palaces'' for an intensive study of such subjects as art, music, drama, and dance. In 1993 the first school for internally displaced persons (IDP schools) opened for elementary, secondary, and high school education. Both the teachers and students are IDPs; 90 percent of students must be IDPs, and the remaining 10 percent are local children.

The school year officially begins in September and ends in June, but the number of official school days is close to 150 due to numerous holidays and breaks throughout the year. Principals may decide to close school altogether during part of the winter due to lack of heat and electricity, or during harvesting season in the agricultural regions. A typical school day generally lasts from seven hours in upper school to as little as three hours in primary school. Schools use a two-semester schedule.

Examinations, Promotions, & Certifications: Students progress to the next grade based on their teachers' recommendations. The decision is made according to written work and participation throughout the year. Instead of being assigned a letter grade, students are rated on a scale of one to five, with five being the best. Students rarely fail or repeat a grade.

Every student in Georgia completing secondary school takes the exit exam, comprised of both oral and

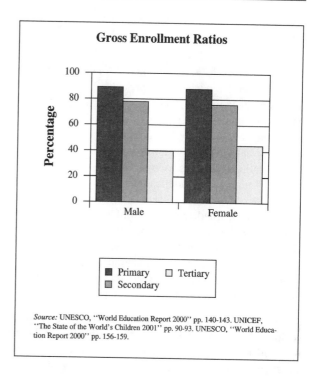

Gross Enrollment Ratios

Legend: Primary, Secondary, Tertiary (Male, Female)

Source: UNESCO, ''World Education Report 2000'' pp. 140-143. UNICEF, ''The State of the World's Children 2001'' pp. 90-93. UNESCO, ''World Education Report 2000'' pp. 156-159.

written assessment on the same day at the same time. The Minister or Deputy Minister of Education announces the essay questions via radio and television to eliminate the possibility of obtaining questions or answers beforehand. Whatever precautions are used before the test to ensure equity are lost in the grading. The exams are graded by members of a panel that includes the student's teacher. Because it is the individual student's teacher who ultimately records the grades and turns them in, the process is ripe for corruption and bribery. Additionally, no school wants to fail students or provide an excuse for further faculty or staff cuts. Annual examinations can also be held after the fourth grade, and many schools use that opportunity to test and evaluate students.

Because Georgia currently lacks national assessment standards for the exit exams, college entrance exams have been instituted. Although passage of exit exams is nearly universal, the rate of students passing the college entrance exams is markedly reduced. Students who want to continue their education thus often hire tutors to prepare for the exam. A World Bank reform project, discussed in detail in the Summary, would ensure national grading standards for exit exams by impartial judges, allowing for the elimination of the unpopular entrance exams. Universal testing at the secondary level and elimination of college entrance exams would improve the quality of students, especially those with financial constraints.

Only about 70 percent of pupils are accepted to higher education institutions. Students who do not successfully move to the next stage after completing secondary or high school can attend vocational and technical schools.

Educational Style & Textbooks: As Georgia tries to distance itself from a Russian curriculum, it still holds on to Soviet educational methodology. Education is content-based and focuses on memorizing facts, lectures, and texts, rather than analyzing subjects and teaching students critical thinking, which is more common in Western educational systems. A typical class begins with the review of homework and the material covered in the previous class, after which students recite the passages read or concepts learned word-for-word from the text. The teacher then explains a new concept and goes over exercises that students will take for homework. Then the teacher may review previous material covered or use the time to talk about what was learned during class. Reading, repeating, and recalling is the standard drill.

Each class lasts about 45 minutes, though in the rural regions classes may be shorter during the winter due to the cold and the lack of fuel to heat school facilities. There is a growing argument that such a curriculum doesn't adequately prepare students for university study and should be modified. Students who go on to study at universities usually have had extensive private tutoring throughout school.

Study of even the most basic topics has become difficult, however, as many students and teachers do not have textbooks. Government policy dictates that students supply their own school texts and supplies. Textbooks are quite expensive and often out of reach for many parents, especially in rural regions. Often the costs of purchasing texts for one child exceed the family's monthly income. The textbooks that are available are often in very poor condition, as the Ministry of Education encourages printers to keep costs low by using inexpensive, poor quality material and smaller type. Students who can afford to may buy several copies of each book because they have such a short life span. Relying on secondhand books is not always an option, as they are often in Russian and do not reflect the new Georgian curriculum and ideas. The Ministry of Education estimates textbook availability to be anywhere from 40 to 75 percent for elementary schools, 40 to 60 percent for secondary, and 25 to 30 percent for upper secondary grades. Plans for textbook reform are also part of the World Bank project.

Enrollment: Accurately estimating the number and percentage of children enrolled in schools is difficult, as no recent official data has been published, and the organizations collecting information use different methods for doing so. Moreover, some poorer families don't register the births of their children until they are old enough to attend school in order to delay the cost of registration.

Estimates for the 1997-1998 school year indicate 926,000 students enrolled in all levels of the Georgia educational system. In 1997, about 87 percent of children eligible for first grade were enrolled. This marks a decline in enrollment since Georgia gained its independence in 1991. Some suggest that the decline might be as large as 20 percent for primary school. The starting age for school was lowered from seven to six years and grade nine is now compulsory, which should raise the level slightly. The dropout rate is about 4.3 to 5 percent in elementary school, 5.4 percent in incomplete secondary, and 9.9 percent at the upper secondary level.

PREPRIMARY & PRIMARY EDUCATION

Preprimary Education: The Georgian government works to develop the personality of children through preschool programs. There are two types of preschool programs: nursery schools for babies age one and two, and kindergarten for children age three to six. In 1989, during the Soviet period, preschool was free, and 42 percent of eligible children attended kindergarten. In that year, there were 2,431 preschool programs with 213,396 pupils, or an average of 87 children per institution.

By 1993, there were 1,921 preschool institutions with 105,975 students, or 55 pupils per institution. By 1995 there was a further decrease to 1,272 institutions serving 79,200 pupils, or 62 pupils per institutions. Prior to the breakup of the Soviet Union, preschool institutions were established at factories and other organizations, and children of employees were cared for during working hours in those institutions. The economic depression following Georgia's independence made that impossible, and the number of preschools in factories and other work sites decreased from 805 to 47. In addition, during the Soviet period, food was given to preschool institutions, while after independence schools were required to pay for their own food.

Private kindergartens have developed to replace the official or governmental schools that existed prior to the change in government and the economic crises. There are also many nonregistered preschool institutions operating in private apartments. The government does not have specific data about these schools, though some estimates of the total enrollment in kindergartens of all kinds suggest that in 1997-1998, approximately 926,000 students were enrolled in public and private kindergartens. By contrast, the government reports its kindergarten enrollment for that year at 75,000. Other sources suggest that kindergarten is much less than universally available, and that it is a sign of prestige and privilege to send one's children to kindergarten.

The preschools are open from September through August. Many charitable organizations are also establishing preschools for younger children. The state-operated preschools receive some subsidy from the government, but parents are expected to pay part of the cost.

Primary Education: The Georgian government attempts to keep records on the percentage of children who enroll in school, compared to the data on births. In 1997, nearly 89 percent of children born in 1991 (and thus of school age) had enrolled in first grade. For the period from 1990 through 1998, there were 512,256 children in grades one through six. That number dropped for the 1995-1996 school year to 429,864. In 1996-1997, primary school enrollments were 435,797. In 1997-1998, the figure was 442,265.

Students in the primary grades study about 7 subjects, compared to 15 in the upper grades. Primary school subjects include native language study, math, fine arts, music, physical education, natural studies, Russian, and literature. All grades also have a free period for extracurricular activities, but the Ministry of Education plans to introduce new courses in religion and culture, which may take up this time. The school day is approximately three hours in the primary grades.

The methodological approach in all disciplines is highly teacher and textbook centered, rather than attempting to engage children through more active learning or research-oriented activities. In the fourth grade, for example, educational strategy focuses on copying, solving exercises with the teacher or individually, applying rules, and recalling.

As Georgia tries to distance itself from its Soviet legacy, the ministry is placing more emphasis on humanities, specifically Georgian history and culture, and less on math, science, and Russian. They have increased the number of hours spent studying foreign languages, humanities, the history and geography of Georgia, and Georgian language and literature. The constitution requires schools to provide education in the Georgian, Russian, Armenian, Azeri, Ossetian, and Abkhazian languages. Georgian is by far the predominant language of instruction, however, especially since many Russians have migrated back to Russia, and South Ossetia and Abkhazia have declared their separation from Georgia.

SECONDARY EDUCATION

In 1997-1998 there were about 275,000 students in the country's two divisions of secondary education. The lower division is called basic, or secondary. The higher level is called upper secondary, or high school. The basic level consists of grades 7 through 9, and the higher level is grades 10 and 11. There is some hope of adding a twelfth grade in the future. Education is compulsory, as mentioned earlier, through ninth grade.

An assessment of the primary teaching activities for ninth graders found that:

- They consist of low cognitive complexity level tasks.

- They are centered on the text and not on transferring potential to other learning activities.

- They do not foster understanding or promote critical and independent thinking.

The typical school day in the secondary school classroom follows a pattern similar to that of the primary schools, as follows:

- Lesson starts by calling the roll and taking note of those absent.

- Teachers check students' homework.

- Teachers propose more exercises or ask questions.

- Teachers introduce a new concept or lesson.

- Teachers make sure students learn the ''right'' answers.

- Lesson ends with the indication of more homework.

- Lesson lasts for 45 minutes.

The school day for basic, or the lower level of secondary education, is five to six hours per day; for the higher level, it is six to seven hours per day. Most students also have two or more hours of homework. History, geography, biology, physics, chemistry, and foreign languages are studied at the secondary level and, at the higher level, students choose an emphasis to study. The choices include humanities, physics and math, chemistry and biology, vocational education, or language. High school is the highest level of education before students reach eligibility for entering higher education.

HIGHER EDUCATION

Post-high school education is diverse in Georgia. The nation's universities used to follow the Soviet five-year program but now have a four-year bachelor's degree program. A master's degree takes two to three years. The next level is called the *aspirantura*, which takes another three to four years and which ends in a candidate degree, a scientific degree that focuses on independent research. The highest degree given is the doctor of science.

Universities administer their own entrance exams. Each state university offers an entrance exam during the same week in August. Students must decide beforehand which university, program, and faculty they want to apply to. Private institutions hold their exams the following week. Reports of corruption are rampant. According to some estimates, about half the students purchase a copy of the test questions beforehand. Faculties have also been implicated in purchasing tests to help their students.

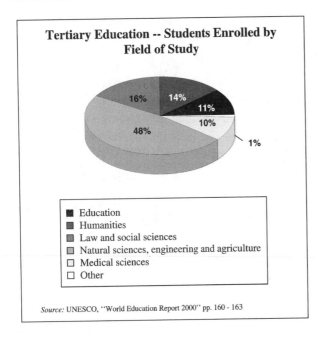

Tertiary Education -- Students Enrolled by Field of Study

- Education
- Humanities
- Law and social sciences
- Natural sciences, engineering and agriculture
- Medical sciences
- Other

Source: UNESCO, "World Education Report 2000" pp. 160 - 163

The nation's total higher education system is made up of 22 institutions, including universities, institutes, *technicums,* and cultural academies. Before independence, the state sponsored more than 100,000 students at these schools, providing a stipend based on school performance. In 1992, approximately 24 percent of Georgians of higher-education age were enrolled in higher education.

University studies typically provide highly specialized, rigid training focusing on a single area of study. Law and medicine students do not attend regular university, but go directly to law and medical school from high school. Law school takes five years to complete and medical schools seven, plus two to three years of *ordinatura,* which is comparable to an internship.

Although the Soviet government ran well-equipped vocational and technical schools, the schools were not popular, and the economic depression that followed independence saw the vocational and technical education system disintegrate. Much of the equipment was stolen and school buildings were occupied by other organizations. There had been 170 vocational technical schools enrolling 70,000 students in 300 branches, but by 1996 there were only 115 schools with 20,000 students and 150 branches.

Since 1996, the government has been working to reestablish vocational and technical education for those who could not attend universities. The programs train specialists in an improved technical system and offer courses for farmers, manufacturers, and businesspersons. Centers for education and industry were established in different parts of the country in the 1990s, and unem-

ployed workers and persons changing professions were given opportunities for retraining.

Study in vocational and technical schools is three to four years. Graduates from those schools receive certificates that permit them to work in their fields of study. Those who pass special advanced courses can continue their education. Graduates of technical schools may acquire certificates as midlevel specialists for work as nurses, teachers, computer operators, and other fields of expertise. There are 32 such schools under the Ministry of Education. There are approximately the same number of schools under other ministries, such as health, culture, and agriculture. These schools are called *technicums,* and their graduates are permitted to enter higher education.

ADMINISTRATION, FINANCE, & EDUCATIONAL RESEARCH

The Ministry of Education is the central governing body and oversees most decisions regarding education throughout the country. The ministry has 10 regions and the city of Tbilisi, which has a separate region. Each region has an education department, with 72 districts comprising the region, and there are local school administrators. The ministry is responsible for approving textbooks, courses, and curricula at all levels. It also licenses and certifies teachers, principals, and schools.

The office of the Ministry of Education experienced a fire several years ago and had insufficient funds to repair the building. Therefore, it works out of two separate buildings. Department heads are often separated from their staff and, with the energy crisis facing Tbilisi, telephones and electricity often do not work, making communication even among officials and staff difficult. The ministry has a few computers, but regional and local offices do not, nor do they have copy machines, so most still fill out forms, registrations, and records by hand.

Funding Sources: In responding to its charge of establishing budgets and overseeing financial matters, the ministry has taken zealous measures. In 1997, Parliament imposed a fee of 10 laris per month (about 8 U.S. dollars) for all but the top 30 percent of students attending public schools. The money is collected at the school level or deposited directly into a bank account set up by the ministry. However, the money does not stay at the school level. Schools are, in fact, forbidden to open their own bank accounts. Because the ministry plays such a significant role in the distribution of funds, having friends and connections at such a level can often increase a district's funding. Some schools have chosen to charge more than the required 10 laris and use the money to purchase heating fuel or pass it along in the form of a teacher's bonus.

A major cause of tight education budgets and inadequate funding for schools is the way the national education budget is spent. All money goes through the Ministry of Education and from there is dispersed to the *rayons*, the substructures of Georgian government. At the rayon level, the funds then go to local districts and finally to the schools. The triangular nature of the system allows for diversion of funds into noneducation functions. The Ministry of Education reportedly uses 40 percent of the national education budget for salaries, social contributions, and the ''miscellaneous'' category. In Tbilisi, the capital, 60 percent of the budget goes to personnel costs at the administrative level.

Other sources of budget disparity are the methods of revenue generation. While each rayon receives some funding from the national level, the rest must be generated locally through taxes and contributions. Rayons in rural areas are much poorer, and in some areas bartering and trading are more common than using money, causing real problems in generating money for schools. Consequently, schools in Tbilisi and other cities are much better equipped and in better condition. Since the Soviet period, local businesses have assisted and sponsored local schools, and some are still able to do this today, which greatly helps schools operate, especially the poorer schools in the regions. Other schools rent out space in the buildings to businesses to generate revenues.

Expenditures: Most school facilities in Georgia are fairly old and have not received much maintenance since the fall of the Soviet Union. The Ministry of Education estimates that over 80 percent of schools are in need of serious repair or reconstruction. Although schools in Tbilisi and other larger cities are in relatively good condition, many schools pose serious threats to students health, with no staircase railings; cracks in walls, ceilings, and hallways; peeling paint; broken windows; no running water; leaking roofs; and decaying, uncomfortable furniture. In rural areas, some schools do not have bathrooms. Fences have not been repaired, allowing animals to roam the schoolyards and creating unsanitary conditions. Some rural schools also lack basic teaching equipment including blackboards, desks, and books.

Lack of teaching materials has forced teachers to become creative in order to carry on their work. A number of teachers make teaching aids in their own homes or ask others to do so. For beginning grades some make alphabet letters and calendars out of cardboard. Most teachers, however, view creating their own teaching materials as something outside their defined roles and responsibilities, and consider it an extra burden forced on them by the lack of funds.

School buildings were constructed during the Soviet period, when energy was well below world price, and many buildings were not insulated. In the cities, there was an underground heating system provided free of charge to schools. In the post-Soviet era energy became scarce, and underground systems are no longer used. Each school is given funding for energy and water, but usually in name only. What money actually makes it to the individual schools is hardly adequate and not enough to install insulation or introduce new technology to conserve water. Consequently, schools are forced to find additional funds or simply close. In the cities, the school budget covers the purchase of some fuel for stoves or space heaters, and parents must provide additional money. In the rural areas, schools usually have wood-burning stoves, and students bring what wood or fuel they can contribute. During the coldest part of the winter schools often close for weeks or months due to lack of heating.

During Soviet times, a certain percentage of the government's funds was allocated for food in the education system. Three meals a day were provided in kindergarten and boarding schools. Meals in primary and vocational schools and university cafeterias were also subsidized. Even though the kindergartens can no longer afford to buy food and provide meals for their students, many still, under contracts, have to pay the kitchen staff. This redundancy of personnel, an ongoing problem at several levels, interferes with the efficiency of the educational system.

NONFORMAL EDUCATION

Under the Soviet system, Georgia had a strong program of adult education and nonformal education, including evening classes and study through correspondence. These systems were very popular because of the small number of people who were allowed to enter formal institutions. In 1996 these programs encountered a reduction in enrollments, largely because adults enrolled instead in private institutions.

Special Education: In Georgia, government has a public policy of providing special education for persons with disabilities as well as appropriate general education and, when it is required, therapeutic training in schools that are established for this purpose. These schools have special syllabi, lesson plans, and teaching methods. Special vocational and technical courses are aimed at enabling students to develop a profession and to be eligible for employment. There is also an effort to help special education students improve their physical and social status.

In 1996, there were 18 special boarding schools in Tbilisi and two preschools for blind children and those with speech defects. There were about 2,000 pupils in those institutions. Duration of study in special schools is based on the ability of the students to learn the subjects offered by the school. Study in special education schools is free and has a high priority in Georgia based on resolutions passed by the Cabinet of Ministers in the mid-1990s. In most cases, there is one institution to correspond with each of the following disabilities: blindness, limited eyesight, limited hearing, cerebral palsy, curvature of the spine, asthma, problems in speech development, and gastric diseases. There are two schools for deaf children, and eight auxiliary schools for children who are mentally retarded. These figures compare similarly to special education institutions in the United States, if one compares Georgia to a state with three to five million people.

TEACHING PROFESSION

Salaries: Teachers' salaries reached their lowest level in 1995, at an amount of US$4 per month. At one time teaching was the lowest paid profession in Tbilisi, a relatively high-paying city: teachers earned 21.8 laris per month, compared to the overall average salary of 61.5 laris per month. Subsequent increases have raised teachers' salaries to about 30 laris (US$24) per month. A lari is worth about 80 U.S. cents. Average teacher salaries are about 55 percent of the average wage for the total economy (54.9 laris) and about 80 percent of that for other public sector employees (37.5 laris). One reason for the low wages is overstaffing: education staffing in Georgia is atypically generous by international standards, and is twice as high per student as in Western nations. Thus already tight budgets must be spread thin over many teachers. Teachers in some rural villages have turned to farming and teach classes in their spare time. Others sell fruit or their remaining household items in Tbilisi market places in order to make ends meet.

The state still controls Georgia's most prominent higher education institutions and is unable to pay professors a living wage. As a result, scholars have been forced to emigrate or "moonlight" at jobs outside their fields. Many now teach at the private colleges and universities that have opened in the country. Although these schools pay decent salaries, the scholars have no time for research and writing, and are sometimes forced to instruct students who do not wish to learn.

An even bigger problem for many teachers, however, has been not being paid at all. Some regions have gone almost a year without paying their teachers, leading to several teacher strikes. In one instance, more than 100 teachers blocked the road in front of the of the regional administration office to demand their wages, which had not been paid for six to eight months.

Parents also complained, noting that teachers were looked at by pupils as poor people who could not even afford to buy proper clothing. This had a negative impact on teacher morale, and some believed that their authority

among students was compromised. Teachers who had to work in the market during the weekend considered that shameful and said that they did not want to be seen by their students. The months without pay, combined with ill-equipped classrooms and limited teaching materials, have made many teachers feel inferior about their jobs.

Training & Qualifications: Teachers in Georgia have been hired not out of necessity, but because of the social prestige associated with teaching and a strong pressure to accommodate the growing number of graduates. The actual abilities and credentials of many candidates played a small role in the process. (An exception is the rural mountainous areas, where most schools lacked even a minimum number of teachers.) Large numbers of teachers cannot teach without a textbook; textbooks have become the main source of knowledge, not a supplement. This is in part due to the practices of the Soviet period, when teachers were compelled to rely heavily on texts; teachers have become accustomed to following them step by step.

The number of teachers has significantly declined since 1990-1991. In 1996, there were 102,073 teachers in Georgia: 69,219 (68 percent) in grades 1-11; 9,368 (9 percent) at preschool; and 18 percent in higher education. In the process of reducing the number of teachers, those teachers who received their posts by merit, as opposed to bribery and nepotism, are most likely to lose their jobs. Another factor is that male teachers were leaving teaching at rates beyond the national average, moving to find work in Russia or Armenia.

The proportion of teachers with complete higher education has increased slightly, to 87 percent in urban schools and 75 percent in rural schools. So far, the impact of low pay and poor conditions has been confined mainly to growing teacher shortages in foreign languages and computer science, where demand is strong outside the teaching profession, and in the remote rural areas, where it has become extremely difficult to replace retiring teachers. Recent measures by the government to consolidate and improve the teaching force have succeeded in raising the pupil-teacher ratio to 10.4 (from 8.3 in 1991), reducing the number of part-time teachers, increasing the full-time working load, and increasing salaries on a performance basis through a national testing and certification process.

Unions & Associations: There are two major trade unions in Georgia. The first is the Education Workers Trade Union of the Georgian Trade Unit Amalgamation, and the second is the Free Trade Union of Teachers of Georgia-Solidarity. Both unions are focused on teachers in the regions. The Education Workers Trade Union is the older organization, and is based in the northeastern region of Tianeti. Many call this union an offshoot of the old Soviet-style unions, although the leaders deny this. The Free Trade Union was established in 1998 and is based out of Kutaisi; it has 2,800 members throughout the regions. Although the trade unions do not have a good working relationship with each other and disagree over methods of change, they appear to have similar goals of improving teachers' working conditions and compensation.

SUMMARY

Georgia faces many problems, but it is also in the process of working to reform its educational system. In that effort, it has the support and participation of the World Bank. The World Bank is working on a 12-year program that will eventually give US$60 million to the government of Georgia. The program is divided into several phases; the first phase goes until 2005 and involves US$25.9 million. If all the triggers are accomplished, the program will advance to the next phase and involve more money. The goal of this project is to realign the educational system and to make it more equitable, effective, and efficient. There are groups at the Georgian Ministry of Education specifically devoted to each component of reform.

There are seven components to the program: curriculum reform, national student assessment, professional development of teachers, development of new textbooks, strengthening policy and administration, efficient use of human resources, and increasing public awareness.

The curriculum component involves developing a national curriculum by 2005 for both primary (grades one through six) and secondary education (grades seven through nine). Students all over the country will study the exact same materials at the same levels.

A national student assessment exam and a national assessment center will be developed. As of 2001, assessment exams were administered and recorded by each local school. Thus students may score the same but be tested on different material. The old system has also been tainted by corruption: because teachers are paid so little and so rarely, some sell test scores, offer private tutoring, or change grades for a little extra money. With a national assessment, the exams will be reviewed and recorded by the national assessment center. The center will also collect and compile data and statistics nationwide for education.

The component for the professional development of teachers has several parts. One important aspect is the development of school networks for sharing information and creating a community of teachers. A program for individual school grants is also planned. The Ministry of Education will be responsible for setting up the regula-

tions and provisions and will also provide support and instruction in grant proposal writing for those without experience in this field. Every school will receive a grant for the purpose of helping children learn. The grant cannot go to books or computers, but to projects engineered by the teachers themselves, in order to involve teachers in the reform process and allow the schools to see immediate results from the project.

The development of new textbooks includes the training of authors and those who will have to make the final decisions about what texts schools should use. Schools will buy the books and then rent them out to students. The first-year students will pay about 50 percent of the cost of the books, and then 30 percent for the next four years. Thus through book rentals the schools will accumulated enough funds to purchase new textbooks every four years and so on. This would make the project self-sustainable and would not require foreign loans or aid in order to provide books for students.

The project also includes a component to strengthen policy and administration. Regional education departments, which were established in the late 1990s, lack clear and defined roles. The Soros Foundation is helping to define the roles of the various departments. Local authorities are responsible for paying teachers' salaries, funding school maintenance and upkeep, however, the management responsibilities have not been plainly articulated.

The next component is a more efficient allocation of resources. Currently there is one teacher for every 10 students, a carryover from the Soviet system in which there was about a 1:5 teacher-student ratio. One of the program's goals is to increase this ratio to 1:14 by 2005. According to current regulations teachers are allowed to teach only certain grades and subjects. Therefore, a village school could have only 5 students but 10 teachers because secondary teachers are not allowed to teach primary classes. Because of this redundancy of teachers, about half of all teachers will have to be laid off. The Ministry of Education and the World Bank are trying to establish a severance package for pensioners. Although teaching pays very little, pensions are even less. It is against World Bank policies to pay severance for teachers, but they are revisiting the policy to look for an interpretation that would allow this. The system would have to retain the most qualified teachers and insure that those receiving severance pay would not return to the education system as consultants or in other capacities.

The Bank's project does not provide for any changes to school buildings, but it will analyze and map schools to eliminate redundancy. If there are two schools in close proximity they may be merged together. These resources will go into a database and the center will develop software and a computerized system for recording this data. Not all schools will have computers—they may still have to fill out their forms by hand—but the data will be computerized. This will allow the government and others access to information about the schools throughout the country.

The final component of the project is increasing public awareness. Sustaining education reform will require the increased dissemination of information and higher levels of parent and teacher involvement in the school system.

This project will help combat corruption through its measures to increase openness, cooperation, community involvement, and organization. Hopefully the example of these reforms will encourage similar changes in higher education, which faces even greater problems of corruption. For example, with nationwide exams throughout secondary schooling, higher institutions of learning might adopt this type of assessment as well, thus minimizing unfair influence and bribery.

Georgia's educational system has a long way to go before it is as effective as its supporters hope it will be. Nonetheless, the country has a plan and the resources to help it achieve major improvements over time.

BIBLIOGRAPHY

Bateman, Graham, ed. *Encyclopedia of World Geography, Vol. 14, Russia and Northern Eurasia.* New York: Marshall Cavendish, 1994.

Ghurchumelia, Manana [Leader of the Free Trade Union of Teachers of Georgia—Solidarity]. Interview by Sara Payne. Kutaisi, Georgia, 13 February 2001.

Grachev, A.S. *Final Days: The Inside Story of the Collapse of the Soviet Union.* Boulder, CO: Westview Press, 1994.

Harbor, Bernard. *The Breakup of the Soviet Union.* New York: New Discovery, 1992.

Imnadze, Elene [Public Sector Management Specialist, World Bank Office]. Interview by Sara Payne. Tbilisi, Georgia, 8 February 2001.

Jones, Stephen F. "Republic of Georgia." In *The Encyclopedia Americana,* 12: 532-537. Danbury, CT: The Grolier Society, 2000.

McGiffert, Carolyn, and Melvin A. Ekedahl. *The Wars of Eduard Shevardnadze.* State College: Pennsylvania State University Press, 1997.

Mikeladze, Mzia [Dean of the Georgian Institute of Public Affairs]. Interview by Sara Payne. Tbilisi, Georgia, 14 February 2001.

Orivel, Francois. *Cost and Finance of Education in Georgia.* Université de Bourgogne: Irédu/CNRS, 1998.

Polazchenko, Pavel, Don Oberdorfer, and P. Polazchenko. *My Years with Gorbachev and Shevardnadze: The Memoirs of a Soviet Interpreter.* State College: Pennsylvania State University Press, 1997.

Read, Tony, Carmelle Denning, Christopher Connolly-Smith, and Kenneth Cowan. *School Textbook Provision in Georgia: A Sub-Sector Study Comprising an Analysis of Current Problem Areas with Options and Recommendations for Future Strategies.* London: International Book Development, 1998.

Rosen, Roger. *Georgia: A Sovereign Country of the Caucasus.* New York: W.W. Norton and Company, 1999.

Shevardnadze, Eduard A. *The Future Belongs to Freedom.* New York: Free Press, 1991.

Specter, Michael. "Letter from Tbilisi: Rainy Days in Georgia." *The New Yorker 76* (December 18, 2000): 54-62.

Topouria, Giorgi. "Science and Education," March 1997. Available from http://www.sakartvelo.com./.

—*Leon Ginsberg*

GERMANY

BASIC DATA

Official Country Name:	Federal Republic of Germany
Region:	Europe
Population:	82,797,408
Language(s):	German, Turkish
Literacy Rate:	99%
Number of Primary Schools:	17,892
Compulsory Schooling:	12 years
Public Expenditure on Education:	4.8%
Foreign Students in National Universities:	165,977
Libraries:	14,372
Educational Enrollment:	Primary: 3,859,490 Secondary: 8,382,335 Higher: 2,131,907
Educational Enrollment Rate:	Primary: 104% Secondary: 104% Higher: 47%

Teachers:	Primary: 224,517
	Secondary: 542,383
	Higher: 274,963
Student-Teacher Ratio:	Primary: 17:1
Female Enrollment Rate:	Primary: 104%
	Secondary: 103%
	Higher: 44%

HISTORY & BACKGROUND

The Federal Republic of Germany, with its population of 80.8 million, lies at the heart of the European Union. It shares borders with nine neighboring countries and is a key member of the European Union. It is a densely populated country, with 230 residents per square kilometer, as compared to only 26 per square kilometer in the United States. Its 143,000 square miles (357,000 square kilometers) measure only 370 miles (640 kilometers) from west to east and about 500 (or 876 kilometers) from north to south. Because the country lacks natural resources, its highly educated workforce constitutes Germany's most important economic asset; thus, education and vocational training enjoy high prestige and financial and administrative support.

Germany's 780,000 teachers in 52,400 schools educate more than 12 million pupils. Over the past decade, the educational institutions of the Federal Republic of Germany have confronted the challenge of increasing numbers of immigrant children. The country's labor force is made up of 12 percent foreigners, and half of them are from Turkey. Approximately 7.4 million non-Germans live within the country's borders, and most of them are in the West. In the 1990s the country experienced an influx of immigrants from the former Soviet Republics, many of them ethnic Germans, although not necessarily proficient in the German language. Because of Germany's citizenship laws, descendants of ethnic Germans may become citizens with relative ease, while those from non-German backgrounds may not, despite generations of residency in the country. As a result, these people, many of them Turks, often retain their own language and culture rather than seeking to assimilate; their presence has obliged schools to confront ethnic and religious diversity. In some urban schools in the West, the proportion of immigrant pupils may be as high as 70 percent.

German public education officially began in 1763, when Frederick the Great of Prussia mandated regular school attendance from the ages of 5 through 13 or 14. The denominational or confessional school remained the norm throughout Prussia (which encompassed the Rhineland and most of modern Germany) during the nineteenth century. Teachers often worked as sextons or church organists, and clergymen served as school inspectors. Catholic and Protestant (Lutheran) areas of Germany were geographically separate, facilitating religious oversight of local schools. In Prussia, efforts to establish schools in which Catholic, Protestant, and Jewish children could receive a common instruction, separated only for classes in religion, failed, despite several serious efforts at reform. In the cities, free, public schools educated children of the working class, while public schools, which charged some fees, attracted children of middle class families and offered a more rigorous curriculum. Women, in low numbers, entered the teaching profession in the late 1800s.

After the Napoleonic era, the responsibilities of the *Gymnasium* (a secondary school preparing boys for university admission) was expanded to include the preparation of civil servants, a task later assumed by the intermediate secondary schools. By 1900 the *Gymnasium* had developed three basic models providing for a specialization in the classical languages, modern languages, or mathematics and science. Girls were not admitted to the *Gymnasium* until 1908 and not admitted to Prussian universities until 1910.

In 1920 Germany introduced the four-year unified public elementary school that provided the same instruction to all children. School attendance until age 18 became compulsory. Another significant change was the requirement that even teachers in the elementary school must have passed the Abitur, the qualifying test for university admission. The basic types of schools in Germany before 1945 were the *Volksschule* (the four-year common elementary school), *Mittelschule* (the six-year middle school) which followed it, and the academically rigorous *Gymnasium*. While non-denominational schools prevailed in Bremen, Hamburg, Baden, Hesse, Saxony, and Thuringia, more than 90 percent of Prussian children attended a denominational school throughout the 1930s. The teaching of history and religion in Prussia aimed to fortify citizens' resistance to the doctrines of the Communists and Social Democrats.

Hitler's National Socialists abolished church-run primary schools. The post World War II influx of 12 million refugees, many of them expelled from German territories assigned to Poland, mixed religious boundaries and further weakened the churches' role in education. In the 1960s West Germany began to phase out small rural schools in favor of larger regional schools where children could be grouped according to age level. This movement effectively ended denominational distinctions in public schooling.

From the renaissance through the nineteenth century, religion played a role in higher education as well. Monasteries became centers of scholarship and learning.

Early universities prepared men for the ministry or priesthood. Heidelberg, the first university on German soil, opened its doors in 1386, followed by the universities of Leipzig in 1409, and Rostock in 1419. During the early centuries of their existence, instruction at these universities occurred in Latin. Traditionally, German universities offered education in theology, law, philosophy (including the natural and social sciences and the humanities), and medicine. During the Hitler era, teachers and university faculty were required to swear a loyalty oath to National Socialism, and freedom of expression was sharply curtailed. About 300 Jewish university professors were driven out, causing a huge loss of scholarly, scientific, and intellectual capacity. Girls were discouraged from pursuing higher education and lost the gains they had made during the first twenty years of the century.

After World War II, the country was divided into the Federal Republic of Germany, consisting of the French, British, and American sectors in the West, and the German Democratic Republic in the east, which was under the dominance of the Union of the Soviet Socialist Republics (USSR). In the west, the Allies undertook a process of removing Nazi ideas from the country's schools. However, West German education did not undergo substantial reforms after World War II because the occupying powers had high respect for the German academic secondary school and universities. Moreover, the differing educational systems of France, Britain, and the United States made it impractical to apply any single new model in the western zone. Colleges of education founded after the war were denominational in character, and the teaching of religion was mandated in the 1949 Basic Law, or constitution, of the Federal Republic of Germany.

Gradually some modest changes made the system more democratic. One such change was the reducing or eliminating the cost of textbooks and school materials to parents and making six years of a common primary education, rather than only four, the norm. By and large, however, the chief features of early twentieth century education were retained through the 1950s: stratification with different types of schools, teachers, and pupils; the dual system of vocational training and general education; centralized decision-making at the state level; and the processes of grading and selection throughout the school system. In 1953 just 3.3 percent of any given age group earned the *Abitur* (the examination certifying satisfactory completion of the academic secondary school) or *Gymnasium*, entitling the graduate to university admission; 90 percent of those so qualified actually entered a university. However, because war veterans received preference for scarce study spaces in the country's war-damaged universities, girls stood a much poorer chance than males; only about half the female recipients of the *Abitur* actually

continued on to university study. Only 6.1 percent of any age cohort completed the elementary school and six-year *Realschule* (an intermediate secondary school preparing civil servants and other administrative employees). The largest number, 63.3 percent, of any age cohort left full-time schooling around the age of 15 and continued with mandatory part-time education until 18, while working or participating in a vocational training program.

Twenty-four new universities sprang up in West Germany in the 1960s and 1970s, including the distance-learning center at Hagen established in 1975. In 1969 the federal government in Bonn assumed some authority over education, which had previously been entirely under the jurisdiction of the 11 federal states. The federal government increased uniformity and standardization in vocational training and the *Abitur*, the university admissions qualifying test.

In 1964 the Social Democratic Party questioned the adequacy of the West German educational system and, after lengthy inquiries, the German Parliament declared it to be in a state of emergency. Compared to similar European industrialized nations, relatively few German youth continued full-time schooling until 18, fewer German youth entered university study, and federal spending on education comprised a relatively small portion of the total national budget. The national investigations also found significant differences in educational opportunity and quality between regions. Some of these differences included class size, provisions for foreign language study, the supply of qualified teachers, and the numbers of school leavers attaining appropriate certificates or diplomas. Educational leaders warned of an anticipated shortfall of skilled workers able to adapt to new developments in technology. Their report recommended reducing the importance of parental status and social connections in decisions about children's secondary education and basing these decisions solely on children's abilities. The report also documented significant gender inequities in education: more girls than boys left full-time schooling at an early age, fewer continued into the *Realschule* or *Gymnasium*, and girls' choices of educational paths were most likely to be based on their fathers' occupations. Girls from rural areas, working-class backgrounds, and from Catholic families fared the worst.

The findings of this nationwide inquiry resulted in a number of significant reforms. A two-year orientation phase in grades five and six was introduced to give schoolchildren more time to consider future educational choices. The number of academic subjects required for the *Abitur* was reduced in 1960; in 1972, students were given the option of concentrating in a few specialized subjects. However, complaints from universities that this step weakened the general preparation of incoming students forced a partial rollback of *Abitur* reforms. The percentage of young people continuing their education into the *Realschule*, *Gymnasium*, or university doubled. However, these increases created a larger supply of better educated workers than the job market could fully absorb.

Further reforms had a more direct effect on the teaching profession. The role of pedagogy in teacher preparation was expanded, and the hours devoted to the study of teaching methods increased to about one-fourth of the total. From the mid-1970s through most of the 1980s, the country experienced an oversupply of teachers, and fewer new teachers were hired. A Federal Ministry of Education and Science, established in 1969, was combined in 1994 with the Ministry of Science and Technology. However, attempts to increase federal authority over planning and coordination disintegrated in the early 1970s, in part due to disagreements between the political parties. In general, the Social Democrats favored greater national oversight, while the more conservative Christian Democrats advocated state autonomy.

Reforms got underway in higher education as well. In 1971 the federal government began providing financial aid to students (which states had done since 1957) in an attempt to democratize higher education. *Hochschulrahmengesetz* (a law for the reform of higher education) passed in 1975 and was aimed at greater nationwide unification of this level of instruction. *Fachhochschulen* (new polytechnic schools) were introduced in the late 1960s and early 1970s. More comprehensive and technical universities were founded. Untenured professors and staff gained a voice in university governance, alongside senior professors who held university chairs. Critics demanded a more practical orientation for courses of university study in the mid-1970s, but effected little change in this area. And, despite objections, universities retained their emphasis on research over student-centered learning.

Nonetheless the balance between higher education and vocational training shifted between 1980 and 1990. In 1980 apprentices outnumbered university students two to one; however, a shortage of apprenticeships in the late 1980s motivated more adolescents to enter universities. By 1990 the number of university entrants surpassed the number of young people beginning an apprenticeship. University enrollment grew by about 75 percent between 1977 and 1992, but increases in faculty, staffing, and facilities failed to keep pace, resulting in serious overcrowding.

In 1981 only about 38 percent of those who actually enrolled in higher education were women (the proportion is 40 percent in West Germany in 2001). Women were still less likely than men to actually begin higher education, more apt to concentrate in the arts and humanities, and more likely to drop out of higher education. At the *Fachhochschulen*, women concentrated chiefly in traditionally female areas such as health professions and social work. Although significantly more young women began to enter apprenticeships, many completed only a two-year course, which was considered inferior to a full course of vocational training.

While the Federal Republic of Germany maintained many features of the system of education inherited from the Weimar Republic, the socialist German Democratic Republic created an entirely new educational system after World War II. The intention of this new educational system was to sever all connections between religion and schooling, eliminating differences between rural and urban areas, the educational opportunities for boys and girls, and social classes.

Schools in the Soviet zone of occupation re-opened in October of 1945. This was quite a feat, given that many school buildings had been damaged, teachers had been killed or displaced, and the region was forced to cope with the influx of ethnic Germans. Eliminating Nazi influence was carried out more rigorously than in the West: three-fourths of the teaching force was fired for having sworn the mandatory oath of loyalty to the National Socialists. Approximately 15,000 new teachers, young and hastily trained, entered the classroom in 1945. Almost 23 years later, 93 percent of the country's teachers had been trained since World War II. The replacement of such a large portion of the teaching profession gave the German Democratic Republic an opportunity to start anew.

Control over the educational system was centralized at the national level, with the Ministry of Education carrying out directives formulated in the Central Committee of the ruling Socialist Unity Party. The Ministry produced textbooks and detailed schedules for their use, including timed lesson plans. Deviation from this centralized curriculum was discouraged by the widespread fear of exposure for failing to promulgate the official doctrines of the socialist state.

A school reform in May 1946 eliminated the three-part secondary education system inherited from the Weimar Republic, which separated students into vocational, managerial, and academic tracks. Further reforms in 1958 and 1959 established 10 years of compulsory education in the polytechnic school, which all pupils attended, following a uniform curriculum, free of militaristic, racist, religious, or imperialist teachings. Pupils in grades 7 through 10 worked a few hours each week to become accustomed to industrial production and to develop solidarity with the working class.

Through the 1950s and early 1960s, East German educators furthered their efforts to utilize education to overturn social class. Achievements of the peasants and working class were highlighted in history, literature, and the social sciences. Children whose parents belonged to the worker and peasant classes received preference in admission to higher education, while those whose parents opposed the Socialist Unity Party might be denied access. Some offspring of white-collar professionals, the landed aristocracy, enemies of the socialist state, and some adherents of organized religion were sent into apprenticeships and factories. *Arbeiter- und Bauern-Fakultäten* (special adult education courses), in existence from 1946 to 1962, were offered for workers, former soldiers, and returning political prisoners. About 25 percent of all university students entered higher education through this path. Gradually, the process of social and political selection was accomplished through polytechnic schools and the *Freie Deutsche Jugend* (socialist Free German Youth groups) present in every educational institution; the *Arbeiter- und Bauern-Fakultäten* were discontinued. Only about 12 percent of the country's pupils continued their education into the university, for the country's leaders guarded against the emergence of an over-educated, under-employed elite, which might foment a rebellion. Not everyone could accept the political restrictions on academic freedom. Between the country's founding in 1949 and the building of the Berlin Wall in 1961, about 2,700 university faculty and 35,000 students moved west.

Nonetheless, the German Democratic Republic did introduce some more democratic elements into its educational system. Schoolbooks and materials were free for all pupils, in contrast to West Germany where the costs of such items as uniforms and school supplies sometimes kept poorer children out of the college-preparatory high school, the *Gymnasium*. From the first, East German schools were coeducational. A 1950 Law for the Promotion of Youth decreed that all children, regardless of gender, should receive the same education, vocational training, higher education, and access to sports. The school day was organized to provide childcare as well as instruction. Children ate a hot noonday meal at school and could remain in school through the late afternoon in the *Schulhort*, where teachers and assistants supervised homework, extra-curricular activities, and sports. All schools included Young Pioneer groups for children under the age of 14 and Free German Youth organizations for older children. While these groups have been depicted, since unification, as a means of political indoctrination, parents acknowledge that they also fostered group work and cooperation and gave children a certain grounding in civic responsibility. They also provided vacation lodgings and summer camps and sponsored a broad range of school and vacation activities. Although the original intent was to equalize education for all children, educators soon recognized the need for

higher levels of instruction for those destined for college or university study. The *Erweiterte Oberschule* (extended secondary school) was introduced in 1960 to provide a three-year course of study beyond the polytechnic school and to prepare students for higher education.

Occupational choices were made in consultation with pupils, parents, school administrators, teachers, and local authorities. In general, pupils were encouraged to choose occupations projected to be needed in the country's economic five-year plans. In balance, however, workers who succeeded in their careers enjoyed a plethora of opportunities to retrain or qualify themselves for entirely different careers. The entire educational system emphasized practical work applications and a solid grounding in Marxism-Leninism, as well as mandatory instruction in Russian. In recompense, citizens were guaranteed life-long employment, a principle that became increasingly difficult to sustain as manufacturing and technology developed through the 1980s. Furthermore, it became evident that the country's educational system emphasized cooperation and productivity at the expense of inventiveness, critical thinking, analytical skills, and creativity. One drawback was a perpetual lag in the development of technological innovation, particularly in engineering and computer science.

During the 1950s and 1960s, the Federal Republic of Germany also introduced a number of reforms to broaden access to its educational system. The number of intermediate secondary schools designed to train managers, civil servants, and white-collar employees increased. New *Fachschulen* (secondary technical schools) were introduced. The numbers of college-preparatory secondary schools in rural areas increased. The new two-year orientation phase for fifth and sixth graders, which appeared in some states, provided more time for teachers and parents to assess whether schoolchildren could best further their education in the *Hauptschule* (general secondary school) and continue into a vocational school to learn a trade or enter the *Realschule* or *Gymnasium*.

Reunified in 1990, the Federal Republic of Germany in 2001 encompasses 16 federal states, 11 in the West (Baden-Württemberg, Bavaria, Rhineland Palatinate, North Rhine-Westphalia, Hesse, Lower Saxony, the Saarland, Schleswig-Holstein, and the 3 city-states— Hamburg, Bremen, and Berlin) and 5 (the so-called new federal states of Thuringia, Saxony, Saxony-Anhalt, Brandenburg, and Mecklenburg-West Pomerania) that formerly made up the German Democratic Republic. With unification, West German law became the law of the land and, thus, a massive restructuring of the East German educational system began. Beginning in the 1992-1993 school year, the West German multi-track system of schooling was introduced into the new federal states to replace the 10-year, homogenous polytechnic school. Retaining the egalitarian ideals of socialism, the new federal states created an educational system less stratified than that of the West; most offer a two-track model of secondary education rather than the tripartite division commonplace in the West. Saxony, for instance, uses the orientation phase in grades 5 and 6, and a *Mittelschule* (middle school) for grades 5 through 10, which combines both the *Hauptschule* and *Realschule*. Pupils can enter either of those institutions or the *Gymnasium* at the end of fourth, fifth, or sixth grade. Courses in Russian were no longer required, and Marxism-Leninism disappeared from the curriculum. Most teachers and university faculty in disciplines such as civics, social studies, history, economics, and political science (about one-fifth of the teaching corps) lost their positions. East Germany soon experienced a need for teachers of English rather than Russian. Rather than the 13 required in the West for a high school diploma, 12 remained the norm. Religious instruction was re-introduced, with some of the new federal states offering courses in ethics as an alternative to Lutheran or Catholic instruction.

Since unification in 1990, Germany's educational system has struggled with new challenges of unifying the radically different philosophies and structures of East and West, equalizing education for both sexes, and adapting a traditional educational system to the demands of a new technological age.

CONSTITUTIONAL & LEGAL FOUNDATIONS

Germany's constitution, which dates from 1949, guarantees all citizens free choice of schooling or a vocational training position, as well as the free choice of occupation. Article Seven of the Basic Law establishes joint federal and state supervision of educational institutions. The federal government establishes compulsory education, the organization of the educational system, the recognition of educational certification, and chiefly holds jurisdiction over higher education and vocational training. West Germany's states established the Standing Conference of Ministers of Education and Cultural Affairs in 1948. The five new East German states became members in 1990. This body, known by its German acronym, KMK (*Kultusminister Konferenz*), facilitates greater standardization of schools and the mutual recognition of certificates awarded by vocational schools and comprehensive schools, and it lays down uniform requirements for the *Abitur*, the entrance examination for university admission. Particularly since the mid-1990s, the Standing Conference of Ministers of Education and Cultural Affairs has moved toward greater standardization, in part to ensure comparable qualifications of pupils who move from one state to another. Previously, school-

children's qualifications would have been judged on the basis of the type of school they attended; now there is more uniformity in these basic subjects, regardless of whether they have attended the *Hauptschule* or *Realschule*.

States retain the chief responsibility for education. They establish general curriculum guidelines, which may specify how many periods of instruction are required at each grade level in each subject. State ministries of education also create a list of approved textbooks and other curriculum materials. In some states, such as Bavaria, there may also be a centralized, statewide *Abitur*, or other achievement testing at designated grade levels.

Local communities have jurisdiction over other aspects of schools and schooling, which are often determined by party dominance. Within municipalities, town or city councils administer schools directly; there are no independent school boards as there are in the United States. Citizens' voices are heard chiefly in the parents' councils attached to individual schools and school classrooms.

Germany's Basic Law also mandates religious instruction in schools, although children may opt not to take it once they reach 14 years. Usually they choose between Lutheran and Catholic instruction, but recent years have witnessed a trend toward more ecumenical instruction, particularly in the East, where courses in ethics (rather than a particular denomination) were introduced in the early 1990s.

Germany's political parties champion significantly different educational policies. The Christian Democrats and their Bavarian allies, the Christian Socialist Union, held power from 1982 to 1998 under the leadership of Helmut Kohl. These parties represent Germany's Catholics and Lutherans, who each comprise about 35 percent of the population. They argue that early and clearly delineated separation into the three tracks (*Hauptschule*, *Realschule*, and *Gymnasium*) is necessary to maintain educational quality. The Social Democratic Party (in power from 1966 to 1969 and again since 1998) champions broader access to education and, therefore, advocates adoption of the *Gesamtschule* (comprehensive high school model) and two-year orientation phase in fifth and sixth grades, rather than separating pupils into prevocational tracks after fourth grade. The Free Democrats, a small swing party, advocate a 12-year path to the *Abitur*, private colleges, independent funding sources for education, and the teaching of tolerance and conflict resolution in schools. Since unification, two other small parties have entered the scene. The former East German Socialist Unity Party, known in 2001 as the Party of Democratic Socialism, wants to abolish the three-part division of secondary education and the providing for

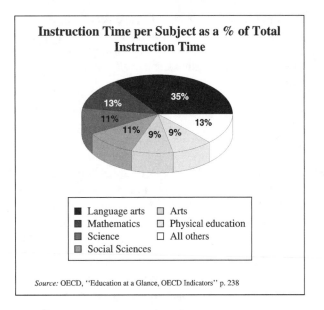

Instruction Time per Subject as a % of Total Instruction Time

35%
13%
11%
11%
9%
9%
13%

■ Language arts □ Arts
■ Mathematics □ Physical education
■ Science □ All others
■ Social Sciences

Source: OECD, "Education at a Glance, OECD Indicators" p. 238

childcare through all-day schooling. East Germany's small revolutionary parties, which arose just before the opening of the Berlin Wall, have allied themselves with Alliance 90/the Greens. Like the Party of Democratic Socialism, they champion a single curriculum for all children through tenth grade. Furthermore, they want schools to teach ecological awareness and a stronger respect for diversity. They advocate mainstreaming children with disabilities and eliminating *Sonderschulen* (special schools) and reducing the pressures of grading and evaluation in schools.

EDUCATIONAL SYSTEM—OVERVIEW

School attendance is compulsory for children between the ages of 6 to 18. Full-time schooling is mandated for either 9 or 10 years (depending on state) and may be followed by part-time attendance at a vocational school, complemented by an apprenticeship. Parents may need to contribute to the cost of textbooks and other materials, depending on the income level of the family.

The school day runs from eight or nine o'clock in the morning until noon or one o'clock in the afternoon and is divided into 45 minute class periods. The school day grows longer as children progress through elementary school, but its length may vary with the day of the week. Children bring a snack to eat at recess, but most return home for a hot noonday meal, a schedule that makes it difficult for mothers to work a full day outside the home. Furthermore, a teacher's absence may result in children being sent home early, since the use of substitute teachers is quite rare. Teachers relinquish their free periods to fill in for absent colleagues, or children are simply sent home early. Few schools have a school nurse on the premises or even a cafeteria. School busses transport children in

the countryside, but the majority ride public transportation, such as streetcars, municipal busses, or trains.

The school year averages 188 days and includes a week of vacation at Christmas, at Easter, and at Pentecost. Schools close for a six-week summer vacation; however, to reduce overcrowding on trains and the Autobahn as families depart for vacations, summer vacation dates are staggered throughout the 16 federal states. Saturday classes are still held two or three times a month in many states. The school week averages 26 to 35 hours, with children attending the *Realschule* or *Gymnasium* spending more hours per week in classes than do children at the *Hauptschule* (general secondary school).

Recently private schools have been growing in importance and, in 1996 and 1997, have educated approximately 600,000 pupils. Private schools are subject to supervision by state agencies to ensure that their facilities, teacher qualifications, and teaching objectives are comparable to those of public schools. They are expressly prohibited from segregating the children from richer families. Generally private schools are viewed not as elite; rather they are seen as innovative and less rigid in structure than public schools. Private institutions must be recognized by the state to administer examinations or to award certifications comparable to those granted by public schools. Those receiving state approval may draw as much as 98 percent of their budgets from public funding, since they help carry the burden of educating for the public good. In times of tight budgets, however, subsidies for private schools may be reduced and remain a topic of highly-charged political debate.

The largest number of private schools, around 1,100, are supported by the Catholic Church, and located chiefly in Bavaria, the Rhineland, or Baden-Württemberg. Most (43.6 percent) operate at the level of the *Gymnasium*. Private schools sponsored by the Protestant Church are fewer in number; because of church involvement in public schools and mandatory religious instruction, parents who want their children to be educated in the Christian tradition need not turn to private schools.

About one-tenth of all German private schools are special schools for the mentally or physically disabled. While the German Democratic Republic prohibited private schools and religious instruction, the churches did play a significant role in caring for people with disabilities and in special education. About 30 elementary schools following the model created by the Italian physician Maria Montessori also exist.

Because the German Democratic Republic did not permit private schools, there are fewer Montessori or Waldorf schools in the east than in the west. Approximately 13 percent of all children attending a private school are in Waldorf schools. Begun by Rudolf Steiner (1861-1925) in Stuttgart in 1919, the Waldorf movement presented an alternative to Germany's socially conservative, stratified school system. Germany's 100 Waldorf schools emphasize the arts and crafts and center around child development. The school day encompasses activities that alternate cognitive and rational exercises, imitative and practical activities, and creative or artistic functions. Eurhythmy, an essential component of the Waldorf curriculum, integrates physical development through movement, dance, recitation, and music. Little importance is attached to testing and formal grading, and children are not separated according to ability or future career path. In these schools, a single teacher usually accompanies the class for several years, creating lasting relationships with pupils.

PREPRIMARY & PRIMARY EDUCATION

Traditionally, the Federal Republic of Germany has not regarded kindergarten as part of the educational system, but rather as a private or familial responsibility. Many kindergartens are run by churches, businesses, municipalities, or private associations. Most offer instruction only in the morning. Attendance is voluntary, and parents are expected to pay part or all of the costs. In 1996 about two-thirds of all three- to six-year-olds attended kindergarten. Nursery schools are administered by state ministries of youth and social affairs rather than ministries of education. About 70 percent depend on some private funding. Private nursery schools receive some state funding, as well as state supervision.

While the German Democratic Republic considered childcare and early childhood education a state responsibility, the Federal Republic did not offer comprehensive free kindergarten placements until 1996; even then the demand exceeded the supply of available spaces. The problem disappeared, at least temporarily, due chiefly to the sharp decline in the East German birthrate between 1990 and 1994. In contrast to both American and East German kindergartens, the West German model emphasizes creative play rather than formal instruction.

At the age of six, children begin *Grundschule* (elementary school), typically holding colorful paper cones filled with candy and treats to assuage the pangs of leaving home to go to school. Children who turn six by June 30 must begin schooling in the fall, provided they are found physically and developmentally ready. For the first two years, teachers do not grade schoolwork, but instead provide evaluations of their pupils' strengths and weaknesses. In the upper grades, a numerical system is used: one means very good, two good, three satisfactory, four passing, and five not passing. The school week may be as short as 20 hours in the early grades, but it gradually

increases in length. Pupils study German and mathematics every day, supplemented by two class periods per week in science, religion, physical education, and art or music. Some children begin foreign language instruction as early as third or fourth grade, not surprising, given Germany's borders with nine countries. By fifth grade virtually all pupils are learning a foreign language, even those planning to enter training for blue-collar trades. Often a lead teacher remains with one class for several years, teaching all subjects except physical education and religion. This arrangement is intended to foster close cooperation and trust and to minimize discipline problems.

The *Grundschule* lasts for six years in Berlin and Brandenburg and for four years in the other federal states. Since 1973 schools in some western states have included a two-year *Orientierungsstufe* (orientation phase) at the end of fourth grade; parents and teachers meet and begin a process of consultation and advisement through which the child's future educational path is determined, with a final decision made at the end of sixth grade. The Social Democratic Party champions the orientation phase, which is opposed by the Christian Democrats, who favor a stricter separation of pupils destined for each of the three secondary education tracks. Thus this two-year adjustment and advisement period is offered in some federal states (such as Hesse, Lower Saxony, Hamburg, and Bremen) but not others, depending on political party dominance.

Some states require a certain grade point average, particularly in German and math, for entrance into the college preparatory secondary school, the *Gymnasium*; others use admissions tests. However, all base their decisions on teachers' recommendations as well as parents' wishes. Because children at the age of 11 or 12 have little basis for choosing a future career, their parents often play a decisive role and, in fact, have a legal right to choose their child's school, even against the recommendations of teachers. It is not uncommon for them to push children into a higher level school than teachers have recommended, perhaps to avoid a general secondary school with a high population of immigrant children, whose presence is assumed to lower the overall quality of instruction.

The general effect of this early division of pupils into three separate tracks is a somewhat conservative reinforcement of the status quo, in which children enter professions fairly closely resembling those of their parents in terms of educational level and socio-economic status. In general, the German educational system is geared toward producing competent, useful members of society. It is not the venue for a soul-searching process of independent self-discovery.

The Standing Conference of Ministers of Education and Cultural Affairs (KMK) passed resolutions in 1994

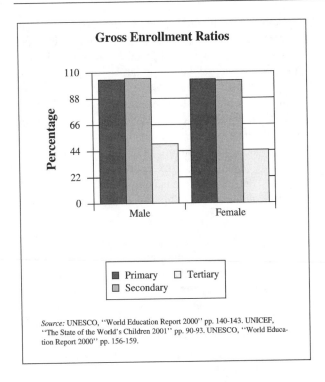

Gross Enrollment Ratios

Primary ■   Tertiary □
Secondary ■

Source: UNESCO, "World Education Report 2000" pp. 140-143. UNICEF, "The State of the World's Children 2001" pp. 90-93. UNESCO, "World Education Report 2000" pp. 156-159.

establishing other responsibilities concerning schools and teaching. Children are to learn critical attitudes toward television and other media, whose excessive use is blamed for their lack of attention in school and the loss of connection to reality. It must be pointed out that West Germany has had private television channels only since 1985, and the German Democratic Republic had none, although most residents could receive West German television. Thus, the distrust of television's impact on children and its deleterious effects in schooling are more widespread than in the United States. On the other hand, these resolutions' statements about over-indulgence in computer games may reveal deep-seated distrust of the computer's potential as an educational tool and may work against the wider use of computers in the classroom. Primary schools are also charged with engendering in children an attachment to their homeland, tolerance, and allegiance to the European Union ideal.

SECONDARY EDUCATION

Upon completion of the *Grundschule*, about one-fourth of pupils enter the *Hauptschule* (secondary general school), where they study German, mathematics, the natural and social sciences, and a foreign language. After unification, the new East German states did not introduce the *Hauptschule*, preferring instead to combine the general and intermediate secondary schools as an alternative to the *Gymnasium*. The Saarland adopted this combined secondary school model in 1997. Some of these schools combining the *Hauptschule* and *Realschule* also exist in

Bremen, Hamburg, Hesse, Lower Saxony, and Schleswig-Holstein and are known by various names: *Mittelschule*, *Regelschule*, and *Sekundarschule*. These developments may call into question the future existence of the *Hauptschule*.

In most West German states, the *Hauptschule* encompasses grades five through nine, but seven through nine in states where the orientation phase remains part of elementary school. Some of the general secondary schools end with ninth grade, some with tenth. Instruction in a foreign language has been required since 1969, and most pupils choose English, although those in border regions may choose French. The upper grades include some computer science and practical work courses. Throughout the past twenty years, the proportion of pupils entering the *Hauptschule* has declined as parents push their children into the more prestigious and more academically oriented *Realschule* and *Gymnasium*. After three to five years of a common curriculum, including German, civics, religion, and physical education, pupils completing the *Hauptschule* earn a *Zeugnis mittlere Reife* (school leaving certificate), which entitles them to enter an apprenticeship. There is no final examination. Those who have earned outstanding marks in the *Hauptschule* and who complete tenth grade may receive the school-leaving certificate normally awarded at the end of the *Realschule*. The dropout rate from the *Hauptschule* is around 9 percent. Successful graduates begin vocational apprenticeships in one of the country's recognized trades, which total around 400. Each year about 600,000 young people enter an apprenticeship. While completion of the *Hauptschule* served for decades as the gateway to an apprenticeship, in 2001 an equal number of beginning apprentices have completed the *Realschule* and around 15 percent have the *Abitur*. This transition has made it increasingly difficult for young people with only the *Hauptschule* certificate to compete for a training position.

Germany's vocational training system has enjoyed a high reputation based on its success in producing skilled craftsmen through the "dual system" of education. Hands-on practical training is supplemented by theoretical instruction in the *Berufsschule* (vocational school), where young people learn theoretical material two or three days a week. These schools usually specialize in one or more areas: industry, commerce, agriculture, home economics, or offer a mixed curriculum. Nearly 60 percent of class time in the vocational school is devoted to training and the remaining 40 percent to specialized subjects. Some discrepancies arise within this dual system because apprenticeships are shaped and supervised by chambers of handicrafts and trades, while vocational schools are administered by state ministries of education. Because the entry level qualification for these schools is the completion of 10 years of schooling, classes have become quite heterogeneous, enrolling graduates of special schools for the disabled as well as those who have earned the *Abitur*.

Students at the vocational school spend the remaining weekdays and their vacations as trainees in the workplace. This system depends upon close cooperation between educational administrators and private industries, which furnish these paid apprenticeships. This system grew out of medieval tradition: during the Middle Ages apprentices traveled from town to town, learning from several masters. Those who passed the first level were recognized as *Geselle* (journeymen) competent to practice their trade. Those who continued through further examinations and produced a *Meisterstück* (masterpiece) were entitled to hire and train apprentices of their own. Today, the examination at the end of vocational school is administered by employers and trainers as well as teachers and includes an oral examination. Those who pass it are then qualified as *Facharbeiter* (skilled workers). Many are then hired by the companies that have trained and observed them for the past two or three years.

The shortage of available apprenticeships that Germany experienced during the mid-1990s was overcome, in part, due to the country's low birthrate and pressure for children to enter the intermediate secondary school or the *Gymnasium*. Most children from immigrant families follow the educational path through the *Hauptschule*, vocational school, and apprenticeship. Today, however, the availability of apprenticeships is limited by the country's economic slump. About one third of all private firms offer apprenticeships, and 90 percent of these are small firms employing 50 people or fewer. Overall, about half a million firms now offer such placements.

Because of the system's dependence on industry to furnish apprenticeships, those in certain trades are frequently oriented either toward girls or toward boys. Thus around 55 percent of girls in the *Berufsschule* choose apprenticeships in just 10 trades. The most popular are doctor's assistant, retail sales, hairdresser, and office worker. Around 40 percent of boys train to become auto mechanics, electricians, industrial mechanics, or business specialists in wholesale or foreign trade. In this way the vocational training system would appear to reinforce, rather than break down, gender stereotyping in vocational choices.

Apprenticeships last for two to three years, with shorter training periods for high achievers or those who have passed the *Abitur*. Apprentices receive a small allowance that increases yearly. What they are taught is determined by federal ministries, based on recommendations from craft associations and trade unions, which thus exercise tight control over the quality of preparation for those entering their field. Apprentices completing their training undergo examinations by chambers of industry or chambers of crafts or trades.

The challenge of providing training in high tech fields assumed critical proportions in the 1990s. In August 2000, for instance, Germany authorized 20,000 new immigrants to enter the country on five-year work permits in order to fill the country's shortfall of skilled computer technicians and software engineers, careers unforeseen in the days of the medieval guild system which gave rise to the dual system of apprenticeships and vocational training.

Around 40 percent of pupils finishing the four or six-year elementary school enter the *Realschule*, which encompasses grades 5 through 10 and is designed to educate mid-level administrators, functionaries, employees in service or commercial sectors, and managers. The number of these intermediate secondary schools increased greatly during the 1950s. They enroll the broadest spectrum of social classes, particularly in rural areas. The Social Democratic Party traditionally supports these schools, and such initiatives as their combining with general secondary schools. This is now the case in most East German states and the Saarland.

The *Realschule* is viewed as a middle class institution, providing a strong grounding in mathematics, modern languages, and technical fields. German and math lessons fill four periods each per week; a foreign language (usually English), geography, physical education, and fine arts for two periods each a week; and science and history for one period each. About one-third of these pupils also study a second foreign language such as French or Russian. Beginning in grades seven and eight, pupils may be separated into pre-vocational tracks. This track, emphasizing business and economics, enrolls about two-thirds of the girls in these schools, while the mathematics, science, and technology track enrolls half the boys. The social science and humanities tracks attract about twice as many girls as boys. Graduates of the *Realschule* (those in Bavaria and Baden-Württemberg must pass a standardized test) are entitled to attend a *Berufsfachschule* (full-time vocational school) or a *Fachoberschule* (vocationally oriented upper secondary school).

The founding of *Berufsfachschulen* is a newer trend. These full-time vocational schools enroll about 300,000 students nationwide. Admission to these institutions requires completion of either the *Hauptschule* or *Realschule*. The *Berufsfachschule* trains students for careers in nursing, bookkeeping, social work, forestry, commerce, the technical trades, tourism, social welfare, home economics, auto mechanics, and medical and dental technology. The course of study lasts from one to three years.

Overall, proper certification of one's education and vocational training is both more complex and far more widespread than in the United States. Job advertisements frequently specify the qualifications required, and both employers and prospective employees recognize a plethora of diplomas, certificates, and licenses, each stamped and validated by professional organizations. Those who lack such documentation stand a far poorer chance in the job market, where the American model for the ''self-made man'' receives little respect. Moreover, this somewhat rigid system means that workers contemplating a career change must invest considerable time and often money in earning new degrees and certificates.

Approximately one-fourth of Germany's pupils completing elementary school enter the *Gymnasium*. Most cities offer several models of *Gymnasium* specializing in modern languages, ancient languages (Greek and Latin), math and the natural sciences, the arts, or humanities. These schools may be further characterized by their religious affiliation, and, until the mid-1970s, many of those in the West were segregated by gender. A student at a modern language *Gymnasium* might have French and mathematics five periods a week; German, Latin, English, chemistry, history, and philosophy for three periods; and physical education for two periods a week. The traditional emphasis on Latin or Greek has declined considerably over the past decades. Today all *Gymnasia* include computer facilities and offer some information technology courses.

These schools are divided into a lower level, grades 5 through 10, and an upper level, grades 11 through 12 or 13, in which students concentrate on fewer subjects. Most require basic or core courses: German, math, civics, sciences, physical education, religion, the arts and music, English, and one other foreign language. Basic or core courses are taught three periods a week, while the courses students choose for their specialty, *Leistungskurse*, meet five periods a week and require higher standards of student mastery. These specialty courses may be chosen from the disciplines listed above, but may also include law, technology, statistics, psychology, sociology, education, astronomy, geology, or computer science, depending on the school. About 9 percent of those students who eventually pass the *Abitur* are enrolled at special economics *Gymnasia* for the three upper grades and concentrate on accounting, law, economics, and information technology. There are other specialized *Gymnasia* for music and the arts. In 1977 North Rhine-Westphalia introduced the *Kolleg*, a school providing vocational education and preparation for the *Abitur* and university admission. Instruction integrates vocational and general subjects. Graduates can also enter the vocationally oriented upper secondary school, sometimes called a polytechnic school *Fachoberschule*.

The increased emphasis on specialized courses in grades 11 through 12 or 13 necessitates choices pointing towards a future career. Some critics believe it weakens the *Gymnasium*'s historical role in providing a liberal arts foundation for university study. Thus the balance between core and specialty courses and how they are weighted in the *Abitur* was debated and revised during the 1990s. These revisions specify that all pupils must study German, mathematics, and a foreign language in depth throughout their *Gymnasium* years, regardless of their choice of specialization. During the 1990s, the nationwide conference of university rectors criticized the structure of the *Abitur*, insisting that science and history, including contemporary history, should be compulsory as well.

Budget tightening in recent years has resulted in *Gymnasium* classes of as much as 30 students. Because teachers enjoy tenure and are assigned to one school, it is difficult to adjust the teaching staff to meet changing demand for more or fewer teachers in a given subject.

High school students are assigned a few hours of homework each afternoon, but testing is fairly infrequent, perhaps two tests per semester in specialty subjects, with just one or none in core subjects. Report cards are issued twice a year, and oral participation weighs heavily in student grades.

At the end of 13 years (12 in the Saarland and most of the new federal states) students at the *Gymnasium* sit for examinations (the *Abitur*) in at least three specialized subjects. Approximately one-fourth of the country's secondary school graduates passes the *Abitur* each year. A half-day of essay questions is followed by a half-hour oral examination. Some states such as Bavaria have a centralized *Abitur*, while other states administer different tests in each school. The Bavarian *Abitur*, requiring examination in four subjects instead of three, is considered the most difficult. About one-fifth of a given year's age group passes the Bavarian *Abitur*, slightly below the national average of 27 percent. That proportion rises as high as 30 to 40 percent in some states, and this leads Bavaria to threaten that it will institute a separate entrance examination for students from other states seeking admission to one of its universities.

Regardless of such disputes, considerable standardization and quality control of the *Abitur* already exist. The Conference of Ministers of Education of the federal states establishes standards for 33 subjects at both the basic level of advanced courses and the advanced level of specialty courses. State ministries of education exchange questions used in written exams, share test results, and disclose their criteria for evaluation. Despite this approach to standardization, there is enough variation in the test's difficulty that students who fail it in one state or city may be able to pass it elsewhere. Questions are submitted by teachers in the schools, so there is some risk that they "teach to the test," although they cannot be certain that the questions they have submitted will be selected. Tests are administered by teachers to their own students, observed by another teacher of the same subject, a recorder, and a chairperson. Students who pass these examinations are awarded the *Abitur* or *Zeugnis der allgemeinen Hochschulreife*. Those who fail may try once more. Because this examination permits admission to any German university, its approach is regarded with considerable trepidation.

In the 1990s many German *Abiturienten* (students who had passed the examination) equipped themselves with formal training in a trade as well. About 15 percent of apprentices now have achieved the *Abitur*. For the most part they seek training in fields such as banking, insurance, communications, and management. Their presence makes it more difficult for candidates who have only the general school-leaving certificate to find apprenticeships.

The chief function of the *Abitur* is to serve as a credential opening the door to university study. Because of overcrowding in desirable specializations such as medicine, veterinary and dental medicine, biology, and chemistry, most universities introduced *numerus clauses* (caps or quotas) in these disciplines in the 1970s. As a result, graduates of the *Gymnasium* may nonetheless need to wait as much as five years to enter a university. Some pursue traineeships, travel to improve their language skills, work as au pairs, or exist as trades people while they await admission. Males may fulfill their 12 months of military service obligation or 15 months of alternative service.

The *Gesamtschule*, emerged as an alternative to Germany's multi-track school system in 1969. Today these schools are found chiefly in Brandenburg, Hesse, North Rhine-Westphalia, Bremen, Hamburg, and Berlin, educating about 13 percent of the country's schoolchildren. Instead of the *Gesamtschule*, some East German states established a middle school (known as a *Sekundarschule*, *Mittelschule*, or *Regelschule*) combining features of the *Hauptschule* and *Realschule* through grades five and six. Most comprehensive schools provide full day instruction, lasting from eight o'clock in the morning until around three o'clock in the afternoon.

The West German *Gesamtschule* of grades 5 or 7 through 10 may house a *Hauptschule*, *Realschule*, and *Gymnasium* under one roof so that pupils can transfer easily from one type of school to another, or it may be integrated so that all pupils follow the same curriculum. The first two years, grades five and six, called the *Förderstufe*, offer maximum flexibility in changing tracks or even transferring to an outside school. From seventh grade upward several levels of difficulty are of-

fered in most subjects, enabling pupils to be grouped by ability. Many comprehensive schools end after tenth grade, and graduates receive certification equivalent to completion of a *Hauptschule* or *Realschule*. They may then continue to a *Gymnasium*. Other comprehensive schools extend through grade 13 and administer the *Abitur* in-house. These schools offer more electives than the traditional schools, and the number of electives increases in the higher grades. Comprehensive schools are intended to be more democratic in governance, more flexible, and employ a more pupil-centered approach to teaching. Although the *Gesamtschule* has been the focus of much educational research, it is still considered experimental and controversial and are opposed by the Christian Democrats and the Bavarian Christian Socialist Union. Therefore, these schools are seldom found in Bavaria and Baden-Württemberg.

Several reports published in the 1990s investigated whether comprehensive schools had achieved their purpose in their first quarter-century of existence. These studies reveal that the comprehensive schools have gradually become alternatives to the general secondary school or *Hauptschule*, with the more able pupils being sent to the *Realschule* or *Gymnasium*. Deprived of the upper strata of student achievement, the *Gesamtschule* has sometimes fallen below initial academic expectations. Furthermore, because these schools draw enrollment from three levels (*Hauptschule*, *Realschule*, and *Gymnasium*), they are often regional, rather than local. They are also considerably larger than other German schools, enrolling as many as 1,000 to 2,000 pupils. Some blame these factors and larger classes for student feelings of anonymity and alienation. And, because of their full day schedule and the broad spectrum of course offerings, these schools may be more expensive to operate than other types.

There are other differences between these three types of schools besides the curriculum they offer. Parents of children at the *Gymnasium* or *Realschule* usually set high expectations for their children's success, monitor their progress, participate in parents' councils, and stay in contact with teachers, all factors which contribute to their children's success. On the other hand, children at the *Hauptschule* may come from homes where there is less support for education, lower expectations, and less assistance with homework. These children are also more likely to bring discipline problems into the classroom, and a very few may need to transfer to a special school. Teachers at this level are apt to need stronger skills in pedagogy and interpersonal relations, while teachers at the *Gymnasium* are more likely to be successful simply with presenting the material.

Students in elementary or secondary schools who receive failing grades are likely to be held back, a decision reached in a conference of teachers. According to most reports, being held back is not stigmatized; rather, it is viewed as a decision made in the best interest of the child. Pupils who fail two subjects also have the option of transferring to a lower level school, for example from the *Realschule* to the *Hauptschule*. In that school, only one year may be repeated; a pupil who is still failing can leave school after the age of 16 with a school-leaving certificate, which is not equal to the normal qualification. About 10 percent of pupils per year take this step; thus the dropout rate from Germany's schools remains very low. A contributing factor may be the difficulty of finding work as an unskilled labor in an economy which places a high value on occupational training and credentials.

Transfer from the *Gymnasium* down into the *Realschule* is not uncommon and leaves children the possibility of earning the *Abitur* later. Pupils may also transfer into the comprehensive school, if there is a *Gesamtschule* in the area, or to a vocational high school (*Gymnasium*).

Nearly 4 percent of the country's school population attends *Sonderschulen* (Germany's special schools) for the physically or mentally handicapped. These institutions, developed out of church-sponsored facilities, are one area where churches continued to play a significant role even in the avowedly atheistic German Democratic Republic. The principle of separate schools was established after World War II, but has been repeatedly questioned. Some expected that children with special needs could be integrated into comprehensive schools. The largest groups of pupils in special schools are those with developmental delays or learning disabilities. At the elementary level, some pupils, usually those with dyslexia or mild learning disabilities, are being mainstreamed. During the first four years of schooling, pupils with disabilities may be sent to these special schools, a decision reached by the local superintendent, teachers, and parents. Almost one fifth of these special schools are private, chiefly those for pupils with hearing or vision impairments. In a few cases, children with disabilities may be schooled in a regular classroom of the *Hauptschule*, but their chances of finding an apprenticeship are slim; Germany has no real anti-discrimination policies comparable to the Americans with Disabilities Act.

Proponents of Germany's separate *Sonderschulen* contend that this system offers two advantages: it provides specialized education efficiently to those with special needs, and it spares other schools the expense of special equipment (wheelchair ramps, elevators) to accommodate such pupils; some *Sonderschulen* are residential institutions. The disadvantages are that separation of these children may not prepare them adequately for integration into the workplace. Furthermore, other children may not learn tolerance or a willingness to accommodate those with special needs. The trend is moving toward increased mainstreaming of physically or mentally challenged pupils.

Significant changes in Germany's three-part secondary school system began in the 1980s. Larger numbers of German children who might otherwise have entered the *Hauptschule* chose the *Realschule* instead, motivated in part by the belief that the quality of instruction in the *Hauptschule* had been compromised by the influx of immigrant children. While the majority of citizens favor the current system of separating pupils after the fourth grade into three separate institutions, many parents aim higher than the school level where their children are placed; for example 52 percent would prefer that their offspring attend the *Gymnasium*, while only about half that number actually do so.

Efforts toward less stratified, more egalitarian structures, such as the orientation phase following fourth grade and the comprehensive secondary school, have gained ground where the Social Democratic Party is strongest, in North Rhine-Westphalia, Hesse, and the three city-states. However, the Christian Democrats and their affiliates, the Christian Socialist Union, form a bulwark preserving the more conservative, traditional three-part division of secondary education in areas where they dominate the political scene, such as Bavaria and Baden-Württemberg.

Germany's public school system presents several contrasts to the American model. Student activities play a far smaller role than is the case in American high schools, although German schools may create their own newspapers. Team sports seldom form part of the school experience; rather children join soccer or swimming clubs, which are sponsored by municipalities or private organizations. Music lessons and school bands are also rare in German schools. Driver education is given through *Fahrschulen* (private schools) where tuition is expensive, and the minimum age for obtaining a driver's license is eighteen. Thus, in contrast to the American pattern, it is rare for high school students to drive to school or to hold part-time jobs at the end of the school day.

German schools offer few special programs for the gifted and talented. It is assumed that these pupils will ascend to the upper tracks within the *Gymnasium*, and this arrangement appears satisfactory, given the system's separation of pupils into tracks based on intellectual ability.

Relatively little career counseling occurs in German schools. For the most part, decisions about which secondary school to enter also encompass decisions about a future occupation. The *Bundesanstalt für Arbeit* (Federal Agency for Work) and its information centers disseminate information about various careers.

At all levels, Germany's educational institutions have been struggling to keep pace with technological innovations. At the turn of the twenty-first century, only about one third of the country's schools had Internet access. In May 2000 Chancellor Gerhard Schroeder announced a new four-year initiative to spend 750 million marks to equip public schools and libraries with Internet connections, to develop educational software, and to expand opportunities to study information technology at colleges and universities over the next five years. In 1999, only 20,000 students began their studies in computer science; at the technical universities of Berlin and Munich about half the applicants had to be turned away due to a lack of financing for such programs. Some universities, such as Hannover and the Free University in Berlin, have responded by introducing newer, shorter information technology programs. In addition, 100 *Fachhochschulen* offered 100 openings each in one-year postgraduate training programs in information technology.

Evidence of the country's serious shortage of computer experts can be seen in Schroeder's initiative to offer 20,000 non-European Union computer specialists a green card entitling them to work in Germany for a five-year period, accompanied by their families. A few months after this initiative was announced in 2000, Germany had received far fewer than the expected number of applications, most from India, Pakistan, Algeria, and Bulgaria. After much debate, German authorities agreed that applicants must either hold an advanced degree or prove a minimum yearly income of 100,000 DM (about US$50,000). German employers found themselves on the horns of a dilemma: while their culture respects and recognizes academic qualifications above any comparable measures of worth, the sudden demand for computer experts has forced them to become more flexible.

HIGHER EDUCATION

Wilhelm von Humboldt (1767-1835) founded the Berlin University in 1810. He insisted that universities should promote both research and teaching and advocated academic freedom, liberating professors from the demand that they submit their lectures for church or state approval and not deviate from the written text. Humboldt insisted that universities must be autonomous, free of political or religious interference, a goal that was not realized for many more decades. Humboldt also introduced less formal instructional settings, seminars, and laboratory sessions.

At the end of World War II, West Germany contained 16 universities and 14 technical colleges. *Fachhochschulen*, offering higher professional training in engineering and scientific fields, appeared in West Ger-

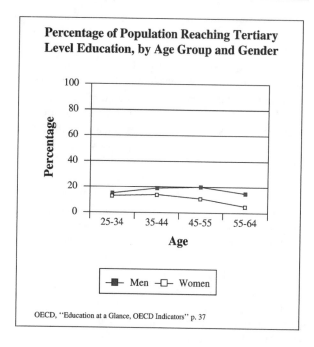

Percentage of Population Reaching Tertiary Level Education, by Age Group and Gender

OECD, "Education at a Glance, OECD Indicators" p. 37

many in the late 1960s. They offer instruction in fields such as business administration, engineering, agriculture, social work, or design. The period of study is usually shorter than at a university and culminates in the award of a *Diplom*.

In East Germany, the research function was transferred from universities to institutes and academies, such as the prestigious Academy of Sciences in Berlin. Both research and academic freedom came under the scrutiny of the Socialist Unity Party in the German Democratic Republic. Many administrators and senior faculty belonged to the Party, and Free German Youth groups existed on all campuses, exercising some control over student access and activities. At the time of unification, East Germany counted 54 institutions of higher education, among them 8 universities and 5 technical colleges. While their physical facilities were often outdated, and laboratory and computer equipment inadequate, these institutions enjoyed a favorable faculty-to-student ratio, with a stronger emphasis on teaching and learning than on research. Since unification, many institutions have been amalgamated and faculties combined or reduced in the East. New universities have been founded at Erfurt, Potsdam, and Frankfurt an der Oder, and new technical colleges at Cottbus and Chemnitz. Over a three-year period, departments of history, social studies, law, and Marxism-Leninism were disbanded and professors' qualifications and personal integrity were examined. New faculty positions were established in the humanities, legal studies, economics, business, and education.

New universities were founded in West Germany throughout the 1970s and 1980s when the population of university students doubled (from a half-million to around 1 million). However, facilities were not expanded to meet the demand. This was because demographers had predicted lower enrollments in the 1980s based on the low birthrates following the advent of oral contraceptives in the early 1960s. Despite these predictions, large numbers of students sought admission to higher education, especially in fields such as computer science, engineering, and business. Expectations that students would complete their studies more expeditiously and leave universities sooner also failed to materialize. In 2000 around one-third of united Germany's young people chose to study at a university or specialized college, and enrollment has remained around 1.8 million. The largest universities are Munich, followed by Berlin's Free University, and the universities in Cologne, Münster, Hamburg, and Frankfurt am Main. The 1980s and 1990s witnessed steady increases in the proportion of students from working class families (now around 15 percent), the proportion of students from immigrant families, and the proportion of women (40 percent in the West and 46 percent in the East) pursuing higher education.

German universities present many contrasts to the American university system. First, admissions to most fields of study are not competitive; high school graduates with the *Abitur* are assured of admission. However, since a period of overcrowding in the 1970s, admissions to fields such as medicine, dentistry, veterinary medicine, biology, management, economics, law, psychology, pharmacy, and nutrition have been restricted. Nearly half of all university admissions are decided on the basis of *Abitur* grades and testing, 10 percent solely on test results, and the remainder on the basis of an interview and other factors such as how long the applicant has been waiting for admission. Decisions for all public universities are made by a central admissions board in Dortmund. The average age for students entering higher education is 22; some have delayed this step because of the difficulty of obtaining a place in high demand fields such as the medical sciences. In 2001 about 25 percent of the students entering higher education have completed vocational training as well as the *Abitur*. Some students have pursued practical training or worked to earn money to finance their education. Because the average length of university study is 7 years, with slightly shorter times for technical colleges, students are 28 or 29 by the time they graduate and are ready to begin their careers. Recently concern has arisen that this places them at a competitive disadvantage among their peers in the European Union.

Tuition is free, but students pay for health insurance and activity fees each semester. Those who need financial assistance to meet living costs receive monthly subsidies known as BAFöG, an acronym for *Bundesausbildungs-förderungsgesetz* (federal law to promote education).

About a quarter of all students in the West and half of those in the East receive this financial assistance. Originally a grant, these subsidies were converted in 1983 to interest-free loans, usually awarded for a maximum of four years. A more recent decision to charge interest on BAFöG loans aroused controversy over the issue of fair access to higher education for all qualified students. About 60 percent of German university students finance their studies through part-time work; however, since Germany values special training and skilled trades, opportunities for entry into low-skilled occupations are limited.

Germany's university faculties have historically been considered attractive and prestigious; indeed those entitled to the honorific "professor" outrank even medical doctors in prestige. At the top of faculty rank are chaired professors; followed by *Privatdozente*, who do not have tenure; temporary and guest faculty; instructors whose role is limited to teaching, *Lehrbeauftragte*; and technical and teaching assistants, *wissenschaftliche Hilfskräfte*. Faculty at technical colleges are expected to bring appropriate practical experience as well as advanced degrees to their teaching posts. In addition to advanced degrees and teaching expertise, those wishing to ascend to a full university professorship must complete a step known as *Habilitation*, research and publication in their field analogous to a second doctoral dissertation, and orally presented to a committee of superiors for discussion and approval. Only after successful completion of this step (which may take as long as ten years) are faculty recommended for permanent appointment to the highest rank.

In 1999 the Conference of University Rectors (*Hochschulrektorenkonferenz*) recommended some changes in the training of new university faculty, maintaining that students should be able to obtain a doctoral degree by 27 or 28 years of age. Qualification for a tenure-track position should not require more than an additional 10 years—still very long by U.S. standards. The present system requires closely supervised research under the auspices of a senior faculty mentor, a procedure which discourages study abroad and may be restrictive, subjective, or unduly dependent on personal interactions. Furthermore, the emphasis on research does nothing to promote effective teaching. Reliance on the support of senior faculty, who are overwhelmingly male, makes it difficult for women to attain tenured university rank. Only about 5 percent of fully tenured university professors are women.

Germany had no private universities until the late twentieth century. In 2001 there are about 65, many church-related, whose total enrollment is about 30,000 students. Even in 2001, there are no noteworthy general-purpose private universities and no significant differences in status or quality among the country's approximately 90 public universities. In 1995 united Germany also counted 17 theological seminaries, 136 polytechnic colleges, and 31 colleges (*Fachhochschulen*) for administrative services. There are almost 50 academies of Music and Art (*Kunsthochschulen, Musikhochschulen*) but only 6 colleges of education (*Pädagogische Hochschulen*), since most have been combined with universities. In the 1960s and 1970s, technical universities and colleges sprang up, for example in Berlin, Munich, Augsburg, Bochum, and Trier. The distance-learning university at Hagen, founded in 1975, enrolls about 50,000 students, most of them part-time, in programs in economics, mathematics, electrical engineering, computer science, and other fields. The last 10 years have witnessed the creation of new bi-national universities, beginning with a joint German-Polish university (Viadrina) in Frankfurt an der Oder. France and Germany founded a new bi-national university in Saarbrücken in 2000, where instruction takes place in both languages; the study of artificial intelligence is a particular emphasis there. Beginning in 2001-2002 a Neisse university founded by the university of Wroclaw in Poland, the university of Liberec in the Czech Republic, and the university of Zittau/Görlitz in Germany will offer bachelors' degrees in information and communication management.

The curriculum at German universities also presents several contrasts to the American model. Germans consider that students at the *Gymnasium* have acquired a broad-based grounding in the liberal arts; thus universities have no core curriculum or general education requirement. Germans do not clearly distinguish graduate and undergraduate education. The period known as *Grundstudium* (basic studies) usually lasts for two years, ending with an examination, the *Zwischenprüfung*, or, in technical fields, the *Diplomvorprüfung*. A period of specialized, in-depth study follows, lasting two or more years longer. An examination is generally required at the end, either for civil service employment, the *Staatsexamen*, or a *Diplomprüfung* in scientific, technical, or engineering fields, or a master's level examination. The *Magister* (Master's degree) may require a thesis, as does the doctorate. There is no formal process for student advisement, nor for selecting an academic major comprised of a recommended curriculum. Instead, most students prepare for examinations by taking a variety of courses and seeking guidance from more experienced students or faculty. About one-fifth change their major during their course of study and as many as one-third drop out. A university degree does not guarantee employment in one's chosen fields: as many as a third of all graduates in languages, culture, social studies, and economics and one-tenth of those in medicine and veterinary medicine failed to find employment in keeping with their qualifications.

Courses of instruction at the university may be divided into various levels. Beginners sit in *Vorlesungen* (large lecture sections) and listen to a professor lecture from his notes or book. Tutorial sessions led by the professor's assistants may be offered in addition. Seminars are designated by their level of specificity and difficulty: *Proseminar*, *Mittelseminar*, and *Hauptseminar*. Students who wish to document their attendance and performance in these courses must make individual arrangements with the professor; generally, research papers and oral reports are required in the seminar courses. Close mentoring relationships between faculty and students are quite rare. Increasing student-faculty ratios make it even more difficult to develop such relationships.

As was the case at the level of high school vocational training, this educational model has proven conservative and somewhat inflexible. Thus new technological fields have found a place in new technical universities and colleges, rather than in the traditional universities. Although these opened their doors to women with the advent of the Weimar Republic, women are under-represented as both students and faculty in the sciences, law, and theology.

Student life at the university also presents several contrasts to the American system. The largest university, in Munich, has about 60,000 students, and many others are nearly as large, although the lack of a centralized campus masks their true size. The winter semester begins in October and extends through mid-February, while the summer semester lasts from mid-April to mid-July. Competitive sports are non-existent. Extra-curricular activities consist of a few groups organized, for example, on the basis of religion. *Bruderschaften* (fraternities) cultivate a rich tradition, but there are no sororities. The university campus may be spread throughout a city, with buildings housing newer faculties scattered on its outskirts. Only about 10 percent of a university's students in the West and 55 percent in the East are housed in dormitories, which usually reserve some space for foreign students. About one-fifth of university students and one-third of those at technical colleges live with their parents. Many students rent rooms or join others in apartments. The *Mensa* (student cafeteria) serves inexpensive meals and provides meeting space for students. Many university libraries have closed stacks, and students rely on their own housing arrangements for study space.

During the late 1990s, some West German students moved east to take advantage of East Germany's less crowded classrooms and lower cost of living. Some differences between East and West German students persist a decade after unification. Easterners are more apt to plan an academic program with a clear career goal in mind. They become financially independent earlier and finish their studies on average one year earlier than West German students.

Change is afoot in Germany's universities, after years of low budgets and high enrollments. In autumn 1997 university students began a series of demonstrations and strikes to protest lack of funding for higher education. While German colleges and universities can accommodate around 1 million students, there are currently about 1.8 million crowding into lecture halls and seminar rooms. From the late 1970s to the late 1990s, the number of students rose 70 percent, but the numbers of college and university faculty increased only 5 percent. Basic federal financial aid (BAFöG) has increased only slightly. In 1997 a proposal made by the University Rector's Conference to charge tuition sparked the largest student protests since 1968 and was ultimately rejected. While these protests attracted media attention and loosened purse strings in a few federal states, they failed to achieve any far-reaching reform of higher education. Other reforms proposed in 1997 would have replaced some aspects of faculty governance with professional administrators, introduced student evaluations of their courses, and prescribed programs of study leading to bachelor's and master's degrees.

On the other hand, different kinds of changes are occurring on the university scene. Over a dozen universities, including Leipzig, Dresden, Reutlingen, Stuttgart, Kaiserslautern, Stralsund, and Duisburg, now offer some instruction in English, particularly in technical fields such as engineering, communications, water resource management, information technology, electronics, and business administration. Some institutions have begun to design curricula that more closely resemble the American model, offering a bachelor's degree after six semesters or a master's degree after nine. Students who have earned a bachelor's degree in their homeland may be able to enter a master's level program directly. Some colleges and universities are considering introducing the credit point system used in the United States. The goal of these innovations is to attract more foreign students and to better prepare German students for internationally recognized degrees. Many of these programs offer study abroad as an integral part of the curriculum. Courses in English are often taught by visiting faculty from the United States, Britain, Asia, or India. A secondary purpose of such programs is to abbreviate the traditional seven years most university students spend passing their examinations and earning a license or diploma. At *Fachhochschulen*, the average is slightly more than five years. Thus far, attempts to shorten these periods of study have proven fruitless. Success could depend on closer monitoring of student progress and better advisement, an area where German universities have traditionally done relatively little.

ADMINISTRATION, FINANCE, & EDUCATIONAL RESEARCH

In general, education is administered and financed by Germany's 16 federal states, with the national government assuming responsibility for the standardization of requirements for the *Abitur*, for teacher training, and for vocational education, as well as for financial support of students in higher education.

The Federal Institute for Vocational Education (*Bundesinstitut für Berufsbildung*), comprised of representatives of state and federal governments, unions, and employers, created educational guidelines for apprenticeships and is responsible for certification. At the local level, chambers of commerce maintain vocational education committees; firms which provide apprenticeships also contribute to their administration and have input.

The Standing Conference of Ministers of Education and Culture sets standards for mutual recognition of teaching certificates, vocational training, the *Abitur*, and other certificates awarded at the completion of secondary education. In 1969 the West German constitution was amended to establish joint federal and state responsibility for higher education. Since the 1980s there has also existed a central office in Dortmund for awarding students admission to a university.

Universities and technical colleges are generally administered by a rector or president, and supported by deans and faculty hierarchies. Governance is shared with an assembly or senate comprised of university faculty. Once restricted to professors holding a university chair, these groups now usually include representatives from other faculty ranks.

Individual schools are under the supervision of a director appointed by the local district. The director, who continues to teach within the school, is responsible for scheduling, the evaluation of teachers, the coordination of grading, and representing the school to the public. A school council comprised of teachers, parents, and pupils discusses school issues such as rules, schedules, space usage, events, textbooks, and field trips. There are also separate teacher and parent councils. Party differences are evident here too: the Christian Democrats oppose the school council as a non-professional interference in educational matters.

Elementary and secondary schools receive around 80 percent of their financing from each of the federal states, with the remainder coming from individual communities; therefore, school quality does not vary significantly between rich and poor towns and cities. Schools may also receive funds or donated equipment from local businesses. Funds are distributed quite evenly among each of the levels of secondary school; the general secondary school does not usually lag behind the *Gymnasium* in the quality of school buildings or adequacy of resources.

With respect to higher education, the federal government provides 65 percent of financial aid to students (BAFöG) and contributes to funding for college and university construction, staffing, and special promotions, such as increasing the numbers of women faculty. However, the states pay 92 percent of higher education costs. About three-fourths of the funding for research comes from the federal government. Adult education funding is shared about equally by the federal, state, and local governments. In 1996 public spending for schools and higher education totaled approximately 159.2 billion DM or about eighty billion U.S. dollars.

The Federal Ministry of Education, Science, Research, and Technology funds educational research (overseen by a joint federal and state council) into topics such as the integration of technology in schools, the role of ecology in the curriculum, and the development of girls and women. The *Wissenschaftsrat* (science council) located in Cologne was established in 1958 to coordinate science and research at the federal and state levels. It makes recommendations on university staffing, finances, and courses of study and played a key role in the reform of East German universities after unification. At that time it had 39 members, and, with additional representatives from East Germany, it now has 54. Members of this highly prestigious council are appointed by the federal president upon recommendation by the Max Planck Society, the University Rectors Conference, and the *Deutsche Forschungsgemeinschaft*. During its first 40 years, only 6 of its members have been women.

The University of Bochum includes a prominent Research Center for Comparative Educational Studies and, since the early 1990s, the University of Marburg has had a center for studies on European developments in education. The Max Planck Institute of Educational Research, established in Berlin in 1963, has worked since unification to analyze East German social networks, in addition to its more general research interests such as psychology and human development, educational development, schools, and teaching. The oldest institution researching international non-university education is the German Institute of International Educational Research at Frankfurt. This organization also assumed responsibility for the former East German Central Educational Library in Berlin, an institution dating back to 1875, now known as the Library for Research into the History of Education. A variety of both federal and state institutes also conduct research in such areas as curriculum development, the effectiveness of comprehensive schools, cooperation between schools, and teaching and learning. The *Deutsche Forschungsgemeinschaft* (German Research Associa-

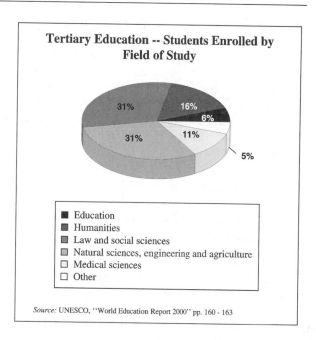

Tertiary Education -- Students Enrolled by Field of Study

- ■ Education
- ■ Humanities
- ■ Law and social sciences
- ◻ Natural sciences, engineering and agriculture
- ◻ Medical sciences
- ◻ Other

Source: UNESCO, ''World Education Report 2000'' pp. 160 - 163

tion), the Volkswagen Foundation, and churches also support specific projects in the area of educational research. Recommendations from the late 1990s would strengthen links between the traditionally independent Max Planck Institute and universities and urge that organization to focus its research efforts on the latest developments in science. The *Deutsche Forschungsgemeinschaft* has a somewhat restrictive peer review process to award grant funding and has been urged to open its review panels to younger researchers and to include more women. Germany ranks seventh among industrialized nations in the proportion of gross domestic product spent on research and development. In Germany as everywhere else, recent years have seen tighter budgets and greater reluctance to fund schools fully. The country taxes its wealthiest citizens at about half their income, in part to defray the high costs of unification.

NONFORMAL EDUCATION

Adults may expand their formal schooling for personal reasons or to develop new job skills. There are more than 1,000 *Volkshochschulen* (adult education centers) in Germany, offering courses in languages, technology, health areas, and arts and crafts. Around 7 million residents take advantage of such offerings each year.

The so-called second path (*zweiter Bildungsweg*) is open to adults over the age of 19 who completed tenth grade and have professional training or a three-year work record. These adults, as well as full-time homemakers, can attend evening courses to earn school completion certificates such as the *Abitur* and the certificate normally awarded upon completion of the *Realschule*. Full-time study for adults is offered in the *Kolleg*, which fills 32 hours a week and can last for three to four years. Participants in these programs can receive BAFöG financial support. Both full-time and part-time instructors teach adult education courses, many of them in the evening. Workers who have been unemployed for a long time may receive subsidies to cover part or most of the cost of such re-training initiatives. The *Bundeanstalt für Arbeit* (Federal Agency for Work) sponsors a retraining program for workers suffering from long-term unemployment. Labor unions, churches, and private businesses also maintain continuing education facilities and programs. A half-dozen universities offer non-degree programs for senior citizens.

While distance learning was widespread in the German Democratic Republic, it did not appear in West Germany until 1975 with the founding of the university at Hagen in North Rhine-Westphalia. Now the university has more than 50,000 students, with more than 50 percent of them part-time; the largest number study economics and education. It operates 60 regional study centers throughout Germany.

TEACHING PROFESSION

In 1990 the nationwide Conference of State Ministers of Education established new standards for teacher education. Those planning to teach in elementary and general secondary schools must study for at three or four years - depending on their state - at the university; those destined for the *Realschule*, *Gymnasium*, vocational schools, or special schools study for five years. Teachers at the elementary level and those in the secondary general school (*Hauptschule*) may study at one of the country's Colleges of Education (*Pädagogische Hochschulen*). In recent years the trend has been to incorporate these institutions into universities, except for Baden-Württemberg, Schleswig-Holstein, and Saxony-Anhalt, where they remain separate. Teachers at the elementary and general secondary schools are required to specialize in German, mathematics, and an additional subject. Those planning to teach in the *Realschule*, *Gymnasium*, or special schools usually specialize in at least two subjects, with relatively less training in pedagogy than is required in the United States. All prospective teachers take a qualifying examination after university study, followed by two years of supervised practice teaching (the *Referendariat*), and then a second state examination. Teachers in vocational schools must have completed an apprenticeship in addition to their academic training. Requirements for teacher education differ among the 16 federal states in length of study, number of specialty subjects, periods of practical experience, and the type of school where one wishes to teach. The result is an inflexible system in which a person prepared to teach at a comprehensive school in Hesse would not be qualified to teach at a *Gymnasium* in Bavaria.

After a three-year probationary period, during which they are further supervised and evaluated, teachers apply to the regional district office for employment. Since 1872 public school teachers in the West have enjoyed lifetime tenure as *Beamtenstatus* (civil servants), a privilege opposed by the Social Democrats. After unification, veteran East German teachers were required to re-apply for their positions and undergo two years of observation and evaluation before receiving the status of *Angestellte* (salaried employees). Since citizens of other countries belonging to the European Union can also work in Germany, they may become salaried employees, but not civil servants, a rank open only to German citizens. Teachers in the *Gymnasium* become eligible for promotion to *Studienrat* (study advisor) and *Oberstudienrat* (head study advisor) and then to assistant principal and principal. An increase in salary accompanies promotion. Most teachers earn between $35,000 and $50,000 per year; however, those in the East still earn around 15 percent less than teachers in the West, although their teaching loads may be heavier and class sizes larger due to school consolidations. Principals continue to teach and come from the ranks of experienced teachers, rather than receiving specialized training. Their salaries are not significantly higher than those of teachers. They observe and evaluate teachers, schedule classes, and organize meetings with parents' councils, but seldom intervene to enforce classroom discipline. Detention or suspension from school are not common disciplinary measures. Few schools employ guidance counselors in the American model; rather, teachers who have received extra training may deal with drug problems or personal issues. Relatively little academic or career counseling occurs in German schools.

Most teachers conduct around 25 classes a week, averaging 45 minutes apiece. At the upper levels, two class periods may be combined for laboratory sessions. Those who supervise student teachers or head departments teach a reduced load, as do those over 55. Teachers retire at 65, or earlier, if they have taught 35 years (5 years of university study may be counted toward that period of service). The largest teachers' union, the *Gewerkschaft Erziehung und Wissenschaft*, enrolls about 65 percent of teachers, followed by smaller unions. Teachers' unions campaign for equal pay for East Germans, reduced teaching loads, and better pay. Because of their civil servant status, teachers may not strike.

Germany's teacher training system has come under scrutiny because of its generally conservative nature. Particularly at the level of the *Realschule* and *Gymnasium*, teachers concentrate on subject matter, the theory being that good scholars will be able to transmit their knowledge effectively. However, as these schools have lost their selectivity and experienced increased enrollments from more diverse and less academically prepared pupils, teachers have sometimes found themselves overwhelmed. Those who have achieved civil servant status may be evaluated every four to six years, but are not obliged to participate in further in-service training, nor does it raise their salaries unless they qualify for teaching at a higher level. It is difficult to remove or dismiss a poor teacher. Teacher training has been slow to respond to changes in the needs of teachers to be familiar with new instructional media and computer technology. In-service training offers teachers many opportunities to up-date their qualifications in methods and instructional media. These retraining courses usually take place during the school day and teachers are excused to participate. Because of the absence of substitutes, however, their participation places hardships on their co-workers. Summer courses for teachers are less common than in the United States.

Because curriculum and textbooks must receive state approval, there is less incentive or opportunity for innovative teaching than in many U.S. schools. It may be difficult to adapt a given text to the abilities of a particular class. And given the secure status of teachers' employment, not all can be motivated to cooperate with their colleagues in creating change. Those who have been promoted to the highest rank have little incentive to further their education or to adopt innovative techniques. Most teachers do not have a "homeroom," but rely on space in a teachers' lounge to prepare classes and do paperwork. Because few schools have cafeterias, most teachers also leave the building when the school day ends around one o'clock, and find little time to compare notes, talk shop, or cooperate with their peers.

Gender imbalance remains in the country's teaching faculties. About three-fourths of all elementary teachers are women. As the educational level rises, the number of males in the classroom increases also. Male kindergarten teachers are virtually unknown, but men and women teach in about equal proportions at the *Gymnasium*. As is true worldwide, women tend to be concentrated in the humanities and social sciences. However, the East German states boast more women teachers of math and science than the West, evidence that the Marxist-socialist education system did achieve some success in overturning gender stereotypes. Unemployment among teachers affects more women than men.

Because of demographics and tight budgets, relatively few new teachers entered the profession in the 1990s. A sharp decline in the birthrate between 1990 and 1994 caused an oversupply of teachers at the elementary level, and this effect is slowly making its way upward through the age cohorts, so that tenured positions have become increasingly difficult to obtain. In the new federal states, school enrollments are expected to remain low through 2010; while in the West they are expected to peak in 2005 and then fall again. In 2000 only 16 percent of Germany's residents were under the age of 15. The greatest oversupply of teachers exists at the *Gymnasium* level. In the East there is an oversupply of elementary teachers, teachers of Russian, humanities, and any social studies areas tainted by Marxism-Leninism. There is a scarcity of teachers in English, French, Latin (which replaced Russian), ethics, and the arts. Class sizes can run as high as 30 pupils; in Saxony in the late 1990s the limit for elementary classes was 32. The birthrate began to rise again in 1994, creating a greater demand for elementary teachers by 2000, but an oversupply of teachers at the secondary level persists. Young teachers who have spent five or more years at the university are often in their late twenties when they begin teaching. As a result, only about one-fifth of the country's teachers are under 35. Since West German teachers hold civil servant status, they cannot be dismissed nor can they be easily displaced from one school to another.

SUMMARY

Public school education in Germany today confronts a spectrum of challenges not unfamiliar to American educators. Some Germans find the school curriculum outdated, as the schools struggle to keep pace with technological innovation. In comparison to other industrialized countries, Germany ranks nineteenth in number of computers per thousand of population, nineteenth in Internet service providers, and seventeenth in the number of Internet users. The high cost of telephone calls makes Internet usage expensive. New training programs and apprenticeships for workers in high tech fields have not kept up with the demand for qualified technicians and software engineers. In addition, the presence of the Internet in schools causes some school children to question the knowledge and authority of their teachers, and opens the door to hundreds of information sources not approved by any state.

Furthermore, since the early 1990s, Germany has suffered from unemployment rates as high as 12 percent in the West and nearly 20 percent in the East. As a result, some Germans question whether a good education guarantees a good job. Particularly in the East, where teachers of Russian, Marxism-Leninism, economics, political science, and the history of the working class were thrown out of work after unification, the value of education has been called into question.

The continuing presence of religion in Germany's schools would appear threatened by the pressures of immigration. Today there are about 28 million Catholics in

Germany and roughly the same number of Lutherans. While these churches have traditionally dominated religious education in schools, they have attracted few believers in the East, where only 25 percent of the population is Lutheran and about 3 percent Catholic. Since the imposition of the church tax (10 percent of the individual's income tax), many East Germans have taken the legal step of disaffiliating themselves from churches, and membership has actually declined. Germany's population now encompasses 2.3 million Moslems, most of them Turks who live chiefly in the West. There are another 370,000 Orthodox Christians, 200,000 evangelical Protestants, and a growing community of 50,000 Jews, most of them immigrants from the former Soviet Union. The 1990s witnessed legal disputes in Germany about the traditional Moslem head covering worn by some schoolgirls and teachers and about the presence of crucifixes in Bavarian classrooms. It seems likely that the most acceptable solution to increasing religious diversity should be a tendency toward courses in ethics rather than religion, a trend strongly opposed by the Christian Democrats and Christian Socialist Union.

The academic success of immigrant children remains uncertain. Bilingual education programs have mostly been abandoned, although some immigrant children may participate in after-school programs or special classes to learn German as a second language. Even Berlin, where about one fifth of the schoolchildren speak a first language other than German, now has only a half-dozen schools still offering some form of bilingual education. The dropout rate for Turkish children is three times that for Germans, and German children are three times as likely as Turks to achieve the *Abitur* and go on to higher education. This hurdle blocks foreigners from entering the teaching profession; thus immigrant children confront teachers who seldom speak their mother tongue. The problem of immigrant children varies with geography; there are fewer foreigners in the new federal states and most of those in the West are concentrated in cities.

Another social issue challenging teachers is that schools have increasingly been expected to assume responsibilities previously held by families and, in the East, by socialist organizations. Such responsibilities have devolved onto the schools as the need increases for women as well as men to work for pay. Moreover, Germany has a high number of single parent families; in the late 1990s, half of all babies in the East were born to unmarried women. The number of single parent families means that schools need to take on some responsibilities for afternoon care, supervision of homework, and enrichment activities such as sports and arts. Some, particularly the *Gesamtschulen*, now offer afternoon programs or a full day of instruction.

The coming decades will bring far-reaching changes, arising from Germany's membership in the European Union. Because teachers from other European Union countries will be eligible to teach in Germany, there must be broad agreement on the qualifications required for effective teaching, such as the balance between subject matter knowledge and practical training.

BIBLIOGRAPHY

Ashwill, Mark A., ed. *The Educational System in Germany: Case Study Findings.* Washington DC: National Institute on Student Achievement, Curriculum, and Assessment, 1999.

Dichanz, Horst, and John A. Zahorik. *Changing Traditions in Germany's Public Schools.* Bloomington, IN: Phi Beta Kappa Educational Foundation, 1998.

Fishman, Sterling, and Lothar Martin. *Estranged Twins; Education and Society in the Two Germanys.* New York: Praeger, 1987.

Fuhr, Christoph. *The German Education System Since 1945; Outlines and Problems.* Bonn: Inter Nationes, 1997.

Geschke, Otti. "Participation and Disadvantage: Women in the Educational System." In *The Federal Republic of Germany; the End of an Era,* ed. Eva Kolinsky, 189-198. New York: Berg, 1991.

Lamberti, Marjorie. *State, Society, and the Elementary School in Imperial Germany.* New York: Oxford University Press, 1989.

Lingens, Hans G. *German Higher Education.* Bloomington, IN: Phi Beta Kappa Educational Foundation, 1998.

Saxony State Ministry of Culture. *Bildungwege in Sachsen.* 8th ed., 2000.

Stevenson, Mark A. "Flexible Education and the Discipline of the Market." *International Journal of Qualitative Studies in Education 12* (May/June 1999): 311-324.

Streitwieser, Bernhard Thomas. "Some Thoughts on Post-Reunification Pedagogical Adjustments." *European Education 31* (Fall 1999): 60-87.

Teichler, Ulrich. "Education in the Federal Republic of Germany: Recollections and Problems." In *The Federal Republic of Germany; the End of an Era,* ed. Eva Kolinsky, 177-188. New York: Berg, 1991.

—Helen H. Frink

GHANA

BASIC DATA

Official Country Name:	Republic of Ghana
Region:	Africa
Population:	19,533,560
Language(s):	English, Akan, Moshi-Dagomba, Ewe, Ga
Literacy Rate:	64.5%
Number of Primary Schools:	12,134
Compulsory Schooling:	8 years
Public Expenditure on Education:	4.2%
Educational Enrollment:	Primary: 2,154,646
Educational Enrollment Rate:	Primary: 79%
Teachers:	Primary: 71,863
Student-Teacher Ratio:	Primary: 30:1
Female Enrollment Rate:	Primary: 74%

HISTORY & BACKGROUND

An Introduction: Ghana, formerly known as the Gold Coast, was the first African country to the south of the Sahara to gain political independence from colonial rule in 1957. This former British colony of 92,000 square miles (about 238,000 square kilometers) shares boundaries with three French-speaking nations: the Côte d'Ivoire to the west, Burkina Faso to the north, and Togo to the east. The Gulf of Guinea of the Atlantic Ocean is to the south of the country. Because much of the Precambrian rocks systems that composed most of the territories have been worn to almost a plain, the country is generally low in its physical relief. The major highlands of the country include the Kwahu Plateau, which lies in the middle section of the country. Several important rivers flow from the plateau. Located to the eastern sector of the country are the Akuampim-Togo Ranges. The Akuapim Range runs from the west of Accra and ends at the gorge at the Volta River, where the Akosombo Dam on the river has been constructed. The southern end of the Togo Range begins at the Volta Dam and runs along the country's border in a northeasterly direction.

Situated just above the equator, Ghana has a tropical climate of high temperatures and heavy rains. The vege-tation in the northern third of the country and a small strip near the coast are classified as savanna, but a heavy forest covers the middle belt of the country. While timber and other forest products (including cocoa) are exported, the country was known as the British Gold Coast because of the county's gold supplies. Ghana continues to export gold in large quantities and it remains an importation foreign exchange earner.

The first post-independent census in 1960 recorded a population of 6.7 million inhabitants. The population grew in the next 10 years to 8.5 million, and in the last official count in 1984, some 12.3 million inhabitants were recorded. Since then, Ghana's population figures have been based on estimates—17.2 million for 1990. At an estimated growth rate of 3 percent for the period 1980 to 1998, the population for 1998 was calculated at 18.5 million. Based on an expected slower rate of growth of 2.2 percent, a population of 26.8 million has been estimated for the year 2015. Of the estimated population, 42 percent are thought to be below 14 years of age, 54 percent are between the ages of 15 and 64, and 4 percent are aged 65 and above. Of this youthful population, about 60 percent of the total number of students are enrolled in primary schools, 35 percent in secondary schools, and only about 5 percent are in the postsecondary institutions including teacher training institutions. In fact, even though the government invested only 5 percent of the money spent during the 1980's Economic Recovery Programs on education, the total national expenditure on education for the same period was as high as one quarter of the total national budget. This national commitment to education is reflected in Ghana's long-standing tradition of demonstrating a commitment to education.

Early History of Education—An Overview: The earliest history of formal, western-style education in Ghana is directly associated with the history of European activities on the Gold Coast. The Portuguese were the first Europeans to arrive at the Guinea coast in 1471. Their intention to establish schools was expressed in imperial instructions that, in 1529, encouraged the Governor of the Portuguese Castle at Elmina to teach reading, writing, and the Catholic religion to the people. While there is no evidence to demonstrate their success, it is amply proven that Dutch, Danish, and English companies operated schools on the Gold Coast, and that instruction in reading, writing, and religious education took place within the castle walls.

The best known Castle Schools on the Gold Coast included the one operated by the Dutch at the former Portuguese fortress at Elmina, the British school at Cape Coast Castle, and the Danish school at Christiansborg, near Accra. In the late eighteenth century and throughout the nineteenth century, children of wealthy African merchants on the coast and relatives of some of the important local chiefs were instructed at castle schools. The historian C. K. Graham has however observed that the majority of students were mulatto children of the European castle staff and their African women.

While pupils received religious instruction as part of their basic training, the primary purpose for educating young people was to prepare them for employment in the European commercial enterprises on the coast. It was, therefore, not unusual that the schools received some funding from the company secretariats overseas. For example, in his history of the Royal African Company, K. G. Davies presented evidence of company sponsorship of education in 1694 and again in 1794 through 1795. But such funding was irregular and, therefore, contributions from other sources were critical to the survival of the school system. Monthly contributions from the salaries of the European men at the Cape Coast Castle created the ''Mulatto Fund,'' from which some financial support for children was drawn. Also, some of the chaplains who served as teachers of the castle schools experimented with imposing fines on the European staff that missed Sunday religious services without a good excuse for doing so. The Rev. Thomas Thompson, who ministered at Cape Coast from 1752 through 1756, was reported to have depended on such revenue to support his school.

Though irregular, overseas beneficiaries also sponsored the education of some African children who traveled to European centers of learning to be schooled. In a 1788 letter to the Privy Council in London, Mayor John Tarleton of Liverpool talked about the 50 or so ''odd West African children, chiefly from the Gold Coast and Sierra Leone, whom parents and British traders had sent over to Liverpool to be educated.'' As much as this was impressive, overseas training for African students was limited to the very few. On the other hand, the castle schools provided only basic education. Company support was limited, and often times the chaplain-turned-teacher had to resort to innovative means of fund-raising to support themselves and the schools.

In comparison to the years before, the nineteenth century witnessed a redoubled effort to improve education on the Gold Coast. The Company of Merchants that took over the activities of the Royal African Company in 1752 appointed Colonel George Torrane in 1805 as its new president of the Cape Coast Castle. While it is not clear if Torrane made any recommendation for the improvement of castle education on the Gold Coast, there is information that the Company of Merchants voted money to hire one Charles Williams as master of the Cape Coast School. Mr. Williams arrived on the Gold Coast in 1815 and reopened the company school at Cape Coast the following year. Schools were also opened at Anomabo, Accra, and Dixcove, and a total of 70 students were attending classes at the facilities by 1822.

The 1820s was a period of conflict between the British and the dominant Asante (Ashanti) kingdom to the hinterland. Between 1815 and 1820, all the major European establishments sent emissaries to the Asante capital of Kumase to negotiate increased commercial relations. However, disagreements between Asante officials and the British led to the war of 1823-1824, in which the newly appointed Governor of the Cape Coast, Castle Sir Charles MacCarthy was killed. Later in 1826, the joint forces of the British, the Danes, and their local allies fought the Asante army in the plains of Accra. While trade into the interior certainly suffered from the conflict, historians are not specific on the extent to which the political instability affected the state of education at the castles. In the 1831 treaty that renegotiated relations among the warring parties, however, two Asante royal youth— Owusu Ansa and Owusu Nkantabisa—were sent to Cape Coast as a sign of the kingdom's commitment to peace. The boys were schooled at the castle school and were later sent to England for a Christian education. It is not surprising that the Dutch, who had competed against the British from their post at Elmina, also sent Akwasi Boakye and Kwamina Poku (also from the Asante royal house) to the Netherlands in the mid-1830s to be educated. In fact, by 1841 some 110 students were reported to be attending English schools on the Gold Coast.

The effort to provide Christian education on the Gold Coast took a decisive turn with the arrival of Wesleyan and Basel missionaries in 1835. The first Wesleyan (Methodist) school was at the Cape Coast Castle. The Rev Thomas B. Freeman reported that nine Wesleyan mission schools had been opened by 1841—six for boys and three for girls. Despite the achievements on the coast, efforts to open schools in the Asante interior did not succeed. Even though Rev. Freeman returned the two royal youth to Kumase in 1841, the Europeans were prevented from opening schools in the territory. Apparently, some of the senior Kumase chiefs expressed fear that western-style education would negatively impact local values. Wesleyan efforts to conduct schools continued to be limited to the coast throughout the nineteenth century.

Unlike the Wesleyan, the Basel (Presbyterian) mission headed for the higher and healthier elevations of the Akuampim Ridge while keeping its headquarters at Christiansborg near Accra. By the 1850s, the Basel missionaries had boarding schools at Christiansborg and schools on the Akuapem Ridge, including one for girls at Aburi. At their school at Akropong (also on the ridge), the Basel missionaries trained teachers, used the schools as agency for the spread of Christianity, and published an elementary grammar book and dictionary in the local

Akan language. To be sure, the popular linkage of western-style education to Christian conversion developed from these experiences.

The Administration of Education on the Gold Coast: 1840-1957: Government attempts to increase educational activities on the Gold Coast began with the signing of the Bond of 1844. This was a political, military agreement between the British and a number of coastal Fanti chiefs. In the agreement, the British were allowed to intervene in criminal cases, provide military protection for the region, and, above all, to collaborate with the chiefs to ''mould the customs'' of the coastal peoples along lines of the ''general principles of English law.'' It was in accordance with the spirit of the bond that Governor Hill proposed his 1852 Ordinance. This recommended that a poll tax be imposed to finance the general improvement of the territories—including the provision of education that could lead to the establishment of a better-educated class of African.

Following the consolidation of the coastal region as the British Gold Coast Colony, the administration became more aggressive in pursuit of its educational policy. This was precipitated by the British purchase of the Danish property at Christiansborg in 1850 and the Dutch Elmina Castle in 1872. To help redress problems faced by the mission schools— such as training local teachers and improving the quality of education—the administration made grants to both the Wesleyan and Basel missions in 1874. In the Educational Ordinance of 1882, government grants to denominational schools were made dependent on an assessment of the level of efficiency. The schools receiving grant-in-aid were defined as ''government assisted schools,'' but their primary funding was to come from the missions themselves and from other private sources. There were also proposals for publicly funded government schools. Industrial schools were identified as important for the Gold Coast, and a Board of Education was recommended to monitor the school system. Rev. Sutter of the respected Fourah Bay College in Sierra Leone was appointed to the position of Inspector of Schools in the Gold Coast Colony.

The administration's desire in the 1880s to provide funds in support of education was interesting, since at the same time it rejected calls to contribute to the construction of rail lines to the gold mines that made the Gold Coast Colony a worthy territory. The support for education must have received an indirect boost from the General Act of the Berlin Conference on Africa, in which education was described as an important European civilizing mission to Africa. Even more important was the fact that the conference gave international recognition to British colonies in Africa, including the Gold Coast. Like other Europeans that had consolidated parts of the Afri-

can coast, aggressive expansion into the hinterlands was also defined as natural by the Neutrality Articles of the Berlin agreement. The government's renewed interest in education in the colony should therefore be evaluated in relation to the perceived benefits to be derived from the colony in the future. Thus, in an Education Ordinance of 1887, the government called for improvements in the school curriculum, teacher certification, and practical education for pupils. It also set the standards by which private schools might qualify for assistance. In F. Wright's 1905 essay on the ''System of Education in the Gold Coast,'' a total of 132 mission schools were said to be in existence by 1901.

Improvements in Education: The First Half of the Twentieth Century: Despite the colonial efforts to assist and regulate schools, the provision of education in the Gold Coast was carried out primarily by Christian denominations. Mostly, the mission schools provided rudimentary teaching at the primary level. In fact, it was still traditional for students seeking higher education to travel to either Europe or the Fourah Bay College in Sierra Leone. It is also significant to note that, because effective colonial authority could not be secured in the Asante interior until after 1904, the provision of education continued to be limited to the coastal areas of the colony and the Akuapem Ridge. Moreover, education for girls and practical training in the field of agriculture and in the crafts continued to be limited in scope.

The inadequacies inherent in the system were observed in the post-World War I appeal made by the Foreign Missions Conference of North America to the Phelps-Stokes Funds for a review of the state of education in Africa. The Phelps-Stokes Commission on Africa issued reports in 1922 and 1925 in which educators were criticized for inadequately catering to the social and economic needs of the continent. The commission called for instructions in the mechanical operations necessary for the improvement of the condition of the mass majority of the people. This included science education and character training.

Certainly, the commission saw the Tuskegee/Hampton program in America as more suitable for Africa than the program that was provided in the castle and mission schools. But the Phelps-Stokes report was not the only source of commentary on education in the colonies. In England, the Education Committee of the Conference of Missionary Societies in Great Britain and Ireland also submitted a memorandum on African education to the Secretary of State. In 1923, the Secretary of State for the Colonies responded with the appointment of an Advisory Committee to study and report on native education. Despite its advisory status, the committee made several major policy recommendations. Between 1925 and 1948, it issued four reports covering such topics as mass education, citizenship education, and guidelines for the overall development of education. Their list of recommendations included the following: greater government supervision of all educational institutions and the creation of local advisory committees, improved funding for education so as to attract the best caliber of people into the colonial education system, equal emphasis on religious and secular subjects, production and use of vernacular textbooks, technical education for natives, training of native teaching staff adequate in qualification and character needs of the territories, and education for girls. For all of the above to be coordinated, the appointment of an Inspector of Schools was deemed necessary.

On the Gold Coast, the appointment of Brigadier General Gordon Guggisberg as governor brought its own advantages. During his tenure from 1919 through 1927, Governor Guggisberg initiated several major developmental programs that included educational improvements as a critical ingredient in his construction of a modern Gold Coast. While the previous administration had seen the provision of elementary schools by the various Christian missions as adequate, Guggisberg was of the conviction that the current system could not sustain future developments. In fact, only a few months after his arrival, the governor presented a 10-year development plan for the Gold Coast. Among other things, funding was aggressively sought for postelementary education for boys and girls. Even though the administration proposed a technical college for Accra, the Prince of Wales College (now Achimota College) was the real trophy of the administration's educational program. This nondenominational school catered to students from kindergarten to the pre-university level. Full teacher training and kindergarten programs opened at the school in January of 1928. The other programs came later, but by the outbreak of World War II, the college was offering a great variety of courses.

Historians have recognized Guggisberg's contributions as a critical government effort in constructing a firm foundation for the future manpower training of the people of the Gold Coast. But the Government College at Achimota was not the only important grammar school to be established before the country's independence in 1957. In fact, schools established by secular as well as the various Christian denominations included many prestigious institutions, such as Adisadel College, Aggrey Memorial College, Mfamtsipim School, Wesley Girls School, St. Augustine College, Prempeh College, Ghana National College, and several Presbyterian institutions in the Akuapem and Kwahu regions. The Catholic Church started missionary activities in the country's northern territories in 1910. Information from the "Gold Coast Report on Education for the Year 1951" indicated that a total of over 300,000 students were enrolled in schools. There were primary and middle schools, teacher colleges, and at least 60 secondary schools already in place, yet the numbers were still considered to be grossly inadequate for the needs of the country when it gained its independence in 1957.

CONSTITUTIONAL & LEGAL FOUNDATIONS

Ghana gained political independence from Great Britain in 1957 but it was the Education Act of 1961 that can be pointed to as the legislative instrument that defined the organization and administration of the country's education. This legislation pertained to pre-university education, and separate legislative acts were passed to define and regulate the functions and administration of the nation's universities. Education was defined as the primary responsibility of the national government. The policy of centralization was consistent with the July 1960 Constitution that declared Ghana a republic. Under the new constitution, the ruling Convention Peoples' Party (CPP) was also designated as the only legal national political party. Consequently, the 1961 Education Act assigned to the Ministry of Education (headquartered in Accra) sole responsibility for pre-university education. It exercised power to make policies regarding planning and curriculum research and development, as well as school inspections. The positions addressed in the Education Act of 1961 have been reaffirmed by the various national constitutions enacted since then. In 2001, the Ministry of Education was assisted by its implementation agency, the Ghana Education Service (GES), which was in charge of pre-university education. Matters of higher education were under the supervision of the National Council on Tertiary Education (NCTC). The Education Ministry listed representative bodies of teachers and students, the Ghana National Association of Teachers (GNAT), and the National Union of Ghanaian Students (NUGS) as "Partners in Education."

The Education Act of 1961 was preceded by the 1951 Legislative Assembly approval of the Accelerated Development Plan for Education. Arguing that the demands on the soon-to-be independent nation required an educated population, the Accelerated Plan aimed at the rapid expansion of the pre-university educational system from 1951 through 1957. The Legislative Assembly declared basic education to be free and compulsory for school-aged children, and the Education Ministry was also empowered to monitor private institutions to ensure educational quality. In fact, by designating the private schools as "government approved" the government qualified these institutions for assisted funding.

The effort to expand basic education was also applied to secondary education. The state absorbed the pre-

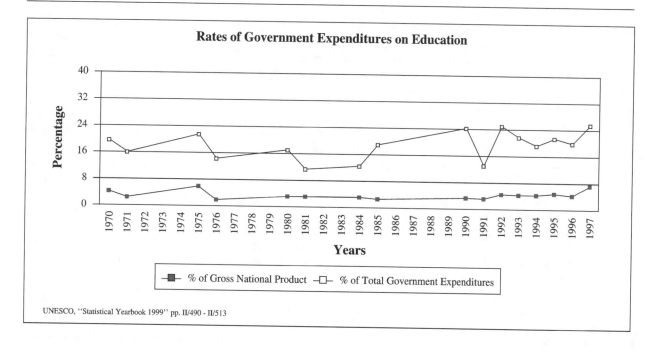

Rates of Government Expenditures on Education

UNESCO, "Statistical Yearbook 1999" pp. II/490 - II/513

viously "unassisted" secondary schools and 66 new secondary schools were added to the system by 1966. Ministry of Education figures showed a tremendous increase in enrollment: the total number of students in secondary schools rose from under 4,000 in 1951 to almost 48,000 in 1966. The number continued to rise to 82,821 in 1971 and to 734,811 in 1985. Following the mid-1980's education reforms that combined some years spent at middle school as part of secondary education, the number of students listed at the secondary level of education rose sharply to 864,300 by 1992.

The rapid expansion of education in the country brought its own problems. The obvious one was the need for the provision of adequately trained teachers. For example, figures from the *Annual Report of the Education Department for the Year 1952* illustrate that over 180,000 new students enrolled in the nation's public primary schools that year alone. The rise continued, and by 1957 there were over 456,000 pupils receiving primary education in public schools. For this same period, there were fewer than 4000 teachers in training. The temporary solution to the teacher shortage was the recruitment of many untrained instructors as "pupil teachers"—their only qualification to teach was their successful completion of elementary school. The government, through the establishment of many teacher training colleges, aggressively tackled the problem of staffing the schools with qualified teachers. The process continued at full speed, and in 1971 alone, 16,000 students were recorded as in training to become teachers. During the same time, however, there were 1,419,838 students enrolled in the primary and middle schools. The rise in the number of students at that level of education remained high, and by 1996, there

were more than 2.3 million students enrolled in primary schools alone. At the secondary level, the need for teachers was first addressed through the recruitment of overseas experts and Peace Corp volunteers. But while some Peace Corp teachers continue to volunteer (especially to teach mathematics and science), trained Ghanaians instructors are available as of 2001.

The establishment of the University of Ghana at Legon (1948), the Kwame Nkrumah University of Science and Technology in Kumase (1952), and the University of Cape Coast (1961) were further indications of the new nation's commitment to meet its developmental needs. Yet, these three institutions could not admit all qualified applicants. In fact, as late as 1992, these universities and two new ones (the University of Developmental Studies at Tamale and the University College of Winneba) had a total enrollment of just above 10,000 students. In other words, as of 2001, there was still a great need for more tertiary institutions, and discussions by the major religious denominations to establish their own universities was consistent with the demand for such programs. Also, with the general increase in the nation's population, there is expected to be a need for more primary and secondary schools, as well as for more trained teachers.

EDUCATIONAL SYSTEM—OVERVIEW

The structure of basic education inherited from the missionaries and the British colonial administration is comprised of six years of primary school and four years of middle school. The official age at which pupils begin schooling is six. Until the introduction of educational reforms in 1987, the 10 years of elementary schooling constituted the first circle of education. All students completing the tenth grade wrote the Middle School Leaving Certificate Examination conducted by the West African Examination Council (WAEC). Established by a 1951 Ordinance, the Examination Council conducts all public examinations for the former British West African countries and Liberia.

The reforms of 1987 reduced the first circle of education to nine years, with the seventh through ninth grades designated as Junior Secondary School (JSS). Successful candidates are admitted to a four-year Senior Secondary School (SSS) system. The rational for reform was originally stated in the Dzobo Committee Report of the mid-1970s, which called for a new type of education that was consistent with national development. Similar to the observations of the Phelps-Stokes Report of 1923, the Dzobo Committee argued for the introduction of more vocational, science, and agricultural courses at the JSS level. Thus, while a general education was provided during the first six years of primary education, it was argued that students attending the JSS should be given the chance to test a variety of practical courses. Those who showed propensity for practical education were to be encouraged to enter vocational and technical institutions, while the others continued with the curriculum associated with the traditional secondary school system. The four-year SSS curriculum is tested in the standardized Senior Secondary School Examination, also conducted by the WAEC. Successful candidates are considered for admission to tertiary institutions for further education in specialized fields.

While some have praised the government's courage to implement reform policies, the new system has also been criticized. The main problem was that the national government called on local governments to provide for the workshop and labs anticipated for the JSS system. Critics feared the increased financial burden on the communities, and it was argued that children in well-to-do communities would fare better than those in the least endowed areas. The reality of the past 10 years, however, has been that many well-to-do parents have sent their wards to the private JSS institutions that opened in the wealthy communities. The rational was that the better-endowed private schools would better prepare children to gain admission to the prestigious secondary schools now designated as part of the new SSS system. On the one hand, it has been observed that the increased establishment of the private JSS was consistent with the privatization of the national economy that characterized the 1980s. On the other hand, critics see the trend in education as favoring the wealthy and widening the gap between haves and the have-nots, since in the end, better preparatory secondary education makes it easier to gain admis-

sion into the nation's universities. Ironically, it has also been argued in some quarters that those with influence have coveted the few government scholarships that are to go only to the very bright students.

There continue to be opportunities, however, for education expansion in Ghana. Advanced vocational and technical education is available through various polytechnic institutes. Nursing and teacher training are now offered exclusively to postsecondary candidates. Professional training in accounting and management courses can also be obtained outside the universities. In fact, the compression of the second circle of education resulting from the reforms has tremendously swollen the university application pool. In the past decade, it was typical for SSS graduates to wait for two years before gaining admission to university programs. The universities responded to the severe bottleneck by admitting more students than they normally would. With limited space available in the old facilities, larger classes and overcrowding in student residence halls occurred, thus creating tension between students, university administrators, and the government. The Ghana University Teachers' Association has also complained about salaries and work conditions. Given the gravity of the problems, it is not surprising that periodic disruptions in the academic year occurred as a result of strikes. These concerns, notwithstanding, Ghana has made great progress in the provision of schools in the past half century. This reality is reflected in the significant reduction in the national adult illiteracy rate—it was 75 percent in 1960, approximately 60 percent in 1970, nearly 57 percent in 1980, about 43 percent in 1990, and almost 30 percent in 2000.

PREPRIMARY & PRIMARY EDUCATION

Preprimary Education: Historically, formal education at the preschool level was not common on the Gold Coast. The inclusion of kindergarten facilities at the Prince of Wales School (Achimota) in the late 1920s as part of the formal education system was therefore innovative. While educators see advantages in kindergarten education for children, there is no formal mandate for the provision of preschool prior to beginning the first grade of primary education. However, some public facilities are available, as well as private nurseries and day care centers, but they have not spread to the rural communities, where close to 70 percent of the nation's population resides. According to *The Education for All Year: 2000 Assessment for UNESCO*, there was a rapid increase in establishing Early Childhood Education establishments in the form of nursery schools and day care centers since 1993. In 1996, there were 5,441 public kindergartens and 3,742 registered private preschool establishments. In 1997, more than 427,000 preschool children were enrolled in public kindergartens, while about 156,000 pupils attended the private preschools. It is important to note that since kindergarten and day care attendance has not been absorbed into the basic education system, it is therefore neither free nor compulsory.

Primary Education: Ministry of Education sources reported more than 2.65 million pupils enrolled in the primary school system in Ghana for the year 1999. The number represented 79.4 percent of the gross possible enrollment for the same year— approximately 3.4 million children of possible primary school age were projected. Observers therefore felt that Ghana would have difficulty reaching its goal of universal primary education from the year 2000 to 2005.

Although the 1951 Accelerated Plan declared the first circle of education to be free and compulsory, some minimal fees were introduced in the 1980s to meet textbook costs. Also, even though the Education Act of 1961 called for universal primary education, this goal has not been met due to the harsh economic realities of the past decades. Despite such problems, all children in Ghana are entitled to primary education and all primary schools in the country are also organized as coeducational institutions. In fact, the female student population of the primary schools has remained at the 40th percentile since the 1970s. It is also important to mention that the number of female teachers in the general education system is highest at the primary level— ranging from 27 percent of the teaching staff in 1970 to 34 percent in 1995.

Though English is the official national language of business, the local vernaculars are used for instruction during the early years of primary education. English, which is taught as a foreign language, rapidly assumes greater use by the third grade of education. This is particularly so because of the diverse linguistic character of both students and teachers. The curriculum at the primary level stresses reading, writing, and basic arithmetic. Sports, agriculture, arts and crafts, and civic education are also part of the primary school curriculum. Upon completing primary education in sixth grade, students enter the Junior Secondary School (JSS) in the seventh grade. JSS admission is based on student performance on curriculum-based examinations and not on any standardized national test. In February 2001, Ghanaian newspaper reports commented on parental concerns about the poor performance of primary school students, especially in mathematics, as reflected by scores on the occasional Performance Monitoring Test. This led to calls for an extension of the academic year. Others have asked that teachers be allowed more authority to discipline pupils as a way of improving performance. No consensus had been reached on the issue by mid-2001.

SECONDARY EDUCATION

The 1987 educational reforms compressed the four-year middle school and the traditional secondary system into the three-year Junior Secondary School (JSS) and four-year Senior Secondary School (SSS). The average age of JSS admissions is twelve. Formerly, student admissions to the secondary schools were based on results of the standardized Common Entrance Examination, which was taken during the middle school years. Successful candidates completed a five-year secondary school program and then wrote the WAEC-conducted examination for the General Certificate of Education at the Ordinary Levels (GCE O-level) in specialized subjects of study. From here, the most successful students gained admission to the few Upper Secondary Schools (Sixth Form) for two more years. Sixth form graduates wrote another standardized examination at the Advanced Levels (GCE A-level) in specialized courses. Admission to the various departments of the national universities then followed, but the majority of students from the old system, who did not continue to the universities, either joined the general workforce or sought admission to postsecondary teacher colleges.

Unlike the former middle schools, the objective for the creation of the JSS included the need to train students in skill development, with a special emphasis on vocational education, science, technology, and creativity. Furthermore, the JSS ensured that girls received greater access to postprimary education. The program called for the inculcation of a healthy appreciation of cultural heritage (history and geography) and the development of sound moral attitudes. The curriculum developed for the achievement of the set goals included courses in mathematics, social studies, cultural studies, Ghanaian languages and English, technical and vocational skills, agriculture, and physical education. The standardized examination conducted by the WAEC evaluates students' achievements at this level and makes it possible for admission into the senior secondary schools, technical institutes, or vocational schools (sometimes referred to as colleges).

For most students, graduation from the JSS marked the end of the formal education process. Students admitted to the post-JSS institutions enter either the academically oriented SSS or opt for entrance to the vocational and technical institutes. Statistical information on secondary education in Ghana in the past 30 years has shown steady increases. In 1970-1971, of the 92,821 students registered in secondary and vocational schools, 28 percent were female; of the 551,439 students at the same level of education in 1980-1981, about 24 percent were female. Student numbers greatly increased to 768,603 (39 percent female) in 1990-1991 and 864,300 (38 percent female) in 1991-1992.

Even though the *UNESCO Statistical Yearbook* (2000) still showed 1992 figures as the most current official numbers for secondary schools, there is no reason to suspect that there has been a decrease in student admissions. Also, it is important to mention that while a small number of Peace Corp teachers still volunteer to teach in Ghana, the schools are almost 100 percent staffed by Ghanaian teachers. Students completing the SSS level are evaluated by the WAEC-conducted Senior Secondary School exams in the core courses of English, mathematics, science, and social studies. The very successful candidates are evaluated for admission to the various departments of the national universities. Others can seek admission to the three-year post SSS teacher training colleges.

HIGHER EDUCATION

The attainment of university education is the ultimate goal of most Ghanaian students. However, the nation's five universities are able to admit only a small fraction of qualified applicants because of limited facilities and faculty. It is also relevant to mention that even though a number of the social science and humanities courses taught at the universities overlap, there is a degree of specialization regarding the courses that each university offers. For example, students seeking degrees in law, medicine, and public administration are most likely to seek admission to the University of Ghana at Legon, while those with interests in architecture, pharmacy, agricultural science, engineering, and the fine art prefer the Kwame Nkrumah University of Science and Technology in Kumase. Both the University of Cape Coast and the University College at Winneba are known for training graduates to teach in the nation's secondary schools. The University of Developmental Studies at Tamale in the Northern Region has courses in rural and community development. These classifications notwithstanding, most graduates performing the compulsory National Service at the end of training are placed in the nation's secondary schools for at least the first two years of their postuniversity employment. The university academic year (two semesters) runs from late September through early July, and the majority of students spend four years working toward their first degree. Of course, the time needed for postgraduate studies and medical training vary. It is also important to mention that Ghana's tertiary education is respected for its quality and relatively peaceful academic environment. In fact, the University of Ghana is one of three sites on the continent where the New York-based Council for International Educational Exchange sends American students for semester studies. The University of Cape Town in South Africa and a summer field study in Tunisia are the other sites. In addition, several European and American universities run ''study abroad'' programs at various Ghanaian sites.

Until the early 1970s, Ghana provided free university education. Due to crisis in the national economy, the provision for free textbooks was revoked. Since then, a loan scheme has been introduced to address students' concerns. But the issue of university funding was revisited again in the 1980s, when the ruling Provisional National Defense Council (PNDC) called for cost sharing in education. Supporters of the plan have reminded critics and protesters that the economic privatization and reforms that characterized the 1980s were consistent with the education policy. Students' protests notwithstanding, the universities announced admission fees for first-year students in the latter part of the 1990s. Many have equated the fees to tuition charges and therefore a revocation of the concept of free university education in Ghana. This, however, has not reduced the enthusiasm for seeking a university degree. The enrollment of 9,609 students in the country's universities in 1990-1991, for example, was almost double the number for 1975. Also, it should be noted that the 1990-1991 figures preceded the addition of Winneba and Tamale to the university system. But despite these enrollment increases, the female representation in the general university student population in Ghana was as low as 22 percent in 1991. Also, 1997 information shows that fewer than 5 percent of the gross national enrollments are at the tertiary level, including teacher training colleges. Certainly, the percentage of students receiving university education is much smaller.

Besides university education, the nation provides opportunities for public higher education through other avenues. For example, there are 7 diploma-granting institutions, 21 technical colleges, 6 polytechnics, and 38 teacher training colleges. Furthermore, a number of private computer-training schools have opened at the major urban centers in the country.

ADMINISTRATION, FINANCE, & EDUCATIONAL RESEARCH

The Ministry of Education and its implementation agency, the Ghana Education Service, have responsibility for policy and curriculum development for the nation's pre-university education. Regional and District Education Officers represent the ministry in the provinces and districts respectively. It is from these offices that education inspectors visit the schools. As it was mandated in the 1961 Education Act, local authorities (i.e., local government) had educational responsibilities. They approved the opening of new public schools, and, as a result of inadequate national funding, were responsible for maintaining school infrastructures. Teacher training remains the duty of the national government, but the religious denominations that have had long histories in the provision of schools also continue to maintain affiliations with their former institutions. They influence the selection of headmasters for these schools and colleges.

The legislation that established the nation's public universities also approved the creation of internal self-governing boards, or University Councils. Representatives from the institutions constituted the various university boards but others, including the council chairs, were appointed by the central government. The universities have broad powers in research and curriculum development.

In the first two decades following independence, a division within the Ministry of Education handled matters concerning higher education. This changed in 1969 when a government decree created the National Council for Higher Education as the advisory body on ''the development of university institutions of Ghana.'' In performing its functions, the council—which included representatives from the universities, some members from the Council for Scientific and Industrial Research, and others appointed by the central government—was to take into account ''the total national resources, needs and development'' programs. Following the educational reforms of 1987, the monitoring of higher education has come under the Ministry of Education agency called the National Council for Tertiary Education. The day-to-day administration of the universities rests with the various vice-chancellors while principals administer the nation's polytechnics.

Research that informs the educational system in Ghana takes place at different levels. The Curriculum Research and Development Division of the Ministry of Education, the National Advisory Committee on Curriculum for Pre-University Education (including representatives of the Ghana National Association of Teachers), and the Bureau of Ghana Languages have all contributed to educational improvements in the country. Also important are the various studies conducted on education at the institutes, centers, and university departments.

In the nation's long history, there has been periodic concern expressed about the adequacy and quality of schools. A consistent complaint, however, has been inadequate educational funding. Ever since the 1951 Accelerated Plan, central government expenditures on education have remained high. In the past 30 years, the average expenditure on education was equal to 25 percent of the total national budget. In 1985, when the government was preparing to introduce educational reforms, the amount of the national budget spent on education rose to as high as 31.5 percent. In 1996, approximately 24 percent of total national expenditures was on education. A considerable portion of this total spending on education has been spent on basic education. Between 1990 and 1998, for example, an average of 67 percent of the total expenditures on education went to support basic education. How much of national funding on education should continue to sup-

port primary and secondary education over tertiary institutions has been a subject of national debate. Some have called on tertiary institutions to improve their financial situations by considering commercialization—that is, by establishing consulting services. In the wake of limited government assistance, a number of ''Educational Funds'' have been created by private organizations—the most advertised is the Asanteman Fund organized by Asantehene Osei Tutu II to assist pre-university institutions. Such support notwithstanding, it should be noted that parents are increasingly called upon to assume more financial responsibility for their children's education in Ghanaian schools. The long-term ramifications of this change are unknown.

NONFORMAL EDUCATION

The Institute of Adult Education was established in 1949 as a department of the University College of the Gold Coast with the responsibility of providing university-based adult education to the nation. The institute opened branch offices in major regional centers to supervise night classes that prepared participants to write the various examinations that qualified them for university admission. It has also conducted correspondence courses for its audience. Another well known institute that conducts correspondence courses in Ghana is the London-based Rapid Result College. Covering courses in all fields that are examined at the GCE O and A levels, participating students receive instructional packages, are assigned exercises, and are graded and prepared for the examinations. Due to the higher foreign exchange cost, more and more Ghanaians seeking preparatory training are likely to use the night class system. With the increase of computer services available in the country, online education opportunities are emerging. For example, it was announced in the late 1990s that Clarke Atlanta University in America now allows students in Ghana to register for its online MBA degree. Also in the 1990s, the University of Cape Coast posted African studies courses online, mostly targeting students in overseas countries.

Another form of nonformal education is the adult literacy program conducted through the Peoples' Education Association. This volunteer organization was first organized in 1949 to teach illiterate adults to read in their local languages. Churches and nongovernmental organizations (NGOs) were the main program supporter, but the government became an active participant in adult literacy education following the 1989 launching of the National Functional Literacy Program (NFLP). The attractiveness of the program is attributed to its combination of skill training with literacy education and, according to the *UNESCO 2000 Assessment*, about 900,000 students graduated from the program between 1992 and 1997. On the whole, however, because of the low availability of technical and vocational training opportunities, informal apprenticeship thrives in Ghana. Traditionally, this is the private nonformal system of providing people with training that allows them to gain the skills necessary for the job market.

TEACHING PROFESSION

According to Ghana Ministry of Education statistical information for 1996, approximately 72 percent of all teachers in the nation's first circle of education are certified. This represents a 34.7 percent increase over the 1990 ratio of 53.2 percent. Of the 1996 total, approximately 86 percent of all female teachers were certified compared to about 64 percent of their male counterparts. This information notwithstanding, 1994-1995 figures showed that, of the 71,863 teachers in public primary schools, only 34 percent were female. However, this was a great improvement over figures from the 1970s, when the average percentage of female teachers employed in the primary school system was in the mid-teens.

Female teaching staff representation at the secondary and tertiary levels of education is comparatively smaller than at the primary school level. In 1970-1971 for example, 17 percent of female teachers were teaching at secondary schools. The number increased to 21 percent in 1980-1981, and 26 percent in 1985-1986. While the percentage for the 1990s was not available in the *UNESCO Statistical Yearbook* (1999), it was still interesting to note that the female student population at the nation's universities was averaging only in the twentieth percentile. Since it was from this pool that secondary school teachers were drawn, there is no reason to believe that the percentages of female teachers in the secondary school system increased significantly during the decade of the 1990s. The percentage of women teachers at the nation's tertiary institutions is much smaller.

Teacher training in Ghana has a history of its own. Historians agree that during the colonial era, teacher training was closely associated with the work of the various religious denominations. In many cases, the headmasters of the schools also acted as caretakers of the village church. The secularization of the teaching profession occurred with the introduction of the 1951 Accelerated Education Plan. Also, because of the rapid expansion of the school system, the need for teachers increased to the extent that many persons whose only qualification was a tenth grade education were recruited as "pupil-teachers." Even as late as 1966, around 63 percent of the nation's primary school teachers were uncertified.

The rapid expansion of teacher training facilities throughout the country took place in the decade of the 1960s. The goal was to provide four-year "Certificate A" training for teachers. But until it was phased out in 1963, two-year "Certificate B" colleges also operated to provide a quick turnover of certified teachers. Students who have completed the traditional five-year secondary education could also be certified to teach in the elementary school system by attending specialized two-year postsecondary teacher institutions.

The rapid expansion of teacher education yielded results, and by 1971, approximately 71 percent of all primary school teachers were certified. Confident that the nation's teacher supply could be met in the near future, many of the teacher training institutions were converted to secondary schools. Of course, this was prior to the severe economic crisis of the late 1970s through the early 1980s that forced many to seek better paying jobs in Nigeria. Furthermore, the educational reforms that began in 1987 have brought further changes in teacher training. All of the remaining 38 teacher training colleges in the country are operated as postsecondary institutions. To address the need for practical training for students in the JSS, more science education has been incorporated into the teacher education curriculum. It has also been proposed that teachers-in-training be required to spend considerable hours doing in-field practice teaching. The plan is to make them more aware of the changing conditions of the communities in which they are to be employed. Teachers for the secondary and teacher training colleges are prepared at the nation's universities.

SUMMARY

The perennial problem facing education in Ghana is the issue of funding. Since the early period when the Europeans opened the castle schools until the present, the question of how much financial support the dominant institutions should bear has been argued. In the 1750s, Rev. Thomas Thompson's school in Cape Coast raised funds from fees imposed on non-Sunday School attendance, but student fees were definitely part of his financial pool. When the Accelerated Education Plan of 1951 was put in place, the fact that the modern state would assume a large portion of the cost of education was seen as necessary. This was due to the fact that national development and the training of an educated population seem to go hand in hand. However, at the same time, the government tradition of making education free and compulsory and of bearing the cost of teacher training and salaries has created the impression that the government should continue to meet those responsibilities. Others have argued that, in a society such as Ghana, where a good portion of the population still faces economic difficulties, the idea of cost sharing in education is untimely.

Progress has, however, been made in Ghana's education development. The rapid expansion of schools under the free and compulsory policy was aimed at an ultimate provision of universal education. While this lofty goal has still not be attained, it is impressive to note that, according to 1999 figures, almost 80 percent of the approximately 3.4 million children of basic education age were actually attending school. Day care and kindergarten programs, while not widespread, are beginning to take shape in the early child education system.

Since the mid-1980s, much of the national attention has been focused on postprimary education, with a greater emphasis on the reformed JSS/SSS programs that reduced the traditional middle schooling and secondary education by four years. While all agree that a strong emphasis on practical training in science and on technical and vocational training is as important as the old system's traditional academic programs, critics have expressed concerns about the availability of appropriate facilities for all schools. As government funding is debated, and as the public questions the quality of available schools, more and more private JSS facilities are being opened as alternatives to public intermediate education. There is every indication that the trend will continue.

At the university level, the nation's five universities are still not able to adequately absorb all qualified applicants. There are efforts on the part of the major religious denominations to expand their tradition of providing schools to the establishment of universities. The success of those efforts means that the private sector will have entered a sphere in the educational system that was traditionally thought to belong strictly to the public sector. Of course that could make it possible for the public universities to impose higher fees to supplement operating costs. As of now, the government continues to bear the full cost of teacher training, and with a pupil-teacher ratio of almost 33:1 in 1996 (an increase of 13.5 percent since 1990), there is no doubt that more teachers need to be trained. Overall, the state bears more than 80 percent of the total cost of education, but the trend shows that parents and communities will be asked in the future to shoulder more of the cost if the nation's quality education system is to be sustained.

In 2001, the government approved the highest budget allocation to the educational sector. It explained this high amount by indicating that it wished to improve school facilities and support the development and maintenance of academic facilities, as well as to supplement funding for scholarship grants to gifted but needy students.

BIBLIOGRAPHY

Apter, David. *Ghana in Transition.* New York: Princeton University Press, 1963.

George, Betty Stein. *Education in Ghana.* Washington, DC: United States Department of Health, Education, and Welfare, 1976.

Government of Ghana. *National Council for Higher Education Decree, 1969.* National Liberation Council Decree 401, Accra-Tema, Ghana: Ghana Publishing Corporation, 1969.

Graham, C. K. *The History of Education in Ghana.* London: Frank Cass & Co. Ltd., 1971.

Kinsey, David C., and John W. Bing, eds. *Nonformal Education in Ghana: A Project Report.* Amherst, MA.: University of Massachusetts, 1978.

Owusu-Ansah, David. ''The Society and Its Environment.'' In *Ghana: A Country Study.* Washington, DC: Library of Congress, 1995.

Owusu-Ansah, David, and Daniel Miles McFarland. *Historical Dictionary of Ghana.* Metuchen, NJ, and London: Scarecrow Press, 1995.

Quist Hubert O. ''Secondary Education in Ghana at the Dawn of the Twenty-first Century: Profile, Problems, Prospects.'' *Prospects XXIX, 3* (1999): 425-442.

Scanlon, David, ed. *Traditions of African Education.* New York: Bureau of Publications of the Teachers College at Columbia University, 1964.

UNESCO. *Statistical Yearbook.* Paris: 1999.

———. *The Education for All Year: 2000 Assessment (EFA).* Paris: 2000.

—David Owusu-Ansah

GIBRALTAR

BASIC DATA

Official Country Name:	Gibraltar
Region:	Europe
Population:	29,481
Language(s):	English, Spanish, Italian, Portuguese, Russian
Literacy Rate:	80%

A British overseas territory since being ceded by Spain in 1713, Gibraltar carries on a peculiar existence sandwiched between the Iberian Peninsula and the mouth of the Mediterranean. English is the official language in the government and the schools, while Spanish remains the language frequently used within most homes. As is the case in much territory with a history of British influence, Gibraltar offers free and compulsory education for citizens aged 5 to 15. This education is provided to the bulk of the nation's 4,000 students by way of 14 schools.

The Gibraltar public school system includes three levels of schools, the first two of which are co-educational. These levels are termed first schools, for ages 5 to 8; middle schools, for ages 8 to 12; and secondary schools, for students age 12 through completion. Although English is the official language of instruction, Spanish is introduced into the curriculum during middle school. Other core subjects required of all students include mathematics, science, English, physical education, and religious education. Religious education varies among the schools with Anglican, Catholic, and Hebrew schools presently functioning.

The nation also supports a technical College of Further Education that grew out of a Royal Navy technical school. With no local higher education facilities, Gibraltar offers scholarships and grants for students seeking university education in Britain.

The constitution charges the minister for education, an elected representative, with responsibility for education in Gibraltar. Managerial oversight is provided through the Department of Education and Training and its director. The department creates and applies the prescribed National Curriculum Regulations, which are modeled closely on the United Kingdom National Curriculum.

—Mark Browning

GREECE

BASIC DATA

Official Country Name:	Hellenic Republic
Region:	Europe
Population:	10,601,527
Language(s):	Greek, English, French
Literacy Rate:	95%
Academic Year:	September-August
Number of Primary Schools:	6,651
Compulsory Schooling:	9 years
Public Expenditure on Education:	3.1%
Libraries:	829
Educational Enrollment:	Primary: 652,040
	Secondary: 817,566
	Higher: 363,150
Educational Enrollment Rate:	Primary: 93%
	Secondary: 95%
	Higher: 47%
Teachers:	Primary: 46,785
	Secondary: 70,682
	Higher: 16,057
Student-Teacher Ratio:	Primary: 14:1
	Secondary: 12:1
Female Enrollment Rate:	Primary: 93%
	Secondary: 96%
	Higher: 46%

HISTORY & BACKGROUND

The Hellenic Republic (Elliniki Dhimocratia), the southernmost country in Europe, lies at the juncture of Europe, Asia, and Africa. A land of mountains and sea, it is simultaneously European, Balkan, and Mediterranean. Mountains occupy about 80 percent of the country and have, at times, restricted internal communications. But the sea opened wider horizons, and Greece has had a naval tradition throughout history.

Greece occupies 131,957 square miles (50,949 square kilometers), approximately the size of Alabama. The Greek Islands make up one-fifth of this territory. Although there are about 2,000 islands, only 170 are inhabited; the largest is Crete. To the east is the Aegean Sea, to the south the Mediterranean, to the west the Ionian. To the north, Greece's continental frontier borders Albania, the former Yugoslav republic of Macedonia, Bulgaria, and Turkey.

Geography has had a big influence on the country's economic, historical, and political development. The landscape has been a strong factor for Greek migration, both internally—from rural to urban areas—and to other countries for employment and a better life. The result over centuries was depopulation of certain areas. In the 1980s, some repatriation occurred.

As of the 1991 census, the population was 10,2590,000, excluding Greeks living in Australia, Canada, and the United States. Of these, 5,055,408 were males and 5,204,492 were females; 58.8 percent lived in urban areas, 12.8 percent in semi-urban, and 28.4 percent in rural. Nineteen percent of the population was 14 years or younger, 67 percent were between 15 and 64, and 14 percent were older than 65.

Between 1991 and 1996, births decreased from 10 per thousand to 9.6, while deaths for the same period increased from 9.3 per thousand to 9.6 (NSSG 1998).

As of the March 18, 2001, census, the population was 10,939,777, an increase of 6.6 percent over 10 years. Women made up 50.4 percent, men 49.6 percent (*Hellas Letter* April 2001). Approximately 6.8 percent of the population is illiterate; of this figure, 9.8 percent are female, 3.7 percent male (NSSG 2000).

Modern Greece is the heir of classical Greece and the Byzantine Empire (300-1453). From ancient Greece it has inherited a sophisticated culture and language that has been documented for almost three millennia. The language of Periclean Athens in the fifth century B.C. and the present language are almost the same. Few languages can demonstrate such continuity. From Sparta (600 B.C.) and Athens (450-350 B.C.) came group teaching, the humanistic curriculum, and the three levels of education. Primary education was for children 7 through 12 years old; secondary was for those 13 through 17; and tertiary, for those 18 and older. Tertiary education was paid by the State. When a boy reached the age of 18, he spent two years training to be a soldier and a citizen. Until the industrial revolution, preprimary education took place within the family.

The Romans adopted this three-level educational system when they conquered Greece in 146 B.C. It was modified and became bilingual—Greek and Latin. In A.D. 364, the Roman Empire was divided into Eastern and Western Roman Empire. The Eastern became the Byzantine Empire, and the educational system was continued. Eventually it became Greek-Christian from the reconciliation and harmonizing of classical Greek humanism with Christian beliefs.

From the Byzantine Empire, Greece inherited Eastern Orthodox Christianity. There was "one holy catholic and apostolic church" until the Great Schism in 1054, when the church was separated into Eastern Orthodox and Roman Catholic.

For nearly 400 years (1453-1821), Greece was under Ottoman rule (*Tourkokratia*). The Ottomans had no provisions to educate their non-Muslim subjects. The Orthodox Church was the only institution where the Greeks could look as a focus. Through the use of Greek in the liturgy and through its modest educational efforts, the church helped to a degree to keep alive a sense of Greek identity. Many times, members of the clergy were executed in reprisal when the Greeks disobeyed orders or tried to revolt.

The most serious disability for the Christian population was the janissary levy (*paidomazoma*). At irregular intervals, Christian families in the Balkans were required to deliver to the Ottoman authorities a given proportion of their most intelligent and handsome male children to serve as elite troops, after they were forced to convert to Islam.

Ottoman rule prevented Greece from experiencing the important historical movements of the Renaissance, the Reformation, the Enlightenment, and the Industrial Revolution, which shaped the destinies of the western European countries. The intellectuals who had fled to the West, especially to Italy, established intellectual centers wherever they settled. They began to publish Greek books in the sixteenth century and send them to the enslaved Greeks to educate and enlighten them.

The eighteenth century saw the emergence of a Greek mercantile middle class in the Ottoman Empire. They were also active in southern Russia, in several central European cities, and in the Mediterranean, where they established communities (*paroikies*), each with its own church. Greeks came in contact with the ordered societies of Western Europe. Their wealth provided for the intellectual revival of the Greeks. Moved by a sense of patriotism they endowed schools and libraries in the occupied mainland and in Asia Minor. They also financed the education of Greek schoolteachers in the universities of Italy and the German states. Influenced by the ideas of the European Enlightenment and the nationalistic beliefs of the French Revolution, these teachers became aware of the reverence in which the language and the culture of ancient Greece were held throughout Europe. This realization sparked an awareness that they were heirs to this same civilization and language.

Greece became a state in 1830, following the War for Independence (1821-1829). The treaty of 1832 between Bavaria and the Great Powers—Britain, Russia, and France—formally recognized Greece's existence as an independent state, although Greece did not participate in the treaty. The Greeks were the first of the subjugated peoples of the Ottoman Empire to gain full independence. Even so, the new state contained only a part of the Greek population, the remaining population in Asia Minor being still under Ottoman rule. The first century of statehood was dominated by the struggle to expand the nation's boarders. It was in 1947 that Greece's present borders were established, after the incorporation of the Dodecanese Islands.

The Great Powers also decided that Greece should be a monarchy. They chose a 17-year-old Bavarian prince, Otto, as king. Because he was a minor, the Great Powers further decided that three Bavarian regents should rule the country. They imported European models of administration without regard to local conditions, consequently, Greece's educational system is heavily influenced by the German and French models.

The past is somewhat a burden to Greeks, who identify themselves as "modern" to differentiate themselves from the ancients. References to Greece are usually to ancient Greece. Greeks, however, are proud of their cultural heritage and have made every effort throughout the centuries to maintain it. The continuity between past and present is an essential element of the Greek self-image and national identity.

Greece became a member of the European Council in 1949, NATO in 1952, and the European Community in 1961. This last relationship helped modernize and democratize Greece's educational system and stabilize its government.

There was a military dictatorship from 1967 to 1974. Since 1974, Greece has been a parliamentary democracy with a president whose powers are restricted. (A plebiscite in 1975 abolished the monarchy.) The president is elected by the parliament (*Vouli*) and may hold office for two five-year terms. The Prime Minister, leader of the majority party, has extensive powers. The parliament consists of 300 deputies elected for four-year terms by direct, universal, and secret ballot.

The parliament has the power to revise the constitution. Incumbent governments, regardless of political affiliation, have amended the electoral law to benefit their own party. The judicial system is essentially the Roman law system prevalent in continental Europe.

The 1980s brought about changes: civil marriage was introduced parallel to religious marriage, divorce was made easier, legal equality between the sexes was recognized. The right to vote also was extended to 18-year-olds.

Greece's unification with the European Community in 1981 (renamed European Union in 1994) reaffirmed its orientation toward Europe. It was the first eastern European country to join EU. Its heritage of Orthodox Christianity and Ottoman rule set it apart from the other European member states.

The 1990s brought economic refugees from Albania and other former Communist countries, from Asia, and from Africa. Repatriated Greeks also came from the former Soviet Union.

Religion is an important aspect of Greek life. In spite of the long Ottoman occupation, most Greeks belong to the Orthodox Church of Greece. A Muslim Turkish minority (3 percent) live mostly in the northeastern part of the country, in Thrace. Roman and Greek Catholics are found primarily in Athens and in the Ionian Islands.

CONSTITUTIONAL & LEGAL FOUNDATIONS

The legal basis of education in Greece is the revised Constitution of 1975. Education is the constitutional responsibility of the State. It is provided free in public institutions at all levels, is controlled by the State, and is compulsory until the age of 15.

Article 16 contains the following provisions:

- Research and teaching in arts and sciences are free, while their development and promotion are obligations of the state.

- Education is the basic mission of the state. Its aims are the moral, intellectual, professional, and physical development of the Greeks, the development in them of a national and religious conscience, and their formation into free and responsible citizens.

- The number of years of compulsory education cannot be less than nine.

- All Greeks have the right to free education in state institutions of all levels. The State supports outstanding students and those in need.

- The state is responsible for providing technical/vocational education in institutes of higher education. It cannot be less than three years duration.

The philosophy underlying the Greek educational system reflects the basic values of the Greek nation, which also constitutes the foundation of Western civilization. The Ministry of National Education and Religious Affairs (MoE), created as the Secretariat for Religious and Public Education by the Constitution of 1832, is in charge of all activities pertaining to education. There is a national curriculum, uniform school timetables, and approved textbooks for each subject in each grade. All these are compulsory for the private schools, also.

The development of education in Greece cannot be seen separate from its turbulent sociopolitical context. In the 170 years since the country emerged as an independent state, it has been involved in more than four wars, a three-year foreign occupation, two long-lasting dictatorships, one bitter and devastating civil war, and numerous *coups d'état*. It also had intermittent civil wars and large influxes of refugees and immigrants, both Greek repatriates and non-Greeks. Such history for a small country weighs heavily on national development and has numerous repercussions on Greek education.

Educational Reforms: Educational reforms have always been a political issue in Greece. Since independence, the educational reforms have been initiated by different political regimes ranging from conservative to center to left. Appropriate laws authorize all educational reforms.

Succeeding governments do not necessarily continue the educational reforms legislated by the government they replaced. They reverse, withdraw, or abolish earlier decisions. This prevents education from moving forward and creates frustration for the pupils and their parents.

The educational system of Greece in the 1950s had three levels: a six-year compulsory primary school; a six-year secondary school (*gymnasium*) with a humanistic curriculum; and the tertiary level consisting of universities and the few tertiary schools of general education, such as the Teacher Training and the Physical Education academies.

There was some preprimary education. Generally the kindergartens were attended by a small number of children. Sixty percent of the kindergartens were in Northern Greece.

In the late 1950s the emphasis on modernization and planned economic development intensified reforms, especially for the expansion of technical/vocational education. In 1958-1959, there were 39,824 pupils attending vocational schools, and 239,648 enrolled in secondary schools (OECD 1980).

The educational reforms that followed were tied to the recognition that education and training are important elements in the economic growth of the country. Without education, the national income could not be increased, nor the social welfare and stability ensured.

Reforms of 1957-1963: The secondary school was divided into two three-year cycles. The first three grades were the lower cycle and emphasized a general and humanistic education. A multi-partisan committee of politicians and educational experts had reaffirmed in 1957 the priority of the humanistic curriculum while adding vocational education.

The upper cycle was divided into separate types of *gymnasia*: classical/literary, commercial, technical, scientific, agricultural, naval, foreign languages, and home economics, with a common core of classes for all.

The *demotic* language (the popular form of the Greek language spoken by the people) was introduced in the first three grades of the primary school, and the *katharevousa* (formal or purist) in the three upper grades. Teacher training of preprimary schoolteachers was increased to two years after secondary education, and made equal to that of primary school teachers (Law 3997 1959).

The occupations of the children included the religious, ethical, and social development, the proper use of the Greek language, introduction of arithmetic (reasoning), exercise of the senses, harmonious and unhindered development of the body, cultivation of dexterity, and development of the sense of good.

The Centre of Planning and Economic Research (KEPE) was established in 1961 to develop scientific programming of resource allocation for economic development, and technical economic training of personnel for key positions in government and industry.

Reforms of 1964: The educational reforms of 1964 promoted educational equality and economic growth after Greece joined the European community in 1961. In 1964, free education was extended to all levels.

The previous two stages of general secondary school were transformed into two successive and autonomous types of schools, three years each: the non-selective lower secondary, or *gymnasium*, and the upper secondary, or *lyceum*. A single *lyceum* was established, its purposes to provide contemporary education to Greek youth and to develop the future leadership of the country. Entrance exams were established to enter the *lyceum,* but entrance examinations from the primary to the *gymnasium* were abolished. The purpose of the *gymnasium* was to provide a comprehensive education for all Greek youth.

The *demotic* Greek language officially replaced the *katharevousa* as a medium of instruction. Also, technical/vocational guidance and the courses of anthropology, ''practical knowledge about professions,'' and ''elements of democracy'' were introduced to the *gymnasium* curriculum.

Compulsory education was extended to nine years (ages 6 to 15), and co-education became mandatory from age 6 to 15. School lunches were introduced as well.

Reforms of 1967-1974: During the military dictatorship, most of the reforms were reversed or withdrawn. The use of the *demotic* language was limited to the first three grades of the primary school. Compulsory education was returned to six years (Law 129, 1967).

New legislation set up a new tertiary level of technical/vocational educational institutions, the Centres for Higher Technical/Vocational Education (KATEE). They would supply vitally needed upper-level technicians, and meet some of the rising demands for university entrance. By 1974, there were five such centers. Law 1404 (1983) transformed them into Technological/Scientific Educational Institutions (TEI). In 1997, there were 14 TEIs throughout Greece.

Reforms of 1975-1981: The country returned to democratic government in 1974. The revision of the Constitution in 1975 reformed and expanded education, and gave it a new direction. Law 309 (1976) restored all the reforms of 1964 and dealt with the organization and function of general education from preprimary to *lyceum*. It also articulated the purpose of each level:

- Preprimary education complements and supports family education by teaching appropriate behavior and correct expression, and provides for the physical and mental development. Attending preprimary is voluntary for children three and a half to five and a half years of age.

- Primary education sets the foundation for learning, enriches pupils' experiences, and stimulates and develops their intellectual and physical abilities.

- The gymnasium completes and consolidates the encyclopedic education of youth.

- The lyceum offers a richer and wider curriculum than that of the gymnasium, for youth who plan either to attend institutions of tertiary education or to enter the job market.

For more effective teaching, the number of students per teacher was reduced from 40 to 30, and the number of teaching hours per week was reduced from 36 to a range of 28 to 34. Additionally, new textbooks were written and published, and seminars were organized for inservice training of teachers.

The new curriculum introduced the course of "technology" and the use of educational television. Adding to this, evening *gymnasia* were started for those students who needed to work during the day to earn their living. *Lyceums* also were established as both three-year day schools and four-year evening schools. A new type of *lyceum,* the three-year Classical Lyceum, was introduced as well. It offered additional hours in ancient Greek, Latin, and history, and introduced German as a second foreign language.

Reforms of 1981-1985: Automatic promotion was established throughout the grades in the primary school, and physical education and school athletics were emphasized in primary school. Entrance exams from the lower secondary to the upper secondary school were abolished. Uniforms for *gymnasium* and *lyceum* pupils were abolished as well. The Integrated Lyceum, or comprehensive school was introduced in secondary education in 1984. It bridged the gap between general and technical education.

The curricula were revised for all grades. They were based on the international bibliography and were adjusted to include Greek traditions. Teachers contributed to the development of the curricula. New textbooks were developed and printed. The new textbooks were no longer merely stores of knowledge, but workbooks to help pupils look for and build knowledge.

Reforms of the 1990s: A new system of postsecondary vocational training was established. The system incorporates the private Centres of Free Studies. The Hellenic Open University was established in 1996-1997 as well.

EDUCATIONAL SYSTEM—OVERVIEW

The first schools in Greece (1834) were patterned on foreign models. The newly independent state had no infrastructure (curricula, books, or organization model). The schools reflected the contemporary ideas prevailing in Western Europe at that time.

The four-year compulsory school was based on the German (Bavarian) tradition that had been influenced by the French educational tradition. It was called *demotico* (primary). The German and French influences resulted in a strong centralized administration, which exists to date.

A three-year Greek school followed the four-year primary. A four-year *gymnasium* (secondary school) followed that. After that came the university for four years. King Otto established the first Greek University in Athens in 1837. Instruction was in Greek in all levels. Attendance in primary and Greek schools was compulsory—a total of seven years.

The curriculum included the humanistic heritage of the classics and the orthodox religion but it was progressive: catechism, elements of Greek reading, writing, arithmetic, measures and weights, drawing, singing and, when possible, elements of geography, Greek history, and physical sciences. It also taught gymnastics, gardening, and silkworm and bee culture. The girls were taught "female arts." At the end of each semester there were examinations.

The number of courses was large and practical, but there were not enough teachers to teach them. To compensate, "mutual instruction" (Lancasterian) was employed: The teacher teaches the students of the upper grades, and they in turn teach the younger students the same subject).

At the same time (1834) a teacher training institution was organized in Naupleion, the provisional capital of Greece. The following year the capital and the institution were moved to Athens.

Modern Structure: The structure of the educational system in Greece in 2001 is organized into three levels: primary, which includes a two-year preprimary since 1985 that is not compulsory; secondary;, and tertiary. Children aged three and a half can enroll in the preprimary.

Compulsory education starts with the primary school at five and a half or six years. Since the 1976 reforms, it includes the three-year lower secondary school (*gymnasium*) lasting 9 years, from age 6 to age 15. By law a pupil who does not complete compulsory education by the age of 15 is obliged to stay on until age 16.

All schools are coeducational. The language of instruction at all levels has been *demotic* Greek since the reforms of 1964.

Ecclesiastical *gymnasiums* and *lyceums* prepare male students for priesthood. In addition to the regular curriculum, they offer extracurricular activities that contribute to the development of appropriate habits and attitudes. Music *gymnasiums* offer, besides the regular curriculum, an additional 15 hours per week of musical education for talented pupils.

Upper secondary education is provided in general *lyceums*, integrated (or comprehensive) *lyceums*, and technical/vocational *lyceums*, as well as technical/vocational schools. Students graduating from the *gymnasium* enroll without exams in the next level, the *lyceum*.

Graduates of the general *lyceum* may attend university and postgraduate studies. Graduates of the integrated and technical/vocational *lyceums* attend technological education institutes. After graduation they can continue to the university or join the job market. Graduates of technical/vocational schools attend institutes of vocational training. After graduation they join the job market.

Tertiary education is provided in universities and technological educational institutes. Entrance is based on exams.

The length of the school year for 1995-1996 was September 11 to June 15 for primary schools, and September 1 to June 30 for secondary. There are five school days a week for both primary and secondary schools for a total of 175 days in a year. There are 12 weeks of summer holidays, two weeks for Christmas and two weeks for Spring/Easter. There are also seven days of national or religious holidays.

Primary school pupils attend 23 to 30 lessons a week. The duration of each lesson is 45 minutes. Pupils in lower secondary attend 33 to 35 lessons per week, each 45 minutes. The number of lessons a week in upper secondary schools varies from 30 in the general *lyceums* to 34 for both the comprehensive and the technical/vocational *lyceums* to 41 for the musical *lyceums*. The duration of one lesson in all secondary schools is 45 minutes.

Primary pupils spend about five hours per day in school, secondary pupils six or seven. The primary school day runs from either 8:15 a.m. to 1:30 p.m., or from 2:00 p.m. to 7:00 p.m. In big cities, a large number

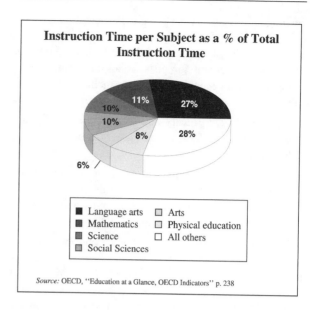

Instruction Time per Subject as a % of Total Instruction Time

- ■ Language arts
- ■ Mathematics
- ■ Science
- ■ Social Sciences
- □ Arts
- □ Physical education
- □ All others

Source: OECD, "Education at a Glance, OECD Indicators" p. 238

of school buildings accommodate more than one school. Therefore pupils attend lessons either in the morning or in the afternoon, or one week in the morning followed by one week in the afternoon. As a result, educational and functional problems are created in these schools ("Organization of School" 1995).

Enrollment by educational level and sex in public and private schools in 1993-1994 was as follows:

- 5,520 preschools with 133,979 pupils (65,511 female); 5,387 were public with 128,627 pupils (62,933 female), and 133 were private schools with 5,352 pupils (2,578 female)

- 7,254 primary schools with 731,500 pupils (354,773 female); 6,851 were public with 678,145 pupils (328,951 female), and 403 private schools with 53,355 pupils (25,822 female)

- 3,069 secondary schools with a total of 719,746 pupils (364,012 female); 2,813 were public with 671,913 pupils (342,778 female), and 159 private schools with 32,214 pupils (16,877 female) (NSSG 2000).

Enrollment in tertiary education for 1993-1994 was 212,525 students. Of these, 110,295 were "active" (enrolled students who have not completed the compulsory period), and 102,226 were "inactive" (students who have continued their studies beyond the normal required time). Among active students, 59,730—or 51.9 percent— were female. Among the inactive students, 45,909—or 48.1 percent— were female (Protopapas 1999).

In 1989-1990, some 57.8 percent of four- and five-year-olds attended public kindergartens, or those supervised by the MoE. Primary school participation was 97 percent, and secondary, 93 percent. Participation rates for boys and girls are equal at preschool and primary levels. At the secondary level the participation rate is 95 percent for boys, 91 percent for girls. Rates may actually be somewhat lower since repeaters are included in the enrollment figures (OECD 1997).

Textbooks for primary and secondary education are published by the Organization of School Textbooks (OEDB).

There are no examinations from the primary to the secondary school. There are nationwide (*Pan-Hellenic*) examinations for entrance to the university and the technological education institutes.

Because education is prized as an end in itself and as a means of upward mobility, there is a great demand to enter universities. Many children attend private ''cramming'' classes (*frontisteria*), after school to prepare for the university entrance exams. Competition for university places is extremely high in spite the creation of new universities between 1960 and 1980.

Law 682 (1977) provides for the operation of private primary and secondary schools. They are under the supervision of the MoE and are required to follow the national curriculum and to use the same textbooks as the public schools. About 6 percent of the students attend private schools. The Constitution forbids the establishment of private universities.

There is educational television in the State television stations. Computers and instructional television were introduced in the classrooms.

Technical/vocational education broadened the base of education and gave pupils more choices. It met the demand for technical personnel and opened venues to the job market, contributing thus to economic development.

Law 309 (1977) abolished the lower vocational schools and replaced them with technical/vocational schools (TES). Intermediate vocational schools were replaced by technical/vocational *lyceums*. General education from this point on was provided by the general *lyceums*.

Graduates of three-year lower secondary schools could enroll in the TES without examinations or, after examinations, enter either the technical/vocational *lyceum* or the general *lyceum*.

Opportunities for technical/vocational training in tertiary education have increased. In 1989-1990, of about 42,000 places available in tertiary education, the TEIs made up approximately 19,000, or 45 percent. In 1991 and 1992 the distribution tended to be 50-50 (Stavrou 1996).

Minority Groups: Greece has a small percentage of linguistic and cultural minorities. By legislation, the Greek government provides a budget and ample facilities to educate minority children. As of 1983, primary schools enrolled 12,000 Muslim students. Four hundred twenty-one Muslim teachers (Greek nationals) taught the classes in these schools, plus 27 temporary instructors who came from Turkey. The Turkish language, as well as religion, is taught in these schools. At the secondary level, three schools offer bilingual instruction, one in Komotini (the Celal-Bayar Lyceum) and two Muslim seminaries in Xanthi. Both cities are in Thrace. The Greek government intends to establish technical/vocational schools for the Muslim minority, provided there is agreement among the Muslim communities. Teachers for the Muslim children are trained in a special program at the Pedagogical Department of the University of Thessaloniki.

There are two primary schools for Armenian children in Athens. Also, in the mid-1980s, a pilot program for itinerant Gypsy children was organized by the University of Thessaloniki.

In 1980-1981, the government developed education programs specifically for the children of repatriated Greeks from Germany, the United States, Canada, and Australia. These children have limited proficiency in the Greek language. The objective of the programs was to ''aid the repatriation of youth by integrating them in school and social milieus and in the Greek way of thinking and behaving'' (OECD 1982). On average, 5,000 children per year were repatriated from Germany, and 4,000 per year from English-speaking countries. Two types of programs were designed for them: special bilingual classes in the regular schools, and out-of-school or ''extra class'' bilingual programs.

In the 1990s, with the influx of economic refugees, the number of foreign pupils attending Greek primary and secondary schools increased to 6 percent of the total. In 1991-1992 in elementary schools, 51.73 percent of these pupils were from the countries of the former USSR, 24.48 percent were from Albania, and 23.78 percent came from all other countries. In the secondary schools, 39.12 percent were from the countries of the former USSR, 22.14 percent were from Albania, and 38.74 percent were from all other countries (Katsikas and Kavadias 1996).

Special Education: Law 1566 (1985) incorporated the education of children with special education needs (SEN) into the central framework of the educational system, based on the philosophy of equal opportunities in education at all levels. Greece, as a member of the international organizations for child protection, has planned the special education program in order to respond to two basic principles: integration and participation.

Pupils with SEN from 3-1/2 to 18 years of age are in the mainstream school. Compulsory education is from six to 15. Special schools share buildings with mainstream schools; they partially integrate the curriculum and totally integrate the social activities. Special education councilors promote the integration of SEN pupils by providing instruction and support programs for teachers in the mainstream schools. The curriculum, "Activities for Learning Preparedness," helps teachers support pupils to develop to the extent of their capacities and to possibly integrate into the mainstream.

There are about 200 special needs school in Greece. In 1995-1996 there were 39 preschools, 138 primary schools, 10 schools for general secondary education, and four for technical/vocational education. Registered SEN students make up less than 1 percent of all pupils (Meijer 1998).

PREPRIMARY & PRIMARY EDUCATION

Preprimary—Kindergarten (*nepiagogeion*): The first interest of the Greek State in preprimary education was in 1895 with a law that allowed Greek citizens to organize private kindergartens after receiving a permit from the MoE. It was for children from three or four years old through age six. The first kindergarten was established in Athens in 1897 by a woman who studied in Germany (like many Greeks did during the nineteenth century). It was private, modeled after the German kindergarten of Froebel (1782-1852). A teacher training institution was part of it.

Until their expansion in the 1970s and 1980s, most kindergartens were private, operating on a fee basis. The teacher and the school's owner determined the curriculum. Teacher training was carried out in separate private institutions.

Children who are three and a half years old by October 1 are accepted and may attend for two years. Attendance is voluntary and participation is continuously increasing.

In 1976 kindergartens became part of primary education. Attendance was still voluntary but can become mandatory in a region if the Minister of Education, the Minister of Health and Welfare, and the Minister of Finance issue a joint resolution according to the needs of the region.

The purpose of kindergarten is to help develop children physically, emotionally, mentally, and socially, and to prepare preschoolers for learning in the elementary schools.

Early childhood education is provided by kindergartens that operate as independent units supervised by the MoE, and within children's centers supervised by the Ministry of Health and Welfare.

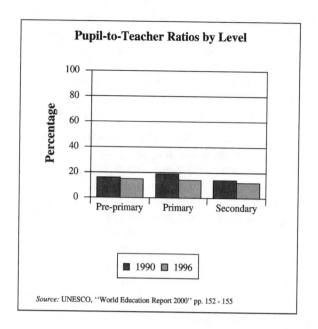

Pupil-to-Teacher Ratios by Level

Percentage

Pre-primary   Primary   Secondary

■ 1990 ■ 1996

Source: UNESCO, "World Education Report 2000" pp. 152 - 155

Kindergarten enrollments vary from region to region. Most rural areas have higher preschool enrollment ratios than Athens, which has one of the lowest.

A kindergarten class can have from 7 to 30 children. In 1993-1994 there were 5,520 kindergartens with 8,706 teachers (8,682 female), and 133,959 pupils (65,511 female). The pupil/teacher ratio was 15:4. The majority of kindergartens (5,387) were public with 8,457 teachers (8,433 female) and 128,627 pupils (62,933 female). The pupil/teacher ratio was 15:2. There were 133 private kindergartens, with 249 teachers, all female, and 5,352 pupils (2,578 female). The pupil/teacher ratio was 21:5. (NSSG 2000) There are almost no male teachers in kindergarten.

In 1989, the MoE issued a national curriculum for kindergarten and a teacher's handbook with guidelines, examples of lesson plans, and activities for implementing the curriculum. Kindergarten teachers, under the guidance of the Pedagogical Institute, developed the curriculum and the handbook. The curriculum is used throughout the country.

Primary education: Elementary school lasts six years. Children who turn six by December 31 can enroll in the first grade. Attendance is obligatory. Pupils graduating from primary school receive a school-leaving certificate that mentions the attainment levels in the various subjects. They enroll in the first grade of the *gymnasium* without examinations. It is part of the compulsory education years.

The new primary education curriculum came into effect by Presidential Decree 583 (1982). It was implemented during the 1982-1983 school year and contains the following features: the aims of the primary school, the goals of each subject taught, the objectives of the major teaching units, prerequisites for achieving the goals, activities through which to attain the objectives of the teaching units, and recommendations as to how much time to assign to the teaching and learning of the units.

Environmental studies, health education, and civic education were added to the existing courses of religion, Greek language, mathematics, history, geography, natural sciences, music, arts and crafts (for aesthetic development), physical education, and a modern language (English or French). The goals and objectives of the new curricula were: a) to gradually familiarize pupils with moral, religious, national, socioeconomic, political, aesthetic, and other values; b) to gradually to introduce pupils to the cognitive sphere; and c) to progressively socialize pupils in an atmosphere of freedom and inquiry.

Specialists teach physical education, music, foreign languages, and arts. Laboratories for physics and chemistry, and school libraries, were introduced in primary schools.

The implementation of the new curricula followed the design and publication of new textbooks by the Organization for Publication of School Textbooks for all subjects taught in the primary school. A teacher's guide was introduced to accompany each textbook. It contains basic methodological principles and suggestions on procedures to follow in organizing the teaching and learning of each unit.

The upper limit of pupils per class is 25 children for a single-room school (one teacher for all children in all grades). Since 1990 there has been an effort to decrease the number of single-room schools. They exist primarily in the islands, in the rural areas, and in isolated mountainous villages. Local authorities, in cooperation with the State, are trying to develop re-allocation solutions so that students may be transported to bigger, better-staffed, and better-equipped schools in a region.

In 1993-1994 there were 7,254 elementary schools with 44,981 teachers (24,418 female) and 731,500 pupils (354,773 female). The pupil/teacher ratio was 16:3. Of these, 6,851 were public elementary schools with 42,207 teachers (22,750 female) and 678,145 pupils (328,951 female). The pupil/teacher ratio was 16:1. There were 403 private elementary schools with 2,774 teachers (1,668 female) and 53,355 pupils (25,822 female). The pupil/teacher ratio was 19:2 (NSSG 2000).

Participation rates for boys and girls are almost equal at the primary level. Primary school participation for 1989-1990 was 97 percent for six- to 11-year-olds. Repeaters at the primary school are extremely few (OECD 1997).

SECONDARY EDUCATION

Secondary education lasts six years, from age 11 and a half to 17 and a half. It is divided into two three-year successive cycles. The lower three grades are the *gymnasium*. The upper three grades are the *lyceum*.

The purpose of the *gymnasium* is to promote pupils' learning potential according to their abilities and the needs of society. The state pursues this goal by offering to all pupils the same curriculum. There are no elective subjects in the *gymnasium* curriculum. The concern for full formal equality of educational opportunities is thus given precedence over that of offering an education that is adapted to particular needs and interests. Attendance is compulsory.

In 1993-1994 there were 1,713 public *gymnasiums* with 32,328 teachers (20,203 female) and 417,752 pupils (201,375 female). The ratio of pupils to teachers was 12:9 (NSSG 2000).

Pupils graduating from the *gymnasium* receive a school-leaving certificate (*apolyterion*), without examination. It mentions the acquired attainment levels in the various subjects and enables the holder to enroll in any of the upper secondary schools without any examination. About 60 percent of the *gymnasium* graduates enroll in the general lyceum, 25 percent in the technical/vocational *lyceum*, 5 percent to the integrated *lyceum*, and about 10 percent to the technical vocational schools (Kallen 1996).

The dropout rate in 1994 was 8.9 percent for all students of the *gymnasium*. It varied from region to region, from 1 to 29 percent. The highest rates were in the Aegean and the Ionian Islands, Crete, and Trace. The dropout rate was higher among boys than among girls, 10.4 and 7.4 percent respectively. This is probably because boys, especially in these regions, are frequently called to work at a young age in their parents' businesses of farming, fishing, or tourism (OECD 1997; Kallen 1996).

The *lyceum* aims to build pupils' character and personality so that they may contribute to the social, economic, and cultural development of the country. It provides students with guidance for further studies or career choice. There are: general, integrated, and technical/vocational *lyceums*, and technical/vocational schools.

The general *lyceum* offers courses preparing students for higher education. There are both day and evening *lyceums*. The latter—for students who must work during the day—last four years. The first- and second-year curriculum covers religion, ancient and modern Greek language and literature, history, psychology, mathematics, physics, chemistry, physical education and foreign languages—a total of 30 hours a week. Third-year subjects are divided into general education and college-preparatory subjects. The latter are divided into four branches(*desmes*), each leading to a certain type of higher education institution. Students are examined in the preparatory subjects on a national level. Branches A and B focus on mathematics and natural sciences. Branch C focuses on ancient Greek, Latin, and history. Branch D focuses on history, sociology, and economics.

In 1993-1994 there were 1,075 day general *lyceums* and 35 evening general *lyceums* with 18,034 teachers (8,937 female). The same teachers teach in both. There were 232,168 day students (129,524 female), and 4,726 evening students (1,991 female) (NSSG 2000).

Graduates of the general *lyceum* receive a leaving-certificate without final examinations. It indicates achievement in the various subjects. They are eligible to compete in the university entrance examinations.

The *integrated lyceum* aims to interconnect and deepen the objectives and curricula of the general and technical/vocational *lyceums*. In 1993-1994 there were 25 public *integrated lyceums* with 2,116 teachers (1,079 female) and 21,993 students (11,859 female). The pupil/teacher ratio was 10.4. (NSSG 2000). Half the curriculum is similar to that of general *lyceum* in all three years. In the second year, half the subjects are electives associated with broad groups of professions. In the third year, more specialized subjects are added.

The technical-vocational *lyceum* aims to teach pupils the necessary technical and vocational knowledge and skills that will enable them to successfully work in the respective technical or vocational fields upon leaving school. In the first year, pupils are introduced to subjects in a technical/vocational field. In the second year, workshops are added. In the third year, students choose any of the four branches, as in the general *lyceum*.

Graduates of the integrated and the technical/vocational *lyceums* either attend non-university higher education (TEIs) or enter the job market in the field of their specialization.

Technical/vocational schools (TES) have a two-year course of study for day students, and three-year study for evening students. Six hours cover general subjects such as modern Greek, mathematics, physics, foreign languages, and civil education. The remaining 24 hours cover specialization subjects and workshop training. Graduates of TES have access to corresponding employment, to the first grade of the general *lyceum*, or to the second grade of the technical/vocational *lyceum*.

Students can move freely from primary school to the *gymnasium* and then to the *lyceum*. Every pupil has a chance to compete for entrance to the institutions of higher learning, both academic and technical. They can also move horizontally between technical/vocational schools and the *lyceum* and, after the first grade of the *lyceum*, between the general *lyceum* and the technical/vocational *lyceum*.

HIGHER EDUCATION

Greece has adopted the international model for higher education suggested by UNESCO, which calls for two main types of institutions for tertiary education—Universities and non-university institutions. In 2001, there were 18 universities in Greece; eight are in the Athens-Piraeus metropolitan area. There are 12 Technological Educational Institutions, two in the Athens-Piraeus area. And there are 61 Higher Professional Schools (the non-university type), 36 in the Athens-Piraeus area (OECD 1997).

Greece's first universities were the National Capodistrian University of Athens (1837), The National Technical University of Athens (*Polytechneion*) (1836), and The Aristotelian University of Thessaloniki (1925). Between 1960 and 1980 new regional universities were established throughout Greece to meet the increased demand for higher education and contemporary fields, such as computer technology and environmental studies. The new universities are in Ioannina, Patra, Thrace, Crete, Corfu, and the Aegean. Even with the new universities, there are not sufficient places for every student who wishes to attend. As a consequence many Greek students go to other European countries or to the United States for study. There are no private universities in Greece.

Under the 1992 law, undergraduate studies leading to a first degree last four years (eight semesters) for the majority of disciplines: five years (ten semesters) for agriculture, engineering, and dentistry, and six years (12 semesters) for medical schools. The various departments grant the degrees (*ptychia*).

Non-university studies (TEIs) last three years in general. Some majors call for additional six-month on-the-job training for a degree. All institutions of higher learning are open five days a week.

Greek universities award doctoral degrees. Earning a doctorate requires submitting an original thesis to a committee of academic experts. The post-graduate programs are in the process of being organized.

A rector and two vice-rectors who are elected for three years by the university general assembly administer each university. The dean, who is elected for three years by the faculty, administers each faculty consisting of relevant departments. The head, who is elected for two years, administers each department. Undergraduates have equal representation in electoral bodies for selecting administrative heads of the universities.

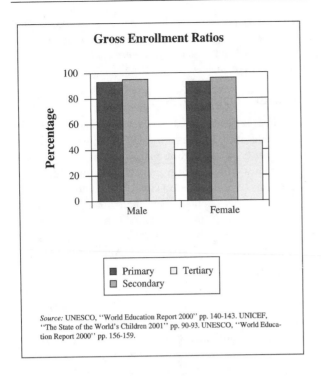

Gross Enrollment Ratios

Source: UNESCO, "World Education Report 2000" pp. 140-143. UNICEF, "The State of the World's Children 2001" pp. 90-93. UNESCO, "World Education Report 2000" pp. 156-159.

The teaching staff has four levels: lecturer, assistant professor, associate professor, and professor. Possession of a doctorate is a prerequisite for all levels.

Women are equally represented in higher education as a whole, though the enrollment of women varies markedly by school or field. In 1993-1994 women exceeded 71 percent in pedagogical sciences, philosophical studies, and social sciences. The fewest women were in engineering, at 23.7 percent (Protopapas 1999).

The demand for tertiary education outstrips supply in the Greek educational system. Admissions are limited by lack of classrooms, staff, and laboratories, and by "inactive" students. Secondary school graduates wishing to enter institutions of higher education must compete in the Panhellenic General Examinations administered yearly by the Central Service of the MoE.

Admissions vary from year to year and from school to school. The are determined by the MoE in consultation with the advisory boards of the National Council of Higher Education and the Council for Technological Education.

Final selection and acceptance to AEIs and TEIs is determined by: the candidate's score on the entrance exam, the AEI/TEI preference stated in the candidate's application, and the number of places available in each institution. Only one in four of the candidates is admitted.

There is a widespread practice among students preparing for tertiary education national exams to take extra courses in *frontisteria* (nonformal, private cramming schools). The students spend the last two years of their *lyceum* studies preparing for the four subjects for the exams at the expense of the rest of the subjects, as well as their school activities and the broader educational purposes of the *lyceum*. The MoE is thinking of modifying the exams system.

Among foreign students studying in Greek universities in 1993-94 were 2,290 from Cyprus, 3,204 compatriots (students whose parents are Greek and live abroad), and 1,263 other foreign students, for a total of 6,757 students (OECD 1997). A large number of students who fail to enter Greek higher institutions go abroad to study. In 1993-1994 there were 21,230. The majority of them prefer Italy (5,494) and Britain (5,272) (NSSG 2000). The expense for study abroad is a drain in the national budget.

Since 1988, the European Union has created programs for inter-university co-operation among member countries. The number of Greek students participating in these programs has increased steadily, from 195 students in 48 programs during the academic year 1988-1989 to 1,765 students in 540 programs during 1993-1994 (OECD 1997).

Centres of Liberal Studies (EES): About 30 private organizations called Centres of Liberal Studies (EES) provide postsecondary education; some are affiliated with foreign universities. Under a 1935 law, these organizations operate as commercial enterprises. As such, they fall under the jurisdiction of the Ministry of Commerce rather than the Ministry of Education, an organizational position that causes some skepticism about the quality of the education they provide.

Applying the organizational structure of foreign universities, some EES have set up courses of two, three, and sometimes four years. In these cases the students of EES are also students of the foreign universities. This means that after two or three years of study in Greece, these students may go to the town or city where the university is located, to complete their studies and obtain a degree. Most of the co-operations are with universities in Britain and the United States, but some are with universities of France, Germany, and Switzerland. Since the MoE is not involved in this kind of education, there is no formal recognition of their degrees (OECD 1997).

ADMINISTRATION, FINANCE, & EDUCATIONAL RESEARCH

The Greek educational system is governed by national laws (passed by the parliament), and by executive acts (decrees, ministerial decisions). Overall responsibility for education rests with the MoE. Its basic functions and responsibilities are:

- Assessment of educational needs.

- Determination of educational goals and objectives.

- Provision of legal framework underlying the educational program.

- Personnel, methods and processes, and schools.

- Coordination and evaluation of the regional education services.

- Financial support and control of educational activities.

The MoE formulates educational policies according to the political orientation of the country's administration. The administration and management of primary and secondary schools is the responsibility of the Directorates of Primary and Secondary Education in the 54 Prefectures, which report directly to the MoE.

Higher education institutions (AEIs, or universities, and TEIs, or technological education institutions) are autonomous according to the Constitution, but are funded and supervised by the MoE. The MoE and the Ministry of Labor share responsibilities for vocational education and training.

The Minister of Education heads the MoE and is appointed by the party in power. He is assisted by a Deputy Minister, a Junior Minister, and a Secretary General. There are also five General Directors and two Special Secretariats. In January 1995, the MoE headquarters comprised 34 directorates.

There are four national councils, one for each section of education: the Council for University Education, the Council for Technological Education, the Central Council for Secondary Education, and the Central Council for Primary Education.

There are two institutes controlled by the MoE, but independent of the Ministry's Central Service—the Pedagogical Institute (PI) and the Institute for Technological Education (ITE).

The PI is responsible for research relating to primary and secondary education, for planning and programming educational policy for primary and secondary education, for developing and implementing educational technology, and for planning and supervising teacher in-service training.

Other central agencies are:

- State Scholarship Foundation (IKY), which administers scholarships to students of higher education.

- Centre for the Recognition of Foreign Academic Degrees (DIKATSA).

- Service for General State Records.

- Organization for School Buildings (OSK).

- Organization for Publication of School Textbooks (OEDB), which publishes textbooks for primary and secondary education.

- Organization of Vocational Education and Training (OEEK), which is responsible for recognizing qualifications awarded by either Greek or foreign vocational education and training, and for allocating all funds from the EU.

There are also two Secretariats: the General Secretariat for Adult Education (GGLE) and the Secretariat for Youth.

The State finances all capital and staff costs of the public education system. Municipalities bear the cost of school maintenance and some operating costs. Recently the school construction has been delegated to the Prefectures.

The primary source of public education is taxation. The state spends 4.2 percent of the GDP for education; the share of public expenditure is 7 percent. Greek families spent large amounts of money—about 2.3 percent of GDP— on private education, cramming schools, and study abroad (OECD 1997).

NONFORMAL EDUCATION

Nonformal education for children takes place outside of school hours, its purpose to supplement and enrich their education. They take instruction in music, foreign languages, arts, dance, and other areas. Their parents pay the fees for this part of their education.

Adult Education: Adult nonformal education is both for enrichment, such as art appreciation, and for vocational training, such as computer literacy. Since 1980 adult education programs were aimed at the unemployed under the age of 25, and the long-term unemployment of those older than 25. They have been financed by the European Social Fund and attended yearly by an estimated 200,000 trainees.

The General Secretariat for Adult Education (GGLE) and its regional agencies—the Regional Committees for Adult Education (NELE) throughout Greece—are the only government services responsible for projects regarding Adult Education. The projects include continuing education, literacy, illiteracy prevention, vocational training, vocational training and rehabilitation of disabled persons, social support activities, health counseling and prevention, and cultural and leisure activities, as well as seminars on intercultural communication, workshops for the preservation of traditional arts and skills, and social integration of unprivileged groups.

GGLE plans and develops projects for such underprivileged groups as Gypsies (education for adults and children, community awareness); offenders/ex-offenders (vocational training and social rehabilitation); the disabled (vocational training and social rehabilitation); repatriated Greeks from Western and Eastern Europe, the former Soviet Republics (Pontian Greeks), and Albania (Greek language, vocational training); and the elderly (new educational opportunities, social support).

EU funding through corresponding programs supports the GGLE activities. The Manpower Employment Organization (OAED) of the Ministry of Labor also runs nonformal training courses and formal apprenticeship programs for young people and adults.

TEACHING PROFESSION

Law 1268 (1982) created pedagogic departments and kindergarten departments in all the Greek universities for the training of teachers in primary and preprimary education respectively. Teacher training lasts four years in both departments and leads to a university degree. The degree is the only qualification to enter the teaching profession. The first pedagogic departments started functioning in 1984-1985. By 1987-1988 pedagogic and kindergarten departments were functioning in all Greek universities. Before 1964 the State had a variety of teacher preparation institutions of diverse lengths of study and curricula that had been in existence since at least the establishment of the new State. In 1964, a third year of studies was added to the pedagogic academies, and the curriculum was enriched with new courses.

There was a movement to make the academies four-year institutions like the other university departments, thus making the status of the primary teachers equal to those of secondary education. Secondary school teachers were always university graduates in the disciplines they taught. An attempt has been made in recent years to provide the secondary school teachers with some pedagogical training before they are appointed to a school. Between 1967 and 1982, students, teaching staff of the academies, the Primary Teachers' Union (DOE), the Federation of Secondary School Teachers (OLME), and the various political parties were all asking for better education for the primary school teachers in particular, but also for all teachers of preprimary and secondary.

The pedagogic academies and the pedagogic departments of the universities co-existed until 1988-1989. Graduates of pedagogic departments are placed on lists (*Epetirida*) each year that are compiled and maintained by the MoE. The lists refer to each category of education. There may be a lapse of about 10 years between graduating from the university and the first appointment. Teachers are taken in serial order out of the lists as needed. The delay in appointment is due to an oversupply of teachers and the appointment system itself. Retraining becomes a necessity. Beginning teachers have to spend a few years in isolated regions before they become eligible to be transferred into a school near home.

Preprimary, primary, and secondary schoolteachers are employed by the MoE. Teacher promotion and increase in salary are entirely related to years of employment. In-service training is mandatory for all teachers. It is done at the universities.

SUMMARY

Greece's educational system has been modernized and democratized steadily during the last 50 years. Many of the reforms resulted from Greece's joining the European Union. One wonders whether the changes were developed from within on imposed from the outside. Greece has to work very hard to maintain its identity within the European identity. There is a need to be balanced. The Greeks also need to keep their religion. It is part of their identity.

The educational reforms seem to lean towards abolishing humanistic education and increasing technical/vocational education. This will be a great detriment to the Greek people. It is humanistic education that provides the values for a person or nation. Even good technocrats need a value system to make sound decisions that will benefit all.

The Greek educational system needs to address the issue of the cramming schools (*frontisteria*). They drain family resources without increasing the quantity of university entrants. It also needs to eliminate the inactive students who prevent more new entrants to higher education.

BIBLIOGRAPHY

Administration and Financial Responsibilities for Education and Training in the European Community. Brussels: EURYDICE European Unit, 1993. (ERIC microfiche ED439970).

Evangelou, Demetra. "Culture and the Greek Kindergarten Curriculum." *Early Childhood Development and Care,* 123: 31-40 (1996).

Evangelopoulos, Spyros. *Hellenike Ekpaideuse (Greek Education),* 2 vols. Athens: Hellinika Gramatta, 1998 (in Greek).

Flogaitis, Eugénie, and Ioanna Alexopoulou. "Environmental Education in Greece." *European Journal of Education* 26, No. 4:339-433 (1991).

Freeman, Kenneth J. *Schools of Hellas.* London: Macmillan, 1907.

"Government Support for Adult Education in Greece." *Journal of Reading* 37:5 (February 1994).

Hellas Letter, April 2001, Monthly Bulletin. Boston: Consulate General of Greece, press office.

Issues in Rural Primary Education in Europe: A Summary of a Symposium on Issues in Rural Education at the European Conference on Educational Research, Seville, Spain, September 25-29, 1997. (ERIC microfiche ED40008116).

Kallen, Denis, Ed. *Secondary Education in Greece. Guide to Secondary Education in Europe.* Strasbourg: Council of Europe Press, 1996. (ERIC microfiche ED399621).

Kazamias, Andreas. "The Curse of Sisyphus in Greek Educational Reform: A Sociopolitical and Cultural Interpretation." *Modern Greek Studies Yearbook* 6: 33-53 (1990).

Kassotakis, Michael. "Greece." In *Handbook of World Education: A Comparative Guide to Higher Education,* ed. Walter Wickremasinghe, 309-323. Houston: American Collegiate Service, 1991.

Katsikas, Christos, and Giorgos Kavvadias. *He Hellenike Ekpaideuse Stonhorizonta Tou 2000* (Greek Education in the Horizon 2000). Athens: Gutenberg, 1996 (in Greek).

Lascarides, V. Celia, and Blythe F. Hinitz. *History of Early Childhood Education.* New York: Falmer Press, 2000, 3-15.

Makrinoti, Kimitra, and Joseph Solomon. "The Discourse of Citizenship Education in Greece: National Identity and Social Diversity." In *Civic Education Across Countries: Twenty-four National Case Studies from the IEA Project,* eds. Judith Torney-Purta, John Schwille, and Jo-"Ann Amadeo, 285-312. Amsterdam: International Association for the Evaluation of Educational Achievement, 1999.

Marrou, Henri I. *The History of Education in Antiquity,* trans. George Lamb. New York: Sheed and Ward, 1956.

Meijer, Cor J. W., ed. *Integration in Europe: Provision for Pupils with Special Education Needs. Trends in 14 European Countries.* Denmark: European Agency for Development in Special Needs Education, 1968. (ERIC microfiche ED426566).

National Statistical Service of Greece (NSSG). *Concise Statistical Yearbook of Greece: 1996, 1997.* Athens: NSSG, 1998 (bilingual Greek-English).

National Statistical Service of Greece (NSSG). *Educational Statistics 1992/93 and 1993/94.* Athens: NSSG, 2000 (bilingual Greek-English).

Organisation for Economic Cooperation and Development (OECD). *Reviews of National Policies for Education: Greece.* Paris: OECD, 1997.

Organisation for Economic Co-operation and Development. *Educational Policy and Planning Educational Reform Policies in Greece.* Paris: OECD, 1980.

Organisation for Economic Co-operation and Development. *The Mediterranean Regional Project: Greece.* Paris: OECD, 1965.

Organization of School Time in the European Union.. Second edition, 1995. (ERIC microfiche ED439971).

Protopapas, Angelos. "Analysis of Data on Higher Education in Greece by Scientific Area." *Higher Education* 37 (April 1999): 295-322.

Saitis, Christos. "Management in the Public Sector in Greece: the Case of the Ministry of Education." *Educational Management and Administration* 18, No. 3 (1990): 53-60.

Starida, Mina. "Issues of Quality in Greek Teacher Education." *European Journal of Teacher Education* 18, No. 1 (1995): 115-121.

Stavrou, Stavros. *Vocational Education and Training in Greece.* Thessaloniki: European Centre for the Development of Vocational Training, 1995. (ERIC microfiche ED394064).

Tsiakalos, Georgios. "Greece: An Approach to Irregular School Attendance." In *Mobility and Young Children, Bernard van Leer Foundation Newsletter* No. 76 (October 1994): 8-9. (ERIC microfiche ED375983).

Vamvoucas, Michael, and George Movroidis. "Greece." In *primary Education in Europe: Evaluation of New Curricula in 10 European Countries,* ed. Lucio Pusci, 55-66. Italy, 1990. (ERIC microfiche ED339546).

—*V. Celia Lascarides*

GREENLAND

BASIC DATA

Official Country Name:	Greenland
Region:	North & Central America
Population:	56,309
Language(s):	Greenlandic, Danish, English, Inuit
Literacy Rate:	similar to Denmark proper

Greenland (*Kalladliit Nunaat*) is a very particular post-colonial country. Its size is like a continent, and it is completely covered by ice. There are approximately 60,000 inhabitants spread on the long coastline in small communities. The country is strongly influenced by the climate and geography; at the same time it has a rather modern society. Eighty percent of the inhabitants are *Inuits* (Eskimos; their origin is closely related to Canadian, Alaskan, and Siberian people, but they have their own *Inuit* mother tongue. The remaining twenty percent is mainly Danish, some settled, some temporarily working, since Greenland is not self-supplying in terms of the work force. The *Inuit* language is now the main official language, but all administration and public communication is bilingual. Greenland is under Danish sovereignty but has a local government, *Grønlands Hjemmestyre*, which, since the 1970s, has gradually taken control of all administration and public services except territorial defense and foreign policy. There has been a move towards increasing the degree of home rule to include international representation in matters of interest specific to Greenland. The local government receives a block grant from Denmark covering a substantial part of public expenditure.

The education system is regarded as a strategic tool to secure sustainability and a self-supplying labor market. It is similar to the Danish educational system but there have been strong efforts to "Greenlandize" it, in terms of staff, language, and adaptation to local circumstances. The instruction is mainly bilingual—but in many specialized domains *Inuit* speaking teachers are sparse and instruction materials only exist in Danish. There is a full general school system including upper secondary education in three locations as well as vocational education in main crafts. The school system is quite centralized in relation to the very widespread population. There is a teacher training college, a school for social work and pedagogy, marine schools of navigation and engineering, and also a small university offering language, cultural, and social studies on a basic university level, as well as specialized research with a local focus. However, advanced higher education and specialized professional education still relies on studies abroad, mainly in Denmark.

—*Henning Salling Olesen*

GRENADA

BASIC DATA

Official Country Name:	Grenada
Region:	Puerto Rico & Lesser Antilles
Population:	89,018
Language(s):	English, French patois
Literacy Rate:	98%

HISTORY & BACKGROUND

Grenada, a tiny island in the Caribbean, occupies the southern-most position in the Windward Islands chain. It is 344 square kilometers (about twice the size of Washington, DC) and, in 2000, the population was estimated at approximately 99,700 persons. English is the official language, but a French patois is also spoken.

The first schools in Grenada were split among religious denominations: Anglican schools, Methodist schools, and, the smallest, Roman Catholic schools. In the mid-part of the nineteenth century, education was not a priority in Grenada. In 1845 only 2.3 percent of the island's budget was spent on education. Although the situation improved, it did so slowly; figures from 1852 show that the percentage of the budget spent on education grew to 5 percent.

During the year 1848, education of the working class in Grenada fell drastically due to the limited financial resources of the government and people. The legislators were reluctant to provide funds for education. Some success was achieved in 1868 when the legislature voted its first grant of 50 pounds for schools.

As the turn of the century approached, interest in schools and education continued to grow. In 1882, the Grenadian legislature enacted a new Education Ordinance that:

1. Made grants-in-aid available to assist schools that reached certain standards in terms of their enrollment and academic results.

2. Provided for the establishment of schools in areas where no assisted schools existed.

3. Doubled the education vote between 1881 and 1882.

4. Allowed funds to be allocated toward the appointment of an Inspector of Schools.

5. Permitted the Roman Catholics to have a 50 percent representation on the Board of Education.

Education in Grenada changed dramatically in 1889; it was during this year that Governor Sendall declared that the financial allocations to education were inadequate and called for the establishment of government-owned and operated schools, the first public schools on the island. The colony continued its financial support for denominational schools, which still remain an important part of the educational system.

CONSTITUTIONAL & LEGAL FOUNDATIONS

In the 1980s, Grenada's education system was deficient in meeting the basic needs of the country. In 1987 it did not produce workers with vocational and administrative skills required of a developing economy. Areas deficient were: training in electricity, electronics, plumbing, welding, construction, and other technical skills.

The People's Revolutionary Government (PRG), which lasted from 1979-1983, made education reform a pillar platform. The leader, Maurice Bishop, initiated and implemented programs to move the curriculum away from the British Model, which was implemented during Grenada's membership to the British Empire from 1784 until its independence in 1974. The goal was to tailor the educational system to meet the needs of the Grenadian society; however, this program was unsuccessful. One problem with the PRG's reform program was that teachers were asked both to instruct students and to attend PRG seminars. The strong political overtones of this attempted reform alienated many teachers and prompted them to drop out of the program. A return to the British school system model was enacted in 1984.

EDUCATIONAL SYSTEM—OVERVIEW

Education is free and compulsory from ages 5 to 16. The majority of the population will at least complete a primary education. Grenada has both public schools and parochial schools, although there may be only one choice in rural areas. Classes are taught in English, and high school students also learn French and Spanish. Students in public schools wear uniforms. The educational environment has many of the same restraints common in poor rural areas as schools in other developing countries. Intentions are good, but classrooms are lacking in resources and trained teachers, and students are not given individualized or well-organized instructions.

Technology: In 1986, an American computer company, the Control Data Corporation (CDC), invited the government of Grenada and the Ministry of Education to install and assess the importance computers have on improving test scores and overall school achievement. Grenada, because of its limited educational budget, accepted the offer. The computers were set up in a small, rural Catholic School in Crochu. The school in Crochu was chosen because it is representative of many Caribbean schools, thus making the experiment transferable. Although the Ministry of Education could not offer long-term assistance for the project, it did pay for extra electricity, provided duty-free import status for the equipment, and lent its general support from the beginning. Difficulties in finances and resources occurred;

however, the people from this small community worked diligently to maintain the computer facilities. The results were positive. By 1989, the effects of the computer-assisted instruction (CAI) resulted in increased performance on the Common Entrance Exam, the exam required to advance to a secondary school. As of 1994, the CAI was still being used in Crochu.

PREPRIMARY & PRIMARY EDUCATION

Preprimary & Special Education: In 1992 there were 75 preprimary schools with 3,916 pupils. In 1991 there were 10 schools for special education and 12 day care centers caring for 249 children.

Primary Education: Statistics available in 1987 show there were 68 primary schools with a total enrollment of approximately 22,100 students. The figures changed slightly in 1992, with the number of primary schools decreasing to 57, and the number of pupils increasing to 22,330.

SECONDARY EDUCATION

The majority of students do not continue on to a secondary school program, according to the last available statistics. The secondary school program in 1987 included 20 schools and 6,250 students. In 1992 there were 18 secondary schools with 6,970 pupils.

HIGHER EDUCATION

Students take a middle-level examination, the Common Entrance Exam, at the age of 16 to determine their eligibility for the final 2 years of preparatory work for university entrance. Few complete these two years. Between 1960-1970 the number of Grenadians trained at the university level increased from 193 to 352 people.

In 1987, Grenada had only three institutions beyond the secondary level for technical or academic training of its citizens: the Institute for Further Education, the Teacher Training College, and the Technical and Vocational Institute. Since 1987 the number of schools has increased. Students who want to continue their education beyond high school may go on to college or university; some may also enter apprenticeship programs to learn a trade. The colleges include Mirabeau Agricultural School, Teacher's Training College, Marryshow College, and the Technical and Vocational Institute. There are also three technical centers in the parishes of St. Patrick, St. David, and St. John. The Grenada National College was established in 1988.

Medical Schools: St. George's Medical School, although administered in Grenada, exists to serve foreign medical students, most of whom come from the United States. St. George's University was originally founded as a School of Medicine, but was authorized to grant additional degrees in 1976. The medical training facilities at St. George's University are highly respected throughout the world. More than two-thirds of the students come from foreign countries including Ireland, Sri Lanka, Swaziland, Kuwait, and Venezuela. Since 1977, more than 2,600 students at the university have been awarded their M.D. degree and currently practice in more than 22 countries around the world. There is also a branch of the Extra-Mural Department of the University of the West Indies (UWI) in St. George's.

ADMINISTRATION, FINANCE, & EDUCATIONAL RESEARCH

Schools in Grenada are funded by the Ministry of Education. Grenada is also part of International Education Policy. In this program, foreign ambassadors visit American schools to promote awareness about the importance of increasing the study of foreign languages and cultures. The ambassadors have the opportunity to foster classroom connections with schools, colleges, and universities, which encourages American students to study overseas. These visits also allow for officials to see the various educational and classroom opportunities available to American students.

NONFORMAL EDUCATION

The Center for Popular Education (CPE) is the main adult education institution. There is a 95 percent literacy rate among the adult population.

TEACHING PROFESSION

Restrictions make finding and retaining trained teachers difficult for rural schools. Stipulations created by the Grenadian National Education Policy prevent prospective teachers from entering the teacher college without three years teaching experience and high marks on their O-level exams. Catholic schools require teachers of the Catholic denomination.

SUMMARY

Grenada needs to make education a priority. Although there have been improvements in awareness and funding, the educational standards in Grenada are not yet where they should be. More funds need to be directed toward technology (as indicated by the Crochu study) and equipment and materials need to be updated so students are learning information before it is outdated. Students, especially those in rural areas, are getting only a basic education that does not always prepare them for higher institutions.

BIBLIOGRAPHY

Bacchus, M.K. "Consensus and Conflict over the Provision of Elementary Education." In *Caribbean Freedom,* eds. Hilary Beckles and Verene Shepherd, 296-312. Princeton: Markus Weiner Publishers, 1996.

Bosch, Andrea. "Computer-Assisted Instruction in Grenada: High-Tech Success and Sustainability Against the Odds." *LearnTech Case Study Series,* no. 3. Washington, DC: Educational Development Center, 1994.

"Citizenship and Immigration Canada." *Cultural Profiles Project,* 15 April 1999. Available from http://cwr.utoronto.ca/cultural/.

Haggerty, Richard A., and John F. Hornbeck. "Grenada." In *Islands of the Commonwealth Caribbean,* eds. Sandra W. Meditz and Dennis M. Hanratty, 349-384. Washington, DC: Library of Congress Cataloging-in-Publication Data, 1989.

Lankshear, Colin, and Peter L. McLaren, eds. *Critical Literacy.* New York: State University of New York Press, 1993.

Turner, Barry, ed. *The Statesman's Yearbook.* New York: St. Martin's Press, 2001.

U.S. Department of Education and the U.S. Department of State. *International Education Policy,* 9 November 2000. Available from http://exchanges.state.gov.

—*Carrie E. Nartker*

GUADELOUPE

BASIC DATA

Official Country Name:	Department of Guadeloupe
Region:	Puerto Rico & Lesser Antilles
Population:	426,493
Language(s):	French, Creole patois
Literacy Rate:	90%

Guadeloupe has been a French possession since 1635 and a department of France since 1946. In July 2000, the population was estimated at 426,493 people. The economy depends heavily on tourism but requires substantial aid from France. In 1998, the unemployment rate was 27.8 percent, and GDP per capita was estimated at \$9,000 in 1996. Although French is the official language, the majority of the population speaks Creole, an important element in the cultural unity of Guadeloupe's society.

Because Guadeloupe is a department of France, the education system is the same as in France. Education is compulsory for 10 years from the ages of 6 to 16. The school year runs from the first week in September to the end of June. The school calendar includes the following holidays: one day at *Mi-Carême* (Mid-Lent) and at the *Abolition de l'esclavage* (the Abolition of Slavery Day) at the end of May, one week at *La Toussaint* (All Saints' Day) in early November and at *Carnaval* in late February, and two weeks at *Noël* (Christmas) and *Pâques* (Easter). French is the language of instruction.

Students may enter the *école maternelle* (preprimary school) at age two, and the *école primaire* (primary school) at age six. In 1998-99, there were 339 *écoles maternelles et primaires* with 63,609 students enrolled.

Secondary education begins at age 11 and lasts for 7 years; it is divided into a premier cycle (first cycle) completed in the *collège* and lasting four years, and a second cycle completed in the *lycée* and lasting three years. In the 1998-99 school year, there were 48 *collèges* enrolling 30,825 students and 31 *lycées* with 20,448 students.

The Guadeloupe campus of the Université des Antilles et de la Guyane has schools of exact and natural sciences, law and economics, sciences and techniques in physical and sporting activities, and medicine. Enrollment in 1998 was about 5,300 students with an academic staff of 130. The *Institut Universitaire de Formation des Maîtres* (University Institute for Teacher Training), affiliated with the university, has a center in Guadeloupe to provide teacher training. The *licence* (bachelor's degree) is required for admission. The program lasts two years, the first for further specialization in a discipline and the second for teacher training in that discipline. Continuing education and training is provided through the *Centre National d'Enseignement à Distance* (The National Center for Distance Education).

Starting in 1947, the school system was under the jurisdiction of the *Recteur of the Académie de Bordeaux* (the Bordeaux Academy). In 1974, an Académie des Antilles-Guyane was created for the departments of Guadeloupe, Martinique, and Guyana. Since January 1997, the school system is headed by the recteur of the newly created Académie de la Guadeloupe.

The new Académie de Guadeloupe implemented a three-year plan in 1999 with a focus on important issues for the schools of Guadeloupe. One of the goals is to reduce the failure and dropout rates, especially in the first

year of the *lycée,* where those rates have been significant. Another objective is the mastery of French: the goal is to improve the effectiveness in the teaching of French and in teaching other subjects in French in Guadeloupe's multilingual society. A final goal encourages teachers to develop activities on the theme of citizenship to include promoting non-violence and the teaching of the skills of democracy: civility, listening to others, and constructing reasonable arguments in support of one's ideas.

BIBLIOGRAPHY

Académie de la Guadeloupe, 15 December 2000. Available from http://www.ac-guadeloupe.fr.

The Central Intelligence Agency (CIA). *The World Factbook 2000.* Directorate of Intelligence, 1 January 2000. Available from http://www.cia.gov.

Europa. *The Europa World Yearbook 2000,* Vol. 1. London: Europa Publications, 1999.

International Association of Universities. *International Handbook of Universities,* Fifteenth Ed. New York: Grove's Dictionaries Inc, 1998.

Michel, C., and G. Pigeon. "Guadeloupe and Martinique: System of Education." In *The International Encyclopedia of Education,* Vol. 6. Tarrytown, NY: Elsevier Science Inc., 1994.

UNESCO. *Statistical Yearbook/Annuaire Statistique 1999.* Lanham, MD: Bernan Press, 2000.

Université des Antilles et de la Guyane, 15 December 2000. Available from http://www.univ-ag.fr.

—*Gilles Labrie*

GUAM

BASIC DATA

Official Country Name:	Guam
Region:	Oceania
Population:	154,623
Language(s):	English, Chamorro, Japanese
Literacy Rate:	99%

History & Background

Guam is the southernmost island of the Marianas archipelago in the western Pacific Ocean, located about three-quarters of the way from Hawaii to the Philippines. The indigenous Chamorros, of Malayo-Polynesian descent, comprise about 42 percent of the population of 154,623 people (2000 estimate). Guam has been an unincorporated territory of the United States since it was ceded by Spain in 1898 by the Treaty of Paris. Japanese forces occupied the island between 1941 and 1944. The government was organized under the Organic Act of Guam, 1950, as amended, which was passed by the U.S. Congress. The local government, elected by resident citizens, is divided into an executive branch (governor and lieutenant governor), a 15-member unicameral legislature (senate), and a judiciary (Guam Superior Court and Guam Supreme Court). The island (212 square miles) is under the jurisdiction of the Office of Insular Affairs, U.S. Department of the Interior; it is subject to U.S. laws under a U.S. Federal District Court. Guam elects one non-voting delegate to the U.S. House of Representatives; it has no representative in the U.S. Senate. Residents (most of whom are U.S. citizens) cannot vote in U.S. national elections.

Educational System—Overview

Guam's public school system is modeled on the U.S. system, and education is compulsory for children between 5 to 16 years of age. Public schools in the system are subject to accreditation by the Western Association of Schools and Colleges. There are 38 public schools— 27 elementary, 7 middle, and 4 high schools. Offering various curricula from elementary through high school are 22 private or independent schools that are operated by religious organizations (14 Catholic and 8 Protestant); four are maintained by other groups. Since 1998 the Department of Defense Education Activity has maintained one high school, two middle schools, and two elementary schools on military bases for dependents of military personnel stationed on Guam.

According to a 1999 estimate, approximately 32,000 students are enrolled in K-12 classes in Guam public schools—an ethnic mix of 54 percent Chamorro, 26 percent Filipino, 11 percent Pacific Islanders, 4 percent mixed ethnic, 2 percent Asian, 2 percent Caucasian, and 1 percent other. The language of instruction is English, except for compulsory classes in Chamorro language and culture. In 1998-1999, Guam spent $5,098.91 on each pupil; however, none of the financing for the island's public school system comes from property taxes. Aside from funding from federal grants and programs, all school-related expenses are appropriated from the legislature's general fund, derived mainly from Guam's in-

come tax, whose code "mirrors" the U.S. income tax code (the income taxes of local residents are combined with taxes returned from the United States for all military personnel stationed in Guam) and from "receipts" taxes on tourism-related businesses. Since these taxes do not provide a stable source of funding (they vary with the number of military personnel assigned and with tourist spending), long-term planning for the public schools is difficult.

Public school teachers are certified by the Guam Department of Education, a highly centralized bureaucracy within the Government of Guam that exercises a great amount of administrative control over the various schools. Although numerous attempts to decentralize the system and to institute site-based management have been made, these efforts have not been successful. The institutions of higher education, Guam Community College and the University of Guam, are semi-autonomous agencies of the government operating under the direction of a board of trustees and a board of regents, respectively. Guam Community College provides vocational classes for high schools, classes for developmental and adult education, two-year college courses, and college transfer courses. The University of Guam offers undergraduate level courses and some graduate school programs leading to a Master's degree. The University has an accredited nursing program and has applied for accreditation of its program in education.

Funding continues to be a problem for the educational system of Guam. The economic downturn in Asia during the 1990s, especially in Japan, and military downsizing have been cited as factors in such difficulties as the failure to purchase needed textbooks and a general lack of maintenance of the physical facilities in the schools. But other sources have contributed to these problems and to the poor scores achieved by Guam students on SAT tests. Guam shares the problems of many inner-city school districts in the United States, including an excessive school dropout rate, a high rate of teen pregnancy, juvenile gangs, and a general lack of academic motivation.

One crippling event for the public schools occurred in 1981, when Guam teachers went on strike over low wages. All the teachers who participated in the strike were fired, and uncertified replacements were hired. The effects of that strike are still being felt—there are not enough certified teachers to fill the classrooms, so teachers' aides and temporary (uncertified) teachers are used extensively. Another disaster for the schools was the loss of military dependents in 1998 when the Department of Defense, after many efforts to improve the public school system, finally opened its own schools on the military bases. Funds previously provided to the Guam Department of Education for teacher recruitment and other uses by the Department of Defense ceased. Another serious problem with implications for the public school system has been the repeated threat of loss of accreditation for the University of Guam's undergraduate program, which was put on "probation" in 1984 and again in 1999 by the Western Association of Schools and Colleges. The University is a major source of recruitment for teachers in the public schools.

BIBLIOGRAPHY

Douglas, Norman, and Ngaire Douglas. *Pacific Island Yearbook, 16th ed.* North Ryde, NSW, Australia: Angus & Robertson, 1989.

Guam Department of Education. "General Information," 20 December 2000. Available from http://www.doe.edu.gu.

Rogers, Robert F. *Destiny's Landfall: A History of Guam.* Honolulu: U of Hawaii Press, 1995.

Roth, Susan. "Governor Plans Territorial Tutoring Program." *Pacific Daily News,* 3 March 2001.

—*Richard E. Mezo*

GUATEMALA

BASIC DATA

Official Country Name:	Republic of Guatemala
Region:	North & Central America
Population:	12,639,939
Language(s):	Spanish, Quiche, Cakchiquel, Kekchi, Mam, Garifuna, Xinca
Literacy Rate:	55.6%
Number of Primary Schools:	12,409
Compulsory Schooling:	6 years
Public Expenditure on Education:	1.7%
Educational Enrollment:	Primary: 1,510,811 Secondary: 375,528 Higher: 80,228
Educational Enrollment Rate:	Primary: 88% Secondary: 26%
Teachers:	Primary: 43,403 Secondary: 22,624
Student-Teacher Ratio:	Primary: 35:1
Female Enrollment Rate:	Primary: 82% Secondary: 25%

HISTORY & BACKGROUND

The Republic of Guatemala is one of seven countries located in Central America. Bordered by Belize, El Salvador, Honduras, Mexico, and the Pacific Ocean, Guatemala has a land area of 108,430 square kilometers (41,865 square miles or approximately the size of Tennessee) and a population of 13 million, representing over one third of Central America's entire population. The climate of Guatemala is primarily tropical, although it contains cool highlands in the north and tropical jungles in the south. The central terrain is largely mountainous, while the coastal region is bordered by plains. There are many active volcanoes in the country, and the area is also subject to hurricanes and earthquakes.

Approximately 40 percent of the population of Guatemala is urban. The most populated area is the country's capital, Guatemala City, which boasts a metropolitan population of over two million people. Guatemala is a leader in Central American's commerce and manufacturing. It produces and exports petroleum, minerals, tobacco, electrical goods, pharmaceuticals, food, and textiles. Tourism in Guatemala also thrives, particularly in Antigua, which is a major cultural center of Guatemala City. Agriculture represents about 25 percent of the Guatemala's income, and farming accounts for nearly half of the nation's workforce. Approximately 36 percent of the country's exports go to the United States, which in turn comprises about 40 percent of Guatemala's imports. Guatemala also exports to other Central American countries, as well as to Japan and Germany.

Guatemala has a rich and culturally distinctive history. More than 50 percent of Guatemala's population descended from Mayan ancestry. Historians believe that the region, which now comprises Guatemala, contained a series of small kingdoms and city-states during whose existence architectural accomplishments, many representations of which can still be found in Guatemala, flourished. In 1521, the area was claimed by Spain, under whose rule the Mayan Indians were suppressed. During the 300 year period which followed, the Mayan Culture diminished, although today it is a celebrated part of Guatemala's heritage. People of Mayan-Spanish descent today are referred to as *Ladinos.*

After winning its independence from Spain in 1821, Guatemala briefly became part of Mexico and later a member of the United Provinces of Central America. From that time until 1944, it was governed by a series of dictatorships until its first civilian president, Juan José Arevalo, was elected and promised to bring democratic political reform. The new form of government, however, was short-lived; many of Arevalo's successors returned the country to a series of dictatorships, military rule, and civil wars until 1985 when Vinico Cerezo was elected to the presidency. Under Cerezo's leadership, the new 1985 Constitution (which was temporarily suspended and amended in 1993) provided for the separation of governmental powers and included provisions for the protection of human rights. Entering the twenty-first century, Guatemala enjoyed a progressive, human rights-oriented government that sought to provide for the protection, education, and cultural advancements of its people. Among the country's agendas in 2000 were the perpetuation of human rights within its borders, the modernization of its schools, and its diplomatic relations with other world governments.

CONSTITUTIONAL & LEGAL FOUNDATIONS

Like the United States, Guatemala's government is comprised of three branches: the *Congreso de la Republica* or Legislative Branch, a unicameral national congress made up of 110 deputies who serve 4 year terms; the Executive Branch, comprised of the president, vice president, and the Council of Ministers, who are appointed by the president; and the Judicial Branch, a hierarchical series of upper and lower courts over which the 13 member *Corte Surpema de Justicia* (Supreme Court) presides. Members of the Supreme Court serve five-year terms, and the president, who acts as both chief of state and as head of government, serves a four-year term.

Guatemala is divided into 22 states or *departmentos*, under which 331 *municipos* (townships) handle local affairs. Each *departmento* is headed by a governor. Under the current constitution, the president and vice president are elected by national vote and may serve only one term. Voting is compulsory for citizens 18 years or older.

EDUCATIONAL SYSTEM—OVERVIEW

Similar to the United States, the educational system in Guatemala is divided into three levels: primary (elementary), secondary (high school), and university. Education in Guatemala is free and compulsory through sixth grade, or between the ages of 7 and 14. Because public schools are often located sparsely in the rural areas of the country, there is an abundance of private schools in Guatemala. Many of these institutions are Marist or Jesuit. In total, there are approximately 9,300 primary schools, which are attended by 1.3 million students. More than

290,000 students attend private secondary schools, and the total university enrollment in Guatemala is approximately 88,000.

Language of Instruction: Although Spanish is the official language spoken in Guatemala, not all of its citizens are fluent in Spanish. Spoken among the nation's high Indian population are over 20 indigenous Mayan Indian languages, including *K'iche'*, *Kakchiquel*, *K'ekchi*, *Mam*, and *Quiche*, which are used primarily in the rural areas of the country. In fact, only 60 percent of Guatemala's population speaks Spanish; the remaining 40 percent speak indigenous Mayan languages. These dialects are spoken in many of the country's rural schools. One of Guatemala's educational goals is to become uni-lingual, which means that ideally all Guatemalans would be able to speak Spanish. However, students who complete all 6 years of primary school and all 5 years of secondary may have as many as 11 years of English instruction, a trend which began around the time of Guatemala's break from dictatorship in the late 1940s. Since that time, school children, at least in the larger cities, may have also received training in other languages, especially French, German, and Italian.

Instructional Technology (Computers): Lack of adequate educational technology remains a problem for the Guatemalan classroom, especially in the mountainous, rural areas. Absence of funding, limited technical access, and lack of operator expertise prevent all schools from being equipped with state-of-the-art computers and distance learning technology. However, these commodities are making their entrance into the universities, particularly the University of San Carlos, which boasts a fully updated website, student access to the Internet, and other interactive features. Students who can afford the required technology and tuition may participate in online education courses offered outside of the country.

Curriculum—Development: The Guatemalan Ministry of Education supports a progressive, globalized curriculum. One of the country's major educational achievements is its focus on globalization and multicultural affairs. Starting in secondary school, students learn about other cultures and nations, including their Latin American neighbors, other Western-hemisphere countries, and countries all over the world. This attention to multiculturalism aids in Guatemala's presence in international affairs, global commerce, and social development. Curriculum in Guatemala also gives attention to the social issues the country faces and encourages its students to be active in helping solve these problems.

PREPRIMARY & PRIMARY EDUCATION

A child's first year in school is pre-kindergarten. Primary or elementary school comprises the next six years.

Students must pass a general examination at each grade level in order to pass to the subsequent level. Students who fail any part of the year-end examination must repeat that entire year. Examinations are prepared under the supervision of Guatemala's Minister of Education, who also presides over the curriculum and administrative functions of the country's public schools.

Students receive instruction in all the "basic" areas, including language, science, mathematics, and history. In most city schools, both Spanish and English are taught at all primary levels, although in more remote areas, indigenous Mayan languages are used exclusively. In some larger urban schools, courses in German, French, Italian, Arabic and Chinese may also be offered. French, German, and English-run schools teach a combination of the national curriculum and their respective country's curriculum.

SECONDARY EDUCATION

Most secondary schools are located in the urban areas of Guatemala and are affiliated with the Roman Catholic Church (Catholicism is the predominant religion of Guatemala, although there are many Protestants and Mayan religions practiced). Several German, French, and American schools also exist. Teachers at these schools use English, rather than Spanish, to deliver instruction.

Since compulsory education ends at the sixth grade, many Guatemalan children do not attend secondary school. In fact, recent estimates hold that only one third of all children continue their education beyond primary school, a problem that may contribute to a high level of illiteracy in adults over age 15. Children may not have easy access to a secondary school, or, if they come from agricultural communities, they are unable to attend because they must work to support their families' farms.

At the secondary level, students receive three years of general education, called *Ciclo Prevocacional*, followed by two years of vocational training, called *Ciclo Diversifacado*, which allows students to "specialize" in one of several professional areas such as education, agriculture, and business. Students who complete the final three years of study receive a *Bachillerato*, the equivalent of a high school diploma, and are eligible to be admitted to university. Instead of attending *Ciclo Diversifcado*, students may opt to devote their following three years of study to specialized studies, resulting in a certificates in *perito* (certification) in *industria* (industry), *agricola* (agriculture), or *contador* (law).

Guatemala faces a rather hefty illiteracy problem with as many as 50 percent of the entire population, especially rural women, being functionally illiterate. To combat this problem and to improve the quality of education,

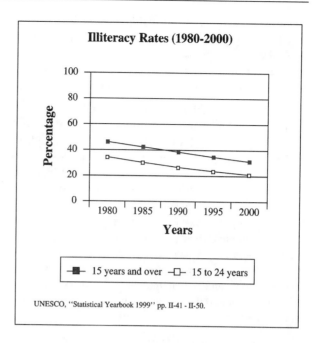

Illiteracy Rates (1980-2000)

UNESCO, "Statistical Yearbook 1999" pp. II-41 - II-50.

Guatemala implemented a requirement into the secondary education requirements for its senior students. Before completing the curriculum necessary for receiving a diploma, secondary students are now required to teach five people to read. This mandate, which went into effect in 2001, seeks to increase citizens' awareness of the need to educate the populace, while simultaneously combating illiteracy. Although this measure was met with some initial resistance by the schools, it has so far proven to be an effective means of reducing the widespread effects of illiteracy in the country.

HIGHER EDUCATION

There are five institutions of higher learning in Guatemala, all located in the capital city. The most prominent of these is the Universidad de San Carlos (USC), the country's largest institution of higher education (and the largest in Central America) with an enrollment of over 60,000 students. As the only public university in Guatemala, USC offers a comprehensive list of degree options in business, education, the arts, medicine, law, agriculture, veterinary, and in other disciplines. The university also operates a number of satellite or complimentary campuses located throughout the country.

The remainder of Guatemala's universities are private: the *Universidad del Valle de Guatemala*, the *Universidad Rafael Landivar*, the *University of Francis Marroquin*, the *University of Mariano Galvez*, and the *University of Galileo*, the country's youngest university. Many of the private universities in Guatemala are linked to the Roman Catholic Church (*la Universidad de Francis Marroquin* was established by an Archbishop, for example), although the *la Universidad de Mariano Galvez* is a Protestant church-governed institution. All institutions offer a variety of degree and certificate programs in all areas of study, including arts and letters, business, medicine, law, engineering, and agriculture.

Admission to universities in Guatemala is based on applicants' holding of the *bachillerato* (equivalent to a high school diploma), a knowledge of Spanish, and, in the case of the private schools, a satisfactory grade on the appropriate *Examen de Admision* (entrance examination). Once enrolled, students must obtain a minimum grade of 51 percent to pass coursework; at some private institutions, a minimum grade of 61 percent is required. When students complete their programs of study, they are issued a diploma by Guatemala's Minister of Education, not by the individual institution. Students from other countries may enter Guatemala's universities provided they have credentials similar to the *bachillerato* and a knowledge of Spanish.

Students may complete many different types of programs at the university level. The first stage is known as the *licenciatura*. This is equivalent to a bachelor's degree in the United States. A student receives this credential after three to seven years of study, depending on the subject area: a technical certificate (*tecnico*) requires three years of study, a degree in Arts and Sciences requires four years; a degree in *ingeniero* (engineering), requires five to six years; and a degree in medicine requires seven years. Usually each degree is accompanied by some type of professional certification. Also as part of their mandatory curriculum, students must complete a seminar in Social Issues, which requires them to write about a significant problem facing Guatemalan society, such as the illiteracy rate. The school year lasts from January to October.

Beyond the *licenciatura* is the *maestrado* (master's degree), which requires two years of additional study and a thesis, and the *doctorado* (doctoral degree), which requires two years' study in addition to the time required for the *maestrado*. Doctoral students must also complete a thesis in one of the following areas: law, humanities, education, economics, or social sciences. To combat the illiteracy problem, each graduating university student must complete an internship which requires them to teach five Guatemalans how to read and write as part of his/her program of academic study.

ADMINISTRATION, FINANCE, & EDUCATIONAL RESEARCH

National policies related to education in Guatemala are handled through the *Ministerio de Educacion* (the Ministry of Education), presided over by the national Minister of Education. The ministry's sphere of influence covers predominantly, but not exclusively, primary (compulsory) schools. The Minister is responsible for such matters as developing proficiency examinations that students are required to pass in order to move from one grade level to the next; ensuring that state curriculum is observed fully in public schools and at least partially in private schools; and managing finances allocated to education, which is approximately 1.8 percent of the country's GDP (Gross Domestic Product). All diplomas are issued to students by the Ministry, not by the individual schools or programs of study. Additionally, programs for non-traditional (older) learners are offered, especially for semi-qualified workers in the agricultural and health sectors.

Educational research in Guatemala covers a spectrum of academic disciplines, including agriculture, business, arts and sciences, social work, engineering, law, and medicine. Each university maintains active research programs in many of these areas, and there are several Guatemalan organizations that support faculty research, including the *Centro de Estudios de Guatemala* (The Center for the Study of Guatemala), the *Centro de Investigaciónes Económicas Nacionales* (The Center for Economic Investigation), and *Facultad Lationamericana de Ciencias Sociales* (Latin American Faculty of Science and Society). Each university also contains a host of institutes which support different research projects, such as *la Universidad de Valle's Centro de Estudios en Salud* (Center for Health Studies), *Centro de Investigaciónes en Ingenieria Civil y Ciencias de la Tierra* (Center for Research in Civil Engineering and Earth Sciences), and *Centro de Investigaciónes Arqueologicas y Anthropologicas* (Center for Archeological and Anthropological Research) to name a few. Additionally, many institutions in other countries work jointly with counterparts in Guatemala to conduct academic research, including the Kaqchikel Resource Center at the University of Kansas, the *Programa Cooperativo para el Desarrollo Sostenible de los Recursos Naturales y la Conservación del Medio Ambiente* (the Cooperative Program for the Continued Development of Natural Resources and the Conservation of the Atmosphere) between the Universidad del Valle and Texas A & M University and the *Instituto de Nutrición de Centro America y Panama* (Central America and Panama Institute for Nutrition). As the effects of globalization continue to impact Guatemala and the surrounding area, the number of collaborative projects will likely increase.

Each university in Guatemala offers a series of conferences, symposia, or other events that allow scholars from within and outside of the country to share insights on problems affecting the region. Seminars related to matters of health, medicine, technology, and natural disasters (particularly earthquakes) can be found at the universities. Moreover, the country's rich Mayan heritage allows for many research projects related to anthropology, archaeology, and cultural studies, which attract researchers from all over the world. The Office of the Ministry of Education also works with institutions from other countries to offer different types of teaching and research exchange programs through its *Departmento de Coordinación con Organismos Internaciónales* (Department of Coordination with International Organizations).

In addition to research and teaching programs which exist primarily for the benefit of citizens in Guatemala, many Spanish language-intensive schools exist, particularly in the capital city. Adult students from the United States, Europe, Asia, and other countries find Guatemala an excellent place to learn or refine their Spanish language skills. Most of these schools, some of which are coordinated through programs in other countries, provide students with immersion in Latin American culture, the opportunity to live with a Guatemalan family, and an excellent way to learn conversational and business Spanish. As of 2000 there were at least five such programs located in Guatemala.

TEACHING PROFESSION

Like the United States and most other progressive countries, Guatemala recognizes the importance of preparing good teachers for the classroom. However, because teachers' salaries in the country are not good, and since teaching conditions are often difficult due to lack of physical resources, the teaching profession does not always attract enough well qualified educators. This problem is also exacerbated by the linguistic differences found in the far northern and southern areas of the country.

All prospective teachers must obtain the *bacherilloto*, with an emphasis on teaching, to enter the classroom. Teachers in Guatemala are referred to as *profesors*.

SUMMARY

Education in Guatemala has undergone much transformation since the ratification of the constitution in 1986. Increased attention to curriculum, multiculturalism, and social responsibility has strengthened the quality of education in Guatemala substantially. However, several future challenges still remain.

First, the government of Guatemala is committed to reducing illiteracy among its populace. Efforts to unify the nation in a common language, Spanish, is part of this directive. Not only does the Ministry of Education seek to improve Guatemalans' reading ability, but it remains determined to enhance students' background in other basics such as mathematics and foreign language.

Second, the government of Guatemala identifies the need to move its schools further into the information age by strengthening instruction in topics related to globalization and multiculturalism. Thanks to the Peace Accord Agreement of 1996 and a constitutional mandate to promote pluralism, the schools in Guatemala are making noteworthy progress toward this goal. Guatemala can continue to move forward by building and maintaining close educational ties with the United States and other countries in the Central America, Europe, and Asia.

Finally, Guatemala recognizes the importance of devoting more resources to its educational endeavors. Like many other countries, teachers in Guatemala are not highly paid, and technological innovations are slow to move into the country's rural schools. The current educational budget is inadequate for advancing widespread educational programs in the smaller cities and mountain areas. Increased internal funding, more participation from parents, more support from the private sector, and continued alliances with other countries will help bring about an even stronger commitment to moving all Guatemalan classrooms into the twenty-first century.

The government and people of Guatemala represent a strong commitment to learning, teaching, and developing. Guatemala's partnership with the United States and the world community at large demonstrate an exceptional willingness to assertively improve the quality of its education. With hard work, ingenuity, and continued support from its neighbors, Guatemala promises to take the lead in educational reform in Central and Latin America.

BIBLIOGRAPHY

Embassy of Guatemala to the United States. *Culture and Education,* 2001. Available from http://www.guatemala-embassy.org/.

Guatemala's Country Profile, 2001. Available from http://www.quetzalnet.com/.

The Latin America Alliance. *Guatemala,* 2001. Available from http://www.latinsynergy.org/.

Latin America Network Information Center, the University of Texas. *Guatemala,* 2001.Available from http://www.lanic.utexas.edu/.

Universidad de Valle de Guatemala, 2001. Available from http://www.uvg.edu.gt/.

U.S. Department of State, Bureau of Western Hemisphere Affairs. *Background Notes: Guatemala,* 2001. Available from http://www.state.gov/.

—*William J. Wardrope*

GUERNSEY

BASIC DATA

Official Country Name:	Guernsey
Region:	Europe
Population:	64,080
Language(s):	English, French, Norman-French
Literacy Rate:	NA

The state of Guernsey comprises not only the English Channel island of that name but also two smaller islands, Sark and Alderney. Like its larger and more populous neighbor, Jersey, Guernsey has drawn benefits from its location between Great Britain and France. Originally a part of Normandy, the Channel Islands became attached to Britain at the time of the Norman Conquest in 1066 and were separated from Normandy in 1204. Guernsey reported a 1998 population of 51,458 people.

Guernsey's education system closely resembles that of the United Kingdom, although a few differences exist. A student's educational career is divided between a primary school, of which there are 10 on the islands, and a secondary school. Education is conducted in English, which is almost universally spoken, although French receives significant emphasis as well. The curriculum includes English, mathematics, science, French, history, geography, art, and music.

Six government-administered secondary schools serve Guernsey's students, although academic accomplishment determines in which of these schools an individual student will be placed. Guernsey, unlike the United Kingdom, still utilizes the 11-plus system through which students performing at a particular level upon completion of middle school are awarded scholarships to the Grammar School or to one of two colleges— Elizabeth College for boys and the Ladies' College for girls. In 2001, the 11-plus system was under review following continued criticism from parents and others.

Students who do not score well enough to earn a scholarship may, after payment of tuition, attend the appropriate college or the Catholic Blanchelande Girls' College. These colleges, although not a part of the government-run education system, do receive their funding from the government.

No institution of higher education exists on the islands aside from the vocationally oriented College of Further Education, which means university-bound students must attend school elsewhere.

—*Mark Browning*

GUINEA

BASIC DATA

Official Country Name:	Republic of Guinea
Region:	Africa
Population:	7,466,200
Language(s):	French
Literacy Rate:	35.9%
Academic Year:	October-July
Number of Primary Schools:	3,723
Compulsory Schooling:	6 years
Public Expenditure on Education:	1.9%
Foreign Students in National Universities:	45
Educational Enrollment:	Primary: 674,732 Secondary: 143,243 Higher: 8,151
Educational Enrollment Rate:	Primary: 54% Secondary: 14% Higher: 1%
Teachers:	Primary: 13,883 Secondary: 4,958 Higher: 947
Student-Teacher Ratio:	Primary: 49:1 Secondary: 29:1
Female Enrollment Rate:	Primary: 41% Secondary: 7% Higher: 0.3%

HISTORY & BACKGROUND

The Republic of Guinea lies on the western coast of Africa. With an area of 94,900 square miles, it is bordered by Senegal and Mali on the north, Côte d'Ivoire on the east, and Liberia and Sierra Leone on the south. The population of 7,600,000 people (January 2001 estimate) is composed of four major tribal groups: 35 percent Peuls (Fulani), 30 percent Malinke, 20 percent Susu, and 14 percent Kissi. French is the official language, but several tribal languages and dialects are also in use. Guinea is 85 percent Muslim, 8 percent Christian, and 7 percent Animist. With a per capita Gross Domestic Product of $1,180 (in 2000), it is one of the poorest nations of Western Africa.

For more than 100 years, Guinea was part of the former French Colonial Empire. It became a protectorate in 1849, a colony in 1898, and a constituent territory of French West Africa in 1904. When France granted independence to its former African colonies in 1958, it also offered a continuing economic, political, and educational relationship with the newly created *Communauté,* the French equivalent of the British Commonwealth. Guinea was the only former colony that refused such a partnership. After a nationwide referendum, it severed all ties with France and proclaimed its independence as the republic of Guinea on 2 October 1958. Its first president-for-life, Achmed Sékou-Touré, established a single party state, where neither political diversity nor any form of opposition were tolerated. To disengage the country from its former colonial past, Sékou-Touré adopted a radical africanization program that rejected Western values. Guinea soon became an isolated, struggling nation that turned to the former Soviet Union for technical aid. In a sense, the history of the educational system of Guinea is closely tied to its political history and efforts to separate itself from its former colonial occupant. But even after 1960, France still loomed large over the economy and cultural life of its former West African colonies. Efforts to abolish French as the official language of instruction to the benefit of local dialects proved to be a failure, as French remained throughout West Africa the language of diplomacy, commerce, and education. Severing ties with Western Europe also had a catastrophic impact on Guinea's economy, and the promotion of a brutally repressive regime controlled by Sékou-Touré did little to foster a climate in which new educational policies and reforms could flourish. Sékou-Touré died in 1984 after 26 years of unopposed dictatorship, having finally restored closer ties with France in 1975. Colonel (later general) Lansana Conté then seized power and has been Guinea's unopposed leader for the past 17 years. The political climate has improved since diplomatic and economic ties were restored with France and Western Europe. Opposition parties were permitted, and free elections were held in the early 1990s. A 114-member National Assembly was democratically installed in June 1995, representing 21 political parties. Though the nation is still poor, Guinea's economy has shown dramatic improvement after French corporations undertook the rehabilitation of the country's infrastructure, and the Paris Club of Creditor Nations agreed to significant debt relief in the late 1990s.

CONSTITUTIONAL & LEGAL FOUNDATIONS

The constitution of 1958 guarantees free, compulsory, and equal education to every citizen until the age of 15. However, the legal and constitutional foundations of the educational system have been undermined by an early Socialist-inspired plan that often resulted in decrees being directly handed down from the executive branch of the government without any consultation or debate with qualified experts.

EDUCATIONAL SYSTEM—OVERVIEW

Guinea set a precedent when it became the only former French colony of West Africa to sever ties completely with its past colonial framework. Everything it did, from its economy to its revolutionary educational system, was closely watched as a new African experiment in the making. The French educational system, which had been in place for more than 100 years was dismantled. Western teachers in the primary and secondary schools (including most Catholic missionaries) and French faculty members in higher education were summarily dismissed. French as an official language of instruction was replaced by native dialects, and the new curriculum reflected the president's predilection for socialist educational philosophy. Only the Koranic schools in this mostly Muslim nation were exempted from this radical restructuring of curriculum and objectives. New pedagogical directives were handed down directly by government officials, such as the 1959 decree (number 49) from the *Ministère de l'Education Nationale* (National Ministry for Education) that spelled out the new ethnocentric policy of radical africanization.

Ultimately, the results proved to be a disaster, and, 20 years later, Guinea lagged behind every other francophone African state that had retained the French pedagogical model. By 1985, a national educational conference held in Conakry, the capital, made public these findings:

- The use of vernacular languages in Guinean education was a failure, mostly because of the lack of standardized syntax and appropriate textbooks.

- The majority of teachers in the primary and secondary schools were poorly trained or unqualified.

- Budgetary restrictions compelled secondary schools to remain open without proper sanitation, equipment, or educational materials.

- Educational planning was ineffective, and the current administration was often unqualified.

Guinea gradually restored its economic and political ties with France in the late 1970s. After Sékou-Touré's death in 1984, most of his socialist educational philosophy and plans for africanization of the curriculum were abruptly abandoned. Though his successor, General Conté, still rules by decree, decisions affecting educational reforms are delegated to qualified professionals. Conté's government has launched two major educational reforms:

Le Plan d'Action Intermédiaire (Intermediate Plan) of 1984 stipulated the following directives:

- A national program of teacher training and in-service training would be immediately implemented.

- Major government funding would be allocated to build new schools and to provide much-needed equipment.

- French was restored as the official language of instruction at all educational levels.

The National Educational Policy Document of 1989 assessed the progress made during the intermediary period between 1984 and 1989 and recommended the implementation of the following steps to meet Guinea's needs: budgetary allocations for education must be increased to represent at least 20 percent of the national budget and, in order to combat illiteracy more effectively, the admission rate for the first year in primary school must be brought up to represent at least 50 percent of the eligible population. Also, by the year 2000, the national education budget was supposed to designate at least 40 percent of its resources for primary education, according to the Policy Document. These reforms were adapted and incorporated in the PASE, or *Programme d'Ajustement Sectoriel de l'Education* (National Education Adjustment Program), which became the reference policy document for the educational reform of Guinea through the year 2000.

PREPRIMARY & PRIMARY EDUCATION

The primary and secondary educational systems are basically carried over from the French national system, which had been implemented in all former colonies of French West Africa. The school year runs from September to July. Officially, primary education begins at the age of seven and lasts for six years. Children from urban areas typically enter primary school around age six, while their counterparts from rural areas may wait until they are almost nine years old.

In 2000, there were 790,497 students enrolled in 4,289 primary schools. Of these, only 39.8 percent were girls. (The disproportionately low percentage of girls and women is an anomaly that is found at every level of public education in Guinea, from primary school to graduate and professional education. The same trend is evidenced among primary and secondary school teachers. It worsens considerably in higher education where the percentage of women shrinks below 5 percent of the faculty. Traditional societal roles, exacerbated by the fact that 85 percent of the population is Muslim, are the most frequently cited explanations for this discrepancy.) These pupils were taught by 17,340 teachers, with 1 teacher for every 45 students. At the primary level, teaching is focused on preparing the majority of students to enter the workforce as quickly as possible. At the end of the sixth grade, the test for the *Certificat d'Etudes Primaires* (Ele-

mentary School Certificate) is administered to all students. Only those who pass the CEP are allowed to continue into the secondary school system (in 2000, the passing rate was 53.2 percent). This elitist system is directly inherited from the French public school system. It creates an early division and orientation between students continuing on to an academic program and those going to technical or vocational schools.

SECONDARY EDUCATION

The secondary school cycle is divided into 2 parts. The first (grades 7-9) leads to the *Brevet d'Etudes du Premier Cycle* or BEPC (Junior High School Certificate). Those who pass this exam are allowed into the next cycle of secondary education (grades 10-13) leading to the *Baccalauréat* (High School Diploma). Those students who fail the BEPC or the *Baccalauréat* are directed into the workforce or to vocational and technical schools. In 2000, there were 129,987 students enrolled in the first part of the secondary school cycle (37.5 percent of them female), taught by 3,782 teachers, with a teacher/student ratio of 1:34 (20 percent female). In the second part of the secondary school cycle (post BEPC), there were 66,665 students enrolled, taught by 1,741 teachers in 399 *lycées* (academic-track high schools) and *colleges* (secondary schools with a more technical orientation for students who will not continue at the university level). At that stage, 21,900 students had left the academic track and were enrolled in 64 vocational schools with a teaching staff of 1,510, including adjunct faculty.

After 12 years of compulsory education, the number of Guinean students eventually accepted into a university represents only 1.8 percent of the total population of primary school students. The secondary school curriculum is diversified. Though it retains a central core of subjects common to both the pre- and post-BEPC cycle (French, geography, history, sciences, mathematics, and principles of economics), it incorporates technical and vocational subjects in grades 7 through 9. This provides an applied source of knowledge and skills that can be utilized by those who do not continue their studies beyond the BEPC. In grades 10 through 13, the curriculum shifts to more academic subjects and incorporates social studies, political science, and philosophy.

HIGHER EDUCATION

Higher education in Guinea closely follows the French national system. The names of the two universities and research institutes in Guinea reflect its political past since the country chose its independence from France in 1958. The largest university, l'Université Gamal Abdel Nasser in Conakry, was founded in 1962 and named after the former Egyptian dictator to whom

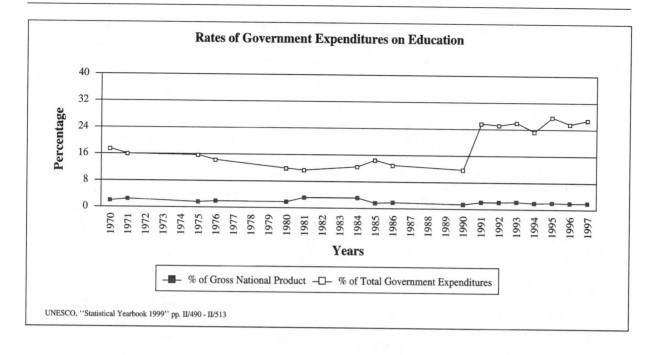

Rates of Government Expenditures on Education

Years

— ■ — % of Gross National Product — □ — % of Total Government Expenditures

UNESCO, "Statistical Yearbook 1999" pp. II/490 - II/513

Sékou-Touré had turned for help during the first republic. In 2001, this university enrolled 8,360 students and employed 401 full-time faculty members (including 24 women). It is composed of the School of Arts and Humanities, the School of Law, the School of Medicine and Pharmacy, the School of Science, and the Polytechnic Institute. It also includes two attached research centers: the Center for Environment Study and Research and the Computer Center. The main diplomas awarded are *Licence* (B.A. or B.S.), *Diplôme d'Etudes Supérieures* (DES) (M.A. or M.S.), and the *Doctorat* (Ph.D., or M.D.). The *Licence* usually takes three years of study, the DES one or two additional years, while the *Doctorat* requires three to four more years beyond the DES. The M.D. degree is a six-year curriculum that begins after the *Baccalauréat*. Admission to the programs of study offered by the university is granted upon successful completion of the *Baccalauréat* and a selective application process.

The University of Kankan is Guinea's second institution of higher education. Initially founded in 1963 as a research institute, it was elevated to university status in 1987. Kankan offers degrees mostly in arts and sciences. In 2001, it enrolled 2,304 students and employed 93 faculty members (including only one woman). At the instructor and assistant professor levels, the teaching staff is mostly comprised of Guinean nationals, while the higher echelon of the faculty is made up of foreigners from France and other French-speaking countries.

There are three main research institutes. One institute is the *Institut Supérieur Agronomique et Vétérinaire "Valéry Giscard d'Estaing,"* (the School of Agricultural Sciences, Forestry, and Veterinary Medicine), founded in 1978 and located in Faranah. In 2001, it enrolled 2,222 students and employed a faculty of 116 (without any women). The Institute was named after the former French president who was instrumental in restoring ties with Guinea. The second is the Advanced Institute of Education at Maneah with 501 students and 71 faculty members (including 4 women). The third institute is the School of Mines, located in Boké, with 769 students and 19 faculty members (no women). Guinea also has eight research institutes, including the *Institut de Recherches en Animaculture Pastoria* (the former Pasteur Institute, founded in 1923 and nationalized in 1965), a National Museum, the National Archives, and a National Library known for its special collection on slavery. All are located in Conakry.

ADMINISTRATION, FINANCE, & EDUCATIONAL RESEARCH

The government of Guinea considers education one of the most important issues facing the nation. In March 1998, the 16-member cabinet of Prime Minister Sidya Touré included cabinet-level posts for national education and scientific research, pre-university teaching, communication and culture, and technical education and training. Supervision of secondary education is carried out by the *Ministère de l'Enseignement Pré-Universitaire et de la Formation Professionelle* (MEPU-FP), which is the National Headquarters for Secondary Education and Vocational Training. It oversees curriculum decisions, administrative and financial affairs, personnel, and the administration of national tests and examinations. Primary schools are inspected by local school inspectors, while secondary schools are inspected by officials from the National Education Institute. There are 5 regional school districts, 33 prefectoral divisions, and 310 sub-prefectoral units. The *Comité National d'Education de Base* (CONEBAT), which is the National Committee on Basic Education, is empowered with the supervision of educational reforms and their implementation until the year 2000. In 1996, the Guinean national budget was $947 million, of which 27.5 percent was allocated for education, with half that amount going to teachers' salaries (68 percent for primary schools, 13 percent for secondary schools, 13 percent for vocational and technical schools, and 6 percent for teacher training.) Of the other half of the educational budget, 25 percent is spent on higher education and 25 percent on administrative costs.

NONFORMAL EDUCATION

Illiteracy is an ongoing problem that the Guinean government addresses through regular nationwide campaigns. While progress has been made, the percentage of illiterates among the adult population is still among the highest in West Africa. In 2000, adult literacy rates were 36 percent for males and 22 percent for females. There has been an effort to promote literacy in the national and tribal dialects, but that rate still does not exceed 50 percent.

TEACHING PROFESSION

Recruitment and training for primary school teachers is carried out at the five normal schools located in each of the five major school districts. Candidates who have successfully passed the BEPC follow a 2- to 3-year curriculum. Vocational school teachers are trained in the *Centres de Formation Professionelle* (Vocational Training Centers), where they enroll in a curriculum preparing them for technical, industrial, or health-related fields. Secondary school teachers are recruited selectively by the National Education Institute located in Goyah and Manarah. In-service training courses for primary school teachers are routinely conducted by local school districts and are planned at the regional level. The number of qualified primary school teachers has increased from 7,165 in 1980; to 11,352 in 1996; and to 17,340 in 2000.

SUMMARY

The educational system of Guinea has experienced many difficulties since the country declared its independence in 1958, with the majority of these being related to ideological and political interferences. With the adoption of more democratic policies, the situation has improved. Now back to an educational system that is largely copied from the French national model, Guinea has accomplished much in the area of research and higher education. However, the top priorities for the next decade remain the improvement of the literacy rate for the adult population, an increase in primary and secondary school enrollments, the adequate training of qualified teachers, proper funding of the educational budget to represent at least 40 percent of the national budget, and an increase in the participation of women at all levels of the educational system, including staff and faculty.

BIBLIOGRAPHY

Annuaire Statistique, 1999-2000. Conakry, Guinée: Service de Statistiques et de Planification. Ministère de l'Enseignement Pré-Universitaire et de l'Education Civique, 2000.

Binns, Margaret. *Guinea.* Santa Barbara: Clio Press, 1996.

Développement de l'Education, 1994-1996: Rapport National de la République de Guinée. Conakry: Ministère de l'Education Nationale, 1996.

Genre et Fréquentation Scolaire au Primaire en Guinée. Brighton, UK: Institute of Development Studies, 1997.

Livre de Référence sur l'Education en Matière de Population en Guinée. Conakry: Institut Pédagogique National, 1992.

—*Eric H. du Plessis*

GUINEA-BISSAU

BASIC DATA

Official Country Name:	Republic of Guinea-Bissau
Region:	Africa
Population:	1,285,715
Language(s):	Portuguese, Crioulo
Literacy Rate:	53.9%

Located primarily on the western coast of Africa (and including the archipelago of Bijagoz), Guinea-Bissau has approximately 1,000,000 inhabitants. As a colony of Portugal, education was originally the province of Roman Catholic missionaries, who followed the governmental policy of assimilating indigenous peoples into European culture. Upon liberation from Portuguese rule in 1974, the *Partido Africano da Independencio da Guine e Cabo Verde* or PAIGC (African Independence Party) established broad educational goals for the country that included the elimination of illiteracy, free compulsory education for ages 7 through 14, and the provision of technical/professional training.

The educational system currently has 2 main levels—primary and secondary. Primary education represents 6 years (ages 7 through 12) of free, compulsory, basic schooling divided into elementary (4 years) and complementary tiers (2 years). In 1994 approximately 64 percent of children were receiving a rudimentary education in primary school. Secondary education consists of two types: a 3-year general-secondary stream (grades 7 through 9) and 2-year postsecondary education (grades 10 through 12); and 3-year vocational programs. The National *lycee* Kwame N'Krumah includes grades 7 through 12, while other *lycees* include only grades 7 through 9. Upon completion of grade 9, students can attend the National School of Physical Education and Sport or the School of Law. Vocational training is available for students who have completed Grade 6 and wish to take courses in vocational-technical training such as mechanics, construction, and agribusiness. Since the agrarian economy is predominant, there is a focus on vocational-technical education to improve the country's economic status and offset the effects of widespread poverty. There is one agricultural college—the residential School of the Comrades Institute in Boe—that offers a three-year course following graduation from Grade 6.

Since there are no universities in the country, students seeking tertiary education must go abroad, typically to Cuba, Portugal, Eastern European, and neighboring African countries. In addition, nonformal night courses in basic education aimed particularly at illiterate adults were added to the formal educational system beginning in the late 1960s. By 1982, literacy courses in Creole and other national languages were being developed.

Although the PAIGC supports education as the right of every citizen, illiteracy remains high. Despite the fact that the official language of instruction is Portuguese, 90 percent of the inhabitants speak Creole and/or other native dialects. In 1991, the illiteracy rate stood at approximately 68 percent. With the introduction of mass literacy programs, UNESCO estimates the average rate of adult illiteracy had declined by 1995 to 45.1 percent.

Educational problems include the lack of educational facilities, teaching resources, and equipment, as well as transportation difficulties. In particular, Guinea-Bissau's inability to hire qualified educational personnel has been detrimental to the PAIGC objective of providing a culturally and economically relevant education that meets national needs. Like many emerging nations, the educational system still displays vestiges of the former colonial system (found most notably in the *lycee*).

The Commissariat of State for National Education and Culture is the chief educational policy-making agency. For the period 1990-1991, the education budget was 300 million pesos (US$60,240), amounting to six percent of the GNP.

BIBLIOGRAPHY

Carneiro, Roberto, and Jeanne Marie Moulton. *An Outline of the Educational System in Guinea-Bissau.* Paris: UNESCO, 1976.

Darcy de Oliveira, Rosiska, and Miguel Darcy de Oliveira. *Guinea-Bissau: Reinventing Education.* Geneva: IDAC, 1976.

Leal Filho, W.D.S. *ronmental Problems and Structural Development in Africa: Cultural Challenge.* Geneva: UNGLS, 1991.

Mendes-Barbosa, Julieta. ''Framework for Educational Reform in Guinea-Bissau: The Choice of Language of Instruction (Africa)''. Ed. D. diss., University of Massachusetts, 1990.

—*Jayne R. Beilke*

GUYANA

BASIC DATA

Official Country Name:	Republic of Guyana
Region:	South America
Population:	697,286
Language(s):	English, Creole, Hindi, Urdu
Literacy Rate:	98.1%
Number of Primary Schools:	420
Compulsory Schooling:	8 years
Foreign Students in National Universities:	38
Educational Enrollment:	Primary: 102,000 Secondary: 62,043 Higher: 8,965
Educational Enrollment Rate:	Primary: 96% Secondary: 75% Higher: 11%
Teachers:	Primary: 3,461

Student-Teacher Ratio:	Primary: 29:1
	Secondary: 29:1
Female Enrollment Rate:	Primary: 96%
	Secondary: 78%
	Higher: 12%

HISTORY & BACKGROUND

The Republic of Guyana, formerly British Guiana, lies between Suriname and Venezuela on the northern coast of South America. Brazil lies on the southern border. More than 90 percent of Guyana's population of almost 800,000 people occupy an arable coastal range 40 miles wide. Guyana's ethnic mixture and educational system are the result of the country's colonial economy. Early plantation owners brought in African slaves. When slavery was abolished in 1838, indentured workers became the main source of cheap labor. The largest number came from India, and their descendants now comprise nearly half the population. Afro-Guyanese make up a third of the population, and the remainder consists of Amerindians, Asians, and Europeans. Nonetheless, Guyana's official language is English.

Public schools, operated by religious organizations, began to appear in the early 1800s. Elementary schools flourished under the direction of the London Missionary Society, and in 1876 primary education became compulsory for children aged 6 to 14. Textbooks were prepared in the United Kingdom favoring continental history and literature. All the examinations were given in Great Britain. Technical education was not available. Trades were learned solely from an apprenticeship to a journeyman. Until the University of Guyana was established in 1963, those seeking higher education had to attend universities abroad.

The educational system underwent major reform in 1961, when the government assumed control of the schools and established the Ministry of Education. Gaining independence in 1966, the country inherited a well-established educational system, but its curricula and educational aims were patterned after the British system. The government introduced changes to align the schools with the country's political goals, ethnic blend, and economic needs. In 1976, private education was abolished and education became free from nursery school through the university. Anyone, no matter their income, could attend school. The Constitution of 1980 guaranteed everyone the right to continuous education and training. Those attending high school would choose between academic, academic and technical, and vocational high schools. The government also established trade schools, which offered job training in such fields as engineering and construction.

With these improvements in place, the literacy rate rose above 95 percent, but conditions in the schools were far from ideal. In the 1970s, schools became overcrowded, and teachers who resisted government efforts to make all teachers teach loyalty to the government and its socialist objectives were fired. Truancy and illiteracy increased. As teachers departed and conditions deteriorated in the schools, scores on the Caribbean-wide examinations vastly dropped.

Guyana's economic troubles in the 1980s, combined with the government's commitment to finance free public education, led to underfunding of the schools. The quality of education declined even further. The school structures were neglected, educational materials became scarce or nonexistent, and equipment deteriorated. Teachers' salaries were poor, and as supply budgets dwindled, so did the number of trained teachers, many of whom sought positions out of the country to escape political oppression and job insecurity. In 1989, the government introduced an Economic Recovery Program, turning from a state-controlled, socialist economy toward a free-market system. By 1999, improvement in education was among the government's top priorities of the government. Teachers' salaries have been raised and new schools are being built, reflecting an upturn in the country's struggling school system.

CONSTITUTIONAL & LEGAL FOUNDATIONS

The mission of the Ministry of Education was to give all Guyanese children equal access to a quality education. The Minister of Education was a political appointee with a seat on the President's cabinet. In 1980, the educational system was decentralized somewhat when it was divided into 10 regions, each with its own council in charge of schools. Each region was headed by a Regional Democratic Council made up of members appointed by various political parties. The Regional Executive Officer was responsible for all the school services in the region, but a Regional Education Officer, appointed by the Ministry of Education, overseen day-to-day operations and prepared the education budget. By 1985, the 10 Regional Democratic Councils were in charge of constructing and maintaining schools, recruiting and paying teachers, and ensuring that schools operated according to regional and national objectives.

The University of Guyana, the country's only university, receives most of its funding from the Minister of Finance and is separate from the rest of the education system. The Guyana School of Agriculture was incorporated in 1962 and empowered to teach the theory and practice of agriculture and to manage, develop, and operate farms. It also conducted experiments and research. The Kuru-

Kuru Co-operative College, founded in 1973, provides courses in cooperative education and management techniques. It also combines technical assistance to Guyana's neighboring countries with courses in business administration, cooperative socialism, and ideological teaching.

The country's educational system has four levels: nursery, primary, secondary, and postsecondary. The government, along with certain private groups, also provides education for the handicapped and mentally deficient and has training programs in several vocational fields, including home economics, automotive mechanics, and other technical fields. All instruction is in English, and the average student must complete the six-year Primary course and two years of secondary education. The statutory age for entering school is five years nine months, and students are usually expected to remain in the school system until age 16. Those who leave the school system early may participate in a number of adult education programs offered by the University of Guyana, the Institute of Adult and Continuing Education, or the Adult Education Association.

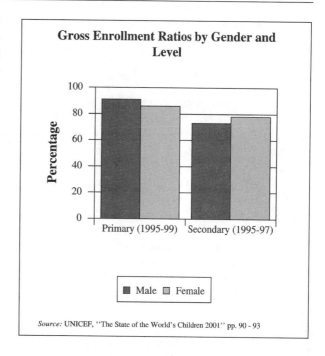

Gross Enrollment Ratios by Gender and Level

Source: UNICEF, "The State of the World's Children 2001" pp. 90 - 93

PREPRIMARY & PRIMARY EDUCATION

Of Guyana's 386 nursery schools, more than 200 are in rural areas. Children are admitted at three years nine months and may remain in the system for two years. Although nursery education is not compulsory, each Guyanese child is guaranteed a place in school, with attendance remaining above 70 percent and continuing to increase. This, despite the fact that transportation is difficult in many cases, fewer than half the teachers are trained, and the school buildings are often makeshift and in poor condition. The nursery program is intended to encourage physical, social, emotional, and intellectual development; teach basic skills; and instill the desire to learn. The hours of school are from 8:30 a.m. to 12:00 noon. Guyana's nursery school teachers are responsible for teaching more than 50,000 children. The student-teacher ratio is 17:1.

In primary school, children receive instruction in basic literacy and arithmetic. Guyana's 426 primary schools administer more than 100,000 pupils who have reached the age of five years and nine months. The student-teacher ratio is 29:1. Students attend school five hours per day from Monday to Friday, usually from 8:30 a.m. to 3:00 p.m., with a lunch period from 11:30 a.m. to 1:00 p.m. The school year lasts from September to July, followed by a six-week vacation at the end of the third term. Each term is 13 weeks long, and a school year has 189 days.

SECONDARY EDUCATION

At the end of primary school, students take the Secondary School Entrance Examination (SSEE) to determine which type of secondary school they will attend; all secondary schools offer an academic program along with prevocational courses. Students who score poorly on the examination continue their education in the secondary department of the primary school, which has a four-year program. Those with higher scores go to a community high school, and top scorers qualify for general secondary school. Both higher schools have a five-year program. Students who continue in secondary departments of primary schools and those who enter community high schools take another proficiency examination at the end of Form 3 (Grade 9). Successful candidates qualify for transfer to a general secondary school; unsuccessful candidates remain in their original placement.

Students in all the secondary schools receive instruction in English language and literature, French, art, Spanish, the sciences, geography, history, nutrition, music, and physical education. In the first three years, they are given prevocational courses as well, such as arts and crafts, agriculture, home economics, and industrial arts. General secondary school gives students a wide choice of educational and professional opportunities while preparing them to take the Caribbean Examination Council (CXC) examination or London General Certificate of Education (GCE), or both. Students who perform well at these examinations qualify for university admission or may pursue studies for the GCE advanced level examination, needed to qualify for higher education out of the country. A multilateral school program within the general high school emphasizes preparation for the CXC examination. It takes an average student five years to prepare for the CXC and an additional two years to prepare for the GCE advanced level examination.

HIGHER EDUCATION

Postsecondary education is provided by the University of Guyana, which has seven faculties besides programs in law and medicine. Full-time classes for the majority of students began in 1973, the same year the first graduate program began. The Faculty of Education offers a Master's degree and a certificate in nursery education. Other faculties include agriculture, arts, health sciences, technology, and social sciences, which has updated its curriculum to include women's studies. An Amerindian unit is now part of the university, and students can earn a Master's degree in Guyanese and West Indian history. Most of these programs are four years long. The semester system became university-wide in 1974, when students began paying tuition. Tuition for two semesters is about US$1,000. Medical school costs about US$2,000, and a year in law school costs about US$3,500. The enrollment today is more than 4,600 students, with a student-teacher ratio of 12:1.

Technical and vocational education may be obtained at a number of institutions. The Georgetown Technical and New Amsterdam Technical Institutes specialize in trade courses, such as carpentry, plumbing, welding, and bricklaying, and courses in mechanical and electrical engineering, building and civil engineering, surveying, and telecommunications. Students may earn a certificate or diploma in commerce and secretarial science as well. The Guyana Industrial Training Center also offers a course in masonry, mechanics, and other trades. The Carnegie School of Home Economics specializes in household management and catering. These adult-education programs are regulated by the University of Guyana and the Adult Education Association, which collaborate with and receive funding from the Ministry of Education.

In 1976, the Institute of Adult and Continuing Education was inaugurated primarily as a center for study and research in adult education and for training teachers of adults and administrators of adult education programs. In 1996, the Institute included distance education in its curriculum to train teachers in Guyana's rural areas. The Guyana School of Agriculture, which prepares students to teach agriculture or to work as managers or field assistants, covers natural science and economics and the practical aspects of farming and animal science. The school accepts students from Guyana and other countries, some of them from Nigeria and Zimbabwe. More than 2,000 students enrolled between 1963 and 1982, about 20 percent of them female. Graduates may continue their education at the University of Guyana, and some obtain employment in the Ministry of Agriculture.

Several non-university institutions accommodate a wide variety of groups with special needs. The Government Technical Institute accepts both males and females and offers full-time, part-time, and evening courses in general education, trade training, and science and technical training.

ADMINISTRATION, FINANCE, & EDUCATIONAL RESEARCH

The largest portion of Guyana's education budget, more than 70 percent from 1992-1994 went to the nursery, primary, and secondary schools. In the same period, the University of Guyana received 16 percent, and the rest of the budget was distributed among teacher training, vocational and technical, and other institutions. Educational institutions also received financial assistance from non-government sources. Many families purchase uniforms, books, and supplies for their children, and in some cases travel and boarding expenses. Community organizations donate cash, and some employers support training outside the workplace. In 1995, for example, the budget for education was 6.6 percent of the national budget. Of this amount, 5.5 percent came from the government; 14.0 percent came from external sources; almost 22.0 percent came from household expenditures, and another 7.4 percent was provided by employers. The educational system also receives loans from the Inter-American Development Bank.

Research remains an important part of Guyana's educational community, which strives to stay up to date on environmental issues, energy sources, social developments, and other concerns of a nation in the process of economic recovery and educational and intellectual growth. At the University of Guyana, research is required for promotion and has focused on local issues, such as environmental radioactivity, oral traditions, socialism, and migration. Subjects relating to the Caribbean area and the Third World generally are researched, and staff members participate in international research projects.

The Institute of Applied Science and Technology and the National Science and Research Council research ways that technology may be used in the handling of the country's natural resources, including solar energy. Researchers at the Guyana School of Agriculture study, among other subjects, the development of egg-grading equipment and foreign livestock feeds. The Institute of Adult and Continuing Education has done research on the needs of the elderly. Many research projects are financed by other countries in the form of donations, student sponsoring, and the support of staff development with scholarships to study or train abroad.

NONFORMAL EDUCATION

Though not part of the formal educational system, several institutions are important adjuncts to it. The Board of Industrial Training, sponsored by the Ministry of Labour, is responsible for the apprenticeship and in-plant training of workers. The Private Aircraft Owners Association operates a training center for pilots and aircraft engineers. Other large and medium-sized companies have established training centers to develop skilled workers in, for example, computing, accounting, business, electronics, and mechanics. A number of schools are devoted to teaching children with learning disabilities and those with physical handicaps. Many churches, parent associations, community groups, and business organizations also have become involved in education. Further education is conducted informally by various government agencies, trade unions, cooperative societies, youth clubs, and adult-education groups. Since the 1980s a parallel system has developed alongside the Ministry-controlled system of education. In response to the shortcomings of the educational system, parents began hiring competent teachers to tutor their children. The practice spread throughout the educational system and has become an important adjunct of the educational system, despite its negative implications.

TEACHING PROFESSION

Teachers are trained principally by the Cyril Potter College of Education, which offers a two-year program for those entering the nursery and primary schools and a three-year program for those aiming to become secondary or vocational teachers. To be accepted, all applicants must pass four subjects (which must include English and mathematics) on the CXC examination or a qualifying level on the General Certificate of Education examination. A fee is required, and each student must agree to serve the government for five years after graduation. Certification requires 85 percent attendance in all subjects, and the course lasts 20 hours a week. Programs include such topics as study skills and the teaching of reading, and lectures are given on the English language, mathematics, music, and moral education and guidance. Gender-free teaching skills and gender sensitivity training are also part of the curriculum.

Graduates earn a teaching certificate from the Cyril Potter College of Education. Between 1995 and 2000, more than 2,200 trained teachers graduated from this college, though many of them chose to teach in private schools or in foreign countries, attracted by higher wages and better working conditions. Female students are the majority in the college, especially in the nursery, primary, and secondary programs. The college also has programs for untrained teachers and programs for upgrading teachers in the remote areas of the republic.

Teachers may also be trained at the University of Guyana, which offers courses in education that lead to a diploma, bachelor's degree, or a master's degree. The university works closely with the Cyril Potter College, and both programs are supervised by the Ministry of Education, which also places graduates. The Lilian Dewar College of Education, which specializes in training secondary teachers, was founded in 1968 in response to the growing need for secondary teachers.

SUMMARY

Throughout the 1980s and 1990s, Guyana's educational system underwent a dramatic decline. As political and economic conditions worsened, many teachers left the country, seeking better pay and greater job security. Schools fell into disrepair and mismanagement became widespread. A democratic government and an improved economy have led to educational reform and many enhancements. Budget allocations to education steadily increased in the 1990s. Teachers were given substantial salary increases, although by the year 2000, teachers were still paid as little as US$100 per month. New schools were being built, and school management has improved.

Although government funding has increased in recent years, the education system is still under funded, and government expenditures on education remain low when compared to education funding in neighboring countries. In 1990, for example, middle-income Latin American countries spent nearly 16 percent of their budget on education, whereas the Guyanese government spent only 4.2 percent. The consequences of under funding are serious. When teachers are poorly paid, the education system cannot attract and keep qualified teachers. Under funding has also been responsible for a lack of learning materials and adequate learning facilities. Nearly a third of the community high schools, when surveyed in 1995, did not have library books. In regional school districts, management is inefficient and poorly supervised. The Ministry does not know how educational funds are actually spent. In the Ministry itself, low pay and understaffing have reduced its efficiency and effectiveness. Teacher training remains the weakest link in the system. As of 1994, approximately 55 percent of the nearly 2,000 nursery school teachers in Guyana had not passed the examinations required of teachers. In the interior regions, the percentage of unqualified teachers was above 80 percent.

The effect of these conditions on student performance is reflected on test scores. On the Secondary School Entrance Examination, scores were consistently low in the 1990s. Performance on the CXC examination was equally disappointing. The number of students qualifying for the University of Guyana has declined to a point where faculty, laboratories, and workshops are underused. Poor attendance is also widespread in primary and secondary schools, and schools face the problem of increasing violence and the lack of discipline, which is said to be the reason for an average attendance of 65 percent. The use of illegal drugs, vandalism, fighting among students, attacks on teachers, and cheating on exams have compounded the problems school officials face. In the remote regions, the language used in school is often not the same as the language spoken in the home. Government expenditures favor secondary and higher education, whereas primary education is in greater need. As a result of these and other weaknesses and inequities, a student entering primary school now has only a 4 percent chance of reaching the university.

The government has employed a number of ways to improve the educational system. One of those measures is the Guyana Education Access Project I, a five-year project funded by the United Kingdom to help provide equal access to all Guyanese children and young people to quality education, focusing on secondary education in two disadvantaged regions. The Secondary School Reform Project is part of a multiphased program whose goals include developing a common curriculum for Forms 1-3, providing textbooks and instructional materials, furnishing school libraries, and promoting community participation. Twelve schools are to be refurbished and others will be given emergency repairs. The project also aims to improve organization and management of schools. The National Plan of Action has also been established to meet the specific needs of Guyana's children by improving the quality of day care centers and primary schools, improving access to them, and teaching literacy and math skills to those who have left school without this education.

At the center of all recommendations for educational reform is the need for adequate funding. With it, teachers would be better trained and those who graduate from the schools would join the public school system and remain. Curricula need to be updated to address the needs of the poor; more women are needed in the technical fields, more schools are needed, and more of the ones in operation need to be repaired. Better management in all areas of the system would help solve many problems associated with funding. Allocating funds equally among the regions is one of the priorities of reform. Perhaps the most promising element in Guyana's struggle to improve its educational system is the willingness on the part of national leaders and educators alike to acknowledge the need to reform. They have identified specific areas where reform is needed and are determined to achieve their goals.

BIBLIOGRAPHY

Abrams, Ovid. *Metegee: The History of Guyana.* New York: Ashanti Books, 1997.

Bacchus, M. K. *Education for Development or Underdevelopment: Guyana's Educational System and Its Implications for the Third World.* Waterloo, Ontario, Canada: Wilfrid Laurier University Press, 1980.

Bray, Mark, ed. *Ministries of Education in Small States: Case Studies of Organization and Management,* 1991.

Brill, Marlene Targ. *Enchantment of the World: Guyana.* Chicago: Children's Press, Inc., 1994.

Country Watch.com, 2000. Available from http://www.countrywatch.com.

"Education Policy Document: State Paper on Education Policy, Guyana." Ministry of Education and Cultural Development, 1995.

Fletcher, Gem, Lynette France, and Iris Sukdeo. *Higher Education in Guyana: University of Guyana.* Venezuela: CRESALC-UNESCO, 1987.

"Guyana: From Economic Recovery to Sustained Growth." Washington, DC: The World Bank, 1993.

Samaroo, Noel K. "The Political Economy of Education in Guyana: Implications for Human Rights." *Journal of Negro Education* 60 (4) (Fall 1991): 512-23.

Singh, Chaitram. *Guyana: Politics in a Plantation Society.* New York and London: Praeger, 1988.

Spinner, Thomas J., Jr. *A Political and Social History of Guyana, 1945-1983.* Boulder and London: Westview Press, Inc., 1984.

Tsang, Mun C. *The Financing of Education in Guyana: Issues and Strategies.* Inter-American Development Bank, 1997.

University of Guyana Home Page, 2001. Available from http://www.sdnp.org.gy/uog/about/html.

Watson, D., and C. Craig, eds. *Guyana at the Crossroads.* New Brunswick and London: Transaction Publishers, 1992.

Wickremasinghe, Walter, ed. *Handbook of World Education: A Comparative Guide to Higher Education & Educational Systems of the World,* 1991.

Williams, David, et al. *Privatization versus Community: The Rise and Fall of Industrial Social Welfare in Guyana,* 1998.

—*Bernard E. Morris*

H

HAITI

BASIC DATA

Official Country Name:	Republic of Haiti
Region:	North & Central America
Population:	6,867,995
Language(s):	French, Creole
Literacy Rate:	45%
Academic Year:	September-October
Number of Primary Schools:	7,306
Compulsory Schooling:	6 years
Educational Enrollment:	Primary: 555,433 Secondary: 143,758 Higher: 6,288
Teachers:	Primary: 26,208 Higher: 654

HISTORY & BACKGROUND

Haiti did not become an independent republic until 1804. The western half of the island that Columbus baptized Hispaniola in 1492 was a French colony known as Saint-Domingue. Haitian education or society cannot be understood today without examining its past, since the sources of all Haitian institutions lie in its history.

At one point there was exclusivity of education in the colony, where all human effort on the plantation was committed to the exploitation of the land. The agrarian economy's awesome demands in time and energy, the roughness of life in an environment deprived of all commodities, and the brutality of a colonial system that depended for survival on oppression precluded any interest in structured education. Creole or freedmen, the rich planters, who themselves rarely laid claim to even an average education, relied on the mother country for the education of their children, while African slaves were forbidden access to literacy.

Anyone who would put a book in the hands of a slave incurred the risk of heavy penalties. Beginning with the Black Code of 1685, in the reign of Louis XIV, the official position of French authorities was that educating servants had the potential to turn loyal servants into rebels. The colonists feared that once educated, the servant population would challenge their authority, would seek reparations, or worse even, would organize to overthrow their régime.

Since sedition had to be stemmed, Africans were kept in a state of abysmal ignorance. Hilliard d'Auberteuil summarizes the rationale behind this attitude: "The interest and safety of the colony demand that we subject the black race to such contempt that anyone whose origins can be traced back to that race will be covered of an indelible stain down to the sixth generation."

The French Governor of Martinique added to this argument: "The safety of the whites demands that we keep the Negroes in the most profound ignorance." In addition to the fear of revolt, there was a pervasive belief that Africans lacked intellectual qualities, as well as the potential for "progress and perfectibility." Montesquieu, the great philosopher of the Enlightenment, who utilized his sharp wit against slavery, alluded ironically to the opinion prevailing among his contemporaries that the people of Africa possessed inferior faculties, that their cognitive apparatus was not open to knowledge on a human scale, and that, consequently, trying to teach them anything would be pointless.

The Black Code in Article 2, nonetheless, provided for some religious instruction, not on humanitarian grounds, but rather from a need to keep the slave population under control. The Black Code did not achieve its goals, however, since only a few colonists chose to use it as a guide. The majority kept all instruction, religious or otherwise, from the slaves. Most administrators in Saint-Domingue believed that the more educated the slaves, the more difficult it was for them to accept their condition. There were, nonetheless, those who defied the oppressive policies and surreptitiously arranged for their slaves to learn how to read and write, not always because it was fair but, above all, because it was practical. The more educated the slave, the more helpful he could be. It is a known fact that some plantation owners not only encouraged practical training with a view to higher productivity, but also favored more than a rudimentary education, especially when their subject was a *nègre à talent* (a talented black). These slaveholders believed their investments would pay off when the servants would fulfill functions beyond the work of the land. This was the case with the master of Habitation Bréda, the plantation on which Toussaint Louverture was born.

Louverture was given not only a religious education in Catholicism, but he also learned French, Latin, geometry, drawing, as well as the medicinal virtues of plants. Thanks to his knowledge of herbs, he was able to serve the plantation as medicine man and veterinarian. Later, Louverture became the steward of the Bréda livestock and coachman to his master and, subsequently, joined the French Army as a scout, where he rose through the ranks to become General and finally Commander-in-Chief of Saint-Domingue.

Another case in point is Henry Christophe, a slave who worked as a waiter in a public hotel of Cap Français in Saint-Domingue and was given an education. Christophe later became king of Haiti. These are only two examples of a small privileged group that was fortunate enough to find educational opportunities in the colony.

The forced process by which the African slaves were integrated into the colonial community is another fact that will help post-independent Haiti. This brutal adaptation aimed to discourage a reversal to the native culture, therefore eliminating any rivalry between the old structure and the new one. Its purpose was to ensure the highest loyalty to Creole society and to subject the African to an internalization of French superiority. It was at once a mechanism of defense and an economy of force. The conquest of the mind was needed to consolidate power over a submissive population that outnumbered the colonists and that might one day revolt.

The colonial authorities created an intricate social system based on complexion and adhesion to French culture. With few exceptions, the lighter-skinned individuals occupied the higher echelons of the social ladder. Since these individuals were also French, French language and culture conferred a higher social status. At the bottom of the ladder, the black population, though more active and productive, was heavily taxed for lacking the qualities of a light complexion and a knowledge of French. Blacks were left with no other option but to pursue the ideals of language and culture that were set for them. They did so more or less enthusiastically. It was a stigmatizing experience that left its mark on Haitian society to this day. What added to the trauma was that, in order to motivate a quick acculturation, plantation owners offered the Africans a system of rewards that ranged from a simple reduction of their duties to the granting of freedom.

Religion was also used in acculturation. Baptism was the first step toward assimilation and, once baptized, African slaves became *nègres créoles* (Creole Blacks), a mark of distinction that carried privileges and denoted their status of being in the colony for some time, and therefore were worthy of everyone's trust. By contrast, the newly arrived, *nègres bossales* (wild, untamed blacks) were supposedly primitive, because they were still attached to traditional African cultures. The most demeaning tasks were assigned to the *bossales* who were constantly derided and harassed by the *nègres créoles* and punished by their masters. Brainwashing, indoctrination, derision, and the whip were the methods used to force Creole culture on the African and to suppress all African traditions brought to the colony.

Acculturation did not entail a systematic teaching or learning of the French language. Having lost their original languages, the Africans were not given opportunities to learn French. Instead, a simplified language that had grown out of the pidgins of triangular trade was adopted by masters and slaves alike. This language, like the people who spoke it, was and is still called Creole. Because of the humiliation associated with its history, it never gained favor with the Haitians, even though it has been the only language available to them throughout their history.

When the Haitians won their independence in 1804, they entered the world with a legacy of ignorance. They had neither a structured system of education nor a strategy to fight illiteracy. Even Toussaint Louverture, when he was Governor of Saint-Domingue, showed no interest in changing the status quo. The Constitution of July 8, 1801, for instance, had no elaborate plans for public instruction. In addition, Haitians had inherited two major handicaps: elitism and the powerful presence of French in their cultural landscape.

CONSTITUTIONAL & LEGAL FOUNDATIONS

Independence completely changed the political outlook of the new republic. At last, Haitians were in power and had the opportunity to build a nation that responded to the needs and aspirations of its citizens. As expected, public instruction was at the top of the new government's priority list. It is interesting to note how consistently thereafter presidents and legislators have attended to this important issue. Indeed, if the short-lived imperial constitution of Jean-Jacques Dessalines reflected no real passion for the subject, all other charts drafted subsequently made education a pressing matter in the country's administrative programs. The reason for this sustained interest is, of course, the realization that progress depends on education.

These decrees, for all their good intentions, never resulted in a real system of education over a period of two hundred years. Several reasons account for this state of affairs:

- political instability

- lack of financial resources

- absence of a pragmatic mentality seeking to identify the public to be served

- a failure to match resources with needs

- discord over the details of an appropriate educational system

To exacerbate these evils, mass education continued to be an object of suspicion, as one dictatorial régime after another felt the need to protect itself against an ignorant populace that, if literate, would be more effective and dangerous. Throughout the nineteenth century and until the 1980s, decrees on education took the character of simple formalities that no one cared to implement or they were drafted without interest in the peasant, Creole-speaking majority of the Haitian population.

Henry Christophe, the King of Haiti, made a serious attempt to organize public instruction, as attested by his constitutional act of February 17, 1807. The single most important item of the act is the mandate to create a central school in every *arrondissement*. The importance of this mandate lies in the fact that it was a proclamation of freedom to teach, and it invited competent individuals to open schools. But the difficulty with this act was that the country lacked competent teachers who could either create the schools or teach in them. Christophe opened an Academy in Cap-Haitien with the help of Haitian and foreign teachers, but it was for the families of public employees.

More interesting was Pétion's Constitution of 1816, which stipulated the universal right to a free education and ordered each *commune* to open free public institutions to the school age population; this constitution was the most durable that Haiti ever had. It lasted until 1843

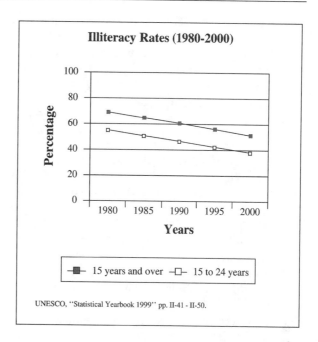

Illiteracy Rates (1980-2000)

UNESCO, "Statistical Yearbook 1999" pp. II-41 - II-50.

and, with a slight modification in 1846, it was still in force in 1867. If one considers that the constitution of Haiti was rewritten at least 20 times in the past 200 years (1801-2001), Pétion's constitution shows an incredible endurance that guaranteed a period of stability and growth for Haitian institutions. It is in this 50-year period that public instruction had the best chance to evolve. With the help of Haitian and foreign educators, Pétion himself had founded a *lycée* in Port-au-Prince as well as a *pensionnat* (boarding school) for girls.

Compulsory education was decreed in July 1852 and again in the constitution of 1874. But at those times, neither the empire of Faustin Soulouque nor the short-lived government of Michel Domingue was able to provide the resources necessary to implement such an ambitious plan. Again, these documents fell in the category of abstractions that served no purpose.

Another important document is the *Concordat* of March 28, 1860, signed by President Geffrard with Pope Pius IX. It involved an agreement with the Vatican to send Catholic educators to Haiti to help with the establishment of parochial schools. Basically, what it entailed was the promotion of the Catholic Church and the education of young men and women who would devote themselves to religious life. This agreement resulted in the establishment of a seminary in Port-au-Prince. Other schools followed and soon there were private Catholic schools in all departments and major cities of Haiti. The Fathers of the Holy Spirit and the Christian Brothers were the first to participate in this missionary endeavor.

The *Concordat* could only go so far to help Haitian children. To be sure, a small number were selected for a general education, whether or not they had a predilection for clerical life. Others were turned away. The private Catholic schools would compete with free public institutions, since parents would be inclined to send their children to the more exclusive schools. Finally, the European could not give young Haitians an education rooted in the reality of their land. The consequence was a widening of the gap between the masses and the educated elite.

Nevertheless, the 1860s witnessed an unprecedented growth in Haitian education. President Geffrard organized the Medical School, founded a School of Music and a Law School. He sent several teacher trainees to Europe to remedy the shortage of teachers. He founded or reorganized several *lycées* around the country, especially in Jacmel and Gonaïves. He created special secondary schools for both genders. By 1872, a remarkable intellectual elite was ready to assume the leadership of the nation. Boards of education were formed as well as a Corps of Public Instruction Inspectors. Primary schools multiplied in the cities and in the countryside.

All these accomplishments were due to a period of economic prosperity in Haiti. The United States, engaged in a war at home (1861-1865), needed cotton and other products, so they bought products for a good price from Haiti. Still, the educational system provided little that could be considered relevant to the masses of Haitians. Vocational schools were not considered necessary at the time, even though it would be helpful in promoting light industry.

The 1880s brought several educational achievements that were decreed and successfully realized. President Salomon reorganized the *lycées,* invited a group of French professors to join the teaching faculty, and opened a sizable number of rural schools for the first time. These schools were so successful that plans were made to promote them further around the country, but the government of Salomon was overthrown.

Apart from the foundation of the State University of Haiti in 1960, no major developments took place either in new constitutions that followed Salomon's government or in occasional decrees. It is now clear that, with regard to education, new governments have only built on their predecessors' accomplishments. Fortunately for the Haitian people, public instruction is the only area where subsequent versions of the constitution have not defeated one another.

The constitution of 1983 brought a fresh set of ideas to the public. For years, there had been a public outcry for relevancy in Haitian education. Since the 1940s, advocates for education in Creole (as the only way out of the linguistic dilemma that plagued Haiti) launched one campaign after another. In the 1970s and 1980s, U.S.

lending institutions eager to see change in Haiti posed certain conditions to the government before they made more money available.

In August 1979, a conference in Port-au-Prince was convened to debate the issue of Haiti's elitist, French system of education, which excluded 90 percent of its population. The question before the conference was whether to relegate French to the background and multiply literacy programs in Creole. In addition, the issue of vocational schools was considered by the conference. Then-minister of education Joseph C. Bernard informed the delegates that the government had approved Creole as a language of instruction. Soon thereafter, a law signed by the head of state formally approved of Creole as a vehicle of communication in the classroom and as a subject matter. Then, with the financial support of the World Bank, the president authorized four years of experimentation to test the idea. This process involved 1,000 children studying all subjects in Creole for the first four years of primary school. French was also offered as an ordinary subject, the first two years being scheduled for the speaking skill in French, while the third and fourth years were reserved for reading and writing. Finally, in the fifth year, the pupils received instruction in French. The program was an absolute success until members of the ruling class, fearing that they would lose privileges associated with proficiency in French, demanded that the program be discontinued. The president, eager to maintain his political base among the ruling class, fired the minister and canceled the Creole program in July 1982. Yet, the new constitution of 1983 made French and Creole national languages even though French remained the official language of administration, law, and education.

EDUCATIONAL SYSTEM—OVERVIEW

In the past decade, school schedules have not been uniform because of the addition of privately run schools modeled on American and other systems and the need for schools to adapt to the recent suburban phenomenon. Also, the increase of the school-age population and the lack of personnel, facilities, and equipment have prompted the schools to switch from a full six-hour day to a half-day of four hours. This strategy enabled the schools to serve two groups of pupils a day.

In general, the academic year begins in October and ends in July. With two vacations at Christmas and Easter, the number of hours in the school year is considerably reduced. Those parents who can afford it pay for private lessons in subjects where their children show the greatest need. Competent teachers who are poorly remunerated depend on tutoring to make ends meet and sometimes earn more this way than by regular means. In the more traditional schools, children are admitted at age six and are expected to complete the primary cycle in six years.

Secondary school takes six more years that lead to the first part of the *baccalauréat* (equivalent of the high school diploma), followed by one more year of study leading to the second part. This system, which is based on the Napoleonic Code, was imported in Haiti by the Concordat and was never reviewed since, even though the French themselves have given it up in the rise of the student protests of May 1968. French remains the language of instruction in the private schools, but Creole and French are used in the public schools.

Students are subject to three sets of trimestrial examinations a year, plus finals in July. The grading system on 10 points is rigid. A grade average of 5 points is required to pass a class. In general, schools are not technologically-equipped. Mediated facilities do exist, however, in a few business and professional schools. Textbooks have always been a concern. Mostly imported, they are often in short supply and their price, like all imported products, can be prohibitive for families who must strive to put food on the table. Many children go to school without books. In addition, the books are not adapted to the Haitian environment. The Haitian system of education is heavily influenced by its French counterpart.

The efforts of Haitian governments to educate their people may seem sincere but, so far, they have not yielded remarkable results. A serious reform is in order that will treat education as a true instrument of progress and development. Education does not appear to be focused on the specific needs of the country. From the outset, the orientation taken by the administration of public education had nothing to do with the reality of Haiti except for the fact that it served the particular interest of an elite who sent their children to study in France and considered themselves French.

In talking about Haitian education, there has been a tendency to focus exclusively on the formal system of education designed for the urban elites who only represent a small minority of the Haitian community, while ignoring the fate of more than 80 percent of the population in the countryside. It is imperative to redefine the scope of Haitian education to rectify this error.

PREPRIMARY & PRIMARY EDUCATION

In formal education, children four to six years of age go to the *jardins d'enfants* (kindergarten) or to the *enfantin* in the private schools. Traditionally, only families that could afford to pay for this stage of their children's education would consider it at all; these families usually live in the city. The decree of 1982 has not changed that situation, even though it stresses the democratic principle of universal accessibility. Once again, the immense majority of children are left out of the process while a generous system of laws is in place. In addition, the 1990s have

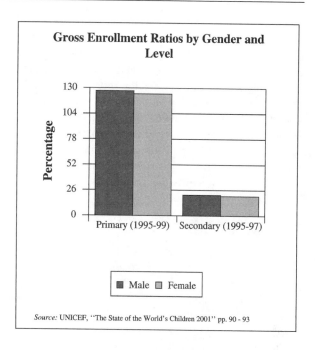

Gross Enrollment Ratios by Gender and Level

Source: UNICEF, "The State of the World's Children 2001" pp. 90 - 93

witnessed a proliferation of preprimary schools, but they were created for the rich and exist purely for mercantile purposes. In the traditional primary schools, pupils study French grammar, arithmetic, world history, world geography, Haitian history, Haitian geography, religion, civic instruction, introduction to sciences, drawing, and physical education. In rural schools, where instruction is given in Creole, a basic reading, writing, and arithmetic package is offered with the other subjects added depending on availability of personnel. Final examinations passed satisfactorily permit access to the next higher grade.

In public schools, classrooms are overcrowded. A class may hold between 70 and 80 children. The facilities are dilapidated and offer no security, comfort, or hygiene. There is often no water, no electricity, and no recreational space. In rural areas, the situation is even worse since children must walk for one or two hours to go to school. The teachers in those areas function irregularly, being often late or absent, because they face the same hurdles as their pupils. In 1998-1999, some 16.44 percent of all schools were public schools and 83.60 percent were private. It should be understood that private schools have outnumbered public schools consistently since 1975, partly because of the Protestant schools created in the country for humanitarian purposes and partly because of the entrepreneurial schools that have sprung like mushrooms in the past two decades.

There are 6,111 primary schools. The school-age population is estimated at 3,000,000 and only 800,000 can be accommodated, although with difficulty. Therefore, 2,200,000 children are left out. These numbers do not take into account the normal evolution of the school-age population, which every year increases by 150,000 to 200,000 people. Out of 100 children who enter the traditional primary school, 67 will finish the fourth year of the cycle. Of these, 42 will give up school entirely to become functionally illiterate for the rest of their lives. A growing number of children are unable to read or write after four years of schooling. Each year 68 percent of school age children (mostly in rural areas) cannot find a school in which to enroll. More boys than girls are enrolled, but enrollment of girls, which has maintained itself at 46 percent across the board for several years, is growing faster than enrollment of boys.

SECONDARY EDUCATION

The traditional secondary cycle either at the secondary public school or at a private college provides six years of study in a track that features the classics or one that emphasizes the sciences with several subject combinations possible. Subjects available in secondary school are French grammar, French literature, Haitian literature, English, Spanish, Latin, Greek, algebra, geometry, human biology, chemistry, physics, zoology, botany, world history, Haitian history, world geography, and Haitian geography. An additional year after the first part of the *baccalauréat* gives instruction in philosophy. This seventh year of study ends with part two of the *baccalauréat*.

The *lycées* and *collèges* of the provinces are as good as those in the capital city, but there are too few secondary schools. In 1998-1999, only 635 institutions, both public and private, all located in urban areas, were open around the country. Of these, 107 were public, and the other 528 were private. To be sure, the needs are not as pressing as they are on the primary level. Out of 100 children who began primary school, only 25 went to secondary school. Less than three reached the year before the *baccalauréat*. Only one (out of 100) ever achieved the second part of the *baccalauréat*. With all levels, classes, and types of schools taken into account, the chance of survival in the Haitian system of education is a little less than 1 percent. Other alarming statistics put the number of graduates at 26 out of 1,000 and the attrition rate at 87.5 percent.

It is interesting to observe that whatever the rate of success at the *baccalauréat,* some schools (private, parochial) always register between 80 and 95 percent success with their candidates. Of these, more than 50 percent are girls. The reason for this success is clear: the system was designed by and for these schools. In addition, they have the resources, the faculty, and the virtues necessary to lead their students to success.

HIGHER EDUCATION

The university system is composed currently of four or five private institutions in addition to the State University of Haiti, which admits 2,000 students every year out of 13,000 to 16,000 applicants. The others receive 3,600 applications a year even though they can only take 1,780 students. The private universities have an attrition rate between 25 and 80 percent. All the institutions are located in the capital city. They offer a degree in law, medicine, pharmacy, dentistry, engineering, agriculture and veterinary sciences, education, social sciences (mainly ethnology and psychology), economics, business administration, linguistics, international studies, and African studies.

At this level, also, relevancy remains a concern. The formation given to young scholars in Haiti seems to prepare them better to live and work in foreign countries than in their own. The content of the curriculum is not defined according to the needs of the nation. In general, the higher education system shows all the faults of the other levels: centralization, French orientation (a conscious effort is made to establish equivalency with the University of Paris for degrees granted by the University of Haiti), elitism, and insufficiency.

TEACHING PROFESSION

Teachers are trained mainly at the *école normale supérieure* of the State University of Haiti where they enroll in a three-year program that includes a concentration on the subject or subjects of their choice and training in teaching strategies. There are at least six teachers colleges around the country. A large number of teachers in the Haitian school system make less than 500 gourdes a month. (The exchange rate is approximately 20 gourdes per US$1.) Another unfortunate fact is that 90 percent of them are not prepared for their task. Teaching is not a very attractive profession in Haiti because it is by all accounts the least appreciated of occupations; those who choose it anyway do so very often because of necessity. Attrition among teachers is extremely high. Yet, teacher colleges are still too few, and their instruction is not uniform. There are no research centers. Testing and assessment instruments are not designed to be of any real help to the system.

SUMMARY

For 200 years, the Haitian system of education has been a failure because it neglected the people it was intended to serve. Instead, it favored an influential minority who identified more with France than with Haiti; it was used as an instrument by politicians and the ruling class to maintain power and privileges at the expense of monolingual Creole speakers. In colonial times, Haitians were stripped of their African identity and were taught in the most violent way to define themselves as sub-products of French culture and society.

Even after independence, the only model Haitians had to start building their new nation was the French model. Even though the majority could hardly speak French, and even though Dessalines and Toussaint Louverture addressed their troops in Creole, the only language Haitians had when talking to the world or negotiating formal situations was French. Creole had not gained the status it enjoys today; those who spoke it were not inclined to use it any other way but informally. Furthermore, Creole had become an object of degradation in the eyes of most Haitians. Later in history, French became an instrument of oppression sustained by the educational system. Citizens had no choice but to play the game. Families that wanted their children to succeed in life sent them to school so they could learn French and other subjects in French, but the children failed because to succeed in the schools they had to be fluent in French. Since most of them spoke no other language than Creole, the system of education sacrificed thousands of them for two centuries.

The tragedy of the Haitian system of education is due for the most part to the linguistic dichotomy that characterizes Haiti. Because the declarations of principles to compulsory education failed to address the language issue, they amount to no more than an exercise in futility. Not until the 1980s were solid measures initiated and supported by the government. In fact, a whole reform was launched in education at that point. It featured education in Creole, a more effective rural school system, a more effective basic education system, better teacher training, a literacy program, the creation of an inspection and supervision agency, rational timetables, and experimentation to test the new ideas. Although the world of education was elated to hear the announcement of these long-overdue reforms in 2001, one still does not see any real change. The *Livre ouvert sur le développement endogène d'Haïti,* a collective work of analysis that tries to tackle the country's problems for ordinary citizens, mentions, among other disappointing statistics in education, the continuing high attrition rate, the extremely high rate of failure in the *baccalauréat,* and the extremely high illiteracy rate.

BIBLIOGRAPHY

Brutus, Edner. *L'instruction publique en Haïti.* Port-au-Prince, 1948.

Desroches, Rosny, and Pierre-Raymond Dumas. "Autour de quelques problèmes du système éducatif Haïtien." (Interview of Rosny Desroches by Pierre Raymond Dumas) in *Conjonction: Revue Franco-Haïtienne, No. 168.*

Girod, François. *La vie quotidienne de la société créole.* Paris, 1972.

Gouraige, Ghislain. *La Diaspora d'Haïti et l'Afrique.* Ottawa, 1974.

Lafontant, Julien J. *Montesquieu et le problème de l'esclavage.* Sherbrooke, 1979.

Pierre, Webster, Gabriel Nicolas, and Wilfrid Joseph. *Livre ouvert sur le développement endogène d'Haïti.* Port-au-Prince, 1999.

Salien, Jean-Marie. "Francophonie et sous-développement: Aspects Historiques et Sociolinguistiques du Français en Haïti." In *Contemporary French Civilization,* 1981.

Trouillot, Hénock. "L'instruction publique sous Pétion." In *Le Nouveau Monde,* December 20-23, 1983.

Vernet, Pierre. "Quelques Réflexions Méthodologiques sur l'enseignement du Français en Haïti." In *Conjonction: Revue Franco-Haïtienne,* No. 168.

Weinstein, Brian, and Aaron Segal. *Haiti: Political Failures, Cultural Successes.* Stanford, CA, 1984.

—*Jean-Marie Salien*

HONDURAS

BASIC DATA

Official Country Name:	Republic of Honduras
Region:	North & Central America
Population:	6,249,598
Language(s):	Spanish
Literacy Rate:	72.7%
Academic Year:	February-November
Number of Primary Schools:	8,114
Compulsory Schooling:	6 years
Public Expenditure on Education:	3.6%
Foreign Students in National Universities:	521
Educational Enrollment:	Primary: 1,008,181 Secondary: 203,192 Higher: 54,106
Educational Enrollment Rate:	Primary: 111% Higher: 10%

Teachers: Primary: 28,888
                                  Secondary: 10,203
                                  Higher: 4,078

Female Enrollment Rate: Primary: 112%
                                  Higher: 9%

HISTORY & BACKGROUND

Honduras is a Central American nation that shares borders with Guatemala, Nicaragua, and El Salvador. It has coasts on both the Atlantic and Pacific oceans. More than three-fourths of the 29,236-square mile country is mountainous. In 1997, its population was over 6 million. Five major cities include Tegucigalpa (the capital), San Pedro Sula, La Ceiba, Puerto Lempira, and Santa Rosa de Copán. Ninety percent of Hondurans are *mestizo* (a mixture of Spanish and Indian), 6 percent are Indian, and more than 2 percent are of African descent. Of these many are Black Caribs (*guarifunas*), who are of both Indian and black stock. The country, which already had one of the lowest per capita incomes in Central America, was decimated in 1998 by Hurricane Mitch, probably its biggest natural disaster ever.

In 1821 Honduras won independence from Spain and joined the Central American Federation, to which it belonged until it became a separate, independent country in 1841. Honduras has shifted from democratic to dictatorial governments, but in 1981 civilian rule returned. There are 18 provinces (*departamentos*) in the country, each with its own governor.

Under Spain, as in most Central American countries, Honduran education was an enterprise of the Roman Catholic Church. Normally, the richest families had access to the best education in or outside the country. For many years, most Hondurans attended universities in nearby Central American countries. Formally, education was recognized as a national enterprise in 1880, when a new constitution was approved; in 1881 an Act of Education was promulgated.

At the end of the nineteenth century, Honduras had already established the nondenominational character of public education, although it did provide some financial support for private (Roman Catholic) schools. Education got another boost at the beginning of the twentieth century when several normal schools (teacher training schools) were established. But advances were minimal from government to government. Recently, at the end of the twentieth century, the government of Ramón Villeda Morales established a more credible educational system and began to construct new schools.

The biggest enemy of both public and private education in Honduras is extreme poverty. Most Hondurans live below the poverty level, and many migrate to the United States and to other Central American nations in search of better living standards. It is unfortunate that one-fifth of the population controls more than half of the combined income of all of the families in Honduras.

CONSTITUTIONAL & LEGAL FOUNDATIONS

The 1982 Honduran constitution stipulates laws and regulations related to education in articles 151 to 171. Primary education is free and obligatory. Honduran nationals must teach the constitution, history, and geography of Honduras in public schools. Public education is nondenominational, and parents can choose whether to send their children to public or private schools. The state charges schools with the tasks of eradicating illiteracy, promoting special education, and insuring adherence to prescribed academic levels. In rural areas, farm or factory owners must establish new primary schools as needed or help support poor schools. Teachers, both active and retired, are tax-exempt.

Articles 160 to 162 address higher education and establish the National Autonomous University of Honduras (*UNAH*) as the official state agency that governs most laws and regulations pertaining to higher education, including setting its own academic standards. By law, the state allocates 8 percent of its national budget to the university. In addition to what is established in the constitution, the government of Honduras has issued other decrees on education, such as the 1966 Organic Law and the 1973 National Commission for Educational Reform Report. All of these reports, laws, and statutes strengthen the central position of the government in the Honduran educational system.

EDUCATIONAL SYSTEM—OVERVIEW

Schools in Honduras fall in four categories: preprimary, primary, lower secondary, and upper secondary. The Secretary of Public Education is the chief administrator. The Ministry of Education supervises the writing and publication of textbooks and is in charge of distributing them throughout the country. The curriculum is the same for the whole country and, following the spirit of the country's constitution, education inspectors make regular visits to insure that syllabi and textbooks are used and implemented properly. The inspectors also visit private schools.

Private education has flourished in the last third of the twentieth century. Unlike in other countries, private schools do not have as much academic prestige in Honduras, where they have the reputation of being little more than moneymaking enterprises. Despite the schools' lower academic standards, wealthy families like to send their children to the private schools because they still convey higher social status.

To pass any academic subject, students must achieve at least the 60 percent mark. They can repeat the same course several times during the year, but low achievers may be required to repeat grades. Education is compulsory from ages 7 to 13, and after finishing primary education, students are required to teach two adults in literacy. Dropout rates are high in both primary and secondary education, especially in the rural areas. While more than 90 percent of students enroll in primary schools, less than half complete their studies. Of those who do finish primary school, only one-third goes on to secondary schools. There are six universities in the country, led by the National Autonomous University in Tegucigalpa.

Although French and German are taught in some private institutions, the most popular language in both the private and the public systems is English. Most students, however, do not achieve the proficiency standards set by the state. The Internet, as a classroom tool, is slowly making its way into many Honduran schools, especially in urban areas. It is used the most at the main university in Honduras.

In the late twentieth century, the educational system in Honduras struggled with a lack of funds, teacher shortages, poor pedagogic training, and antiquated curricula. These problems were compounded in 1998 when Hurricane Mitch hit the country. An estimated one-fourth of schools were destroyed.

PREPRIMARY & PRIMARY EDUCATION

At age four, children may attend either a public or a private school, and they do so for a period of three years (ages four to six). Preprimary education is divided into three stages: prekindergarten, kindergarten, and preparatory. The Honduran constitution stipulates that preprimary education must be both free and compulsory. In fact, however, very few children (less than 13 percent in the early 1990s) do go to school at this early age, and those who do go come mostly from urban areas. This is because the law forcing compulsory attendance is more strictly enforced in urban areas.

As one might expect, primary school students get a smattering of academics: they learn a few numbers and the alphabet. Most youngsters spend their time playing games and singing songs that are appropriate for their age. However, preprimary teaching goes further than babysitting. Teachers emphasize good behavior and disposition for study.

Primary school lasts six years, and the age level ranges from 7 to 13. More than 90 percent of Honduran children attend primary school, despite a scarcity of

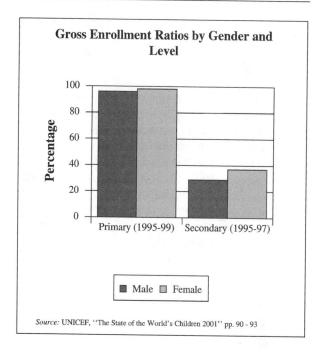

Gross Enrollment Ratios by Gender and Level

Source: UNICEF, "The State of the World's Children 2001" pp. 90 - 93

teachers and inadequate classroom space. In addition, most elementary schoolteachers have poor backgrounds themselves, having had very little preparation in the sciences and in teaching methodology. Primary school teachers concentrate on teaching basic skills, though many instruct students in practical subjects such as agriculture and physical education.

SECONDARY EDUCATION

There are two stages in secondary education: lower and upper. To be accepted in the lower level (equivalent to the American middle school or junior high) students must have completed six years of primary education. In the lower level there are two tracks, called common cycles: the common cycle of general culture and the prevocational common cycle. Both tracks last two years and enroll students from ages 13 to 16. The common cycles prepare students with basic knowledge that they can use either for a vocational career or to move on to the next academic level.

The upper secondary level is called diversified education. It lasts two years, from 16 to 18 years of age. To be accepted, students at this upper level must have completed the general culture common cycle. They can specialize in either sciences or letters. They are awarded the high school degree (*bachillerato*) upon completion of their studies.

Students who opt out of diversified education can enroll in a three-year technical secondary school program, for students ages 16 to 19. Students learn practical skills that prepare them for more vocational training, or they try to get a job. The technical track awards certificates in public accounting, primary teaching, or business. By choosing this option, students can enter the workforce more quickly.

Private secondary schools compete with public ones. There are more than 150 private secondary schools in Honduras, and they cater to the rich and the middle class. A lack of both private and public schools at this level explains why more than two-thirds of students who graduate from primary schools do not continue on to secondary education. Nonetheless, those who do not have access to centers of secondary learning have the option of enrolling in a distance education system. Many who do so, as might be expected, come from rural areas.

There are many specialized secondary schools in the country. They include the School of Fine Arts, the National School of Forestry, the National School of Agriculture, and the National School of Music. Admission to these schools depends upon completion of primary studies.

HIGHER EDUCATION

The National Autonomous University of Honduras, founded in 1847, is the premier institution of higher learning. It became autonomous in 1847, and in the 1990s, more than 30,000 students were enrolled. In addition to the main campus in Tegucigalpa, it has branches in San Pedro Sula and La Ceiba. Other universities include JoséCecilio del Valle University (founded in 1977), Central American Technological University (1986), and the National Pedagogic University Francisco Morazán (1989). This latter institution trains mainly secondary teachers. There is low morale among university professors, as they are poorly paid and receive little encouragement to do research. Most professors are not full time.

To be accepted at the university, students must finish high school and take a general orientation course. There are three stages, or university levels. In the first stage students can, after three or four years of study, earn a university first degree (*bachillerato universitario*) or a licentiate (*licenciatura*). The university usually does not offer master's or doctoral programs, although there are doctoral degrees for medicine, chemistry, and dental surgery.

Most students at the university choose careers in medicine, law, or engineering. To specialize in medicine, students have to work for three years after they complete six years of undergraduate work. Because they have to work full- or part-time, many college students take even longer to finish their degree programs. In addition, many do not get their diplomas at all because they fail the final comprehensive examination.

ADMINISTRATION, FINANCE, & EDUCATIONAL RESEARCH

The Ministry of Education controls all facets of primary and secondary education, although the universities enjoy autonomy. This centralization contributes to the ineffectiveness of the educational system. Too much power is concentrated in Tegucigalpa, and few initiatives are left to provincial (departmental) school officials. The government enacts educational legislation that is handed down to the Ministry to implement in the whole country.

Traditionally, both primary and higher education get a bigger slice of the money allocated. Higher education, by constitutional mandate, gets 6 percent of the national budget. Money for education at the end of twentieth century stood at about one-sixth of the national budget, fluctuating between 14 and 17 percent. Usually, over 90 percent of the education budget is allocated to teacher salaries.

Research activities are very limited in Honduras. And, for the most part, funding comes from outside sources, like UNESCO or other United Nations agencies. Research grants from government sources are very rare. At the universities, professors are not offered any incentives to conduct research activities. A few scientific research projects take place at the primary and secondary levels. Were there more computers, laboratories, and release time, as well as more access to the Internet, teachers and professors could engage in more research.

NONFORMAL EDUCATION

As in most Central American countries, adult education programs focus on three areas: literacy programs, agrarian education and community development programs, and vocational courses. The illiteracy rate in Honduras at the end of the twentieth century stood at about 73 percent. In the rural areas, more than 80 percent of the population was illiterate. Literacy classes are offered by government agencies, the private sector, and religious organizations. The Ministry of Education established an accelerated literacy program for adults so that they can complete their primary education in four years. Agrarian education programs are administered by governmental and international agencies and by private organizations. Honduras has many nongovernmental organizations that offer vocational training and literacy classes. These programs are carried out in cooperation with the appropriate state agencies.

Vocational education spans the three levels: the common cycle, the diversified level, and the university level. The complexity of this education increases from the lower to the higher levels. Also, distance learning is administered by the National Autonomous University of

Honduras and by the National Pedagogic University Francisco Morazán. The courses offered tend to be more academic than vocational. Distance learning students are required to do the same work as students who attend the main campuses.

TEACHING PROFESSION

Primary school teachers must attend three years of the upper secondary cycle in the teacher training schools (*escuelas normales*). After completing the program they are awarded the teaching certificate (*Maestro de educación primaria*). Aspiring teachers for secondary schools have obtained either a *bachillerato* or a Normal School Certificate. Then they go to the *Escuela Superior del Profesorado* (Higher School for Teacher Training), or to the National Pedagogic University Francisco Morazán, or to both. But because there are only a few centers to train secondary professionals, the majority of secondary teachers do not receive proper training, though some seek academic development via correspondence courses.

SUMMARY

The Honduran education system faces several challenges in the twenty-first century. For much of the twentieth century, Honduran students were required to memorize useless or impractical data at the expense of sharpening their reasoning powers and critical thinking skills. To address this issue, educators must update the curriculum and conduct better assessment of student performance. Teacher training and the selection and hiring of teaching professionals are other crucial needs facing significant obstacles. Teachers are paid low wages, they do not have access to effective instructional materials, and their training often does not include the latest technologies and current teaching methods. In addition, there is a scarcity of teachers and many parents prefer to send their children to private schools to gain social status.

Hondurans must also contend with the more immediate and practical difficulties that arose in the aftermath of Hurricane Mitch. The Education Ministry building was flooded, and computers and school records were destroyed. Classes were cancelled for more than three months, and one-fourth of all Honduran schools were lost. Teachers spent their time distributing medicine, working as census takers, and cleaning the streets. Building new schools will remain a high priority for the Honduran education system for some time, and both teachers and students will have to adjust to the new challenges posed by starting over.

BIBLIOGRAPHY

The Economist Intelligence Unit. *Country Report: Nicaragua, Honduras.* London: 1999. Available from http://www.eiu.com/.

Merrill, Tim L., ed. *Honduras, A Country Study.* Washington, DC: Federal Research Division, The Library of Congress, 1995.

Pineda Portillo, Noé, and José Luis Luzón Benedicto. *Honduras.* Madrid: Ediciones Anaya, 1988.

Waggoner, George R., and Barbara Ashton Waggoner. *Education in Central America.* Lawrence, KS: University of Kansas Press, 1971.

World Higher Education Database 2000. Available from http://www.usc.edu/.

WRAL5Online. "Hurricane Wipes Out Much of Honduras' Education System." Available from http://www.wral-tv.com/.

—*Jorge Rodríguez-Florido*

HONG KONG

BASIC DATA

Official Country Name:	Hong Kong
Region:	East & South Asia
Population:	7,116,302
Language(s):	Chinese (Cantonese), English
Literacy Rate:	92.2%
Number of Primary Schools:	860
Compulsory Schooling:	9 years
Public Expenditure on Education:	2.9%
Libraries:	56
Educational Enrollment:	Primary: 467,718 Secondary: 473,817 Higher: 97,392
Educational Enrollment Rate:	Primary: 94% Secondary: 73%
Teachers:	Primary: 19,710 Secondary: 23,536 Higher: 6,504
Student-Teacher Ratio:	Primary: 24:1 Secondary: 20:1
Female Enrollment Rate:	Primary: 95% Secondary: 76%

HISTORY & BACKGROUND

Hong Kong's 646 square miles (1,040 square kilometers) are mostly small, uninhabited islands. Ninety percent of the 7 million people live on about 97 square miles (156 square kilometers) of land—Hong Kong Island, Kowloon peninsula, and the New Territories. The Mongkok section of Kowloon has more than 250,000 people per square mile, making it the most crowded area in the world. About 98 percent of the people are Chinese, most of whom have roots in the Guangzhou area, about 84 miles northwest across the channel on China's mainland.

During the last three decades of the twentieth century, Hong Kong developed into one of the world's leading financial capitals. Hong Kong claims to be the world's eighth largest trading economy, the world's busiest container port, Asia's leading air cargo hub, and the financial and banking center of Asia. Even before its return to the People's Republic of China (PRC) on July 1, 1997, Hong Kong was China's leading trading partner; this relationship has continued to expand. By the opening of the twenty-first century, Hong Kong employed more than 3 million workers in China and was a major investor in the Chinese economy.

After it took control of Hong Kong in 1843, the British colonial government never made much effort to educate the Chinese beyond training clerks and servants. Missionaries, however, did establish schools early. St. Paul's College opened in 1849 to train Chinese to become teachers and clergy. During the remaining of the century, only a small number of Chinese children attended government-sponsored schools. Most attended either private Chinese schools or no school at all.

In 1887, the College of Medicine was founded and, in the early twentieth century, this became a part of the first university in Hong Kong. The colony, however, remained a minor economic extension of the British empire until the 1950s. The victory of communists on mainland China transformed the colony into a dynamic center of economic activity. By 1960, about 2 million refugees from the mainland had escaped to Hong Kong. Some were educated, wealthy business leaders, especially in industries such as textiles and shipbuilding, but the vast majority were poor, uneducated peasants. Living in cardboard shacks in refugee camps and on boats in Hong Kong harbor, the majority of refugees provided a huge pool of workers for basic industries that needed unskilled labor. By the 1970s, Hong Kong businesses were converting from low-skilled industries to electronics, banking, and international trade, which required some basic literacy.

As a result, in 1971 Hong Kong authorities passed the first law requiring compulsory education for children between the ages of 6 and 11. By 1980, free education was guaranteed for children through grade nine, or junior secondary school. Three types of schools were established: government-operated public schools, privately owned and operated but with government aid (aided schools), and privately owned and operated without government aid.

Following the British system, Hong Kong's secondary students (seventh grade) were placed in classes according to their tests scores. This "banding" separated students into academic (science and humanities) and vocational tracks. Band 1 consists of students scoring in the highest 20 percent, and Band 5 is made up of students with scores in the lowest 20 percent. Also taken from the British system was the 6-3-2-2 system: primary school is six years; junior secondary school is three years; senior secondary school is two years; and Form Six (preparation for university entry exams) is two years.

Before the 1980s, there were very few institutions of higher education. The oldest is the University of Hong Kong (HKU) founded in 1911, closely followed by the Chinese University of Hong Kong (CUHK), which was established in 1963. Several universities that existed earlier than the 1980s were originally postsecondary institutions, but not degree-granting university institutions.

In the 1960s about 15 percent of the population had completed senior secondary school. By 1991, the percentage had grown to 44 percent. Attendance at universities also experienced rapid growth, from 15,381 students in 1975 to 60,289 students in 1995. Even with the rapid expansion of education in the late 1990s, about 45 percent of the population aged 25 years and older had not received any secondary schooling.

CONSTITUTIONAL & LEGAL FOUNDATION

Free and compulsory primary school education in Hong Kong began in 1971. By 1978 the government had expanded free education to children up to 15-years-old, covering primary and junior secondary school, grades one through nine. Then in the 1990s, the Hong Kong government analyzed the educational system and set down detailed plans for the twenty-first century. The Hong Kong Board of Education (BoE), which is a statutory advisory body of the Education Department (EdD), reported that "the aims of Hong Kong education were not made explicit until a formal document *School Education in Hong Kong: A Statement of Aims* was published by the Education and Manpower Branch (EMB) in 1993."

The EMB is the top governmental agency responsible for education and training. In addition to supervising policies, budgets, and programs, the EMB prepares reports and proposals for Hong Kong's ruling Legislative

Council. Established in 1984, the EdD manages daily educational affairs. Its committees and subcommittees investigate, research, and propose policies to the EMB. Schools are evaluated regularly by the department's Advisory Inspectorate to make sure they are following official policies.

In 1992 the Curriculum Development Institute (CDI) was created as a wing of the EdD to develop curriculum for primary and secondary schools. Its major role is developing and supporting the transition to the new curriculum that stresses independent and analytical thinking skills; the use of new technology, including computers; the new ties with the mainland; and life-long learning skills. The CDI works closely with the Curriculum Development Council (CDC), which evaluates and proposes curriculum from the preprimary through secondary school levels. The CDC reports directly to the Chief Executive of Hong Kong.

Vocational and technical training fall under the responsibility of the Vocational Training Council (VTC), founded in 1982. This organization offers courses for technical and vocational careers. The VTC sponsors programs in a wide variety of occupations, from Chinese cuisine and hospitality to seaman and welding training.

The Hong Kong Examination Authority (HKEA) was created in 1975 to develop and administer a variety of examinations, ranging from testing for professional and commercial licenses to the two major secondary school city-wide examinations: The Hong Kong Certificate of Education (HKCEE) and the Hong Kong Advanced Level Examination (HKALE).

On December 19, 1984, the People's Republic of China (PRC) and Great Britain signed the Sino-British Joint Declaration of the Question of Hong Kong (Joint Declaration). China instituted the "One Country, Two Systems" policy. Article 5 states that "the socialist system and policies will not be practiced in the Hong Kong Special Administrative Region (HKSAR) and Hong Kong's previous capitalist system and life-style will remain unchanged for 50 years." The PRC further protected Hong Kong's educational system through the Basic Law, which went into effect on July 1, 1997, the date that Hong Kong was officially handed over to the PRC. Article 136 of the Basic Law guarantees that ". . .the Government of the Hong Kong Special Administrative Region shall, on its own, formulate policies on the development and improvement of education, including policies regarding the. . .examination system."

EDUCATIONAL SYSTEM—OVERVIEW

In order to compete in international commerce, the government places a strong emphasis on education.

When free, compulsory primary school education was initiated in 1971, only about 40 percent of the male population had six years of education. By 1999, that figure stood at 75 percent. The figures for females throughout the same period jumped from 35 to 60 percent.

Until 2000, Hong Kong authorities continued citywide examinations for placement into preferred schools from kindergarten through Sixth Form. Examination scores were used to stream students into the major fields of science, humanities, or vocational training. Examinations have also been used to determine which secondary schools students will attend. In 2000, Hong Kong began to switch away from using examination scores to stream and place students. The HKCEE in the final year of senior secondary school and the HKALE in the final year of Sixth Form remain critical examinations for all students hoping to continue their education.

The government subsidizes education at all levels. Primary and junior secondary school fees for students attending government or government-aided schools are paid completely by the government. At the senior secondary and tertiary levels, students must pay fees, but the government offers many grant and loan programs that help students with financing their education. In addition, the government funds most of the costs for students attending certain public-funded tertiary institutions. Annually, government spending ranges between 18 percent and 23 percent of its public spending budget.

Although preschool is not mandatory, 90 percent of all children aged four to six attend preschool. Kindergartens are privately owned and operated, but they must register with the government and follow strict guidelines. The competition for finding good schools begins at the primary level. Until 2000, students in primary grade six took examinations that determined where they attended junior secondary school; the placement scheme has recently been revised. More than 80 percent of those aged 12 to 14 enroll in junior secondary school.

Once students finish grade 9 or are 15-years-old, school attendance is no longer mandatory. The government, however, guarantees openings for 85 percent of junior secondary finishers who want to continue to senior secondary or another type of education. The government also has committed itself to guaranteeing subsidized openings for all students who want to continue their education either in senior secondary or vocational training schools beginning in the 2002-2003 academic year.

The two years at senior secondary school prepare students for a broad range of options, but the main goal is to prepare students for the HKCEE. In their second year (S5), they take the HKCEE to determine who gets into the limited number of places in Sixth Form schools for a two-year college preparatory program. About a third of the students who begin senior secondary school qualify for openings in Sixth Form. Only 18 percent of Sixth Form students can attend universities in Hong Kong because of the limited number of openings.

Some students go from primary six (P6) into technical secondary schools. These schools offer five-year programs, although after the first three years, students are no longer required to attend school. Many students in technical secondary schools take the HKCEE with hopes of scoring high enough to obtain a place in Sixth Form. A small percentage of students finish junior secondary school and decide to take vocational courses offered by the VTC that lead to a Certificate in Vocational Studies (CVS). This prepares them for a broad range of jobs.

Although mainly attended by expatriates' children, the international schools, often run by religious groups, are popular with the affluent Chinese population. These schools are very expensive, with fees ranging from $5,000 Hong Kong dollars (US$641.05 in March 2001) to HK$20,000 (US$2,564.20) a year. Because they emphasize problem-solving and creative thinking, many Chinese parents consider the education superior to public schools. In 2000, there was already a two-year waiting period for openings in the international schools.

Students with special needs have several options. In 1999-2000 there were 74 special education schools, including practical schools and skills opportunity schools. Hong Kong also has separate schools for the blind, the deaf, the physically handicapped, and a school for students with social adjustment problems. Some of these schools are residential. All of the special education schools provide nurses, social workers, educational psychologists, speech therapists, and other specialists. In 1999-2000, nearly 9,500 students were enrolled in special schools. The government offers testing, screening, and checklists for teachers to identify and serve students with special needs. From these tests, students are placed into regular schools if possible.

The institutions at the tertiary level consist of degree granting institutions, teacher training, and postsecondary training institutions. The government guarantees subsidized, first-year university places for 18 percent of 17-to 20-year-olds, approximately 14,500 students in 2000. In addition, the government guarantees subsidized openings in postsecondary training at technical institutions for 8 percent of this age group.

University education is not totally free, however, even at the public-funded institutions. Students do have to pay their tuition, which amounted to HK$5,500 in 2000 (US$705.16). Tuition fees account for about 20 percent of the total budget per student for universities. The remaining money comes from the government.

With the transfer of Hong Kong to the PRC, significant curriculum changes have been instituted in the primary and secondary school curriculum. New courses in civics and Putonghua (Mandarin) are being taught. The civics courses cover information on China and its culture, the basic law that governs Hong Kong, and the meaning of the "one country, two system" policy. Mandarin is the common spoken language of the majority of people in China. In the ideal situation, students will be fluent in their "mother tongue"—Cantonese, English, and Mandarin. All primary schools teach in Cantonese but, until the 1990s, secondary schools had used mostly English. Since 1997, the government has implemented the "mother-tongue" policy, requiring all but about 100 secondary schools to use Cantonese as their language of instruction.

A new government education policy instituted in the late 1990s addresses the critical issue of the thousands of newly arrived children (NAC) from mainland China. The policy is to provide 60 hours of orientation, including courses in Cantonese, Hong Kong life, and Hong Kong culture. The government hopes to integrate these children into the mainstream educational system as soon as possible. For this purpose, the government has organized and given grants to hundreds of schools to conduct programs for these children.

In the late 1990s, Hong Kong's first Chief Executive Tung Chee-wah began a public campaign to reform education in Hong Kong. He, and other officials, wanted to make sure the citizens of Hong Kong were prepared to compete in a world that required constant changing and updating of skills. One of Tung's major projects was to make schools at all levels more accountable to the people and government. To do this, he introduced School-Based Management (SBM). Tung and other education officials believed that many schools lacked strong management goals and assessment methods for growth and improvement. Since the late 1990s, Hong Kong has proposed many reforms. Some have remained in place, some have evolved into new plans, and some have been tabled for lack of public support.

Target-Oriented Curriculum (TOC) is one of the reforms being promoted. Begun in 1995, TOC was supposed to redirect the primary and secondary curriculum away from academic, teacher- and textbook-centered, and driven by competitive, norm-referenced examinations to a curriculum that will encourage "individualism and whole-person growth, child-centered and task-based learning, and criterion-referenced assessment." Three core subjects make up TOC: Chinese, English, and Mathematics. The vagueness and subjectivity of assessment standards and the extra time required to create and evaluate student activities, however, has caused some teachers to question TOC. The general idea, however, of focusing on skills in these three subjects continues to provide the foundation for Hong Kong education reform in the twenty-first century.

In line with the movement to encourage more creative thinking in the classroom, the government launched major reform in methods of assessing students. Since the mid-1990s, the trend is to replace rigid, competitive testing with more individual student assessment and guidance. The major assessment tool being used in the early twenty-first century is the Hong Kong Attainment Test (HKAT).

PREPRIMARY & PRIMARY EDUCATION

Nursery schools and kindergartens are privately owned, but they must register with the government and follow its regulations. In 1999-2000, some 756 kindergartens were registered and taught 171,138 students. The government provides financial assistance to needy families who cannot afford kindergarten fees. In 1999-2000, the Student Financial Assistance Agency (SFAA) received 72,436 applications for kindergarten fee remission. From this total, 65,128 received half fee remission and 3,741 received full fee remission. The pupil-teacher ratio in 1999-2000 was 12.6 children per teacher, but individual class sizes vary.

There were 819 primary schools with 491,181 students enrolled in 1999-2000. About 6 percent of these schools were operated entirely by the government, about 84 percent were operated by nonprofit groups that received government aid, and about 10 percent were privately owned and funded.

Most primary schools operate half day sessions. One group of children attends the morning sessions, and another group attends the afternoon sessions. The government plans to convert all primary schools to full-day schools in the future. In September 2000, about 39 percent of all primary students attended full-day schools. By the 2002-2003 school year, government plans call for 60 percent of the students to be in full-day primary schools and, by 2007-2008, all primary students should be attending full-day schools. The pupil-teacher ratio was 22.4:1 in 1999-2000, but class size is usually in the mid-thirties. The government has promoted a teaching method called "Activity Classes," a system that encourages student-centered learning. These classes are usually smaller than normal classes.

Before 2000, parents competed to get their children into prestigious primary schools, even if those schools were outside their "NET" (Hong Kong is divided into 58 primary school NETS or home districts). Parents often moved, rented, or even cheated to get their children into one of the higher rated schools. The government began a new policy in 2000 for the Primary One Admission (POA) System that restricts the competition for primary school openings. Parents are allowed to apply to any school anywhere but are only guaranteed places in their home district. There are two stages of selection. In the first, each primary school selects 65 percent of its entering primary one students from applications, but 30 percent of these must come from their district. Those children still waiting for placement are then assigned by the government to schools within their home districts.

For decades Hong Kong education officials have proposed different plans to assess student learning and to evaluate each school's performance. One was the Academic Aptitude Test (AAT), put into place in 1978. It measured verbal and numerical reasoning in Chinese and consisted entirely of multiple choice questions. In the 1990s it came under increased criticism for not measuring higher order thinking skills and for not testing more of the actual subjects from the curriculum. It was also used to compare each school's relative success at educating students. As of September 2000, the AAT was abolished. Authorities are attempting to devise tests that will allow them to assess student competency, individual school performance compared to other schools, and the city-wide school system as whole. In the meantime, a temporary three-part method will be used that combines the school's average AAT results from 1997-2000, each student's grades, and parents' preferences.

Besides the core subjects of Chinese, English, and mathematics, primary schools teach courses in general studies, including sciences and health; civics; music and art; physical education; English; and Mandarin. Instruction in computer use is also being added to the curriculum.

Although Cantonese is the language of instruction, English is taught in every primary grade. Overall, each student receives between 180 and 210 hours per year in English instruction.

SECONDARY EDUCATION

Hong Kong's secondary schools are operated by three separate groups: the government (about 8 percent of students); voluntary groups largely funded by the government (about 77 percent of students); and private schools that raise their own finances (about 15 percent of students). Secondary education is divided into three years of junior secondary (S1-S3) and two years of senior secondary (S4-S5) school. Senior secondary students take the HKCEE, and about 30 percent usually score high enough to qualify for places in Sixth Form (Secondary Sixth or S6-S7), a two-year program that prepares students to take the university qualifying exam (HKALE).

There are three types of secondary schools: grammar, which concentrates on academic subjects; technical/

vocational, which prepares students to enter the workforce after their ninth year but also offers academic preparation if students wish to continue their education; and prevocational/special schools, which are for students with disabilities. In 1999-2000, there were 433 grammar, 20 technical, and 27 prevocational schools, with more than 450,000 students: 235,974 in S1-S3; 159,343 in S4-S5; and 58,248 in S6-S7. Although the pupil-teacher ratio is about 19 to 1, class size in 1998-1999 averaged in the upper thirties, not much lower than in 1985-1986, when there were slightly fewer than 40 students per class.

Where students attend school has always been a controversial issue. Certain secondary schools established superior reputations, and parents competed to place their children in these schools. Until 1978, the availability of openings in secondary schools was limited, so students had to take a competitive exam called the Secondary School Entrance Examination (SSEE) to get into S1. After 1978, the government guaranteed a subsidized place for everyone through S3 or the age of 15. Therefore, the SSEE was not needed and it was eliminated. To determine which junior secondary school students attended, the Secondary School Places Allocation (SSPA) was introduced. Under the SSPA, there was no competitive examination. Allocation was based on a student's academic record, the Academic Aptitude Test (AAT) used to weigh the academic standards at each school, parental choice of secondary schools, and school NETS or districts.

In the late 1990s, the Education Commission began an extensive review of the SSPA system and eliminated the ATT. In 2001 they began looking at alternative plans, but the interim system is similar to the former SSPA except with less dependence on public examination scores. The end result is that most students must attend secondary schools in their own secondary school NET. The government has encouraged primary and secondary schools to link together in a system called "Through Train" so that students will pass directly from P6 (sixth year of primary school) to specified junior secondary schools for S1. The commission plans to have a new system in place by 2004 or 2005.

Gaining a place in senior secondary schools is also competitive. Because there were limited places in senior secondary schools, the government created the Junior Secondary Education Assessment (JSEA) in 1980. In 1993, the present system called Secondary Four Places (SFP) was adopted. It combines student performance in school with a formula called Mean Eligibility Rate (MER), which determines the success of each junior secondary school in placing students in S4.

The government subsidizes places for 85 percent of the S3 leavers in grammar and technical schools and an other 10 percent for places in vocational subsidized schools. In 1999, approximately 78,000 students finished S3. Almost all of them sought further education. In addition, a few thousand former S3 finishers sought some form of post S3 education. The government offered subsidized places for 73,749 students. Courses taught by other agencies and subsidized by the Department of Education covered 2,240 more students. The Vocational Training Council (VTC) subsidized 4,192 full time openings in vocational and industrial training, including study with the Construction Industry Training Authority and the Clothing Industry Training Authority. Other programs with private schools took 3,498 students in 1999. So in effect, almost everyone who wanted to continue schooling beyond junior secondary had the opportunity.

There are few expenses for students attending junior secondary school other than transportation, books, and uniforms. The government Student Financial Assistance Agency (SFAA) offers textbook assistance for needy families. Students attending senior secondary school, however, must pay an annual fee. For the academic year 2000-2001, this amounted to HK$5,050 (US$647.48). For Sixth Form the fee was HK$8,750 (US$1,121.80).

The SFAA provides fee remission and other assistance for needy S4-S7 students from families with average monthly incomes of under HK$23,200 (US$2,974.37). In 2001, the government promised that subsidized S4 places would be available in the future for everyone who wanted to further his or her education beyond the required nine years.

Getting into senior secondary school puts students on track to take the HKCEE and qualify for Sixth Form, but openings are limited. There were 23,956 guaranteed places in S6 for the 1999-2000 academic year. In recent years the percentage of students going on to post S5 study has been around 33 percent. Many of those who take the HKCEE are not associated with a school; they are retaking the exam to try to increase their scores. In 2000, of the 130,303 examinees, 41,267 were private candidates.

To prepare students for the HKCEE, senior secondary schools dedicate about 50 percent of the curriculum to the three core subjects: Chinese, English, and mathematics. In all, the HKCEE covers 42 subjects, and most students choose 7 or 8 for examination. Chinese, English, and mathematics must be taken by all students, then students select either humanities exams in subjects such as world history, Chinese history, geography, and economics; or science exams in subjects such as physics, chemistry, biology, and additional mathematics. The tests are scored on an A through F basis: A, 5 points; B, 4 points; C, 3 points; D, 2 points; E, 1 point; and F, not passing. The best six grades are counted, and they must total 14 or higher if a student hopes for a place at a subsidized

Sixth Form. HKCEE scores are also used in the workforce for mid-level hiring. To get a civil service position as a clerical officer, for example, an applicant must have five grade Es, two of which must be in Chinese and English languages.

Annually, from 60 to 68 percent of the exams are scored E or above. In 2000, the four most popular subjects were Chinese language with 78,975 examinees (66.0 percent scored E or higher); mathematics with 78,658 (74.7 percent scored E or higher); additional math with 21,479 (84.6 percent scored E or higher); English language with 66,064 (64.6 percent scored E or higher); and economics with 38,494 examinees (68.4 percent scored E or higher).

To qualify for university level education, students must take the HKALE. Most students take the exam in the late spring during their second year of Sixth Form. To be eligible to take the HKALE, students must have a grade of E or above in six HKCEE subjects, two of which must be Chinese and English. Because more than 25 percent of those who take the HKALE annually are no longer students, they are classified as private candidates. To be eligible for the exam, private candidates must meet one of three criteria: (1) have taken the HKCEE 18 months before the HKALE examination; scored a grade of E or above in six subjects, including Chinese and English; have a C or above in at least one subject; and a point total from the exams of at least 10 (using the same A through F point system as the HKCEE); (2) have taken the HKALE before; or (3) be 21-years-old by January 1 of the year of the examination.

In 2000, some 35,549 students sat for the exams, 75.7 percent for the first time. Of this total, 16,868 (48.7 percent) scored high enough to qualify for admission to tertiary institutions: 7,586 males (47.1 percent) and 9,282 females (50 percent). Only about 14,500 government subsidized openings were available, however. This shortage of places leads many students to study overseas. The Hong Kong government estimated that in the late 1990s, a total of about 40,000 Hong Kong university students were studying overseas. The most popular countries were the United States (13,000 students), the United Kingdom (10,000), Australia (9,000), and Canada (6,500). Another 2,000 studied in other places such as Mainland China and Taiwan.

The HKALE tests subjects at two levels: 20 subjects at the A or advanced level and 20 subjects at the AS or advanced supplementary level. Both require two years of study, but the AS courses are half the classroom time as the A level courses. Universities consider two AS exams to be equal to one A-level exam when figuring scores on the HKALE. AS subjects were introduced in 1994 as a part of the government's attempt to encourage students to study outside the narrow course offerings in their majors.

Prior to 1994, the only mandatory language exam on the HKALE was English. Following the government's initiative, tertiary institutions began requiring a passing grade in both English and Chinese on the HKALE as prerequisite for acceptance. However, except for the AS-level English and Chinese exams, AS-level subjects have not become popular. In general, students take examinations that will enable them to meet entry requirements into specific university programs. As a result, more than 50 percent of the students never take AS level exams except in language.

To enter universities, candidates must score a grade of E or above in both "Use of English" and "Chinese Language and Culture," and a minimum of two more A-level or one A-level plus two AS-level subjects. Particular university programs might require additional requirements.

Instead of university study, thousands of students enter technical and prevocational secondary schools. The prevocational schools concentrate more on crafts for industry at the lower range of difficulty, while the technical schools offer three years of courses that also prepare students for possible senior secondary school. Therefore, the first three years in technical secondary schools include concentrations in academic subjects similar to grammar schools. A few technical schools offer S4 and S5 level courses that prepare students for the HKCEE. Technical openings go unfilled, however. In the late 1990s, only half of the 10 percent of subsidized openings were being filled.

HIGHER EDUCATION

Higher education generally covers two major types of institutions: degree-granting and technical/vocational education (postsecondary). Both are under the general supervision of the University Grants Council (UGC). The UGC fully subsidizes eight institutions offering bachelor's degrees. These include City University of Hong Kong (City U), Hong Kong Baptist University (HKBU or Baptist University), Lingnan University (LU), Chinese University of Hong Kong (CUHK), Hong Kong Polytechnic University (Poly U), Hong Kong University of Science and Technology (HKUST), University of Hong Kong (HKU), and most recently Hong Kong Institute of Education (HKIEd).

The oldest university in Hong Kong is the University of Hong Kong, formed in 1912 when the Medical College (founded in 1887) joined with the new Technical Institute. In recent decades, HKU has established itself as a major research institution with international acclaim. The

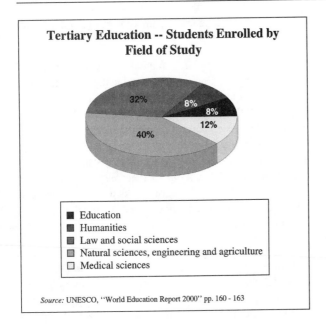

Tertiary Education -- Students Enrolled by Field of Study

- ■ Education
- ■ Humanities
- ■ Law and social sciences
- ▨ Natural sciences, engineering and agriculture
- □ Medical sciences

Source: UNESCO, "World Education Report 2000" pp. 160 - 163

next development came 50 years later, in 1963, when three colleges joined to form the Chinese University of Hong Kong, which also has developed into a highly respected teaching and research university. CUHK is home of the other medical school in Hong Kong.

In the 1970s and 1980s, several new higher educational institutions opened. Hong Kong Baptist University, which offers university degrees through the doctoral level, opened as Baptist College in 1970. Today, Baptist University has no formal affiliation with the church. In 1978, a branch of Guangzhou's Lingnan University opened with a strong emphasis on the liberal arts. LU has expanded into programs offering a Master of Philosophy and Doctor of Philosophy in Chinese, cultural studies, English, philosophy, translation, business, and social sciences. Hong Kong Polytechnic University began in 1972 as Hong Kong Polytechnic and became a fully-accredited university in 1994. In 1984, City University of Hong Kong began as City Polytechnic. It also was fully accredited in 1994. The Hong Kong Academy for Performing Arts (APA) started up in 1984 and, in the late 1990s, began offering first degree level programs, in addition to advanced diplomas and certificates in the fine arts (dance, drama, music, and technical arts). It has about 700 full-time students. In 1989, the Open University of Hong Kong (OUHK) began as the Open Learning Institute, and in 1996 OUHK became accredited as a university. OUHK offers university degrees, but it is funded independently, mostly from student fees. It is Hong Kong's major institution offering distance learning. Half of OUHK's 18,000 students are between 26- and 35-years-old, and most of these students attend part time.

The Hong Kong University of Science and Technology (HKUST) opened in 1991 and immediately offered university and graduate level courses. In 1994, the Hong Kong Institute of Education was formed from four colleges of education. At first it offered professional certificates and training, but in 1997, HKIEd became fully funded by the government under the sponsorship of the University Grants Committee; in the following year, HKIEd offered its first degree programs.

Most bachelor's degree programs take three years. Unlike programs in the United States, Hong Kong university degree programs focus on a single major and closely related subjects, rather than requiring a broad range of core courses across disciplines. There is a strong movement to change to the broader-based education system used by U.S. universities, which would require most Hong Kong universities to restructure course requirements.

Business and related fields are the most popular university degree subjects. In 1999-2000, business and management accounted for 23 percent of the majors in UGC funded institutions. Almost a third of these were studying accounting. About 16 percent studied science and mathematics, and another 19 percent chose engineering as their major field. Other popular majors include economics, medicine, and computer science.

In an attempt to expand their resources and international reputation, several universities have formed partnerships with universities overseas and on the China mainland. For example, Poly U has ties with Tianjin Medical University and Peking Union Medical College for teaching health science research. Baptist University offers a long-distance MBA degree program jointly with Scotland's University of Strathclyde.

A number of private institutions provide education at the tertiary level. They are self-supporting, so they depend on private funding. One is Caritas Francis Hsu College (CFHC) which targets people who are mainly working in the commercial fields and want to continue their formal education. In coordination with universities in Great Britain and Australia, Francis Hsu College's Centre for Advanced and Professional Studies (CAPS) offers bachelor and master programs in a variety of fields, including accounting, business management, and hospitality management.

Higher vocational and technical education in the nongovernment sponsored schools must register with the government under the Post Secondary College Ordinance. Currently, only Shue Yan College (SYC) is registered. Opened in 1976, SYC offers four-year secondary diploma courses and a few first degree and masters programs. SYC has ties to universities in China and overseas.

The other type of postsecondary education consists of institutions that provide technical and vocational courses, called sub-degree levels. These programs tend to be vocational, more specifically targeted to teaching work-related skills. They are not equivalent to a bachelors degree from a university. Typically, candidates need passing scores on at least five HKCEEs to qualify for sub-degree programs. Upon completion of these programs, students receive a higher certificate, a diploma, or higher diploma. As a rule, these students usually attend part time since they normally work full time. The length of study ranges from two to four years. A variety of these programs are offered through several colleges and universities, including Poly U, APA, HKIEd, City U, OUHK, and the Hong Kong Institute of Vocational Education (IVE).

The major government sponsor of technical and vocational training is the Vocational Training Council (VTC), founded in 1982, which offers programs through its IVE. Although officially these are not classified as secondary education, they do include some senior secondary courses that help prepare some students for the HKCEE. IVE has nine different institutes around Hong Kong that teach a wide range of vocational courses in coordination with industry, from commerce to textiles. In 1999-2000, some 54,781 full- and part-time students studied with IVE. Some of the curriculum is designed for higher level technical positions in industry and commerce. Upon completion, students receive certificates and associate degrees.

Students must pay for their higher education. For needy students attending the University Grants Council (UGC) subsidized institutions, financial assistance is available from government grants and loans. Besides the eight universities listed earlier, other subsidized institutions are IVE, APA, and Prince Philip Dental Hospital. In 1999-2000, the UGC processed 32,085 applications and offered assistance to almost all applicants. In many cases, students received a combination of grants and loans to cover their higher education expenses. The average amount offered was HK$47,223 (US$6,054.60).

In the early 1980s, total enrollment in UGC funded tertiary institutions for full time, first degree students numbered 2,000 and 3,000, or approximately 3 to 4 percent of the 17- to 20-year-old population. Then Hong Kong authorities began to build more institutions of higher education. The percentage of the 17- to 20-year-old population entering as full time, first degree students more than doubled between 1984 and 1990, to more than 9 percent, or approximately 7,000 full-time students. From 1991 to 1997, full-time students increased by 32 percent in UGC funded institutions (46 percent if the VTC technical colleges are included). By the late 1990s, there were approximately 14,500 (about 19 percent) of 17- to 20-year-olds entering UGC funded bachelor degree level institutions full time each year. The total enrollment at all levels for full-time students at UGC institutions in 1999-2000 was 69,948 students. The total enrollment for all of the 11 major tertiary institutions was 112,473 students. Another 150,000 people were taking some kind of continuing training and education.

ADMINISTRATION, FINANCE, & EDUCATIONAL RESEARCH

For the 2000-2001 fiscal year, Hong Kong's government expenditure on education was approximately HK$54.4 billion (US$7 billion). This total was 22.3 percent of the total government expenditure, an increase over previous annual budgets. The total was divided fairly evenly among primary, secondary, and tertiary levels. The agency responsible for education throughout Hong Kong is the Education and Manpower Bureau (EMB). The Education Commission (EC), however, carries out much of the daily planning, developing, and monitoring of all the schools. The EC is composed of 19 members, most of whom are appointed from the field of education, not government officials.

The UGC oversees the distribution of government money to tertiary institutions. Much of this money is allocated as a triennial block grant to each of the eight public funded institutions, and these institutions determine how to spend the money to provide the best educational services for their students. The UGC committee is made up of members appointed by Hong Kong's chief executive from outside the government, including representatives from the business and academic communities. Their mission is two-fold: one is to protect the academic freedom and independence of the institutions that they fund, and the other is ensure that the government's money is used effectively for the benefit of the people.

High quality research in Hong Kong universities is a relatively new activity. Until the mid-1990s, the government was mainly concerned with expanding educational opportunities. Since that time, however, Hong Kong educators have worked toward international respectability in research. The government's Research Grants Council (RGC), a subsidiary of the UGC, has four subject area panels that evaluate research proposals and recommend grants for research to academic staff members at UGC funded institutions. The subject areas are physical sciences, engineering, biology and medicine, and humanities and social sciences. Members of the panels are independent of government. Most are academics from Hong Kong and overseas institutions, while some are from nonacademic sectors of Hong Kong.

The VTC is made up of 22 members, 4 of whom come from government. The remaining are appointed

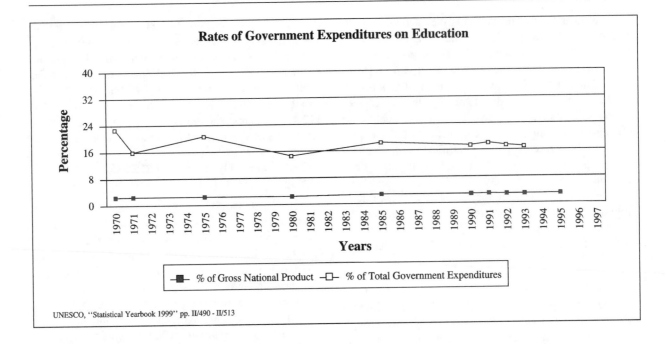

Rates of Government Expenditures on Education

UNESCO, "Statistical Yearbook 1999" pp. II/490 - II/513

from industry, business, and universities. VTC's main function is to advise government on the manpower requirements in Hong Kong, especially as it pertains to future development. Through its 20 Training Boards—covering areas such as accounting, banking and finance, hotel, catering and tourism, maritime services, textile and clothing, apprenticeship and trade testing, and disability training—the VTC offers training and skill upgrading to tens of thousands of workers annually. VTC also operates two technical colleges that offer diploma and higher certificate courses.

NONFORMAL EDUCATION

In the late 1990s, Hong Kong's government made a strong commitment to promoting "life-long learning" skills. The rationale behind this movement is that people in the fast-pace changing world of the twenty-first century must be prepared to learn new skills throughout their lifetime. One type of learning involves professional and career upgrading. Another involves knowledge for improving lifestyle so that people can appreciate the arts or pursue new hobbies.

Hong Kong has extensive continuing and professional education (CPE) programs. In the UGC supported institutions alone, continuing studies has grown from about 20,000 students in 1970 to more than 160,000 in 1996. In 1997, the 20- to 64-year-old age group in Hong Kong was estimated to be 4,214,300 people. From this group alone, the number of people taking some form of continuing education was 872,360 (even higher if the under 20 working group was included). Among the institutions with large CPE enrollments are HKU (School of Profes-

sional and Continuing Education), CUHK (the School of Continuing Studies), City U, Poly U (Centre for Professional and Continuing Education and the Centre for Professional & Business English), HKBU (School of Continuing Education), HKIEd, and the OUHK.

Several other agencies offer different forms of CPE, including the Caritas Adult and Higher Education Service at Caritas Francis Hsu College, the Hong Kong Management Association, the Hong Kong College of Technology through its Information Service Centre of Professional Studies (ISCOPS), and dozens of private firms and government departments.

TEACHING PROFESSION

Qualifications to teach in Hong Kong schools vary according to the level of teaching. Until September 2001, the minimum qualification to teach kindergarten was completion of S5 with two or more passes on the HKCEE, one of which had to be in either Chinese language or Chinese literature. In September 2001, the minimum number of passes was raised to five, including both Chinese and English languages. In 1999-2000, about 54 percent of the 8,855 kindergarten teachers were qualified kindergarten trained (QKT) and another 19 percent were in training. A person must take 360 hours of in-service training offered by the HKIEd to receive the QKT endorsement.

Only about 15 percent of primary teachers held university degrees in 1999-2000, but the vast majority had received professional teacher training. By 2004-2005 all the teaching programs at HKIEd will offer the Certificate of Education (CEd) university degree. Students with the

HKCEE can enter HKIEd and take a three-year program leading to the CEd, the general qualification for teaching in primary schools in the future. Students who possess the HKAL can take a two-year program to get the CEd. Secondary school teachers are also trained at the HKIEd for their CEd. Those with degrees from a university but without teacher training take a year-long postgraduate course at HKIEd, UHK, CUHK, or BU to qualify for a postgraduate certificate in education. In 1999-2000, of a total of 24,453 secondary school teachers, 72 percent were graduates with degrees, while another 10 percent had special teacher training.

The HKIEd was created in 1994 by statute that combined Northcote College of Education, Grantham College of Education, Sir Robert Black College of Education, the Hong Kong Technical Teachers' College, and the Institute of Language in Education. In 1997, HKIE became fully funded by the government under the sponsorship of the UGC. Besides the CEd, HKIEd offers a Postgraduate Diploma in Education (PGDE) and Bachelor of Education for primary teachers. By 1999-2000 HKIEd was offering more than 50 courses and had nearly 10,000 students. HKIEd also has added a School of Creative Arts, a School of Sciences and Technology, a School of Early Childhood Education, a School of Languages in Education, and a School of Foundations in Education.

Masters- and doctoral-level degrees are prerequisites for most full time, university teaching positions. Like universities in the West, graduate level students also teach. To encourage postgraduate research in all fields, the government is increasing its positions for postgraduate research by 11 percent each academic year between 2001 and 2004.

The Hong Kong Professional Teachers Union (PTU) represents more than 60,000 teachers, or 90 percent of all teachers from kindergarten through university. It is active in all aspects of education, including protecting academic freedom, offering teacher workshops, publishing newsletters to keep teachers informed. In addition, the PTU sponsors services such as a cooperative supermarket, an optometric center, a dental center, and health project medical center.

Salaries for teachers vary greatly from primary to university level. In 1999, a full time academic professor near the top of the pay scale made about US$190,000 annually. A senior lecturer/reader with several years experience makes around US$125,000. The pay for an assistant lecturer/lecturer varies from US$50,000 to US$120,000. Primary and secondary school teachers with several years experience average around US$42,000 annually, but the scale varies considerably with experience. A teacher/administrator/coordinator position pays more, as much as US$60,000 annually. In 2000, the government was re-cruiting secondary school teachers for its native English-speaking teacher scheme (NET) for salaries ranging from US$26,000 to more than US$70,000, depending on qualifications. All of these full-time positions offer health and retirement benefits.

SUMMARY

The most prominent feature in Hong Kong life and culture is the tension between the people's traditional Chinese respect for authority and conformity, and their need for more flexible and creative problem-solving skills. The two potential changes most often debated are eliminating the total reliance on citywide, standardized examinations for placing students and switching to a more open curriculum that resembles the American model of education, with its broad span of offerings. The government has taken steps to open up the curriculum, but moving to the American 6-3-3-4 system of education (6 years of primary, 3 of junior high, 3 of senior high, and 4 of university) and abolishing "banding" in secondary schools is running into opposition.

Another major reform movement in Hong Kong's educational system involves languages. Hong Kong has begun an intensive campaign to promote "biliterate and trilingual" skills in the curriculum. The first change has been to require most public schools to use Cantonese as the teaching language in primary and secondary schools. Officials believe that students are more comfortable learners when they are taught in their native language. With Hong Kong's heritage of English as the language of commerce, however, educators realize that they have the opportunity to retain and increase the numbers and quality of English speakers so that Hong Kong will remain a center of international finance and trade. To accomplish this goal, the government initiated the NET scheme to recruit 750 native English teacher/coordinators (NETs) for the public schools by the early years of the twenty-first century. The government provides extra funding for schools who hire NETs. The third language requirement comes with the handover of Hong Kong to the People's Republic of China. Mandarin, the language spoken in most of China, is a Chinese dialect not understood by most people in Hong Kong. All the schools now teach Mandarin as a standard course.

The reform that is succeeding with little opposition is the campaign to extend education and use of information technology (IT) from primary schools through universities. As a city without any natural resources, Hong Kong's success is tied to its people's ability to gather and manage information.

The Secretary for Education and Manpower Branch reported that by May 2001 all public supported schools would have computers, and the plan is to supply each primary school with 40 computers and each secondary school with 82 computers. In addition, all secondary and almost all primary schools had Internet access by the spring of 2001. Ultimately, the government wants all publicly supported schools to teach 25 percent of their curriculum through the Internet. To accomplish this, the government has instituted a comprehensive training program for all teachers. By late 2000, 75 percent of the teachers had finished basic information technology training (IT). The goal is to have 75 percent of all teachers trained at the intermediate level by 2002-2003. Another prominent feature of the IT crusade is the online learning tool for public schools and life-long learning projects called Hong Kong Education City. In the spring of 2001, the e-class site listed 294 science courses, 146 language courses, 123 art/music/physical education/vocational/library courses, and 117 social studies courses for students.

BIBLIOGRAPHY

Bray, M. "Hong Kong: System of Education." *The International Encyclopedia of Education.* Vol. 5, 2nd ed. Torsten Husen and T. Neville Postlewaite, eds. New York: Elsevier Science Ltd., 1994.

Board of Education. "Report on Review of 9-year Compulsory October 1997 Education (Revised Version)," October 1997. *Hong Kong Special Administrative Region [HKSAR].* Available from http://www.info.gov.hk/emb/eng/public/rep_table.html.

The Central Intelligence Agency (CIA). *The World Factbook 2000.* Directorate of Intelligence, 1 January 2000. Available from http://www.cia.gov/.

Chee-Cheong, Choi. "Public Examinations in Hong Kong." *Assessment in Education: Principles, Policy & Practice,* no. 3, November 1999. Available from http:e-hostvgw1.epnet.com.

Cheung, Michael. "Spotlight on Hong Kong: Reading, Writing, and Rote Learning. . .Drive Students to Western Schools." *Business Week International Editions,* 14 August 2000. Available http://www.businessweek.com/.

Education Commission. HKSAR, March 2001. Available from http://www.e-c.edu.hk/eng/main.html.

Education Department. HKSAR, March 2001. Available from http://www.ed.gov.hk/ednewhp/text_sitemap_link.htm.

Hong Kong Examinations Authority. HKSAR, March 2001. Available from http://www.hkea.edu.hk/.

"Recruiting Students in Asia: Hong Kong: Local and International Education," March 2001. Available from http://home.school.net.hk/üiie/hked/hkeducation.htm.

—*John A. Zurlo*

HUNGARY

BASIC DATA

Official Country Name:	Republic of Hungary
Region:	Europe
Population:	10,138,844
Language(s):	Hungarian
Literacy Rate:	99%
Number of Primary Schools:	3,596
Compulsory Schooling:	10 years
Public Expenditure on Education:	4.6%
Foreign Students in National Universities:	6,399
Libraries:	3,518
Educational Enrollment:	Primary: 508,003 Secondary: 1,128,911 Higher: 170,147
Educational Enrollment Rate:	Primary: 103% Secondary: 98% Higher: 24%
Teachers:	Primary: 44,585 Secondary: 109,902 Higher: 19,103
Student-Teacher Ratio:	Primary: 11:1 Secondary: 10:1
Female Enrollment Rate:	Primary: 102% Secondary: 99% Higher: 26%

HISTORY & BACKGROUND

The Republic of Hungary is one of the oldest nations in Europe, tracing its roots to the invasion of the vast Hungarian plain from the east by King Árpád the First around A.D. 1000. This cultural group, the Magyars, was the forerunner of today's ethnic Hungarian population that constitutes more than 90 percent of the current population. In addition to a long settlement history, Hungary also boasts a long history of formal education. The University of Pécs was established in 1367 to study law and medicine, and a number of other universities were established as early as the fifteenth and sixteenth centuries. In

1777 the first university was established in the capital Budapest. The blossoming of the Austro-Hungarian Empire between 1848 and 1920 saw significant achievements in the educational, scientific, and cultural life of the nation. This period also saw significant exchanges with other European universities that contributed to the vitality of the Hungarian educational system. The end of the Austro-Hungarian Empire and the significant reduction in the territorial area of Hungary in 1920, as a result of the conditions of the Treaty of Trianon, created a large diaspora of ethnic Hungarians outside the present boundaries of Hungary. The welfare of these people, particularly in the preservation of their Hungarian identity, has been an issue since 1920. Education has played a significant role in preserving this identity; for example, the demand by the Hungarian government for the creation of Hungarian language universities in present day Romania has been a feature of inter-ethnic and international relations.

Language is the single most unifying feature of Hungarian identity. Hungarian is a language of the Finno-Ugrian group of Uralic languages. It is therefore a non Indo-European tongue with its nearest linguistic relatives being Finnish and Estonian. As a result speech, writing, and comprehension are more difficult for Indo-European speakers. Thus the Hungarian education system is marked not only by an emphasis on studying the mother tongue but also on preparing students to communicate in the Indo-European tongues, particularly English and German, of the nations that surround them. Religion is also important in Hungary, and the Catholic Church in particular plays a large role in the educational system. More than two-thirds of the population are Roman Catholic, 20 percent are Calvinists, and 5 percent are Lutheran. A major exception to the Hungarian linguistic and religious majority is the presence of 500,000-700,000 Roma, often called "Gypsies," representing approximately 5 percent of the population. The educational system and achievements of this cultural group represent a major exception to the overall excellent standard of education in Hungary.

The other significant development in the Hungarian educational system has been the effects of demographic trends. Demographically, Hungary is one of the few nations in the world experiencing a negative natural increase. In other words, the death rate is higher than the birth rate. This pattern has been present for more than 20 years and as such has important repercussions for school enrollment and ultimately the future labor force.

All of these cultural and historical trends must be seen in the light of political change in Hungary in the twentieth century from a European system between 1920 and 1948 to a socialist system between 1948 and 1990. From 1990 to the present, the restructuring of the system to reflect a more democratic system of government and privatization of property and the demands of a market economy occurred.

For many years the Hungarian system of education was seen as one of the finest in the world. Indeed at one point Hungary had produced more Nobel Prize winners per capita than any other nation. It particularly excelled in science, where such important figures as Dr. Leó Szilárd and Dr. Edward Teller, atomic scientists on the Manhattan project, and Van Kaman, the helicopter pioneer, were all Hungarian born and trained. Perhaps more recognizable are Ernö Rubik, the Hungarian mathematician who invented the Rubik's cube, and József Bíró, who invented the Biro disposable pen. Finally, Andy Grove, the CEO of Intel Corporation and the 1998 Time magazine Man of the Year was born in Budapest. Today the challenge presented by the need to restructure the Hungarian educational system puts this legacy of educational excellence at serious risk.

CONSTITUTIONAL & LEGAL FOUNDATIONS

Constitutional Provisions & Laws Affecting Education: An understanding of the laws and regulations that currently guide Hungarian education requires an understanding of the changes wrought by the imposition of the socialist system in 1948. The socialist government in the years following 1948 placed a great emphasis on education and significantly increased the number of schools, colleges, scientific institutes, and universities. They also made all the institutes of higher education separate and distinct from other institutions within the higher education community. Thus, for example, medical schools were separate institutions from law schools, which in turn were separate from technical schools, schools of veterinary medicine, teacher training colleges, art colleges, and physical education colleges. Yet all of these could be located in the same city and often on the same campus. At the highest level of the system were the Academies of Sciences that functioned as supreme educational, yet predominantly research institutes.

Reform of this system commenced in 1993 with the Law on Higher Education (Act LXXX). All education was placed under the jurisdiction of the Ministry of Education (previously education had been the responsibility of five ministries). Two advisory bodies were formed to guide, and in some cases control, institutions and their curricula. These bodies were the Hungarian Accreditation Committee (HAC) and the Higher Education and Scientific Council (HESC). The law also established budgeting procedures for student support, facility support, program development, and research.

In 1996 the Law on Higher Education was amended to integrate postsecondary vocational institutions into an overall system of higher education. In addition the law proscribed what constituted a higher education degree namely:

- A 3- or 4-year degree (equivalent to an undergraduate degree)

- A 3-year doctoral program (The Ph.D.)

- A further 2-year program for a specialized postgraduate degree

This amendment also initiated the integration of the universities. The goal was to reduce the number of state institutions of higher education from 55 to 30 (17 universities and 13 state colleges). However many of the existing colleges refused to forgo their autonomy, and the process of integration was slow and resented.

Further amendments were made in 1999 (Act LII) to expedite this consolidation, and further proposals to amend the Act in 2000 were produced that would affect quality assurance, admissions to higher education, distance learning, the credit system, and regional cohesion.

Educational Philosophies: Since 1990, the Hungarian educational philosophy has been concerned with access, equality of opportunity, quality (or, given the standard of excellence prior to 1990, maintenance of quality), and applicability to the needs of the twenty-first century workforce and in particular to its integration into the European Union philosophy of educational development. The Ministry of Education in 2000 enunciated the following goals:

- To provide the opportunity of having access to educational institutions of guaranteed quality to every child and youth

- To make the standard and efficiency of the educational work visible to all partners and interested parties

- To improve the quality of the professional work of maintainers of schools and kindergartens

- To enhance the flexibility of the structure of training and its orientation towards the labor market in secondary vocational education

The educational policy of the Ministry of Education is based on three pillars, namely: strengthening the role of the state in the field of financing (increasing the ratio of state funding to local funding), supplementing the regulation of content by framework curricula, and developing the national system of assessment and quality control. As part of the latter, the COMENIUS 2000 Program for Quality Improvement in Public Education was launched in 2000.

EDUCATIONAL SYSTEM—OVERVIEW

Compulsory Education & Age Limits: Education in Hungary is compulsory between the ages of 6 and 16. The child may have had the benefit of a kindergarten (*óvoda*) experience prior to school entry but formally begins school (*általános iskola*) at 6 and remains in that school until 14. At 14 the child will attend a secondary school, either a grammar school devoted primarily to academic studies (*gimnázium*) or a vocational school (*szakközépiskola*). While the pupil is permitted to leave school at 16, most continue to 18 years of age. Further study in institutes of higher education is by competitive entry and less than one fifth of all students go on to colleges and universities.

Academic Year: The school academic year runs from September to mid-June while institutes of higher education are finished by the end of May. Schools generally use two semesters, but religious holidays (Christmas and Easter) are times of extended school breaks.

Enrollment: In 1996 enrollment in primary schools was 97 percent of the relevant age group and enrollment in compulsory secondary school was 87 percent. Enrollment for males (98 percent) was similar to females (97 percent) in primary schools but female enrollment was higher in secondary schools (87 percent) than males (85 percent). Overall school enrollment has risen since 1990, probably as a result of a dedicated effort on the part of the government and population to adjust to economic change.

Females & Minority Enrollments: Unlike many nations, Hungary has full equality in education as a legacy of the Socialist system. As a result school enrollment is around 98 percent for the nation. The most significant obstacle to full enrollment is enrollment of Roma children into the school system.

Language of Instruction: In the primary and secondary schools of Hungary, Hungarian is the predominant language of instruction. However, in areas of significant ethnic minorities (Croats, Serbs, and Roma), bilingual education is present. This is particularly so in southern Hungary (areas of Croat and Serbian ethnicity) and in the northeast region (an area of Roma concentration). Language training in English and/or German (sometimes Italian) commences around the age of ten, but, in schools specializing in languages, it can be as early as the third grade or age eight. Language training continues through the four years of secondary school. In institutes of higher education, classes are often taught in German or English to improve student familiarity with these languages and also to attract foreign students to study in Hungarian institutions.

Examinations: Students at the primary and secondary levels are examined at the end of the year with the summer examination acting as the judge of whether the student advances to the next grade. Examinations at the end of secondary school are set by the state and partly used as university entrance examinations, in conjunction with examinations set by the individual university for the faculty in which the aspiring student wishes to enter. Examinations in universities and colleges are at year's end and can be both written and oral.

Grading System: When graded at primary and secondary school, the grading is on a one (failure) to five (excellent) system.

Private Schools: Private schooling is not a major part of the Hungarian educational system. This is because the state has consistently reaffirmed its commitment to full funding (albeit an increasingly diminishing amount). In 1996 only 2 percent of all preprimary students were in private schools, 3 percent of primary school children were in school, and 5 percent of secondary students were in school.

Religious Schools: During the period of Socialist government, the church as a vehicle in the education system was totally repressed. With the coming of democracy, the church sought to recover its role in the system, culminating in Law LXX of July 1999 that established the role of the Catholic Church in the financing of the public and religious activities of the schools. In 1999 the church ran 74 kindergartens, 177 primary schools, 7 schools for special education, 15 vocational schools, and 79 general secondary schools. At the tertiary level in 2000, there were 26 institutions of higher education sponsored by the church, mostly theological colleges but some universities. One example is Pázmány Péter Catholic University, which was established in 1993 following the change of government. Other religions were less impactful. The Károlyi Gáspár University of the Hungarian Reform church was formed in 1993 though.

It should also be noted that there are six ''foundation'' colleges in Hungary specializing in such subjects as education for the handicapped, business, and entrepreneurial activity. They receive their funding from tuition fees and educational foundation grants and attempt to provide educational services to defined market niches.

Instructional Technology (Computers): There is a growing availability of computers in the schools of Hungary, usually for administrators and within the library. Most students commence computer training at the age of 11 or 12, but voluntary instruction at an even earlier age is not unknown. Most of the institutions of higher educa-

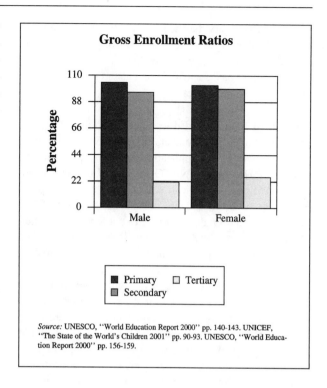

Gross Enrollment Ratios

Source: UNESCO, ''World Education Report 2000'' pp. 140-143. UNICEF, ''The State of the World's Children 2001'' pp. 90-93. UNESCO, ''World Education Report 2000'' pp. 156-159.

tion have computer labs but state institutions, particularly in the outlying cities, have a serious lack of computers for instructional technology. Access to the Internet is thus restricted.

Textbooks—Publication & Adoption: The state of school libraries is generally considered poor notwithstanding their heavy use in the curriculum. Budget difficulties in education have meant that new textbooks have not been produced or purchased, and hence the concern is not necessarily content but quantity and the physical condition of the existing inventory. Most socialist texts have disappeared though this was never a major feature of Hungarian libraries. In the area of tertiary education the situation seems a little better. As the institutions merge their holdings and expand, new libraries are being built to cater to the larger institutions. The World Bank has been a major supporter in the revitalization of libraries at the tertiary level.

Audiovisuals: There is a serious deficiency in the provision of audio-visual services in the classrooms at all levels. In large part this is a legacy of the socialist pedagogical method of instruction by means of lecture. Budget restrictions since the collapse of the Socialist system has made the provision of audio-visual as a modern teaching aid even more problematic. Audio-visual aids are limited to overhead projectors and slide projectors.

Curriculum—Development: The state is responsible for the development of the schools' curriculum and, in the case of Hungary, has been very active in the attempted transformation to a more western or global perspective. Teachers have some freedom to decide on their course content based usually on local and regional topics, opportunities, and issues.

Foreign Influences on Educational System: With the granting of associate membership in the European Union (EU) in 1994, the full application to join in 1997, and the joining of Hungary to NATO in 1999, European influences on Hungarian education have become more apparent. In particular Hungary was required to fulfill a number of requirements in order to conform to EU standards, which involved significant foreign involvement. Specific EU influences include Hungarian participation in the Socrates (K1-12 student exchanges), Erasmus (youths and student exchanges in higher education), and Leonardo da Vinci (development of vocational education) projects. Hungary is a partner in the EU European Voluntary service initiative established in 2000 and is also part of the "Fifth framework program" in which research and technological development are coordinated with the EU through the Ministry of Education. Finally, by becoming part of NATO, Hungary could take part in the NATO Science Fellowships Program that links Hungarian research in higher education to scientific institutes within all NATO countries.

Role of Education in Development: Education is very important to the Hungarian economy with more than 297,000 persons employed in this sector in 1997 or 8.14 percent of the labor force, making it a very significant employer in the country. Moreover, education has been touted as a major contributor to the bringing of Hungary into the world economy. To this end there has been a great emphasis placed on the role of the education system in fostering innovative thinking and entrepreneurship—two major areas that are seen as very important for the future of Hungary but were completely lacking in the socialist system of education. This emphasis must be reconciled with the concern that since the high literacy rates and technological achievements in the socialist era, the educational system has regressed. The reasons for this regression are readily apparent: lack of funding for teachers, equipment, and buildings; a movement out of the teaching profession of teachers; and a move away from a teaching career of the best and brightest graduates.

PREPRIMARY & PRIMARY EDUCATION

General Survey: Prior to 1990 Hungary had an extensive system of *crèches* and kindergartens that provided preschool care from the age of one up to the time children started primary school. This system was state-run and was an excellent preparation for school system entry.

Mass privatization and the divesting of kindergarten facilities by the state and "new" private enterprises has led to a reduction in the number of preschool facilities. By the year 2000, *crèches* were still in use, but children could only enter kindergarten at age three and then move into the primary school at six. In 1999 to 2000 there were 4,643 kindergartens with 365,704 students and 31,409 teachers. The children are taught songs, games, and nursery rhymes in the first year and then language, basic mathematics skills, communication skills, and music in subsequent years.

In 1999 to 2000 there were 3,696 primary schools with 960,601 students being taught by 82,829 teachers, a ratio of 11:1 that ranks it amongst the best in the developed world. Enrollments in primary schools are in a state of decline as a result of the overall decline in birth rates. Primary enrollments are falling by about 4 percent per annum, and the decline in enrollments is exacerbated in rural areas as a result of migration into the cities as young people pursue employment opportunities.

One area that has received significant attention in the provision of education has been the attempt by the government to more fully integrate the Roma population into the educational system. Most often these efforts have been directed at the primary level of schooling for, as noted below, the dropout rate for Roma children is particularly high at this level. The official government policy that attempts to give the Roma population a more sedentary lifestyle has created a large number of predominantly Roma villages, and the educational result has been a series of special schools. There are 134 special schools in Hungary, but they are unevenly distributed in the country. In some parts of the country, particularly the northeast, this proportion is as high as 94 percent. The Hungarian Ombudsman for Ethnic and Minority Rights notes that such a disproportionate number of Roma pupils is a sign of institutional prejudice and discrimination and in particular the education of these pupils suffers because of this spatial concentration. Moreover the schools have great difficulty in finding teachers who will and can teach in such schools in part because of discrimination but also because of the need to speak Romany, the Roma language. The government responds that such a concentration helps disadvantaged Roma children but has appointed an Ombudsman for Educational Affairs to study the issue. The issue of Roma education remains a difficult issue. For example in 2000 the Hungarian courts found in favor of Roma students whose primary school had organized a separate graduation ceremony for Roma students, and the local government was required to pay compensation. The issue of Roma education will remain at the forefront of Hungarian educational policy as the EU views respect for minority rights as a major criterion for admittance.

Curriculum—Examinations: The curriculum for all students is set by the state, and teachers generally teach this curriculum though departures are possible. The most important subjects, not prioritized, are mathematics, history, Hungarian language and grammar, physical education, a foreign language of choice, physics, biology and chemistry (the latter 3 only ages 12-14), music, arts, geography, and environmental skills. Music and art lessons only take place in one or two classes per week. At the conclusion of each lesson period of some 45 minutes, the teacher is required to record in a centralized book what was taught to each student. The student will typically have 5 to 6 classes per day. Students are not usually examined in primary schools but are required to do essays and homework and interact during creative problem solving exercises. They are graded on their work on a scale of one (failure) to five (the best) and these cumulative assessments at the end of the school year determine whether they will be advanced to the next grade level.

Urban & Rural Schools: Data on the ratio of urban to rural schools is difficult to obtain. It is known that 25 percent of all primary schools are in the central region of Budapest and Pest County. If rural settlements are defined as those below 10,000 people, then 58.7 percent of schools are in rural areas and 41.3 percent in urban areas. Rural primary schools exhibit lower results in all performance measures than urban schools as enrollments are decreasing as a direct result of state support that is less than urban schools. This is because the amount of state subsidy is directly based on number of enrollments.

Teachers: Most teachers are women. They are usually trained at the regional teachers training institute and in rural areas usually teach in a former collective school building. In preprimary Hungarian schools, 100 percent of the teachers are women while in primary schools 92 percent are women. The average monthly salary in 2001 was approximately 50,000 Hungarian Forints or less than $200. In urban and suburban areas, teaching conditions are better than rural areas with greater access to equipment and supplies. Moreover local city governments are relatively more wealthy than rural governments and hence the buildings are in a better state of repair and thus more conducive to teaching. Overall, including secondary education, teacher numbers in the labor force per capita at 50 per 1,000 is amongst the highest in the world.

Repeaters & Dropouts: The number of repeaters in any one school year in Hungary was reported in 1990 at 3 percent (4 percent males and 2 percent females). Officials suggest that this has not changed significantly over the years. Total numbers of dropouts are not available but it is known that in 1999 the proportion of those reaching the age of 15 but not finishing primary school was 6.3 percent. This is up from 5 percent in 1997 and 5.1 percent in 1998. It is also known that a disproportionate number of these school dropouts are Roma children. In 2000 the EU indicated less than 46 percent of Roma youth completed their primary school education.

SECONDARY EDUCATION

General Survey: In 1999 to 2000 there were 14,155 secondary school teachers in the 1,533 general grammar schools and 26,512 teachers in the 990 secondary vocational schools. In total there were 503,617 students at the secondary level with females in the majority in general secondary schools (87,569 females and 57,641 males). In vocational schools males outnumber females (195,268 males and 162,035 females). The number of enrollments in secondary schools increased on average 3 percent per year between 1997 and 2000, but the decrease in primary and preprimary enrollments should reverse this trend in coming years.

Curriculum—Examinations & Diplomas: The most important diploma a student obtains is his or her Secondary School Certificate, which forms the basis for entering higher education or a profession. It is supplemented by an official book in which the school has recorded all courses taken and the grades received in the various examinations that are a part of the courses.

Teachers: Of the teachers in the secondary school system, most have received a university education, which is a necessary prerequisite to teaching in the school system. In secondary schools teachers tend to teach specialized subjects such as music, physical education, science, and art. With the falling number of teachers and the rising enrollment rate, class sizes are invariably increasing.

Vocational Education: As was noted earlier, a student, upon completing the lower level of primary education at age 14, can either continue in the secondary school or begin specialized technical or vocational study at a vocational school. In 1999 to 2001 there were 357,303 students and 26,512 teachers in 990 secondary vocational schools teaching 350 subjects. In 1999 the number of students in different types of secondary vocational schools were as follows: teacher training (1,684), arts (4,916), journalism and media (114), business administration (41,891), computers/MIS (7,229), engineering (27,929), manufacturing (7,909), architecture (4,939), agriculture (6,055), health (5,851), social services (2,535), human resources (8,445), transportation (4,137), environmental programs (1,996), security (3,100), and pre-vocational training (112,639). Since 1999 the government has dedicated a significant portion of its efforts to reforming the system of vocational education to create conformity with

EU practices and objectives. The first measure was to provide a network of Public Evaluation and Examination Centers to standardize vocational education and training. The National Institute for Vocational Education, in conjunction with these centers, undertook an assessment of the needs of economy and recommended changes to the qualifications a student should obtain to reflect the changing labor marketplace. Finally, in January 2000 these qualifications were transferred from the Ministry of Economic Affairs to the Ministry of Education such that such qualifications were part of the educational attainment of the individual. By 2001, some 460 qualifications or 50 percent were under the Ministry of Education. Further progress in this area is being driven by Hungary's participation in the Leonardo da Vinci program that assists in aligning vocational education with future EU labor needs.

Education Outside the School System: In order to fight illiteracy and upgrade the workforce, Hungary has an extensive system of training outside the school system delivered primarily through regional job centers. In 1998 there were 103,675 participants in 5,363 vocations of which government or some other external financial source supported 36 percent. A total of 43 percent of these students were completing secondary school qualifications and 46 percent primary school qualifications. Of the fields of study of the vocational training establishments, 23 percent were in business administration; 20 percent in hospitality, trade, and tourism; 19 percent in the acquisition of computer skills; 16 percent in the industrial sector; 5 percent in health industries; and 17 percent in 7 miscellaneous fields. The institutions providing this type of private training are predominantly private companies (45 percent), autonomous bodies of existing educational institutions (47 percent), and non-profits (8 percent).

HIGHER EDUCATION

Types of—Public & Private: There are no private institutions of higher education with the exception of the 6 foundation universities noted above and the 26 church universities that are run with some support from the state.

Admission Procedures: Admission to Hungarian institutions of higher education commences with the publication of an admissions guide on or around December 15 each year. A central body, the National Office of Higher Education Admissions (NOHEA), publishes this guide. This body also provides information on the criteria required for admission, and sets national university entrance examinations. Their booklet also contains the application forms, which must be submitted by March 1 in the proposed year of entry. (There are two other less

significant application periods but these are only for a limited number of subjects and institutions.) This body receives and processes the application forms after March 1 and sets entrance exams. It then acts as a liaison with the institutions of higher education.

Individual institutions have a significant role in the selection and admission of students. Applicants are generally scored on a combination of their scores in the final examination at secondary school, their overall GPA in secondary school, and their score on the NOHEA national examinations. However in practice the individual institutions have significant autonomy in the criteria they use in ranking an applicant. In some cases NOHEA scores alone may be used or the examinations waived (particularly for outstanding students). Language ability is often an important criterion, as is previous professional training. Health and artistic abilities may also be used. Finally a parent who graduated in the proposed profession, particularly law and medicine, may also be a factor. These subjective criteria for admission are awarded as "extra points" when creating an applicant's total score for admission. Essentially the institutions control their entry numbers and choose their entry-level class.

Applicants, on their application form, may apply for several majors and institutions but must rank their choices as they can only be admitted to one institution. The national scores for the NOHEA tests are published in July, and the applicant can then see if he or she has passed the standard for university or college admission. If this is so, at that time the prospective student's secondary or lower choices for colleges are dropped. It is also at this time that the "extra points" are awarded to place students.

It should be noted that in 2000 the Ministry of Education began a process to reform this admissions process, particularly to standardize admissions and make the system more equitable, transparent, and fair. To do this it is expected that greater emphasis will be placed on overall performance in the secondary school system and the final secondary school score and the NEOHA test will be made more responsive to specific applications to specific disciplines. The Ministry hopes to have reformed the secondary school examinations by 2002 and the university entrance exams by 2005. Finally, as part of this overall change, the admittance of more students into higher education is planned. At present only 17 percent of all eligible students are in higher education (up from 12 percent in 1995). The system is therefore seen as elitist and discriminatory.

Administration & Governance: Administration of higher education establishments is conducted by the individual institution with the state acting in an oversight capacity and enforced by granting an accreditation license to award degrees. The senior administrator is the rector (or the director general in a small number of colleges) who is elected by the university faculty for a period of five years, which is a renewable term. The rector reports to an institutional council and a senate that ratifies his decisions but who can also veto his decisions. The state can only intervene in university affairs in theevent of legal irregularities. Thus a university is essentially autonomous in regard to its inner workings. The composition of the governance boards is specified in the Higher Education Act of 1993-1996.

Enrollment: In 1999 there were 62 institutes of higher education in Hungary serving 280,000 students. Most are located in and around Budapest. With the amalgamation of the former Socialist institutions, there has been a move to provide regional centers of educational excellence that in turn will create economic development. Thus the cities of Debrecen, Miskolc, Szeged, and Pécs have taken on importance in not only regional education but also regional economic development. Eötvös Loránd University, with 18,500 students and more than 1,000 faculty; the Technical University of Budapest, with 12,300 students and more than 1,000 faculty members; and the Budapest University of Economic Science and Public Administration, with 3,700 students and 375 full time faculty, are the largest institutions of higher education in Budapest. Budapest is also the center for universities and colleges concentrating on music, fine arts, and applied arts. The University of Pécs, with 407 full-time faculty members and 19,500 students; the University of Debrecen, which will have 1,600 full-time faculty members and 14,000 students when 4 institutions are fully amalgamated into 1; and the University of Szeged, catering to 6,000 students with approximately 500 full-time faculty members, have the most students outside Budapest. Highly specialized studies (veterinary medicine, dentistry, pharmaceutics, forestry, and horticulture) tend to be located in only one institution, usually in the city and institution that provided that specialization in socialist times. Of all the institutions of higher education, the ecclesiastical institutions catered to 10,303 full-time students and 5,511 evening and correspondence students in 1999 while the foundations catered to 7,582 full-time students and 15,743 evening and correspondence students.

Teaching Styles & Techniques: The principal language of instruction in the institutions is Hungarian. Teaching pedagogy is in the process of slow change from primarily a standard lecture format to a more varied style with wider use of source material. Thus the use of overheads is becoming increasingly common but PowerPoint presentations and the use of Internet sources is still rare.

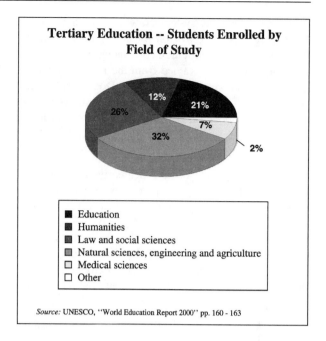

Tertiary Education -- Students Enrolled by Field of Study

- Education
- Humanities
- Law and social sciences
- Natural sciences, engineering and agriculture
- Medical sciences
- Other

Source: UNESCO, "World Education Report 2000" pp. 160 - 163

Finance (Tuition Costs): Typical tuition fees for Hungarian nationals for university courses range from US$75.00 (20,000 HUF) per course rising to $2,200 per semester, but fees for all Hungarian colleges and universities are generally paid for in full by the state in the form of fee waivers. In addition the state may give scholarships for living expenses or support in the form of meals and accommodations. In addition the Hungarian government has substantially increased the number and amount of scholarships for Roma students in higher education in order to increase the number of Roma in higher education. Data indicates only 0.24 percent of the Roma population obtained a degree in higher education in 1999.

Courses, Semesters, & Diplomas: Higher education in Hungary depends on the institution and the level of study. At the college level the length of study is either three or four years. The student receives the equivalent of a baccalaureate degree. For a university degree, the length of study is between four and five years and is equivalent to obtaining a master's degree. The exception to these degrees are degrees in law and medicine in which the law degree can be obtained in four and a half years and medicine is typically of six years duration with significant practical work in the latter part of the prospective lawyer or doctors study.

During the socialist regime, upon completion of the university education, a student could undertake further post-graduate work, usually of a scientific nature. Thus a person could get a *doctor universitatis* (university doctor or dr. univ) from a university or a *candidatus scientiarium* (candidate of sciences or C.Sc.) or *doctor scientarium* (doctor of sciences or D.Sc.) as part of the

Academy of Sciences system. However within the Act of 1993 there was the provision for universities to grant a Ph.D. There has been a dramatic change in the number of doctoral degrees awarded from the former system to the new Ph.D. qualification (or a Doctor of Liberal Arts—DLA —in the case of liberal arts) allowed under the law. In all doctoral programs the student is required to pursue a proscribed course of study, undertake original research, and write and defend a dissertation.

Upon completion of their degree program students receive a college graduate degree (*fõiskolai oklevél*) or a university graduate degree (*egyetemi oklevél*) that may be referred to as a Bachelor of or Master of, depending on their study program and its length in order to facilitate comparison with international degrees. In the case of medical doctors, dentists, veterinary doctors or lawyers, their degrees are dr. med, dr. med. dent., dr. vet., and dr. jur., respectively.

All higher education institutes work in a two semester system that commences in September and ends in May with a one-month winter recess.

Professional Education: Universities and colleges can also provide certification programs of shorter duration than typical university courses. This is called Accredited Higher Vocational Training (AHVT) and is typically in a specialized area of applied study. These programs are usually two years in length, taught at colleges (though not exclusively), and in cooperation with secondary vocational schools. The graduate receives a certificate upon graduation, not a diploma. In addition university and college courses may be taught at other campuses to extend the reach of an institute's course offerings. This represents an important source of supplementary income for both institutions and their faculty.

Postgraduate Training: There is a long history in Hungary of post-graduate teaching in the various Academies of Science that was usually linked with the award of the doctorate degree. Out of necessity, this training was highly specialized and found in those specialized institutes established under the socialist system to produce an intellectual elite. This system is gradually being replaced by a system where university professors undertake both research and teaching while former academicians in academies must make their living by teaching as well as undertaking research.

Foreign Students: There are a number of foreign students in Hungarian universities primarily studying at the baccalaureate level. Typical of the extent of foreign students was the University of Pécs with 95 foreign students or 0.5 percent of their total student body in 2001. Seventy-five came from Europe, primarily under the EU Socra-

tes program, and the remainder were American. Many of the students classified as foreign are ethnic Hungarians granted scholarships to study at Hungarian institutions. Thus, for example, ethnic Hungarians living as Croatian citizens in Croatia or Romanian citizens living in Transylvania often study in Hungary. The number of students from Western Europe and the United States is considerably less owing to the difficulty in understanding Hungarian, which is the language of instruction. Many universities provide lectures in English in part to offset this problem, and these courses are often linked to the Socrates/Erasmus program of the EU. Elementary language instruction in Hungarian is also a significant part of Hungarian higher education course offerings. In 1999 there were 448 Americans studying in Hungary.

Students Abroad: Given the difficulty of transition and the uncertain future of the nation, any ability to speak a foreign language, particularly English, and the resultant opportunity to study abroad has become a major incentive to students in higher education completing their studies overseas. This incentive is unfortunately accompanied by a reluctance to return to Hungary to become part of the labor force. Essentially a brain drain is occurring—albeit on a small scale, but enough to warrant concern. In 1999 there were 1,166 Hungarian students in the United States with a little more in Europe, the majority being in Germany. The major deterrent for Hungarian students to study abroad is the high cost of tuition and living expenses outside Hungary. Hence most students studying outside Hungary are on some kind of scholarship. It should also be noted that in 2000, a total of 479 Hungarian scholars were also studying in the United States, the largest of any eastern European country except Poland.

Role of Libraries: As was noted above, libraries have received serious attention since the change from a socialist government. In addition the historic importance placed on education throughout the last 500 years has left an impressive legacy of historic documents and literature that is available for consultation.

ADMINISTRATION, FINANCE, & EDUCATIONAL RESEARCH

Government Educational Agencies: There are essentially two levels of educational responsibility in Hungary. At the local level, elected administrative bodies (village and city councils) are responsible for school provision, maintenance, and teaching materials, including teachers. At the state level the Ministry of Education sets the curriculum for all primary and secondary public schools while institutions of higher education set their own curriculum with approval from the Higher Education and

Scientific Council. Control over education policy is exercised by the state through the HESC by means of allocating finances, certification, and licensing of educational bodies.

At the local level schools are funded through a portion of tax revenue that is provided to schools by the local municipality and supplemented by state funds.

In Hungary, local teachers elect school principals. However, the election is a formality since the local government appoints school leaders in the end. School boards exist but without power or decision-making authority—policy and appointments are thus made by the local mayors and councils. Thus a school principal may not be a professional educator but rather a political appointee.

Ministry of the Department of Education: Daily responsibility for state education resides in the Ministry of Education based in Budapest. There were 700 public servants working in the Ministry of Education in 2001—613 ministry employees, 5 for the secretariat of UNESCO, and 82 working for the National Public Education and Examination Board.

Educational Budgets: State budgeting is still the primary source of funds for education in Hungary. Hungary's Gross National Product was $46.6 billion in 1998, and while only 1992 data on contribution to education is available (in 1992 education contributed 7.5 percent to the GDP), it is estimated that the percentage has remained approximately the same.

In 1996, some 308 billion forints (US$1,029 million) of government expenditures were spent on education. By 2001 spending on education represented 4.6 percent of the gross national product and had fallen since 1996 when it was just over 6 percent. Of the monies spent on education, 0.74 percent of the GNP went to kindergarten education, 2.38 percent to primary, 1.47 percent to secondary, 0.81 percent to higher education, and 0.28 percent to other forms of education. Education spending represented 9.56 percent of all government expenditures in 1990, and it fell at an average annual rate of 5.2 percent between 1990 and 1996. In 1996 education represented 8.66 percent of all state expenditures. Inflation over the years has also eroded significantly the purchasing power of these expenditures and notwithstanding the commitment to funding education, it is apparent that education spending is falling.

Types of Expenditures: Preprimary and primary education consumed 36.8 percent, secondary education consumed 46.3 percent and tertiary education consumed 15.5 percent of the national education budget in 1996. Howev-

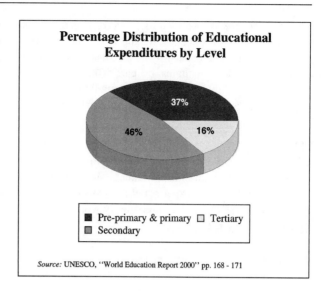

Percentage Distribution of Educational Expenditures by Level

37%

16%

46%

■ Pre-primary & primary □ Tertiary
■ Secondary

Source: UNESCO, "World Education Report 2000" pp. 168 - 171

er expenditures per pupil as a percentage of GNP indicate only 18 percent was spent on primary and preprimary education (down from 23 percent in 1990), 49 percent was spent on the secondary sector, and 33 percent on tertiary education. Teacher and professional salaries take up approximately 70 percent of the total education budget.

National Education Organizations: There are a large number of committees and advisory bodies that advise the Minister of Education. The presence of advisory bodies such as HÖOK, the Association of Hungarian Students, the House of Professors, the Hungarian Academy of Sciences, and the Hungarian Rectors Conference are important independent bodies guiding Hungarian educational policy. Moreover the two major committees that guide policy and programming, the Hungarian Accreditation Committee and the Higher Education and Scientific Council, have representatives from all interest groups. For example, the HAC has a board of 30 members chosen from higher education, research institutes, and professional organizations. There are also non-voting members on the HAC from unrepresented groups and also a non-voting student representative. The HESC has 21 members on its board of which 10 are academics, 10 are from user organizations (employers, municipalities, academic bodies, and unions), and 1 is from the Ministry of Education.

Educational Research: There are two bodies conducting educational research in Hungary; the Hungarian Institute for Educational Research (*Oktataskutato Intezet*), which deals with sociological and other social science issues associated with education. They also publish a periodical called "Education." This institute provides for a doctorate in education through the University of Debrecen. The second body, the National Institute of Public Education (*Orszagos Kozoktatasi Intezet*), carries out research at all levels of education and across the spectrum of educational issues usually by means of surveys on education topics. Both institutes are part of the Ministry of Education but they also receive external funding from private sources both Hungarian and international.

Project specific research is also undertaken by the HAC and the HESC. As part of their mandates to provide educational policy and program development, they may see the need to research a particular issue. To that end they frequently utilize experts and professional committees to undertake research as preparatory work for the decisions of the bodies.

NONFORMAL EDUCATION

Adult Education: Adult education has been recognized as a priority in Hungary in order for adults to adjust to the new socio-economic system. However the requirement that students (or businesses) pay for this learning seems to be a major obstacle to its success in difficult economic times. Invariably, if the individual wishing to upgrade his or her skills is unemployed, the government, through the job-center network, will pay for or subsidize the training. Costs vary on the type of training but the average in 2001 was between 70,000 and 120,000 HUF (US$230 to US$400). Foreign languages, bookkeeping and accounting, marketing and market economics, management and particularly human resource management, and computer literacy have been identified as priorities, but few establishments outside the larger cities of Budapest, Debrecen, Miskolc, Szeged, and Pécs offer these programs at present. In 1999 there were 132,789 persons registered as undertaking 6,743 types of adult education courses.

Open Universities & Distance Education: There are no open university-type opportunities. Distance learning in the form of correspondence courses through existing universities is possible but these are supplementary to the universities' normal in-residence structure. Correspondence courses with major universities are a significant contributor to the part time student body. There are distance education courses delivered through TV, radio, or Internet. These are becoming more and more popular but a dramatic growth in online courses is limited owing to the limited availability or scarcity of Internet links.

TEACHING PROFESSION

Training & Qualifications: Seven universities and colleges offer teacher training either as distinct faculties of teacher training or integrated into schools of natural, humanities, or social science. Those teachers who are trained in colleges graduate after four years and are qualified to teach in kindergartens and primary schools. Those trained in universities train for five years and are then qualified to teach in secondary schools. In 1999 some 21 percent of the total tertiary student population in teacher training colleges were education majors. This was down from 35 percent in 1994 probably reflecting the poor salaries to be expected upon graduation. In 1999 to 2000, there were 44,500 students studying in teacher training institutes, and if one assumes one-sixth of these graduated, there would be 6,500 new teachers in 2000. Eighty percent of all new graduates were women. In view of the low birth rates it might be expected that the demand for teachers in the twenty-first century will be reduced but this must be balanced with a teaching force that has a high median age. Moreover the loss of teachers, particularly in rural areas as a result of urbanization, will be cause for concern. This process will be exacerbated by the fact that urban schools have a higher prestige attached to teaching in them so they are preferred by teachers. It is also known that while 37 percent of the Hungarian population is considered rural, only 8 percent of students leaving secondary schools are from rural areas. As a result the challenge is to persuade urban teachers to move to rural areas—a policy that is in conflict with the urban migration trend of the rural population. Finally, upon the transformation away from a socialist economy to a more western system in 1990, there was a shortage of English language teachers in particular. By 2000 there was no teacher shortage and in some subject areas a surplus.

Salaries: Education is generally considered by Hungarians to be one of the worst paying employment sectors in the nation. The average teacher salary has increased every year since 1990 but has been grossly inadequate both in purchasing power and in its ability to keep up with inflation. It remains one of the most problematic areas of Hungary's educational system. In 2001 a typical salary of a person working in the education sector would be 72,710 HUF gross and 48,533 HUF net. There is no official discrimination in salary between men and women. More detailed data from the Ministry of Education reveal that salaries for women can range from 67,644 HUF to 46,162 HUF and for men 90,122 HUF to 56,714 HUF. This probably reflects the lower salaries for women who tend to occupy the more menial tasks (cleaners and canteen workers) in the education system. The typical salary scale quoted above is for all persons in education. Specifically for teachers, in 1998 a kindergarten teacher received 1.14 times the average salary, primary teachers earned 1.38 times, a secondary school teacher 1.67 times, and a university teacher 1.9 times. At the rate of exchange in 2001, a primary school teacher would take home approximately US$160.00 per month, while a university assistant professor could be expected to receive US$300.00

(In 2001, $1.00 was approximately 300 forints). The amount of salary usually depends on the years spent in the job, educational background, degree, and number of languages spoken, but not on gender. These salaries should be seen in light of daily living expenses in Hungary in 2001 that invariably exceeded salary by a significant amount. Indeed the average salary of a teacher or university professor in Hungary is such that supplemental sources of income must actively be sought. In rural areas it is estimated that 80 percent of teachers make extra money in addition to their teaching salary while in Budapest the figure is 79 percent of primary school teachers. In secondary schools the figure is 88 percent. This supplemental work usually involves private tutoring, supplemental teaching or consulting or even separate and different employment outside school hours, especially during the long summer recess.

Unions & Associations: Teachers are represented in Hungary by a union called The Democratic Union of Higher Education Employees (*Pedagógusok Szakszervezete*). However, the role and influence of this trade union, as those of all other trade unions, is weakening. In the socialist era they were not, nor could be, real organs of interest or representation, and after the systemic change in 1990, they were unable to adjust to the new political and economic system. The Union of Higher Education that represents employees in other areas of education (*Felsõoktatási Dolgozók Szakszervezete*) is not an exception, either. It is too weak to have a strong negotiating position.

There are also a number of student and administration bodies that are actively making representation in the process of changing the Hungarian educational system. For example there is a students' union that represents students' interests; it is represented at the national level by an association of students' unions with the acronym HÖOK.

SUMMARY

General Assessment: The Hungarian educational system is currently in a state of rapid and dramatic change. Up until the collapse of the eastern Bloc, it was a model of literacy, availability, and accomplishment. Since 1990 it has been required to transform to a more global orientation, conform to a more European system, and make provision in its graduates for a student that must function in a market economy and democratic system. The adjustment has been often slow, painful, and problematic. The principal challenges appear to be:

- The desire to retain the standard of excellence that has characterized Hungarian education for many years

- The ongoing ability of the Central government to find the financial means to provide complete funding for education

- The need to pay teachers in the public schools and universities a living wage

- The need for curriculum change to reflect the move away from a centralized economy to a market-driven privatized economy

- A decreasing birth rate, particularly in the urban areas, that will put pressure on the educational system to adjust to a diminution in students entering the school system in the coming years

- The removal of administrative appointments from the political sphere and its replacement by a system based on competition and merit.

It is also common practice that people who have not undergone educational leadership training, nor studied organizational development, make all education decisions at the local and regional level. It appears that there is the need for the installation of a professional educational leadership system of school principals and superintendents to provide professional leadership at the local and regional level. This in turn would suggest the need for more power for school boards made up of parent representatives.

International Programs: Upon the fall of the Soviet Union, the countries of the eastern Bloc embarked on a rapid program of opening up their educational system to the influences of western educational institutions. Many of these links were established by expatriate Hungarians who were located in the west as refugees or descendants of refugees from the 1956 Hungarian uprising. Hungarian institutions therefore invariably have a network of partners that are former socialist states as well as European and American partners. More specifically, the desire of the Hungarian government to join the European Union also created an extensive liaison with western institutions. Thus, for example, the HAC has an international advisory board of nine European Union and U.S. academics that meet yearly to advise and recommend changes to Hungary's educational system. The overall result today is vibrant and active exchanges between Hungarian educators and international educational institutions.

Needs for Changes—Future: It would therefore appear that the most significant changes required for Hungary's educational system to stabilize would be for the country to enjoy economic stability and prosperity from which education could take its place as a significant contributor to the country's viability. This kind of stabilization and growth is anticipated upon the accession of Hungary to the EU and at that time a revitalization of Hungarian education might be said to be complete.

BIBLIOGRAPHY

Europa Publications 2001. *The Europa World Yearbook 2000.* 41st ed. Vol. 2. London: Europa Pub.

International Association of Universities 1998. *International Handbook of Universities.* 15th ed. New York: Groves Dictionaries, 1998.

United Nations Educational, Scientific and Cultural Organization. (UNESCO). *The Right to Education.* World Education Report 2000. Paris: UNESCO, 2000.

Government of Hungary, Ministry of Education, 2001. Available from http://www.om.hu/jg.html.

—*Richard W. Benfield and Zoltán Raffay*